House of
Commons
Procedure
and Practice

House of Commons Procedure and Practice

Robert Marleau

Camille Montpetit

House of Commons
OTTAWA

Chenelière/McGraw-Hill
MONTRÉAL • TORONTO

House of Commons Procedure and Practice

edited by Robert Marleau and Camille Montpetit

© 2000 House of Commons

Coordination : Gertrude Gillich D'Urso
Proofreading : Licia Canton
Typesetting : Claude Bergeron
Cover and design : Norman Lavoie

Canadian Cataloguing in Publication Data

Canada. Parliament. House of Commons

House of Commons Procedure and Practice

Issued also in French under title : La procédure et les usages de la Chambre des communes.

ISBN 2-89461-378-4
Cat. no. X9-2/5-1999E

1. Parliamentary practice – Canada – Handbooks, manuals, etc.
2. Legislation – Canada – Handbooks, manuals, etc. 3. Canada.
Parliament. House of Commons – Rules and practices –
Handbooks, manuals, etc. I. Marleau, Robert. II. Montpetit,
Camille. III. Title.

JL164.C32 1999   328.71'05   C99-980478-2

Chenelière/McGraw-Hill
7001 Saint-Laurent Blvd.
Montréal (Québec)
Canada H2S 3E3
Telephone : (514) 273-1066
Fax: (514) 276-0324
chene@dlcmcgrawhill.ca

ISBN 2-89461-378-4

Legal deposit: 1st quarter 2000
Bibliothèque nationale du Québec
National Library of Canada

Every effort has been made to trace the source of copyright material contained in this book. The publisher will appreciate any additional information regarding rights and will rectify any errors or omissions in future editions.

Printed and bound in Canada
1 2 3 4 5   IQE   04 03 02 01 00

ECOLOGO CERTIFIED PAPER
MADE IN CANADA

Preface

Those who have a comprehensive enough genius to be able to give laws to their own nation or to another should pay certain attentions to the way they are formed.

MONTESQUIEU (*The Spirit of the Laws*, Book XXIX, Chapter XVI)

In 1980, the Clerk of the House, Dr. C.B. Koester (1979-1987), supported by Speaker Jeanne Sauvé (1980-1984), established the Table Research Branch at the House of Commons. The Table Research Branch was mandated to provide information and advice on parliamentary procedure to the Chair, the Table, Members of Parliament, public servants, academics and the general public. In addition, Dr. Koester envisaged the Table Research Branch producing an original, comprehensive manual of procedure and practice in the House of Commons—not that there had never been a book on Canadian parliamentary procedure.

Sir John George Bourinot, Clerk of the Canadian House of Commons from 1880 to 1902, was the first person to write a book on parliamentary procedure from the Canadian perspective. *Parliamentary Procedure and Practice in the Dominion of Canada,* first published in 1884, with a fourth edition in 1916, is still recognized as a fundamental, if somewhat outdated, authority on Canadian practice. Following in Bourinot's footsteps, Arthur Beauchesne, Clerk of the House of Commons from 1925 to 1949, published four editions of *Rules and Forms of the House of Commons of Canada,* a collection of notes with annotations, comments and precedents to provide Members with a quick reference whenever questions of procedure arose. In particular, the fourth edition, published in 1949, is still highly regarded by proceduralists. Two more editions were published, the fifth in 1978 and the sixth in 1989, under the direction of Alistair Fraser, a former Clerk of the House (1967-1979). However, because the copyrights for these earlier publications are held privately, it proved difficult for the House of Commons to provide Parliamentarians with timely and accurate updated editions.

Before setting out to publish a procedural reference book, the Table Research Branch first developed a database to consolidate procedural information at the House of Commons and to serve as a reference tool for future publications. Once this undertaking was completed, procedural research officers began drafting *The Annotated Standing Orders of the House of Commons of Canada* which focussed on the written rules and included a concise commentary and brief history of each Standing Order. Upon its publication in 1989, this work became a solid foundation of reliable information on Canadian procedure and practice.

With the success of *The Annotated Standing Orders,* John A. Fraser, Speaker of the House of Commons from 1986 to 1993, and Gilbert Parent, the Speaker since 1994, embraced the idea that the time had come for a distinctly Canadian reference work on the procedure and practice of the House of Commons. They committed the resources and encouraged the efforts of the team of researchers, writers and editors brought together for this purpose.

House of Commons Procedure and Practice represents a milestone in the evolution of Canadian parliamentary jurisprudence. Parliamentarians, proceduralists, academics and interested Canadians should find this book an essential guide to understanding the House of Commons and its Members.

Although it touches on constitutional, political and historical matters, this reference book is primarily a procedural work which examines the many forms, customs and practices which have been developed and established since Confederation in 1867. While shedding light on the Westminster model of parliamentary government, it provides a distinctive Canadian perspective in describing procedure in the House of Commons up to the end of the First Session of the Thirty-Sixth Parliament in September 1999.

The material is presented with full commentary on the historical circumstances which have shaped the current approach to parliamentary business. Key Speakers' rulings and statements are also documented and the considerable body of practice, interpretation and precedents unique to the House of Commons of Canada is amply illustrated. A wealth of references in the footnotes support the text and offer additional insights into the development of the current rules and practices. The book is complemented further by the figures found throughout the text and by many appendices.

In many ways, *House of Commons Procedure and Practice* is a continuation of Bourinot's work, documenting Canadian parliamentary procedure from the early years of the House to the start of a new millenium. It is our hope that in offering a clear exposition of our procedures and practices, this book will serve as a reference guide for Parliamentarians in their daily work and for all those who study and are intrigued by the House of Commons and how it functions.

Robert Marleau
Clerk of the House of Commons
September 1999

Acknowledgements

As the Senior Editors of *House of Commons Procedure and Practice,* Robert Marleau and I take great pride in this comprehensive study of Canadian parliamentary jurisprudence. As hard as some have laboured on this project, it must be pointed out that this book is the culmination of several years of work by many talented, experienced and dedicated people. I wish to acknowledge their efforts in bringing this milestone project to fruition.

I particularly wish to salute Debra Manojlovic Ford, Joann Garbig and Johan Fong who assiduously worked on this project from the laborious beginnings in 1993 to the rewarding end in 1999. I also want to give special thanks to an esteemed colleague, Deputy Principal Clerk Michael Lukyniuk, who, for the last two years, was responsible for the management of all the resources assigned to this project. His contribution to the final stages of the drafting and editing of the English and French texts was crucial in meeting the production deadlines.

It all began in earnest in late 1993. The planning of this project commenced in the Table Research Branch of the House of Commons under the direction of Principal Clerk Audrey O'Brien and Deputy Principal Clerks Marc Bosc and Marie-Andrée Lajoie, with the support of Deputy Clerk Mary Anne Griffith. The planning exercise involved several aspects, among them: the creation of chapter outlines, the identification of research methodology, and the collection of research material. Joann Garbig, Suzanne Kinsman and Debra Manojlovic Ford were the key procedural researchers involved in this early phase of the project.

By early 1996, several rough drafts of chapters had been written by the team of Joann Garbig, Debra Manojlovic Ford, John Phillips and Pat Steenberg under the direction of Deputy Principal Clerk David Gussow. As the project advanced, I became more directly involved, as one of the Senior Editors, in reviewing the texts and providing procedural feedback and criticism on substance and form. Terry Moore was asked to assist in the review exercise. With the impending retirement of David Gussow, Deputy Principal Clerk Michael Lukyniuk took over direction of the team in late 1997 and saw the project to completion.

By this time, the work had advanced to the point where chapters were being sent to the Clerk of the House for review and publication objectives were being set. In order to meet the approaching deadline of February 2000, additional researcher-writers were added to the team: Wayne Cole, Diane Deschamps, Jean-Jacques Gariépy, Patrice Martin and Terry Moore; in addition to their other duties, some procedural clerks in other services were asked to assist in the drafting of specific chapters: Deputy Principal Clerk Marc Bosc, Monique Hamilton and Beverley Isles; still others were asked for assistance in research support: Paulette Nadeau and Suzanne Verville, as well as administrative assistant Fiona Bladon. The unstinting work on the inputting, revising and formatting of the text by Johan Fong, assisted later by Dany Lamarque, has been a tremendous boost throughout the life of this project.

Besides researching and writing, this project involved other resources. The indexing in both languages was undertaken by the dedicated team in the Index Service of the House under the direction of Michel Boileau. The Translation Bureau assigned a team of seasoned translators to handle the heavy demands of the project under the supervision of Dominique Chauvaux: Ghislain Dion, Jacques Dubé, Laurent Fillion, Patricia Galbraith, Frèdelin Leroux Jr. and Denis Samson. In keeping with its reputation, the Library of Parliament provided a prompt and efficient service in responding to our numerous requests for reference material. English and French texts were reviewed in the Table Research Branch by Pierre Couture and Diane Deschamps before being sent to the publisher. Aspects relating to the production of the book—finance, relations with the publisher, arrangements for indexing, and distribution—were handled by Diane Diotte and Lucile McGregor under the supervision of Deputy Principal Clerk Eric Janse.

Such a project also required a corporate commitment and contribution from various services of the House of Commons. Of great use to the project were written documents and reference material from the following branches: Legal Services, Curator's Services, Committees and Legislative Services, Financial Services and the Table Research Branch. In addition, logistical support was regularly provided by the House Proceedings and Parliamentary Exchanges Directorate. Throughout this project, valuable information and advice were received from procedural clerks not directly involved in researching or writing; workloads may also have been increased for others because colleagues were given special assignments on this project. The indirect contribution of these individuals is much appreciated.

A number of "strangers"[1] also made important contributions to this project and I wish to take this opportunity to thank Judith A. LaRocque and Anthony P. Smyth from the Office of the Secretary to the Governor General, Antonine Campbell from the Office of the Auditor General, and Judy Charles from the Office of the Chief Electoral Officer for reviewing portions of the text.

Though "strangers" in the parliamentary sense of the term but certainly no strangers to the world of parliamentary procedure, two other truly professional individuals were key contributors to the editing phase of the manual. Both Lynda Chapin, a former public servant with practical knowledge and experience in parliamentary affairs, and Queen's University Professor C.E.S. Franks, a recognized authority in Canada's parliamentary system, gave us invaluable feedback and provided an essential service in pointing out minor and not-so-minor errors and omissions.

---

1. The procedural term "strangers" refers to those not normally found on the floor of the House. In keeping with the style of the book, might I add: For further information on "strangers", see Chapter 6, "The Physical and Administrative Setting".

I wish to thank them for having read the entire manuscript with such close attention and for providing concrete suggestions on how it could be improved.

Finally, I wish to acknowledge the special contribution of the Clerk of the House who, after setting the daring publication date of February 2000, gave his full support to the resourcing requirements and, despite the many claims on his time, managed to fully respect the deadlines which the team imposed for the final review of the draft chapters.

A work of this kind requires vision and a long-term commitment since it attempts to encapsulate the wisdom of generations of parliamentarians. The participants in this project were well aware of the dimensions of this daunting task and they are to be congratulated on having produced such a fine record. As is the usual practice with publications of this nature, any errors or omissions in the text remain the responsibility of the Senior Editors.

Camille Montpetit
Deputy Clerk of the House of Commons
September 1999

Photo Credits

Inside Cover and Chapter Opening Photos
(also details at end of chapter)

Aerial view of Parliament Buildings; Stone Sculptures: pages 1, 35 (47), 49, 139, 209, 225, 255, 307 (334), 335 (353), 355, 415 (446), 447, 503 (552), 553 (573), 575 (602), 603 (684), 685 (696), 697, 769 (796), 797 (887), 889 (921), 923 (938), 939, 961: Reproduced with the consent of the Library of Parliament.

Appendix 1   Governors General of Canada Since 1867

Pages 985-9: Portrait Images of the Governors General—Copyright 1999—Irma Coucill.

Appendix 2   Speakers of the House of Commons Since 1867

Pages 990-6: All credits with National Archives of Canada except for John Bosley (Ron DeVries); Jeanne Sauvé (Proulx Studio); Lloyd Francis (Mitchell House of Portraits); John Fraser and Gilbert Parent (House of Commons).

Appendix 8   Government Ministries and Prime Ministers of Canada Since 1867

Pages 1012-7: All credits with National Archives of Canada except for Pierre E. Trudeau (House of Commons); Joseph Clark, Brian Mulroney, Kim Campbell (Progressive Conservative Party of Canada); John Turner and Jean Chrétien (Jean-Marc Carisse, Office of the Prime Minister).

Jacket Flaps

Robert Marleau and Camille Montpetit (studio von dulong); Gilbert Parent (Thies Bogner Master Photographer).

Table of Contents

CHAPTER 1

Parliamentary Institutions   1

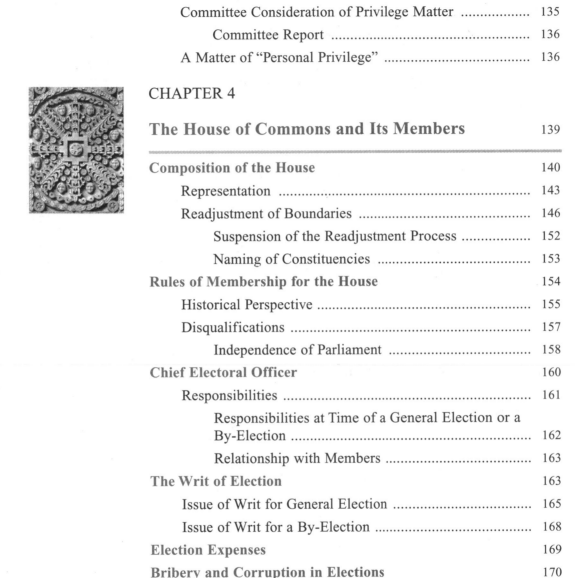

CHAPTER 4

The House of Commons and Its Members   139

CHAPTER 5

Parliamentary Procedure   209

CHAPTER 6

The Physical and Administrative Setting   225

CHAPTER 7

The Speaker and Other Presiding Officers of the House   255

CHAPTER 8

The Parliamentary Cycle   307

CHAPTER 9

Sittings of the House   335

CHAPTER 10

The Daily Program   355

CHAPTER 11

Questions

CHAPTER 12

The Process of Debate   447

CHAPTER 13

CHAPTER 14

The Curtailment of Debate

The Previous Question

CHAPTER 15

Special Debates   575

CHAPTER 16

The Legislative Process   603

CHAPTER 17

Delegated Legislation

CHAPTER 18

Financial Procedures   697

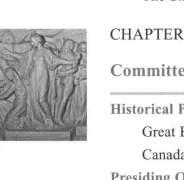

CHAPTER 19

Committees of the Whole House   769

CHAPTER 20

Committees   797

CHAPTER 21

Private Members' Business   889

CHAPTER 22

Public Petitions   923

CHAPTER 23

CHAPTER 24

List of Figures

List of Abbreviations

References to certain procedural authorities and other frequently cited sources are abbreviated in the notes as follow:

Beauchesne	Beauchesne, A., *Rules and Forms of the House of Commons of Canada,* 1st ed., Toronto: Canada Law Book Company, 1922; 2nd ed., 1927; 3rd ed., 1943; 4th ed., Toronto: Carswell, 1958.
	Beauchesne, A., *Beauchesne's Rules and Forms of the House of Commons of Canada,* 5th ed., edited by A. Fraser, G.A. Birch and W.F. Dawson, Toronto: Carswell, 1978; 6th ed., edited by A. Fraser, W.F. Dawson, and J.A. Holtby, 1989.
Bourinot	Bourinot, J.G., *Parliamentary Procedure and Practice in the Dominion of Canada,* South Hackensack: Rothman Reprints Inc., 1971 (reprint of 1st ed., 1884); 2nd ed., Montreal: Dawson Brothers, 1892; 3rd ed., edited by T.B. Flint, Toronto: Canada Law Book Company, 1903; 4th ed., edited by T.B. Flint, 1916.
Dawson	Dawson, W.F., *Procedure in the Canadian House of Commons,* Toronto: University of Toronto Press, 1962.
Dawson's The Government of Canada	Dawson, R.M., *Dawson's The Government of Canada,* 6th ed., edited by N. Ward, Toronto: University of Toronto Press, 1987.
Debates	Canada, Parliament, House of Commons, *House of Commons Debates: Official Report.*
Franks	Franks, C.E.S., *The Parliament of Canada,* Toronto: University of Toronto Press, 1987.
Fraser	Fraser, J.A., *The House of Commons at Work,* Montreal: Les Éditions de la Chenelière inc., 1993.
Griffith and Ryle	Griffith, J.A.G., and M. Ryle, *Parliament: Functions, Practice and Procedure,* London: Sweet & Maxwell, 1989.

Hatsell	Hatsell, J., *Precedents of Proceedings in the House of Commons,* 4 vols., South Hackensack: Rothman Reprints Inc., 1971 (reprint of 4th ed., 1818).
Hogg	Hogg, P. W., *Constitutional Law of Canada,* 4th ed., Toronto: Carswell, 1997.
House of Representatives Practice	*House of Representatives Practice,* 1st ed., edited by J.A. Pettifer, Canberra: Australian Government Publishing Service, 1981; 2nd ed., edited by A.R. Browning, 1989; 3rd ed., edited by L.M. Barlin, 1997.
Jackson and Jackson	Jackson, R. J., and D. Jackson, *Politics in Canada: Culture, Institutions, Behaviour and Public Policy,* 4th ed., Scarborough: Prentice-Hall Allyn and Bacon Canada, 1998.
Jerome	Jerome, J., *Mr. Speaker,* Toronto: McClelland and Stewart, 1985.
Journals	Canada, Parliament, House of Commons, *Journals of the House of Commons.*
Kaul and Shakdher	Kaul, M.N., and S.L. Shakdher, *Practice and Procedure of Parliament (with particular reference to Lok Sabha),* 4th ed., edited by S.C. Kashyap, New Delhi: Metropolitan, 1991, reprinted 1995.
Laundy	Laundy, P., *The Office of Speaker in Parliaments of the Commonwealth,* London: Quiller, 1984.
Maingot	Maingot, J.P. Joseph, *Parliamentary Privilege in Canada,* 1st ed., Toronto: Butterworths, 1982; 2nd ed., House of Commons and McGill-Queen's University Press, 1997.
May	May, T.E., *Erskine May's Treatise on the Law, Privileges, Proceedings and Usage of Parliament,* South Hackensack: Rothman Reprints Inc., 1971 (reprint of 1st ed., 1844); 2nd ed., 1851; 3rd ed., 1855; 4th ed., 1859; 5th ed., London: Butterworths, 1863; 6th ed., 1868; 7th ed., 1873; 8th ed., 1879; 9th ed., 1883. Beginning with the 10th edition, it has been edited by officers of the United Kingdom House of Commons: 10th ed., 1893; 11th ed., 1906; 12th ed., 1917; 13th ed., 1924; 14th ed., 1946; 15th ed., 1950; 16th ed., 1957; 17th ed., 1964; 18th ed., 1971; 19th ed., 1976; 20th ed., 1983; 21st ed., 1989; 22nd ed., 1997.

McGee	McGee, D., *Parliamentary Practice in New Zealand,* 1st ed., Wellington: Government Printer, 1985; 2nd ed., GP Publications, 1994.
McMenemy	McMenemy, J., *The Language of Canadian Politics: A Guide to Important Terms and Concepts,* rev. ed., Waterloo: Wilfrid Laurier University Press, 1995.
O'Brien	O'Brien, G., "Pre-Confederation Parliamentary Procedure: The Evolution of Legislative Practice in the Lower Houses of Central Canada 1792-1866", Ph.D. dissertation, Carleton University, 1988.
Odgers	Odgers, J.R., *Australian Senate Practice,* 1st ed., Canberra: 1953; 2nd ed., 1959; 3rd ed., 1967; 4th ed., 1972; 5th ed., 1976; 6th ed., 1991. Beginning with the 7th edition, it has been edited by H. Evans: 7th ed., 1995; 8th ed., Australian Government Publishing Service, 1997.
Redlich	Redlich, J., *The Procedure of the House of Commons,* 3 vols., translated by A. Steinhal, New York: AMS Press, 1969 (reprint of 1908 edition).
R.S.C.	Canada, *Revised Statutes of Canada,* Ottawa, 1985.
S.C.	Canada, *Statutes of Canada,* Ottawa.
Stewart	Stewart, J.B., *The Canadian House of Commons: Procedure and Reform,* Montreal: McGill-Queen's University Press, 1977.
Wilding and Laundy	Wilding, N., and P. Laundy, *Encyclopaedia of Parliament,* 4th ed., London: Cassell, 1972.

1

Parliamentary Institutions

Separated from the British Isles by a three thousand mile ocean, situated next to the United States, living in a country which covers half of the North American continent, with our heterogeneous population, our two cultures and our two languages, we have developed a parliamentary practice of our own based on British principles and yet clearly Canadian.

ARTHUR BEAUCHESNE
(*Beauchesne,* 4th ed., p. 8)

The Parliament of Canada consists of the Crown, the Senate and the House of Commons. Canada's Parliament was created by the *Constitution Act, 1867,*[1] a statute of the British Parliament[2] uniting the provinces of Nova Scotia, New Brunswick and Canada (Ontario and Quebec).[3] The legislation which gave birth to this new political confederation, to be known as the

---

1. Originally named the *British North America Act, 1867,* it was renamed the *Constitution Act, 1867*, in 1982 (*Constitution Act, 1867*, R.S.C. 1985, Appendix II, No. 5). For consistency, all references will be to its new title.

2. "From the earliest colonial times, the Parliament at Westminster had the power not only to make laws for the United Kingdom, but also to make laws for the overseas territories of the British Empire. In performing the latter function it was known as the imperial Parliament and its enactments were known as imperial statutes" (*Hogg*, p. 44).

3. The Preamble of the Constitution begins with "Whereas the Provinces of Canada, Nova Scotia and New Brunswick have expressed their Desire to be federally united into One Dominion ..." and goes on to say, "And whereas such a Union would conduce to the Welfare of the Provinces ..." (*Constitution Act, 1867*, R.S.C. 1985, Appendix II, No. 5).

Dominion of Canada, was passed by Westminster[4] on March 29, 1867, and came into force on July 1 of that year. The Dominion's first general elections were held later that summer and the House of Commons assembled at Ottawa for the first time on November 6, 1867. Members proceeded to elect James Cockburn, M.P., as their Speaker[5] and the next day, November 7, the Dominion Parliament met to hear the Governor General, Lord Monck, read Canada's inaugural Speech from the Throne.[6]

While the law enacting Canada's Parliament came into force on July 1, 1867, it would be misleading to conclude that Canadian parliamentary institutions were created at Confederation; they were then neither new nor untried. The provinces of Canada (Ontario and Quebec), Nova Scotia and New Brunswick each possessed sophisticated systems of governance, including legislative assemblies and upper houses, functioning according to historic, well-understood principles of parliamentary law and practice. While these parliamentary traditions were largely British in origin, they had been adapted over the years as the local political situation required. This body of domestic practices, traditions, customs and conventions grew with the result that, at Confederation, Canada's parliamentary system was well adapted to meet the needs of governing a young, diverse and growing nation.[7]

The oldest of Canada's institutional structures, those found in the Maritime Provinces, evolved out of the myriad instructions and commissions issued by the

---

4. "A reference to the British Parliament, which is built on the site of Westminster Palace in London. Thus, references to "Westminster" or "the Westminster model" are references to the British Parliament and its practices" (*McMenemy*, p. 320).

5. See *Journals*, November 6, 1867, p. 2. For further information on the election of the Speaker, see Chapter 7, "The Speaker and Other Presiding Officers of the House".

6. *Journals*, November 7, 1867, pp. 3-4. For further information on the Speech from the Throne, see Chapter 15, "Special Debates".

7. The following are some of the sources consulted on the evolution and function of Canadian parliamentary institutions: John George Bourinot, *Parliamentary Procedure and Practice, with a Review of the Origin, Growth and Operation of Parliamentary Institutions, in the Dominion of Canada*, 2nd ed., Montreal: Dawson Brothers, 1892; John George Bourinot, *Parliamentary Procedure and Practice in the Dominion of Canada*, 4th ed., edited by Thomas Barnard Flint, Toronto: Canada Law Book Co., 1916; Robert MacGregor Dawson, *The Government of Canada*, 6th ed., Toronto: University of Toronto Press, 1987; Eugene A. Forsey, *How Canadians Govern Themselves*, 4th ed., Ottawa: Her Majesty the Queen in Right of Canada, 1997; C.E.S. Franks, *The Parliament of Canada*, Toronto: University of Toronto Press, 1987; Peter W. Hogg, *Constitutional Law of Canada*, 4th ed., Toronto: The Carswell Company Limited, 1997; Robert J. and Doreen Jackson, *Politics in Canada: Culture, Institutions, Behaviour and Public Policy*, 4th ed., Scarborough: Prentice-Hall, Allyn and Bacon, Canada, 1998; J.R. Mallory, *The Structure of Canadian Government*, rev. ed., Toronto: Gage, 1984; John McMenemy, *The Language of Canadian Politics: A Guide to Important Terms and Concepts*, rev. ed., Waterloo: Wilfrid Laurier University Press, 1995; John B. Stewart, *The Canadian House of Commons: Procedure and Reform*, McGill-Queen's University Press, 1977; Richard Van Loon and Michael Whittington, *The Canadian Political System: Environment, Structure and Process*, 4th ed., Toronto: McGraw-Hill Ryerson, 1987; Richard Van Loon and Michael Whittington, *Canadian Government and Politics: Institutions and Processes*, Toronto: McGraw-Hill Ryerson, 1996; and Norman Wilding and Philip Laundy, *An Encyclopaedia of Parliament*, 4th ed., London: Cassell, 1972.

imperial government to successive governors over the years of British colonial rule.[8] By contrast, the institutional structure which emerged in the territory comprising present-day Ontario and Quebec was from the beginning laid out in statutes, a practice continued at Confederation with the enactment of the *Constitution Act, 1867.*

The Canadian System of Government

Canada is a parliamentary democracy: its system of government holds that the law is the supreme authority. The *Constitution Act, 1867,* which forms the basis of Canada's written constitution, provides that there shall be one Parliament for Canada, consisting of three distinct elements: the Crown, the Senate and the House of Commons. However, as a federal state, responsibility for lawmaking in Canada is shared among one federal, ten provincial and three territorial governments.

The power to enact laws is vested in a legislature composed of individuals selected to represent the Canadian people. Hence, it is a "representative" system of government. The federal legislature is bicameral: it has two deliberative "houses" or "chambers"—an upper house, the Senate, and a lower house, the House of Commons.[9] The Senate is composed of individuals appointed by the Governor General to represent Canada's provinces and territories. Members of the House of Commons are elected by Canadians who are eligible to vote.[10] The successful candidates are those who receive the highest number of votes cast among the candidates in their electoral district in this single-member, simple-plurality system.

Canada is also a constitutional monarchy, in that its executive authority is vested formally in the Queen through the Constitution.[11] Every act of government is carried out in the name of the Crown, but the authority for those acts flows from the Canadian people.[12] The executive function belongs to the Governor in Council, which is, practically speaking, the Governor General acting with, and on the advice of, the Prime Minister and the Cabinet.[13]

---

8. See, for example, B. Murdoch, *A History of Nova-Scotia, or Acadie Volume II,* Halifax: James Barnes Printer and Publisher, 1866, pp. 351-4.

9. Although this was not always so, all provincial legislatures are now unicameral. For more information, see G. William Kitchin, "The Abolition of Upper Chambers," *Provincial Government and Politics: Comparative Essays*, 2nd ed., edited by Donald C. Rowat, Ottawa: Department of Political Science, Carleton University, Reprinted, 1974, pp. 61-82.

10. For more information, refer to the sections in this chapter on the "Governor General", the "Senate" and the "House of Commons". See also Chapter 4, "The House of Commons and Its Members".

11. *Constitution Act, 1867*, R.S.C. 1985, Appendix II, No. 5, s. 9. In practical terms, however, the powers belonging to the Crown are exercised through an executive committee of ministers (Cabinet), chosen and led by a Prime Minister, and "responsible" to the House of Commons for their policies and for the activities of government (see section in this chapter on "Responsible Government and Ministerial Responsibility").

12. *Forsey*, p.1.

13. For more information, refer to the section in this chapter on "The Executive".

Political parties play a critical role in the Canadian parliamentary system.[14] Parties are organizations, bound together by a common ideology, or other ties, which seek political power in order to implement their policies. In a democratic system, the competition for power takes place in the context of an election.

Finally, by virtue of the Preamble to the *Constitution Act, 1867*, which states that Canada is to have "a Constitution similar in Principle to that of the United Kingdom", Canada's parliamentary system derives from the British, or "Westminster", tradition. The Canadian system of parliamentary government has the following essential features:

- Parliament consists of the Crown and an upper and lower legislative Chamber;

- Legislative power is vested in "Parliament"; to become law, legislation must be assented to by each of Parliament's three constituent parts (i.e., the Crown, the Senate and the House of Commons);

- Members of the House of Commons are individually elected to represent their constituents within a single electoral district; elections are based on a single-member constituency, first-past-the-post or simple-plurality system (i.e., the candidate receiving more votes than any other candidate in that district is elected);

- Most Members of Parliament belong to and support a particular political party;[15]

- The leader of the party having the support of the majority of the Members of the House of Commons is asked by the Governor General to form a government and becomes the Prime Minister;

- The party, or parties, opposed to the government is called the opposition (the largest of these parties is referred to as the "official" opposition);

- The executive powers of government (the powers to execute or implement government policies and programs) are formally vested in the Crown, but effectively exercised by the Prime Minister and Cabinet, whose membership is drawn principally from Members of the House belonging to the governing party;

- The Prime Minister and Cabinet are responsible to, or must answer to, the House of Commons as a body for their actions; and

- The Prime Minister and Cabinet must enjoy the confidence of the House of Commons to remain in office. Confidence, in effect, means the support of a majority of the House.

---

14. For more information, refer to the section in this chapter on "Political Parties".

15. A political party may be defined as "... any group, however loosely organized, seeking to elect governmental office holders under a given label" (Leon Epstein, quoted in Van Loon and Whittington, *The Canadian Political System*, p. 305). Official party designation for the purposes of the electoral system is made by the Chief Electoral Officer, while official party status, for the purposes of parliamentary procedure, has been associated with having at least 12 Members in the House of Commons. (For more detailed information, refer to the section in this chapter on "Political Parties".)

Canadian Parliamentary Institutions

HISTORICAL PERSPECTIVE

The Years Preceding Confederation

The history of Canadian parliamentary institutions begins in Nova Scotia. In 1758, the colony was granted an elected assembly,[16] becoming the first Canadian colony to enjoy a representative political institution.[17] No limit was set for the duration of a legislature; in fact, the Assembly elected in 1770 sat until 1785. In 1792, legislation was passed limiting the duration to seven years and subsequently to four years in 1840. Following the example of Nova Scotia, Prince Edward Island was granted a popular assembly in 1773[18] and the newly designated province of New Brunswick in 1784.[19] Each of the three maritime colonies continued to be administered by a British governor and an appointed executive council. Upper chambers (called "Legislative Councils") were introduced as distinct legislative bodies in New Brunswick in 1832 and in Nova Scotia in 1838.[20]

The situation was considerably different in New France, where there was no legislature and virtually no popular participation in political affairs. For a short period, residents of the settlements now known as Quebec City, Montreal and Trois-Rivières elected representatives or "syndics" to sit as members of the colonial council. The Council, however, remained responsible to the King of France or the governor of New France, not to the people. The office of syndic was disbanded in 1674 by Jean-Baptiste Colbert, then secretary of state for colonial affairs.[21]

In 1760, as a result of the Seven Years' War between Britain and France, New France was ceded to England under the terms of the *Treaty of Paris*.[22] In 1763, King George III of England issued a proclamation establishing governments for each of Britain's recently acquired territories in the New World, including the territory known as Quebec.[23]

---

16. Twenty-two members were elected and met at Halifax in October of that year to take their seats in the House of Assembly. *Journals*, March 1, 1883, Sessional Paper No. 70 (Provincial Charters), Appendix, pp. 8, 14.

17. Representative government is a political system with an elected legislature (*McMenemy*, pp. 259-60).

18. *Bourinot*, 2nd ed., pp. 73-4.

19. *Journals*, March 1, 1883, Sessional Paper No. 70 (Provincial Charters), Appendix, pp. 46-52, and *Bourinot*, 2nd ed., pp. 72-3. Until 1784, New Brunswick was part of Nova Scotia (*Forsey*, p. 3).

20. See John George Bourinot, *Constitutional History of Canada,* Toronto: Copp Clark Co. Ltd., 1901, p. 69; *The Nova Scotia Legislature*, Nova Scotia Information Service, rev. 1990, p. 12.

21. For a short history of the "syndics", see *A History of the Vote in Canada,* published by Minister of Public Works and Government Services Canada for the Chief Electoral Officer, 1997, p. xiv.

22. The historic Battle of the Plains of Abraham took place on September 13, 1759; Quebec surrendered on September 18. Montreal fell nearly a year later and the capitulation was signed on September 8, 1760 (*Bourinot*, 2nd ed., p. 5).

23. *The Royal Proclamation, 1763* (R.S.C. 1985, Appendix II, No. 1) defined the boundaries of Quebec.

Chronological Development of Canadian Parliamentary Institutions

1758	Nova Scotia was granted an elected assembly, becoming the first colony in what was to become Canada to enjoy a representative political institution. The assembly met on October 2 in Halifax.
1773	Prince Edward Island (known as Saint John's Island until 1799) was granted a popular assembly.
1774	The *Quebec Act* defined a new constitutional form for Quebec but made no provision for an elected assembly; government was entrusted to a governor and a legislative council, both appointed by the Crown.
1784	New Brunswick was granted a popular assembly which first met in Saint John.
1791	The original province of Quebec was divided by the *Constitutional Act, 1791*, into two provinces— Lower Canada (now Quebec) and Upper Canada (now Ontario). Each was provided with a legislative council (upper house) and an elected assembly.
1792	Upper Canada's elected assembly met for the first time on September 17 at Newark, now Niagara-on-the-Lake.
1792	Lower Canada's elected assembly met for the first time on December 17 at Quebec.
1824	Newfoundland officially received colonial status and was administered by a governor.
1826	Newfoundland's governor was granted the power to appoint the Board of Council to advise him. This Council would eventually evolve into the upper house and was known as the Legislative Council from 1833 to 1855.
1832	New Brunswick was given a legislative council (upper house).
1832	Newfoundland held its first election of Members to a Representative Assembly.
1833	Newfoundland's House of Assembly (lower house) met for the first time on January 1.
1838	Nova Scotia was given a legislative council (upper house).
1840	Upper and Lower Canada were united through the *Union Act, 1840*, which provided for a single appointed legislative council, and a single elected legislative assembly for the newly constituted Province of Canada.
1841	The Province of Canada's Legislative Assembly met for the first time on June 14 at Kingston.
1849	Vancouver Island obtained the authority to elect an assembly upon its creation.

A governor was commissioned and authorized to appoint a local executive council and summon a popular (elected) assembly, modelled on the one in Nova Scotia.[24] Together, they were empowered to make laws for the peace, welfare and good government of the colony.[25] However, before they could sit in the assembly, elected representatives were required to swear allegiance to the British Crown and to make a declaration against transubstantiation,[26] a fundamental tenet of the Roman Catholic faith.[27] Few of the original inhabitants were willing to make the declaration, with the result that no assembly ever met. The *Royal Proclamation* also imposed British civil and criminal law, which upset many of the original inhabitants who had believed their traditional civil and property rights were secured under the terms of the *Treaty of Paris*.[28] For the next 11 years, the "Province of Quebec", as it was then known, was ruled by the Governor General with the assistance of his executive council.

In 1774, the British Parliament passed the *Quebec Act,* which defined a new constitutional form for Quebec.[29] The Act enlarged the boundaries of the province[30] and no longer required Roman Catholics to take the oath of abjuration, should they wish to assume public office. The new Act, however, made no provision for an elected assembly; government was entrusted to a governor and a legislative council, both appointed by the Crown.[31] The council, with the assent of the governor, had the right to make laws but had no authority to impose taxes or duties except those authorized by local inhabitants for roads and other ordinary services. The costs of the civil administration were covered by revenues from duties on spirits and molasses, with any deficiencies made up out of the Imperial treasury.[32]

---

24. In the instructions to Governor Murray, dated December 7, 1763, there are specific references to the Nova Scotian constitutional documents (see *Journals*, 1907, Sessional Papers, Vol. 7, Third Session of the Tenth Parliament of the Dominion of Canada; 1906-7, Vol. XLI, No. 18, p. 137). In "The Early Provincial Constitutions", J. E. Read states that the early constitutional documents of the Province of Quebec "provide a constitutional position substantially identical to that of Nova Scotia ..." (*Canadian Bar Review*, 1948, p. 630).

25. *Royal Proclamation, 1763*, R.S.C. 1985, Appendix II, No. 1, p. 3.

26. A belief that during the sacrament of Holy Communion, the consecrated bread and wine are wholly converted into the body and blood of Christ; only the appearance of the bread and wine remain.

27. The "oath of abjuration", along with oaths of allegiance and supremacy, were then required of every member of the British House of Commons (*Bourinot*, 2nd ed., p. 8, note 1).

28. *Bourinot*, 2nd ed., p. 9.

29. R.S.C. 1985, Appendix II, No. 2.

30. *Quebec Act, 1774*, R.S.C. 1985, Appendix II, No. 2, Preamble.

31. Section XII of the *Quebec Act, 1774*, states that "whereas it is inexpedient to call an Assembly", and went on to provide for an appointed "Council for the Affairs of the Province of Quebec" of 17 to 23 members. As a rule, the Council sat behind closed doors, debates were conducted in both French and English, and ordinances were drawn up in both languages (quoted in *Bourinot*, 2nd ed., p. 13).

32. *Bourinot*, 2nd ed., p. 12, note 1.

Chronological Development of Canadian Parliamentary Institutions *(continued)*

1855	Newfoundland was granted responsible government with a parliament consisting of the elected House of Assembly and the appointed Legislative Council (upper house).
1856	The Province of Canada's Legislative Assembly passed an act providing for an elected upper house; the first election of Members to the upper house took place later that year.
1856	Vancouver Island held its first election for an Assembly. The first Assembly met on August 12.
1858	Mainland British Columbia was constituted as a colony and a governor was empowered to make laws for the colony.
1866	The colonies of mainland British Columbia and of Vancouver Island were united and administered by a Governor and a legislative council; there was no provision for an elected assembly.
1867	The *British North America Act, 1867,* was passed by the British Parliament on March 29 and came into force on July 1. The Confederation of Nova Scotia, New Brunswick, Ontario and Quebec created the Dominion of Canada; appointed upper and elected lower houses were created for the federal parliament and the provincial legislatures (except for Ontario, which only had an elected lower house).
1867	The House of Commons assembled at Ottawa for the first time on November 6.
1868	The *Rupert's Land Act* was passed by the British Parliament permitting the Crown to purchase all lands from the Hudson's Bay Company.
1869	The *Temporary Government of Rupert's Land Act* was passed by the Canadian Parliament authorizing the creation of a temporary government for Rupert's Land (later known as the Northwest Territories).
1870	The province of Manitoba was created and given upper and lower houses; the legislative assembly first met on March 15, 1871, in Fort Garry, now Winnipeg.
1870	The *Rupert's Land and North-Western Territory Order* declared that Rupert's Land became part of Canada on July 15.
1871	British Columbia joined Confederation on July 20.
1872	British Columbia's legislative assembly met for the first time on February 15 in Victoria.
1873	Prince Edward Island joined Confederation.

The passage of the *Quebec Act* represented the first time that the British Parliament had intervened directly in Canadian affairs; previous constitutional arrangements had been imposed by royal prerogative (i.e., the King acting unilaterally).[33]

In 1776, the United States declared its independence from Britain and over the next 20 years, thousands of British loyalists emigrated to Canada, many settling in what are now Ontario and Quebec. The dramatic rise in settlers of British descent increased the demand for political representation. However, it was not until 1791, when the *Quebec Act* was replaced by the *Constitutional Act,* that representative institutions were finally acquired.[34]

The *Constitutional Act, 1791,* divided the original Province of Quebec into two provinces—Lower Canada (now Quebec) and Upper Canada (now Ontario). Each was provided with both an upper house, or legislative council, and an elected assembly. Members of the legislative council were to be appointed by the Sovereign for life;[35] those of the assembly were to be elected. To sit either in the council or in the assembly, Members had to be at least 21 years of age and subjects of the British Crown. Provision was made for the Governor to appoint a Speaker for the legislative council; none was made for selecting Speakers for the assemblies. Each question coming before the legislatures would be decided by a majority of votes cast; in the event of a tie, the Speaker would have the deciding voice.[36] As well, provision was made for the Crown to appoint, in each province, an executive council to advise and assist the Governor in the administration of the province.[37] The legislature of Upper Canada met for the first time on September 17, 1792, at Newark, now Niagara-on-the-Lake; that of Lower Canada on December 17, 1792, at Quebec. The Governor was authorized to fix the time and place of meetings of the legislature and to prorogue or dissolve it when deemed expedient, provided the legislature met at least once in every year and that

---

33. Colonial legislation could be enacted by the British Parliament or, in the case of conquered colonies, by the British monarch acting alone. However, once a colony had been granted a legislature, new colonial laws or changes to colonial laws could no longer be made by the Sovereign unilaterally: they now required the consent of the Imperial Parliament or the colonial assembly (*Hogg*, p. 35).

34. *Constitutional Act, 1791*, R.S.C. 1985, Appendix II, No. 3. Like the *British North America Act* almost a century later, the *Constitutional Act, 1791*, was framed with the intention of "assimilating the constitution of Canada to that of Great Britain, as nearly as the difference arising from the manners of the people, and from the present situation of the province, will admit" (quoted in *Bourinot*, 2nd ed., p. 20).

35. The *Constitutional Act, 1791*, also provided that the Sovereign could make the right to sit in the legislative council hereditary although no titles were ever conferred under the authority of this Act (*Constitutional Act, 1791*, R.S.C. 1985, Appendix II, No. 3, s. VI. See also *Bourinot*, 2nd ed., p. 16).

36. *Constitutional Act, 1791*, R.S.C. 1985, Appendix II, No. 3.

37. *Constitutional Act, 1791*, R.S.C. 1985, Appendix II, No. 3, s. XXXIV. Section L further provided that the Governor and a majority of the Members of the Executive Council could make temporary laws when the legislature was prorogued and that such laws would remain in force for a period no longer than six months following the date on which the legislature subsequently assembled.

Chronological Development of Canadian Parliamentary Institutions *(continued)*

1876	Manitoba's upper house was abolished.
1881	The Northwest Territories' legislative assembly was fully elected.
1892	New Brunswick's upper house was abolished.
1893	Prince Edward Island's upper house was abolished.
1898	The Yukon Territory was created out of the Northwest Territories.
1905	Saskatchewan became a province of Canada on September 1.
1905	Alberta became a province of Canada on September 1.
1905	The Northwest Territories' elected legislative assembly was replaced by an appointed council.
1906	Alberta's legislative assembly met for the first time on March 15.
1906	Saskatchewan's legislative assembly met for the first time on March 29.
1909	The Yukon Territory's legislative assembly met for the first time on July 15.
1928	Nova Scotia's upper house was abolished.
1931	The *Statute of Westminster* removed the legislative authority of the British Parliament over Canada, Australia, New Zealand, South Africa and Newfoundland.
1934	Newfoundland's responsible government was suspended on February 16 with the Parliament (House of Assembly and Legislative Council) and Executive Council temporarily abolished. From 1934 to 1949, Newfoundland was ruled by a Commission of Government consisting of three Newfoundland and three British Members with the Governor as Chair.
1949	Newfoundland joined Confederation on March 31; general elections were held and Members elected to the House of Assembly; the Legislative Council was not re-established.
1968	Quebec's upper house was abolished.
1975	The Northwest Territories' legislative council (known as the Legislative Assembly after 1976) was fully elected.
1999	Nunavut was created out of the Northwest Territories and given its own legislature effective April 1.

each legislative assembly continued for a period of no longer than four years.[38] The Governor was empowered to give, as well as withhold, the Royal Assent[39] for bills and to "reserve"[40] bills for the further consideration and approval of the Crown.[41]

Legislation was enacted by way of bills which were first considered and passed by both houses of the legislature—the assembly and the legislative council—then assented to by the Governor on behalf of the Crown. This reflected the structure of the British Parliament at Westminster, with the Governor representing the Sovereign, and the assembly and legislative council assuming the roles and functions of the House of Commons and the House of Lords, respectively.

There was, however, endless conflict between the appointed Governors and the elected representatives over who should control public spending (Supply)[42] and who should appoint public officials (the civil list).[43] "For years, colonial reformers had argued that the only way to ensure harmony between the executive and the legislature was for the Governor to appoint to his Executive Council those who had the confidence of, and were responsible to, the Assembly".[44] This, in effect, suggested the implementation of responsible government.

Ultimately, discontent led to rebellions in both Upper and Lower Canada during the period 1837-38.[45] The Lower Canadian Assembly formulated its grievances in the form of ninety-two resolutions, including a demand for an elected legislative council.[46] In 1838, Lord Durham arrived in Canada as High Commissioner and

---

38. *Constitutional Act, 1791*, R.S.C. 1985, Appendix II, No. 3, ss. XXVI and XXVII. See also *Bourinot*, 2nd ed., pp. 16-9. A dissolution ends a legislature, the period of time when a legislature is "sitting", to make way for a general election. A legislature, in turn, may be divided into one or more sessions, each beginning with a new legislative agenda, presented as the Speech from the Throne. A session ends either with a dissolution, followed by a general election, or with a prorogation, which does not terminate the legislature but establishes that a new session will begin with a Speech from the Throne (see also Chapter 8, "The Parliamentary Cycle").

39. To become law, bills required the consent of both houses and the Sovereign. The Royal Assent signifies the approval of the bill by the latter.

40. The power to delay giving Royal Assent so that the legislation could be approved or disallowed by the British government (*McMenemy*, p. 260).

41. *Constitutional Act, 1791*, R.S.C. 1985, Appendix II, No. 3, ss. XXX-XXXII. See also the section in this chapter on the "Governor General".

42. See also Chapter 18, "Financial Procedures".

43. Technically, the Civil List referred to a list of the sums appropriated out of the public revenue to pay members of the civil government (*Gage Canadian Dictionary*, Toronto: Gage Educational Publishing Company, 1997, p. 284), i.e., those individuals occupying official positions in government administration, the precursors of the modern Public Service. At the time, they were patronage appointments made by the governor, often for life (see also *O'Brien*, pp. 48-9; *Wilding and Laundy*, pp. 131-3).

44. *Mallory*, p. 11.

45. For further information on the rebellions, see R. Douglas Francis, Richard Jones and Donald B. Smith, *Origins: Canadian History to Confederation*, 3rd ed., Harcourt Brace & Company, Canada, 1996, pp. 224-48, 264-76.

46. *Bourinot*, 4th ed., p. 8.

Governor General of British North America.[47] He produced an elaborate report for the British Parliament outlining the difficulties, as he saw them. Among his recommendations, Durham proposed that Upper and Lower Canada be reunited under one legislature and called for the institution of responsible government.[48] Under a system of responsible government, the governor could act only on the advice of ministers who were supported by members of the elected assembly, in other words, by those who represented the interests of the local citizenry most directly.

In July 1840, *An Act to re-unite the Provinces of Upper and Lower Canada and for the Government of Canada,* known as the *Union Act, 1840,*[49] was adopted by the British Parliament and came into effect on February 10, 1841. The Act provided for a single Legislative Council, composed of no less than 20 members appointed by the Crown,[50] and a single Legislative Assembly, with equal representation from each part of the newly constituted "Province of Canada".[51] Passage of the Act also signalled acceptance of the principle of responsible government by the colonial administration. Lord Sydenham, the first Governor General of Canada following the *Union Act, 1840,* introduced two practices which were essential prerequisites for responsible government. First, he reorganized the executive, creating departments and placing each under the direction of a single political head, transforming his council into a genuine policy-making body. Secondly, he created a government party, using his powers and patronage to ensure his ministers had support in the legislature. Although his system broke down, it paved the way for the introduction of responsible or cabinet government of the type which still exists. In 1847, the new Colonial Secretary in the British Government, Lord Grey, instructed Governors Sir John Harvey (Nova Scotia) and Lord Elgin (Canada) that, in future, they should choose their Councils from the leaders of the majority party in the Assembly. Shortly thereafter, in 1848, the principle was tested in Nova Scotia where the ministry resigned following its defeat on a motion of confidence in the Assembly and the Governor called upon the leader of the majority party to form a new government. Within a few weeks, similar changes of government had taken place in Canada and in New Brunswick, and the principle of responsible government was firmly established in British North America.[52]

In 1854, the British Parliament had passed, in response to an address (a formal request) from the Legislative Assembly of Canada, an act empowering the legislature to alter the constitution of the Legislative Council. Two years later, the legislature

---

47. His responsibilities also included "the adjustment of certain important questions respecting the form and future government of the two provinces" (*The Report of The Earl of Durham, Her Majesty's High Commissioner and Governor General of British North America*, London: Metheun and Co., 1902).

48. *Bourinot*, 2nd ed., p. 25.

49. R.S.C. 1985, Appendix II, No. 4.

50. *Union Act, 1840*, R.S.C. 1985, Appendix II, No. 4, ss. III and IV.

51. *Union Act, 1840*, R.S.C. 1985, Appendix II, No. 4, ss. III and XII.

52. *Mallory*, pp. 12-3.

passed an act providing for an elected upper house,[53] and the first election of Members to the upper house took place later that year. Until 1862, the Speaker of the Legislative Council continued to be appointed by the Crown, after which time the Councillors elected their own.[54]

The development of Newfoundland's parliamentary institutions followed a different path. Until 1824, the territory was not even recognized as a colony. From 1729 until 1829, the commander of the British naval convoy served as governor during the months the convoy was stationed in Newfoundland to protect the English fishing boats. In 1824, it was recognized as a true colony administered by a governor assisted by an appointed council. An election for a legislative assembly was called by the governor in 1832.[55] As had been done previously in Nova Scotia and New Brunswick, an upper chamber was created in 1855[56] and, at the same time, the province was granted responsible government.

The only other part of the country having pre-Confederation experience with British representative institutions was British Columbia,[57] which was created in 1866 out of an amalgamation of two English colonies: Vancouver Island and mainland British Columbia. While Vancouver Island had authority to elect an assembly when it was created in 1849,[58] in mainland British Columbia, only the Governor was empowered to make laws for the colony when it was constituted in 1858. With the union of the two colonies in 1866, government was exercised by the Governor and legislative council; there was no provision for an elected assembly. When British Columbia joined Confederation in 1871, the terms of union[59] provided for an elected provincial assembly although responsible government was not realized until the following year.[60]

Confederation

Beginning in the late 1850s and continuing into the early 1860s, there was increasing pressure on the provinces of British North America to unite.[61] The movement was

---

53. *Statutes of the Province of Canada*, 19-20 Victoria, c. 140. See also *Bourinot*, 2nd ed., pp. 38-9. An elected upper chamber had been a long-standing demand of the House of Assembly of Lower Canada. (Resolution No. 27, *Journals*, House of Assembly of Lower Canada, February 21, 1834, pp. 310-38, and in particular p. 316.) A total of 48 councillors were to be elected, one quarter every two years, each to serve for a period of eight years. Existing members were allowed to retain their seats during their lifetimes (*Bourinot*, 2nd ed., p. 38).

54. *Bourinot*, 2nd ed., pp. 38-9.

55. Paul G. Cornell, Jean Hamelin, Fernand Ouellet, and Marcel Trudel, *Canada: Unity in Diversity*, Toronto: Holt, Rinehart and Winston, 1967, pp. 109-17.

56. *Consolidated Statutes of Newfoundland* (Third Series), 1916, Appendix, p. 47.

57. All relevant constitutional documents relating to British Columbia may be found in the *Royal Statutes of British Columbia*, 1979, Vol. 7 (Appendices), Part B. See also the *British Columbia Terms of Union*, R.S.C. 1985, Appendix II, No. 10.

58. The first election took place in 1856 (see *A History of the Vote in Canada*, published by Minister of Public Works and Government Services Canada for the Chief Electoral Officer, 1997, pp. 34-5).

59. *British Columbia Terms of Union*, R.S.C. 1985, Appendix II, No. 10.

60. For further information on the pre-Confederation history of British Columbia, see Hubert Howe Bancroft, *History of British Columbia, 1792-1887,* San Francisco: The History Company Publishers, 1887, pp. 582-604.

61. For historical accounts of the initiation of Confederation, see *Bourinot*, 2nd ed., pp. 39-45; 4th ed., pp. 15-6, and the *Confederation Debates*, 1865.

prompted by political difficulties in the Province of Canada[62] and fuelled by collective prospects for economic advantage and improved military security.

Such a federal union had been recommended by Lord Durham in his report and discussed more than once in the legislatures of British North America.[63] On September 1, 1864, delegates from the Maritime Provinces met in Charlottetown to discuss the union of Nova Scotia, New Brunswick and Prince Edward Island. They were joined by representatives from both parts of the Province of Canada with the result that a decision was made to consider a larger union of all the provinces.[64] A second meeting was held in Quebec City beginning on October 10, 1864, attended by 33 delegates representing the provinces of Canada, Nova Scotia, New Brunswick, Prince Edward Island and Newfoundland. After 18 days of deliberation, the delegates unanimously approved 72 resolutions embodying the terms of a federal union.[65]

The resolutions were debated in the legislature of the Province of Canada from February 3 to March 14, 1865, culminating in the agreement of both houses to proceed with the union. Maritime opposition, however, delayed the process for over a year.[66] In the fall of 1866, delegates from Canada, Nova Scotia and New Brunswick travelled to London, England, to meet with the Colonial Secretary and make their case to legislators in the British Parliament. Sixty-nine resolutions were drafted and introduced in

---

62. Under Section 12 of the *Union Act, 1840*, Upper and Lower Canada were equally represented in the legislature of the United Province. In the beginning, this arrangement favoured Upper Canada whose population was then smaller. However, the large number of immigrants flowing into Upper Canada following the union soon gave it the preponderance of the population. Demands for increased representation were resisted by Lower Canada on the grounds that this would contravene one of the conditions under which they had agreed to unite (R.S.C. 1985, Appendix II, No. 4).

To manage the ongoing political conflict, the legislature embraced the principle of a double majority: in short, no administration should continue in power unless it enjoyed the support of a majority of the Members from each part of the province, and no measure affecting the interests of a particular section should be passed without the consent of the majority of its representatives. However attractive in theory, the principle was not terribly practicable and was abandoned in the early 1860s.

With the opposing interests in the legislature so evenly balanced, the vote of a single member could decide the fate of a ministry. Between May 21, 1862, and June 30, 1864, there were no less than five different ministries and legislation was virtually deadlocked (*Bourinot*, 2nd ed., p. 42).

63. See *Bourinot*, 2nd ed., p. 42.

64. See *Bourinot*, 2nd ed., p. 43.

65. The Quebec Resolutions, 1864, may be found in the *British North America Acts, 1867-1962,* by M. Ollivier, Ottawa: Queen's Printer, 1962, pp. 39-49.

66. See *Bourinot*, 2nd ed., pp. 44-5.

the form of the *British North America Act* on February 12, 1867.[67] The legislation received Royal Assent a little over a month later, on March 29, and came into force on July 1 of the same year.

The preamble of the Act expressed the desire of the founding provinces to be federally united, with a constitution similar in principle to that of the United Kingdom.[68] The Act entrenched the three principal elements of British parliamentary tradition—monarchy, representation and responsibility—in a new federal form of government. A central government was created for national purposes, and provincial governments for matters of regional or local concern. The provincial governments were not to be subordinate to the national government; rather, within its own jurisdiction, each was to be largely autonomous.

Although only Nova Scotia, New Brunswick, and the Province of Canada (subsequently named Ontario and Quebec) initially chose to be included in the new Dominion of Canada, the *Constitution Act, 1867* made provision for the admission of Newfoundland, Prince Edward Island, British Columbia and "Rupert's Land and the North-western Territory" (subsequently designated the Northwest Territories) at a later date.[69] The Northwest Territories became part of Canada in 1868,[70] the province of Manitoba was established in 1870,[71] British Columbia joined the federation in 1871[72] and Prince Edward Island in 1873.[73] The provinces of Saskatchewan and Alberta were formed in 1905.[74] Following provincial boundary changes, only the Northwest Territories and the Yukon (created out of the Northwest Territories in 1898) were left as "territories" within Canada.[75] Newfoundland joined Confederation, becoming the tenth Canadian province in 1949.[76] In 1999, Nunavut was created out of the Northwest Territories and given its own legislature.[77]

---

67. The London Resolutions, 1866, may be found in *British North America Acts, 1867-1962*, by M. Ollivier, pp. 50-60. In 1982, the *British North America Act, 1867* was renamed the *Constitution Act, 1867* (R.S.C. 1985, Appendix II, No. 5).

68. *Constitution Act, 1867*, R.S.C. 1985, Appendix II, No. 5, Preamble.

69. *Constitution Act, 1867*, R.S.C. 1985, Appendix II, No. 5, ss. 146 and 147.

70. *Rupert's Land Act, 1868*, S.C. 1869, pp. iii-v; and *An Act for the temporary Government of Rupert's Land and the North-Western Territory when united with Canada*, S.C. 1869, c. 3.

71. *Manitoba Act, 1870*, R.S.C. 1985, Appendix II, No. 8.

72. *British Columbia Terms of Union*, R.S.C. 1985, Appendix II, No. 10.

73. *Prince Edward Island Terms of Union*, R.S.C. 1985, Appendix II, No. 12.

74. *Alberta Act* and *Saskatchewan Act*, R.S.C. 1985, Appendix II, Nos. 20 and 21 respectively.

75. See *Constitution Act, 1867*, R.S.C. 1985, Appendix II, No. 5, s. 146.

76. *Newfoundland Act*, R.S.C. 1985, Appendix II, No. 32.

77. See *Nunavut Act*, S.C. 1993, c. 28; *An Act to amend the Nunavut Act and the Constitution Act, 1867*, S.C. 1998, c. 15.

INSTITUTIONAL FRAMEWORK

The Constitution

In Canada, the Constitution is not found in one single document.[78] The *Constitution Act, 1867,* did not codify all of the new Dominion's constitutional rules, stating simply that Canada was to have a "constitution similar in principle to that of the United Kingdom".[79] Apart from changes needed to establish the new federation, the old rules governing the exercise of public authority continued in form and substance virtually unchanged from those operating in the colonies at the time of Confederation. For this reason, much of Canadian constitutional law is found outside the Constitution Acts. In fact, some of Canada's most important rules are not matters of law at all, but conventions.[80]

The Constitution prescribes which powers—legislative, executive and judicial—may be exercised by which organs of the state, and sets limits on those powers. Canada being a federal state, the Constitution also describes how powers will be distributed among the national and provincial governments.[81] Finally, constitutional amendments enacted in 1982 included a *Charter of Rights and Freedoms* with which all subsequent legislation would have to conform.[82]

---

78. *Hogg*, p. 4. The Constitution of Canada is defined in section 52(2) of the *Constitution Act, 1982*, as including: (1) the *Canada Act, 1982*; (2) all acts and orders referred to in the schedule of the *Constitution Act, 1982* (includes the *Constitution Act, 1867*, and its amendments and orders in council and statutes admitting or creating new provinces or altering boundaries; and the *Statute of Westminster*); and (3) any amendments to any act or order referred to in (1) and (2). The *British North America Act* was an act of the British Parliament which established Canada as a federal union. It was renamed the *Constitution Act, 1867*, in 1982. Until 1982, with some exceptions, the *BNA Act* could only be amended by the British Parliament at the request of the Canadian Parliament. In 1982, the Canadian Parliament asked Britain to amend the Act so that all subsequent amendments would be carried out, according to a variety of amending formulae, solely by Canadian legislatures (*Canada Act, 1982*, and its schedules, including the *Constitution Act, 1982*, ss. 38-49, which contains the amending formulae). The amendments to the *Constitution Act, 1867*, which were contained in the *Constitution Act, 1982*, included the *Charter of Rights and Freedoms* (*McMenemy*, pp. 63-5).

79. *Constitution Act, 1867*, R.S.C. 1985, Appendix II, No. 5, Preamble.

80. See *Hogg*, p. 19.

81. *Constitution Act, 1867*, R.S.C. 1985, Appendix II, No. 5, ss. 91 and 92.

82. *Constitution Act, 1982*, R.S.C. 1985, Appendix II, No. 44, Schedule B, ss. 1-34.

The Crown

In Canada, the state is commonly referred to as "the Crown",[83] the country's supreme executive authority.[84] On the other hand, the Crown is constitutionally conferred in the person of the Sovereign. In order to distinguish the notion of the Canadian "Crown" from the Crown in other countries that recognize the British Monarch as their formal head of state, it is usual to speak of "the Crown in right of Canada".[85]

Much of Britain's constitutional development revolved around Parliament's efforts to limit or appropriate royal prerogative power. Today, with very few exceptions, no act of the monarch (or Governor General as the monarch's representative) is carried out without the formal advice and consent of the Prime Minister and Cabinet. The Crown does retain the right to be consulted, to encourage and to warn.[86]

Because Canada is a federal state, the Crown is represented in each of the provinces by a Lieutenant Governor.

The Governor General

Although the Sovereign is the formal head of state, almost all of the Sovereign's powers over Canada have been assigned to the Governor General,[87] with the notable exception of the power to appoint or dismiss Governors General. The Queen

---

83. A usage which dates from the time "when all powers of government were vested in the monarch and were exercised by delegation from the monarch" (*Hogg*, p. 268).

84. Section 9 of the *Constitution Act, 1867*, provides that "Executive Government and Authority of and over Canada ... be vested in the Queen".

    "This power is placed above and outside the governmental structure and political parties of the day; power is given to them temporarily and in trust by the Crown on behalf of the people." D. Michael Jackson, *The Canadian Monarchy in Saskatchewan*, 2nd ed., Regina: Government of Saskatchewan, 1990, p. 12.

    "... one institution (the government) does not possess power but exercises it; while the other institution (the Crown) possesses power but does not exercise it." Frank MacKinnon, *The Crown in Canada,* Calgary: Glenbow–Alberta Institute, McClelland and Stewart West, 1976.

    "The government rules. It does not reign. The Crown reigns ... the power of the state is held in a non-partisan office above the conflicts and divisions of the political process." Jacques Monet, *The Canadian Crown,* Toronto/Vancouver: Clarke, Irwin and Company, 1979.

85. *Hogg*, p. 269. In 1953, the Canadian Parliament adopted *An Act respecting the Royal Style and Titles* to reflect the fact that the Sovereign was the Sovereign not only of the United Kingdom but also of Canada (S.C. 1952-53, c. 9).

86. Walter Bagehot, *The English Constitution,* 4th ed., London: Fontana, 1965, p. 111.

87. *Letters Patent Constituting the Office of the Governor General of Canada, 1947*, R.S.C. 1985, Appendix II, No. 31, Art. II, and *Governor General's Act*, R.S.C. 1985, c. G-9 (see also *Mallory*, pp. 15-22, 33-75). See Appendix 1, "Governors General of Canada Since 1867".

appoints the Governor General by Commission under the Great Seal of Canada[88] on the recommendation of the Prime Minister. The term of office begins with the Governor General's installation in the Senate Chamber by the Chief Justice of Canada or any other of the *Puisne* Judges of the Supreme Court of Canada. Tenure is "at pleasure" usually lasting five years, although terms have been extended to as long as seven years.[89] The incumbent bears the title "Governor General and Commander-in-Chief in and over Canada".[90]

The Governor General may name one or more deputies, usually justices of the Supreme Court, to exercise on his or her behalf, any of the lawful powers, functions and authorities in respect of Canada that he or she deems necessary or expedient to assign.[91] A common example is the power to grant Royal Assent.[92] In the case of a Governor General's death, incapacity, removal or absence from the country, the Chief Justice of the Supreme Court (or, in the case of death, incapacity, removal or extended absence of the Chief Justice, the senior judge of the Court) becomes "Administrator of the Government" and assumes the powers of the Governor General.[93] If the Governor General is to be absent for less than 30 days, he or she designates the Deputy Governor General to act on his or her behalf.[94] Deputy Administrators are named as a matter of course each time an Administrator assumes office.[95]

Until the 1950s, the office of Governor General of Canada had always been held by a citizen of the United Kingdom—in the early years of Confederation, by members

---

88. The Great Seal of Canada signifies the power and authority of the Crown. It has both a ceremonial and an administrative purpose. Although the Governor General has formal custody of the seal, its actual custodian is the Registrar General of Canada whose incumbent has been, since 1967, the Minister of Industry (formerly Consumer and Corporate Affairs). Prior to that time, it was the Secretary of State. The seal is affixed to official documents in accordance with the provisions of the *Seals Act*, R.S.C. 1985, c. S-6, and the *Public Officers Act*, R.S.C. 1985, c. P-30, and the *Formal Documents Regulations,* Consolidated Regulations of Canada, 1978, Vol. XIV, c. 1331. The Great Seal of Canada came into official use as of July 1, 1867 (Consumer and Corporate Affairs Canada, *The Great Seal of Canada*, Supply and Services Canada, Ottawa, 1988).

89. *Dawson's The Government of Canada*, p. 181. The appointment being made at the discretion of the Sovereign, the term or the extension of the term is not for a fixed period. Extensions were made for The Earl of Minto (1898-1904), Earl Grey (1904-11), The Viscount Alexander (1946-52), Vincent Massey (1952-59), Georges Vanier (1959-67), Roland Michener (1967-73), and Jeanne Sauvé (1984-89). See also Appendix 1, "Governors General of Canada Since 1867".

90. *Letters Patent Constituting the Office of the Governor General, 1947*, R.S.C. 1985, Appendix II, No. 31, Art. I.

91. *Letters Patent Constituting the Office of the Governor General of Canada, 1947*, R.S.C. 1985, Appendix II, No. 31, Art. VII.

92. To become law, a bill must be agreed to in the same form by all three of Parliament's constituent parts: the House of Commons, the Senate and the Crown. Royal Assent signifies the agreement of the Crown.

93. *Letters Patent Constituting the Office of the Governor General of Canada, 1947*, R.S.C. 1985, Appendix II, No. 31, Art. VIII.

94. Prior to 1947, the Sovereign appointed the Administrator as each occasion arose. The continuing designation of the Chief Justice or next senior judge of the Supreme Court in the 1947 *Letters Patent* makes that practice no longer necessary.

95. Usually these are the judges of the Supreme Court, along with the Secretary and Assistant Secretary to the Governor General, the latter two for the purpose of signing documents.

of the British royal family or nobility, and later by retired senior military officers. In 1952, Vincent Massey became the first Canadian to assume the office; since that time all Governors General have been Canadian citizens.

Origins

The Office of the Governor General is one of Canada's oldest institutions. The Governor General was the chief dignitary in New France and was appointed by the King.[96] In the eighteenth century, the highest ranking official in the British North American colonies was given the title of "Captain General and Governor in Chief".[97] At that time, wars and other hostilities were frequent occurrences and the Governor General truly exercised a military function in addition to his executive responsibilities. Over time, the powers of the office have declined or have been undertaken by the Prime Minister and Cabinet.[98]

At the time of Confederation, the Governor General was both the Sovereign's personal representative and an agent of the British government.[99] This meant that, in matters deemed to be of "imperial" concern, the Governor General acted on the instructions of the British Colonial Office.[100] Between 1887 and 1937, the principal means of high-level consultation between representatives from the United Kingdom, Canada, and other self-governing parts of the British Empire/Commonwealth were the colonial and imperial conferences. The report on the conclusions of the 1926 conference (the Balfour Report) led directly to the recognition of dominion autonomy.[101] The Governor General ceased to be a representative of the British government and ceased to be appointed on the advice of the British Cabinet.[102]

In addition to the powers and jurisdiction of successive Governors General cited in the *Constitution Act, 1867,* others have been enumerated in a series of commissions, instructions and letters patent,[103] issued initially by the Sovereign, and later by the British Colonial Office. Of these, the letters patent issued in 1947 and still effective today

---

96. *Cornell, Hamelin, Ouellet and Trudel*, p. 60.

97. For example, the Commission of James Murray designated him "Captain General & Governor in Chief" of the Province of Quebec, dated November 28, 1763 (*Journals*, 1907, Sessional Paper No. 18, p. 126).

98. Van Loon and Whittington, *The Canadian Political System*, p. 183.

99. *Mallory*, pp. 15-22.

100. The Colonial Office was the department of the British Civil Service which managed the affairs of the colonies. The Colonial Secretary was responsible to Parliament for the government of British Colonies, Protectorates and Trust Territories, and was usually a member of the Cabinet (*Wilding and Laundy*, pp. 143-4).

101. M. Ollivier, *The Colonial and Imperial Conferences from 1887 to 1939, Volume III,* Ottawa: The Queen's Printer, 1954, pp. 147-8, 249-50.

102. In 1931, the *Statute of Westminster* gave legal effect to the principle that Great Britain and the dominions of Canada, Australia, New Zealand and South Africa were autonomous communities within the British Empire, equal in status, and in no way subordinate to one another in any aspect of their domestic or external affairs, although united by a common allegiance to the Crown and freely associated as members of the British Commonwealth of Nations. See *McMenemy*, pp. 288-9, and *Canadian Encyclopaedia*, pp. 131, 375.

103. Letters patent are statutory instruments which give some power to act or to confer some right.

were the most crucial. The *Letters Patent Constituting the Governor General of Canada, 1947*[104] replaced all prior commissions, instructions and letters patent and established the right of the Governor General to exercise, with the advice of the duly elected government, all the powers and authorities of the Sovereign in right of Canada. However, not all the powers conferred by the 1947 instrument were exercised immediately. Canadian diplomatic appointments, for example, have been made by the Governor General, rather than by the Sovereign, only since 1977.[105]

Legislative and Executive Powers
The Constitution Act, 1867, accords the Governor General certain basic powers of government. In administering the executive authority of the government, the Governor General exercises his or her powers, almost without exception, upon the advice of the federal Cabinet.[106] A recommendation from the Governor General must accompany all spending measures[107] and it is the Governor General who gives Royal Assent to legislation adopted by both the Senate and the House. Under the Constitution, the Governor General (or Lieutenant Governor, in the case of a province) may also withhold Royal Assent.[108]

---

104. R.S.C. 1985, Appendix II, No. 31.

105. Although the authority to appoint Canadian representatives abroad was transferred to the Governor General in the 1947 *Letters Patent*, that power was not exercised before 1977. Evidently, there was no particular reason why the change was made in 1977; it was merely part of an ongoing process of transference of practice from the Sovereign to the Governor General. The change was announced in a news release issued by the Prime Minister's Office on December 30, 1977, and a question about the change was asked subsequently in the House (*Debates*, January 23, 1978, p. 2088).

106. The Governor General is kept fully informed of Cabinet business and public affairs and receives minutes of all Cabinet meetings. It is very rare that a Governor General has gone against the advice of a Prime Minister. In 1896, Governor General Lord Aberdeen refused to agree to a number of senatorial and judicial appointments made by the defeated government of Sir Charles Tupper. Again, in 1926, Governor General Lord Byng refused to grant Prime Minister Mackenzie King's request for a dissolution and asked the Conservative Leader Arthur Meighen to form a government (see *McMenemy*, p. 151).

107. *Constitution Act, 1867*, R.S.C. 1985, Appendix II, No. 5, s. 54. These are legislative initiatives (typically bills) that will require a disbursement from the Consolidated Revenue Fund. Appropriations set aside, or "appropriate" from the fund, the amount that Parliament has authorized the government to spend. A proposal to spend public money may only be initiated by the Crown (see also Chapter 18, "Financial Procedures").

108. *Constitution Act, 1867*, R.S.C. 1985, Appendix II, No. 5, ss. 55, 56 and 57. Under the Act, Governors General were given the power to refuse or delay the Royal Assent until the British Parliament approved of or disallowed the bill. By the same token, provincial Lieutenant Governors were empowered to reserve a bill for the pleasure of the Governor in Council (i.e., the Governor General acting with the advice of the federal cabinet). Since 1926, it has been unconstitutional for the British government to interfere in Canadian legislation rendering the Governor General's power to reserve effectively moot. However, the disallowance power in section 56 remains unchanged (see *Hogg*, pp. 48 and 120). Federal powers to disallow provincial legislation also remain, although proposals for constitutional amendments have included their abolition (*McMenemy*, pp. 260-1). The Governor General has never refused assent for a government bill (as opposed to reserving) and convention dictates a Governor General will always give assent to a bill which has passed both Houses of Parliament. Refusals clearly would be in competition with the principles of responsible government. It is less clear whether the powers of disallowance have been nullified by convention (see *Hogg*, p. 253, and *Mallory*, p. 23).

The Canadian Constitution stipulates that only Parliament can authorize the expenditure of public funds. However, under exceptional circumstances, the Governor General may be asked to issue a Special Warrant permitting the government to make expenditures which are not otherwise authorized.[109] This provision, for example, makes it possible for the government to meet its expenditures when Parliament is dissolved for a general election. Governor General's "Special" Warrants are to be distinguished from Governor General's Warrants which are issued and signed by the Governor General each time funds are withdrawn from the Consolidated Revenue Fund.

The Governor General appoints Senators to the Upper House,[110] as well as the Speaker of the Senate,[111] summons Parliament into session[112] and prorogues and dissolves Parliament.[113] At the start of every new session of Parliament, the Governor General reads the Speech from the Throne which sets out the government's agenda. All Privy Councillors,[114] which include Ministers, are appointed and may be removed by the Governor General, who also appoints court judges.[115] The Governor General is also Commander-in-Chief of the Armed Forces,[116] performs a number of ceremonial functions, and represents Canada in state visits abroad and in other international events.

The Governor General appoints provincial Lieutenant Governors.[117] As well, various officers, including commissioners, justices of the peace, and diplomats, may be appointed and likewise removed from office by the Governor General.[118] By the same authority, the Governor General presides over the administration of oaths of allegiance and oaths of office, issues *exequaturs* (i.e., instruments for the recognition of foreign diplomatic representatives) and grants pardons.[119]

The Governor General also enjoys certain prerogative or discretionary powers.[120] One of the duties of the Governor General is to choose the Prime Minister. The individual

---

109. *Financial Administration Act*, R.S.C. 1985, c. F-11, s. 30; S.C. 1997, c. 5, s.1.

110. *Constitution Act, 1867*, R.S.C. 1985, Appendix II, No. 5, ss. 24, 26.

111. *Constitution Act, 1867*, R.S.C. 1985, Appendix II, No. 5, s. 34.

112. *Constitution Act, 1867*, R.S.C. 1985, Appendix II, No. 5, s. 38.

113. *Constitution Act, 1867*, R.S.C. 1985, Appendix II, No. 5, s. 50. See also Chapter 8, "The Parliamentary Cycle".

114. The Privy Council is the formal body, provided for under section 11 of the *Constitution Act, 1867*, to advise the Crown.

115. *Constitution Act, 1867*, R.S.C. 1985, Appendix II, No. 5, s. 96.

116. *Constitution Act, 1867*, R.S.C. 1985, Appendix II, No. 5, s. 15.

117. *Constitution Act, 1867*, R.S.C. 1985, Appendix II, No. 5, s. 58. Lieutenant Governors are not subordinate to the Governor General and the federal government but are as much the representative of Her Majesty for all purposes of the provincial government as the Governor General is for all purposes of the federal government (see Van Loon and Whittington, *The Canadian Political System*, pp. 180-1).

118. *Letters Patent Constituting the Office of Governor General of Canada, 1947*, R.S.C. 1985, Appendix II, No. 31, Arts. IV and V.

119. *Letters Patent Constituting the Office of Governor General of Canada, 1947*, R.S.C. 1985, Appendix II, No. 31, Arts. XI, XII and XIII. Under the provisions of the *Letters Patent, 1947*, the right to exercise the prerogative of mercy was delegated to the Governor General. However, while this remains a personal decision on the Governor General's part, the prerogative is exercised only upon the advice of the Solicitor General.

120. See *Hogg*, pp. 256-63.

selected must be someone who is willing to form a government and seek the confidence of the House of Commons. By convention, this is the leader of the political party that has won a majority of seats in the House of Commons in a general election. Where no party is given a majority, the defeated Ministry may choose to stay in office until defeated in the House, or it may resign. If it resigns, the Governor General will ask the leader of the opposition party most likely to enjoy the confidence of the House to form a government.[121] However, it is still correct to refer to the Governor General's prerogative or discretionary powers in appointing a Prime Minister, subject of course to the selection being sustained in the House of Commons, as this remains one of the few decisions the Governor General makes without ministerial advice.[122]

Among the other discretionary prerogatives is the power to dissolve Parliament for a general election, which is done normally at the request of the Prime Minister. Conventionally, where the government is in a majority position, the Governor General grants the Prime Minister's request. However, when the Prime Minister leads a minority government (i.e., one that does not hold an absolute majority of the seats in the House of Commons), the Governor General may exercise personal discretion in whether or not to accede to the Prime Minister's request.[123]

The discretionary prerogatives are invoked rarely and only in the most exceptional circumstances. The overwhelming majority of the Governor General's powers are invariably exercised on the advice of the Prime Minister and Cabinet.

The Legislature

Section 17 of the *Constitution Act, 1867,* states that "there shall be one Parliament for Canada consisting of the Queen, an Upper House styled the Senate and the House of Commons". Thus, the legislative arm of Canada's Parliament is bicameral. Each house has equal status as regards to its immunities, privileges and powers,[124] but each is far from being a duplicate of the other. Confidence in the government is tested in the lower house (called the confidence chamber) where by custom members of the

---

121. See *Forsey*, pp. 4-5. See also Chapter 2, "Parliaments and Ministries".

122. As Governor General, Lord Aberdeen was twice placed in the position of having to select a Prime Minister. The first occasion followed the sudden death of Sir John Thompson in 1894, when several cabinet ministers were considered qualified to be successors (Sir Mackenzie Bowell was invited and accepted to become Prime Minister). The second occurred when Bowell resigned in 1896; Lord Aberdeen chose Sir Charles Tupper as his successor (*Dawson's The Government of Canada*, pp. 183-4).

Ostensibly, the Governor General also has the power to dismiss the Prime Minister. However, no Canadian Governor General has ever done so. When the Australian Governor General dismissed the Prime Minister in 1975, his power to do so under the Australian constitution was upheld (see *House of Representatives Practice*, 3rd ed., pp. 5-6).

123. This happened in 1926 when Governor General Lord Byng refused Prime Minister Mackenzie King's request for a dissolution and asked Opposition Leader Arthur Meighen to form a government (see *McMenemy*, p. 151, and *Mallory*, pp. 52-7).

124. *Constitution Act, 1867,* R.S.C. 1985, Appendix II, No. 5, s. 18.

Ministry sit. Furthermore, although the same legislation must be adopted by both houses before being given Royal Assent, bills for the appropriation of public revenues or for imposing any tax must originate in the House of Commons.[125] Another marked difference between the two houses is that the Speaker in the Senate is appointed by the Governor General,[126] while the House of Commons elects its own Speaker.[127] Each Chamber functions in accordance with its own traditions, powers and practices.

The Senate

The Senate is the appointed upper house of the Parliament of Canada. It exercises all the powers of the House of Commons with the exception of the right to initiate financial legislation.[128] Senators are "summoned" or appointed by the Governor General on the recommendation of the Prime Minister. They must be at least 30 years of age, reside in the province for which they have been summoned and have real and personal property worth $4,000, in excess of any debts and liabilities.[129] Quebec Senators must both reside in and hold their property in the electoral division of appointment.[130] A Senator may resign by advising the Governor General in writing to this effect.[131] A Senator's place becomes vacant if the Senator is absent for two consecutive sessions; becomes bankrupt or insolvent or a public defaulter; becomes a citizen or subject of any foreign power; is attainted of treason or convicted "of any

---

125. *Constitution Act, 1867,* R.S.C. 1985, Appendix II, No. 5, s. 53. See also Chapter 18, "Financial Procedures".

126. *Constitution Act, 1867,* R.S.C. 1985, Appendix II, No. 5, s. 34.

127. *Constitution Act, 1867,* R.S.C. 1985, Appendix II, No. 5, s. 44.

128. *Constitution Act, 1867,* R.S.C. 1985, Appendix II, No. 5, s. 53. "Financial legislation" refers to any bill proposing government spending or imposing taxes. See also Chapter 18, "Financial Procedures".

129. *Constitution Act, 1867,* R.S.C. 1985, Appendix II, No. 5, s. 23.

130. *Constitution Act, 1867,* R.S.C. 1985, Appendix II, No. 5, s. 23. Although Quebec now has more than 24 electoral districts or ridings, Quebec Senators are still appointed from the original 24 electoral divisions of Lower Canada as set out in the *Constitution Act, 1867.*

131. *Constitution Act, 1867,* R.S.C. 1985, Appendix II, No. 5, s. 30. In December 1997, the Senate suspended Senator Andrew Thompson's use of Senate resources, including his telecommunication expense allowance and his travel allowance (except that required for travel between his Ontario residence and the Senate in Ottawa), and ordered him to appear in his place when the Senate resumed sitting after the Christmas recess (Seventh Report of the Standing Senate Committee on Internal Economy, Budgets and Administration, *Senate Journals*, December 9, 1997, pp. 305-6; December 12, 1997, pp. 358-9; December 15, 1997, p. 369; and December 16, 1997, pp. 378-81). When the Senator did not obey the order, the Senate passed another motion requiring him to appear before the Standing Committee on Privileges, Standing Rules and Orders (*Senate Journals*, February 11, 1998, pp. 426-8). On February 19, 1998, the Senate concurred in the committee's Second Report, which found the Senator in contempt, and suspended him for the remainder of the session (*Senate Journals*, February 19, 1998, pp. 457-8). On March 23, 1998, Senator Thompson resigned.

infamous crime"; or ceases to be qualified in respect of property or residence.[132] Unless they die, resign, are disqualified or their seat is declared vacant, Senators hold office until they retire at age 75.[133]

At Confederation, provision was made for 72 Senators.[134] This number has been adjusted several times, mainly to accommodate the addition of new provinces and territories. For the purposes of Senate representation, Canada is deemed to be divided into four divisions: the Western Provinces, the Maritime Provinces, Ontario and Quebec. To these four divisions have been added Newfoundland, the Yukon, the Northwest Territories and Nunavut.[135] The *Constitution Act, 1867,* now provides for 105 members[136] of the Senate with the membership distributed as follows:

Western Provinces	24
British Columbia (6)	
Alberta (6)	
Saskatchewan (6)	
Manitoba (6)	
Ontario	24
Quebec	24
Maritime Provinces	24
New Brunswick (10)	
Nova Scotia (10)	
Prince Edward Island (4)	
Newfoundland	6
Yukon Territory	1
Northwest Territories	1
Nunavut	1

---

132. *Constitution Act, 1867*, R.S.C. 1985, Appendix II, No. 5, s. 31. The last time a Senator's seat was declared vacant pursuant to section 31, occurred in 1915 (see *Senate Journals*, April 13, 1915, pp. 224-5).

133. Until 1965, the term of the appointment was for life (*Constitution Act, 1867*, R.S.C. 1985, Appendix II, No. 5, s. 29). The *Constitution Act, 1965*, provided that Senators would henceforth be required to retire at age 75. Senators appointed prior to the coming into force of the Act would retain the right to remain in office past age 75, should they so choose (*Constitution Act, 1965*, R.S.C. 1985, Appendix II, No. 39, s. 1).

134. *Constitution Act, 1867*, R.S.C. 1985, Appendix II, No. 5, ss. 21, 22.

135. *An Act to amend the Nunavut Act and the Constitution Act, 1867*, S.C. 1998, c. 15, ss. 43(3), 45.

136. *An Act to amend the Nunavut Act and the Constitution Act, 1867*, S.C. 1998, c. 15, s. 43(1).

The Constitution also allows for the appointment of four or eight additional Senators, equally representing the four divisions.[137] When additional Senators have been so appointed, there may be no further appointments in a division until Senate representation for that division falls below 24.[138] At no time may the maximum number of Senators exceed 113.[139]

The House of Commons

The House of Commons, or lower house, is the elected assembly of the Parliament of Canada. The *Constitution Act* provides for the size and distribution of representation in the Commons, as well as for future readjustments, or "redistributions".[140] With the 1997 redistribution and the creation of Nunavut in 1999, the House consists of 301 members distributed as follows:

Alberta	26
British Columbia	34
Manitoba	14
New Brunswick	10
Newfoundland	7
Northwest Territories	1
Nova Scotia	11
Nunavut	1
Ontario	103
Prince Edward Island	4
Quebec	75
Saskatchewan	14
Yukon Territory	1

Further information on the composition of the House can be found in Chapter 4, "The House of Commons and Its Members".

The Executive

In Canada, executive authority is vested in the Sovereign and carried out by the Governor in Council.[141] Formally, this is the Governor General acting by and with the

---

137. *Constitution Act, 1867*, R.S.C. 1985, Appendix II, No. 5, s. 26. The only time this provision has been used was in 1990. Prime Minister Brian Mulroney invoked sections 26 through 28 of the *Constitution Act, 1867*, to recommend the appointment of eight additional Senators to ensure passage of government legislation implementing a Goods and Services Tax.

138. *Constitution Act, 1867*, R.S.C. 1985, Appendix II, No. 5, s. 27.

139. *Constitution Act, 1867*, R.S.C. 1985, Appendix II, No. 5, s. 28, and *An Act to amend the Nunavut Act and the Constitution Act, 1867*, S.C. 1998, c. 15, s. 43(2).

140. *Constitution Act, 1867*, R.S.C. 1985, Appendix II, No. 5, ss. 37, 51; *Representation Act*, S.C. 1986, c. 8, s. 2; *An Act to amend the Nunavut Act and the Constitution Act, 1867*, S.C. 1998, c. 15, s. 30. For more information on representation, see Chapter 4, "The House of Commons and Its Members".

141. *Dawson's The Government of Canada*, pp. 198-9; *Constitution Act, 1867*, R.S.C. 1985, Appendix II, No. 5, ss. 12, 13.

advice and consent of the Queen's Privy Council for Canada; in practice, it is the Governor General acting with the advice and consent of the Prime Minister and Cabinet.[142] As provided for under the *Constitution Act, 1867,* the Privy Council is composed of individuals chosen by the Governor General to advise the Crown;[143] in practice, Privy Council nominations are made on the advice of the Prime Minister. Privy Councillors are given the title "Honourable", which they retain for life.[144] They serve "at pleasure"[145] but their term is effectively for life. Prime Ministers are designated "Right Honourable" for life from the moment they assume office.[146]

Once appointed, the Prime Minister selects a number of confidential advisors (usually from among the Members of the government party) who are first made members of the Privy Council. The selected confidential advisors are then sworn

142. *Constitution Act, 1867*, R.S.C. 1985, Appendix II, No. 5, ss. 9, 12, 13; *McMenemy*, pp. 124-5. Cabinet comprises the Prime Minister and Ministers and constitutes the government of the day. Ministers are individuals chosen by the Prime Minister to provide policy advice, as well as administrative leadership for the various government departments and agencies (*McMenemy*, pp. 17 and 178-9). At the time Britain acquired the Canadian colonies, the Monarch ruled at the head of an autonomous executive—a select group of Privy Councillors in whom the Crown placed its trust. In Parliament, the Lords represented the great landed interests and the Commons the interests of the propertied middle and commercial classes. Under this system, the Crown was presumed to operate as a check on the power of the legislature and Parliament on the power of the Crown. Over time, as more and more of the Sovereign's executive powers shifted to the Ministers (now chosen increasingly from among the influential Members of Parliament), the contemporary model of Cabinet government began to emerge. In effect, the Crown's business was carried out by Ministers who retained office by virtue of their ability to control and manage the House of Commons. From this emerged the modern notion of a Cabinet which fuses executive powers with those of the legislature to produce a government continuously responsive to the elected House (*Mallory*, pp. 8-11).

143. *Constitution Act, 1867*, R.S.C. 1985, Appendix II, No. 5, s. 11. Originally, the Privy Council was a more or less permanent executive body of nobles chosen by the Sovereign as counsellors. The Council was separate from the legislative body, or Parliament, of which the Sovereign was a constituent part. When the Council became too large for the practical purpose of consultation, the Sovereign selected from among its members his or her most trusted and intimate counsellors. The practice of forming from the larger group of Privy Councillors a small, specialized committee to advise the Crown has continued to this day (*Wilding and Laundy*, pp. 66, 602-4).

144. The *Table of Titles for Use in Canada*, approved by Queen Victoria in 1868, conferred the title of "Honourable" on Privy Councillors for life.

145. The term "at pleasure" means at the will, desire or discretion. A Privy Councillor serves at the pleasure of, and may be removed at the discretion of, the Crown or Governor General.

146. Until 1968, Canadian Prime Ministers, with the exception of Alexander Mackenzie, John Abbott, Mackenzie Bowell and Charles Tupper, were made Members of the Privy Council of Great Britain, which carried with it the lifetime title of "Right Honourable". In 1967, and again in 1968, the *Table of Titles for Use in Canada* was revised, with the result that Canadian Governors General, Prime Ministers and Supreme Court Chief Justices now all acquire the title of "Right Honourable" for life. Lester Pearson was the last Canadian Prime Minister to be a member of the British Privy Council (Library of Parliament, *The Origin of the Title "The Right Honourable"*, 1989).

in as Ministers. Collectively, they are known as the "Ministry" or Cabinet.[147] Privy Councillors are active in their capacity as advisors to the Crown only as part of a Ministry.[148] However, not all Privy Councillors are part of a Ministry and some may never have been Ministers.[149]

A Prime Minister's choice of Ministers is influenced by political considerations respecting, for example, geography, gender and ethnicity. However, the Prime Minister alone decides on the size of the Ministry and what constitutes an appropriate balance of representation.

By custom, members of the Ministry have seats in Parliament and, apart from the Leader of the Government in the Senate, normally sit in the House of Commons.[150] Persons appointed to the Ministry from outside Parliament are expected to stand for election at the earliest possible opportunity. If they are unsuccessful at the polls, custom requires they resign from the Ministry.[151]

Although the terms "Ministry" and "Cabinet" are commonly used interchangeably, in fact a Ministry is composed of both Cabinet Ministers and Secretaries of State. Most Cabinet appointees are designated Ministers in charge of government

---

147. Originally, Ministry was the *term* applied to Ministers holding office at the pleasure of the Crown while the Cabinet was a *place*, provided by the Prime Minister, in which the Ministry met (Privy Council Office, *Responsibility in the Constitution*, Supply and Services Canada, Ottawa, 1993, p. 26). The Ministry and the Cabinet are not always identical; not all Ministers are members of Cabinet. For a large part of Canadian history, the Cabinet and the Ministry have been the same (*Dawson's The Government of Canada*, p. 196).

148. For more information on the Privy Council, see *Dawson's The Government of Canada*, Chapters 10 and 11.

149. There are two main categories of Privy Councillor: one group includes current and former Cabinet Ministers; the other includes those appointed as an honour but who have never been Cabinet Ministers. Among those in the second group have been leaders of opposition parties, Chief Justices and distinguished Canadians. Certain exceptions have been made: during the 1991 Persian Gulf War, New Democratic Party leader Audrey McLaughlin was sworn in as a Privy Councillor so that she could be given highly secret information; members of the Security Intelligence Review Committee must, by statute, be Privy Councillors, and several have been appointed solely for that reason (*Canadian Security Intelligence Service Act*, R.S.C. 1985, C-23, s. 34(1)).

150. *Forsey*, pp. 35-6. In the past, there have been Senators who were appointed to the Cabinet as Ministers of departments (for example, Robert de Cotret was Minister of Industry, Trade and Commerce in the Twenty-First Ministry) and ministers without portfolio (for example, Andrew Olson was Minister of State for Economic Development in the Twenty-Second Ministry). It is exceptional for a Minister who is head of a department to be in the Senate, and typically the only Senator in the Cabinet is the Leader of the Government in the Senate.

151. General Andrew George McNaughton was Minister of National Defence from November 2, 1944 until August 20, 1945, without a seat in either House. After failing to win a seat both in a by-election and, subsequently, a general election, he resigned. He appeared, with permission, three times on the floor of the House during the period he served as Minister (*Forsey*, p. 35). In 1975, Pierre Juneau was appointed as Minister of Communications. He subsequently contested and lost a by-election, following which he resigned from Cabinet (Privy Council Office, *A Guide to Canadian Ministries Since Confederation: July 1, 1867 to February 1, 1982*, Government of Canada, Ottawa, 1982).

departments (or ministries) although some may be given responsibility for an important policy portfolio.[152] Secretaries of State are assigned to assist Cabinet Ministers in specific areas within their portfolios.[153] They are members of the Ministry (sworn to the Privy Council) but not of Cabinet.[154] In addition, the *Parliament of Canada Act* provides for the appointment of Parliamentary Secretaries (Members who assist Cabinet Ministers but who are not members of the Ministry).[155] Finally, provision may be made for the appointment of an Acting Minister in the event a Minister is absent or incapacitated, or the office is vacant.

A Minister's tenure in office depends solely on the Prime Minister. The Prime Minister may replace or ask for a Minister's resignation at any time. The Governor General will not accept a Minister's resignation without the approval of the Prime Minister. After the Prime Minister, members of Cabinet and Secretaries of State are accorded precedence[156] or seniority according to the date they were sworn in as Privy Councillors, regardless of portfolio.

The duration of a Ministry is measured by the tenure of its Prime Minister, which is calculated from the day the Prime Minister takes the oath of office to the day he or she resigns. The resignation of a Prime Minister brings about the resignation of the Ministry as a whole.[157] A Prime Minister who resigns but is subsequently restored to office is said to form a new Ministry.[158]

Responsible Government and Ministerial Responsibility

Responsible government has long been considered an essential element of government based on the Westminster model.[159] Despite its wide acceptance as a cornerstone of the Canadian system of government, there are different meanings attached

---

152. For example, in the Twenty-Sixth Ministry, Ministers were assigned responsibility for "International Cooperation" and "Intergovernmental Affairs". In the Twenty-Fifth Ministry, Ministers were assigned responsibility for "Small Business" and "Small Communities and Rural Areas". During the Twentieth Ministry, a number of Ministers were appointed "Without Portfolio" (Privy Council Office, *A Guide to Canadian Ministries Since Confederation: July 1, 1867 to February 1, 1982*, Supply and Services Canada, Ottawa, 1982; and *Supplement to Guide to Canadian Ministries, 1980 to Date*, Library of Parliament, May 1998).

153. The position "Secretary of State" has been included in earlier Ministries, designated as Minister of State. Ministers and Secretaries of State are paid out of the Consolidated Revenue Fund in accordance with the provisions of the *Salaries Act* (R.S.C. 1985, c. S-3, ss. 2, 4, 5).

154. See Release issued by the Office of the Prime Minister, November 4, 1993.

155. R.S.C. 1985, c. P-1, ss. 46-7.

156. The order of precedence of Canadian dignitaries and Officials is set by the Governor General on the advice of the Prime Minister. The Prime Minister, in turn, is advised on this matter by the Minister of Canadian Heritage. The Ministry of Canadian Heritage is custodian of the *Table of Precedence of Canadian Dignitaries and Officials*, as well as of the *Table of Titles to Be Used in Canada*.

157. See also Chapter 2, "Parliaments and Ministries".

158. There have been 26 Ministries since 1867. See Appendix 8, "Government Ministries and Prime Ministers of Canada Since 1867".

159. In Canada, responsible government had been well established by the time of Confederation. See the section in this chapter entitled "Historical Perspective–The Years Preceding Confederation".

to the term "responsible government". In a general sense, responsible government means that a government must be responsive to its citizens, that it must operate responsibly (i.e., be well organized in developing and implementing policy) and that its Ministers must be accountable or responsible to Parliament. Whereas the first two meanings may be regarded as the ends of responsible government, the latter meaning—the accountability of Ministers—may be regarded as the device for achieving it. [160]

In terms of ministerial responsibility, Ministers have both individual and collective responsibilities to Parliament. The individual or personal responsibility of the Minister derives from a time when in practice and not just in theory the Crown governed; Ministers merely advised the Sovereign and were responsible to the Sovereign for their advice. The principle of individual ministerial responsibility holds that Ministers are accountable not only for their own actions as department heads, but also for the actions of their subordinates; individual ministerial responsibility provides the basis for accountability throughout the system. Virtually all departmental activity is carried out in the name of a Minister who, in turn, is responsible to Parliament for those acts. Ministers exercise power and are constitutionally responsible for the provision and conduct of government; Parliament holds them personally responsible for it. [161]

The principle of collective ministerial responsibility, [162] which is of a much more recent vintage, evolved when Ministers replaced the Sovereign as the decision-makers of government. Ministers are expected to take responsibility for, and defend, all Cabinet decisions. [163] The principle provides stability within the framework of ministerial government by uniting the responsibilities of the individual Ministers under the collective responsibility of the Crown. [164]

---

160. See comments of Anthony Birch in *Responsible Government*, Canadian Study of Parliament Group, Ottawa, October 1989, p. 5.

161. "Parliament used to bring Ministers to account by a semi-judicial process. The King could do no wrong in the eyes of the law ... and it was more satisfactory and expedient to attack his advisers for their evil counsel by charging them with high crimes and misdemeanours. The Commons were the accusers; the Lords the judges; the process was impeachment.... During the 18th century votes of censure against Ministers and Governments gradually replaced the cumbersome machinery of impeachment.... The process has never been abolished but it is in practice obsolete." It survives in the United States (de Smith, quoted in *Responsibility in the Constitution*, pp. 14-5).

162. Commonly referred to as "cabinet solidarity".

163. A number of Ministers have resigned over disagreements with government policy. For example: Minister of Transport Paul Hellyer resigned because he disagreed with the government's housing policy (*Debates*, April 24, 1969, p. 7893; *Journals*, April 24, 1969, p. 939); Eric Kierans, Minister of Communications and Postmaster General, resigned in disagreement over the government's economic priorities (*Debates*, April 29, 1971, p. 5339; *Journals*, April 29, 1971, p. 515, Sessional Paper No. 283-1/190B); and Minister of the Environment Lucien Bouchard resigned in disagreement over matters concerning the Meech Lake Accord on the Constitution (*Debates*, May 22, 1990, pp. 11662-4).

164. Ministers and Secretaries of State are bound by their Privy Council oath of secrecy not to reveal the nature of Cabinet proceedings.

Political Parties

Political parties[165] have been variously described as groups which seek to elect governmental office holders under a given label;[166] "as an organization of people who share a common political ideology and who together establish a constitution, elect a leader and other officers and act toward a common goal";[167] as bodies which compete "to obtain political power in legislative and executive institutions and the subsequent political debate and enactment of public policy in those institutions";[168] and as organizations designed to gain control of the levers of government in order to realize their policies or programs.[169]

Political parties are not mentioned in the *Constitution Act*. However, they are defined in other selected statutes for certain administrative purposes. For example, political parties may seek registration under the *Canada Elections Act*[170] which, among other things allows them to issue official receipts entitling contributors to a tax credit under the federal income tax system;[171] to have their candidates' affiliation reflected on the ballot in an election; to incur election expenses; and to claim their share of free air time from network broadcasters during a general election campaign.[172] Certain other provisions of the Act require a party to have representation in the House of Commons as one of the criteria used when deciding whether or not a party retains its official registered status at the time of a general election.[173]

The *Parliament of Canada Act* and the *By-laws* of the Board of Internal Economy (the administrative governing body of the House of Commons) make a distinction between political parties which are "recognized" in the House of Commons and those with less than 12 sitting Members. With regard to financial benefits, the *Parliament of Canada Act* provides additional allowances to the Leader, the Whip and the House Leader of a party that has a recognized membership of 12 or more persons in the House of Commons.[174] The Board of Internal Economy also provides financial

---

165. Originally, the Sovereign along with the prominent nobles selected to advise the Crown were effectively both the Government and the "party" permanently in power. It was generally the case that certain factions opposed the Crown; the strength of that opposition depended in large part on the personality of the Monarch and varied from reign to reign. The first recognizable political parties emerged as a result of the Civil Wars in England when, in 1679, the Cavaliers and the Roundheads became the Tories and the Whigs, respectively (see *Wilding and Laundy*, pp. 545-6).

166. Leon D. Epstein, quoted in Van Loon and Whittington, *The Canadian Political System*, p. 305.

167. Elections Canada Backgrounder, "Registration of Federal Political Parties", p. 1.

168. *McMenemy*, pp. 214-5.

169. *Jackson and Jackson*, p. 434.

170. There is no limitation on the formation of political parties; however, parties must satisfy certain criteria in order to be registered under the *Canada Elections Act* (R.S.C. 1985, c. E-2, ss. 25-32).

171. Revenue Canada Information Circular No. 75-2R4.

172. Elections Canada Backgrounder, "Registration of Federal Political Parties", pp. 4-5.

173. *Canada Elections Act*, R.S.C. 1985, c. E-2, s. 28. See also Elections Canada Backgrounder, "Registration of Federal Political Parties".

174. R.S.C. 1985, c. P-1, s. 62(*b*), (*d*) and (*f*). This was first included in 1963 in the precursor to the *Parliament of Canada Act*, namely the *Senate and House of Commons Act*.

support to the caucus research units of "recognized parties", again defined as parties with a membership of at least 12 Members.[175] With regard to procedure, recognized parties are also extended certain considerations,[176] though the definition of what constitutes a "recognized party" is not as clear in this case as it is with financial benefits. Since the Standing Orders have never provided a definition for recognized parties, Speakers have relied on practice or a decision by the House.[177] However, in recent practice, a procedural interpretation of the definition "recognized party" has come to mean any party with 12 or more Members in the House. The number 12 has assumed an authenticity of its own.

Parliamentary Caucuses

Throughout Canada's history, most parliamentarians have been members of political parties. In fact, Canada's system of responsible government is predicated on the ability of the governing party (usually the party with the most seats in the House of Commons) to win votes in the legislature. Members of the House of Commons belonging to the same party, together with their counterparts in the Senate, are collectively referred to as that party's parliamentary caucus. The government retains the confidence of the House mainly through the support of its caucus.

Parliamentary caucuses meet regularly, typically on Wednesday morning when Parliament is in session, and at other times when the party's parliamentary leadership deems it necessary.[178] Although each caucus operates differently, most limit attendance to parliamentarians.

Because they are held *in camera,* caucus meetings allow Members to express their views and opinions freely on any matter which concerns them.[179] Policy positions are elaborated, along with, in the case of the government party, the government's legislative

---

175. See Board of Internal Economy *By-law* 302, ss. 2 and 3(2). In 1990, a question of privilege was raised relating to a request refused by the Board for funding to a political party with fewer than 12 Members. In his reply, Speaker Fraser stated that the decision of the Board stood unless the House itself wished to overrule the decision (*Debates*, December 13, 1990, pp. 16703-7).

176. For example, the order of participation in debate and Question Period (see Chapter 13, "Rules of Order and Decorum" and Chapter 11, "Questions"); the allocation of opposition Supply days (see Chapter 18, "Financial Procedures"); and the deferral of recorded divisions by Whips (see Standing Order 45(7) and Chapter 12, "The Process of Debate").

177. In 1963, Speaker Macnaughton cautioned that the recognition of parties in the Chamber must ultimately be resolved by the House itself (*Journals*, September 30, 1963, pp. 385-8). On February 18, 1966, Speaker Lamoureux was asked to pronounce on the right of a party with fewer than 12 Members to respond to a Statement by a Minister. In his ruling, he concluded that until the House defined more precisely who could respond, the Chair would be guided by practice (*Journals*, February 18, 1966, pp. 158-60). For further information on Minister's Statements, see Chapter 10, "The Daily Program". In 1979 and 1994, Speakers Jerome and Parent also made some remarks on the issue of the recognition of parties in the House (*Debates*, October 10, 1979, pp. 49-51; October 11, 1979, p. 69; June 16, 1994, pp. 5437-40).

178. On Wednesday, because of caucus meetings, the House does not sit until 2:00 p.m. (see Chapter 9, "Sittings of the House").

179. In 1973, a question of privilege was raised in the House concerning the discovery of a bugging device in a caucus meeting room (*Debates*, October 17, 1973, pp. 6942-4).

proposals. Caucus provides a forum in which Members can debate their policy differences among themselves without compromising party unity.

The Whip enforces "party discipline". This party official ensures that Members discharge their caucus responsibilities (e.g., attendance at committee meetings and in the Chamber, and voting with the party).[180] Whips manage committee membership, allocate office space and choose who will represent the party at various special activities or functions. They are the critical communication link between the party leadership and the backbenchers.[181]

In addition to a Whip, each party has a House Leader[182] who is responsible, in conjunction with the other House Leaders, for co-ordinating the day-to-day business of the House. The House Leaders of all the recognized parties meet regularly to consult one another on the sequence and transaction of parliamentary business. This practice has evolved over time to ensure that the business of the House is conducted in an organized manner. Should the House Leaders not agree on a schedule, the government retains the right, subject to the rules of the House, to decide unilaterally the order of its business.[183]

The Opposition

Functionally, the House is divided into three groups: the Ministry and its Parliamentary Secretaries, Members who support the government, and Members who oppose the government.[184] The role of the opposition is key to our system of parliamentary democracy. Prime Minister Wilfrid Laurier put it succinctly when he said: "… it is indeed essential for the country that the shades of opinion which are represented on both sides of this House should be placed as far as possible on a footing of equality and that we should have a strong opposition to voice the views of those who do not

---

180. See *McMenemy*, p. 214.

181. Backbenchers are Members of the House of Commons who are neither Ministers, Parliamentary Secretaries or one of their party's House officials.

182. The Government House Leader is a Minister, officially titled Leader of the Government in the House of Commons. From 1867 until 1944, Prime Ministers usually organized the business of the House by themselves, their contacts being the Whips of the other parties. In October 1944, Prime Minister Mackenzie King chose to delegate those duties and openly recognized the position of Government House Leader in July 1946. In 1968, it became a full-time position. Until 1997, all Government House Leaders had held at least one other portfolio concurrently; between 1963 and 1990, the Government House Leader typically was also President of the Privy Council (Library of Parliament, *Leaders of the Government in the House of Commons*, Compilation No. 78, November 21, 1997). The position of Opposition House Leader evolved gradually in the 1950s and has been remunerated since 1974 (*An Act to amend the Senate and House of Commons Act, the Salaries Act and the Parliamentary Secretaries Act,* S.C. 1974-75-76, c. 44, s. 3). The House Leaders of parties with 12 or more Members have been remunerated since 1981 *(An Act to amend the Senate and House of Commons Act, the Salaries Act, the Parliamentary Secretaries Act and the Members of Parliament Retiring Allowances Act,* S.C. 1980-81, c. 77, s. 3).

183. See also Chapter 10, "The Daily Program".

184. *Stewart*, p. 17. There are often occasions where opposition Members or parties will vote the same way as the government on a particular issue.

think with the majority."[185] Members in opposition may belong to registered parties or they may be independent of any party affiliation.[186]

By convention, the opposition party with the largest number of seats in the House is designated as the Official Opposition (and referred to as "Her Majesty's Opposition"[187]), although nowhere is this set down in any Canadian rule or statute.[188] The Official Opposition is pre-eminent among the other recognized parties in opposition. On all government bills and motions, a representative of the Official Opposition is usually the first to be recognized in debate following the lead speaker from the government. Debating time in the Chamber is typically allocated among the remaining recognized parties roughly in proportion to the number of seats each holds in the House.[189] When parliamentary committees present reports in the House which are accompanied by supplementary or dissenting opinions or recommendations, a committee member from the Official Opposition, representing those who supported the opinions or recommendations, may rise and offer a succinct explanation.[190]

Should an equality of seats among the largest opposition parties occur, the Speaker may be called upon to decide which party should be designated as the Official Opposition. In 1996, when a tie occurred between the two largest opposition parties during the course of a Parliament, the Speaker ruled that incumbency was the determining factor and that the *status quo* should be maintained.[191]

---

185. *Debates*, July 17, 1905, col. 9729-30.

186. Members of registered parties with fewer than 12 sitting members are entitled to have their party affiliation noted, along with their name, on the television screen and in official House records. They are also permitted to be seated together in the Chamber (see Speakers' rulings, *Debates*, December 13, 1990, pp. 16705-6; June 16, 1994, pp. 5437-40). There have been instances where parties which did not have 12 sitting members claimed the status of a recognized party. Speakers have been clear in rulings that it is up to the House itself to decide such matters (see Speakers' rulings, *Journals*, September 30, 1963, pp. 385-8; February 18, 1966, pp. 158-60; and *Debates*, October 11, 1979, p. 69; November 6, 1979, p. 1009; June 16, 1994, p. 5439).

187. See *Wilding and Laundy*, pp. 509-10. Also referred to as "Her Majesty's Loyal Opposition" to emphasize the notion that an opposition is loyal to the Crown (see Gerald Schmitz, "The Opposition in a Parliamentary System", Library of Parliament Backgrounder, December 1988).

188. The only exception to this in the history of the House of Commons came in 1922 when the Progressive party won the second highest number of seats but declined to assume the role of official opposition (see also Appendix 9, "Leaders of the Official Opposition in the House of Commons Since 1873"; Appendix 10, "Party Leaders in the House of Commons Since 1867"; and Appendix 11, "General Election Results Since 1867").

189. See also Chapter 13, "Rules of Order and Decorum".

190. Standing Order 35(2).

191. See ruling of Speaker Parent, *Debates*, February 27, 1996, pp. 16-20. In the United Kingdom, the Speaker has statutory authority to determine who shall be designated as Leader of the Opposition in the House. See the *Ministerial and Other Salaries Act*, 1975, U.K., s. 2(2). See also ruling of Speaker Amerongen, *Alberta Hansard*, March 11, 1983, pp. 9-11, and November 6, 1984, p. 1381; the ruling of Speaker Dysart, *Journal of Debates*, Legislative Assembly, Province of New Brunswick, December 16, 1994, pp. 3749-53; and the ruling of Speaker Bruce, *Votes and Proceedings of the Yukon Legislative Assembly*, December 9, 1996, pp. 15-9.

If the leader of the party designated as the Official Opposition holds a seat as a Member of the House, he or she automatically becomes Leader of the Opposition.[192] If that party leader does not have a seat in the House, the caucus of the Official Opposition may designate another of its members to act as Opposition Leader.[193]

The office of Leader of the Opposition has been formally recognized since 1905, when Parliament voted to give the incumbent an additional salary allowance, equal to that provided to Cabinet Ministers.[194] The Opposition Leader is accorded certain rights and privileges, including the right to a seat on the Board of Internal Economy,[195] the right to a seat in the front row of the Chamber directly across the floor from the Prime Minister, and the right to unlimited time to participate in debates.[196] Traditionally, the Speaker recognizes the Leader of the Opposition as the first to ask a question during the daily Question Period, should the latter rise to seek the floor.[197] The rules also empower the Opposition Leader to extend a committee's consideration of the Main Estimates of a specific department or agency.[198]

The leaders of the other recognized opposition parties usually also sit in the front row of the Chamber[199] and are the first member of their party to be given the floor should they rise to ask a question during Question Period.[200] Some statutes require that the government consult with the Leader of the Opposition, as well as other party leaders, when certain actions are contemplated or prior to making certain sensitive appointments.[201] The Standing Orders of the House provide an opportunity for recognized opposition parties to respond to Ministers' statements,[202] to propose motions on allotted or opposition days[203] and to participate in the leadership of the standing committees.[204]

---

192. Party leaders who did not hold a seat and who did not automatically become Leader of the Opposition include, among others: Robert Stanfield in 1967, Brian Mulroney in 1983 and Jean Chrétien in 1990, all of whom sought and won a seat in a by-election before assuming that office (see also Appendix 9, "Leaders of the Official Opposition in the House of Commons Since 1873").

193. See, for example, references to the Hon. Eric Nielsen and to the Hon. Herb Gray in Appendix 9, "Leaders of the Official Opposition in the House of Commons Since 1873".

194. *An Act to amend the Act respecting the Senate and House of Commons*, S.C. 1905, c. 43, s. 2, now the *Parliament of Canada Act*, R.S.C. 1985, c. P-1, s. 62(a). Canada was the first of the Commonwealth parliaments to fund the office of Leader of the Opposition.

195. *Parliament of Canada Act*, R.S.C. 1985, c. P-1, s. 50(2).

196. Standing Orders 43(1), 50(2), 74(1), 84(7), and 101(3).

197. See also Chapter 11, "Questions".

198. Standing Order 81(4)(*a*). The Main Estimates are the government's projected annual spending plan (see also Chapter 18, "Financial Procedures").

199. For some time during the Thirty-Fifth Parliament (1994-97), the Leader of the Reform Party, Preston Manning, chose not to sit in the front row.

200. See also Chapter 11, "Questions".

201. See, for example, *Canadian Security Intelligence Service Act,* R.S.C. 1985, c. 23, s. 34(1); *International Centre for Human Rights and Democratic Development Act,* S.C. 1988, c. 64, s. 7(2); *Referendum Act*, S.C. 1992, c. 30, s. 5(2).

202. Standing Order 33(1).

203. Standing Order 81(13).

204. Standing Order 106(2). Typically, a Member from the Official Opposition chairs the Standing Committee on Public Accounts and the Standing Joint Committee for the Scrutiny of Regulations (see also Chapter 20, "Committees").

2

Parliaments and Ministries

In the United States, president and Congress can be locked in fruitless combat for years on end. In Canada, the government and the House of Commons cannot be at odds for more than a few weeks at a time. If they differ on any matter of importance, then, promptly, there is either a new government or a new House of Commons.

EUGENE A. FORSEY
(*How Canadians Govern Themselves*, 3rd ed., p. 26)

The relationship between the House of Commons and the executive can affect both the lifespan of a Ministry and the duration of a Parliament. The end of a Ministry always has an impact on the proceedings of the House of Commons; the consequences may range from the simple interruption of a sitting to the dissolution of a Parliament. It is from that perspective that any procedural events leading to or brought about by the end of a Ministry are examined, whether the end is triggered by death, by resignation following a defeat in a general election, by resignation due to the loss of confidence in the House of Commons, by resignation for other reasons, or by dismissal.

Majority Supporting the Government

Governments must be supported by the majority of Members in the House of Commons whether or not they are majority governments or minority governments. A majority government is supported by the party or the coalition of parties holding the majority of the seats in the House of Commons. (Canada has never been governed by a coalition of parties.) A minority government is supported by the party or the coalition of parties holding a minority of the seats in the House of Commons. Within each Parliament, party standings can and do fluctuate because of deaths, resignations, by-elections, floor crossings or other changes in the status of individual Members. As a result, the government's ability to retain the support of the majority of Members can be increased or diminished.

All questions arising in the House are to be decided by a majority vote of those Members present.[1] Even the rules by which the House governs its own proceedings are adopted by simple majority vote. It is therefore obvious that the government's ability to command the support of a majority of the House allows it to exercise control over the management of the business of the House and, by extension, of its committees. The government's powers in this regard are counterbalanced by its responsibility to the House to account for its actions.

The government's role in the management of House business is established in several Standing Orders, which refer either to the government or a Minister as the initiator of certain types of proceedings.[2] Likewise, there are many Standing Orders that recognize the House's role in holding the government to account for its actions.[3] Parliamentary procedure must balance the government's power to manage the business of the House, against the opposition's responsibility to hold the government accountable. The crucial test of the government's power comes in votes of confidence, for in Canada's parliamentary democracy, a government must enjoy the confidence of the House.

The Confidence Convention

An essential feature of parliamentary government is that the Prime Minister and the Cabinet are responsible to, or must answer to, the House of Commons as a body for

---

1. *Constitution Act, 1867,* R.S.C. 1985, Appendix II, No. 5, s. 49. See also Chapter 12, "The Process of Debate".

2. For example, the bulk of House time is allocated to government business, which is called in such sequence as the government determines (Standing Orders 30 and 40). Furthermore, to name but a few examples, it is the government that requests a recall of the House when it stands adjourned (Standing Order 28); that moves the extension of sitting hours in June (Standing Order 27); that causes a special *Order Paper* to be issued (Standing Order 55); that initiates time allocation (Standing Order 78) and closure (Standing Order 57); that proposes the referral to committees of the government's Estimates (Standing Order 81); that gives notice of and designates Orders of the Day for the consideration of Ways and Means motions (Standing Order 83); and that initiates debate on the Standing Orders at the beginning of each Parliament (Standing Order 51).

3. Examples may be found in the rules governing Supply (Standing Order 81); questions (Standing Orders 37, 38 and 39); petitions (Standing Order 36); and the tabling of documents (Standing Order 32).

their actions and must enjoy the support and the confidence of a majority of the Members of that Chamber to remain in office. This is commonly referred to as the confidence convention. This complex constitutional subject, a matter of tradition that is not written into any statute or Standing Order of the House, is thoroughly reviewed in other authorities more properly concerned with the subject.[4]

Simply stated, the convention provides that if the government is defeated in the House on a confidence question, then the government is expected to resign or seek the dissolution of Parliament in order for a general election to be held. This relationship between the executive and the House of Commons can ultimately decide the duration of each Parliament and of each Ministry. The confidence convention applies whether a government is formed by the party or the coalition of parties holding the majority of the seats in the House of Commons, or by one or more parties holding a minority of seats. Naturally, it is more likely that the government will fail to retain the confidence of the House when the government party or parties are in a minority situation.

What constitutes a question of confidence in the government varies with the circumstances. Confidence is not a matter of parliamentary procedure, nor is it something on which the Speaker can be asked to rule.[5] It is generally acknowledged, however, that confidence motions may be:[6]

- explicitly worded motions which state, in express terms, that the House has, or has not, confidence in the government;

- motions expressly declared by the government to be questions of confidence;

- implicit motions of confidence, that is, motions traditionally deemed to be questions of confidence, such as motions for the granting of Supply (although not necessarily an individual item of Supply[7]), motions concerning the budgetary policy of the government[8] and motions respecting the Address in Reply to the Speech from the Throne.

---

4. See in particular Eugene A. Forsey and G.C. Eglington, "The Question of Confidence in Responsible Government", study prepared for the Special Committee on the Reform of the House of Commons (Ottawa: 1985). Also of interest are the First and Third Reports of the Special Committee on the Reform of the House of Commons (the McGrath Committee), respectively presented on December 20, 1984 (*Journals*, p. 211), and June 18, 1985 (*Journals*, p. 839).

5. See, for example, Speaker Lamoureux's rulings, *Journals*, May 4, 1970, pp. 742-3, and March 6, 1973, pp. 166-7. See also *Debates*, October 20, 1981, p. 11974, and March 4, 1988, p. 13400.

6. See Philip Norton, "Government Defeats in the House of Commons: The British Experience", *Canadian Parliamentary Review*, Winter 1985-86, pp. 6-9.

7. See, for example, *Journals*, March 26, 1973, pp. 212-3. Certain opposition motions have been adopted on days allotted for the Business of Supply which were not framed as confidence matters; see, for example, *Journals*, February 12, 1992, pp. 1010-2, and March 8, 1994, pp. 220-3.

8. See statement of Prime Minister Clark, *Debates*, December 13, 1979, p. 2362.

CONFIDENCE AND THE STANDING ORDERS

When the Standing Orders respecting Supply were amended in 1968, it was specified that, in each of the three Supply periods, the opposition could designate not more than two of the motions proposed on allotted days as motions of non-confidence in the government.[9] This was the first time the notion of confidence found expression in the Standing Orders. This rule was modified provisionally in March 1975 to remove the no-confidence qualification; the motions would still be brought to a vote but the vote would not automatically be considered an expression of confidence in the government.[10] The provisional Standing Orders lapsed at the beginning of the following session and the term "no-confidence" found its way back into the 1977 version of the Standing Orders. No further changes were made until June 1985, when the Standing Orders were again modified to remove the no-confidence provision with regard to Supply.[11]

Meanwhile, in 1984, a recommendation was made that a change be made in the manner of electing a Speaker.[12] This proposal found favour and a variant of it was adopted by the House in 1985.[13] One of these new rules still provides that the election of a Speaker shall not be considered to be a question of confidence in the government.[14]

Duration of a Parliament and a Ministry

The duration of a Parliament—the period of time between elections during which the institution of Parliament exercises its powers—is calculated from the date set for the return of the writs following a general election to its dissolution by the Governor General.[15] At the same time, the *Constitution Act* provides that, subject to dissolution, five years is the maximum lifespan of the House of Commons between general

---

9. *Journals*, December 20, 1968, pp. 554, 557 (1968 Standing Order 58(9)).

10. See the Second Report of the Standing Committee on Procedure and Organization, presented on March 14, 1975 (*Journals*, p. 372-6), and concurred in on March 24, 1975 (*Journals*, p. 399). The House adopted a Supply motion for the first time under this rule on February 12, 1976 (*Journals*, p. 1016). See also the comments of the President of the Privy Council, Mitchell Sharp, *Debates*, February 12, 1976, p. 10902.

11. *Journals*, June 27, 1985, pp. 910-9. This change had been proposed in the First Report of the Special Committee on the Reform of the House of Commons (*Journals*, December 20, 1984, p. 211), and the government had expressed support for the proposal (*Debates*, April 18, 1985, pp. 3868-9).

12. See the First Report of the Special Committee on the Reform of the House of Commons, presented on December 20, 1984 (*Journals*, p. 211), and the government response to the First Report, tabled on April 18, 1985 (*Journals*, p. 486).

13. *Journals*, June 27, 1985, pp. 910-9. These are now Standing Orders 2, 3, 4, 5 and 6.

14. Standing Order 6.

15. For a detailed description of the practicalities of convocation and dissolution of Parliament, see Chapter 8, "The Parliamentary Cycle".

elections, calculated from the date fixed for the return of the writs, and that there must be a sitting of Parliament at least once every 12 months.[16]

The Ministry, which exercises the practical functions of government, has no fixed maximum duration. Its duration is measured by the tenure of its Prime Minister and is calculated from the day the Prime Minister takes the oath of office to the day the Prime Minister dies, resigns or is dismissed.

These two time lines—the parliamentary one, which has a maximum duration, and the prime ministerial one, which is open-ended—do not always coincide perfectly.

DURATION OF PARLIAMENTS

About one third of the Parliaments since 1867 have lasted between four and five years, about another third have lasted between three and four years and a final third, less than three years (see Figure 2.1)[17]. Three Parliaments (i.e., the Seventh (1891-96), Seventeenth (1930-35) and Nineteenth (1940-45)) have gone near the limit of the five-year maximum constitutional lifespan, within days of when the House of Commons would have expired by effluxion of time. One Parliament, the Twelfth (1911-17), was extended.[18] Four Parliaments (i.e., the Fifteenth (1925-26), Twenty-Third (1957-58), Twenty-Fifth (1962-63) and Thirty-First (1979)) have lasted less than one year.

DURATION OF MINISTRIES

Since Confederation, there have been 26 Ministries, although only 20 individuals have served as Prime Minister. A Prime Minister whose party is re-elected in successive general elections simply continues in office as the head of the same government. For example, Sir Wilfrid Laurier, who became Prime Minister in 1896, continued in office through the general elections of 1900, 1904 and 1908 before resigning after his party was defeated in the 1911 general election. On the other hand, a Prime Minister who resigns from office following a party defeat in a general election, but who is later returned to power, forms a new Ministry. For example, Pierre E. Trudeau, who first became Prime Minister in 1968 forming the Twentieth Ministry, resigned from office in 1979, only to be re-elected with a majority in 1980, thus again

---

16. *Constitution Act, 1867*, R.S.C. 1985, Appendix II, No. 5, s. 50; *Constitution Act, 1982*, R.S.C. 1985, Appendix II, No. 44, ss. 4(1), 5. The question of the duration of Parliament was thoroughly discussed in the talks leading to Confederation. In the end, it was decided to follow the New Zealand example of a five-year maximum. (See comments of Sir John A. Macdonald in *Confederation Debates*, 1865, p. 39.)

17. For the actual dates for the return of the writs and of dissolution for each Parliament, see Appendix 12, "Parliaments Since 1867 and Number of Sitting Days".

18. This was accomplished by way of a constitutional amendment (*British North America Act, 1916,* R.S.C. 1985, Appendix II, No. 24). Since 1949, the Constitution has provided for an extension if no more than one third of the Members oppose it (*British North America Act (No. 2), 1949,* R.S.C. 1985, Appendix II, No. 33; see also *Constitution Act, 1982,* s. 4(2)).

Figure 2.1   *Duration of Parliaments*

PARLIAMENT	YEARS	DURATION		
		years	months	days
1	1867-1872	4	9	8
2	1872-1874	1	3	30
3	1874-1878	4	5	26
4	1878-1882	3	5	27
5	1882-1887	4	5	8
6	1887-1891	3	8	27
7	1891-1896	4	11	29
8	1896-1900	4	2	26
9	1900-1904	3	9	24
10	1904-1908	3	9	2
11	1908-1911	2	7	26
12*	1911-1917	5	11	29
13	1918-1921	3	7	7
14	1922-1925	3	7	22
15	1925-1926		6	25
16	1926-1930	3	6	28
17	1930-1935	4	11	27
18	1935-1940	4	2	16
19	1940-1945	4	11	30
20	1945-1949	3	8	21
21	1949-1953	3	9	19
22	1953-1957	3	6	4
23	1957-1958		5	24
24	1958-1962	3	11	20
25	1962-1963		6	19
26	1963-1965	2	4	
27	1965-1968	2	4	14
28	1968-1972	4	1	7
29	1972-1974	1	4	9
30	1974-1979	4	7	26
31	1979		6	3
32	1980-1984	4	3	29
33	1984-1988	4		7
34	1988-1993	4	8	19
35	1993-1997	3	5	12
36	1997-			

* Extended by constitutional amendment

becoming Prime Minister, forming the Twenty-Second Ministry. There can, as well, be several Ministries within the same Parliament. This was the case for the Seventh Parliament. Prime Minister Sir John A. Macdonald died in office not long after being re-elected in 1891. From the time of his death to the 1896 general election, no less than four more administrations took office. Figure 2.2 illustrates the sometimes ephemeral, sometimes lengthy duration of Ministries.[19]

Figure 2.2   *Duration of Ministries*

MINISTRY	PRIME MINISTER	YEARS	DURATION		
			years	months	days
1	Macdonald	1867-1873	5	4	4
2	Mackenzie	1873-1878	4	11	30
3	Macdonald	1878-1891	12	7	20
4*	Abbott	1891-1892	1	5	8
5	Thompson	1892-1894	2		7
6*	Bowell	1894-1896	1	4	6
7	Tupper	1896		2	7
8	Laurier	1896-1911	15	2	25
9	Borden	1911-1917	6		2
10	Borden**	1917-1920	2	6	28
11	Meighen	1920-1921	1	5	19
12	King	1921-1926	4	5	30
13	Meighen	1926		2	27
14	King	1926-1930	3	10	13
15	Bennett	1930-1935	5	2	16
16	King	1935-1948	13		23
17	St-Laurent	1948-1957	8	7	6
18	Diefenbaker	1957-1963	5	10	1
19	Pearson	1963-1968	4	11	29
20	Trudeau	1968-1979	11	1	14
21	Clark	1979-1980		8	26
22	Trudeau	1980-1984	4	3	27
23	Turner	1984		2	18
24	Mulroney	1984-1993	8	9	8
25	Campbell	1993		4	10
26	Chrétien	1993-			

* Senator
** Unionist government

19. For actual dates of terms of office for each Ministry, see Appendix 8, "Government Ministries and Prime Ministers of Canada Since 1867".

The End of a Ministry

The end of a Ministry is triggered by the death, resignation or dismissal of the Prime Minister.[20] It does not necessarily entail the end of a Parliament. While, on one hand, the operation of the confidence convention can lead and has led to early dissolution of a Parliament,[21] there are, on the other hand, examples of multiple Ministries during the same Parliament.[22] The procedural consequences of the end of a Ministry vary depending on how the Ministry ends. The procedural effect of dissolution is of course well known: sittings cease immediately and all proceedings in Parliament are quashed. A new Parliament, once summoned, begins with a clean slate.[23]

Death of a Prime Minister

The death of a Prime Minister holds few procedural implications. If death occurs during a session of Parliament while the House is sitting, tributes may be made in the House or the House may adjourn for an extended period.[24] Since Confederation, only two Prime Ministers have died in office: Sir John A. Macdonald, in 1891, during a session, and Sir John Thompson, in 1894, while Parliament was prorogued.[25]

Resignation of a Prime Minister

Resignation may be prompted by a defeat in a general election, by the operation of the confidence convention alone, by the operation of the confidence convention followed by a defeat in a general election, or by other reasons, including the Prime Minister's desire to retire from public life.

---

20. Failure to be re-elected as a Member of the House does not result in the Prime Minister being obliged to resign automatically. Prime Ministers Macdonald and King both suffered personal defeat but not party defeat and were subsequently elected in by-elections. (See *The Canadian Directory of Parliament 1867-1967*, edited by J.K. Johnson, Ottawa: Public Archives of Canada, 1968, pp. 305-6, 399.)

21. See, for example, *Journals*, December 13, 1979, pp. 345-7; December 14, 1979, p. 350.

22. See, for example, the Seventh, Twenty-Seventh, and Thirty-Fourth Parliaments.

23. For a full description of the procedural effects of prorogation and dissolution, see Chapter 8, "The Parliamentary Cycle".

24. *Journals*, June 8, 1891, p. 208. See also the Speaker's statement to the House, *Debates*, June 8, 1891, col. 883. In keeping with ancient practice, when the House stands adjourned during a session, the Speaker, in robes, can attend the funeral procession or the state funeral accompanied by the Mace, as authorized by an express resolution of the House, or by reliance on parliamentary usage. The Mace may not be used for such a purpose when Parliament is prorogued. See *Bourinot*, 4th ed., p. 176, footnotes c) and e). The organization of state occasions, such as state funerals, is the responsibility of the Department of Canadian Heritage.

25. For descriptions of the circumstances of these two deaths, see Donald Creighton, *John A. Macdonald, The Old Chieftan*, Toronto: MacMillan Co. of Canada, 1955, pp. 564-78 and P.B. Waite, *The Man From Halifax, Sir John Thompson, Prime Minister*, Toronto: University of Toronto Press, 1985, pp. 415-31.

• Defeat in a General Election

If Parliament is dissolved when the Ministry resigns, there are of course no procedural implications. This is typically the case for majority governments which, at a moment of their own choosing, seek a dissolution, are defeated at the polls and subsequently resign in the days that follow.[26] It falls to the new government to meet the new House.

An election may be triggered by the Prime Minister of a minority government, in the same manner as a Prime Minister of a majority government. For example, throughout the Sixteenth Parliament (1926-30), Prime Minister Mackenzie King headed a minority government but was able to retain the support of the third party in the House and thus govern for almost four years. He then sought and obtained a dissolution in the usual manner, was defeated at the polls and resigned.

In an unusual and controversial case, following the general election of 1925, the Mackenzie King government lost its majority status when the Liberals received fewer seats than the former Official Opposition party, the Conservatives.[27] Nevertheless, it decided to meet the House to test its confidence, and did so successfully until June 1926. For further details of this case, see below.

• Operation of the Confidence Convention

The role of procedure in the operation of the confidence convention revolves around the decision-making process in the House of Commons. When the government is defeated on a vote on a question of confidence in the House, the Prime Minister must either resign[28] or seek a dissolution. The Speaker does not decide what constitutes a matter of confidence. Successive Speakers have stated that it is not for the Chair to interfere to prevent debate, or a vote, on a question relating to the issue of confidence, unless the motion being put forward is clearly defective or irregular on procedural grounds.[29] Naturally, when numbers are close, the procedural implications of pairing and the manner in which a vote is recorded become critically important. The rules and practices governing these areas of parliamentary procedure are discussed in Chapter 12, "The Process of Debate".

---

26. See, for example, the Turner (1984) and Campbell (1993) Ministries.

27. See Appendix 11, "General Election Results Since 1867". A similar case occurred in Ontario in 1985 when the Progressive Conservative government of Frank Miller won the largest number of seats, but resigned in favour of the second-place Liberals who, with the support of the New Democrats, were able to govern with the confidence of the Legislature. The numbers were PC: 52; Lib.: 48; NDP: 25 (*Canadian Parliamentary Guide*, 1986, edited by Pierre G. Normandin, Ottawa, pp. 979, 1066-7).

28. *Forsey and Eglington* list a large number of pre- and post-Confederation examples of provincial government resignations without dissolution (pp. 253-8).

29. See, for example, Speaker Lamoureux's ruling, *Journals*, March 6, 1973, pp. 166-7. See also, *Debates*, October 20, 1981, p. 11974.

Four governments have been defeated in a vote in the House on a clear, uncontested question of confidence. In 1926, the three-day old Meighen minority government lost a vote (96-95) on what amounted to a motion of censure of the government.[30] In 1963, the Diefenbaker minority government was defeated by a wide margin (142-111) on a Supply motion.[31] In 1974, the Trudeau minority government and, in 1979, the Clark minority government both lost a vote on a Budget motion sub-amendment, by votes of 137-123 and 139-133 respectively.[32] All four Prime Ministers sought and obtained a dissolution following defeat in the House. Of the four governments, the Meighen, Diefenbaker and Clark governments were subsequently defeated in general elections and, in each case, the Prime Minister resigned without meeting the new House. The Trudeau government was returned with a majority and met the new House.

The government of Mackenzie King in 1925-26 faced a more complex set of circumstances and ultimately resigned without a dissolution. The case has been cited by some as one of a resignation due to the operation of the confidence convention,[33] although Mackenzie King himself stated that he resigned because he did not obtain the dissolution he had sought.[34] In any case, the events leading to the government's resignation illustrate that it is not always clear what constitutes a question of confidence.

A general election was held on October 29, 1925. Prior to the election, Prime Minister Mackenzie King held a bare majority of 118 of 235 seats. (The number of seats he held had fluctuated throughout the Fourteenth Parliament, giving him sometimes a majority, sometimes a minority.)[35] The 1925 election returned 101 Liberals (supporters of the King government), 116 Conservatives, 24 Progressives, 2 Labour and 2 Independents.[36] Parliament met on January 7, 1926. The King government did not resign but instead chose to meet the House, despite having received fewer seats than the Conservative Party. It retained the support of the House until June 1926 when the official opposition moved an amendment to a motion to concur in a committee report that amounted to a censure of the government; at that time, the King government was not able to command the support of the House on a series of

---

30. *Journals*, July 1, 1926, pp. 508-9.

31. *Journals*, February 5, 1963, pp. 474-5.

32. *Journals*, May 8, 1974, pp. 175-6, and December 13, 1979, pp. 345-7.

33. *Forsey and Eglington*, pp. 253, 261-3.

34. *Journals*, June 28, 1926, p. 483.

35. See Appendix 11, "General Election Results Since 1867", footnote 8.

36. See Appendix 11, "General Election Results Since 1867".

procedural motions meant to set aside the censure amendment.[37] Before the censure amendment was ever put to a vote, Prime Minister King announced his resignation to the House on the afternoon of Monday, June 28, 1926. He stated that, having sought and been refused a dissolution, he was resigning.[38] After the announcement, the House adjourned. The next morning, Arthur Meighen, the Leader of the Opposition, was asked by the Governor General to form a new government. When the House convened later the same day, the government and the official opposition had changed sides in the House and acting House Leader Sir Henry Drayton made a statement announcing changes to the Ministry.[39] The House then resumed the transaction of its business. Two days later, the Meighen government lost a vote on a motion of censure.[40]

Not all government defeats on a vote are automatically considered matters of confidence.[41] On February 19, 1968, a motion for the third reading of a tax bill was defeated by a vote of 82-84.[42] Prime Minister Pearson did not agree that this defeat constituted an expression of non-confidence in the government, as some were arguing. The government introduced a motion "That this House does not regard its vote on February 19th in connection with third reading of Bill C-193, which had carried in all previous stages, as a vote of non-confidence in the Government". This motion was carried on February 28 by a vote of 138-119.[43] From February 20 to February 28, all House business was concerned with the resolution of this matter, and in fact the House transacted no business at all from February 20 to 22.[44]

Similarly, on December 20, 1983, a clause of a bill amending the Income Tax Act and other acts was defeated in a Committee of the Whole by a vote of 28-67.[45] The Official Opposition claimed that this constituted a defeat on a question of confidence and demanded that the government resign or seek a dissolution. The

---

37. *Journals*, June 18, 1926, pp. 444-9; June 22, 1926, pp. 461-2; June 23, 1926, p. 465; June 25, 1926, pp. 475-81.

38. *Journals*, June 28, 1926, p. 483.

39. *Journals*, June 29, 1926, pp. 485-6.

40. *Journals*, July 1, 1926, pp. 508-9.

41. In 1973, Prime Minister Trudeau stated that his minority government would not consider every defeat on a vote as a matter of confidence (*Debates*, January 8, 1973, p. 61). The government did, in fact, lose several votes in the 1973-74 period (see, for example, *Journals*, March 26, 1973, pp. 212-3).

42. *Journals*, pp. 702-3.

43. *Journals*, February 28, 1968, pp. 719-21.

44. See *Journals*, February 20, 1968, to February 28, 1968, pp. 705-21.

45. *Debates*, December 20, 1983, p. 352.

government disagreed.[46] As in other, similar circumstances, this was not a procedural matter upon which the Chair could rule.[47]

• Resignation Due to Other Causes

Several Prime Ministers have resigned for reasons other than those referred to above. Most have done so out of a stated desire to retire from public life.[48] There are, however, a few cases where the departure was prompted by other reasons.

In one case, the government of Prime Minister Sir John A. Macdonald (Second Parliament, 1873), embroiled in a scandal, resigned rather than face near-certain defeat on a no-confidence motion.[49] According to an eyewitness, on November 5, 1873, "… Sir John got up and briefly announced that the Government had resigned. The announcement was received in perfect silence. The Opposition, directly [after] it was over, crossed the House to their new desks."[50] The Leader of the Opposition, Alexander Mackenzie, formed a new government and Parliament was prorogued on November 7, 1873. On January 2, 1874, he sought and obtained a dissolution without having met the House with a legislative program.

In 1896, the Prime Minister, Senator Sir Mackenzie Bowell, faced a serious Cabinet revolt (seven Ministers resigned) and ultimately resigned himself on April 27 of that year, three days after he had been granted a dissolution.[51] He was succeeded by Sir Charles Tupper, who in turn resigned after his defeat in the election.[52]

Dismissal of a Prime Minister

Since Confederation, no Prime Minister has been dismissed.[53] The circumstances that might give rise to dismissal have nevertheless been the subject of considerable academic debate.

Ministerial Crisis

If the House is sitting when the composition of the Ministry is being changed in circumstances of ministerial crisis, it is normal for the House to adjourn from day to

---

46. See *Debates*, December 20, 1983, from p. 352, especially pp. 354-6.

47. *Debates*, December 20, 1983, pp. 367-8.

48. See, for example, *Debates*, June 16, 1993, pp. 20890-4.

49. See *Debates*, November 5, 1873, p. 781, and *Forsey and Eglington*, p. 258. See also *Journals*, November 4 to 7, 1873, pp. 139-42.

50. Marchioness of Dufferin and Ava, *My Canadian Journal, 1872-78*, New York: D. Appleton and Company, 1891, p. 133. See also *Debates*, November 6 and 7, 1873, pp. 783, 785.

51. *"We Twa", Reminiscences of Lord and Lady Aberdeen*, Volume II, London: W. Collins Sons & Co., 1925, pp. 32-4.

52. See *"We Twa"*, pp. 35-7, for a description of the circumstances from the Governor General's point of view.

53. For an Australian example, see *House of Representatives Practice*, 3rd ed., p. 87.

day (unless it decides otherwise) until such time as the changes are complete.[54] In such cases, the House normally transacts only routine business on the days it meets and questions may be asked concerning the progress being made in reconstituting the Ministry.[55] When a new Ministry is to be formed following the death, resignation or dismissal of the Prime Minister, it is likewise appropriate for the House to adjourn from day to day (again, unless it decides otherwise),[56] but no questions may be asked as to the progress being made, there being no Ministry.[57] However, party leaders may make statements.[58] When the ministerial crisis is resolved, it is usual for a leading Member of the government caucus to make a statement explaining the ministerial changes to the House.[59]

54. In early 1896, seven Ministers (half the Cabinet) resigned and it took several days to reconstruct the Cabinet (see *Debates*, January 7 to 15, 1896, cols. 5-71). The death or dismissal of several Ministers could result in similar circumstances for the government, and thus a similar adjournment of the proceedings in the House, should it be sitting at the time.

55. See, for example, *Journals*, January 7 to 15, 1896, pp. 7-13, and *Debates*, January 7 to 15, 1896, cols. 5-71. See also *Bourinot*, 2nd ed., pp. 795-6.

56. See, for example, *Debates*, November 5 to 7, 1873, pp. 781-7, and June 8, 1891, cols. 888-91. See also *Journals*, June 28, 1926, p. 483.

57. See *Debates*, November 5 to 7, 1873, pp. 781-7, and June 28, 1926, pp. 5096-7.

58. See Speaker's ruling, *Debates*, June 28, 1926, p. 5096. See also *Bourinot*, 4th ed., p. 355.

59. See, for example, *Debates*, November 7, 1873, pp. 785-6 (following resignation of Macdonald); June 16, 1891, cols. 891-2 (following death of Macdonald); January 15, 1896, cols. 69-71 (following resolution of Bowell Cabinet crisis); and *Journals*, June 29, 1926, pp. 485-6 (following resignation of Mackenzie King).

3

Privileges and Immunities

Privilege is that which sets hon. members apart from other citizens giving them rights which the public do not possess. . . . In my view, parliamentary privilege does not go much beyond the right of free speech in the House of Commons and the right of a member to discharge his duties in the House as a member of the House of Commons.

SPEAKER LUCIEN LAMOUREUX
(*Debates,* April 29, 1971, p. 5338)

T he practices and precedents of the House of Commons of Canada regarding parliamentary privilege stretch far back into colonial times. At an early stage, the young assemblies of the colonies, modelling themselves on Westminster, claimed the privileges of the British House, though without statutory authority. At Confederation, the privileges of the British House were transferred in the *Constitution Act, 1867*[1] to the Canadian Parliament, and for many years the Canadian House continued to look to the experience of the British House for guidance in matters of parliamentary privilege.[2]

The origins of the privileges enjoyed by the House of Commons in the United Kingdom were a product of a direct and real threat from the Crown and the House of Lords. As the threat subsided, the thrust of the history of

---

1. R.S.C. 1985, Appendix II, No. 5, s. 18.

2. In fact, this was reflected in the wording of Standing Order 1, which until 1986 stated with minor variations over time: "In all cases not provided for hereafter or by sessional or other orders, the usages and customs of the House of Commons of the United Kingdom of Great Britain and Northern Ireland as in force at the time shall be followed so far as they may be applicable to this House."

privilege has been towards defining those rights and immunities in their narrowest sense, reflecting the reality that all privileges enjoyed by the House and its Members ultimately derive from the electorate. Fortunately, the privileges of the Canadian House of Commons were inherited without the need to overcome physical threats and challenges. They enable the institution of Parliament to flourish and individual Members to fulfil the functions for which they were elected.

In modern parlance, the term "privilege" usually conveys the idea of a "privileged class", with a person or group granted special rights or immunities beyond the common advantages of others.[3] This is not, however, the meaning of privilege in the parliamentary context. "Parliamentary privilege" refers more appropriately to the rights and immunities that are deemed necessary for the House of Commons, as an institution, and its Members, as representatives of the electorate, to fulfil their functions. It also refers to the powers possessed by the House to protect itself, its Members, and its procedures from undue interference, so that it can effectively carry out its principal functions which are to inquire, to debate, and to legislate.[4] In that sense, parliamentary privilege can be viewed as special advantages which Parliament and its Members need to function unimpeded.

This chapter will briefly summarize the evolution of privilege in the United Kingdom and in Canada, discuss the rights and immunities of the House and its Members, and describe the procedures by which matters of privilege are raised and dealt with in the Canadian House. For an in-depth treatment of the subject, the reader is referred to two principal sources. The first is *Erskine May's Treatise on The Law, Privileges, Proceedings and Usage of Parliament,*[5] which lays out the practice and precedents of the British House of Commons. The second is *Parliamentary Privilege in Canada* by Joseph Maingot,[6] which focusses on the history and workings of privilege in Canada.

Parliamentary Privilege: A Definition

The classic definition of parliamentary privilege is found in *Erskine May's Treatise on the Law, Privileges, Proceedings and Usage of Parliament:*

> *Parliamentary privilege is the sum of the peculiar rights enjoyed by each House collectively . . . and by Members of each House individually, without which they could not discharge their functions, and which exceed those*

---

3. *Black's Law Dictionary,* 6th ed., 1990, p. 1197, defines privilege as, "A particular and peculiar benefit or advantage enjoyed by a person, company, or class, beyond the common advantages of other citizens. An exceptional or extraordinary power or exemption. A peculiar right, advantage, exemption, power, franchise, or immunity held by a person or class, not generally possessed by others."

4. *Odgers,* 8th ed., pp. 27-8.

5. *May,* 22nd ed., edited by Sir Donald Limon and W.R. McKay, London: Butterworths, 1997.

6. *Maingot,* 2nd ed., Ottawa: House of Commons and McGill-Queen's University Press, 1997.

possessed by other bodies or individuals. Thus privilege, though part of the law of the land, is to a certain extent an exemption from the general law.[7]

These "peculiar rights" can be divided into two categories: those extended to Members individually, and those extended to the House collectively. Each grouping can be broken down into specific categories. For example, the rights and immunities accorded to Members individually are generally categorized under the following headings:

- freedom of speech;
- freedom from arrest in civil actions;
- exemption from jury duty;
- exemption from attendance as a witness.

The rights and powers of the House as a collectivity may be categorized as follows:

- the power to discipline, that is, the right to punish (by incarceration) persons guilty of breaches of privilege or contempts, and the power to expel Members guilty of disgraceful conduct;
- the regulation of its own internal affairs;
- the authority to maintain the attendance and service of its Members;
- the right to institute inquiries and to call witnesses and demand papers;
- the right to administer oaths to witnesses;
- the right to publish papers containing defamatory material.

These two groupings represent all the privileges extended to Members of Parliament and the House of Commons collectively. Each of these privileges will be examined in greater detail and illustrated with relevant cases later in this chapter.

The House has the authority to invoke privilege where its ability has been obstructed in the execution of its functions or where Members have been obstructed in the performance of their duties. It is only within this context that privilege can be considered an exemption from the general law. Members are not outside or above the law which governs all citizens of Canada. The privileges of the Commons are designed to safeguard the rights of each and every elector.[8] For example, the privilege of freedom of speech is secured to Members not for their personal benefit, but to enable them to discharge their functions of representing their constituents without

---

7. *May*, 22nd ed., p. 65. For other definitions of privilege, see *Maingot*, 2nd ed., pp. 12-3.

8. This point was forcefully made by Sir Barnett Cocks, Clerk of the House of Commons of the United Kingdom, in a memorandum to the Select Committee on Parliamentary Privilege. United Kingdom, House of Commons, Select Committee on Parliamentary Privilege, *Minutes of Evidence*, November 23, 1966, p. 1.

fear of civil or criminal prosecution for what might be said in the House and committees. When a constituency has returned a candidate, it is the electors' right that
this chosen representative should be protected from any kind of improper pressure,
and particularly from crude violence.[9]

> *The distinctive mark of a privilege is its ancillary character. The privileges
> of Parliament are rights, which are "absolutely necessary for the due exe-
> cution of its powers". They are enjoyed by individual Members because the
> House cannot perform its functions without unimpeded use of the services
> of its Members; and by each House for the protection of its Members and
> the vindication of its own authority and dignity.[10]*

Privilege essentially belongs to the House as a whole; individual Members can only
claim privilege insofar as any denial of their rights, or threat made to them, would
impede the functioning of the House. In addition, individual Members cannot claim
privilege or immunity on matters that are unrelated to their functions in the House.[11]

Any conduct which offends the authority or dignity of the House, even though
no breach of any specific privilege may have been committed, is referred to as a contempt of the House. Contempt may be an act or an omission; it does not have to actually obstruct or impede the House or a Member, it merely has to have the tendency
to produce such results.

What Parliament has considered as "absolutely necessary" privileges has varied
over the centuries. Nevertheless, certain basic principles relating to privilege have
become established. Neither House individually can extend its privileges, though
either House can, formally by resolution, decide not to claim or apply privileges it
has hitherto claimed.[12] No one House of Parliament has a right to claim for itself new
privileges; new privileges can only be created or old privileges extended by Act of

9. United Kingdom, House of Commons, Select Committee on Parliamentary Privilege, *Minutes of Evidence*,
November 23, 1966, p. 1.

10. *May*, 20th ed., pp. 70-1.

11. See *Griffith and Ryle*, pp. 85-6.

12. With the possible exception of the relinquishment of its power to try controverted elections, the Canadian
House of Commons has never formally renounced any of the basic rights and immunities it claims for itself
and its Members. See *Bourinot*, 4th ed., pp. 122-7; *Maingot*, 2nd ed., pp. 187-90; *Dominion Controverted
Elections Act, 1874*, S.C. 1874, c. 10. See also Chapter 4, "The House of Commons and Its Members". In
British practice, the authors of *May* note that since the eighteenth century a number of privileges have been
surrendered or modified (*May*, 22nd ed., pp. 81-2).

Parliament.[13] Either House can apply its rights to new circumstances, thereby in some cases creating new instances of contempt.[14] And finally, each House can individually adjudicate and punish breaches of its privileges.

Historical Perspective

Parliamentary privileges were first claimed centuries ago when the English House of Commons was struggling to establish a distinct role for itself within Parliament. In the earliest days, Parliament functioned more as a court than as a legislature, and the early claims to some of these privileges were originally made in this context.[15] In any case, these privileges were found to be necessary to protect the House and its Members, not from the people, but from the power and interference of the King and the House of Lords. Over time, as the House of Commons gained stature and power as a deliberative assembly, these privileges were established as part of the statute and common law of the land.

The House of Commons in Canada has not had to challenge the Crown, its executive, or the Upper House in the same manner as the British House of Commons. The privileges of the British House of Commons were formally transferred to the Canadian Parliament at the time of Confederation through the *Constitution Act, 1867* and were put into force by the enactment of a statute now known as the *Parliament of Canada Act*.[16] Nonetheless, the privileges enjoyed by the House and its Members are of the utmost importance; they are in fact vital to the proper

---

13. *Maingot*, 2nd ed., p. 20. An example of the extension of privilege was the adoption by the British Parliament of the *Parliamentary Papers Act, 1840* and the enactment by the Canadian Parliament of virtually the same provisions in 1868. The British legislation followed the famous *Stockdale v. Hansard* case of 1837. The Act of 1840 provided that the publication of reports, papers, votes or proceedings of either House of Parliament by order was essential to the functions and duties of Parliament and thus privileged. The same provisions were adopted in Canada in 1868 as *An Act to define the privileges, immunities and powers of the Senate and House of Commons, and to give summary protection to persons employed in the publication of Parliamentary Papers* (S.C. 1868, c. 23). This Act is now sections 7, 8 and 9 of the *Parliament of Canada Act* (R.S.C., 1985, c. P-1) and corresponds exactly to sections 1, 2 and 3 of the *Parliamentary Papers Act, 1840*. For a full discussion of the case and its consequences, see *Maingot*, 2nd ed., pp. 63-75, and *May*, 22nd ed., pp. 86-8.

14. The advent of the broadcasting of the proceedings of the House illustrates such an application. In the Donahoe case referred to below, the Supreme Court affirmed that the Nova Scotia House of Assembly, in exercising its rights to control its internal proceedings and to exclude strangers from the House and its precinct, could exclude cameras from its galleries.

15. Charles H. McIlwain, *The High Court of Parliament and its Supremacy*, New Haven: Yale University Press, 1910, reprinted 1962; and Carl Wittke, *The History of English Parliamentary Privilege*, Ohio State University, 1921.

16. *Constitution Act, 1867*, R.S.C. 1985, Appendix II, No. 5, s. 18; *Parliament of Canada Act*, R.S.C. 1985, c. P-1, ss. 4-5.

functioning of Parliament. This is as true now as it was centuries ago when the English House of Commons first fought to secure these privileges and rights.

PRIVILEGE IN THE UNITED KINGDOM

Centuries ago, the British House of Commons began its struggle to win its basic rights and immunities from the King.[17] The earliest cases go back to the fourteenth and fifteenth centuries when several Members and Speakers were imprisoned by the King who took offence at their conduct in Parliament, despite the claims of the House that these arrests were contrary to its liberties. In the Tudor and early Stuart periods, though Parliament was sometimes unable to resist the stronger will of the Sovereign, the conviction continued to be expressed that Parliament, including the House of Commons, was entitled to certain rights. Sir Thomas More, when elected Speaker of the House of Commons in 1523, was among the first Speakers to petition the King to seek the recognition of certain privileges for the House.[18] By the end of the sixteenth century, the Speaker's petition to the King had become a fixed practice.[19]

Despite these early petitions of the Speaker, the King was not above informing the Commons that their privileges, particularly freedom of speech, existed by his sufferance. James I did this in 1621. In protest, the Commons countered "that every Member of the House of Commons hath and of right ought to have freedom of speech . . . and . . . like freedom from all impeachment, imprisonment and molestation (other than by censure of the House itself) for or concerning any speaking, reasoning or declaring of any matter or matters touching the Parliament or parliament business".[20] In rebuke, James ordered that the *Journals* of the House be

---

17. See F.W. Maitland, *The Constitutional History of England*, Cambridge: Cambridge University Press, 1908; and A.F. Pollard, *The Evolution of Parliament*, 2nd ed., London: Longmans Green, 1926.

18. It has been argued that Sir Thomas More did not consider his petition a petition of right, as free speech was not yet a formal privilege. "Parliament is the king's court; he may be displeased with what members say, and as discipline is his to maintain, he may punish the too bold or too rash for their speeches . . . More wants liberty of speech, whereas his predecessors wished to avoid punishment, thereby tacitly renouncing the liberty which More claims." John Neale, "The Commons Privilege of Free Speech in Parliament", *Historical Studies of the English Parliament*, Cambridge: Cambridge University Press, 1970, Vol. 2, pp. 157-8.

19. This ceremony is also part of Canadian practice. When the newly elected Speaker is presented to the Governor General prior to the Speech from the Throne, the Speaker claims on behalf of the House " . . . all their undoubted rights and privileges, especially that they may have freedom of speech in their debates, access to Your Excellency's person at all reasonable times, and that their proceedings may receive from Your Excellency the most favourable construction". See, for example, *Senate Debates*, September 23, 1997, p. 3. See also Chapter 8, "The Parliamentary Cycle".

20. *May*, 22nd ed., p. 70.

sent to him; he tore out the offending page of protest and then summarily dissolved Parliament.[21]

Nor was privilege able to prevent the detention or arrest of Members at the order of the Crown. On several occasions in the early seventeenth century, Members were imprisoned without trial while the House was not sitting or after the dissolution of Parliament. In 1626, Charles I arrested two Members of the House while it was in session and, in 1629, judgements were brought against several Members for sedition. These outrages by the Crown were denounced after the Civil War and in 1667 both Houses agreed that the judgement against the arrested Members had been illegal and contrary to the privileges of Parliament.[22]

In 1689, the implementation of the *Bill of Rights* confirmed once and for all the basic privilege of Parliament, freedom of speech. Article 9 states "that the freedom of speech and debates or proceedings in Parliament ought not to be impeached or questioned in any court or place out of Parliament".[23] Free speech in the House was now finally established and protected from interference either by the Crown or the courts.

In the late seventeenth century and the first half of the eighteenth century, some claims of the House as to what constituted privilege went too far. The privilege of freedom from arrest in civil matters was sometimes applied not only to Members themselves, but also to their servants. In addition, Members sought to extend their privilege from hindrance or molestation to their property, claiming a breach of privilege in instances of trespassing and poaching. Such practices were eventually curtailed by statute because they clearly became a serious obstruction to the ordinary course of justice.[24] Thus, privilege came to be recognized as only that which was absolutely necessary for the House to function effectively and for the Members to carry out their responsibilities as Members.

In the midst of their occasional excesses, the House of Lords and the House of Commons both acknowledged that a balance had to be maintained between the need to protect the essential privileges of Parliament and, at the same time, to avoid any risk that would undermine the interests of the nation. In this connection, it was agreed in 1704 that neither House of Parliament had any power, by any vote or declaration, to create for themselves any new privileges not warranted by the known laws and customs of Parliament.[25] Since then, neither House alone has ever sought to lay claim to any new privilege beyond those petitioned for by Speakers or already established by precedent and law.[26]

---

21. Godfrey Davies, *The Early Stuarts 1603-1660*, Oxford: Clarendon Press, 1938, pp. 26-7.

22. *May*, 22nd ed., pp. 70-1.

23. *May*, 22nd ed., p. 72.

24. *Maitland*, pp. 322-3; *May*, 22nd ed., p. 75.

25. *May*, 22nd ed., p. 81.

26. *May*, 22nd ed., p. 81.

The nineteenth century witnessed numerous cases of privilege, which helped to determine the bounds between the rights of Parliament and the responsibility of the courts. [27] Perhaps the most famous of the court cases was *Stockdale versus Hansard*. In 1836, a publisher, John Joseph Stockdale, sued Hansard, the printer for the House of Commons, for libel on account of a report published by order of the House. [28] Despite numerous resolutions of the House protesting the court proceedings and the committal to prison of Stockdale by the House, the courts refused to acknowledge the claims of the House. "Lord Denman denied . . . that the *lex parliamenti* [the Law of Parliament] was a separate law, unknown to the judges of the common law courts. Either House considered individually was only a part of the High Court of Parliament, and neither could bring an issue within its exclusive jurisdiction simply by declaring it to be a matter of privilege. Any other proposition was 'abhorrent to the first principles of the constitution.'" [29] In the end, the situation was partially resolved by the enactment of the *Parliamentary Papers Act 1840,* which gave statutory protection to papers published by order of either House. [30]

Modern Practice in the United Kingdom

While the late eighteenth and nineteenth centuries saw, for the first time, the systematic study of the history of privilege and contempt, [31] the culmination of these efforts to understand and elucidate better the constitutional history of Parliament was achieved in 1946 with the publication of the fourteenth edition of *May*. This edition presented a thorough and elaborate examination of parliamentary privilege based on an exhaustive examination of the *Journals* and the principles of the law of Parliament. [32] It also cited instances of misconduct of strangers or witnesses, disobedience

---

27. *May,* 22nd ed., pp. 160-2.

28. *May,* 22nd ed., pp. 161-3. For the importance of this case in Canada, see *Maingot,* 2nd ed., pp. 63-74.

29. *May,* 22nd ed., p. 162.

30. The results of this case have been applied to Canada through the *Parliament of Canada Act.* The right of the courts to take notice of the privilege of Parliament is declared in section 5: "The privileges, immunities and powers held, enjoyed and exercised in accordance with section 4 are part of the general and public law of Canada and it is not necessary to plead them but they shall, in all courts in Canada, and by and before all judges, be taken notice of judicially" (*Parliament of Canada Act*, R.S.C. 1985, c. P-1, s. 5). At the same time, sections 7 through 9 grant statutory protection to any person who has printed a publication by or under the authority of the Senate or the House of Commons.

31. See John Hatsell, *Precedents of Proceedings in the House of Commons*, 4 vols., London, 1776-96, reprinted 1971; S.A. Ferrall, *An Exposition of the Law of Parliament, as It Relates to the Power and Privileges of the Commons' House*, London: Sweet, 1837; and Thomas Erskine May, *A Treatise upon the Law, Privileges, Proceedings and Usage of Parliament*, 1st ed., London: 1844, reprinted 1971, now in its 22nd edition.

32. This edition concluded that any "act or omission which obstructs or impedes either House of Parliament in the performance of its functions, or which obstructs or impedes any member or officer of such House in the discharge of his duty, or which has a tendency, directly or indirectly, to produce such results may be treated as a contempt even though there is no precedent of the offence" (*May,* 14th ed., p. 108).

to the rules or orders of the House or committees, attempts at intimidation or bribery and molestation of Members or other Officers of the House as cases that more properly involve a contempt of Parliament rather than an explicit breach of an established privilege.

The British House of Commons now takes a more narrowly defined view of privilege than was formerly the case. The change became apparent in 1967 when the Select Committee on Parliamentary Privilege issued a report on the entire subject of privilege. In its report, the Committee noted that the law, practice and procedure relating to privilege at Westminster at that time had been the subject of much criticism.[33]

The general thrust of the Committee's view of privilege was evident from a recommendation to forsake the term "privilege" for "rights and immunities". In justifying this proposal, the Committee wrote:

> *Your Committee have reached the conclusion that the word "privilege" has in modern times acquired a meaning wholly different from its traditional Parliamentary connotation. In consequence its use could convey to the public generally the false impression that Members are, and desire to be, a "privileged class". It is out of keeping with modern ideas of Parliament as a place of work and of the status of its Members as citizens who have been elected to do within that place of work their duty as representatives of those who elected them. Your Committee cannot too strongly emphasise the fundamental principle that "privileges" are not the prerogative of Members in their personal capacities. Insofar as the House claims and Members enjoy*

---

33. United Kingdom, House of Commons, Select Committee on Parliamentary Privilege, 1967, Report, (reprinted 1971), p. vi, para. 9. The report laid down six major criticisms from the public of the way privilege was used. These were:

(i) Members are too sensitive to criticism and invoke too readily the penal jurisdiction of the House; they do so not merely in respect of matters which are too trivial to be worthy of that jurisdiction, but also on occasions when other remedies (e.g., in the courts or by way of complaint to the Press Council) are available to them as citizens;

(ii) the procedure for invoking the penal jurisdiction encourages its use for the purposes of publicity, is inequitable to persons whose conduct is under scrutiny and fails to accord with the ordinary principles of natural justice;

(iii) the scope of Parliament's penal jurisdiction is too wide, too uncertain and too dependent upon precedent; the Press and the public are wrongly inhibited from legitimate criticism of Parliamentary institutions and of Members' conduct by fear that the penal jurisdiction may be invoked against them;

(iv) there is too great uncertainty about the defences which may legitimately be raised by those who are subjected to the penal jurisdiction; in particular it is a matter of doubt whether a person who has made truthful criticisms should be allowed to testify to their truth; this should be an undoubted right;

(v) it is contrary to principle that Parliament should be "both prosecutor and judge"; its penal powers should be transferred to some other tribunal;

(vi) the rules which govern the reporting of debates in the House and Standing Committee are obsolete and disregarded; those which govern the reporting of proceedings in Select Committee are obsolete, anomalous, uncertain and contrary to the public interest. (Report, pp. vi-vii, para.10.)

> *those rights and immunities which are grouped under the general descrip-*
> *tion of "privileges", they are claimed and enjoyed by the House in its cor-*
> *porate capacity and by its Members on behalf of the citizens whom they*
> *represent. Your Committee therefore strongly favour the discontinuance of*
> *the use of the term "privilege" in its traditional Parliamentary sense. They*
> *believe that if the basic concept of "privileges" or "privilege" is abolished,*
> *it will be easier to understand and to concentrate upon the provision of*
> *the essential protection which is required by the House, its Members and*
> *Officers.*[34]

The Select Committee accepted the need for the radical reform of the law, practice and procedure relating to privilege and especially contempt, agreeing that they
required to be simplified and clarified and to be brought into harmony with contemporary thought. The Committee went further to express the conviction that the recognized rights and immunities of the House "will and must be enforced by the courts
as part of the law of the land".[35] However, with respect to contempts which can
extend far beyond the boundaries of those recognized rights and immunities, the
Committee proposed that, as a general rule, the House should exercise its authority
"... as sparingly as possible and only when it is satisfied that to do so is essential
in order to provide reasonable protection for the House, its Members or its Officers,
from such improper obstruction or attempt at or threat of obstruction as is causing,
or is liable to cause, substantial interference with the performance of their respective
functions".[36]

The general thrust and conclusions of the 1967 report were reiterated in a subsequent report of the Committee of Privileges in 1977. This Committee again
reviewed the meaning of privilege and contempts and again made recommendations to limit their application to cases of clear necessity. Another recommendation
concerned a new procedure for raising complaints in the British House. The practice
was for matters of privilege to be raised at the earliest opportunity and for the
Speaker to be satisfied that a *prima facie* (on the first impression or at first glance)
case had been established. Failing either of these two requirements, the alleged
question of privilege forfeited its claim to priority of consideration before all other
matters in the House.[37] Under the new scheme proposed by the Committee, Members seeking to raise a privilege complaint would give written notice to the Speaker
as soon as was practicable after the Member had become aware of the offending

---

34. Report, p. vii, para. 12. It is interesting to note that the use of the term "privilege" remains an issue in the
British Parliament. In the parliamentary session of 1997-98, a Joint Committee on Parliamentary Privilege
was struck to review parliamentary privilege. One of the matters being investigated was whether or not there
existed a more modern and better phrase to replace "parliamentary privilege". See United Kingdom, House
of Commons, *Debates*, July 30, 1997, col. 423.

35. Report, pp. xiii-xiv, para. 38.

36. Report, p. viii, para. 15.

37. *May*, 14th ed., pp. 356-7. This practice has become the method by which the Canadian House of Commons
treats claims to breaches of privilege following the incorporation of this procedure into the fourth edition of
Beauchesne's Parliamentary Rules and Forms in 1958 (pp. 94-6).

incident. If, however, after consideration, the Speaker did not find that the complaint warranted precedence in the House, the Member would be informed by letter and any attempt to raise the matter of privilege in the House would be out of order. If the Speaker did decide in favour of the complaint, the decision was made known to the House and, on the following day, a motion to refer the matter to committee could be considered.[38]

This recommendation, among others, was implemented. The new procedure had a dramatic effect on the number of claims to privilege raised in the British House.[39] Because a question of privilege first must be cleared through the Speaker privately before it can be brought to the attention of the House at all, there has been a marked decrease in the claims of breaches of privileges. "The use of the word 'privilege' to gain the Speaker's ear and to secure the chance to raise a political issue unrelated to real privilege . . . is now almost unknown."[40] There are now far fewer trivial cases referred to the Committee of Privileges. In particular, since 1978, there have been no cases of privilege involving what is often referred to as "constructive contempts", that is, rude or derogatory reflections on Members. In this sense, the new privilege practice has helped to cure a problem first suggested in the 1967 report that Members of the British House of Commons were too sensitive in their reaction to press criticism. In addition, the total number of privilege matters of all kinds referred to committee has been significantly reduced. Finally, the House usually accepts without debate most of the reports now presented by the Committee of Privileges. Only when the Committee finds that there has been a serious breach of privilege or contempt requiring further action does the House consider the report.[41]

PRIVILEGE IN CANADA

Privilege in the Pre-Confederation British North American Colonies

From the establishment in 1758 of the first legislative assembly in Nova Scotia, the common law accorded the necessary powers to the legislature and its Members to perform their legislative work. "Members had freedom of speech in debate and the right of regulating and ordering their proceedings, and were protected from being arrested in connection with civil cases, because the legislature had first call on their services and attendance."[42] As to the power of an Assembly in the colonies to punish

---

38. United Kingdom, House of Commons, Select Committee of Privileges, 1977, Third Report, pp. vi-vii, para. 9. For details on the way privilege complaints are raised and dealt with in the British House, see *May*, 22nd ed., pp. 144-52, and *Griffith and Ryle*, pp. 95-8.

39. *Griffith and Ryle* (pp. 98-104) surveys the results of the new procedure in its first 10 years in effect. See also *May*, 22nd ed., p. 82.

40. See *Griffith and Ryle*, p. 98.

41. See *Griffith and Ryle*, pp. 97-8.

42. *Maingot*, 2nd ed., p. 3. See also p. 198.

and more especially imprison for contempt, the situation was not at all clear.[43] In effect, the rights enjoyed by the Assemblies in the pre-Confederation period were quite limited.[44] However, as early as 1758, the House of Assembly of Nova Scotia had an individual arrested and briefly confined because of threats made against a Member of the Assembly.[45]

In Upper and Lower Canada, the *Constitutional Act, 1791,* adopted by the British Parliament, was silent on the privileges of the Legislatures, although by 1801 the Speaker of the Legislative Assembly in Upper Canada claimed "by the name of the Assembly, the freedom of speech and generally all the like privileges and liberties as are enjoyed by the Commons of Great Britain our Mother Country".[46] Although it had no statutory authority, the Assembly of Upper Canada proceeded to fight for and assert many of the same privileges, such as freedom from arrest while sitting and freedom from jury duty, claimed by the British Commons. The Assembly also claimed the power to send for and question witnesses and to punish any individual who refused to appear or answer questions, using its power of imprisonment to ensure obedience of its orders. Although challenged on occasion, the Assembly was successful in enforcing its privileges, "which though not recognized *de jure,* were at least recognized *de facto*".[47] In the period prior to responsible government, the Assembly in Upper Canada guarded its reputation by punishing libels against it in the newspapers and also fought for the right to initiate money bills, that is, bills for appropriations and taxation.[48] In general, the Assembly of Upper Canada was satisfied that it could discharge its functions with the privileges it had.[49]

In the same period, the Assembly of Lower Canada also asserted both individual and corporate privileges—freedom from arrest and freedom from the obligation to appear in court with respect to civil suits brought against Members, and the right of the Assembly to punish for contempt, no matter the offender.[50] The Assembly was not afraid to put forward its claims of privilege against the Crown. In 1820, it blocked the conduct of business at the opening of a new Parliament because of a dispute over the return of election writs and again in 1835 over comments made by the Governor about the privileges of the Assembly.[51]

---

43. *Maingot*, 2nd ed., p. 3, and in particular note 8.
44. *Maingot*, 2nd ed., p. 3.
45. *Maingot*, 2nd ed., p. 198.
46. *O'Brien*, p.109.
47. *O'Brien*, p. 110.
48. *O'Brien*, p. 111. See also Chapter 18, "Financial Procedures".
49. *O'Brien*, pp. 112-3.
50. *O'Brien*, pp. 191-2.
51. *O'Brien*, pp. 195-6.

With the *Union Act, 1840* which created the Province of Canada out of Upper and Lower Canada, and especially following the achievement of responsible government, issues of privilege were less frequent or serious. This can be attributed to the fact that responsible government acknowledged the supremacy of the Assembly. The Assembly no longer felt threatened by outside bodies and thus was less sensitive to criticism. Members were less likely to be upset when their rights were unintentionally interfered with, and most infractions of privilege were committed by inadvertence.[52] "With respect to individual claims, the Assembly became more careful not to use privilege to gain rights for its members over and above the rights belonging to all."[53]

As had been the case in the old colonial assemblies, the power to commit or imprison for contempt claimed by the Assembly of the Province of Canada remained an issue. In 1842, it was held "that colonial legislatures had no power to commit for contempt outside the assembly, and in 1866 it was held that they had no power to commit for contempt even when committed in the assembly."[54]

Privilege Since Confederation

As has already been stated, the privileges of the British House of Commons were transferred to Canada in the *Constitution Act, 1867*. Section 18 of the Act was quite explicit in limiting the privileges that can be claimed in Canada to those of the British Parliament. It read:

> *The Privileges, Immunities, and Powers to be held, enjoyed, and exercised by the Senate and by the House of Commons and by the Members thereof respectively shall be such as are from Time to Time defined by Act of the Parliament of Canada, but so that the same shall never exceed those at the passing of this Act held, enjoyed, and exercised by the Commons House of Parliament of the United Kingdom of Great Britain and Ireland and by the Members thereof.*[55]

---

52. *O'Brien*, pp. 303-4, 377.

53. *O'Brien*, p. 379.

54. *Maingot*, 2nd ed., p. 3.

55. *Constitution Act, 1867*, R.S.C. 1985, Appendix II, No. 5, s. 18. The original section was repealed and substituted by the *Parliament of Canada Act*, 1875, 38-39 Vict., c. 38 (U.K.) (R.S.C. 1985, Appendix II, No. 13):

    The privileges, immunities, and powers to be held, enjoyed, and exercised by the Senate and by the House of Commons, and by the Members thereof respectively, shall be such as are from time to time defined by Act of the Parliament of Canada, but so that any Act of the Parliament of Canada defining such privileges, immunities, and powers shall not confer any privileges, immunities, or powers exceeding those at the passing of such Act held, enjoyed, and exercised by the Commons House of Parliament of the United Kingdom of Great Britain and Ireland, and by the Members thereof.

    See also *Bourinot*, 1st ed., pp. 187-8.

The privileges, immunities and powers of the House are also embodied in sections 4 and 5 of the *Parliament of Canada Act*.[56]

The manner in which questions of privilege were raised following Confederation was vastly different from today's procedure. Dozens of cases between 1867 and 1913 followed the same, simple course. A Member would rise, explain the matter of privilege and conclude with a motion calling on the House to take some action— usually that someone be called to the Bar or that the matter be referred to the Standing Committee on Privileges and Elections for study and report. At that point, without any intervention on the part of the Speaker, debate would begin on the motion, amendments might be moved and, finally, the House would come to a decision on the matter.[57] The House would then take whatever further action was required by the motion. Perhaps because of the immediate recognition given to Members rising on "questions of privilege", it was also common throughout this time for Members to take the floor ostensibly to raise such a question, but really to make personal explanations. Members used the claim of a breach of privilege as a ready means to be recognized by the Speaker and to gain the floor in order to state a complaint or grievance of whatever kind.[58] Here, too, they met with little interference from Chair occupants.[59] From 1913 to 1958, while the number of "questions of privilege" blossomed for such purposes as the recognition of school groups in the gallery, congratulatory messages, complaints, grievances and a plethora of procedural matters, in addition to the continued "personal explanations",[60] the number of legitimate matters of privilege dealt with the House declined dramatically.[61]

Modern practice in matters of privilege first took root following the publication of the fourth edition of Beauchesne's *Parliamentary Rules and Forms* in 1958.

---

56. R.S.C. 1985, c. P-1. Sections 4 and 5 read as follows:

    4. The Senate and the House of Commons, respectively, and the members thereof hold, enjoy and exercise

       (a) such and the like privileges, immunities and powers as, at the time of the passing of the *Constitution Act, 1867*, were held, enjoyed and exercised by the Commons House of Parliament of the United Kingdom and by the members thereof, in so far as is consistent with that Act; and

       (b) such privileges, immunities and powers as are defined by Act of the Parliament of Canada, not exceeding those, at the time of the passing of the Act, held, enjoyed and exercised by the Commons House of Parliament of the United Kingdom and by the members thereof.

    5. The privileges, immunities and powers held, enjoyed and exercised in accordance with section 4 are part of the general and public law of Canada and it is not necessary to plead them but they shall, in all courts in Canada, and by and before all judges, be taken notice of judicially.

57. For a good example, see *Debates*, February 28, 1884, pp. 542-66. In two rare cases, the Speaker decided the matters raised were not urgent enough to be accorded precedence as matters of privilege (*Debates*, March 21, 1892, cols. 287-9; April 6, 1892, cols. 1032-5).

58. *Beauchesne*, 3rd ed., pp. 82-3.

59. See, for example, *Debates*, May 18, 1883, pp. 1281-3. For examples of interference from the Speaker, see *Debates*, February 20, 1877, pp. 122-3; April 11, 1878, pp. 1867-72; April 24, 1883, pp. 785-6.

60. See, for example, *Debates*, June 9, 1936, p. 3528; May 16, 1947, p. 3159; March 7, 1955, p. 1761.

61. For examples of legitimate questions of privilege, see *Journals*, April 20, 1921, p. 199; May 22, 1924, p. 299; February 8, 1932, pp. 15-6; June 30, 1943, pp. 565-6; *Debates*, June 7, 1928, pp. 3868-74.

Beauchesne included a new section, taken from *May*, 14th edition, published in 1946, on the manner of raising questions of privilege.[62] This description of the British procedure soon became a handy reference seized upon by successive Speakers, beginning with Speaker Michener, as a way to curtail spurious interventions by Members on non-privilege matters. It introduced two guiding conditions: whether on the first impression (*prima facie*) the matter raised appeared to be a matter of privilege, and whether the matter was raised as soon as it could have been. Both were to be determined by the Speaker before a debate could proceed.[63] Nonetheless, on occasion the House adopted motions on matters of privilege without a ruling of the Speaker.[64]

In the years that followed, successive Speakers kept a tighter rein on "questions of privilege", even though practice required that the interventions at least be heard, however briefly, before being ruled on. The *prima facie* condition was invoked most often, although a number of other cases were refused because they were not raised at the proper time.[65] Several cases arose which permitted the Speaker to find that debate on a matter of privilege should go forward, with the result that a body of precedents began to take shape. For example, a 1959 case (known as the Pallett case) led the Speaker to declare that a proposed motion in which the conduct of a Member was alluded to was not, *prima facie*, a matter of privilege and could not be given precedence because the proposed motion was not a specific complaint against the Member,[66] a ruling frequently cited in subsequent years.[67] In 1964, the Deputy Speaker ruled that questions of privilege could not be raised during proceedings on the adjournment motion,[68] while in 1975 the House adopted a report which recommended that such matters should not be taken up during Question Period.[69] Divisions were also judged an inopportune time for raising questions of privilege on matters

---

62. *Beauchesne*, 4th ed., pp. 94-6; *May*, 14th ed., pp. 356-7.

63. For a list of questions of privilege ruled *prima facie* by the Speaker since 1958, see Appendix 14.

64. See, for example, motion moved by Stanley Knowles (Winnipeg North Centre): *Debates*, April 27, 1964, pp. 2582-3; April 28, 1964, pp. 2645-7; *Journals*, April 28, 1964, p. 251; June 15, 1964, pp. 425-6; August 17, 1964, pp. 623-4; question raised by Erik Nielsen (Yukon): *Debates*, May 14, 1970, pp. 6949-51; *Journals*, May 14, 1970, p. 803; June 3, 1970, pp. 917-8; June 10, 1970, p. 977; motion moved by Jerry Pringle (Fraser Valley East): *Debates*, March 14, 1972, p. 795; *Journals*, March 14, 1972, p. 61; May 24, 1972, pp. 321-6; motion moved by Allan J. MacEachen (President of the Privy Council): *Debates*, December 22, 1976, pp. 2241-2; *Journals*, December 22, 1976, p. 270; and motion moved by Lloyd Axworthy (Minister of Employment and Immigration): *Debates*, April 22, 1980, pp. 285-8; *Journals*, April 22, 1980, p. 66; July 10, 1980, pp. 347-8.

65. See, for example, *Debates*, May 15, 1964, pp. 3299-302.

66. *Journals*, June 19, 1959, pp. 581-6.

67. See, for example, *Journals*, March 11, 1966, pp. 279-81; October 7, 1970, pp. 1423-4; May 16, 1972, pp. 300-1.

68. *Debates*, April 30, 1964, pp. 2799-802. See also *Debates*, May 17, 1973, p. 3903.

69. The Second Report of the Standing Committee on Procedure and Organization was presented on March 14, 1975 (*Journals*, p. 373), and concurred in on March 24, 1975 (*Journals*, p. 399).

not related to the business then before the House.[70] Finally, a number of Speakers, in deciding that a *prima facie* case did not exist, suggested to the Members concerned that the matter might instead be brought forward through the normal procedure, that is, as a substantive motion after proper notice.[71] By definition, a matter of privilege also involves a substantive proposal which, because it involves the privileges of the House or of its Members, is given precedence with the usual notice requirements being waived.

Privilege Challenged in Court

An examination of privilege in the Canadian context shows that the constitutionally guaranteed privileges of the House have rarely, if ever, been seriously challenged. Indeed, there have been only two significant court actions; one relating to freedom of speech in the House of Commons and the other concerned with the right of a provincial legislature to control its proceedings.

The first matter, dealing with freedom of speech, arose in a judicial setting, rather than in the House of Commons itself. In the case of the *Roman Corporation Limited versus Hudson's Bay Oil and Gas* in 1971, an action was brought against the Prime Minister and the Minister of Energy, Mines and Resources for announcements made in the House of Commons. In its ruling, the Ontario Supreme Court disavowed any jurisdiction over statements made in Parliament based on Article 9 of the English *Bill of Rights* of 1689.[72] However, Speakers have always urged Members not to abuse their privilege in light of the damage that can result through the wide dissemination of their remarks through the official printed reports of the House and the television broadcasts of House proceedings.[73]

The second matter involved the right of the House of Assembly in the province of Nova Scotia, in light of the Canadian *Charter of Rights and Freedoms*,[74] to exclude strangers from its proceedings. The case involved a claim by the Canadian Broadcasting Corporation (CBC) that its reporters had a constitutional right to film the proceedings of the Nova Scotia House of Assembly with their own cameras. CBC applied to the Nova Scotia Supreme Court for an order allowing it to film the proceedings based on Section 2(b) of the Charter which guarantees freedom of expression, including freedom of the press. The Trial Division and the Court of Appeal both ruled in favour of the CBC and the Speaker of the House of Assembly appealed to the Supreme Court of Canada.[75] The Supreme Court allowed the appeal and overturned the decisions of the lower courts, upholding the absolute authority of

---

70. *Debates*, April 12, 1962, p. 2909.

71. See, for example, ruling of Speaker Lamoureux, *Debates*, October 29, 1970, p. 686.

72. *Maingot*, 2nd ed., pp. 29-31.

73. See ruling of Speaker Fraser, *Debates*, December 3, 1991, p. 5681; and ruling of Speaker Parent, *Debates*, September 30, 1994, p. 6371. See also *Debates*, April 1, 1998, p. 5653.

74. *Constitution Act, 1982*, R.S.C. 1985, Appendix II, No. 44, Schedule B.

75. The case was known as *New Brunswick Broadcasting Co. v. Nova Scotia (Speaker of the House of Assembly)* (it is also referred to as *Donahoe v. Canadian Broadcasting Corporation*) and the Speakers of the House of Commons, the Senate and the provincial legislatures were interveners.

the Houses of Parliament and of the legislative assemblies to control their proceedings and reasserting the independence of the different branches of government.[76]

Reviews of Rights, Immunities and Privileges

On only three occasions has a committee of the House been specifically charged with a direct order of reference to examine the rights, immunities and privileges of the House. The first of these studies took place in the Thirtieth Parliament (1974-79) when the Special Committee on Rights and Immunities of Members was created under the chairmanship of Speaker James Jerome. The Committee presented two reports, one on privilege in the First Session[77] and one on the *sub judice* convention in the Second Session.[78] In its report on privilege, the Special Committee stated that the purpose of privilege was "to allow Members of the House of Commons to carry out their duties as representatives of the electorate without undue interference". Echoing the recommendation of the 1967 British Select Committee, it also found that the term "privilege" was likely to give rise to misconceptions on the part of the public and so preferred the use of the term "rights and immunities". The Report also stated that a question of privilege is a serious matter, when validly raised, but was frequently resorted to when no real question of privilege was actually involved. It suggested that another mechanism might be devised to enable Members to challenge reports or to correct statements. The Committee further pointed out that when matters of privilege are raised, the Member involved cannot devote full attention to his or her parliamentary duties until the case is disposed of. Therefore, it was considered desirable that cases of privilege be dealt with as swiftly as possible. The Committee also reported on the advisability of arriving at precise definitions for the terms "parliamentary precinct" (particularly taking into account the fact that parliamentary committees meet outside of Ottawa) and "proceedings in Parliament". It also proposed to examine the premature publication of confidential reports of parliamentary committees and the *sub judice* convention. In the First Session, the Special Committee did not pursue these matters further. In the succeeding session, the Committee focussed on the *sub judice* convention.[79]

The second committee charged with the examination of the rights, immunities and privileges of the House was the Standing Committee on Elections, Privileges, Procedure and Private Members' Business in the Second Session (1989-91) of the

---

76. See *Maingot*, 2nd ed., pp. 303-50, for an explanation of the relationship between the *Canadian Charter of Rights and Freedoms* and parliamentary privilege. See also Diane Davidson, "Parliamentary Privilege and Freedom of the Press: A Comment on Donahoe v. Canadian Broadcasting Corporation (1993)", *Canadian Parliamentary Review*, Vol. 16, No. 2 (Summer 1993), pp. 10-12, for a summary of the Supreme Court Decision.

77. *Journals*, July 12, 1976, pp. 1421-3.

78. *Journals*, April 29, 1977, pp. 720-9.

79. For further information on the *sub judice* convention, see Chapter 13, "Rules of Order and Decorum".

Thirty-Fourth Parliament (1988-93).[80] While the Committee did take up consideration of the matter,[81] no report on this topic was tabled in the House.

In December 1989, a third committee was created to review the *Parliament of
Canada Act* regarding the powers, duties and obligations of Members, and regarding
the authority, responsibilities and jurisdiction of the Board of Internal Economy.[82]
While this Special Committee focussed its attention on the provisions of the Act and,
in particular, on those provisions governing the expenditure of public funds under
the authority of the Board of Internal Economy, it also explored the role and responsibilities of Members of Parliament and the nature of financial controls and accountability, among other matters.[83] In its Second Report, the Special Committee stated
that it accepted and endorsed the principle that Members of the House of Commons
were not above the law. "Laws must be applied equally to all. Members are not
entitled to special treatment, but they deserve assurance that their rights will not be
jeopardized or sacrificed. It must be recognized that Members and their activities
will be subject to intense public scrutiny."[84] The Special Committee recommended
that the House reaffirm a number of principles which applied to its Members, one of
which was " . . . that a Member has the constitutional rights and immunities applicable to that office and independence in the performance of the activities and functions of that office free from interference or intimidation. . . . "[85]

In its Third Report which focussed on the execution of search warrants within the
parliamentary precinct, the Special Committee stated as part of its recommendations:

*The privileges, immunities and powers of the House of Commons and its
Members are established by section 18 of the* Constitution Act, 1867, *and
section 4 of the* Parliament of Canada Act. *These privileges are intended to
enable Members of Parliament to carry out their functions and activities
and to represent Canadians. These privileges, immunities and powers must
be considered and respected in the execution of search warrants. . . .* [86]

Privilege Versus Contempt

Any disregard of or attack on the rights, powers and immunities of the House and its
Members, either by an outside person or body, or by a Member of the House, is

---

80. This order of reference to the Committee arose out of discussions among the House Leaders following tes-
    timony given before the Standing Committee on Justice and the Solicitor General relating to police investi-
    gations of certain Members (*Debates*, December 14, 1989, pp. 6939-40). See also Standing Committee on
    Justice and the Solicitor General, *Minutes of Proceedings and Evidence,* December 12, 1989, Issue No. 21,
    pp. 5-12, 20-42.
81. See Standing Committee on Elections, Privileges, Procedure and Private Members' Business, *Minutes of
    Proceedings and Evidence,* January 30, 1990, Issue No. 20.
82. *Debates*, December 14, 1989, pp. 6939-40; *Journals*, December 14, 1989, p. 1011.
83. Special Committee on the Review of the Parliament of Canada Act, Second Report, *Minutes of Proceedings
    and Evidence,* Issue No. 7, p. 5. The Report was presented to the House on February 16, 1990 (*Journals*,
    p. 1233), and concurred in on March 7, 1990 (*Journals*, p. 1301).
84. Second Report, p. 6.
85. Second Report, p. 7.
86. Special Committee on the Review of the Parliament of Canada Act, Third Report, presented to the House
    on May 29, 1990, and concurred in on the same day (*Journals*, pp. 1775-6).

referred to as a "breach of privilege" and is punishable by the House.[87] There are, however, other affronts against the dignity and authority of Parliament which may not fall within one of the specifically defined privileges. Thus, the House also claims the right to punish, as a contempt, any action which, though not a breach of a specific privilege, tends to obstruct or impede the House in the performance of its functions; obstructs or impedes any Member or Officer of the House in the discharge of their duties; or is an offence against the authority or dignity of the House, such as disobedience of its legitimate commands or libels upon itself, its Members, or its Officers.[88] "The rationale of the power to punish contempts, whether contempt of court or contempt of the Houses, is that the courts and the two Houses should be able to protect themselves from acts which directly or indirectly impede them in the performance of their functions."[89] In that sense, all breaches of privilege are contempts of the House, but not all contempts are necessarily breaches of privilege.

Contempts, as opposed to "privileges", cannot be enumerated or categorized. As Speaker Sauvé explained in a 1980 ruling, " . . . while our privileges are defined, contempt of the House has no limits. When new ways are found to interfere with our proceedings, so too will the House, in appropriate cases, be able to find that a contempt of the House has occurred."[90]

Just as it is not possible to categorize or to delineate what may fall under the definition of contempt, it is not even possible to categorize the "severity" of contempt. Contempts may vary greatly in their gravity; matters ranging from minor breaches of decorum to grave attacks against the authority of Parliament may be considered as contempts.[91]

---

87. *May*, 22nd ed., p. 65.
88. *May*, 22nd ed., pp. 65, 108.
89. *Odgers*, 8th ed., p. 53.
90. See *Debates*, October 29, 1980, p. 4214. Speakers Fraser and Parent also reiterated this explanation. See *Debates*, October 10, 1989, p. 4459; October 9, 1997, p. 687.
91. M.N. Kaul and S.L. Shakdher, *Practice and Procedure of Parliament*, 4th ed., edited by Subhash C. Kashyap, New Delhi: Metropolitan Book Co., 1991 (Reprinted 1995), p. 225. For a listing of the main types of contempt established in the United Kingdom, see *Griffith and Ryle,* pp. 93-4. No such list exists for the Canadian House. Of the *prima facie* cases of contempt raised in the House since 1867, only one motion containing the word "contempt" has been adopted by the House. This occurred in 1873 when the House found an article printed in the *Morning Freeman* newspaper to be a "high contempt of the privileges and the Constitutional authority of this House" (see *Journals*, April 17-18, 1873, pp. 167-72). In the 1996 Jacob case, the wording of the motion moved by Jim Hart (Okanagan–Similkameen–Merritt) referred to the actions of Jean-Marc Jacob (Charlesbourg) as constituting a "contempt of Parliament". However, the motion as adopted by the House had been amended to delete the reference to contempt (see *Journals*, March 12, 1996, p. 79; March 13, 1996, pp. 88-9; March 14, 1996, pp. 94-6; March 18, 1996, pp. 107-10). It has been the practice of the House in such instances to refer the matter to committee for investigation to determine if a contempt has been committed and therefore not prejudge the findings of the committee. Actual mention of the word "contempt" is usually found in the remarks made by Members during debate (see, for example, the remarks of Jesse Flis (Parkdale–High Park) in moving his motion summoning Ian Waddell (Port Moody–Coquitlam) to the Bar of the House (*Debates*, October 31, 1991, pp. 4271-2)); in the remarks by the Speaker in ruling on the *prima facie* nature of the issue (see *Journals*, October 24, 1966, pp. 911-3; December 6, 1978, pp. 221-3); in the report of the Committee on the matter (see Standing Committee on Elections, Privileges and Procedure, Seventh Report, *Journals*, December 18, 1987, p. 2016; Standing Committee on Privileges and Elections, Twenty-Fourth Report, *Minutes of Proceedings and Evidence*, March 7, 1991, Issue No. 39, p. 5); or in the wording of motions which the House adopted subsequent to a committee report (see *Journals*, September 29, 1891, p. 561).

By far, most of the cases of privilege in the Canadian House relate to matters of contempt challenging the perceived authority and dignity of Parliament and its Members.[92] Other cases have involved charges made between Members[93] or media allegations concerning Members.[94] The premature disclosure of committee reports and proceedings has frequently been raised as a matter of privilege.[95] However, in those instances where no specific individual has been identified, the matter has not been pursued even though it might appear to involve contempt.[96]

92. In 1973, for example, Flora MacDonald (Kingston and the Islands) and her staff were questioned in her West Block office by the Ottawa police and the RCMP respecting the disappearance of certain files from a government department. The matter was raised as a question of privilege and referred to committee for study. The committee reported that the question of privilege was well founded and asked the Speaker to remind outside police forces to follow established practice and obtain authorization from the Speaker before seeking access to a Member's office. See *Debates*, September 4, 1973, pp. 6179-81; *Journals*, September 21, 1973, p. 567.

93. In March 1996, for example, Jim Hart (Okanagan–Similkameen–Merritt) accused Jean-Marc Jacob (Charlesbourg) of sedition for a 1995 communiqué sent by him to members of the Armed Forces in Quebec concerning the October 30, 1995 referendum in that province. The Speaker ruled the matter *prima facie*, Mr. Hart moved a motion, which after debate was amended, and the House referred the matter to committee for study. See *Debates*, March 12, 1996, pp. 557-67; March 13, 1996, pp. 648-74; March 14, 1996, pp. 680-703, 716-47; March 18, 1996, pp. 854-9. On June 18, 1996, the Standing Committee on Procedure and House Affairs presented its Twenty-Ninth Report which found that although Mr. Jacob's actions had been ill advised, there was no contempt of the House. On June 20, 1996, Chuck Strahl (Fraser Valley East) moved a motion of concurrence in the report. After debate, Don Boudria (Glengarry–Prescott–Russell) moved the adjournment of the debate. This was adopted, debate was adjourned and, pursuant to the Standing Orders, the concurrence motion was transferred to Government Orders. It was not debated again. See *Journals*, June 18, 1996, pp. 565-6; June 20, 1996, pp. 592-3.

94. In 1975, for example, the Standing Committee on Privileges and Elections found the *Montreal Gazette* to have fallen short of accepted journalistic standards in a story claiming that a Member, John Reid (Kenora–Rainy River), had advance knowledge of the budget and that he had passed on that information to businessmen. See *Debates*, July 24, 1975, pp. 7886-9; July 25, 1975, pp. 7937-41, 7946-8; *Journals*, July 25, 1975, pp. 742-3; October 17, 1975, pp. 781-2. A similar finding was made in 1983 when the same newspaper suggested that Bryce Mackasey (Verdun) had acted as a paid lobbyist while still a Member of the House. See *Debates*, March 16, 1983, pp. 23834-5; March 17, 1983, pp. 23880-1; March 22, 1983, pp. 24027-30; *Journals*, March 22, 1983, p. 5736; November 23, 1983, p. 6588. In March 1998, Peter MacKay (Pictou–Antigonish–Guysborough) rose on a matter concerning an article in the March 8 edition of the *Ottawa Sun* newspaper which attributed to Members of the House statements which might bring into question the integrity of the House and the Speaker. This matter was found *prima facie*, Mr. MacKay moved a motion, and after debate the matter was referred to committee for study. See *Debates*, March 9, 1998, pp. 4560-75; March 10, 1998, pp. 4592-8, 4666-8. On April 27, 1998, the Standing Committee on Procedure and House Affairs presented its Twenty-Ninth Report which found that the statements made by the Members did not bring into question the integrity of the House or the Speaker. On May 5, 1998, the House concurred in the report. See *Journals*, April 27, 1998, p. 706; April 29, 1998, p. 722; May 5, 1998, pp. 744-5.

95. The most notable instance occurred in 1987 when the Speaker accepted as a *prima facie* question of privilege a matter involving John Parry (Kenora–Rainy River), who divulged the result of an *in camera* vote. See *Debates*, April 28, 1987, pp. 5299, 5329-30; May 5, 1987, pp. 5737-42; May 14, 1987, pp. 6108-11; December 18, 1987, pp. 11950-1; *Journals*, May 14, 1987, p. 917; December 18, 1987, pp. 2014-6.

96. See, for example, rulings of Speakers Jerome and Parent, *Journals*, October 22, 1975, pp. 791-2; *Debates*, December 9, 1997, p. 2945; November 26, 1998, p. 10467.

The reluctance to invoke the House's authority to reprimand, admonish or imprison anyone found to have trampled its dignity or authority and that of its Members appears to have become a near constant feature of the Canadian approach to privilege. Though the power of the House to imprison remains, it is difficult to foresee circumstances arising that would oblige the House to invoke it.[97] Members have proven themselves to be fairly thick-skinned when it comes to criticism, even when it appears hard and unfair. They seem willing to endure such treatment from the press and other media rather than raise a potential conflict between the authority of the House and the freedom of the press.[98] There is, however, no doubt that the Canadian House of Commons remains capable of protecting itself from senseless abuse should the occasion ever arise.

In only a very few cases in Canadian practice has the House, or a procedure committee report, recommended a punishment. A 1976 committee report did chastise a former Member (Auguste Choquette) who claimed that many parliamentarians had obtained undue financial considerations. After the former Member maintained his allegation under questioning, the committee concluded that his attitude was intemperate and irresponsible, but recommended no further consideration be given to the matter.[99] In the 1987 Parry case, the Committee also did not recommend punishment[100] and the Member's apology to the House put an end to the matter. In the 1996 Jacob case, the Committee noted that while the Member's actions were ill advised, they did not amount to contempt or a breach of parliamentary privilege.[101] This was also true in the 1998 case concerning the integrity of the House and the Speaker, following comments that were made on the Speaker's ruling on displaying the flag in the House. In its report, the Standing Committee on Procedure and House

---

97. This was noted by the Special Committee on the Rights and Immunities of Members in its First Report to the House presented on July 12, 1976 (*Journals*, p. 1422).

98. *Maingot*, 2nd ed., pp. 247-55. See also rulings of Speakers, *Debates*, June 18, 1964, p. 4434; June 9, 1969, pp. 9899-900; April 9, 1976, p. 12668; August 12, 1988, p. 18272; March 24, 1994, pp. 2705-6. The Speaker has noted, however, that, as a citizen, a Member who has a complaint about media coverage of his or her own words or actions has access to the courts. Speaker Fraser stated in 1988: "Past Speakers have consistently argued that freedom of the press is one of the fundamental rights of our society which ought to be interfered with only if it is clearly in contempt of the House. Members who have complaints about reporting of their positions or activities should seek remedy in the courts" (*Debates*, August 12, 1988, p. 18272). See also Speaker Jerome's ruling, *Debates*, June 23, 1977, pp. 7044-5.

99. *Debates*, May 7, 1976, pp. 13269-71, 13280-1; *Journals*, May 7, 1976, p. 1275; May 21, 1976, pp. 1305-7.

100. Standing Committee on Elections, Privileges and Procedure, Seventh Report, presented on December 18, 1987 (*Journals*, pp. 2014-6).

101. Standing Committee on Procedure and House Affairs, Twenty-Second Report, *Minutes of Proceedings*, June 18, 1996, Issue No. 1, p. 50. The report was presented to the House on June 18, 1996 (*Journals*, pp. 565-6).

Affairs found that the statements attributed to the Members quoted in the *Ottawa Sun* newspaper did not bring into question the integrity of the House or the Speaker.[102]

The Structure of Privilege

The privileges of the House can be examined from two vantage points: the rights and immunities of its individual Members and the rights of the House in its collective capacity. Within this framework, the individual Member's rights are subordinate to those of the House as a whole in order to protect the collectivity against any abuses by individual Members. For instance, a Member's individual privileges may be considered suspended if the House orders that Member to attend in his or her place and answer questions demanded by the House. It is extremely rare, however, that the rights of the House collectively will be used to override those of an individual.[103] Some of these immunities are applicable to officials of the House and to individuals summoned by the House on official business.[104]

In addition, both the House in its collective capacity and Members individually have the responsibility to protect from abuse their rights and immunities, particularly freedom of speech.[105] Members should avoid any arrangement which might limit their independence as Members:[106] they should not raise trivial matters as matters of privilege or contempt; and they should not use the privilege of freedom of speech to be unfairly critical of others in debate.[107] The House should exercise its powers with regard to privilege and contempt sparingly and ensure that when exercising its power to punish for contempt, the action it orders is appropriate to the offence.

102. Standing Committee on Procedure and House Affairs, Twenty-Ninth Report, presented to the House on April 27, 1998 (*Journals*, p. 706, Sessional Paper No. 8510-361-51).

103. The most recent example of such an action was the reprimand of Ian Waddell (Port Moody–Coquitlam). See *Journals*, October 31, 1991, pp. 574, 579; *Debates*, October 31, 1991, pp. 4271-85, 4309-10.

104. *Maingot*, 2nd ed., p. 160.

105. This responsibility has been described in the Australian *House of Representatives Practice* and is pertinent to the Canadian House of Commons. See *House of Representatives Practice*, 3rd ed., pp. 724-6.

106. It is for this reason that section 327 of the *Canada Elections Act*, R.S.C. 1985, c. E-2, was enacted to forbid pledges. This section makes it illegal for any candidate for election as a Member of Parliament to sign any written document by way of a demand or claim on the candidate if it requires the candidate to follow any course of action that will prevent him or her from exercising freedom of action in Parliament, if elected, or to resign as a Member if called on to do so by those who present the pledge. See also Chapter 4, "The House of Commons and Its Members".

107. See section below, "Freedom of Speech".

Rights and Immunities of Individual Members

The rights, privileges and immunities of individual Members of the House are finite, that is to say, they can be enumerated but not extended except by statute or, in some cases, by constitutional amendment, and can be examined by the courts. Moreover, privilege does not exist "at large" but applies only in context, which usually means within the confines of the parliamentary precinct and a "proceeding in Parliament". With the role of the courts to uphold the *Canadian Charter of Rights and Freedoms* as well as the *Canadian Bill of Rights,* Members must avoid creating unnecessary conflicts with private rights and thereby having issues of parliamentary privilege brought before the courts.

FREEDOM OF SPEECH

By far, the most important right accorded to Members of the House is the exercise of freedom of speech in parliamentary proceedings. It has been described as:

> . . . *a fundamental right without which they would be hampered in the performance of their duties. It permits them to speak in the House without inhibition, to refer to any matter or express any opinion as they see fit, to say what they feel needs to be said in the furtherance of the national interest and the aspirations of their constituents.*[108]

Much has been written about this over the centuries—in Great Britain, Canada and throughout the Commonwealth.[109]

In *Odgers' Australian Senate Practice,* this privilege is expressed in broader terms as immunity of proceedings from impeachment and question in the courts.[110] It is also stated that this is the only immunity of substance possessed by the Houses of Parliament and their Members and committees.[111] There are two aspects to the immunity. "First, there is the immunity from civil or criminal action and examination in legal proceedings of members of the Houses and of witnesses and others

---

108. Special Committee on the Rights and Immunities of Members, First Report, presented to the House on April 29, 1977 (*Journals*, pp. 720-9).

109. See, for example, *May*, 22ⁿᵈ ed., Chapter 6, pp. 83-107; *Maingot*, 2ⁿᵈ ed., Chapters 3-5 and 7, pp. 25-105, 115-23; *Redlich*, Vol. III, Part IX, Chapter 1, pp. 42-50.

110. *Odgers*, 8ᵗʰ ed., pp. 30-2.

111. *Odgers*, 8ᵗʰ ed., p. 30.

taking part in proceedings in Parliament. . . . Secondly, there is the immunity of parliamentary proceedings as such from impeachment or question in the courts."[112]

The statutory existence of parliamentary privilege in relation to freedom of speech dates from the adoption of the English *Bill of Rights* in 1689. Though meant to counter the challenge of the Crown, it also prohibited actions of any kind by any person outside the House against Members for what they might say or do in Parliament. Section 9 of that statute declares, "That the freedom of speech and debates or proceedings in Parliament ought not to be impeached or questioned in any court or place out of Parliament".[113]

Proceedings in Parliament

No definition of "proceedings in Parliament" is contained in the English *Bill of Rights* and, as is noted in *May,* although the courts both in the United Kingdom and elsewhere have commented on the term, no comprehensive lines of decision have emerged and an exhaustive definition has not been achieved.[114] *Maingot* has also devoted considerable attention to the term.[115] In a supplementary memorandum to the 1967 United Kingdom Select Committee on Parliamentary Privilege, the Clerk of the British House of Commons wrote of the term:

> *The primary meaning, as a technical parliamentary term of "proceedings" (which obtained at least as early as the seventeenth century) is some formal action, usually a decision, taken by the House in its collective capacity. This is naturally extended both to the forms of business on which the House takes action and to the whole process, the principal part of which is debate, by which the House reaches a decision.*
>
> *An individual Member takes part in proceedings usually by speech, but also by various recognised kinds of formal action, such as voting, giving notice of a motion, etc., or presenting a petition or a report from a Committee, most of such actions being time-saving substitutes for speaking. Officers of the House take part in its proceedings principally by carrying out its orders, general or particular. Strangers can also take part in the proceedings of the House, e.g., by giving evidence before one of its committees, or by presenting petitions for or against private bills.*

---

112. *Odgers*, 8th ed., p. 31.
113. *May,* 22nd ed., p. 83.
114. *May,* 22nd ed., p. 95. See also pages 95-7 for a discussion of the term.
115. *Maingot*, 2nd ed., pp. 77-105.

While taking part in the proceedings of the House, Members, officers and strangers are protected by the same sanction as that by which freedom of speech is protected, namely, that they cannot be called to account for their actions by any authority other than the House itself.

By the insertion of the term "proceedings" in the Bill of Rights, *Parliament gave statutory authority to what was implied in previous declarations of the privilege of freedom of speech by the Commons, e.g. in the Protestation of 1621, where it is claimed:*

> *that in the handling and proceeding of those businesses every member of the House of Parliament hath and of right ought to have freedom of speech to propound, treat, reason and bring to conclusion the same ... and that every member of the said House hath like freedom from all impeachment, imprisonment and molestation (other than by censure of the House itself) for or concerning any speaking, reasoning or declaring of any matter or matters touching the parliament or parliament business (1 Rushworth, 53).*

A general idea of what the term covers is given in the Report of the Select Committee on the Official Secrets Acts *in Session 1938-39.*

> *It covers both the asking of a question and the giving written notice of such question, and includes everything said or done by a Member in the exercise of his functions as a member in a committee of either House, as well as everything said or done in either House in the transaction of Parliamentary business.*[116]

In Australia, the Commonwealth Parliament has enacted the *Parliamentary Privileges Act 1987* which defines "proceedings in Parliament" as follows:

> *. . . all words spoken and acts done in the course of, or for purposes of or incidental to, the transacting of the business of a House or of a committee, and, without limiting the generality of the foregoing, includes*
>
> *(a) the giving of evidence before a House or a committee, and evidence so given;*

---

116. United Kingdom, House of Commons, Select Committee on Parliamentary Privilege, 1966-67, Report, p. 9. In its Third Report to the House, the United Kingdom, House of Commons, Select Committee on Privileges in 1976-77 recommended that a definition of "proceedings in parliament" be legislated, though this did not occur. The proposed definition had originally been suggested by the United Kingdom, Joint Committee on the Publication of Proceedings in Parliament (1969-70). In its Report presented to both Houses on March 30, 1999, the United Kingdom Joint Committee on Parliamentary Privilege again recommended that a statutory definition be enacted (para. 129, p. 38.)

(b) the presentation or submission of a document to a House or a committee;

(c) the preparation of a document for purposes of or incidental to the transacting of any such business; and

(d) the formulation, making or publication of a document, including a report, by or pursuant to an order of a House or a committee and the document so formulated, made or published.[117]

There is no statutory definition of "proceedings in Parliament" in Canada. From the numerous court cases where the law of parliamentary privilege has been applied, it is clear that the courts understand the meaning of the term and see it as part of the law of Canada. However, the courts have been reluctant to extend the immunity deriving from the rule of free speech beyond the context of parliamentary proceedings. In other words, despite the fact that the role of a Member of the House of Commons has evolved considerably since the seventeenth century when the rule was formulated in the *Bill of Rights,* the courts have, with few exceptions, confined the scope of this immunity to the traditional role of Members as debaters and legislators in Parliament.[118]

Importance of Freedom of Speech

Freedom of speech permits Members to speak freely in the Chamber during a sitting or in committees during meetings while enjoying complete immunity from prosecution for any comment they might make.[119] This freedom is essential for the effective working of the House. Under it, Members are able to make statements or allegations about outside bodies or persons, which they may hesitate to make without the protection of privilege. Though this is often criticized, the freedom to make allegations which the Member genuinely believes at the time to be true, or at least worthy of investigation, is fundamental. As in courts of justice, the House of Commons could not work effectively unless its Members were able to speak and criticize without having to account to any outside body. There would be no freedom of speech if everything had to be proven true before it were uttered. Speaker Bosley was required

---

117. *House of Representatives Practice*, 3rd ed., pp. 683-4.

118. See *Maingot*, 2nd ed., pp. 90, 92-4, 101-2, for an analysis of the scope of this privilege in relation to the role of the modern Member of Parliament, and the reasons of Hugessen A.C.J., for the Superior Court of Québec in *Re Ouellet (No. 1),* (1976) 67 D.L.R. (3) 73 (English version) or [1976] C.S. 503 (French version); confirmed by the Court of Appeal of Québec at (1976) 72 D.L.R. (3d) 95 (English version) or [1976] C.A. 788 (French version). See also the ruling given by Speaker Jerome, *Debates*, May 15, 1978, p. 5411.

119. See *Maingot*, 2nd ed., pp. 33-6, for a discussion of freedom of speech and the criminal law.

to rule on such a situation in 1984, following a question of privilege. [120] While finding that there was no *prima facie* question of privilege, the Speaker affirmed that "the privilege of a Member of Parliament when speaking in the House or in a committee is absolute, and that it would be very difficult to find that any statement made under the cloak of parliamentary privilege constituted a violation of that privilege." [121] Paraphrasing Speaker Michener, he went on to note that, unless such conduct has led to the obstruction of other Members or of the House, "the conduct of a Member of Parliament even though reprehensible, cannot form the basis of a question of privilege although it can form the basis of a charge by way of a substantive motion. . . ." [122] It should be borne in mind that this right is also extended to individuals summoned to appear before the House or its committees. [123]

Limitations on Freedom of Speech

Remarks Made Outside of Debate

The privilege of freedom of speech is not limitless and grey areas remain. Members may be confident of the protection given to their speeches in the House and other formal proceedings, but can never be certain how far their freedom of speech and parliamentary action extends. [124] The parliamentary privilege of freedom of speech applies to a Member's speech in the House and other proceedings of the House itself, but may not apply to reports of proceedings or debates published by newspapers or

---

120. On December 7, 1984, John Nunziata (York South–Weston) rose on a question of privilege to claim that comments made by Svend Robinson (Burnaby) in committee constituted a contempt of Parliament. Mr. Robinson had alleged United States Central Intelligence Agency penetration at senior management levels of Petro-Canada and had named several individuals as CIA agents. In his ruling, Speaker Bosley noted that the statements made by Mr. Robinson did not constitute a contempt of Parliament in that no Member or official of the House had been obstructed or impeded in the discharge of his or her duty. On December 21, 1984, Mr. Robinson rose in the House to retract his remarks in the committee. He said that he had relied upon a confidential source of information and had availed himself of parliamentary immunity to accuse the Petro-Canada employees of spying for the CIA. He then went on to state: "While the tradition of parliamentary immunity is a long and important one, in retrospect I regret that I used my immunity to name these individuals. I have written to both men to express unreservedly my regret for having publicly named them in the Justice Committee. As well, Mr. Speaker, I wish at this time to issue a complete and unequivocal retraction of the allegations I made and unreservedly apologize to the two individuals involved. . . . " (see *Debates*, December 7, 1984, pp. 1004-7; December 11, 1984, pp. 1114-5; December 21, 1984, p. 1447).

121. *Debates*, December 11, 1984, p. 1114.

122. *Debates*, December 11, 1984, p. 1115.

123. *Maingot*, 2nd ed., p. 160.

124. *Griffith and Ryle*, p. 90.

others outside Parliament. Parliamentary privilege may not protect a Member publishing his or her own speech separate from the official record.[125]

Members are therefore cautioned that utterances which are absolutely privileged when made within a parliamentary proceeding may not be when repeated in another context, such as in a press release, a householder mailing, a telegram, on an Internet site, a television or radio interview, at a public meeting or in the constituency office. Members also act at their peril when they transmit otherwise libellous material for purposes unconnected with a parliamentary proceeding. Thus, comments made by a Member at a function as an elected representative—but outside the forum of Parliament—would not be covered by this special privilege, even if the Member were quoting from his or her own speech in the *Debates* of the House of Commons.[126] Telecommunications, including new technology such as electronic mail, facsimile machines and the Internet, should therefore not be used to transmit otherwise libellous material.

The publication of libellous material has been considered by most courts to be beyond the privileges of Parliament when such publication was not part of the parliamentary process to begin with.[127] Courts take a distinctly "functional" approach to the interpretation of parliamentary privilege by relating any novel situation in which a Member may become involved back to the function and purpose that parliamentary privilege was originally intended to serve: the need for Members of Parliament to be able to fearlessly debate issues of public policy in Parliament. Thus even correspondence between one Member and another on a matter of public policy may not be considered to be privileged.[128]

Misuse of Freedom of Speech

The privilege of freedom of speech is an extremely powerful immunity and Speakers have on occasion had to caution Members about its misuse. In a ruling following a question of privilege,[129] Speaker Fraser urged Members to take the greatest care in framing questions concerning conflict of interest guidelines. Since the question

---

125. For protection provided to the media, see *Maingot*, 2nd ed., pp. 44-6, 50-9.

126. *Maingot*, 2nd ed., pp. 39, 41, 44-6, 90-4.

127. This was one of the main issues in the famous case of *Stockdale v. Hansard*. See *May*, 22nd ed., pp. 86-7, 161-3; *Maingot*, 2nd ed., pp. 63-75.

128. *Maingot*, 2nd ed., pp. 82-94.

129. On April 14, 1987, Otto Jelinek (Minister of State for Fitness and Amateur Sport) raised a question of privilege regarding oral questions asked about an alleged conflict of interest involving himself. Speaker Fraser ruled that the Minister's capacity to function as a Minister and a Member was not impaired. See *Debates*, April 14, 1987, pp. 5124-34; May 5, 1987, pp. 5765-6.

raised affected the very nature of Members' rights and immunities, he spoke at length about the importance of freedom of speech and the need for care in what Members said:

> *There are only two kinds of institutions in this land to which this awesome and far-reaching privilege [of freedom of speech] extends—Parliament and the legislatures on the one hand and the courts on the other. These institutions enjoy the protection of absolute privilege because of the overriding need to ensure that the truth can be told, that any questions can be asked, and that debate can be free and uninhibited. Absolute privilege ensures that those performing their legitimate functions in these vital institutions of Government shall not be exposed to the possibility of legal action. This is necessary in the national interest and has been considered necessary under our democratic system for hundreds of years. It allows our judicial system and our parliamentary system to operate free of any hindrance.*
>
> *Such a privilege confers grave responsibilities on those who are protected by it. By that I mean specifically the Hon. Members of this place. The consequences of its abuse can be terrible. Innocent people could be slandered with no redress available to them. Reputations could be destroyed on the basis of false rumour. All Hon. Members are conscious of the care they must exercise in availing themselves of their absolute privilege of freedom of speech. That is why there are long-standing practices and traditions observed in this House to counter the potential for abuse.* [130]

In a ruling following a point of order, Speaker Parent also emphasized the need for Members to use great care in exercising their right to speak freely in the House: "… paramount to our political and parliamentary systems is the principle of freedom of speech, a member's right to stand in this House unhindered to speak his or her mind. However when debate in the House centres on sensitive issues, as it often does, I would expect that members would always bear in mind the possible effects of their statements and hence be prudent in their tone and choice of words". [131]

Speakers have also stated that although there is a need for Members to express their opinions openly in a direct fashion, it is also important that citizens' reputations

---

130. *Debates*, May 5, 1987, pp. 5765-6.

131. *Debates*, September 30, 1994, p. 6371. On September 27, 1994, Svend Robinson (Burnaby–Kingsway) raised a point of order concerning remarks made by Roseanne Skoke (Central Nova) during second reading debate on Bill C-41 (Criminal Code Amendment (sentencing)) on September 20, 1994. Speaker Parent gave his ruling on September 30, stating that although he realized there existed a profound difference of opinion between the two Members, he acknowledged that the remarks made by Ms. Skoke were within the context of debate and not directed at any particular Member. See *Debates* September 20, 1994, pp. 5912-3; September 27, 1994, pp. 6183-4.

are not unfairly attacked. In a ruling on a question of privilege,[132] Speaker Fraser expressed his concern that an individual who was not a Member of the House had been referred to by name and noted that this concern had also been shared by some Members who had participated in the discussion of the question of privilege. He then went on to say: "But we are living in a day when anything said in this place is said right across the country and that is why I have said before and why I say again that care ought to be exercised, keeping in mind that the great privilege we do have ought not to be abused."

In a later ruling following a point of order,[133] Speaker Fraser observed that the use of suggestive language or innuendo with regard to individuals or an individual's associations with others can provoke an angry response which inevitably leads the House into disorder. The Speaker stated that he was heartened by Members' comments and a general sense of the necessity to maintain decorum, for the sake of the House and the viewing public. Specifically referring to individuals outside the Chamber, he agreed with a suggestion that the House consider constraining itself ". . . in making comments about someone outside this Chamber which would in fact be defamatory under the laws of our country if made outside the Chamber. . . ."[134]

Sub judice *Convention*

There are other limitations to the privilege of freedom of speech, most notably the *sub judice* convention.[135] It is accepted practice that, in the interests of justice and fair play, certain restrictions should be placed on the freedom of Members of Parliament to make reference in the course of debate to matters awaiting judicial decisions and that such matters should not be the subject of motions or questions in the House. Though loosely defined, the interpretation of this convention is left to the Speaker. The word "convention" is used as no "rule" exists to prevent Parliament from discussing a matter which is *sub judice* ("under the consideration of a judge or court of record"). The acceptance of a restriction is a voluntary restraint on the part of the House to protect an accused person or other party to a court action or judicial inquiry

---

132. The Speaker ruled on a question of privilege raised by Harvie Andre (Minister of Consumer and Corporate Affairs) on May 21, 1987, concerning questions asked by Ian Waddell (Vancouver–Kingsway) which, in the Minister's view, implied that he was in a possible conflict of interest situation. The Speaker ruled that he was satisfied that there was no accusation directed against the Minister. See *Debates*, May 21, 1987, pp. 6299-306; May 26, 1987, pp. 6375-6.

133. This ruling was given on December 3, 1991, following a point of order raised by Nelson Riis (Kamloops) on November 28, 1991, concerning remarks about the President of the Public Service Alliance of Canada made by Felix Holtmann (Portage–Interlake) during "Statements by Members". See *Debates*, November 28, 1991, pp. 5498-9, 5509-10; December 3, 1991, pp. 5679-82.

134. *Debates*, December 3, 1991, p. 5681.

135. For a complete discussion of the *sub judice* convention, see Chapter 13, "Rules of Order and Decorum".

from suffering any prejudicial effect from public discussion of the issue.[136] While certain precedents exist for the guidance of the Chair, no attempt has ever been made to codify the practice in Canada.[137]

The *sub judice* convention is important in the conduct of business in the House. It protects the rights of interested parties before the courts, and preserves and maintains the separation and mutual respect between the legislature and the judiciary. The convention ensures that a balance is created between the need for a separate, impartial judiciary and free speech.

The practice has evolved so that it is the Speaker who decides what jurisdiction the Chair has over matters *sub judice*. In 1977, the First Report of the Special Committee on the Rights and Immunities of Members[138] recommended that the imposition of the convention should be done with discretion and, when there was any doubt in the mind of the Chair, a presumption should exist in favour of allowing debate and against the application of the convention. Since the presentation of the report, Speakers have followed these guidelines while using discretion.

Authority of the Speaker

A further limitation on the freedom of speech of Members is provided by the authority of the Speaker under the Standing Orders to preserve order and decorum, and when necessary to order a Member to resume his or her seat if engaged in irrelevance or repetition in debate, or to name a Member for disregarding the authority of the Chair and order him or her to withdraw.[139]

FREEDOM FROM ARREST IN CIVIL ACTIONS

Freedom from arrest in civil actions[140] is the oldest privilege of the House of Commons, pre-dating freedom of speech in the United Kingdom.[141] The immunity exists because the House has the pre-eminent claim to the attendance and service of its Members, free from restraint or intimidation particularly by means of legal arrest in civil process. It has only applied to arrest and imprisonment under civil process and

---

136. See Special Committee on the Rights and Immunities of Members, First Report, *Minutes of Proceedings and Evidence*, April 4, 1977, Issue No. 1, Appendix "C","The *Sub Judice* Convention in the Canadian House of Commons", pp. 1A: 11-2. See also Philip Laundy, "The *Sub Judice* Convention in the Canadian House of Commons", *The Parliamentarian*, Vol. 57, No. 3 (July 1976), pp. 211-4.

137. The practice has been codified in some jurisdictions either by the adoption of Standing Orders (Alberta, Ontario, Quebec, India (Lok Sabha), New Zealand) or by way of resolution (United Kingdom (House of Commons)). See also *May,* 22nd ed., pp. 333, 383-4.

138. The report was presented to the House on April 29, 1977 (see *Journals*, pp. 720-9).

139. Standing Orders 10 and 11. See also Chapter 7, "The Speaker and Other Presiding Officers of the House", and Chapter 13, "Rules of Order and Decorum".

140. See *Bourinot,* 4th ed., pp. 42-7; *May,* 22nd ed., pp. 100-7; *Maingot,* 2nd ed., pp. 151-8.

141. For its origins and history in the United Kingdom and Canada, see *May,* 1st ed., pp. 86-7, and *Maingot,* 2nd ed., pp. 152-5.

does not interfere with the administration of criminal justice. It is not claimable for any incident having a criminal character or a criminal nature, for treason, felony,[142] breach of the peace, matters including criminal offences under federal statutes, breaches of provincial statutes (considered quasi-criminal) which involve the summary jurisdiction of the *Criminal Code,*[143] or any indictable offence.[144]

It goes without saying that if Members are charged with infractions of the law, then they must abide by the due process of law just like any other citizen. To do otherwise would be contemptful of the justice system. While a Member is protected from arrest for civil contempt of court, there is no protection from arrest for criminal contempt of court.[145] If a Member is arrested on a criminal charge or is committed for a contempt of court, the House should be notified by the authorities if it is in session. If a Member is committed for high treason or any criminal offence, the House is informed by way of a letter addressed to the Speaker by the judge or magistrate.[146]

Whatever privilege of freedom from arrest a Member may claim, it exists from the moment of the execution of the return of the writ of election by the returning officer. It continues while the House is sitting and also applies 40 days before and after a session of Parliament and 40 days after a dissolution of Parliament.[147]

EXEMPTION FROM JURY DUTY

Since the House of Commons has first claim on the attendance and service of its Members, and since the courts have a large body of individuals to call upon to serve on juries, it is not essential that Members of Parliament be obliged to serve as jurors.

---

142. For a discussion of the meaning of the term "felony", see Edward McWhinney, "Forfeiture of Office on Conviction of an 'Infamous Crime'," *Canadian Parliamentary Review*, Vol. 12, No. 1 (Spring 1989), pp. 2-6.

143. On February 16, 1965, G.J. McIlraith (President of the Privy Council) raised a question of privilege concerning the effects on the privileges of the House of the arrest of Gilles Grégoire (Lapointe) outside the Parliament Buildings on two warrants for traffic offences. The Speaker ruled the matter *prima facie,* and it was subsequently referred to the Standing Committee on Privileges and Elections. On March 19, 1965, the Committee presented its Fourth Report which found that the privilege of freedom from arrest of the Member had not been infringed (*Journals*, February 16, 1965, pp. 1035-6; March 19, 1965, pp. 1141-2).

144. *Bourinot*, 4ᵗʰ ed., p. 43; *Maingot*, 2ⁿᵈ ed., pp. 151, 156-7.

145. *Maingot*, 2ⁿᵈ ed., pp. 157-8. *Bourinot*, 4ᵗʰ ed., p. 44, notes that while the House will not normally interfere if a Member is committed for contempt, it does reserve the right to inquire into the nature of the offence and protect Members in proper cases.

146. *Bourinot*, 4ᵗʰ ed., pp. 46-7. *Bourinot* also notes, based on English practice, that failure to inform the Speaker has not been viewed as a matter of privilege (p. 47).

147. *Maingot*, 2ⁿᵈ ed., p. 155.

This was the tradition in the United Kingdom long before Confederation and this has been the Canadian practice since 1867.[148] The duty of Members to attend to their functions as elected representatives is in the best interests of the nation and is considered to supersede any obligation to serve as jurors. It has also been recognized in law.[149]

One of the rights of the House is to provide for the protection of its officers so that they may assist in its deliberations. Therefore, officers of the House are exempt from jury duty under the same circumstances as Members, as are individuals summoned to appear before the House or its committees.[150]

EXEMPTION FROM APPEARING AS A WITNESS

The right of the House to the attendance and service of its Members exempts a Member, when the House is in session,[151] from the normal obligation of a citizen to comply with a subpoena to attend a court as a witness.[152] This exemption applies in civil, criminal and military matters before the courts.[153] However, this claim is not intended to be used to impede the course of justice and, therefore, is regularly waived, particularly for criminal cases.[154] When the House is in session, should a subpoena be served on a Member, the Member may wish to appear in court where he or she feels that absence from court might affect the course of justice. However, the Member still has a right to claim the privilege of exemption from appearing as a

---

148. *Maingot*, 2nd ed., p. 159; *May*, 22nd ed., p. 106.

149. Jury selection is a matter of provincial jurisdiction. While exemption from jury duty is claimed as a right by the House of Commons, provincial jury legislation usually includes Members of Parliament as one of the exempt categories. In some provincial statutes, the staff of Members of the Legislative Assembly as well as officers of the Assembly are also exempted from jury duty. See, for example, *The Jury Act, Revised Statutes of New Brunswick, 1973*, c. J-3.1, s. 3; *Juries Act, Revised Statutes of Ontario, 1990*, c. J-3, s. 3; *Jurors Act, Revised Statutes of Québec*, c. J-2, s. 4; *The Jury Act, 1981, Statutes of Saskatchewan, 1980-81*, c. J-4.1, s. 4.

150. *Maingot*, 2nd ed., p. 160.

151. A session is one of the fundamental periods into which a Parliament is divided, usually consisting of a number of separate sittings. Sessions are begun by a Speech from the Throne and are ended by prorogation. Adjournments, whether they be for a few minutes or several months, are considered to be within a session.

152. See *Bourinot*, 4th ed., pp. 45-6; *May*, 22nd ed., pp. 105-6; *Maingot*, 2nd ed., pp. 158-9. For a recent discussion of the issue, see *Debates*, November 25, 1998, pp. 10453-62.

153. *Maingot*, 2nd ed., p. 158.

154. *Maingot*, 2nd ed., p. 159.

witness.[155] A Member may give evidence voluntarily without any formality, even on a day when the House is sitting or scheduled to meet,[156] but if he or she does so, no claim of privilege may be made and the Member is required to give evidence.[157]

If a subpoena is to be served in a Member's parliamentary office, the permission of the Speaker must be sought in advance. This was most forcefully stated by Speaker Fraser in a ruling given in May 1989, following a question of privilege raised by David Kilgour (Edmonton–Strathcona) involving the rights of Members appearing as witnesses in court.[158] In his submission, Mr. Kilgour stated that in March 1989, while Parliament was prorogued, a subpoena authorized by a British Columbia Supreme Court Justice was served on him in his Centre Block office in connection with a defamation action then under way. Much correspondence followed, including a letter from the Law Clerk and Parliamentary Counsel of the House of Commons in which the Member's right to be exempt from attending as a witness in a court of law was affirmed. Subsequent to a letter from one of the counsel indicating that Mr. Kilgour was ordered by the Judge to appear, the Member complied and attended in the Kelowna Court. Mr. Kilgour refused to give evidence upon being questioned, and just prior to his being cited for contempt, the counsel for the plaintiff withdrew the subpoena.[159]

In his ruling, Speaker Fraser spoke first about the manner in which the subpoena had been served on the Member and noted that since the permission of the Speaker had not been sought nor obtained for this service, it had been improperly carried out. The Speaker cautioned Members not to accept service of their own accord within the parliamentary precinct. If they wished to waive their parliamentary immunity, they could do so by leaving the precinct and accepting the service elsewhere. He noted that to do otherwise was "to put at risk our ancient privileges ... [which] are part of the law of Canada". Furthermore, he cautioned "... those who attempt to further improper service of subpoenae, that they may be acting in a manner that is in

---

155. *Maingot*, 2nd ed., p. 159. *Maingot* also notes that while the service of a subpoena would not normally be raised in the House, the counsel who authorized the service should be advised by the Member or by general legal counsel of the House of Commons of the lawful claim of this privilege. In the United Kingdom, in certain cases when this has been raised by the Member concerned, the British Speaker has communicated with the court drawing attention to the privilege and asking that the Member be excused (*May*, 22nd ed., p. 105).

156. *May*, 22nd ed., p. 106.

157. See also David Kilgour and Jef Bowdich, "A serious question of immunity", *The Parliamentarian*, October 1989, pp. 233-5.

158. *Debates*, May 19, 1989, pp. 1951-3.

159. *Debates*, April 4, 1989, p. 39.

contempt of the House".[160] With regard to the privilege of exemption from attending as a witness in a court of law, the Speaker pointed out that although Parliament was prorogued, according to *May* and *Bourinot,* the Member's immunity persisted throughout this period. However, since Mr. Kilgour had accepted to attend in the court, he had essentially waived that privilege. The Speaker noted: "By waiving his privilege, being sworn and answering some questions, he appears to have voluntarily submitted to the jurisdiction of the court. Once this privilege is waived, the Member surrenders the protection implicit in it." The Speaker had been very disturbed by the fact that the counsel for the plaintiff in this case had questioned Mr. Kilgour's right "to claim his parliamentary immunity, alleging that this was a matter for the court to decide". He then stated " . . . for the record that the right of a Member of Parliament to refuse to attend court as a witness during a parliamentary session and during the 40 days preceding and following a parliamentary session is an undoubted and inalienable right supported by a host of precedents". He urged Members " . . . to refuse to accept any writ of summons within the precincts and to report to the Speaker should such an attempt be made".

Just as in the case of jury service, House officials or individuals summoned to appear before the House or its committees are also exempt from appearing as witnesses if their services are needed by the House.[161]

FREEDOM FROM OBSTRUCTION, INTERFERENCE, INTIMIDATION AND MOLESTATION

> *Members are entitled to go about their parliamentary business undisturbed. The assaulting, menacing, or insulting of any Member on the floor of the House or while he is coming or going to or from the House, or on account of his behaviour during a proceeding in Parliament, is a violation of the rights of Parliament. Any form of intimidation (it is a crime to commit "an act of violence in order to intimidate the Parliament of Canada") of a person for or on account of his behaviour during a proceeding in Parliament could amount to contempt.[162]*

Members of Parliament, by the nature of their office and the variety of work they are called upon to perform, come into contact with a wide range of individuals and groups. Members can, therefore, be subject to all manner of influences, some legitimate and some not. Certain matters, most notably bribery, the acceptance of fees and

---

160. *Debates*, May 19, 1989, pp. 1952-3. In connection with Mr. Kilgour's claim that communications between a Member of Parliament and a member of the public are privileged in the same manner as those between lawyer and client, the Speaker indicated that there are no precedents to support this claim. He then referred to comments made by Speakers Lamoureux and Jerome, as well as to his own ruling on November 17, 1987, to explain that the House cannot create new or extend existing privileges.

161. *Maingot*, 2nd ed., p. 160.

162. *Maingot*, 2nd ed., pp. 230-1.

corrupt electoral practices are dealt with in law.[163] Over the years, Members have brought to the attention of the House instances which they believed were attempts to obstruct, impede, interfere, intimidate or molest them, their staffs or individuals who had some business with them or the House. In a technical sense, such actions are considered to be contempts of the House and not breaches of privilege.[164] Since these matters relate so closely to the right of the House to the services of its Members, they are often considered to be breaches of privilege.

Speakers have consistently upheld the right of the House to the services of its Members free from intimidation, obstruction and interference. Following a question of privilege, Speaker Lamoureux ruled that, while in the particular case before him there was no *prima facie* question of privilege, he had "… no hesitation in reaffirming the principle that parliamentary privilege includes the right of a member to discharge his responsibilities as a member of the House free from threats or attempts at intimidation".[165] In ruling on another question of privilege, Speaker Bosley stated further that the threat or attempt at intimidation cannot be hypothetical, but must be real or have occurred.[166]

---

163. See Chapter 4, "The House of Commons and Its Members". For a discussion of bribery and the acceptance of fees by Members, see *Maingot*, 2nd ed., pp. 59-61, 250-1. For a discussion of the 1994 United Kingdom questions for payment case and the resulting institution of a Code of Conduct for Members, see *May*, 22nd ed., pp. 112-5, 419-20.

164. *Maingot*, 2nd ed., p. 15. See also *May*, 22nd ed., pp. 121-30.

165. On September 19, 1973, Otto Jelinek (High Park–Humber Valley) raised a question of privilege claiming that an employee of the Canadian Broadcasting Corporation, in telephone conversations with the Member, had advised Mr. Jelinek to stop asking questions about television coverage of the Olympic games during Question Period or else it would be alleged that the Member had a contract with the CTV network and was in a conflict of interest. Mr. Jelinek claimed that these calls were an attempt to intimidate him. As the Member did not know the name of the caller, no specific charge could be made and therefore there was no *prima facie* question of privilege (*Debates*, September 19, 1973, p. 6709).

166. On May 14, 1986, Herb Gray (Windsor West) rose on a question of privilege concerning the proposed inquiry into conflict of interest allegations against the former Regional Industrial Expansion Minister (Sinclair Stevens). The Opposition had maintained that such an inquiry should be carried out by the House itself through one of its committees. The Deputy Prime Minister (Erik Nielsen) had indicated that the inquiry would be undertaken by a person or persons outside the House, and that the inquiry's terms of reference would include the various statements and allegations made in the House of Commons. Mr. Gray argued that the government was seeking, through executive action, to call into question statements made by Members in the House of Commons, a course of action which would infringe upon their freedom of speech. Mr. Gray also accused the Deputy Prime Minister, through his comments, of attempting to intimidate Members in the exercise of their duties. In his ruling, the Speaker noted that no court or inquiry may call into question or pass judgement on statements made by Members in the House, although it must remain possible to investigate the substance of an allegation once it has been made in the House. It was difficult for the Chair to determine whether the purposes of an inquiry were improper in advance of the inquiry being created since a breach of privilege could not be hypothetical. The Chair could not find an expressed intention to be a breach unless it were of itself a threat. No threat, real or implied, that Members be called to account for anything they said in the House had been made (*Debates*, May 16, 1986, p. 13362). See also *Debates*, May 12, 1986, pp. 13171-2; May 13, 1986, p. 13225; May 14, 1986, pp. 13270-3; May 16, 1986, pp. 13361-2.

Physical Obstruction, Assault and Molestation

In circumstances where Members claim to be directly obstructed, impeded, interfered with or intimidated in the performance of their parliamentary duties, the Speaker is apt to find that a *prima facie* breach of privilege has occurred. This may be physical obstruction, assault or molestation.

On October 30, 1989, Speaker Fraser ruled that a *prima facie* case of privilege existed when Herb Gray (Windsor West) raised a question of privilege, claiming that a RCMP roadblock on Parliament Hill, meant to contain demonstrators, constituted a breach of Members' privileges by denying them access to the House of Commons.[167]

On February 17, 1999, a number of questions of privilege were raised resulting from picket lines set up by members of the Public Service Alliance of Canada at strategic locations of entry to Parliament Hill and at entrances to specific buildings used by parliamentarians. Jim Pankiw (Saskatoon–Humboldt) in his submission stated that the strikers had used physical violence and intimidation to stop him from gaining access to his office. On this matter, Speaker Parent ruled immediately that there was a *prima facie* case of privilege. Mr. Pankiw moved that the matter of his molestation be referred to the Standing Committee on Procedure and House Affairs and it was agreed to without debate.[168] Other questions of privilege, raised by John Reynolds (West Vancouver–Sunshine Coast), Roy Bailey (Souris–Moose Mountain) and Garry Breitkreuz (Yorkton–Melville), focussed on the difficulties Members had had in gaining access to their offices. The picket lines, it was claimed, impeded Members from performing their duties and meeting their obligations as Members of Parliament in a timely fashion. The next day, noting that the Speaker is the guardian of the rights of Members, Speaker Parent stated in his ruling that he had been

---

167. Herb Gray (Windsor West) rose on a question of privilege pertaining to access by certain Members by taxi to Parliament Hill. During a demonstration on Parliament Hill, which included taxi drivers protesting the Goods and Services Tax, several Members entered taxi cabs and asked to be driven to the main entrance of the Centre Block. However, their way was barred by a roadblock of RCMP cars. Some of the Members proceeded on foot, while others eventually reached the Centre Block by taxi after the roadblock was lifted. Mr. Gray submitted that the actions of the RCMP constituted a breach of Members' privileges since they were denied access to the House of Commons. The Speaker ruled immediately, finding that a *prima facie* matter of privilege existed, and Mr. Gray moved that the matter be referred to the Standing Committee on Elections, Privileges, Procedure and Private Members' Business. The motion was adopted. The Committee never reported on the matter. See *Debates*, October 30, 1989, pp. 5298-302; *Journals*, p. 773.

168. See *Debates*, February 17, 1999, pp. 12011-2; *Journals*, February 17, 1999, p. 1517.

persuaded by the interventions made by the three Members who had raised the matter and had decided that their concerns were sufficiently serious for the Chair to act. Therefore, he found that the incident of the previous day of impeding access to the parliamentary precinct constituted a *prima facie* case of contempt of the House and invited Mr. Reynolds to move the appropriate motion. The Member moved that the matter be referred to the Standing Committee on Procedure and House Affairs, and the motion was adopted without debate.[169]

Other Examples of Obstruction, Interference and Intimidation

The unjust damaging of a Member's good name might also be seen as constituting an obstruction. In ruling on a question of privilege,[170] Speaker Fraser stated: "The privileges of a Member are violated by any action which might impede him or her in the fulfilment of his or her duties and functions. It is obvious that the unjust damaging of a reputation could constitute such an impediment. The normal course of a Member who felt himself or herself to be defamed would be the same as that available to any other citizen, recourse to the courts under the laws of defamation with the possibility of damages to substitute for the harm that might be done. However, should the alleged defamation take place on the floor of the House, this recourse is not available."[171]

In finding a *prima facie* case of privilege on March 21, 1978, Speaker Jerome ruled that the electronic surveillance of a Member beyond the parliamentary precinct " . . . could be regarded as a form of harassment or obstruction or molestation or

---

169. *Debates*, February 17, 1999, pp. 12009-12; February 18, 1999, p. 12134; *Journals*, February 18, 1999, p. 1525. On April 14, 1999, the Standing Committee on Procedure and House Affairs presented its Sixty-Sixth Report to the House (*Journals*, p. 1714). The Committee suggested that measures be taken to address certain concerns raised in committee. These included better co-ordination between police forces and the House of Commons Security Service, a clearer legal definition of the parliamentary precinct, and an increased public awareness of the importance of the parliamentary precinct (paras. 18-22). The Committee concluded that there was no deliberate intention to contravene parliamentary privilege, that any contempt of Parliament that had occurred was "technical and unintended", and that there was no need for sanctions (para. 23). No further action was taken on the report.

170. On April 14, 1987, Otto Jelinek (Minister of State for Fitness and Amateur Sport) raised a question of privilege regarding oral questions asked about an alleged conflict of interest involving him. On May 5, 1987, Speaker Fraser ruled that the Minister's capacity to function as a Minister and a Member was not impaired. See *Debates*, April 14, 1987, pp. 5124-34; May 5, 1987, pp. 5765-6.

171. *Debates*, May 5, 1987, p. 5766.

intimidation of a Member, all of which phrases have been used in our precedents to support the position that such conduct is a contempt of the House." [172]

On May 6, 1985, Speaker Bosley ruled that there was a *prima facie* question of privilege in a case where a newspaper advertisement identified another person as a Member of Parliament rather than the sitting Member. [173] He stated: "It should go without saying that a Member of Parliament needs to perform his functions effectively and that anything tending to cause confusion as to a Member's identity creates the possibility of an impediment to the fulfilment of that Member's functions. Any action which impedes or tends to impede a Member in the discharge of his duties is a breach of privilege. There are ample citations and precedents to bear this out." [174]

On December 6, 1978, in finding that a *prima facie* contempt of the House existed, Speaker Jerome ruled that a government official, by deliberately misleading a Minister, had impeded a Member in the performance of his duties and consequently obstructed the House itself. [175]

---

172. On February 22, 1978, John Rodriguez (Nickel Belt) rose on a question of privilege complaining of possible surveillance activities undertaken against him. The matter was raised again on March 1 when Mr. Rodriguez argued that a bugging operation had taken place and that it was a breach of privilege since it called into question the privacy of communications between a Member and his constituents. On March 21, after the Speaker had found the question of privilege *prima facie*, Mr. Rodriguez moved his motion, which was negatived on a recorded division. See *Journals*, March 21, 1978, pp. 520-2, 525-6; *Debates*, February 22, 1978, p. 3129; March 1, 1978, pp. 3348-9; March 2, 1978, pp. 3384-5; March 8, 1978, pp. 3571-6; March 9, 1978, pp. 3607-9; March 16, 1978, pp. 3831-2; March 21, 1978, pp. 3975-7, 3988-9.

173. On April 25, 1985, Andrew Witer (Parkdale–High Park) rose on a question of privilege relating to an advertisement which appeared in a Toronto-based Ukrainian-language newspaper. The ad in question identified Jesse Flis, the incumbent's predecessor, as Member of Parliament for Parkdale–High Park, listing the address and phone number of Mr. Flis' former constituency office. In his ruling, the Speaker noted that, based on the evidence available, a *prima facie* case of privilege must be found. Mr. Writer's motion to refer the matter to the Standing Committee on Privileges and Elections was then agreed to. On May 30, 1985, the Committee presented its report which found that the advertisement had been published in error and that there had been no intention on the part of any of the parties involved to misrepresent Mr. Flis as the sitting Member of Parliament. It concluded that no further action was necessary. See *Debates*, April 25, 1985, pp. 4111-3; May 6, 1985, p. 4439; *Journals*, May 30, 1985, pp. 676-7.

174. *Debates*, May 6, 1985, p. 4439.

175. On November 3, 1978, Allan Lawrence (Northumberland–Durham) raised a question of privilege and charged that he had been deliberately misled by a former Solicitor General. Acting on behalf of a constituent who suspected that his mail had been tampered with, Mr. Lawrence had written in 1973 to the then Solicitor General who assured him that as a matter of policy the RCMP did not intercept the private mail of anyone. However, on November 1, 1978, in testimony before the McDonald Commission, the former commissioner of the RCMP stated that they did indeed intercept mail on a very restricted basis and that the practice was not one which had been concealed from Ministers. Mr. Lawrence claimed that this statement clearly conflicted with the information he had received from the then Solicitor General some years earlier. On December 6, Speaker Jerome dealt with a number of points raised in the presentations on the question of privilege and ruled the matter *prima facie*. Mr. Lawrence then moved that the matter be referred to the Standing Committee on Privileges and Elections for investigation and report. The motion was debated over the course of two days and was negatived on a recorded division. See *Journals*, November 9, 1978, pp. 125-9; December 6, 1978, pp. 221-4; December 7, 1978, pp. 228-9; *Debates*, November 3, 1978, pp. 777-92; November 8, 1978, p. 924; November 9, 1978, pp. 964-6; December 6, 1978, pp. 1856-77; December 7, 1978, pp. 1892-925.

In another example involving a government official, Speaker Francis found a *prima facie* case of privilege involving the intimidation of an employee of a Member. In a ruling given on February 20, 1984, the Speaker stated: "A threat emanating from any government department or public corporation to withhold information or co-operation from a Member of Parliament would undoubtedly hinder that Member in the fulfilment of his or her parliamentary duties and therefore constitute a breach of privilege. By the same token, an offer of favourable treatment on condition that questions are first cleared with the office concerned would also violate privilege in an equally fundamental way. . . . It is therefore the view of the Chair that an action which amounts to a form of intimidation does not need to be directed at the Member in person in order to constitute an offence in terms of privilege."[176]

Just as *prima facie* cases of privilege have been found for the intimidation of Members and their staff, the intimidation of a committee witness was also found to be *prima facie* contempt by Speaker Fraser on December 4, 1992. The matter was referred by the House to the Standing Committee on House Management for consideration.[177] The Committee presented its Sixty-Fifth Report to the House on February 18, 1993, and the Report was concurred in by the House on February 25.[178] In its report, the Committee reaffirmed the principles of parliamentary privilege and the

---

176. *Debates*, February 20, 1984, p. 1560. On February 6, 1984, Albert Cooper (Peace River) had risen on a question of privilege arising out of a telephone conversation between a member of his staff and an official in the office of the President of Canada Post Corporation. Mr. Cooper, Opposition critic for Canada Post, alleged that the official had been abusive. The official had complained that Mr. Cooper's office had not cleared questions asked by the Member in the House with the President's office and warned that if this was not done in the future, Mr. Cooper could expect little co-operation from Canada Post. Mr. Cooper argued that this was an attempt to inhibit his freedom of speech, influence his actions in the House and hamper him in his role as spokesman for the Official Opposition. On February 9, 1984, the Minister of Labour (André Ouellet), who was also responsible for Canada Post, reported to the House that he had spoken to the official involved who denied making any such threats. The Minister also challenged the validity of Mr. Cooper's question of privilege since it was based on a conversation between his assistant and the officer at Canada Post and did not directly involve the Member. On February 20, 1984, the Speaker ruled that a *prima facie* question of privilege had been established. Mr. Cooper then moved a motion to refer the matter to the Standing Committee on Privileges and Elections. The question was put and the motion was negatived on a recorded division. See *Debates*, February 6, 1984, pp. 1101-6; February 9, 1984, pp. 1234-5; February 14, 1984, pp. 1382-4; February 20, 1984, pp. 1559-61; *Journals*, February 20, 1984, pp. 188-9.

177. Don Boudria (Glengarry–Prescott–Russell) rose on a question of privilege concerning alleged threats to a witness who had appeared before a sub-committee. Mr. Boudria contended that witnesses before committees enjoy the same privileges as Members of the House and are accorded the temporary protection of the House. In the Member's opinion, if such threats were to go unchallenged, it would imply that witnesses before committees could not testify without the threat of being sued or intimidated (*Debates*, December 4, 1992, pp. 14629-31).

178. *Journals*, February 18, 1993, p. 2528; February 25, 1993, p. 2568.

extension of privilege to witnesses. The report stated: "The protection of witnesses is a fundamental aspect of the privilege that extends to parliamentary proceedings and those persons who participate in them. It is well established in the Parliament of Canada, as in the British Parliament, that witnesses before committees share the same privileges of freedom of speech as do Members. Witnesses before parliamentary committees are therefore automatically extended the same immunities from civil or criminal proceedings as Members for anything that they say before a committee.... The protection of witnesses extends to threats made against them or intimidation with respect to their presentations before any parliamentary committee."[179]

Intimidation of the Speaker and Other Chair Occupants

As with the intimidation of a Member or witness, the intimidation or attempted intimidation of the Speaker or any other Chair occupant is viewed very seriously by the House. On three occasions, the House has viewed criticisms of the impartiality of the Chair as attempts at intimidation and, therefore, as privilege matters.[180] On December 22, 1976, the House adopted a motion finding that a statement made in a newspaper article about Speaker Jerome was a gross libel on the Speaker and that the publication of the article was a gross breach of the privileges of the House.[181] On March 23, 1993, Speaker Fraser ruled that a question of privilege regarding comments on the impartiality of a Chair occupant by a Member of the House was a *prima facie* case of privilege, noting that an attack against the integrity of an officer of the

---

179. Standing Committee on House Management, Sixty-Fifth Report, *Minutes of Proceedings and Evidence*, February 18, 1993, Issue No. 46, p. 9. The Report also quoted *May*, 21st ed., p. 131: "Any conduct calculated to deter prospective witnesses from giving evidence before either House or a committee is a contempt [of Parliament]. . . . On the same principle, molestation of or threats against those who have previously given evidence before either House or a committee will be treated by the House as a contempt."

180. See also Chapter 7, "The Speaker and Other Presiding Officers of the House".

181. The matter was raised by Allan MacEachen (President of the Privy Council) on a motion on matters of urgency moved without notice. The text of the motion read: "That the statement 'Let it be said of James Jerome that he is not a Speaker but a gambler who plays incredible odds for the popularity of his party' contained in the editorial in the *Globe and Mail* on December 22, 1976, is a gross libel on Mr. Speaker, and that the publication of the article is a gross breach of the privileges of this House." See *Debates*, December 22, 1976, p. 2241.

House was also an attack against the House.[182] On March 9, 1998, Peter MacKay (Pictou–Antigonish–Guysborough) rose on a question of privilege to claim that quotations attributed to certain Members of the House in a newspaper article constituted an attempt to intimidate the Speaker and, collectively, the House. The Member was concerned that comments, attributed by the media to Members about matters which were before the Chair for adjudication and suggesting that if the Speaker ruled a particular way he should be removed, were attempting to influence the ruling of the Chair. Speaker Parent ruled that there was a *prima facie* case of privilege.[183]

Constituency or Politically Related Instances

In instances where Members have claimed that they have been obstructed or harassed, not directly in their roles as elected representatives but while being involved in matters of a political or constituency-related nature, Speakers have consistently ruled that this does not constitute privilege.

On July 15, 1980, in finding that there was no *prima facie* case of privilege in relation to a Member's constituency work, Speaker Sauvé stated: "While I am only too aware of the multiple responsibilities, duties, and also the work the member has to do relating to his constituency, as Speaker I am required to consider only those matters which affect the member's parliamentary work. That is to say, whatever duty a member has to his constituents, before a valid question of privilege arises in respect of any alleged interference, such interference must relate to the member's parliamentary duties. In other words, just as a member is protected from anything he does

---

182. On March 16, 1993, Gilles Bernier (Beauce) rose on a question of privilege regarding comments made by Benoît Tremblay (Rosemont) and reported in a newspaper, which cast doubts on the integrity and impartiality of Charles DeBlois (Beauport–Montmorency–Orléans), Assistant Deputy Chairman of Committees of the Whole. The Speaker ruled that the matter was a *prima facie* case of privilege; Mr. Bernier then moved a motion to refer the matter to the Standing Committee on House Management and the motion was adopted. On March 25, 1993, Mr. Tremblay rose in the House and withdrew the offending comments. No further action was taken and the Committee did not report on the matter. See *Debates*, March 16, 1993, p. 17027; March 23, 1993, pp. 17403-5; March 25, 1993, p. 17537; *Journals*, March 23, 1993, p. 2688.

183. Mr. MacKay moved a motion that the matter be referred to the Standing Committee on Procedure and House Affairs. Debate on the motion ensued, continuing the next day, and the motion was adopted with an amendment on a recorded division. See *Debates*, March 9, 1998, pp. 4560-75; March 10, 1998, pp. 4592-8, 4666-8; *Journals*, March 9, 1998, p. 540; March 10, 1998, pp. 548, 550-2. On April 27, 1998, the Committee presented its Twenty-Ninth Report, which was concurred in by the House on May 5, 1998 (*Journals*, April 27, 1998, p. 706; April 29, 1998, p. 722; May 5, 1998, pp. 744-5). In its report, the Committee noted that the Members involved were adamant that they had not intended to intimidate or threaten the Speaker in any way or show disrespect for the House or the Speaker. It concluded that the statements attributed to the Members "were not intended to be contemptuous of the House of Commons or the Speaker" (Standing Committee on Procedure and House Affairs, Twenty-Ninth Report, April 27, 1998, p. 5).

while taking part in a proceeding in Parliament, so too must an interference relate to the member's role in the context of parliamentary work."[184]

This view was further reinforced in a ruling given on November 17, 1987, by Speaker Fraser, following a question of privilege on a matter involving the staff of a Member, a constituent, and an officer of the Correctional Services. The Speaker ruled that there was no *prima facie* case of privilege explaining ". . . I am sure Hon. Members will appreciate that this matter does not fall within the restricted scope of the concept of parliamentary privilege. . . . Indeed, I can go further and state that even without the direct involvement of the staff person and with the direct involvement of the Member himself, I could not find that a *prima facie* case of privilege exists."[185]

Importance of Relationship to Parliamentary Duties

In some cases where *prima facie* privilege has not been found, the rulings have focussed on whether or not the parliamentary duties of the Member were directly involved. While frequently noting that Members raising such matters might have

---

184. *Debates*, July 15, 1980, pp. 2914-5. On July 3, 1980, Bill Domm (Peterborough) rose on a question of privilege to protest that not only had the Department of the Secretary of State been ordered not to send him a list of the new Canadian citizens in his constituency, but moreover, he had been deliberately misled by officials and personally supplied with false documents. In finding that there was no *prima facie* question of privilege, the Speaker noted that the documents submitted by the Member did not clearly indicate inaccuracies. Furthermore, even if they had been shown to be incorrect, falsified or altered, which they had not, there was no indication that the intent had been to deceive the House. See also *Debates*, July 3, 1980, pp. 2540-6; July 14, 1980, pp. 2855-7.

185. *Debates*, November 17, 1987, p. 10888. On October 26, 1987, John Nunziata (York South–Weston) rose on a question of privilege regarding the alleged interception by the Correctional Service of Canada of a telephone conversation between the Member's office and an inmate of Joyceville Penitentiary who was also a constituent. Mr. Nunziata alleged that "As a result of this conversation the inmate was transferred to the maximum security penitentiary at Millhaven and put in segregation". The Member contended that his privileges as a Member had been breached with regard to his ability to deal with constituents "in an unfettered fashion" and his privileges as an Opposition critic for the Solicitor General had been breached with regard to access to inmates and conducting conversations with them in private. The Member also contended that, although he did not speak personally with the inmate, his privileges as a Member must also extend to any staff working on his behalf. On November 17, 1987, in his ruling, the Speaker noted that the House cannot create new privileges. Quoting a 1971 Speaker Lamoureux ruling, the Speaker reiterated that the House should not construe circumstances in such a way as to add to the privileges which have been recognized over the years. The Speaker indicated that he was unable to find anything which would extend parliamentary privilege to the actions of the staff of a Member. Indeed, the Speaker contended, even with the direct involvement of the Member, he could not find that a *prima facie* case of privilege existed. With regards to the Member's status as an Opposition critic to the Solicitor General, the Speaker stated that, although the position may bring extra responsibilities, it does not afford any special privileges above those of any other Member. See *Debates*, October 26, 1987, pp. 10385-7; October 27, 1987, pp. 10447-9; November 17, 1987, pp. 10887-9.

legitimate complaints, Speakers have regularly concluded that Members have not been prevented from performing their parliamentary duties. The following cases illustrate this.

In two 1978 cases, the Speaker ruled that since the Members' parliamentary duties had not been directly infringed upon, no *prima facie* breach of privilege existed. In the first case, involving Ron Huntington (Capilano), the Speaker had difficulty in accepting that the Member's complaint concerning a civil suit brought against him constituted harassment or obstruction in the narrow sense and further expressed concern about extending the definition of privilege. In ruling that he could find no *prima facie* case of privilege, Speaker Jerome noted: "It seems quite clear that this matter has caused the member certain difficulties in the performance of his duties as a member of parliament, but I have trouble in accepting the argument that these difficulties constitute obstruction or harassment in the narrow sense in which one must construe the privilege of freedom from molestation, particularly in the face of what must be construed as being ordinary access to the courts of the land, which surely ought to be something parliament would interfere with only upon the most grave and serious grounds." [186]

The second 1978 case was raised by Simma Holt (Vancouver–Kingsway) on November 2, 1978. In ruling that there was no *prima facie* question of privilege, Speaker Jerome stated: "Since the member was not in the circumstances acting in the official capacities which are surrounded by privilege—that very narrow category—it would, I think, be unwarranted extension of the precedents to extend privilege with respect to an act which was directed to her person in the circumstances". [187] In ruling, the Speaker noted that society demands much of Members but

---

186. *Debates*, May 15, 1978, p. 5411. On May 2, 1978, Ron Huntington (Capilano) raised a question of privilege. He explained that the Canadian Union of Postal Workers (CUPW) (Vancouver) had brought a civil suit against him because of remarks he had made on a radio talk show in which he repeated sentiments originally expressed in a committee of the House. Mr. Huntington complained that he was the victim of harassment and attempted intimidation and that the actions of the union were calculated to obstruct him in the performance of his parliamentary duties. Mr. Huntington based his question of privilege upon two points: a Member's right to protection from obstruction and the concept of a parliamentary proceeding. Mr. Huntington claimed that his remarks, since they had been made originally in committee, fell within the ambit of a parliamentary proceeding. In his ruling, the Speaker pointed out that while there may be circumstances in which a matter arising outside Parliament can properly be considered as an extension of a proceeding in Parliament, and therefore be covered by privilege, a radio talk show would not be one. See *Debates*, May 2, 1978, pp. 5069-73; May 15, 1978, p. 5411.

187. *Debates*, November 2, 1978, p. 730. On October 31, 1978, Simma Holt (Vancouver–Kingsway) had risen on a question of privilege claiming that she had been verbally insulted and had had a protest button pulled from her hand by a commissioner at a Canadian Radio-television and Telecommunications Commission hearing in British Columbia. The Member had been attending the CRTC hearing to intervene on behalf of constituents over cable television service in Vancouver. The actions taken against her, she argued, interfered with her right as a Member of Parliament to appear and discharge her responsibilities to her constituents before a federal commission. She claimed that the actions of the commissioner against her constituted a breach of privilege and a contempt of Parliament. See *Debates*, October 31, 1978, pp. 645-50; November 2, 1978, pp. 729-31.

not all demands strictly impose a parliamentary duty. Every Member has duties as a representative of the electorate. A Member may only claim the protection of privilege relating to his or her parliamentary duties, "particularly in his primary duty or service to this House of Commons here", though the line distinguishing these duties might blur. However, as *Maingot* has pointed out, while assaults on Members that occur outside the precinct and that are unrelated to the Member's parliamentary duties do not amount to contempt, the same assault occurring within the precinct, yet unrelated to a proceeding in Parliament, would constitute contempt of the House.[188]

On May 15, 1985, Douglas Frith (Sudbury) rose on a question of privilege claiming that his ability to serve his constituents was being infringed or impeded by a departmental directive restricting the release of information about a government program. In ruling that, while the Member did have a complaint, there was no *prima*

---

188. *Maingot*, 2nd ed., p. 256; see also pp. 165-6. Maingot cites the case of the physical assault on J.B.E. Dorion (Drummond and Arthabaska) by Elzéar Gérin Lajoie, editor of the newspaper, *Le Canada,* which took place in the Library of the Legislative Assembly of the Province of Canada while the Assembly was sitting on July 31, 1866. An argument had taken place over an article about Mr. Lajoie published in the newspaper, *Le Défricheur,* owned by Mr. Dorion. Ultimately, blows were exchanged. After the matter was raised in the House, the House adopted an order that the Speaker issue a warrant to the Sergeant-at-Arms to take Mr. Lajoie into custody and bring him to the Bar of the House forthwith (*Journals*, July 31, 1866, p. 257). On August 1, 1866, Mr. Lajoie appeared at the Bar and explained his actions. The House then resolved that Mr. Lajoie was guilty of a breach of the privileges of the House and ordered that he be reprimanded at the Bar by the Speaker and committed to the custody of the Sergeant-at-Arms during the pleasure of the House. Mr. Lajoie was then reprimanded by the Speaker as follows:

> Mr. *Gérin Lajoie* — It is a power incidental to the constitution of this House to preserve peace and order within its precincts, and protect the Members of it from insults and assault. This power is necessary, not only to insure the freedom of action of Members, but that freedom of discussion which is one of their fundamental rights.

> You, *Elzéar Gérin Lajoie*, pretending a cause of complaint against a Member of this House, sought him out, and came within the precincts of this Building, and within a part thereof to which you are entitled to resort—not by right, but by favour only—grossly insulted that Honorable Member, and concluded by violently assaulting him. For these gross breaches of privilege you have not even thought it judicious or becoming to offer any apology; you have mistaken your rights and position in reference to Honorable Members and in this Building. The place in which this insult was offered and assault committed greatly aggravates the criminality of your conduct.

> Having been found guilty of a breach of the privileges of this House, in having assaulted *Jean Baptiste Eric Dorion*, Esquire, a Member thereof, you have rendered yourself liable to such punishment as this House might award; and this House having ordered that you be reprimanded, you are reprimanded accordingly.

> The Order of the House directs that you be committed to the custody of the Sergeant-at-Arms, during the pleasure of this House (*Journals*, August 1, 1866, pp. 263-6).

facie question of privilege, Speaker Bosley noted that the purpose of parliamentary privilege was to protect freedom of speech in the House and to protect the institution from threats, obstructions and intimidations.[189]

Again on May 1, 1986, Speaker Bosley ruled that there was no *prima facie* case of privilege on a matter raised by Sheila Copps (Hamilton East). Reiterating the reasons invoked in previous rulings, the Speaker stated: "If an Hon. Member is impeded or obstructed in the performance of his or her parliamentary duties through threats, intimidation, bribery attempts or other improper behaviour, such a case would fall within the limits of parliamentary privilege. Should an Hon. Member be able to say that something has happened which prevented him or her from performing functions, that he or she has been threatened, intimidated, or in any way unduly influenced, there would be a case for the Chair to consider."[190]

On December 9, 1986, in ruling on a question of privilege raised by Nelson Riis (Kamloops–Shuswap), claiming that the information provided by the government at a press conference concerning a bill not yet introduced in the House amounted to a breach of privilege, Speaker Fraser stated that in no way had the actions of the Minister impeded or obstructed any Member in the discharge of his or her duties.[191]

On March 24, 1994, Speaker Parent ruled on a question of privilege raised by Jag Bhaduria (Markham–Whitchurch–Stouffville) who had claimed he was being intimidated by the media and had received blackmail threats as a result of media reports concerning the authenticity of the Member's academic credentials. In finding that there was no *prima facie* question of privilege, the Speaker stated: "Threats of blackmail or intimidation of a Member of Parliament should never be taken lightly. When such occurs, the very essence of free speech is undermined. Without the guarantee of freedom of speech, no Member of Parliament can do his duty as is expected. . . . While the Chair does not in any way make light of the specifics that

---

189. *Debates*, May 15, 1985, pp. 4768-9.

190. On April 29, 1986, Sheila Copps (Hamilton East) rose on a question of privilege arguing that her privileges had been adversely affected in that the office of the Deputy Prime Minister (Erik Nielsen) had improperly monitored communications between Members of Parliament and the Assistant Deputy Registrar General with the intention of interfering with the exercise of their duties and attempting to intimidate them. This focussed on Members' inquiries of the Assistant Deputy Registrar General about compliance with conflict of interest guidelines. In his ruling, the Speaker felt that the fact that the Deputy Prime Minister had inquired whether Members of Parliament had been in communication with the Assistant Deputy General did not seem to constitute an interception of those communications. See *Debates*, April 29, 1986, p. 12756; April 30, 1986, p. 12791; May 1, 1986, p. 12847.

191. *Debates*, November 6, 1986, p. 1147; December 9, 1986, p. 1903.

have been raised . . . I cannot, however, say that he has sufficiently demonstrated that a case of intimidation exists such that his ability to function as a member of Parliament has been impeded." [192]

In another instance involving written questions on the *Order Paper,* John Williams (St. Albert) claimed that an unnamed official in the office of the Leader of the Government in the House had deliberately tried to interfere with the Member by denying him a response to his questions. Based on quotations by the media, the Member claimed that the official's "arrogance and insolence . . . in the face of Parliament" were contemptuous. In a ruling given on May 6, 1996, Speaker Parent noted: " . . . it is very difficult to accept the veracity of the remarks allegedly made by an unidentified person in the government House leader's office. As such, I cannot find that the member has been obstructed in performing his duties and hence there is no question of privilege." [193]

Rights of the House as a Collectivity

In contrast to the privileges and immunities of individual Members, which are finite, the privileges and powers of the House of Commons as a collectivity do not lend themselves to specific definition. The privileges needed by the House to perform its constitutional duties require the power to protect itself and punish any transgressions against it. [194] Much like a court of law, the House of Commons enjoys very wide latitude in maintaining its dignity and authority through its exercise of contempt power, which is inherent to any superior court. In other words, the House may through its orders consider any misconduct to be contempt and may deal with it

---

192. *Debates*, March 24, 1994, p. 2706. Jag Bhaduria (Markham–Whitchurch–Stouffville) had raised the matter on February 15, 1994, claiming that media accounts of a dispute he had had with the Toronto Board of Education over his academic credentials while in their employ impeded his ability to function effectively and efficiently as a Member of Parliament. He also stated that he had been threatened by an anonymous caller. See *Debates*, February 15, 1994, pp. 1387-8; February 16, 1994, p. 1431; February 17, 1994, pp. 1507-8; February 23, 1994, p. 1728; March 23, 1994, p. 2677; March 24, 1994, pp. 2705-6.

193. *Debates*, May 6, 1996, p. 2367. On April 24, 1996, John Williams (St. Albert) rose on a question of privilege to argue that statements by an official in the Government House Leader's office quoted in the media to the effect that the Member's questions were outrageous and that the Government was not going to divert personnel to answer the questions were a contempt of the House. On May 6, 1996, stressing the importance of written questions as a tool for Members which help to hold the government accountable for its actions, the Speaker ruled that there was no question of privilege since the Deputy House Leader had indicated that answers to the questions were being prepared. See *Debates*, April 24, 1996, pp. 1894-7; May 6, 1996, pp. 2366-7.

194. *Maingot*, 2nd ed., p. 179. For a full description of the corporate rights, privileges and powers of the House and of the Senate, see *Maingot*, 2nd ed., pp. 179-215.

accordingly. This area of parliamentary law is therefore extremely fluid and most valuable for the Commons to be able to meet novel situations.

As a collectivity, the House of Commons has a certain number of rights which it claims or which have been accorded to it by statute. For example, the House claims the right to institute inquiries into any matter, requires the attendance of witnesses, and orders the production of documents; the *Parliament of Canada Act* confers the right to administer oaths to witnesses.[195]

The rights and powers of the House as a collectivity may be categorized as follows:

- the power to discipline;
- the regulation of its own internal affairs;
- the authority to maintain the attendance and service of its Members;
- the right to institute inquiries and to call witnesses and demand papers;
- the right to administer oaths to witnesses;
- the right to publish papers containing defamatory material.

The two most dominant rights or powers are the power to discipline and the right of the House to regulate its own internal affairs.

POWER TO DISCIPLINE

Whether it is against its own Members, staff or "strangers", the House has the power to discipline whoever is guilty of a misconduct, which it considers to amount to a breach of privilege or contempt. Article 9 of the *Bill of Rights* gives both Members and strangers protection from outside interference when engaged in the business of the House; it also subjects them to the disciplinary power of the House for their conduct during proceedings.[196] This power affords the House a wide range of penalties for dealing with misconduct: non-Members may be removed from the galleries of the Chamber or from the parliamentary precinct, be given a reprimand, or incarcerated; Members may be called to order, directed to cease speaking because of persistent repetition and irrelevance in debate, "named" for disregarding the authority of the Chair, suspended from the service of the House, incarcerated or even expelled. The disciplinary power of the House is to some extent regulated through the Standing Orders so that each case need not be raised formally in the House in order to be dealt with efficiently.[197] For example, this disciplinary power allows the House,

---

195. R.S.C. 1985, c. P-1, ss. 10-13.

196. *Maingot*, 2nd ed., p. 180.

197. Power is delegated to the Speaker, particularly in relation to discipline within the Chamber, under the provisions of Standing Orders 10, 11 and 16. Power is also delegated to the Sergeant-at-Arms in the case of "strangers" under Standing Orders 157 and 158.

through its Officers, to refuse entry to a stranger who has on previous occasions been guilty of misconduct in the public galleries or corridors.

Individuals who come within the jurisdiction of the House, whether strangers, staff or Members themselves, are subject to its discipline for any form of misconduct not only within the parliamentary precinct but also outside.[198] For example, sittings of a committee outside the precinct would be covered by the disciplinary power of the House.

Though a keystone of parliamentary privilege, the power of the House to discipline is nevertheless limited: the House has the right to reprimand and to imprison only until the end of the session; it does not have the power to impose fines.[199] In Canada, Parliament has been reluctant to use these powers and such cases have been rare. With the adoption of the *Charter of Rights and Freedoms,* there is even some question as to the constitutionality of Parliament's right to impose incarceration.[200]

Censure, Reprimand and the Summoning of Individuals to the Bar of the House

On a number of occasions in the late nineteenth and early twentieth centuries, individuals were summoned to appear before the Bar of the House. The Bar is a brass rod extending across the floor of the Chamber inside its south entrance beyond which strangers are not allowed. Individuals who are in contempt of the House—that is, are guilty of an offence against the dignity or authority of Parliament—may be formally summoned by the House to appear before it, if the House adopts a motion to that effect. When summoned, the individual stands at the Bar. The House has ordered Members to attend in their places in the House and has summoned others to the Bar of the House, to answer questions or to receive censures, admonitions or reprimands. Although, at first view, this may not appear to be a punishment, the summoning of a Member to attend in his or her place or of an individual to the Bar is an extraordinary event which places the Member or individual under the authority of the House vested with its full disciplinary powers.

In 1873, James Bell, a Returning Officer, was summoned to appear before the Bar to answer for his actions in a contested election. He appeared, asked and received permission to have counsel, and answered questions. The House adopted a

---

198. *Maingot,* 2nd ed., pp. 193-5.

199. *May,* 22nd ed., p. 138, notes that the last time the British House of Commons imposed a fine was in 1666 and its power to do so was denied by Lord Mansfield in *R v Pitt* in 1762.

200. For further elaboration, see section below entitled "Privilege and the Constitution". See also *Maingot,* 2nd ed., pp. 334-41.

resolution criticizing Mr. Bell's actions. He was recalled to the Bar, the resolution was read out to him and he was discharged.[201]

Again in 1873, the editor of the *Courrier d'Outaouais* newspaper, Elie Tassé, who was also a sessional employee of the House of Commons, was ordered to appear before the Bar of the House to answer questions about an article reflecting on two Members of the House. Mr. Tassé appeared, answered questions and was then allowed to withdraw.[202]

In November 1873, the Sergeant-at-Arms was ordered to take Ottawa Alderman John Heney into custody and bring him to the Bar of the House for attempting to bribe a Member. Mr. Heney was held in custody from November 4 to 7, 1873, but never appeared at the Bar as Parliament was prorogued on November 7.[203]

On March 31 and April 1, 1874, Louis Riel (Provencher) was ordered to attend in his place in the House for having fled from justice in the matter of the murder of Thomas Scott. He failed to attend and was later expelled from the House. Three witnesses were summoned to appear at the Bar (the Attorney-General of Manitoba and two police officers of Ottawa) in relation to the Riel matter. All three appeared and were questioned.[204]

In 1879, a visitor in the gallery, John Macdonnell, directed offensive remarks to a Member and, having been removed from the gallery, repeated the remarks in a note delivered to the Member at his place in the House. As a result, he was summoned to appear at the Bar, whereupon he apologized. He was asked to withdraw and the House then adopted a motion stating that Mr. Macdonnell had breached the privileges of the House, but that no further action was necessary in light of the apology. Mr. Macdonnell was recalled and the resolution read to him before he was discharged.[205]

In May 1887, John Dunn, a Returning Officer, was asked to appear before the Bar to answer for his conduct during an election. Mr. Dunn received the permission of the House to have counsel and answered many questions. He was discharged and no further action was taken.[206]

In 1891, Michael Connolly, a witness before the Privileges and Elections Committee, attended as requested with certain documents which he refused to put into the hands of the Committee. The Committee reported this to the House and requested "the action of the House". A motion was then moved and adopted for

---

201. *Journals*, March 10, 1873, pp. 10-12; March 26, 1873, pp. 70-3; March 27, 1873, pp. 75-7; March 28, 1873, p. 84.

202. *Journals*, April 7, 1873, pp. 133-4. According to *Bourinot*, 4th ed., p. 53, the Speaker subsequently informed the House that Mr. Tassé had been dismissed.

203. *Journals*, November 3, 1873, pp. 134-5; November 4, 1873, p. 139; November 7, 1873, p. 142.

204. *Journals*, March 30, 1874, p. 8; March 31, 1874, pp. 10-3; April 1, 1874, pp. 14, 17-8; April 9, 1874, pp. 32-9; April 15, 1874, pp. 64-5; April 16, 1874, pp. 67-71; April 17, 1874, p. 74.

205. *Journals*, May 13, 1879, p. 423; May 15, 1879, p. 436; February 16, 1880, p. 24; February 24, 1880, pp. 58-9.

206. *Journals*, May 12, 1887, p. 121; May 30, 1887, pp. 187-93.

Mr. Connolly to appear before the Bar. He appeared, was questioned, granted counsel, and ordered to produce the books of account requested by the Committee.[207]

Again in 1891, the Public Accounts Committee reported that André Senécal, an employee of the Government Printing Bureau, had failed to appear when called as a witness. The House adopted a motion summoning him to appear at the Bar. When he failed to do so, the House ordered that he be taken into the custody of the Sergeant-at-Arms, who could not locate him. No further action was taken.[208]

In 1894, two witnesses (Messrs. Provost and Larose) failed to appear when summoned as witnesses before the Privileges and Elections Committee. The Committee reported this and asked for "the action of the House". A motion was adopted summoning the two witnesses to appear before the Bar. They failed to comply and the House ordered them to be taken into the custody of the Sergeant-at-Arms in order to be brought to the Bar of the House. They later appeared, answered questions and were discharged.[209]

In 1906, William T. Preston, Inspector of Canadian Immigration in Europe, was a witness before the Agriculture and Colonization Committee as well as the Public Accounts Committee and refused to answer certain questions. Both committees reported this to the House. A motion was moved, based on the report of the Agriculture Committee, that he should be summoned to appear before the Bar of the House. However, the motion was amended to the effect that Preston was not required to appear, and the motion was adopted as amended.[210]

Also in 1906, a Member complained about a newspaper article; it was read and a motion was adopted summoning its author, E.E. Cinq-Mars, to appear before the Bar of the House. Mr. Cinq-Mars appeared and answered questions during that sitting of the House and at another sitting. The House then adopted a motion of censure against him, which was read to him before he was discharged. [211]

In 1913, R.C. Miller, a witness before the Public Accounts Committee, refused to answer questions. This was reported to the House, whereupon it adopted a motion summoning Mr. Miller to appear before the Bar and answer questions. Mr. Miller made two appearances before the Bar and on both occasions was permitted to have

---

207. *Journals*, June 5, 1891, p. 205; June 16, 1891, pp. 211-2.

208. *Journals*, August 27, 1891, p. 454; September 1, 1891, p. 467.

209. *Journals*, June 7, 1894, p. 242; June 11, 1894, p. 288; June 13, 1894, pp. 298-300.

210. At a later date, a Supply motion attempted to remove Mr. Preston from office but it was not adopted by the House. See *Journals*, May 30, 1906, p. 316; June 1, 1906, p. 323; June 4, 1906, pp. 331-3; July 3, 1906, pp. 475-6.

211. *Journals*, June 6, 1906, p. 342; June 7, 1906, pp. 345-6; June 14, 1906, pp. 370-7.

counsel. He was directed to withdraw after he refused to give the information requested by the Committee. The House then adopted a motion stating that Mr. Miller was in contempt of the House and that he should be imprisoned. Mr. Miller was again brought before the Bar and the resolution was read to him.[212]

In 1991, a Member rose on a question of privilege to allege that a contempt of the House had occurred at the adjournment of the previous sitting, when a Member, Ian Waddell (Port Moody–Coquitlam), had attempted to take hold of the Mace as it was carried out of the Chamber. The Speaker found a *prima facie* case of contempt, and the House adopted an order finding Mr. Waddell guilty of contempt and calling him to the Bar of the House to receive a reprimand from the Chair. Accordingly, the Member appeared at the Bar, was admonished by the Chair and declared guilty of a breach of privilege and a gross contempt of the House.[213]

Taking Individuals into Custody and Imprisonment

The House of Commons possesses the right to confine individuals as a punishment for contempt.[214] On occasion, it has ordered the Sergeant-at-Arms to take individuals into custody and has ordered the imprisonment of others. In May 1868, a Member who was chosen Chairman of a Select Committee failed to appear when the committee was sworn in and a motion was adopted in the House ordering him to be taken into custody by the Sergeant-at-Arms. The Sergeant-at-Arms informed the House that he had been unable to comply with the order and no further action was taken.[215] In 1873, two Members, Sir John A. Macdonald and Frederick Pearson, were members of a committee and failed to appear when they were to be sworn in. A motion was adopted in the House to have them taken into the custody of the Sergeant-at-Arms. When Mr. Macdonald appeared, another Member read an affidavit stating that he was unable to perform his duties for medical reasons. Mr. Macdonald was discharged. No further action was taken against Mr. Pearson, the Sergeant-at-Arms having informed the House that he had been unable to comply with the order, due to Mr. Pearson's absence from the city.[216] In the November 1873 Heney case, the alderman was held in custody from November 4 to 7.[217] In 1913, the House ordered

---

212. *Journals*, February 14, 1913, p. 249; February 17, 1913, p. 254; February 18, 1913, pp. 266-7; February 20, 1913, pp. 274-8.

213. *Journals*, October 31, 1991, pp. 574, 579; *Debates,* October 31, 1991, pp. 4271-85, 4309-10. As a sitting Member, the individual could have received the admonishment at his assigned place, which would have been the normal practice. In this case, however, the motion did specifically call for the Member to appear at the Bar.

214. *Maingot*, 2nd ed., pp. 193-209.

215. *Journals*, May 1, 1868, pp. 267-8; May 2, 1868, p. 271.

216. *Journals*, May 10, 1873, pp. 317-8; May 12, 1873, pp. 327-8.

217. *Journals*, November 3, 1873, p. 134-5; November 4, 1873, p. 139; November 7, 1873, p. 142.

the imprisonment of R.C. Miller after he appeared at the Bar and refused to answer questions. He remained in prison for some four months until the end of the session.[218]

Expulsion

Parliamentary privilege holds Members responsible for acting in character with the function they fulfil as elected representatives. Disobedience to orders of the House, and actions such as making threats, offering or taking bribes, or intimidating persons are offences for which Members can be reprimanded or even expelled. Under Section 18 of the *Constitution Act, 1867,* which endowed the Canadian House with the same privileges, immunities, and powers as enjoyed by the British House of Commons, the Canadian House of Commons possesses the power of expulsion. A serious matter, expulsion has a twofold purpose as explained in *May:*

> *The purpose of expulsion is not so much disciplinary as remedial, not so much to punish Members as to rid the House of persons who are unfit for membership. It may justly be regarded as an example of the House's power to regulate its own constitution. But it is more convenient to treat it among the methods of punishment at the disposal of the House.[219]*

Even this most drastic power has its limits as is noted in *Bourinot:*

> *The right of a legislative body to suspend or expel a member for what is sufficient cause in its own judgement is undoubted. Such a power is absolutely necessary to the conservation of the dignity and usefulness of a body. Yet expulsion, though it vacates the seat of a member, does not create any disability to serve again in parliament.[220]*

The House may expel a Member for offences committed outside his or her role as an elected representative or committed outside a session of Parliament. As *Maingot* explains, it "extends to all cases where the offence is such as, in the judgement of the House, to render the Member unfit for parliamentary duties."[221]

---

218. *Journals,* February 14, 1913, p. 249; February 17, 1913, p. 254; February 18, 1913, pp. 266-7; February 20, 1913, pp. 274-8.

219. *May,* 20th ed., p. 139.

220. *Bourinot,* 4th ed., p. 64. For a discussion of expulsion and in particular the possible role of the *Canadian Charter of Rights and Freedoms,* see Gwenn Ronyk, "The Power to Expel", *The Table,* Vol. 53 (1985), pp. 43-50, and Andrew Heard, "The Expulsion and Disqualification of Legislators: Parliamentary Privilege and the Charter of Rights", *Dalhousie Law Journal,* Vol. 18 (Fall 1995), pp. 380-407.

221. *Maingot,* 2nd ed., p. 211; see also pp. 212-5.

The House has expelled Members on four occasions. Louis Riel (Provencher) was expelled from the House twice. Riel had fled from justice after being charged with the murder of Thomas Scott. In the spring of 1874, the House ordered Mr. Riel to attend in his place. He failed to do so and the House expelled him.[222] In the autumn of that year, he was re-elected as Member for Provencher. Mr. Riel's second expulsion occurred in February 1875. On February 22, an "Exemplification of Judgement Roll of Outlawry in the case of *Regina vs. Riel*" was tabled in the House. On February 24, after this document was read to the House, the House adopted two orders, one noting that Mr. Riel had been judged an outlaw for felony and the other ordering the Speaker to issue his warrant for a new writ of election for the electoral district of Provencher, thus expelling Mr. Riel.[223]

In 1891, Thomas McGreevy (Quebec West) was accused by Israel Tarte (Montmorency) of corrupt practices concerning construction work in the Quebec Harbour, and the matter was referred by the House to the Select Standing Committee on Privileges and Elections. Mr. McGreevy refused to answer questions put to him while appearing before the Committee. The Committee reported this to the House on August 12, 1891, and requested that the House take action. On August 13, Mr. McGreevy was ordered by the House to attend in his place on August 18. On that day, Mr. McGreevy was found not to be in attendance and the Sergeant-at-Arms was ordered to take the Member into custody. On August 19, Mr. McGreevy sought to resign his seat, but the House refused to accept the resignation as his seat was being contested at the time. On September 29, the House adopted a resolution finding Mr. McGreevy guilty of contempt of the authority of the House by not attending in his place when ordered, as well as being guilty of certain other offences. The House then adopted a second resolution expelling Mr. McGreevy.[224]

On January 30, 1947, the House resolved that, since Fred Rose (Cartier) had been convicted of violating the *Official Secrets Act* and had been sentenced to serve six years in prison, he had become incapable of sitting or voting in the House. The motion also ordered the Speaker to issue a warrant to the Chief Electoral Officer to make out a writ of election to fill the vacancy. Although expulsion was not explicitly referred to in the motion, the House declared his seat vacant.[225]

---

222. *Journals*, April 15, 1874, pp. 64-5; April 16, 1874, pp. 67-71; April 17, 1874, p. 74.

223. *Journals*, February 4, 1875, p. 42; February 22, 1875, p. 111; February 24, 1875, pp. 118-25.

224. *Journals*, May 11, 1891, pp. 55-60; August 12, 1891, p. 402; August 13, 1891, p. 407; August 18, 1891, p. 414; August 19, 1891, pp. 417, 419; August 20, 1891, p. 422; September 1, 1891, pp. 466-7; September 4, 1891, p. 477; September 16, 1891, p. 512; September 24, 1891, pp. 527-31; September 29, 1891, p. 561.

225. *Journals*, January 30, 1947, pp. 4-8. The matter of the expulsion of Members is also treated in Chapter 4, "The House of Commons and Its Members".

REGULATION OF INTERNAL AFFAIRS

The exclusive right of the House of Commons to regulate its own internal affairs refers especially to its control of its own agenda and proceedings.[226] For example, courts or other institutions cannot direct the affairs of the Commons,[227] even when it may be in the interests of justice that cases pending before the courts not be discussed in a manner that might prejudice the outcome of such cases. The House of Commons is not obliged to restrain itself in matters *sub judice* so as to accommodate

---

226. See *Maingot*, 2nd ed., pp. 183-7. *Maingot* states: "The right to regulate its own internal affairs and procedures free from interference includes:

   1. The right to enforce discipline on Members of the House of Commons by suspension, commitment, and expulsion. However, this creates no disability to stand for re-election.

   2. The right to secure the attendance of persons on matters of privilege, and to deliberate and examine witnesses, and to do so behind closed doors (*in camera*). This latter aspect may properly be considered to be included with the right to exclude strangers from the precincts.

   3. The right to control the publication of its debates and proceedings and those of its committees by prohibiting their publication.

   4. The right to administer that part of the statute law relating to its internal procedure without interference from the courts.

   5. The right to administer its affairs within the precincts and beyond the debating Chamber, such as regulating the sale of intoxicating beverages within the precincts, and appointing and managing its staff.

   6. The right to settle its own code of procedure.

   7. The power to send for persons in custody."

227. Members have objected to what they considered unfair interference by the judiciary. For example, on February 3, 1998, John Bryden (Wentworth–Burlington) raised a question of privilege concerning remarks made by Justice Marcel Joyal of the Federal Court. During a court proceeding, Justice Joyal had criticized the behaviour of Members during a Question Period, when Members had cheered and applauded the announcement of the dismissal of the chairman of the Canadian Labour Relations Board by Lawrence MacAulay (Minister of Labour). (Justice Joyal had compared them to the crowds around the guillotine during the French Revolution.) The Chairman had initiated court proceedings to prevent his dismissal, and it was during these proceedings that Justice Joyal had made his comments. Mr. Bryden argued that Justice Joyal was in contempt of the House. In a statement on February 11, 1998, Speaker Parent noted that there is a necessary constitutional divide between the legislative and judicial branches. He also noted that the practice of the House is to treat as unparliamentary and a breach of order any reference to a judge or court which is a personal attack or censure. He went on to state that the House of Commons deserved at least the same respect from the courts. As the Clerk of the House had received correspondence from the Chairman of the judicial conduct committee of the Canadian Judicial Council that Justice Joyal's remarks were being investigated, the Speaker decided to await the outcome of the review before taking further action on Mr. Bryden's question of privilege (*Debates*, February 11, 1998, pp. 3737-8). On April 21, 1998, the Speaker tabled correspondence and documentation from the Judicial Council. The Council's committee had found that Justice Joyal's comments were inappropriate and outside the sphere of proper judicial expression. It also noted that the Justice had acknowledged publicly the inappropriateness of his remarks. The committee concluded that the Judge's conduct did not warrant a formal investigation. Speaker Parent stated that with the tabling of these documents he considered the matter closed (*Debates*, April 21, 1998, p. 5910; *Journals*, April 21, 1998, p. 682). See also Robert Marleau, "Relationship Between Parliament and the Courts in Canada: The Joyal Affair," *The Table*, Vol. 66 (1998), pp. 15-21.

the interests of justice. While, by convention, parliamentarians often exercise caution in deference to the courts, there is no legal obligation to do so. That is because there may be an equally important public interest in the public debate of issues which happen also to be before the courts.[228] Indeed, the passage of legislation by Parliament is often deliberately intended to influence the outcome of court cases.

The House of Commons is normally free from judicial review of its decisions when these are made pursuant to Standing Order, sessional order or resolution.[229] This is also true of Speakers' rulings interpreting such orders or resolutions. Thus, if Members feel that the rules of the House are not being applied as they would wish, there is no appeal to the courts.[230] If Standing Orders are breached, the only place to

---

228. On March 8, 1990, Speaker Fraser ruled on a point of order raised on March 5, 1990 by Nelson Riis (Kamloops). The Member had asked the Speaker to consider whether debate on the Budget, presented on February 20, 1990, should be allowed to continue and whether the House should suspend any proceedings in relation to a bill on notice based on the government's budget policy, given the action taken by the government of British Columbia to challenge in the courts the federal government's decision to cap its contributions to the Canada Assistance Plan. In his ruling, the Speaker pointed out that "as the debate on the budget is generally wide-ranging and touches upon all aspects of the government's budgetary policy, members are at liberty to debate or not debate whatever aspect of the motion they choose. Therefore I must rule that the *sub judice* convention does not apply in the present circumstances" (*Debates*, March 8, 1990, p. 9007). See also *Debates*, March 5, 1990, pp. 8767-70; March 8, 1990, pp. 9006-9.

229. For discussion of the possible role of the courts, see *Maingot*, 2nd ed., pp. 185-7. On January 22, 1999, Justice Chadwick of the Ontario Court (General Division) did rule on a matter brought before the Court which arose from an order of the House. On June 4, 1998, the House adopted the following order: "That this House order that Ernst Zundel be denied admittance to the precinct of the House of Commons during the present Session" (see *Journals*, June 4, 1998, p. 937; *Debates*, June 4, 1998, pp. 7608-9, 7616). The House had adopted this order to prevent Mr. Zundel from holding a press conference in the Canadian Parliamentary Press Gallery's Conference Room in the Centre Block of the Parliament Buildings. Mr. Zundel had brought an action against the political parties represented in the House of Commons, as well as a number of Members of Parliament, seeking a declaration that the defendants had violated his right to freedom of expression guaranteed under section 2(b) of the *Canadian Charter of Rights and Freedoms* which was not justified under section 1 of the Charter, and seeking damages against each defendant for, among other reasons, wrongfully and maliciously violating his right to freedom of expression with intent to injure him. In dismissing the action, Justice Chadwick found, among other reasons, that the House of Commons was exercising its parliamentary privilege in restricting the precinct of the House of Commons and did not prohibit Mr. Zundel from speaking. The Justice also stated: "Although there is no reference to the reason behind the decision, it is obvious it was to preserve the dignity and integrity of Parliament." (*Ernst Zundel v. Liberal Party of Canada et al.*, Reasons for Decision, Ontario Court (General Division), Court File No. 98-CV-7845, January 22, 1999.)

230. For example, although Standing Order 109 confers a right upon demand to a comprehensive response from the government to a committee report within 150 days of its presentation, the "right", which belongs to the committee requesting the response and not to individual Members, is not a legal right of which the courts may take any notice.

raise the point of order is in the House of Commons. Neither is a Speaker's ruling on such a point of order reviewable by the courts.

The exclusive right of the House of Commons to regulate its own internal affairs has also been construed to mean that local or provincial regulatory legislation does not ordinarily apply within the parliamentary precinct. Thus, for example, liquor permits are not required in order to operate a bar within the precinct, and elevators need not be certified safe by provincial authorities. [231] Process servers ordinarily may not enter the precinct in order to serve civil process on anyone. [232] Although the precinct of Parliament is not intended to be a sanctuary, the dignity of the House of Commons requires also that police forces not enter the precinct to investigate the commission of an offence without permission from the Speaker or the Sergeant-at-Arms. [233]

THE AUTHORITY TO MAINTAIN THE ATTENDANCE AND SERVICE OF ITS MEMBERS

The Standing Orders of the House provide that every Member is bound to attend the sittings of the House unless otherwise occupied with parliamentary activities or functions or on public or official business. [234] Ordinarily, the attendance of Members to their duties is not enforced by the House, and alluding to the presence or absence of Members in the Chamber is considered to be out of order. [235]

The attendance of Members is seen to be a function of the party leadership usually through the Whip or as a matter of personal obligation if the Member is without party affiliation. *May* notes: "Attendance upon the service of Parliament includes the

---

231. *Maingot*, 2nd ed., p. 165. However, *Maingot* notes: "Generally speaking, the ordinary civil and criminal laws of the Province of Ontario and of Canada respectively apply on Parliament Hill and within the precincts in the same way as elsewhere in Ontario" (p. 172).

232. On June 4, 1993, Brian Tobin (Humber–St. Barbe–Baie Verte) rose on a question of privilege complaining of intimidation and interference as he attempted to perform his parliamentary duties. The Member explained that he had been served with a notice of intention to bring action against him unless he made certain withdrawals concerning an individual, Mr. Ralfe. The Member was disturbed by the fact that the document had been served to him in the lobby of the House of Commons. On June 10, 1993, Deputy Speaker Champagne delivered a ruling in which she referred to the long-standing tradition that process cannot be served in the precinct of the House of Commons without the permission of the Speaker. She also made reference to the ruling of Speaker Fraser of May 19, 1989, on a question of privilege raised by David Kilgour (Edmonton Southeast) who had been served in his Centre Block Office. (See *Debates*, May 19, 1989, pp. 1951-3. See also above section entitled "Exemption from Appearing as a Witness".) The Deputy Speaker noted that the letter delivered to Mr. Tobin did not fall under the definition of process (implying an issuance from a court of law) as legal proceedings had not begun. She commented that, in this instance, there was no requirement to inform the Speaker and ruled that there was no *prima facie* case of privilege. See *Debates*, June 4, 1993, pp. 20375-7; June 10, 1993, pp. 20693-4. See also *Debates*, June 4, 1993, pp. 20371-2.

233. *Parliament of Canada Act*, R.S.C. 1985, c. P-1, s. 5.

234. Standing Order 15.

235. See Chapter 4, "The House of Commons and Its Members", and Chapter 13, "Rules of Order and Decorum".

obligation to fulfil the duties imposed upon Members by the orders and regulations of the House".[236]

THE RIGHTS TO INSTITUTE INQUIRIES, TO REQUIRE THE ATTENDANCE OF WITNESSES AND TO ORDER THE PRODUCTION OF DOCUMENTS

The ability of Parliament to institute its own inquiries, to require the attendance of witnesses and to order the production of documents is fundamental to its proper functioning. It is as old as Parliament itself. Much of this power is now exercised by committees pursuant to powers delegated to them in the Standing Orders.[237] "The only limitations, which could only be self-imposed, would be that any inquiry should relate to a subject within the legislative competence of Parliament, particularly where witnesses and documents are required and the penal jurisdiction of Parliament is contemplated. This dovetails with the right of each House of Parliament to summon and compel the attendance of all persons within the limits of their jurisdictions."[238]

THE RIGHT TO ADMINISTER OATHS TO WITNESSES

The right of the House and of its committees to examine witnesses under oath,[239] a right that was not part of the ancient custom of Parliament, has been conferred by legislation and is now contained in the *Parliament of Canada Act.*[240] The provisions of the Act allow witnesses to be examined under oath and authorize the Speaker, committee Chairs and anyone appointed by the Speaker to administer an oath or affirmation. It also stipulates that any person examined under oath who wilfully gives false evidence is liable to the penalties for perjury.

THE RIGHT TO PUBLISH PAPERS CONTAINING DEFAMATORY MATERIAL

The *Parliament of Canada Act*[241] provides protection for the publication, by order of the House, of any parliamentary paper which may contain or have appended to it

---

236. *May*, 22nd ed., p. 179.
237. Standing Order 108 (1)(*a*).
238. *Maingot*, 2nd ed., p. 190. See also p. 191. For a more detailed examination of the functioning of committees, see Chapter 20, "Committees".
239. See *Maingot*, 2nd ed., pp. 191-2.
240. R.S.C. 1985, c. P-1, ss. 10-13.
241. R.S.C. 1985, c. P-1, ss. 7-9.

defamatory material.[242] This includes all documents published by a committee acting under the authority of the House. This right is not intended to protect the publication of libels that may be contained in other documents, such as the householder mailings of Members.

The Inherent Limitations of Privilege

The collective privileges of the House of Commons and the individual privileges of its Members are subject to limitations. The courts have certain powers to delineate the rights claimed by Parliament, and statutory law has been used in some Parliaments to codify these rights, immunities and privileges. This section will examine the role of the courts in limiting privilege, the impact of codifying privilege into statutory law, and the relationship between privilege and the Constitution.

THE IMPACT OF THE COURTS ON PRIVILEGE

It is frequently stated that Parliament is the highest court in the land. This is true in that it is the high court of public opinion where the concerns of the electorate are voiced by their chosen representatives. It is also true that, in the medieval period, the English Parliament had a judicial role, where Parliament was seen primarily as a court of justice, the High Court of Parliament, a court of last resort consisting of the King and the lords temporal.[243] This role has all but disappeared in the United Kingdom.[244] The Canadian Parliament has never had a judicial role.[245]

The privileges enjoyed by Parliament are a part of the general and public law of Canada. As such, the courts may judicially take notice of and interpret these privileges as they would any branch of law, as noted in the *Parliament of Canada Act*:

> *The privileges, immunities and powers held, enjoyed and exercised in accordance with section 4 are part of the general and public law of Canada and it is not necessary to plead them but they shall, in all courts in Canada, and by and before all judges, be taken notice of judicially.*[246]

---

242. The famous case of *Stockdale v. Hansard* in the 1830s resulted in a decision by the British courts that parliamentary privilege did not provide the authority to publish defamatory material with impunity (see *Maingot*, 2nd ed., pp. 281-7). As a result, legislation was adopted throughout the British Empire in the nineteenth century to grant assemblies the right to publish documents which contained such material.

243. *Maingot*, 2nd ed., p. 16.

244. For the role of the House of Lords as a Court of Judicature, see *May*, 22nd ed., pp. 60-3.

245. For a history of the courts and parliamentary privilege, see *Maingot*, 2nd ed., pp. 271-302; *May*, 22nd ed., pp. 153-72.

246. R.S.C. 1985, c. P-1, s. 5.

A unique characteristic of privilege is that, although it may not appear to be the case, the rights and immunities claimed by elected representatives are controlled in large part by the courts. Though Parliament lays claim to sole control of its privileges, such claims have gone largely unchallenged because both courts and Parliaments are reluctant to deal definitively with such matters. However, in cases where privileges of Parliament have been challenged, the courts have on occasion more narrowly defined the privileges while on other occasions have supported the rights of Parliament. Thus, to some extent, the courts may determine or defend what are the privileges of Parliament.[247]

A part of the justification for the privileges of the United Kingdom's Parliament has rested upon the analogy with judicial practice.[248] A court has privileges auxiliary to the due execution of its powers. Just as witnesses and judges must speak freely, be protected from molestation and be released from other conflicting tasks and obligations, so it might be thought necessary to make similar provisions for "the Court of Parliament, the first and the highest court in the kingdom".[249]

The extensive power to punish contempts has a judicial flavour and origin in the United Kingdom, yet in reality the English Parliament in the twentieth century is not a court.[250] It has been British practice that where the House commits an individual to prison for contempt without stating the grounds, or commits generally, it appears that the courts will not inquire into the nature of the contempt.[251] However, where facts are stated in the warrant, the courts would be free to inquire into the grounds and, in suitable cases, declare the committals to be defective as arbitrary or unrelated to any known privilege of the House.[252]

CODIFICATION: THE AUSTRALIAN CASE

In order to alleviate some of the uncertainty traditionally inherent in the exercise of their privileges, some Parliaments based on the Westminster model have opted to codify their privileges.[253] In 1987, the Australian Parliament passed legislation

---

247. For a discussion of this matter, see *Odgers*, 8th ed., pp. 35-8, 40-2.

248. *May*, 22nd ed., pp. 65-6; *Maingot*, 2nd ed., p. 16.

249. *Hatsell*, Vol. 1, p. 1.

250. Geoffrey Marshall, "The House of Commons and Its Privileges," *The House of Commons in the Twentieth Century*, edited by S.A. Walkland, Oxford: Clarendon Press, 1979, p. 205; *May*, 22nd ed., pp. 131-2.

251. *Marshall*, p. 207; *May*, 22nd ed., p. 133.

252. *Marshall*, p. 207; *May*, 22nd ed., pp. 133, 135-6.

253. For a list of Commonwealth countries which had codified their privileges in statute as of 1966, see United Kingdom, House of Commons, Select Committee on Parliamentary Privilege, 1966-67, Report, pp. 184-5.

declaring, clarifying and substantially changing its law of parliamentary privilege. [254] Partly in consequence of the legislation, the Australian Senate passed a series of resolutions substantially codifying its practices in matters related to privilege. [255]

The Australian Parliament, finding that the courts were severely restricting its freedom of speech, enacted statutory remedies to protect its proceedings. The *Australian Parliamentary Privileges Act 1987* provides definitions for a number of concepts including contempt. By restricting the category of actions which may be treated as contempts, the Act could be seen as either limiting the right of action of either Australian House or of opening up the actions of both Houses to judicial interpretation. For example, a person punished for a contempt of Parliament could bring an action to attempt to establish that the conduct for which he or she was punished did not fall within the statutory definition. This could lead to a court overturning a punishment imposed by a House for contempt of Parliament. [256]

A number of concerns have been expressed in relation to the Australian statutory definition of privilege: the right of a House to expel a Member or the protection of witnesses before committees might be challenged in court; [257] the statute might unduly restrict the rights of litigants and defendants in using evidence given before parliamentary committees for the purposes of their court proceedings; the resulting statutory interpretation would further restrict the powers and immunities of Parliament; affirming privileges in statute would result in challenges to the right of the public and the media to comment on what happens in Parliament; [258] and should serious problems arise, they may be corrected only by further codification of the law through legislative amendment. [259] As the function of the courts is to consider and apply statutes, not to investigate the proceedings leading to the passage of laws, it has been seen that both the courts and Parliament have expressed the need to avoid conflict in interpreting the scope of privilege. [260]

254. Australia, Parliament, *Parliamentary Privileges Act 1987*. See also *Odgers*, 8th ed., pp. 27-8.

255. For the text of the Senate resolutions, see *Odgers*, 8th ed., pp. 537-52. See also Harry Evans, "Parliamentary Privilege: Legislation and Resolutions in the Australian Parliament", *The Table*, Vol. 56 (1988), pp. 21-2. This was done as a matter of necessity. The legislation was occasioned by two judgements of the Supreme Court of New South Wales, which severely restricted Parliament's privilege of freedom of speech. As Evans noted, there has always been great reluctance on the part of Parliaments, which have inherited their privilege, practices and traditions from Britain, to legislate for parliamentary privilege. The basic reason for this reluctance is the danger of unduly restricting the powers and immunities of Houses of Parliament by tying them to precise legislative terms. It was thought better to rely on common law and the broad terms of the old statutes such as the Bill of Rights.

256. *Evans*, p. 30.

257. *Evans*, pp. 31-3.

258. Sylvia Song, "The Reform of Parliamentary Privilege: Advantages and Dangers," *Legislative Studies*, Vol. 12, No. 1 (Spring 1997), p. 39.

259. *Evans*, p. 35.

260. *Song*, p. 31.

CODIFICATION: THE UNITED KINGDOM EXPERIENCE

Where Australia has opted to legislate codification of privilege, the United Kingdom has not, though it continues to review its practice and has altered its way of dealing with matters of privilege. The whole scope and application of privilege was reviewed by the Select Committee on Parliamentary Privilege in 1967-68; re-examined again in the Third Report of the same Committee in 1976-77; and revisited by the Joint Committee on Parliamentary Privilege in 1998-99. Prior to the 1967-68 Committee's appointment, some concern had been expressed about the number of occasions when criticisms had been raised in the House of breaches of privilege or contempt regarding relatively trivial matters.[261]

Having examined all aspects of privilege in the House, the 1967-68 Committee came down against any major changes in the law of privilege, especially the suggestion that jurisdiction in privilege cases should be transferred to the courts through statute.[262] The Committee did recommend that legislation be promoted to extend and clarify the scope of privilege.[263] It also recommended a number of significant reforms in the way privilege complaints should be considered.[264] It modified the procedure for their examination and, to a certain extent, codified procedures for dealing with matters of privilege.[265] Other reforms served to bring the House's formal rules into line with the practice of nearly 200 years.[266] The 1976-77 Committee re-examined the findings of the earlier committee and recommended the adoption of many of its recommendations.[267]

In his memorandum to the British Select Committee in 1976-77, the Clerk of the House cautioned against too rigidly codifying the House's options in dealing with matters of privilege. He wrote:

> *It would be a mistake first and foremost because it would introduce an element of inflexibility into the manner in which the House upholds its privileges and punishes contempts. It is true that the House would be in no*

---

261. United Kingdom, House of Commons, Select Committee on Parliamentary Privilege, 1966-67, Report, pp. v-vii, viii-xi, paras. 5-10, 16-24.

262. United Kingdom, House of Commons, Select Committee on Parliamentary Privilege, 1966-67, Report, p. xxxix, para. 146.

263. United Kingdom, House of Commons, Select Committee on Parliamentary Privilege, 1966-67, Report, p. xxvii, para. 87.

264. United Kingdom, House of Commons, Select Committee on Parliamentary Privilege, 1966-67, Report, pp. xlii- xliv, paras. 162-75.

265. United Kingdom, House of Commons, Select Committee on Parliamentary Privilege, 1966-67, Report, pp. xliv-xlvii, paras. 176-91.

266. See "Summary of Principal Recommendations", United Kingdom, House of Commons, Select Committee on Parliamentary Privilege, 1966-67, Report, pp. xlix-li, para. 205.

267. United Kingdom, House of Commons, Select Committee on Parliamentary Privilege, 1976-77, Third Report, pp. ix-x, paras. 16-8.

danger of abridging its privileges or powers by a mere resolution setting out the sort of cases upon which it normally proposed to act. But formulas which may appear precise and faultless at the time at which they are drafted, may be found to be defective at a later stage owing to some undis-covered loophole or developments which could not be envisaged at an ear-lier stage. It would certainly seem undesirable to have to ask the House to amend its resolutions on privileges with any frequency.[268]

Following the 1976-77 Report, the focus of the House in such matters appeared to shift to the conduct of Members. Allegations of misconduct by Members of the British House were dealt with as matters of conduct or standards and not as privilege. The development of the Register of Members' Interests institutionalized this approach, and this continued into the 1990s with the first report of the Committee of Privileges in 1994-95 and the Nolan Committee on Standards in Public Life which led to the establishment of the Select Committee on Standards in Public Life. This Committee made a number of recommendations pertaining to Members' conduct which resulted in the adoption of a Code of Conduct for Members, the remodelling of the Committee of Privileges as the Committee on Standards and Privileges, and the appointment of a Parliamentary Commissioner for Standards.[269]

In the 1997-98 session, the British Parliament created a Joint Committee on Par-liamentary Privilege with the broad mandate to review parliamentary privilege and make recommendations. Reappointed with the same terms of reference and member-ship in the 1998-99 session, the Committee presented its report to both Houses on March 30, 1999, and made a number of recommendations calling for the codification of various matters of privilege in statutory law.[270] The Committee recommended that "place out of Parliament" and "proceedings in Parliament" be defined in statute and that Members of both Houses be included within the scope of forthcoming legisla-tion on corruption. It called for the codification in statute of contempt of Parliament, for the abolition of Parliament's power to imprison for contempt and for the transfer of Parliament's penal powers over non-Members to the courts. It recommended the termination of Members' exemption from attendance in court as witnesses and the abolition of Members' freedom from arrest in civil cases. It also recommended the replacement of the *Parliamentary Papers Act 1840* by a modern statute and sug-gested that a Parliamentary Privileges Act be passed bringing together all the changes in the law it recommended and codifying parliamentary privilege as a whole.

---

268. United Kingdom, House of Commons, Select Committee on Parliamentary Privilege, 1976-77, Third Report, p. xiv, para. 16.

269. *May*, 22nd ed., p. 82.

270. See "Summary of Recommendations", United Kingdom, Joint Committee on Parliamentary Privilege, 1998-99, Report, pp. 1-7.

PRIVILEGE AND THE CONSTITUTION[271]

Section 18 of the *Constitution Act, 1867* provides that Parliament may not confer on itself any greater privileges than those enjoyed at the time by the House of Commons of the United Kingdom. "Clearly the courts could not review the manner in which Parliament exercised its privileges, for example, in punishing a person for contempt of Parliament. But it has long been held that the courts can ascertain whether the privilege asserted by Parliament is one recognized by the law. Therefore, the courts could in a proper case test any statute pursuant to Section 18 [of the *Constitution Act, 1867*] to determine whether the privilege it created was one which the Canadian Parliament was entitled to claim for itself. Such an issue might be raised by means of a reference or by proceedings such as *habeas corpus,* or by damage actions on behalf of individuals who had suffered at the hand of Parliament in the exercise of its alleged privileges."[272]

The adoption of the *Canadian Charter of Rights and Freedoms* in 1982, "ushered in a flood of constitutional litigation, gave Canadian courts a greater degree of superintendence over government, and dramatically changed the form and forum of politics. It was thus inevitable that the Canadian legislative assemblies and Houses of Parliament would become implicated in the *Charter*."[273]

As part of the general and public law of Canada,[274] parliamentary privilege, like any law, is now subject to the provisions of the *Charter*.[275] In 1993, the Supreme Court of Canada in *New Brunswick Broadcasting Co v. Nova Scotia (Speaker of the House of Assembly)* addressed the issue of whether and how the *Charter* applies to the provincial legislative assemblies and their proceedings, which had a direct impact on the powers, privileges and immunities of the House of Commons.[276] *Maingot* summarizes the decision as follows:

> *The majority held that the act of the House of assembly in excluding television cameras from the public galleries was an exercise of a constitutionally inherent privilege to exclude strangers from the House and its precinct. The basis of this inherent privilege is the preamble to the* Constitution Act, 1867 *in context of historical tradition and the pragmatic principle of necessity: the legislature must be presumed to possess such constitutional powers as are necessary for its proper functioning.*

---

271. See *Maingot*, 2nd ed., pp. 303-50.

272. Barry L. Strayer, *The Canadian Constitution and the Courts: The Function and Scope of Judicial Review*, 3rd ed., Toronto: Butterworths, p. 224.

273. *Maingot*, 2nd ed., p. 303.

274. *Parliament of Canada Act*, R.S.C. 1985, c. P-1, s. 5.

275. *Maingot*, 2nd ed., p. 306.

276. *Maingot*, 2nd ed., p. 306.

The majority affirmed the existence of two categories of privilege: (1) con-stitutionally inherent privilege; (2) privilege that is not constitutionally inherent. Both the Charter *and the first category of privilege are part of the Constitution. The first category of privilege is therefore not subject to judi-cial review under the* Charter, *because one part of the Constitution may not abrogate another part of the Constitution. Therefore, once it is established that the privilege is constitutionally inherent, as in this case, the exercise of that privilege is not subject to judicial scrutiny. If, however, it is not so established, the privilege is subject to such scrutiny.*[277]

The situation is far from clear as to when the courts can and should review ques-tions, which have primarily been assigned by the Constitution or the law for decision by other instruments of government. "It is, of course, clear that actions of both the executive and the legislative branches can be reviewed on jurisdictional grounds. It is also clear that administrative law permits review of executive decisions on a wide range of procedural grounds, but that substantive decisions may not be reviewed where the matter is one clearly left in the discretion of the executive to decide. It is more debatable to what extent Parliament's internal processes, and the exercise of its historic privileges with respect to determining its own composition and the conduct of its members, can be reviewed."[278]

Members' Privileges and the Criminal Law

PRIVILEGE AND THE CRIMINAL CODE

The special privileges of Members never were intended to set them above the law; rather, the intention was to give them certain exemptions from the law in order that they might properly execute the responsibilities of their position. Members of Par-liament are subject to the criminal law except in respect of words spoken or acts done in the context of a parliamentary proceeding. However, it would be difficult to envis-age a criminal act which would fit into or be a part of a parliamentary proceeding.[279] Therefore, it goes without saying that if Members are charged with infractions of the criminal law, they must abide by the due process of law. To do otherwise would show contempt for the Canadian system of justice.[280]

---

277. *Maingot*, 2nd ed., p. 307.

278. *Strayer*, p. 224.

279. *Maingot*, 2nd ed., pp. 122-3.

280. *Maingot*, 2nd ed., p. 123: "The *Criminal Code* applies to the internal regulation of the Houses of Parliament, including the alleged criminal misuse of Members' budgets".

In determining whether there is a *prima facie* breach of privilege, the Speaker must differentiate between actions which directly affect Members in the performance of their duties, and actions which affect Members but do not directly relate to the performance of their functions. For example, if a Member is summoned to court for a traffic violation or if the income tax return of a Member is under investigation, one might say at first glance that the Member may be hampered in the performance of his or her duties—for the Member may have to defend himself or herself in court instead of attending to House or committee duties. However, in these cases, the action brought against a Member is not initiated as a result of his or her responsibilities as an elected representative, but rather as a result of actions taken by the Member as a private individual. In these situations, the protection afforded by parliamentary privilege does not and should not apply.[281]

Freedom from arrest has been confined to civil cases and does not entitle a Member to evade criminal law. This is in accordance with the principle laid down by the British House of Commons in a conference with the House of Lords in 1641 where it was stated: "Privilege of Parliament is granted in regard of the service of the Commonwealth and is not to be used to the danger of the Commonwealth."[282]

Any incident of a criminal nature in which a Member has been charged is not a matter where immunity from arrest will protect that Member.[283] Matters of a criminal nature would include treason, felonies, all indictable offences, forcible entries, kidnapping, printing and publishing seditious libel, and criminal contempt of court (though not civil contempt).[284] Members cannot claim freedom from arrest or imprisonment on a criminal charge. A Member of the House of Commons is in exactly the same position as any other citizen if he or she is suspected of, charged with, or found guilty of a crime, provided that it is unrelated to proceedings in Parliament.[285]

In Canada, the 1965 case of Gilles Gregoire (Lapointe) would suggest that a Member could be arrested within the precinct of Parliament with the permission of the House and that the grounds surrounding the Parliament buildings do not constitute a part of the precinct of Parliament.[286]

The House of Commons cannot be used to give a Member sanctuary from the application of the law. Even the floor of the Chamber of the House is not a sanctuary

---

281. *Maingot*, 2nd ed., pp. 234-5.

282. United Kingdom, House of Commons, Select Committee on Parliamentary Privilege, 1966-67, Report, p. 1.

283. *Maingot*, 2nd ed., p. 155.

284. See above section entitled "Rights and Immunities of Individual Members".

285. *Maingot*, 2nd ed., p. 156.

286. See Special Committee on Rights and Immunities of Members, First Report, presented to the House on July 12, 1976 (*Journals*, pp. 1421-3), for a summary of the case. See also *Maingot*, 2nd ed., p. 174. See also above section entitled, "Rights and Immunities of Individual Members". In the United Kingdom, a Member may even be arrested in the House itself, and writs may be served on Members in the precinct of Westminster Palace provided, in both cases, that the House gives leave if it is a sitting day *(May*, 22nd ed., pp. 98, 100-1, 131n).

and the application of the law, particularly in criminal matters, is foremost.[287] It is not the precinct of Parliament but the function that the precinct serves which is sacred.[288] The only special procedure relating to the arrest or the imprisonment of a Member of Parliament is that if he or she is detained for any significant time (for example, if remanded in custody), the police or court concerned must notify the Speaker. Similarly, if a Member is sent to prison after a conviction, the House is informed.[289] Thus, should the police arrest a Member outside the House on some criminal matter, the House of Commons is not entitled to intervene. In Canada, the administration of justice is a provincial responsibility. The Crown Attorney for the particular judicial district where the offence occurred would therefore prosecute any breach of the *Criminal Code*.[290] In its 1967 report, the British House of Commons Select Committee on Parliamentary Privilege noted that it could see no reason why, unless the circumstances are exceptional, a Member should be able to claim immunity from the normal process of the courts.[291]

THE EXECUTION OF SEARCH WARRANTS IN THE PRECINCT OF PARLIAMENT

The privileges of the House of Commons include "such rights as are necessary for free action within its jurisdiction and the necessary authority to enforce these rights if challenged".[292] It is well established that, by extension, the House has complete and sole authority to regulate and administer its precinct, without outside interference.

As custodian of the rights and privileges of the House of Commons and head of its administrative structure, the Speaker oversees the management of the precinct of the House. The Standing Orders delegate to the Sergeant-at-Arms some duties and responsibilities in this regard, including the maintenance of order in the galleries, corridors, lobbies and other areas of the House, and the arrest and custody of any person who misconducts himself or herself while in the precinct of the House.[293]

The right of the House to control its precinct extends to considerations of security and policing. The House of Commons maintains its own protective service, the House of Commons Security Service, under the direction of the Sergeant-at-Arms.

---

287. *May,* 22nd ed., p. 98.
288. *Maingot,* 2nd ed., pp. 164-5, 171-2.
289. *May,* 22nd ed., pp. 100-2.
290. *Maingot*, 2nd ed., p. 171.
291. United Kingdom, House of Commons, Select Committee on Parliamentary Privilege, 1966-67, Report, p. xvi, para. 47.
292. *Bourinot*, 4th ed., p. 37.
293. Standing Orders 157 and 158.

Beyond the precinct, the RCMP is responsible for security on the grounds of Parliament Hill,[294] as well as for the security of the Prime Minister and any visiting dignitary up to the entrance of the Parliament Buildings. Inside the buildings, it then becomes the responsibility of the House of Commons Security Service.

Authorization of the Speaker

Cases have arisen where representatives of outside police forces have wanted to enter the precinct of Parliament for purposes of making an arrest, conducting an interrogation or executing a search warrant. The Speaker has the authority, on behalf of the House, to grant or deny outside police forces permission to enter the precinct, and oblige police to seek this permission prior to conducting their business.

This authority was established in two separate incidents which occurred in the 1970s. The first case occurred in 1973 and involved Flora MacDonald (Kingston and the Islands). At that time, her parliamentary office was visited by the Ottawa City Police and the RCMP, who were inquiring about documents missing from the Department of Indian Affairs, without having previously sought permission from the Speaker to do so. Miss MacDonald raised a question of privilege which was found *prima facie,* and the matter was referred to committee for study. In its report to the House, the committee stated: "It is well-established that outside police forces on official business shall not enter the precincts of Parliament without first obtaining the permission of Mr. Speaker who is custodian of the powers and privileges of Parliament. . . . The Committee must find that the question of privilege of the House of Commons is well founded."[295] The committee stopped short of finding the police force in contempt of the House, on the grounds that they acted in good faith. Rather, they recommended to the Speaker that he " . . . remind outside police forces and the security staff of the House of Commons of their respective obligations in this regard, and that no further action be taken. . . . "[296] While the report of the committee confirmed the necessity for outside police forces to seek the permission of the Speaker prior to entering the precinct of the House, it was not until six years later, in another Parliament, under another Speaker, that the House was to hear confirmation that the permission police forces were obliged to seek was not in any way a mere formality, but indeed involved a very conscious exercise of discretion on the part of the Speaker.

The second case occurred in 1979 and involved Terry Sergeant (Selkirk–Interlake). The Member raised a question of privilege regarding a RCMP request to the

---

294. This has been made clear by Speakers in rulings over the years. See, for example, *Debates*, May 15, 1970, p. 7007; May 25, 1970, p. 7255; May 21, 1981, pp. 9769-70; May 26, 1981, pp. 9920-1; May 27, 1981, pp. 9983-4; June 4, 1986, p. 13961.

295. *Journals*, September 21, 1973, p. 567.

296. *Journals*, September 21, 1973, p. 567.

Speaker to conduct a search of the Member's Parliament Hill offices for copies of a leaked document. Having confirmed that the RCMP had indeed requested permission from the Speaker to search Mr. Sergeant's office, Speaker Jerome found that there was no *prima facie* breach of privilege and indicated to the House that he had exercised his discretion against the execution of the warrant: "To my understanding, the reason for the presence of any discretion in the Speaker is because, in this situation, the rights of the police force, which may be legitimate, come into collision with the rights of the member which are obviously equally legitimate. . . . What I have done, therefore, is to take the position that, where no charge has been laid against a member and there does not appear to be the investigation of an actual offence against him, but rather an investigation which may be part of another set of circumstances, initially I have exercised my discretion against the execution of the warrant in these premises in the office of a member. On the other hand, I would think that in the more extreme cases, where there is an allegation of an offence by a member and it is in the enforcement or investigation of a specific and formal charge against a member, I might be facing a different situation. Obviously that would depend on the nature of the charge and the actual circumstances." [297]

In such cases, the Speaker is always in a difficult position: the Speaker must ensure that Members' parliamentary privileges are protected without leaving the Speaker open to accusations of obstructing justice. However, as Speaker Jerome explained in 1979, if no charge has been laid or there is no evidence of an investigation against a Member, the Chair may exercise its discretion against the execution of a warrant. If there is an allegation of an offence by a Member, and the enforcement of the charge necessitates a warrant, the Speaker may give permission for its execution. [298]

In making this statement, Speaker Jerome underscored the limits of the Speaker's authority in matters of privilege. It is not the Speaker, but the House itself, which determines the extent of Members' privileges and decides when a breach has occurred. It would appear that the role that the Speaker plays in deciding whether a *prima facie* case of privilege exists constitutes a close parallel to the exercise of discretion in granting police forces entry to the precinct of the House. In both cases, the Speaker must keep in mind that the final authority on such matters rests with the House itself, which by its disposition of the matter will reflect on the Speaker's preliminary determination.

---

297. *Debates*, November 30, 1979, pp. 1890-2.

298. *Debates*, November 30, 1979, p. 1891.

Investigation of Matters Involving Members' Budgets and Services

In 1989, a number of search warrants were executed on Parliament Hill involving investigations related to Members' use of their office budgets and other services available to them. These investigations led to much media speculation and were the cause of great concern to Members. As a result, the House established a special committee to " . . . review the *Parliament of Canada Act* regarding the powers, duty and obligations of the Members of the House in relation thereto and regarding the authority, responsibilities and jurisdiction of the Board of Internal Economy".[299]

On May 29, 1990, the House unanimously approved the Special Committee's Third Report.[300] This Report dealt exclusively with procedures surrounding the execution of search warrants within the parliamentary precinct. By unanimously adopting the report, the House reaffirmed the following principles respecting the execution of search warrants:

1. Well-established parliamentary tradition provides that search warrants may only be executed within the precinct of Parliament with the consent of the Speaker.

2. The Speaker may withhold or postpone giving his or her consent if it is determined that the execution of the search warrant will violate the collective and individual privileges, rights, immunities and powers of the House of Commons and its Members by interfering with the proper functioning of the House of Commons.

3. A search warrant must be executed in the presence of a representative of the Speaker who ensures that a copy of it is given to any Member whose affairs are subject of the search, at the time of the search or as soon as practicable thereafter.[301]

On June 1, 1990, the Committee presented its Fourth Report, which the House concurred in on the same day.[302] The report contained proposed amendments to the *Parliament of Canada Act,* primarily dealing with the Board of Internal Economy. It also proposed to prohibit any criminal process respecting the way Members used House of Commons money, goods or services unless the authorities had previously requested and obtained from the Board a ruling or opinion on the propriety of the

299. *Journals*, December 14, 1989, p. 1011. See also James R. Robertson and Margaret Young, "Parliament and the Police: The Saga of Bill C-79," *Canadian Parliamentary Review*, Vol. 14, No. 4 (Winter 1991-92), pp. 18-21.

300. *Journals*, May 29, 1990, pp. 1775-6. See also Special Committee on the Review of the Parliament of Canada Act, *Minutes of Proceedings and Evidence,* March 11, 1990, Issue No. 7, pp. 5-9.

301. *Journals*, May 29, 1990, pp. 1775-6.

302. *Journals*, June 1, 1990, pp. 1797-804.

Member's action.[303] In particular, the Special Committee wanted to ensure that Members would not be exposed to charges or proceedings based on a misunderstanding of the nature of their work or the structure and rules of the House of Commons.

On June 26, 1990, Bill C-79, *An Act to amend the Parliament of Canada Act*, was introduced,[304] which closely followed the draft provisions of the Fourth Report. Bill C-79 was designed to give the Board of Internal Economy exclusive authority to determine whether any past, present or proposed use of funds, goods, services or premises available to Members had been, was or would be improper. The Bill received Royal Assent on April 11, 1991.[305]

The *Parliament of Canada Act* empowers the Board to make by-laws governing the use by Members of funds, goods, services and premises made available to them to carry out their parliamentary functions.[306] The Board determines the terms and conditions of managing and accounting for such funds by the Members and has exclusive authority to determine whether such use is or was proper.[307] Members may request from the Board an opinion with respect to such use.[308]

In investigating the use by a Member of these funds, goods, services or premises, a law enforcement authority may request the Board's opinion whether such use is or was proper.[309] The Board can respond by interpreting an existing by-law or regulation, or if none exists by examining the issue. Similarly, the Board may provide the peace officer with an opinion on its own initiative.[310] The Board has explicit authority to include in its opinions any comments that it considers relevant.[311] A peace officer who receives an opinion and then makes an application for a criminal process is under an obligation to place the opinion before a provincial court

---

303. *Journals*, June 1, 1990, pp. 1798-9.

304. *Journals*, June 26, 1990, p. 1956.

305. These provisions were incorporated into the Act as sections 52.6 to 52.9. See the *Parliament of Canada Act*, R.S.C 1985, c. P-1 as amended by S.C. 1991, c. 20, s. 2.

306. *Parliament of Canada Act*, R.S.C. 1985, c. P-1 as amended by S.C. 1991, c. 20, s. 2 (s. 52.5(1)). Such by-laws must be tabled by the Speaker within 30 days (s. 52.5(2)). "Parliamentary functions" include duties and activities related to the position of Member of the House of Commons wherever performed and includes public and official matters and partisan political activity. The Board may also issue general opinions regarding the proper use of funds, goods, services and premises (s. 52.8).

307. *Parliament of Canada Act*, R.S.C. 1985, c. P-1 as amended by S.C. 1991, c. 20, s. 2 (s. 52.6(1)).

308. *Parliament of Canada Act*, R.S.C. 1985, c. P-1 as amended by S.C. 1991, c. 20, s. 2 (s. 52.6(2)).

309. *Parliament of Canada Act*, R.S.C. 1985, c. P-1 as amended by S.C. 1991, c. 20, s. 2 (s. 52.7(1)).

310. *Parliament of Canada Act*, R.S.C. 1985, c. P-1 as amended by S.C. 1991, c. 20, s. 2 (ss. 52.7(1), 52.9(4)).

311. *Parliament of Canada Act*, R.S.C. 1985, c. P-1 as amended by S.C. 1991, c. 20, s. 2 (s. 52.9(1)).

judge.[312] The Board can also publish its opinions, in whole or in part, for the guidance of the Members, although the Board must ensure that privacy is maintained.[313]

Execution of a Search Warrant Once Obtained

The criminal law of Canada provides for the execution of search warrants within the terms of the *Criminal Code*. However, both parliamentary privilege and the criminal law are part of the general and public law of Canada. The Speaker, therefore, is placed in a sensitive position when police officers attend at the Parliament Buildings in order to execute a search warrant. The Speaker must ensure that the corporate privilege of the House to administer its affairs within the precinct, as well as the privileges of individual Members to participate freely in the proceedings, are not infringed. At the same time, the Speaker must be careful not to obstruct the administration of criminal justice.

In practice, the police recognize that the law does not allow them to enter the Parliament Buildings without the permission of the Speaker. For the police to bypass the Speaker in order to execute a search warrant (even if the Speaker would in the end have allowed them to enter for that purpose) could amount to a breach of privilege and possibly a contempt of the House. The Speaker, therefore, personally examines every search warrant that the police wish to execute within the precinct. It has been established in law that the police must produce a search warrant upon request so that an occupier of property may satisfy himself that the search is lawful.[314] Indeed, Section 29(1) of the *Criminal Code* provides that: "It is the duty of every one who executes a process or warrant to have it with him, where it is feasible to do so, and to produce it when requested to do so."

An obvious distinction exists between the Speaker acting on behalf of the House and its Members and other citizens faced with the same situation when the police wish to execute a search warrant. Whereas the police must produce a warrant upon request in the ordinary case, the law requires the police to present themselves to the Speaker before entering a particular Member's office within the parliamentary precinct which is to be searched, in order for the Speaker to be satisfied that the search is lawful.

It is essential to understand that throughout this process, the Speaker can do no more than ensure that the search warrant is lawful "on its face" and that it is executed according to its terms. In no sense does the Speaker enjoy the right to review the decision to issue the warrant in the first instance. To do so could amount to an

---

312. *Parliament of Canada Act*, R.S.C. 1985, c. P-1 as amended by S.C. 1991, c. 20, s. 2 (ss. 52.7(2) and (4)). Criminal process is defined as wiretap authorizations, search warrants, seize or freeze orders relating to the proceeds of crime and the laying of criminal charges (see s. 52.7(3)).

313. *Parliament of Canada Act*, R.S.C. 1985, c. P-1 as amended by S.C. 1991, c. 20, s. 2 (ss. 52.9(2) and (3)).

314. *Ho Quong v. Cuddy* (1914) 7 *Western Weekly Reports*, pp. 797-802 (Alta C.A).

obstruction of justice and would undeniably blur the distinctions between Parliament as a legislative body on the one hand and the judicial and executive functions in respect of the issuance of the search warrant and the administration of justice on the other.

In the examination of a search warrant, there are two major considerations which the Speaker takes into account: the procedural sufficiency of the search warrant and the precise description of the documents sought under the search warrant.[315] Essentially, the Speaker's role in reviewing a search warrant is restricted to an examination based on form and content.

Ultimately, a Member of the House of Commons is not "above the law". The Member is, however, entitled to the full protection of the law, including the application of both corporate and individual parliamentary privilege and is subject to the criminal law and the protection it provides. Parliamentary privilege is not the privilege of an élite group but rather a necessary component of what is required for the Canadian electorate's representatives to conduct public business on behalf of all Canadians free from interference and intimidation.

Procedure for Dealing with Matters of Privilege

The House of Commons is certainly the most important secular body in Canada. It is said that each House of Parliament is a "court" with respect to its own privileges and dignity and the privileges of its Members. The purpose of raising matters of "privilege" in either House of Parliament is to maintain the respect and credibility due to and required of each House in respect of these privileges, to uphold its powers, and to enforce the enjoyment of the privileges of its Members. A genuine question of privilege is therefore a serious matter not to be reckoned with lightly and accordingly ought to be rare, and thus rarely raised in the House of Commons.[316]

Any claim that privilege has been infringed or a contempt committed is raised in the House by means of a "question of privilege". The procedure with respect to raising a question of privilege is governed by both the Standing Orders and practice. A question of privilege is a matter for the House to determine. The decision of the House on a question of privilege, like every other matter which the House has to decide, can

---

315. Re: *Bell Telephone Co. of Canada* (1947), 89 C.C.C. 196, 4 C.R. 162 (Ont. H.C.), in *Canadian Criminal Procedure*, 6th ed., edited by Justice R.E. Salhany, Aurora: Canada Law Book Inc., 1998, paras. 3.1250, 3.1330. See generally Delisle and Stuart, *Learning Canadian Criminal Procedure*, 2nd ed., Carswell, 1991, pp. 57-92.

316. *Maingot*, 2nd ed., p. 217.

be elicited only by a question put from the Chair by the Speaker and resolved either in the affirmative or in the negative, and this question is necessarily founded on a motion made by a Member.

This section will describe the manner in which such matters are dealt with by the House.[317] (See Figure 3.1 at the end of this chapter depicting the path of a question of privilege from the time it is raised until it is disposed of.)

MANNER OF RAISING MATTERS OF PRIVILEGE

Great importance is attached to matters involving privilege. A Member wishing to raise a question of privilege in the House must first convince the Speaker that his or her concern is *prima facie* (on the first impression or at first glance) a question of privilege. The function of the Speaker is limited to deciding whether the matter is of such a character as to entitle the Member who has raised the question to move a motion which will have priority over Orders of the Day; that is, in the Speaker's opinion, there is a *prima facie* question of privilege. If there is, the House must take the matter into immediate consideration.[318] Ultimately, it is the House which decides whether a breach of privilege or a contempt has been committed.

Matters relating to privilege may also arise in standing, special, legislative and joint committees, and in a Committee of the Whole House. However, the procedures for dealing with such situations in committee differ from the general procedure followed in the House.

If a Member believes that a breach of privilege or a contempt has occurred, but does not feel that the matter should have priority in debate, the Member may follow an alternate route for bringing the matter before the House. He or she may place a written notice of a motion on the *Notice Paper*.

In the House

A complaint on a matter of privilege must satisfy two conditions before it can be accorded precedence over the Orders of the Day. First, the Speaker must be convinced that a *prima facie* case of breach of privilege has been made and, second, the matter must be raised at the earliest opportunity. If in the opinion of the Speaker these two conditions have been met, then the Speaker informs the House that, in his or her opinion, this matter is entitled to take precedence over the notices of motions and Orders of the Day standing on the *Order Paper*. The Speaker's ruling does not extend to deciding whether a breach of privilege has in fact been committed—a question which can only be decided by the House itself.

Time of Raising and Notice Requirements

A question of privilege arising out of the proceedings during the course of a sitting may be raised immediately without notice. However, Speakers have disallowed

---

317. See also *Maingot*, 2nd ed., pp. 217-70.

318. Standing Order 48(1).

questions of privilege during Statements by Members and Question Period,[319] the process of Royal Assent,[320] as well as during the Adjournment Proceedings,[321] and divisions.[322] In such circumstances, the question of privilege may be raised at the end of the time provided for such business on that day.[323] A matter of privilege related to the Adjournment Proceedings would be raised at the next sitting, following the proper notification to the Speaker.[324]

A Member wishing to raise a question of privilege which does not arise out of the proceedings during the course of a sitting must give notice before bringing the question to the attention of the House. The Member must provide a written statement to the Speaker at least one hour before raising the question of privilege in the House. If such notice is not given, the Speaker will not allow the Member to proceed.[325] Speakers have also ruled that oral notice is neither necessary nor sufficient.[326] Questions of privilege for which written notice has been given are raised at specific times, namely on the opening of the sitting, following Routine Proceedings but before Orders of the Day, immediately after Question Period, and, occasionally, during a debate.

The notice submitted to the Speaker should contain four elements:

1. It should indicate that the Member is writing to give notice of his or her intention to raise a question of privilege.

2. It should state that the matter is being raised at the earliest opportunity.[327]

---

319. This is based on recommendations in the Second Report of the Standing Committee on Procedure and Organization, presented on March 14, 1975, and concurred in by the House on March 24, 1975. See *Journals*, March 14, 1975, pp. 372-6; March 24, 1975, p. 399; April 14, 1975, p. 441. See also *Debates*, April 19, 1983, pp. 24624-6; December 20, 1983, p. 355. See also Chapter 11, "Questions".

320. *Debates*, December 17, 1990, p. 16830.

321. *Debates*, April 30, 1964, pp. 2799-802; November 25, 1985, p. 8795. See also Chapter 11, "Questions".

322. *Debates*, April 12, 1962, p. 2909.

323. See Speaker Parent's ruling, *Debates*, December 7, 1995, p. 17392.

324. For example, Jesse Flis (Parkdale–High Park) raised a question of privilege concerning the behaviour of Ian Waddell (Port Moody–Coquitlam) who interfered with the Mace upon the adjournment of the House on October 30, 1991. At the next meeting of the House on October 31, 1991, the Speaker recognized Mr. Flis on a question of privilege immediately following Prayers. See *Debates*, October 30, 1991, pp. 4269-70; October 31, 1991, p. 4271.

325. See, for example, *Debates*, March 22, 1971, p. 4451; March 7, 1972, p. 591; April 27, 1972, p. 1675; December 17, 1990, p. 16830.

326. See, for example, *Debates*, March 10, 1966, p. 2477; February 18, 1982, p. 15144; March 18, 1982, p. 15557; May 12, 1982, p. 17338; May 19, 1982, p. 17596; October 31, 1986, pp. 955-6; March 2, 1995, p. 10273; December 7, 1995, p. 17392.

327. See, for example, *Debates*, May 20, 1982, p. 17643.

3. It should indicate the substance of the matter that the Member proposes to raise by way of a question of privilege. [328]

4. It should include the text of the motion which the Member must be ready to propose to the House should the Speaker rule that the matter is a *prima facie* case of privilege.

By providing the Chair with a context for the question of privilege and a proposed remedy for the problem, the Member will assist the Speaker to deal with the issue in an informed and expeditious manner. The inclusion of the text of the proposed motion allows the Speaker the opportunity to suggest changes to avoid any procedural difficulties in the wording; otherwise, the Member might be prevented or delayed from moving the motion should the Speaker rule the matter a *prima facie* question of privilege. [329]

Raising at the First Opportunity

The matter of privilege to be raised in the House must have recently arisen and must call for the immediate action of the House. Therefore, Members must satisfy the Speaker that the matter has been raised at the earliest opportunity. When a Member does not fulfil this important requirement, the Speaker has ruled that the matter is not a *prima facie* question of privilege. [330] In instances where more than one Member is involved in a question of privilege, the Speaker may postpone discussion until all concerned Members can be present in the House. [331]

Multiple Notices

Should the Speaker receive more than one notice of a question of privilege, or should more than one Member seek the floor on a specific question of privilege, the Speaker will determine the order in which the Members will be recognized. [332] Generally, the Speaker will recognize Members in the order in which the notices were received, or recognize the first Member who catches the Speaker's eye. If more than one matter is being raised, the Speaker will hear Members on one question of privilege at a time.

---

328. See Speakers' comments, *Debates*, April 4, 1973, p. 2947; February 18, 1982, p. 15144; May 20, 1982, p. 17643.

329. See, for example, *Debates*, February 17, 1999, pp. 12011-2.

330. *May*, 15th ed., p. 365. See, for example, Speakers' rulings rejecting questions of privilege because they were not raised at the earliest opportunity: *Debates*, May 10, 1966, pp. 4923-4; October 12, 1966, pp. 8553-5; November 28, 1967, pp. 4773-4; June 9, 1969, pp. 9899-900; September 27, 1971, p. 8174. In 1983, Speaker Sauvé did allow a Member (Bill Domm (Peterborough)) to raise a question of privilege, even though the Member could have raised the matter earlier (see *Debates*, October 4, 1983, pp. 27726-7; October 12, 1983, pp. 27944-5).

331. See, for example, *Debates*, February 15, 1985, pp. 2398-9; April 23, 1990, pp. 10528-30; October 12, 1990, pp. 14106-10; October 15, 1990, pp. 14148-9; October 18, 1990, pp. 14367-8; February 24, 1993, pp. 16393-4; September 30, 1997, pp. 293-5; February 1, 1999, p. 11174; April 26, 1999, pp. 14326-7.

332. See, for example, the questions of privilege raised by John Reynolds (West Vancouver–Sunshine Coast), Jim Pankiw (Saskatoon–Humboldt), Garry Breitkreuz (Yorkton–Melville) and Roy Bailey (Souris–Moose Mountain) concerning picket lines blocking access to Parliament Hill and entrances to certain buildings on February 17, 1999 (*Debates*, pp. 12009-12).

Initial Discussion of Matter Raised

A Member recognized on a question of privilege is expected to be brief and concise in explaining the event which has given rise to the question of privilege and the reasons why consideration of the event complained of should be given precedence over other House business.[333] Generally, the Member tries to provide the Chair with relevant references to the Standing Orders, precedents and citations from procedural authorities. In addition, the Member demonstrates that the matter is being brought to the House's attention at the first opportunity. Finally, the Member should state what corrective House action is being sought by way of remedy and indicate that, should the Speaker rule the matter a *prima facie* question of privilege, he or she is prepared to move the appropriate motion.[334]

The Speaker will hear the Member and may permit others who are directly implicated in the matter to intervene. The Speaker also has the discretion to seek the advice of other Members to help him or her in determining whether there is *prima facie* a matter of privilege involved which would warrant giving the matter priority of consideration over all other House business. When satisfied, the Speaker will terminate the discussion.[335]

The decision as to the existence of a *prima facie* question of privilege belongs exclusively to the Speaker who may take the matter under advisement to permit a considered judgement in all but the clearest of cases. When a question of privilege has required an immediate decision of the Chair, the Speaker has, without objection, suspended the sitting for a short time to deliberate on the matter, and has then returned to the House with a ruling.[336] In deliberating upon the matter, the Chair will take into account the extent to which the matter complained of infringed upon any Member's ability to perform his or her parliamentary duties or appears to be a contempt against the dignity of Parliament.

If the Speaker is satisfied that the necessary conditions have been met and finds a *prima facie* breach of privilege or contempt, the decision is announced to the House. As soon as the Chair has apprised the House that a *prima facie* case of privilege has been found, the Member raising the matter is immediately allowed to move a motion.

In the vast majority of cases, the Chair decides that a *prima facie* case of privilege was not made. In informing the House of such a decision, the Chair customarily explains (often in some detail) the factors which resulted in this finding. However, in such cases, the Chair will often acknowledge the existence of a genuine grievance and may recommend avenues of redress.[337] If the Speaker rules that there is not a

---

333. See, for example, *Debates*, March 9, 1972, p. 661; February 1, 1973, p. 850.

334. See, for example, *Debates*, February 17, 1999, pp. 12009-10; April 26, 1999, pp. 14326-7.

335. *Debates*, March 31, 1981, pp. 8800-6.

336. See, for example, *Debates*, February 7, 1990, p. 7953; March 12, 1996, pp. 561-2.

337. See, for example, *Debates*, May 23, 1989, pp. 2051-2; September 24, 1990, pp. 13216-7; June 13, 1991, pp. 1644-6; December 8, 1992, pp. 14807-8; June 10, 1994, pp. 5160-1; November 16, 1998, pp. 10020-1.

prima facie question of privilege, the matter ends there. However, if in the future additional information comes to light, the Member who raised the question of privilege or any other Member may raise the matter again.[338]

Debate on a Privilege Motion

After the Speaker has decided that a matter is a *prima facie* question of privilege, it is left to the Member raising the matter to move the appropriate motion;[339] like all motions, it must be seconded. Occasionally, the Member will propose a motion at the end of his or her arguments when initially raising the question of privilege. Under these circumstances, the Speaker may advise the Member on the proper form of the motion.[340] In cases where the motion is not known in advance, the Speaker may provide assistance to the Member if the terms of the proposed motion are substantially different from the matter originally raised.[341] The Speaker would be reluctant to allow a matter as important as a privilege motion to fail on the ground of improper form.[342] In Canadian practice, the terms of the motion have generally provided

---

338. See, for example, the questions of privilege raised by Jag Bhaduria (Markham–Whitchurch–Stouffville) on February 15, 1994 (*Debates*, pp. 1387-8); February 23, 1994 (withdrawn by the Member, *Debates*, p. 1728); and March 23, 1994 (reintroduced by Mr. Bhaduria, *Debates*, p. 2677); and the Speaker's ruling on March 24, 1994 (*Debates*, pp. 2705-6). See also the questions of privilege raised by Judy Wasylycia–Leis (Winnipeg North Centre) on October 1, 1997 (*Debates*, pp. 336-7, and the Speaker's ruling on October 9, 1997, *Debates*, pp. 689-90); and on November 25, 1997 (*Debates*, pp. 2190-1, and the Speaker's ruling on December 4, 1997, *Debates*, pp. 2695-6).

339. "Until the motion is actually put to the House, the House is not seized of it, and therefore, the Member may amend or withdraw his proposed motion without the consent of the House" (*Maingot*, 2nd ed., p. 261).

340. In the Allan Lawrence (Northumberland–Durham) case in December 1978, there was a difference between the first motion proposed and the one actually moved in the House (see *Debates*, November 3, 1978, p. 780; December 6, 1978, p. 1857). In October 1990, Albert Cooper (Peace River) proposed to move a motion which implicated another Member in a demonstration in the public gallery of the House. When Speaker Fraser ruled on the matter some days later, he stated that because the accused Member had denied any advance knowledge of the demonstration, the Chair could not find a question of privilege in that respect. However, the Speaker allowed that, without the reference to the Member, the matter of the demonstration would be a *prima facie* question of privilege. Mr. Cooper changed his motion which was then adopted by the House. See *Debates*, October 18, 1990, p. 14360; November 6, 1990, pp. 15177-81.

341. In the Jim Pankiw (Saskatoon–Humboldt) case in February 1999, concerning the obstruction of Members by picket lines blocking the entrances to parliamentary buildings, the motion proposed by Mr. Pankiw, following Speaker Parent's ruling that there was a *prima facie* question of privilege, differed substantially from what the Member had raised in his submission. With the Speaker's assistance, Mr. Pankiw rephrased the motion which was then moved and adopted by the House. See *Debates*, February 17, 1999, pp. 12011-2.

342. *Debates*, April 19, 1977, p. 4766. See also *Maingot*, 2nd ed., pp. 260-1. For examples of the wording of some privilege motions, see *Maingot*, 2nd ed., pp. 261-2.

that the matter be referred to committee for study or have been amended to that effect.[343]

Once the motion is properly moved and proposed to the House, it is subject to all the procedures and practices relating to debate on a substantive motion. The speeches are limited to 20 minutes, followed by a 10-minute questions and comments period.[344] Only the Prime Minister and the Leader of the Opposition are permitted unlimited debating time (with no period for questions or comments). Members are subject to the rules of relevance and repetition and the Speaker must ensure that the debate is focussed on the terms of the motion.

When the motion being considered touches on the conduct of a Member, he or she may make a statement in explanation and then should withdraw from the Chamber.[345] The Chair has interpreted "conduct" to refer to actions which, if proven, could result in the expulsion of a Member from the House on the grounds that he or she is unfit for membership, as opposed to actions which could lead to a Member being "named" by the Speaker.[346] However, it is not always clear that Members whose conduct was under consideration actually withdrew from the Chamber.[347] In some circumstances, a Member may be allowed to return to the Chamber in order to clarify or explain particular matters.

A privilege motion once under debate has priority over all Orders of the Day including Government Orders and Private Members' Business. However, the debate does not interfere with the regular holding of Routine Proceedings, Statements by Members, Question Period, Royal Assent and the adjournment of the House.[348]

---

343. In March 1966 during the Munsinger affair, having ruled that Douglas Harkness (Calgary North) did have a *prima facie* question of privilege, Speaker Lamoureux ruled out of order the motion proposed by the Member condemning the behaviour of the Minister of Justice. Other motions proposed by other Members were also ruled out of order because they were couched in terms which were too general or because they were substantive motions requiring notice. Speaker Lamoureux more than once pointed out that it was Canadian practice to refer such matters to committee for study and suggested that this should be the avenue pursued. It was not, however, and no motions were put to the House. See *Journals*, March 10 to March 15, 1966, pp. 267-93. See also *Maingot*, 2nd ed., p. 263.

344. Standing Order 43.

345. Standing Order 20.

346. *Debates*, May 25, 1956, p. 4348.

347. See *Debates*, May 17, 1894, cols. 2931-3; July 22, 1903, cols. 7095-103; March 6, 1911, cols. 4645-56; May 22, 1924, pp. 2401-7. In 1996, Jean-Marc Jacob (Charlesbourg) was present in the House during debate on the motion concerning his behaviour. He voted on a motion to adjourn the debate (see Division List No. 7, *Debates*, March 12, 1996, pp. 566-7), made a comment recorded in *Hansard* (*Debates*, March 13, 1996, p. 673) and voted on the motion that the debate not be further adjourned (see Division List No. 10, *Debates*, March 14, 1996, pp. 680-1).

348. See, for example, *Debates*, March 13, 1996, pp. 635-48, 674-8; March 14, 1996, pp. 679-80, 703-16; March 10, 1998, pp. 4591-4.

Once the privilege motion is before the House, it may be amended by the House, even if the amendment results in the text of the motion differing from the one originally accepted by the Speaker and proposed to the House.[349]

During the proceedings on a privilege motion, motions to adjourn the debate, to adjourn the House, or to proceed to Orders of the Day are in order,[350] as are motions for the previous question ("that this question be now put"), for the extension of the sitting, or "that a Member be now heard". However, should the previous question be negatived, or a motion to proceed to Orders of the Day be adopted, then the privilege motion is superseded and dropped from the *Order Paper*. Closure may also be moved on the privilege motion by a Minister.[351]

Should debate on a privilege motion not be completed by the time of adjournment, then on the next sitting day the item will take priority over all other Orders of the Day and will appear on the *Order Paper* before all other Orders of the Day.[352]

When debate has concluded on the motion, the Speaker will put the question to the House. If the motion is adopted, then the terms of the motion will be implemented. If the motion is defeated, the proceedings are ended.[353]

In Standing, Special, Legislative and Joint Committees

Since the House has not given its committees the power to punish any misconduct, breach of privilege, or contempt directly, committees cannot decide such matters; they can only report them to the House. Only the House can decide if an offence has been committed.[354] Speakers have consistently ruled that, except in the most extreme situations, they will only hear questions of privilege arising from committee proceedings upon presentation of a report from the committee which directly deals with the matter and not as a question of privilege raised by an individual Member.[355] Most matters which have been reported by committees concerned the behaviour of Members, witnesses or the public. Committees have reported to the House on the refusal

---

349. During the proceedings on the Jacob case on March 13, 1996, Jim Hart (Okanagan–Similkameen–Merritt) challenged the acceptability of an amendment stating that it was "trying to completely gut the spirit of the motion". The Speaker ruled the amendment procedurally in order (*Debates*, March 13, 1996, p. 649).

350. See, for example, *Debates*, March 12, 1996, pp. 566-7.

351. See, for example, *Debates*, March 13, 1996, p. 666; March 14, 1996, pp. 680-1.

352. See, for example, *Order Paper and Notice Paper*, March 13, 1996, p. 9; March 10, 1998, p. 13.

353. See, for example, *Journals*, October 24, 1966, pp. 915-6; March 21, 1978, pp. 525-6; December 7, 1978, pp. 228-9; February 20, 1984, pp. 188-9.

354. For the House to give penal powers to committees would be an extension of the privileges of the House requiring legislation. See United Kingdom, House of Commons, Select Committee on Procedure, 1977-78, First Report, Vol. I, Appendix C, "Powers of Select Committees to Send for Persons, Papers and Records (PPR)", Memorandum by the Clerk of the House, p. 26, para. 55.

355. See, for example, *Debates*, June 30, 1987, p. 7822; December 9, 1987, p. 11628; April 2, 1990, pp. 10074-6; November 28, 1990, pp. 15854-5; June 19, 1991, p. 2070; November 7, 1991, pp. 4772-3; May 18, 1995, p. 12760; September 16, 1996, pp. 4233-4; December 9, 1997, p. 2945.

of witnesses to appear when summoned;[356] the refusal of witnesses to answer questions;[357] the refusal of witnesses to provide papers or records;[358] the refusal of individuals to obey orders of a committee;[359] and the divulging of events during an *in camera* meeting.[360] Committees could report on instances of contempt, such as behaviour showing disrespect for the authority or activities of a committee, the intimidation of members or witnesses, or witnesses refusing to be sworn or lying to the committee.

Unlike the Speaker, the Chair of a committee does not have the power to censure disorder or decide questions of privilege. Should a Member wish to raise a question of privilege in committee, or should some event occur in committee which appears to be a breach of privilege or contempt, the Chair of the committee will recognize the Member and hear the question of privilege, or in the case of some incident, suggest that the committee deal with the matter. The Chair, however, has no authority to rule that a breach of privilege or contempt has occurred.[361] The role of the Chair in such instances is to determine whether the matter raised does in fact touch on privilege and is not a point of order, a grievance or a matter of debate. If the Chair is of the opinion that the Member's interjection deals with a point of order, a grievance or a matter of debate, or that the incident is within the powers of the committee to deal with, then the Chair will rule accordingly, giving reasons. The committee cannot then consider the matter further as a question of privilege. Should a Member disagree with the Chair's decision, then the Member can appeal to the committee, which can sustain or overturn the Chair's decision.

If in the opinion of the Chair the issue raised relates to privilege (or if an appeal should overturn a Chair's decision that it does not touch on privilege), then the

356. See, for example, *Journals*, April 26, 1878, pp. 218-20; August 27, 1891, p. 454; September 1, 1891, p. 467; September 24, 1891, p. 532; June 7, 1894, p. 242; June 11, 1894, p. 288; June 13, 1894, pp. 298-300; November 22, 1990, pp. 2280-1.

357. See, for example, *Journals*, August 12, 1891, p. 402; August 13, 1891, p. 407; August 18, 1891, p. 414; August 19, 1891, p. 417; September 29, 1891, p. 561; May 30, 1906, p. 316; June 1, 1906, p. 323; June 4, 1906, pp. 331-3; July 3, 1906, pp. 475-6; March 27, 1907, p. 371; April 4, 1907, pp. 388-9; February 14, 1913, p. 249; February 17, 1913, p. 254; February 18, 1913, pp. 266-7; February 20, 1913, pp. 274-8.

358. See, for example, *Journals*, June 5, 1891, p. 205; June 16, 1891, pp. 211-2; December 19, 1990, p. 2508; February 28, 1991, p. 2638; May 17, 1991, p. 42; May 29, 1991, pp. 92-9.

359. See, for example, *Journals*, May 1, 1868, pp. 267-8; May 2, 1868, p. 271; May 10, 1873, pp. 317-8; May 12, 1873, pp. 327-8.

360. See, for example, *Journals*, April 28, 1987, p. 791; May 14, 1987, p. 917; December 18, 1987, pp. 2014-6.

361. See Chapter 20, "Committees". See also *Maingot*, 2nd ed., pp. 221-2.

committee can proceed to the consideration of a report on the matter to the House.[362] The Chair will then entertain a motion which will form the text of the report. It should clearly describe the situation, summarize the events, name any individuals involved, indicate that privilege may be involved or that a contempt may have occurred, and request the House to take some action.[363] The motion is debatable and amendable, and will have priority of consideration in the committee. If the committee decides that the matter should be reported to the House, it will adopt the report which will be presented to the House at the appropriate time during the Daily Routine of Business.

Once the report has been presented, the House is formally seized of the matter.[364] After having given the appropriate notice,[365] any Member may then raise the matter as a question of privilege. The Speaker will hear the question of privilege and may hear other Members on the matter, before ruling on the *prima facie* nature of the question of privilege. As Speaker Fraser noted in a ruling, " . . . the Chair is not judging the issue. Only the House itself can do that. The Chair simply decides on the basis of the evidence presented whether the matter is one which should take priority over other business."[366] Should the Speaker rule the matter a *prima facie* question of privilege, the next step would be for the Member who raised the question of privilege to propose a motion asking the House to take some action.[367] Should the Speaker rule that there is no *prima facie* question of privilege, no priority would be given to the matter. As with any committee report, any Member may still seek concurrence in the report by following the normal procedures during the Daily Routine of Business.[368]

---

362. In the 1987 case involving John Parry (Kenora–Rainy River), the Standing Committee on Aboriginal Affairs and Northern Development met *in camera* to deal with the matter as noted in its Third Report to the House. See Standing Committee on Aboriginal Affairs and Northern Development, Third Report, *Minutes of Proceedings and Evidence*, April 28, 1987, Issue No. 25, p. 3. See also *Journals*, April 28, 1987, p. 791.

363. The Third Report of the Standing Committee on Aboriginal Affairs and Northern Development, concerning the disclosure of *in camera* proceedings of the Committee, presented to the House on April 28, 1987, serves as an excellent model of such a report. Having described the events, the Report concluded: "Your Committee feels it is their duty to place these matters before you at this time since privilege may be involved and to give the House an opportunity to reflect on these matters." See Standing Committee on Aboriginal Affairs and Northern Development, Third Report, *Minutes of Proceedings and Evidence*, April 28, 1987, Issue No. 25, p. 3. See also *Journals*, April 28, p. 791.

364. See Speaker Fraser's ruling, *Debates*, May 14, 1987, p. 6108.

365. Standing Order 48(2). On April 28, 1987, the Standing Committee on Aboriginal Affairs and Northern Development presented its Third Report, relating to the disclosure of *in camera* proceedings, to the House during Routine Proceedings. The question of privilege based on that report was raised the same day immediately after Question Period. See *Debates*, April 28, 1987, pp. 5299, 5329.

366. *Debates*, May 14, 1987, p. 6110.

367. See above for the procedure for dealing with questions of privilege in the House.

368. See Chapter 10, "The Daily Program" for the procedures for concurring in committee reports.

In a Committee of the Whole

Given that the House infrequently sits as a Committee of the Whole, and that when it does, the proceedings are typically completed in a matter of minutes, questions of privilege are not often raised today in a Committee of the Whole.[369] The practice regarding the raising of questions of privilege in a Committee of the Whole is virtually identical to that for standing, special, or legislative committees.

When the House sits as a Committee of the Whole, a Member may raise a question of privilege only on matters which have occurred in the Committee. The question of privilege must be relevant to the proceedings in the Committee. A Member may not raise as a question of privilege matters affecting the privileges of the House in general or something which has occurred outside the Chamber. In a Committee of the Whole, a Member wishing to raise a question of privilege about something that does not concern the Committee may move a motion that the Committee rise and report progress in order that the Speaker may hear the question of privilege.[370] If the motion is adopted, the Chairman will rise and report to the Speaker who will then hear the Member.[371]

If a Member rises on a question of privilege which is relevant to the proceedings in a Committee of the Whole, the Chairman will hear the question of privilege. As in a standing, special, or legislative committee, the role of the Chairman is to decide whether the matter raised does in fact relate to privilege.[372] Again, that decision may be appealed. However, such an appeal is not to the Committee of the Whole, but rather to the Speaker.[373] If the matter raised by the Member touches on privilege and relates to events in the Committee of the Whole, the Chairman will entertain a motion that the events be reported to the House. The motion is debatable and amendable, and has priority of consideration in the Committee. If the Committee agrees to

---

369. For a description of the functioning of a Committee of the Whole, see Chapter 19, "Committees of the Whole House".

370. See, for example, *Debates*, April 30, 1964, p. 2782; October 29, 1964, pp. 9561-2; June 2, 1966, pp. 5908-9.

371. An example of such a situation occurred on April 30, 1964. In a Committee of the Whole, Lawrence Kindt (Macleod) rose on a question of privilege which, he stated, affected every Member of the House. The question of privilege concerned remarks made by the Minister of Transport (Walter Pickersgill) outside the House which the Member claimed should have been made in the House. The Chairman of the Committee of the Whole pointed out that the Member could only raise such a question of privilege when the Speaker was in the Chair. Another Member, Erik Nielsen (Yukon), then moved that the Committee rise and report progress and seek leave to sit again in order that Mr. Kindt might raise his question of privilege. The Committee adopted the motion, the Chairman rose, reported progress, and Mr. Kindt presented his question of privilege. The Deputy Speaker ruled that the matter was not a *prima facie* question of privilege and the House then went back into a Committee of the Whole. See *Debates*, April 30, 1964, pp. 2782-3.

372. See, for example, *Debates*, November 23, 1970, p. 1373; November 8, 1971, p. 9435; October 23, 1974, p. 665; May 22, 1975, pp. 6012-3; December 20, 1983, pp. 379-90.

373. Standing Order 12. See also Chapter 19, "Committees of the Whole House".

report the matter, the Chairman then rises, the Speaker resumes the Chair and the Chairman reports.[374] The text of the report to the House should summarize the events, indicate that privilege may be involved, and include a request for the Committee to sit again to consider its business.[375]

Only after the Chairman has reported to the House, may the matter be properly brought before the House and the Speaker deal with it. A Member should rise on a question of privilege and put the matter before the Speaker, who may allow interventions on the matter. When satisfied, the Speaker will rule whether or not it is a *prima facie* question of privilege. If a *prima facie* case of privilege is found, the Member may move a motion dealing with the matter.[376] If the Speaker finds that there is no *prima facie* question of privilege, then the House will resume its regular business. Under "Orders of the Day", the House may sit again as a Committee of the Whole to resume consideration of the matter originally before it, or the House may proceed to another Order of the Day.

The Speaker will entertain a question of privilege in regard to a matter that occurred in a Committee of the Whole only if the matter has been dealt with first in the Committee of the Whole and reported accordingly to the House.[377]

By Way of Written Notice on the Notice Paper

If a Member believes that a breach of privilege or a contempt has occurred, but does not feel that the matter should have priority in debate, in a procedure very rarely resorted to, the Member may place a written notice of motion on the *Notice Paper*.

---

374. A question of privilege was raised in a Committee of the Whole in 1987 by John Nunziata (York South–Weston) who rose to complain that a Member had assaulted him because he was not in his own seat. He requested an apology, but the Member refused. Although the Chairman advised that he would report on the matter to the full House, only the bill under consideration in the Committee was reported later that day (*Journals*, October 15, 1987, pp. 1688-9). The following day, Mr. Nunziata raised his question of privilege in the House. The Member about whom Mr. Nunziata had complained rose in the House and apologized to Mr. Nunziata and to the House, and the Speaker declared the matter closed (*Debates*, October 15, 1987, p. 10064; October 16, 1987, pp. 10089-90).

375. Although from a Standing Committee, the Third Report of the Standing Committee on Aboriginal Affairs and Northern Development, presented to the House on April 28, 1987, can serve as a model for a report on a privilege matter. Having described the events, the Report concluded: "Your Committee feels it is their duty to place these matters before you at this time since privilege may be involved and to give the House the opportunity to reflect on these matters" (Standing Committee on Aboriginal Affairs and Northern Development, Third Report, *Minutes of Proceedings and Evidence*, April 28, 1987, Issue No. 25, p. 3). See also *Journals*, April 28, 1987, p. 791.

376. See above for the procedure for dealing with questions of privilege in the House.

377. See *Debates,* June 12, 1980, pp. 2030-1; December 20, 1983, pp. 364-9. In the 1983 instance, a Member argued that because the Committee had risen and reported progress, the House was apprised of the circumstances surrounding the question of privilege. The Speaker ruled that the Committee had only risen, reported progress and asked for leave to sit again. The Committee had not reported the bill nor any concerns to the House.

In this instance, at the conclusion of the required notice period, the motion is placed under the appropriate heading on the *Order Paper*. When sponsored by a Minister, the motion requires a 48 hours' notice period and will be considered by the House when called under Government Orders.[378] When sponsored by a private Member, the motion requires a notice period of two weeks and will be placed under Private Members' Business.[379]

However, following the appropriate notice period, the Member in whose name the item stands may decide to seek priority in debate for the motion (e.g., if new information were to come to light). The Member must then seek to convince the Speaker that the matter raised in the motion should be considered a *prima facie* question of privilege. In such a case, the Member would be required to notify the Speaker at least one hour before raising the matter in the House.[380]

Historically, there have been a number of occasions when Members have chosen to give written notice of their motions of privilege, particularly in cases where the matter stemmed from events occurring outside the House. In 1874, for instance, a motion for which written notice had been given, and which was not likely to arise on a particular day, was taken up before its turn, displacing scheduled business.[381] A similar case in 1886 saw a motion taken up before its turn at the request of the Member attacked in the motion.[382] Yet, it was not always so easy and, in two rare cases in 1892, motions for which written notice had been given were refused precedence as the Speaker judged them not to contain true matters of privilege.[383] Furthermore, in cases involving a motion amounting to a charge against a Member, etiquette required that the sponsor of such a motion privately advise the Member concerned when the motion would be moved.[384]

These practices endured into the twentieth century, and oral and written notices, although not required, were both common when questions of privilege were raised. In 1911, for example, a matter of privilege was raised following oral notice,[385] while in 1932, a motion regarding charges which had been made against the Prime Minister was taken up after written notice had been given.[386] There were other cases where matters were raised without any notice.[387]

---

378. Standing Orders 48(2), 54 and 56(1).

379. Standing Orders 48(2), 86(2) and 87.

380. Standing Order 48(2).

381. *Journals,* April 15, 1874, p. 64. See also *Bourinot,* 4th ed., pp. 304-5.

382. *Debates*, April 5, 1886, p. 488.

383. *Debates*, March 18, 1892, cols. 245-9; March 21, 1892, cols. 287-9; April 6, 1892, cols. 1032-5.

384. See, for example, *Debates*, April 25, 1877, p. 1810; May 11, 1891, cols. 156-7.

385. *Debates*, March 3, 1911, cols. 4566-7.

386. *Debates*, February 8, 1932, p. 8.

387. See, for example, *Debates*, May 22, 1924, p. 2401.

Eventually, an attempt was made to convince the Speaker to take a notice of motion out of sequence because it appeared to involve privilege. In June 1959, the Leader of the Opposition gave notice of a motion in which he questioned the conduct of a Member on the government side. The Speaker, who had not ruled on whether or not it should be given precedence, sought the advice of the House.[388] After a lengthy discussion on this point, the Speaker was able to arrive at the conclusion, in keeping with the recently established criteria guiding Speakers on questions of privilege, that, *prima facie,* no matter of privilege appeared to exist and that therefore he would not allow other business to be set aside to debate the motion.[389] As a result, the motion stayed on the *Order Paper* and was never reached.

A written notice of motion, dealing with an alleged contempt of the House, was placed on the *Notice Paper* on February 27, 1996. The text of the motion, sponsored by Don Boudria (Glengarry–Prescott–Russell), accused Ray Speaker (Lethbridge) of attempting to put pressure on the Speaker to recognize the Reform Party as the Official Opposition. The motion further declared that this constituted a contempt of Parliament and ordered that the Member for Lethbridge be admonished at the Bar of the House by the Chair. The motion had been placed on the *Order Paper* under Private Members' Business[390] and had subsequently been chosen for debate after a random draw on March 4, 1996. The Standing Committee on Procedure and House Affairs had not, however, selected the motion to come to a vote.

On May 9, 1996, the day before the motion would, in accordance with the order of precedence for Private Members' Business, be called for debate, Mr. Speaker (Lethbridge) raised a point of order in the House to question whether a motion which was not votable could be used to make a charge against another Member. The Acting Speaker informed the House that the motion would not be called the next day because Mr. Boudria could not be present, and that in the meantime the Chair would consider the point of order.[391]

On June 18, 1996, Speaker Parent ruled that the motion was procedurally acceptable under the rules for Private Members' Business. He stated, "The hon. Member is quite correct in his assertion that the conduct of a member can be brought before the House only by way of a specific charge contained in a substantive motion. Often, in such cases, members will choose to raise the matter on the floor of the House without giving the required 48-hour or two-week notice and ask the Speaker to give it priority or right of way for immediate consideration by the House, thus putting all other regular House business aside…. In the current circumstances, I find that the rules for Private Members' Business have been followed and that there is

---

388. *Debates*, June 16, 1959, p. 4761.

389. *Journals*, June 19, 1959, pp. 581-6.

390. See *Order Paper and Notice Paper*, February 28, 1996, p. VI. Mr. Boudria's motion was designated Private Members' Notice of Motion M-1.

391. *Debates*, May 9, 1996, pp. 2523-4.

therefore no point of order." [392] The Chair also noted that it did not have the authority to make the motion votable. He further pointed out that there were "procedures at the disposal of the House to ensure that a sense of fair play prevails in all its proceedings". [393] The Member for Lethbridge immediately raised a question of privilege which would provide a way of resolving the charge made against him by permitting the matter to come to a vote. He argued that allowing the charge to remain unresolved would seriously affect his reputation. After hearing from other Members, the Speaker reserved his decision. [394]

When he returned to the question on June 20, 1996, the Speaker reminded the House that motions regarding the conduct of Members had in the past been placed on the *Order Paper* under Private Members' Business without ever being voted on by the House. Although he could not find there was a *prima facie* question of privilege, the Speaker suggested that the Member consider pursuing the matter of the non-votable motion with the Standing Committee on Procedure and House Affairs. [395]

On October 23, 1996, the Speaker announced to the House that Mr. Boudria had advised the Chair in writing that he could no longer move private Members' motions because of his recent appointment to Cabinet. The Speaker, who has the duty under the Standing Orders of making arrangements for the orderly conduct of Private Members' Business, thus directed that Mr. Boudria's motion be removed from the *Order Paper*. [396]

COMMITTEE CONSIDERATION OF PRIVILEGE MATTER

If the terms of the privilege motion stipulate that the matter be referred to the Standing Committee on Procedure and House Affairs, then the adoption of the motion by the House constitutes an order of reference to the Committee. The Standing Orders empower the Committee to enquire into all such matters referred to it and to send for persons, papers and records. While the Committee is free to determine its own agenda, both the Committee and the House take such enquiries very seriously. The Committee does not have the power to punish. This power rests with the House. The Committee may only study the matter and report to the House. The conduct of the Committee in investigating a privilege matter is the same as for other business considered by any committee of the House, though the nature of the order of reference would encourage the Committee to proceed cautiously. [397]

---

392. *Debates*, June 18, 1996, p. 4028.

393. *Debates*, June 18, 1996, p. 4028.

394. *Debates*, June 18, 1996, pp. 4029-31.

395. *Debates*, June 20, 1996, pp. 4183-4.

396. *Debates*, October 23, 1996, p. 5630. See also *Journals*, October 23, 1996, p. 768.

397. See *Maingot*, 2nd ed., pp. 267-9.

Committee Report

The form of a report of the Standing Committee on Procedure and House Affairs on a matter of privilege is no different from a report of any other committee of the House on a substantive matter. It may or may not contain recommendations for action or punishment[398] and, if the Committee so orders, it may also have appended to it dissenting or supplementary opinions or recommendations.[399] Frequently, the report itself may be sufficient to put an end to the matter and no further action is required by the House.[400] A report may, on the other hand, recommend that the Speaker take some action or that some administrative action be taken.[401] Just as with most committee reports, following appropriate notice, a Member may move for concurrence which the House may debate.[402]

A MATTER OF "PERSONAL PRIVILEGE"

The Chair may occasionally grant leave to a Member to explain a matter of a personal nature although there is no question before the House.[403] This is commonly

---

398. See, for example, Standing Committee on Elections, Privileges and Procedure, Seventh Report, presented to the House on December 18, 1987, *Journals*, pp. 2014-6; Standing Committee on Privileges and Elections, Twenty-Fourth Report, *Minutes of Proceedings and Evidence,* March 7, 1991, Issue No. 39, pp. 3-8; Standing Committee on House Management, Sixty-Fifth Report, *Minutes of Proceedings and Evidence,* February 18, 1993, Issue No. 46, pp. 7-11.

399. See, for example, Standing Committee on Procedure and House Affairs, Twenty-Second Report, *Minutes of Proceedings,* June 18, 1996, Issue No. 1, pp. 46-55; Standing Committee on Procedure and House Affairs, Twenty-Ninth Report, presented to the House on April 27, 1998, *Journals*, p. 706.

400. See, for example, Standing Committee on Privileges and Elections, Twenty-Fourth Report, *Minutes of Proceedings and Evidence,* March 7, 1991, Issue No. 39, pp. 3-8. In the case involving John Parry (Kenora–Rainy River), following the presentation of the Seventh Report of the Standing Committee on Elections, Privileges and Procedure on December 18, 1987, which criticized the Member but called for no punishment, Mr. Parry rose in the House and apologized for his actions (see *Debates*, December 18, 1987, p. 11951).

401. See, for example, Standing Committee on House Management, Sixty-Fifth Report, *Minutes of Proceedings and Evidence,* February 18, 1993, Issue No. 46, pp. 7-11, which recommended that the Speaker write a letter to the CBC and a named individual advising them of the content of the report; Standing Committee on Procedure and House Affairs, Sixty-Sixth Report, presented to the House on April 14, 1999, *Journals*, p. 1714, Sessional Paper No. 8510-361-152, which suggested improvements for handling demonstrations around the parliamentary precinct and other parliamentary buildings (see especially paras. 16-23).

402. See, for example, the motion for concurrence in the Sixty-Fifth Report of the Standing Committee on House Management, adopted on February 25, 1993 (*Debates*, p. 16440); the motion for concurrence in the Twenty-Second Report of the Standing Committee on Procedure and House Affairs, debated in the House on June 20, 1996, superseded by a motion to adjourn the debate and transferred to Government Business on the *Order Paper* (see *Journals*, pp. 592-3); the motion for concurrence in the Twenty-Ninth Report of the Standing Committee on Procedure and House Affairs, adopted on a recorded division (see *Journals*, May 5, 1998, pp. 744-5). See also *Journals*, April 29, 1998, p. 722.

403. See also Chapter 13, "Rules of Order and Decorum".

referred to by Members as "a point of personal privilege" and is an indulgence granted by the Chair. There is no connection to a question of privilege, and as Speaker Fraser once noted, "There is no legal authority, procedural or otherwise, historic or precedential, that allows this."[404] Consequently, such occasions are not meant to be used for general debate, and Members have been cautioned to confine their remarks to the point they wish to make.[405] The Speaker has also stated that, as these are generally personal statements and not questions of privilege, no other Members will be recognized to speak on the matter.[406] Members have used this procedure to make personal explanations,[407] to correct errors made in debate,[408] to apologize to the House,[409] to thank the House or acknowledge something done for the Member by the House,[410] to announce a change in party affiliation,[411] to announce a resignation,[412] or for some other reason.[413]

---

404. *Debates*, November 21, 1990, p. 15526.

405. In 1996, Speaker Parent advised the House that Jean-Marc Jacob (Charlesbourg) would be rising to make a solemn declaration to the House. The Speaker cautioned Members that the statement was not to incite debate. The Speaker subsequently interrupted Mr. Jacob and ruled that "the words being used [in the statement] tend more toward a debate than a solemn declaration". The Member was not allowed to continue (see *Debates*, June 18, 1996, p. 4027). See also *Debates*, May 11, 1989, pp. 1571-3, when a Minister rose on a matter of personal privilege to clarify a statement he had made the previous day. Following the statement of the Minister, the Speaker recognized the critic from the Official Opposition to respond to the statement. However, when the Minister began to engage in a debate with the opposition Member, the Speaker closed off the remarks and advised the House that Members could seek further information from the Minister on another occasion.

406. *Debates*, March 17, 1997, p. 9060.

407. See, for example, *Debates*, June 13, 1977, pp. 6584-5; October 8, 1987, p. 9827; June 18, 1996, p. 4027.

408. See, for example, *Debates*, May 11, 1989, pp. 1571-3.

409. See *Debates*, December 18, 1987, pp. 11950-1; March 19, 1991, p. 18710; October 9, 1991, pp. 3515-6; January 24, 1994, p. 197; October 31, 1996, pp. 5948-9; April 28, 1999, p. 14448.

410. See, for example, *Debates*, November 26, 1992, pp. 14113-5.

411. See, for example, *Debates*, November 21, 1990, pp. 15526-8; March 17, 1997, pp. 9059-60.

412. See, for example, *Debates*, March 15, 1984, pp. 2138-9; May 12, 1986, p. 13149; February 3, 1988, p. 12581.

413. See *Debates*, January 26, 1990, p. 7495; December 12, 1990, pp. 16635-6; May 27, 1991, p. 610.

Figure 3.1 *The Path of a Question of Privilege*

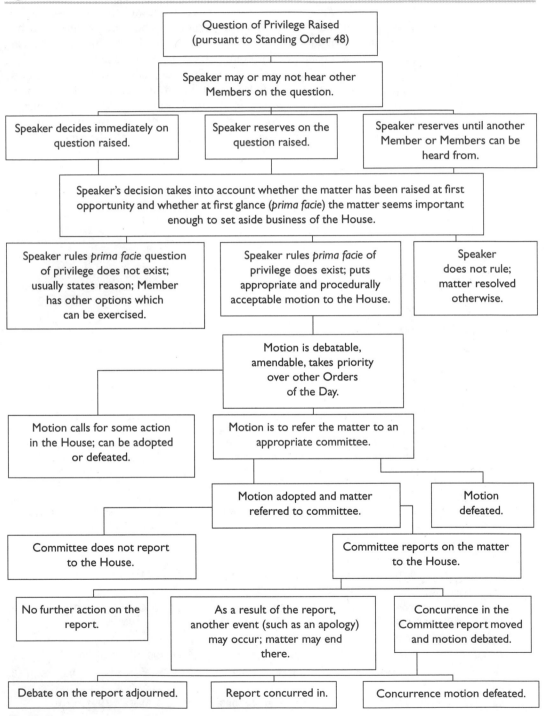

4

The House of Commons and Its Members

We use the words "House of Commons" very often without pausing to reflect upon what those words mean…. The word "Commons" means the people. This is the house of the people. Sitting on both sides of this house and on both sides of the Speaker are representatives of every constituency of Canada. Collectively, those of us who meet in this chamber represent all Canadians. That is our responsibility; that is our duty.

THE HON. GEORGE DREW, Leader of the Opposition
(*Debates,* June 4, 1956, p. 4644)

The House of Commons is the elected assembly of the Parliament of Canada. Its 301 Members are elected by popular vote at least once every five years to sit in the House of Commons. For that purpose, the country is divided into electoral districts, also known as ridings or constituencies, and each is entitled to one seat in the House of Commons. The composition of the House has grown considerably since 1867 when 181 Members sat in the House for the very first time.

The Canadian electoral system is known as the single-member, simple-plurality voting system, or "first past the post" system.[1] In this system, Canadian citizens 18 years of age or older are eligible to vote. Elections at the federal level are simultaneous and nation-wide. Voting is by secret ballot and a voter may cast only one vote and vote for

---

1. For a description of various electoral systems, see *Jackson and Jackson,* pp. 426-34.

only one person on the ballot. To be elected, the candidate who gains the most votes wins, even if he or she has received fewer than half of the votes.[2]

The electoral process, rules regarding membership, and the number and distribution of seats are governed by various acts of Parliament. The main body of Canadian election law is found in the *Canada Elections Act,* which sets down the conditions in which parties and candidates engage in the election process and ensures the free expression of political choice by electors. Other statutes such as the *Criminal Code* and the *Dominion Controverted Elections Act* also contain provisions governing the electoral process. The *Representation Act* and the *Electoral Boundaries Readjustment Act* establish the processes for determining the number of Members each province is entitled to and the boundaries of each electoral district. The *Constitution Act, 1867* and the *Parliament of Canada Act* include provisions governing membership in the House and the various responsibilities and obligations of Members. The Standing Orders of the House of Commons and the By-laws of the Board of Internal Economy also set down rules and regulations affecting the conduct and responsibilities of Members of the House of Commons. These matters are discussed in detail in this chapter.

Composition of the House

Canada is divided into 301 electoral districts, each of which sends one Member to the House of Commons.[3] An electoral district can be defined as any place or territorial area in Canada entitled to return a person to serve in the House of Commons. The boundaries of an electoral district are determined by an electoral boundaries commission following each decennial census when the number of seats to be apportioned among the provinces is decided. These districts or constituencies are grouped by province and territory, and the population serves as the main basis for assigning the seat total to each.

The composition of the House has expanded greatly since 1867. At the time of Confederation, representation was based on Quebec having the same number of seats that it had in the Legislature of the Province of Canada, with the other provinces being granted representation in proportion to that number. At the opening of

---

2. Indeed, the number of Members a party elects does not necessarily reflect the proportion of votes it received at the national level, as has been clearly demonstrated in numerous general elections. As an example, in the election of 1968, the Liberal Party polled 45% of the votes cast and won 59% of the seats in the House; in 1984, the Progressive Conservative Party polled 50% of the votes cast and won 75% of the seats in House. See *Dawson's The Government of Canada*, 5th ed., pp. 314-5; 6th ed., p. 85.

3. *Constitution Act, 1867*, R.S.C. 1985, Appendix II, No. 5, s. 40. Until the 1968 general election, some electoral districts were entitled to return two Members to the House of Commons. In each two-Member constituency, voters were entitled to cast two votes; the two candidates with the most votes won. See Norman Ward, "Voting in Canadian Two-Member Constituencies", in *Voting in Canada* (ed. John C. Courtney), Scarborough: Prentice-Hall of Canada Ltd., 1967, pp. 125-9, for a historical perspective of two-Member constituencies.

the First Parliament, 181 Members sat in the House of Commons, representing the following provinces: 82 for Ontario, 65 for Quebec, 19 for Nova Scotia, and 15 for New Brunswick.[4]

Soon after, new provinces began to seek admittance to Confederation; representation in Parliament was considered negotiable and often did not reflect representation by population.[5] When Manitoba joined Canada in 1870, four Members were added to the membership of the House.[6] British Columbia and Prince Edward Island each got six Members upon joining Confederation in 1871 and in 1873 respectively.[7] In 1886, the Northwest Territories received four seats and in 1902, the Yukon Territory was granted one seat.[8] When Saskatchewan and Alberta were established out of the Northwest Territories in 1905, they were allotted 10 and seven Members respectively.[9] The Northwest Territories no longer had a seat in the House. Newfoundland joined Confederation in 1949 and was granted seven seats.[10] In 1952, the Mackenzie district of the Northwest Territories was granted one seat and, in 1962, the *Representation Act* was amended to give the entire Northwest Territories one seat.[11] In 1975, the number of seats in the Northwest Territories grew to two. On April 1, 1999, the Nunavut Territory was established out of the eastern portion of the Northwest Territories and was given one of the two seats.[12]

Today, there are 301 Members from 10 provinces and three territories: 34 for British Columbia, 26 for Alberta, 14 for Saskatchewan, 14 for Manitoba, 103 for Ontario, 75 for Quebec, 10 for New Brunswick, 11 for Nova Scotia, four for Prince Edward Island, seven for Newfoundland, and one each for the Yukon Territory, the Northwest Territories, and Nunavut. (See Figure 4.1 for changes in representation from 1867 to the present.)

---

4. *Constitution Act, 1867*, R.S.C. 1985, Appendix II, No. 5, s. 37.

5. See Norman Ward, "A Century of Constituencies", *Canadian Public Administration* 10 (1967) as reprinted in *Representation and Electoral Systems Canadian Perspectives*, J. Paul Johnson and Harvey E. Pasis (editors), Scarborough: Prentice-Hall Canada Inc., 1990, p. 207.

6. *An Act to amend and continue the Act 32 and 33 Victoria, chapter 3, and to establish and provide for the Government of the Province of Manitoba*, S.C. 1870, c. 3.

7. See *Journals*, March 31, 1871, p. 198; May 20, 1873, p. 402.

8. *Northwest Territories Representation Act, 1886*, S.C. 1886, c. 24; *The Yukon Territory Representation Act, 1902*, S.C. 1902, c. 37.

9. See *An Act to readjust the representation of the provinces of Saskatchewan and Alberta in the House of Commons and to amend the Representation Act*, S.C. 1907, c. 41.

10. *An Act to approve the terms of the union of Newfoundland with Canada*, S.C. 1949, c. 1.

11. *An Act to amend the British North America Acts, 1867 to 1951, with respect to the Readjustment of Representation in the House of Commons*, S.C. 1952, c. 15; *An Act to amend the Representation Act*, S.C. 1962, c. 17.

12. *Nunavut Act*, S.C. 1993, c. 28; *An Act to amend the Nunavut Act and the Constitution Act, 1867*, S.C. 1998, c. 15, ss. 25, 45.3.

Figure 4.1   *Representation Since 1867*

Year	Canada	Ont.	Que.	N.S.	N.B.	Man.	B.C.	P.E.I.	Sask.	Alta.	Nfld.	N.W.T.	Y.T.	Nunavut
1867	181	82	65	19	15									
1870	185	82	65	19	15	4								
1871	191	82	65	19	15	4	6							
1872	200	88	65	21	16	4	6	6						
1873	206	88	65	21	16	4	6	6						
1882	211	92	65	21	16	5	6	6						
1886	215	92	65	21	16	5	6	6				4		
1892	213	92	65	20	14	7	6	5				4		
1902	214	92	65	20	14	7	6	5				4	1	
1903	214	86	65	18	13	10	7	4				10	1	
1905	221	86	65	18	13	10	7	4	10	7			1	
1914	234	82	65	16	11	15	13	3	16	12			1	
1915	235	82	65	16	11	15	13	4	16	12			1	
1924	245	82	65	14	11	17	14	4	21	16			1	
1933	245	82	65	12	10	17	16	4	21	17			1	
1947	255	83	73	13	10	16	18	4	20	17			1	
1949	262	83	73	13	10	16	18	4	20	17	7		1	
1952	265	85	75	12	10	14	22	4	17	17	7	1	1	
1966	264	88	74	11	10	13	23	4	13	19	7	1	1	
1975	265	88	74	11	10	13	23	4	13	19	7	2	1	
1976	282	95	75	11	10	14	28	4	14	21	7	2	1	
1987	295	99	75	11	10	14	32	4	14	26	7	2	1	
1997	301	103	75	11	10	14	34	4	14	26	7	2	1	
1999	301	103	75	11	10	14	34	4	14	26	7	1	1	1

REPRESENTATION

The Fathers of Confederation adopted the principle of representation by population. Each province was allotted a number of seats on the basis of its share of the total population in relation to that in the province of Quebec, which had been guaranteed 65 seats, the same number it had in the Province of Canada legislature. [13] On the basis of this principle, a formula was derived to calculate the number of seats each province would be allocated in the House of Commons. The *Constitution Act, 1867* stipulated that in order for the population of each province to be accurately represented in the House of Commons, the number of seats for each province was to be recalculated after each decennial census, starting with the census of 1871. [14] The total number of seats was to be calculated by dividing the population of each province by a fixed number referred to as the "electoral quota" or "quotient". This quotient was determined by dividing the population of the province of Quebec by 65. There was one exception to this formula, the one-twentieth rule as it was known, whereby no province could lose seats unless its share of the national population had decreased by at least 5% (one-twentieth) between the last two censuses.

Because of the growing population of the country, the one-twentieth clause caused no problems for the first 25 years of Confederation. In 1872, representation in the House increased after the decennial census of 1871: Ontario received six additional Members, Nova Scotia two, and New Brunswick one. With the readjustment of representation in 1882, Ontario received four extra seats and Manitoba one, bringing the total to 211 Members. However, in 1892, the three Maritime provinces lost four seats in total, causing some concern, particularly in Prince Edward Island. Although the population was growing in the Maritime provinces, it was becoming relatively smaller in proportion to the national total. In 1903, the readjustment of representation saw the number of seats in Prince Edward Island reduced. In arguments before the Supreme Court, Prince Edward Island claimed that it should be entitled to the six seats it was allocated when it joined Confederation. The Supreme Court subsequently upheld that representation must be based on the total population of Canada and that no exception could be made for Prince Edward Island. [15]

Despite the Supreme Court ruling, there was dissension among some of the provinces whose population was declining. A constitutional amendment was proposed in 1914 and adopted the following year. Still in effect today, the "senatorial

---

13. In 1865, at the time of the Confederation debates, then Attorney General John A. MacDonald (later Canada's first Prime Minister) explained that Quebec was chosen as the pivotal province because it was "the best suited for the purpose, on account of the comparatively permanent character of its population and from its having neither the largest nor the least number of inhabitants ..." (*Confederation Debates*, February 6, 1865, p. 38).

14. *Constitution Act, 1867*, R.S.C. 1985, Appendix II, No. 5, s. 51. A less detailed census takes place every five years.

15. See Norman Ward, *The Canadian House of Commons: Representation*, Toronto: University of Toronto Press, 1950, pp. 39-41.

clause", as it is referred to, guarantees that no province can have fewer seats in the House of Commons than it has in the Senate and was added to the Constitution to protect the smallest provinces from losing any more seats because of a declining population.[16]

Following the census of 1941, a constitutional amendment was adopted to postpone the redistribution process until the first session of Parliament after the end of the war.[17] This constitutional amendment came about because the Western provinces were concerned that the dislocation of population caused by the war would affect their representation. There was also widespread dissatisfaction among the provinces with the rules for redistribution, which would have seen four of the nine provinces being allocated representation in accordance with their population; the other five provinces would have been guaranteed extra seats either because of the senatorial clause or the one-twentieth formula.[18] The demand for representation by population, in particular by Quebec, led to the repeal of the one-twentieth clause in 1946.[19] The total number of seats was fixed at 255, one for the Yukon and the other 254 divided among the provinces on the basis of their share of the country's total population, rather than on the average population per electoral district in Quebec.[20]

However, under this new formula, it was soon discovered that with provincial populations not increasing at the same rate, representation in some provinces declined. With Nova Scotia, Manitoba and Saskatchewan all scheduled to lose seats after the 1951 census, the *Constitution Act, 1867* was amended again to prevent a

---

16. *Constitution Act, 1867*, R.S.C. 1985, Appendix II, No. 5, s. 51A. This clause was enacted as the *Constitution Act, 1915,* R.S.C. 1985, Appendix II, No. 23. Prince Edward Island was guaranteed four seats and Nova Scotia and New Brunswick 10 each. At the time of Confederation, the Senate had 72 appointed members, 24 members each from Quebec, Ontario and the Maritimes (12 for Nova Scotia and 12 for New Brunswick). When Manitoba joined Confederation in 1870, it was given two Senators; in 1871 British Columbia received three and Prince Edward Island four (two from each of the other Maritime Provinces; see s. 147 of the *Constitution Act, 1867*); Alberta and Saskatchewan were granted four Senators each in 1905. The Senate was reconstituted at 96 by the *Constitution Act, 1915.* Six more Senators were added when Newfoundland joined Canada in 1949 and one Senator each was added for the Yukon Territory and the Northwest Territory in 1975. In 1999, one Senator was added for the new territory of Nunavut. The Senate ordinarily has 105 members.

17. *Journals*, July 5, 1943, pp. 582-4.

18. Only the provinces of Quebec, Manitoba, Saskatchewan and British Columbia would have had seats in proportion to their population. See Ward, *The Canadian House of Commons: Representation*, p. 53.

19. See the *Constitution Act, 1946*, R.S.C. 1985, Appendix II, No. 30. For additional information, see Ward, *The Canadian House of Commons: Representation*, pp. 54-5.

20. The entry of Newfoundland in 1949 increased this total to 262.

rapid decline in the number of seats of some provinces.[21] In this instance, the amendment stipulated that no province could lose more than 15% of the number of seats it was entitled to under the last readjustment, nor could a province have fewer seats than a province with a smaller population. Nonetheless, after the 1961 census, these same three provinces as well as Quebec lost seats, and following the 1971 census, Newfoundland was added to the list of provinces scheduled to lose seats.

In 1974, legislation was introduced to remedy this problem. A new formula, the amalgam formula, was proposed in the *Representation Act, 1974* to ensure that no province lost any seats.[22] As in the original representation formula, Quebec was allocated a set number of seats, 75, and its average constituency population was used to calculate the number of seats in the other provinces. In each subsequent readjustment, there would be an automatic increase of four seats for Quebec to compensate for population growth and decrease the average constituency population in Quebec, the basis on which the allocation of seats among the other provinces would be calculated. In addition, three categories of provinces were created: large provinces (population of 2.5 million or more); intermediate provinces (population between 1.5 and 2.5 million); and small provinces (population under 1.5 million). Only the large provinces would be allocated seats in strict proportion to Quebec; separate rules for calculating the number of seats were established for the small and intermediate provinces.[23] The amalgam formula was applied only once, in 1976, establishing 282 seats in the House.

Following the 1981 census, calculations revealed that there would be substantial increases in the representation in the House both immediately and after subsequent censuses. Indeed, it was projected that, by the year 2001, there would be 396 Members in the House. The Standing Committee on Privileges and Elections was mandated to study the issue of representation in both the Thirty-Second (1980-84) and Thirty-Third (1984-88) Parliaments[24], and new representation legislation was passed

---

21. See the *Constitution Act, 1952*, S.C. 1952, c. 15, s. 1. This was the first constitutional amendment passed by the Parliament of Canada after the amending procedure for the Constitution was modified in 1949.

22. S.C. 1974-75-76, c. 13. The President of the Privy Council, Mitchell Sharp, noted during second reading of this bill: "The amalgam method was devised as a means of ensuring that the population size of constituencies in Canada would not grow to a point where a Member's ability to represent his constituents would be impaired, nor the access of constituents to their Member unduly restricted." See *Debates*, December 2, 1974, p. 1846. For additional information, see *Dawson's The Government of Canada,* 6ᵗʰ ed., p. 91.

23. See *Debates*, December 2, 1974, pp. 1845-7, where Mitchell Sharp, President of the Privy Council, outlines the amalgam formula.

24. See *Journals*, January 13, 1981, pp. 1138-9; Standing Committee on Privileges and Elections, *Minutes of Proceedings and Evidence,* July 6, 1982, Issue No. 21, pp. 5-7 (Fifth Report presented on July 8, 1982 (*Journals*, pp. 5132-3)). See also *Journals*, October 1, 1985, p. 1051; November 21, 1985, p. 1251.

in 1986. The *Representation Act, 1985*[25] set down a new formula for calculating representation, starting with 282 seats, the number of Members resulting from the previous distribution (see Figure 4.2):

1. One seat each is allocated to the Northwest Territories, Nunavut[26] and the Yukon.

2. The total population of the 10 provinces is divided by 279 to obtain the electoral quotient.

3. The number of seats to be allocated to each province is calculated by dividing the total population of the province by the electoral quotient. If the result leaves a remainder higher than 0.50, the number of seats is rounded off to the next whole number.

4. Once the number of seats per province is obtained, adjustments are made by applying the senatorial and grandfather clauses. The senatorial clause guarantees that no province has fewer Members than it has Senators, while the grandfather clause ensures that no province has fewer seats than it had in 1986 when this legislation came into force.[27]

As a result of this new formula, the House grew to 295 seats after the 1988 federal election and to 301 seats following the 1997 election.

READJUSTMENT OF BOUNDARIES

While Section 51 of the *Constitution Act, 1867,* sets out the formula for the allocation of seats in the House of Commons among the provinces after each decennial census, the *Electoral Boundaries Readjustment Act* provides for the drawing of the constituency or electoral district boundaries within each province. The boundaries of electoral districts need to be adjusted whenever a province's representation changes or when there have been significant population fluctuations within a province, such as movement from rural to urban areas. The readjustment of boundaries is a federal matter controlled by Parliament.

---

25. S.C. 1986, c.8, s. 2.

26. As enacted by *An Act to amend the Nunavut Act and the Constitution Act, 1867*, S.C. 1998, c. 15, s. 25.

27. In April 1994, the Standing Committee on Procedure and House Affairs was instructed to prepare and bring in a bill respecting the system of readjusting electoral boundaries and to consider a formula to cap or reduce the number of seats in the House of Commons (*Journals*, April 19, 1994, pp. 368-70). In its Fifty-First Report (presented on November 25, 1994 (*Journals*, p. 939)), the Committee concluded that a cap or reduction in the size of the House would not be feasible because of certain constraints set out in the Constitution, notably the senatorial clause, which can only be changed with the unanimous agreement of all provinces. Capping or reducing the size of the House, while maintaining the senatorial floor, would lead to certain provinces losing a significant number of seats while others would be protected. In addition, capping the size of the House would require repealing the grandfather clause which guarantees that provinces with declining populations maintain the same number of seats they had in 1986. See the Standing Committee on Procedure and House Affairs, *Minutes of Proceedings and Evidence,* November 25, 1994, Issue No. 33, pp. 5-11.

Figure 4.2   *Calculating Representation in the House of Commons*

$$282 \text{ SEATS} - \text{N.W.T.} - \text{NUNAVUT} - \text{YUKON} = 279$$

$$\text{POPULATION OF PROVINCES} \div 279 = \text{ELECTORAL QUOTIENT}$$

$$\text{PROVINCIAL POPULATION} \div \text{ELECTORAL QUOTIENT} = \text{PROVINCIAL SEAT ALLOCATION}$$

In the early years of Confederation, the government would introduce a bill describing the boundaries of each electoral district and then have the bill adopted like any other piece of legislation. This was subject to criticism as being a highly biased task focussed on maximizing the governing party's electoral successes, often referred to as "gerrymandering".[28] In 1903, this legislative process was altered by Sir Wilfrid Laurier when the readjustment of constituency boundaries was placed in the hands of a special committee of the House of Commons on which Members from all parties were represented.[29] Each time a redistribution was to occur, as provided for by the *Constitution Act, 1867* and the latest census, the government brought in a bill which would not contain any details on individual ridings. After the bill was read a second time, it would be referred to a special committee instructed to "prepare schedules to contain and describe the several electoral divisions entitled to return Members to this House".[30] This process remained highly partisan and was lacking

---

28. Gerrymandering is the manipulation of riding boundaries by the government party to ensure that the opposition's vote is concentrated in as few constituencies as possible. John McMenemy explains in *The Language of Canadian Politics*, Waterloo: Wilfrid Laurier University Press, 1995, p. 122, that the term "gerrymander" comes from such a manipulation in Massachusetts in 1812 by the party of Governor Elbridge Gerry, which resulted in constituencies whose configurations resembled those of a salamander. In his book, *The Canadian House of Commons: Representation*, Professor Norman Ward briefly describes the 1872, 1882 and 1892 redistributions as being affected by gerrymandering (see pp. 26-9).

29. *Journals*, April 14, 1903, p. 116.

30. See *Journals*, February 19, 1914, p. 153; March 25, 1924, p. 81; November 25, 1932, p. 148; February 24, 1947, pp. 122-3; June 28, 1952, p. 618.

guidelines to instruct Members on how to base their decisions.[31] This system remained in place until 1964 when non-partisan electoral boundaries commissions were established to draw and readjust the boundaries of electoral constituencies.

Even before Confederation, suggestions had been made to place the drawing of electoral boundaries into the hands of an impartial body, and not with Members.[32] This continued to be a concern after Confederation and, on a number of occasions, it was recommended that the process be moved away from Members into the hands of judges.[33] In 1963, the decision was taken to assign the drawing of electoral boundaries to non-partisan commissions operating under specified general principles and, in 1964, the *Electoral Boundaries Readjustment Act* was passed.[34] Today, there is an electoral boundaries commission appointed for each province. No commission is appointed for the Yukon Territory, the Northwest Territories or Nunavut. Each commission consists of a chairman, normally a provincial court judge, who is appointed by the chief justice of the province,[35] and two other individuals appointed by the Speaker of the House of Commons "from among such persons resident in that province as the Speaker deems suitable".[36] No sitting member of the Senate or of the House of Commons or of a provincial or territorial legislature can be appointed to a commission.[37]

As soon as possible after the completion of each decennial census, the Chief Statistician provides the Chief Electoral Officer, an officer of Parliament who is

---

31. For a more detailed look at the history of readjustment up to the 1960s, see Ward, "A Century of Constituencies", pp. 207-20.

32. See Ward, "A Century of Constituencies", p. 211.

33. See, for example, *Debates*, May 25, 1933, pp. 5468-9; February 21, 1947, pp. 698-9. Between 1958 and 1962, a private Member, Frank Howard (Skeena), annually introduced a bill to assign this task to an independent body.

34. S.C. 1964-65, c. 31. The bill took over a year to get through Parliament because of disagreements over some of the major clauses. See Ward, "A Century of Constituencies", pp. 212-6.

35. If the chief justice of the province does not or cannot appoint someone for whatever reason, the Chief Justice of the Supreme Court may make the appointment (*Electoral Boundaries Readjustment Act*, R.S.C. 1985, c. E-3, s. 5). This occurred in 1993 when the Chief Justice of the Supreme Court appointed the chairman of the British Columbia electoral boundaries commission. Originally, there was a fourth person appointed to each commission, a representation commissioner. The Office of Representation Commissioner was abolished in 1979, when the incumbent retired and most of his duties were transferred to the Chief Electoral Officer.

36. *Electoral Boundaries Readjustment Act*, R.S.C. 1985, c. E-3, ss. 4-6. After the *Electoral Boundaries Readjustment Act* was passed in 1964, many Members expected the Speaker to consult with party leaders prior to making appointments to the electoral boundaries commissions. Instead, the Speaker consulted with the chief justice in each province and the chairman of each commission, and generally appointed an university professor in political science and a citizen whose professional employment indicated some semblance of impartiality, such as the clerk of a legislature. See Ward, "A Century of Constituencies", p. 216.

37. *Electoral Boundaries Readjustment Act*, R.S.C. 1985, c. E-3, s. 10.

responsible for the administration of federal elections, with the population figures.[38] The Chief Electoral Officer then calculates the total number of House of Commons seats and their distribution among the provinces and territories.[39] This information is published in the *Canada Gazette*[40] and then the process begins to appoint the chairman and members of each commission. When the electoral boundaries commissions have been established, the Chief Electoral Officer provides the chairman of each electoral boundaries commission with the population figures. The commission has up to one year from that date to recommend constituency boundaries.[41]

Each commission is required to draw constituency boundaries in such a way that the population of each constituency is as close as possible to the quotient obtained by dividing the provincial population by the number of seats allocated to the province. No constituency is permitted to have a population smaller than 75% of this figure or greater than 125%, although in extraordinary circumstances a commission may exceed this limit. Commissions may vary the size of constituencies within this range on the basis of special geographic considerations, such as density of population in various regions of the province, and the accessibility, size and shape of such regions. Because accessibility, transportation and communications are often seen as obstacles both to effective representation and to ease of campaigning, electoral boundaries commissions generally draw boundaries so that there are fewer voters in rural constituencies than in urban constituencies. Variations may also occur on the basis of a special community of interest or the historical background of a particular district.[42]

Before writing its report, each commission publishes in the *Canada Gazette,* as well as in newspapers in the province, a map or drawing showing the proposed electoral boundaries for the province and invites electors and Members of Parliament to public meetings held in locations that will encourage the attendance of as many interested people as possible. The commission's proposals must be published at least 60 days before the date of the first hearing. Interested persons wishing to make a representation must submit their notice in writing to the commission within 53 days after the date of publication of the commission's advertisement.[43]

Following the hearings, each commission reviews its proposals, prepares a report and forwards it to the Chief Electoral Officer before the end of its one-year

---

38. The Office of the Chief Electoral Officer is discussed in detail later in this chapter.

39. *Electoral Boundaries Readjustment Act*, R.S.C. 1985, c. E-3, ss. 13-4.

40. The *Canada Gazette* is a periodical publication of the Government of Canada containing orders in council and proclamations, regulations and other statutory instruments, and Acts of Parliament.

41. *Electoral Boundaries Readjustment Act,* R.S.C. 1985, c. E-3, s. 20(1) as amended by c. 6 (2nd supp.), s. 4.

42. *Electoral Boundaries Readjustment Act*, R.S.C. 1985, c. E-3, s. 15 as amended by c. 6 (2nd supp.), s. 2.

43. *Electoral Boundaries Readjustment Act*, R.S.C. 1985, c. E-3, s. 19 as amended by c. 6 (2nd supp.), s. 3.

mandate, unless the Chief Electoral Officer has granted an extension of not more than six months.[44] The Chief Electoral Officer transmits a copy of each report to the Speaker of the House of Commons who tables them in the House and ensures that they are referred to a committee designated to deal with electoral matters.[45] If reports are received between sessions, the Speaker of the House will have the reports published in the *Canada Gazette,* and a copy of that *Canada Gazette* will be sent to the Members representing the electoral districts in that province.[46]

Members of Parliament have 30 days following the tabling or publication to file objections in writing with the clerk of the committee designated to deal with electoral matters. Members must specify the provisions objected to in the reports and the reason for the objection. These representations are made in the form of a motion signed by at least 10 Members.[47] Following the filing deadline, the committee has 30 sitting days to review the Members' representations,[48] unless the committee asks the House for an extension.[49] At the conclusion of its consideration of the reports and the objections thereto, the committee returns the reports to the House along with a copy of the objections and its minutes of proceedings. The reports and attached documents are then sent by the Speaker to the Chief Electoral Officer for distribution to

---

44. *Electoral Boundaries Readjustment Act*, R.S.C. 1985, c. E-3, s. 20(2). The Chief Electoral Officer noted in an appearance before the Procedure and House Affairs Committee on February 3, 1994, that no extension had been given in the previous redistribution nor did he anticipate that it would in the 1993-94 redistribution process (Standing Committee on Procedure and House Affairs, *Minutes of Proceedings and Evidence,* February 3, 1994, Issue No. 1, p. 15).

45. *Electoral Boundaries Readjustment Act*, R.S.C. 1985, c. E-3. s. 21(1) as amended by c. 6 (2nd supp.), s. 5. See, for example, *Journals*, June 22, 1995, p. 1867. If the House is not sitting, the reports are tabled on any of the first five sitting days when the House returns. On June 10, 1994, the Standing Orders were amended to designate the Standing Committee on Procedure and House Affairs as the parliamentary committee responsible for electoral matters (see *Journals*, June 10, 1994, p. 563; Twenty-Seventh Report, Standing Committee on Procedure and House Affairs, *Minutes of Proceedings and Evidence,* June 9, 1994, Issue No. 16, pp. 7-8. See also Standing Order 108(3)(*a*)(vi)).

46. *Electoral Boundaries Readjustment Act*, R.S.C. 1985, c. E-3, s. 21(2).

47. *Electoral Boundaries Readjustment Act*, R.S.C. 1985, c. E-3, s. 22 as amended by c. 6 (2nd supp.), s. 6.

48. *Electoral Boundaries Readjustment Act*, R.S.C. 1985, c. E-3, s. 22 as amended by c. 6 (2nd supp.), s. 6. In 1995, because of the large number of objections filed, the Standing Committee on Procedure and House Affairs established four regional sub-committees to hear from Members and to make recommendations to the Committee (see Standing Committee on Procedure and House Affairs, *Minutes of Proceedings and Evidence,* October 17, 1995, Issue No. 52, pp. 25-6).

49. See, for example, *Journals*, October 4, 1995, p. 1990; *Debates*, October 4, 1995, p. 15222. See also Standing Committee on Procedure and House Affairs, *Minutes of Proceedings and Evidence,* October 17, 1995, Issue No. 52, p. 17.

the various electoral boundaries commissions.[50] No discussion of the reports or the objections thereto takes place in the House.[51]

The commissions must consider the objections but they are not compelled to make any changes as a result of the objections. Each commission then submits a final report, with or without amendment, to the Chief Electoral Officer who forwards it to the Speaker of the House.[52] Tabled in the House by the Speaker,[53] the commission's decision is final and without appeal.

After each commission has submitted its final report, the Chief Electoral Officer prepares a draft representation order. The draft representation order specifies the number of Members to be elected in each province and territory, divides each province and territory into electoral districts, describes the boundaries of each district and specifies the population of and the name to be given to each district.[54] Within five days after its receipt by the Minister designated by the Governor in Council as being responsible for implementing the *Electoral Boundaries Readjustment Act,* the draft representation order must be proclaimed by the Governor in Council.[55] The new boundaries cannot be used at the time of an election unless one year has passed between the date the representation order was proclaimed and the date that Parliament is dissolved for a general election.[56]

The *Electoral Boundaries Readjustment Act* also requires the Chief Electoral Officer to publish maps showing the new electoral district boundaries resulting from the readjustment process.[57]

---

50. *Electoral Boundaries Readjustment Act*, R.S.C. 1985, c. E-2, s. 22 as amended by c. 6 (2nd supp.), s. 6. See, for example, *Journals*, November 29, 1995, p. 2188. For the Committee's final report on this matter in regard to the 1995 readjustment of electoral boundaries, see Standing Committee on Procedure and House Affairs, *Minutes of Proceedings,* November 28, 1995, Issue No. 53, pp. 16-118, in particular pp. 18-26.

51. Until 1986, the *Electoral Boundaries Readjustment Act* contained provisions which allowed Members to discuss their objections to a report of an Electoral Boundaries Commission on the floor of the House. Four debates—in 1966, 1973, 1976 and 1983—were held under the Act's provisions (S.C. 1964-65, c. 31, s. 20). Within 30 days of the tabling in the House of such a report, a motion for consideration of an objection to the report signed by not less than 10 Members could be filed with the Speaker. The motion would detail the provisions of the report objected to and the reasons for the objection. Within 15 days of the filing of the motion, time would be set aside under Government Orders for Members to voice their concerns about the report. Upon the conclusion of consideration of the objections, the Speaker was required to refer the objections and the relevant *Debates* pages back to the Commission. In 1986, the Act was amended to provide for the current procedure (*Representation Act, 1985*, S.C. 1986, c. 8, ss. 9-10).

52. *Electoral Boundaries Readjustment Act*, R.S.C. 1985, c. E-3, s. 23(1).

53. *Electoral Boundaries Readjustment Act*, R.S.C. 1985, c. E-3, s. 23(2). See, for example, *Journals*, March 4, 1996, p. 36.

54. *Electoral Boundaries Readjustment Act*, R.S.C. 1985, c. E-3, s. 24 as amended by c. 6 (2nd supp.), s. 7.

55. *Electoral Boundaries Readjustment Act*, R.S.C. 1985, c. E-3, s. 25(1).

56. *Electoral Boundaries Readjustment Act*, R.S.C. 1985, c. E-3, s. 25(1).

57. *Electoral Boundaries Readjustment Act*, R.S.C. 1985, c. E-3, s. 28.

Suspension of the Readjustment Process

In each decade since the 1960s, Parliament has adopted legislation either to suspend or to amend the redistribution process for one reason or another. After both the 1971 and 1981 censuses, the readjustment process was suspended to permit amendments to Section 51 of the *Constitution Act, 1867,* setting out the formula for representation in the House and to make some changes to the readjustment process itself.[58] The redistribution process has been suspended twice since the 1991 census.

In 1992, Parliament agreed that in light of the proposed changes to the *Canada Elections Act* made by the Royal Commission on Electoral Reform and Party Financing, as well as the probability that the readjustment process could not be completed before the next federal election, the Act should be suspended.[59] In 1994, the government believed that it was time for a full review of the Act, given the dissatisfaction being expressed by Members about certain aspects of the process and the continual increase in the number of seats in the House after each census.[60] The readjustment process was subsequently suspended by the *Electoral Boundaries Readjustment Suspension Act, 1994,* which provided for the suspension of the readjustment process until the earlier of the enactment of new electoral boundaries readjustment legislation or June 22, 1995. It also temporarily discharged the existing electoral boundaries commissions of their duties once their reports to the House of Commons on electoral districts had been completed.[61] In the interim, the Standing Committee on Procedure and House Affairs was instructed to draft a bill respecting the system of readjusting electoral boundaries.[62] The Committee was also asked to consider a formula to cap or reduce the number of seats in the House and to review the method of appointing members for electoral boundaries commissions, the rules surrounding their powers and methods of proceeding, and the involvement of the public and the House of Commons in the work of the commissions.

---

58. *Representation Act, 1974,* S.C. 1974-75-76, c. 13; *Representation Act, 1985*, S.C. 1986, c. 8.

59. See *Debates*, May 1, 1992, pp. 9995-8. Bill C-67, the *Electoral Boundaries Suspension Act* was subsequently granted Royal Assent on June 18, 1992.

60. See *Debates*, March 21, 1994, pp. 2518-20.

61. Initially, when the House passed Bill C-18, the *Electoral Boundaries Readjustment Suspension Act, 1994,* at the third reading stage, the legislation stipulated that the electoral boundaries commissions would cease to exist and the operation of the *Electoral Boundaries Readjustment Act* would be suspended for 24 months on the day the Act was assented to. However, the Senate amended the legislation to allow the commissions to hold public hearings on their proposals and fixed February 6, 1995, as the date on which the suspension would end (*Journals*, May 25, 1994, p. 478). The House concurred in the amendments proposed by the Senate with the exception of the February 6, 1995 date. The date was pushed back to June 22, 1995 and the legislation was eventually adopted by both Houses and assented to on June 15, 1994. See *Journals*, June 3, 1994, p. 528; June 9, 1994, p. 557; June 14, 1994, p. 585. See also *Debates*, June 3, 1994, pp. 4811-2.

62. *Journals*, April 19, 1994, pp. 368-70.

On November 25, 1994, the Standing Committee on Procedure and House Affairs presented its report which included draft legislation to repeal the existing statute and to abolish the electoral boundaries commissions.[63] While the Committee did not recommend a change in the manner of assigning seats among the provinces after each decennial census nor a formula for capping the number of seats in the House, it did propose a new method of drawing electoral boundaries. As a result, Bill C-69, *Electoral Boundaries Readjustment Act, 1995,* was introduced by the government on February 16, 1995.[64] The objective of the bill was to stop the redistribution plans and to start the process all over again, allowing the next election to be held on the basis of the 1981 boundaries. The bill would have also brought about a redistribution every five years in provinces where the shift in population warranted it, a new triggering mechanism for holding a decennial redistribution which would have eliminated an unnecessary redistribution in provinces without a significant change in population, and parliamentary oversight of appointments to electoral boundaries commissions. However, amendments subsequently proposed to the bill by the Senate and rejected by the House prevented the bill from being passed.[65] Since new electoral boundaries readjustment legislation had not been passed by the stipulated June 22, 1995 deadline, the Speaker tabled the reports of all the electoral boundaries commissions in the House as required and the electoral boundaries were adjusted accordingly.[66] The general election of 1997 was held on the basis of the post-1991 redistribution and revision of boundaries.

Naming of Constituencies

At the time of Confederation, the electoral districts for each province were established in the *Constitution Act, 1867.*[67] The electoral districts existing at that time were named after counties, cities, parts of cities, and towns in each province. From 1872 to 1964, the names of the ridings were provided in legislation to enact seat redistributions and to fix electoral boundaries.

---

63. *Journals*, November 25, 1994, p. 939; Standing Committee on Procedure and House Affairs, *Minutes of Proceedings and Evidence,* November 25, 1994, Issue No. 33, pp. 5-40.

64. *Journals*, February 16, 1995, p. 1141.

65. *Journals,* June 8, 1995, pp. 1600-1; June 14, 1995, pp. 1748-9; June 19, 1995, pp. 1786-8; June 20, 1995, pp. 1817-21. See also *Debates*, June 14, 1995, pp. 13854-5. The Senate objected to the provision whereby a commission would not be established in a province where there had not been a significant change in population, the reduction of the maximum deviation from the electoral quotient to 15% from 25%, parliamentary oversight of appointments to electoral boundaries commissions and the proposed definition for "community of interests". The Senate also opposed the next election being held on the basis of electoral boundaries drawn after the 1981 census and not on the basis of electoral boundaries required to be redrawn after the 1991 census. See also *Minutes of the Proceedings of the Senate*, June 8, 1995, pp. 998-1001; *Senate Debates*, June 8, 1995, pp. 1725-7, 1730-5.

66. *Journals*, June 22, 1995, p. 1867.

67. *Constitution Act, 1867*, R.S.C. 1985, Appendix II, No. 5, s. 40. See also Schedules 1 through 4.

Since 1964 and the adoption of the modern process for drawing electoral boundaries, the names of electoral districts are decided by the electoral boundaries commissions and included in their reports. The names are set down in the representation orders giving legal effect to those reports. The alteration to the name of an electoral district after the publication of the representation order can be effected by the passage of a private Member's bill. A Member usually introduces legislation to change the name of the electoral district in response to concerns expressed by constituents that the name does not accurately describe the boundaries of the riding.[68] Such a bill is typically entitled "An Act to change the name of the electoral district of (electoral district)". Once the bill is before the House for second reading, it is dealt with quickly, typically being read a second time, considered in a Committee of the Whole, reported without amendment, concurred in at the report stage, read a third time and adopted in the same sitting by unanimous consent.[69]

Rules of Membership for the House

With few exceptions, anyone who is qualified to vote can run for a seat in the House of Commons. The qualifications and disqualifications for candidacy in a federal election are set down in the *Canada Elections Act,*[70] the *Parliament of Canada Act*[71] and the *Constitution Act, 1982.*[72]

As stated in the *Charter of Rights and Freedoms,* "every citizen of Canada has the right to vote in an election of members of the House of Commons or of a legislative assembly and to be qualified for membership therein".[73] Thus, any Canadian citizen at least 18 years of age on polling day, who is qualified as an elector, is eligible to be a candidate in an election.[74] A candidate must have established residency

---

68. See, for example, *Debates*, June 27, 1989, pp. 3730-3.

69. See, for example, *Journals*, June 27, 1989, pp. 468-70; September 16, 1992, pp. 2000-1. See also *Journals*, November 8, 1996, p. 856, and December 12, 1996, pp. 1007, 1010, where one bill altered the names of 22 electoral districts (*An Act to change the names of certain electoral districts*, S.C. 1996, c. 36). In 1998, a private Member introduced a similar bill to alter the names of a number of electoral districts. By unanimous consent, the bill was deemed introduced, read a first time and printed, deemed read the second time and referred to a Committee of the Whole, deemed reported without amendment, deemed concurred in at report stage and deemed read the third time and passed without debate or amendment. See *Journals*, May 28, 1998, p. 902; *Debates*, May 28, 1998, pp. 7317-8.

70. R.S.C. 1985, c. E-2, ss. 76.1-78 as amended by S.C. 1989, c. 28, s. 1; and S.C. 1993, c. 19, ss. 34-5.

71. R.S.C. 1985, c. P-1, ss. 21-4.

72. R.S.C. 1985, Appendix II, No. 44, s. 3.

73. *Constitution Act, 1982*, R.S.C. 1985, Appendix II, No. 44, s. 3.

74. *Canada Elections Act*, R.S.C. 1985, c. E-2, s. 76.1 as amended by S.C. 1989, c. 28, s. 1(1). See also s. 50.

somewhere in Canada but not necessarily in the constituency where he or she is seeking election.[75] A candidate may seek election in only one electoral district.[76]

HISTORICAL PERSPECTIVE

The qualifications for candidacy for persons seeking election to the House of Commons have been revised on numerous occasions and have always been closely linked with the right to vote. During periods when groups of citizens were disenfranchised, they were also disqualified from seeking election.[77] In 1867, the *Constitution Act* stated that all laws in force in the provinces respecting qualifications and disqualifications of persons seeking election to provincial legislatures would apply to the election of Members to the House of Commons until the Parliament of Canada

---

75. This usually occurs when a seat must be found for a party leader who is not a Member of Parliament. In these instances, the incumbent Member resigns his or her seat and a by-election takes place. For example, in 1983, Brian Mulroney was named leader of the Progressive Conservative Party of Canada. Later that year, Elmer McKay resigned his Central Nova seat and Mr. Mulroney won a by-election in the riding. In 1990, Jean Chrétien was elected to the leadership of the Liberal Party of Canada. Fernand Robichaud resigned his Beauséjour seat shortly thereafter and Mr. Chrétien won the seat in a by-election.

76. *Parliament of Canada Act*, R.S.C. 1985, c. P-1, s. 21. Until 1919, candidates were permitted to contest more than one seat in a general election (*An Act to amend the House of Commons Act*, S.C. 1920, c. 18. s. 1). If a Member was returned for two constituencies, he had to formally resign one of the seats. It was the practice of party leaders routinely to seek two seats in an election. In the general election of 1878, at a time when the polls were not confined to one day exclusively due to geographic and other factors, Sir John A. Macdonald contested three seats. He was defeated in Kingston, Ontario, on September 17, yet was elected two days later in Marquette, Manitoba. Pursuant to the law at that time, upon his acceptance of the office of Prime Minister, he vacated that seat and was subsequently elected to represent Victoria, British Columbia, on October 21. In 1896, Sir Wilfrid Laurier won his own safe seat in Quebec East and also captured Saskatchewan (NWT) from the Opposition. He resigned the latter seat. In 1908, Sir Robert Borden won a safe seat in Carleton and a doubtful one in Halifax. He relinquished Carleton. In only 6 of the 14 instances where party leaders were candidates in more than one riding did the Member resign one of the seats immediately. See Ward, *The Canadian House of Commons: Representation*, pp. 81-2. However, if one of the elections was contested, the Member could not resign from either. This happened to Sir John A. Macdonald in 1882 and to Sir Wilfrid Laurier who held two seats from 1911 to 1917. In the case of a double return, when returning officers were unable to determine which of two or more candidates had been elected, each of the Members-elect was entitled to be sworn in, but neither could sit in the House nor vote until the matter had been resolved. See *Bourinot*, 4th ed., pp. 135-40, where special and double returns are described. See also *Journals,* March 27, 1871, p. 152; April 19, 1872, p. 27; April 25, 1872, pp. 44-6; May 13, 1872, p. 104; May 18, 1872, pp. 124-5.

77. Between 1867 and 1885, five federal general elections were held with the electorate varying from province to province under the provincial election laws then in force. In all provinces, there were nonetheless three basic conditions: electors had to be male, 21 years of age and a British subject either by birth or naturalization (see *A History of the Vote in Canada,* Ottawa: Minister of Public Works and Government Services for the Chief Electoral Officer of Canada, 1997, p. 45). In 1885, control of the federal franchise was shifted to the federal level (*Electoral Franchise Act*, S.C. 1885, c. 40) and then back to the provinces in 1898 (*The Franchise Act, 1898*, S.C. 1898, c. 14). It was only in 1920 that Parliament regained control (see p. 40).

enacted its own legislation. [78] Although the *Constitution Act, 1867* did stipulate (as did the provincial laws) that candidates had to be male, British subjects, 21 years of age and property owners, [79] the qualification provisions in each province were not necessarily the same and there was no uniformity of qualifications for the first Members returned to the House. Indeed, candidates did not have to reside in the country. For more than one session in the First Parliament, some Members sat not only in the House of Commons, but also in the legislative assemblies of Ontario and Quebec. [80] In 1873, a private Member successfully sponsored a bill to make the practice of dual representation illegal. [81] In 1874, Parliament passed its own legislation providing for the election of Members. The *Dominion Election Act* abolished the property qualification for candidates and declared that any British-born or naturalized male subject of Great Britain, Ireland, or Canada or one of its provinces was eligible for candidacy in an election. [82] In 1919, women received the franchise and the right to be candidates

---

78. *Constitution Act, 1867*, R.S.C. 1985, Appendix II, No. 5, s. 41. See *Confederation Debates*, February 6, 1865, p. 39, where Sir John A. Macdonald said: "Insuperable difficulties would have presented themselves if we had attempted to settle now the qualification for the elective franchise."

79. *Constitution Act, 1867*, R.S.C. 1985, Appendix II, No. 5, s. 41. Property qualifications in terms of real estate ranged at Confederation from $100 in New Brunswick to $150 in Nova Scotia to $300 in Ontario and Quebec. Citizens were allowed to vote in each area in which they owned property. See Ward, *The Canadian House of Commons: Representation,* pp. 63-5.

80. See *Bourinot*, 1st ed., pp. 124-8. Twenty-five Members from Ontario and Quebec also sat in their provincial legislatures and, in both provinces, a majority of the Cabinet held federal seats.

81. *An Act to render Members of the Legislative Councils and Legislative Assemblies of the Provinces now included, or which may hereafter be included within the Dominion of Canada, ineligible for sitting or voting in the House of Commons of Canada,* S.C. 1873, c. 2. Two Members of Prince Edward Island's legislative assembly were elected to the House after dual representation was abolished: S.F. Perry in 1874 and J. E. Robertson in 1883. Mr. Perry was allowed to maintain his seat in the House while the House rejected Mr. Robertson's election. For a historical perspective, refer to Ward, *The Canadian House of Commons: Representation*, pp. 65-9.

82. *Dominion Elections Act*, S.C. 1873-74, c. 9, s. 20. These provisions were so widely accepted that they were only included in the statute when the Senate insisted on an amendment to the legislation stipulating that candidates be British subjects by birth or naturalization.

in an election.[83] In 1948, the election laws were amended to ensure that candidates were Canadian residents and qualified electors; amendments also eliminated disqualification from voting on the basis of race (status Indians excepted), which in turn opened up candidacy to people of Oriental origin, in particular to Japanese-Canadians.[84] In 1955, revisions to the Act gave the franchise to various religious groups, in particular to Doukobours, who had previously been disenfranchised.[85] Aboriginal persons received the right to vote and seek election in 1960.[86] In 1970, the voting age was lowered to 18 and, as an extension, so was the age requirement for candidacy.[87]

DISQUALIFICATIONS

The *Canada Elections Act* sets out a series of disqualifications that apply to electoral candidacy. Inmates of penal institutions serving sentences of two or more years are disqualified from seeking election.[88] Until 1993, patients suffering from mental

---

83. *Dominion By-Election Act*, S.C. 1919, c. 48, s. D. See also *Dominion Elections Act*, S.C. 1920, c. 46, s. 38, which provided universal access to the vote without reference to property ownership. In 1917, when Parliament passed the *Military Voters Act* (S.C. 1917, c. 34), some 2000 military nurses received the right to vote. The *War-time Elections Act* (S.C. 1917, c. 39) conferred the right to vote on spouses, widows, mothers, sisters, and daughters of any persons who had served or were serving in the Canadian forces provided they met the age, nationality and residence requirements for electors in their respective provinces or the Yukon. Women received the franchise to vote in provincial elections in the following sequence: Manitoba (January 28, 1916); Saskatchewan (March 14, 1916); Alberta (April 19, 1916); British Columbia (April 5, 1917); Nova Scotia (April 26, 1918); Ontario (April 24, 1919); Prince Edward Island (May 3, 1922); Newfoundland (May 13, 1925); New Brunswick (March 9, 1934); Quebec (April 24, 1940). The general election of 1921 was the first one open to all Canadians, men and women, over the age of 21. Four women ran but only one was elected. Agnes Campbell MacPhail became the first woman elected to the House of Commons when she won a seat as an Independent for the riding of Grey South East in Ontario. She was re-elected four times. Between 1920 and 1945, only five women sat in the House (see *Fraser*, p. 67). Ellen Louks Fairclough became the first female Cabinet Minister on June 21, 1957, when she was appointed Secretary of State. For additional information on women and the franchise, see *A History of the Vote in Canada*, pp. 58-9, 61-8.

84. *Dominion Elections Act*, S.C. 1948, c. 46, ss. 6, 12. For additional information on racial exclusions, see *A History of the Vote in Canada*, pp. 80-3. The residency requirement had long been a matter of concern in the House. See, for example, *Debates*, April 11, 1890, cols. 3197-8, where a Member explained to the House that although he had moved his residence to England, he did not intend to resign his seat in the House.

85. *An Act to amend the Canada Elections Act*, S.C. 1955, c. 44, s. 4(1). For additional information on religious exclusions, see *A History of the Vote in Canada*, pp. 83-5.

86. *An Act to amend the Canada Elections Act*, S.C. 1960, c. 7, s. 1. The first Aboriginal person to be elected to the House of Commons was Leonard S. Marchand (Kamloops–Caribou) on June 25, 1968. Peter Ittinuar (Nunatsiaq) was the first Inuit elected to the House in the general election of May 22, 1979. For additional information on aboriginals and the vote, see *A History of the Vote in Canada*, pp. 85-9.

87. *Canada Elections Act*, S.C. 1969-70, c. 49, s. 14.

88. *Canada Elections Act*, R.S.C. 1985, c. E-2, s. 77 as amended by S.C. 1993, c. 19, s. 34(5)(*j*).

disease were ineligible to be candidates during the period of confinement or while under the protection and supervision of a guardian.[89] Certain officials such as sheriffs, clerks of the peace, or county or judicial district crown attorneys may not seek election.[90] Similarly, federally appointed judges (citizenship judges excepted) and election officials are disqualified from voting and seeking election.[91] Members of provincial legislatures and territorial councils are also ineligible to run in federal elections.[92] An appointment to the Senate disqualifies a person from being a Member; no violation of this has occurred, although Senators have resigned their seats on occasion to seek election to the House.[93]

A person found guilty of any corrupt electoral practice under the *Canada Elections Act* within the previous five years, such as knowingly making a false declaration respecting election expenses, exerting undue influence upon a voter at an election, or inducing voters by promises of valuable consideration, food or drink, is disqualified from seeking election for seven years following the date of the conviction.[94] A person guilty of any illegal electoral practice under the *Canada Elections Act,* such as wilfully exceeding the legal spending limit, failing to submit a return respecting election expenses, or consenting to be a candidate when ineligible, is disqualified from seeking election for five years from the date of conviction.[95]

Independence of Parliament

As noted by Professor Norman Ward, "It is an ideal of democratic government that representation should be independent of undesirable forces that might bias their judgement on public matters. In particular, they should be free of the executive, at least insofar as direct pecuniary benefit is concerned."[96] In order to preserve its independence, the Parliament of Canada re-enacted 1857 legislation from the Province of Canada which disqualified from eligibility as a Member of the Assembly or from

89. *Canada Elections Act*, R.S.C. 1985, c. E-2, ss. 51(*f*), 77(*h*) as amended by S.C. 1993, c. 19, s. 23(3).

90. *Canada Elections Act*, R.S.C. 1985, c. E-2, s. 77(*e*).

91. *Canada Elections Act*, R.S.C. 1985, ss. 51(*d*), 77(*h*) as amended by S.C 1993, c. 19, ss. 23(1), 34(5).

92. *Canada Elections Act*, R.S.C. 1985, c. E-2, s. 77(*d*), (*g*). This prohibition can also be found in the *Parliament of Canada Act*, R.S.C. 1985, c. P-1, s. 22.

93. *Constitution Act, 1867*, s. 39. As an example, Robert de Cotret was appointed to the Senate on June 5, 1979. He resigned from the Senate on January 14, 1980, to run, unsuccessfully, as a candidate in the February 18, 1980 general election.

94. *Canada Elections Act*, R.S.C. 1985, c. E-2, s. 269. See also s. 77 as amended by S.C. 1993, c. 19, s. 34. A person found guilty of any corrupt practice is also disqualified from voting or holding office in the nomination of the Crown or of the Governor in Council.

95. *Canada Elections Act*, R.S.C. 1985, c. E-2, s. 269. See also s. 77 as amended by S.C. 1993, c. 19, s. 34. If found guilty, the person cannot sit in the House of Commons, hold office in the nomination of the Crown or of the Governor in Council or vote in a federal election for five years.

96. Ward, *The Canadian House of Commons: Representation*, p. 83.

sitting or voting, any person who had accepted or held "any office, commission or employment in the service of the Government of Canada at the nomination of the Crown, to which an annual salary or any fee, allowance, or emolument in lieu of an annual salary from the Crown [was] attached."[97] This disqualified Members appointed to the Cabinet: Cabinet Ministers had to resign their seats and seek re-election in order to obtain the approval of the electors in their constituencies. Also disqualified from eligibility were government contractors and officers of the navy and militia. In 1878, the Act was amended to exempt from disqualification Members already holding a ministerial position and to further disqualify sheriffs, registrars of deeds, clerks of the peace, and county Crown attorneys.[98] In 1931, an amendment to the *Senate and House of Commons Act* freed Ministers appointed after an election from the necessity of vacating their seats and seeking re-election.[99]

In 1992, the Royal Commission on Electoral Reform and Party Financing, also known as the Lortie Commission, recommended the removal of the office of profit or emolument disqualification from the *Canada Elections Act,*[100] arguing that public officers and employees had the right to a leave of absence to seek a nomination and contest an election.[101] Once elected to the House of Commons, the individual's employment with the Crown would then be deemed terminated in order to avoid any conflict of interest issues. In regard to the eligibility of a candidate holding a government contract, the Lortie Commission recommended the removal of this disqualification, reasoning that, if elected, the Member would then have to bring the contractual relationship in line with the rules governing the conduct of Members. In 1993, these recommendations were included in legislation introduced, and subsequently passed, to amend the *Canada Elections Act.*[102]

---

97. *An Act further securing the independence of Parliament,* S.C. 1867, c. 25. In 1871, the words "permanent or temporary" were added after the phrase "office, commission or employment" (*Independence of Parliament Act,* S.C. 1871, c. 19).

98. *An Act further securing the Independence of Parliament,* S.C. 1878, c. 5. For a historical perspective, see *Bourinot,* 1ˢᵗ ed., pp. 128-37.

99. *Senate and House of Commons Act,* S.C. 1931, c. 52.

100. *Canada Elections Act,* R.S.C. 1985, c. E-2, s. 77(*c*), (*f*).

101. In November 1989, the federal government appointed a five-person Royal Commission on Electoral Reform and Party Financing to inquire into and report on the process for electing Members to the House of Commons and the financing of political parties and candidates' campaigns. Its report was tabled in the House on February 13, 1992, and contained 267 recommendations, including draft legislation. See *Journals,* February 13, 1992, p. 1016.

102. In 1992, the Special Committee on Electoral Reform, which had been established to conduct a comprehensive review of the Lortie Commission's report and to report its recommendations for changes in the *Canada Elections Act,* presented its report. The report comprised a draft bill which included these changes (see Special Committee on Electoral Reform, *Minutes of Proceedings and Evidence,* December 11, 1992, Issue No. 7, pp. 3-5, 29). Bill C-114, *An Act to amend the Canada Elections Act,* received Royal Assent on May 6, 1993 (*Journals,* p. 2935).

However, pursuant to the *Parliament of Canada Act,* any person holding an office of emolument or profit and any person holding government contracts are still ineligible to be a Member of the House and to sit and to vote therein.[103]

Chief Electoral Officer

The Chief Electoral Officer is an officer of Parliament, appointed by resolution of the House of Commons, responsible for the administration of federal elections and referendums, and the registration of political parties and electors. This officer also provides support to the independent electoral boundaries commissions which carry out the periodic readjustment of electoral boundaries. The Chief Electoral Officer heads Elections Canada, an independent, non-partisan agency responsible, among other things, for the conduct of federal elections and referendums.

The position of Chief Electoral Officer was created in 1920 with the adoption of the *Dominion Elections Act*.[104] The post was created largely to prevent political partisanship in the administration of elections. (Prior to 1920, election officials were appointed by the government of the day.) The first incumbent of the position was specifically named in the Act: Oliver Mowat Biggar held the position of Chief Electoral Officer until 1927.[105] In 1927, when Mr. Biggar announced his intention to vacate the office, the law was amended to remove any reference to a specific office holder and to establish that the Chief Electoral Officer would be appointed by resolution of the House rather than by the government of the day.[106] Since that time, the position has been independent of the government and political parties, with the incumbent reporting directly to the House of Commons. The Chief Electoral Officer communicates with the Governor in Council through a member of the Queen's Privy Council designated by the Governor in Council for that purpose.[107]

---

103. See *Parliament of Canada Act*, R.S.C. 1985, c. P-1, ss. 32-4 as amended by c. 1 (4th supp.), s. 29.

104. *Dominion Elections Act*, S.C. 1920, c. 46, ss. 18-9. Prior to 1920, the *Dominion Elections Act, 1874* (S.C. 1874, c. 9, ss. 64-7) assigned to the Clerk of the Crown in Chancery some of the duties now carried out by the Chief Electoral Officer. The Clerk of the Crown in Chancery was always present at the Table of the House of Commons at the commencement of a new Parliament to hand to the Clerk of the House the roll or return book containing the list of Members elected. He issued writs for elections, made certificates to the House of the return of Members and performed other functions relating to elections. For additional information on the role of the Clerk of the Crown in Chancery, see *Bourinot*, 4th ed., pp. 188-9.

105. *Dominion Elections Act*, S.C. 1920, c. 46, s. 19.

106. *An Act to amend the Dominion Elections Act*, S.C. 1927, c. 53, s. 1. See also *Canada Elections Act*, R.S.C. 1985, c. E-2, s. 6(2). The Senate plays no role in the appointment.

107. *Canada Elections Act*, R.S.C. 1985, c. E-2, s. 4(3).

There have been five incumbents of this office.[108] With the exception of Mr. Biggar who was appointed by the government, all the incumbents have been chosen by way of a resolution of the House after consultations among the various parties in the House.[109] A motion setting out the appointment was moved by the Prime Minister in 1927 and 1949, after written notice appeared on the *Order Paper*.[110] A motion was moved by unanimous consent on behalf of the Prime Minister in 1966[111] and by the Minister of Justice and Attorney General in 1990.[112] In all four cases, the motion was debated only briefly and agreed to by all parties.

The Chief Electoral Officer's appointment is without term. He or she serves until the age of 65, unless he or she retires or is removed for cause by the Governor General, following a joint address of the House of Commons and Senate.[113]

RESPONSIBILITIES

The Chief Electoral Officer has the rank and power of a deputy minister.[114] While the original focus of the job was the general direction and supervision of federal elections, today the Chief Electoral Officer also administers federal referendums, provides support to commissions established to study the readjustment of electoral boundaries, monitors election spending by candidates and political parties, examines and discloses their financial reports and reimburses their expenses, and is responsible for the registration of political parties and the establishment and maintenance of an automated register of Canadians who are qualified electors.[115] In addition, the Chief Electoral Officer oversees the work of the Commissioner of Canada Elections who ensures that all provisions of the *Canada Elections Act* and *Referendum Act* are complied with and enforced,[116] as well as that of the Broadcasting Arbitrator who allocates paid and free broadcasting time for political parties during a general election and for referendum committees during a referendum.[117]

---

108. Oliver Mowat Biggar (1920-27), Jules Castonguay (1927-49), Nelson J. Castonguay (1949-66), Jean-Marc Hamel (1966-90) and Jean-Pierre Kingsley (1990 to present).

109. See, for example, *Debates*, April 12, 1927, pp. 2313-5; April 14, 1927, p. 2499; October 4, 1949, pp. 489-91; June 6, 1966, pp. 6049-51; February 16, 1990, pp. 8453-6.

110. *Journals*, April 14, 1927, p. 560; October 4, 1949, p. 61.

111. *Journals*, June 6, 1966, p. 615.

112. *Journals*, February 16, 1990, p. 1234.

113. *Canada Elections Act*, R.S.C. 1985, c. E-2, s. 6(1).

114. *Canada Elections Act*, R.S.C. 1985, c. E-2, s. 4(2). His or her salary is equivalent to that of a judge of the Federal Court and cannot be raised or reduced without legislation (*Canada Elections Act*, R.S.C. 1985, c. E-2, s. 5(1)).

115. *Canada Elections Act*, R.S.C. 1985, c. E-2, ss. 8, 71 as amended by S.C. 1996, c. 35, s. 22.

116. *Canada Elections Act*, R.S.C. 1985, c. E-2, s. 255. The Commissioner is appointed by the Chief Electoral Officer.

117. *Canada Elections Act*, R.S.C. 1985, c. E-2, s. 304.

The Chief Electoral Officer chairs an advisory committee composed of representatives of registered political parties and Elections Canada officials. The advisory committee is a forum for sharing information, fostering good working relationships and resolving administrative issues that do not require legislative change but that may have an impact on parties and candidates.

Responsibilities at Time of a General Election or a By-election

The Chief Electoral Officer supervises and directs the conduct of federal elections and by-elections when vacancies occur in the House. As soon as the election date is known, the Chief Electoral Officer issues a writ of election to each returning officer who is ultimately responsible for conducting the election within the electoral district.[118] The Chief Electoral Officer directs each returning officer to hire staff and prepare for an election.

Following polling day, each time the Chief Electoral Officer receives a writ of election of a Member from a returning officer, he or she enters it in a book kept for that purpose and immediately gives notice of the name of the candidate elected in either an ordinary or special issue of the *Canada Gazette*.[119]

Within 60 days of the date set for the return of the writs, the Chief Electoral Officer prepares a narrative report to Parliament containing information on the conduct of the election and recommendations for improvements to the electoral system.[120] The report is submitted to the Speaker of the House who tables it in the House.[121] It is then referred permanently to the Standing Committee on Procedure and House Affairs.[122] The Chief Electoral Officer prepares a similar report within 60 days of the date set for the return of the writ for any by-election.[123]

After each general election, the Chief Electoral Officer also prepares and publishes a report of official voting results. This report contains, poll by poll, the number of votes cast for each candidate, the number of rejected ballots and the number of names on the final list of electors together with any other relevant information.[124] A similar report is prepared for any by-elections held during the year.[125]

---

118. *Canada Elections Act*, R.S.C. 1985, c. E-2, s. 12(3).

119. *Canada Elections Act*, R.S.C. 1985, c. E-2, s. 192(1) as amended by S.C. 1993, c. 19, s. 100.

120. *Canada Elections Act*, R.S.C. 1985, c. E-2, s. 195(1) as amended by S.C. 1993, c. 19, s. 101(1) and (2).

121. *Canada Elections Act*, R.S.C. 1985, c. E-2, s. 195(3). See, for example, *Journals*, January 19, 1994, p. 28; September 24, 1997, p. 19.

122. Standing Orders 32(5) and 108(3)(*a*)(vi).

123. See, for example, *Journals*, April 24, 1995, p. 1350; September 16, 1996, p. 619; November 20, 1998, p. 1281; May 31, 1999, p. 1968.

124. *Canada Elections Act*, R.S.C. 1985, c. E-2, s. 193(*a*) as amended by S.C. 1996, c. 35, s. 49.

125. *Canada Elections Act*, R.S.C. 1985, c. E-2, s. 193(*b*).

When an automatic recount occurs, a candidate may apply to the Chief Electoral Officer for reimbursement of any costs incurred as a result of the recount. The Chief Electoral Officer determines the amount of the costs actually incurred by the candidate and submits a certificate showing the amount of the costs to the Receiver General who reimburses the candidate out of the Consolidated Revenue Fund. [126]

Relationship with Members

The Chief Electoral Officer provides advice and assistance to the Standing Committee on Procedure and House Affairs which is responsible for reviewing and reporting on matters relating to the election of Members. [127] The Chief Electoral Officer and his staff provide the Committee with research material and, at the Committee's request, assist in the drafting of amendments to the *Canada Elections Act* [128] and the *Electoral Boundaries Readjustment Act*. [129] The Chief Electoral Officer also appears before the Committee at its invitation to discuss the Main Estimates of Elections Canada [130] and the reports on general elections. [131]

The Writ of Election

A writ is a formal written order instructing the returning officer in each electoral district to hold an election to elect a Member of Parliament. The writ specifies the day by which the names of candidates must be entered into nomination, and sets a polling date and a date on which the writ, with the name of the successful candidate noted on the back, is to be returned to the Chief Electoral Officer. (See Figure 4.3.) The returning officer is responsible for the conduct of an election within an electoral district. One returning officer is appointed by the Governor in Council for each electoral district. The returning officer receives instructions from the Chief Electoral Officer and holds office as long as he or she meets the requirements of residency within the electoral district, competency and non-partisanship, or until the electoral boundaries for the riding are changed.

The election process has evolved considerably since 1867. In 1867 and in 1872, polling days were held on different days in different locations over several weeks, so

---

126. *Canada Elections Act*, R.S.C. 1985, c. E-2, s. 171(3)-(5) as amended by S.C. 1993, c. 19, ss. 96(2), 98.

127. Standing Order 108(3)(*a*)(vi). See, for example, Standing Committee on Procedure and House Affairs, *Minutes of Proceedings*, December 14, 1995, Issue No. 54, p. 18.

128. See, for example, Standing Committee on Procedure and House Affairs, *Minutes of Proceedings*, October 3, 1995, Issue No. 52, pp. 30-1.

129. See, for example, Standing Committee on Procedure and House Affairs, *Minutes of Proceedings and Evidence*, March 24, 1994, Issue No. 6, pp. 7-8; June 7, 1994, Issue No. 15, pp. 5-6.

130. See, for example, Standing Committee on Procedure and House Affairs, *Minutes of Proceedings and Evidence*, May 9, 1995, Issue No. 50, pp. 4-5; *Minutes*, April 28, 1998, Meeting No. 22.

131. See, for example, Standing Committee on Procedure and House Affairs, *Minutes*, November 20, 1997, Meeting No. 6; February 26, 1998, Meeting No. 14.

Figure 4.3 *The Writ of Election*

WRIT OF ELECTION

. . . .

Deputy of the Governor General

ELIZABETH THE SECOND, by the Grace of God of the United Kingdom, Canada and Her other Realms and Territories, QUEEN, Head of the Commonwealth, Defender of the Faith

To . . . .

of . . . .

GREETING:

WHEREAS, by and with the advice of OUR PRIME MINISTER OF CANADA, We have ordered a PARLIAMENT TO BE HELD AT OTTAWA, on the . . . . day of . . . . next. (*Omit the foregoing preamble in case of a by-election.*)

WE COMMAND YOU, that notice of the time and place of election being duly given,

YOU DO CAUSE election to be made according to law of a member to serve in the House of Commons of Canada for the said electoral district in the Province aforesaid (*in case of a by-election: in the place of* . . . . .);

AND YOU DO CAUSE the nomination of candidates to be held on . . . . ;

And if a poll becomes necessary, that the poll be held on . . . . ;

AND YOU DO CAUSE the name of such member when so elected, whether present or absent, to be certified to Our Chief Officer, as by law directed (*in case of a by-election, omit the following*) as soon as possible and not later than the . . . . day of . . . . 19. . . .

Witness: . . . . , Deputy of Our Right Trusty and Well-beloved . . . . , Chancellor and Principal Companion of Our Order of Canada, Chancellor and Commander of Our Order of Military Merit upon whom We have conferred Our Canadian Forces' Decoration, GOVERNOR GENERAL AND COMMANDER-IN-CHIEF OF CANADA.

At Our City of Ottawa, on . . . . and in the . . . year of Our Reign.

BY COMMAND,

Chief Electoral Officer

Source: *Canada Elections Act*, c. E-2.

that the government could control the timing of elections in each region.[132] For example, in 1867, elections were held on different dates in different ridings over a period of six weeks; during the next election in 1872 the process lasted three months.[133] In 1874, Parliament passed a law stipulating that votes had to be cast on the same day in all electoral districts.[134] Since 1929, polling day is always on Monday, unless that day is a statutory holiday, in which case the election is held the next day.[135] In 1996, amendments to the *Canada Elections Act* rectified the long-standing grievance of western voters who heard election results from eastern and central Canada while the polls in the west were still open. The hours for voting are now staggered across Canada's six time zones with polling stations open 12 hours in each region.[136]

ISSUE OF WRIT FOR GENERAL ELECTION

The Prime Minister begins the process of calling a general election by presenting the Governor General with an Instrument of Advice recommending that the House of Commons be dissolved. The Governor General then issues a proclamation dissolving Parliament.[137] Subsequently, the Prime Minister presents an Order in Council addressed to the Chief Electoral Officer requesting the issuance of writs of election, and the Governor General issues a Proclamation for the issuance of writs of election.[138]

After having been notified by the Prime Minister that an election has been called, the Chief Electoral Officer sends a writ of election to each returning officer.[139] The writs cannot be issued or dated later than the 36th day before polling day, making

---

132. See *Jackson and Jackson*, p. 435. This system even allowed a candidate who lost in one riding to run again in another riding. See *A History of the Vote in Canada*, p. 43.

133. See *A History of the Vote in Canada*, p. 43. See also Appendix 11, "General Election Results Since 1867".

134. *An Act respecting the Elections of Members of the House of Commons*, S.C. 1874, c. 9.

135. *Canada Elections Act*, R.S.C. 1985, c. E-2, s. 79(3). See also *An Act to amend the Dominion Elections Act*, S.C. 1929, c. 40, s. 15.

136. *Canada Elections Act*, R.S.C. 1985, c. E-2, s. 105(5) as amended by S.C. 1996, c. 35, s. 44.1. However, a problem arose in Saskatchewan during the 36th general election when the polls were required to stay open later than elsewhere because the province remains on standard time in the summer. See *A History of the Vote in Canada*, p. 98.

137. See, for example, *Journals*, Second Session, Thirty-Fifth Parliament (February 1996-April 1997), p. 1561. For information on the discretionary powers of the Governor General, see Chapter 1, "Parliamentary Institutions".

138. *Canada Elections Act*, R.S.C. 1985, c. E-2, s. 12(2) as amended by S.C. 1993, c. 19, s. 3. See, for example, *Journals*, First Session, Thirty-Fifth Parliament (January 1994-February 1996), p. v.

139. *Canada Elections Act*, R.S.C. 1985, c. E-2, s. 12(3) as amended by S.C. 1993, c. 19, s. 3.

the minimum length of a federal election campaign 36 days.[140] After the returning officer receives the writ, he or she prepares a public proclamation notifying the electors of the important dates and other details related to the election, such as the date by which nomination papers must be filed and the time and date for the official addition of the votes.[141] (See Figure 4.4.)

No later than 2:00 p.m. on nomination day, which is Monday, the 21st day before polling day,[142] each candidate must file with the returning officer several documents, including the nomination paper, a declaration signed by the candidate stating that he or she accepts the nomination, a declaration of acceptance signed by the candidate's official agent and a statement of acceptance signed by the candidate's auditor. A $1,000 deposit is also required to ensure the candidate's intention to stand as an official candidate.[143] Candidates who change their mind have until 5:00 p.m. on nomination day to withdraw.[144]

Where only one candidate has been officially nominated for an electoral district, the returning officer immediately returns the writ of election to the Chief Electoral Officer stating that the candidate is duly elected for that electoral district.[145]

Before polling day, each returning officer issues a proclamation stating, among other things, the time and date for the official addition of the votes.[146] That date must not be later than seven days following the polling date.[147] Normally, no later than six days following the date set for the official addition, the returning officer is required

---

140. *Canada Elections Act*, R.S.C. 1985, c. E-2, s. 12(4) as amended by S.C. 1996, c. 35, s. 2. Until 1982, the *Canada Elections Act* did not provide for a minimum campaign period, although campaigns averaged about 60 days. Since 1982, the minimum length of election campaigns has gone from 50 days (*Canada Elections Act*, S.C. 1980-81-82, c. 96, s. 2) to 47 days (*Canada Elections Act*, R.S.C. 1985, c. E-2, s. 12(4) as amended by S.C. 1993, c. 19, s. 3) to 36 days. See also *Final Report of the Royal Commission of Electoral Reform and Party Financing*, Vol. 2, 1991, p. 79. Prior to the passage of the 1996 amendments, the enumeration or collection of names of voters was done after an election was called. Since mid-campaign enumeration is no longer required because of the establishment of a permanent register of electors, it was feasible to shorten the election campaign period to 36 days.

141. *Canada Elections Act*, R.S.C. 1985, c. E-2, ss. 12(5), 73(1)(*c*).

142. *Canada Elections Act*, R.S.C. 1985, c. E-2, ss. 79(5), 85 as amended by S.C. 1996, c. 35, s. 41.

143. *Canada Elections Act*, R.S.C. 1985, c. E-2, s. 81(1)(*j*) as amended by S.C. 1993, c. 19, s. 38(4). Fifty percent of the deposit will be returned if the candidate's election expenses and unused official receipts are submitted within the required time. The other 50% is returned if the candidate receives at least 15% of the valid votes cast in his or her electoral district (*Canada Elections Act*, R.S.C. 1985, c. E-2, s. 84(2)-(3) as amended by S.C. 1993, c. 19, s. 41).

144. *Canada Elections Act*, R.S.C. 1985, c. E-2, s. 88 as amended by S.C. 1993, c. 19, s. 42.

145. *Canada Elections Act*, R.S.C. 1985, c. E-2, s. 92.

146. *Canada Elections Act*, R.S.C. 1985, c. E-2, s. 73(1)(*b*) as amended by S.C. 1996, c. 35, s. 40.

147. *Canada Elections Act*, R.S.C. 1985, c. E-2, s. 73(1)(*c*) as amended by S.C. 1993, c. 19, s. 32(1) and S.C. 1996, c. 35, s. 40.

Figure 4.4   *Public Proclamation Issued by Returning Officer*

PROCLAMATION

of which all persons are asked to take notice and to govern themselves accordingly and in obedience to Her Majesty's writ of election directed to me for the electoral district of	dont chacun est requis de prendre connaissance et d'agir en conséquence. En conformité avec le bref de Sa Majesté m'ordonnant de tenir une élection pour la circonscription de

for the purpose of electing a person to serve in the House of Commons of Canada, public notice is hereby given of the following.	d'un député pour siéger à la Chambre des communes du Canada, un avis public est par les présentes donné de ce qui suit:

NOMINATIONS OF CANDIDATES WILL BE RECEIVED BY ME AT	JE RECEVRAI LES PRÉSENTATIONS DES CANDIDATS À

ADDRESS DATE TIME	ADRESSE DATE HEURE

IF A POLL IS GRANTED POLLING DAY WILL BE	SI UN SCRUTIN EST OCTROYÉ LE SCRUTIN SE TIENDRA

MONDAY — LUNDI

DATE HOURS	DATE HEURES

AT LOCATIONS TO BE PUBLISHED BY ME AT A LATER DATE	AUX ENDROITS DONT JE DONNERAI SUBSÉQUEMMENT AVIS

I HAVE ESTABLISHED MY OFFICE for the conduct of the election at the following location, where I shall add up the votes cast for each candidate as taken from the statements of the poll and declare the name of the person who obtained the largest number of votes as noted.	J'AI ÉTABLI MON BUREAU pour la conduite de l'élection à l'endroit suivant où j'additionnerai les votes déposés en faveur de chaque candidat d'après les relevés du scrutin et déclarerai le nom du candidat ayant obtenu le plus grand nombre de votes.

ADDRESS DATE TIME	ADRESSE DATE HEURE

DESCRIPTION OF URBAN OR RURAL AREAS	INDIQUER LES ENDROITS URBAINS OU RURAUX

GIVEN UNDER MY HAND	DONNÉ SOUS MON SEING

AT À	DATE	RETURNING OFFICER/PRÉSIDENT D'ÉLECTION

OFFENCE: It is an offence with severe penalties to take, deface or otherwise tamper, with any publicly posted election notice.	INFRACTION: Quiconque enlève, détériore ou altère de quelque façon un avis d'élection affiché publiquement commet une infraction entraînant des peines sévères.

Source: *Canada Elections Act,* c. E-2.

to complete the form on the back of the writ, declaring a candidate elected.[148] The returning officer returns the writ of election, along with a post-election report and other documentation, to the Chief Electoral Officer.[149]

A judicial recount of the ballots is automatically requested by the returning officer if there is an equality of votes between two or more candidates with the highest number of votes, or if the winning candidate is separated from any other candidate by less than one one-thousandth of the total votes cast.[150] A recount may also take place when, within four days of the official addition, someone who witnessed that addition applies to a judge claiming that there were irregularities in the addition of the ballots.[151] The judicial recount is conducted by a judge and must take place no later than four days after the application has been received by the judge.[152]

As soon as the recount is done,[153] the returning officer completes the back of the writ, indicating the name of the successful candidate, and returns the writ to the Chief Electoral Officer.[154]

The Chief Electoral Officer publicizes the results of the election in the *Canada Gazette,*[155] provides Parliament with a report on the conduct of the election,[156] and retains all electoral documents in the event an election is contested.[157] The Chief Electoral Officer also provides the Clerk of the House with a certified list of Members returned to serve in the House of Commons. The list is tabled in the House by the Clerk at the beginning of the first session of the new Parliament and is included in the *Journals.*[158]

ISSUE OF WRIT FOR A BY-ELECTION

Whenever a vacancy in the representation of the House occurs, for whatever reason, the Speaker addresses a warrant (a written authorization) to the Chief Electoral

---

148. *Canada Elections Act*, R.S.C. 1985, c. E-2, s. 189. If the date set for the official addition of the votes is the day immediately following the polling day, then the earliest the writs could be returned would be seven days following the general election. When the returning officer is, for some reason, not in receipt of all the necessary information, the count may be postponed for a period not exceeding two weeks (s. 172).

149. *Canada Elections Act*, R.S.C. 1985, c. E-2, ss. 189-90.

150. *Canada Elections Act*, R.S.C. 1985, c. E-2, s. 171(1) as amended by S.C. 1993, c. 19, s. 96(1).

151. *Canada Elections Act*, R.S.C. 1985, c. E-2, s. 177.

152. *Canada Elections Act*, R.S.C. 1985, c. E-2, ss. 177-85.

153. In the event of a tie after a judicial recount, the returning officer casts the deciding vote (*Canada Elections Act*, R.S.C. 1985, c. E-2, s. 184(2)).

154. *Canada Elections Act*, R.S.C. 1985, c. E-2, s. 189.

155. *Canada Elections Act*, R.S.C. 1985, c. E-2, s. 192(1)(*b*) as amended by S.C. 1993, c. 19, s. 100.

156. *Canada Elections Act*, R.S.C. 1985, c. E-2, s. 195.

157. *Canada Elections Act*, R.S.C. 1985, c. E-2, s. 196(1).

158. See, for example, *Journals*, January 17, 1994, pp. 2-9; September 22, 1997, pp. 1-7.

Officer for the issue of a writ of election to fill the vacancy.[159] The writ for a by-election must be issued between the 11th day and the 180th day after the receipt of the warrant by the Chief Electoral Officer.[160] While the *Parliament of Canada Act* requires by-elections to be called within six months of a seat becoming vacant, there is no limit on how far in the future the actual date of the by-election may be set. The date of the by-election is fixed by the Governor in Council.[161]

A writ for a by-election would be superseded and withdrawn when a by-election has been ordered for a day subsequent to the dissolution of Parliament and the calling of a general election.[162]

Election Expenses

Legislation on election expenses was first incorporated into the *Canada Elections Act* in 1974.[163] Election expenses are defined as those costs incurred "for the purpose of promoting or opposing, directly and during an election, a particular registered party, or the election of a particular candidate".[164] Sections of the *Canada Elections Act* require all registered federal political parties and candidates to disclose the details of their election campaign financing.[165] The Act sets down guidelines to control election spending by both parties and candidates according to a formula based on the number of names on the preliminary voters list for each constituency.[166] The amount of election expenses a candidate or political party may incur is limited, thereby ensuring that no one candidate dominates due to wealth and that any eligible Canadian may consider becoming a candidate. Under the Act, only the candidate and the candidate's official agent may pay the candidate's personal expenses, whereas only the official agent may pay all other campaign-related expenses.

---

159. *Parliament of Canada Act*, R.S.C. 1985, c. P-1, s. 28(1). See, for example, *Journals*, December 12, 1988, pp. 7-8; February 6, 1995, p. 1075; June 1, 1999, p. 2033. In the absence of the Speaker, any two Members may address the warrant to the Chief Electoral Officer (see s. 28(2)). See also section entitled "Vacancies in Representation".

160. *Parliament of Canada Act*, R.S.C. 1985, c. P-1, s. 31(1) as amended by S.C. 1996, c. 35, s. 87.1.

161. *Canada Elections Act*, R.S.C. 1985, c. E-2, s. 79(1).

162. *Canada Elections Act*, R.S.C. 1985, c. E-2, s. 329. See also *Parliament of Canada Act*, R.S.C. 1985, c. P-1, s. 31(3).

163. *Election Expenses Act*, S.C. 1973-74, c. 51.

164. *Canada Elections Act*, R.S.C. 1985, c. E-2, s. 2.

165. *Canada Elections Act*, R.S.C. 1985, c. E-2, ss. 208-47 as amended by S.C. 1993, c. 19, ss. 106-8, and S.C. 1996, c. 35, ss. 53-4. See also sections 14 and 15 of the Thirty-Fifth Report of the Standing Committee on Procedure and House Affairs, presented in the House on June 18, 1998 (*Journals*, September 21, 1998, p. 1039), where election expenses and spending limits are discussed.

166. *Canada Elections Act*, R.S.C. 1985, c. E-2, s. 210.

Within four months after polling day, all candidates, whether successful or not, must submit both a return and a declaration respecting election expenses.[167] If the elected Member fails to submit his or her report and declaration of election expenses within the prescribed time, the Member will not be permitted to sit or vote in the House until the declaration is filed.[168] Candidates who get at least 15% of the valid votes cast in their electoral district are reimbursed 50% of their maximum allowed election expenses out of the Consolidated Revenue Fund.[169]

In 1974, the position of Commissioner of Election Expenses was created to ensure that the election expenses provisions of the *Election Expenses Act* were complied with and enforced.[170] In December 1977, the statute was amended to extend the Commissioner's responsibilities to cover all provisions of the *Canada Elections Act*.[171] The Commissioner ensures that candidates and their official agents fulfil their obligations under the legislation, such as submitting their election expenses returns and official receipts within the legal time frame and ensuring that corrective action is taken promptly when minor transgressions occur. When requested to do so by the Chief Electoral Officer, the Commissioner also investigates complaints of alleged infractions by election officers.[172]

Bribery and Corruption in Elections

Over the years, Parliament has passed several statutes touching on bribery and corruption in elections, delegating to the courts the authority to decide breaches of this kind when they occur.[173] These laws ensure that fair elections are held, free from

---

167. *Canada Elections Act*, R.S.C. 1985, c. E-2, ss. 228, 230(1).

168. *Canada Election Act*, R.S.C. 1985, c. E-2, s. 236(1). In 1966, a question of privilege was raised in regard to the validity of votes cast by a Member who had failed to file his return of election expenses on time. A few days later the court issued a ruling excusing the Member for having failed to file his election expenses return. Speaker Lamoureux subsequently ruled that the House is the judge of its own proceedings regardless of any court order. The Speaker added that it was the House, not the Speaker, which had the authority to make decisions regarding the exercise of Members' rights (*Debates*, February 21, 1966, pp. 1509-11; February 28, 1966, pp. 1843-4; March 1, 1966, pp. 1939-40).

169. *Canada Elections Act*, R.S.C. 1985, c. E-2, ss. 241-3. Fifty percent of the candidate's deposit is also returned if he or she obtains 15% of the valid vote cast in his or her electoral district.

170. *Election Expenses Act*, S.C. 1973-74, c. 51, s. 11.

171. *An Act to amend the Canada Elections Act*, S.C. 1977-78, c. 3, s. 45.

172. *Canada Elections Act*, R.S.C. 1985, c. E-2, s. 257.

173. The principal statute is the *Dominion Controverted Elections Act*, R.S.C. 1985, c. C-39. Others include the *Corrupt Practices Inquiries Act*, R.S.C. 1985, c. C-45; *Disfranchising Act*, R.S.C. 1985, c. D-3; *Canada Elections Act,* R.S.C. 1985, c. E-2. The *Corrupt Practices Inquiries Act* was adopted in 1876 and provides for the establishment of a commission of inquiry to investigate the existence of corrupt or illegal practices at the election of Members of the House of Commons (see S.C. 1876, c. 9 and c. 10). The *Disfranchising Act* was enacted in 1894 and provides for the presentation to the courts of a petition alleging bribery in an election and provides for the disenfranchisement of electors who have taken bribes (see S.C. 1894, c. 14).

corruption, intimidation and other actions which may deter an elector, a candidate or an official involved in the election process. As such, where a candidate has engaged in bribery or some other form of corruption in being elected, severe penalties are provided for, including: several years' disqualification from candidacy and voting in subsequent elections; fines, imprisonment, or both; a voided election; the loss of the right to sit or vote in the House. [174] Still, the House has never relinquished its power to act in matters affecting its membership in instances other than those related to controverted elections. In addition, the House can always "receive petitions setting forth grievances and praying for a remedy, provided they do not question the return of a Member ..." [175]

Since 1926, the House has not been asked to investigate claims of corruption or bribery in elections, although suggestions have been made from time to time to do so. [176] On at least one occasion, leave was granted for an emergency debate to discuss corruption in a specific election. [177]

Dominion Controverted Elections Act

An election may be contested or controverted (i.e., challenged) if the announced results of the election in an electoral district are very close, if there are allegations of irregularities in voting or in the counting of ballots, or if there are allegations of

---

174. *Canada Elections Act*, R.S.C. 1985, c. E-2, s. 269; *Dominion Controverted Elections Act*, R.S.C. 1985, c. C-39, ss. 50, 51, 54, 57; *Criminal Code*, R.S.C. 1985, c. C-46, s. 750 as amended by S.C. 1995, c. 22, s. 6.

175. *Bourinot*, 4th ed., p. 134. See also *Corrupt Practices Inquiries Act*, R.S.C. 1985, c. C-45. Any 25 or more electors of a district may sign a petition stating that no petition charging the existence of corruption or illegal practices has been presented under the *Dominion Controverted Elections Act* and that corrupt or illegal practices have, or there is reason to believe that corrupt or illegal practices have, prevailed at the election of a Member (s. 3(*b*)). The petition must be presented to the House of Commons either within 60 days after publication in the *Canada Gazette* of the notice of the return of the writ of election by the Chief Electoral Officer, if Parliament is sitting at the expiration of the 60 days, or if Parliament is not sitting, within the first 14 days of the meeting of Parliament (s. 4). The petition would be presented to the House by a Member. If the House agrees that corrupt practices did take place or may have taken place, or that the matter should be further investigated, the Act provides that the House may by Address represent to the Governor General that a petition in the proper form has been presented to the House and that the House prays the Governor General to cause an inquiry to be made by one of the persons listed in the Act (s. 3).

176. See, for example, *Debates*, February 2, 1938, p. 105.

177. *Debates*, July 20, 1943, pp. 5092-103.

corrupt or illegal practices. An election petition[178] may be filed by a candidate or by any qualified elector who alleges irregularities or corruption in the election that would disqualify an elected Member of the House of Commons. Such petitions are investigated and tried under the *Dominion Controverted Elections Act*.[179] Trials are conducted without jury by two superior court justices for the province in which the disputed election took place. The judges' report is transmitted to the Speaker of the House of Commons and may result in the election being awarded to a candidate other than the one who was declared elected by the returning officer; or the election could be declared null and void; or the petition could be dismissed by the court.

Prior to Confederation, Nova Scotia, New Brunswick and the Province of Canada followed the example of the British Parliament in dealing with electoral matters in their own legislatures. After Confederation, between 1867 and 1873, the Speaker of the House of Commons regularly appointed six Members to serve on the General Committee of Elections to adjudicate controverted elections.[180] This committee routinely passed judgement on cases of bribery and corruption in electoral contests, usually on partisan grounds and regardless of any findings of corrupt practices. Indeed, only one election was ever voided.[181] In 1873, the House transferred to the provincial courts exclusive jurisdiction over matters relating to the election of its Members.[182] The following year a new law was passed establishing the provincial supreme courts as election courts.[183] With the introduction of the secret ballot, simultaneous elections across the country, and the enactment of new election laws, the

---

178. An election petition is "a petition complaining of an undue return or undue election of a member, of no return or a double return, of matters contained in a special return made or of any unlawful act by any candidate not returned by which he is alleged to have become disqualified to sit in the House of Commons" (*Dominion Controverted Elections Act*, R.S.C. 1985, c. C-39, s. 2(1)). See section below, "The Election Petition".

179. *Dominion Controverted Elections Act*, R.S.C. 1985, c. C-39. See also the Thirty-Fifth Report of the Standing Committee on Procedure and House Affairs, presented in the House on June 18, 1998 (*Journals*, September 21, 1998, p. 1039). The Committee recommended that this Act be repealed and its provisions incorporated into the *Canada Elections Act* (see section 10 of the report).

180. See *Journals*, November 21, 1867, pp. 26-7; May 4, 1869, p. 57; March 1, 1871, p. 39; October 27, 1873, pp. 120-1.

181. For a historical perspective on controverted elections, see *Bourinot*, 1st ed., pp. 117-23, and Norman Ward, "Electoral Corruption and Controverted Elections", *Canadian Journal of Economics and Political Science*, Vol. 15, No. 1, February 1949, pp. 74-86.

182. *Controverted Elections Act*, S.C. 1873, c. 28.

183. *Dominion Controverted Elections Act, 1874*, S.C. 1874, c. 10.

number of contested elections gradually dropped.[184] Since 1949, only five elections have been declared void, all on the grounds that a number of ballots were unlawfully cast.[185]

THE ELECTION PETITION

A candidate or any qualified elector who wishes to contest the result of an election must file an election petition with the office of the clerk of the provincial or territorial court designated in the *Dominion Controverted Elections Act* to hear such cases.[186] The election petition includes the particulars of the complaint whether it be of an undue (i.e., illegal or improper) return or election of a Member,[187] of no return,[188] of a double return,[189]

---

184. Patrick Boyer notes in *Election Law in Canada,* Vol. 2, Toronto: Butterworths, 1987, p. 1067: "The offences which have traditionally given rise to election petitions—bribery, treating, conveying voters to the poll and the like—have been on the statute books for quite some time, and those in the election process have generally become aware of the tolerable levels for campaign activities and the limits of the law in this regard."

185. In 1949: Annapolis–Kings, Nova Scotia (*Journals*, March 6, 1950, pp. 68-84); in 1957: Yukon (*Journals*, October 23, 1957, pp. 37-44); in 1962: St. John's West, Newfoundland (*Journals*, November 8, 1962, pp. 231-46); in 1968: Comox–Alberni, British Columbia (*Journals*, February 14, 1969, pp. 701-6); in 1988: York North, Ontario (*Journals*, June 7, 1990, pp. 1850-1). In the latter case, the Progressive Conservative candidate, Michael O'Brien, had initially been declared the winner in the riding of York North in the 1988 federal election. Three days later, as a result of a recount, the Liberal candidate, Maurizio Bevilacqua, was declared the winner. Mr. O'Brien sought a judicial recount, was declared the winner by 99 votes, was sworn in, and participated in the Canada-U.S. free-trade agreement debate in the short-lived First Session of the Thirty-Fourth Parliament. Mr. Bevilacqua appealed the recount and was subsequently declared the sitting Member by 77 votes (see *Journals*, April 3, 1989, pp. 2-3). Mr. O'Brien then filed an election petition. Two Ontario supreme court judges found that the number of irregularly cast ballots in the 1988 election had exceeded Mr. Bevilacqua's 77-vote plurality over Mr. O'Brien. The election was subsequently voided. In a by-election held December 10, 1990, Mr. Bevilacqua was declared the winner.

186. *Dominion Controverted Elections Act,* R.S.C. 1985, c. C-39, ss. 5(1), 11. See also s. 2(1) for a list of the designated courts. An election petition once filed can be withdrawn only with the leave of the court or the trial judges (see s. 78).

187. Any type of wrongdoing or lack of legal capacity which can be said to have resulted in an election that is not valid (Boyer, *Election Law in Canada*, p. 1062).

188. When the returning officer fails to return the writ of election. This would be unlikely to happen today because the returning officer is specifically required by the *Canada Elections Act* to return the writ of election.

189. Where the votes given to two candidates in a constituency are equal and the returning officer returns the writ with both names endorsed on the back. This happened in the early years of Confederation when the returning officer did not have a casting vote to break a tie. Today, returning officers have the right to cast a deciding ballot between two candidates.

of a special return,[190] or of a corrupt or illegal practice pursuant to the *Canada Elections Act*.[191] The petition must be signed by the petitioner or petitioners and a security deposit of $1000 must be left with the court when the petition is filed.[192]

The *Parliament of Canada Act* provides that a Member, who has been declared elected, may not resign his or her seat while his or her election is being contested.[193] However, if the Member gives notice to the court or trial judges that he or she does not intend to oppose the election petition, the Member cannot sit or vote in the House of Commons until the trial judges have reported to the Speaker.[194]

TRIAL OF THE ELECTION PETITION

The election petition is heard by two superior court judges in the province and the electoral district where the election has been challenged.[195] The trial of the election petition is to determine whether a Member was duly elected or not, whether another candidate should have been duly elected instead, or whether the election should be declared void. The judges conduct an inquiry, scrutinizing the ballots for irregularities and investigating any claims of illegal or corrupt electoral practices. The judges may also call and examine witnesses.

At the conclusion of the trial of an election petition, the trial judges render a decision which is transmitted to the Speaker of the House of Commons by means of a certificate within 12 days of the decision being rendered.[196] If any party to the case

---

190. Patrick Boyer notes in *Election Law in Canada* (p. 1065) that the statutes are silent as to what constitutes a special return. He writes: "A special return would presumably involve a writ returned under anything but the normal circumstances of the returning officer certifying the name of the member elected on the writ after the official addition of votes and dispatching it to the Chief Electoral Officer. There are basically three cases where a return might be made other than in the normal course: (1) on the death of a nominated candidate; (2) where there has been a delay in the official addition due to the loss of ballot boxes or inability to obtain poll statements; or (3) following an official recount where the result in the original writ as returned has been changed."

191. *Dominion Controverted Elections Act,* R.S.C. 1985, c. C-39, s. 9(2).

192. *Dominion Controverted Elections Act,* R.S.C. 1985, c. C-39, s. 12. The deposit is security for the payment of all costs, charges, and expenses that the petitioner may have to pay.

193. *Parliament of Canada Act*, R.S.C. 1985, c. P-1, s. 27(2). In 1981, Speaker Sauvé informed the House that she had received a certificate of judgement from the trial judges appointed for the trial of a petition in the matter of the election in the Electoral District of Spadina. The judges found that the petition had abated by reason of the seat being vacated and by the Speaker directing the Chief Electoral Officer to issue a writ for a by-election. In this instance, the Member (Peter Stollery) had resigned his seat upon being appointed to the Senate. See *Journals*, October 14, 1981, pp. 2875-6.

194. *Dominion Controverted Elections Act,* R.S.C. 1985, c. C-39, s. 82.

195. *Dominion Controverted Elections Act,* R.S.C. 1985, c. C-39, s. 37(1) and (2). Notice of the time and place at which an election petition will be tried must be given not less than 14 days before the trial date (s. 37(3)).

196. *Dominion Controverted Elections Act,* R.S.C. 1985, c. C-39, s. 58(1).

is dissatisfied with the court's decision, he or she may appeal to the Supreme Court of Canada within eight days of the date on which the trial judges' decision was given.[197]

If the trial judges determine that corrupt or illegal practices have occurred, the judges also provide the Speaker with a report indicating the corrupt practice committed and naming the individuals involved; at the same time, they may submit a special report outlining any matters which ought to be referred to the House of Commons.[198] It is up to the House of Commons to deal with the matter as it sees fit. No new writ for an election can be issued unless the House orders it.[199]

ROLE OF THE SPEAKER

As soon as the Speaker receives the certificates and reports of the trial judges (or the Supreme Court if an appeal had been made), he or she communicates the decision to the House.[200] The Speaker then takes the necessary steps to confirm or alter the return or to issue a writ for a new election.[201]

If the trial judges find that an election was a valid election and that the Member was duly elected, the Speaker informs the House accordingly and the certificate of judgement appears in that day's *Journals*.[202] If the court has awarded the election to another candidate, the Speaker must take the necessary action to alter the return[203] and the other candidate takes the necessary steps to claim his or her seat. If the trial judges find that the successful candidate or his or her agent has committed any corrupt or illegal practice, the election is void.[204] The seat becomes vacant when the Speaker receives the certificate of the trial judges or the Supreme Court. Until that time, the person elected is entitled to all the benefits, services and allowances that come with being a Member of Parliament. The Speaker addresses a warrant to the Chief Electoral Officer for the issue of a new writ of election in the electoral district

197. See *Dominion Controverted Elections Act,* R.S.C. 1985, c. C-39, ss. 64-9.

198. *Dominion Controverted Elections Act,* R.S.C. 1985, c. C-39, ss. 60-1.

199. *Dominion Controverted Elections Act*, R.S.C. 1985, c. C-39, s. 72.

200. *Dominion Controverted Elections Act*, R.S.C. 1985, c. C-39, s. 71.

201. *Dominion Controverted Elections Act,* R.S.C. 1985, c. C-39, s. 70.

202. See, for example, *Journals*, December 12, 1968, pp. 517-27; February 23, 1976, pp. 1043-4.

203. *Dominion Controverted Elections Act,* R.S.C. 1985, c. C-39, s. 70.

204. *Dominion Controverted Elections Act,* R.S.C. 1985, c. C-39, ss. 50, 57. Note also ss. 52-4.

in question.[205] A by-election must be held to fill the vacancy, and the Prime Minister has six months from the date on which the Chief Electoral Officer receives the Speaker's warrant to announce the date of the by-election.[206]

The Oath or Solemn Affirmation of Allegiance

Before a duly elected Member may take his or her seat and vote in the House of Commons, the Member must take an oath or make a solemn affirmation of allegiance or loyalty to the Sovereign and sign the Test Roll (a book whose pages are headed by the text of the oath). When a Member swears or solemnly affirms allegiance to the Queen as Sovereign of Canada, he or she is also swearing or solemnly affirming allegiance to the institutions the Queen represents, including the concept of democracy. Thus, a Member is making a pledge to conduct him- or herself in the best interests of the country. The oath or solemn affirmation reminds a Member of the serious obligations and responsibilities he or she is assuming.

The obligation requiring all Members of Parliament to take the oath is found in the *Constitution Act, 1867,* with the text of the oath itself outlined in the Fifth Schedule.[207] The Act states: "Every Member of the … House of Commons of Canada shall before taking his Seat therein take and subscribe before the Governor General or some Person authorized by him … the Oath of Allegiance contained in the Fifth Schedule to this Act …" The wording of the oath is as follows: "I, (Member's name), do swear, that I will be faithful and bear true Allegiance to Her Majesty Queen Elizabeth the Second."[208] As an alternative to swearing the oath, Members may make a solemn affirmation, by simply stating:[209] "I, (Member's name), do solemnly, sincerely, and truly declare and affirm that I will be faithful and bear true allegiance to Her Majesty Queen Elizabeth the Second."

---

205. *Dominion Controverted Elections Act*, R.S.C. 1985, c. C-39, s. 70. See, for example, *Journals*, June 7, 1990, pp. 1850-1. In 1877, in response to questions concerning the power of the House to order the issue of writs when seats become vacant by a decision of the courts, Speaker Anglin confirmed in a ruling that it was the express duty of the Speaker to order the issue of a writ (*Journals*, March 1, 1877, pp. 84-6; *Debates*, March 5, 1877, p. 436).

206. *Parliament of Canada Act*, R.S.C. 1985, c. P-1, s. 31(1) as amended by S.C. 1996, c. 35, s. 87.1.

207. *Constitution Act, 1867*, R.S.C. 1985, Appendix II, No. 5, s. 128.

208. *Constitution Act, 1867*, R.S.C. 1985, Appendix II, No. 5, Fifth Schedule. Found below the Fifth Schedule is a note which reads as follows: "The Name of the King or Queen of the United Kingdom of Great Britain and Ireland for the Time being is to be substituted from Time to Time, with proper Terms of Reference thereto."

209. Affirmation is not mentioned in the Constitution. See *Beauchesne*, 4th ed., pp. 13-4.

HISTORICAL PERSPECTIVE

Great Britain

During the Middle Ages, there was no legal requirement for the taking of oaths of allegiance in the British Parliament.[210] The taking of an oath by a Member of Parliament as a legal prerequisite first arose as a result of the political and religious conflicts in Great Britain in the sixteenth century, in particular the breach with Rome and the struggle between Protestants and Catholics for power. The first oath was imposed upon Members in 1563 following the adoption of the *Act of Supremacy* during the reign of Queen Elizabeth I. The *Act of Supremacy* appointed the Sovereign the head of the Church: before taking their seat in the House of Commons, Members of Parliament were required to testify to their belief that the Sovereign was the only supreme governor of the realm, both in ecclesiastical and in temporal matters.[211] Indeed, the oath of supremacy was primarily directed at preventing Roman Catholics from holding public office. To this was added, in 1678, a declaration against transubstantiation which, with the oath of supremacy, effectively barred Roman Catholics from Parliament.[212]

In 1701, in an attempt to strengthen Protestantism in response to the attempt by Jacobites, supporters of James II, to restore Catholicism in England, English authorities devised three oaths of state designed to exclude Catholics and Jacobites from public office. The first was one of allegiance to the King of England; the second, known as the oath of supremacy, denounced Catholicism and papal authority; and the last, the oath of abjuration, repudiated all rights of James II and his descendants to the English throne.[213]

More than one hundred years later, the British Parliament passed the *Roman Catholic Relief Act of 1829,* which replaced the declaration against transubstantiation with a simple declaration of allegiance to the Crown and provided a special form of oath acceptable to members of the Roman Catholic Church. In 1858, the oaths of supremacy, allegiance and repudiation were replaced by a single oath for Protestants, and later the same year the British Parliament passed another law allowing Jews to

---

210. See R.W. Perceval and P.D.G. Hayter, "The Oath of Allegiance", *The Table*, Vol. XXXIII, 1964, pp. 85-90. The authors state that the oath of allegiance taken by barons during the Middle Ages is not historically connected to the oath of allegiance now required before a Member may take his seat in the Commons.

211. *Redlich*, Vol. II, p. 62.

212. *Redlich*, Vol. II, p. 63. Transubstantiation, according to the Roman Catholic church, is the conversion in the Eucharist of the whole substance of the bread into the body and of the wine into the blood of Christ, with only the appearance of bread and wine remaining. See *An Act for the More Effectual Preserving the King's Person and Government by Disabling Papists from Sitting in Either House of Parliament* found in *English Historical Documents 1660-1714*, Andrew Browning (ed.), London: Eyre and Spottiswoode, 1953, pp. 391-4.

213. *A History of the Vote in Canada*, p. 7. The oath of abjuration also included the words "on the true faith of a Christian", which prevented Jews from taking the oath. See *Wilding and Laundy*, p. 503. See *May*, 1ˢᵗ ed., pp. 461-3, for the wording of the three oaths.

be admitted as Members of Parliament.[214] By 1866, the British Parliament had established a single oath for Members of all religious beliefs and, by 1888, it permitted those objecting to the taking of the oath on religious grounds to make a solemn affirmation.[215]

Canada

The requirement that Members of the Canadian House of Commons take an oath of allegiance before assuming their seats in the Chamber stems from British practice; however, the oath taken in the Canadian colonies was a very different one from the anti-papal oath taken by Members in the British House of Commons.

In 1758, the first election for a popular Assembly was held in Nova Scotia; Catholics and Jews were not allowed to vote or seek election.[216] The legislative assembly abolished religious discrimination in voter eligibility criteria in 1789, enabling Catholics and Jews to vote.[217] In 1823, the Nova Scotia Assembly adopted a resolution which granted the right to Catholics to take a seat in the Assembly without taking the Declaration against Transubstantiation.[218] The *Quebec Act, 1774,* which was passed by the British Parliament provided, among other matters, that Roman Catholics no longer had to take the Oath of Supremacy, substituting an oath of allegiance, should they wish to assume public office.[219] The *Constitutional Act, 1791* divided the original province of Quebec into two provinces—Lower Canada and Upper Canada. Each was provided with a Legislative Council and an elected Assembly; Members had to swear an oath of allegiance to the King before sitting in either the Legislative Council or Assembly.[220] When the United Province of Canada was established, the provisions of the *Constitutional Act, 1791* regarding the oath of allegiance were

---

214. *Redlich*, Vol. II, p. 63. Twenty-seven years earlier, in 1831, the Legislative Assembly of Lower Canada had passed a bill allowing Jews who were natural-born British subjects the right to seek public office and the following year, the legislation was approved by the British Parliament. See *O'Brien*, pp. 139-42.

215. *Redlich*, Vol. II, pp. 63-4. According to *Wilding and Laundy*, the right to make an affirmation was given by the *Promissory Oaths Act, 1868*. However, there were some objections when a new Member, Charles Bradlaugh, who had no religious beliefs, attempted to affirm instead of taking an oath on the Bible. The Member was excluded from the House. On three separate occasions, he was re-elected to the House and subsequently excluded when he attempted to affirm. On the fifth occasion in 1886, the Speaker would not listen to any objections when the Member took the oath in the ordinary form. In 1888, the Member succeeded in having the *Oaths Act* adopted. See *Wilding and Laundy*, pp. 10-11, 53-4.

216. See John Garner, *The Franchise and Politics in British North America 1755-1867*, Toronto: University of Toronto Press, 1969, pp. 131-2.

217. See *A History of the Vote in Canada*, pp. 10-2.

218. See *Garner*, pp. 141-3. See also J. Murray Beck, *The Government of Nova Scotia*, Toronto: University of Toronto Press, 1957, pp. 51-2. See also *Journal and Proceedings of the House of Assembly*, Nova Scotia, April 3, 1823, pp. 292-3.

219. R.S.C. 1985, Appendix II, No. 2, s. 7. The Act made no provision for an elected assembly; government was entrusted to a governor and a legislative council, both appointed by the Crown.

220. R.S.C. 1985, Appendix II, No. 3, s. 29.

carried over into the *Union Act, 1840.*[221] At Confederation, the requirement for Members of the House of Commons, Senate and provincial legislative assemblies to swear an oath of allegiance was included in the *Constitution Act, 1867.*

While provisions for a solemn affirmation existed in the Province of United Canada pursuant to the *Union Act, 1840*[222] and were later duplicated in section 5 of the *Oaths of Allegiance Act*[223] passed in 1867, these provisions did not apply to Members of the House of Commons and the Senate. Members of Parliament were not permitted to make a solemn affirmation until 1905 when the Governor General was "authorized to administer the oath of allegiance or affirmation to persons who shall hold places of trust in Canada in the form provided by an Act passed in the thirty-first and thirty-second years of the Reign of Queen Victoria intituled *An Act to amend the law in relation to Promissory Notes*".[224]

SWEARING-IN PROCESS

Following a general election, the Chief Electoral Officer files a certificate with the Clerk of the House of Commons which lists Members duly elected to serve in the new Parliament. Once this certificate is received by the Clerk of the House, the process of administering the oath of allegiance commences.[225]

According to Section 128 of the *Constitution Act, 1867,* the Governor General *"or some person authorized by him"* may administer the oath of allegiance. Commissioners for this purpose are appointed through Orders in Council. Up until August 1949, this was accomplished by naming specific persons to hold this commission but since that time, the appointment has been made by virtue of office, thus avoiding the need to repeat the Order in Council. The offices of Clerk of the House

---

221. R.S.C. 1985, Appendix II, No. 4, s. 35.

222. R.S.C. 1985, Appendix II, No. 4, s. 36.

223. S.C. 1867-68, c. 36. Section 3 of the Act specified that the form of the oath described in the Act did not supersede the oath described in the *Constitution Act, 1867* for Members of Parliament. Section 5 further clarified that the affirmation could be made in lieu of the oath in civil cases. No mention is made of the solemn affirmation for Members of Parliament. See also *Oaths of Allegiance Act*, R.S.C. 1985, c. O-1.

224. Beauchesne, 4th ed., p. 13.

225. When the House meets for the first time for the despatch of business, the Clerk lays upon the Table the list of duly elected Members certified by the Chief Electoral Officer. The certificate and list are printed in the *Journals* (see, for example, *Journals*, September 22, 1997, pp. 1-7). Prior to 1888, Members were permitted to take the oath and their seats on production of the certificate of the Returning Officer in advance of the certificate of the Clerk of the Crown in Chancery, but this practice was discontinued owing to the risk of numerous legal difficulties (see *Bourinot*, 4th ed., p. 149).

of Commons, Deputy Clerk, Clerk Assistant, and Sergeant-at-Arms have been given this authority, although this function is normally carried out by the Clerk.[226]

The present swearing-in procedure followed by the House is not governed by rules but has always been defined by practice and precedent. Traditionally, Members have been sworn in on an individual, rather than collective, basis.[227] The Clerk of the House invites each Member to make an appointment to be sworn in and sign the Test Roll, a book whose pages are headed by the text of the oath or affirmation, prior to the opening day of the new Parliament. The Test Roll is signed by the Member in witness to his or her having taken the oath of allegiance as required by the *Constitution Act, 1867* or made the solemn affirmation. The Test Roll is signed immediately after the oath or affirmation has been taken.[228]

Most Members take the oath either in the office of the Clerk or in another room in the parliamentary precinct designated for the ceremony. Members may invite guests to attend the short private ceremony and arrange for pictures to be taken. Members who have not been sworn in prior to the opening day of a new Parliament may do so on the opening day itself. This ceremony is performed in the Commons Chamber at the Clerk's Table prior to the time designated for all the Members to assemble for the opening of Parliament. On this occasion, guests are not invited nor are pictures taken. After the first day of a new Parliament, the swearing-in ceremony takes place in the Clerk's Office. Following by-elections, new Members take the oath and sign the Test Roll in the office of the Clerk.

---

226. For a recent example of appointments for the purpose of administering the oath, see *Journals*, September 22, 1997, p. 1.

227. Following the 36th general election and prior to the opening of Parliament, three of the opposition parties (i.e., the Reform Party, the New Democratic Party and the Progressive Conservative Party) opted to have a collective swearing-in ceremony for their Members. Each ceremony took place in a committee room in the Centre Block. The leader of the party was sworn in first and then the Members recited the oath of allegiance or solemn declaration. Each Member was then invited by the Clerk to sign the Test Roll. The ceremonies were broadcast on the parliamentary channel. In June 1985, the Special Committee on the Reform of the House of Commons had recommended that public awareness of the swearing-in ceremony be increased by broadcasting the ceremony on national television in a similar fashion as is done for the swearing-in of a new cabinet. Members would also be required to take the oath individually. (See pp. 57-8 of the Third Report of the Special Committee on the Reform of the House of Commons, presented on June 18, 1985 (*Journals*, p. 839)). In its response to the Committee's report, the government suggested that the House refer this matter to the Board of Internal Economy for consideration and decision (see p. 10 of the Response of the Government of Canada to the Second and Third Reports of the Special Committee on the Reform of the House of Commons (*Journals*, October 9, 1985, p. 1082)). No subsequent action was taken at that time.

228. There is an interesting anecdote about the swearing-in of Louis Riel. Louis Riel was duly elected in the riding of Provencher, first in a by-election in 1873 and then in the general election of 1874. While avoiding arrest, he travelled to Ottawa and succeeded in taking the oath of allegiance and signing the Test Roll before the Clerk noticed the signature on the Roll. See Marc Bosc (ed.), *The Broadview Book of Canadian Parliamentary Anecdotes*, Peterborough: Broadview Press Ltd., 1988, pp. 22-3.

If a Member fails or refuses to swear the oath of allegiance or make a solemn affirmation, the Member may not be allowed to take his or her seat in the Chamber and may be deprived of any entitlements.[229] Thus, it is the taking of the oath or affirmation which enables a Member to take his or her seat in the House and to vote.[230]

BREACH OF THE OATH OF ALLEGIANCE

Breaking the oath of allegiance is a serious offence and any Member whose conduct has been determined by the House to have violated the oath could be liable to punishment by the House.[231] Although there have been no cases of a Member having been found guilty of breaching the oath of allegiance, the Speaker was asked in 1990 to rule on the sincerity of a Member's solemn affirmation.[232] Speaker Fraser ruled

---

229. *Beauchesne*, 4th ed., p. 14. There do not appear to be any cases of Members refusing to take the oath of allegiance. In 1988, following the 34th general election, one Member-elect, John Dahmer (Beaver River) was hospitalized. Arrangements were made to have the Deputy Clerk fly to his bedside to swear him in. Unfortunately, the Member-elect died before the swearing-in ceremony could take place.

    In the British House of Commons, on May 14, 1997, in regard to the election of Sein Fein members, Speaker Betty Boothroyd remarked: "The services that are available to all other Members from the six Departments of the House and beyond will not be open for use by Members who have not taken their seats by swearing or by affirmation". See British House of Commons Debates, May 14, 1997, cols. 35-6. See also *May*, 22nd ed., pp. 242-3, which states that a Member who has not taken the oath may not sit and vote in the House, is fined and the seat is vacated in the same manner as if the Member were deceasd. In addition, the Member would not receive a salary.

230. In 1875, the Speaker brought to the attention of the House that a Member who had been duly elected in a by-election had sat and voted in the Chamber without having first taken and subscribed the oath of allegiance (*Debates*, February 22, 1875, p. 260). George Turner Orton (Centre Wellington) had first been elected in the general election and had been sworn in. Subsequently, his election was overturned. The Member explained that, because he had already sworn the oath, he did not realize he had to be sworn in again upon his re-election (*Bourinot*, 4th ed., pp. 150-1). The matter was referred to the Select Standing Committee on Privileges and Elections (*Journals*, February 25, 1875, p. 129). See *Debates*, February 24, 1875, pp. 322-3; February 25, 1875, pp. 324-5. In its report presented on March 8, 1875, the Committee noted that since neither the *British North America Act* nor any other statute provided a penalty in the event a Member omitted to take and subscribe the oath, the Member's seat was not affected by the oversight. However, the Committee recommended that the votes taken by the Member before he took the oath be struck from the records *(Journals*, March 8, 1875, p. 176). The report was never considered by the House.

231. *Beauchesne*, 4th ed., p. 14. *Beauchesne* expounds further that, for example, if a Member, during a state of war, were to make a statement, either outside of the House or on the floor of the Chamber, that was damaging to Canada, but favourable to the enemy, the House as a whole could decide to suspend or even expel the Member. Indeed, the House did expel a Member in 1947 when he was found guilty of treason (*Journals*, January 30, 1947, pp. 4-8). Expulsions from the House of Commons are discussed later in the chapter and in Chapter 3, "Privileges and Immunities".

232. That year, a new political party, the Bloc québécois, was founded and its first Member was elected in a by-election. As required, Gilles Duceppe (Laurier–Sainte-Marie) made a solemn affirmation and signed the Test Roll before taking his seat in the House; he also made another statement, similar to the oath required to be sworn by Members of the Quebec National Assembly, outside the Chamber expressing his loyalty to the people of Quebec. Jesse Flis (Parkdale–High Park) rose on a question of privilege concerning the meaning of the oath of allegiance and the duties and obligations of Members relating thereto. See *Debates*, October 3, 1990, pp. 13736-42.

that the Chair was "not empowered to make a judgement on the circumstances or the sincerity with which a duly elected Member takes the oath of allegiance. The significance of the oath to each Member is a matter of conscience and so it must remain." Since the Member stated very clearly in the House that he had "never mocked the Canadian Parliament nor the Queen", the Speaker concluded that, in keeping with convention that the House accepts as true the word of the Member, there was no breach of privilege. He did note, however, that "only the House can examine the conduct of its Members and only the House can take action if it decides action is required".[233] No further action was taken.

Entrance in the House

After a Member's election certificate has been received by the Clerk of the House and he or she has sworn the oath of allegiance or made an affirmation and signed the Test Roll, the Member is ready to take his or her seat in the Chamber. Members, whether they be newly elected or not, are not formally introduced to the House at the opening of a new Parliament. Customarily, only when Members have been elected to the House in by-elections do they receive formal introduction to the House.[234] The introduction of a Member is ceremonial[235] and a convention not mandated by any

---

233. *Debates*, November 1, 1990, pp. 14969-70. Since 1990, private Members have introduced bills to require newly elected Members to swear an oath of allegiance to Canada and the Constitution as well as swearing allegiance to the Queen (see, for example, *Debates*, October 16, 1990, p. 14189; September 18, 1991, p. 2320; February 12, 1993, p. 15850; January 20, 1994, p. 72; June 18, 1996, p. 3989; September 25, 1997, p. 57).

234. See *Bourinot*, 4th ed., pp. 149-53. For examples of introductions, see *Debates*, February 22, 1995, p. 9941; April 21, 1998, p. 5901. In a departure from this tradition, a newly elected Member from the Northwest Territories was formally introduced to the House on the fourth sitting day of the First Session of the Thirty-Fourth Parliament. Because the House had come back early from a general election, the Member's election return had not arrived at the Office of the Chief Electoral Officer in time for the opening (see *Debates*, December 15, 1988, pp. 92-3). In 1980, when the election return of another Member from the Northwest Territories was received late, the Member was not introduced in the House, although the notice of the election return is indicated in the *Journals* (April 18, 1980, p. 47). In 1989, on the opening day of the Second Session of the Thirty-Fourth Parliament, the Speaker informed the House that the Clerk had received a substitute return of election. The successful candidate was subsequently introduced in the House (*Journals*, April 3, 1989, pp. 2-3; *Debates*, p. 1).

235. This is a very old practice dating back to the seventeenth century in England (see *Hatsell*, Vol. II, p. 85).

statute of Canada or rule of the House of Commons.[236] The right of a Member to sit and vote in the House is in no way affected if an introduction does not take place.[237]

Introductions typically are done at the beginning of a sitting or before Question Period. When a Member is to be introduced, the Speaker begins by advising the House that: "I have the honour to inform the House that the Clerk of the House has received from the Chief Electoral Officer a certificate of the election and return of (Member's name), Member for the electoral riding of (Member's riding)." The Member, escorted by two Members of the House (generally the leader of the Member's party and the senior party representative from his or her province), is then ushered from the Bar of the House up the centre aisle of the Chamber to the Table.[238] At this point, the party leader will state: "Mr. (Madam) Speaker, I have the honour to present to you (Member's name), Member for the Electoral District of (Member's riding), who has taken the oath (or made an affirmation), signed the Roll and now claims the right to take his (her) seat." The Speaker directs: "Let the Member take his (her) seat." The Member then approaches the Chair and exchanges greetings with the Speaker. The Member is directed, by the party whip, to his or her seat.[239] If other Members are to be introduced during the same sitting, the process is repeated.[240] Customarily, if the Member being introduced is a party leader, he or she is escorted by two leading Members of the party and the House allows the other party leaders to offer some brief words of welcome.[241]

Assignment of Seats in the House

Members are allocated their seats and desks in the House under the authority of the Speaker but on the advice of the whips of the recognized parties (usually those parties with 12 or more Members[242]) following negotiations. In order to be recognized

---

236. See *Beauchesne*, 4th ed., p. 17.

237. In 1878, Speaker Anglin resigned his seat between sessions. He was re-elected in a by-election held before the new session began. When the new session opened, Mr. Anglin, along with several other Members, took the oath, signed the Roll and was in his seat for the election of the Speaker. When the Prime Minister, Alexander Mackenzie, moved that Mr. Anglin be elected Speaker, the Leader of the Opposition, Sir John A. Macdonald, protested the validity of the proceeding, claiming that Mr. Anglin had not been introduced to the House and could not be introduced until a Speaker had been elected and, thus, Mr. Anglin was not a Member and could not be elected Speaker. Mr. Mackenzie contended that, contrary to British practice, the practice in Canada had been that once a Member had been sworn in and signed the Roll, he was entitled to enter the House and take his seat. This view prevailed and the motion to elect Mr. Anglin was adopted shortly thereafter (see *Debates*, February 7, 1878, pp. 2-12).

238. In the case of an independent Member, Members of one of the opposition parties assume the ceremonial duties.

239. See, for example, *Debates*, September 16, 1996, p. 4222; April 21, 1998, p. 5901.

240. See, for example, *Debates*, April 15, 1996, p. 1461. The Members are usually introduced in alphabetical order.

241. See, for example, *Debates*, February 20, 1969, pp. 5741-3; January 15, 1991, pp. 16981-3.

242. For more information on recognized parties, see Chapter 1, "Parliamentary Institutions".

by the Speaker to participate in the business of the House and to vote in any recorded division, a Member must be in his or her designated seat.[243]

Members representing the governing party traditionally occupy those seats to the right of the Chair, with the Prime Minister and the other Ministers seated in the front rows. Private Members, otherwise known as backbenchers, representing the governing party are customarily seated according to their seniority or length of service in the House within their caucus. If the number of Members representing the governing party exceeds the number of desks on the right side, the overflow, or "rump", of government Members occupies those seats across the aisle. This section may, at the discretion of the Speaker, be near the Chair or at the far end of the Chamber.[244]

Members who represent parties in opposition to the government are seated to the left of the Chair.[245] The Leader of the Official Opposition is seated immediately opposite the Prime Minister and is flanked by Members of his or her party. Other opposition Members sit, according to party, in the remaining seats: the second-rank opposition party gets the first choice of seats after the Official Opposition, the third-rank party the next choice and so on.[246] The leading Members of the opposition parties, including House Leaders, whips and critics, sit in the front rows of their designated area.[247]

Those Members who do not have a party designation or who represent a party not recognized by the House are seated subject to the discretion of the Speaker in whatever seats are remaining. These Members typically occupy the desks to the left of the Speaker along the back rows, often but not necessarily near the end of the Chamber. The Speaker allocates the seats for these Members pursuant to their

---

243. This rule does not apply when the House is conducting its proceedings as a Committee of the Whole where Members may sit and speak from any seat in the House. For additional information, see Chapter 13, "Rules of Order and Decorum", and Chapter 19, "Committees of the Whole House".

244. For example, during the Thirty-Fifth Parliament (1994-97), the overflow of government Members sat to the immediate left of the Speaker. During the Twenty-Fourth Parliament (1958-62), the overflow of government Members sat to the left of the Speaker at the far end of the Chamber. During the Thirty-Third Parliament (1984-88) when there were 211 government Members, the overflow of government Members was situated both immediately to the left of the Chair and in the desks at the far end of the left-hand side of the Chamber, effectively splitting the overflow of government Members to book-end those Members of the opposition parties.

245. During the Twenty-Fifth Parliament (1962-63), 19 Members of the New Democratic Party sat on the government side of the House at the far end of the Chamber. During the Second Session of the Twenty-Seventh Parliament (1967-68), two independent Members sat on the government side of the House at the far end of the Chamber. During the Thirty-First Parliament (1979), the five Members of the Social Credit Party sat on the government side of the House at the far end of the Chamber.

246. In response to a point of order, Speaker Parent explained the process followed in assigning seats to parties (*Debates*, September 30, 1998, pp. 8584-5).

247. In 1994, at the beginning of the Thirty-Fifth Parliament (1994-97), the leader of the Reform Party (Preston Manning) chose to sit in the second row of seats; he eventually moved to the front benches.

seniority as elected Members, while at the same time retaining a degree of latitude in determining these arrangements.[248]

Three desks immediately to the left of the Chair are reserved for the Deputy Speaker and the other Chair occupants when they are not presiding over the House. There is no seat reserved for the Speaker.[249]

The seating plan is modified frequently during a Parliament, sometimes following changes within a party, sometimes as a result of negotiations among the parties. Any changes in the seating of a Member or Members within a party are made by the whip who then notifies the Speaker. If a Member is expelled from his or her party, or chooses to leave to sit as an independent, then the Speaker reassigns a new seat to the Member.[250]

---

248. See Speaker Fraser's ruling, *Debates*, September 24, 1990, pp. 13216-7. In 1963, a number of Social Credit Party Members from Quebec formed a new party, the *Ralliement des Créditistes*. As a result, Speaker Macnaughton was asked to decide a number of issues, including the recognition of parties and a new seating arrangement for the Chamber. In a statement given September 30, 1963, the Speaker informed the House that he believed the Chair should not be placed in a position to decide matters affecting the character or existence of a party because those decisions could be mistaken as political decisions. He concluded that the House itself had to resolve the various issues which had arisen as a result of the emergence of a new party. The House subsequently adopted a motion to refer these matters to the Standing Committee on Privileges and Elections (*Journals*, September 30, 1963, pp. 385-8). In its Second Report to the House, the Committee recommended that the NDP (which had become the third largest party in the House) be seated next to the Official Opposition; that the Social Credit Party be seated to the left of the New Democratic Party; and that the new party occupy the seats to the left of the Social Credit Party (*Journals*, October 9, 1963, p. 423). The report was concurred in on October 21, 1963 (*Journals*, pp. 465-6). At the beginning of the Thirty-Fifth Parliament (1994-97), "independent Members" included representatives of the New Democratic Party (nine Members), the Progressive Conservative Party (two Members), and independent Members (originally just one Member, but the numbers grew to four over the life of the Parliament). The Speaker assigned each independent Member a seat according to his or her precedence in the House. Later as the result of a point of order regarding the party status of the NDP, the Speaker modified the seating plan to allow the NDP and Progressive Conservative caucuses each to be seated together and identified as such. The other independent Members were assigned the remaining seats according to their seniority. See *Debates*, June 16, 1994, pp. 5437-40, in particular p. 5439.

249. It appears from seating plans for the Chamber that the Speaker, normally a government Member, used to be assigned a desk on the government side near the Chair. No desk has been assigned to a Speaker since the Thirty-First Parliament (1979) when, following a change of government, Speaker Jerome was elected to a second term, becoming the first opposition Member to be nominated by the governing party to preside over the House. See *Beauchesne*, 6th ed., p. 37.

250. See, for example, *Debates*, February 18, 1965, p. 11457; August 29, 1966, pp. 7731-2; December 3, 1969, p. 1532; May 4, 1971, p. 5470; June 27, 1978, pp. 6777-8; November 21, 1990, pp. 15526-9. In many instances, no record of the change in the party affiliation or status appears in the *Debates* or the *Journals*. The Speaker is advised of the change through correspondence or by means of a press release issued by the Member. During the Thirty-Third Parliament (1984-88), one government Member became an independent Member, and then a member of the New Democratic Party before finally sitting again as an independent Member (see *Debates*, May 14, 1986, p. 13268; December 16, 1986, p. 2152; October 26, 1987, p. 10384). During the Thirty-Fourth Parliament (1988-93), a government backbencher, Gilbert Chartrand (Verdun–St. Paul), chose to sit as an independent with other Members who had formed a new party, the Bloc Québécois; a year later, the same Member received permission to return to the Progressive Conservative Party caucus and sit with its Members (see *Debates*, May 22, 1990, p. 11631; April 9, 1991, pp. 19231-2).

CROSSING THE FLOOR

Although most Members are elected with a party affiliation (a very small percentage of Members are elected as independents), Members are not obliged to retain that party label during the whole of their mandate. "Crossing the floor" is the expression used to describe a Member's decision to break all ties binding him or her to a particular political party.[251] A Member who changes party allegiance is under no obligation to resign his or her seat and stand for re-election; entitlement to sit as a Member is not contingent upon political affiliation. If a Member decides to cross the floor and sit with another party, the Member's new party whip determines the seating arrangement for the Member.

Responsibilities and Conduct of Members

Members sit in the House of Commons to serve as representatives of the people who have elected them to that office. They have wide-ranging responsibilities which include work in the Chamber, committees, their constituencies and political parties. As Professor C.E.S. Franks has noted:

> *The member of parliament represents his constituency through service in the House of Commons. This does not mean, however, that he spends most of this time sitting in the House, or even that attendance there is the most important part of his work. An MP spends far more of his working life outside the House than in it.... The job is people-oriented, involving talking about and listening to ideas, proposals, and complaints, reconciling opposing viewpoints, explaining party or government policy to citizens and citizens' views to party and government, getting action out of the government on problems of constituents, and examining how the government uses or abuses the power it exercises on behalf of the people of Canada.*[252]

---

251. For examples of Members changing parties, see *Debates*, March 13, 1972, p. 745; March 7, 1979, p. 3910. On April 20, 1977, an Opposition Member, Jack Horner (Crowfoot), crossed the floor to the governing party and was appointed Minister without Portfolio the following day. The decision of Members to leave the party under which they were elected to form a new group has occurred on at least three occasions since Confederation. In February 1943, three Members from Quebec left the Liberal Party to form the *Bloc populaire canadien* in response to the introduction of conscription (see *Debates*, February 10, 1943, pp. 309-13; February 18, 1943, pp. 532-7, 542-5). In 1963, members of the Quebec wing of the Social Credit Party broke away to form a new group called the *Ralliement des Créditistes* (see *Journals*, September 30, 1963, pp. 385-8). In 1990, in response to the failure of the Meech Lake Accord, eight Members of different political affiliations formed a new party, the *Bloc québécois* (see *Debates*, May 18, 1990, pp. 11615-7; May 22, 1990, pp. 11631, 11662-4; June 26, 1990, pp. 13087-8, 13121-3).

252. *Franks*, p. 87. For additional information on the role of the Member, see *Fraser*, pp. 58-63, and *Supporting Democracy*, Commission to Review Allowances of Members of Parliament, Ottawa: Minister of Public Works and Government Services, Vol. 2, 1998, pp. 59-83.

Besides participating in debates in the Chamber and in committees, and conveying their constituents' views to the government and advocating on their behalf, Members also have responsibilities in many other areas:

- They act as ombudsmen by providing information to constituents and resolving problems.

- They act as legislators by either initiating bills of their own or proposing amendments to government and other Members' bills.

- They develop specialized knowledge in one or more of the policy areas dealt with by Parliament, and propose recommendations to the government.

- They represent the Parliament of Canada at home and abroad by participating in international conferences and official visits.

Members, once elected and sworn in, are bound to observe certain rules of conduct in carrying out their parliamentary functions. Although there is no statute which dictates a code of conduct for parliamentarians at the federal level, some provisions regarding conduct for Members and conflict of interest matters exist in the Standing Orders of the House,[253] the *Parliament of Canada Act*[254] and the *Criminal Code*.[255] Also in place is the *Conflict of Interest and Post-Employment Code for Public Office-Holders*, in particular for Cabinet Ministers and Parliamentary Secretaries, issued by the Prime Minister's Office. A number of these provisions are discussed later in this chapter.

ATTENDANCE

One of the Member's primary duties is to attend the sittings of the House when it is in session, unless the Member has other parliamentary or official commitments, such

---

253. See Standing Orders 15 to 23. The Standing Orders contain provisions requiring Members to attend the business of the House, register foreign travel in certain instances, and disclose any pecuniary interest in a question before a vote. A number of other obligations, including dress code and decorum, are discussed in Chapter 13, "Rules of Order and Decorum".

254. R.S.C. 1985, c. P-1 as amended by c. 31, 42 (1st supp.), c. 38 (2nd supp.), c. 1 (4th supp.), S.C. 1991, c. 20 and c. 30, S.C.1993, c. 13 and c. 28, S.C. 1994, c. 18, S.C. 1996, c. 16 and c. 35, and S.C. 1997, c. 32. For example, the *Parliament of Canada Act* prohibits Members from entering into a contract directly with the Government of Canada or from receiving any benefit under contract with the Government of Canada.

255. R.S.C. 1985, c. C-46 as amended by S.C. 1995, c. 22, s. 6. The most serious breaches of ethical behaviour are dealt with in the *Criminal Code* by making offences of bribery, influence peddling and breach of trust.

as committee meetings, constituency work or parliamentary exchanges.[256] Indeed, the Speaker has traditionally discouraged Members from signalling the absence of another Member from the House because "there are many places that Members have to be in order to carry out all of the obligations that go with their office".[257]

The *Parliament of Canada Act* provides for deductions for non-attendance from the Member's sessional allowance.[258] At the end of each month and at the end of each session, each Member is required to provide the Clerk of the House with a statement of the number of days of attendance during the month or session, as the case may be, for which they are entitled to receive their sessional and expense allowances.[259] For the purposes of this declaration, those days on which a Member was absent due to illness, a military commitment, the adjournment of the House or because the Member was on "public or official business", are considered days of attendance.[260] Since there is no regulatory mechanism to monitor Members' attendance, calculations of Members' allowances are made on the basis of their statements and deductions are made only when absences exceed 21 sitting days.[261]

---

256. Standing Order 15: "Every Member, being cognizant of the provisions of the *Parliament of Canada Act*, is bound to attend the sittings of the House, unless otherwise occupied with parliamentary activities and functions or on public or official business". Prior to 1994, Standing Order 15 read as follows: "Except as otherwise provided in these Standing Orders, every Member is bound to attend the service of the House, unless leave of absence has been given him or her by the House." This Standing Order had remained unchanged since 1867. During the early years of Confederation, a Member who wanted permission to be absent from the House sought the necessary leave through another Member, who moved a motion to that effect. The usual reason for seeking leave was illness, but other family and personal reasons were commonly given (see, for example, *Journals*, May 8, 1868, p. 301; February 15, 1871, p. 10; April 13, 1877, p. 257). The last time a Member was granted a formal leave of absence was in 1878 when it was done by means of a resolution (*Journals*, April 26, 1878, p. 220). After 1878, the rule was no longer applied; the House chose to rely instead on statutory provisions which provided for monetary penalties for non-attendance (see *An Act respecting the Senate and the House of Commons*, R.S.C 1884, c. 10, s. 26). In 1994, this Standing Order was considered by the Standing Committee on Procedure and House Affairs. Members of the Committee expressed concern that the Standing Order was obsolete and did not reflect that Members are often prevented from attending a sitting of the House because of committee meetings or other parliamentary or constituency commitments. See Standing Committee on Procedure and House Affairs, *Minutes of Proceedings and Evidence,* March 24, 1994, Issue No. 5, pp. 32-4; May 24, 1994, Issue No. 12, p. 6. See also the transcript of the meeting of May 3, 1994, pp. 1-10. On June 10, 1994, the House concurred in the Twenty-Seventh Report of the Standing Committee on Procedure and House Affairs which included the amended wording for Standing Order 15 (*Journals*, June 8, 1994, p. 545; June 10, 1994, p. 563). See also Standing Committee on Procedure and House Affairs, *Minutes of Proceedings and Evidence,* June 9, 1994, Issue No. 16, p. 3.

257. *Debates*, April 3, 1987, p. 4875. See also *Debates*, February 18, 1994, pp. 1553-4; June 21, 1994, p. 5674; December 5, 1995, pp. 17207-8.

258. R.S.C. 1985, c. P-1, s. 57(1).

259. *Parliament of Canada Act*, R.S.C. 1985, c. P-1, s. 65(1).

260. *Parliament of Canada Act,* R.S.C. 1985, c. P-1, ss. 57(3), 58 as amended by c. 31 (1st supp.), s. 61.

261. *Parliament of Canada Act,* R.S.C. 1985, c. P-1, s. 57(1).

While the *Parliament of Canada Act* gives the House the power to impose more stringent regulations respecting Members' attendance or deductions from sessional allowances,[262] the presence of Members in the Chamber is largely a function of politics, not procedure or law. Consequently, it has fallen to the whips to ensure an adequate representation of Members in the Chamber for debates and votes. Thus, through the use of a roster system and other controls, the party whips are able to regulate the attendance of Members in the Chamber, in committees and in other parliamentary functions.

CONFLICT OF INTEREST MATTERS

On being elected, Members of the House of Commons become trustees of public confidence. Members must be seen to be impartial and to derive no personal benefit or gain from their decisions. Various attempts have been made over the past 25 years to define what constitutes a conflict of interest and to devise rules regarding Members improperly using their influence, using insider information, and furthering their private interests.

Historical Perspective

In 1973, the Federal Government issued a Green Paper on Members of Parliament and Conflict of Interest.[263] During the next Parliament, the Green Paper was referred to the Standing Committee on Privileges and Elections.[264] The Committee reported it back to the House with numerous recommendations.[265] In 1978, the government introduced Bill C-6, *An Act respecting the independence of Parliament and conflicts of interests of Senators and Members of the House of Commons and to amend certain other Acts in relation thereof or in consequence,* which would have extended the provisions in the Green Paper and incorporated some of the recommendations made by the Committee.[266] The bill was referred to the Standing Committee on Elections and Privileges after second reading,[267] but Parliament was dissolved before the Committee could report back to the House.

In 1983, the government established a Task Force on Conflict of Interest to devise a regime dealing with conflict of interest whereby public confidence would be ensured and the integrity of the political process protected. In May 1984, the Task Force identified nine activities as involving conflicts of interest and recommended that these forms of conduct be dealt with, depending on the severity of the conflict, by using a code of conduct.[268]

---

262. R.S.C. 1985, c. P-1, s. 59.

263. *Journals*, July 17, 1973, p. 485.

264. *Journals*, November 27, 1974, p. 149; December 10, 1974, pp. 183-4.

265. *Journals*, June 10, 1975, pp. 615-8.

266. *Journals*, October 16, 1978, p. 22.

267. *Journals*, March 8, 1979, pp. 454-5.

268. See Report of the Task Force on Conflict of Interest entitled *Ethical Conduct in the Public Sector* (the Starr-Sharp Report) tabled on May 28, 1984 (*Journals*, p. 484).

In 1985, the Standing Committee on Management and Members' Services was asked to consider matters related to the establishment of a Register of Members' Interests.[269] The Committee concluded that such a Register was not warranted and that the current laws regarding conflict of interest were adequate.[270]

At the end of 1987 came the Report of the Parker Commission on Conflict of Interests regarding the allegations of conflict of interest involving the Hon. Sinclair Stevens. Mr. Justice Parker made a number of recommendations, and in particular the requirement that conflict of interest guidelines include public disclosure of a Minister's assets, interests and activities. In 1988, the government introduced Bill C-114, *Members of the Senate and House of Commons Conflict of Interest Act,* which was referred to a legislative committee after the second reading,[271] but Parliament was dissolved before the committee could report back.

Another conflict of interest bill (Bill C-46, *Members of the Senate and House of Commons Conflict of Interest Act)* was introduced during the Second Session (April 1989-May 1991) of the Thirty-Fourth Parliament[272] but was not proceeded with. Two similar bills were introduced during the Third Session (May 1991-September 1993): Bill C-43, *Members of the Senate and House of Commons Conflict of Interest Act;*[273] and Bill C-116, *Conflict of Interests of Public Office Holders Act.*[274] The House of Commons gave second reading to Bill C-116 and referred it to the Special Joint Committee of the Senate and the House of Commons on Conflict of Interests on March 30, 1993.[275] On June 3, 1993, the Special Joint Committee recommended to the House that the bill not be proceeded with.[276] The Thirty-Fourth Parliament was dissolved shortly thereafter.

Each conflict of interest bill provided for an annual declaration of the private interests of Senators, Members of the House of Commons, their spouses and dependent children to an independent three-member conflict of interests commission. The bills also contained rules against using confidential information to further one's own private interests and against trying to influence others' decisions from one's own private interests; rules on gifts and on post-employment conduct;

---

269. *Journals,* November 25, 1985, pp. 1266-7.

270. *Journals,* March 26, 1986, p. 1926. See also Standing Committee on Management and Members' Services, *Minutes of Proceedings and Evidence,* March 19, 1986, Issue No. 4, pp. 5-7.

271. *Journals,* September 1, 1988, p. 3508.

272. *Journals,* November 9, 1989, p. 842.

273. *Journals,* November 22, 1991, pp. 715-6, 717-8; June 10, 1992, p. 1677. See also the Special Joint Committee of the Senate and House of Commons on Conflict of Interests, *Minutes of Proceedings and Evidence,* June 9, 1992, Issue No. 17.

274. *Journals,* March 11, 1993, pp. 2618-9.

275. *Journals,* March 30, 1993, pp. 2742-3.

276. *Journals,* June 3, 1993, p. 3107.

and special rules for Ministers regarding outside activities. Proposed penalties for non-compliance ranged from fines to loss of the Member's or Senator's seat, but their imposition remained in the hands of the Member's Chamber.

During the First Session (January 1994 - February 1996) of the Thirty-Fifth Parliament, a special joint committee of the Senate and of the House of Commons was established to develop a code of conduct to guide parliamentarians in reconciling their official responsibilities with their personal interests, including their dealings with lobbyists.[277] The Committee was re-established during the Second Session (February 1996 - April 1997)[278] and reported to the House on March 20, 1997[279] with the recommendation that the Senate and the House of Commons adopt a "Code of Official Conduct".[280] The Thirty-Fifth Parliament was dissolved a month later without the report being concurred in.

Governing Prohibitions

Statutory provisions and guidelines governing aspects of conflict of interest presently exist. The *Parliament of Canada Act* contains several conflict of interest prohibitions. A number of them govern the eligibility of Members to sit in the House of Commons and accept any other office, commission or employment in the service of the Government of Canada, with exceptions such as the offices of Cabinet Minister, Parliamentary Secretary or active service in the Armed Forces in wartime.[281] Anyone who contracts with the government or who works for such a contractor is not eligible to be a Member of the House of Commons and may not sit or vote in the House, although a Member may be a shareholder with a company having a government contract that does not involve building any public work.[282] If a Member contravenes these provisions, his or her seat is vacated, his or her election is declared void, and the Member forfeits the sum of $200 for each day he or she sat or voted.[283]

All public office holders are subject to the *Criminal Code's* general provisions on corruption, including bribery, influence-peddling and breach of trust.[284] For example, breach of trust occurs when a Member pays a person for work not performed, accepts payment from a person in return for hiring that person as an

---

277. *Journals*, June 19, 1995, pp. 1801-3.

278. *Journals*, March 12, 1996, pp. 83-4.

279. *Journals*, March 20, 1997, p. 1325.

280. See the Second Report of the Special Joint Committee on a Code of Conduct (*Proceedings,* March 20, 1997, Issue No. 6, pp. 7-21).

281. *Parliament of Canada Act*, R.S.C. 1985, c. P-1, ss. 32-3 as amended by R.S.C. 1985, c. 1 (4th supp.), s. 29.

282. *Parliament of Canada Act*, R.S.C. 1985, c. P-1, ss. 34-5, 38, 40. The contracting provisions in the *Parliament of Canada Act* date back to the days when a major activity of the government was the construction of public buildings.

283. *Parliament of Canada Act*, R.S.C. 1985, c. P-1, ss. 34-36(1).

284. R.S.C. 1985, c. C-46, ss. 121, 122, 124, 125.

employee or contractor, and uses public funds for private travel. Should a person be convicted of one of these offences and sentenced to more than two years of imprisonment, that person is incapable of being elected or sitting or voting as a Member of Parliament.[285] Nonetheless, in terms of its membership, the House of Commons retains the right to regulate its own internal affairs and procedures, free from any interference from the courts. This includes the right to enforce discipline on its Members by suspension or expulsion. Even where a Member has been convicted of bribery, or sentenced to imprisonment for an indictable offence for a period longer than the life of the Parliament, the Member cannot be deprived of his or her seat unless the House decides so.[286]

In addition to statutory prohibitions, Prime Ministers have issued conflict of interest guidelines for Ministers and other public office holders (*Conflict of Interest and Post-Employment Code for Public Office Holders*).[287] The code is voluntary and applies to Cabinet Ministers, Secretaries of State, Parliamentary Secretaries and other senior public office holders (full-time Governor in Council appointees). It requires that, on appointment to one of these offices, the office holders are to arrange their private affairs so as to prevent real, potential or apparent conflicts from arising.[288] They are not to solicit or accept money or gifts; not to assist individuals in

---

285. *Criminal Code*, R.S.C. 1985, c. C-46, s. 748 as amended by S.C 1995, c. 22, s. 6.

286. See *Maingot*, 2nd ed., pp. 187-90. See also Chapter 3, "Privileges and Immunities". Since 1960, a number of Members have been charged under the *Criminal Code* with either fraud, bribery, influence-peddling or breach of trust in their official capacity as a Member. In many instances, the charges were either dropped, the Member was acquitted, or the Member was found not guilty. In the few cases where a Member was found guilty of one of these charges (in some instances only after the Parliament in which they were charged had been dissolved), only one Member resigned his seat (see *Debates*, May 30, 1989, p. 2321); the others chose either not to seek re-election or were defeated in the following general election. See also *Debates*, May 24, 1989, pp. 2095-7.

287. The first conflict of interest code was issued by Prime Minister Pierre Trudeau in the early 1970s, while another version was introduced by Prime Minister Joe Clark in 1979. Prime Minister Brian Mulroney issued *The Conflict of Interest and Post-Employment Code for Public Office Holders* in September 1985 (see *Debates*, September 9, 1985, pp. 6399-402), and it was modified by Prime Minister Jean Chrétien in 1994.

288. In 1994, a Reform Party Member, Ed Harper (Simcoe Centre), raised concerns in the House that a Parliamentary Secretary, Herb Dhaliwal (Vancouver South), had not complied with the conflict of interest guidelines for public office holders because a company in which he was part owner had government contracts. Mr. Dhaliwal denied the allegations and claimed that he had resigned as an officer and director of the company when he was named Parliamentary Secretary to the Minister of Fisheries and Oceans. Speaker Parent ruled that this was a disagreement as to facts which did not fulfil the conditions of parliamentary privilege. See *Debates*, June 13, 1994, pp. 5217-8; June 16, 1994, p. 5437.

their dealings with government in such a way as to compromise their own professional status; not to take advantage of information obtained because of their positions as insiders; and, after they leave public office, not to act so as to take improper advantage of having held that office. After leaving office, Ministers are prohibited for two years, and other public office holders for one year, from certain activities in order to ensure impartiality while in office and to avoid preferential treatment upon leaving office. These guidelines are administered by an ethics councillor who is a public servant reporting directly to the Prime Minister.[289]

Bribery

Bribery, the most extreme form of conflict of interest, is a criminal offence. One of the parliamentary privileges or rights Members enjoy is the freedom to carry out their parliamentary duties without fear of intimidation or interference. An attempt to tamper with this privilege through bribery undermines the independence of Members and, by extension, the independence of the House itself. The Standing Orders define any attempt to offer a Member any advantage for promoting any matter before Parliament as a "high crime and misdemeanour", which "tends to the subversion of the Constitution".[290]

There are few recorded instances of attempted bribery. In 1873, a Member rose in the House to say that someone had attempted to buy his vote. The House immediately ordered the accused party taken into custody, but Parliament prorogued before the individual could be questioned at the Bar and the matter was never again taken up.[291] In 1964, it was alleged that a bribe had been offered to a Member on condition that he change his party allegiance by crossing the floor of the House. The Standing Committee on Privileges and Elections was ordered to study and report on the charge, but on investigation concluded that the allegation was unfounded and the matter went no further.[292]

Instances where a Member accepts the offer of a bribe or even arranges for one in consideration of his or her work in Parliament are not foreseen by the rules of the House. However, there have been many cases in which allegations of accepting bribes in exchange for favours or influence formed the substance of motions against

---

289. See Press Release issued by the Prime Minister's Office on June 16, 1994. Prior to June 1994, the Assistant Deputy Registrar of Canada performed the functions of the Ethics Counsellor.

290. Standing Order 23(1).

291. *Journals*, November 3, 1873, pp. 134-5; November 7, 1873, p. 142.

292. *Debates*, April 27, 1964, pp. 2582-3; April 28, 1964, pp. 2645-7; *Journals*, June 15, 1964, pp. 425-6. A related example can be found in *Debates*, February 20, 1984, pp. 1559-61, where the Speaker ruled on a question of privilege in which a Member alleged that a Canada Post employee had attempted to influence the Member's actions in the House by way of threats and insults. The Minister of Labour had investigated the matter and determined that there was no foundation for the allegation. Because there was a conflict of opinion as to what had happened, the Speaker found that there was a *prima facie* question of privilege. The motion to have the matter referred to the Standing Committee on Privileges and Elections was subsequently defeated.

Members by their colleagues.[293] The *Parliament of Canada Act* prohibits a Member from receiving outside compensation for services rendered on any matter before the House, the Senate or their committees.[294] Pursuant to that Act, a Member found guilty of such an offence is liable to a fine of $500 to $2000 and is disqualified from being a Member of the House of Commons and from holding any office in the public service of Canada for five years after conviction of that offence.[295] In addition, the *Criminal Code* provides for 14 years' imprisonment for a parliamentarian who accepts or attempts to obtain any form of valuable consideration for doing or omitting to do anything in his or her official capacity.[296]

Pecuniary Interests

While no legislation exists to enforce the disclosure of a Member's financial interests, the Standing Orders of the House provide that Members may not vote on questions in which they have direct pecuniary interests; any such vote will be disallowed.[297] The pecuniary interest must be immediate and personal, and belong specifically to the person whose vote is contested. Measures with a wide application, such as matters of public policy, are not generally considered in this light. Even voting a pay increase to Members themselves does not constitute direct monetary interest because it applies to all Members.[298]

A Member with a pecuniary interest in a matter simply refrains from voting. In the event the Member votes, the vote may be questioned and eventually disallowed. When a Member's vote is questioned, his or her word usually prevails,[299] although

---

293. See, for example, *Journals*, April 5, 1886, pp. 112-5; May 28, 1886, p. 322; May 11, 1891, pp. 55-60; August 20, 1891, pp. 422-4. In each of these instances, the allegations were referred to a committee. In the first case, the committee reported back but its report was not printed (see *Journals*, May 18, 1886, p. 283); in the second case, Parliament was dissolved before the committee reported back; the August 20, 1891 allegation was not substantiated (see *Journals*, September 15, 1891, pp. 507-11). In the May 11, 1891 case, Thomas McGreevy (Quebec West) was expelled from the House (see *Journals*, September 29, 1891, p. 561). This matter is discussed in greater detail later in the chapter. In 1976, a former Member was quoted as saying before a court that a substantial number of Members of Parliament received bribes. A Member raised the matter as a question of privilege. The Speaker ruled that it was a *prima facie* matter of privilege and the House adopted a motion to refer the matter to the Standing Committee on Privileges and Elections (see *Debates*, May 7, 1976, pp. 13269-71 and 13280-1). The Committee invited the former Member to appear before it. In its report to the House, the Committee concluded that the former Member's comments were "intemperate and irresponsible". The Committee recommended that "the dignity of the House of Commons would be best served by giving the matter no further consideration". See *Journals*, May 21, 1976, pp. 1305-7.

294. R.S.C. 1985, c. P-1, s. 41(1).

295. *Parliament of Canada Act*, R.S.C. 1985, c. P-1, s. 41(2).

296. R.S.C. 1985, c. C-46, s. 119.

297. Standing Order 21. This topic is also discussed in Chapter 12, "The Process of Debate".

298. *Bourinot*, 4th ed., pp. 387-8.

299. See, for example, *Debates*, June 4, 1900, cols. 6607-8.

the Member's vote may be challenged by way of a motion to disallow it.[300] While no Member's vote has ever been disallowed by the House on grounds of direct pecuniary interests, several Members have either voluntarily refrained from voting[301] or have had their votes questioned.[302]

Registry of Foreign Travel

Members are sometimes called upon to travel outside Canada in their capacity as Members of the House of Commons. When visits are made outside of Canada and are not paid for out of the Consolidated Revenue Fund (i.e., paid by individuals or organizations other than the Member personally, any registered Canadian political party, or an inter-parliamentary association or friendship group recognized by the House of Commons), the Member must register the trip and the name of the sponsoring individual or organization with the Clerk of the House who keeps a public record of this information.[303] The Member may register the trip before or after it takes place by sending the Clerk of the House a personally signed letter[304] and the Clerk enters the information into the registry. Staff members or other representatives may not provide the information to the Clerk for the registry in the Member's place.

Remuneration, Pensions and Entitlements

The compensation package for Members of the House of Commons consists of three main components: a sessional indemnity (also known as a sessional allowance or salary), an incidental expense allowance, and a pension plan. In addition, Members are provided with other benefits and allowances related to travel between Ottawa

---

300. The only time this was ever attempted, the question was not proposed to the House (*Debates*, May 22, 1956, pp. 4244-5).

301. See, for example, *Debates*, September 10, 1985, p. 6473; November 25, 1985, p. 8794; May 27, 1996, p. 3041. In December 1997, the Minister of Finance (Paul Martin) rose on a point of order to indicate that in the process of the House agreeing to apply the results of one vote to another vote, he had been registered as voting for a bill at third reading (Bill C-9, *Canada Marine Act*). He asked for the unanimous consent of the House to have his vote deleted from the record. Consent was granted. See *Debates*, December 9, 1997, pp. 3007-9, 3011.

302. See, for example, *Debates*, May 3, 1886, p. 1011; June 21, 1982, pp. 18708-9.

303. Standing Order 22. This Standing Order was adopted on February 3, 1986, after the Government House Leader addressed the House on the desirability of keeping a registry of the foreign travel of Members. See *Debates*, November 4, 1985, pp. 8323-7; *Journals*, February 6, 1986, p. 1664; February 13, 1986, p. 1710.

304. In March 1986, five Members travelled to South Korea at that country's expense. Certain Members raised objections when it was discovered that some of the travellers had not registered the trip before departing. It became clear in the ensuing discussion that the Standing Order did not specify when the registration should be done and the matter was left to the House Leaders to decide. See *Debates*, March 18, 1986, pp. 11618, 11624-7.

and their constituency and within the constituency, a budget to staff the Parliament Hill and the constituency offices, and goods and services provided for the Members' use.

THE SESSIONAL INDEMNITY AND INCIDENTAL EXPENSE ALLOWANCE

The sessional indemnity, the equivalent of a salary, is stated as an annual amount and is paid monthly.[305] Additional salaries are payable to Members of the House of Commons occupying certain offices and positions. These include the Prime Minister, Cabinet Ministers, the Speaker and other Chair occupants, the Leaders of recognized opposition parties, House Leaders, Whips, and Parliamentary Secretaries.[306] Members also receive an incidental expense allowance which is non-accountable (i.e., Members do not have to document their use of the allowance with receipts) and is not subject to income tax. Members representing remote or difficult-to-access constituencies (as listed in the *Canada Elections Act*) receive a slightly larger expense allowance.[307]

In 1990, an accountable travel expense allowance (often referred to as the housing allowance) was introduced to compensate Members for the cost of meals, incidentals and accommodation expenses incurred while on official business more than 100 kilometres from their principal residence. The accountable expense allowance helps Members to offset some of the costs involved in maintaining two households, one in their constituency and one in Ottawa. Expenses claimed under the travel status expenses provision cannot exceed the amount set by the Board of Internal Economy.[308]

PENSION

The pension plan for Members was first established in 1952. At that time, Prime Minister Louis St. Laurent expressed concern about the reluctance of some people to run for a seat in the House of Commons because of their belief that long years spent in public service would not allow them to provide adequately for their later

---

305. *Parliament of Canada Act*, R.S.C. 1985, c. P-1, ss. 55, 56 as amended by R.S.C. 1985, c. 38 (2nd supp.), s. 1; S.C. 1991, c. 30, s. 23; S.C. 1993, c. 13, s. 11; S.C. 1994, c. 18, s. 10; and S.C. 1998, c. 23, s. 1. In 1999, Members of the House of Commons received a basic annual salary of $66,900 and an annual tax free expense allowance of between $22,100 and $29,200 (depending on the size of the constituency they represented). In 1867, Members received a sessional indemnity of six dollars a day if a session did not extend beyond 30 days; if the session continued longer, Members received a sessional allowance of $600 (see *Bourinot*, 4th ed., pp. 153-6). For an overview of the evolution of the sessional indemnity, see *Supporting Democracy*, Vol. 2, pp. 32-3.

306. *Parliament of Canada Act*, R.S.C. 1985, c. P-1, ss. 60-2 as amended by S.C. 1998, c. 23, ss. 2-4. The amount of the indemnity varies with the position.

307. *Parliament of Canada Act*, R.S.C. 1985, c. P-1, s. 63(3).

308. *Parliament of Canada Act*, R.S.C. 1985, c. P-1, ss. 50-4 as amended by S.C. 1991, c. 20, s. 2 (s. 52.5(1)). In 1998, the Board of Internal Economy increased the limit for Members' Travel Status Expenses from $6,000 to $12,000 for the 1998-99 fiscal year. See By-law 501 of the *By-laws of the Board of Internal Economy*.

years. The Prime Minister believed that the establishment of a pension plan would strengthen the parliamentary institution and attract the right kind of person to public service.[309] Under the *Members of Parliament Retiring Allowances Act,* a retiring allowance (pension) is payable to former Members who have contributed to the pension plan for a minimum of six years and who have attained age 55.[310] Should a Member retire with less than six years of service, the Member receives a withdrawal allowance in a single payment.[311]

A former Member who is not entitled to a pension and who was a Member on the day of dissolution, but is not re-elected or did not seek re-election, is entitled to a severance allowance equal to 50% of the total of the basic annual sessional indemnity and any annual salary payable to Members occupying certain offices (such as that of a Minister, House Leader, Whip, or Parliamentary Secretary).[312] The severance allowance is also payable to a Member who is not eligible for a pension and who resigned during an election period, following the dissolution of Parliament, or who resigned during a Parliament because of permanent illness or disability which in the opinion of the Speaker prevented the Member from performing his or her duties.[313]

The provisions of the *Members of Parliament Retiring Allowance Act* continue to apply between the day of dissolution and election day. Contributions cease as of the day of the election for Members who are not re-elected.

COMMISSION ON MEMBERS' SALARIES AND INDEMNITIES

Since 1975, the law has required that a commission be appointed by the Governor in Council after each general election, within two months after the date fixed for the return of the writs, to determine the adequacy of indemnities and various allowances

---

309. See *Debates*, June 25, 1952, pp. 3678-80.

310. R.S.C. 1985, c. M-5 as amended by S.C. 1992, c. 46, s. 81, and S.C. 1995, c. 30, s. 11. Contributions under the Act are ordinarily mandatory, but were made optional for Members of the Thirty-Fifth Parliament (1994-97) (see S.C. 1995, c. 30, s. 2). In 1998, amendments to the *Members of Parliament Retiring Allowance Act* permitted Members who opted out of the pension plan during the Thirty-Fifth Parliament to opt back in (see S.C. 1998, c. 23, s. 10). For Members who chose not to opt back in, a supplementary severance allowance is provided. For additional information, see *Manual of Allowances and Services*, Chapter F-2, "Retirement Benefits".

311. *Members of Parliament Retiring Allowance Act*, R.S.C. 1985, c. M-5, s. 15 as amended by S.C. 1992, c. 46, s. 81.

312. *Parliament of Canada Act*, R.S.C. 1985, c. P-1, ss. 70(1), 70(4), 71, as amended by S.C. 1998, c. 23, s. 6.

313. *Parliament of Canada Act*, R.S.C. 1985, c. P-1, s. 70(2).

payable to Members of the Senate and the House of Commons and to report back with recommendations, if deemed necessary, within six months.[314]

Commissions to review Members' allowances are generally known by the name of their chairs or members. Since 1979, reports have been received from the Hales Commission (1979),[315] the McIsaac-Balcer Commission (1980),[316] the Clarke-Campbell Commission (1985),[317] the St. Germain-Fox Commission (1989),[318] the Lapointe Commission (1994)[319] and the Blais Commission (1998).[320] The Report of the Commission to Review Allowances of Members of Parliament is tabled in the House by a Minister, typically the Government House Leader,[321] and permanently referred to the Standing Committee on Procedure and House Affairs.[322]

Every commission has recommended that the sessional indemnity be increased, but they have differed in how the increase should be made and how much the increase should be. The incidental expense was treated differently by each commission with no consensus on the amount, its status or how it should be changed. Similarly, each commission has recommended changes to the amount of other allowances and services, but recommendations were not consistent from one commission to another.[323] Since 1980, following the tabling of each commission's report, the

---

314. *Parliament of Canada Act*, R.S.C. 1985, c. P-1, s. 68(1). This provision was added to the *Parliament of Canada Act* following the 1970 recommendations of an advisory committee appointed to review parliamentary salaries and expenses. For a history and overview of the recommendations of these commissions since 1979, see *Supporting Democracy*, Vol. 2, pp. 7-17. Budgetary entitlements and other allowances are reviewed annually by the Board of Internal Economy.

315. *Report of the Commission to Review Salaries and Allowances of Members of Parliament and Senators*, Ottawa, 1979. Alfred D. Hales was the sole commissioner appointed to look into this matter.

316. *Report of the Commission to Review Salaries of Members of Parliament and Senators*, Ottawa, 1980. Cliff McIsaac and Léon Balcer were the two commissioners.

317. *Report of the Commission to Review Salaries of Members of Parliament and Senators*, Ottawa, 1985. William H. Clarke and Coline Campbell, former Members of the House of Commons, were appointed to this Commission.

318. *Commission to Review Allowances of Members of Parliament*, Ottawa, 1989. Gerry St. Germain and Francis Fox, both former Cabinet Ministers, sat on this commission.

319. *Democratic Ideals and Financial Realities,* Commission to Review Allowances of Members of Parliament, Ottawa: Minister of Supply and Services, 1994. This Commission was composed of Charles Lapointe (chair), Jean Pigott (a former Member of the House of Commons) and C.E.S. Franks (a professor of political studies at Queen's University).

320. *Supporting Democracy*, Jean-Jacques Blais (chair and former Cabinet Minister), Monique Jérôme-Forget (a public policy expert) and Ray Speaker (a former Member of the House of Commons) were the members.

321. *Parliament of Canada Act*, R.S.C. 1985, c. P-1, s. 68(2). See, for example, *Journals*, May 14, 1985, p. 614; October 13, 1989, p. 623; September 19, 1994, p. 690; February 4, 1998, p. 413.

322. Standing Order 32(5). Pursuant to Standing Order 108(3)(*a*)(i) which mandates the Standing Committee on Procedure and House Affairs to review and report on the administration and provision of services and facilities to Members, the Committee considered the Blais report in 1998 and submitted a response to the House. See the Thirty-Fourth Report of the Standing Committee on Procedure and House Affairs, presented to the House on June 3, 1998, and concurred in later that day (*Journals*, p. 929).

323. See *Supporting Democracy*, Vol. 2, pp. 13-5.

government has subsequently introduced legislation respecting the indemnities and allowances of Members of Parliament. [324]

Budgetary Entitlements

The *Parliament of Canada Act* authorizes the Board of Internal Economy to make by-laws with regard to the use of funds, goods, services and premises provided to Members. [325] The *Members' Manual of Allowances and Services,* produced in accordance with the *By-laws of the Board of Internal Economy,* contains administrative guidelines on the availability and use of all the funds, goods, services and premises to which Members are entitled.

The Thirty-Fifth Parliament (1993-97) was the first Parliament to operate with a complete set of by-laws. The By-laws were first enacted by the Board of Internal Economy in 1993 and are a series of guidelines concerning the handling by Members of public funds put at their disposal to help them carry out their parliamentary functions. Parliamentary functions are defined as duties and activities related to the position of Member of the House of Commons and includes public and official business and partisan matters but does not include the private business interests of a Member or of a Member's immediate family. [326] Each year, the Board of Internal Economy publishes a Finance By-law (By-law 501) which establishes the financial provisions for the fiscal year (April 1 to March 31). These include the Members' Budget (including the Member's Office Budget, the Constituency Furniture and Equipment Allowance and Members' Travel Expenses), House Officers' Budgets [327] and Committees' Budgets. [328] The other By-laws set out the terms governing

324. See *An Act to amend the Senate and House of Commons Act, the Parliamentary Secretaries Act and the Members of Parliament Retiring Allowances Act,* S.C. 1980-81-82-83, c. 77; *An Act to amend the Senate and House of Commons Act,* S.C. 1986, c. 50; *An Act to amend the Parliament of Canada Act,* S.C. 1991, c. 20; *An Act to amend the Members of Parliament Retiring Allowances Act and to provide for the continuation of a certain provision,* S.C. 1995, c. 30; *An Act to amend the Parliament of Canada Act, the Members of Parliament Retiring Allowances Act and the Salaries Act,* S.C. 1998, c. 23. See also *Debates,* July 9, 1981, pp. 11370-6; November 19, 1986, pp. 1337-9; May 4, 1995, pp. 12151-6; June 11, 1998, pp. 8060-2.

325. R.S.C. 1985, c. P-1 as amended by S.C. 1991, c. 20, s. 2 (ss. 52.3 and 52.5(1)(*b*)). For more information on the Board of Internal Economy, see Chapter 6, "The Physical and Administrative Setting".

326. By-law 101 of the *By-laws of the Board of Internal Economy of the House of Commons.*

327. House Officers include leaders of parties, House leaders, whips, the Speaker and other presiding officers.

328. See By-law 501 of the *By-laws of the Board of Internal Economy of the House of Commons.*

Members' use of their budgets and other benefits provided by the House including travel points, printing privileges, staff, and the purchase of goods.

The Board determines the terms and conditions of managing and accounting for the funds by the Members and has exclusive authority to determine whether their use is or was proper.[329] In the event the By-laws are contravened, the Board of Internal Economy may pursue a number of options, including withholding money from one of the Member's budgets or allowances, or freezing any budget or allowance or payment that may be available to the Member.[330]

Each Member is entitled to an office in the precinct of Parliament, office furniture and furnishings and equipment for this office.[331] Every Member is also entitled to establish one or more offices in his or her respective constituency and is provided with furniture and equipment for these offices. Furniture and equipment provided to Members are the property of the House of Commons. Each Member is provided with several budgets, including an Office Budget and a Constituency Furniture and Equipment Allowance.[332] Members may spend their budgets as they choose so long as they conform to the regulations prescribed by the Board of Internal Economy. The Members' Office Budget is used to pay expenses for the Member's parliamentary precinct office, including staff remuneration. This budget also pays expenses incurred in establishing and operating a constituency office, including staff remuneration, office rent and utilities, and office furnishings, supplies and equipment.[333]

329. *Parliament of Canada Act*, R.S.C. 1985, c. P-1, as amended by S.C. 1991, c. 20, s. 2 (s. 52.6(1)). In its Fourth Report presented and adopted on June 1, 1990, the Special Committee on the Review of the *Parliament of Canada Act* proposed amendments to the *Parliament of Canada Act* to clarify the jurisdiction and the authority of the Board of Internal Economy (*Journals*, June 1, 1990, pp. 1797-1804). In particular, the Special Committee wanted to ensure that Members would not be exposed to charges or proceedings based on a misunderstanding of the nature of their work or the structure and rules of the House of Commons.

330. See s. 7 of By-law 102 of the *By-laws of the Board of Internal Economy of the House of Commons*.

331. In 1991, Louis Plamondon (Richelieu) rose on a question of privilege after his parliamentary precinct offices had been entered and all his documents, files and personal effects, and those of his staff, had been removed to another building without his consent. The Speaker ruled that it was an administrative matter to be settled outside the Chamber (*Debates*, April 8, 1991, pp. 19126-7). See also *Debates*, April 9, 1991, pp. 19232-3; April 11, 1991, p. 19340.

332. Electoral and geographic supplements, where applicable, are made available to Members and are integrated into the Member's Office Budget. The electoral supplement is a graduated supplement available to eligible constituencies where the number of electors exceeds 70,000. The geographic supplement is also a graduated supplement for constituencies where the geographic area to be served is 8,000 sq. km. or more. See *Parliament of Canada Act*, R.S.C. 1985, c. P-1, s. 63(3)(*b*). See also By-law 501 of the *By-laws of the Board of Internal Economy of the House of Commons*.

333. See By-law 301 of the *By-laws of the Board of Internal Economy of the House of Commons*.

Each Member is the employer of all his or her employees and each Member has the prerogative to recruit, hire, promote and release employees.[334] A Member is allowed full discretion in the direction and control of the work performed on his or her behalf by employees and is subject only to the authority of the Board of Internal Economy and the House of Commons in the exercise of that discretion. Members determine the duties to be performed, hours of work, job classifications and salaries, and are responsible for employee relations. Subject to specific terms and conditions, Members may enter into contracts for services with individuals, agencies or organizations and use a portion of the Member's Office Budget for the payment of these contractors. Members may not hire or enter into a contract for consulting and professional services with members of their immediate family (spouses and children and their spouses and children).

The House covers the cost of printing newsletters, commonly known as "householders", sent by the Member to all constituents. Members have free mailing privileges to send out householders and other materials.[335] These mailing privileges are often referred to as "franking" privileges. "Franking" is the process by which Members of the House of Commons, by affixing their signatures to an addressed piece of mail, may have that mail delivered postage-free anywhere in the country. It is available only for mail that is addressed to places in Canada and may not be used for parcels, special delivery or other special services offered by Canada Post. Mail addressed to Members of the House is also delivered free of charge if sent to a Parliamentary Hill address. These mailing privileges begin on the day the notice of the Member's election is published by the Chief Electoral Officer in the *Canada Gazette* and end 10 calendar days after a dissolution of Parliament or 10 days after that person ceases to be a Member.[336]

The House of Commons provides Members with modern office equipment and services such as extensive long-distance calling, electronic mail and internet facilities,

---

334. In 1913, secretarial assistance was first made available to Members for a few days at a time. Beginning in 1916, Members shared a pool of secretaries who were laid off during periods of recess and dissolution. In 1958, secretaries became dedicated to individual Members. In 1968, each Member was authorized to hire one full-time secretary. In 1974, a second full-time secretary was authorized for each Member. The same year, constituency offices were established. In 1978, each Member received a staff budget of $58,000, including at least $12,000 for constituency staff, to be used at the Member's discretion for staffing requirements. For the 1999-2000 fiscal year, the base Office Budget was set at $190,000.

335. *Canada Post Corporation Act*, R.S.C. 1985, c. C-10, s. 35.

336. For additional information, see the *Members' Manual of Allowances and Services*. On occasion, questions of privilege have been raised alleging the misuse of these privileges. See, for example, *Debates*, March 9, 1987, pp. 3958-66; April 13, 1989, p. 458. The Speaker has ruled that the breach of mailing and householder guidelines does not obstruct in any way a Member from carrying out the activities for which he or she was elected (*Debates*, March 18, 1987, pp. 4301-2; April 13, 1989, p. 458). The Chair has indicated, however, that a question of privilege could exist if the content of the communication sent out under the frank "worked against the right of Members to free expression and the carrying out of their obligations as Members" (*Debates*, October 16, 1986, pp. 405-6). See also *Debates*, April 23, 1990, pp. 10522-8, and May 17, 1990, pp. 11561-3, where a question of privilege was raised alleging the misuse of parliamentary stationery by a former Member. The Speaker ruled that the matter was arguably one of contempt rather than privilege.

internal mail and messenger services, printing, security and language training. The Library of Parliament, through its research and reference services, provides Members, upon request, with research papers, background information and press clippings.

Members are allowed regular return trips to travel between Ottawa and the constituency and on occasion elsewhere in Canada.[337] Members or persons representing the Member can be reimbursed for travel costs while travelling within the constituency or within the province or territory in which the constituency is situated to a maximum amount established by the Board of Internal Economy.[338] Receipts must be submitted and the amount reimbursed is deducted from the Member's office budget.

When Parliament is dissolved, Members of the House of Commons are discharged from their responsibility to attend the sittings of the House and cease to be Members of Parliament. However, the *Parliament of Canada Act* provides for the continuation of a number of provisions upon dissolution. For purposes of the allowances payable, a Member is deemed to continue to be a Member of the House until the date of the following election.[339] Between the date Parliament is dissolved and the day of the election, budgetary funds, goods, services and premises made available by the House to its Members are to be used to carry out Members' parliamentary functions.

Members who are defeated or who did not seek re-election are provided with travel benefits to come to Ottawa to close their office. If a Member resigns before Parliament is dissolved, his or her travel benefits cease as of the day of resignation. Household moving expenses from the constituency to Ottawa and back are covered once per Parliament.

On behalf of the Board of Internal Economy, the Speaker tables in the House an annual report of Members' expenses. Members receive a copy of their annual expenditures prior to disclosure.[340]

---

337. Travel provisions have changed dramatically since Confederation. In 1867, travel expenses were authorized at $0.10 per mile for a return trip, once per session, between Ottawa and the constituency and in 1903, free rail transportation, without limitation, was made available to Members, their spouses and dependent children. Access to free rail transportation ended as of July 1, 1996, with the repeal of the *Canadian National Railway Act*. Nonetheless, Members, their spouses and dependants are entitled to free VIA train transportation in Canada in accordance with VIA Rail Canada's policy. For information on air transportation provisions, which were first authorized in 1948, see Commission to Review Allowances of Members of Parliament, *Democratic Ideals and Financial Realities*, 1994, pp. 57-9.

338. See By-law 303 of the *By-laws of the Board of Internal Economy of the House of Commons*.

339. *Parliament of Canada Act*, R.S.C. 1985, c. P-1, s. 69. See also By-law 305, of the *By-laws of the Board of Internal Economy of the House of Commons*.

340. See, for example, *Journals*, October 10, 1997, p. 105.

Vacancies in Representation

Once elected, Members are expected to serve for the duration of a parliament. Nonetheless, vacancies in representation may, and often do, occur. A person ceases to be a Member of the House of Commons when:

- that person dies;
- that person resigns his or her seat;
- that person has accepted an office of profit or emolument under the Crown;
- that person has been elected to sit in a provincial legislative assembly;
- the Member's election has been overturned in accordance with the *Dominion Controverted Elections Act*;
- the House has, by order, declared that the Member's seat is vacant and has ordered the Speaker to address a warrant to the Chief Electoral Officer for the issue of a writ of election for a new Member.[341]

DEATH OF A MEMBER

Should a Member die while in office, the Speaker is informed of the vacancy in one of two ways. A Member may rise in his or her place and advise the House of the death;[342] alternatively, two Members may notify the Speaker in writing.[343] Typically at the beginning of the sitting, the Speaker informs the House that a communication has been received giving notice of a vacancy in representation and that a warrant has been addressed to the Chief Electoral Officer for the issue of a writ for the election.[344]

In the absence of the Speaker, or if there is no Speaker, or if the seat vacated is that of the Speaker, two Members may alert the Chief Electoral Officer in writing of the death of the Member. The Chief Electoral Officer is then authorized to issue a new writ for the election of a Member to fill the vacancy.[345]

Death of a Member Following a General Election

If, following a general election but before the first session of the new Parliament and before the election of a Speaker, a vacancy occurs in the representation of the House

---

341. *Maingot*, 2nd ed., pp. 22-3.

342. See, for example, *Debates*, September 19, 1994, pp. 5811-4; September 20, 1994, p. 5900; February 3, 1997, pp. 7581-3; February 4, 1997, p. 7615.

343. *Parliament of Canada Act*, R.S.C. 1985, c. P-1, s. 28(1).

344. See, for example, *Debates*, November 23, 1989, p. 6067; February 26, 1993, p. 16511. On December 9, 1998, Shaughnessy Cohen (Windsor–St. Clair) collapsed on the floor of the House of Commons and later died in hospital. The following day, tributes were paid to the Member (*Debates*, December 10, 1998, pp. 11123-6) and an entry announcing the vacancy was published in the *Journals* (December 10, 1998, p. 1431). Four Members have died on the parliamentary precinct: Bowman Law (in 1916 during the fire which destroyed the Centre Block; see *Debates*, February 7, 1916, pp. 590-1), John L. MacDougall (*Debates*, June 6, 1956, p. 4786), Owen Trainor (*Debates*, November 28, 1956, pp. 114-5), and Joseph Gour (*Debates*, March 24, 1959, p. 2209; March 25, 1959, pp. 2213-5).

345. *Parliament of Canada Act*, R.S.C. 1985, c. P-1, s. 28(2).

because of the death of a Member, any Member may alert the Chief Electoral Officer in writing of this vacancy.[346] The Chief Electoral Officer is then authorized to issue a new writ for the election of a Member to fill the vacancy. On the opening day of the first session, after the election of a Speaker and after the House has returned from hearing the Speech from the Throne in the Senate, the House is advised of the vacancy at some point during the day's proceedings.[347]

RESIGNATION OF A MEMBER

A Member may give notice of his or her intention to resign by making a statement on the floor of the House.[348] Immediately upon the recording of this notice in the *Journals* of the House, the Speaker addresses a warrant to the Chief Electoral Officer for the issue of a writ for the election of a Member to fill the vacancy.[349] A Member may also resign his or her seat by delivering to the Speaker a written declaration of intention to resign signed before two witnesses. On receiving the declaration, the Speaker addresses a warrant to the Chief Electoral Officer for the issue of a writ for the election of a Member to fill the vacancy.[350]

A Member who wishes to resign when there is no Speaker or when the Speaker is absent from Canada may deliver to any two Members his or her signed declaration of intention to resign. The same applies when a Speaker wishes to resign as a Member.[351] On receiving the declaration, these two Members address a warrant to the Chief Electoral Officer for the issue of a writ for the election of a Member to fill the vacancy.[352]

Once a Member has tendered his or her resignation, the seat is deemed to be vacated and the individual ceases to be a Member of Parliament.[353] No Member, however, may tender his or her resignation while his or her election is being contested or until after the expiration of the time during which the election may be contested on grounds other than corruption or bribery.[354]

---

346. There have been 10 instances since Confederation where a Member has been elected to the House but has died before the opening of Parliament: Adelbert Edward Hanna (1918); Peter McGibbon (1921); Joseph Marcile (1925); Benoit Michaud (1949); John Ernest McMillan (1949); Gordon Graydon (1953); Azra Clair Casselman (1958); Colin Cameron (1968); Rt. Hon. John Diefenbaker (1979); and John Dahmer (1988).

347. See, for example, *Debates*, October 9, 1979, p. 7; December 12, 1988, p. 11.

348. See, for example, *Debates*, September 24, 1990, p. 13215.

349. *Parliament of Canada Act*, R.S.C. 1985, c. P-1, s. 25(1)(*a*). See, for example, *Journals,* September 24, 1990, pp. 1975-6.

350. *Parliament of Canada Act*, R.S.C. 1985, c. P-1, s. 25(1)(*b*). See, for example, *Journals*, February 3, 1997, p. 1025; October 1, 1997, p. 55.

351. *Parliament of Canada Act*, R.S.C. 1985, c. P-1, s. 26(1).

352. *Parliament of Canada Act*, R.S.C. 1985, c. P-1, s. 26(2). See, for example, *Debates*, October 1, 1986, p. 15; *Journals*, p. 25.

353. *Parliament of Canada Act*, R.S.C. 1985, c. P-1, s. 27(1).

354. *Parliament of Canada Act*, R.S.C. 1985, c. P-1, s. 27(2).

Acceptance of an Office of Profit or Emolument Under the Crown

No person may hold an office of profit or of emolument under the Crown and become or remain a Member of Parliament. Thus, the seat of a Member who has accepted an appointment to the Senate, the office of the Governor General, a judgeship or any other such public office is automatically vacated.[355] This provision does not apply to Members who occupy positions as Ministers or who are appointed to the Ministry in the course of a session.[356] A Member must also resign if he or she becomes a member of a provincial legislature.[357] In the event a Member accepts an office after a general election but before Parliament first meets, any other Member may notify the Chief Electoral Officer of the vacancy. The Chief Electoral Officer will then issue a writ for an election of a Member to fill the vacancy.[358]

CONTROVERTED ELECTION RESULT

A vacancy in the representation of the House may occur as a result of a controverted election. As discussed earlier in this chapter, a judicial decision concerning a controverted election may void the election result, depriving the person first declared elected of his or her seat. In this case, the Speaker informs the House of the decision and then addresses a warrant to the Chief Electoral Officer to issue a writ for the election of a Member to fill the vacancy.[359]

EXPULSION

Once a person is elected to the House of Commons, there are no constitutional provisions and few statutory provisions for removal of that Member from office. The statutory provisions rendering a Member ineligible to sit or vote do not automatically cause the seat of that Member to become vacant.[360] Indeed, the laying of a

---

355. *Parliament of Canada Act*, R.S.C. 1985, c. P-1, ss. 28(1), 32(1). See, for example, *Debates*, October 1, 1986, p. 15 (appointment to the office of Lieutenant Governor of Newfoundland); June 1, 1988, p. 16010 (acceptance of public office); November 23, 1994, p. 8165 (appointment to the Senate). In 1984, Speaker Sauvé resigned her seat upon her appointment as Governor General. She addressed her resignation letter to the Clerk of the House (*Journals*, January 16, 1984, p. 72). Following the election of Lloyd Francis as Speaker, the vacancy in the representation was announced to the House (*Journals*, January 16, 1984, p. 74).

356. *Parliament of Canada Act*, R.S.C. 1985, c. P-1, s. 33(2).

357. *Parliament of Canada Act*, R.S.C. 1985, c. P-1, s. 23(1). See, for example, *Debates*, February 1, 1993, p. 15167.

358. *Parliament of Canada Act*, R.S.C. 1985, c. P-1, s. 29. See, for example, *Journals*, October 9, 1979, pp. 17-8.

359. *Dominion Controverted Elections Act*, R.S.C. 1985, c. C-39, ss. 70-1. See, for example, *Debates*, June 7, 1990, p. 12459.

360. See *Maingot*, 2nd ed., pp. 22-3.

criminal charge against a Member has no effect on his or her eligibility to remain in office. By virtue of parliamentary privilege, the House has the inherent right to decide matters affecting its own membership: the House decides for itself if a Member should be permitted to sit on committees, receive a salary or even be allowed to keep his or her seat. [361] The power of the House to expel one of its Members derives from its traditional authority to determine whether Members are qualified to sit. A criminal conviction is not necessary for the House to expel a Member; the House may judge a Member unworthy to sit in the Chamber for any conduct unbecoming the character of a Member. Even if convicted of an indictable offence, a formal resolution of the House is still required to unseat a Member. [362] Expulsion terminates the Member's mandate: the House of Commons declares a seat vacant and orders the Speaker to address a warrant to the Chief Electoral Officer for the issue of a writ of election. [363]

The determination of whether a Member is ineligible to sit and vote is a matter initiated without notice and would be given precedence by its very nature. [364] When there has been a criminal conviction, the House of Commons has acted only when sufficient evidence against a Member has been tabled (i.e., judgements sentencing the Member and appeals confirming the sentence). [365] Any Member may move to examine the conduct of another Member, and the Member whose conduct is in question is permitted to make a statement and then withdraw from the Chamber while the motion to expel him or her is being debated. [366]

Since Confederation, there have been four cases where Members of the House of Commons were expelled for having committed serious offences. [367] Three cases involved criminal convictions: Louis Riel (Provencher) was expelled twice, in

---

361. *Maingot*, 2nd ed., pp. 188, 247. See also Speaker Lamoureux's ruling, *Debates*, March 1, 1966, pp. 1939-40.

362. *Maingot*, 2nd ed., p. 188. See also *Criminal Code*, R.S.C. 1985, c. 46, s. 750 as amended by S.C. 1995, c. 22, s. 6.

363. See, for example, *Journals*, April 16, 1874, p. 71; February 24, 1875, pp. 124-5; September 29, 1891, p. 561; January 30, 1947, p. 8.

364. *Maingot*, 2nd ed., p. 247.

365. See *Maingot*, 2nd ed., pp. 188-9, 212. See, for example, *Journals*, February 22, 1875, p. 111; January 30, 1947, pp. 4-8. In 1874, only an indictment for Riel's arrest was tabled (*Journals*, March 31, 1874, pp. 11-2).

366. Standing Order 20.

367. For additional information, see Chapter 3, "Privileges and Immunities". The last time a Member was expelled from a Canadian legislature was in 1986 in Nova Scotia by reason of the Member's conviction on four counts of using forged documents in respect of money received by him in his capacity as a Member. In that case, the Court held that the Legislature had the power to expel a Member by resolution and that this was not normally reviewable by the Courts. It was also held that the establishment and enforcement of proper standards for Members of the House was not a breach of section 3 of the *Charter of Rights and Freedoms* (*MacLean v. A.G. Nova Scotia (1987) 35 D.L.R. (4th) 306 (N.S.S.C.)*).

1874[368] and in 1875,[369] for being a fugitive from justice; and Fred Rose (Cartier) was expelled in 1947 after having been found guilty of conspiracy under the *Official Secrets Act*.[370] In 1891, Thomas McGreevy (Quebec West) was expelled after having been found guilty of contempt of the authority of the House.[371]

Expulsion does not disqualify a Member from standing for re-election, unless the cause of the expulsion constitutes in itself a disqualification to sit and vote in the House (for example, such as being convicted of an illegal or corrupt election practice).[372] Indeed, on two occasions a Member who had been expelled from the House sought re-election: following his first expulsion from the House in April 1874, Louis Riel was re-elected in a by-election in September 1874; Thomas McGreevy was re-elected to the House in a by-election on April 17, 1895.[373]

---

368. In April 1874, the House ordered that Louis Riel, "having been charged with murder, and a Bill of Indictment for said offence having been found against him, and warrants issued for his apprehension, and the said Louis Riel having fled from justice, and having failed to obey an Order of this House that he should attend in his place on Thursday, the 9th day of April, 1874, be expelled [from] this House". A second motion was subsequently adopted ordering the Speaker to issue a warrant for an election to fill the vacancy. See *Journals*, April 15, 1874, pp. 64-5; April 16, 1874, pp. 67-71. See also *Journals*, March 31, 1874, pp. 10-3; April 1, 1874, pp. 17-8; April 8, 1874, pp. 25-6; April 9, 1874, pp. 32-9.

369. In the by-election held to fill the vacancy resulting from the expulsion of Louis Riel, he was once again elected. On February 22, 1875, the Prime Minister tabled a court ruling finding Mr. Riel guilty of murder (*Journals*, p. 111). Two days later, motions were adopted to effect the expulsion of Mr. Riel. First, the Prime Minister moved that the court ruling tabled two days earlier be read. After the motion was adopted, the Clerk read the judgement into the record (*Journals*, February 24, 1875, pp. 118-22). The Prime Minister then moved that "it appears from the said Record that Louis Riel, a Member of this House has been adjudged an outlaw for felony". The House adopted the motion. This motion was followed by another motion ordering the Speaker to issue a warrant for a new writ of election (*Journals*, February 24, 1875, pp. 122-5).

370. On January 30, 1947, the Speaker tabled court judgements, including copies of court of appeal judgements, in connection with the imprisonment of Fred Rose (Cartier). The Prime Minister then moved that the Member had become incapable of fulfilling his parliamentary duties and that the Speaker be ordered to issue a warrant to the Chief Electoral Officer to make out a writ of election to fill the vacancy. The motion was adopted. See *Journals*, January 30, 1947, pp. 4-8.

371. In this instance, there was no conviction before a criminal court. In 1891, a private Member moved a motion to establish a select committee to enquire into allegations of corruption against the Member for Quebec West, Thomas McGreevy (*Journals*, May 11, 1891, pp. 55-60). The Member refused to answer questions in the committee and the committee subsequently found the Member guilty of the charges made against him (*Journals*, September 16, 1891, p. 512). After adopting the committee's report (*Journals*, September 21, 1891, pp. 522-3; September 22, 1891, p. 523; September 24, 1891, pp. 527-31), the House resolved, on September 29, 1891, that Thomas McGreevy be expelled from the House. This resolution was followed by the adoption of a motion ordering the Speaker to issue a new writ of election (*Journals*, September 29, 1891, p. 561).

372. Any disqualification imposed by the *Criminal Code* ceases when the sentence has been served or a pardon has been granted. See *Maingot*, 2nd ed., p. 212.

373. Unlike Louis Riel, Thomas McGreevy did not suffer a further expulsion, but was defeated in the general election of 1896.

5

Parliamentary Procedure

The authority of the Chair is no greater than the House wants it to be. When the rules are clear and offer precise guidance to the Speaker, the authority of the Chair is absolute and unquestioned, for this is the will of the House. On the other hand, when there are no rules to fall back on, the Speaker must proceed very cautiously indeed. The most the Chair can do is to lay the matter before the House which can then itself create a new precedent.

SPEAKER JEANNE SAUVÉ
(*Debates*, March 18, 1982, p. 15556)

Parliamentary procedure has been described as a "means of reaching decisions on when and how power shall be used".[1] According to such a definition, procedure is at once the "means" used to circumscribe the use of power and a "process" that legitimizes the exercise of, and opposition to, power. Parliamentary procedure has also been described as "a combination of two elements, the traditional and the democratic".[2] In other words, parliamentary procedure based on the Westminster model stems not only from an understanding and acceptance of how things have been done in the past, but is embedded in a particular culture that evolves along democratic principles. These principles, known as "parliamentary law",[3] were summarized in the

---

1. *Franks*, p. 116.

2. *Wilding and Laundy*, p. 605.

3. *Black's Law Dictionary*, 6th ed., St. Paul, Minn.: West Publishing Co., 1990, p. 1005, defines parliamentary law as, "The general body of enacted rules and recognized usages which governs the procedure of legislative assemblies. ..."

following manner by John George Bourinot, an authority on parliamentary procedure and Clerk of the Canadian House of Commons from 1890 to 1902:

> *The great principles that lie at the basis of English parliamentary law have ... been always kept steadily in view by the Canadian legislatures; these are: To protect the minority and restrain the improvidence and tyranny of the majority, to secure the transaction of public business in a decent and orderly manner, to enable every member to express his opinions within those limits necessary to preserve decorum and prevent an unnecessary waste of time, to give full opportunity for the consideration of every measure, and to prevent any legislative action being taken heedlessly and upon sudden impulse.*[4]

Commentators on Canadian parliamentary history have argued that, over the years, the ideal of "protecting the minority" has had to adapt to the modern dictates of an efficient legislative body.[5] Closure and time allocation rules, adopted in 1913 and 1969 respectively, as well as other rules adopted by the House, have long since given the government majority greater ability to advance its legislative program over the objections of the minority. Nevertheless, it remains true that parliamentary procedure is intended to ensure that there is a balance between the government's need to get its business through the House, and the opposition's responsibility to debate that business without completely immobilizing the proceedings of the House. In short, debate in the House is necessary, but it should lead to a decision in a reasonable time.

The proceedings of the House of Commons are regulated by a vast body of parliamentary rules and practices—practice being that part of procedure which developed spontaneously and became regarded as the usual or regular way of proceeding, though not written into the rules (the Standing Orders).[6] As described in Chapter 1, many of these rules and practices originated in the United Kingdom, others were inspired by pre-Confederation legislative assemblies[7] and subsequently adopted in Canada. According to Erskine May, "... some [of the forms and rules of practice] were no doubt invented in Parliament itself, but others have been traced to analogies in the medieval courts of law and in the councils of the Church".[8] Some rules have

---

4. *Bourinot*, 2nd ed., pp. 258-9.

5. According to C.E.S. Franks, three modern developments have led to a more rigid set of rules: the ever increasing amount of business before the House; the Member's job becoming a full-time occupation; and the increasing willingness on the part of the opposition to use dilatory tactics (*Franks*, pp. 128-9).

6. *May*, 22nd ed., p. 4.

7. In testimony to the validity of pre-Confederation experiences, a few days into the First Parliament, a special committee was appointed to assist the Speaker in framing permanent rules and regulations for the House and, in its deliberations, was to study the "Rules and Standing Orders of the Imperial House of Commons, of the Legislative Assembly of the late Province of Canada, and of the Houses of Assembly of the Provinces of Nova Scotia and New Brunswick" (*Journals*, November 15, 1867, p. 16).

8. *May*, 22nd ed., p. 4.

remained virtually unchanged for the last four hundred years,[9] others have evolved to become, in time, conventional practices. Finally, the origins of some of the earliest practices of parliamentary procedure "are lost in history".[10]

As will be seen in this chapter, the parliamentary procedures and practices of the Canadian House of Commons are founded on the Constitution and Statutes, the Standing Orders of the House, Speakers' rulings and House practice.

The Constitution and Statutes

Canadian parliamentary institutions took shape well over two hundred years ago. Successive British statutes adopted specifically for the colonies which were to form Canada came to prescribe, in increasing detail, several basic procedural provisions.[11] Many of these provisions were later included in the *Constitution Act, 1867,* which stated that Canada shall have a constitution similar in principle to that of the United Kingdom, which is what each of the founding provinces had before Confederation.

Those sections of the *Constitution Act, 1867* which can be traced back to earlier constitutional documents stipulate that on first assembling, the House must elect a Speaker,[12] that it must also proceed to elect a Speaker in the case of a vacancy in that office due to death, resignation or some other cause,[13] that the Speaker shall preside at all meetings of the House,[14] that the quorum of the House shall be 20 Members,[15] and that all requests for the raising or spending of money must originate in the House of Commons and must be recommended to the House by the Governor General.[16] These provisions are also found in the *Union Act, 1840.*[17] Other sections of the *Constitution Act, 1867* may be traced back even further. The provisions which stipulate that all questions arising in the House are to be decided by a simple majority,

---

9. See, for example, Sir Thomas Smith's 1560 "De Republica Anglorum", which contains an impressive list of procedural rules and practices that, after more than 430 years, have barely changed. Quoted in *Redlich*, Vol. I, pp. 26-51.

10. *Griffith and Ryle*, p. 176.

11. Most notably the *Constitutional Act, 1791,* R.S.C. 1985, Appendix II, No. 3, and the *Union Act, 1840,* R.S.C. 1985, Appendix II, No. 4.

12. *Constitution Act, 1867,* R.S.C. 1985, Appendix II, No. 5, s. 44. For more information on the election of the Speaker, see Chapter 7, "The Speaker and Other Presiding Officers of the House".

13. *Constitution Act, 1867,* R.S.C. 1985, Appendix II, No. 5, s. 45.

14. *Constitution Act, 1867,* R.S.C. 1985, Appendix II, No. 5, s. 46.

15. *Constitution Act, 1867,* R.S.C. 1985, Appendix II, No. 5, s. 48. For more information on the quorum, see Chapter 9, "Sittings of the House".

16. *Constitution Act, 1867,* R.S.C. 1985, Appendix II, No. 5, s. 54. For more information, see Chapter 18, "Financial Procedures".

17. R.S.C., 1985, Appendix II, No. 4, ss. XXXIII-IV, LVII.

with the Speaker having a casting vote in the case of a tie,[18] and that all Members must take a prescribed oath before being allowed to take their seat in the House[19] date back to the *Constitutional Act, 1791.*[20]

In some cases, the inclusion of a constitutional provision was predated by a practice already in place. Beginning in 1758, the Nova Scotia House of Assembly, for example, followed the practice of electing a Speaker as the first order of business of a new legislature, despite the absence of a constitutional provision to that effect.[21] Similarly, both Upper and Lower Canada's legislative assemblies followed the same practice of electing a Speaker[22] and had quorum provisions in their rules before a quorum of 20 was statutorily provided for in the *Union Act, 1840.*[23]

In other cases, a procedural difficulty experienced in a previous assembly led to the inclusion of specific constitutional provisions. For example, section 47 of the *Constitution Act, 1867,* which provided for the House to elect another of its Members to exercise the functions of the Speaker during the latter's absence, sought to anticipate the possible recurrence of a situation that had arisen when, on at least one occasion between 1840 and 1866, the Assembly of the Province of Canada had to adjourn due to the illness of the Speaker.[24]

Perhaps the most procedurally significant part of the *Constitution Act, 1867,* however, is that which provides a statutory basis for the privileges enjoyed by the House. *The Constitution Act* provides that "the privileges, immunities, and powers to be held, enjoyed and exercised" by the House and its Members are to be "defined by Act of the Parliament of Canada", with the proviso that such privileges, immunities and powers may not exceed those enjoyed by the British House of Commons and its Members.[25] The Canadian House of Commons thus acquired, as one of its more

---

18. *Constitution Act, 1867,* R.C.S. 1985, Appendix II, No. 5, s. 49. For more information on the casting vote, see Chapter 7, "The Speaker and Other Presiding Officers of the House".

19. *Constitution Act, 1867,* R.C.S. 1985, Appendix II, No. 5, s. 128. For more information on the oath taken by Members, see Chapter 4, "The House of Commons and Its Members".

20. *Constitutional Act, 1791,* R.C.S. 1985, Appendix II, No. 3, ss. XXVIII-IX.

21. At the first sitting of the Nova Scotia House of Assembly on October 2, 1758, a Speaker was chosen as the first item of business before the Speech from the Throne was read (*Votes of the House of Assembly,* p. 1). This was repeated in the following legislature (*Votes of the House of Assembly,* July 1, 1861, p. 1). No formal constitution was conferred on the colony of Nova Scotia; the constitution was always considered as being derived from the terms of the Royal Commissions to the Governors (see *Journals,* 1883, Sessional Paper No. 70 (Provincial Charters) pp. 7-8).

22. *Lower Canada Journals,* December 18, 1792, pp. 10-4; *Upper Canada Journals,* September 17, 1792, p. 1.

23. *Lower Canada Journals,* January 11, 1793, pp. 86-90; *Upper Canada Journals,* September 18, 1792, p. 3.

24. *Bourinot,* 2nd ed., p. 210.

25. R.S.C. 1985, Appendix II, No. 5, s. 18. For more information on parliamentary privilege, see Chapter 3, "Privileges and Immunities".

important privileges, the exclusive right to regulate its own internal affairs and to control its own agenda and proceedings.

The Parliament of Canada has therefore the constitutional authority not only to regulate its internal proceedings and establish rules of procedure, but also to enact a large number of procedurally important statutory provisions, many of which are found in the *Parliament of Canada Act*.[26] Of procedural significance for the House, this Act, for instance, provides for: the power of the House and its committees to administer oaths to witnesses appearing either at the Bar of the House or before a committee;[27] procedures to be followed when Members resign or when seats are otherwise vacated;[28] conflict of interest rules applicable to Members;[29] a Deputy Speaker's ability to act in the Speaker's absence;[30] the existence and remuneration of parliamentary secretaries;[31] the remuneration of Members of Parliament;[32] the existence and management of the Library of Parliament;[33] and the establishment of the Board of Internal Economy to act on all financial and administrative matters respecting the House.[34] There are, in addition to the *Parliament of Canada Act,* dozens of other statutes which oblige the House to undertake some action or which regulate some aspect of the proceedings of the House.[35]

The Standing Orders

The permanent written rules under which the House regulates its proceedings are known as the Standing Orders.[36] The continuing or "standing" nature of rules means that they do not lapse at the end of a session or parliament. Rather, they remain in effect until the House itself decides to suspend, change or repeal them. There are at present more than 150 Standing Orders, each of which constitutes a continuing order of the House for the governance and regulation of its proceedings. The detailed

---

26. R.S.C. 1985, c. P-1. Major amendments to the Act were adopted in 1991. See S.C. 1991, c. 20.

27. *Parliament of Canada Act*, R.S.C. 1985, c. P-1, s. 10.

28. *Parliament of Canada Act*, R.S.C. 1985, c. P-1, s. 25.

29. *Parliament of Canada Act*, R.S.C. 1985, c. P-1, s. 32.

30. *Parliament of Canada Act*, R.S.C. 1985, c. P-1, s. 42.

31. *Parliament of Canada Act*, R.S.C. 1985, c. P-1, s. 46.

32. *Parliament of Canada Act*, R.S.C. 1985, c. P-1, s. 55.

33. *Parliament of Canada Act*, R.S.C. 1985, c. P-1, s. 73.

34. *Parliament of Canada Act*, R.S.C. 1985, c. P-1, s. 50. For further information on the Board, see Chapter 6, "The Physical and Administrative Setting".

35. See, for example, *Access to Information Act*, R.S.C. 1985, c. A-1; *Canada Elections Act*, R.S.C. 1985, c. E-2; *Canadian Security Intelligence Service Act*, R.S.C. 1985, c. 23; *Electoral Boundaries Readjustment Act*, R.S.C. c. E-3; *International Centre for Human Rights and Democratic Development Act*, S.C. 1988, c. 64; *Official Languages Act*, R.S.C. 1985, c. 31, (4th Supp.) and *Referendum Act*, S.C. 1992, c. 30.

36. The Standing Orders are found in Appendix 15, "Standing Orders of the House of Commons".

description of the legislative process, the role of the Speaker, the nature of the parliamentary calendar and the rules governing the work of committees and private Members' business are some of the topics covered in the Standing Orders. The House declares these continuing orders to be Standing Orders when it formally adopts them, and it periodically issues them as a publication for the guidance and use of all Members.

When the House of Commons first met in 1867, the rules it adopted were largely those of the Legislative Assembly of the Province of Canada, itself created in 1840.[37] While it can be said that the Legislative Assembly of the Province of Canada obtained its rules from the assemblies of Upper and Lower Canada, created in 1791, the vast majority of these came from the House of Assembly of Lower Canada.[38] Of the many rules the Assembly of Lower Canada adopted in the first years of its existence, particularly in 1793,[39] more than 35 have survived virtually unchanged and are still in effect today in the House of Commons. A further 40 also pre-date Confederation.[40]

Since 1867, there have been countless reviews of the Standing Orders.[41] New Standing Orders have been adopted, while others have been significantly modified or deleted, leading on occasion to substantial renumbering. Furthermore, interpretations given to the older rules have been adapted over time to fit the modern context.[42] Occasionally, the adoption of a new Standing Order merely represents the codification of a long-standing practice of the House[43] or the permanent adoption of a provisional, sessional or special order. At other times, a rule is changed or added as a

---

37. The House adopted the following motion: "That until otherwise provided, the Rules, Regulations and Standing Orders of the Legislative Assembly of the late Province of Canada, be those of this House" (*Journals*, November 7, 1867, p. 5, and *Debates*, November 6, 1867, p. 4). See also *Journals*, December 20, 1867, pp. 115-25, and *Debates*, December 20, 1867, p. 333, for the first written rules of the House of Commons.

38. See *Province of Canada Debates*, June 15, 1841, pp. 22-3, and June 19, 1841, pp. 72-81. An analysis of these rules confirms their Lower Canadian origin. See *O'Brien,* pp. 255-6. For a description on how the customs and practices of Upper and Lower Canada were transformed into constitutional provisions, see David Hoffman and Norman Ward, *Bilingualism and Biculturalism in the House of Commons*, Ottawa: Queen's Printer, 1970, pp. 2-20.

39. *Lower Canada Journals,* January 1793.

40. A comparative analysis of the rules of the various assemblies may be found in *O'Brien*, Table 6.1, pp. 439-45.

41. The first amendments to the written rules occurred as early as four months after the adoption of the first Standing Orders (*Journals*, March 19, 1868, p. 144).

42. For example, in reply to a point of order arguing that the motion "When shall the bill be read a second time?" was a votable motion, Speaker Fraser ruled that it would not be appropriate to apply to current practices what may well have been appropriate one hundred years ago (*Debates*, May 24, 1988, pp. 15706, 15719-23).

43. For example, a long-standing practice had been for the House to arrange for longer hours of sitting prior to the start of the summer adjournment in order to complete or advance its business. In 1982, this practice was codified by adopting Standing Orders for the extension of sitting hours during the last 10 days in June. See Standing Order 27.

result of an incident or event which convinced the House to seek a way to avoid its repetition.[44]

As an indicator of the importance the House attaches to reviewing the Standing Orders, at the beginning of each Parliament a debate must be held on the following motion: "That this House takes note of the Standing Orders and procedures of the House and its committees".[45] In addition, the permanent mandate of the Standing Committee on Procedure and House Affairs[46] includes "the review of and report on the Standing Orders, procedure and practice in the House and its committees".[47] The Committee can make rule change recommendations as part of its continuing mandate or as the result of a specific order of reference.[48]

Although the means by which the House reviews the Standing Orders vary greatly, the Standing Orders may be added to, changed or repealed only by a decision of the House, which is arrived at either by way of consensus or by a simple majority vote on a motion moved by any Member of the House.[49]

---

44. There are two notable examples: First, when in December 1912, the government of Sir Robert Borden introduced a resolution on the Naval Aid Bill, it triggered one of the most bitter debates known to Parliament. After a particularly acrimonious two-week continuous sitting during a filibuster of the Bill early in 1913, the government brought forward a motion on April 9, 1913, to amend the Standing Orders. As a result of this incident, rules were adopted which, among other things, introduced closure. After an uncharacteristically long debate on the motion, the rules were adopted on April 23, 1913 (*Journals*, April 9, 1913, pp. 451-2; April 23, 1913, pp. 507-9; *Debates*, April 9, 1913, cols. 7388-414). Second, decades later, in what is known as the "Bell ringing" episode, changes were made to the Standing Orders in order to prevent a recurrence of the situation that took place in March 1982 when division bells were rung continuously for two weeks. For a detailed account of the political causes and procedural consequences of the Bell ringing episode, see Charles Robert, "Ringing in Reform: An Account of the Canadian Bells Episode of March 1982," *The Table*, Vol. LI, 1983, pp. 46-53.

45. Standing Order 51. For an example of such a debate, see *Debates*, April 21, 1998, p. 5863. For more detailed information about this proceeding, see Chapter 15, "Special Debates".

46. The Standing Committee on Procedure and Organization, as it was first called, was created on December 20, 1968 (*Journals*, December 20, 1968, pp. 554-74). Up to that point, it had not been uncommon for the Prime Minister, the Leader of the Opposition and the Speaker to sit on a special (or select) committee created to revise the rules or to chair such a committee. For example, Prime Minister Alexander Mackenzie sat on such a select committee in 1876, as did Prime Minister Sir Wilfrid Laurier in 1906 and 1909 (*Journals*, February 14, 1876, pp. 58-9; March 16, 1906, p. 61; December 14, 1909, p. 130). It was also common for the Prime Minister to take an active role in the process of amending the Standing Orders (see, for example, *Journals*, February 11, 1938, p. 60; September 18, 1945, p. 52).

47. Standing Order 108(3)(*a*)(iii).

48. See, for example, *Journals*, June 8, 1989, p. 340. On November 4, 1998, a report of the Standing Committee on Procedure and House Affairs concerning rule changes to Private Members' Business was concurred in (*Journals*, p. 1238). The next day, a point of order was raised concerning the implementation of those recommendations. Speaker Parent ruled that certain recommendations contained in the report would be implemented immediately since they were matters of practice or administration, but that other recommendations required substantive amendments to the Standing Orders which involved technical interpretations. He stated that when the House pronounced itself on a specific text, the Chair would be governed accordingly (*Debates*, November 5, 1998, p. 9923). The House adopted such a motion to amend the Standing Orders on November 30, 1998 (*Journals*, pp. 1327-9).

49. See Speaker Fraser's ruling, *Debates*, April 9, 1991, pp. 19236-7.

On many occasions, a special committee has been established with a mandate to suggest revisions to the rules and report its recommendations to the House. These recommendations, presented in the House in the form of a report, were often debated on a motion to concur in the report. If the House concurred in such a report, the Standing Orders were immediately modified. The content of the report was sometimes also used as the basis for further discussions leading to changes to the rules.[50]

In other cases, the Standing Orders have been amended through the adoption of a government motion by unanimous consent; such a motion can at times resemble the recommendations of a procedure committee.[51] The motion can also be a government initiative for which proper notice has been given and which appears on the *Order Paper* under "Government Business".[52] More often than not, however, procedural changes are the result of a broad consensus among Members of all parties and are readily adopted without debate.[53] That being said, since 1867, there have been occasions when controversial proposals have led to lengthy debates where the government used its majority to amend the Standing Orders.[54]

Finally, changes to the Standing Orders have also been made through the adoption of a motion by a private Member[55] and the concurrence in a report presented by a joint committee of the Senate and House of Commons.[56]

Besides the permanent Standing Orders, the House may adopt other types of written rules for limited periods of time. Provisional Standing Orders are individual Standing Orders adopted for a specific period of time which does not correspond to

---

50. See, for example, the Special Committee on Procedure, *Journals*, September 24, 1968, pp. 67-8 (Committee established), and December 20, 1968, pp. 554-79 (Fourth and Fifth Reports concurred in), and the Special Committee on the Reform of the House of Commons, *Journals*, December 5, 1984, pp. 153-4 (Committee established), and June 27, 1985, pp. 903, 910-9 (amendments to Standing Orders adopted).

51. See, for example, *Journals*, June 27, 1985, pp. 910-9, and *Debates*, June 27, 1985, pp. 6325-7. This government motion, adopted by unanimous consent, was inspired by the First Report of the Special Committee on the Reform of the House of Commons, presented on December 20, 1984 (*Journals*, p. 211).

52. See, for example, *Journals*, February 7, 1994, pp. 112-20; June 12, 1998, pp. 1027-8.

53. For examples of changes adopted by unanimous consent without debate, see *Journals*, October 10, 1997, p. 107; March 10, 1998, p. 549; and November 30, 1998, pp. 1327.

54. Examples include the adoption of the closure rule in 1913 (*Journals*, April 23, 1913, pp. 507-9), the time allocation provisions in 1969 (*Journals*, July 24, 1969, pp. 1393-1402) and a series of procedural changes in 1991 (*Journals*, April 11, 1991, pp. 2898-932). In the 1969 and 1991 examples, closure was imposed to bring the debate to an end and force a decision. In 1913, the previous question was moved, thus precluding amendments and limiting debate to the main motion.

55. See, for example, *Journals*, April 9, 1997, pp. 1366-8.

56. See Senate *Journals*, June 3, 1903, p. 156, and House of Commons *Journals*, June 11, 1903, p. 270; October 10, 1903, p. 644.

the duration of a Parliament or a Session.[57] They may be adopted on an experimental basis,[58] extended provisionally, dropped, or eventually made permanent.

Sessional Orders are intended to be temporary and remain in effect only for the duration of the session in which they are adopted. Sessional Orders may be renewed from session to session, and some eventually become Standing Orders.[59]

The House may also adopt special orders in addition to the Standing, Provisional, and Sessional Orders which form the collected body of written rules. A frequently used instrument for the conduct of House business, special orders do not modify the "written" Standing Orders. Since they routinely concern the business of the House and are thus often moved without notice, following consultations, they are often adopted without debate by unanimous consent. They may apply to a single occasion or to such period of time as may be specified.[60] Some special orders over time have become Standing Orders.[61]

Finally, some Standing Orders explicitly allow the House to suspend the operation of other Standing Orders.[62] It is also common for the House, at any given time, to set aside its rules with the unanimous consent of all Members then present in the House, so that something can be done which would otherwise be inconsistent with the Standing Orders.[63] The House does this, for example, when it wants a bill to pass

---

57. See, for example, *Journals*, November 29, 1982, p. 5400.

58. Speaking to a motion to adopt provisional Standing Orders in 1982, the President of the Privy Council summed up the nature of procedural reform: "I would like to invite all Members of Parliament to make this experiment a success and not to look for anomalies or weaknesses in this proposal, since it is not perfect as we recognize ourselves and as I think our friends opposite and the members of the Committee also recognize. The rules proposed to this House have weaknesses and unclear elements, and I believe that for a destructive mind, it would be very easy although childlish [sic] to prevent this experiment from being positive and successful. I therefore call on the intellectual honesty of all Members and I want to assure them of the sincerity of the Government in implementing the proposed changes so that this experiment can be a success and result in fact in permanent changes to which adjustments may be made" (*Debates*, November 29, 1982, pp. 21071-2).

59. As an example, from 1867 to 1876 the present Standing Order 23, concerning bribery in elections, was put forward at the beginning of each session as a Sessional Order, before finally becoming a permanent rule. See *Debates*, February 10, 1876, p. 3.

60. See, for example, *Journals*, February 2, 1994, p. 96.

61. Standing Order 86.1, concerning the reinstatement of private Members' bills, adopted in November 1998, is essentially the same as the special order adopted in March 1996 (see *Journals*, March 4, 1996, pp. 34-5; November 30, 1998, pp. 1327-9).

62. Standing Order 53, for example, states: "In relation to any matter that the government considers to be of an urgent nature, a Minister of the Crown may, at any time when the Speaker is in the Chair, propose a motion to suspend any Standing or other Order of this House relating to the need for notice and to the hours and days of sitting."

63. Typically, a motion seeking to circumvent the provisions of existing Standing Orders is worded thus: "That notwithstanding any Standing Order or usual practice of this House ..." See, for example, *Journals*, June 22, 1994, p. 657; June 8, 1998, pp. 947-8; February 2, 1999, p. 1457.

all stages in one day, a procedure which would otherwise contravene the rules.[64] Furthermore, the House can adopt a Special Order to supersede a previously adopted Special Order.[65] The Standing Orders also provide for the House to proceed in situations where unanimous consent has been denied, but where the overwhelming majority of Members nevertheless agree to proceed with the action contemplated.[66]

In the hierarchy of parliamentary procedure, just as statutory provisions cannot set aside constitutional provisions, Standing Orders cannot set aside statutory law. Only Parliament can enact or amend statutory provisions; the House of Commons can adopt its own rules as long as they respect the written constitution and statutory law.

Speakers' Rulings

The Speaker has been duty-bound to decide all questions of procedure since representative assemblies were first established in the colonies which were to form Canada.[67] Just as case law (the body of judge-made law) is an important part of the common-law system, rulings (the body of Speaker-made parliamentary law) are an important part of our parliamentary system. Over the years, the sum total of rulings from Speakers has helped shape the way in which the House conducts its business.[68] Successive Speakers have been called upon to decide how rules should apply and, through rulings, have either settled issues or encouraged the House,[69] the Government,[70] or the Board of Internal Economy[71] to take steps to resolve them. Prior to 1965, the rulings of Speakers were subject to an appeal and could be overturned by

---

64. Standing Order 71. See *Journals*, October 1, 1997, p. 56; November 24, 1997, p. 249; May 28, 1998, p. 902.

65. In June 1998, for example, the House adopted a Special Order to undo the provisions of a previously adopted Special Order and, in so doing, to revert to the provisions of the Standing Orders. The motion read: "That, notwithstanding the Special Order of Monday, February 9, 1998, the length of speeches and the rotation between parties during the consideration of the Business of Supply on Tuesday, June 9, 1998, shall be as provided in the Standing Orders and in the usual practice of the House in considering Government Orders" (*Journals*, June 8, 1998, p. 948).

66. Standing Order 56.1. For further information, see Chapter 14, "The Curtailment of Debate".

67. Standing Order 10. The Canadian origins of this British-inspired rule can be traced back to the rules of the Legislative Assembly of Lower Canada in 1793: "The Speaker shall preserve Order and Decorum, and shall decide Questions of Order, subject to an appeal to the House" and "When the Speaker is called upon to explain a point of order or practice, he is to state the rule applicable to the case, without argument or comment."

68. While the totality of Speakers' rulings from 1867 onward has not been compiled in any systematic way, a collection of selected decisions has been published for every Speaker since 1966. The collection includes Speakers Lamoureux, Jerome, Sauvé, Francis, Bosley and Fraser.

69. See, for example, *Debates*, March 1, 1966, pp. 1939-40; December 1, 1986, p. 1647; June 16, 1994, pp. 5437-40; March 16, 1998, pp. 4902-3.

70. See, for example, *Debates*, February 2, 1982, p. 14899; November 16, 1982, pp. 20702-3; October 12, 1983, pp. 27944-5.

71. See, for example, *Debates*, May 2, 1995, pp. 12072-4; April 23, 1998, pp. 6035-7; December 3, 1998, pp. 10826-31.

the House;[72] since then, Members have not been allowed to question a decision of the Chair.[73]

A distinction must be made between "rulings" and "statements" made by the Speaker. Rulings deal with the procedural acceptability of some matter before the House which, unless otherwise specified, serve as precedents to govern future proceedings. They, more often than not, address procedural issues raised on a point of order or a question of privilege and seek to give directions to the House. Statements, on the other hand, seek to convey information or clarification to Members of the House.[74] Not every statement is a ruling and Speakers have often explicitly stated that certain procedures, although permitted in certain circumstances, should not be interpreted as precedents.[75] Speaker Fraser summed up the fine balancing act that is often involved in adapting old rules to new situations: "When interpreting the rules of procedure, the Speaker must take account not only of their letter but of their spirit and be guided by the most basic rule of all, that of common sense."[76]

In arriving at a decision on a procedural point, the Speaker may draw on a full range of procedural information and examine the precedents to determine how the Standing Orders have been applied and interpreted in the past. The Standing Orders, though a vital reference, constitute a comparatively small part of the much larger body of House of Commons procedure and practice that the Speaker will consult in preparing a ruling. The primary records of the House, the *Journals* and *Debates,* are the richest repository of information on precedents, practices and usages as well as being the most reliable.[77] Finally, while Speakers must take the Constitution and

---

72. For further information, see Chapter 7, "The Speaker and Other Presiding Officers of the House".

73. Standing Order 10.

74. See Chapter 7, " The Speaker and Other Presiding Officers of the House".

75. In 1987, in a ruling on the acceptability of a motion moved during Routine Proceedings, the Speaker ruled the motion in order but then went on to say that this ruling should not "be regarded as a precedent for all time, and that in other circumstances the Chair might well disallow such a motion" (*Debates*, April 14, 1987, pp. 5119-24). For other examples, see *Debates*, October 1, 1987, p. 9528; October 16, 1987, pp. 10091-2; March 14, 1988, p. 13685; February 17, 1999, p. 12046.

76. *Debates*, April 14, 1987, p. 5121.

77. In the 1781 preface to the first edition of his *Collection of Precedents of the British Parliament,* Hatsell wrote: "It is unnecessary again to put the Reader in mind, that this Work, as well as the former of "Cases of Privilege of Parliament," are to be considered in no other light than as Indexes to refer him to the Journals at large, and to other Historical Records; from whence alone can be derived a perfect knowledge of the Law and Proceedings of Parliament" (*Hatsell*, p. v). Josef Redlich wrote: "It is no mere chance that the journals of the House began from the end of the sixteenth century to be compiled with increasing care and detail. It was the outcome of the anxiety of the Commons to maintain their practice in each individual case and, above all, to take care that precedents as to procedure and privilege were safeguarded against forgetfulness and preserved for future use" (*Redlich*, Vol. I, p. 44).

statutes into account when preparing a ruling, numerous Speakers have explained that it is not up to the Speaker to rule on the "constitutionality" or "legality" of measures before the House.[78]

While good procedure requires that there be consistency in the interpretation of practice and in the application of the Standing Orders,[79] Speakers have never shied away from creating new precedents when faced with an apparent contradiction between Standing Orders and contemporary values. In this way, Speakers have declared past rules or Standing Orders to be redundant[80] and have often invited the House to ponder the consequences of things such as new technologies on Members' privileges.[81]

In arriving at a decision, Speakers will also review cornerstone events of the past, known as precedents, which may be useful in applying to a new situation. Precedent has been defined as "a previous decision by the Chair, or a well-established procedure or usage which serves as an authority or guide when a similar point or circumstance arises in Parliament".[82] Determining what is or is not a precedent is not always straightforward. Speaker Fraser once said that "a precedent is something that happened once upon a time and that everyone decided to follow ... in legal terms, it is usually the consequence of a decision made after argument has been proffered to

78. In a 1991 ruling, Speaker Fraser made that point abundantly clear: "The Speaker has no role in interpreting matters of either a constitutional or legal matter." See *Debates*, April, 9, 1991, pp. 19233-4. See also, for example, *Debates*, July 8, 1969, p. 10955, and October 1, 1990, p. 13620.

79. While it is for the House to determine what constitutes a "good" rule, good procedure must be binding and "have mandatory effect on those persons or parties to which they apply"; must be "predictable and no business should be sprung on the House without adequate notice" and, finally, must be "clear and readily comprehensible by all those whom they effect, including those charged with their interpretation and enforcement" (*Griffith and Ryle*, pp. 172-4).

80. In a ruling concerning the use of Standing Order 39(6) which deals with written questions, Speaker Fraser suggested that the said Standing Order might have "survived so long unchanged because it had remained unused for the past 60 years; that its use in today's context may not be what was intended; and that it no longer fits the conditions of the present House of Commons." He went on to add that new elements "which were incorporated in the Standing Orders ... have practically eliminated the kind of abuse" Standing Order 39(6) sought to address. See *Debates*, June 14, 1989, pp. 3023-6, and in particular p. 3025.

81. Over the last few years, for example, there have been a number of points of order and questions of privilege dealing with noted discrepancies between printed and electronic official records. In one case, the Speaker ruled that the difference between the printed and electronic *Hansard* was an editorial error and did not constitute a question of privilege, but also pointed out that because the larger issue of the status of the electronic *Hansard* had never been investigated, the issue warranted an examination by the Standing Committee on Elections, Privileges and Procedure. See *Debates*, June 6, 1986, pp. 14055-6. The Speaker has also ruled on the use of cellular phones in the House (*Debates*, April 27, 1993, p. 18495).

82. *Wilding and Laundy*, p. 570.

the Chair [...] on a certain point".[83] The mere occurrence of an event does not make it a precedent, and Speakers have on occasion ruled that a special circumstance justifies a deviation from a known precedent.[84]

At times, the Speaker will allow Members to address the issue raised to give them an opportunity to present facts that might help shed some light on the case at hand. At other times, a ruling will be made immediately without Members' intervention. It is left to the Speaker to determine what method he or she will use.

While previous rulings and statements always serve as important and reliable guides, and while Speakers invariably rely on the decisions of their predecessors, every new situation is different and is examined on its own merits. A great many practices remain uncodified, although some are frequently defined and made explicit in Speakers' rulings and statements.

Practice

The House's often unique methods of proceeding are the result of centuries of practice[85]—the unwritten rules of procedure which developed over time and came to be accepted as the normal way of proceeding. The first representative assemblies on Canadian soil were inspired mainly by British parliamentary tradition,[86] and to a lesser degree by American practice.[87] Until recently, the British influence was

---

83. *Debates*, November 6, 1986, p. 1153.

84. Often, by unanimous consent, the House agrees to proceed in a way which would otherwise be ruled inadmissible by the Speaker (see, for example, *Debates*, October 1, 1987, p. 9528; March 14, 1988, p. 13685). Occasionally, the Speaker may make a decision which breaks with past rulings but which is not to be regarded as a precedent (see, for example, Speaker Fraser's ruling, *Debates*, April 14, 1987, pp. 5119-24, and in particular pp. 5120-2).

85. *May* distinguishes between modern and ancient pratice and describes in the following terms their relationship: "[T]he function of modern practice, besides that of applying ... the rules of the ancient usage to changing conditions, is to supplement the standing orders and to harmonize them with each other and with the general body of practice" (*May*, 22nd ed., p. 5).

86. Soon after their establishment, the assemblies of both Lower and Upper Canada chose to be guided by British practice in unprovided cases. See *Lower Canada Journals*, December 22, 1792, p. 48, and January 16, 1793, p. 124, and *Upper Canada Journals*, June 22, 1802, p. 286.

87. With regard to American influence in Upper Canada, *O'Brien* explains: "Jefferson's *Manual*, disguised as Thomson's *Manual*, became the Assembly's chief procedural textbook in 1828. The Speaker was not wigged, as in Britain: instead he wore a cocked hat." Other examples of American influence include the use of pages in the Chamber, roll-call votes and desks for Members (*O'Brien*, p. 114, see also pp. 62-4 and 407-8). It is important to note that in 1793, when Lower Canada's Assembly adopted 71 rules, the British House had a mere six Standing Orders dealing with public business, only one of which was adopted as is by the Lower Canadian Assembly. The rules were not copied from any one source, but rather were inspired by such authorities as Hatsell's *Precedents* (British), Jefferson's *Manual* (American) and Petyt's *Lex Parliamentaria* (British) (see *O'Brien*, Chapter 3, note 40).

explicitly recognized by the House in its Standing Orders[88] and, to this day, in instances where internal precedents do not provide the necessary guidance, the Speaker is given full authority to go beyond the House's jurisprudence "in cases not provided for hereinafter".[89] The Speaker may thus turn to provincial or foreign precedents, typically those of Commonwealth legislative bodies, "so far as they may be applicable to the House".[90]

In some areas (e.g., the conduct of Question Period), almost all procedures are based on practice augmented by decisions of the Chair;[91] in other areas, some practices are born without the active participation of the Speaker.[92]

There has been a tendency for the House to codify in the Standing Orders many procedures which have originated and evolved as unwritten practices. In many ways, this has resolved issues which for many years had to be revisited by the Speaker periodically. For example, although, for many years, representatives of the recognized parties had been permitted to respond to ministerial statements, it was only in 1964 that the practice was written into the Standing Orders.[93] A more recent example is the adoption of a Standing Order incorporating a practice that can be traced back to the earliest days of Confederation: the pairing of Members unable to be present in the House for recorded decisions.[94]

The Authorities

The rules and procedures of the House are far more complex than they would appear to be on the surface. This complexity, illustrated by the growth in the number of Standing Orders, an ever-increasing number of Speakers' rulings and statements, and the whole body of unwritten practice, has led to the publication over the years of various works on parliamentary procedure which have come to be referred to as

---

88. Until 1986, Standing Order 1 read as follows: "In all cases not provided for hereafter or by sessional or other orders, the usages and customs of the House of Commons of the United Kingdom of Great Britain and Northern Ireland as in force at the time shall be followed so far as they may be applicable to this House."

89. Standing Order 1.

90. Standing Order 1. In March 1998, in the course of ruling on a question of privilege, Speaker Parent stated: "I have looked carefully at practice here in the House of Commons and in other Canadian legislatures: in the House of Commons of the United Kingdom and in other Westminster-style Parliaments." See *Debates*, March 16, 1998, p. 4902.

91. See Chapter 11, "Questions".

92. The division of speaking time between two Members provides a good illustration of a practice which became a Standing Order without much intervention from the Speaker. See, for example, *Debates*, March 14, 1991, p. 18439. Standing Order 43(2) was adopted on April 11, 1991 (*Journals*, p. 2910).

93. See the Special Committee on Procedure and Organization, Third Report, concurred in on May 7, 1964 (*Journals*, p. 297, and *Debates*, pp. 3007-10, particularly the comments of Stanley Knowles).

94. See Standing Order 44.1, which was adopted by the House on April 11, 1991 (*Journals*, pp. 2910-1). For historical information on the former practice of pairing, see *Dawson*, pp. 188-90.

"the Authorities". In their own time, these books have attempted to collect and organize the traditions, precedents and procedures of our Parliament. The House has relied primarily on Arthur Beauchesne's *Parliamentary Rules and Forms of the House of Commons of Canada* and Sir John George Bourinot's *Parliamentary Procedure and Practice in the Dominion of Canada* (last published in 1916). Other works have also proved useful in understanding the procedures of the House, notably William F. Dawson's *Procedure in the Canadian House of Commons*, C.E.S. Franks' *The Parliament of Canada*, Joseph Maingot's *Parliamentary Privilege in Canada*, John B. Stewart's *The Canadian House of Commons: Procedure and Reform*, and Norman Ward's *Dawson's The Government of Canada*. When these and other sources have been insufficient to help with a problem, reference may be made to Erskine May's *Treatise on the Law, Privileges, Proceedings and Usage of Parliament* as a guide to relevant current British procedures.

The Relationship Between Procedural Sources

Within parliamentary procedure, a distinction is made between those procedures the House may alter alone, and those it may not. Procedural provisions contained in the *Constitution Act* and in various statutes cannot be modified by the House acting independently. A change to the constitutional provisions affecting any part of the House must be made in accordance with the amending formulae contained in the *Constitution Act, 1982* and requires, at a minimum, the passage of an Act of Parliament.[95] Similarly, only Parliament may enact or amend a statutory provision which affects House procedure. Therefore, where the written constitution applies in relation to the House, it takes priority over statutory provisions applicable to the House. Statutory provisions, in turn, may not be set aside in favour of rules or orders made by the House alone. The same reasoning applies to standing, sessional and special orders, which necessarily override practices and precedents, always provided that such orders must be interpreted not in isolation but in the context of their past application. Where there are no express rules or orders, the House turns to its own jurisprudence, as interpreted by the Speaker, who examines the *Journals* and *Debates* of the House to determine which rulings of past Speakers and which practices and precedents should be applied. In situations not provided for by the practices and precedents of the House, the Standing Orders permit the Speaker to have recourse to the practices and precedents of other jurisdictions, both in and outside Canada, so far as they may be applicable.[96] More and more, the Speaker and procedural advisors are looking to the practices of the provinces, the United Kingdom and those countries possessing Westminster-style Parliaments, particularly Australia, India and New Zealand.

---

95. *Constitution Act, 1982,* R.S.C. 1985, Appendix II, No. 44, Part V.

96. Standing Order 1.

6

The Physical and Administrative Setting

There is no such thing as a bad seat in the House of Commons.
SPEAKER GILBERT PARENT
(*Debates*, September 30, 1998, p. 8585)

While the House of Commons conducts its business in accordance with established procedures and practices, it does so in its own unique physical setting and under administrative structures of its own making. These two factors are an important backdrop to the procedural operations of the House. This chapter provides information about Ottawa as the seat of government, the Parliament Buildings, the House of Commons Chamber and the administrative framework through which are provided an array of facilities and services dedicated to the operations of the House and the needs of its Members.

Ottawa as the Seat of Government

In 1857, Queen Victoria chose Ottawa as the seat of government for the Province of Canada. This followed years of intense rivalry among the elected representatives of the pre-Confederation colonies of Upper and Lower Canada, who could not agree on a permanent site.[1] The itinerant Legislative Assembly of the Province of Canada met in several different cities, beginning with Kingston in 1841. In 1844, it moved to Montreal where it remained until

---

1. For a complete history of the selection of Ottawa as a capital city, see Wilfrid Eggleston, *The Queen's Choice,* Ottawa: Queen's Printer, 1961, ch. 5.

1849 when the legislative building was burned by rioters.[2] Thereafter a system was adopted under which the assembly met alternately at Quebec and Toronto before finally settling into its permanent home in Ottawa, where it met for the first time in 1866. With the advent of Confederation the following year, the capital of the Province of Canada became the national capital, in compliance with the *Constitution Act, 1867,* Section 16 of which states that "the seat of Government of Canada shall be Ottawa".[3] Accordingly, the Parliament of Canada assembled in Ottawa on November 6, 1867, for the First Session of the First Parliament.

The Parliament Buildings and Grounds

LOCATION AND DISPOSITION

The Parliament Buildings are situated on a cliff, originally a primeval forest of beech and hemlock whose southern approach consisted of dense cedar swamps and a beaver meadow. The site,[4] which was formerly the location of a military barracks, overlooks the Ottawa River. It is bounded by Wellington Street to the south (the Wellington Wall, which was built in 1872, stands on the north side of Wellington Street, separating the lawns and buildings of Parliament Hill from the city street), the Rideau Canal to the east, the Ottawa River to the north and Bank Street to the west, and has the legal name of Parliament Hill.[5] (See Figure 6.1, The Parliamentary Precinct.) The original complex of buildings comprised the Parliament Building—fronted by a tower and backed by the Library of Parliament, a 16-sided polygonal structure—as well as two extant departmental buildings styled East Block and West Block. The Parliament Building, including the tower, was destroyed by fire on February 3, 1916.[6] Only the library survived intact, thanks to an employee who closed the great iron doors connecting the

---

2. During a time of political and economic crisis, protest coalesced against the Governor's assent to the Rebellion Losses Bill (compensating losses suffered in Lower Canada during the 1837 rebellion). There were days of rioting, in the course of which an angry mob invaded the House of Assembly. The building burned on April 25, 1849, and very little was saved. (See J.M.S. Careless, *The Union of the Canadas,* Toronto: McClelland and Stewart Limited, 1967, pp. 122-6.)

3. The choice of Ottawa as national capital is reflected in the Quebec resolutions of 1864, adopted by delegates from the provinces of Canada, Nova Scotia and New Brunswick, and the colonies of Newfoundland and Prince Edward Island and the London resolutions of 1866, adopted by delegates from the provinces of Canada, Nova Scotia and New Brunswick. (The Quebec Resolutions, 1864, and the London Resolutions, 1866, may be found in M. Ollivier, *British North America Acts and Selected Statutes, 1867-1962*, Ottawa: Queen's Printer, 1962, p. 47, s. 52, and p. 58, s. 51, respectively.)

4. For a description of the original site, see *Eggleston*, p. 83.

5. *Parliament of Canada Act*, R.S.C. 1985, c. P-1, s. 80.

6. The report of a Royal Commission, appointed to inquire into the origin of the fire, was presented to the House later that year (*Journals*, May 16, 1916, p. 388). The commissioners were "... of the opinion that there are many circumstances connected with this fire that lead to a strong suspicion of incendiarism", but as the inquiry was taken no further, the true cause of the fire remains a mystery. The report noted that the fire started in the Reading Room, which was furnished and fitted in "highly inflammable" varnished white pine, and where many newspapers and files were kept. See also Jane Varkaris and Lucile Finsten, *Fire on Parliament Hill!* The Boston Mills Press, 1988.

Figure 6.1   *The Parliamentary Precinct*

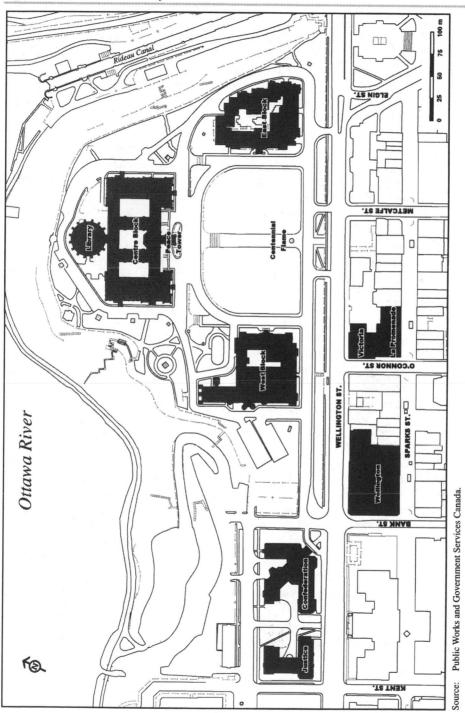

Source: Public Works and Government Services Canada.

library to the rest of the building. For the next four years, both Houses of Parliament met several city blocks south of Parliament Hill in the Victoria Memorial Museum, now called the Canadian Museum of Nature.[7] In 1920, sittings resumed in the new Centre Block, which was built on the same site as the old building.[8] A new tower, called the Peace Tower in commemoration of Canada's human and material contributions to the First World War, was also built.[9]

While originally sufficient to house the entire parliamentary and governmental apparatus, the Centre, East and West Blocks ceased to provide adequate accommodation as the size, complexity and functions of Parliament and government multiplied. Today, government departments are housed in office buildings throughout the National Capital Region and elsewhere in the country. The parliamentary precinct—those premises which both Houses of Parliament "occupy from time to time for their corporate purposes"[10]—has expanded to include several other buildings in the immediate vicinity of Parliament Hill.[11]

The House of Commons and Senate Chambers are located in the Centre Block. Offices for Members of Parliament are located in the Centre Block, East Block and West Block, as well as the Confederation Building, the Justice Building and the Wellington Building. Committee rooms are found in the Centre Block, East and West Blocks, La Promenade Building and Wellington Building. Offices for House staff and parliamentary services are found in these and other locations in the capital.

The grounds around Parliament Hill have undergone several stylistic transformations since Confederation but have always included a wide central walk leading from the gateway at the south end of the grounds to the main entrance at the base of the tower. At the southern end of the walkway is a fountain; in its centre burns the Centennial Flame, which was lit on New Year's Eve 1966, to mark the first hundred years of Confederation (1867-1967).[12] The fountain is a 12-sided truncated pyramid, each side holding a bronze shield bearing the coat of arms of a province or territory.

---

7. Arrangements were quickly made and remarkably the House began sitting in the Museum's auditorium the day after the fire (*Journals*, February 4, 1916, p. 53). The Senate, which was not sitting at the time of the fire, was accommodated in what had been the Geological Department (*Senate Debates*, February 8, 1916, p. 50).

8. When the session opened on February 26, 1920, the Senate Chamber was not ready. The Senate met in the House of Commons, where the Speech from the Throne was read, and the House met in the Railway Committee Room; thereafter, until the Senate Chamber was ready, the Commons met in its Chamber and the Senate in the Railway Committee Room (*Senate Debates*, February 26, 1920, p. 1; February 27, 1920, p. 2; see also pages 5 and 6 of the *Report of the Minister of Public Works for the Fiscal Year Ended March 31, 1919*, tabled on March 10, 1920 (*Journals*, p. 39)).

9. On being occupied in 1920, the building was still in an unfinished state. It was completed in 1922, the Peace Tower in 1927.

10. *Maingot*, 2nd ed., p. 163.

11. The principal ones are the Confederation, Justice, Wellington, Victoria and La Promenade buildings.

12. The design and the construction of the fountain were the work of the then Department of Public Works. The flame was originally conceived as a project for the Centennial year and the intention was to extinguish it at the end of 1967. However, in response to popular demand, the government decided to continue the flame in perpetuity (*Debates*, December 11, 1967, p. 5260; December 12, 1967, pp. 5358-9).

Water flows continuously around the shields; the flame, fed by natural gas, burns through the water and gives the impression of the flame dancing over the water. Coins tossed into the fountain are retrieved to fund the Centennial Flame Research Award Fund. [13]

The grounds of Parliament Hill are the site of 14 bronze portrait statues, erected between 1885 and 1992. [14] Represented are seven former Prime Ministers (John A. Macdonald, Alexander Mackenzie, Wilfrid Laurier, Robert Borden, William Lyon Mackenzie King, John Diefenbaker and Lester B. Pearson), five Fathers of Confederation (George-Étienne Cartier, a joint memorial to Robert Baldwin and Louis-Hippolyte Lafontaine, George Brown and Thomas D'Arcy McGee) and two monarchs (Victoria and Elizabeth II). [15]

Title, Management, Care and Control

Given Parliament's right to administer its own affairs free from interference, including overseeing the areas used in the performance of official parliamentary functions, the Speakers of the two Houses have traditionally held authority and control over accommodation and services within the parliamentary precinct. [16] At Confederation, Parliament Hill (including the adjacent parcel of land on which the Confederation Building stands) was transferred by the imperial government to Canada as "ordnance property". [17] As such, control of the grounds and construction, repair and maintenance of the buildings fell under the general mandate of the government department responsible for federal buildings and property. [18] The National Capital Commission, a federal body whose mandate is the improvement and beautification of the national

---

13. *Centennial Flame Research Award Act*, S.C. 1991, c. 17. The Act originated as a private Member's bill introduced by Patrick Boyer (Etobicoke–Lakeshore); it established the Fund which is administered by the parliamentary committee whose mandate includes matters relating to the status of disabled persons. The Fund provides awards to disabled persons to conduct research and prepare reports on the contributions of disabled persons to the public life of Canada. Reports prepared by award recipients are presented in the House by the Chair of the committee. See *Journals*, June 14, 1993, p. 3204; December 13, 1994, p. 1043; April 23, 1997, pp. 1515-6; May 12, 1998, p. 775; June 10, 1999, p. 2090.

14. Originally planned for Parliament Hill, the statue of Louis St-Laurent (Prime Minister from 1948 to 1957) was erected in 1975 in front of the Supreme Court of Canada building and looks towards Parliament Hill, which is nearby. This location was considered to be in keeping with St-Laurent's distinguished legal career and service as Minister of Justice and Attorney General prior to becoming Prime Minister. For further information about the statues on and near Parliament Hill, see *Statues of Parliament Hill*, National Capital Commission, 1986.

15. The monument to Elizabeth II is the only monument on Parliament Hill which was not erected posthumously. It was unveiled in 1992, the year of the fortieth anniversary of her accession to the Throne.

16. For information on Parliament Hill and the precincts of the Houses of Parliament, see *Maingot*, 2nd ed., pp. 163-78.

17. *Constitution Act, 1867*, R.S.C. 1985, Appendix II, No. 5, s. 108, The Third Schedule, clause 9. See also *Maingot*, 2nd ed., pp. 168-9.

18. Formerly the Department of Public Works, it was reorganized and renamed in 1993-94; see *Department of Public Works and Government Services Act*, S.C. 1996, c. 16.

capital region,[19] is charged with the landscaping and upkeep of the grounds of Parliament Hill.

THE CENTRE BLOCK

Built in a modern Gothic revival style, the rectangular Centre Block is some 144 metres long by 75 metres deep, and six stories high.[20] More than 25 different types of stone and marble were used in the building's construction; however, much of the exterior is Nepean sandstone, quarried near Ottawa, and its interior walls are sheeted with Tyndall limestone from Manitoba. Inside, the history and traditions of Canada are reflected in many stone carvings which have been the ongoing work of over 60 sculptors and carvers since 1916.

The main entrance to the Centre Block is located at the base of the Peace Tower, where a broad flight of steps leads into a stately Gothic archway. The main doors open onto stairs leading up into the octagonal Confederation Hall (also called the Rotunda) and the Hall of Honour leading to the Library of Parliament (see Figure 6.2, Floor Plan of the Centre Block). In the centre of the Confederation Hall is a massive stone column inscribed in memory of the Canadian soldiers who fought in World War I. On the eastern end of the Centre Block is found the Senate Chamber and on the western end, the House of Commons Chamber. Each House has a distinct entrance to the building for its Members.

PEACE TOWER

The Peace Tower with its four-faced clock is the focal point of the Parliament Buildings. It commemorates Canada's contributions to World War I and houses on its third floor the Memorial Chamber, which holds the books of remembrance naming those Canadians who gave their lives in each of the wars in which Canada has been involved. An enclosed observation deck below the clock offers a view in all directions of the National Capital Region. The Tower, which is 92.2 metres high, is surmounted by a mast from which the flag is flown.[21]

The Peace Tower also contains a carillon of 53 bells, inaugurated on July 1, 1927, in honour of the Diamond Jubilee of Confederation. Regular recitals are given by the carillonneur. The bells chime every quarter-hour, controlled by a mechanism connected to the clock.

---

19. *National Capital Act*, R.S.C. 1985, c. N-4, s. 10.

20. Arthur Beauchesne, *Canada's Parliament Buildings: The Senate and House of Commons, Ottawa,* Ottawa: 1948, p. 24. Figures converted from imperial to metric.

21. When the Sovereign or the Governor General is present on Parliament Hill for a state or public function, the Canadian flag is replaced by Her Majesty's Personal Canadian Flag or by the Governor General's Flag, as the case may be (*The Arms, Flags and Emblems of Canada*, 2nd ed., Deneau Publishers, 1981).

Figure 6.2   *Floor Plan of the Centre Block*

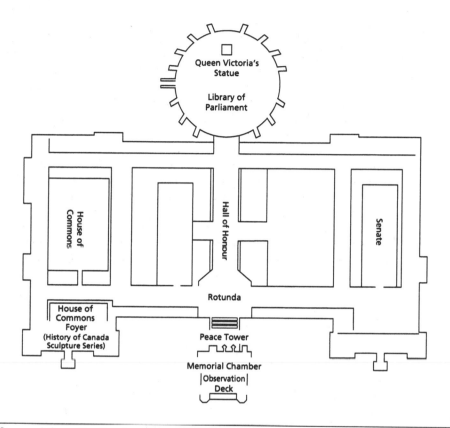

Source: Information Service, Library of Parliament.

LIBRARY OF PARLIAMENT

At the north end of the Centre Block's Hall of Honour, opposite the main entrance, are the doors to the Library of Parliament. Its style of architecture is High Victorian Gothic Revival; its interior is circular in form and richly ornamented with carved white pine panelling. The Library survived the fire of 1916, but in 1952 a fire broke out in the cupola of the Library, causing extensive smoke and water damage. The Library serves Parliament using state-of-the-art information technologies, and housing a collection of well over 1,000,000 items (books, periodicals, brochures and microforms), of which over 400,000 titles are catalogued in the integrated Library system. Comprehensive information, research and analysis services are provided by the Library to parliamentarians, their staff, parliamentary committees, parliamentary associations and delegations and senior officials of both Houses. It also provides information about Parliament to the general public.[22] Apart from the main Library and the Parliamentary Reading Room, there are branch libraries in some of the other buildings used by Parliament.[23]

The Chamber

The South Corridor, hung with portraits of former Prime Ministers, links the Confederation Hall to the Commons Chamber. At the west end of the corridor is the spacious, high-ceilinged foyer of the House of Commons, which may also be accessed from the Members' entrance at the western end of the Centre Block. On the four walls of the foyer, just below the balcony which overlooks it from the floor above, is a series of 10 bas-relief sculpture panels depicting 25,000 years of Canadian history from the arrival of the aboriginal peoples to that of the United Empire Loyalists in the late eighteenth century.[24] Opening off the foyer are the doors to an antechamber which leads into the Chamber itself.[25] The doors are made of white oak and trimmed with hand-wrought iron. Members tend to use the smaller doors to either side of the main doors; these lead into the antechamber and then into the government and opposition lobbies, rooms behind the government and opposition benches, which also open onto the Chamber.

Each day when the House meets to conduct business, the Speaker's parade[26] moves from the Speaker's chambers through the halls of the Centre Block, entering the antechamber through the large centre doors and proceeding into the Chamber through a second set of doors.

The Chamber itself is rectangular in shape, measuring approximately 21 metres in length and 16 metres in width; it is also sheeted with Tyndall limestone as well as white oak and, like its counterpart at Westminster, it is decorated in green.[27] (See Figure 6.3,

---

22. For additional information on the services offered by the Library of Parliament, see *Library of Parliament, A Guide to Services*, December 1997.

23. For further information on the history of the Library of Parliament, see Audrey Dubé and Mike Graham, *Chronology of a Building, the Library of Parliament* (1995), and Kenneth Binks, *Library of Parliament*, Canada, KCB Publications, 1979.

24. The "History of Canada" series was begun in 1962 by Eleanor Milne and her team of stonecarvers, and completed in 1974. The Loyalists were American colonists of diverse ethnic backgrounds who supported the British cause during the American revolution, and who left the United States at the end of the War of Independence or soon thereafter. (For further information on the United Empire Loyalists, see Wallace Brown and Hereward Senior, *Victorious in Defeat: The Loyalists in Canada,* Methuen Publications, 1984.)

25. Antechambers for the House and Senate were part of the design for the new Parliament Building constructed after the fire of 1916; the original building had no antechamber.

26. For information on the Speaker's parade, see Chapter 9, "Sittings of the House".

27. The predominance of the colour red in the Senate Chamber and the British House of Lords can be explained by its history as a royal colour used in the room where the Sovereign met his Court and nobles, as was the case in Parliament's earliest days. The association of the colour green with the Commons is not so easily determined. The colour green has been linked to the Commons' meeting places at least since 1663 (date of the first authoritative written reference to green in the House of Commons). See J.M. Davies, "Red and Green" in *The Table*, Vol. XXXVII for 1968, pp. 33-40; as well as "House of Commons Green", Factsheet No. 13, Public Information Office, House of Commons, London, 1987.

Figure 6.3   *The House of Commons Chamber*

House of Commons

1. Speaker
2. Pages
3. Government Members
4. Opposition Members
5. Prime Minister
6. Leader of the Official Opposition
7. Leader of second largest party in opposition
8. Clerk and Table Officers
9. Mace
10. Hansard Reporters
11. Sergeant-at-Arms
12. Interpreters
13. Press Gallery
14. Public Gallery
15. Official Gallery
16. Reserved Gallery
17. MPs' Gallery
18. Special Gallery
19. MPs' Gallery
20. Speaker's Gallery
21. Senate Gallery

Source: Information Service, Library of Parliament.

The House of Commons Chamber.) The 14.7-metre high ceiling is made of linen canvas, hand-painted with the provincial and territorial coats of arms.

The floral emblems of the ten provinces and two territories are depicted in 12 stained-glass windows on the east, west and north walls of the Chamber.[28] On the east and west walls, above the Members' galleries and between the stained-glass windows, is the noted British North America Act series of sculptures. It consists of 12 separate bas-relief sculptures in Indiana limestone. Each one depicts, in symbolic and story form, the federal roles and responsibilities arising out of the BNA Act (now called the *Constitution Act, 1867*).[29]

SEATING

The Chamber is divided by a wide central aisle and is furnished on either side with tiered rows of desks and chairs, facing into the centre. Government Members sit to the Speaker's right, opposition Members to the left. The Prime Minister and Cabinet sit in the front rows of the government side; directly across the floor from the Prime Minister sits the Leader of the Opposition who is flanked by Members of his or her party. The second-ranked opposition party and all other recognized parties in the House sit with their leaders usually to the left of the Official Opposition, closer to the Bar of the House. Traditionally, the front-row seats to the left of the Speaker are reserved for leading members of the opposition parties, and opposition parties are allocated front-row seats in proportion to their numbers in the House.[30] The distance across the floor of the House between the government and opposition benches is 3.96 metres, said to be equivalent to two swords' length.[31] When there are more government Members than can be accommodated on the Speaker's right, some are seated on the left, usually nearest the Speaker. Members of parties not recognized in the House and independent Members are assigned seats at the discretion of the Speaker, usually at the rear of the House on the Speaker's left.

---

28. The windows were a special project, undertaken in 1967 by Speaker Lamoureux to mark Canada's centennial. They were designed by Parliamentary Sculptor Eleanor Milne. The project was completed in 1973. See *The Stained Glass Windows of Canada's House of Commons*, Ottawa, published under the authority of the Speaker of the House of Commons; see also *Debates*, September 7, 1971, p. 7545.

29. This 11-year project, completed in 1985, was undertaken by Parliamentary Sculptor Eleanor Milne and her team. On the east wall are featured civil law, freedom of speech, the Senate, the Governor General, Confederation, the vote; on the west wall are bilingualism, education, House of Commons, taxation, criminal law and communication. R. Eleanor Milne, *The British North America Act Series*, Ottawa: Department of Public Works, 1983.

30. This is said to originate with the formation of political parties and party government. In the parliaments of seventeenth century Britain, according to Redlich, the division into right and left was "… quite unknown." For information on the origins of this and other traditions associated with seating in the British House, see *Redlich*, Vol. II, pp. 23-7.

31. This relates to times gone by in the British House; its Members no longer wear swords, but red lines marked on the carpet two swords' length apart serve as a reminder to seek resolutions by peaceful means.

The allocation of seats in the House is the responsibility of the Speaker and is carried out in collaboration with the party Whips.[32] Seat assignments may change from time to time, but the Prime Minister and Leader of the Opposition are always seated in the same places. It is customary for seats to be assigned near the Chair for the use of the Deputy Speaker and other Chair occupants when they are not presiding over the House; no such allocation is made for the Speaker.[33]

THE CHAIR

The Speaker's Chair stands on a dais[34] at the north end of the Chamber with the flag displayed on either side.[35] In the years after Confederation, it was the custom for departing Speakers to take their chairs with them and a new Chair to be made for the new Speaker;[36] this custom ceased in 1916 when the Chair then in use was destroyed in the fire. A new Chair arrived in 1921 as a gift from the British branch of what is now the Commonwealth Parliamentary Association.[37] This Chair is an exact replica of the original Speaker's Chair at Westminster, made *circa* 1849, and then destroyed when the British House of Commons was bombed in 1941. It is approximately four metres high, surmounted by a canopy of carved wood and the Royal coat of arms. The oak used for the carving of the Royal arms was taken from the roof of Westminster Hall, which was built in 1397.

In recent years, the Chair has undergone some minor renovations. Microphones and speakers have been installed and lights placed overhead. The armrests now offer a writing surface and a small storage space, as well as document holders onto which can be fixed the seating plan for the House. A hydraulic lift was also installed to permit more comfortable seating for the various occupants of the Chair.[38] At the foot of the Chair, visible only to its occupant, are two screens. The first, which was installed

---

32. In response to a point of order, Speaker Parent explained the process followed in assigning seats to parties and stated, "There is no such thing as a bad seat in the House of Commons" (*Debates*, September 30, 1998, pp. 8584-5). For further information on assignment of seats, see Chapter 4, "The House of Commons and Its Members".

33. Seating plans for the House indicate that at one time the Speaker, a government Member, was assigned a desk on the government side near the Chair. It appears the practice was discontinued in the Thirty-First Parliament (1979) when, following a change of government, Speaker Jerome was elected to a second term, becoming the first opposition Member to be nominated by the governing party to preside over the House.

34. This design element may be related to the fact that the Chair is a replica of the original Speaker's Chair at Westminster, which is also raised above floor level. In St. Stephen's Chapel, the home of the British Commons from 1547 to 1834, the Speaker's Chair was located atop the steps leading to the altar.

35. In 1973, the House adopted a motion authorizing the Speaker to "display the Canadian Flag in the House of Commons in such location as he chooses" (*Journals*, February 14, 1973, p. 119). For some years the flag was displayed on the Speaker's right. Since the Thirty-Fifth Parliament (1994-97), the flag has been displayed to either side of the Chair.

36. *Debates*, May 20, 1921, p. 3691.

37. *Journals*, June 8, 1920, p. 324; see also *Debates*, May 20, 1921, pp. 3689-96.

38. The lift was installed in 1981 during the tenure of Speaker Sauvé.

during the Thirty-Fourth Parliament (1988-93), is a television monitor, enabling the Speaker to see the House as the camera sees it. The other is a computer screen, installed during the Thirty-Fifth Parliament (1994-97), by which the Speaker can receive information from the Table, which is equipped with laptop computers. During debate, for example, or when other time limits apply, a Table Officer activates the digital "count-down clock" and the Speaker is able to monitor the length of speeches and interventions.

At the foot of the dais below the Speaker's Chair is a bench where some of the House of Commons pages are stationed during sittings of the House. The pages are university students employed by the House of Commons to carry messages and deliver documents to Members during sittings of the House.[39]

A door behind the Speaker's Chair opens onto a corridor, called the Speaker's corridor, leading directly to the Speaker's chambers. Hanging in this hallway are portraits of past Speakers of the House.[40]

THE TABLE

A short distance in front of the dais and the Speaker's Chair is a long oak table where the Clerk of the House, chief procedural advisor to the Speaker, sits with other Table Officers.[41] The Clerk sits at the north end of the Table, with Table Officers along the right- and left-hand side of the Table. The Clerk's chair was made in 1873. After the death in 1902 of the then Clerk, Sir John Bourinot, the chair was presented to his widow; in 1940 it was donated back to the House by the family. The Table is equipped with microphones, small television monitors and laptop computers. The laptop computers are used to keep the records,[42] to relay information to the Chair and, as they are connected to the House network, to send and receive information via electronic mail to and from other branches of the House. The Mace rests at the south end of the Table. Also on the Table is a collection of parliamentary reference texts for consultation by Members and Table Officers, a pair of bookends, a calendar stand, inkstand and seal press.[43]

---

39. See comments of Speaker Jerome on the Page Programme, *Debates,* March 22, 1978, pp. 4026-7; October 10, 1978, p. 6953.

40. The portraits are normally commissioned before a Speaker leaves office, but hung only after a Speaker has left office; a hanging ceremony is held when a new portrait is added to the collection.

41. The Table, with its elaborately carved base, was designed by J.A. Pearson, one of the architects of the reconstructed Centre Block.

42. The scroll is the (traditionally handwritten) record of proceedings in the House, kept by the Table Officers. It is the basis of the *Journals.* The time book, also kept by Table Officers, is an account of how time is used in the House.

43. The calendar stand, inkstand and seal press are the handiwork of ironmaster Paul Beau; they were placed on the Table in 1926 to replace items lost in the fire of 1916 (*Debates*, May 26, 1926, p. 3731). For a description of their design, see *Journals*, May 28, 1926, pp. 364-5. Mr. Beau was also responsible for many of the ironwork items found elsewhere in the Centre Block (see *Paul Beau* by Rosalind Pepall, Musée des beaux-arts de Montréal, 1982).

THE MACE

The Mace is the ornamental staff, symbol of the authority of the Speaker, which rests on the Table during sittings of the House. In the Middle Ages, the mace was an officer's weapon; it was made of metal with a flanged or spiked head and was used to break through chain-mail or plate-armour.[44] In the twelfth century, the Sergeants-at-Arms of the King's Bodyguard were equipped with maces. These maces, stamped with the Royal Arms and carried by the Sergeants in the exercise of their powers of arrest without warrant, became recognized symbols of the King's authority. Maces were also carried by civic authorities.

Royal Sergeants-at-Arms began to be assigned to the Commons early in the fifteenth century. By the end of the sixteenth century, the Sergeant's mace had evolved from a weapon of war to an ornately embellished emblem of office. The Sergeant-at-Arms' power to arrest without warrant enabled the Commons to arrest or commit persons who offended them, without having to resort to the ordinary courts of law.[45] This penal jurisdiction is the basis of the concept of parliamentary privilege and, since the exercise of this privilege depended on the powers vested in the Royal Sergeant-at-Arms, the Mace—his emblem of office—was identified with the growing privileges of the Commons and became recognized as the symbol of the authority of the House and of the Speaker through the House.[46]

At Confederation, the House of Commons' Mace was that of the former Legislative Assembly of the Province of Canada.[47] It had survived the burning of the Parliament building in Montreal in 1849,[48] as well as two fires in Quebec City in 1854,[49] but was lost in the great fire of February 3, 1916. When the House met in the Victoria Memorial Museum (as it was then known) in the immediate aftermath of the fire, the Senate lent the House its mace. For the following three weeks, the mace belonging

---

44. The Mace developed from the club (prehistoric weapon) and the staff (ancient symbol of age, wisdom and authority). See Erskine Grant-Dalton, "The Mace", *The Table*, Vol. XXV for 1956, pp. 15-20; see also Peter Thorne, "Maces: Their Use and Significance", *The Parliamentarian*, Vol. 44, 1963, pp. 25-30. It is said that the mace rather than the sword was carried into battle by the medieval warrior bishops, in conformity with canonical rule forbidding priests to shed blood (Beauchesne, *Canada's Parliament Buildings*, p. 55).

45. *May*, 22nd ed., pp. 136-7.

46. At this time, the British Commons was at the start of its centuries-long struggle to assert and win the privileges essential to establishing its distinct role in Parliament. In the Ferrers case of 1543, the House of Commons successfully challenged the City of London authorities, securing the release of an arrested Member (Ferrers) "by their Serjeant without writ, only by shew of his mace, which was his warrant"; see the account in *Hatsell*, Vol. I, pp. 53-9. See also Chapter 3, "Privileges and Immunities".

47. The legislative assemblies of the other provinces joining Confederation did not use maces (*Bourinot*, 2nd ed., pp. 277-8, note 5). Nova Scotia and New Brunswick obtained maces in 1930 and 1937 respectively. In Upper and Lower Canada (now Ontario and Quebec), maces were used in the houses of assembly from the time of their first meetings in 1792.

48. *Bourinot*, 2nd ed., pp. 277-8, note 5.

49. John McDonough, "The History of the Maces of the British and Canadian Parliaments," *Canadian Parliamentary Review*, Vol. II, No. 2, June 1979, p. 29.

to the Ontario Legislature was used until a temporary mace, made of wood, was fashioned. The Mace currently in use is a replica of the original. Made of silver covered with heavy gilt, it is 1.47 metres long and weighs 7.9 kilograms. It was a gift from the Lord Mayor and the Sheriffs of London and was presented in May 1917.[50] The wooden mace was kept; it is displayed in the foyer of the House of Commons and is used in the Chamber on the anniversary of the date of the fire.[51]

    The Mace is integral to the functioning of the House; since the late seventeenth century it has been accepted that the Mace must be present for the House to be properly constituted.[52] The guardian of the Mace is the Sergeant-at-Arms,[53] who carries it on the right shoulder in and out of the Chamber at the beginning and end of each sitting of the House. At the opening of a sitting of the House, the Mace is laid across the foot of the Table with its crown pointing to the government side of the House. When the House sits as a Committee of the Whole, it is placed on brackets below the Table;[54] and during the election of a Speaker, the Mace rests on a cushion on the floor beneath the Table. The Mace is kept in the Speaker's Chambers when the House is adjourned. During the longer adjournments and recesses, it is on display in or near the Commons Chamber.

THE BAR OF THE HOUSE

The Bar is a brass rod extending across the floor of the Chamber inside its south entrance. It is a barrier past which uninvited representatives of the Crown (as well as other non-Members) are not welcome.[55] When the House sits as a Committee of the

---

50. *Journals*, May 16, 1917, p. 216. For a description of the design of the Mace, see *Debates*, May 16, 1917, pp. 1468-9. See also *Wilding and Laundy*, pp. 455-6 for information on maces in other Commonwealth parliaments.

51. This has taken place on each anniversary since 1977 (see, for example, *Debates*, February 3, 1994, p. 847). The tradition began in 1961 during the tenure of Speaker Michener (*Debates*, February 3, 1961, p. 1701) and was revived by Speaker Jerome in 1977 (*Debates*, February 3, 1977, p. 2665).

52. "The Mace in the House of Commons", House of Commons Library Document No. 3, London: Her Majesty's Stationery Office, 1957, p. 7. See also *Hatsell*, Vol. II, p. 141.

53. Standing Order 157(1).

54. This long-standing custom may have originated in the Elizabethan period, when the large committees of the time began to meet in the Chamber as an alternative to less-convenient locations outside the precinct. The position of the Mace—on the Table or below it—would have provided a clear indication as to whether Members were sitting as a House or as a committee ("The Mace in the House of Commons", House of Commons Library Document No. 3, pp. 9-10).

55. In 1642, in a conflict over the respective rights and authority of the monarch and the British Parliament, Charles I issued a warrant for the arrest of five Members of the British House of Commons. The King himself went to the Commons Chamber, crossed the Bar—the first and last monarch to do so—and took the Speaker's Chair, demanding the presence of the five wanted Members. The King's intentions were foiled by Speaker Lenthall whose famous words ("May it please Your Majesty, I have neither eyes to see, nor tongue to speak in this place, but as the House is pleased to direct me, whose servant I am here, and I humbly beg Your Majesty's pardon that I cannot give any other answer than this to what Your Majesty is pleased to demand of me.") established the precedence of the privileges of the Commons over the authority of the Crown (*Wilding and Laundy*, pp. 708-9).

Whole, departmental officials are permitted onto the floor of the House in order to assist the Minister. The Sergeant-at-Arms, or an assistant, sits at a desk on the opposition side of the Chamber and inside the Bar.

Individuals may be summoned to appear before the Bar of the House in order to answer to the authority of the House, or to respond to questioning. If someone is judged to be in contempt of the House—that is, guilty of an offence against the dignity or authority of Parliament—the House may summon the person to appear and order that he or she be reprimanded by the Speaker in the name of and with the full authority of the House. On a number of occasions in the late nineteenth and early twentieth centuries, individuals were summoned to appear before the Bar of the House. Since 1913, there has been just one instance of the House requiring someone to appear at the Bar.[56] Witnesses to be examined by the House will also stand at the Bar and reply to questions posed by Members.[57]

THE GALLERIES

Overlooking the floor of the House on both sides and both ends of the Chamber are galleries which can accommodate more than 500 people. (See Figure 6.3, The House of Commons Chamber.) In the gallery facing the Speaker's Chair, called the Ladies Gallery,[58] the first rows are reserved for the diplomatic corps and for other distinguished guests; the remaining rows are reserved for the visiting public. At the opposite end of the Chamber, immediately above the Speaker's Chair, is the Press Gallery. Admittance is restricted to members of the Parliamentary Press Gallery[59] (one of the galleries in which note-taking is permitted). Immediately behind the Press Gallery is another public gallery. On the side of the Chamber facing the government benches are three galleries: one for guests of government Members, another for Senators and their guests, and another one for guests of the Prime Minister and the Speaker. Only from the Speaker's gallery can distinguished visitors (such as heads of state, heads of government and parliamentary delegations invited to Canada) be recognized and introduced to the House by the Speaker.[60] On the other side of the Chamber, facing

---

56. On October 30, 1991, angry at having missed a vote, Ian Waddell (Port Moody–Coquitlam) attempted to take hold of the Mace as it was borne out of the Chamber at the end of the sitting. The Member's actions were judged to be an attempt to obstruct the House, as well as a challenge to the Chair's authority to adjourn the sitting. A *prima facie* breach of privilege was found and a motion was adopted calling the Member to the Bar to be admonished by the Speaker (*Debates*, October 30, 1991, pp. 4269-70; October 31, 1991, pp. 4271-85, 4309-10). As a sitting Member, the individual could have received the admonishment at his assigned place, which would have been the normal practice. In this case, however, the motion adopted by the House specifically requested the Member to appear at the Bar.

57. For further information, see Chapter 3, "Privileges and Immunities".

58. At one time the Ladies' Gallery was reserved for women (who tended to be the wives and daughters of Members), as is the Ladies' Gallery in the British House. See *Wilding and Laundy*, p. 424; *Redlich*, Vol. II, pp. 22, 35.

59. The Parliamentary Press Gallery is a non-profit corporation whose membership comprises journalists assigned by media organizations to cover Parliament.

60. For further information on this custom, see Chapter 7, "The Speaker and Other Presiding Officers of the House".

the opposition benches, a gallery is reserved for departmental officials (the other gallery in which note-taking is permitted), another for guests of the Leader of the Opposition, and two others for guests of Members of other opposition parties.

The doors to the galleries are opened at the start of each sitting of the House, after prayers are read. For reasons of decorum and security, photography, reading and sketching materials, and note-taking (with the above exceptions) are not permitted in the galleries. Coats, briefcases, notebooks, photographic equipment and the like may not be carried into the galleries.[61] Guests seated in the private galleries must be appropriately attired.[62]

Strangers

"Stranger" is a term of longtime use in the procedural lexicon; it refers to anyone who is not a Member or an official of the House of Commons (for example, Senators, diplomats, government officials, journalists or members of the general public). It underlines the distinction between Members and non-Members and gives emphasis to the fact that strangers or outsiders may be present in the galleries or within the parliamentary precinct only under the authority of the House.[63] Strangers are not permitted on the floor of the House of Commons when the House is sitting.[64]

The right of the House to conduct its proceedings in private—that is, without strangers present—is centuries old. Until 1845 in the British House, sessional orders excluded strangers from every part of its premises (while in practice the presence of strangers came to be tolerated in areas not appropriated to the exclusive use of Members).[65] In Canada, at Confederation, the House adopted a rule giving individual

---

61. In March 1997, the House was made aware that an aboriginal visitor carrying an eagle feather had been refused admission to the public galleries. The House took note of the sacred character of the eagle feather for aboriginal peoples, and the Speaker stated that it is permissible for an aboriginal person to bring an eagle feather into the House (*Debates*, March 12, 1997, pp. 8946, 8954-5).

62. This has traditionally been interpreted as conservative business dress; for example, jackets and neckties for male guests. Appropriate national costume and traditional aboriginal dress are also acceptable. The dress code is not applied in the public galleries.

63. For further information on the authority of the House over its precinct, see Chapter 3, "Privileges and Immunities". When it came to the attention of the House in June 1998 that Ernst Zundel (notorious for having published his claims that the Holocaust never occurred) had been granted use of the Centre Block press conference facility managed by the Parliamentary Press Gallery (*Debates*, June 4, 1998, pp. 7608-9), the House agreed that, for the remainder of the session, Mr. Zundel would be denied admission to the House of Commons precinct (*Journals*, June 4, 1998, p. 937).

64. There have been rare exceptions. In 1944, the House twice agreed to permit the Minister of National Defence, who was newly appointed and not an elected Member, to address the House during a sitting (*Journals*, November 23, 1944, p. 926; November 24, 1944, p. 928). In addition, the House met in a secret session at which the Minister was present and participated (*Journals*, November 28, 1944, p. 931; *Debates*, November 28, 1944, p. 6634).

In 1996 and 1998, the House sat as a Committee of the Whole for ceremonies recognizing the national Olympic and Paralympic teams of the 1996 Summer Games and 1998 Winter Games, for which the athletes were brought onto the floor of the House (*Journals*, October 1, 1996, p. 699; *Debates*, October 1, 1996, pp. 4944-6; *Journals*, April 22, 1998, p. 691; *Debates*, April 22, 1998, pp. 5959-60).

65. For historical background, see *May*, 1st ed., pp. 163-4; 5th ed., pp. 238-40; *Redlich*, Vol. II, pp. 34-5.

Members the power to order the galleries cleared.[66] In 1876, the rule was substantially amended,[67] allowing Members only to move a motion "that strangers be ordered to withdraw"; this non-debatable and non-amendable motion was then left for the House to decide.[68] The present rule, which was adopted in 1994,[69] provides that the Speaker may order the withdrawal of strangers, and also that if a Member notices the presence of strangers, the Speaker "may" allow the non-debatable and non-amendable motion to be put. The House thus retains the power to order the removal of strangers and to meet privately.[70] In practice such occurrences are not frequent and strangers are welcome so long as there is space to accommodate them and proper decorum is observed.

Disorder in the Galleries

The Sergeant-at-Arms, one of the senior officials of the House, is responsible for maintaining order and decorum in the galleries.[71] From time to time there have been instances of misconduct in the galleries and the Sergeant-at-Arms and security staff have acted to remove demonstrators or strangers behaving in a disruptive way. In cases of extreme disorder, the Speaker has directed that the galleries be cleared.[72] In addition, should the House adopt the motion "That strangers be ordered to withdraw", it would be the duty of the Sergeant-at-Arms and security staff to clear the galleries of strangers.

LOBBIES

Adjacent to the government and opposition sides of the Chamber is a long, narrow room known as a lobby. The one behind the government benches is reserved for government Members; the other, on the opposition side, is for Members of the opposition

---

66. See *Rules and Forms of Proceedings of the House of Commons of Canada*, 1868, Rule 6; and *Debates*, March 27, 1871, col. 655, for an example of its use.

67. *Debates*, March 29, 1876, p. 905.

68. No such motion was ever adopted, although attempts were made (see, for example, *Journals*, September 7, 1950, p. 38; *Debates*, April 4, 1990, pp. 10186-7). In the 1990 example, Speaker Fraser ruled that a Member could not propose the motion on a point of order.

69. Standing Order 14 (*Journals*, June 10, 1994, p. 563).

70. See the section on secret sittings in Chapter 9, "Sittings of the House".

71. Standing Orders 157(2) and 158.

72. See, for example, *Debates*, May 11, 1970, p. 6796; November 28, 1989, pp. 6342-3. On October 18, 1990, a question of privilege was raised accusing a Member of complicity in a demonstration in the galleries on the previous day, when some 20 individuals identified as students had shouted and pelted Members with macaroni and messages of protest before being escorted from the galleries by security staff (*Debates*, October 18, 1990, pp. 14359-68). The Speaker ruled out the allegation of complicity, but found a *prima facie* breach of privilege in the demonstration. The matter was referred to committee, which recommended that participants in such demonstrations be charged or otherwise punished for their actions (*Debates*, November 6, 1990, pp. 15177-81; *Journals*, November 6, 1990, p. 2228; March 6, 1991, pp. 2666-7). For text of the report, see Standing Committee on Privilege and Elections, *Minutes of Proceedings and Evidence*, March 6, 1991, Issue No. 39, pp. 3-8. The report was not taken up by the House.

parties. Connected by doors to the Chamber, the lobbies are furnished with tables and armchairs and equipped with telephones, fax machines, photocopiers, computer terminals and the like for Members' use. Members attending the sitting of the House use the lobbies to converse, discuss matters, make telephone calls, attend to correspondence or other business and are able to return to the Chamber at a moment's notice. The party Whips assign staff to work from the lobbies and pages are stationed in the lobbies to answer telephones and carry messages. The lobbies are not open to the public. The House of Commons security staff control access to the lobbies in accordance with guidelines set by the Whips.

SOUND REINFORCEMENT AND INTERPRETATION SYSTEMS

In 1951, a special committee of the House recommended the installation of a sound reinforcement system "similar to the one in the House of Commons Chamber at Westminster".[73] For some years, there had been complaints about the acoustics in the Chamber and the difficulty that Members and those in the galleries had in following the proceedings. The challenge in providing effective sound amplification lay in devising a system for use in an assembly where members speak from their places (rather than from a rostrum) and only when recognized by the Speaker. The committee's report was adopted, the system was installed during a recess and used for the first time in the session which opened on November 20, 1952.[74] Each Member's desk, as well as the Speaker's Chair, is equipped with a microphone. A microphone switching console, staffed by console operators, is located at the front of the gallery at the south end of the Chamber. Individual microphones are activated when a Member is recognized by the Speaker. Only the Speaker has the power to activate his or her own microphone (it may also be activated by the console operator); when the Speaker's microphone is activated, the Members' microphones will not function.

In 1958, the House agreed to the installation in the Chamber of a system for simultaneous interpretation in both official languages.[75] Members were of the opinion that this would give further expression to the Constitution, which provides for the equal status of the official languages and for their use in parliamentary debate.[76]

Enclosed booths for interpreters are located in the corners of the Chamber opposite the Speaker's Chair. Members' desks are equipped with interpretation devices in order to receive simultaneous interpretation of the proceedings into French or

---

73. The development of the system in the British House was watched with interest; see reports tabled by the Speaker in *Journals*, December 5, 1947, pp. 7, 30-2; March 15, 1951, pp. 177-9. The special committee's report was presented and adopted on June 19, 1951 (*Journals*, pp. 517-8).

74. See *Journals*, February 29, 1952, p. 9 (tabling of an Order in Council authorizing the Minister of Public Works to contract for the supply, installation and operation of a sound system); *Debates*, June 25, 1952, p. 3732 (questioning of the Minister in the Committee of Supply); *Debates*, November 21, 1952, p. 11; November 26, 1952, p. 123 (Members' comments on the new system).

75. *Journals*, August 11, 1958, p. 402.

76. See the discussion in the House when the decision was taken (*Debates*, August 11, 1958, pp. 3331-40) and on an earlier occasion when a motion seeking the establishment of simultaneous interpretation was debated (*Debates*, November 25, 1957, pp. 1456-99).

English. Visitors in the galleries also have access to the sound reinforcement and interpretation systems and may choose to listen to the proceedings with interpretation in the official language of their choice, or without interpretation.

BROADCASTING ARRANGEMENTS

Following the decision in 1977 to broadcast the proceedings of the House of Commons,[77] the Chamber became the site of extensive construction to equip it for this purpose. During the summer adjournment, the Chamber was refitted: the sound systems were upgraded, appropriate lighting installed, cameras were added (operated manually and later replaced with remote-controlled cameras), and a control room was constructed above the Ladies' Gallery situated at the south end of the Chamber.[78] (The subject of broadcasting as an "electronic Hansard" is addressed in Chapter 24, "The Parliamentary Record".)

Provision for Still Photography

Before the advent of broadcasting of House of Commons' proceedings, photographs of the House during a sitting were taken with the permission of the House.[79] In the late 1970s, once the House had dealt with the question of broadcasting, the matter of still photography arose. There were no provisions for print media to take pictures of the House at work, except by special arrangement, whereas the electronic media now had access to images of every sitting of the House.[80] On a trial basis, and later to become standard practice,[81] a photographer was allowed behind the curtains on each side of the House during Question Period. The photographers are employed by a news service agency which supplies other news organizations under a pooling arrangement. When in the Chamber, they operate in accordance with the principles governing the use of television cameras, described in Chapter 24, "The Parliamentary Record".

OTHER USES OF THE CHAMBER

At times, the House of Commons Chamber is used for purposes other than a parliamentary sitting. Some are recurring events such as addresses by distinguished

---

77. *Journals*, January 25, 1977, p. 287.

78. See the Speaker's statement when the House began broadcasting its proceedings (*Debates*, October 17, 1977, pp. 8201-2).

79. See, for example, the special order adopted on May 11, 1961 (*Journals*, p. 535). On another occasion, when a Member objected, the Speaker sought the consent of the House for photographs to be taken during a sitting (*Debates*, November 27, 1964, p. 10597; December 17, 1964, p. 11263). In January 1967, the Speaker wrote to all Members, informing them of arrangements made in consultation with the House Leaders for photographs to be taken of the House in session.

80. See *Debates*, October 24, 1979, p. 557.

81. See *Debates*, January 25, 1983, p. 22194.

visitors,[82] orientation sessions for new Members,[83] and annual programs.[84] At other times, the Chamber has been used for special events.[85] Since these events are not actually sittings of the House, the Mace is not on the Table.

Committee Rooms

The House of Commons delegates much of its work to committees which are composed of Members (and in the case of joint committees, Members and Senators).[86] Aside from Committees of the Whole House which meet in the Chamber,[87] committees meet in rooms outside the Chamber, often while the House is sitting. Committee rooms are located principally in the Centre Block, East Block, West Block, Wellington Building and La Promenade Building. They are outfitted with sound amplification systems as well as the necessary equipment to record the proceedings and to provide simultaneous interpretation in both official languages. One room is set up for television broadcasting, with an adjoining control room and cameras operated by remote control. Although certain rooms are designated and equipped as committee rooms, they are all multifunctional and are used for other purposes. Committees may

---

82. From time to time, the House of Commons Chamber is the site for an address by a distinguished visitor to assembled Members and Senators. In order for such a meeting to take place, the House first adopts a motion to that effect (see, for example, *Journals*, June 9, 1992, pp. 1660-1). When a joint address takes place, an established protocol is followed. It does not constitute a sitting of the House and the House is not in session. For further information on joint addresses to Members of both Houses, see Chapter 9, "Sittings of the House".

83. Orientation sessions, usually given for Members after a general election and before the opening of Parliament, were held in the Chamber following the general elections of 1993 and 1997.

84. For example: The Teachers' Institute on Canadian Parliamentary Democracy, a professional development seminar held annually since 1996; the annual meetings of the Forum for Young Canadians, a program operated by the non-profit Foundation for the Study of Processes of Government in Canada, for students of secondary school age to learn about the workings of government and the responsibilities of citizenship; and the annual swearing-in ceremony for the parliamentary pages.

85. In 1921, Members and Senators assembled in the House of Commons Chamber for a ceremony to receive the Speaker's Chair, a gift to replace the Chair lost in the fire of 1916. The gathering was not a sitting of the House and the Mace was not laid on the Table. When the House sat later the same day, special orders were adopted to prefix the remarks made at the ceremony to that day's *Debates* (*Journals*, May 20, 1921, pp. 305-6).

    Sessions were held in the House of Commons Chamber when the Parliament of Canada hosted the XIth and XVIIIth General Assemblies of the *Association internationale des parlementaires de langue française* in 1980 and 1991 respectively (since renamed *l'Assemblée parlementaire de la Francophonie (APF)*) and the XXVth General Assembly of the *Assemblée parlementaire de la Francophonie* in 1999.

    In 1996, Members and Senators past and present gathered in the Chamber and galleries to witness a ceremony unveiling the first of a series of plaques commemorating the service of individual parliamentarians since Confederation. The event was not a sitting of the House. (The ceremony was televised but the official documents contain no written record; see references in *Debates*, May 29, 1996, pp. 3124, 3133.)

86. For further information, see Chapter 20, "Committees".

87. See Chapter 19, "Committees of the Whole House".

meet anywhere in the parliamentary precinct provided the requirements for interpretation and recording are met.

Typically a committee room is set up with several tables placed in a rectangular formation. The Chair sits at the centre of one end with the Committee Clerk and other committee advisors. The Members take seats on either side; as in the House, the government Members normally sit to the Chair's right and the opposition Members to the left. Witnesses are seated at the end opposite the Chair. Tables are available for representatives of the press, usually behind the witnesses' chairs, together with additional seating for individuals viewing the proceedings.

While a committee may tend to hold its meetings in a particular room, no such formal room assignments are made. In the years immediately following Confederation, committees were fewer and larger and much business was conducted in Committees of the Whole. Certain rooms were set aside for committee meetings. For example, the room known informally as the Railway Committee Room came to be so called because (although it was used by other committees) it was the home of the standing committee dealing with railways.[88] Committees book rooms as needed; priority of use may be established from time to time by the Standing Committee on Procedure and House Affairs.[89]

Members' Offices

Members are accommodated in suites of offices located in the Centre Block, East Block, West Block, Confederation Building, Justice Building and Wellington Building. Ministers have offices on Parliament Hill as well as in their departments. Office space is assigned to Members in consultation with their party Whips.[90] Members of parties not officially recognized in the House and Members with no party affiliation (usually referred to as independent Members) are then allocated offices by the Speaker.[91]

At Confederation, the newly built Centre Block, or "Parliament Building" as it was then known, housed the entire Parliament of Canada. The East and West Blocks, or "departmental buildings", were occupied by government departments and

---

88. The Standing Committee on Railways, Canals and Telegraph Lines was in existence from 1867 to 1965, when its name was changed. The Railway Committee Room opens off the Hall of Honour. It is one of the largest committee rooms, and it has been equipped to broadcast committee proceedings.

89. Standing Order 115(4). The priority system is based on the Committee's report (see Standing Committee on Procedure and House Affairs, *Minutes of Proceedings and Evidence*, June 10, 1994, Issue No. 16, pp. 9-10), which was adopted by the House on September 19, 1994 (*Journals*, p. 682). See also Chapter 20, "Committees".

90. *Members' Manual of Allowances and Services*, House of Commons, March 1998, Vol. I, Chapter B-1, p. 1.

91. In 1991, Louis Plamondon (Richelieu), a Member of a non-recognized party, raised a question of privilege about the reassignment of his office by the Speaker without his authorization. The Speaker ruled that the Member's complaint was an administrative rather than procedural matter (*Debates*, April 8, 1991, pp. 19126-7; April 9, 1991, pp. 19232-3; April 11, 1991, p. 19340). Prior to the opening of the Thirty-Sixth Parliament in 1997, John Nunziata (York South–Weston), a former Member of a recognized party who had been re-elected as an independent Member, was reassigned office space by the Speaker against his will.

included offices for Cabinet Ministers. The Speaker was the only Member to have an office in the parliamentary building. Members were provided with desks in the Chamber, lockers nearby, and facilities for dressing, reading and smoking; the nature of the Members' work and the length of sessions were such that this was considered adequate to their needs.[92]

The Centre Block was designed for the Legislative Assembly of the Province of Canada, which was composed of 130 members; at Confederation in 1867, it was required to house 181 Members of the House of Commons. By the 1880s, the basements and attics were fully utilized and parliamentarians demanded improvements in their accommodations. By 1916, the year in which fire destroyed the building, some Members were allocated private offices (i.e., the Speaker, Cabinet Ministers, leading Opposition Members); others shared rooms. Conditions for Members were improved in the new Centre Block, though not to the extent of offering private offices for all.[93] Over the years, the membership of the House increased and so did Members' requirements for space and staff, in line with the evolving role and worklife of Parliament and its elected representatives. Gradually, additional space became available as administrative services were moved to other locations, and as other buildings were converted to House of Commons use.[94]

Administrative Structures and Services

The House of Commons is one of three constituent elements of the Parliament of Canada.[95] The other two elements are the Senate and the Sovereign, represented in Canada by the Governor General. The House of Commons is not a department of the Government of Canada, although its administrative structure may be described as generally comparable to that of a government department. One of the privileges of the House is its right to independent regulation of its own internal affairs.[96] The

---

92. At that time, sessions of Parliament were on average well under six months in length; see Appendix 12, "Parliaments Since 1867 and Number of Sitting Days".

93. The original building had residences for the Speaker and Sergeant-at-Arms as well as living quarters for housekeepers, servants and messengers. The new building was two storeys higher and additional space was made available by eliminating the residences, though the Speaker retained a suite of rooms in order to offer the traditional hospitality (J. D. Livermore, "A History of Parliamentary Accommodation in Canada, 1841-1974", published as Appendix III of the *Report of the Advisory Commission on Parliamentary Accommodation*, which was tabled on December 17, 1976 (*Journals*, p. 254)).

94. The West Block was renovated and reopened for Members in 1963, and the Confederation Building in 1973. Since 1980, the East Block (which had always been used by the Prime Minister) has been used by other Members. Office space is also available to Members in the Wellington Building, which the House of Commons began to use in 1977 (*Maingot*, 2nd ed., p. 169). More space will be made available to Members in the Justice Building.

95. *Constitution Act, 1867*, R.S.C. 1985, Appendix II, No. 5, s. 17.

96. *Maingot*, 2nd ed., pp. 183-5. See also Chapter 3, "Privileges and Immunities".

House may voluntarily follow administrative policies of the government, but it cannot be compelled to do so, and it is also free to develop new policies and practices.[97]

The House administration exists to support the activities of Members individually and collectively in their various roles as legislators in the House and in committees, as representatives of their constituents, and as members of their respective party caucuses. As well as serving Members elected for the duration of a Parliament, the administration also serves the House as an institution.[98]

In 1964, the administrative structure of the House of Commons was the subject of an important review which noted significant changes in the nature, volume and complexity of House services and recommended an administrative reorganization.[99] The origins of the modern administrative structure of the House may be traced to a major comprehensive audit carried out by the Auditor General in 1979 and 1980. In 1978, wishing to support a program of expenditure restraint undertaken by the government, the Speaker asked the Standing Committee on Management and Members' Services to suggest possible economy measures for the House.[100] Out of this came a recommendation from the Committee for a complete and independent review of the House administration.[101]

At the Speaker's request, the Auditor General reviewed the administration of the House of Commons, submitting an interim report in October 1979 and a final report early in 1981.[102] The Auditor General noted that services to Members were of high quality; however, fundamental weaknesses and a number of significant deficiencies were identified.[103] These findings led to a major realignment of the administrative structure of the House, which has continued to evolve to meet changing circumstances and demands. Another comprehensive audit undertaken by the Auditor General in 1990-91 found a greatly improved quality of general and financial administration.[104]

---

97. An example would be the House-wide program of environmental awareness and conservation, known as "Greening the Hill", established in 1990 by Speaker Fraser, well in advance of other such initiatives in the public sector.

98. See page 3 of the *Report on Plans and Priorities 1998-99*, tabled on March 25, 1998 (*Journals*, p. 620).

99. See the Sixth Report of the Special Committee on Procedure and Organization, presented on May 20, 1964 (*Journals*, pp. 331-7).

100. For a description of the administrative review, see comments of the Speaker in *Debates*, November 1, 1979, pp. 841-3.

101. See the exchange of correspondence between the Speaker of the House and the Auditor General, tabled on November 1, 1979 (*Journals*, p. 162) and printed by order of the House (*Journals*, November 2, 1979, p. 168) as an appendix to the *Debates* (*Debates*, November 2, 1979, pp. 922-6).

102. The interim report was tabled in the House (*Journals*, November 1 and 2, 1979, pp. 162, 168) and a summary report appeared as Chapter 5 of the Auditor General's report for the fiscal year ended March 31, 1980 (tabled on December 11, 1980; see *Journals*, p. 840). The full audit report was filed as an exhibit with the Standing Committee on Public Accounts (*Minutes of Proceedings*, February 10, 1981, Issue No. 21, p. 3).

103. See paragraphs 5.8-5.10 of the Report of the Auditor General for the fiscal year ended March 31, 1980.

104. See page 9 of the Report of the Audit of the House of Commons Administration, tabled on November 21, 1991 (*Journals*, p. 703; *Debates*, pp. 5158-9).

The administrative structure of the House is not set out in any single text or piece of legislation. The organization required to support the activities of the House has evolved and expanded over the years in response to the needs of an increasingly complex system of government. Provisions for various aspects of the administration are found in legislation,[105] the Standing Orders,[106] by-laws made by the Board of Internal Economy, internal policy manuals and in the unwritten practices developed over time.

OVERALL AUTHORITY OF THE SPEAKER

Elected by the Members of the House, the Speaker holds a position of authority and represents the Commons in all its powers, proceedings and dignity.[107] The Speaker is guardian of the rights and privileges of the House, and spokesperson for the House in its relations with the Senate, the Sovereign and other authorities outside Parliament; when in the Chair, he or she is responsible for regulating debate and preserving order in accordance with the rules of the House.[108]

In addition to the more visible roles as representative of the House and presiding officer in the Chamber, the Speaker is at the head of the administration of the House of Commons and holds extensive responsibilities in that regard. The Speaker is responsible for the overall direction and management of the House of Commons administration,[109] much as a Cabinet Minister is responsible for a department.

The House has a number of unique characteristics that have a direct impact on how it functions and is managed. As part of its corporate rights and privileges, the House of Commons, through the Speaker, holds exclusive jurisdiction over its premises and the people within. The administrative activities of the House are numerous and diverse. All matters of finance and administration are overseen by the Board of Internal Economy, a statutory body of Members of Parliament. The House is accommodated for the most part in heritage buildings, which are recognized national symbols. These and other characteristics inevitably produce a necessarily complex administrative decision-making process.

---

105. For example, the *Parliament of Canada Act*, R.S.C. 1985, c. P-1; *Salaries Act*, R.S.C. 1985, c. S-3; *Official Languages Act*, R.S.C. 1985, c. 31 (4th Supp.); and *Canada Post Corporation Act*, R.S.C. 1985, c. C-10, s. 35.

106. See, for example, Standing Orders 22, 107, 121, 148-59.

107. *May*, 22nd ed., p. 188.

108. For further information on the role of the Speaker, see Chapter 7, "The Speaker and Other Presiding Officers of the House".

109. In 1998-99, the House of Commons administration under the Speaker's jurisdiction comprised some 1,340 person-years (not including Members' staff) and had a budget of approximately $235.2 million. Person-year figures were presented to the Procedure and House Affairs Committee by the Clerk of the House on April 30, 1998 (see Issue 23 of the Committee proceedings). For budget figures, see 1998-99 Estimates, Part I and II, *The Government Expenditure Plan and the Main Estimates*, p. 18–2, tabled in the House on February 26, 1998 (*Journals*, p. 534).

BOARD OF INTERNAL ECONOMY

The Board of Internal Economy is the governing body of the House of Commons. It has a long statutory history, originating in 1868 with the passage of *An Act respecting the internal Economy of the House of Commons, and for other purposes.*[110]

Membership

The membership of the Board consists of the Speaker, who acts as its Chair, two Ministers of the Crown (appointed to the Board by the Governor in Council), the Leader of the Opposition or his or her representative, and additional Members appointed in numbers resulting in an overall equality of government and opposition representatives (apart from the Speaker). All recognized opposition parties (i.e., those holding at least 12 seats in the House) are given representation on the Board. When there is only one recognized opposition party in the House of Commons, the caucus of that party appoints two members of the Board and the government caucus appoints one. When there is more than one recognized opposition party, each opposition caucus appoints one member of the Board; the government caucus appoints a number of members of the Board that is one less than the total number appointed by the opposition caucuses.[111] The Speaker informs the House of appointments within 15 sitting days after they are made.[112] Each Member of the Board is required to take an oath or affirmation "of fidelity and secrecy", administered by the Clerk of the House.[113]

The Clerk of the House is the Secretary to the Board of Internal Economy.[114] When Parliament is dissolved, members of the Board retain their functions until they are replaced.[115] This ensures continuity in the administrative leadership of the House; the practice has been that decisions taken by the Board while Parliament is dissolved are confined to those of a housekeeping nature.

---

110. S.C. 1867-68, c. 27.

111. Until November 1997, when these provisions came into effect (Bill C-13, *An Act to amend the Parliament of Canada Act (composition of the Board of Internal Economy)* received Royal Assent on November 27, 1997), the Deputy Speaker was automatically a Member of the Board of Internal Economy. Peter Milliken (Kingston and the Islands), who was Deputy Speaker at the time, was subsequently appointed to the Board as one of the government's representatives (*Journals*, December 11, 1997, p. 391).

   Following the adoption of these provisions early in the First Session of the Thirty-Sixth Parliament (1997-99), the composition of the Board was as follows: the Speaker, two Cabinet Ministers, the nominee of the Leader of the Opposition, one representative from each of the four opposition caucuses (Reform Party, Bloc Québécois, New Democratic Party and Progressive Conservative Party) and three Members appointed by the government caucus.

112. *Parliament of Canada Act*, R.S.C. 1985, c. P-1, s. 50 as amended by c. 42 (1st supp.), s. 2 and S.C. 1991, c. 20, s. 2 (s. 50(4)). See, for example, *Journals*, January 18, 1994, p. 18 (appointment of several Members at the beginning of a Parliament); September 18, 1995, p. 1882 (appointment of one Member to replace another).

113. *Parliament of Canada Act*, R.S.C. 1985, c. P-1, s. 50 as amended by S.C. 1991, c. 20, s. 2. The text is set out as Form 3 of the Schedule to the Act.

114. *Parliament of Canada Act*, R.S.C. 1985, c. P-1, s. 51 as amended by S.C. 1991, c. 20, s. 2.

115. *Parliament of Canada Act*, R.S.C. 1985, c. P-1 as amended by c. 42 (1st supp.), s. 2 and S.C. 1991, c. 20, s. 2 (s. 53).

Chairperson

Meetings of the Board of Internal Economy are chaired by the Speaker of the House. Five members, including the Speaker, constitute a quorum.[116] In the event of the death, disability or absence of the Speaker, five members of the Board constitute a quorum; one must be a Minister. The members present then designate one of themselves to chair the meeting.[117]

Mandate and Authority

The powers and authority of the Board flow from provisions of the *Parliament of Canada Act,* the Standing Orders of the House of Commons, and the *Parliamentary Employees and Staff Relations Act.* Under the *Parliament of Canada Act,* the Board has legal authority to "act on all financial and administrative matters respecting the House of Commons, its premises, its services and its staff; and the Members of the House of Commons".[118] The Board examines and approves the annual budget estimates of the House before the Speaker transmits them to the President of the Treasury Board, who will then lay them before the House with the estimates of the government.[119] All sums of money voted for the House by Parliament are released by order of the Board. In other words, the Board of Internal Economy manages all operating and administrative expenses of the House, including employee salaries and amounts payable to Members (i.e., their sessional indemnities, expense allowances, travel and communications costs). In administrative matters, the Board is responsible for managing the premises, services and staff of the House as well as those goods, services and premises made available to Members to carry out their parliamentary duties.

Pursuant to the Standing Orders of the House, the Board approves and controls the budget expenditures of the committees of the House of Commons, and must table an annual financial report outlining the expenses incurred by each committee.[120] The rules further require that when the Board has reached a decision concerning any budget presented to it, the Speaker shall lay upon the Table the record of the Board's decision.[121]

In accordance with the *Parliamentary Employee and Staff Relations Act,* the Board is deemed to be the employer of the staff of the House of Commons, as defined in the Act (the chief exception being Members' staff, who are deemed to be

---

116. *Parliament of Canada Act*, R.S.C. 1985, c. P-1, s. 50 as amended by c. 42 (1st supp.), s. 2 and S.C. 1991, c. 20, s. 2 (s. 52.1).

117. *Parliament of Canada Act*, R.S.C. 1985, c. P-1 as amended by S.C. 1991, c. 20, s. 2 and S.C. 1997, c. 32, s. 2 (s. 52(2)). Formerly, the Deputy Speaker or a person designated by the Speaker or Deputy Speaker was required to be present and to chair the meeting.

118. *Parliament of Canada Act*, R.S.C. 1985, c. P-1 as amended by S.C. 1991, c. 20, s. 2 (s. 52.3).

119. *Parliament of Canada Act*, R.S.C. 1985, c. P-1 as amended by S.C. 1991, c. 20, s. 2 (s. 52.4).

120. Standing Order 121.

121. Standing Order 148(2).

employed by the Members).[122] As employer, the Board approves salary scales for non-unionized employees and authorizes officials of the House to negotiate the renewal of the collective agreements of unionized employees and ratifies such agreements.

Pursuant to the Standing Orders, a member of the Board is designated to be responsible for answering any questions pertaining to the administration of the House which may be put during Question Period.[123]

By-laws and Decisions of the Board

The Board is authorized by the *Parliament of Canada Act* to make by-laws governing Members' use of the funds, goods, services and premises made available to them. When the Board makes a by-law, it must be tabled in the House within 30 days of its making, or deposited with the Clerk if the House is not sitting.[124]

The Standing Orders require the Speaker to table at the beginning of each new session of Parliament a report of decisions of the Board of Internal Economy for the previous session.[125] Early in the Thirty-Fifth Parliament (1994-97), a new practice was instituted whereby records of the Board's decisions (typically, in the form of minutes) are tabled in the House as soon as they have been approved by the Board.[126]

EXECUTIVE COMMITTEE

The Executive Committee is responsible for management policy and major decision-making involving general administrative practices, security, and financial and personnel administration of the House. It is chaired by the Speaker and composed of the Deputy Speaker, the Clerk, the Sergeant-at-Arms and a senior official responsible for financial services and human resources.

STANDING COMMITTEE ON PROCEDURE AND HOUSE AFFAIRS

Some of the duties of the Standing Committee on Procedure and House Affairs also deal with the administration of the House. The Committee's mandate includes,

---

122. R.S.C. 1985, c. 33 (4th Supp.), ss. 3, 4(2). The Board of Internal Economy issues guidelines to Members in connection with their role as employers (*Manual of Allowances and Services,* House of Commons, January 1999).

123. Standing Order 37(2). See, for example, *Debates,* February 5, 1986, p. 10473. See also Chapter 11, "Questions".

124. *Parliament of Canada Act,* R.S.C. 1985, c. P-1 as amended by S.C. 1991, c. 20, s. 2 (s. 52.5(3)).

125. Standing Order 148(1).

126. See *Debates,* February 17, 1994, p. 1507. See, for example, the minutes of the Board's meeting of November 5, 1996, tabled on December 6, 1996 (*Journals,* p. 975); March 18, 1997, tabled on April 25, 1997 (*Journals,* p. 1557); May 26, 1998, tabled on June 11, 1998 (*Journals,* p. 1021).

among other things, reviewing and reporting to the House and to the Board of Internal Economy on:

- issues concerning the management of the House and the provision of services and facilities to Members;

- the effectiveness and management of operations under the joint control of the House of Commons and the Senate;

- radio and television broadcasting of proceedings of the House and its committees; and

- matters relating to the election of Members.

In addition, the Committee considers the budgetary estimates of the House of Commons, including the *Report on Plans and Priorities* and the *Performance Report,* just as other committees consider departmental estimates.[127]

OFFICE OF THE CLERK OF THE HOUSE

Members are supported in their parliamentary functions by services administered by the Clerk of the House[128] who, as the chief executive of the House administration, reports to the Speaker. The Clerk is appointed by Order-in-Council[129] and is the senior permanent official of the House. The Clerk advises and supports the Speaker, the House and its committees in all procedural and administrative matters, and acts as Secretary to the Board of Internal Economy. The staff and administration of the House come under the control of the Clerk.[130] The Standing Orders establishing the procedural and administrative functions of the Clerk have changed little since

---

127. Standing Order 108(3)(*a*). For further information on this Committee, see Chapter 20, "Committees". See, for example, statements of the Speaker in appearances before the Standing Committee on Procedure and House Affairs: *Minutes and Evidence of Proceedings*, April 12, 1994, Issue No. 7, pp. 5-10; April 4, 1995, Issue No. 48, pp. 6-11; October 26, 1995, Issue No. 91; May 30, 1996, Issue No. 16; April 8, 1997, Issue No. 39; April 30, 1998, Issue No. 23; March 11, 1999, Issue No. 54.

128. Since Confederation, 10 Clerks have served the House of Commons (see Appendix 6, "Clerks of the House of Commons Since 1867"). The office of Clerk has a long history in British parliamentary tradition. The first official appointment of a Clerk to the Commons took place in 1363, though from much earlier times kings had employed officials to record their decisions and those of their advisors. In the language of the time, the word "clerk" simply indicated a person who could read and write. Thus, the early Clerks of the House were servants of the Crown appointed to assist the Commons with its business. Their duties included reading petitions and bills. As the Commons gained in stature and recognition, its Clerk became more identified with the institution. In the mid-sixteenth century, Clerks began keeping notes on proceedings in the House, and these evolved into the *Journals*. During the tumultuous sittings of the Long Parliament (1640-53), the role of Clerk grew to include advising the Chair and the House on procedural matters (*Wilding and Laundy,* pp. 134-5). For a historical account, see Philip Marsden, *The Officers of the Commons 1363-1978,* London: Her Majesty's Stationery Office, 1979.

129. For examples of recent appointments, see *Journals*, October 9, 1979, p. 18; September 18, 1987, p. 1485. The appointment of the Clerk is provided for by the *Public Service Employment Act* (R.S.C. 1985, c. P-33, s. 40(*d*)).

130. Standing Order 151.

Confederation; however, the responsibilities of the office have evolved considerably as the administrative apparatus of the House has become more complex.

The Clerk is responsible for maintaining records of the proceedings of the House and for keeping custody of these records and other documents in the possession of the House.[131] The Standing Orders also require the Clerk to provide the Speaker, prior to each sitting of the House, with the official agenda for the day's proceedings, published under the title *Order Paper and Notice Paper*.[132] This rule has traditionally been interpreted to mean that the Speaker must be in possession of the current *Order Paper and Notice Paper* in order for the day's proceedings to begin.

All decisions of the House are authenticated by signature of the Clerk. At the beginning of a Parliament, the Clerk administers the oath of allegiance to all duly elected Members. The Clerk also administers an oath to Members joining the Board of Internal Economy.[133] In addition, the Clerk is responsible for administering the oath of allegiance to all employees of the House administration.[134]

Reporting to the Clerk are senior officials who are responsible for the various organizational units of the House administration (i.e., parliamentary precinct services, procedural services in the House and committees, and corporate resources). The Sergeant-at-Arms, the Deputy Clerk and the Clerks Assistant have duties in the Chamber when the House is sitting as well as administrative responsibilities.

The Sergeant-at-Arms[135] assists the Clerk as head of parliamentary precinct services, performing certain ceremonial functions and being responsible for security and building services. The ceremonial role of the Sergeant-at-Arms entails accompanying the Speaker, as Mace-bearer, on all parliamentary functions.[136] When engaged in ceremonial functions and when attending sittings of the House, the Sergeant-at-Arms is attired formally in black tailcoat and cocked hat, with a sword signifying the authority of the office.[137]

---

131. Standing Order 151.

132. Standing Order 152.

133. *Parliament of Canada Act*, R.S.C. 1985, c. P-1 as amended by S.C. 1991, c. 20, s. 2 (s. 50(5)).

134. *Parliament of Canada Act*, R.S.C. 1985, c. P-1, s. 49(1). This section of the Act also requires the Clerk to swear the oath before the Speaker of the House.

135. The office of Sergeant-at-Arms originated in the early years of the British Parliament, when mace-bearing members of the Royal bodyguard were assigned to attend the Speaker at sittings of the House of Commons. With the Sergeant-at-Arms and the Mace, the House could exercise its powers of arrest, trial and imprisonment and pursue its lengthy struggle to establish its rights and privileges. (See the section in this chapter on the Mace. For a detailed history of the office, see *Marsden*.) See Appendix 7 for a list of Sergeants-at-Arms of the House of Commons since Confederation.

136. For example, in the parade escorting the Speaker to and from the Chamber, or to the Senate Chamber for the reading of the Speech from the Throne.

137. In 1849, when rioters entered the Parliament Building in Montreal, the Sergeant-at-Arms reportedly drew his sword while attempting to protect the Mace (Beauchesne, *Canada's Parliament Buildings*, pp. 56-7).

As regards security, the Sergeant-at-Arms is responsible for the protection and security of Members, employees, visitors and property within the parliamentary precinct.[138] This includes personal security for the Prime Minister in the precinct of Parliament, and maintaining order in the Chamber and all the parliamentary buildings. The Sergeant-at-Arms is also responsible for parking control on Parliament Hill by agreement with the Royal Canadian Mounted Police, and for maintaining accommodation for Members and staff of the House of Commons.

From time to time since Confederation, the Clerk of the House has also been assisted by a Deputy Clerk and one or more Clerks Assistant,[139] who act as Table Officers and assume various responsibilities in the administration of the House of Commons.[140] Appointments to the position of Clerk Assistant have been made at various times either by the Speaker;[141] by Order-in-Council;[142] or, more recently, some have been made under the administrative authority of the Executive Committee on the recommendation of the Clerk of the House.

---

138. Since 1920, the House of Commons has had its own security service under the Sergeant-at-Arms. Prior to this, security was the responsibility of the Dominion Police, which in 1920 was merged with the Royal North West Mounted Police to create a new national force, the Royal Canadian Mounted Police (RCMP). (For further information, see *History of the House of Commons Security Services 1920-1995*, Security Services Directorate, House of Commons, 1995.) With the Speaker's permission, other police forces (such as the Royal Canadian Mounted Police or the City of Ottawa police force) may enter the buildings on official business (*Maingot*, 2nd ed., pp. 171-3).

139. The appointment to the position of Deputy Clerk has been made by Order in Council (Mary Anne Griffith: see *Journals*, September 18, 1987, p. 1485; Camille Montpetit: see *Canada Gazette, Part I,* November 7, 1998, p. 3036; *Journals*, February 11, 1999, p. 1498). In Britain, the post of Clerk Assistant is second to that of Clerk and dates from 1640, when the first such appointment was made (*May*, 22nd ed., p. 198; for historical background, see *Marsden,* pp. 45-8).

140. Table Officers are part of a corps of procedural staff, trained by means of an established career structure which provides experience in a variety of procedural fields. See "The Clerkship as a Profession" by C. S. Koester in *The Table*, Vol. LVII for 1989, pp. 35-43.

141. See, for example, the appointments of John George Bourinot (*Journals*, February 17, 1879, p. 8; *Debates*, February 17, 1879, cols. 5-6) and Arthur Beauchesne (*Journals*, February 15, 1916, pp. 79-80; February 17, 1916, p. 85).

142. See, for example, the appointments of Thomas Munro Fraser (*Journals*, February 5, 1925, p. 1); Charles Beverley Koester (*Journals*, October 14, 1975, p. 754); Philip A.C. Laundy (*Journals*, March 4, 1983, p. 5672); Robert Marleau (*Journals*, March 4, 1983, p. 5672); and Mary Anne Griffith (*Journals*, January 21, 1985, p. 224).

7

The Speaker and Other Presiding Officers of the House

You know what we demand of you, Mr. Speaker. Perfection! We want fairness, independence, decisiveness, patience, common sense, good humour, upholding the traditions of the House, knowledge of the rules and an intuition for the changing mood and tone of the House as we move through our days.

JOHN N. TURNER, Leader of the Opposition
(*Debates,* September 30, 1986, p. 9)

The Speaker of the House of Commons holds a position which is not only one of historical significance but also one of important responsibility. The incumbent of the office performs several functions falling into three main categories. First, the Speaker presides over debate in the House and is responsible for enforcing and interpreting all rules and practices and for the preservation of order and decorum in the proceedings of the House. Second, the Speaker is the chief administrative officer of the House of Commons. Third, the Speaker is the representative or spokesperson for the House in its relations with authorities or persons outside Parliament. This chapter describes the speakership from a general point of view and enumerates the specific powers, duties and responsibilities attached to the office of Speaker.

The Speaker of the House

HISTORICAL PERSPECTIVE

No other office or position is more closely linked to the history of the House of Commons than that of the Speaker. The office dates back at least 600 years, almost to the very beginnings of Parliament itself.

Great Britain

The first Speaker to be so designated was Sir Thomas Hungerford in 1377.[1] His predecessor, Sir Peter de la Mare, was elected in 1376 and was the first Commons spokesperson known to have been selected by the House membership.[2] Originally, the Speaker's principal function was to act as the spokesperson of the House in its dealings with the House of Lords and the Crown.[3] In an era when the influence and power of the King was great and that of the House still tentative and subordinate, the Speaker was as much an agent of royal interests (seen as "the King's man") as a servant of the House.[4] The year 1642 marked the end of the Crown's influence over the Speaker, when Charles I, accompanied by an armed escort, crossed the Bar of the House, sat in the Speaker's chair and demanded the surrender of five parliamentary leaders on a charge of treason. Falling to his knees, Speaker William Lenthall replied with these now famous words which have since defined the Speaker's role in relation to the House and the Crown:

> *May it please Your Majesty, I have neither eyes to see, nor tongue to speak in this place, but as the House is pleased to direct me, whose servant I am here; and I humbly beg Your Majesty's pardon that I cannot give any other answer than this to what Your Majesty is pleased to demand of me.*[5]

While Speaker Lenthall's words heralded the end of the Crown's influence over the Speakership, it was the beginning of the government's authority over the Chair. The Speakership then became an appointment much coveted by members of the

---

1. Earlier presiding officers were called "parlour", "prolocutor" and "procurator" (*Wilding and Laundy*, p. 707).

2. *May*, 22nd ed., p. 9.

3. The task of communicating the resolutions of the Commons to the King was not an enviable one. At least nine Speakers are known to have died violently—four during the stormy period of the Wars of the Roses (mid-fifteenth century) (Philip Laundy, *The Office of Speaker in the Parliaments of the Commonwealth*, London: Quiller Press, 1984, pp. 19-20).

4. This is exemplified by the remark of Speaker Finch, in 1629, to an angry House which did not wish to comply with a royal command to adjourn: "I am not less the King's servant for being yours!" (*Laundy*, p. 31).

5. *Laundy*, p. 34.

party in power and used to advance its policies. The House allowed Speakers, who often held government posts, to participate routinely in debate and to set the agenda of the sitting by selecting when and what bills should be considered. However, with his advent to the Chair, Speaker Arthur Onslow (1728-61) loosened the ties to government and established the standards of independence and impartiality which have come to be associated with the office of Speaker. Believing that widespread corruption in government was destroying the dignity of Parliament, he became a strict proceduralist and impartial arbiter of the House's proceedings. By the mid-1800s and the tenure of Speaker Shaw-Lefevre (1839-57), the principle of Speakers abstaining from all political activity became established. Throughout the nineteenth century and into the twentieth, the House altered its rules to invest the Speaker with considerable authority to curtail obstruction and disorder, thereby firmly entrenching the tradition of a non-partisan Chair.

It was also during the Speakership of Shaw-Lefevre that the principle of continuity of office began. Upon election, the Speaker renounces all party affiliation and, when seeking re-election to the House, runs as Speaker. No Speaker of the British House of Commons seeking re-election in his or her constituency has been defeated; it has happened that Speakers have faced one or more opponents nominated by other parties.[6] Upon retirement, the Speaker is appointed to the House of Lords with a pension as compensation for the sacrifice of active partisan political life.[7]

Canada

As in the British parliamentary system, the Speaker of the Canadian House of Commons functions as its spokesperson and as the presiding officer of its proceedings. However, the historic position and character of the British and Canadian speakerships are distinctly different.

In Canada, the relationship between the Crown, the Senate and the House of Commons was clearly established by the time of Confederation. The Canadian Speaker has not, therefore, been involved in constitutional disputes relating to the role of the Speaker, as took place in Britain over a period of several centuries. The appointment and role of the Speaker were clearly defined in the *Constitution Act, 1867* and subsequently in the *Parliament of Canada Act* and the Standing Orders of

---

6. *Laundy,* pp. 68-71.

7. In Canadian practice, a retiring Speaker is not guaranteed a position or posting. In recent years, Speakers Lamoureux (1966-74) and Francis (1984) were appointed Ambassadors; Speaker Michener (1957-62) was appointed High Commissioner to India and, in 1967, was named Governor General; Speaker Macnaughton (1963-66) was appointed to the Senate; Speaker Sauvé (1980-84) was named Governor General; Speaker Jerome (1974-80) was appointed a Judge to the Federal Court; Speaker Bosley (1984-86) continued as a private Member; Speaker Fraser (1986-94) was appointed Canada's Ambassador for the Environment.

the House of Commons.[8] In addition, political parties and party government have always been a part of the Canadian House. The British Commons, on the other hand, saw the development of the system of party government over 150 years of its history, beginning in the late seventeenth century.[9] By the end of the nineteenth century, it had conferred on its Speaker discretionary powers to overcome determined obstruction by minorities in the House.

In contrast to the established British practice of continuity in the Speakership, the experience in Canada has seen the length of tenure limited normally to one or two Parliaments.[10] The issue of the continuity of the Speakership has often been raised in the House and its committees;[11] only two of the more than 30 Speakers since Confederation have served more than two Parliaments (i.e., Speaker Lemieux (1922-30) and Speaker Lamoureux (1966-74) each served in three Parliaments).[12] The longest tenure, that of Speaker Lamoureux, lasted nine years.

The Speaker has almost always been elected from among the Members of the governing party,[13] and although the Speaker eschews partisan political activity, he or she does not make a complete break. Only one Speaker has chosen to sever himself from all party affiliation and to present himself as an independent candidate in general elections. Speaker Lamoureux (1966-74) resigned from the Liberal Party and, as an independent candidate, ran and won in the general elections of 1968 and 1972. In 1968, the Liberal Party and the Progressive Conservative Party did not nominate candidates to oppose him; the New Democratic Party had already nominated a

---

8. See next section, "Governing Provisions".

9. For a description of this process, see *Redlich*, Vol. I, pp. 52-72.

10. See Appendix 2, "Speakers of the House of Commons Since 1867".

11. An example is the recurring proposal for the establishment of a special constituency for the Speaker, designated as Parliament Hill, with the electorate being the Members of the House of Commons. A private Members' bill with this objective was introduced on October 20, 1970 (*Journals*, p. 40) and debated on October 29, 1971 (*Debates*, pp. 9186-92). See also the Fourth Report of the Special Committee on Standing Orders and Procedure, presented on December 3, 1982 (*Journals*, p. 5420) and paragraph 11 of the First Report of the Special Committee on the Reform of the House of Commons, presented on December 20, 1984 (*Journals*, p. 211).

12. Seven Speakers have served in two Parliaments: Cockburn (1867-74), Anglin (1874-79), Rhodes (1917-22), Michener (1957-62), Jerome (1974-80), Fraser (1986-94) and Parent, who was first elected in 1994 (see Appendix 2, "Speakers of the House of Commons Since 1867").

13. Speaker Jerome (1974-80), elected to a second term to serve as Speaker during the minority government of Prime Minister Clark in 1979, was the first and only Speaker to be elected from an opposition party. Prior to 1986, Speakers were elected on a motion proposed by the Prime Minister and the practice of alternating between anglophone and francophone Speakers was well entrenched (see Appendix 2, "Speakers of the House of Commons Since 1867"). Following rule changes adopted in 1985 (see *Journals*, June 27, 1985, pp. 910-9), the election has been conducted as a secret ballot. See the section of this chapter entitled "Election of the Speaker as Presiding Officer".

candidate prior to his decision to run as an independent. In 1972, both the New Democratic Party and the Progressive Conservative Party ran candidates against him.

Certain developments in recent years have served to strengthen and enhance the office of Speaker. In 1968, the official Order of Precedence of Canada[14] was amended to move the Speaker of the House of Commons from tenth position to seventh, immediately after the Governor General, the Prime Minister, the Chief Justice of Canada, former Governors General, former Prime Ministers and the Speaker of the Senate.[15] Since the mid-1970s, the salary and allowances attached to the office of Speaker have been comparable to those of a Cabinet Minister.[16] A long-standing rule providing for appeals to the House from decisions of the Speaker was removed from the Standing Orders in 1965.[17] Provisional rules, adopted on June 27, 1985, and made permanent in June 1987, provide for the election of the Speaker by secret ballot.[18]

GOVERNING PROVISIONS

The *Constitution Act, 1867* establishes the office of Speaker, the requirement for the election of the Speaker, certain of the Speaker's duties and the right of the Speaker to vote only in case of a tie, referred to as a "casting vote".[19]

The *Parliament of Canada Act* fixes the Speaker's salary and enumerates certain administrative responsibilities such as chairing the Board of Internal Economy, the body which is by statute responsible for all matters of financial and administrative policy affecting the House of Commons.[20] The Act also provides for the Deputy Speaker, or any other Member called upon by the Speaker, to preside over the House during the Speaker's absence.[21] The *Parliament of Canada Act* further provides that following a dissolution of Parliament, the Speaker and the other members of the Board of Internal Economy will remain in office, for administrative purposes, until the opening of the new Parliament.[22]

---

14. Precedence (the right to precede others) in ceremonies and matters of protocol is governed by the Table of Precedence for Canada. See "Official Precedence" in successive editions of the *Canadian Parliamentary Guide*.

15. Order in Council approved on December 19, 1968.

16. See the *Salaries Act* for salaries of Cabinet Ministers and the *Parliament of Canada Act* for the Speaker's salary.

17. *Journals*, June 11, 1965, p. 224.

18. See Standing Orders 2, 3, 4, 5 and 6.

19. *Constitution Act, 1867*, R.S.C. 1985, Appendix II, No. 5, ss. 44-47, 49.

20. See *Parliament of Canada Act*, R.S.C. 1985, c. P-1, ss. 13(1), 23(2), 25(1), 28, 42-4, 50-3, 60, 70(2) and (3), 74.

21. *Parliament of Canada Act*, R.S.C. 1985, c. P-1, ss. 42, 43.

22. *Parliament of Canada Act*, R.S.C. 1985, c. P-1 as amended by S.C. 1991, c. 20, s. 2 (s. 53).

A number of other statutes have an impact on the role and responsibilities of the Speaker of the House. For example, the *Electoral Boundaries Readjustment Act* establishes the Speaker's role in appointing two members to each provincial Electoral Boundaries Commission,[23] in tabling the reports of these commissions and in the filing of possible objections.[24] The *Official Languages Act* provides that in the event of the absence or incapacity of the Commissioner of Official Languages, the Governor in Council may appoint a replacement, following consultation by the Prime Minister with the Speakers of both Houses.[25]

Certain statutes require the Speaker to receive reports and other documents and to table them in the House.[26] Other statutes, such as the *Western Grain Transportation Act*, the *Emergencies Act,* the *Energy Administration Act,* the *Energy Supplies Emergency Act,* the *Old Age Security Act,* the *International Development (Financial Institutions) Assistance Act* and the *Special Economic Measures Act,* which provide for Parliament to confirm, revoke or amend instruments of delegated legislation by means of resolutions adopted after debate in the House, also require the Speaker to perform a specific role in this process.[27]

The Standing Orders provide for the Speaker's duties as presiding officer in the House, and outline further administrative duties, most of which are carried out by the Clerk and the Sergeant-at-Arms under the direction of the Speaker.[28]

PROCEDURAL ROLE OF THE SPEAKER

The House devises its own rules, develops its own practices and is master of its own proceedings. The office of the Speaker derives its authority from the House and the holder of the office can accurately be described as its representative and authoritative counsellor in all matters of form and procedure.[29] The office of the Speaker is to be distinguished from its incumbent, who requires the support and goodwill of the House in order to carry out the duties of the office. The Speaker's authority and responsibilities as Presiding Officer in the House of Commons flow in large part from the Constitution and from the written rules of the House.

The duties of the Speaker of the House of Commons require balancing the rights and interests of the majority and minority in the House to ensure that the public

---

23. *Electoral Boundaries Readjustment Act*, R.S.C. 1985, c. E-3, s. 6.
24. *Electoral Boundaries Readjustment Act*, R.S.C. 1985, 2nd Supp., c. 6, ss. 5, 6.
25. *Official Languages Act*, R.S.C. 1985, 4th Supp., c. 31, s. 49(4).
26. For further details, see the section of this chapter entitled "Tabling of Documents".
27. For further information and examples, see the section on statutory debates in Chapter 15, "Special Debates".
28. See, for example, Standing Orders 9 to 14 and 19. For examples of administrative responsibilities set out in the Standing Orders, see Standing Orders 22, 107, 121 and 148 to 159.
29. *Redlich*, Vol. II, pp. 143-4.

business is efficiently transacted and that the interests of all parts of the House are advocated and protected against the use of arbitrary authority.[30] It is in this spirit that the Speaker, as the chief servant of the House, applies the rules. The Speaker is the servant, not of any part of the House or any majority in the House, but of the entire institution and the best interests of the House as distilled over many generations in its practices.

Despite the considerable authority the Speaker holds, he or she may exercise only those powers conferred by the House, within the limits established by the House itself. In ruling on matters of procedure, the Speaker adheres strictly to this principle, delineating the extent of the Speaker's authority and in some cases offering a suggestion as to matters which the House may see fit to pursue.[31]

Guardian of Rights and Privileges

It is the responsibility of the Speaker to act as the guardian of the rights and privileges of Members and of the House as an institution.[32] At the opening of each Parliament, the House is summoned to the Senate Chamber and the newly elected Speaker addresses the Crown or its representative and claims for the Commons all its rights and privileges.[33] The claim holds good for the life of the Parliament and is not repeated in the event of a new Speaker being elected during the course of a Parliament.[34] Freedom of speech may be the most important of the privileges accorded to Members of Parliament; it has been described as:

> . . . *a fundamental right without which they would be hampered in the performance of their duties. It permits them to speak in the House without inhibition, to refer to any matter or express any opinion as they see fit, to say what they feel needs to be said in the furtherance of the national interest and the aspirations of their constituents.*[35]

The right to freedom of speech is not absolute; there are restrictions, derived from practice, convention, and the rules agreed to by the House. For example, the Standing Orders provide for time limits on speeches, and according to the *sub judice*

---

30. *Redlich*, Vol. II, pp. 149-50. See also Speaker Fraser's ruling, *Debates*, April 14, 1987, pp. 5119-24.

31. See, for example, *Debates*, January 26, 1967, pp. 12271-2; October 11, 1979, p. 69; May 3, 1990, pp. 10941-2; October 25, 1995, pp. 15812-3.

32. Parliamentary privilege is the "sum of the peculiar rights enjoyed by each House collectively as a constituent part of the High Court of Parliament, and by Members of each House individually, without which they could not discharge their functions, and which exceed those possessed by other bodies or individuals" *(May*, 22nd ed., p. 65). See also Chapter 3, "Privileges and Immunities".

33. See, for example, *Debates of the Senate*, September 23, 1997, p. 3.

34. *Bourinot*, 4th ed., pp. 49-50. See later sections of this chapter for information on the election of the Speaker during the course of a Parliament.

35. See paragraph 3 of the First Report of the Special Committee on the Rights and Immunities of Members, presented on April 29, 1977 (*Journals*, pp. 720-9).

convention, it is accepted that Members will restrict themselves from discussion of matters which are under the consideration of a judge or court.[36] The duty of the Speaker is to ensure that the right of Members to free speech is protected and exercised to the fullest possible extent; this is accomplished in part by ensuring that the rules and practices of the House are applied and that order and decorum are maintained.[37] Whenever a Member brings to the attention of the House a possible breach of a right or privilege, the responsibility of the Speaker is to determine whether or not *prima facie* a breach of privilege has occurred.[38] In practice the Speaker, in hearing an alleged question of privilege, may intervene to remind Members of the Speaker's role and to request that the Member's remarks be directed to providing facts to establish the existence of a *prima facie* case.[39] At the Speaker's discretion, other Members may be permitted to participate. Only when the Speaker has ruled the matter to be a *prima facie* question of privilege is it before the House for its consideration.[40]

Order and Decorum

As the arbiter of House proceedings, the Speaker's duty is to preserve order and decorum in the House and to decide any matters of procedure that may arise. When a decision on a matter of procedure or a question of order is reached, the Standing Orders provide that the Speaker identify which Standing Order or authority is being applied to the case.[41]

Sometimes, a ruling is given quickly and with a minimum of explanation.[42] At other times, circumstances do not permit an immediate ruling. The Speaker may allow discussion of the point of order before he or she comes to a decision.[43] The Speaker might also reserve on a matter, returning to the House at a later time to deliver the ruling.[44] Once the Speaker has ruled, the matter is no longer open to

---

36. For further information, see Chapter 13, "Rules of Order and Decorum".

37. Speaker Fraser has observed that there can be no freedom of speech without order in the House (*Debates*, March 24, 1993, pp. 17486-8).

38. *Prima facie* means "at first sight" or "on the face of it". *Maingot* offers the following definition: "A *prima facie* case of privilege in the parliamentary sense is one where the evidence on its face as outlined by the Member is sufficiently strong for the House to be asked to debate the matter and to send it to a committee to investigate whether the privileges of the House have been breached or a contempt has occurred and report to the House" (2nd ed., p. 221).

39. *Maingot*, 2nd ed., p. 220.

40. Standing Order 48(1). The wording of the rule is unchanged since Confederation. For further information on the role of the Speaker in deciding on a question of privilege, see Chapter 3, "Privileges and Immunities".

41. Standing Order 10.

42. See, for example, *Debates,* March 9, 1992, pp. 7840-1.

43. Standing Order 19. See, for example, *Debates*, October 16, 1986, pp. 402-6.

44. See, for example, *Debates*, October 27, 1986, pp. 767-8; October 29, 1986, p. 864.

debate or discussion. On some occasions, the Speaker has chosen to amend or clarify a previous ruling.[45]

The duty to maintain order and decorum in the House[46] confers on the Speaker a wide-ranging authority extending to such matters as Members' attire and behaviour in the Chamber, the conduct of House proceedings, the rules of debate, and disruptions on the floor of the House and in the galleries. There are a number of ways in which the Speaker ensures that order and decorum are preserved:

- The rules governing the conduct of debate empower the Speaker to call a Member to order if the Member persists in repeating an argument already made in the course of debate, or in addressing a subject which is not relevant to the question before the House.[47] The Speaker may intervene directly to address an individual Member or the House in general;[48] or, the Speaker may respond to a point of order raised by another Member.[49] The Speaker can call to order any Member whose conduct is disruptive to the order of the House. For example, if it is a question of unparliamentary language, the Speaker requests an unequivocal withdrawal of the word or expression.[50]

- If the Speaker has found it necessary to intervene in order to call a Member to order, he or she may then choose to recognize another Member, thus declining to give the floor back to the offending Member.[51] On occasion, a Member who is called to order by the Speaker may not immediately comply with the Speaker's instructions; in such a case, the Speaker has given the Member time to reflect on his or her position and upon the duty of the Chair, exercising in the meantime the prerogative of the Chair not to "see" the Member if he or she should rise to be recognized.[52]

- The strongest sanction available to the Speaker for maintaining order in the House is "naming", a disciplinary measure invoked against a Member who persistently disregards the authority of the Chair.[53] If a Member refuses to heed the Speaker's requests to bring his or her behaviour into line with the rules and practices of the House, the Speaker has the authority to name that Member (i.e., address the Member by name rather than by constituency or title, as is the usual practice) and, without putting the question to the House, order his or her withdrawal from the Chamber for the remainder of the sitting day.[54] During debate in a Committee of

---

45. See, for example, *Journals*, March 28, 1916, pp. 201-2; June 1, 1956, pp. 678-9; *Debates*, May 13, 1999, pp. 15108-9.

46. Standing Order 10. Matters of order and decorum are addressed in greater detail in Chapter 13, "Rules of Order and Decorum".

47. Standing Order 11(2).

48. See, for example, *Debates*, September 25, 1989, p. 3818; September 26, 1996, p. 4715.

49. See, for example, *Debates*, August 11, 1988, p. 18232; April 22, 1997, pp. 10103, 10106.

50. See, for example, *Debates*, March 22, 1971, pp. 4467-9; October 26, 1998, p. 9396.

51. See, for example, *Debates*, December 4, 1998, pp. 10914-5, 10922.

52. See, for example, *Debates*, November 18, 1987, pp. 10927-8.

53. Standing Order 11(1).

54. Standing Order 11(1)(*a*). For further information on naming, see Chapter 13, "Rules of Order and Decorum".

the Whole House, if a Member persists in disorderly conduct and refuses to obey the warning of the Chair to discontinue his or her unparliamentary behaviour, the Chair of the Committee rises and reports the conduct of the Member to the Speaker. The Chair may do this on his or her own initiative without recourse to a motion from the Committee.[55] The Speaker will then follow the procedure for naming the Member.[56] The power to name a Member extends to the Deputy Speaker and Acting Speaker.[57]

- Another means of preserving order in the Chamber is the Speaker's discretionary power to order the withdrawal of strangers:[58] that is, anyone who is not a Member or an official of the House of Commons (e.g., Senators, diplomats, government officials, journalists or members of the general public). This has been used to clear the galleries of individuals whose presence has been a cause of disruption.[59] From time to time, the Speaker has also seen fit to remind spectators in the galleries of the expected standard of behaviour.[60] In addition, the rules provide that, should a Member take note of the presence of strangers (or should the House wish to proceed *in camera*[61]), the Speaker may put the question "That strangers be ordered to withdraw".[62] This motion is not debatable or amendable, and if decided in the affirmative, the Speaker—with the help of the Sergeant-at-Arms, if necessary—then ensures that the galleries are cleared.[63]

---

55. Standing Order 11(2). See, for example, *Debates*, March 16, 1962, pp. 1888-90.

56. For further information on naming in a Committee of the Whole, see Chapter 19, "Committees of the Whole House".

57. *Parliament of Canada Act*, R.S.C. 1985, c. P-1, s. 44. For instances of Members being named by the Deputy Speaker, see *Debates*, February 23, 1981, pp. 7586-8; May 20, 1983, pp. 25628-31. For examples of Members being named by the Acting Speaker, see *Debates*, March 24, 1983, pp. 24109-10; May 25, 1984, pp. 4078-9.

58. Standing Order 14.

59. See, for example, *Debates*, May 11, 1970, p. 6796. On this occasion, the Speaker ordered the galleries cleared and then obtained the agreement of the House to suspend the sitting, which resumed 34 minutes later. On another occasion, by order of the Speaker, the galleries were entirely cleared and reopened to the public within 10 minutes (*Debates*, November 28, 1989, pp. 6339, 6342-3). In other cases when a disturbance arises, the security staff on duty in the galleries proceed to remove the individual responsible and there is little or no disruption of the sitting (see, for example, *Debates*, May 7, 1974, p. 2114; April 14, 1986, p. 12188; November 26, 1992, p. 14108).

60. See, for example, *Debates*, May 10, 1899, col. 2897; September 12, 1983, p. 26987; November 17, 1992, p. 13501.

61. See the section on secret sittings of the House in Chapter 9, "Sittings of the House".

62. Standing Order 14. In 1990, Nelson Riis (Kamloops) attempted to move the motion but was ruled out of order on the grounds that the motion cannot be moved by a Member who has been given the floor on a point of order (*Debates*, April 4, 1990, pp. 10186-7). For further information on this rule, see Chapter 6, "The Physical and Administrative Setting".

63. Traditionally, and in accordance with Standing Orders 157(2) and 158, the Sergeant-at-Arms is responsible for preserving order and decorum in the galleries and other parts of the House and for removing strangers who "misconduct" themselves. For further information on the role of the Sergeant-at-Arms, see Chapter 6, "The Physical and Administrative Setting".

No Appeals

The present Standing Orders prohibit any debate on decisions of the Speaker and prohibit any appeal of a decision to the House.[64] From Confederation until 1965, however, it was possible for any Member who disagreed with a Speaker's decision on a question of order to appeal it immediately to the House (i.e., to move a non-debatable motion on the question of whether or not the House upheld the Speaker's ruling).[65] In the early years of Confederation, this was rarely done.[66] After the turn of the century, however, Members began asserting their right to an appeal to the House.[67] By the 1920s and thereafter, hardly a session passed that did not see at least one appeal.[68] The practice reached a peak in the session of 1956 when 11 appeals were made, mostly during the very contentious "Pipeline Debate".[69] Similar numbers of appeals were made in the Parliaments of 1962-63 and 1963-65.[70] In 1965, as part of a series of amendments to the Standing Orders, the opportunity to appeal rulings of the Speaker was abolished.[71] Former Speaker Lambert supported the abolition of appeals because "one of the chief difficulties with the business of Parliament over the past 10 years has been the somewhat indiscriminate use of appeals against Speaker's rulings, not on points of jurisprudence or points of procedure but for political effect".[72]

Before 1965, there were several instances where the decision of the Speaker was appealed and not sustained by the House. The first of these came in 1873 when the House overruled the Speaker on the acceptability of a petition.[73] In 1926, another ruling was rejected, and three more in 1963 were not sustained.[74] The vote on a fourth ruling in 1963 resulted in a tie and was sustained when the Speaker declined

---

64. Standing Order 10.

65. See 1867 rule 8, and 1962 rule 12(1).

66. See, for example, *Debates*, May 20, 1868, p. 750; *Journals*, March 24, 1873, pp. 58-9. Although Members were sometimes openly critical of a ruling, few formal challenges were made (see the comments of Sir John A. Macdonald, *Debates*, March 5, 1877, p. 485).

67. Between 1907 and 1917, for example, six appeals took place (*Journals*, April 3, 1907, p. 381; April 6, 1910, pp. 418-20; May 12, 1913, pp. 576-7; March 25, 1914, pp. 301-2; May 10, 1916, pp. 353-5; September 8, 1917, pp. 639-40, 641).

68. See entries in the *Journals* indexes under the heading "Speaker's Rulings and Statements".

69. For text of the rulings and votes on the appeals, see *Journals* for 1956 as follows: March 21, pp. 323-8; May 10, pp. 517-23; May 14, pp. 536-43; May 15, pp. 554-7; May 17, pp. 568-70; May 23, pp. 602-4, 604-9; May 25, pp. 628-32; May 31, pp. 662-9; June 1, pp. 675-7; June 5, pp. 705-10.

70. See *Journals* indexes for this period.

71. *Journals*, June 11, 1965, p. 224.

72. *Debates*, June 8, 1965, p. 2140.

73. *Journals*, March 24, 1873, pp. 58-9.

74. *Journals*, June 25, 1926, p. 477; January 31, 1963, pp. 462-3 (two rulings); October 28, 1963, p. 493.

to give a casting vote and ruled that his decision should stand "since the decision has not been negatived".[75]

Impartiality of the Chair

When in the Chair, the Speaker embodies the power and authority of the office, strengthened by rule and precedent. He or she must at all times show, and be seen to show, the impartiality required to sustain the trust and goodwill of the House. The actions of the Speaker are not to be criticized in debate or by any means except by way of a substantive motion. Such motions have been moved against the Speaker[76] or other presiding officers[77] on rare occasions. Reflections on the character or actions of the Speaker—an allegation of bias, for example—could be taken by the House as breaches of privilege and punished accordingly.

On two occasions, newspaper editorials were found to contain libellous reflections on the Speaker and were declared by the House, in one instance, to be a contempt of its privileges[78] and, in the other, a gross breach of its privileges.[79]

In 1981, a Minister complained that remarks directed to the Speaker by the Leader of the Opposition constituted an attack on the authority and impartiality of the Speaker. The following day, the Minister tabled a motion in the House calling for the remarks to be referred to the Standing Committee on Privileges and Elections.

---

75. *Journals*, December 4, 1963, pp. 621-2.

76. In June 1956, during the "Pipeline Debate", Speaker Beaudoin ruled to revert the House to a position it had been in 24 hours earlier. On June 4, the Leader of the Opposition moved a motion of censure against the Speaker for his actions and rulings of June 1. The motion was defeated on June 8, 1956. See *Debates*, June 1, 1956, pp. 4537-40; *Journals*, June 4, 1956, pp. 692-3; June 8, 1956, pp. 725-6.

77. On March 13, 1964, the Prime Minister moved, without notice, a motion calling for Canadian peacekeeping forces to be sent to Cyprus. Even though the motion appeared to have the general support of the House, some opposition Members objected to the fact that no notice of motion had been given. Stating that the Prime Minister had in fact obtained the proper "permission", Deputy Speaker Lamoureux dismissed the objections and directed the House to consider the motion in question. On March 18, 1964, a Member introduced a motion of non-confidence in the Deputy Speaker, alleging that he had violated the Standing Orders and deprived certain Members of their rights and privileges. The motion was put to a vote on March 19, 1964, and was rejected (*Debates*, March 13, 1964, pp. 910-26; *Journals*, March 18, 1964, pp. 103-4; March 19, 1964, pp. 106-7).

On May 4, 1992, a Member tabled a motion of non-confidence (under the heading "Motions" and printed in the *Order Paper and Notice Paper* of May 4, 1992) in the Deputy Chairman of Committees of the Whole and Acting Speaker (Steve Paproski) for not allowing, on April 30, 1992, full time for debate on a bill. The debate gave rise to a question of privilege on May 1, 1992. The Speaker found that there was "no *prima facie* case of privilege in this matter" (*Debates*, April 30, 1992, p. 9945; May 1, 1992, pp. 9963-72, 9990-1). On February 12, 1993, at the request of the Member who had sponsored it, the motion of non-confidence was withdrawn (*Debates,* February 12, 1993, p. 15851).

78. *Journals*, April 25, 1894, pp. 108-9.

79. *Journals*, December 22, 1976, p. 270.

However, the Leader of the Opposition withdrew his remarks and the matter was taken no further.[80]

In another incident, occurring in 1993, a question of privilege was raised concerning disparaging remarks made by a Member about the impartiality of the Assistant Deputy Chairman of Committees of the Whole. When the Member refused to withdraw the comments, the Speaker stated that the comments "affect[ed] the dignity of [the] House" and were "an attack against the integrity" of an officer of the House. He ruled that *prima facie* there was a case of privilege and the matter was referred to a Committee. Two days later, the Member rose in the House and withdrew the remarks.[81]

In 1996, a private Member's motion on the *Order Paper* alleged that another Member and his party were guilty of a contempt of the House for attempting to rally public opinion with a view to influencing an upcoming decision of the Speaker. The motion was selected for debate in the House but was later withdrawn without having been considered.[82]

In 1998, a Member raised a question of privilege, alleging that statements attributed to other Members in a newspaper article (concerning an upcoming ruling of the Chair) constituted an attempt to intimidate the Speaker and the House itself. The Speaker found a *prima facie* case and the matter was referred to a committee, which investigated and concluded that the statements attributed to the Members "were not intended to be contemptuous of the House of Commons or the Speaker" and that "they did not bring into question the integrity of the House of Commons and its servant, the Speaker".[83]

In order to protect the impartiality of the office, the Speaker abstains from all partisan political activity (for example, by not attending caucus meetings), does not participate in debate and will vote only in the case of an equality of voices, normally referred to as the "casting vote" of the Chair.[84] Since 1979, the Speaker, unlike all other Members, has not had an assigned desk in the Chamber; this is a further indication that it has become an accepted practice that the Speaker has no role whatsoever in debate, whether in the House or in a Committee of the Whole.[85]

Although the requirement that Speakers remain mute in debate has existed since 1867, it has not always been applied when the House met in a Committee of the Whole. During the first 60 years after Confederation, there were many instances of participation by the Speaker in this forum.[86] By 1927, however, the practice had

---

80. *Debates*, January 21, 1981, p. 6410; January 22, 1981, pp. 6455-7.

81. See *Debates*, March 16, 1993, p. 17027; March 23, 1993, pp. 17403-5; and March 25, 1993, p. 17537.

82. *Order Paper and Notice Paper*, March 5, 1996, p. 15; *Journals*, October 23, 1996, p. 768.

83. *Debates*, March 9, 1998, pp. 4560-75; March 10, 1998, pp. 4592-8, 4666-8. See also the Twenty-Ninth Report of the Standing Committee on Procedure and House Affairs, presented on April 27, 1998 (*Journals*, p. 706), and adopted by the House on May 5, 1998 (*Journals*, pp. 744-5).

84. *Constitution Act, 1867*, R.S.C. 1985, Appendix II, No. 5, s. 49; Standing Order 9.

85. See Chapter 6, "The Physical and Administrative Setting".

86. Speaker Anglin (1874-78), for example, was an active participant during proceedings in a Committee of the Whole. See, for example, *Debates*, April 26, 1878, p. 2216; May 3, 1878, pp. 2402-3.

become rare, and when Speaker Lemieux spoke in Committee, Members objected.[87] After this, Speakers did not intervene in a Committee of the Whole except on occasion to defend their Estimates.[88] Since 1968, these Estimates have been referred to standing committees for study and the Speaker, as a witness, continues to defend the Estimates of the House of Commons in this forum.[89]

In the past, Speakers have appeared before, and have sometimes chaired, House committees, usually when matters of procedure and reform of the rules have been considered.[90] In recent years, however, Speakers have limited themselves to appearing before standing committees as witnesses on matters within their jurisdiction, such as the spending Estimates of the House.

Casting Vote

The Speaker does not participate in debate and votes only in cases of an equality of voices; in such an eventuality, the Speaker is responsible for breaking the tie by casting a vote.[91]

In theory, the Speaker has the same freedom as any other Member to vote in accordance with his or her conscience; however, the exercise of this responsibility could involve the Speaker in partisan debate, which would adversely affect the confidence of the House in the Speaker's impartiality. Therefore, certain conventions have developed as a guide to Speakers (and Chairmen in a Committee of the Whole) in the infrequent exercise of the casting vote.[92] Concisely put, the Speaker would normally vote to maintain the *status quo*. This entails voting in the following fashion:

- whenever possible, leaving the matter open for future consideration and allowing for further discussion by the House;

---

87. *Debates*, April 7, 1927, pp. 2034-8.

88. The last to do so was Speaker Macnaughton on November 27, 1964 (*Debates*, pp. 10623-9).

89. See, for example, the appearances of Speaker Parent before the Standing Committee on Procedure and House Affairs in connection with the Estimates of the House of Commons, on April 12, 1994; April 4, 1995; May 30, 1996; April 8, 1997; April 30, 1998.

90. For example, Speaker Bosley (1984-86) appeared before the Special Committee on the Reform of the House of Commons on January 22, 1985; Speaker Fraser (1986-94) appeared before the Standing Committee on Elections, Privileges, Procedure and Private Members' Business on November 29, 1989, before the Special Committee on the Review of the *Parliament of Canada Act* on September 25, 1990, and before the Standing Committee on Environment on November 5, 1991. The latter appearance was in connection with "Greening the Hill", the program of environmental conservation launched by the Speaker. In 1977-78, Speaker Jerome (1974-80) chaired the Special Committee on TV and Radio Broadcasting of Proceedings of the House and Its Committees.

91. *Constitution Act, 1867*, R.S.C. 1985, Appendix II, No. 5, s. 49; Standing Order 9.

92. An equality of voices is a rarity, having occurred on just five occasions in the House: May 6, 1870 (*Journals*, p. 311; *Debates*, cols. 1401-2); February 28, 1889 (*Journals*, pp. 113-4; *Debates*, p. 368); March 31, 1925 (*Journals*, pp. 180-2; *Debates*, pp. 1714-5); March 11, 1930 (*Debates*, pp. 502-3, 527); December 4, 1963 (*Journals*, pp. 621-2; *Debates*, pp. 5405-6); and on four occasions in a Committee of the Whole: *Debates*, June 20, 1904, col. 5164; April 15, 1920, p. 1265; June 23, 1922, p. 3473; March 26, 1928, p. 1681.

- whenever no further discussion is possible, taking into account that the matter could somehow be brought back in the future and be decided by a majority of the House;

- leaving a bill in its existing form rather than having it amended.[93]

In 1863, these conventions were acknowledged in the Legislative Assembly of the Province of Canada when the Speaker was called upon to give a casting vote, and gave as his reason "that in the case of an equal division, the practice was, that the Speaker should keep the question as long as possible before the House in order to afford a further opportunity to the House of expressing an opinion upon it".[94] The application of this convention has not always been consistent and there are very few examples where Speakers or Chairmen of Committees of the Whole gave reasons when casting a vote. For instance, on one occasion, the Speaker voted in favour of a hoist amendment[95] to the motion for third reading of a bill in order "to keep the Bill before the House";[96] on another, the Speaker voted against a hoist amendment for the same reason ("to give the House a further opportunity for consideration").[97]

The manner in which the Speaker casts a deciding vote is as follows: typically, a recorded vote is demanded, taken and, when an equality of voices is discerned at the announcement of the result, the Speaker then votes and may give reasons. Any given reasons are recorded in the *Journals*. On one occasion, an equality of voices was announced, the Speaker cast his vote and it later came to light that no tie had occurred. The next day, the Speaker made a brief statement and declared his vote invalidated.[98] On another occasion, prior to the abolition of appeals from Speakers' rulings, the voices were equal on the motion to sustain the ruling of the Chair. The Speaker declined to vote, stating that "Since the decision has not been negatived, I declare my ruling sustained" and no objection was raised.[99]

93. For an elaboration of these conventions in the British context, see *May*, 22nd ed., pp. 357-61.

94. *Journals of the Legislative Assembly*, August 19, 1863, p. 33. See also *Bourinot*, 4th ed., p. 384.

95. If adopted, the hoist amendment has for effect the rejection of the bill. See Chapter 16, "The Legislative Process".

96. *Debates*, May 6, 1870, col. 1401; in this case, no reasons were entered in the *Journals*.

97. *Debates*, February 28, 1899, p. 368.

98. *Debates*, March 11, 1930, pp. 502-3; March 12, 1930, p. 527. The casting vote was not noted in the *Journals* (see *Journals*, March 11, 1930, pp. 83-4). The disposition of the motion was not changed as it had in fact been defeated by one vote before the Speaker cast his vote with the "nays". In New Zealand, the converse has occurred; a question thought to have been carried by one vote was discovered to have been a tie; the Speaker gave a casting vote at that time and declared the motion defeated (*McGee*, 2nd ed., pp. 71, 180-2).

99. *Journals*, December 4, 1963, pp. 621-2.

Specific Duties

Specific duties of the Speaker in the Chamber are described below; many of the procedural topics referred to are explored in greater detail in other chapters.

Opening the sitting: It is the Speaker's responsibility to open the sittings of the House once it has been determined that a quorum is present.[100] When opening a sitting, the Speaker takes the Chair, calls the House to order, reads prayers, directs that the doors to the public galleries be opened, and then calls the first item of business. If, as sometimes happens, the Speaker is absent at the opening of a sitting, the House is so informed by the Clerk and the Deputy Speaker takes the Chair.[101]

Reading motions, putting questions, announcing results of votes: Before debate begins on a matter, the Speaker proposes the question by reading the motion on which the House is to decide. When no Member rises to be recognized in debate, the Speaker asks if the House is "ready for the question", thus ascertaining whether or not the debate has concluded. When debate on a question is closed, it is the Speaker's responsibility to put the question, that is, to put the matter for a decision of the House, and afterwards to announce the result to the House.[102]

Recognizing Members to speak in the House: No Member may speak in the House until called or recognized by the Speaker; any Member so recognized may speak during debate, questions and comments periods, Question Period, and other proceedings of the House. Various conventions and informal arrangements exist to ensure the participation of all parties in debate; nevertheless, the decision as to who may speak is ultimately the Speaker's.[103]

Deciding questions of order and questions of privilege: In presiding over the deliberations of the House, the Speaker is responsible for deciding questions of order and questions of privilege, and for ensuring that the rules and practices of the House are respected.[104] The Speaker rules on questions of order and questions of privilege as they occur and not in anticipation.[105] A question of order may be brought to the Speaker's attention by a Member, or the Speaker may intervene when he or she observes an irregularity.[106] In ruling on questions of order and questions of privilege,

---

100. A quorum of 20 Members, including the Speaker, is required for the House to conduct business (*Constitution Act, 1867*, R.S.C. 1985, Appendix II, No. 5, s. 48; Standing Order 29(1)). For further information on quorum, see Chapter 9, "Sittings of the House".

101. *Parliament of Canada Act*, R.S.C. 1985, c. P-1, s. 43(1). See, for example, *Journals*, December 7, 1998, p. 1401.

102. For further information, see Chapter 12, "The Process of Debate".

103. *Bourinot*, 4th ed., p. 334. See also *Debates*, May 20, 1986, p. 13443; May 5, 1994, p. 3925. For further information, see Chapter 13, "Rules of Order and Decorum".

104. Standing Order 10. See the section above entitled "Order and Decorum" and see also Chapter 3, "Privileges and Immunities".

105. *Bourinot*, 4th ed., p. 178.

106. *Bourinot*, 4th ed., p. 178.

the Speaker cites the Standing Order or other applicable authority.[107] At times, the Speaker may be called upon to deal with situations not provided for in the Standing Orders of the House; in such cases, the rules give authority to the Speaker to consider parliamentary tradition in jurisdictions outside the House of Commons of Canada.[108] *Decisions on motions:* The Standing Orders confer on the Speaker certain responsibilities in connection with motions coming before the House for consideration. The Speaker has the responsibility to act, in the event that he or she judges a motion to be "contrary to the rules and privileges of Parliament".[109] In such a case, it is the Speaker's responsibility to inform the House at the earliest opportunity, before the question is put, and to refer to the applicable rule or authority. This is to be distinguished from the Speaker's general power to rule authoritatively on matters of procedure. While the Speaker is guardian of the rules and privileges of the House, he or she is its servant as well; the Members of the House retain control of their collective actions. Thus, if the Speaker were to inform the House that a proposed motion, though correct as to its form, runs counter to established parliamentary principles, customs or privileges, the House would then be in a position to take a decision on the matter, with the benefit of the information provided and the authorities cited by the Speaker. This rule was first adopted after Confederation[110] and has never been invoked by the Speaker, although there have been attempts to persuade the Chair to invoke it. [111]

Other rules of the House give the Speaker the power to select which report stage amendments will be considered by the House, and to group these for purposes of debate and division.[112] In addition, in the event that notice of more than one opposition motion is given when a Supply day has been designated, the Speaker is responsible for selecting the one which will have precedence for consideration by the House.[113]

Conduct of Private Members' Business: It is the overall responsibility of the Speaker to make all the necessary arrangements to ensure the orderly conduct of the hour of each sitting day devoted to Private Members' Business.[114] This includes ensuring that the House has 24 hours' notice of the item to be considered in each

---

107. Standing Order 10.

108. Standing Order 1. For further information on the rule and practice pertaining to unprovided cases, see Chapter 5, "Parliamentary Procedure".

109. Standing Order 13.

110. *Journals*, December 20, 1867, pp. 115-25.

111. See, for example, point of order raised in *Debates*, December 9, 1968, pp. 3639-43, and Speaker Lamoureux's ruling in *Journals*, December 10, 1968, pp. 511-3; point of order raised in *Debates*, July 24, 1969, pp. 11551-68, and Speaker Lamoureux's ruling in *Journals*, July 24, 1969, pp. 1398-9.

112. Standing Order 76(5) and 76.1(5). The text of these rules includes guidelines for the Speaker on the selection of amendments. See also Chapter 16, "The Legislative Process".

113. Standing Order 81(14)(*b*). See Chapter 18, "Financial Procedures".

114. Standing Order 94(1)(*a*). For further information, see Chapter 21, "Private Members' Business".

sitting,[115] seeing to the arrangement of exchanges when a sponsoring Member is unable to be present when his or her item is scheduled for consideration,[116] and refusing a notice of an item of Private Members' Business which is deemed to be substantially the same as another.[117]

Private bills: When private bills[118] are to be brought before Parliament, those wishing to act as parliamentary agents (i.e., employed in promoting or opposing a private bill) must be granted authority to do so by the Speaker.[119] The Speaker also has the power to issue a temporary or absolute prohibition on an individual acting as a parliamentary agent, in cases where he or she has failed to act in accordance with parliamentary rules and practice.[120]

Tabling of documents: Statutory provisions, as well as rules of the House, state that the Speaker receives and tables certain reports and documents in the House. When the Speaker tables a document, he or she may do so during the sitting;[121] alternatively, the document may be deposited with the Clerk of the House.[122] In either case, the tabling is noted in the *Journals* and the item tabled is deemed permanently referred to the appropriate standing committee.[123] The specific documents tabled by the Speaker are as follows:

- As Chair of the Board of Internal Economy (the body responsible for all financial and administrative matters affecting the House of Commons) the Speaker is responsible for tabling reports of the Board's proceedings.[124] The reports consist of minutes of the Board's meetings, which are tabled as they are approved by the Board.[125] The Speaker is also responsible for tabling the annual reports of the Board's decisions respecting the budgets of parliamentary committees.[126] In addition, the *Parliament of Canada Act* requires the Speaker to table any by-laws

---

115. Standing Order 94(1)(*a*).

116. Standing Order 94(2)(*a*).

117. Standing Order 86(5).

118. For further information, see Chapter 23, "Private Bills Practice".

119. Standing Order 146(1).

120. Standing Order 146(4).

121. Typically, this is done during Routine Proceedings under the rubric "Tabling of documents" (see, for example, *Debates*, April 15, 1986, p. 12221; *Journals*, April 5, 1989, p. 26; March 12, 1990, p. 1323). The Speaker has also tabled documents immediately prior to Statements by Members (see, for example, *Debates*, December 11, 1984, p. 1102; September 26, 1996, p. 4740).

122. See, for example, *Journals*, September 21, 1998, p. 1056.

123. Standing Order 32(5). For further information on the tabling of documents, see Chapter 10, "The Daily Program".

124. Standing Order 148(1). See, for example, *Journals*, January 27, 1994, p. 71.

125. The rule requires the Speaker to table, within 10 days of the opening of a session, a report of the Board's proceedings for the previous session; the practice of more frequent tablings throughout the session began in the Thirty-Fifth Parliament (see *Debates*, February 17, 1994, p. 1507).

126. Standing Order 148(2). See, for example, *Journals*, September 30, 1994, p. 758.

made by the Board within 30 days of their making; typically, these are deposited with the Clerk.[127]

- Statutory requirements exist whereby designated officers of Parliament[128] and the Canadian Human Rights Commission transmit their annual reports and any special or investigatory reports to the Speaker, who then tables them in the House.[129]

- In the decennial process to readjust electoral boundaries, reports of the provincial and territorial electoral boundaries commissions are transmitted by the Chief Electoral Officer to the Speaker, who tables them when the House is sitting.[130]

- When election results are contested under the *Dominion Controverted Elections Act,* reports are made to the Speaker, who then informs the House; typically, this is done at or shortly after the opening of the sitting.[131] The legislation also requires the Speaker to inform the House of amendments to the rules of the provincial Supreme Courts, which are the courts of appeal in such cases.[132] In accordance with the *Corrupt Practices Inquiries Act* (which provides for investigation of alleged or suspected corrupt or illegal practices during elections), commissions of enquiry are appointed and their reports are made to Parliament—that is, to the Speakers of both Houses—and it would be the Speaker's responsibility to inform the House of the reports.[133]

---

127. *Parliament of Canada Act*, S.C. 1991, c. 20, s. 52.5(2), (3). See, for example, *Journals*, December 4, 1998, p. 1399.

128. They are the Auditor General, the Chief Electoral Officer, the Commissioner of Official Languages, the Information Commissioner and the Privacy Commissioner.

129. *Auditor General Act*, R.S.C. 1985, c. A-17, ss. 7(3), 8(2), 19(2); *Canada Elections Act*, R.S.C. 1985, c. E-2, s. 195(3); *Official Languages Act*, R.S.C. 1985, 4ᵗʰ Supp., c. 31, ss. 65(3), 66, 67(1), 69(1); *Access to Information Act*, R.S.C. 1985, c. A-1, ss. 38, 39(1), 40; *Privacy Act*, R.S.C. 1985, c. P-21, ss. 38, 39(1), 40(1); *Canadian Human Rights Act*, S.C. 1998, c. 9, s. 32.

130. *Electoral Boundaries Readjustment Act*, R.S.C. 1985, c. E-3, s. 21; *An Act to amend the Electoral Boundaries Readjustment Act*, R.S.C. 1985, c. 6 (2ⁿᵈ Supp.), s. 5. See, for example, *Journals*, June 22, 1995, p. 1867. The legislation provides an alternative course for the Speaker, should a report arrive during an intersession. For further information on the role of the House of Commons in the redistribution process, see Chapter 4, "The House of Commons and Its Members".

131. *Dominion Controverted Elections Act*, R.S.C. 1985, c. C-39, ss. 58(1), 60, 61, 71. For examples of the Speaker informing the House, see *Debates*, March 6, 1950, p. 468; February 23, 1976, p. 11139; October 14, 1981, p. 11731. For further information on contested or controverted elections, see Chapter 4, "The House of Commons and Its Members".

132. *Dominion Controverted Elections Act*, R.S.C. 1985, c. C-39, s. 84(3). This is a rare occurrence; in 1950, for example, the Speaker tabled such an amendment (*Journals*, June 5, 1950, p. 471).

133. *Corrupt Practices Inquiries Act*, R.S.C. 1985, c. C-45, s. 30. No commissions of enquiry have been struck; nor have any reports been made under the terms of the Act.

Emergency debates: When a Member has made a request to move the adjournment of the House in order to debate a matter requiring urgent consideration (an emergency debate), the Speaker is responsible for deciding whether or not the request will be granted. [134] When the Speaker has granted an application for an emergency debate, the rules provide for it to take place the same day, but the Speaker may also exercise a discretionary power to defer the debate to a specific time on the next sitting day. [135] An emergency debate ends at the times provided in the Standing Orders, but again, the Speaker has discretion to declare the motion carried and adjourn the House to the next sitting day if, in his or her opinion, debate has concluded before those times. [136] Once it is underway, an emergency debate takes precedence over all other business; in the event of conflict or incompatibility with regard to other rules or other business of the House, the Speaker has complete discretion in reconciling the difficulty. [137]

Recall of the House: When the House stands adjourned during a session, the Speaker has the power to recall the House to meet prior to the date it is scheduled to reconvene. [138] The request to recall the House is always initiated by a Minister (usually the Government House Leader), and the Speaker has no authority to consider such a request from any other Member. In these circumstances (or while Parliament stands prorogued, or prior to the first session of a new Parliament), upon receipt of a written request from the government, the Speaker will cause to be published a *Special Order Paper* which informs the House of any measure the government wishes the House to consider immediately. [139] A notice for recall of the House is not usually withdrawn; but on one occasion, after receiving a request from all the recognized parties in the House, the Speaker issued a formal statement cancelling an earlier notice for recall. [140]

Parliamentary publications: The official publications of the House of Commons are published under the authority of the Speaker. These include, among others, the *Journals,* the *Debates,* the indexes to the *Journals* and *Debates,* the *Order Paper and Notice Paper,* the Standing Orders of the House of Commons, bills and the minutes and reports of parliamentary committees. [141]

---

134. Standing Order 52(4). For further information on emergency debates, see Chapter 15, "Special Debates".

135. Standing Order 52(9). For example, an application was made on Friday, November 27, 1998. The Speaker granted it and ruled that the debate would take place on Monday, November 30 at 8:00 p.m. (*Journals*, November 27, 1998, p. 1323).

136. Standing Order 52(12).

137. Standing Order 52(15).

138. Standing Order 28(3).

139. Standing Order 55(1). For further information on recall of the House and publication of a *Special Order Paper*, see Chapter 8, "The Parliamentary Cycle", and Chapter 12, "The Process of Debate".

140. The original notice was given on June 26, 1992, for the House to meet on July 15, 1992; the notice of cancellation was issued on July 11 and tabled when the House met on September 8, at which time the Speaker made a statement to the House (see *Journals*, September 8, 1992, p. 1924; *Debates*, September 8, 1992, p. 12709).

141. For further information on parliamentary publications, see Chapter 24, "The Parliamentary Record".

Chairs of Legislative Committees: The Speaker also has responsibilities with regard to Chairs of legislative committees.[142] It is the Speaker's duty at the start of each session, and thereafter as necessary, to select Members to form a Panel of Chairmen. The Speaker exercises a certain amount of discretion in the choice of Members; the rules specify only that a proportionate number of Members be appointed from the government and opposition parties and that the other Presiding Officers of the House be members of the Panel.[143] Whenever the House agrees to proceed with the appointment of a legislative committee, it is the Speaker's responsibility to select from the Panel of Chairmen a Member to chair that legislative committee.[144]

ADMINISTRATIVE ROLE OF THE SPEAKER

The Speaker is the head of the House of Commons administration and is responsible for its overall direction and management.[145] The House administration supports Members of Parliament, individually and collectively, in their parliamentary roles as well as the House itself as an institution.

One of the fundamental privileges of the House is to regulate its own internal affairs, holding exclusive jurisdiction over its premises and the people within.[146] By virtue of the *Parliament of Canada Act,* all matters of administrative and financial policy affecting the House of Commons are overseen by the Board of Internal Economy,[147] which is composed of Members of the House from the government and opposition parties. The Speaker chairs the Board of Internal Economy.

The day-to-day management of the staff of the House of Commons rests with the Clerk[148] and the senior officials reporting to the Clerk, subject to orders of the House or of the Speaker.[149] The Speaker, as Chair of the Board of Internal Economy and senior authority in matters of House management, retains a major interest in issues of human resources management.

Spending Estimates[150] for the House of Commons are prepared at the request of the Board of Internal Economy and once they have been approved by the Board, it is the Speaker's responsibility to transmit them to the President of the Treasury Board for tabling with the government's departmental Estimates for the fiscal year.

---

142. See Standing Orders 112 and 113. For further information about legislative committees, see Chapter 20, "Committees".
143. Standing Order 112.
144. Standing Order 113(2).
145. See Chapter 6, "The Physical and Administrative Setting".
146. *Maingot,* 2nd ed., pp. 183-5.
147. *Parliament of Canada Act*, R.S.C. 1985, c. P-1, s. 52.3.
148. The Clerk of the House serves as Secretary to the Board of Internal Economy, as provided in the *Parliament of Canada Act.*
149. Standing Order 151.
150. See Chapter 18, "Financial Procedures".

The Speaker also chairs the Executive Committee, which is established by the Board of Internal Economy. The Executive Committee is responsible for management policy and major decision-making affecting general administrative practices, security, and financial and human resources administration.[151]

The right of each House of Parliament to regulate its own internal affairs also extends to the management of the premises "within the precincts and beyond the debating Chamber ...".[152] As guardian of the rights and privilege of the House, the Speaker ensures that they are respected within and outside the House.[153] Within the precincts, the Speaker oversees matters of security and policing. Security within the buildings occupied by Members and staff of the House is the responsibility of the Sergeant-at-Arms, who acts under the Speaker's authority.[154] For this purpose, the House maintains its own security service. Arrangements are in place whereby the Royal Canadian Mounted Police (RCMP) is charged with security of the grounds outside the buildings. There are occasions when the House security staff request and receive assistance from outside police forces, whether the RCMP or the local police. It is also well established that outside police forces wishing to enter the parliamentary precincts must first have permission from the Speaker to do so, and that the authority to grant or withhold permission rests with the Speaker, who exercises sole discretion in this regard.[155]

The Speaker as the chief administrator of the House oversees all its dealings with government departments in matters of administration. Public Works and Government Services Canada (PWGSC) is the primary provider of central and common services to the Government of Canada and to the Parliament of Canada. Officials of the House of Commons, under the Speaker's authority, work in close co-operation with PWGSC for the delivery of professional and technical services such as translation and interpretation, printing and publishing, as well as the management of the Parliament Buildings and leased properties. The National Capital Commission (NCC) is a Crown corporation whose objective is to plan and assist in "the development, conservation and improvement of the National Capital Region in order that the

---

151. The Executive Committee exists by virtue of By-Law 201 of the Board of Internal Economy. The Board's power to make by-laws is conferred by section 52.5(1) of the *Parliament of Canada Act*.

152. *Maingot*, 2nd ed., p.183.

153. An incident in 1998 illustrates the authority of the Speaker over access to the precinct. On February 26, 1998, a Member's employee, carrying a large flag, accosted a Member in the House of Commons foyer, and security staff intervened. The Speaker investigated the incident and the employee in question was required, for a minimum period of one year, to confine his activity in the Centre Block to the public entrance and the party offices on one floor of the building.

154. See Standing Orders 157 and 158.

155. See, for example, the Second Report of the Standing Committee on Privileges and Elections, presented on September 21, 1973 (*Journals*, p. 567). See also the Speaker's comments in *Debates*, November 30, 1979, pp. 1890-2; May 19, 1989, pp. 1951-3. For further information, see Chapter 3, "Privileges and Immunities".

nature and character of the seat of the Government of Canada may be in accordance with its national significance".[156] The NCC has the responsibility for maintaining the grounds on Parliament Hill[157] and this historic site is the focal point of much other NCC-sponsored activity. The Speaker is naturally interested to ensure that all such activity takes place with due regard to the dignity and authority of the institution and the privileges of Members, such as the right to have access to the House of Commons and the parliamentary precinct at all times.

CEREMONIAL/DIPLOMATIC ROLE OF THE SPEAKER

Certain responsibilities of the Speaker may be categorized as being of a traditional, ceremonial or diplomatic nature, highlighting the role of the Speaker as a representative of the Commons. The Speaker is the representative and spokesperson for the House of Commons in its relations with the Senate, the Crown and other bodies outside the House of Commons. Messages, correspondence and documents addressed to the House of Commons are communicated to it by the Speaker.[158]

When entering or leaving the House, the Speaker is always preceded by the Sergeant-at-Arms, who carries the Mace.[159] The opening of a sitting of the House is preceded by a ceremonial event known as the Speaker's parade, in which the Speaker walks in procession through the halls of the Centre Block to the House of Commons Chamber.[160]

Whenever the House is summoned to the Senate Chamber to attend the Queen, the Governor General, or the representative of the Governor General, the Speaker leads the procession. This happens at the opening of a Parliament and of a session,[161] or whenever there is to be a ceremony to grant Royal Assent to bills.[162] When a new Parliament or new session opens and a Speech from the Throne is read in the Senate Chamber, it is then officially communicated to the House by the Speaker. When the House has debated the Address in Reply to the Speech from the Throne, the text of

---

156. *National Capital Act*, R.S.C. 1985, c. N-4, s. 10(1).

157. *National Capital Act*, R.S.C. 1985, c. N-4, s. 10(2)(*d*).

158. An example would be messages to the House from the Senate, which are read by the Speaker in the course of the sitting (see, for example, *Debates*, December 3, 1998, p. 10888).

159. *Bourinot*, 4th ed., p. 176. For further information about the Mace, see Chapter 6, "The Physical and Administrative Setting".

160. In the absence of the Speaker, the Presiding Officer for the sitting takes the Speaker's place in the parade. For further information on the Speaker's parade, see Chapter 9, "Sittings of the House".

161. For further information on the opening of a Parliament or a session, see Chapter 8, "The Parliamentary Cycle".

162. For further information on the Royal Assent ceremony, see Chapter 16, "The Legislative Process".

the Address is engrossed, signed by the Speaker and personally presented to the Governor General.[163]*

The Parliament of Canada maintains relations with the provincial and territorial legislatures as well as with most foreign parliaments. Many of these relationships are carried on by, or in the name of, the Speaker of the House of Commons and the Speaker of the Senate. Contacts between the Parliament of Canada and other parliaments and legislative assemblies may range from exchanges of correspondence, to formal visits conducted on a reciprocal basis, to training and development sessions for parliamentary officers.

The Parliament of Canada is an active participant in the international exchange of ideas, information and experiences among world parliaments, and holds membership in several inter-parliamentary associations and friendship groups.[164] The Speaker of the House is an honorary president of each of them and, with the Speaker of the Senate, authorizes the budgetary allocations for each association.[165] Parliamentarians (as delegates, members or participants) attend national, bilateral and international meetings, conferences and seminars arranged through the parliamentary associations and friendship groups.

Outside the framework of the inter-parliamentary associations, the Parliament of Canada also participates in exchanges and programs of parliamentary co-operation with other parliaments throughout the world, authorized and overseen by both Speakers. Parliamentary exchanges offer parliamentarians the opportunity to broaden their knowledge, to discuss problems of mutual interest and issues of the day. The Speaker's involvement may include accepting invitations from other parliaments, hosting visiting delegations of parliamentarians, and participating in the meetings of Speakers from Canada and abroad.

During a sitting, the Speaker may draw the attention of the House to the presence of distinguished visitors seated in the gallery of the House.[166] Generally, this takes place immediately following Question Period, though the Speaker has also

---

163. For further information on the Address in Reply to the Speech from the Throne, see Chapter 15, "Special Debates".

164. The associations are: Canada-China Legislative Association; Canada-France Inter-parliamentary Association; Canada-Japan Inter-parliamentary Group; Canada-United Kingdom Inter-parliamentary Association; Canada-United States Inter-parliamentary Group; *L'Assemblée parlementaire de la Francophonie;* Canada-Europe Parliamentary Association; Commonwealth Parliamentary Association; Inter-parliamentary Union; and the North Atlantic Assembly (Canadian NATO Parliamentary Association).

   The friendship groups are the Canada-Germany Friendship Group, the Canada-Israel Friendship Group, and the Canada-Italy Friendship Group.

165. The Speakers of the Senate and the House of Commons are members of the Joint Inter-parliamentary Council, which is responsible for budget allocation among the associations.

166. Other Members who have attempted to direct the attention of the House to the presence of visitors have been ruled out of order (see, for example, *Debates*, February 6, 1992, p. 6550). See also Speaker Fraser's remarks in *Debates*, October 5, 1990, pp. 13867-8. It has also happened that the practice has been departed from (see, for example, *Debates*, November 28, 1989, p. 6359).

recognized visitors prior to Question Period and even during Question Period.[167] In most cases, the visitors recognized are seated in the Speaker's Gallery.[168] No written rules or formal guidelines exist to define what type of visitors the Speaker shall recognize. The practice has been to recognize:

- heads of state and leaders of foreign governments, and official guests of the Governor General or of the Prime Minister;

- parliamentary delegations, presiding officers and cabinet ministers from provincial and territorial legislative assemblies, or from foreign countries;

- Canadians who have distinguished themselves in any field of endeavour by their achievements, deeds or success of national or international scope.[169]

From time to time, a distinguished visitor (usually a head of state or of government) has given a joint address to Members of the House of Commons and Senators in the House of Commons Chamber. The Speaker, as host, takes a pre-eminent role in such events, which are organized in accordance with an established protocol.[170]

ELECTION OF THE SPEAKER AS PRESIDING OFFICER

The election of the Speaker of the House of Commons is a constitutional requirement.[171] An election must take place at the beginning of the first session of a Parliament, when the House is without a Speaker. Should the Speaker resign or state his or her intention to resign in mid-Parliament, election proceedings again take place; a vacancy occurring for any other reason also leads to the election of a new Speaker.[172] This constitutional requirement is the basis of the Standing Orders which specify when and under what circumstances the election of a Speaker takes place.[173] Although the Speaker has in most cases been elected at the opening of the first session of a Parliament, several Speakers have been elected in mid-session or at the

---

167. See, for example, *Debates*, December 13, 1994, p. 9003 (recognition following Question Period); March 23, 1994, p. 2666 (recognition prior to Question Period); June 3, 1992, p. 11294 (recognition during Question Period).

168. On one occasion, however, a group of World War II veterans seated in the Diplomatic Gallery was recognized by the Speaker (*Debates*, June 6, 1994, p. 4858).

169. In 1996 and 1998, the House sat as a Committee of the Whole for ceremonies recognizing the national Olympic and Paralympic Teams of the 1996 Summer Games and the 1998 Winter Games, for which the athletes were brought onto the floor of the House (*Journals*, October 1, 1996, p. 699; *Debates*, October 1, 1996, pp. 4944-6; *Journals*, April 22, 1998, p. 691; *Debates*, April 22, 1998, pp. 5959-60).

170. For further information on joint addresses to Parliament, see Chapter 9, "Sittings of the House".

171. *Constitution Act, 1867*, R.S.C. 1985, Appendix II, No. 5, s. 44.

172. *Constitution Act, 1867*, R.S.C. 1985, Appendix II, No. 5, s. 45.

173. Standing Order 2(1), (2).

opening of the second or later session of a Parliament.[174] In any case, the election takes precedence over all other business and is not to be considered as a question of confidence in the government.[175] If necessary, the election continues beyond the ordinary hour of daily adjournment until a Speaker is elected. No other business can come before the House until the election has taken place and the new Speaker has taken the Chair.[176]

Although the time at which a Speaker is to be elected is described in the Constitution, no Standing Order before 1985 ever indicated by what means this should be accomplished. From 1867 to 1985, the Clerk of the House conducted the election. The general practice was for the Prime Minister to propose the name of a Member to become Speaker. This debatable motion was usually seconded by a leading Minister, although starting in 1953, the nomination typically was seconded by the Leader of the Opposition.[177] After debate on the motion, the question was put by the Clerk and the Member was elected by a majority of the Members present; in almost all cases, the motion was carried unanimously.[178] The Speaker-elect, showing mock reticence, was then escorted to the Chair by the mover and seconder, after which he or she accepted the nomination and the Mace was placed on the Table. It has been customary for the Speaker-elect to make a pretence of reluctance while being escorted to the Chair. This has its origin in the genuine reluctance with which early British Speakers assumed their duties.[179]

In 1982, the Special Committee on Standing Orders and Procedure (known after its chairman as the Lefebvre Committee) recommended a new procedure to be followed in electing a Speaker by secret ballot.[180] The recommendation was acted upon in 1985, when the government responded favourably to a re-issue of the recommendation

---

174. Of the 33 Speakers who have served the House since Confederation, 26 were elected at the opening of a Parliament; another two were re-elected at the opening of a Parliament, having first been elected in the course of the previous Parliament. See Appendix 2, "Speakers of the House of Commons Since 1867".

175. Standing Orders 2 and 6.

176. Standing Order 2(3).

177. Of the Speakers elected at the beginning of a Parliament (as opposed to those elected in the course of a session), the nominations of eight have been seconded by the Leader of the Opposition, starting in 1953.

178. For a typical example, see the election of Speaker Michener on October 14, 1957 (*Journals*, pp. 7-8; *Debates*, pp. 1-4). No more than one name was ever proposed at any election. Occasionally, there was opposition to the name put forward. For example, Speaker Anglin was elected on a recorded division in 1878 (*Journals*, February 7, 1878, pp. 9-10). In 1936, Speaker Casgrain was elected "on division"—meaning it was not unanimous (*Journals*, February 6, 1936, p. 8). The House "divided" on the question, but no recorded vote was requested.

179. *Wilding and Laundy,* pp. 706-7. *Laundy* (pp. 14, 64) identifies Sir Richard Waldegrave as the founder of this tradition in 1381: "In all probability he anticipated a dispute between the King and the Commons which could result in embarrassment for himself. Little could he have known that in expressing his own genuine reluctance to serve as Speaker he was founding a tradition which was to endure for centuries, long after it had become completely meaningless".

180. See the Fourth Report of the Special Committee on Standing Orders and Procedure, presented on December 3, 1982 (*Journals*, p. 5420).

by the Special Committee on the Reform of the House of Commons (known after its chairman as the McGrath Committee). [181] In its response, the government suggested changes to the recommendation that were later reflected in proposed amendments to the Standing Orders. The amendments were adopted by the House in June 1985. [182] The new procedure went into effect in September of that year on a provisional basis and was first invoked in 1986 when Speaker Bosley resigned the Speakership and, after 11 ballots, the House elected John Fraser as the new Speaker. [183] The protracted election prompted calls for changes in the process; to that end, the Standing Orders were amended in 1987, to exclude from a subsequent ballot candidates receiving five percent or less of the total votes cast. At the same time, the secret ballot procedure became permanent. [184] In 1988, Speaker Fraser was re-elected on the first ballot. In 1994, Speaker Parent was elected after six ballots, and re-elected in 1997 after four ballots.

Election of the Speaker by Secret Ballot

When the House meets at the beginning of a new Parliament, Members are summoned to the Senate Chamber through a message delivered to the House by the Usher of the Black Rod. [185] Preceded by the Clerk of the House, the Members go to the Senate Chamber where they are informed by a Deputy of the Governor General [186] that the causes of summoning will not be divulged (meaning that the Speech from the Throne will not be read) "until the Speaker of the House of Commons shall have been chosen according to Law ...". The Members then return to the House and proceed immediately to the election of a Speaker.

All Members of the House, except for Ministers and party leaders, are automatically considered candidates for the Speakership. [187] The Standing Orders designate who shall preside over the election of a Speaker [188] but are silent as to whether the Member presiding could also be a candidate. In all four elections to date, the

---

181. See the First Report of the Special Committee on the Reform of the House of Commons, presented on December 20, 1984 (*Journals*, p. 211); and the Government Response to the First Report, tabled on April 18, 1985 (*Journals*, p. 486).

182. The proposed amendments to the Standing Orders were tabled on June 27, 1985, and adopted the same day (*Journals*, pp. 910-9).

183. *Journals*, September 30, 1986, pp. 2-8; see also *Debates*, September 30, 1986, pp. 1-10.

184. *Journals*, June 3, 1987, p. 1016. After the Standing Orders were reorganized and renumbered in 1988, the original Standing Order on the election of the Speaker was divided into the present Standing Orders 2, 3, 4, 5 and 6.

185. The Usher of the Black Rod is an officer of the Senate whose responsibilities include delivering messages to the House of Commons when its Members' attendance is required in the Senate Chamber by the Governor General or a Deputy of the Governor General. (In November 1997, the title of the office was changed to Usher of the Black Rod from Gentleman Usher of the Black Rod. See *Senate Debates*, November 6, 1997, pp. 333-43.)

186. A Deputy to the Governor General is a person, usually a Justice of the Supreme Court, who exercises the powers of the Governor General on certain occasions.

187. Standing Order 5.

188. Standing Order 3.

Member presiding took the prescribed action to remove himself from the list of candidates. Any eligible Member who does not wish to be considered must so inform the Clerk in writing by 6:00 p.m., at the latest, on the day before the election is to take place.[189] The notice of withdrawal must be signed by the Member.[190] After the deadline has passed, the Clerk draws up an alphabetical list of the names of Members who do not wish to be considered or who are ineligible by virtue of being Ministers or party leaders. A Member who has withdrawn may, before the deadline, recall the letter of withdrawal and allow his or her name to go forward.[191]

The rules providing for the Speaker's election by secret ballot are silent on many aspects of the election process. In 1986, when preparations began for the first secret-ballot election, matters not covered by the written rules were settled by the Clerk in consultation with the House Leaders, and have since then become part of the practice associated with an election of the Speaker.[192]

The Chamber is set up somewhat differently from normal when a Speaker is to be elected. The Table is cleared of its usual accoutrements and, while the Clerk's chair remains at its head, the chairs of the Table Officers are removed. A ballot box is placed on a stand at the foot of the Table and portable voting booths are placed on either side of the Table. While the election proceeds, the Mace rests under the Table as no Speaker is in the Chair.

When the election of a Speaker takes place at the beginning of a Parliament, it is presided over by the so-called "dean of the House", the Member with the longest unbroken record of service who is neither a Minister nor a holder of any office within the House.[193] After the return of the House from the Senate Chamber, the Clerk invites the dean of the House to take the Chair as the Member presiding. When an election is held during a Parliament to replace a Speaker who has given notice of his or her intention to resign, as was the case in 1986, the outgoing Speaker presides.[194] In the absence of an outgoing Speaker at an election taking place in the course of a Parliament, the Deputy Speaker and Chairman of Committees of the Whole would preside.[195] The Member presiding is vested with all the powers of the Chair and votes in the election; however, he or she may not cast an additional ballot in the event of a tie.[196]

---

189. Standing Order 4(1).

190. See, for example, *Debates*, September 30, 1986, p. 2. In practice, the Clerk sends a written reminder of these provisions to all Members.

191. This occurred in 1986; the Member who did so, John A. Fraser, was eventually elected Speaker.

192. See Philip Laundy, "Electing a Speaker—Canadian Style", *The Table*, Vol. LV for 1987, pp. 42-50. The author was a Clerk Assistant at the House of Commons at the time of the first secret-ballot election of a Speaker.

193. Standing Order 3(1)(*a*). Length of service is determined by reference to the *Canada Gazette*, which publishes the names of Members elected in the order in which the returns are received by the Chief Electoral Officer.

194. Standing Order 3(1)(*b*).

195. Standing Order 3(1)(*c*).

196. Standing Order 3(2).

The Standing Orders require the Member presiding to inform the House that the list of Members who do not wish to be considered for election to the office of Speaker, or who are ineligible, is available for consultation at the Table.[197] This is done before balloting begins; at the same time, the Member presiding reads out (in alphabetical order) the names of the Members appearing on the first ballot, and informs the House that this list is available in each voting booth. Both these lists will also have been distributed to Members at their desks. It has happened that Members not wishing to be considered have sought to remove their names before having passed the start of voting. The Member presiding has responded that, the deadline having passed (6:00 p.m. of the previous day), the list for the first ballot cannot be amended, but doubtless the House would take note of any such request.[198] The voting begins when the Member presiding asks those who wish to cast their ballots to leave their desks, proceed along the corridors behind the curtains in the direction of the Chair, and come to the Table through the doorways at the left and right of the Chair, according to whether the Members sit on the Speaker's left or right.

At these doorways, Members have their names recorded and are issued ballot papers by Table Officers assisting the Clerk.[199] Members must enter through the doorway on the side of the House where they are seated. Once provided with a ballot paper, Members then proceed to the voting booth on the appropriate side of the Table. Members print the first and last names of a candidate on the ballot paper,[200] deposit the paper in the ballot box[201] and then leave the area around the Table in order to ensure the confidentiality of the vote for other Members.

When the Member presiding is satisfied that all Members wishing to vote have done so, the Clerk withdraws from the Chamber to count the ballots, with the assistance of other Table Officers, in a nearby room. The Sergeant-at-Arms carries the ballot box, and pauses by the Chair while the Member presiding deposits his or her ballot paper. The Member presiding then signifies that the proceedings are suspended while the counting of the ballots takes place.

The ballots are counted in secret. Once the Clerk is satisfied as to the accuracy of the count, all ballot papers and related records are destroyed. The Clerk is enjoined by the Standing Orders not to divulge in any way the number of ballots cast for any candidate.[202] When the count is complete, the bells are rung for a few minutes to call the House to order and the Clerk re-enters the Chamber.

---

197. Standing Order 4(3).
198. See, for example, _Debates_, December 12, 1988, pp. 1-2; January 17, 1994, p. 1.
199. Standing Order 4(2).
200. Standing Order 4(4).
201. Standing Order 4(5).
202. Standing Order 4(6). Those assisting the Clerk in the ballot-counting will have taken an oath of secrecy.

If any Member has received a majority of the votes cast, the Clerk gives the Member presiding the name of the successful candidate, which is then announced from the Chair.[203] If no Member has received a majority of the votes cast, then the Clerk provides the Member presiding with a list of the candidates in alphabetical order for the next ballot. The list is drawn up as follows: from the original list of candidates, the Clerk deletes the name of the last-place candidate (or names, in the case of a tie vote for last place), as well as the name of any Member who received five percent or less of the total votes cast.[204] The rule further provides that no names be deleted in the event that every candidate receives the same number of votes. The Member presiding announces that a second ballot will be necessary and reads out the names of the candidates. At this point, any candidates on the second ballot who do not wish to be further considered may rise and withdraw, stating their reasons.[205] The Clerk is then instructed to remove from the list the names of Members who have thus withdrawn. When an alphabetical list of eligible Members is available in each voting booth, the Member presiding asks Members who wish to vote to proceed in the same manner as for the first ballot.

The voting procedure for the second ballot is the same as for the first, except that the ballot papers are a different colour. When the Member presiding is satisfied that all Members wishing to vote have done so, he or she instructs the Clerk to proceed with the count of the second ballot. When the count is complete, the Clerk destroys all the ballot papers and related records, again to ensure the secrecy of the count as required by the Standing Orders.

The Member presiding then calls the House to order and either announces the name of the successful candidate, or that a third ballot will be necessary, in which case the names of the candidates eligible for the third ballot will be read from the list prepared by the Clerk. Members who wish to withdraw their candidacy at this point or on any subsequent ballot may do so and are not required to give reasons.[206] The names of those who withdraw are then removed from the list of eligible candidates and, when the list is made available, the Members proceed to vote.

Balloting continues in this fashion until one candidate has received a majority of the votes cast or until only one name remains. If necessary, the House may continue to sit beyond its usual adjournment time until a Speaker is declared elected.[207]

After announcing the name of the successful candidate from the Chair, the Member presiding invites the Speaker-elect to take the Chair. The Member presiding steps down and escorts the Speaker-elect from his or her seat to the dais. The Speaker-elect may make a token show of resistance.[208]

---

203. Standing Order 4(7).

204. Standing Order 4(8)(*a*).

205. Standing Order 4(8)(*b*). In 1986 (the only election in which Members withdrew after the first ballot), three Members withdrew their names (*Debates*, September 30, 1986, p. 3).

206. Standing Order 4(9). See, for example, *Debates*, September 30, 1986, p. 4. To date, this is the only instance of a withdrawal following the second or a later ballot.

207. Standing Order 2(3). This occurred once: in 1986, the House met at 3:00 p.m., the election process concluded after 11 ballots, and the House adjourned at 2:30 a.m.

208. For the historical background to this practice, see *Laundy*, pp. 14, 64.

Standing at the top of the steps, the first official act of every Speaker elected since Confederation has been to thank the House for the honour it has bestowed. The opening words follow a pattern established over time: "Honourable Members, I beg to return my humble acknowledgements to the House for the great honour you have been pleased to confer upon me in choosing me to be your Speaker".

Speakers have typically included in their remarks a pledge to carry out their duties with firmness and impartiality, an acknowledgement of the great responsibilities of the office, a request to the House for its continued support and goodwill, and acknowledgements and commendations directed to predecessors, other candidates (in the case of secret-ballot elections), constituents, family and fellow Members.[209] The Speaker then takes the Chair. The voting booths and ballot box having been removed, the Sergeant-at-Arms takes the Mace (symbol of the authority of the House) from under the Table, where it sits during the election, and places it on the Table, signifying that now with the Speaker in the Chair, the House is properly constituted.

Since the Speaker has been elected by secret ballot, the party leaders have risen on occasion to offer congratulations and good wishes, and to pledge their support once the newly elected Speaker has taken the Chair and the Mace has been laid on the Table.[210] Before 1986, when the Speaker was nominated on a motion moved by the Prime Minister and elected when the motion was adopted by the House, it was the custom for the individual nominated to be warmly spoken of in the nomination speeches of the Prime Minister and Leader of the Opposition, and congratulatory remarks after the election did not occur as a rule.[211]

By the time the new Speaker has taken the Chair and heard from any Members wishing to offer congratulations, the House may have gone beyond its usual time of adjournment as set out in the Standing Orders; under these circumstances, the

---

209. See, for example, the remarks of Speaker Sutherland, the first to make his remarks in both official languages (*Debates*, January 11, 1905, cols. 3-4); Speaker Lamoureux (*Debates*, January 18, 1966, pp. 5-6); and Speaker Fraser (*Debates*, September 30, 1986, pp. 7-8). This is a convention of the British Parliament as well, where in addition the Speaker-elect must seek Royal approbation (*May*, 22nd ed., p. 239). Redlich describes the ancient custom of the Speaker-elect making repeated and exaggerated declarations of unworthiness, which prevailed long before the modern, non-partisan Speakership, when the office of Speaker was political and dependent on the Crown, and the attitude of its incumbent was characterized as "subservient" (*Redlich*, Vol. II, pp. 156-8).

210. This occurred in 1986, 1988 and 1994; in 1994, congratulatory remarks were also made by a private Member on behalf of the independent Members, by the Member who presided over the election, and by one other private Member (*Debates*, September 30, 1986, pp. 8-10; December 12, 1988, pp. 5-7; January 17, 1994, pp. 6-7). In 1997, a Member sought the unanimous consent of the House to deem the Speaker unanimously elected, and it was granted (*Journals*, September 22, 1997, p. 9; *Debates*, September 22, 1997, p. 4).

211. In 1963 and 1966, the Prime Minister briefly congratulated the newly elected Speaker (Macnaughton and Lamoureux, respectively) prior to making the usual suggestion for the suspension of the sitting (*Debates*, May 16, 1963, p. 5; January 18, 1966, p. 6). In 1874, after the election of Speaker Anglin, the Leader of the Opposition offered congratulations but went on to express misgivings about the government's choice. In 1878, in speaking to the motion to elect Speaker Anglin (who had served as Speaker earlier in the same Parliament, resigned his seat and then was re-elected), the Leader of the Opposition questioned the choice of the government and raised a lengthy argument—in which the Prime Minister and another Member intervened—as to the right of Mr. Anglin to take his seat in the House prior to the election of the Speaker (*Debates*, February 7, 1878, pp. 2-11).

Speaker adjourns the House until the next sitting day.[212] This occurred in 1986 when the House adjourned at 2:30 a.m. to reconvene later the same day for the opening of the session.[213] In 1988, the Speaker was elected after a single ballot, and the sitting was suspended for several hours until the opening of Parliament later the same day.[214] At other times, the Speaker was elected before the House reached its usual adjournment time, and the House then adjourned to the following day at the time fixed for the opening of Parliament.[215]

During the election of a Speaker, debate is not permitted, no motions are accepted and the Member presiding may not entertain any question of privilege.[216] On one occasion, a point of order was raised and settled by the Chair.[217]

At the time fixed for the formal opening of Parliament with a Speech from the Throne, the House receives the Usher of the Black Rod and goes in procession to the Senate Chamber. At the Bar of the Senate, the newly elected Speaker stands on a small platform, removes his or her three-cornered hat and receives an acknowledgement from the Governor General, who is seated on the Throne. The Speaker addresses the Governor General by an established formula, as follows:

> *May it please Your Excellency,*
>
> *The House of Commons has elected me their Speaker, though I am but little able to fulfil the important duties thus assigned to me. If, in the performance of those duties, I should at any time fall into error, I pray that the fault may be imputed to me, and not to the Commons, whose servant I am, and who, through me, the better to enable them to discharge their duty to their Queen and Country, humbly claim all their undoubted rights and privileges, especially that they may have freedom of speech in their debates, access to Your Excellency's person at all seasonable times, and that their proceedings may receive from Your Excellency the most favourable construction.[218]*

The Speaker of the Senate, on behalf of the Governor General, makes the traditional reply:

> *Mr./Madam Speaker,*
>
> *I am commanded by His/Her Excellency the Governor General to declare to you that he/she freely confides in the duty and attachment of the House of*

---

212. Standing Order 2(3). For daily meeting and adjournment times, see Standing Order 24.

213. *Journals*, September 30, 1986, pp. 8-9.

214. *Journals*, December 12, 1988, p. 3.

215. See *Journals*, January 17, 1994, p. 11; September 22, 1997, p. 9.

216. Standing Order 4(10).

217. *Debates*, September 30, 1986, p. 2.

218. See, for example, *Debates of the Senate*, September 23, 1997, p. 3.

Commons to Her Majesty's Person and Government, and not doubting that their proceedings will be conducted with wisdom, temper and prudence, he/she grants, and upon all occasions will recognize and allow, their constitutional privileges. I am commanded also to assure you that the Commons shall have ready access to His/Her Excellency upon all seasonable occasions and that their proceedings, as well as your words and actions, will constantly receive from him/her the most favourable construction.[219]

A new Speaker always presents himself or herself to the Governor General; however, the claiming of privileges by the Speaker on behalf of the House takes place only at the opening of a Parliament and is not repeated in the event that a new Speaker is elected before the end of the Parliament.[220]

Election of the Speaker During a Session

When a Speaker is to be elected during a session, the Members assemble in the House at the usual time for the start of the sitting. The Chair is taken either by the Speaker who has already indicated his or her intention to resign the office,[221] or, in the absence of the Speaker, by the Deputy Speaker and Chairman of Committees of the Whole.[222] Because the office of Speaker is vacant, the Mace is not on the Table.[223] The Prime Minister informs the Members that the Governor General has given leave to the House to elect a Speaker. The Chair occupant then presides over the usual proceedings for the election of a Speaker. Once a successful candidate is announced, the Speaker-elect is escorted from his or her place and makes some brief remarks from the upper steps before taking the Chair for the first time. The Mace is then placed on the Table and the sitting is suspended for a few minutes pending the arrival of the Usher of the Black Rod. Once summoned, the House proceeds to the Senate Chamber where the Speaker presents himself or herself and receives the Governor General's acknowledgement, in the traditional wording.[224] On its return from the Senate, the House proceeds to the business of the sitting.

Only two of the 33 Speakers elected since Confederation were elected during a session.[225] Both cases predate the current rules providing for the election of the Speaker by secret ballot. In 1899, Speaker Bain succeeded Speaker Edgar, the only

---

219. See, for example, *Debates of the Senate*, September 23, 1997, p. 4.

220. *Bourinot*, 4th ed., pp. 49-50. See, for example, the presentation of Speaker Francis, elected during the Second Session of the Thirty-Second Parliament, and of Speaker Fraser, elected at the opening of the Second Session of the Thirty-Third Parliament (*Journals*, January 16, 1984, pp. 72-3; October 1, 1986, p. 12).

221. Standing Order 3(1)(*b*).

222. Standing Order 3(1)(*c*).

223. In 1984, the Mace was on the Table and was moved beneath it after the Speaker's letter of resignation had been read by the Clerk.

224. No claim of privileges is made; this is done only at the beginning of a Parliament.

225. For the election of Speaker Bain, see *Journals*, August 1, 1899, pp. 488-9, and *Debates*, August 1, 1899, cols. 9062-4. For the election of Speaker Francis, see *Journals*, January 16, 1984, pp. 72-3; *Debates*, January 16, 1984, pp. 421-4.

Speaker to have died while in office, and presided over the House for the remainder of the Eighth Parliament, until 1901. Speaker Francis was elected during the Thirty-Second Parliament (1984) to succeed Speaker Sauvé, who resigned to become Governor General of Canada. Speaker Bain and Speaker Francis presided over the House for the balance of the session and the Parliament in which they were elected.

Election of the Speaker at the Opening of a Second or Later Session Within a Parliament

When the House is to proceed to the election of a Speaker immediately at the opening of the second or subsequent session within a Parliament, the House meets for the opening of the session on the date fixed by proclamation. As for the election of a Speaker during a session, the Chair is taken either by the Speaker who has already indicated his or her intention to resign the office, or by the Deputy Speaker, and the Mace is not on the Table. The Prime Minister is recognized and signifies the consent of the Governor General to proceed to the election of a new Speaker.[226] The House then goes through the usual proceedings for the election of a Speaker. The Speaker-elect is escorted from his or her seat to the dais where he or she makes the usual remarks and acknowledgements and takes the Chair for the first time. The Mace is then placed on the Table. The sitting would normally be adjourned at this point or shortly thereafter, and the presentation of the Speaker to the Governor General and the reading of the Speech from the Throne would take place the following day.[227]

The election of a Speaker on the opening day of the second or subsequent session of a Parliament has occurred six times since 1867.[228] Each time, the vacancy in the Speakership arose through resignation. In 1986, the most recent example,

---

226. In 1986, when the Speaker was elected at the opening of the Second Session of the Thirty-Third Parliament, the House met, prayers were read and, after some remarks by the outgoing Speaker who was to preside over the election of a successor, the Prime Minister was recognized (*Debates*, September 30, 1986, pp. 1-10).

227. In 1904, the Leader of the Opposition asked a question of the Prime Minister, and the sitting was then adjourned (*Debates*, March 10, 1904, cols. 1-5). In 1916, a new Member took his seat after the Mace had been placed on the Table (*Debates*, January 12, 1916, pp. 1-4); in other instances, this had occurred prior to the election of the Speaker (*Debates*, February 7, 1878, pp. 1-2; March 10, 1904, cols. 1-3). In 1917, the Speaker announced the appointment of a Deputy Sergeant-at-Arms, there were tributes to deceased Members, Orders in Council were tabled by the Prime Minister and a question asked of the Prime Minister before the sitting adjourned (*Debates*, January 18, 1917, pp. 1-5). In 1935, the only instance in which the Speech from the Throne was read later the same day, the Mace was placed on the Table and, immediately thereafter, the Speaker read the letter informing the House of the arrival of the Governor General in the Senate Chamber (*Debates*, January 17, 1935, pp. 1-2).

228. Speaker Anglin, who had earlier resigned his seat and the Speakership, was re-elected in a by-election and re-elected Speaker at the opening of the Fifth Session of the Third Parliament (*Journals*, February 7, 1878, pp. 9-10). Speaker Belcourt was elected at the opening of the Fourth Session of the Ninth Parliament (*Journals*, March 10, 1904, p. 10). Speaker Sévigny was elected at the opening of the Sixth Session of the Twelfth Parliament (*Journals*, January 12, 1916, p. 6). Speaker Rhodes was elected at the opening of the Seventh Session of the Twelfth Parliament (*Journals*, January 18, 1917, pp. 6-7). Speaker Bowman was elected at the opening of the Sixth Session of the Seventeenth Parliament (*Journals*, January 17, 1935, p. 2). Speaker Fraser was elected at the opening of the Second Session of the Thirty-Third Parliament (*Journals*, September 30, 1986, pp. 2-8).

Speaker Bosley's resignation took effect on the opening day of the Second Session of the Thirty-Third Parliament, and Speaker Fraser then became the first to take the Chair under the new rules for the election of the Speaker by secret ballot.

In all six cases, the House met for the opening of the session on the date fixed by proclamation. In the five cases preceding 1986, the House was immediately summoned to the Senate and advised (as at the opening of a Parliament) that a Speaker must be chosen before the Speech from the Throne could be read.[229] On its return from the Senate, the House proceeded to the election of a Speaker; a Member was nominated by the Prime Minister, seconded by a leading Minister, and (with one exception[230]) after a brief intervention by the Leader of the Opposition, the person nominated was unanimously elected.

Campaigning for the Speakership

The rules for the election of the Speaker by secret ballot contain no provision for a nomination process and are silent on the matter of campaigning for the office.[231] The special procedure committee which recommended the secret-ballot process sought to give control of the choice of Speaker to the House and its Members (away from what it called the "exclusive control" of the Prime Minister), noting that the Speaker belongs not to the government or opposition but to the House.[232] Speaker Bosley, appearing before the committee in 1985, expressed reservations about the success of a secret-ballot system should political-style campaigning be resorted to.[233]

In each of the four secret-ballot elections held to date (1986, 1988, 1994, 1997), campaign activity occurred but took place informally, outside the Chamber, because the rules do not permit debate during the election process.[234] In recent years, Members have noted the difficulty faced by those newly elected to the House who are called upon to choose a Speaker with little time or opportunity to become informed

---

229. In 1878, the Gentleman Usher of the Black Rod arrived with a message from the Deputy Governor General for the immediate attendance of the House in the Senate Chamber. In 1904, 1916, 1917 and 1935, the arrival of Black Rod was preceded by the Clerk reading a letter informing the House of the date and time of the Deputy Governor General's arrival at the Senate for the opening of the session. For pre-Confederation examples and British precedents, see *Bourinot*, 4th ed., pp. 172-3.

230. In 1878, Speaker Anglin's nomination was not supported by the opposition. He is the only Speaker whose election was the subject of a recorded vote (*Debates*, February 7, 1878, pp. 2-12).

231. All Members apart from party leaders and Cabinet Ministers are considered candidates, unless they take the prescribed action to remove themselves from consideration (Standing Orders 4(1) and 5).

232. See paragraphs 8-16 of the First Report of the Special Committee on Reform of the House of Commons, presented on December 20, 1984 (*Journals*, p. 211).

233. The Special Committee on Reform of the House of Commons, *Minutes of Proceedings and Evidence,* January 22, 1985, pp. 3:14-7.

234. Standing Order 4(10). For further information on campaigning, see Marcel Danis, "The Speakership and Independence: A Tradition in the Making" in *Canadian Parliamentary Review*, Vol. 10, No. 2, Summer 1987; John Holtby, "Secret Ballot in the Canadian Commons Elects New Speaker" in *The Parliamentarian*, Vol. XVIII, No. 1. It has also been noted that because the 1986 election took place in the course of a Parliament, there was prior opportunity for the House membership to become acquainted with the individuals on the ballot.

about all the candidates.[235] Prior to the election for the Speaker in 1994, some of the parties in the House organized caucus meetings to which individual candidates were invited.[236] Prior to the 1997 election, it was suggested that candidates should declare themselves and attend an all-party question-and-answer session organized by one of the four opposition parties.[237]

TENURE

A Speaker is elected as the first item of business at the start of each Parliament, and presides over the House for the life of the Parliament.[238] When the Parliament is dissolved, the Speaker is deemed to remain in office for administrative purposes until a new election takes place.[239] Should a vacancy in the Speakership occur during a Parliament, another Speaker must be elected forthwith;[240] no other business can come before the House until a new Speaker has been chosen.

A vacancy in the Speakership can arise through death or resignation of the office. Speaker Edgar (1896-99) died while in office, in July 1899, during a session. Speaker Edgar had been away from the House for some time, due to indisposition. In his absence, the Chair was taken by the Deputy Speaker.[241] Speaker Edgar's death was announced to the House on July 31, 1899, by the Prime Minister, who then moved a motion for the adjournment of the House. After a brief intervention by a Member of the opposition, the motion was adopted and the sitting was adjourned.[242] The next day, the House met at its usual time and immediately proceeded to elect a new Speaker.[243]

A vacancy in the Speakership may occur when the Speaker expresses an intent to resign the office or if the House were to take action to remove the Speaker from office. It has also happened that the office of Speaker has been vacated when the incumbent accepted a position which necessitated an automatic relinquishing of his or her seat in the House.

235. See references in *Debates*, April 21, 1998, pp. 5867-8, 5876. Following the general election of 1993, an unprecedented degree of turnover occurred, such that 205 of the 295 Members sent to the House of Commons were first-time Members called upon to elect a Speaker. (See *Report on the Administration of the House of Commons for the 35th Parliament*, p. 7, tabled on October 23, 1997 (*Journals*, p. 139).)

236. Press reports indicate that some candidates attended these sessions, and some did not; see, for example, *Times-Colonist*, January 15, 1994.

237. See reference in *Debates*, April 21, 1998, pp. 5867-8.

238. *Constitution Act, 1867*, ss. 44, 46.

239. *Parliament of Canada Act*, R.S.C. 1985, c. P-1, s. 53.

240. *Constitution Act, 1867*, s. 45.

241. See, for example, *Journals*, July 13, 1899, p. 426.

242. *Debates*, July 31, 1899, cols. 9060-1.

243. *Journals*, August 1, 1899, pp. 488-9. See also the account in *Bourinot*, 4th ed., pp. 171-2.

On three occasions, a vacancy in the Speakership arose after the Speaker gave written notice of intent to resign. The resignations were those of Speaker Black in 1935, Speaker Sauvé in 1984 and Speaker Bosley in 1986.

The resignation of Speaker Black (1930-35) as Speaker was tendered in a letter to the Prime Minister dated January 15, 1935, during a prorogation. This was announced to the House by the Prime Minister when the House met on January 17, the date set for the opening of the session. The House then proceeded to elect a new Speaker.[244]

Speaker Sauvé (1980-84), having been designated to become Governor General of Canada, resigned as a Member and as Speaker by letter to the Clerk of the House dated January 6, 1984. The letter stated that her resignation would take effect as of midnight, January 15, 1984. The House, which had adjourned on December 21, reconvened on January 16, and the Clerk read the letter. The House then proceeded to the election of Speaker Francis.[245]

Speaker Bosley (1984-86) resigned the Speakership in 1986. His concern about the "erosion of public respect for Parliament" was known, and it was his opinion that he could best contribute to the reform of the institution as a private Member, giving the House an "unfettered" choice of Speaker by the new secret-ballot process.[246] He wrote to the Clerk on September 5, 1986, while Parliament was prorogued, tendering his resignation to take effect with the election of a successor on the date set by proclamation for the opening of the new session. When the House met on September 30, the Speaker tabled copies of the correspondence and expressed his acknowledgements to the House for the honour of having served as its Speaker. Then, pursuant to Standing Order, he presided over the election by secret ballot of Speaker Fraser.[247]

In three further instances, Speakers accepted other positions, by virtue of which their seats in the House (and thus the Speakership) were relinquished. Speaker Brodeur (1901-04) and Speaker Sévigny (1916-17) were appointed to Cabinet[248] and

---

244. *Journals*, January 17, 1935, pp. 1-2; *Debates*, January 17, 1935, p. 1. It was reported that ill health had forced the Speaker's resignation. Mr. Black continued to sit as a private Member, but was later hospitalized and did not contest the general election of October 1935; he recovered and, in 1940, was elected to his old seat in the House of Commons, where he remained until 1949 (Gary Levy, *Speakers of the House of Commons*, Ottawa: Library of Parliament, 1996, pp. 56-7). See also "Vacancy in the Office of Presiding Officer", *The Table*, Vol. XXIV for 1955, in particular pp. 31-3.

245. *Journals*, January 16, 1984, p. 72; *Debates*, January 16, 1984, p. 421.

246. These views were expressed in letters written by the Speaker on September 5, 1986, to the leaders of the three recognized parties in the House.

247. *Debates*, September 30, 1986, p. 1; *Journals,* September 30, 1986, p. 2. Former Speaker Bosley sat as a private Member until the end of the Thirty-Fourth Parliament (1988-93).

248. Until 1931, Members who accepted certain positions in Cabinet were required, pursuant to sections of the *Senate and House of Commons Act*, to resign their seats and seek re-election (*Senate and House of Commons Act*, R.S.C. 1927, c. 147, ss. 13, 14). The Act (now called the *Parliament of Canada Act*) was amended to remove this requirement (R.S.C. 1930, c. 52, s. 1).

Speaker Sproule (1911-15) was appointed to the Senate.[249] In each case, the appointment took effect during the interval between two sessions and, therefore, no formal indication of intent to resign was communicated to the House. On those occasions, when the House reconvened, it met without a Speaker. The letter informing the House of the Deputy Governor General's arrival for the opening of the new session, normally read by the Speaker, was instead read by the Clerk. Later, when in accordance with usual practice, the Clerk announced the list of electoral districts for which notifications of vacancy had been received, among them were those of Speaker Brodeur in 1904,[250] Speaker Sproule in 1916[251] and Speaker Sévigny in 1917.[252]

There is also the unusual example of Speaker Anglin, who was twice elected Speaker in the course of the Third Parliament (1874-78). First elected at the opening of Parliament in 1874, he vacated his seat in the House during the intersession.[253] A by-election was held, in which Mr. Anglin was re-elected. Thus, when the new session opened on February 7, 1878, the House was informed both of the vacancy in the riding held by the former Speaker, and of his re-election to the House.[254] He was again nominated for the Speakership, and re-elected.[255]

Few examples exist in Canada where the resignation of a Speaker was secured following the action of a legislative body to effect a removal.[256] In 1875, in the House

---

249. The Speaker of the House is an elected Member, and Section 39 of the *Constitution Act, 1867* provides that "A Senator shall not be capable of being elected or of sitting or voting as a Member of the House of Commons".

250. *Journals*, March 10, 1904, pp. 1-2, 5. The notification of vacancy was dated January 19, 1904; Mr. Brodeur was then re-elected in a by-election and took his seat in the House as a Cabinet Minister on March 10, 1904 (*Journals*, p. 10).

251. *Journals*, January 12, 1916, pp. 1-2, 4. The notification of vacancy was dated December 3, 1915, the date of his appointment to the Senate (*Journals of the Senate*, January 12, 1916, pp. 1-2).

252. *Journals*, January 18, 1917, pp. 2, 6. The notification of vacancy was dated January 8, 1917. Mr. Sévigny was re-elected in a by-election and took his seat in the House as a Cabinet Minister on April 19, 1917 (*Journals*, p. 90).

253. A notification of vacancy was submitted, dated June 5, 1877. Speaker Anglin was known to have had business dealings with the government of the day, and this became the subject of study by a privilege committee. On April 28, 1877, the last day of the session, the committee presented a report stating that, in its view, the Speaker was in violation of the *Independence of Parliament Act* and thus his election was void. (The Act provided that individuals could not be Members of the House of Commons if they held offices of emolument under the Government of Canada, or were contractors with the Government of Canada (31 Vict., c. 25, amended in 1871 by 34 Vict, c. 19). For background, see *Bourinot*, 4ᵗʰ ed., pp. 140-8.) The report was not considered by the House (*Journals*, April 28, 1877, p. 357; for the text of the report, see item No. 8 in the *Appendix* to the *Journals* for the Fourth Session of the Third Parliament).

254. *Journals*, February 7, 1878, pp. 2, 5.

255. This occurred over the objections of the opposition, who forced a recorded vote on the question (see *Journals*, February 7, 1878, pp. 9-10).

256. On two occasions in the seventeenth century, the British House pronounced itself on the question of the continuance of its Speaker in the Chair. In 1673, a motion for the removal of Speaker Seymour was defeated (*Hatsell*, Vol. II, pp. 214-5). In 1694, a parliamentary committee found that Speaker Trevor had accepted a bribe, and he resigned after the House resolved that he was guilty of a high crime and misdemeanor (*Laundy*, pp. 39-40).

of Assembly of the province of Nova Scotia, a motion was moved which proposed that the Speaker's resignation be requested and that a new Speaker be elected.[257] The motion was adopted on a recorded division, and the House then adjourned to the following day when, as the first item of business, the Speaker rose, tendered his resignation and left the Chair.[258] The House then adopted a motion, moved by a member of the cabinet, that the resignation be accepted and that a committee of Ministers be struck to inform the Lieutenant Governor that the House was without a Speaker.[259] When the House next met, the Committee reported that it had communicated with the Lieutenant Governor; a new Speaker was then elected.[260]

In July 1956, in the House of Commons, Speaker Beaudoin (1953-57) offered his resignation, but this offer was not taken up by the House. This occurred on the heels of the political controversy and procedural disputes of what has since become known as the Pipeline Debate.[261] During the consideration of the pipeline bill, numerous points of order were raised and the Chair faced many challenges. There were 25 appeals from rulings of the Chair (allowed under the rules in effect at that time), all of which were sustained.[262] A motion of censure against the Speaker was moved and defeated.[263] This is the only instance of a motion of censure against a Speaker of the House of Commons of Canada. Three weeks after passage of the bill by the House, a question of privilege was raised which called into question the

---

257. *Journal and Proceedings of the House of Assembly of the Province of Nova Scotia*, April 30, 1875, p. 109. There was a preamble to the motion which stated, first, that past Speakers had been selected on the basis of their parliamentary experience; second, that the incumbent had no parliamentary experience or previous training indicating fitness for the "onerous and sometimes technical" duties of Speaker; and third, that the "present state of things is not calculated to elevate the dignity and preserve the decorum of this Legislature". See also the account in *Bourinot,* 4th ed., p. 177.

258. *Journal and Proceedings of the House of Assembly of the Province of Nova Scotia*, April 30, 1875, pp. 109-10; May 1, 1875, p. 110.

259. *Journal and Proceedings of the House of Assembly of the Province of Nova Scotia*, May 1, 1875, pp. 110-1.

260. *Journal and Proceedings of the House of Assembly of the Province of Nova Scotia*, May 3, 1875, pp. 111-2.

261. In May and June of that year, the government (having concluded an agreement to provide assistance on or before June 7 for the building of a pipeline) was seeking to obtain passage of Bill No. 298, *An Act to establish the Northern Ontario Pipe Line Crown Corporation*. The opposition did not favour the bill and, for the first time in 24 years, closure was invoked; moreover, it was applied to each stage in the passage of the bill. Debate was acrimonious and punctuated by procedural argument (for background and details, see J. Gordon Dubroy, "Canada: House of Commons: Relations between Chair and Opposition in 1956," *The Table*, Vol. XXV for 1956, pp. 39-53).

262. Of the 25 appeals, 11 were from rulings of the Speaker and the remainder were from rulings of the Chair in a Committee of the Whole. Appeals from rulings of the Speaker were abolished in 1965.

263. On June 1, 1956, which later became known as "Black Friday", the Speaker ruled to revert the House to its position of the day before (with respect to its deliberations on the pipeline bill); the ruling was sustained on appeal (*Journals*, June 1, 1956, pp. 678-80). On Monday, June 4, the Leader of the Opposition moved a motion of censure against the Speaker (*Journals*, pp. 692-3). The motion was defeated on June 8 (*Journals*, pp. 725-6). See also *Debates*, June 4, 1956, pp. 4643-60; June 6, 1956, pp. 4783-6; June 7, 1956, pp. 4794-831; June 8, 1956, pp. 4845-70.

Speaker's impartiality.[264] On July 2, at the opening of the sitting, the Speaker made a statement and placed his resignation before the House to take effect at the pleasure of the House.[265] However, no resolution of the House was forthcoming and no objection was registered when the Speaker continued to fulfil his official duties. Speaker Beaudoin served for the balance of the Twenty-Second Parliament.

There have been other cases where motions of censure were brought against Speakers of the Senate and other legislatures in Canada; however, none were adopted.[266]

Other Presiding Officers

HISTORICAL PERSPECTIVE

At Confederation, the constitutional responsibility of the Speaker to "preside at all meetings" of the House[267] was fulfilled by the Speaker alone, as there were no provisions allowing another Member to take the Chair.[268] After just a few months, the

---

264. On June 29, 1956, the Leader of the Opposition rose on a question of privilege to allege that the Speaker had improperly impugned the motives of certain Members; the allegation was based on extracts of private correspondence of the Speaker, which were published in a newspaper (*Debates*, pp. 5509-15).

265. *Journals*, July 2, 1956, p. 838. For the full text of the Speaker's remarks, see pp. 835-8.

266. For examples of motions of censure brought against Speakers of the Senate and other legislatures in Canada, see: in the Senate, against Speaker Charbonneau (*Journals of the Senate*, December 30, 1990, p. 1997); in British Columbia, against Speaker Smith (*Journals of the Legislative Assembly of British Columbia*, July 21, 1977, pp. 213-4; July 22, 1977, p. 214); in Manitoba, against Speaker Walding *(Journals of the Legislative Assembly of Manitoba*, December 13, 1982, pp. 27-8) and six against Speaker Dacquay (*Journals of the Legislative Assembly of Manitoba*, November 2, 1995, pp. 379-80; June 3, 1996, p. 339; November 21, 1996, pp. 874-7; March 3, 1997, pp. 16-7; December 1, 1997, pp. 19-20; December 3, 1997, p. 33); in Nova Scotia, against Speaker MacLean (*Nova Scotia Assembly Debates*, March 14, 1975, p. 1270; March 18, 1975, pp. 1350-6), and against Speaker Donahoe (*Journals of the Legislative Assembly of Nova Scotia*, March 9, 1981, pp. 77-80); in Ontario, against Speaker Turner (November 16, 1981, *Journals of the Legislative Assembly of Ontario*, pp. 187-8; *Debates of the Legislative Assembly of Ontario*, pp. 3531-46); in Quebec, two against Speaker Lavoie (*Debates*, March 20, 1974, pp. 69-84; December 21, 1974, pp. 3935-73), and one against Speaker Bertrand (*Debates of the National Assembly of Quebec*, February 3, 1995, pp. 1353-73; March 14, 1995, pp. 1381-5); in Saskatchewan, against Speaker Agar (*Journals of the Legislative Assembly of Saskatchewan*, March 15, 1944, pp. 125-7), against Speaker Brockelbank (*Journals of the Legislative Assembly of Saskatchewan*, April 29, 1980, p. 421), and against Speaker Rolfes (*Journals of the Legislative Assembly of Saskatchewan*, July 21, 1992, p. 160); and in the Yukon Territory, against Speaker Bruce (April 1, 1998, *Votes and Proceedings of the Yukon Legislative Assembly*, pp. 215-6; *Debates of the Yukon Legislative Assembly*, pp. 2657-60).

267. *Constitution Act, 1867*, R.S.C. 1985, Appendix II, No. 5, s. 46.

268. Section 47 of the *Constitution Act, 1867* called for the election of an interim Speaker only if the Speaker was absent for more than 48 hours. This section had been included in the Constitution because, on one occasion, the Legislative Assembly of the Province of Canada was not able to meet over a period of days because the Speaker was ill and unable to attend (*Journals*, March 22, 1858, p. 161); in another case, after Confederation, the House began its sitting late because the Speaker missed his train and was not present at the hour of meeting (*Debates*, April 19, 1870, p. 1065).

First Parliament passed an Act which allowed the Speaker to choose any Member to occupy the Chair in the Speaker's absence during the course of a sitting.[269] When the House formed itself into a Committee of the Whole, the Speaker had the authority to select a Member to act as Chairman.[270] Many Members were called upon to fulfil this task.[271] There could be no guarantee that Members selected *ad hoc* to preside over the House or a Committee of the Whole would be conversant with the rules or able to arrive at a satisfactory resolution of questions of order. There were no set adjournment times for the daily sittings, and the House typically sat late into the evening. All this tended to add to the burden of responsibility carried by the Speaker.

In 1885, having cited the British practice as an example to follow, the Prime Minister put forward the proposition that the House would be better served if the positions of Speaker and Chairman of Committees of the Whole were divided into two offices so that a permanent Chairmanship of Committees of the Whole would be established. The salaried incumbent could also act as Speaker both at the beginning of and during a sitting when the Speaker was absent.[272] The Speaker would retain the right to call any Member to take the Chair temporarily during a sitting and would still be obliged, in the absence of the Chairman, to select another Member to chair any Committee of the Whole. The House was not entirely convinced of the need;[273] nevertheless, the Prime Minister pursued the matter. After debate, rules were adopted providing for a Chairman of Committees of the Whole to hold office for the duration of a Parliament[274] and, later that year, a bill was passed enabling this

---

269. *An Act respecting the Office of Speaker of the House of Commons of the Dominion of Canada*, S.C. 1867, c. 2. These provisions are now found in the *Parliament of Canada Act*, R.S.C. 1985, c. P-1, s. 42. The Speaker used this new power for the first time on March 30, 1868 (see *Journals*, p. 167). Substitutions of this nature were not recorded in the *Journals* after 1870, although they continued to take place.

270. See 1867 Rule 76.

271. See, for example, *Journals*, May 14, 1868, pp. 353-64.

272. *Debates*, February 10, 1885, pp. 67-8. In the British Parliament, the office of Deputy Speaker came into existence in 1855 (see *May*, 22nd ed., pp. 194-5).

273. The Opposition objected, claiming there were no provisions for such a position in the Constitution and alleging it was intended to create a salaried office for political patronage; the question of language requirements was also raised (*Debates*, February 10, 1885, pp. 68-70).

274. *Journals*, February 10, 1885, pp. 53-5; see also *Debates*, February 10, 1885, pp. 67-72. An amendment, later to become a Standing Order (the current Standing Order 7(2)), concerned the language requirement for the position. Malachy B. Daly, selected Chairman of Committees of the Whole on February 10, 1885, became the first incumbent of the newly created office (*Journals*, p. 55).

Chairman to act as Speaker in the Speaker's absence.[275] The provisions of that Act are now found in the *Parliament of Canada Act* and were the basis for subsequent changes in the Standing Orders, which vested in the Deputy Speaker and Chairman of Committees of the Whole all the legal powers of the Speaker when he or she is absent from the House.

In the years that followed, it became accepted practice for the Deputy Speaker, on occasion, to delegate the powers of Chairman to other Members.[276] In 1938, when it was foreseen that the Deputy Speaker and Chairman of Committees of the Whole would be absent from the House for a period of time, the House adopted an amendment to the rules to provide for the selection of a Deputy Chairman of Committees of the Whole who would have all the powers of the Chairman.[277] The rule codified the power of the Chairman to open a sitting of the House in the Speaker's absence, a power that up to then had not been shared.[278] It was suggested that the new position would not be permanent but would be filled only as required;[279] the rule provided for the office of Deputy Chairman to be filled on a sessional basis or as the need arose. After the initial appointment for a single session in 1938, the post was left vacant for nine years and not filled until 1947.[280] From 1947 to 1953, subsequent appointments were made as the need arose.[281] When nominating a Deputy Chairman of Committees of the Whole in 1953, the Prime Minister referred to the appointment as "completing the organization of the personnel of the House"[282] and, thereafter,

---

275. The Opposition had argued that the office of Speaker was governed by legislation (the Constitution) and that, while Parliament might alter its provisions, this had to be done by way of legislation rather than a resolution of the House. The Prime Minister accepted this argument and the bill, *An Act to provide for the Appointment of a Deputy Speaker of the House of Commons*, S.C. 1885, c. 1, received Royal Assent on May 1, 1885. (See *Debates*, February 10, 1885, pp. 73-4.) Malachy B. Daly took the Chair as Deputy Speaker for the first time on May 2, 1885 (*Journals*, p. 357). See also Appendix 3, "Deputy Speakers and Chairmen of Committees of the Whole House Since 1885".

276. The practice was at first controversial (see, for example, *Debates*, April 26, 1888, pp. 1005-6, and April 8, 1896, cols. 5732-7, when objections were raised about a Member taking the Chair in the absence of the Deputy Speaker and Chairman of Committees of the Whole; *Debates*, June 6, 1899, cols. 4445-57, and June 7, 1899, cols. 4553-4, when, in reporting from a Committee of the Whole, the Chairman replaced the absent Speaker and named another Member to make the report; and *Debates*, July 15, 1903, cols. 6630-8, when the Member acting as Chairman of the Committee took the Chair to receive its report and later went on to adjourn the House); however, no such objections appear to have been raised after 1903, and it seems the practice was accepted.

277. *Journals*, February 11, 1938, p. 60.

278. The Opposition Leader expressed doubts that the statute allowed for this particular delegated power, but did not object further when the Minister of Justice responded that it was a satisfactory way of providing for the case at hand (*Debates*, February 11, 1938, pp. 370-1).

279. *Debates*, February 11, 1938, pp. 370-1.

280. *Debates*, March 28, 1947, pp. 1826-7.

281. See Appendix 4, "Deputy Chairmen of Committees of the Whole House Since 1938".

282. *Debates*, December 16, 1953, p. 963.

the practice of selecting a Deputy Chairman for the duration of each session was established.

As the work of the House and the length of its sessions continued to increase, the House identified a need for the services of an additional Presiding Officer. The position of Assistant Deputy Chairman of Committees of the Whole was created in 1967, through an amendment to the rules pursuant to the recommendation of a special committee on procedure.[283] Again, the rule enabled the incumbent to exercise all the powers of the Chairman of Committees of the Whole, including those of Deputy Speaker, during the Speaker's absence. There was no suggestion that the position should be temporary, and since 1971 it has been routinely filled.[284]

The written rules on other Presiding Officers have undergone little change over the years. In 1906, the rule obliging the Speaker to appoint a Member to preside at any Committee of the Whole ("shall appoint") was relaxed so as to remove the element of obligation ("may appoint").[285] In 1927, the term "Deputy Speaker", which had for some time been in common use among Members in referring to the Chairman of Committees of the Whole, began to be used in the written rules.[286] The original rules governing the selection of the Deputy Speaker and Chairman of Committees of the Whole explicitly required the selection to take place at the start of each Parliament, after the Address in Reply from the Speech from the Throne had been agreed to. However, this rule was not always adhered to[287] and, in 1955, it was amended so that the selection could be made early in a new Parliament, regardless of whether or not the Address had yet been agreed to.[288] In 1968, a reference to its British antecedents was dropped from the rule providing for the appointment of the Deputy Speaker.[289]

---

283. The special committee's mandate included reporting to the House on possible rule changes which it might "deem suitable to promote the more expeditious dispatch of the business of the House". The committee's first report, presented on March 20, 1967 (*Journals*, p. 1549), and adopted without debate on April 26, 1967 (*Journals*, p. 1769; *Debates*, p. 15489), stated that the appointment of an Assistant Deputy Chairman of Committees of the Whole would be "desirable", and went on to recommend the necessary amendment to the Standing Orders.

284. See Appendix 5, "Assistant Deputy Chairmen of Committees of the Whole House Since 1967".

285. See 1906 Rule 13(4).

286. *Journals*, March 22, 1927, pp. 324-5.

287. In 1887, for example, the Deputy Speaker was not selected until almost a month after the Address had been agreed to (*Journals*, May 11, 1887, pp. 370-1); in 1891, the Address was agreed to on May 4 (*Journals*, p. 17), and the Deputy Speaker was chosen on May 22 (*Journals*, p. 159). In 1949 and 1953, the House agreed to waive the rule and the Deputy Speaker was selected before the Address was agreed to (*Journals*, September 15, 1949, p. 17; November 12, 1953, p. 16).

288. *Journals*, July 12, 1955, pp. 920-1.

289. *Journals*, December 20, 1968, p. 572. Until then, the duties of the office holder had been described in the Standing Order as "in accordance with the usages which regulate the duties of a similar officer, generally designated the Chairman of the Committee of Ways and Means, in the House of Commons of the United Kingdom of Great Britain and Northern Ireland".

AUTHORITY

Every action of the Deputy Speaker, when acting in the Speaker's place, has the same effect and validity as if the Speaker had acted; or, in the terms of the *Parliament of Canada Act:*

> *Every act done and warrant, order or other document issued, signed or published by a Deputy Speaker ... that relates to any proceedings of the House of Commons or that, under any statute, would be done, issued, signed or published by the Speaker, if then able to act, has the same effect and validity as if it had been done, issued, signed or published by the Speaker.*[290]

At the start of a sitting, the *Parliament of Canada Act* provides that when the Speaker's unavoidable absence is announced to the House by the Clerk,[291] the Deputy Speaker takes the Chair. If the Speaker is still absent at the start of the next sitting, the Deputy Speaker again assumes the Speaker's role and may continue to do so from day to day until the Speaker's return. If the House should adjourn for longer than 24 hours, the Deputy Speaker can continue to act as Speaker only for 24 hours from the time of adjournment.[292]

From time to time, the Speaker has been absent at the beginning of a sitting; more rarely, the Speaker has been absent over several consecutive sittings.[293] It has happened that in the absence of both the Speaker and the Deputy Speaker, the Deputy Chairman and Assistant Deputy Chairman, as alternates to the Deputy Speaker and Chairman of Committees of the Whole, have opened a sitting of the House.[294] In such cases, they are entitled to exercise all the powers vested in the Deputy Speaker during the Speaker's absence.[295]

---

290. *Parliament of Canada Act*, R.S.C. 1985, c. P-1, s. 44(2). See also *Debates*, June 4, 1985, p. 5387.

291. Typically, the House is informed of the unavoidable absence of the Speaker by the Clerk of the House before prayers are read; but exceptions have taken place. For example, on one occasion after the sitting was underway, the announcement was made by the Assistant Deputy Chairman (*Journals*, March 3, 1995, p. 1999; *Debates*, March 3, 1995, p. 10313).

292. *Parliament of Canada Act*, R.S.C. 1985, c. P-1, s. 43.

293. For example, in 1885, the Speaker was replaced over three sittings due to illness in the family (*Journals*, May 2, 4 and 5, pp. 357-9); in 1899, Speaker Edgar fell ill and was replaced at the start of 16 sittings (*Journals* Index for 1899 under "Deputy Speaker"). In two more recent cases (Speaker Sauvé in 1983 and Speaker Fraser in 1993), the Speaker was absent from the House for a period of time due to illness and was replaced over several consecutive sittings.

294. In 1983, for example, the Deputy Chairman and the Assistant Deputy Chairman of Committees of the Whole, acting as Speaker, each opened sittings of the House (*Journals*, June 28, 1983, p. 6098 (Assistant Deputy Chairman); December 20, 1983, p. 60 (Deputy Chairman)). When the Speaker became ill that year, the Deputy Speaker and Assistant Deputy Chairman alternated days on which they took responsibility for opening the sitting. For more recent examples, see *Journals*, October 24, 1997, p. 145 (Assistant Deputy Chairman); October 26, 1998, p. 1183 (Deputy Chairman).

295. Standing Order 8.

ROLE

The primary roles of the Deputy Speaker and the other Presiding Officers are to support the Speaker in the Chamber as presiding officers, to take the Chair when the House sits as a Committee of the Whole and, on occasion, to chair legislative committees. In addition, the Deputy Speaker has certain administrative responsibilities.

In the House, the Speaker is generally in the Chair at specific times: at the opening of the sitting and during Members' Statements, Oral Questions and Routine Proceedings. The remaining time in the Chair is shared by the Deputy Speaker and the other Presiding Officers.[296] On occasion, the Speaker or one of the other Presiding Officers may choose another Member to replace them for a short period.

When the House forms itself into a Committee of the Whole, it is the duty of the Chairman of Committees of the Whole to take the Chair if present in his or her place in the House.[297] The fact that the rules now provide for the selection of a Deputy and Assistant Deputy Chairman of Committees of the Whole does not, in theory, affect the Speaker's power to appoint another Member to preside as Chairman in the absence of the Deputy Speaker;[298] however, in keeping with the practice established at the turn of the twentieth century, the task of filling the acting chairmanship typically falls to the Member presiding as Speaker.[299] It has rarely been necessary for the Speaker to call upon another Member.

As regards administrative responsibilities, the Deputy Speaker may be asked to serve on the Board of Internal Economy[300] and is usually a member of the Executive Committee. With the Deputy and Assistant Deputy Chairman of Committees of the Whole, the Deputy Speaker is a member of the Panel of Chairmen for legislative committees, and may thus be appointed by the Speaker to chair a legislative committee, or act in place of the Speaker to appoint Members to chair legislative committees.[301] On

---

296. *Parliament of Canada Act*, R.S.C. 1985, c. P-1, s. 42.

297. Standing Order 7(1). See also Chapter 19, "Committees of the Whole House".

298. Standing Order 7(4).

299. See, for example, *Debates*, March 11, 1971, pp. 4177-8, when the Deputy Speaker appointed another Member (Mr. Richard) to act as Chairman of a Committee of the Whole.

300. Formerly, the *Parliament of Canada Act* explicitly included the Deputy Speaker in the membership of the Board of Internal Economy (R.S.C. 1985, c. P-1, s. 50(2)). When the Act was amended in 1997 (S.C. 1997, c. 32) to give additional representation on the Board to opposition parties, the Deputy Speaker was removed; but the government then appointed the Deputy Speaker as one of its representatives on the Board (*Journals*, December 11, 1997, p. 391).

301. Standing Order 112. See, for example, *Journals*, March 11, 1988, p. 2280; November 23, 1989, p. 78 (appointments of the Deputy Speaker to chair legislative committees); March 24, 1988, p. 2416 (appointment of the Deputy Chairman to chair a legislative committee); February 23, 1990, p. 1278 (appointment of the Assistant Deputy Chairman to chair a legislative committee); May 25, 1993, p. 2999 (Deputy Speaker appointing Members to act as chairmen of legislative committees).

one occasion, the House adopted a special order establishing a special committee to be chaired by the Deputy Speaker.[302]

While the Standing Orders provide for the Speaker's impartiality and independence by enjoining him or her not to participate in any debate before the House,[303] there is no such clear statement as to whether the Deputy Speaker and other Presiding Officers should take part in debate. Until the 1930s, it was not unusual for the Deputy Speaker to participate actively in debate,[304] and there has been controversy from time to time over the extent to which the Chair occupants (other than the Speaker) should remain aloof from partisan politics.[305]

In 1931, when a question arose as to the propriety of the Deputy Speaker speaking in debate, it was generally felt that the actions of the Deputy Speaker must be governed by "good taste and judgement".[306] Since then, and in the absence of any rule or guideline governing the political activities of Presiding Officers of the House or limiting their participation in debate or voting, the degree of participation has been an individual decision. In 1993, Deputy Speaker Champagne agreed to act as co-Chair of her party's leadership convention. A question of privilege was raised in the House by a Member who argued that this decision affected the appearance of impartiality attached to the office of Deputy Speaker and that she was therefore guilty of a contempt of the House. Speaker Fraser ruled that, given the existing practice and the absence of clear direction from the House, Deputy Speakers have used varying degrees of discretion in terms of their party involvement. He clarified that they remain members of their political parties and, unlike the Speaker, may attend caucus meetings, participate in debate and vote. The Speaker ruled that the

---

302. *Journals*, December 14, 1989, p. 1011. When the Deputy Speaker (Marcel Danis) was later appointed to the Cabinet, the House agreed that he should continue to chair the special committee (*Journals*, March 6, 1990, p. 1290).

303. Standing Order 9.

304. When reproached for indulging in politics, Deputy Speaker LaVergne declared, "A deputy speaker is not supposed to be impartial when he is not in the chair. Truth holds a greater place in the house than the opinion of the hon. friend" (*Debates*, June 19, 1931, p. 2840).

305. In 1914, for example, the involvement of Pierre-Édouard Blondin (Deputy Speaker) in a by-election campaign gave rise to a motion moved in the House by Sir Wilfrid Laurier (Leader of the Opposition) "That in the opinion of this House, in the discharge of the duties and responsibilities of the Deputy Speaker toward this House, he is bound by and subject to the same rules as apply to Mr. Speaker, and that, therefore, he is disbarred from taking part in electoral contests" (*Debates*, March 5, 1914, p. 1362). Prime Minister Borden opposed the motion, arguing that the status of both the Speaker and Deputy Speaker was based on custom and should the House find it necessary to set rules for the Deputy Speaker, it would surely be necessary to do likewise for the Speaker. No decision was taken and the motion was withdrawn (*Debates*, March 5, 1914, pp. 1362-70).

306. *Debates*, March 20, 1931, pp. 173-80.

Deputy Speaker is not "cloaked with the same exigencies that are expected of the Speaker" and that the matter did not constitute a *prima facie* case of privilege.[307]

In accordance with recent practice, the Deputy Speaker and other Presiding Officers generally avoid taking part in debate, but do for the most part maintain their right to vote when not presiding over the House.[308] In 1985, when the Assistant Deputy Chairman participated in debate on a bill before the House, an objection was raised.[309] Presiding Officers (with the exception of the Speaker) have presented petitions[310] and made Members' Statements,[311] and no objection has been made. On occasion, a Presiding Officer has taken the opportunity to offer a comment from the Chair, and again no objection was made.[312] In general, occupants of the Chair have not sponsored or pursued private Members' bills or motions,[313] or placed written questions on the *Order Paper*.[314]

---

307. *Debates*, March 8, 1993, pp. 16577-81; March 9, 1993, p. 16685.

308. See, for example, *Debates*, October 12, 1979, p. 134. Some recent occupants of the Chair have taken the decision to abstain entirely from voting (David Kilgour, Deputy Speaker and Chairman of Committees of the Whole in the Thirty-Fifth Parliament (1994-97); Ian McClelland, Deputy Chairman of Committees of the Whole in the First Session (1997-99) of the Thirty-Sixth Parliament).

309. *Debates*, November 25, 1985, pp. 8777-81. Assistant Deputy Chairman Jean Charest took part in debate and a question of privilege was raised the next day. The Speaker ruled that there is no rule that would prevent a Presiding Officer (other than the Speaker) from speaking; "whether one should or should not do so," he said, "is a question of judgment that various deputy Speakers have exercised in various ways" (*Debates*, November 26, 1985, pp. 8821-4).

310. See, for example, *Journals*, October 26, 1994, p. 829 (petition presented by the Assistant Deputy Chairman); June 19, 1995, p. 1784 (petition presented by the Deputy Chairman).

311. See, for example, *Debates*, February 27, 1985, p. 2542 (Assistant Deputy Chairman); February 25, 1993, p. 16461 (Deputy Speaker); April 21, 1997, p. 9986 (Deputy Chairman).

312. On one occasion, following the passage of a bill, the Deputy Speaker spoke briefly on it from the Chair (*Debates*, June 11, 1992, pp. 11870-1).

313. There have been exceptions. In the 1976-77 session, a private Members' bill was sponsored by Gérald Laniel, then Deputy Speaker. The bill dealt with readjustment of electoral boundaries and (with several other such bills) passed through the legislative process in the House without debate, which could be taken as an indication that its contents were of a non-partisan nature (*Journals*, June 29, 1977, p. 1267; June 30, 1997, pp. 1279-80; *Debates*, June 30, 1977, p. 7236).

Peter Milliken was selected during a session to be Deputy Chairman of Committees of the Whole (*Journals*, October 29, 1996, p. 785-9); on November 28, a private Members' bill, sponsored by him prior to his becoming a Chair occupant, came before the House for consideration at report stage. The bill, an amendment to the *Financial Administration Act*, was concurred in, read a third time and passed without debate (*Journals*, November 28, 1996, p. 935; *Debates*, November 28, 1996, pp. 6889-90). The sponsorship of another of Mr. Milliken's bills was, by leave of the House, transferred to another Member after his appointment as a Presiding Officer (*Journals*, February 19, 1997, p. 1151).

314. On February 6, 1997, Peter Milliken, Deputy Chairman of Committees of the Whole, placed a question on the *Order Paper* and it was answered on April 15, 1997 (*Debates*, p. 9702).

METHOD OF SELECTION

The rules of the House provide for the selection of the Deputy Speaker and Chairman of Committees of the Whole.[315] The Deputy Speaker is selected at the start of every Parliament and holds office for the duration of the Parliament. The selection generally occurs after the Speaker's report to the House on the Speech from the Throne, at the opening of the first session.[316] A Member, usually the Prime Minister,[317] moves a motion proposing that a certain Member assume the office of Deputy Speaker and Chairman of Committees of the Whole House. With a few exceptions, the proposed Member has been from the government side of the House[318] and the motion has been seconded by a government Member.[319] The rules require the Deputy Speaker to be fluent in the official language which is not that of the Speaker "for the time being".[320] The names put forward have rarely met with opposition.[321]

The rules provide similarly for the selection of a Deputy Chairman and Assistant Deputy Chairman of Committees of the Whole for a session.[322] The appointments are made at the start of each session, or from time to time as necessary, by means of a

---

315. Standing Order 7.

316. For further information on the opening of a Parliament, see Chapter 8, "The Parliamentary Cycle".

317. In 1891, 1896, 1901 and 1935, the motion was moved by another leading Minister instead of the Prime Minister. See *Journals*, May 22, 1891, p. 159; August 27, 1896, p. 15; February 11, 1901, p. 20; March 11, 1935, p. 209.

318. Three Deputy Speakers have been opposition Members: George Henry Boivin (*Debates*, March 21, 1918, pp. 73-4), Robert McCleave (*Debates*, January 4, 1973, pp. 11-2) and Gérald Laniel (who served in two Parliaments, over a change of government—1974-79 and 1979; see *Debates*, October 9, 1979, p. 15).

319. The nominations of Robert McCleave (an opposition Member) and Gérald Laniel (an opposition Member going into his second term as Deputy Speaker) were seconded by the Leader of the Opposition (*Journals*, January 4, 1973, p. 13; October 9, 1979, p. 20). The nomination of Andrée Champagne (a government Member) was seconded by the Opposition House Leader (*Journals*, May 15, 1990, p. 1705).

320. Standing Order 7(2). The language requirement has been met in each Parliament since 1885. In 1918, Prime Minister Borden nominated an opposition Member (George Henry Boivin) for the position, citing in his remarks the paucity of experienced francophone Members on the government benches (see *Debates*, March 21, 1918, pp. 73-4). Since the late 1950s, a similar linguistic balance has also been met with regard to the Deputy Chairman and Assistant Deputy Chairman of Committees of the Whole, although no such requirement exists.

321. The motion to select Malachy Daly in 1885 was adopted on division (*Debates*, February 10, 1885, pp. 72-3). In 1911, the motion nominating Pierre Blondin was debated and then adopted without division (*Debates*, November 29, 1911, cols. 519-25). In 1918, a Member objected to the nomination of George Henry Boivin; but again, the motion was adopted without division (*Debates*, March 21, 1918, pp. 73-5). Only once has a recorded division been taken on the motion to select a Deputy Speaker and Chairman of Committees of the Whole; this was in 1962, on the motion to select Paul Martineau (*Journals*, January 18, 1962, pp. 6-7; *Debates*, January 18, 1962, pp. 5-6).

322. Standing Order 8.

motion moved and seconded by Members from the government side of the House. [323] In some recent cases, adoption of the motion has been preceded by debate and a recorded division. [324]

With just one exception, the Members selected to the offices of Deputy Chairman and Assistant Deputy Chairman of Committees of the Whole have come from the government benches. [325]

TENURE

The selection of a Deputy Speaker and Chairman of Committees of the Whole is effective for the life of the Parliament; in the event of a vacancy in the office "by death, resignation, or otherwise", the House is required to proceed "forthwith" to the selection of a successor. [326]

Vacancies in the office of Deputy Speaker have occurred between sessions as well as during a session. Vacancies have occurred four times between sessions (1889, 1914, 1959 and 1961), when Members who were occupying the Chair as Deputy Speaker were appointed to Cabinet positions. Charles Carroll Colby and Pierre-Édouard Blondin were appointed to Cabinet in 1889 and 1914 respectively. As was the law at the time, they resigned their seats as Members, thus vacating the

---

323. With few exceptions, the motion has been moved by the Prime Minister; exceptions in this practice occurred in the selection of Deputy Chairman William Henry Golding in 1947 (*Journals*, March 28, 1947, p. 258) and Peter Milliken in 1996 (*Journals*, October 28, 1996, p. 778); and in the selection of Assistant Deputy Chairman Charles DeBlois in 1990 (*Journals*, October 2, 1990, p. 2050). In most cases, the motion is also seconded by a government Member; instances of seconding by opposition Members occurred in the nominations of Gérald Laniel as Deputy Chairman in 1973 (his fourth of five sessional appointments—*Journals*, January 4, 1973, p. 13), Ian McClelland as Deputy Chairman in 1997 (Mr. McClelland was himself an opposition Member—*Journals*, September 23, 1997, p. 13); the nomination of Charles DeBlois as Assistant Deputy Chairman was jointly seconded by two opposition Members (*Journals*, October 2, 1990, p. 2050).

324. The motion for the selection of the Assistant Deputy Chairman has twice been the object of a recorded division. In 1990, an objection was raised on the grounds that the opposition Bloc Québécois party had not been consulted (*Debates,* October 2, 1990, pp. 13657-8; *Journals*, October 2, 1990, p. 2050). In 1996, the opposition parties contended that the office should be held by an opposition Member; the motion nominating Pierrette Ringuette-Maltais was debated and adopted on a recorded division (*Journals*, February 27, 1996, p. 4; February 28, 1996, pp. 9-10; *Debates*, February 27, 1996, pp. 9-16; February 28, 1996, pp. 70-1). Also in 1996, the motion nominating a Deputy Chairman was decided on a recorded division, after opposition Members argued that at least one Chair occupant should be selected from the opposition; a government Member, Robert Kilger, was selected (*Journals*, February 27, 1996, p. 3; *Debates*, February 27, 1996, pp. 6-9). Later in the session, the nomination of Peter Milliken as Deputy Chairman was debated at length, closured and agreed to following a recorded division; in addition, the opposition moved an amendment (which was defeated) in order to have one of its members appointed to the position (*Journals*, October 28, 1996, pp. 778-9; October 29, 1996, pp. 785-9).

325. In 1997, Ian McClelland became the first opposition Member to assume the office of Deputy Chairman of Committees of the Whole (*Journals*, September 23, 1997, p. 13).

326. Standing Order 7(3).

office of Deputy Speaker and Chairman of Committees of the Whole.[327] Each was re-elected in by-elections between sessions and in each case, on the first day of the new session, the Speaker informed the House of the vacancy in representation and then announced the certificate of election and return of the Member.[328] On the fourth and third sitting day of the new session respectively, a new Deputy Speaker was selected;[329] in accordance with the rules in effect at the time, the selection could not take place until after the Address in Reply to the Speech from the Throne had been agreed to.[330] Pierre Sévigny and Jacques Flynn were appointed to Cabinet in 1959 and 1961 respectively. In each case, on the first day of the new session, following the Speech from the Throne, the Prime Minister informed the House of changes to the Cabinet and then moved a motion to appoint a Deputy Speaker and Chairman of Committees of the Whole.[331] In none of the foregoing cases do the official publications mention a resignation or letter of resignation communicated to the House by the Speaker.

There have also been vacancies during a session (in 1935, 1952, 1970, 1984 and 1990). The death of Armand LaVergne in 1935 is the only instance of the death of a Deputy Speaker while in office.[332] A successor was chosen four sitting days after news of his death was brought to the House.[333] J.A. Dion was appointed a judge in 1952 and resigned as a Member, thus creating a vacancy in the Deputy Speakership.[334] Hugh Faulkner was appointed a Parliamentary Secretary in 1970, and his resignation was communicated to the House by the Speaker.[335] Lloyd Francis, selected as Deputy Speaker at the opening of the Thirty-Second Parliament in 1980,[336] vacated that office by virtue of his election to the Speakership following the resignation of Speaker Sauvé in the Second Session of the Parliament.[337] In the latter three cases, the new Deputy Speaker was selected on the day on which the House was informed of the change in status of the Members. A less typical case is that of Deputy Speaker Marcel Danis, who was appointed to the Cabinet on February 23,

---

327. Until 1931, Members who accepted certain positions in Cabinet were required, pursuant to the *Senate and House of Commons Act*, to resign their seats and seek re-election (*Senate and House of Commons Act*, R.S.C. 1927, c. 147, ss. 13, 14). The Act (now called the *Parliament of Canada Act*) was amended in 1931 to remove this requirement (see R.S.C. 1930, c. 52, s. 1).

328. *Journals*, January 16, 1890, pp. 2-4; February 4, 1915, pp. 2, 4.

329. *Journals*, January 21, 1890, p. 15; February 9, 1915, p. 20.

330. This part of the rule was amended in July 1955 to remove the reference to the Address in Reply (*Journals*, July 12, 1955, pp. 920-1).

331. *Debates*, January 14, 1960, pp. 3-5; January 18, 1962, pp. 4-6.

332. The House was informed of the death on March 5, 1935 (*Debates*, pp. 1415-7).

333. *Journals*, March 11, 1935, p. 209.

334. *Journals*, April 9, 1952, pp. 197-8.

335. *Journals*, October 5, 1970, p. 1192.

336. *Journals*, April 14, 1980, p. 22.

337. *Journals*, January 16, 1984, p. 72.

1990. Following his Cabinet appointment, he did not preside over the House, but remained in office as Deputy Speaker and Chairman of Committees of the Whole until May 15, 1990, when his official resignation was communicated to the House and a new Deputy Speaker was elected.[338]

The offices of Deputy Chairman and Assistant Deputy Chairman of Committees of the Whole may be filled "at the commencement of every session, or from time to time as necessity may arise".[339] Thus, a vacancy during a session would not necessarily be filled immediately, or at all. For example, after the initial appointment of a Deputy Chairman of Committees of the Whole for a single session in 1938, the post was left vacant until 1947.[340] In December 1967, the Deputy Chairman of Committees of the Whole, Maurice Rinfret, died, and the position remained vacant for the balance of the session. However, since 1974 (First Session, Thirtieth Parliament), the House has operated with the full complement of Presiding Officers as the statutes and rules provide, and current practice has been that when such vacancies arise they are filled without undue delay.[341]

Vacancies during a session in the offices of Deputy Chairman and Assistant Deputy Chairman have occurred for various reasons. In more than one case, a Member serving as Deputy Chairman or Assistant Deputy Chairman was appointed to fill a vacancy among the other Presiding Officers,[342] or accepted an appointment of another kind.[343] In 1961, the Prime Minister informed the House that the Deputy Chairman of Committees of the Whole wished to be replaced, due to illness, and

---

338. *Journals*, May 15, 1990, pp. 1704-5. In his capacity as Deputy Speaker, Mr. Danis had been appointed Chairman of the Special Committee on the Review of the Parliament of Canada Act (*Journals*, December 14, 1989, p. 1011). After his appointment to Cabinet, he continued, by leave of the House, to chair the Committee which continued meeting until November 1990 (*Journals*, March 6, 1990, p. 1290).

339. Standing Order 8.

340. *Debates*, March 28, 1947, pp. 1826-7.

341. See Appendix 4, "Deputy Chairmen of Committees of the Whole House Since 1938", and Appendix 5, "Assistant Deputy Chairmen of Committees of the Whole House Since 1967".

342. In 1952, Louis-René Beaudoin, then Deputy Chairman, became Deputy Speaker and Chairman of Committees of the Whole. In 1980, Rod Blaker, then Assistant Deputy Chairman, became Deputy Chairman. In 1990, Andrée Champagne, then Assistant Deputy Chairman, was selected to be Deputy Speaker and Chairman of Committees of the Whole, as had Eymard Corbin in 1984.

343. In 1970, Albert Béchard was appointed a Parliamentary Secretary, and the Speaker announced to the House that Mr. Béchard had submitted his resignation as Deputy Chairman of Committees of the Whole; the Prime Minister then moved a motion appointing another Member to fill the position (*Debates*, October 5, 1970, p. 8705; *Journals*, October 5, 1970, p. 1192). On June 30, 1986, Jean Charest, the Assistant Deputy Chairman of Committees of the Whole, was appointed Minister of State (Youth); no formal resignation was communicated to the House and a replacement was selected in the next session. In 1996, the Deputy Chairman of Committees of the Whole, Robert Kilger, was appointed Chief Government Whip and was replaced on October 29; no formal resignation was communicated to the House.

immediately moved a motion naming a successor.[344] In 1996, the Deputy Chairman was appointed to the Senate and resigned as a Member, thus vacating the Deputy Chairmanship.[345] On other occasions, vacancies have occurred as the result of resignations.[346] In some cases where the Deputy Chairman of Committees of the Whole stepped down, the fact of the resignation was announced to the House by the Speaker.[347]

The selection of a particular individual as Chairman, Deputy Chairman or Assistant Deputy Chairman has been renewed from Parliament to Parliament or from session to session as the case may be.[348] It has also happened that individuals have moved from one presiding officer position to another, either through filling vacancies during a session or through selection to other positions in a new session of Parliament; however, there is little evidence to suggest that this experience has created a path to the Speakership. Of the 33 Speakers who have occupied the Chair since Confederation, eight had prior experience as a Presiding Officer in the House of Commons.[349]

---

344. The Prime Minister indicated to the House that the Deputy Chairman (Charles Edward Rea) was seriously ill and that his wife, speaking for him, had requested that he be replaced (*Debates*, June 8, 1961, p. 6015). The motion proposed the appointment of Gordon Campbell Chown, "in the place of Charles Edward Rea . . . who is unable to carry on this duty because of illness" (*Journals*, June 8, 1961, p. 640).

345. Shirley Maheu was appointed to the Senate on February 1, 1996, during the intersession.

346. In 1982, the Deputy Chairman, Denis Ethier, resigned in protest against procedural tactics employed by the Official Opposition (*Debates*, July 8, 1982, pp. 19164-5; July 14, 1982, pp. 19321-6; July 21, 1982, p. 19555), and in 1990, the Assistant Deputy Chairman, Denis Pronovost, resigned following controversial remarks he had made (see *Debates*, May 31, 1990, pp. 12110, 12123-4; June 1, 1990, p. 12163).

347. Keith Penner and Rod Blaker were appointed Parliamentary Secretaries on October 10, 1975, and January 13, 1984, respectively. The Speaker informed the House of their resignations on October 14, 1975 (*Debates*, p. 8091; *Journals*, p. 754), and January 16, 1984 (*Debates*, p. 443; *Journals*, p. 74).

348. See Appendix 3, "Deputy Speakers and Chairmen of Committees of the Whole House Since 1885"; Appendix 4, "Deputy Chairmen of Committees of the Whole House Since 1938"; and Appendix 5, "Assistant Deputy Chairmen of Committees of the Whole House Since 1967".

349. Speakers Brodeur, Marcil, Sévigny, Rhodes, Macdonald, Beaudoin, Lamoureux and Francis had all served as Deputy Speaker and Chairman of Committees of the Whole prior to becoming Speaker. Speaker Beaudoin had, in addition, served as Deputy Chairman of Committees of the Whole. In 1942, Thomas Vien was serving as Deputy Speaker when he was appointed to the Senate, and became Speaker of the Senate shortly thereafter.

8

The Parliamentary Cycle

I believe [the parliamentary calendar] has been responsible for bringing order to our proceedings and has encouraged and fostered negotiation and compromise between the Parties in the days leading up to the automatic adjournments. Without that co-operation and constant negotiation and compromise, our system of government ceases to operate smoothly.

SPEAKER JOHN A. FRASER
(*Debates*, June 13, 1988, p. 16379)

The life cycle of a Parliament is regulated by constitutional provisions as well as Standing Orders. The most fundamental of these are the *Constitution Acts, 1867 to 1982,* which provide first, that only the Crown may "summon and call together the House of Commons";[1] second, that subject to a dissolution, five years is the maximum lifespan of the House between general elections;[2] and third, that "there be a sitting of Parliament at least once every twelve months".[3]

At the same time, the financial requirements of the government render a meeting of Parliament every year a practical necessity for the annual granting of Supply by Parliament for a fiscal year (April 1 of one year to March 31

1. *Constitution Act, 1867*, R.S.C. 1985, Appendix II, No. 5, s. 38.

2. *Constitution Act, 1867*, R.S.C. 1985, Appendix II, No. 5, s. 50; *Constitution Act, 1982*, R.S.C. 1985, Appendix II, No. 44, s. 4(1).

3. *Constitution Act, 1982*, R.S.C. 1985, Appendix II, No. 44, s. 5.

of the following year).[4] As such, the date selected for the opening of each new Parliament following a general election and of each new session within a Parliament, can and does vary—within constitutional limitations—according to the political and financial priorities of the government.

Against this backdrop, the Standing Orders of the House provide for a predetermined annual calendar of sittings, known as the parliamentary calendar, which applies only when the House is in session.[5] In this way, within each session, the days on which the House is likely to meet are known long in advance, thus allowing for a more orderly planning of House business.

The complex procedures and practices surrounding financial matters are addressed in Chapter 18, "Financial Procedures". The present chapter focusses on the life of a Parliament and its sessions; namely, the opening and closing of a Parliament and a session, and the sitting and non-sitting periods within a session, as determined by the parliamentary calendar.

Terminology

Several recurring terms and phrases associated with the parliamentary cycle require explanation for the purpose of clarity.

Parliament

A Parliament is a period of time, during which the institution of Parliament (comprising the Sovereign, the Senate and the House of Commons) exercises its powers. The process of starting a Parliament begins with the proclamation of the Governor General calling for the formation of a new Parliament and setting the date for a general election. A Parliament ends with its dissolution. A House of Commons has a constitutionally determined maximum lifespan of five years.[6]

Session

A session is one of the fundamental time periods into which a Parliament is divided, and usually consists of a number of separate sittings. A session begins with a Speech from the Throne when Parliament is summoned by proclamation of the Governor General; it ends with a prorogation or dissolution of Parliament. There may be any number of sessions in a Parliament; the numbers have ranged from one to seven.[7] There is no set length for a session.

Sitting

A sitting is a meeting of the House within a session. The Standing Orders provide times and days for the sittings of the House.[8] A sitting is not necessarily synonymous

---

4. Section 53 of the *Constitution Act, 1867*, R.S.C. 1985, Appendix II, No. 5, and Standing Order 80(1) stipulate that all financial legislation must originate in the House of Commons. The fiscal year is defined in the *Financial Administration Act,* R.S.C. 1985, c. F-11, s. 2.

5. Standing Order 28(2).

6. *Constitution Act, 1867*, R.S.C. 1985, Appendix II, No. 5, s. 50; *Constitution Act, 1982*, R.S.C. 1985, Appendix II, No. 44, s. 4(1).

7. See Appendix 12, "Parliaments Since 1867 and Number of Sitting Days".

8. Standing Order 24.

with a "day". Some sittings are very brief; some have extended over more than one calendar day.[9]

Adjournment

An adjournment is the termination of a sitting (pursuant to Standing or Special Order, or by motion). An adjournment covers the period between the end of one sitting and the beginning of the next. It can be of varying duration—a few hours, overnight, over a weekend, a week or longer.[10] While prorogation and dissolution are prerogative acts of the Crown, the power to adjourn rests solely with the House.

Parliamentary Calendar

The parliamentary calendar, as laid out in the Standing Orders, provides a fixed timetable of sittings and adjournments for a full calendar year.[11] In effect, once a session begins, the calendar alternates *sitting periods* with *adjournments* at set points throughout the year. Each year consists of seven sitting periods of approximately three to five weeks in length, and seven adjournments of varying lengths.

Prorogation

Prorogation of Parliament is the ending of a session, with a special ceremony held in the Senate Chamber or with the issuance of a Governor General's proclamation to that effect. Prorogation also refers to the period of time a Parliament stands prorogued.

Recess

The time between the ending of one session and the opening of the next can be called a recess. In practice, the term "recess" is also used in reference to a lengthy adjournment.

Dissolution

Dissolution is the formal ending of a Parliament by proclamation of the Governor General. This has always occurred prior to the five-year time limit set by the Constitution for the expiration of the House of Commons by effluxion of time. Dissolution is followed by a general election.

---

9. For example, on March 30, 1973, there were two sittings in a single day (*Journals*, March 30, 1973, p. 229). For an example of the House sitting continuously over two days, see *Journals*, December 18 and 19, 1980, pp. 951-1130. For an example of the House sitting continuously over several days, see *Journals,* March 10-15, 1913, pp. 326-40. In 1982, the division bells were rung continuously, resulting in a two-week sitting (*Journals*, March 2-17, 1982, p. 4608).

10. Standing Order 24 provides for adjournments overnight and over weekends. Standing Order 28 provides for periodic adjournments of a week or more. Occasionally, there are brief adjournments of a few hours' duration. See, for example, *Journals,* September 9, 1992, p. 1957; June 15, 1995, p. 1768.

11. Standing Order 28(2).

Opening of a Parliament and a Session

SUMMONING PARLIAMENT

Section 38 of the *Constitution Act, 1867* provides for the summoning of Parliament: "The Governor General shall from Time to Time, in the Queen's Name, by Instrument under the Great Seal of Canada, summon and call together the House of Commons."

The "Instrument" consists of two forms of proclamation issued by the Governor General on the advice of the Prime Minister[12] and published in the *Canada Gazette*. The first form sets the date for which Parliament is summoned (the date can later be advanced or put back). It is issued at the end of the preceding session, in keeping with the principle of the continuity of Parliament, whereby a session ends with provision made for its next meeting. The second form confirms the date and sets the time at which Parliament is summoned to meet for the transaction of business. For example, prior to the opening of the First Session of the Thirty-Sixth Parliament, a series of proclamations was initially issued summoning Parliament to meet on June 23, 1997, then to meet on August 1 and later to meet on August 29, 1997. On August 27, a final proclamation summoned Parliament to meet "for the DESPATCH OF BUSINESS" at 11:00 a.m. on September 22, 1997.[13]

PROCEEDINGS ON OPENING DAY

The opening of a Parliament is also the opening of the first session of that Parliament. Two procedures distinguish it from the opening of subsequent sessions. These are the taking and subscribing of the Oath of Allegiance by Members, and the election of a Speaker.

Members Sworn In

Following a general election, the Clerk of the House receives from the Chief Electoral Officer the names of Members elected to serve in the House of Commons.[14] In order for the elected Members to take their seats in the House, it is required by the

---

12. See Privy Council minute, P. C. 3374, dated October 25, 1935, a "Memorandum regarding certain of the functions of the Prime Minister", which stated that recommendations (to the Crown) concerning the convocation and dissolution of Parliament are the "special prerogatives" of the Prime Minister.

13. See proclamations in the *Canada Gazette*, Part II, Vol. 131, Extra No. 3 (April 28, 1997), Extra No. 5 (June 20, 1997), Extra No. 6 (July 31, 1997) and Extra No. 7 (August 28, 1997).

14. When the House meets for the despatch of business, the Clerk lays upon the Table a list of the elected Members certified by the Chief Electoral Officer. The certificate and list are printed in the *Journals*. See, for example, *Journals*, January 17, 1994, pp. 2-9.

Constitution Act, 1867, that they first subscribe to an Oath of Allegiance.[15] As an alternative to swearing the oath, the Member may make a solemn affirmation.[16]

The oath or affirmation is administered by the Clerk of the House or another designated Commissioner.[17] At this time, the newly sworn-in Member signs the Test Roll, a book whose pages are headed by the text of the oath or affirmation. The general practice now is for Members to be sworn in prior to opening day, after the Clerk receives the certificates of election returns from the Chief Electoral Officer.[18]

Matters relating to the oath, the affirmation and the signing of the Test Roll are covered in greater detail in Chapter 4, "The House of Commons and Its Members".

Election of the Speaker

Section 44 of the *Constitution Act, 1867* provides for the election of a Speaker as the first item of business when Members assemble following a general election. The Standing Orders provide for the manner in which the Speaker is elected.[19] On the day appointed by proclamation for the meeting of a new Parliament, the Members are summoned by the division bell to assemble in the Chamber, where they receive the Usher of the Black Rod,[20] who reads a message requesting the immediate attendance of the House in the Senate Chamber.

---

15. *Constitution Act, 1867*, R.S.C. 1985, Appendix II, No. 5, s. 128. The requirement stems from British practice dating back to the sixteenth century. Amid the political and religious conflicts of the time, the *Act of Supremacy* was adopted, requiring all Members to declare their belief in the Sovereign as supreme governor in matters both temporal and ecclesiastical. See *Redlich*, Vol. II, pp. 62-4.

16. Affirmation is not mentioned in the Constitution. Instructions issued by the Crown in 1905 allowed for Members to take the oath or make an affirmation. See *Beauchesne*, 4th ed., p. 13. For further information on the affirmation, see Chapter 4, "The House of Commons and Its Members".

17. Section 128 of the *Constitution Act, 1867*, states that the oath is to be taken before "the Governor General or some person authorized by him". For the Thirty-Sixth Parliament, the Clerk of the House of Commons, the Deputy Clerk and the Sergeant-at-Arms were so authorized (*Journals*, September 22, 1997, p. 1).

18. For the opening of the Thirty-Sixth Parliament in 1997, group swearing-in ceremonies were organized for Members of the Reform, New Democratic and Progressive Conservative parties. In 1985, the McGrath Committee recommended, in the interest of increasing awareness of parliamentary institutions, a televised collective swearing-in of all Members, in addition to the customary private swearing-in for individual Members (see pages 57 and 58 of the Third Report of the Special Committee on Reform of the House of Commons, June 1985).

19. Standing Order 2.

20. The Usher of the Black Rod is an officer of the Senate whose responsibilities include delivering messages to the House of Commons when its Members' attendance is required in the Senate Chamber by the Governor General or a Deputy of the Governor General. (On November 6, 1997, the title of the Office was changed from the "Gentleman Usher of the Black Rod" to the "Usher of the Black Rod". See the *Journals of the Senate*, pp. 165-7 and the *Debates of the Senate*, pp. 333-43.)

In a procession led by the Clerk of the House, the Members go to the Senate. There, a Deputy of the Governor General[21] is seated at the foot of the Throne, and the Speaker of the Senate addresses the Members on the Deputy's behalf, informing them that "... the Deputy ... does not see fit to declare the causes of his (her) summoning of the present Parliament of Canada until the Speaker of the House shall have been chosen according to Law ...".[22] This means that the Speech from the Throne will not be read until a Speaker has been elected. The Members then return to the House and proceed to elect a presiding officer. (For further details on the election of the Speaker, refer to Chapter 7, "The Speaker and Other Presiding Officers of the House".)

Presentation of Speaker to Governor General

Following the election of the Speaker, at the time fixed for the purpose of appearing for the formal opening of Parliament with a Speech from the Throne, the House again receives the Usher of the Black Rod, who conveys the message of the Governor General requesting the presence of the House in the Senate.[23] The procession is led by the Usher of the Black Rod, followed by the Sergeant-at-Arms (bearing the Mace), the Speaker, the Clerk and the Members. At the Bar of the Senate, the newly elected Speaker stands on a small platform, removes his or her hat and receives an acknowledgement from the Governor General, who is seated on the Throne.[24] The Speaker addresses the Governor General by an established formula, as follows:

> *May it please Your Excellency,*
>
> *The House of Commons has elected me their Speaker, though I am but little able to fulfil the important duties thus assigned to me. If, in the performance of those duties, I should at any time fall into error, I pray that the fault may be imputed to me, and not to the Commons, whose servant I am, and who, through me, the better to enable them to discharge their duty to their Queen*

---

21. A Deputy to the Governor General is a person, usually a Justice of the Supreme Court, who exercises the powers of the Governor General on certain occasions (*Constitution Act, 1867*, R.S.C. 1985, Appendix II, No. 5, s. 14; see also Part VII of *Letters Patent Constituting the Office of Governor General of Canada*, effective October 1, 1947).

22. Since the opening of the Fifth Session of the Third Parliament in 1878, a Deputy of the Governor General rather than the Governor General has received the House in the Senate prior to the election of a Speaker (*Bourinot*, 2ⁿᵈ ed., pp. 274-5). See also *Beauchesne*, 4ᵗʰ ed., p. 19.

23. This message can be delivered on the same day as the election of the Speaker, or on another day. See, for example, *Journals*, December 12, 1988, pp. 3-4 (the sitting was suspended following the election of the Speaker, and resumed some hours later); September 22, 1997, p. 9 (after the election of the Speaker, the House adjourned to the following day).

24. The tradition of meeting in the Senate accords with the practice established in the United Kingdom whereby the rightful place of the Sovereign in Parliament is in the Upper House—no monarch, or monarch's representative, having entered the British House of Commons since King Charles I in 1642 (see *Redlich*, Vol. II, pp. 89-90). During the rebuilding of the Canadian Parliament following the great fire of 1916, the first session in the new building opened on February 26, 1920. Because the Senate Chamber was not ready, the Senate occupied the House of Commons Chamber on opening day, thereafter moving to the Railway Committee Room elsewhere in the building (*Debates of the Senate*, February 26, 1920, p. 1; February 27, 1920, p. 2).

and Country, humbly claim all their undoubted rights and privileges, especially that they may have freedom of speech in their debates, access to Your Excellency's person at all seasonable times, and that their proceedings may receive from Your Excellency the most favourable construction. [25]

The Speaker of the Senate, on behalf of the Governor General, makes the traditional reply: [26]

Mr. Speaker, I am commanded by His/Her Excellency the Governor General to declare to you that he/she freely confides in the duty and attachment of the House of Commons to Her Majesty's Person and Government, and not doubting that their proceedings will be conducted with wisdom, temper and prudence, he/she grants, and upon all occasions will recognize and allow, their constitutional privileges. I am commanded also to assure you that the Commons shall have ready access to His/Her Excellency upon all seasonable occasions and that their proceedings, as well as your words and actions, will constantly receive from him/her the most favourable construction. [27]

The claiming of privileges by the Speaker on behalf of the House occurs only at the opening of a Parliament, and is not repeated in the event a Speaker is elected during the course of a Parliament. [28] After the claiming of privilege, the session is formally opened by the reading of the Speech from the Throne.

OPENING OF A SESSION

The swearing-in of Members and the election of a Speaker are the distinguishing features of the summoning of a new Parliament for the opening of its first session; in sessions subsequent to the first, there are no preliminary proceedings in the House. The opening of a session—whether it is the first or a subsequent session—is marked by the reading of the Speech from the Throne. On each opening of a session, the House assembles with the Speaker in the Chair, receives the Usher of the Black Rod

---

25. See, for example, *Debates of the Senate*, September 23, 1997, p. 3.

26. See also Chapter 3, "Privileges and Immunities". There is not now any question of the choice of Speaker by the House being subject to approbation, confirmation or ratification by the Crown. In the pre-1841 legislatures of Upper and Lower Canada, however, it was customary for the new Speaker to seek the approval of the governor. In 1827 Lord Dalhousie, then Governor General of Lower Canada, refused to accept Louis-Joseph Papineau as Speaker of the Legislative Assembly. The Assembly passed resolutions declaring this action unconstitutional, and expunged the proceedings from their Journals. The Governor General prorogued Parliament and in a subsequent session Mr. Papineau received the approval of Sir James Kempt, Lord Dalhousie's successor. The practice of ratifying the Assembly's choice of Speaker was discontinued in the first session following union in 1841, the *Act of Union* being silent on the matter (*Bourinot*, 4th ed., pp. 92-3).

27. See, for example, *Debates of the Senate*, September 23, 1997, p. 4.

28. *Bourinot*, 4th ed., pp. 49-50.

and proceeds in due course to the Senate for the reading of the Speech from the Throne.

The Speech imparts the causes of summoning Parliament, prior to which neither House can embark on any public business.[29] It marks the first occasion Parliament meets in an assembly of its three constituent parts: the House of Commons, the Senate and the Sovereign, or Sovereign's representative.

Opened by the Sovereign

When a session is opened by the Sovereign, as occurred in 1957 and 1977, the message communicated to the House by the Usher of the Black Rod is "Mr. (Madam) Speaker, The Queen (King) commands this Honourable House to attend Her (His) Majesty immediately in the chamber of the Honourable the Senate".[30]

Opened by the Governor General

When, as in most cases, the Speech from the Throne is read by the Governor General,[31] the Usher of the Black Rod delivers a message to the effect that His (or Her) Excellency the Governor General of Canada "desires" the immediate attendance of the House in the Senate chamber.[32]

Opened by the Administrator

In the event of the death, incapacity, removal or absence from the country of the Governor General, the powers of the office devolve upon the Chief Justice of Canada. When acting in this capacity, the Chief Justice is known as the Administrator of the Government of Canada.[33] The Speech from the Throne has been read on occasion by the Administrator.[34] The message conveyed to the House by the Usher

---

29. See Speaker's ruling respecting the first day of a session, *Journals,* March 24, 1873, p. 58. In this ruling, the Speaker referred to the procedural authorities Hatsell, Dwarris, May and Todd. An exception to this established procedure occurred in October 1995, when the First Session of the Fifty-Third Legislative Assembly of New Brunswick was called, pursuant to proclamation, and the Administrator made a short statement after the election of the Speaker; whereupon the Assembly proceeded to consider a resolution concerning the distinct-society status of Quebec. When this was disposed of, a message was read calling the Assembly to the formal opening of the session on February 6, 1996. At that time the Speech from the Throne was read by the Lieutenant-Governor (*Journals of the Legislative Assembly,* October 25, 1995, pp. 1-6; February 6, 1996, pp. 7-27).

30. *Journals,* October 14, 1957, p. 8; October 18, 1977, p. 2.

31. On two occasions, the wife of the Governor General shared in the reading of the Speech from the Throne. Jules Léger took office as Governor General in January 1974; in June of that year, he suffered a debilitating stroke which affected his speech. During his tenure, four sessions of Parliament were opened: on September 30, 1974, the Speech from the Throne was read by the Administrator; on October 18, 1977, it was read by the Sovereign; on October 12, 1976, and October 11, 1978, the Governor General and Madame Léger shared the reading of the Speech from the Throne.

32. See, for example, *Journals,* September 23, 1997, p. 11.

33. *Letters Patent Constituting the Office of Governor General of Canada* (1947), R.S.C. 1985, Appendix II, No. 31, art. VIII.

34. See, for example, *Journals,* March 12, 1931, p. 3; May 16, 1940, p. 9; May 16, 1963, p. 9; September 30, 1974, p. 8.

of the Black Rod in these cases is "His (Her) Excellency the Administrator desires the immediate attendance of this Honourable House in the chamber of the Honourable the Senate".[35]

SPEECH FROM THE THRONE AND SUBSEQUENT PROCEEDINGS IN THE HOUSE

The Speech from the Throne usually sets forth in some detail the government's view of the condition of the country and provides an indication of what legislation it intends to bring forward. After hearing the Speech, the Speaker and Members return to the House. If the session is the first of a new Parliament, the newly elected Speaker will have made the traditional statement claiming for the House all its "undoubted rights and privileges". This is reported by the Speaker to the House on returning from the Senate.[36] The business for the day's sitting then proceeds.

There are certain items which normally are dealt with by the House on the first day of a session. These are described below, in the order in which they are normally brought before the House. As will be noted, variations can and do occur.

Formal Business

Pro forma bill: Before proceeding to the consideration of the Speech from the Throne, the House gives first reading to the *pro forma* Bill C-1, *An Act respecting the Administration of Oaths of Office*.[37] Typically, the bill is introduced by the Prime Minister; it receives first reading but is not proceeded with any further during the session. Its purpose is to assert the independence of the House of Commons and its right to choose its own business and to deliberate without reference to the causes of summons as expressed in the Speech from the Throne.[38]

---

35. See, for example, *Journals*, September 30, 1974, p. 8.

36. See, for example, *Journals*, September 23, 1997, p. 11.

37. See, for example, *Journals*, September 23, 1997, p. 11. For an example of an occasion on which the practice was not adhered to, see *Journals*, August 29, 1950, p. 4. The House had been recalled to a special session that day, to deal with a labour dispute, among other matters. Instead of the usual *pro forma* bill, the government introduced back-to-work legislation which was read the first time and ordered for a second reading later that day. See also *Debates*, August 29, 1950, pp. 1-2.

38. The introduction of a *pro forma* bill as a ritual act of independence has existed as a practice of the House since prior to Confederation. It originated in the British House of Commons in 1571, being confirmed in the following resolution adopted on March 22, 1603: "That the first day of sitting, in every Parliament, some one Bill, and no more, receiveth a first reading for form's sake" (*Hatsell*, Vol. II, p. 81). The custom is observed in other parliaments where, in most cases, the bill is read a first time and not heard of again until the start of the next session: the Australian House of Representatives refers to its "formal" or "privilege" bill (*House of Representatives' Practice*, 3rd ed., pp. 234-5); in the British House, it is called the Outlawries Bill (*May*, 22nd ed., p. 245). In the Legislative Assembly of British Columbia, the *pro forma* bill is Bill 1, *An Act to ensure the Supremacy of Parliament* (see, for example, *Votes and Proceedings* for March 17, 1992, and March 26, 1998).

Report of Speech from the Throne: The Speaker reports to the House on the Speech from the Throne, informing the House that "to prevent mistakes" a copy of the Speech has been obtained; its text is printed in the *Debates*.[39] A motion is then moved, usually by the Prime Minister, and adopted for the Speech from the Throne to be considered either "later this day" or on a future day,[40] at which time debate takes place on a motion for an Address in Reply to the Speech from the Throne (for further information on the Address in Reply, see Chapter 15, "Special Debates").

Routine Opening Day Motions and Announcements

Traditionally, certain other items of business have been attended to following the Speech from the Throne. These are described below, in the order in which they are customarily taken up.

Board of Internal Economy: The Speaker may make an announcement to the House with regard to Members appointed to sit for the duration of the Parliament on the Board of Internal Economy, the body responsible for all matters of administrative and financial policy affecting the House of Commons.[41]

Membership of Standing Committees: At the start of the first session of each Parliament, the membership of the Standing Committee on Procedure and House Affairs is appointed and charged with the selection of Members for all standing committees and standing joint committees.[42] This is effected by

---

39. The text of the Speech from the Throne used to be printed in the *Journals* as well as the *Debates*. However, beginning in 1996, at the opening of the Second Session of the Thirty-Fifth Parliament, the text was tabled and printed in the *Debates* but not in the *Journals* (*Debates*, February 27, 1996, pp. 1-6; September 23, 1997, pp. 5-12; *Journals*, February 27, 1996, pp. 1-2; September 23, 1997, p. 12).

40. The motion is debatable and amendable. In 1988, for example, the motion was debated and adopted on recorded division (*Journals*, December 12, 1988, pp. 6-7). In 1926, an amendment was moved, debated at length and eventually negatived on recorded division (*Journals*, January 8, 1926, pp. 12-3; January 15, 1926, pp. 28-9).

41. See, for example, *Journals*, December 12, 1988, p. 8. The announcement is made pursuant to s. 50(4) of the *Parliament of Canada Act*, R.S.C. 1985, c. P-1 as amended by S.C. 1991, c. 20, s. 2. For further information on the role and functions of the Board of Internal Economy, see Chapter 6, "The Physical and Administrative Setting".

42. Standing Order 104(1). See, for example, *Journals*, January 18, 1994, p. 18. Formerly, this Standing Order provided for the appointment of a seven-member Striking Committee at the commencement of the first session of each Parliament. In 1991, the rule was amended (see *Journals,* April 11, 1991, pp. 2904-5, 2922) and the task of selecting committee membership became one of the duties of a new standing committee, since renamed Procedure and House Affairs. The practice has been that a motion to appoint a committee to designate standing and joint committee membership is moved and disposed of on the opening day of the Parliament. In 1962, however, such a motion was moved and adopted by unanimous consent on the eleventh sitting day (*Journals*, October 12, 1962, p. 63).

motion moved without notice by a Minister, usually the Government House Leader.[43]

Election of Other Chair Occupants: At the beginning of a Parliament, a Chairman of Committees of the Whole (who is also Deputy Speaker) is selected for the duration of that Parliament.[44] This is done by a government Member (usually the Prime Minister) moving without notice that a particular Member, usually also from the government side,[45] be Chairman of Committees of the Whole. The Deputy Chairman and the Assistant Deputy Chairman of Committees of the Whole are selected in the same manner;[46] their terms extend for the duration of the session in which they are chosen (for further information on the roles and functions of these Presiding

43. A well-entrenched practice exists whereby, on opening day, Ministers move certain motions without notice and the House disposes of them. Normally, the *Order Paper and Notice Paper* is not produced for the first day of the session. Bourinot's first edition (1884) describes the practice of moving a formal resolution for the appointment of committees without notice (pp. 231-2).

Standing Order 55(1) provides for a *Special Order Paper* during a prorogation or when the House stands adjourned and the Government wishes a matter requiring notice to be considered when the House reconvenes. A *Special Order Paper and Notice Paper* was produced for the opening of the Second Session of the Thirty-Fifth Parliament on February 27, 1996, and for the opening of the Thirty-Sixth Parliament on September 23, 1997; they contained notices of items of Government Business. In 1997, the notice included among other matters, the proposed membership of the committee charged with selecting members for committees.

In Australia, there is no *Notice Paper* for the first day of sitting and notice would normally be required for first day business, though examples exist of business proceeding by leave of the House or suspension of the rules (*House of Representatives Practice*, 3rd ed., pp. 235-6). In New Zealand, an *Order Paper* is produced and notice is required for opening day motions (*McGee*, 2nd ed., p. 99).

44. Standing Order 7(1). Standing Order 7(3) provides for the selection of a successor should a vacancy arise during the course of the Parliament.

45. However, in 1973 and 1979, for example, the Deputy Speakers (Robert McCleave and Gérald Laniel) were chosen from among the Members of the Official Opposition.

46. They are usually from the government side; however, in 1997, for example, the Deputy Chairman of Committees of the Whole (Ian McClelland) was chosen from among the Members of the Official Opposition.

Officers, see Chapter 7, "The Speaker and Other Presiding Officers of the House"[47]). The motions have generally been adopted without dissent.[48]

Order for Supply: The Standing Orders require the House at the start of each session to designate, by means of a motion, a continuing Order of the Day for the consideration of the business of Supply.[49] The designation of a continuing order for Supply follows on the statement usually found in the Speech from the Throne informing Members that they "will be asked to appropriate the funds required to carry out the services and expenditures authorised by Parliament".[50] The wording of the motion is generally as follows: "That this House at its next sitting consider the business of Supply". Once the motion is adopted, a continuing order to deal with Supply is placed on the *Order Paper* under Government Orders and any Supply item to be considered by the House during the session will appear on the *Order Paper* under this Order of the Day.

Other Items

Other items of business have been included from time to time on opening day. For example, in 1996, Speaker Parent responded to a point of order raised in the previous session on the first day of the new session after all the usual business items had been dealt with.[51]

---

47. See also Appendix 3, "Deputy Speakers and Chairmen of Committees of the Whole House Since 1885"; Appendix 4, "Deputy Chairmen of Committees of the Whole House Since 1938"; Appendix 5, "Assistant Deputy Chairmen of Committees of the Whole House Since 1967".

48. Exceptions occurred in 1962 when the motion to select the Deputy Speaker was adopted after a recorded division (*Journals*, January 18, 1962, pp. 6-7); in 1990 when the motion to select the Assistant Deputy Chairman of Committees of the Whole was adopted on recorded division (*Journals*, October 2, 1990, p. 2050); in 1996, when the motion to select the Deputy Chairman of Committees of the Whole was adopted on recorded division (*Journals,* February 27, 1996, p. 3) and the motion to select the Assistant Deputy Chairman of Committees of the Whole was also adopted on a recorded division (*Journals*, February 27, 1996, p. 4; February 28, 1996, pp. 9-10). Later in the session, the post of Deputy Chairman of Committees of the Whole was vacated and a motion was moved selecting a successor. It was debated, an amendment was moved and negatived on recorded division, the motion was closured and later adopted on recorded division (*Journals*, October 28, 1996, pp. 778-9; October 29, 1996, pp. 784-9).

49. Standing Order 81(1). An Order of the Day is an item of business on the House agenda (the *Order Paper*). "Continuing" means that the Order for the Business of Supply will remain on the *Order Paper* for every sitting of the session thereafter.

50. See, for example, *Journals*, May 13, 1991, p. 11; January 18, 1994, p. 17. For further information on the Supply process, see Chapter 18, "Financial Procedures". On occasion the statement has not been made in the Speech from the Throne (see *Journals*, September 8, 1930, p. 9; January 25, 1940, p. 8; October 9, 1951, pp. 2-4; December 12, 1988, pp. 5-6; April 3, 1989, pp. 3-12). The Speaker ruled on May 2, 1989, that the Standing Orders do not specify that a request for funds must appear in the Speech from the Throne (*Debates*, pp. 1175-7).

51. *Debates*, February 27, 1996, pp. 16-20. The point of order concerned the designation of the Official Opposition, when events had resulted in an equality of seats between the two main opposition parties. Although prorogation normally puts to an end any outstanding business, the Speaker determined that the recent equality of seats had created a new context and required an immediate statement on the issue. For further information on the point of order and the Speaker's ruling, see Chapter 1, "Parliamentary Institutions".

Vacancies: From time to time, the Speaker is notified that a sitting Member has vacated his or her seat in the House. When this occurs prior to the opening of the session (whether the first or a subsequent session of a Parliament), the Speaker so informs the House at some point during the day's proceedings.[52]

New Members: Members elected in by-elections prior to the opening of a session have been introduced to the House on the first day of the new session.[53]

Tributes: When a Member, former Member or distinguished individual has died during a period when the House is not in session, tributes have been offered on the first day of the new session, often at the point in the proceedings following the adoption of the motion to consider the Speech from the Throne.[54] Such tributes have also been offered early in the session but not as part of the proceedings on the opening day.[55]

Appointment of House Officials: In the event that senior officials of the House are appointed between sessions, it has been customary for the Speaker to inform the House of the appointment or appointments on the first day of the new session.[56]

"SPECIAL" SESSIONS

A small number of sessions (see Figure 8.1) have been termed "special sessions" in the *Debates* or *Journals* of the House of Commons. From a procedural standpoint, there is nothing special about a "special" session. The elements required for the opening and closing of a session are present. If the special session is the first of a Parliament (as occurred in 1930), a Speaker of the House must first be elected.

It will readily be noted that the "special" sessions were short-lived. They also shared certain characteristics. However, other sessions of short duration, though not

---

52. See, for example, *Journals*, September 15, 1949, pp. 10-3; October 9, 1979, pp. 17-8; October 1, 1986, pp. 24-5; December 12, 1988, pp. 7-8; February 27, 1996, p. 2. For further information, see Chapter 4, "The House of Commons and Its Members".

53. See, for example, *Journals*, August 29, 1950, p. 4; April 3, 1989, p. 3. For matters relating to a new Member's entrance in and introduction to the House, see Chapter 4, "The House of Commons and Its Members".

54. For example, on the opening day of the Third Session of the Twenty-First Parliament, tributes were offered in memory of former Prime Minister W.L. Mackenzie King, two Members (Mr. Mitchell and Mr. Belzile) and former Speaker Casgrain (*Debates*, August 29, 1950, pp. 5-10). For other examples of tributes given on the opening day of a session, see *Debates*, September 12, 1968, pp. 10-1; January 4, 1973, pp. 8-11; September 30, 1974, pp. 8-9; October 12, 1976, pp. 4-5; October 9, 1979, pp. 7-8; December 12, 1988, pp. 11-2.

55. See, for example, the tributes made on the second day of the session in *Debates*, January 5, 1973, p. 14; May 14, 1991, pp. 55-8; and on the fourth and fifth days of the session in *Debates*, January 20, 1994, pp. 108-12; January 21, 1994, pp. 157-8; September 25, 1997, pp. 104-6; September 26, 1997, pp. 153-6.

56. See, for example, announcements informing the House of the appointment of a new Clerk (*Journals*, February 5, 1925, p. 1; October 9, 1979, p. 18) and of a new Sergeant-at-Arms (*Journals*, March 18, 1918, p. 7; January 14, 1960, p. 8).

Figure 8.1 *Sessions Identified as "Special" in House of Commons* Debates *or* Journals

Parliament. session	Opening day of the session	Last sitting day of the House	Number of days on which the House sat	Specific purpose
12.4	1914-08-18	1914-08-22	5	Outbreak of World War I
17.1	1930-09-08	1930-09-22	12	Exceptional economic conditions
18.5	1939-09-07	1939-09-13	6	Outbreak of World War II
21.3	1950-08-29	1951-01-29	17	Disruption of railway transportation facilities and fighting in Korea
22.4	1956-11-26	1957-01-18	5	Hostilities in Middle East and events in Hungary

officially termed "special" in the *Debates* or *Journals* of the House of Commons, have shared the same characteristics:

- Parliament was called to meet for a specific purpose, which was the principal focus of what was in each case a comparatively short Speech from the Throne;[57]
- The five sessions specifically designated as "special" took place during a period when sessions were generally shorter, with a fairly predictable annual rhythm of sitting and non-sitting periods; the special sessions were called in late summer or autumn, times of the year when the House did not usually sit;[58]

---

57. *Journals*, August 18, 1914, pp. 2-3; September 8, 1930, p. 9; September 7, 1939, p. 2; January 25, 1940, p. 8; March 19, 1945, pp. 2-3; August 29, 1950, pp. 4-5; November 26, 1956, p. 2; December 12, 1988, pp. 5-6.

58. At the time of the short-lived First Session of the Thirty-Fourth Parliament, which is not specifically designated as "special" in the *Debates* or *Journals* of the House of Commons, the situation had evolved to where Parliament was sitting year-round. It is worth noting that in this case Parliament was summoned to meet only three weeks after the general election of November 21, 1988. Parliament met on December 12, 1988, and this was also the date set for the return of the writs. The list of Members elected and the accompanying certificate of the Chief Electoral Officer, usually tabled by the Clerk immediately when the House meets for the despatch of business, was in this instance not tabled until December 15, 1988, the fourth sitting day of the session (*Journals*, pp. 26-33). The session started on December 12, 1988, and dealt with a bill to implement a free trade agreement between Canada and the United States. On December 23, the House passed the bill and pursuant to Special Order, adjourned, reconvened for the Royal Assent on December 30 and adjourned until March 6, 1989. Parliament was prorogued by proclamation dated February 28, 1989.

- The House in each of the "special" sessions approved a temporary suspension of certain Standing Orders, with the aim of expediting the business before it.[59]

The Parliamentary Calendar

The parliamentary calendar, as laid out in the Standing Orders and reproduced as Figure 8.2, sets out a schedule of adjournments of a week or more and thereby provides for sittings, or sitting periods, throughout a year.[60] It comes into effect once a session starts; in other words, the government is not bound by the Standing Orders in considering plans for the timing and length of sessions.[61] The calendar works in conjunction with other Standing Orders providing for daily meeting and adjournment times,[62] and providing for the House not to sit on certain days, most of the days in question being statutory holidays or days deemed to be non-sitting days.[63]

HISTORICAL PERSPECTIVE

In late 1982, the House agreed for the first time to operate under a fixed parliamentary calendar specifying exactly when longer adjournments would take place and thereby when the House would sit during a session.[64] For much of its history, however, the House operated differently. There were no written rules specifying when the House would not sit. If the House wished to adjourn for a period of time during a session, it was necessary to adopt a special adjournment motion, even for a statutory holiday.[65]

Until 1940, sessions tended to be short, beginning in January or February and ending in May or June of the same calendar year. During the years of the Second

---

59. *Journals*, August 18, 1914, p. 3; September 8, 1930, p. 10; September 7, 1939, p. 5; August 29, 1950, p. 5; November 26, 1956, p. 3. Rules were also suspended in two other sessions of short duration not designated as "special" in the *Debates* or *Journals* of the House of Commons: in 1945 (Sixth Session of the Nineteenth Parliament), the House agreed to give precedence to Government Business for the balance of the session and to treat Wednesdays (then a day of early adjournment) as other sitting days (*Journals*, March 19, 1945, p. 3); in 1988 (First Session of the Thirty-Fourth Parliament), a motion was adopted (and deemed rescinded on completion of the business at hand) to extend the hours of sitting and suspend the operation of certain Standing Orders (*Journals*, December 16, 1988, pp. 46-9; December 30, 1988, p. 87).

60. Standing Order 28(2).

61. In 1986, for example, the House was recalled for a day during the summer adjournment (July 24) in order to consider a Senate amendment to a government bill. Parliament was prorogued on August 28 and the new session opened on September 30, some three weeks after the date provided in that year's calendar for the resumption of sittings.

62. Standing Order 24.

63. Standing Order 28(1).

64. *Journals*, November 29, 1982, p. 5400.

65. See, for example, *Journals*, March 19, 1894, p. 15; *Debates*, March 19, 1894, cols. 78-9 (adjournment over Easter).

World War, the burden of government business grew and session length increased; a pattern of long and irregularly timed sessions established itself.[66]

In 1964, the House adopted a Standing Order specifying certain days (mainly statutory holidays) during a session when the House would not sit.[67] Despite this, sessions continued to be long and adjournments and prorogations unpredictably timed.

The notion of scheduled adjournments again came to the fore in the early 1980s when the motion to adjourn for the summer became the occasion for extended and rancorous debate.[68] In November 1982, in accordance with recommendations of a special procedure committee (the Lefebvre Committee), the House adopted a series of measures intended to better organize the time of the House and of Members who, along with responsibilities in the House, were occupied with work in committees and in their constituencies. Chief among the measures was the parliamentary calendar, providing for the first time a fixed schedule of sittings and adjournments for the House and adding some degree of predictability to the scheduling of sitting and non-sitting periods.[69]

The calendar as adopted in 1982 divided the session into three parts (assuming the House to be in session through an entire calendar year), separated by adjournments at Christmas, Easter and the summer months. Since its implementation, the calendar has undergone some modification. The Christmas and summer adjournments were extended slightly in 1991 and, within the three main sitting periods, additional brief adjournments were added in 1983 and 1991.[70] These are for the most part clustered around existing statutory holidays observed by the House, with the result that each trimester is further broken down into two to three sitting periods.

---

66. For session dates, see Appendix 12, "Parliaments Since 1867 and Number of Sitting Days". In 1947, responding to "complaints ... that protracted sessions of Parliament are caused by deficiencies in the rules of procedure ...", the Speaker put forward a Report on Procedure containing (among other items) a suggestion that sessions be divided into three sections, or sitting periods (*Journals*, December 5, 1947, pp. 7, 24-5). This recommendation was not acted on; nor were later proposals of a similar nature (see Appendix "J" to the Report of the Sub-Committee on the Use of Time, Standing Committee on Procedure and Organization, *Minutes of Proceedings and Evidence*, September 30, 1976, Issue No. 20, pp. 53-4. See also pages 4 and 5 of the document entitled "Position Paper: The Reform of Parliament", tabled on November 23, 1979 (*Journals*, p. 260)).

67. *Journals*, October 9, 1964, pp. 780-1.

68. *Journals*, July 18, 1980, p. 488; July 21, 1980, pp. 492-5; July 22, 1980, pp. 498-9; July 10, 1981, pp. 2848-50; July 16, 1981, pp. 2864-5 (notice of closure); July 17, 1981, pp. 2868-71.

69. See Part II of the Third Report of the Special Committee on Standing Orders and Procedure, presented on November 5, 1982 (*Journals*, p. 5328). The recommendations were adopted on November 29, 1982 (*Journals*, p. 5400). For an example of comments on the anticipated effect of the new parliamentary calendar, see *Debates*, November 29, 1982, p. 21069. See also certain interventions in the *Debates* of June 1988, when the government sought to introduce a motion proposing the temporary suspension of certain Standing Orders, including the parliamentary calendar (*Debates*, June 9, 1988, pp. 16296-7, 16301; June 10, 1988, pp. 16322-3; June 13, 1988, pp. 16379 (Speaker's ruling), 16389; June 20, 1988, p. 16626).

70. *Journals*, December 19, 1983, pp. 55-6 (see also the First Report of the Special Committee on Standing Orders, presented on December 15, 1983, *Journals*, p. 47); April 11, 1991, pp. 2902-7.

SITTING AND NON-SITTING PERIODS

The House calendar as it appears in the Standing Orders, reproduced in Figure 8.2, sets out the pattern of adjournments and thereby sittings during a calendar year.[71] Each adjournment begins at the end of the sitting on the days listed in column A. If such a sitting carries over to another day, the adjournment would still begin at the end of the sitting. In each case the session resumes on the corresponding day listed in column B. In order for the adjournment provisions to take effect, the House must sit on the day listed in column A, unless special arrangements are previously agreed to by the House.[72]

The House may be recalled, or Parliament may be summoned for the opening of a new session, during what would normally be an adjournment period. The House would then transact its business in the usual way and, unless a special adjournment motion is adopted, would continue to sit during the remaining days of that adjournment period and into the following sitting period as set out in the parliamentary calendar. The next adjournment period would then begin at the end of that sitting period as specified in column A.

Figure 8.2   *The House Calendar (Standing Order 28(2))*

When the House meets on a day, or sits after the normal meeting hour on a day, set out in column A, and then adjourns, it shall stand adjourned to the day set out in column B.	
A	**B**
The Friday preceding Thanksgiving Day	The second Monday following that Friday
The Friday preceding Remembrance Day	The second Monday following that Friday
The second Friday preceding Christmas Day	The first Monday in February
The Friday preceding the week marking the midway point between the first Monday in February and the Friday preceding Good Friday	The second Monday following that Friday
The Friday preceding Good Friday	The Monday following Easter Monday
The Friday preceding the week marking the midway point between the Monday following Easter Monday and June 23	The second Monday following that Friday or, if that Monday is the day fixed for the celebration of the birthday of the Sovereign, on the Tuesday following that Monday
June 23 or the Friday preceding if June 23 falls on a Saturday, a Sunday or a Monday	The second Monday following Labour Day

---

71. Standing Order 28(2).

72. See, for example, *Journals*, April 21, 1994, p. 380.

The House meets five days a week, from Monday to Friday.[73] Assuming that the House is in continuous session for the full calendar year, the parliamentary calendar provides for about 135 sitting days and seven adjournment periods at set times throughout the year. This may be described as creating three distinct sitting periods: September to December, February to Easter, and Easter to June. Three major adjournments are scheduled at Christmas (approximately 7 weeks), Easter (2 weeks) and the summer season (approximately 12 weeks). Four additional adjournments, each about a week in duration, occur in mid-October, mid-November and at the mid-points of the second and third trimesters.

Although the span of time in which the House has operated under the fixed parliamentary calendar is relatively brief, it may be said that since its institution, the parliamentary calendar has enjoyed an appreciable level of compliance. Departure from the calendar can and does occur, however. The royal prerogatives of prorogation and dissolution, for example, are not in any way compromised by the existence of the parliamentary calendar. On occasion the House has been recalled during an adjournment, pursuant to Standing Order.[74] The House has also agreed to vary the calendar, both by unanimous consent[75] and by the adoption of a motion following notice and debate.[76]

STATUTORY HOLIDAYS AND OTHER NON-SITTING DAYS

For most of its history, the House had no written rule identifying days during a session when it would not meet. This gave rise to a practice of irregular—if not haphazard—adjournments, mainly for observance of statutory holidays. The question of whether or not the House would adjourn on a particular day was dependent on such variables as:

The Length and Timing of Sessions

In the early post-Confederation years, sessions tended to begin in mid- to late winter and end in late spring; consequently, the question of adjourning over Christmas, for example, did not arise.[77]

---

73. Standing Order 24(1). Weekend sittings take place infrequently and in unusual circumstances; for example, in 1995, pursuant to a Special Order, the House met on Saturday and Sunday to consider back-to-work legislation (*Journals*, March 23, 1995, p. 1265).

74. Standing Order 28(3) provides for recall during an adjournment. For examples, see Appendix 13, "Recalls of the House of Commons During Adjournment Periods Since 1867".

75. See, for example, *Journals*, December 10, 1991, pp. 909-10.

76. *Journals*, June 20, 1988, pp. 2925-7. Following the appearance of the government's notice of a motion to suspend the operation of certain Standing Orders—including the parliamentary calendar—points of order were raised as to the receivability of the motion. See *Debates*, June 13, 1988, pp. 16376-9 for the text of the Speaker's ruling.

77. See Appendix 12, "Parliaments Since 1867 and Number of Sitting Days".

The Development of Provisions for Statutory Holidays

In the absence of any written rule, the House tended to make its own decisions with regard to statutory or non-statutory holiday observances (for example, Dominion Day[78] has been a statutory holiday since 1879, but this has not prevented the House from sitting on that day[79]).

Prevailing Customs

In the early post-Confederation years, the House adjourned for the day when informed of the death of a sitting Member during the session; by the late nineteenth century this practice had all but disappeared[80], and in the 1970s and 1980s, it was accepted practice that an adjournment for the remainder of the day would take place when news of the death of a sitting Member reached the House in the course of the sitting.[81] Another example of a prevailing custom is the practice whereby the House agrees not to sit on certain days to accommodate Members who wish to attend a policy or leadership convention of their political party.[82]

In 1964, the Standing Orders were amended to include a list of the days on which the House would not sit during a session.[83] There are nine: New Year's Day, Good Friday, Victoria Day (celebration of the birthday of the Sovereign), St. John the Baptist Day, Canada Day (Dominion Day), Labour Day, Thanksgiving Day, Remembrance Day and Christmas Day.[84] All, except St. John the Baptist Day, are statutory holidays as defined by the *Interpretation Act*.[85] The Standing Order further provides that when St. John the Baptist Day (June 24) and Canada Day (July 1) fall on Tuesday, the House does not sit on the preceding day; similarly, when they fall on Thursday, the House does not sit on the following day. Since these non-sitting days typically fall within the periods of long adjournments, this Standing Order rarely

---

78. *An Act to make the first day of July a Public Holiday, by the name of Dominion Day*, S.C. 1879, c. 47. Dominion Day was renamed Canada Day in an amendment to the *Holidays Act* (S.C. 1980-83, c.124), assented to October 27, 1982 (*Journals*, p. 5288).

79. See, for example, *Journals*, July 1, 1891, 1919, 1931, 1947, 1958 and 1961.

80. *Bourinot*, 4ᵗʰ ed., pp. 211-2. See also *Debates*, June 3, 1872, cols. 947-9, concerning the evolution of the practice.

81. *Debates,* November 17, 1970, p. 1228. For example, in 1976 when evening sittings were routine, a Member died at "supper hour", and when the House reconvened, a motion to adjourn was immediately moved and adopted (*Journals*, December 16, 1976, p. 251; *Debates*, December 16, 1976, pp. 2088-9).

82. See, for example, *Debates*, January 11, 1958, p. 3187 and *Journals*, January 11, 1958, p. 337; *Debates*, October 27, 1977, p. 324 and *Journals*, October 27, 1977, p. 42; *Debates*, June 7, 1993, p. 20462 and *Journals*, June 7, 1993, p. 3136; *Debates*, February 17, 1998, p. 4033; February 26, 1998, pp. 4505, 4512-3 and *Journals*, February 17, 1998, p. 497.

83. *Journals*, October 9, 1964, pp. 780-1.

84. Standing Order 28(1).

85. *Interpretation Act*, R.S.C. 1985, c. I-21.

comes into play.[86] It will, of course, come into play if the House meets outside the parliamentary calendar.

EXCEPTION TO THE CALENDAR

From time to time, the House may be called to reassemble during an adjournment period pursuant to the calendar for the sole purpose of participating in the ceremony granting Royal Assent to a bill or bills.[87] (For further information, see Chapter 9, "Sittings of the House"; for further information on Royal Assent, see Chapter 16, "The Legislative Process").

Recall of the House During an Adjournment

When the House stands adjourned during a session, the rules provide the means by which the House may be recalled prior to the date originally specified, to transact business as if it had been duly adjourned to the earlier date.[88] The decision to recall is taken by the Speaker, after consultation with the government and once the Speaker is satisfied that the public interest would be served by an earlier meeting of the House.[89] The rule makes no reference to criteria other than the public interest. Should the Speaker be satisfied of the need for the recall, the rule further provides for the Speaker to give notice of the day and hour of the resumption of the session. Normally, the Speaker requests a period of time following the notice (the practice is a minimum of 48 hours) in which to notify Members individually and allow for their travel time. Depending on the circumstances, a *Special Order Paper and Notice Paper* (in addition to the regular *Order Paper and Notice Paper*) may be published at the request of the government.[90]

---

86. Within the parliamentary calendar, the only day not specifically covered in all cases by a long adjournment would be Victoria Day (celebration of the birthday of the Sovereign).

87. Standing Order 28(4). See, for example, *Journals*, July 7, 1994, pp. 672-3. The rule, which was adopted on June 10, 1994, codifies a pre-existing practice whereby the House would adopt an order enabling it to reconvene for the sole purpose of granting Royal Assent (see, for example, *Journals*, June 23, 1992, pp. 1833-4).

88. Standing Order 28(3). See also Appendix 13, "Recalls of the House of Commons During Adjournment Periods Since 1867".

89. See, for example, *Journals*, September 8, 1992, p. 1924. On July 3, 1987, the government requested a recall, citing pressing legislation then in the Senate. The House was not recalled; it was reported that the government and the Senate were pursuing an agreement on the handling of the bills in question. On August 7, 1987, citing different reasons, the government again requested a recall; the Speaker granted the request and the House was recalled on August 11 (*Journals*, p. 1308). During the 1991 crisis in the Persian Gulf, the House adopted a motion allowing two of its standing committees to request that the Speaker recall the House, with Standing Order 28(3) temporarily modified to provide for 12-hour notice (*Journals,* January 21, 1991, pp. 2587-8).

90. Standing Order 55. See also Chapter 12, "The Process of Debate".

For the first 70 years after Confederation, the practice was to end the session by prorogation rather than have a lengthy adjournment.[91] In 1940, however, given the uncertainty of the wartime situation, it was deemed advisable to adjourn rather than to prorogue, in order to enable the House to reconvene quickly if necessary. The House adopted a motion to adjourn which empowered the Speaker to recall the House if, after consultation with the government, it was concluded that it was in the public interest to do so.[92] Similar motions were adopted in subsequent sessions and became routine when the House adjourned for an extended period of time.

The first recall under these circumstances occurred in 1944, when the government wished to apprise the House of the situation arising from the resignation of the Minister of National Defence.[93] Several other recalls took place before 1982,[94] at which time the practice was codified by the adoption of a Standing Order worded similarly to the adjournment motions used before 1982.[95] The rule further provides that should the Speaker be unable to act due to illness or other reason, deputy presiding officers may act in the Speaker's place for the purpose of this particular Standing Order.

Consultation between the Speaker and the government regarding a recall of the House usually begins with a government request made in writing to the Speaker, setting out reasons why it is in the public interest to recall the House. The request may be made at any time.[96] When a decision is taken to recall the House, the Speaker advises the Clerk of the House and asks that the necessary steps be taken to resume the session. The Clerk then ensures that all is made ready for the resumption of the sittings.

---

91. See Appendix 12, "Parliaments Since 1867 and Number of Sitting Days".

92. *Journals*, August 3, 1940, p. 325.

93. *Journals*, November 22, 1944, p. 921. See also *Debates*, November 22, 1944, p. 6505. The recall of 1944 was the first to take place pursuant to an Order of the House.

94. Recalls from adjournment took place in 1951, 1966, 1972, 1973, 1977 and 1980.

95. Standing Order 55. See page 12 of the Third Report of the Special Committee on Standing Orders and Procedure, presented on November 5, 1982 (*Journals,* p. 5328). The Standing Order came into effect on December 22, 1982 (*Journals,* November 29, 1982, p. 5400). The House was later recalled pursuant to Standing Order in 1986, 1987, 1991 (twice) and 1992. See Appendix 13 for a list of recalls and the reasons for the recalls.

96. In 1991, for example, the letter requesting the January recall was dated Saturday, January 12, 1991 (*Journals*, January 15, 1991, p. 2556).

House officials are responsible for the logistics of the recall, including informing the Members and publishing the *Order Paper and Notice Paper* (and a *Special Order Paper and Notice Paper,* if the government so requests).[97]

CANCELLING RECALL ORDER

No mechanism exists to cancel an order to recall the House. However, on one occasion, after receiving such a request from all the recognized parties in the House, the Speaker issued a formal statement in which he cancelled an earlier notice for recall. The original notice was given on June 26, 1992, for the House to meet on July 15, 1992; the notice of cancellation was given on July 11, 1992, and tabled on September 8, 1992, at which time the Speaker made a statement to the House.[98]

TABLING OF PERTINENT CORRESPONDENCE BY SPEAKER

It is usual practice, when the House reassembles following a recall, for the Speaker to inform the House of the reason for the recall, the various steps taken to effect the recall and, if a *Special Order Paper and Notice Paper* was requested, the steps taken for its publication and circulation.[99] Since 1980, the Speaker has also tabled correspondence received from the government concerning the recall.[100]

ORDER OF BUSINESS UPON RESUMPTION OF SITTING

A recall has no effect on the ordinary daily order of business of the House. When the House first meets following a recall, Routine Proceedings, Question Period and other

---

97. A message is sent to all Members over the Speaker's signature advising of the date and time of the recall. Since 1986, these messages have been sent via electronic mail; see, for example, *Debates*, July 24, 1986, p. 15011; *Journals*, January 15, 1991, p. 2556. Prior to this, telegrams were used (see, for example, *Debates*, November 22, 1944, p. 6504; August 9, 1977, p. 8129). In cases where special transportation arrangements are required, House officials may work with the Department of National Defence and will include in the notice to Members details of routing and scheduling of aircraft. In 1977, for example, travel by military aircraft was arranged when the House was recalled due to a nation-wide strike which had the effect of closing down the commercial air transportation industry.

The party Whips' offices are also notified of the recall and of any special transportation arrangements. As well, the necessary steps are taken to ensure that Members travelling on parliamentary business at the time of a recall are informed of the recall and provided assistance in returning to Ottawa.

In the past, a notice of recall was published over the Speaker's signature in a special or "extra" edition of the *Canada Gazette.* There is no statutory requirement for this measure, and the practice was abandoned with the recall of February 1991. See also Appendix 13.

98. *Journals*, September 8, 1992, p. 1924; *Debates*, September 8, 1992, p. 12709.

99. See, for example, *Debates*, November 22, 1944, p. 6504; January 29, 1951, p. 755; August 30, 1973, p. 6059; January 15, 1991, p. 16981.

100. *Journals*, October 6, 1980, p. 504; July 24, 1986, p. 2474; August 11, 1987, p. 1308; January 15, 1991, p. 2556; February 25, 1991, p. 2602; September 8, 1992, p. 1924.

proceedings are all held in the usual manner depending on the time of meeting of the House, which is set out in the notice of recall.[101] Unless a motion to adjourn to a later date is adopted, or the session is ended by prorogation, the House merely continues on subsequent days with its regular sittings as if it had been adjourned to the recall date. In such cases, the House may well operate outside the parliamentary calendar for some time, as it did in 1987 when the House was recalled in early August and did not again adjourn for an extended period until the December break, which was in accordance with the calendar.[102]

"Recall" During a Prorogation

When Parliament is prorogued, the proclamation issued by the Governor General on the advice of the Prime Minister and Cabinet includes a date for the opening of the new session. This date can be changed by means of a further proclamation, resulting not in a recall as such but in an opening of the session at an earlier date than that given in the initial proclamation. The new session commences and is conducted as an ordinary session.[103] It is also possible to prorogue Parliament and end a session by proclamation during an adjournment.[104] Parliament would then meet for a new session in the normal manner on the date set in the proclamation.

Prorogation and Dissolution

PROROGATION

Prorogation of a Parliament results in the termination of a session. Parliament then stands prorogued until the opening of the next session. Like the summoning and dissolution of Parliament, prorogation is a prerogative act of the Crown, taken on the advice of the Prime Minister.[105] Parliament is actually prorogued either by the Governor General (or Deputy of the Governor General) in the Senate Chamber, or

---

101. On Mondays, for example, the usual time of meeting is 11:00 a.m. (Standing Order 24(1)); when the House was recalled at 2:00 p.m. on Monday, February 25, 1991, the Speaker made the usual statement as to the recall, and the House proceeded with the daily program for Monday afternoon as set out in the Standing Orders (*Journals*, February 25, 1991, pp. 2602-21).

102. *Journals*, August 11, 1987, p. 1308; December 18, 1987, pp. 2018-9.

103. See, for example, the so-called special sessions, described elsewhere in this chapter.

104. For example, during the First Session of the Thirty-Third Parliament, the House adjourned on July 24, 1986, until September 8, 1986. On August 28, 1986, the session was ended by prorogation and the Second Session was set to begin on October 1, 1986. On September 25,1986, a new proclamation was issued, fixing September 30, 1986, as the date of the opening of the new session.

105. See Privy Council minute, P. C. 3374, dated October 25, 1935, a "Memorandum regarding certain of the functions of the Prime Minister", which stated that recommendations (to the Crown) concerning the convocation and dissolution of Parliament are the "special prerogatives" of the Prime Minister.

by proclamation published in the *Canada Gazette*. When Parliament stands prorogued to a certain day, a subsequent proclamation (or proclamations) may be issued to advance or defer the date.[106]

Effects of Prorogation

The principal effect of ending a session by prorogation is to terminate business. Members are released from their parliamentary duties until Parliament is next summoned. All unfinished business is dropped from or "dies" on the *Order Paper* and all committees lose their power to transact business, providing a fresh start for the next session. No committee can sit during a prorogation.[107] Bills which have not received Royal Assent before prorogation are "entirely terminated" and, in order to be proceeded with in the new session, must be reintroduced as if they had never existed.[108]

On occasion, however, bills have been reinstated by motion at the start of a new session at the same stage they had reached at the end of the previous session; committee work has similarly been revived. This has been accomplished in various ways:

- The House has given unanimous consent to a motion to reinstate a bill in a new session at the same stage it had reached before prorogation.[109]

- The House has adopted amendments to its Standing Orders to carry over legislation to the next session, following a prorogation.[110]

- In 1991, Parliament was prorogued for one day, ending the Second Session of the Thirty-Fourth Parliament. The Third Session started a day later. Two standing committees were then revived by unanimous consent so that they might terminate mandates from the previous session, provided that these committees would cease to exist once their reports were presented in the House. A special joint committee was likewise revived and two bills were reinstated.[111] However, when unanimous consent was withheld to reinstate a further six bills, the government sought and achieved reinstatement by adoption of a motion, following notice.[112]

---

106. For example, the opening of the Fifth Session of the Twenty-Fourth Parliament, originally set for November 7, 1961, was changed by successive proclamations to December 16, 1961, then to January 25, 1962, and finally to January 18, 1962.

107. For further details, see Chapter 20, "Committees".

108. *Bourinot*, 4th ed., pp. 102-3.

109. See, for example, *Journals*, October 21, 1970, p. 46; May 9, 1972, p. 281; March 8, 1974, pp. 25-6; October 3, 1986, pp. 47-8. In 1986, the special order included a provision to bring forward from committee any evidence adduced and documents received in relation to the revived bills. A bill has also been reinstated after a dissolution; see *Journals,* October 1, 1997, p. 56, and *Debates,* October 1, 1997, p. 338.

110. *Journals,* July 22, 1977, p. 1432; March 22, 1982, pp. 4626-8.

111. *Journals*, May 17, 1991, pp. 42-5; May 23, 1991, p. 59.

112. *Debates*, May 28, 1991, pp. 702-3; May 29, 1991, pp. 733-5; *Journals*, May 29, 1991, pp. 102-9.

- In the Second Session of the Thirty-Fifth Parliament (1996-97), the first item of government business (laid out in a special *Order Paper and Notice Paper*) was a motion "to facilitate the conduct of the business of the House", which included a mechanism for reinstatement of bills—private Members' as well as government bills.[113]

For further information about the reinstatement of bills in a new session, see Chapter 16, "The Legislative Process".

There is also a provision in the Standing Orders for any outstanding Orders or Addresses of the House for returns or papers to be presented to the House. They are considered to have been readopted at the start of the new session without a motion to that effect.[114] The Speaker has ruled that outstanding government responses to committee reports and to petitions are also given the status of returns ordered by the House and therefore would be tabled in the House in the new session.[115]

Prorogation in Practice

Prorogation practices have varied over time. Two methods have been used. Parliament has in recent years been prorogued by proclamation while the House is adjourned, with the date of the new session being fixed by proclamation.[116] The House has also in the past adjourned for a period of time, reconvened, and Parliament has been prorogued shortly thereafter with the new session opening soon afterward.[117] On several occasions, the session was ended by prorogation in the morning, with the new session starting in the afternoon of the same day.[118]

Traditionally, the House was summoned to the Senate to hear the Governor General (or the Deputy of the Governor General) deliver a speech reviewing the

---

113. If, when proposing a motion for the first reading of a bill during the first 30 sitting days of the new session, the mover stated that the bill was in the same form as a bill at the time of prorogation, and if the Speaker was so satisfied, then the bill was deemed to have reached the same stage as the previous bill at prorogation. The motion was moved on the second sitting day of the session, and closured and adopted on the third day (*Journals*, March 1, 1996, pp. 23-5; March 4, 1996, pp. 33-5, 39-41).

114. Standing Order 49.

115. *Debates*, June 27, 1986, p. 14969.

116. For example, during the First Session of the Thirty-Fourth Parliament, the House adjourned on December 30, 1988, to resume on March 6, 1989; Parliament was prorogued on February 28, 1989, with the opening of the Second Session fixed for April 3, 1989. During the Second Session of the Thirty-Fourth Parliament, the House adjourned to the call of the Chair on May 8, 1991. Parliament was prorogued on May 12, 1991, with the opening of the Third Session fixed for May 13, 1991.

117. For example, the 1940-42, 1942-43, 1943-44, 1977-78 and 1978-79 sessions (the first four sessions of the Nineteenth Parliament and the Second, Third and Fourth Sessions of the Thirtieth Parliament) were in each case adjourned, reconvened, ended by prorogation with the new session starting the next day.

118. See, for example, *Journals*, January 8, 1957; May 8, 1967; October 12, 1976.

accomplishments of the session, and to hear the Speaker of the Senate read a message containing the date for the opening of the new session. At the end of the ceremony, the House of Commons delegation would leave the Senate Chamber, but the procession would not return to the House of Commons Chamber. The Speaker would return to the Speaker's chambers and other Members would simply disperse. The prorogation ceremony is a convention and is not required by any Standing Order or statute.[119]

It is the prerogative of the Crown, on the advice of the Prime Minister, to determine which method to use for prorogation.

DISSOLUTION

A dissolution terminates a Parliament and is followed by a general election.[120] The date of the election is set in accordance with the provisions of the *Canada Elections Act*.[121] Like the summoning and prorogation of a Parliament, dissolution is a prerogative act of the Crown, normally taken on the advice of the Prime Minister and proclaimed under the Great Seal of Canada by the Governor General.[122]

Usually three proclamations are issued at the time of dissolution. The first is for the dissolution itself, stating that Parliament is dissolved and declaring that "the Senators and Members of Parliament are discharged from their meeting and attendance". A second proclamation usually appears simultaneously; it calls the next Parliament and informs with regard to the issuance of writs of election, the date set for polling and the date set for the return of the writs. The third proclamation fixes the date on which Parliament is summoned to meet, sometime following the return of the writs.[123] The date of this summons may be changed through the issuance of a further proclamation.[124]

A Parliament may be dissolved at any time. If the House is sitting and there is not to be a prorogation ceremony in the Senate Chamber, the dissolution is usually

---

119. Prorogation has not taken place in this manner since 1983, the end of the First Session of the Thirty-Second Parliament (*Journals*, November 30, 1983, pp. 6632-46).

120. The Constitution provides for a maximum five-year lifespan for the House, and for a sitting of Parliament at least once every 12 months (see *Constitution Act, 1867*, R.S.C. 1985, Appendix II, No. 5, s. 50; *Constitution Act, 1982*, , R.S.C. 1985, Appendix II, No. 44, ss. 4(1), 5). For comments on this issue, see J. Patrick Boyer, *Election Law in Canada*, Vol. 1, Toronto: Butterworths, 1987, pp. 164-6.

121. *Canada Elections Act*, R.S.C. 1985, c. E-2, s. 79.

122. In June 1926, Governor General Byng refused to dissolve Parliament, whereupon Prime Minister Mackenzie King resigned and the leader of the opposition, Arthur Meighen, was invited to form a government (*Journals*, June 28-9, 1926, pp. 483-6; *Debates*, June 28-9, 1926, pp. 5096-7). For further details, see Chapter 2, "Parliaments and Ministries".

123. *Bourinot*, 4th ed., pp. 104-5.

124. In 1997, for example, the proclamation of April 27, summoning Parliament to meet on June 23, was superseded by proclamations which changed the date of summons to August 1, then to August 29 and finally September 22.

announced to the House by the Prime Minister or another Minister.[125] The Speaker then leaves the Chair without further ado.

The demise of the Crown does not have the effect of dissolving Parliament.[126] In ancient British practice and until 1843 in Canada, however, the demise of the Crown resulted in an automatic dissolution of Parliament. Because the summoning of Parliament is a royal prerogative and Parliament sits at the pleasure of the Crown, its demise meant a lapsing of the summons and thus dissolution.[127] In 1843, an act was passed in the Province of Canada providing that a parliament in existence at the time of any future demise of the Crown should continue as it would have otherwise, unless dissolved by the Crown.[128] Similar legislation existed in other provinces prior to Confederation.[129] The law was re-enacted in the First Session of the First Parliament of Canada.[130]

Effects of Dissolution

With dissolution, all business of the House is terminated. The Speaker, the Deputy Speaker and the Members of the Board of Internal Economy continue in office for the acquittal of certain administrative duties until they are replaced in a new Parliament.[131] For the purposes of certain allowances payable to them, Members of the House of Commons at the time of dissolution are deemed to remain so until the date of the general election.[132]

Expiration of the House of Commons

The Constitution states that no House "shall continue for longer than five years".[133] Mindful of this deadline, all governments since Confederation have resorted to

---

125. See, for example, *Journals*, February 1, 1958, p. 398, and *Debates*, February 1, 1958, pp. 4199-202; *Journals*, December 14, 1979, p. 350, and *Debates*, December 14, 1979, p. 2363 (announced by the Prime Minister); *Journals*, March 26, 1979, p. 594, and *Debates*, March 26, 1979, p. 4517 (announced by the Deputy Prime Minister and President of the Privy Council).

126. *Parliament of Canada Act*, R.S.C. 1985, c. P-1, s. 2. A demise of the Crown can occur on the death, deposition or abdication of the sovereign, at which time the Kingdom is transferred or demised to a successor.

127. *Wilding and Laundy*, pp. 202-3.

128. *An Act for continuing the Provincial Parliament, in case of the demise of the Crown*, S.C. 1843, c. 3.

129. *Bourinot*, 4th ed., pp. 103-4.

130. *An Act for continuing the Parliament of Canada, in case of the demise of the Crown*, S.C. 1867-68, c. 22. See also *Bourinot*, 4th ed., pp. 103-4.

131. *Parliament of Canada Act*, R.S.C. 1985, c. P-1 as amended by S.C. 1991, c. 20, s. 2 (s. 53).

132. *Parliament of Canada Act*, R.S.C. 1985, c. P-1, s. 69.

133. *Constitution Act, 1982,* , R.S.C. 1985, Appendix II, No. 44, s. 4(1). See also *Constitution Act, 1867*, R.S.C. 1985, Appendix II, No. 5, c. 50.

dissolution. In some cases, the dissolution took place within days of when the House would have expired through effluxion of time.[134]

Extension of Life of the House of Commons

Since 1949, the Constitution has provided that in time of war, invasion or insurrection, the five-year limit of the lifetime of the House of Commons "may be continued by Parliament" if no more than one third of the Members oppose the continuation.[135] Prior to the existence of this provision, such an extension required a constitutional amendment, a means resorted to only once. Due to circumstances relating to World War I, the life of the Twelfth Parliament (1911-17) was extended in this way for one year—from 1916 to 1917.[136]

---

134. The Seventh and Seventeenth Parliaments extended almost to the five-year limit. In the first case, the date set for the return of the writs was April 25, 1891 (*Journals*, Vol. XXV (1891), p. x) and dissolution took place on April 24, 1896 (*Journals*, Vol. XXXI (1896), p. v). In the second case, the writs were returnable on August 18, 1930 (*Journals*, Vol. LXVIII, Special Session (1930), p. iv) and Parliament was dissolved on August 15, 1935 (*Journals*, Vol. LXXIV (1936), p. iii).

In Australia, the Third Parliament (the only instance of the expiration of the House of Representatives through effluxion of time) had its final sitting on December 8, 1909, was prorogued to January 26, 1910, and on January 18 was again prorogued to February 19, 1910, at which time it expired. Election writs were issued on February 28, 1910 (*House of Representatives Practice*, 3rd ed., p. 238).

The expiration of New Zealand's twenty-seventh Parliament in 1946 went unnoticed due to an earlier departure from the country's usual electoral timetable, and a proclamation dissolving the Parliament was made and acted on. The forty-second Parliament was dissolved in 1990 on the day it was due to expire. According to the practice in New Zealand, when Parliament expires, the procedures for holding a general election operate as if a dissolution had taken place on the date of expiration (*McGee*, 2nd ed., pp. 128-30).

135. *British North America (No. 2) Act, 1949*, R.S.C. 1985, Appendix II, No. 33; see also *Constitution Act, 1982*, R.S.C. 1985, Appendix II, No. 44, s. 4(2).

136. *British North America Act, 1916*, R.S.C. 1985, Appendix II, No. 24. The writs for the general election electing the Twelfth Parliament were returnable on October 7, 1911 (*Journals*, Vol. XLVI (1910-11), p. 563). Dissolution occurred on October 6, 1917 (*Journals*, Vol. LIV (1918), p. iii). The Act was repealed by the *Statute Law Revision Act, 1927*.

9

Sittings of the House

. . . there is nothing wrong in trying to improve the life style of parliamentarians, many of whom are men and women with family responsibilities. . . . The fact that Members of Parliament would not have to sit in the evening will upgrade their role in the sense that . . . they would be free to come and go as they please, to look after the interests of their constituents, to sit on the standing committees of the House, to participate actively in the special caucuses of their respective parties, [and] to go and address the Canadian people in many communities located within a reasonable distance from Ottawa.

YVON PINARD, President of the Privy Council
(*Debates,* November 29, 1982, p. 21070)

A meeting, or "sitting", of the House begins when the Speaker takes the Chair and, seeing that a quorum is present, calls the House to order. A sitting ends upon the adjournment of the House. On days when the House meets, it does so in accordance with a predetermined daily schedule or timetable.[1] Within this context, the House retains a large measure of flexibility in the timing and duration of its sittings, and departures from the usual daily timetable do occur.

This chapter provides an outline of the manner in which a sitting commences, the requirements for quorum, and the way that the hours of sitting are set or altered, as well as an examination of unusual or special types of sittings of the House.

---

1. See Chapter 10, "The Daily Program".

Opening of a Sitting

Before a sitting commences, a ceremonial procession known as the Speaker's parade makes its way from the Speaker's chambers via the Hall of Honour to the House of Commons Chamber. The procession is led by the Sergeant-at-Arms bearing the Mace,[2] followed by the Speaker, a page carrying documents for the Speaker's use during the sitting, the Clerk of the House and other Table Officers. As the parade enters the Chamber, Members rise while the Speaker proceeds to the Chair. The Sergeant-at-Arms pauses at the end of the Table until the Speaker has taken the Chair, then places the Mace on the Table, bows and takes his or her seat at the Bar of the House. Once satisfied that a quorum is present, the Speaker reads the prayer and opens the sitting.

In the absence of the Speaker, the Presiding Officer for the sitting takes the Speaker's place in the parade.[3] Once the Presiding Officer has entered the Chamber, the Clerk will inform the House of the unavoidable absence of the Speaker and the Presiding Officer will then take the Chair as Speaker. When a quorum is present, the Presiding Officer will then read the prayer[4] and open the sitting.

At the end of a sitting, the Speaker adjourns the House and then exits the Chamber, this time, through the doors at the rear of the Chair, preceded by the Sergeant-at-Arms bearing the Mace.

Quorum

Under the *Constitution Act, 1867*, a quorum of 20 Members, including the Speaker, is required "to constitute a meeting of the House for the exercise of its powers".[5] This constitutional requirement is reiterated in the Standing Orders, which also set out the procedure to be followed in cases where the House lacks a quorum.[6] Although there have been several attempts to increase the size of quorum, it has remained unchanged since Confederation.[7] Modern-day demands on Members' time are such that attending the sittings of the House is only one of many duties. Party whips have

---

2. When entering or leaving the Chamber, the Speaker is always preceded by the Sergeant-at-Arms, who carries the Mace (*Bourinot*, 4th ed., p. 176).

3. *Parliament of Canada Act*, R.S.C. 1985, c. P-1, s. 43(1). The Presiding Officer would be either the Deputy Speaker, the Deputy Chairman or Assistant Deputy Chairman of Committees of the Whole.

4. For further information on the prayer, see Chapter 10, "The Daily Program".

5. *Constitution Act*, 1867, R.S.C. 1985, Appendix II, No. 5, s. 48. A quorum of 20 Members had previously been established for the Legislative Assembly of the Province of Canada (see *Union Act, 1840*, R.S.C. 1985, Appendix II, No. 4, Art. xxxiv).

6. Standing Order 29.

7. There have been attempts in the past to change the quorum from 20 to 30 and even 50 (see, for example, *Journals*, May 29, 1925, p. 348). As well, between 1952 and 1980, Stanley Knowles (Member from 1942-58 and 1962-84) repeatedly introduced private Members' bills to increase the quorum to 30 and to 50. None of these bills was passed.

thus traditionally been responsible, through the use of roster systems, for ensuring that the required number of Members is present to maintain the quorum.[8]

QUORUM BEFORE A SITTING BEGINS

Should a quorum appear not to exist at the time the House is scheduled to meet, a count of the House is taken by the Speaker. If fewer than 20 Members are present, the Speaker adjourns the House until the next sitting day.[9] The Speaker may take such an initiative only before the House has been called to order.[10] Once the sitting has begun, "control over the competence of the House is transferred from the Speaker to the House itself. ... The Speaker has no right to close a sitting at his own discretion."[11] There are no known instances of this having happened at the beginning of a sitting and, in practice, the bells summoning Members to the House at the start of a sitting are not silenced until a quorum exists, often some minutes after the appointed meeting time.[12]

QUORUM DURING A SITTING

During a sitting, any Member may draw the attention of the Speaker to the lack of a quorum, requesting a "count" of the Members present. Such a request may be made while another Member is speaking. If a quorum is obviously present, the Speaker may simply announce that there is a quorum, dispense with the count and proceed with the business. If there is some doubt as to there being a quorum, a count is made by the Speaker. If a quorum is present, business continues.[13] However, if no quorum exists after the first count, the bells are ordered to be rung for no longer than 15 minutes. Within that time period, if a second count determines that a quorum is present, the Speaker will order the bells silenced and the House will proceed with

---

8. In 1990, Nelson Riis (Kamloops) argued, among other things, that it was the responsibility of the Government to maintain quorum when dealing with government supply (see *Debates*, April 2, 1990, p. 10083). In the subsequent ruling, Speaker Fraser stated that it was difficult for the Chair to conclude that the government must bear sole responsibility for the House adjourning for want of quorum (see *Debates,* April 3, 1990, p. 10119).

9. Standing Order 29(2).

10. On November 16, 1982, when the House resumed sitting following the evening meal interruption, the Acting Speaker, not seeing a quorum, took the initiative to order the bells to be rung. When the ringing of the bells failed to produce a quorum, he adjourned the House (see *Debates*, November 16, 1982, p. 20729; *Journals*, November 16, 1982, p. 5353).

11. *Redlich*, Vol. II, p. 74.

12. In practice, the bells summoning Members to the House at the start of a sitting are not in fact interrupted until a quorum exists, occasionally 5 to 10 minutes after the stated hour of meeting. On Wednesday, the practice is to start the bells a few minutes before the stated hour of meeting so that prayers can be said earlier without time being lost from Members' Statements and Oral Question Period (see *Debates*, March 27, 1991, p. 19068, and December 4, 1991, p. 5762).

13. See, for example, *Debates*, December 6, 1984, p. 969.

the business before it.[14] If at the end of the 15 minutes a second count reveals that there is still no quorum, the Speaker adjourns the House until the next sitting day;[15] the names of the Members present are recorded in the *Journals*.[16]

As in the House, the quorum in a Committee of the Whole is 20 Members. If notice is taken by a Member that there is not a quorum present in a Committee of the Whole, the Chairman counts the Members. If there is not a quorum, the Committee rises and the House resumes its sitting.[17] On a report from the Chairman of the Committee, the Speaker counts the House. If there is not a quorum, the bells are rung for a maximum of 15 minutes.

Usually, quorum is quickly restored so that the House may proceed with the business before it.[18] Should the House be required to adjourn for lack of quorum, any Order of the Day under consideration at the time, with the exception of an item of Private Members' Business not selected to come to a vote, retains its precedence on the *Order Paper* for the next sitting.[19]

A number of practices govern how the determination of a quorum is made. A Member who calls quorum need not remain in the House.[20] Furthermore, a Member who calls quorum while speaking and who subsequently leaves the House may, upon returning after a count that confirmed a quorum, resume speaking.[21] As well,

---

14. Standing Order 29(3). See, for example, *Journals*, August 25, 1987, p. 1378; May 24, 1990, p. 1755; December 6, 1990, p. 2390; June 11, 1991, p. 163; April 2, 1993, p. 2790; April 11, 1994, p. 323; June 15, 1995, p. 1756; October 29, 1996, p. 786; April 24, 1997, p. 1537; May 26, 1998, p. 892.

15. Standing Order 29(3).

16. Standing Order 29(4). See, for example, *Journals*, March 30, 1990, p. 1477; October 19, 1995, p. 2032.

17. See *Journals*, June 6, 1899, p. 239. See also Chapter 19, "Committees of the Whole House".

18. Prior to December 1982, if the first count requested during a sitting confirmed the lack of a quorum, the Speaker was compelled to adjourn the House. On November 29, 1982, the House adopted the current text of Standing Order 29(3) in accordance with a recommendation made by the Special Committee on Standing Orders and Procedure, which provided for the ringing of the bells for not more than 15 minutes. The Standing Order came into effect at the end of Government Business on December 22, 1982. See *Journals*, November 29, 1982, p. 5400. There have been instances since 1867 when the House has been adjourned during a sitting for want of a quorum: see *Journals*, June 14, 1869, p. 244; June 29, 1917, p. 402; March 11, 1919, pp. 49-50; June 9, 1938 (Supply Committee), p. 434; July 10, 1969, pp. 1329-31; December 17, 1974, pp. 217-8; March 23, 1979, pp. 588, 590; May 5, 1982, p. 4797; November 16, 1982, p. 5353; March 30, 1990, pp. 1477-8; October 19, 1995, p. 2032.

19. Standing Order 41(2). Prior to the adoption of this Standing Order on May 13, 1991, any item under consideration at the time of a lack of quorum would drop from the *Order Paper,* and the House could be asked at a subsequent sitting to revive any item that may have lapsed because of the lack of quorum. See, for example, *Journals*, March 30, 1990, p. 1477; April 3, 1990, p. 1486. See also *Debates*, April 2, 1990, pp. 10076-89; April 3, 1990, pp. 10119-21. Since the adoption of Standing Order 41(2), there has only been one instance of the House being adjourned during a sitting for want of a quorum: October 19, 1995. The business before the House at that time was a votable item of Private Members' Business in its second hour of debate. This item was dropped to the bottom of the order of precedence on the *Order Paper* (see *Order Paper*, October 20, 1995, pp. 22-3). The lack of quorum only meant that the House adjourned for the day.

20. See, for example, *Debates*, December 13, 1990, p. 16724.

21. See, for example, *Debates*, April 19, 1982, pp. 16368-70.

Members need not be in their seat in order to be counted.[22] While the count is taking place, no point of order or question of privilege will be considered by the Chair.[23]

When the Speaker adjourns the House for want of a quorum, either at the start of a sitting or during a sitting, Members present are asked to come to the Table and sign the scroll in order that their names may be recorded in the *Journals*. Logically, only the names of those Members counted ought to appear in the scroll, although in practice this has not always been the case, given that Members are free to enter or leave the Chamber during and after a count. As such, the list of Members entered in the *Journals* may exceed 20 names.[24] Thus, to adjourn the House, it is the count which is decisive, not the list of names.[25]

LACK OF QUORUM DURING DIVISIONS

During a recorded division, if the Speaker's attention is drawn to the fact that the sum of the votes and the number of Members present who did not vote (including the Speaker) do not total at least 20, then the question remains undecided; the usual quorum procedure is then triggered. If no objection is raised at the time the result of the vote is read to the House, the Speaker simply confirms the result and business proceeds as though there were a quorum.[26]

QUORUM WHEN THE ATTENDANCE OF THE HOUSE IS REQUESTED IN THE SENATE

A quorum is deemed to exist, regardless of the number of Members in attendance, whenever a message is received for the attendance of the House in the Senate.[27] The constitutional requirement for a quorum of 20 Members does not apply when the House is summoned to the Senate, since the House is not, in fact, exercising any of its powers in responding to the message; it is simply acting as a witness to the proceedings about to take place in the Upper Chamber.

Most messages requiring the attendance of the House in the Senate Chamber are, by prior arrangement, delivered by the Usher of the Black Rod at times when the House is sitting and thus when a quorum is likely to be present. In those instances, the message is received by the Speaker as soon as it arrives and the House, led by the

---

22. See, for example, *Debates*, February 12, 1997, pp. 8022-3.

23. See, for example, *Debates*, May 5, 1982, p. 17067.

24. For examples where the list of Members in the *Journals* exceeded 20 names, despite the fact that the House adjourned because of the lack of quorum, see *Journals*, May 5, 1982, p. 4797, and November 16, 1982, p. 5353.

25. *Journals*, July 10, 1969, pp. 1329-30.

26. For examples where recorded votes did not total 20 Members and no objection was taken in the House, see *Journals*, June 15, 1988, p. 2893, and May 26, 1989, p. 274. See also Speaker Sauvé's ruling of July 12, 1982, where it was stated that since no one, according to the record of the proceedings, had asked for a quorum call, "a quorum did exist" (*Debates*, July 9, 1982, p. 19201; July 12, 1982, pp. 19214-5).

27. Standing Order 29(5).

Speaker, proceeds to the Senate.[28] However, there are occasions when the House stands adjourned and its attendance is required for Royal Assent ceremonies. In such cases, the Speaker may, at the request of the government, cause the House to meet during a period of adjournment for the sole purpose of giving Royal Assent to a bill or bills, following which the House stands further adjourned.[29] In such circumstances, when it is known that the attendance of the House in the Senate will be desired, the Speaker causes the House to meet at an appointed hour. When the Usher of the Black Rod arrives, the Speaker receives the message and, with the Members then present (often less than a quorum), proceeds to the Senate.

Daily Sitting

Each sitting of the House customarily occurs on a separate day. However, in the nineteenth century, the holding of two or more sittings on a single day was used in an effort to expedite the business of the House by creating a mechanism to circumvent the rule prohibiting a bill receiving more than one "reading" on a single day.[30] Generally, some time prior to the prorogation or dissolution of Parliament, the House would adopt an order specifying that there would be two sittings a day, stating the times of meeting and adjournment.[31] This practice was abandoned with the extension of sittings, the introduction of extended hours prior to the June adjournment, and time limits for debate on certain items of legislation through time allocation or agreements to suspend the rules. In the twentieth century, the holding of two sittings on one day has occurred for entirely different reasons, such as the end and opening of successive sessions of a Parliament;[32] and to allow Members to attend special ceremonies.[33]

---

28. See, for example, *Journals*, May 12, 1994, pp. 459-60; *Debates*, May 12, 1994, p. 4300.

29. Standing Order 28(4). On occasion, points of order have been raised concerning the proceedings in the House when Members have assembled in anticipation of being summoned to the Senate Chamber for Royal Assent during an adjournment of the House. On December 30, 1988, and on June 29, 1989, Marcel Prud'homme (Saint-Denis) rose to suggest that as the House was being convened for the sole purpose of awaiting the arrival of the Usher of the Black Rod who would summon the House to the Senate, the House should not have proceeded with Prayers nor should the Speaker have taken the Chair prior to the announcement of the arrival of Black Rod by the Sergeant-at-Arms (see *Debates*, December 30, 1988, pp. 851-2, and June 29, 1989, pp. 3803-6. See also *Debates*, July 13, 1995, p. 14499).

30. Standing Order 71.

31. See, for example, *Journals*, July 18, 1895, p. 300. On June 21, 1869, the House conducted three separate sittings throughout the course of one day. This is the only known example of this occurrence (*Journals*, pp. 292-308).

32. See, for example, *Journals*, October 9, 1951; November 20, 1952; January 8, 1957; May 8, 1967; October 12, 1976.

33. See, for example, *Journals*, March 8, 1955, pp. 245-7 (unveiling memorial to the late Agnes Macphail, the first female Member elected to the House of Commons); *Debates*, March 29, 1973, pp. 2726-7; and *Journals*, March 30, 1973, p. 229 (joint address by the President of Mexico).

The Standing Orders provide for the House to meet on Monday at 11:00 a.m., Tuesday, Thursday and Friday at 10:00 a.m., and Wednesday at 2:00 p.m.[34] Once the House meets and begins its proceedings, it generally does not adjourn until the scheduled adjournment time: 6:30 p.m. on Monday, Tuesday, Wednesday and Thursday, and 2:30 p.m. on Friday.[35] On Monday, Tuesday, Wednesday and Thursday, a motion to adjourn the House is deemed to have been made and seconded. Officially referred to as the Adjournment Proceedings and informally as the "late show",[36] this motion is debatable for not more than 30 minutes, after which the Speaker deems the motion to adjourn to have been carried and adjourns the House until the next sitting day.[37] On Friday, no motion to adjourn the House is proposed; the Speaker adjourns the House without question put.

ALTERING DAYS AND HOURS OF SITTING

Notwithstanding the rules, the House may alter days or times of sittings, through special orders. Special orders have been adopted for many reasons: to eliminate a sitting in order to allow some Members to attend a political convention;[38] to start a sitting earlier on given days in order to consider government business;[39] to begin a sitting later in order for a visiting leader or head of state to address both Houses;[40] not to sit on days on which the House would otherwise sit;[41] and to sit on days on which the House would not otherwise sit, including Saturdays and Sundays.[42] If the special order adopted to sit on a Saturday or Sunday does not designate the order of

---

34. Standing Order 24(1).

35. Standing Order 24(2). Until 1906, there was no requirement for the House to adjourn automatically on any sitting day. That year, the House agreed to adjourn the proceedings of the House at 6:00 p.m. on Wednesday in order to provide for one night in the week when the House would not sit (*Debates*, July 9, 1906, cols. 7463-5). It was not until 1927 that the House adopted a mandatory time of adjournment for all sitting days (*Journals*, March 22, 1927, pp. 318-9).

36. Since the Adjournment Proceedings normally take place at the end of the sitting, they thus became known as the "late show" at the time of late evening sittings.

37. Standing Order 38. For further information on the Adjournment Proceedings, see Chapter 11, "Questions".

38. See, for example, *Debates*, June 7, 1993, p. 20462.

39. See, for example, *Journals*, May 30, 1977, p. 874.

40. See, for example, *Debates*, June 9, 1992, p. 11622.

41. See, for example, *Debates*, June 22, 1994, p. 5767.

42. See, for example, *Journals*, December 19, 1975, p. 970; December 20, 1975, p. 971; March 23, 1995, p. 1265.

business, it will be that of a Friday sitting.[43] At one time, sittings of the House conducted on a Saturday were common towards the end of a session or prior to the summer adjournment when the government wished to expedite the passage of legislation. However, since the adoption of Standing Orders to accommodate extended hours of sitting within the regular parliamentary timetable, the House rarely sits on a Saturday or Sunday.[44]

SUSPENDING A SITTING

Although the proceedings of the House run continuously from the beginning of a sitting through to its adjournment, the House may agree to a pause, called a "suspension". Suspensions are common and may be initiated for any number of reasons, as they are a simple method by which the House is able to manage its time as it sees fit. Upon the suspension of a sitting, the Speaker leaves the Chair but the Mace remains on the Table, thus indicating that the House is still constituted. Sittings of the House are routinely suspended with the intention of resuming the proceedings sometime later that day. There are no Standing Orders which explicitly govern the suspension of a sitting. Provision for a suspended sitting may be contained within the wording of a motion or special order of the House;[45] or, the House may suspend its proceedings simply through an agreement by unanimous consent.[46]

Sittings are most frequently suspended when the House, having terminated the consideration of an item of business, halts its proceedings to the call of the Chair or to the time when the next order of business is scheduled to begin. This is achieved either through the suggestion of a Member, who asks for the unanimous consent of

---

43. An unusual situation occurred in 1961 when the House, having adopted an opposition amendment to a government motion extending the hours of sitting, agreed to Saturday sittings without providing for their order of business (*Journals*, April 24, 1961, p. 468). The government attempted to introduce a motion covering the omission but failed to receive the consent of the House to do so (*Debates*, May 5, 1961, p. 4443). As a result, the *Order Paper* for Saturday, May 6, included the items available for consideration, ordered as for a Friday sitting. (See Speaker Michener's ruling, *Journals*, May 6, 1961, pp. 511-4.) On March 23, 1995, the House adopted an order to sit at 9:00 a.m. on Saturday, March 25, 1995, and at 1:00 p.m. on Sunday, March 26, 1995, for the purpose of considering Government Orders and attending a Royal Assent ceremony. On these two days, the House considered Bill C-77, *An Act to provide for the maintenance of railway operations and subsidiary services*, at the report and third reading stages. Royal Assent also took place on the Sunday (see *Journals*, March 23, 1995, p. 1265; March 25, 1995, pp. 1277-88; March 26, 1995, pp. 1289-91).

44. The last occasion of a continued period of Saturday sittings was in 1961, prior to the summer adjournment of the House. The House sat on every Saturday in the months of May, June and July, prior to the adjournment of the House for the summer on July 13, 1961, pursuant to a sessional order to that effect adopted on April 24, 1961 (*Journals*, April 24, 1961, pp. 467-8). The House has conducted a Sunday sitting only once, on March 26, 1995 (*Journals*, pp. 1289-91).

45. See, for example, *Journals*, November 7, 1990, pp. 2239-40; October 10, 1991, p. 471; and February 19, 1992, p. 1042.

46. See, for example, *Journals*, November 21, 1994, p. 905; February 9, 1995, p. 1109.

the House to suspend the sitting;[47] or, through the action of the Speaker who, seeing that debate on an item has come to a conclusion, suspends the sitting.[48] In the latter case, it is generally understood that the Speaker is acting with the concurrence of the House.

In recent years, the House has suspended its sittings for a variety of reasons: to await a specified time ordered by the House for a recorded division;[49] to allow for Royal Assent;[50] to allow the Speaker to deliberate on a ruling;[51] to await the time ordered for a Budget presentation;[52] because of a fire alarm;[53] to allow specific Members to be present in the Chamber for debate;[54] in order to await a message from the Senate regarding an amendment to a bill;[55] to allow for negotiations between parties on an item of legislation;[56] to allow copies to be made of motions introduced without notice;[57] to await an anticipated statement by the Prime Minister;[58] to allow

---

47. As in the case of motions to adjourn earlier than scheduled, suggestions to suspend the sitting are often proposed by House officers such as the House Leaders, the Whips or their deputies. This is done either after consultation with the other parties, to facilitate negotiations on a matter, or because there has been co-operation among the parties over House business. See, for example, *Debates*, December 2, 1991, p. 5627; April 21, 1994, p. 3340; June 20, 1994, p. 5597; February 7, 1995, p. 9299.

48. This is true particularly in the case of Private Members' Hour. It has become the practice that when proceedings on an item of Private Members' Business have been completed before the end of the time provided in the rules, as there can be no further business before the House at that moment, the Chair will suspend the sitting until the time for Government Orders (on a Monday) or the Adjournment Proceedings (on a Tuesday, Wednesday or Thursday). This has been proposed both by Members and the Chair, or the Chair has suspended the sitting with the tacit consent of the House. See, for example, *Debates*, October 23, 1989, p. 5026; October 24, 1989, p. 5074; April 23, 1990, p. 10508; October 28, 1991, p. 4070; February 4, 1992, p. 6406; February 6, 1992, p. 6530; December 7, 1992, p. 14701; June 1, 1993, p. 20192; March 21, 1994, p. 2518; September 26, 1994, p. 6116; October 3, 1994, p. 6416; October 17, 1994, p. 6753. It also is frequently proposed by Members that the House by consent proceed immediately without a suspension to the next scheduled order of business, if the House is ready to do so. See, for example, *Debates*, September 27, 1991, p. 2867; October 28, 1991, p. 4121; December 4, 1991, p. 5806; November 19, 1992, p. 13676; June 3, 1993, p. 20341; April 21, 1994, p. 3340; May 24, 1994, p. 4377; March 3, 1995, p. 10346.

49. See, for example, *Debates*, June 19, 1991, pp. 2130-1.

50. See, for example, *Debates*, November 26, 1986, pp. 1551-2; October 10, 1991, p. 3618; October 29, 1991, pp. 4203-4.

51. See, for example, *Debates*, February 7, 1990, p. 7953; October 31, 1991, pp. 4277-9; March 12, 1996, pp. 651-2.

52. See, for example, *Debates*, May 23, 1985, pp. 5011-2; February 26, 1986, p. 10979; February 25, 1992, p. 7593; April 26, 1993, pp. 18464, 18470.

53. See, for example, *Debates*, May 25, 1990, p. 11910; April 6, 1992, p. 9359; March 15, 1993, p. 16964; September 29, 1994, p. 6348; April 25, 1997, p. 10218.

54. See, for example, *Debates*, March 11, 1993, p. 16893.

55. See, for example, *Debates*, July 24, 1986, pp. 15011-2, 15061.

56. See, for example, *Debates*, December 11, 1989, p. 6784.

57. See, for example, *Debates*, June 14, 1990, p. 12788.

58. See, for example, *Debates*, January 17, 1991, pp. 17268-70.

Members to attend the funeral of a Member;[59] to allow Members to attend the unveiling of a statue on Parliament Hill;[60] to rectify a technical problem with the simultaneous interpretation in the Chamber;[61] and due to a Member taken ill in the Chamber.[62]

To resume the sitting, the Speaker takes the Chair and has the bells rung briefly. The proceedings of the House recommence without a count of the House, or pursuant to the terms of the special order adopted by the House, or according to the agreement or understanding reached by the House prior to the suspension.

CONTINUING OR EXTENDING A SITTING

Under certain conditions, it is possible for any Member to move a motion, without notice, to continue or extend a sitting beyond the fixed daily adjournment time in order to continue the consideration of a specific item of business at one or more stages.[63] From the time the fixed adjournment rule came into effect in 1927 until 1965, a multitude of motions were agreed to, many with unanimous consent, to continue or extend sittings through mealtimes or beyond the ordinary hour of daily adjournment. By the early 1960s, however, it had become increasingly difficult to secure agreements to extend a sitting beyond the obligatory adjournment time on any given day.[64] This kind of inflexibility undoubtedly led to the introduction of a new Standing Order in 1965 which put forward a different sitting extension mechanism.[65]

Since then, a motion to continue or extend a sitting of the House may be proposed, provided it is while the item to be considered is under discussion,[66] and at some time during the hour preceding the time at which consideration of the item would customarily be interrupted by Private Members' Business or the fixed daily adjournment time.[67] A motion of this nature is neither debatable nor amendable[68] and

---

59. See, for example, *Debates*, November 20, 1989, p. 5853; *Journals*, November 21, 1989, p. 862.

60. See, for example, *Debates*, September 26, 1990, pp. 13452-3, 13455.

61. See, for example, *Debates*, January 24, 1994, p. 246.

62. See, for example, *Debates*, December 9, 1998, p. 11122.

63. Standing Order 26(1).

64. On one occasion, the refusal of unanimous consent to extend a sitting to complete the consideration of an item of business indirectly resulted in the holding of a sitting on Good Friday (see *Journals*, March 27, 1964, p. 137).

65. See Standing Order 6(2) in *Journals*, June 11, 1965, p. 224.

66. On November 7, 1986, a motion was adopted to sit beyond the ordinary hour of daily adjournment for the purpose of continuing the rubric "Introduction of Bills" under Routine Proceedings (see *Journals*, November 7, 1986, p. 190).

67. Standing Order 26(1)(*a*) and (*b*). See, for example, the ruling of Acting Speaker Milliken (*Debates,* November 27, 1996, pp. 6813-4).

68. Standing Order 26(1)(*c*). On one occasion, a motion was amended by unanimous consent to provide a dinner hour (see *Debates*, August 31, 1966, pp. 7862-3).

may not be moved during Private Members' Business.[69] Such a motion can be moved by any Member in the course of debate but not on a point of order,[70] nor during the period reserved for questions and comments following a Member's speech,[71] nor when the House is bound to complete a proceeding by a specific time. For example, a motion to extend the sitting beyond the normal hour of adjournment may not be proposed when votes are scheduled on days allotted for the Business of Supply and during debate on the Address in Reply to the Speech from the Throne or on the Budget, when time allocation or closure is applied to a bill or motion, or when any special order of the House prescribes a precise time to dispose of a proceeding.

When a motion to continue or extend the sitting is moved, the Speaker puts the question to the House and specifically requests those Members who object to rise. If 15 or more Members do so, the motion is deemed to have been withdrawn; otherwise, the motion is adopted.[72] The motion has been moved more than once in the same hour.[73]

When the House is in a Committee of the Whole, it is necessary for the Committee to rise briefly so the motion can properly be moved and disposed of with the Speaker in the Chair.[74] When a motion to extend a sitting is adopted on a Tuesday, Wednesday, Thursday or Friday prior to the consideration of Private Members' Business, the debate on the item is continued after Private Members' Hour.

When a motion to continue or extend the sitting has been adopted, the House may be adjourned by the Speaker only upon the completion of the item of business in question or by the adoption of a motion to adjourn made by a Minister if the item of business is not yet completed.[75]

EXTENDING SITTING HOURS IN JUNE

Since 1982, and the advent of a fixed parliamentary calendar, the Standing Orders have provided for the extension of sitting hours during the last 10 sitting days in

69. On June 3, 1987, the House prohibited the moving of such motions during Private Members' Business (*Journals*, pp. 1016-28, and in particular p. 1017). See, for example, *Debates*, December 14, 1990, pp. 16797-8. From 1965 to 1985, six motions to extend the sitting on Private Members' Business were moved and two were adopted. See *Journals*, February 13, 1976, p. 1021; February 9, 1983, p. 5587; February 16, 1983, p. 5612; *Debates*, February 23, 1983, pp. 23153-4; *Journals*, February 7, 1984, p. 149; March 18, 1985, p. 387.

70. See, for example, *Debates*, February 14, 1969, p. 5560; November 5, 1991, pp. 4513-4; May 20, 1992, p. 10968; June 8, 1992, pp. 11596-7; March 9, 1993, p. 16747.

71. See, for example, *Debates*, February 17, 1987, p. 3541; March 26, 1991, pp. 19010-1.

72. Standing Order 26(2).

73. See, for example, *Debates*, June 1, 1993, pp. 20176-7, 20181-2.

74. Standing Order 26(1)(*a*). See, for example, *Debates*, March 13, 1969, p. 6606; November 17, 1970, p. 1270. See also Chapter 19, "Committees of the Whole House".

75. Standing Order 25.

June.[76] This rule represented a codification of a long-standing practice whereby, prior to the prorogation of the Parliament or the start of the summer recess, the House would arrange for longer hours of sitting in order to complete or advance its business. These longer hours of sitting were generally provided for by the House sitting on Saturdays;[77] meeting earlier in the day;[78] sitting during evenings that the House was not otherwise scheduled to sit;[79] or suspending lunch and dinner breaks.[80]

In order to extend the hours of sitting in June, a motion, for which no notice is required, must be moved by a Minister during Routine Proceedings on the tenth sitting day preceding June 23.[81] The motion, which must propose to extend sittings to a specific hour, but not necessarily for every day during that period,[82] is subject to a maximum two-hour debate before the question is put by the Speaker.[83]

Although the Standing Order to provide for the extension of the hours of sitting in June has been in effect since 1982, it has not been used at every opportunity. On a number of occasions, special orders have been moved instead and adopted, usually by unanimous consent.[84]

---

76. Standing Order 27.

77. See, for example, *Journals*, April 24, 1961, pp. 467-8.

78. In the nineteenth century, the House occasionally met earlier each day, usually at 11:00 a.m., and arranged to hold two distinct sittings each day. This allowed the House to advance certain business, such as the completion of several stages of a bill, on the same day. By 1900, however, longer hours were provided for almost entirely through earlier meeting times. See, for example, *Journals*, June 8, 1897, p. 222; June 22, 1900, p. 359.

79. See, for example, *Journals*, July 20, 1956, p. 911.

80. See, for example, *Journals*, June 27, 1950, p. 600.

81. Until 1991, the rule permitted a motion of this nature to be moved by any Member. On June 15, 1988, Nelson Riis (Kamloops–Shuswap), the House Leader for the New Democratic Party, moved a motion to extend the hours of sitting pursuant to the Standing Order, as was permitted at that time. Debate on the motion was adjourned before the maximum two hours of debate had taken place. See *Journals,* June 15, 1988, p. 2894. See also *Debates*, June 15, 1988, pp. 16498-501. The rule was amended on April 11, 1991, limiting the moving of the motion to Ministers (*Journals*, p. 2906).

82. In June 1991, the motion to extend the hours of sitting omitted two sitting days: Wednesday, June 12, and Friday, June 14, 1991 (*Journals*, June 10, 1991, p. 157). In June 1992, the motion did not refer to the sitting day of Tuesday, June 16, 1992 (*Journals*, June 9, 1992, p. 1661). In June 1994, the motion omitted two sitting days: Friday, June 10, and Friday, June 17, 1994 (*Journals*, June 9, 1994, p. 557). In June 1996, the motion omitted four sitting days: Thursday, June 13; Friday, June 14; Thursday, June 20; and Friday, June 21, 1996 *(Journals,* June 5, 1996, p. 490). On these days, regular hours of sitting remained in effect.

83. Standing Order 27.

84. When sitting hours have been extended in June by special order, it has generally been before the date on which, had the rule been invoked, such motions could have been moved. See *Journals*, June 14, 1984, p. 566; June 13, 1985, pp. 803-4; June 11, 1986, p. 2301; June 12, 1987, p. 1089; June 13, 1989, pp. 360-1; May 31, 1990, p. 1791; June 5, 1990, p. 1821. On June 20, 1988, the House adopted a government motion to extend both the days and hours of sitting of the House into the summer (see *Journals*, pp. 2925-7).

A SITTING WHICH LASTS MORE THAN ONE DAY

A sitting of the House is not necessarily confined to a single calendar day as one sitting may consume more than one day. Prior to the establishment in 1927 of fixed hours of adjournment for all days of the week,[85] sittings often extended over more than one day.[86] Since that time, these types of sittings have occurred infrequently and mainly as the result of events such as the prolonged ringing of the division bells;[87] the extension of a sitting beyond the ordinary hour of daily adjournment for the purpose of considering a specified item of business;[88] the continuation of an emergency debate past the hour of adjournment stipulated in the Standing Orders;[89] and the decision to complete all remaining stages of a bill[90] or to allow all Members wishing to do so to speak on an item.[91] At the conclusion of an extended sitting, the House stands adjourned until the regular commencement time of the next sitting, which is either later the same day if that time has not yet been reached, or the next day if the extended sitting has gone beyond that time.[92]

ALTERING THE ADJOURNMENT TIMES

There are times when the House may wish to temporarily set an adjournment time earlier or later than the time prescribed in the Standing Orders. The House may do this by adopting a special order to this effect.[93] At other times, when debate on an item of business concludes shortly before the specified adjournment, the House may adjourn earlier than the usual hour of adjournment by unanimous consent; Members

---

85. *Debates*, March 22, 1927, pp. 318-9.

86. There are numerous examples of single sittings consuming many days at a time (see *Bourinot*, 4th ed., pp. 213-4).

87. A notable example occurred in 1982, when division bells were rung continuously for several days resulting in a two-week sitting (see *Journals*, March 2-17, 1982, p. 4608). See, for example, *Journals*, March 19, 1984, pp. 260-3; March 28, 1984, pp. 314-6.

88. See, for example, *Journals*, October 31, 1983, p. 6383; February 3, 1987, pp. 433, 443; November 28, 1990, pp. 2312, 2316; June 18, 1991, pp. 216, 223; February 19, 1992, pp. 1043-4; May 25, 1993, pp. 2993, 3004.

89. Standing Order 52. See, for example, *Journals*, April 4, 1989, pp. 23-4; December 18, 1989, pp. 1034-5; May 5, 1992, pp. 1398-9; June 22, 1992, pp. 1825, 1829. For further information on emergency debates, see Chapter 15, "Special Debates".

90. See, for example, *Journals*, March 23, 1999, pp. 1650-3, 1656-7.

91. See, for example, *Journals*, January 16, 1991, p. 2571.

92. See, for example, *Journals*, April 28-29, 1987, pp. 796-7.

93. For examples of the House adopting special orders to adjourn earlier than the regular time of daily adjournment, see *Journals*, February 19, 1992, p. 1042, and June 19, 1992, p. 1811. For examples of the House adopting special orders to sit later and adjourn at a time later than the regular time of daily adjournment, see *Journals*, January 25, 1994, p. 62; February 1, 1994, p. 89; April 21, 1994, pp. 381-2; and May 6, 1994, p. 435.

ask that the Speaker "call it 6:30" (or "2:30" on Friday). This request is usually met and thus the need for a motion to adjourn is avoided.[94]

The adjournment of the House may also take place under other conditions. Any Member may propose a motion to adjourn the House without notice except when specifically prohibited by the Standing Orders;[95] the motion "That this House do now adjourn" is not debatable and not amendable. The adoption of such a motion immediately concludes a sitting.

Furthermore, when the House has extended its sitting beyond the fixed hour of adjournment for the completion of a specific item of business,[96] a motion to adjourn the House before the item is completed may only be proposed by a Minister.[97] When the business for which the House has extended its proceedings beyond the hour of daily adjournment is completed, the Speaker adjourns the House until the next sitting day in the usual manner.[98] When a sitting has been extended for a "take note" debate, the Speaker adjourns the House when no Member seeks the floor unless the special order governing the "take note" debate provides for a specific mechanism for adjournment.[99]

Special or Unusual Sittings

The House sometimes alters its normal schedule of sittings to accommodate special events or ceremonies. These "special" or "unusual" sittings have included: sitting for the sole purpose of attendance at the Royal Assent ceremony; sitting for the purpose of electing a Speaker; conducting a secret sitting; and sitting to hear addresses by distinguished visitors.

---

94. Such suggestions are usually made by the government, either the Chief Government Whip or the Parliamentary Secretary to the Government House Leader. See, for example, *Debates*, February 4, 1994, p. 956; November 4, 1994, p. 7697; December 2, 1994, p. 8604; December 5, 1994, p. 8658; February 13, 1995, p. 9562. Occasionally, when an item of business has been concluded, the Chair, sensing the mood of the House, will suggest that it be called 6:30 or 2:30 (see, for example, *Debates*, March 11, 1994, p. 2188).

95. Standing Order 60. For example, the motion is prohibited during the election of a Speaker (Standing Order 2(3)). For further information on the restrictions on the use of this Standing Order, see Chapter 12, "The Process of Debate".

96. For example, by special order or pursuant to Standing Orders 26 or 57.

97. Standing Order 25. Ministers have rarely moved the adjournment of the House before the completion of proceedings under this rule. See, for example, *Journals*, October 31 to November 1, 1983, pp. 6383, 6388-9. However, on several occasions, motions to adjourn the House have been refused on days when a special or Standing Order required completion or disposition of an item or items of business. See, for example, *Debates*, January 31, 1983, p. 22341; February 1, 1983, pp. 22400-1; May 23, 1985, pp. 4984, 5011-2; December 7, 1990, p. 16470.

98. Standing Order 24(2). See, for example, *Journals*, October 20, 1997, pp. 119, 122; February 17, 1998, p. 497; February 18, 1998, p. 503; June 8, 1998, pp. 947-8, 951.

99. See, for example, *Journals*, April 12, 1999, p. 1687. For further information on "take note" debates, see Chapter 15, "Special Debates".

SITTING FOR THE SOLE PURPOSE OF ATTENDING ROYAL ASSENT

In the late 1980s, the House followed the practice of adopting special orders permitting the Speaker, during periods of adjournment, to recall the House for the sole purpose of attending Royal Assent.[100] The Standing Order authorizing the Speaker to recall the House, if it is deemed to be in the public interest, has also been invoked to recall the House for the sole purpose of attending Royal Assent.[101] In 1994, the House codified in the Standing Orders the practice of recalling the House, at the request of the government for the sole purpose of Royal Assent.[102]

A sitting for the sole purpose of Royal Assent is treated as a recall of the House with proper notice given so that the Speaker may make the necessary preparations to reopen the House. The House does not need a quorum for the Speaker to take the Chair when the Usher of the Black Rod appears in the Chamber to request the attendance of Members in the Senate.[103] In responding to a summons of the Crown, the House is simply being asked to witness an event, rather than to make a decision. At the conclusion of the ceremony, the Speaker returns to the House and, once in the Chair, reports that the Governor General was pleased to give, in Her Majesty's name, Royal Assent to certain bills. The Chair then immediately adjourns the House[104] without proceeding to any other business.[105]

ELECTION OF A SPEAKER

At the first sitting of a new Parliament or at any time during the course of a Parliament when the Speakership becomes vacant, the House may, if necessary, sit beyond the regular hour of adjournment until such time as a Speaker is declared elected. The election of a Speaker takes precedence over all other business. No other business

---

100. See, for example, *Journals*, December 23, 1988, p. 80; June 27, 1989, p. 463; December 20, 1989, p. 1060; December 19, 1990, pp. 2513-5; June 16, 1993, pp. 3321-2.

101. Standing Order 28(3). See also *Debates*, June 23, 1994, pp. 5781-2. For further information on recalls of the House, see Chapter 8, "The Parliamentary Cycle".

102. Standing Order 28(4). See Standing Committee on Procedure and House Affairs, Twenty-Seventh Report, June 8, 1994, Issue No. 16, p. 3, adopted by the House on June 10, 1994 (*Journals*, p. 563).

103. Standing Order 29(5). Though a "sitting" for the sole purpose of Royal Assent is not a regular sitting, it has become practice for the Speaker's parade to be held and for the Speaker to read Prayers prior to receiving the message from the Governor General for the House's attendance in the Senate. See also section above, "Quorum When the Attendance of the House Is Requested in the Senate".

104. See, for example, *Journals*, December 10, 1998, p. 1440.

105. This also precludes the deposit of any document with the Clerk of the House and the reading of any Senate message except for those regarding Royal Assent. See, for example, *Journals*, June 23, 1994, pp. 668-70; July 7, 1994, pp. 672-3; July 13, 1995, pp. 1877-9; December 15, 1995, pp. 2267-8; February 2, 1996, p. 2269; December 18, 1997, pp. 399-400; June 18, 1998, pp. 1029-32; December 10, 1998, pp. 1439-40.

may be addressed and no motion for adjournment, nor any other motion, may be entertained. If the House has continued to sit beyond the regular hour of adjournment, the Speaker, upon being elected and taking the Chair, adjourns the House until the next sitting day. [106]

SECRET SITTINGS

Although not explicitly provided for in the Standing Orders, the House has the right and authority to conduct its proceedings in private. This has been referred to as a "secret sitting". The House may conduct an entire sitting or a portion of a sitting where "strangers" (anyone who is not a Member or an official of the House of Commons) are either not admitted or asked to withdraw from the galleries of the House. [107] These meetings are regarded as sittings and are noted as such in the documents of the House. To conduct a secret sitting, the House has either adopted a special order to initiate the proceeding, [108] or has simply not opened the doors of the House to the public following the prayers at the beginning of a sitting. [109]

The House has met in secret on four occasions, all during wartime. [110] As well, in the years shortly after Confederation, the House would, upon the commencement of a sitting but prior to the doors being opened to the public, conduct a portion of its sittings out of public view in order to discuss internal or "domestic" matters. [111]

ADDRESSES BY DISTINGUISHED VISITORS

From time to time, the House of Commons Chamber is the site for a joint address to Parliament by a distinguished visitor (usually a head of state or head of government). Since the early 1940s, numerous distinguished visitors have addressed Members of the Senate and the House of Commons from the floor of the Chamber. (See Figure 9.1.)

---

106. Standing Order 2. The election of John Fraser as Speaker in September 1986 serves as an excellent example of the operation of this Standing Order. The House met at 3:00 p.m. on Tuesday, September 30, and proceeded with the election process. After 11 ballots, John Fraser was elected Speaker and, after taking the Chair, adjourned the House at 2:30 a.m. on the morning of October 1 (see *Journals*, September 30, 1986, pp. 1-9). For further information on the election of the Speaker, see Chapter 7, "The Speaker and Other Presiding Officers of the House".

107. For further information on "strangers", see Chapter 6, "The Physical and Administrative Setting".

108. *Journals*, April 15, 1918, p. 151.

109. *Journals*, November 28, 1944, p. 931. Prior to the adjournment of the House on the day preceding the secret sitting, Members discussed various ways by which the House could conduct a sitting in secret. It was decided, on the invitation of the Speaker, that, upon commencing the sitting the following day, the prayers would be read but the doors would not be opened. The Speaker then indicated that he would leave it to the House, at that point, to proceed as it deemed fit (*Debates*, November 27, 1944, pp. 6632-3).

110. See *Journals*, April 17, 1918, p. 160; February 24, 1942, p. 93; July 18, 1942, p. 553; November 28, 1944, p. 931.

111. See, for example, *Debates*, December 6, 1867, p. 199; December 19, 1867, p. 317.

Figure 9.1   *Joint Addresses to Parliament Since 1940*

December 30, 1941	Winston Churchill, Prime Minister, Great Britain
June 16, 1943	Madame Chiang Kai-shek
June 1, 1944	John C. Curtin, Prime Minister, Australia
June 30, 1944	Peter Fraser, Prime Minister, New Zealand
November 19, 1945	Clement R. Attlee, Prime Minister, Great Britain
June 11, 1947	Harry S. Truman, President, United States
October 24, 1949	Pandit Jewaharlal Nehru, Prime Minister, India
May 31, 1950	Liaquat Ali Khan, Prime Minister, Pakistan
April 5, 1951	Vincent Auriol, President, French Republic
November 14, 1953	Dwight D. Eisenhower, President, United States
February 6, 1956	Sir Anthony Eden, Prime Minister, United Kingdom
March 5, 1956	Giovanni Gronchi, President, Republic of Italy
June 5, 1956	Dr. Sukarno, President, Republic of Indonesia
March 4, 1957	Guy Mollet, Prime Minister, French Republic
June 2, 1958	Dr. Theodor Heuss, President, Federal Republic of Germany
June 13, 1958	Harold Macmillan, Prime Minister, United Kingdom
July 9, 1958	Dwight D. Eisenhower, President, United States
July 21, 1958	Dr. Kwame Nkrumah, Prime Minister, Ghana
May 17, 1961	John F. Kennedy, President, United States
May 26, 1964	U Thant, Secretary General, United Nations
April 14, 1972	Richard M. Nixon, President, United States
March 30, 1973	Luis Echeverria, President, Mexico
June 19, 1973	Indira Gandhi, Prime Minister, India
May 5, 1980	Masayoshi Ohira, Prime Minister, Japan
May 26, 1980	José Lopez Portillo, President, Mexico
March 11, 1981	Ronald W. Reagan, President, United States
September 26, 1983	Margaret Thatcher, Prime Minister, United Kingdom
January 17, 1984	Zhao Ziyang, Premier, State Council, People's Republic of China
May 8, 1984	Miguel de la Madrid, President, Mexico

Figure 9.1   *Joint Addresses to Parliament Since 1940 (continued)*

March 7, 1985	Javier Perez de Cuellar, Secretary-General, United Nations
January 13, 1986	Yasuhiro Nakasone, Prime Minister, Japan
April 6, 1987	Ronald W. Reagan, President, United States
May 25, 1987	François Mitterand, President, French Republic
May 10, 1988	Her Majesty Queen Beatrix of the Netherlands
June 16, 1988	Dr. Helmut Kohl, Chancellor, Federal Republic of Germany
June 22, 1988	Margaret Thatcher, Prime Minister, United Kingdom
February 27, 1989	Chaim Herzog, President, State of Israel
October 11, 1989	His Majesty King Hussein Bin Talal, Hashemite Kingdom of Jordan
June 18, 1990	Nelson Mandela, Deputy President, African National Congress
April 8, 1991	Carlos Salinas de Gortari, President, Mexico
June 19, 1992	Boris Yeltsin, President, Federation of Russia
February 23, 1995	William J. Clinton, President, United States
June 11, 1996	Ernesto Zedillo, President, Mexico
September 24, 1998	Nelson Mandela, President, Republic of South Africa
April 29, 1999	Vaclav Havel, President, Czech Republic

Since the 1970s, the practice has normally been for the House to adopt a motion for a joint address, without debate, prior to the delivery of the address.[112] In addition to the order to append the address and related speeches to *Hansard*,[113] the motion has also included the date and time of the adjournment of the House, as well as other conditions for the order of business on the day of the address. By 1980, the motion also included permission for the transmission of the address and related speeches by the media.[114]

When a joint address takes place, Senators and Members of the House of Commons assemble in the House of Commons Chamber. However, the assembly does not constitute a sitting and the Mace is not on the Table. An established protocol is nonetheless followed.

---

112. See, for example, *Journals*, March 29, 1972, p. 232; March 11, 1999, p. 1593. Prior to the 1970s, the motions to append the text of the address and introductory and related speeches were normally adopted at the sitting following the delivery of the address by distinguished visitors (see *Journals*, January 21, 1942, p. 654; May 18, 1961, p. 561).

113. The joint address by U Thant, Secretary-General of the United Nations, on May 26, 1964, was not printed in *Hansard*.

114. See, for example, *Journals*, April 29, 1980, p. 94; April 1, 1987, p. 689; March 11, 1999, p. 1593.

The seating arrangements in the House are not what they would be for a regular sitting. The Speaker of the House takes the Chair, with the Speaker of the Senate seated in a chair to his or her right. The Table is cleared of the usual paraphernalia and a lectern placed at its head. The Prime Minister and the distinguished visitor are seated along the side of the Table to the Speaker's right; the Clerk of the Senate and the Clerk of the House of Commons are seated along the other side of the Table. Seating for the rest of the official party, the Justices of the Supreme Court and the Senators is arranged on the floor of the House in front of the Table.

On arrival at the Centre Block, the distinguished visitor is met in the Rotunda by the Prime Minister and the Speakers of both Houses, and signs the Senate and House of Commons' visitors books. At the appointed hour, the official party enters the House of Commons Chamber. The Prime Minister provides an official welcome and invites the visitor to address the assembly. Afterwards, the visitor is thanked by the Speaker of the Senate, followed by the Speaker of the House of Commons who will then conclude the assembly. At this point, the official party exits the Chamber and proceeds to the House of Commons Speaker's Chambers.

10

The Daily Program

Routine Proceedings are an essential part of the House business and if they are not protected the interests of the House and the public it serves are likely to suffer.

SPEAKER JOHN A. FRASER
(*Debates,* April 14, 1987, p. 5120)

While Chapters 8 and 9 describe the parliamentary calendar and the hours of sitting of the House respectively, this chapter provides an outline of the recurring sequence of business for each sitting day, that is, the daily order of business, and gives details of the major categories of daily business.

The daily business of the House is taken up according to a predetermined sequence outlined in the rules of the House.[1] In 1867, the program of the House varied according to the days of the week.[2] Afterwards, almost every time major rule revisions took place, the order of business was affected. The majority of alterations came about as a result of the changing nature of the business coming before the House, the growing volume of government business to be transacted and changes to the hours of sitting.

All items of business that can be dealt with on a given day are listed on the daily *Order Paper,* the official agenda of the House. See Figure 10.1 which depicts the day by day

---

1. Standing Order 30(6).
2. See *Rules, Orders and Forms of Proceeding of the House of Commons of Canada*, 1868, Rule No. 19.

Figure 10.1   *Daily Order of Business*

Hours	Monday	Tuesday	Wednesday	Thursday	Friday	Hours
10:00 – 11:00		Routine Proceedings		Routine Proceedings	Government Orders	10:00 – 11:00
11:00 – 11:15	Private Members' Business (4)	Government Orders (2)		Government Orders (2)	Members' Statements	11:00 – 11:15
11:15 – 12:00					Oral Questions	11:15 – 12:00
12:00 – 1:00	Government Orders		Review of Delegated Legislation (5)		Routine Proceedings (1) — Government Orders (2)	12:00 – 1:00
1:00 – 1:30					Government Orders (2)	1:00 – 1:30
1:30 – 2:00	Members' Statements	Members' Statements	Members' Statements	Members' Statements	Private Members' Business (4)	1:30 – 2:00
2:00 – 2:15	Oral Questions	Oral Questions	Oral Questions	Oral Questions		2:00 – 2:15
2:15 – 2:30						2:15 – 2:30
2:30 – 3:00	Routine Proceedings (1) — Government Orders (2)	(1) — Government Orders (2)	Routine Proceedings (1) — Notices of Motions for the Production of Papers — Government Orders (2)	(1) — Government Orders (2)		2:30 – 3:00
3:00 – 5:30						3:00 – 5:30
5:30 – 6:30		Private Members' Business (4)	Private Members' Business (4)	Private Members' Business (4)		5:30 – 6:30
6:30 – 7:00	Adjournment Proceedings (3)	Adjournment Proceedings (3)	Adjournment Proceedings (3)	Adjournment Proceedings (3)		6:30 – 7:00

(1) Possible extension of Routine Proceedings to complete Introduction of Government Bills pursuant to Standing Order 30(4).

(2) Possible extension pursuant to Standing Order 33(2) respecting Ministerial Statements.

(3) Possible delay pursuant to Standing Order 33(2) respecting Ministerial Statements.

(4) Possible delay or rescheduling pursuant to Standing Order 30(7) to compensate for a delay or an interruption of more than 30 minutes, and pursuant to Standing order 33(2) respecting Ministerial Statement.

(5) If required, House to sit at 1:00 p.m. for the review of Delegated Legislation pursuant to Standing Order 128(1).

order of business. The daily activities of the House are generally grouped into five categories:

- Daily Proceedings;
- Routine Proceedings;
- Government Orders;
- Private Members' Business;
- Adjournment Proceedings.

The Daily Proceedings include three events in the daily schedule: Prayers (followed by the National Anthem on Wednesdays), Statements by Members and Oral Questions. The Daily Routine of Business, or Routine Proceedings as it is more commonly known, consists of separate categories of business usually referred to as rubrics and includes, among other items, tabling of documents, statements by Ministers and the introduction of bills sponsored by either the government or private Members. Government Orders include any item of business proposed by a Minister which the House has ordered for consideration. Each day one hour of House time is set aside for Private Members' Business during which bills and motions sponsored by Members who are not Ministers are considered. The Adjournment Proceedings are the final category of business considered on a sitting day (Fridays excepted).

Daily Proceedings

Each of the three events in the Daily Proceedings—Prayers, Statements by Members and Oral Questions—is covered separately in the Standing Orders. (On Wednesday, the National Anthem is also included in the Daily Proceedings.)

PRAYERS

Prior to the doors of the Chamber being opened to the public at the beginning of each sitting of the House, the Speaker takes the Chair and proceeds to read the prayer, after it has been determined that a quorum of 20 Members including the Speaker is present, and before any business is considered.[3] While the prayer is being read, the Speaker, the Members and the Table Officers all stand. When the prayer is finished, the House pauses for a moment of silence for private thought and reflection. At the end of the moment of silence, the Speaker orders the doors opened and the proceedings of

---

3. Standing Order 30(1). The reading of the prayer is considered the first stage of the proceedings of the House (*Debates*, February 19, 1877, p. 94). Objection has been raised in the House that the practice of reciting prayers is in violation of the Charter of Rights and Freedoms. In response, the Speaker noted that it was not for the Chair to rule on the constitutionality of this practice or make any decision concerning the laws of the nation. The Speaker further stated that the jurisdiction of the Chair extended only to decisions concerning the procedural rules, and if any changes were contemplated regarding the practice of prayers, it was a matter for the House and not the Chair to decide (*Debates*, June 19, 1990, pp. 12927-9).

the House then begin. At this point, television coverage of the proceedings commences and the public enters the galleries.[4]

Although the practice of reading a prayer at the start of each sitting was not codified in the Standing Orders until 1927,[5] it has been part of the daily proceedings of the House since 1877. At that time, the House charged a committee to consider the desirability of using a form of prayer in the Chamber.[6] In its report, the committee recommended that the proceedings of the House should be opened each day with the reading of a prayer and included therein a suggested form of prayer.[7] In a discussion that immediately followed the adoption of the committee report, it was determined that the prayer would be read prior to the doors of the House being opened, as was the practice of the Senate of Canada and the British House of Commons.[8]

Much later, suggestions were made to rewrite or reword the prayer in a nonsectarian form and to have the prayer read by a chaplain instead of the Speaker.[9] Recommendations have also been made to change the way the House takes up the prayer. Over the years, many Members have expressed the view that the public should be admitted before the prayer is read.[10] In 1976, the House adopted a motion recommending that the Standing Orders be changed in order to allow the public to enter the galleries before the prayer is read. However, the motion was worded as a recommendation, not as an order, and provided no instruction for implementing the change. For that reason, the Speaker indicated that the practice of reciting the prayer prior to the admission of the public would continue until the Standing Committee on Procedure and Organization considered the matter and reported to the House;

---

4. Standing Order 30(2) states: "Not more than two minutes after the reading of prayers, the business of the House shall commence." This excludes any private business that may have to be conducted *in camera* before the doors are opened to the public. This Standing Order came into force in 1975 and has not been amended since (see Item No. 9 of the Second Report of the Standing Committee on Procedure and Organization, presented on March 14, 1975 (*Journals*, p. 373) and concurred in on March 24, 1975 (*Journals*, p. 399)). Although not recently, there have been occasions, following prayers but before the public was allowed into the galleries, when the House has met *in camera* to discuss internal matters or matters of privilege (*Bourinot*, 4th ed., p. 219). See also *Debates*, February 19, 1877, p. 94. References to *in camera* discussions can be found in *Debates*, December 6, 1867, p. 199; December 19, 1867, p. 317; and *Journals*, April 16, 1929, p. 245. See a related discussion in *Debates*, April 12, 1929, pp. 1508-11.

5. *Journals*, March 22, 1927, pp. 330, 333.

6. *Journals*, February 13, 1877, p. 26. See also *Debates*, February 12, 1877, pp. 26-8.

7. *Journals*, February 19, 1877, p. 42.

8. *Debates*, February 19, 1877, p. 94. Although not specified in the report, when two sittings occur on the same day, the prayer must be read at the opening of each (see *Bourinot*, 4th ed., p. 216).

9. See *Debates*, November 12, 1957, p. 991; April 21, 1978, p. 4734; Item Nos. 16 and 17 of the Tenth Report of the Special Committee on Standing Orders and Procedure, presented on September 30, 1983 (*Journals*, p. 6250); Item No. 7.12 of the Third Report of the Special Committee on the Reform of the House of Commons, presented on June 18, 1985 (*Journals*, p. 839).

10. See *Debates*, February 1, 1944, p. 65; Item No. 15 of the Tenth Report of the Special Committee on Standing Orders and Procedure, presented on September 30, 1983 (*Journals*, p. 6250); Item No. 7.12 of the Third Report of the Special Committee on the Reform of the House of Commons, presented on June 18, 1985 (*Journals*, p. 839).

however, no further action was taken on this matter. [11] There have been, nonetheless, rare instances when the public has heard the prayer. [12]

Until 1994, no major change to the form of the prayer [13] was made aside from references to royalty. [14] At that time, the House adopted a report recommending a new form of prayer more reflective of the different religions embraced by Canadians. [15]

---

11. *Debates*, November 9, 1976, p. 881; November 10, 1976, pp. 939-40.

12. On March 19, 1984, for example, the sitting was suspended and resumed the following day. That sitting ended at 11:30 a.m. on March 20 and was immediately followed by the opening of the next sitting. The public was in the galleries when the prayer was read since the galleries had remained opened (see *Debates*, March 19, 1984, pp. 2219-21; March 20, 1984, p. 2223). See also *Debates*, February 21, 1994, p. 1581, when the Speaker requested the "agreement" of the House to read the prayer in public.

13. The text of the prayer was as follows:

O Lord our heavenly Father, high and mighty, King of kings, Lord of lords, the only Ruler of princes, who dost from thy throne behold all the dwellers upon earth: Most heartily we beseech thee with thy favour to behold our most gracious Sovereign Lady, Queen Elizabeth; and so replenish her with the grace of thy Holy Spirit that she may always incline to thy will and walk in thy way; Endue her plenteously with heavenly gifts: grant her in health and wealth long to live; strengthen her that she may vanquish and overcome all her enemies; and finally, after this life, she may attain everlasting joy and felicity; through Jesus Christ our Lord— Amen.

Almighty God, the fountain of all goodness, we humbly beseech thee to bless Elizabeth the Queen Mother, the Prince Philip, Duke of Edinburgh, Charles, Prince of Wales, and all the Royal Family: Endue them with thy Holy Spirit; enrich them with thy Heavenly Grace; prosper them with all happiness; and bring them to thine everlasting kingdom; through Jesus Christ our Lord—Amen.

Most gracious God, we humbly beseech thee, as for the United Kingdom, Canada and Her Majesty's other Realms and Territories, so especially for Canada, and herein more particularly for the Governor General, the Senate, and the House of Commons, in their legislative capacity at this time assembled; that thou wouldst be pleased to direct and prosper all their consultations, to the advancement of thy glory, the safety, honour, and welfare of our Sovereign and Her Realms and Territories, that all things may be so ordered and settled by their endeavours, upon the best and surest foundations, that peace and happiness, truth and justice, religion and piety, may be established among us for all generations. These, and all other necessaries for them, and us, we humbly beg in the name, and through the mediation of Jesus Christ, our most blessed Lord and Saviour—Amen.

Our Father who art in heaven, Hallowed by thy Name. Thy Kingdom come. Thy will be done on earth as it is in heaven. Give us this day our daily bread; And forgive us our trespasses, as we forgive those who trespass against us. And lead us not into temptation. But deliver us from evil—Amen.

A shorter version of the prayer was initiated by Speaker Sauvé in the early 1980s; there is no record of the change in the *Journals* or the *Debates*, nor is there any indication that objections were raised.

14. For examples of the House being informed of changes in reference to royalty, see *Journals*, March 22, 1957, p. 303; July 28, 1958, p. 311.

15. On February 18, 1994, the House concurred in the Sixth Report of the Standing Committee on Procedure and House Affairs, which contained the text of the new prayer. See Standing Committee on Procedure and House Affairs, *Minutes of Proceedings and Evidence,* March 15, 1994, Issue No. 3, pp. 5, 12; *Debates*, February 18, 1994, pp. 1559-60, 1563-5.

This prayer was read for the first time when the House met to open its proceedings on February 21, 1994: [16]

> *Almighty God, we give thanks for the great blessings which have been bestowed on Canada and its citizens, including the gifts of freedom, opportunity and peace that we enjoy. We pray for our Sovereign, Queen Elizabeth, and the Governor General. Guide us in our deliberations as Members of Parliament, and strengthen us in our awareness of our duties and responsibilities as Members. Grant us wisdom, knowledge, and understanding to preserve the blessings of this country for the benefit of all and to make good laws and wise decisions. Amen.*

The prayer is followed by a moment of silence for private reflection and meditation.

There has been no explicit pronouncement on when French and English are to be used in reading the prayer. When the reading of the prayer was first sanctioned in 1877, it was agreed that the prayer would be read in the language most familiar to the Speaker. [17] It was only two years later that Speaker Blanchet, the Commons' first bilingual Speaker, inaugurated the practice of reading the prayer in French and English on alternate days. [18] From then until the 1970s, many Speakers, depending on their fluency in the two languages, followed this practice. Since then, some Speakers have alternated between the two languages, while others have used a bilingual version.

When the House convenes on the first day of a new Parliament or on any day when the House is to elect a Speaker, the prayer is not read until a Speaker has been elected. [19] Indeed, at that time, the election of a Speaker must be the first order of business and has precedence over all other matters. [20] Only after a Speaker has been elected is the House properly constituted to conduct its business. [21] After the House reconvenes following the election of the Speaker, the prayer is read before the House proceeds to the Senate to inform the Governor General of its choice. [22]

---

16. *Debates*, February 21, 1994, p. 1581.

17. *Debates*, February 19, 1877, pp. 94-6.

18. *Bourinot*, 4th ed., pp. 215-6.

19. *Bourinot*, 4th ed., p. 216.

20. Standing Order 2.

21. *Bourinot*, 4th ed., pp. 88-9.

22. See, for example, *Journals*, October 9, 1979, p. 11; April 14, 1980, p. 11; November 5, 1984, p. 10. Neither the *Journals* nor the *Debates* makes reference to the prayer before the House proceeded to the Senate for the opening of Parliament on December 12, 1988. In 1994 and 1997, the Speaker was elected the day prior to the opening of Parliament; the prayer was read on the day Parliament opened (*Journals*, January 18, 1994, p. 14; September 23, 1997, p. 11).

NATIONAL ANTHEM

Although not provided for in the Standing Orders, it has become the practice for the House of Commons to sing the national anthem each Wednesday at the opening of the sitting. After the prayer has been read, but before the doors are opened to admit the public, the Speaker recognizes a Member to lead the House in singing the national anthem.[23]

The practice of singing *O Canada* at the beginning of each Wednesday sitting began during the Thirty-Fifth Parliament (1994-97). Members had discussed the possibility of singing the national anthem in the House, and the matter was raised in the Standing Committee on Procedure and House Affairs. In a report presented in the House on November 10, 1995, the Committee recommended that a Member lead the House in singing the national anthem at the beginning of each Wednesday sitting; later in the sitting, the House concurred in the Committee's report.[24]

STATEMENTS BY MEMBERS

The second activity grouped under Daily Proceedings is "Statements by Members". At 2:00 p.m. on Monday, Tuesday, Wednesday and Thursday, and at 11:00 a.m. on Friday, the Speaker calls "Statements by Members".[25] Members who are not Ministers, when recognized by the Speaker, are permitted to address the House for up to one minute on virtually any matter of international, national, provincial or local concern.[26] This one-minute time limit is rigorously enforced by the Speaker.

---

23. Members wishing to lead the House in the singing of the anthem advise the Speaker through their whip of their interest and the Speaker recognizes one of them (see Standing Committee on Procedure and House Affairs, *Evidence*, November 9, 1995, Issue No. 95, p. 2). On December 4, 1996, a visiting choir led the House in the singing of the anthem. After the reading of the prayer, the Sergeant-at-Arms was ordered to admit the choir into the gallery facing the Speaker before the doors were opened to the public (*Debates*, December 4, 1996, p. 7077). Again, on December 10, 1997, and on December 9, 1998, a school choir participated in the singing of the national anthem (*Debates*, December 10, 1997, p. 3021; December 9, 1998, p. 11107). On April 23, 1997, the Speaker invited the pages to lead the House in the singing of the anthem (*Debates*, April 23, 1997, p. 10111).

24. See Standing Committee on Procedure and House Affairs, *Minutes of Proceedings*, November 10, 1995, Issue No. 53, p. 10; *Journals*, November 10, 1995, pp. 2124-5. The singing of the national anthem is televised. There was consensus among the members of the Committee that the television coverage would begin immediately after the prayers had been read. See Standing Committee on Procedure and House Affairs, *Evidence*, November 9, 1995, pp. 1-6. Deborah Grey (Beaver River) led the House in singing the national anthem for the first time on November 22, 1995. See *Debates*, November 22, 1995, p. 16659. See also *Debates*, October 30, 1995, pp. 15975-6.

25. Standing Order 30(5).

26. When "Statements by Members" was first established in 1983, Speaker Sauvé stated that this period was intended to provide Members with an opportunity "to voice serious issues of international, national or local concern" (*Debates*, January 17, 1983, p. 21873). During this period, Members have, on occasion, given part or all of their statement to the House in a language other than English or French (for example, Inuktitut, Cree, Slavey, Italian, Hebrew, Creole, Croatian and Armenian). See, for example, *Debates*, October 2, 1991, p. 3134; March 26, 1992, p. 8856; April 10, 1992, p. 9644; February 8, 1993, p. 15550; March 31, 1993, pp. 17837, 17840; March 10, 1994, p. 2120; May 27, 1998, p. 7269. A Member has also used sign language to make a statement (*Debates*, May 13, 1998, pp. 6918-9). When using another language, Members usually provide the interpreters with a copy of the text in English or French. See also Chapter 13, "Rules of Order and Decorum".

If "Statements by Members" begins promptly at 2:00 p.m. (11:00 a.m. on Friday),[27] the entire 15 minutes provided for these proceedings is used; a minimum of 15 Members is typically recognized. If the start of these proceedings is delayed, the time is reduced accordingly and could even be eliminated entirely for that sitting. Question Period begins promptly at 2:15 p.m. (or 11:15 a.m. on Friday), regardless of whether or not a full 15 minutes was allotted to "Statements by Members". If not enough Members rise to use all the time provided for, then the Speaker would proceed to call "Oral Questions", although there is no record of this having occurred.[28]

Historical Perspective

The procedures regarding "Statements by Members" came into force with the adoption of provisional rule changes in 1982.[29] However, what is now used to give Members an opportunity to make statements on issues of current interest had its genesis in another rule, which existed for the first 60 years of Confederation, allowing Members to seek the unanimous consent of the House to move a motion without notice.[30] In 1925, a special committee reported that "The unanimous consent of the House is usually granted with such readiness and so little opposition that in many cases motions are passed before the House has had time to understand them" and recommended that the rule be changed so that a satisfactory explanation could be given as to why notice should be waived.[31] In 1927, the House finally agreed to the recommendation that the Standing Orders be amended so that unanimous consent could be sought only "in case of urgent and pressing necessity previously explained by the mover".[32] It was not until 1968 that this rule was invoked with any frequency when more and more Members began to rise daily under its provisions before Question

---

27. For the convenience of the House, the Speaker has occasionally proceeded to "Statements by Members" before 2:00 p.m. (or 11:00 a.m. on Friday) (see, for example, *Debates*, November 28, 1997, p. 2432; June 9, 1998, p. 7803). The House has also unanimously agreed to proceed to "Statements by Members" before the appointed time (see, for example, *Debates*, November 30, 1990, p. 16031; March 27, 1992, p. 8923).

28. Occasionally, when proceedings have been delayed, the time allotted for "Statements by Members" and Question Period has been extended accordingly so that Members have the full amount of time allotted (see *Debates*, September 18, 1991, p. 2300; June 16, 1995, p. 14011; November 1, 1995, p. 16063; November 29, 1996, p. 6903). Once before a Christmas adjournment, the Speaker allowed "Statements by Members" to exceed the time limit by five minutes (*Debates*, December 19, 1990, p. 16939). Question Period was also extended accordingly. More recently, the House unanimously agreed to dispose of this proceeding and proceed directly to Question Period after Members paid tribute for more than 30 minutes to the Rt. Hon. Brian Mulroney (see *Debates*, February 24, 1993, pp. 16379-83).

29. *Journals*, November 29, 1982, p. 5400.

30. The Standing Order read: "A motion may be moved by unanimous consent of the House without previous notice". See also *Bourinot*, 4th ed., pp. 301-2.

31. *Journals*, May 29, 1925, p. 356.

32. *Journals*, March 22, 1927, pp. 334-5.

Period, often in regard to cases where no "urgent and pressing necessity" appeared to exist.

This trend continued until 1975 when a further limitation was instituted whereby such motions could be moved only by Members not of the Ministry during a restricted time period before "Oral Questions" were called.[33] Nonetheless, throughout the 1970s and early 1980s, it became a common, though misused and often time-consuming, feature of the proceedings of the House.[34] In 1982, a special procedure committee concluded that "… the Standing Order is used for purposes for which it was never intended. It is also open to objection because the refusal of unanimous consent to waive notice can frequently be misunderstood as a declaration of opposition to a well-intentioned motion." The committee's recommendation to abolish this Standing Order was endorsed by the House, which also adopted the committee's proposal to institute a new Standing Order that "would enable Members to make statements on current issues on a daily basis during the first 15 minutes of the sitting."[35] Originally Members were allowed to speak for not more than 90 seconds; this rule was amended in 1986 when the time for each Member's statement was reduced to not more than one minute.[36]

Guidelines

In presiding over the conduct of this daily activity, Speakers have been guided by a number of well-defined prohibitions. In 1983, when the procedure for "Statements by Members" was first put in place, Speaker Sauvé stated that[37]

- Members may speak on any matter of concern and not necessarily on urgent matters only;

- Personal attacks are not permitted;[38]

- Congratulatory messages, recitations of poetry and frivolous matters are out of order.

These guidelines are still in place today, although Speakers tend to turn a blind eye to the latter restriction.[39]

---

33. *Journals*, March 14, 1975, p. 373; March 24, 1975, p. 399.

34. See *Jerome*, pp. 104-6. See also Speaker's ruling, *Debates*, February 13, 1979, pp. 3164-6.

35. Third Report of the Special Committee on Standing Orders and Procedure, *Minutes of Proceedings and Evidence*, November 4, 1982, Issue No. 7, p. 19, presented in the House on November 5, 1982 (*Journals*, p. 5328), and agreed to on November 29, 1982 (*Journals*, p. 5400).

36. *Journals*, February 6, 1986, p. 1648; February 13, 1986, pp. 1709-10.

37. *Debates*, January 17, 1983, pp. 21873-4.

38. In a 1990 ruling, Speaker Fraser clarified that a statement about another Member's political position would be acceptable, but a personal attack against a Member would not be allowed (*Debates*, November 26, 1990, p. 15717). Speaker Parent further cautioned in a 1996 decision that "once they [the words] have been uttered, it is very difficult to retract them and the impression they leave is not always easily erased" (*Debates*, November 29, 1996, p. 6899). See also *Debates*, September 22, 1994, pp. 6032-3; December 3, 1997, p. 2646.

39. See, for example, *Debates*, November 26, 1990, p. 15705; March 8, 1994, p. 1992; September 29, 1997, p. 204; December 11, 1997, pp. 3107-8.

Since 1983, additional restrictions have been placed on these statements. The Speaker has cut off an individual statement and asked the Member to resume his or her seat when

- offensive language has been used;[40]
- a Senator has been attacked;[41]
- the actions of the Senate have been criticized;[42]
- a ruling of a court has been denounced;[43] and
- the character of a judge has been attacked.[44]

The Speaker has also cautioned Members not to use this period to make defamatory comments about non-Members,[45] nor to use the verbatim remarks of a private citizen as a statement,[46] nor to make statements of a commercial nature.[47]

The opportunity to speak during "Statements by Members" is allocated to private Members of all parties. In according Members the opportunity to participate in this period, the Chair is guided by lists provided by the whips of the various parties and attempts to recognize those Members supporting the government and those Members in opposition on an equitable basis.[48] While Ministers are not permitted to

---

40. See, for example, *Debates*, October 20, 1986, p. 510; March 25, 1987, p. 4541; October 29, 1997, p. 1278. Speaker Fraser ruled that it is inappropriate for a Member to use this proceeding to attack another Member for offensive language when that Member has already been admonished by the Chair (*Debates*, October 29, 1986, p. 864).

41. See, for example, *Debates*, October 1, 1990, pp. 13607, 13621-2; October 3, 1997, pp. 456-7. See also *Debates*, February 13, 1998, p. 3853; February 19, 1998, p. 4156.

42. See, for example, *Debates*, December 20, 1989, pp. 7247-8; June 8, 1990, p. 12522; September 22, 1994, pp. 6031-2, 6040.

43. See, for example, *Debates*, November 19, 1986, p. 1315; December 1, 1986, pp. 1636, 1651-2. In the latter ruling, Speaker Fraser noted that "it is often the obligation of Members of Parliament to criticize a law. However ... it is not their place to castigate a court or judge or the decisions rendered under a law ..." (p. 1636).

44. See, for example, *Debates*, November 28, 1996, pp. 6853-4.

45. See, for example, *Debates*, December 3, 1991, pp. 5679-82. See also *Debates*, November 28, 1991, pp. 5509-10.

46. See, for example, *Debates*, April 27, 1995, p. 11878.

47. See, for example, *Debates*, September 16, 1996, pp. 4221-2; September 17, 1996, pp. 4309-10.

48. At the start of the Thirty-Fifth Parliament (1994-97), the Speaker informed the House that, after consultation, the party whips had agreed on a format regarding party representation and the number of Members to be recognized to offer statements during this period: nine interventions by government Members, three by the Official Opposition (Bloc Québécois), three by the Reform Party; the independent Members would be recognized on an *ad hoc* basis (*Debates*, January 19, 1994, p. 17). Five months later, Speaker Parent observed that Members not belonging to a recognized party had participated almost daily during "Statements by Members" (*Debates*, June 16, 1994, p. 5439). At the beginning of the Thirty-Sixth Parliament in 1997, the breakdown was established as follows: eight interventions by government Members, three by the Official Opposition (Reform Party), two by the Bloc Québécois, one each by the NDP and the Progressive Conservative party.

use this period to address the House, Parliamentary Secretaries may.[49] Leaders of parties in opposition have availed themselves of this rule.[50] Chair occupants other than the Speaker, in their capacity as Members, have also made statements.[51]

Points of order arising from "Statements by Members" are normally dealt with after Question Period,[52] although in some cases, unparliamentary language is dealt with immediately.[53]

The Speaker retains discretion over the acceptability of each statement and has the authority to order a Member to resume his or her seat if improper use is being made of this Standing Order.[54] As Speaker Parent noted, however, in a 1996 ruling, "the Chair is often caught between respect for freedom of speech and the rapid delivery of 60-second statements".[55] It is often difficult for the Chair to determine the direction a Member is going to take and thus the acceptability or otherwise of the remarks before the Member completes the statement.

ORAL QUESTIONS

The third event under the Daily Proceedings is "Oral Questions". Each sitting day, following "Statements by Members", at no later than 2:15 p.m. (11:15 a.m. on Friday), Question Period begins.[56] It lasts no longer than 45 minutes. At this time, Members may seek information from the Ministry by asking questions on matters falling within the jurisdiction of the federal government. Question Period is discussed extensively in Chapter 11, "Questions".

Routine Proceedings

The daily routine of business, commonly referred to as "Routine Proceedings", is a time in the daily schedule when business of a basic nature is considered, providing Members with an opportunity to bring a variety of matters to the attention of the House, generally without debate. The House proceeds to Routine Proceedings at the

---

49. See, for example, *Debates*, March 9, 1994, pp. 2036-7.

50. See, for example, *Debates*, November 27, 1997, p. 2379; February 26, 1998, p. 4495; June 9, 1998, p. 7807.

51. See, for example, *Debates*, February 27, 1985, p. 2542; February 25, 1993, p. 16461.

52. Standing Order 47. See, for example, *Debates*, November 28, 1991, pp. 5509-10; February 25, 1998, pp. 4406-7.

53. See, for example, *Debates*, June 19, 1992, pp. 12437, 12448; March 19, 1998, p. 5126.

54. Standing Order 31. On at least one occasion, the Speaker has allowed a Member who was initially asked to resume his seat to revise his statement and present an acceptable version at the conclusion of the period for "Statements by Members" (*Debates*, December 8, 1992, pp. 14849-51).

55. *Debates*, November 29, 1996, p. 6899.

56. Standing Order 30(5). On occasion, if "Statements by Members" has been delayed or extended, or if the Speaker has delivered a ruling that could impact on Question Period, the start of Question Period has been delayed. Under these circumstances, the Speaker has typically extended the time allotted for "Oral Questions". See, for example, *Debates*, May 2, 1994, pp. 3762-3; September 19, 1994, p. 5811.

opening of the sitting on Tuesday and Thursday (immediately after the Speaker has read the prayer and ordered the doors opened), at 3:00 p.m. on Monday and Wednesday, and at 12:00 noon on Friday (immediately following Question Period). [57]

This segment of the daily program consists of separate headings or rubrics called by the Speaker each day and considered in succession. These headings include:

- Tabling of Documents;
- Statements by Ministers;
- Presenting Reports from Inter-parliamentary Delegations;
- Presenting Reports from Committees;
- Introduction of Government Bills;
- Introduction of Private Members' Bills;
- First Reading of Senate Public Bills;
- Motions;
- Presenting Petitions;
- Questions on the *Order Paper.*

After Routine Proceedings on Wednesday, "Notices of Motions for the Production of Papers" is considered immediately after "Questions on the *Order Paper*". (For further details, see the relevant section later in this chapter.) Applications for emergency debates are also considered after Routine Proceedings, prior to the calling of Orders of the Day. (For further information, see Chapter 15, "Special Debates".)

As the Speaker calls each rubric in Routine Proceedings, Members who wish to bring forward matters rise in their place and are recognized. Usually they will have previously indicated to the Chair or the Table their wish to raise an item. [58] The amount of time required to complete Routine Proceedings varies from day to day depending on the number of items dealt with under each rubric.

All rubrics up to and including "Introduction of Government Bills" must be called each sitting day. Thus, at 2:00 p.m. on Tuesday and Thursday, "Statements by Members" interrupts Routine Proceedings if the rubric "Introduction of Government Bills" has not yet been completed. The ordinary daily routine of business then continues at 3:00 p.m., immediately after Question Period, until all items under "Introduction of Government Bills" are completed, suspending as much of the hour set

---

57. Standing Order 30(3). Routine Proceedings may be delayed if the Speaker delivers a ruling or is asked to consider a question of privilege or point of order.

58. On occasion, a Minister or Member is not present during Routine Proceedings to participate under a specific rubric, or a document is not available for presentation at the time. Later in the sitting, the Minister or Member may seek unanimous consent to revert to a specific rubric under Routine Proceedings to table a document or present a committee report, make a statement, present a petition or move a motion. See, for example, *Debates*, February 9, 1995, p. 9390; September 19, 1995, pp. 14622-3.

aside for Private Members' Business as necessary.[59] Obviously, this does not apply on Monday, Wednesday and Friday, since on those days "Statements by Members" and Question Period take place before Routine Proceedings. If the proceedings are not completed by the ordinary hour of daily adjournment on any sitting day, the House continues to sit until such time as all rubrics under Routine Proceedings up to and including "Introduction of Government Bills" have been called and completed. The Speaker then adjourns the House until the next sitting day.[60] However, on days when time remains for Routine Proceedings after "Introduction of Government Bills" is completed, Routine Proceedings could possibly continue until interrupted either by the normal adjournment of the sitting on Monday,[61] by "Statements by Members" on Tuesday and Thursday,[62] or by Private Members' Business on Wednesday and Friday.[63]

Historical Perspective

Since Confederation, the Standing Orders have provided for a daily routine of business. What has varied over time is its composition, its timing in the parliamentary day and the classes of items that could be dealt with under each rubric. For almost 40 years beginning in 1867, there were just four rubrics: "Presenting Petitions", "Reading and Receiving Petitions", "Presenting Reports by Standing and Select (later Special) Committees", and "Motions".[64] In 1906, the rubric "Introduction of Bills" was added after "Motions" in the sequence (bills having previously been presented under "Motions").[65] A few years later, in 1910, another rubric styled "First Reading of Senate Bills" was added after "Introduction of Bills," while at the same time the two rubrics dedicated to petitions were dropped.[66] The order of rubrics under Routine Proceedings did not change again until 1955 when "Government Notices of Motions" was added.[67] Twenty years later, in 1975, "Tabling of Documents"

---

59. Standing Order 30(4)(*a*). On September 25, 1989, a question of privilege was raised at the commencement of the sitting. The House was unable to proceed to Routine Proceedings until after Question Period later that afternoon. The House completed Routine Proceedings up to and including "Introduction of Government Bills" before proceeding to Government Orders. See *Debates*, September 25, 1989, p. 3842; *Journals*, pp. 492-505.

60. Standing Order 30(4)(*b*).

61. Standing Order 24(2).

62. Standing Order 30(5).

63. Standing Order 30(6). See, for example, *Journals*, April 23, 1997, p. 1519.

64. *Rules, Orders and Forms of Procedure of the House of Commons of Canada*, 1868, Rule No. 19.

65. *Rules, Orders and Forms of Procedure of the House of Commons of Canada*, 1906, Rule No. 25.

66. *Rules of the House of Commons of Canada*, 1910, Rule No. 25. Although the rubric for presenting petitions was removed, any Member wishing to present a petition in the House (as opposed to filing it with the Clerk) could do so anytime during Routine Proceedings before the introduction of bills (Rule No. 75). See also *Debates*, April 29, 1910, cols. 8365-7.

67. *Journals*, July 12, 1955, pp. 886-7. "Government Notices of Motions" had previously been an item set down in the order of business to be called after the daily routine of business.

and "Statements by Ministers" were added to Routine Proceedings to reflect and codify long-standing practices which had previously been dealt with under the rubric "Motions".[68] In 1986, the rubric "Presenting Reports from Inter-parliamentary Delegations" was created and the item "Presenting Petitions" was reinstated.[69]

In late 1986 and early 1987, the moving of motions "to proceed to Orders of the Day"[70] and "to proceed to the next item of Routine Proceedings"[71] during Routine Proceedings, combined with requests for recorded divisions on what would normally have been *pro forma* proceedings,[72] resulted not only in the House failing to reach Government Orders on occasion, but also prevented the government from introducing its legislation.[73] In the fall of 1986, a government bill to amend the *Patent Act* was placed on the *Order Paper*. The strong opposition to the bill led to the use of these motions during Routine Proceedings to delay introduction, first reading and

68. *Journals*, March 14, 1975, p. 373; March 24, 1975, p. 399. The headings under Routine Proceedings were reordered as follows: "Presenting Reports from Standing or Special Committees", "Tabling of Documents", "Statements by Ministers", "Introduction of Bills", "First Reading of Senate Public Bills", "Government Notices of Motions" and "Motions".

69. *Journals*, February 6, 1986, pp. 1663, 1665; February 13, 1986, p. 1710.

70. Standing Order 59 states that such a motion has preference over any other motion before the House. For examples of this motion being moved under different rubrics, see *Debates*, November 24, 1986, p. 1437 (moved under "Presenting Petitions"); March 20, 1997, pp. 9241-2 (moved under "Tabling of Documents"); March 19, 1997, pp. 9230-1; April 1, 1998, pp. 5649-50; June 2, 1998, pp. 7452-6 (moved during debate on a motion to concur in a committee report under "Motions"). On January 30, 1990, a motion to proceed to Orders of the Day was moved under "Tabling of Documents". A question of privilege was raised concerning the use of this motion to prevent Members from presenting petitions; the Chair ruled that this was not a matter of privilege (*Debates*, pp. 7588-9).

71. See, for example, *Debates*, November 7, 1986, pp. 1192-3; November 25, 1986, pp. 1485-8; April 8, 1987, p. 4983; April 9, 1987, pp. 4996-7. In all four examples, the motion was moved under "Presenting Petitions", which at that time preceded "Introduction of Bills".

72. For example, at that time motions for introduction and first reading of a public bill, even though not debatable, were votable, and recorded divisions were frequently demanded.

73. The moving of such motions during Routine Proceedings is a procedural tactic used by both the government and the opposition parties either to delay the progress of an item of business (for example, the introduction of bills, or the concurrence in a committee report) or to accelerate consideration of some matter by abruptly ending Routine Proceedings so that the House can proceed immediately to Orders of the Day. Indeed, the government often uses such motions to proceed as quickly as possible to Government Orders while the opposition employs them to delay the introduction of certain government bills, or the moving of government motions under the rubric "Motions", or even to prevent altogether the calling of "Orders of the Day".

second reading of the bill.[74] After the bill was considered by a legislative committee and reported back to the House with amendments,[75] the government gave notice of a time allocation motion respecting the report stage of the bill.[76] The government intended to move the time allocation motion under the rubric "Motions" during Routine Proceedings; however, the use of procedural tactics prevented the House from reaching this rubric.[77] On April 13, 1987, the government attempted to skip over certain rubrics under Routine Proceedings when the Parliamentary Secretary to the Deputy Prime Minister moved that the House proceed from "Tabling of Documents" to "Motions" which, if carried, would have had the effect of superseding all intervening rubrics. The Speaker had ruled out of order a similar motion only a few months earlier.[78] A point of order arose, a debate ensued and the Speaker reserved judgement.[79]

In his ruling,[80] Speaker Fraser expressed concern about the disruption which these procedural tactics had on Routine Proceedings and the inappropriate use of the rules of procedure as a substitute for debate: "It is a practice which can supersede the presentation of petitions, delay indefinitely the introductions of Bills—those of Private Members as well as those of the Government—and completely block debate on motions for concurrence in committee reports as well as on allocation of time motions."[81] Speaker Fraser stated that, in light of the various obstruction tactics

---

74. On November 6, 1986, at the conclusion of "Presenting Petitions", an Opposition Member moved that the House proceed to Orders of the Day. After the motion was negatived on a recorded division, a Minister moved the introduction of the bill; the motion was adopted on a recorded division. The following day, during "Presenting Petitions", an Opposition Member again moved the motion that the House proceed to the Orders of the Day, and the motion was again negatived on a recorded division. An Opposition Member then moved the motion "That a Member be now heard", which was agreed to without a recorded vote. The government subsequently moved that "The House do now proceed to the next item of Routine Proceedings" ("Introduction of Bills"); the motion was adopted on a recorded division. After motions for the introduction of two private Members' bills were negatived on recorded divisions, Bill C-22, *An Act to amend the Patent Act*, was finally read a first time and printed following a recorded division. See *Journals*, November 6, 1986, pp. 180-2; November 7, 1986, pp. 188-91. Also see *Debates*, November 7, 1986, pp. 1187-1202. Eight more recorded divisions, the majority of them resulting from the moving of these two motions, took place during Routine Proceedings before the bill was read a second time on December 8, 1987. See *Journals*, November 21, 1986, p. 224; November 24, 1986, pp. 229-30; November 25, 1986, pp. 234-5; December 3, 1986, p. 269-70; December 5, 1986, p. 280; December 8, 1986, pp. 286-8.

75. *Journals*, March 16, 1987, pp. 586-91.

76. *Journals*, April 7, 1987, p. 719.

77. See *Debates*, April 8, 1987, pp. 4983-8; April 9, 1987, pp. 4990-7.

78. *Debates*, November 24, 1986, p. 1435. The Speaker ruled that it is not in order to propose a motion that would exclude certain rubrics from consideration on a given sitting day (for example, to go from "Tabling of Documents" to "Motions").

79. *Debates*, April 13, 1987, pp. 5071-82.

80. See *Debates*, April 14, 1987, pp. 5119-22.

81. *Debates*, April 14, 1987, p. 5120.

which had been used by the opposition parties over the course of a few weeks in response to the controversial legislation and which had completely blocked debate on that and other government legislation, the interests of the House would be served best if the government were allowed to proceed, in this instance only, with its motion, which would supersede certain rubrics under Routine Proceedings. He cautioned, however, that the use of motions to supersede business during Routine Proceedings needed to be examined and "that no procedures should be sanctioned which would permit the House to be brought to a total standstill for an indefinite period."[82] He elaborated further that the decision was circumscribed by events for which the rules of procedure offered no solution and was not to be regarded as a precedent.

In June 1987, through amendments to the Standing Orders, the items under Routine Proceedings were reordered to their present form, the rubric "Introduction of Bills" was divided to create separate ones for the introduction of government bills and of private Members' bills, and the procedure for the completion of "Introduction of Government Bills" was adopted.[83] In addition, the rubric "Questions on the *Order Paper*" was inserted into the list of items, and "Government Notices of Motions" was dropped from Routine Proceedings.

TABLING OF DOCUMENTS

The first rubric called by the Speaker under Routine Proceedings is "Tabling of Documents". This rubric was added to Routine Proceedings in 1975.[84] Prior to that time, there was no set time for Ministers to table documents, although they would usually do so during Routine Proceedings under the rubric "Motions". The 1975 rule changes codified the practice already being followed in the presentation of papers.

The presentation of reports and returns[85] is one method by which the House obtains information. For many years if a paper to be tabled was in answer to an Order or Address of the House or in pursuance of a statute requiring its production, a Minister had only to rise, usually during Routine Proceedings, and formally present the document to the House. A record of its presentation was then printed in the *Journals*. If the government wished to table a document that had not been ordered, it was necessary to adopt a motion in order to allow its presentation.[86] In 1910, in response to the ever-increasing amount of House time taken to consider these motions, the House adopted a new rule in order to regulate their use.[87] The rule allowed Ministers simply to seek leave of the House to table these documents, a request customarily

---

82. *Debates*, April 14, 1987, p. 5121.
83. *Journals*, June 3, 1987, pp. 1017-8.
84. *Journals*, March 14, 1975, p. 373; March 24, 1975, p. 399.
85. Documents for which an order or address of the House for tabling has been made, or which are required by statute to be tabled.
86. See, for example, *Debates*, May 9, 1892, col. 2268; *Journals*, June 5, 1899, pp. 227-8.
87. *Journals*, April 29, 1910, pp. 536-7.

granted.[88] In 1968, the Standing Orders were amended to allow a Minister, or his or her Parliamentary Secretary, to table any report or paper so long as it dealt with a matter within the administrative competence of the government.[89] Since 1982, the government has also been required to table a comprehensive response to a committee report if the committee so requests,[90] and since 1986, to table responses to petitions referred to it[91] as well as announcements of Order-in-Council nominations or appointments.[92]

In addition to the administrative documents that may be tabled in the House by Ministers, certain returns, reports and other papers are required to be laid before the House each year or session by statute, by order of the House, or by Standing Order.[93] A number of statutes set forth the specific circumstances for tabling; for example, some statutes require Ministers to table annual reports of the departments, agencies and commissions which fall under their administrative responsibilities.[94]

A Minister or Parliamentary Secretary acting on behalf of the Minister may table documents in the House during Routine Proceedings when the rubric "Tabling of Documents" is called.[95] This method of tabling is often referred to as "front door" tabling.

As an alternative, the Standing Orders provide that papers required by statute, by order of the House, or by Standing Order may be deposited by a Minister with the Clerk of the House.[96] This is known as "back door" tabling. It is entirely at the discretion of the Minister involved as to which method to use for those documents that are required to be tabled; however, if a Minister wishes to table a document which is

---

88. See, for example, *Debates*, March 2, 1920, pp. 85-7; December 4, 1968, p. 3472.

89. Standing Order 32(2). See also *Journals*, December 20, 1968, pp. 569-70.

90. Standing Order 109. See *Journals*, November 29, 1982, p. 5400.

91. Standing Order 36(8). See *Journals*, February 6, 1986, p. 1665; February 13, 1986, pp. 1709-10.

92. Standing Order 110. See *Journals*, February 6, 1986, p. 1664; February 13, 1986, pp. 1709-10.

93. In April 1993, the Speaker ruled that a *prima facie* breach of privilege occurred when the government failed to table a document required by statute in a timely manner. The matter was subsequently referred to the Standing Committee on House Management. See *Debates*, February 24, 1993, pp. 16393-4; March 29, 1993, p. 17722; April 19, 1993, pp. 18104-6. In its report to the House, the Committee stated its belief that "... the statutory and procedural time limits must be complied with. If a document cannot be tabled within the prescribed time, the responsible Minister should advise the House accordingly before the deadline; it is not acceptable that the deadline is ignored." See Standing Committee on House Management, *Minutes of Proceedings and Evidence,* June 15, 1993, Issue No. 56, pp. 13-5 (One Hundred and First Report), presented on September 8, 1993 (*Journals*, p. 3338). The Thirty-Fourth Parliament (1988-93) was dissolved before the report could be considered by the House. See also *Debates*, February 3, 1992, pp. 6289-93; February 5, 1992, pp. 6425-8, when a related question of privilege was raised and ruled on.

94. Standing Order 153. At the beginning of each session of Parliament, the Clerk of the House has a list printed and delivered to all Members of all the reports and periodical documents which certain public officers, government departments and private corporations must have tabled in the House.

95. A Minister will often table a document under this rubric and then proceed to speak on its subject matter under the next rubric, "Statements by Ministers" (see, for example, *Journals*, May 25, 1994, pp. 472-3).

96. Standing Order 32(1). This Standing Order was implemented in 1955 as a time-saving procedure (see *Journals*, July 12, 1955, pp. 916-7).

not required to be tabled, it can only be tabled in the House during Routine Proceedings. Each sitting day, an entry is recorded in the *Journals* of all papers presented in the House or deposited with the Clerk.[97]

When a report, return or other paper is required to be laid before the House or an Order-in-Council appointment or nomination is tabled, it is automatically referred to an appropriate standing committee of the House by the Minister, usually according to its subject matter.[98] The referrals are permanent so that committees are not required to examine the documents by a specific deadline.[99]

All documents tabled in the House by a Minister or, as the case may be, by a Parliamentary Secretary, whether during a sitting or deposited with the Clerk, are required to be presented in both official languages.[100] Alternative versions (such as computer disks, audio cassettes, video cassettes or CD-ROMs, or documents in Braille or large print) have also been tabled along with the required document in both official languages.[101]

Any document quoted by a Minister in debate, or in response to a question, must be tabled.[102] This practice is examined in Chapter 13, "Rules of Order and Decorum".

97. Standing Order 32(3).

98. Standing Order 32(5) and (6). There have been instances when motions have been adopted, notwithstanding any order or practice of the House, to refer a report to more than one committee (see, for example, *Debates*, June 27, 1990, pp. 13172-3; February 27, 1991, p. 17715).

99. For further details, see Chapter 20, "Committees".

100. Standing Order 32(4). In 1988, a private Member's motion moved by Jean-Robert Gauthier (Ottawa–Vanier), calling on the House to require that official documents tabled or distributed in the House be in both French and English, was adopted, thus leading to the addition of this Standing Order to the rules of the House (*Journals*, September 16, 1988, p. 3556). See also *Debates*, June 8, 1989, pp. 2812-3; December 17, 1990, p. 16824.

101. See, for example, *Journals*, November 8, 1990, p. 2244 (audio cassette); May 12, 1992, p. 1445 (Braille summary and audio cassette); December 11, 1996, p. 991 (CD-ROM). See also *Debates*, November 8, 1990, pp. 15289-90; November 19, 1992, pp. 13604-5 (computer disk).

102. See, for example, *Debates*, October 17, 1995, p. 15488; October 2, 1997, p. 415; October 29, 1997, p. 1287; April 29, 1998, p. 6293. See also *Debates*, February 19, 1998, p. 4125, when the Parliamentary Secretary to the Government House Leader sought unanimous consent to table a newspaper article which was quoted by a Minister and which was available in English only. Consent was given.

Tabling of Documents by Private Members

There has been a long-standing practice in the House that private Members may not table documents, official or otherwise,[103] even with the unanimous consent of the House.[104] Unlike Ministers who must table documents required by statute or in respect to their administrative responsibilities,[105] the Standing Orders contain no provisions for private Members to table documents. Another reason against the tabling of documents by private Members relates to the availability of the document in both official languages as required by the rules.[106] However, since the 1980s, Members have been allowed on occasion to table documents with the unanimous consent of the House;[107] the documents have typically been tabled in only one language.[108] Private Members have sometimes placed on the Table material for the information of Members, although this is not considered an official tabling.[109]

103. *Journals*, April 6, 1971, pp. 475-6. Speaker Lamoureux submitted that while Ministers must table official documents cited in debate in support of an argument, this rule has never been interpreted to apply to a document, official or otherwise, referred to by private Members. In 1974, when a Member attempted to seek unanimous consent to table a document, Speaker Lamoureux stated that there was "no provision in the rules for a private Member to table or file documents in any way." The Speaker concluded by suggesting that Members "could presumably make them public in a number of other ways" (*Debates*, December 3, 1974, p. 1882). See also *Debates*, February 1, 1985, p. 1914; May 14, 1985, p. 4744; January 28, 1987, p. 2821.

104. Speakers have occasionally refused to put to the House a request by a private Member for unanimous consent to table a document. See, for example, *Debates*, March 25, 1985, pp. 3326-7; June 27, 1986, p. 15006.

105. Standing Order 32(1) and (2).

106. Standing Order 32(4).

107. See, for example, *Debates*, June 8, 1989, pp. 2812-3; December 5, 1990, p. 16330; November 30, 1992, p. 14276; February 1, 1994, p. 690; March 16, 1994, p. 2369; October 2, 1997, p. 415; February 13, 1998, p. 3866. By special order of the House, private Members tabled documents during debate on the reform of the Constitution in 1992 (*Journals*, February 5, 1992, p. 975; *Debates*, pp. 6429-30). The first time a private Member was allowed to seek unanimous consent to table a document occurred on November 15, 1978, although it appears that there may have been consultation or agreement with the government to do so (*Debates*, pp. 1160-1). Speaker Sauvé tried twice to discourage Members from tabling material by unanimous consent, but allowed the request to be made (*Debates*, January 18, 1983, pp. 21954-5; May 6, 1983, p. 25229). Speaker Francis allowed unanimous consent to be sought on two separate occasions (*Debates*, February 14, 1984, pp. 1362-3; April 18, 1984, p. 3185). Speaker Bosley regularly refused such requests (see, for example, *Debates*, February 13, 1985, p. 2313; September 23, 1985, p. 6864). In 1986, in allowing a Member to table a document by unanimous consent, Speaker Fraser advised the House that while he would abide by its wishes, "the House has quite clearly decided to move outside the usual practice" (*Debates*, October 24, 1986, pp. 709-10).

108. See, for example, *Journals*, December 5, 1990, p. 2379; November 30, 1992, p. 2254; February 1, 1994, p. 88; March 16, 1994, p. 260; October 2, 1997, p. 70.

109. See, for example, *Debates*, June 13, 1991, p. 1646. See also Speaker's comments, *Debates*, February 24, 1992, p. 7531.

Tabling of documents by private Members is also examined in Chapter 13, "Rules of Order and Decorum".

Tabling of Documents by the Speaker

The Speaker tables documents pertaining to the administrative or ceremonial functions of the office of the Speaker or to the procedural affairs of the House itself.[110] As chairman of the Board of Internal Economy, the Speaker also tables:

- Minutes of Proceedings of the Board of Internal Economy;[111]

- Annual reports on committee activities and expenditures;[112]

- The By-laws, and amendments thereto, of the Board of Internal Economy;[113]

- The annual *Report on Plans and Priorities* of the House of Commons Administration as approved by the Board of Internal Economy;[114]

- The annual *Performance Report* on the House of Commons Administration as approved by the Board of Internal Economy.[115]

The Speaker also tables the annual report of the Parliamentary Librarian.[116]

---

110. See, for example, *Journals*, April 5, 1989, p. 26 (*Annotated Standing Orders of the House of Commons*); February 4, 1992, p. 970 (report of an official visit); September 8, 1992, p. 1924 (documentation concerning a recall of the House); June 1, 1993, p. 3091 (report concerning initiatives undertaken by the House to serve Canadians with disabilities); September 23, 1997, pp. 11-2 (letter from government concerning notice of two government motions for a *Special Order Paper*; copy of the Speech from the Throne); September 24, 1997, p. 19 (Standing Orders of the House of Commons); October 1, 1997, p. 56 (Estimates of the House of Commons); October 23, 1997, p. 139 (Report of the Administration of the House for the Thirty-Fifth Parliament).

111. Standing Order 148(1) requires the Speaker to table, within 10 calendar days after the opening of each session, a report containing the minutes of the Board's meetings for the previous session (see, for example, *Journals*, May 16, 1991, p. 36; January 27, 1994, p. 71). Since June 1994, the minutes have been tabled as soon as they are approved by the Board (see *Debates*, June 8, 1994, p. 5030). They are typically deposited with the Clerk of the House and recorded in the *Journals* (see, for example, *Journals*, October 10, 1997, p. 109; February 13, 1998, p. 464).

112. Standing Order 121(4). See, for example, *Journals*, September 30, 1994, p. 758; September 18, 1995, p. 1908; October 10, 1997, p. 109; October 9, 1998, p. 1145. Standing Order 148(2) also requires the Speaker to table any Board of Internal Economy decision concerning committee budgets. See, for example, *Journals*, January 15, 1991, pp. 2560-1; June 10, 1993, p. 3197. Since the Thirty-Fifth Parliament (1994-97), these decisions are part of the Board minutes which are now laid upon the Table as soon as they are approved.

113. *Parliament of Canada Act*, R.S.C. 1985, c. P-1 as amended by S.C. 1991, c. 20, s. 2 (sbs. 52.5(2)). Any by-laws made by the Board are to be tabled within 30 calendar days of their making. They are typically deposited with the Clerk of the House and recorded in the *Journals* (see, for example, *Journals*, December 2, 1996, p. 950; October 10, 1997, p. 109; February 13, 1998, p. 464).

114. See, for example, *Journals*, March 25, 1998, p. 620; March 5, 1999, p. 1561.

115. See, for example, *Journals*, November 18, 1998, p. 1271.

116. See, for example, *Journals*, February 2, 1999, p. 1455.

In addition, various statutes identify the Speaker as the individual through whom reports are to be laid before the House.[117] In particular, statutory requirements exist whereby five designated officers of Parliament transmit their annual reports and any special investigative reports to the Speaker who then tables them in the House: the Chief Electoral Officer, the Auditor General, the Commissioner of Official Languages, the Access to Information Commissioner and the Privacy Commissioner.[118] The Speaker also tables the annual report of the Canadian Human Rights Commission,[119] and reports of the provincial and territorial electoral boundaries commissions in the decennial process to readjust constituency boundaries after the reports have been forwarded to him by the Chief Electoral Officer.[120]

Tabling of Documents During Periods of Adjournment or Prorogation

Since 1994, the Standing Orders have contained provisions allowing Ministers during periods of adjournment to deposit once a month with the Clerk of the House, on the Wednesday following the 15th day of any month during the period of adjournment, any returns, reports or other papers required to be laid before the House pursuant to statute, Special Order, or Standing Order of the House, including responses to petitions and to committee reports.[121] On the first sitting day following the adjournment, these documents are then entered in the *Journals* as having been deemed tabled on that Wednesday.[122] However, even if a document is technically due during the adjournment period, a Minister still has the option of waiting until the first sitting day following the adjournment to table it in the House or deposit it with the Clerk.[123]

---

117. See, for example, *Journals*, September 24, 1997, p. 20 (Proceedings of the Royal Society of Canada for 1995); May 26, 1998, p. 891 (Report of the Commissioner of the Environment and Sustainable Development to the House for the year 1998).

118. *Canada Elections Act*, R.S.C. 1985, c. E-2, s. 195(3); *Auditor General Act*, R.S.C. 1985, c. A-17, ss. 7(3), 8(2), 19(2) as amended by S.C. 1994, c. 32; *Official Languages Act*, R.S.C. 1985, 4th Supp., c. 31, ss. 65(3), 66, 67(1), 69(1); *Access to Information Act*, R.S.C. 1985, c. A-1, ss. 38, 39(1), 40; *Privacy Act*, R.S.C. 1985, c. P-21, ss. 38, 39(1), 40(1). See, for example, *Journals*, November 26, 1996, p. 918; April 8, 1997, p. 1351; September 24, 1997, pp. 19-20; September 29, 1997, p. 40.

119. The *Canadian Human Rights Act*, S.C. 1998, c. 9, s. 32. See, for example, *Journals*, March 23, 1999, p. 1649.

120. *Electoral Boundaries Readjustment Act*, R.S.C. 1985, c. E-3, s. 21(1) as amended by c. 6 (2nd Supp.), s. 5. See, for example, *Journals*, June 22, 1995, p. 1867. If Parliament is not sitting, the reports are tabled on any of the first five sitting days when the House returns. See Chapter 4, "The House of Commons and Its Members", for additional information.

121. Standing Order 32(1). See the Twenty-Seventh Report of the Standing Committee on Procedure and House Affairs, presented on June 8, 1994 (*Journals*, p. 545), and concurred in on June 10, 1994 (*Journals*, p. 563). See also Standing Committee on Procedure and House Affairs, *Minutes of Proceedings and Evidence*, June 9, 1994, Issue No. 16, pp. 3-4.

122. See, for example, *Journals*, September 18, 1995, pp. 1894, 1904; February 3, 1997, p. 1034; February 2, 1998, p. 404; September 21, 1998, pp. 1040, 1053.

123. See, for example, *Journals*, September 18, 1995, p. 1908 (deposited with Clerk on first sitting day).

As a general principle, a prorogation puts an end to all proceedings pending in Parliament. Sometimes, however, various papers and documents requested by the House (also referred to as returns) cannot be prepared for tabling in the same session in which they were requested. As these papers and documents are obtained either by a direct Order of the House or by an Address to the Governor General, the ordinary effect of a prorogation would be to force a renewal, in the next session, of these Orders and Addresses for which returns are not yet ready. However, pursuant to the Standing Orders of the House, they are considered to have been readopted at the start of the new session without a motion to that effect. [124] The Speaker has ruled that outstanding responses to committee reports and to petitions are also given the status of returns ordered by the House and therefore would be tabled in the House in the new session. [125]

Tabling of Documents After a Dissolution

After a dissolution, the Clerk of the House does not accept in advance for tabling in the next Parliament any returns, reports or other papers required to be tabled pursuant to an Act of Parliament or a resolution or Standing Order of the House. During the period when Parliament is dissolved, however, Ministers or government departments may authorize the release of any return, report or other paper required to be laid before the House. When the new Parliament opens, returns, reports and papers are tabled as required by Ministers on the opening day of Parliament. [126]

STATEMENTS BY MINISTERS

The second rubric under Routine Proceedings is "Statements by Ministers". Under this rubric, Ministers make announcements or statements on government policy or matters of national interest. [127] Following the ministerial statement, a spokesperson from each recognized party in opposition is permitted to respond. [128]

---

124. Standing Order 49.

125. *Debates*, June 27, 1986, p. 14969.

126. See, for example, *Journals*, January 18, 1994, pp. 19-26; September 23, 1997, pp. 15-7.

127. Frequently, a Minister will first table a document under the rubric "Tabling of Documents". The subsequent statement will expand on the context of the tabled document (see, for example, *Journals*, May 25, 1994, pp. 472-3; *Debates*, pp. 4395-400). Prime Ministers have also used this proceeding to make announcements in the House (see, for example, *Debates*, November 27, 1989, pp. 6229, 6234-39 (visit to U.S.S.R); June 11, 1990, pp. 12590, 12604-10 (Meech Lake Accord); September 24, 1991, pp. 2585-91 (proposals to renew Canadian federation); February 8, 1994, pp. 1029-32 (tobacco smuggling); June 16, 1994, pp. 5395-7 (integrity in government); November 22, 1994, p. 8097 (appointment of new Governor General); June 10, 1999, pp. 16195-6 (Kosovo)). The Leaders of the recognized parties in opposition customarily respond to the Prime Minister's statement.

128. Standing Order 33(1).

Historical Perspective

This rubric is of recent origin, though the practice of receiving statements from Ministers has been well established for years. At Confederation, no provision existed in the written rules for the kind of ministerial statements that are now possible. Nonetheless, beginning in 1867, Ministers rose from time to time just before Orders of the Day to make presentations on matters of government policy or public interest.[129] In addition, until at least 1915, Prime Ministers frequently made statements to explain changes in the membership of the Cabinet.[130] Representatives of the opposition parties routinely responded to policy statements, while ministerial changes traditionally elicited comments from the Leader of the Opposition.

As the number of policy statements increased, House practice became more defined; by the early 1950s it had become customary to allow only party leaders to respond to the statements. By 1959, not only had the practice reverted from allowing responses only from party leaders to allowing responses from one speaker from each of the opposition parties, but statements took place under the rubric "Motions" during Routine Proceedings, instead of just before Orders of the Day. A further modification to the practice occurred that year when the Speaker advised the House that he considered unacceptable any opposition responses which "went beyond the length of the statement itself ...".[131]

In 1964, a Standing Order was adopted both to formalize the tradition of making statements under "Motions" and to provide guidelines by which the procedure could be regulated. The new rule allowed for factual pronouncements of government policy which did not provoke debate. It also codified the existing practice of responses by opposition parties.[132] This last aspect of the rule later provoked a discussion on the question of what constituted a party for the purposes of the Standing Order, with some Members citing the *Senate and House of Commons Act* (now known as the *Parliament of Canada Act*) which provided additional allowances to leaders of parties with more than 12 Members. In the end, the Speaker concluded that, until the House defined more precisely who could respond to a ministerial statement, the Chair would be guided by practice, which had long allowed each party, but not independent Members, an opportunity to comment on ministerial statements.[133]

---

129. See, for example, *Debates*, December 12, 1867, pp. 257-63; September 12, 1919, pp. 242-58; April 19, 1932, pp. 2150-4; June 4, 1940, pp. 482-5.

130. See, for example, *Debates*, February 12, 1877, pp. 32-3; February 16, 1915, pp. 207-8.

131. *Debates*, March 24, 1959, pp. 2177-8.

132. See the Third Report of the Special Committee on Procedure and Organization, concurred in on May 7, 1964 (*Journals*, p. 297); see also *Debates*, May 7, 1964, pp. 3007-10, in particular the comments of Stanley Knowles (Winnipeg North Centre).

133. See *Journals*, February 18, 1966, pp. 158-60. See also *Debates*, February 15, 1966, pp. 1224-7; *Senate and House of Commons Act*, S.C. 1963, c. 14, s. 3.

These guidelines remained in effect until 1975 when, on the recommendation of a procedure committee, the way in which ministerial statements were commented upon was modified to allow both comments by opposition representatives and questions by Members in general. At the same time, the Speaker was given full discretion in limiting the time taken up by such proceedings, which would now be conducted under a newly created item in Routine Proceedings called "Statements by Ministers".[134] In the beginning, the new procedure worked well, although before long it became lengthy and difficult to regulate—so much so that the making of policy statements and announcements in the House fell into disuse in order, it seems, to preserve valuable House time for other government business.[135] Following the recommendations of two special committees examining procedural reforms in the early and mid-1980s, the House made several changes to the conduct of "Statements by Ministers". Rules were introduced to encourage Ministers to make public through the House any announcements of government policy by eliminating the "mini-question period" that generally followed a statement, permitting only a comment by a representative of each opposition party.[136] These changes were finally adopted on a provisional basis in June 1985 and in February 1986, and made permanent in June 1987.[137] The new rules also adjusted the schedule of the sitting so as to preserve the amount of time reserved for Government Orders and Private Members' Business, by extending the sitting if necessary beyond the ordinary hour of daily adjournment by the amount of time taken by the statement.[138]

Guidelines

During "Statements by Ministers", Ministers are expected to make brief and factual statements on government policy or announcements of national interest.[139] Only Members speaking on behalf of parties recognized by the House are

---

134. See the Second Report of the Standing Committee on Procedure and Organization, presented on March 14, 1975 (*Journals*, p. 373) and concurred in on March 24, 1975 (*Journals*, p. 399). See also *Journals*, April 18, 1975, pp. 459-60, for a statement by the Speaker on the operation of this new rule.

135. See *Debates*, February 10, 1983, pp. 22716-7.

136. See Special Committee on Standing Orders and Procedure, *Minutes of Proceedings and Evidence,* September 29, 1983, Issue No. 24, pp. 3-5, and *Journals*, September 30, 1983, p. 6250; Special Committee on the Reform of the House of Commons, *Minutes of Proceedings and Evidence,* December 19, 1984, Issue No. 2, pp. 18-9, and *Journals*, December 20, 1984, p. 211.

137. *Journals*, June 27, 1985, pp. 912-3, 919; February 6, 1986, p. 1647; February 13, 1986, p. 1710; June 3, 1987, pp. 1018-9.

138. Prior to 1994, the extension of the sitting could take place during the lunch hour (see, for example, *Debates*, February 27, 1992, p. 7682; May 14, 1992, p. 10695). If necessary, any additional time was added to the end of the day (see, for example, *Debates*, March 12, 1987, pp. 4085, 4098; September 24, 1991, pp. 2605-6).

139. Standing Order 33(1). On one occasion, two Ministers made a joint statement (see *Debates*, March 24, 1999, pp. 13442-4).

permitted to speak in response to a Minister's statement.[140] However, with the unanimous consent of the House, other Members have been allowed to respond.[141] In responding to the statement, Members are not permitted to engage in debate or ask questions of the Minister.[142] The length of each response may not exceed the length of the Minister's statement; Members who exceed this length are interrupted by the Speaker.[143] The rules provide no explicit limitation of time allotted to the Minister or the overall time to be taken for these proceedings, although the duration of the proceedings can be limited at the discretion of the Chair.[144]

A Minister is under no obligation to make a statement in the House. The decision of a Minister to make an announcement outside of the House instead of making a statement in the House during Routine Proceedings has been raised as a question of privilege, but the Chair has consistently found there to be no grounds to support a claim that any privilege has been breached.[145]

It is customary that as a courtesy, a Minister advises opposition critics in advance of his or her intention to make a statement in the House. However, should no such warning be given, custom does not prohibit the Minister from making a statement.[146]

The length of time taken up by a Minister's statement and opposition replies is added to the time provided for government business on the day on which the statement is made. Accordingly, the hour for Private Members' Business, where applicable, and the ordinary hour of daily adjournment, including the Adjournment Proceedings, may be delayed.[147]

PRESENTING REPORTS FROM INTER-PARLIAMENTARY DELEGATIONS

"Presenting Reports from Inter-parliamentary Delegations" is the third rubric under Routine Proceedings. This rubric was created in 1986 following a recommendation

---

140. See, for example, *Debates*, October 25, 1990, pp. 14665-9. See also *Debates*, June 19, 1991, p. 2084; June 1, 1992, p. 11166; June 3, 1992, pp. 11306-7.

141. See, for example, *Debates*, March 10, 1992, pp. 7883-4; November 24, 1992, pp. 13905-6; February 8, 1994, p. 1034; April 27, 1995, p. 11843; March 8, 1996, p. 489. On one occasion, the chairman of a standing committee received unanimous consent to respond to a ministerial statement (*Debates*, March 16, 1994, p. 2364). Government backbenchers have also been granted unanimous consent to respond to ministerial statements (*Debates*, February 8, 1994, p. 1035; March 12, 1997, p. 8955).

142. See, for example, *Debates*, April 11, 1994, p. 2867.

143. Standing Order 33(1). See, for example, *Debates*, May 25, 1994, p. 4400; June 9, 1994, p. 5059.

144. Standing Order 33(1).

145. See, for example, *Debates*, November 1, 1974, p. 957; March 2, 1977, pp. 3578-9; February 17, 1978, p. 2972; February 8, 1982, p. 14755; December 2, 1985, p. 9027; October 4, 1989, p. 4309; February 18, 1998, p. 4073; December 3, 1998, pp. 10826-31.

146. See, for example, *Debates*, March 18, 1987, p. 4305; April 2, 1987, p. 4810; April 8, 1987, p. 4982; April 12, 1988, pp. 14357-62; April 11, 1994, p. 2867; October 27, 1994, pp. 7273-4.

147. Standing Order 33(2). There have been occasions when the consideration of Government Orders has been extended by more than 60 minutes: *Debates*, March 12, 1987, pp. 4085, 4098 (71 minutes); September 24, 1991, pp. 2605-6 (107 minutes); October 29, 1991, p. 4141 (67 minutes); February 7, 1995, p. 9253 (80 minutes).

of a special committee to provide a means by which inter-parliamentary delegations could report their work to the House.[148]

Members frequently travel abroad or within Canada on officially recognized inter-parliamentary delegations as representatives of both the House and Parliament. An officially recognized inter-parliamentary delegation is a delegation, composed in whole or in part of Members of the House, which has either been appointed and funded by the Speaker or by a recognized parliamentary association to represent the House or that association at an official inter-parliamentary activity either in Canada or abroad.

A parliamentary association is an international association, whose Canadian component is composed of both Members and Senators, which provides a forum for the exchange of ideas and information and for the sharing of knowledge and experience through person-to-person contact.[149] The main activities of these associations include exchanges, conferences and seminars on various subjects. The Canadian Parliament is a participant in 10 official parliamentary associations:

- Canada-China Legislative Exchange;
- Canada-France Inter-parliamentary Association;
- Canada-Japan Inter-parliamentary Group;
- Canada-United Kingdom Parliamentary Association;
- Canada-United States Inter-parliamentary Group;
- *Assemblée parlementaire de la Francophonie (APF)*;
- Canada-Europe Parliamentary Association;
- Commonwealth Parliamentary Association (CPA);
- Inter-parliamentary Union (IPU);
- North Atlantic Assembly (Canadian NATO Parliamentary Association).

---

148. See page 47 of the Third Report of the Special Committee on the Reform of the House of Commons, presented on June 18, 1985 (*Journals*, p. 839). The proposed amendments to the Standing Orders were tabled on February 6, 1986 (*Journals*, p. 1663), and adopted on February 13, 1986 (*Journals*, p. 1710). Similar concerns had been expressed as early as 1973, when a Member proposed a motion aimed at "bringing to the attention of the House of Commons ... some of the deliberations that are held at the various meetings of the IPU" (*Debates*, March 1, 1973, pp. 1803-9). This idea was also mentioned in 1977 (*Debates*, December 20, 1977, p. 2054).

149. On one occasion, a question of privilege was raised in regard to the announcement by a Minister of the creation of a new parliamentary association. The Member who raised the matter argued that the creation of inter-parliamentary groups is not an executive matter to be decided by Cabinet. In his ruling, Speaker Parent agreed that the Minister overreached his authority. He stressed that the creation of parliamentary associations is governed by certain administrative bodies within the House of Commons and the Senate. See *Debates*, April 21, 1998, pp. 5910-4; April 23, 1998, pp. 6035-7.

These associations choose delegates to participate in and host meetings, seminars and international conferences with counterpart countries. Each association, operating under established constitutions, elects a number of parliamentarians from its membership to form an Executive Committee. Staff support and funding are provided by the Senate and the House of Commons.

In addition to these parliamentary associations, the Canadian Parliament also participates in three formally recognized friendship groups, whose Canadian component is composed of both Members and Senators, established to increase mutual understanding between Canada and another country through bilateral exchanges. The three formally recognized friendship groups are:

- Canada-Germany Friendship Group;
- Canada-Israel Friendship Group;
- Canada-Italy Friendship Group.

Friendship groups receive administrative assistance from the House and Senate but do not receive funds to cover meetings and travel expenses. Their sole source of revenue is membership fees they receive from individual parliamentarians.

Each inter-parliamentary delegation is required to present to the House a report on its activities on any trip taken in fulfillment of its duties, either in Canada or abroad, within 20 sitting days of its return.[150] The report typically includes the names of the Members who participated on the delegation, the travel dates, and information on the delegation's activities and on the cost of the trip. When "Presenting Reports from Inter-parliamentary Delegations" is called by the Speaker during Routine Proceedings, the head of the delegation, or a Member acting on his or her behalf, rises and presents the report.[151] The Member may comment briefly on the content of the report at this time; no debate is permitted.[152] The Speaker has also presented reports after official visits abroad by parliamentary delegations headed by a presiding officer.[153] The report is recorded as a sessional paper and as such is open to public scrutiny.[154] No other action is taken.

PRESENTING REPORTS FROM COMMITTEES

Any information to be transmitted to the House from standing, special or legislative committees and standing or special joint committees of the House must be

---

150. Standing Order 34(1). The Standing Order was amended in 1987 to increase from 10 to 20 the number of sitting days within which delegations must present a report (*Journals*, June 3, 1987, p. 1026).

151. On occasion, Members have been granted unanimous consent to present a report from an unofficial delegation (see, for example, *Debates*, February 25, 1998, p. 4407; March 5, 1999, p. 12504; April 21, 1999, p. 14162).

152. Standing Order 34(2).

153. See, for example, *Debates*, February 4, 1992, p. 6376; May 16, 1996, p. 2851; March 10, 1997, p. 8842.

154. Any document tabled in the House or filed with the Clerk during a session of Parliament is given a sessional paper number. All documents tabled or filed are open to public scrutiny.

presented by way of a report. Committees submit reports on a variety of subjects, including:

- bills;
- Estimates;
- subject matter inquiries;
- matters concerning the mandate, management and operation of the departments assigned to them;
- Order-in-Council appointments and nominations;
- delegated legislation;
- provisions in statutes requiring a review.

This is done under "Presenting Reports from Committees", the fourth rubric under Routine Proceedings and one of the four original rubrics provided for in the rules of the House at the time of Confederation. When the Speaker calls this rubric, the committee chair, or in his or her absence a Member of the committee, once recognized by the Speaker, rises in his or her place to present the report and to provide "a succinct explanation of the subject matter of the report".[155] If the committee has adopted a motion to request a response from the government to its report, that request is communicated orally at the time.[156] Provided that a report is tabled in printed format in both official languages, it may also be tabled in alternative forms of media, such as on computer disk, audio cassette, video cassette or CD-ROM, or in Braille or large

155. Standing Order 35(1). In 1985, a special committee recommended that Members presenting reports to the House be allowed to give a brief explanation thereof in order to bring the reports to the attention of the House (see page 22 of the Third Report of the Special Committee on the Reform of the House of Commons, presented on June 18, 1985 (*Journals*, p. 839)). The present Standing Order was adopted on February 13, 1986 (see *Journals*, February 6, 1986, p. 1663; February 13, 1986, p. 1710). If a chair's remarks go beyond the scope of the report, the Speaker may interrupt the Member (see, for example, *Debates*, December 4, 1992, pp. 14654-5). On occasion, an opposition Member has received unanimous consent to comment on a report (*Debates*, October 18, 1994, p. 6816; October 31, 1994, p. 7430). Until 1955, each report presented in the House was read in its entirety by a Table Officer, and the text was also included in the *Journals* for that day. If the report was lengthy, its reading was often dispensed with. After 1955, this practice was abandoned and the only reports read were those for which the Member presenting had stated his or her intention to move concurrence later the same day (*Journals*, July 12, 1955, p. 944). Still the texts of all reports, both read and not read, were included in the *Journals*. This arrangement remained in effect until 1981 when it was decided to include only the texts of reports on bills and Estimates in the *Journals* (see *Debates*, December 11, 1981, pp. 13973-4). Reports for which the Member presenting stated an intention of moving concurrence later the same day continued to be read by a Table Officer during the 1980s. The practice now is to have such reports read by a Table Officer only when so requested by the Speaker before the House is asked for unanimous consent to proceed immediately with the concurrence motion. See, for example, *Debates*, September 27, 1991, p. 2848.

156. Standing Order 109. The government is obliged to table the response within 150 calendar days of the tabling of the report. The Speaker has ruled that a committee may request a response to only part of its report, but the whole of the report nonetheless remains open to comment by the government (*Debates*, May 13, 1986, p. 13232).

print. [157] All related *Minutes of Proceedings* of the committee are also tabled with the report.

While there is no provision in the rules for the tabling of minority reports, [158] since April 1991 committees have been permitted to append supplementary or dissenting opinions or recommendations to their reports. [159] Following the presentation of the report and any statement offered by the chair or presenting Member, a committee member representing the Official Opposition, speaking on behalf of those who support the opinions expressed in the appended material, may provide a brief explanation of these views. [160] No other Member may comment on the report at this time. [161]

---

157. See, for example, *Journals*, June 14, 1993, p. 3204; June 16, 1993, p. 3318; September 8, 1993, pp. 3338-9.

158. See *Journals*, July 24, 1969, pp. 1397-9; March 16, 1972, pp. 194-5; *Debates*, November 24, 1994, pp. 8252-3.

159. Standing Order 108(1)(*a*). Standing committees are permitted to "... report from time to time and to print a brief appendix to any report, after the signature of the chairman, containing such opinions or recommendations, dissenting from the report or supplementary to it, as may be proposed by committee members ..." Such material is only appended following the adoption of a motion to do so by the committee prior to the presentation of the report to the House. In 1994, a point of order was raised in the House regarding the printing of dissenting opinions in a report by the Special Joint Committee Reviewing Canada's Foreign Policy. The dissenting opinions were printed in a second volume instead of being appended after the signature of the chair. Although the Speaker ruled that the report as presented would be accepted by the House, he stated that the dissenting opinions should have been printed after the signature of the chair pursuant to the wording of the Standing Order. In addition, Speaker Parent cautioned committees to observe carefully the terms of Standing Order 108(1)(*a*) in the future (see *Debates*, November 24, 1994, pp. 8252-3). While this Standing Order refers only to standing committees, it has become the practice of the House to also apply the Standing Order to special committees (see *Debates*, November 24, 1994, p. 8252). See also Chapter 20, "Committees", for additional information on the format of committee reports.

160. Standing Order 35(2). A committee member from the Official Opposition has an equal amount of time as that of the presenter of the committee report (*Debates*, October 18, 1994, p. 6816; November 7, 1997, pp. 1715-6). Since the introduction of this rule in April 1991 (*Journals*, April 11, 1991, pp. 2905, 2908), some inconsistency has surrounded its implementation. Members often refer to "dissenting opinions" as minority reports and, at times, Members have sought and have been permitted to "table minority reports" following the presentation of the main committee report (see, for example, *Debates*, December 12, 1991, pp. 6171-2; June 16, 1993, p. 20921). However, as Speaker Parent noted in a 1994 ruling: "Regardless of how the media or members themselves may label such dissent, the House has never recognized or permitted the tabling of minority reports. Speaker Lamoureux twice condemned the idea of minority reports, explaining to the House that what is presented to the House from a committee is a report from the committee, not a report from the majority" (see *Debates*, November 24, 1994, p. 8252).

161. On occasion, however, Members not belonging to the Official Opposition have sought and received unanimous consent to speak (see, for example, *Debates*, April 13, 1994, p. 2980; November 7, 1997, p. 1716; December 1, 1997, p. 2503). When two dissenting opinions are appended to a report, a Member from a party other than the Official Opposition may only comment on the appended material with the consent of the House (see *Debates*, May 14, 1992, p. 10692). If the Official Opposition does not append a dissenting opinion, but a third party does, a Member from the third party may only give an explanation of these views with the unanimous consent of the House (see *Debates*, June 18, 1992, p. 12322; June 21, 1995, p. 14322).

A motion to concur in a committee report may be moved during Routine Proceedings under "Motions", following the 48-hour written notice requirement. However, after presenting a report, usually on a non-controversial matter, a committee
chair may advise that he or she intends to move concurrence in it later in the sitting,
with the unanimous consent of the House. When "Motions" is called, the chair rises
and seeks the unanimous consent of the House to move concurrence. If requested, a
Table Officer will typically read the report aloud because printed copies of the report
are not readily available to Members in the House.[162] Concurrence is often granted
without debate.

Further information on committee reports is found in Chapter 20, "Committees".

INTRODUCTION OF GOVERNMENT BILLS

"Introduction of Government Bills" comes immediately after the presentation of
committee reports. Prior to June 1987, all public bills sponsored either by the government or private Members were introduced under the rubric "Introduction of
Bills". As a result of amendments to the Standing Orders, the rubric was divided into
"Introduction of Government Bills" and "Introduction of Private Members' Bills".[163]

Legislation emanating from the Ministry is first presented for the consideration
of the House during Routine Proceedings under this rubric. Following a minimum
48-hour notice period,[164] any public bill sponsored by the government is placed on
the *Order Paper* in chronological order. When "Introduction of Government Bills"
is called by the Speaker, the Minister wishing to introduce a bill signals his or her
desire to proceed with the bill (advance notice having been given to the Chair of the
Minister's desire to introduce a bill), thereupon the Speaker proposes the motion for
leave to introduce the bill. The following formula is used: *"(name of Minister),
seconded by (name of Member), moves for leave to introduce a bill intitled: 'An Act
to ...'."*[165] A motion for leave to introduce a bill is deemed carried, without debate,

---

162. See, for example, *Debates*, September 27, 1991, p. 2848.

163. See *Journals*, June 3, 1987, pp. 1016, 1018.

164. Standing Order 54(1). On occasion, the 48-hour notice requirement for the introduction of a government bill
has been waived with the unanimous consent of the House (see, for example, *Debates*, December 19,
1990, p. 16951; October 10, 1991, pp. 3557, 3559; February 14, 1992, p. 7056; May 5, 1992, pp. 10145-6;
February 8, 1994, p. 1035). The notice requirement has also been waived pursuant to Standing Order 53
(*Journals*, March 15, 1995, p. 1219). See Chapter 12, "The Process of Debate", for additional information
on notice requirements.

165. Standing Order 68(1). This Standing Order has remained unchanged since its adoption in 1867. See
Rule No. 39 in *Rules, Orders and Forms of Proceeding of the House of Commons of Canada*, 1868. See
Chapter 16, "The Legislative Process", for additional information on the introduction and first reading of
government bills.

amendment or question put.[166] After the motion has been agreed to, the Minister may give a succinct explanation of the bill.[167]

Immediately after the motion for leave to introduce a bill is adopted, the Speaker proposes to the House that the bill be read a first time and be printed.[168] This motion is also deemed carried, without debate, amendment or question put.[169] A Table Officer then rises and declares, *"First reading of this bill/ Première lecture de ce projet de loi"*.[170] The Speaker completes the process by routinely asking, *"When shall*

---

166. Standing Order 68(2). From 1867 to 1913, the motion for leave to introduce a bill was debatable and amendable. In April 1913, in an attempt to define and lessen the number of motions considered debatable, the Standing Orders were amended. Among those motions no longer held to be debatable was the motion for leave to introduce a bill (*Journals*, April 23, 1913, pp. 507-9). However, Members could still negative the motion for leave to introduce, although this usually happened only in regard to private Members' bills (see, for example, *Debates*, February 22, 1932, pp. 380-4; August 3, 1964, p. 6285; November 13, 1967, pp. 4165-6; December 5, 1967, pp. 5035-6; November 7, 1986, p. 1193). In April 1991, the Standing Order was amended to provide that the motion for leave would automatically be deemed carried, without debate, amendment or question put (*Journals*, April 11, 1991, p. 2913).

167. Standing Order 68(2). Ministers rarely take this opportunity to explain the purpose of the bill, preferring to wait until the bill is called for second reading. There have been occasions, however, when a Minister has given a brief explanation of a bill (see *Debates*, December 1, 1987, pp. 11343-4; September 27, 1990, pp. 13481-2; February 27, 1992, p. 7681; April 10, 1992, p. 9655; June 18, 1992, p. 12323; February 5, 1998, pp. 3402-3).

168. Standing Order 69(1). The original version of this Standing Order, adopted in December 1867, provided only for the first reading of bills. In 1968, a special procedure committee recommended that the first reading motion be amended to read "That this bill be read a first time and printed". The committee felt that adoption of this motion would imply that the House had agreed to the introduction of the bill without any commitment beyond the fact that it should be made generally available for the information of Parliament and the public (see Item Nos. 10 and 11 of the Third Report of the Special Committee on Procedure of the House, presented on December 6, 1968 (*Journals*, pp. 432-3)).

169. The wording of the original Standing Order prohibited debate on or amendments to the main motion, although the motion could be voted on. Speakers were strict in enforcing the rule and in asserting that no discussion could take place at first reading except by unanimous consent, and that the House had the option only of accepting or rejecting the bill's first reading (see, for example, remarks by the Speaker in *Debates*, February 27, 1912, col. 3902; February 13, 1933, pp. 2016-7; February 26, 1934, p. 927; April 2, 1962, p. 2383; April 6, 1982, p. 16202). During the Second Session of the Thirty-Fourth Parliament (April 1989 - May 1991), the opposition parties frequently forced recorded divisions on the introduction and first reading motions for both government and private Members' bills as a means of delaying the proceedings. As voting procedures could take up to 45 minutes per recorded vote, the time available for Government Orders was reduced. In April 1991, the Standing Orders were amended to provide for these motions being deemed carried without question put (see *Journals*, April 11, 1991, pp. 2913-4).

170. The ancient practice of the British Parliament to read bills at length was obsolete by the time of Confederation. Since the earliest Canadian Parliament, it was considered sufficient at first reading merely to read the title of the bill in English and French (*Bourinot*, 1st ed., p. 518). In April 1878, at the request of a Member, a bill was read in its entirety at the first reading stage by the Assistant Clerk. In his remarks concerning this proceeding, the Speaker emphasized that, although there was no rule against it, the practice of reading the text of bills had entirely disappeared (*Debates*, April 2, 1878, pp. 1582-4).

the bill be read a second time?" and responds *"At the next sitting of the House."* The House agrees to this without the adoption of a motion. [171] The expression "next sitting of the House", when used to state the time that a question is ordered to stand over, means the bill is placed on the *Order Paper* in its proper place for a second reading at a future sitting according to the precedence given to it by the Standing Orders, the government determining the order in which government legislation is called. No bill can be read a second time on the same day as introduction and first reading without a special order or the unanimous consent of the House. [172] Following first reading, the bill is then placed on the *Order Paper* under "Orders of the Day" for a second reading at some future sitting of the House. The one exception to this rule is for the passage of appropriation bills at all stages on the last allotted day in a Supply period. [173]

A government bill may only be introduced by a Minister. A government bill standing on the *Order Paper* in one Minister's name may be moved on his or her behalf by another Minister since the bill is considered an initiative of the entire Cabinet. [174] If the Minister does not wish to introduce the bill when the rubric is called, the bill remains on the *Order Paper* for introduction and first reading at a later date. Although the usual practice is for the government to have a Minister second a motion to introduce a government bill, it is not mandatory; [175] another Member may be chosen as the seconder for a bill.

INTRODUCTION OF PRIVATE MEMBERS' BILLS

Any public bill sponsored by a Member who is not a Minister may be introduced under this rubric. This rubric was created in June 1987 when "Introduction of Bills" was divided into "Introduction of Government Bills" and "Introduction of Private Members' Bills". [176] The procedures here are exactly the same as for bills introduced

---

171. On one occasion, a Member argued that this question was a votable motion which could be put to the House. The Speaker ruled, however, that the practice had fallen into disuse and that without clear directions from the House to the contrary, it would not be appropriate to apply to current practices what may well have been an appropriate ruling over 100 years ago (*Debates*, May 24, 1988, pp. 15706, 15719-23).

172. See, for example, *Journals*, February 8, 1994, pp. 130-2; October 29, 1997, p. 166. Note also that Standing Order 71 provides for the reading of a bill at two or more stages on one sitting day, on urgent or extraordinary occasions; this would be accomplished by unanimous consent or special order. See also Chapter 16, "The Legislative Process".

173. Standing Order 81(17), (18)(*c*). See, for example, *Journals*, December 8, 1994, pp. 1008-9.

174. In respect to points of order raised about a Minister introducing legislation in relation to another Minister's administrative responsibilities, Speaker Jerome ruled that there was no prohibition against the practice (*Debates*, July 20, 1977, pp. 7836-7).

175. See, for example, *Debates*, January 31, 1985, p. 1845; October 28, 1991, pp. 4070-2, 4076.

176. *Journals*, June 3, 1987, pp. 1016, 1018.

by the government under the previous rubric: the notice period is the same;[177] the Speaker reads the rubric "Introduction of Private Members' Bills" from the *Order Paper*; a Member wishing to introduce a bill signals his or her desire to proceed at that point. If the Member is not in the House or is not ready to introduce the bill, the bill remains on the *Order Paper*. However, with the unanimous consent of the House, a Member other than the sponsor of the bill may move the introduction of the bill on behalf of the sponsor.[178] After the Speaker identifies a seconder for the bill, the motion for leave to introduce is deemed carried without debate, amendment or question put.[179] Where a Minister generally foregoes the opportunity of commenting briefly on a bill at this stage, a private Member will invariably do so.[180] The Chair may interrupt the explanation if the Member is engaging in debate.[181]

After the Member has commented briefly on the bill, the Speaker proposes to the House that the bill be read a first time and printed. This motion is also deemed carried without debate, amendment or question put.[182] A Table Officer then rises and declares, *"First reading of this bill/ Première lecture de ce projet de loi"*. The bill is then placed on the *Order Paper* under "Private Members' Business" where it is set down for a second reading.[183]

FIRST READING OF SENATE PUBLIC BILLS

Under Routine Proceedings, "First Reading of Senate Public Bills" comes after "Introduction of Private Members' Bills" and before "Motions". Prior to 1910, public bills emanating from the Senate were read a first time under the rubric "Motions". The rubric "First Reading of Senate Public Bills" was created in April 1910 and immediately followed "Introduction of Bills".[184]

When a Senate public bill has been passed by the Senate, a message is sent so informing the House and requesting its concurrence in the measure. This message is received by the Clerk of the House, and the Speaker makes the announcement of its contents at the first convenient opportunity.[185] The Speaker reads the message,

---

177. They are listed in chronological order on the *Order Paper* after 48 hours' written notice. The 48-hour notice period can be waived with the unanimous consent of the House (see, for example, *Debates*, April 22, 1993, pp. 18278-9).

178. See, for example, *Debates*, January 27, 1981, p. 6616; June 15, 1993, p. 20795.

179. Standing Order 68(2).

180. Standing Order 68(2). On April 22, 1997, a Member introduced and commented on 29 bills (see *Journals*, April 22, 1997, pp. 1502-6). The same Member introduced 38 bills on February 13, 1998 (*Journals*, pp. 458-63).

181. See, for example, *Debates*, March 28, 1996, p. 1329; October 22, 1997, p. 974; November 7, 1997, p. 1717.

182. Standing Order 69(1).

183. See Chapter 21, "Private Members' Business", for detailed information on the consideration and passage of a private Member's bill.

184. *Journals*, April 29, 1910, p. 537.

185. *Bourinot*, 4th ed., p. 272.

stating, *"I have the honour to inform the House that a message has been received from the Senate informing this House that it has passed the following bill to which the concurrence of the House is desired: An Act to ..."*. There is no need for a motion for leave to introduce the bill since it is already available in printed form. The bill is then placed on the *Order Paper* under the heading "First Reading of Senate Public Bills" in Routine Proceedings. [186]

If the Member or Minister[187] sponsoring the bill in the House of Commons signals his or her desire to proceed with the bill when the rubric "First Reading of Senate Public Bills" is called by the Chair during Routine Proceedings, the question, *"That this bill be now read a first time"*, is deemed carried without debate, amendment or question put. [188] Since a Senate public bill is already printed when it is introduced in the House, there is no need to order that it be printed again. If the Member or Minister sponsoring the bill in the House is not present or is not ready to move first reading of the bill when the rubric is called, then the bill remains on the *Order Paper* for first reading at a later sitting. In the case of private Members' bills, with the unanimous consent of the House, a Member other than the sponsor of the bill may move first reading of the bill on behalf of the sponsor; in the case of government

---

186. See, for example, *Order Paper*, June 10, 1998, p. 10; June 11, 1998, p. 11. On one occasion, the notice of first reading of a Senate public bill was struck from the *Order Paper* because the bill was found to infringe upon the royal prerogative in financial matters (*Journals*, November 12, 1969, pp. 79-80). In 1998, in response to a point of order raised concerning the procedural acceptability of a Senate public bill which had been read a first time, the Speaker ruled that the bill imposed a tax and therefore should have originated in the House of Commons and been preceded by the adoption of a Ways and Means motion. The first reading proceedings on the bill were declared null and void, and the bill was withdrawn from the *Order Paper*. See *Debates*, December 2, 1998, pp. 10788-91. See also Chapter 16, "The Legislative Process", and Chapter 21, "Private Members' Business".

187. There have been a number of Senate bills sponsored by the Ministry. See, for example, *Journals*, June 18, 1992, p. 1793; November 19, 1992, p. 2079; March 10, 1993, p. 2611; March 23, 1994, p. 296; June 14, 1995, p. 1723: November 26, 1997, p. 270; February 2, 1998, p. 403; February 11, 1998, p. 444; March 25, 1998, p. 622; May 28, 1998, p. 901; June 3, 1998, p. 929.

188. Standing Order 69(2). Prior to September 1994, the question was put on the motion for first reading of a Senate public bill, and on occasion Senate bills were defeated on recorded division at this stage (see, for example, *Journals*, December 20, 1989, pp. 1059-60; June 18, 1990, pp. 1920-1). The Standing Order was amended in June 1994 when the House concurred in a committee report recommending a number of changes to the rules of the House (see *Journals*, June 8, 1994, p. 545; June 10, 1994, p. 563; Standing Committee on Procedure and House Affairs, *Minutes of Proceedings and Evidence,* June 9, 1994, Issue No. 16, p. 5).

Between 1968 and 1998, there were three occasions when a private Member commented on a Senate public bill at the first reading stage (see *Debates*, September 21, 1971, p. 8029; June 29, 1987, p. 7715; November 18, 1998, p. 10145).

bills, a bill standing in the name of one Minister may be moved on his or her behalf by another Minister. If no Member chooses to sponsor a bill emanating from the Senate, no further action is taken following the reading of the message from the Senate. The bill remains on the *Order Paper* under "First Reading of Senate Public Bills".

After the motion for first reading is adopted, the Speaker routinely asks, *"When shall the bill be read a second time? At the next sitting of the House?"* The House agrees to this without a formal motion and the order for second reading is placed on the *Order Paper* under Government Orders if the bill is sponsored by a Minister,[189] or under "Private Members' Business" at the bottom of the list in the Order of Precedence if the bill is sponsored by a private Member.[190]

MOTIONS

"Motions" was one of four rubrics provided for in Routine Proceedings at the time of Confederation.[191] Over the years, various kinds of motions, once considered under this rubric, have been categorized and assigned their own place in the Daily Program, including private Members' motions, motions to introduce bills, and motions to adjourn under Standing Order 52 (emergency debates). For example, until 1906, bills were introduced under this rubric.[192] And it was only in 1964 that the House adopted a new Standing Order to provide a separate rubric for ministerial statements which had been taking place under "Motions".[193] In 1975, the items under Routine Proceedings were reordered so that "Government Notices of Motions"[194] and "Motions" were the last two rubrics to be considered each day. By moving "Motions" to the bottom of the list, the House was no longer prevented from reaching other

189. A Senate public bill sponsored by a Minister has been read a first time and subsequently considered at all stages on the same sitting day (see *Journals*, June 18, 1992, pp. 1793, 1803).
190. See Chapter 21, "Private Members' Business".
191. See *Rules, Orders and Forms of Proceeding of the House of Commons of Canada*, 1868, Rule No. 19.
192. See *Rules, Orders and Forms of Proceeding of the House of Commons of Canada*, 1906, Rule No. 25.
193. *Journals*, May 7, 1964, p. 297.
194. Until 1955, government notices of motions had been considered and debated outside of Routine Proceedings as a separate item of business, when and if that category were reached. In 1955, the Standing Orders were amended to allow any government notice of motion to be transferred to Government Orders automatically when called from the Chair during Routine Proceedings. By being included as a routine proceeding, government notices of motions could be called daily by the Speaker and, as the rule made clear, were no longer subject to debate because they were immediately transferred to the *Order Paper* under Government Orders for consideration in due course (*Journals*, July 12, 1955, pp. 886-7, 900).

routine items because of lengthy debates.[195] In 1987, the rubric "Government Notices of Motions" was dropped and the others were reordered to their present form.[196]

Different categories of business have developed over the years in response to the need to adapt to the organization of House business. Some categories are now uniquely reserved for the government or the opposition, some are reserved for private Members, and still others are reserved for items which affect the transaction of routine business of the House. As a general rule, motions dealing with matters of substance or government policy are moved either by Ministers under Government Orders or private Members under Private Members' Business. The kinds of motions permissible under "Motions" has been narrowed to consist primarily of motions for concurrence in committee reports and motions relating to the sittings and proceedings of the House.[197]

The Chair has consistently ruled that any motion pertaining to the arrangement of the business of the House should be introduced by the Government House Leader[198] and may be considered under "Motions" or under Government Orders,

195. Item No. 9 of the Second Report of the Standing Committee on Procedure and Organization, presented on March 14, 1975 (*Journals*, p. 373), and concurred in on March 24, 1975 (*Journals*, p. 399). Until 1965, if debate under "Motions" did not conclude at one sitting, it was resumed at the next sitting (and possibly subsequent sittings) when the rubric "Motions" was reached. This meant that the House would not be able to consider any routine proceeding following "Motions" nor Orders of the Day nor Question Period. For example, the House debated the motion for concurrence in the report of the Special Committee on a Canadian Flag for two weeks before a decision was taken (only after closure was used). For 11 days, the House did not consider any rubric following "Motions" and there was no Question Period (see *Stewart*, pp. 63-4). The Standing Orders were amended so that the order for resuming debate begun under "Motions" was concluded the next day under Government Orders as the first item of business (*Journals*, June 11, 1965, pp. 224, 226). In 1968, the rules were again amended to permit the government to call such business in the order it chose without restriction (*Journals*, December 20, 1968, p. 571).

196. *Journals*, June 3, 1987, pp. 1017-8. Debatable government notices of motions are now placed on the *Order Paper* under Government Orders after the normal 48 hours' notice (Standing Order 56(1)). It becomes an order of the day, similar to any other government business ordered for consideration by the House.

197. *Bourinot*, 4th ed., p. 219; *Beauchesne*, 4th ed., p. 79. See also *Journals*, May 2, 1961, p. 494; *Debates*, July 13, 1988, p. 17506; June 18, 1996, pp. 3981-2.

198. See, for example, various Speakers' rulings, *Journals*, May 30, 1928, p. 476; May 11, 1944, p. 365; May 2, 1961, pp. 493-5; and the Speaker's comments in *Debates*, April 28, 1982, p. 16701.

depending on where the Minister giving notice has decided to place it.[199] The Chair has also ruled that while the rubric "Motions" "usually encompasses matters related to the management of the business of the House and its committees, it is not the exclusive purview of the government, despite the government's unquestioned prerogative to determine the agenda of business before the House".[200] Accordingly, the Chair accepts certain motions put on notice by private Members for consideration under the rubric "Motions", such as motions of instruction to committees and for concurrence in committee reports.[201] When private Members give written notice of other substantive matters, these motions are placed under "Private Members' Business" on the *Order Paper*.[202]

When the Speaker calls "Motions" during Routine Proceedings, any Member or Minister may rise and move a motion, if it has been placed on the *Notice Paper* 48 hours in advance. Otherwise, a Member or Minister must seek unanimous consent to move the motion.[203] If a Member or a Minister who has given notice of a motion is not in the House or does not wish to move it, the matter will stand on the *Order Paper* until a subsequent sitting.

The motions which are considered under this rubric are often moved without notice by unanimous consent and adopted without debate. Examples of motions moved under this rubric include those to:

- manage the proceedings and business of the House or its committees;[204]
- change the order of business of the House;[205]

---

199. See *Debates*, May 16, 1985, pp. 4821-2, where Speaker Bosley was called upon to rule on whether a time allocation motion had to be moved under "Motions" during Routine Proceedings, or whether it could be placed under "Government Notices of Motions" and then transferred to Government Orders. The Speaker ruled that the government has the right to proceed in the manner it chooses. Speaker Fraser explained in 1988: "The question then becomes, what is the distinction between a Government Notice of Motion and a motion? I would suggest a Government Notice of Motion is any motion that the Government gives notice of. In other words, a Government Notice of Motion is not based on the content of the motion, but rather upon the mover. In many cases, therefore, a notice of motion could go under more than one heading and it is up to the Minister giving notice to decide which heading should be chosen. Clearly a Government Notice of Motion can only be moved by the Government, but the Government can choose to place it either under Motions or Government Notices of Motions" (*Debates*, June 13, 1988, pp. 16376-9, and in particular p. 16377).

200. *Debates*, July 13, 1988, p. 17506.

201. See Speaker Fraser's ruling, *Debates*, July 13, 1988, pp. 17504-9. A private Member was allowed to place a notice of motion under this rubric to deal with the reporting back of a private Member's bill from committee (see Speaker Parent's rulings, *Debates*, September 23, 1996, pp. 4560-2; November 21, 1996, pp. 6519-20).

202. See Speaker Parent's ruling, *Debates*, June 18, 1996, pp. 3981-2.

203. *Bourinot*, 4th ed.: "As a rule these motions require notice, but some are of such a purely formal nature that by general consent notice is not insisted upon" (p. 301).

204. See, for example, *Journals*, June 27, 1989, p. 463; February 5, 1992, p. 975; March 11, 1992, p. 1124; November 24, 1994, pp. 927-8.

205. See, for example, *Journals*, November 4, 1987, p. 1831; June 2, 1988, pp. 2778-9; May 6, 1994, p. 435.

- arrange the times or days of sitting of the House;[206]
- amend the Standing Orders;[207]
- suspend the Standing Orders;[208]
- discharge an Order of the House;[209]
- concur in a committee report;[210]
- authorize a committee to travel;[211]
- establish a special committee;[212]
- instruct a committee to do something;[213]
- alter the membership of a committee;[214]
- appoint officers of the House (such as the Commissioner of Official Languages, the Privacy Commissioner, the Chief Electoral Officer and the Information Commissioner);[215]
- extend messages to another country;[216] and
- censure Chair occupants.[217]

---

206. See, for example, *Journals*, April 21, 1994, p. 380; May 6, 1994, p. 435.

207. See, for example, *Journals*, April 5, 1989, pp. 40-2; March 23, 1990, p. 1397; January 25, 1994, pp. 58-61.

208. See, for example, *Journals*, June 8, 1994, p. 545.

209. See, for example, *Journals*, June 10, 1992, p. 1678; April 5, 1995, p. 1334.

210. See, for example, *Journals*, April 29, 1992, pp. 1336-7; April 13, 1994, p. 339.

211. See, for example, *Journals*, June 8, 1994, p. 545; September 27, 1995, p. 1959.

212. See, for example, *Journals*, September 18, 1991, p. 363; October 30, 1991, p. 568; February 14, 1992, p. 1026.

213. See, for example, *Journals*, October 16, 1985, p. 1107; July 13, 1988, pp. 3174-5; June 22, 1994, p. 655.

214. See, for example, *Journals*, May 17, 1991, p. 45; September 27, 1995, p. 1959; September 23, 1996, p. 666.

215. See, for example, *Journals*, June 19, 1991, p. 239; December 2, 1997, p. 313; April 22, 1998, pp. 692-3. See also *Debates*, June 6, 1990, pp. 12339-40, where Speaker Fraser ruled that the motions concerning the appointment of the Information Commissioner and the appointment of the Privacy Commissioner could be filed either under the rubric "Motions" or the rubric "Government Motions". In 1998, the appointment of the Information Commissioner was debated under Government Orders (*Journals*, June 10, 1998, pp. 999-1000).

216. See, for example, *Journals*, November 28, 1990, p. 2311; October 30, 1991, p. 568; December 10, 1991, p. 908.

217. See, for example, *Journals*, June 4, 1956, pp. 691-3; June 6, 1956, pp. 713-4; June 7, 1956, pp. 719, 723; June 8, 1956, pp. 725-6; March 18, 1964, pp. 103-4; March 19, 1964, pp. 106-7; *Order Paper and Notice Paper*, May 4, 1992, pp. 11, III-IV. See also *Journals*, May 28, 1956, pp. 645-7, where the Speaker instructed the Clerk that if a motion of censure against the Chair was received, it was to be put under "Motions" in Routine Proceedings.

Although motions of congratulations have been moved under this rubric, the Speaker has warned against this practice.[218]

After a motion has been read to the House by the Chair, debate begins and amendments may be moved to it; the normal rules of debate apply. During debate, if a motion to proceed to the Orders of the Day is moved and adopted, the motion being debated would be superseded and dropped from the *Order Paper*.[219] When debate on any motion considered during Routine Proceedings is adjourned[220] or interrupted (either by the normal adjournment of the sitting on Mondays, for "Statements by Members" on Tuesdays and Thursdays, or for Private Members' Business on Wednesdays and Fridays),[221] the order for resumption of the debate is transferred to Government Orders.[222] The motion will be considered again only under Government Orders in such sequence as the government determines.[223]

Motions for Concurrence in Committee Reports

Motions that call for concurrence in committee reports are listed under "Motions" on the *Order Paper* after a 48-hour notice period. Any Member may give notice of a motion for concurrence in a committee report, and more than one Member may give notice of a motion to concur in the same committee report.[224] Generally, the Chair of the committee will give notice of a motion to concur in a report of his or her committee and move the motion. However, as with any notice of motion not sponsored by a Minister, the Member who placed the notice on the *Order Paper* is the only one who may move the motion. In the absence of the sponsor, another Member may move the motion on the sponsor's behalf only with the unanimous consent of the House.[225]

---

218. On February 1, 1993, during Routine Proceedings, a private Member moved a motion with the consent of the House congratulating a Canadian recording artist who had received a musical award (*Journals*, p. 2422). Later in the sitting, another Member rose to question whether or not this type of motion was appropriate and if it should be raised under "Motions" without notice. The Speaker responded that a problem could have arisen if the motion had been on a more divisive matter, placing the Chair in a difficult position. Speaker Fraser undertook to bring the matter to the attention of the Standing Committee on House Management (*Debates*, February 1, 1993, pp. 15213, 15220-2).

219. See, for example, *Journals*, March 25, 1993, p. 2720; June 22, 1994, p. 655; April 1, 1998, p. 659; June 2, 1998, pp. 920-1.

220. See, for example, *Journals*, December 13, 1994, pp. 1026-7; June 20, 1996, pp. 592-3; March 26, 1998, pp. 633-4.

221. See, for example, *Journals*, April 23, 1997, pp. 1518-9; April 26, 1999, pp. 1766-7.

222. Standing Order 66.

223. Standing Order 40(2). The government rarely resumes debate during Government Orders on a motion first proposed by a private Member during Routine Proceedings.

224. *Journals*, January 20, 1970, pp. 327-9, in particular p. 328.

225. *Debates*, October 17, 1983, pp. 28078-9. Unanimous consent is not required for motions sponsored by a Minister; motions for which notice was given by one Minister may be moved by any member of the Cabinet.

As noted above, such a motion may be moved, without prior notice, with the unanimous consent of the House during the sitting in which the committee report is presented.[226] Normally, the Member presenting the report states that he or she will seek the leave of the House to move concurrence in the report later that day when the rubric "Motions" is called; the report of the committee may be considered, with leave of the House, at that time. These reports often pertain to the powers, sittings or membership of a committee and are typically adopted without debate.

Routine Motions for Which Unanimous Consent Has Been Denied

A rule adopted in April 1991 allows the House to consider any routine motion for which written notice has not been provided and whose presentation requires, but has not been granted, unanimous consent.[227] A routine motion is defined in the Standing Orders as one *"which may be required for the observance of the proprieties of the House, the maintenance of its authority, the management of its business, the arrangement of its proceedings, the establishing of the powers of its committees, the correctness of its records or the fixing of its sitting days or the times of its meetings or adjournment"*.[228] When consent has previously been denied for the moving of such a motion, a Minister may rise under the rubric "Motions" during Routine Proceedings to request that the Speaker propose the question to the House.[229] The Chair puts the question without debate or amendment.[230] The Speaker then asks those opposed to the motion to rise in their places. If 25 Members or more rise to object, the motion is deemed withdrawn;[231] otherwise, the motion is adopted.[232] Since 1991,

---

226. See, for example, *Journals*, February 6, 1995, pp. 1080-1. In one instance in 1985, the Member presenting a report explained that it contained a recommendation to change the name of the committee and that he intended to seek concurrence in the report later in the sitting. The Speaker advised the House that the report appeared to go beyond the committee's order of reference and that it would not be in order to proceed with the concurrence motion. The Member argued that it could be concurred in by unanimous consent. The Speaker ruled immediately that the House could not concur in a report that had been found to be out of order (*Debates*, February 28, 1985, pp. 2602-4). Later in the sitting under "Motions", the Member sought leave to propose a motion to simply amend the Standing Orders, effecting the change the Member originally had wanted in the report which was ruled not in order. The House gave its consent and the motion was adopted (*Debates*, pp. 2604-5).

227. See *Journals*, April 11, 1991, pp. 2905, 2912-3. This rule is also examined in Chapter 12, "The Process of Debate", and in Chapter 14, "The Curtailment of Debate".

228. Standing Order 56.1(1)(*b*).

229. Standing Order 56.1(1)(*a*).

230. Standing Order 56.1(2).

231. See, for example, *Journals*, September 30, 1994, pp. 756-7; June 9, 1998, p. 954; March 19, 1999, p. 1640; March 22, 1999, p. 1645.

232. Standing Order 56.1(3). See, for example, *Journals*, December 10, 1992, pp. 2387-8; October 7, 1994, p. 780; March 16, 1995, p. 1226; June 8, 1995, p. 1594; June 15, 1995, p. 1754; April 24, 1997, pp. 1524-5; December 1, 1997, pp. 290-1; February 9, 1998, p. 430; April 12, 1999, p. 1687.

motions proposed pursuant to this Standing Order have fixed the hours of sitting of the House, dealt with the adjournment of the House and the management of its business, and authorized certain committees to travel.

PRESENTING PETITIONS

A Member wishing to present petitions in the House may do so in one of two ways: at any time during a sitting of the House, a Member may file a petition with the Clerk of the House who enters it into the *Journals* for that sitting day;[233] or a Member may present the petition in the House during Routine Proceedings when "Presenting Petitions" is called by the Speaker.[234] Before being presented, a petition must be examined and certified correct as to form and content by the Clerk of Petitions.[235] If the petition meets the requirements specified in the rules of the House, a Member, after being recognized by the Chair under this rubric during Routine Proceedings, presents the petition and gives a brief statement to inform the House of its content.

The period provided for the presentation of petitions is not to exceed 15 minutes.[236] The Speaker recognizes a Member only once during "Presenting Petitions"; if a Member has more than one petition to present, he or she must present them all when given the floor.[237] In his or her statement, the Member may summarize the prayer (or request) of the petition, state the parties from whom it comes and the number of signatures it contains.[238] The Member may not make a speech or enter into debate on or in relation to the petition.[239] The petition itself is not read.[240]

Historical Perspective

For the first 40 years of Confederation, the only method available to Members for presenting a petition was for them to rise during Routine Proceedings under a rubric called "Presenting Petitions". In 1910, substantial changes were made to the rules on petitions. The rubric "Presenting Petitions" was removed from Routine Proceedings and Members wishing to present petitions from their places did so before "Introduction of Bills". A second procedure, copied from Great Britain, was also adopted to allow Members merely to file their petitions with the Clerk of the House during the hours of sitting.[241] The rules respecting the presentation of petitions remained intact until 1986 when the rubric "Presenting Petitions" was restored to

---

233. Standing Order 36(5).

234. Standing Order 36(6).

235. Standing Order 36(1).

236. Standing Order 36(6).

237. See ruling of Speaker Sauvé, *Debates*, October 28, 1983, pp. 28457-8.

238. See, for example, *Debates*, June 10, 1998, p. 7935.

239. Standing Order 36(7). See, for example, *Debates*, February 25, 1998, pp. 4408-9; October 2, 1998, p. 8709.

240. See, for example, *Debates*, October 24, 1997, p. 1103; February 13, 1998, p. 3867; March 18, 1998, p. 5055.

241. *Journals*, April 29, 1910, pp. 535-6.

Routine Proceedings.[242] However, on occasion, the presentation of petitions took up long periods of House time, thus preventing the House from reaching other business.[243] This led, in part, to changes in 1987 to the order of the rubrics under Routine Proceedings; "Presenting Petitions" is now the second to last rubric considered.[244] In 1991, the period for presenting petitions was restricted to 15 minutes to prevent Members from using petitions as a means to delay the House from proceeding to other routine business and the Orders of the Day.[245]

A number of conditions, conventions and practices apply to the certification and presentation of petitions. These matters as well as the history of presenting petitions in the House are examined in detail in Chapter 22, "Public Petitions".

QUESTIONS ON THE *ORDER PAPER*

This is the last rubric considered during the daily routine of business. The rules of the House have always provided a mechanism for responses to written questions.[246] However, between 1867 and 1975, the rubric "Questions on the *Order Paper*" was not necessarily considered on each sitting day for two reasons. At one time, the rubric had precedence over the Orders of the Day only on certain days of the week and, on the other days, the House typically never reached the rubric. At other times, the rules provided for the rubric to be called only on certain days of the week, such as Mondays and Wednesdays. After 1975, a rule change ensured that the House would reach this rubric daily; indeed, it was the first item of business every day following the daily routine of business and before the Orders of the Day were called.[247] In June 1987, as a result of amendments to the Standing Orders, the rubric "Questions on the *Order Paper*" was added to the list of items considered during Routine Proceedings.[248]

Members may place on notice no more than four questions "relating to public affairs" at any one time to a Minister.[249] A Member may ask the government to respond to a specific question within 45 calendar days by so indicating when filing the question;[250] a Member may also ask that an oral answer be provided by attaching

---

242. *Journals*, February 6, 1986, pp. 1646, 1665; February 13, 1986, p. 1710.

243. See, for example, *Journals*, May 19, 1983, pp. 5910-1; October 27, 1983, pp. 6356-9; October 28, 1983, pp. 6362-7; December 19, 1985, pp. 1444-8.

244. *Journals*, June 3, 1987, pp. 1017-8.

245. *Journals*, April 11, 1991, pp. 2905-6, 2908-9.

246. Indeed, from 1867 until 1964 when certain procedures for oral questions were codified, the rules of the House only provided for written questions.

247. *Journals*, March 14, 1975, pp. 372-6, and in particular pp. 373-4; March 24, 1975, p. 399.

248. *Journals*, June 3, 1987, pp. 1017-8.

249. Standing Order 39(4).

250. Standing Order 39(5)(*a*).

an asterisk to no more than three questions.[251] After the notice requirement has been fulfilled, the question appears on the *Order Paper*.

When "Questions on the *Order Paper*" is called during Routine Proceedings, a Minister, or more usually the Parliamentary Secretary to the Government House Leader, rises in his or her place to announce which questions the government intends to answer on that particular day. The government may answer written questions in one of two ways. First, the Parliamentary Secretary may simply indicate to the House the number of the question being answered,[252] and the text of the answer appears in the *Debates* of that day as if the Minister to whom the question was directed had actually stood in the House and given a full reply.[253] If an oral reply has been requested, the Parliamentary Secretary may give the answer orally, or may seek the consent of the House to deem the question answered without actually reading aloud the text of the answer; the answer will be printed in the *Debates*.[254] The second method is that the government may request the House to transform a certain question into an "order for return"; that is, the House orders the government to table a document which will serve as a response to the question. This is normally done when the reply is too lengthy to be easily printed in the *Debates*. If there is agreement from the House to proceed in this way, the tabled response is filed with the Clerk as a sessional paper, open to public scrutiny; the text of the response does not appear in the *Debates*.[255] If there is no agreement, the government would proceed to read the answer in the case of a starred question; in the case of a request for tabling, the government may choose not to proceed with the question on that day[256] or have the Minister table the answer under "Tabling of Documents".

After the designated Parliamentary Secretary or Minister has enumerated the questions which are to be answered on a given day, he or she will then ask the House to stand the remaining unanswered questions. This permits the questions to retain their position on the *Order Paper*; otherwise the unanswered questions would be struck from the *Order Paper*.[257]

---

251. Standing Order 39(3)(*a*).

252. This procedure began on July 17, 1963 (see *Debates*, July 17, 1963, p. 2295). Prior to this, the procedure was very time-consuming: the Speaker went through the entire list of questions each Monday and Wednesday, with the Minister or Parliamentary Secretary interrupting on occasion to say "Answered" when they wished to table a reply (see *Stewart*, p. 65).

253. See, for example, *Debates*, June 16, 1992, pp. 12116-7; March 14, 1995, pp. 10430-1; February 2, 1998, pp. 3195-6; October 28, 1998, pp. 9522-3.

254. See, for example, *Debates*, May 15, 1989, p. 1694; May 14, 1990, pp. 11372-3; February 2, 1998, p. 3196; September 21, 1998, pp. 8174-7; April 30, 1999, p. 14549.

255. Standing Order 39(7). See, for example, *Journals*, September 23, 1994, p. 725; December 13, 1996, pp. 1018-9. See *Journals*, April 2, 1998, p. 664, for an example of a revised return being tabled.

256. See, for example, *Debates*, March 13, 1995, p. 10397; March 17, 1995, p. 10671.

257. Standing Order 42(1).

It is at this time that Members raise any concerns they have about their questions, typically seeking information about the status of the reply. If a Member has requested that a question be answered within 45 days and it remains unanswered after that time, he or she may rise during "Questions on the *Order Paper*" and give notice of his or her intention to transfer the question and raise the matter during the Adjournment Proceedings of the House.[258] The question is then removed from the *Order Paper*.

Procedures regarding written questions and responses to them are examined in greater detail in Chapter 11, "Questions".

NOTICES OF MOTIONS FOR THE PRODUCTION OF PAPERS

The rubric "Notices of Motions for the Production of Papers" is called only on Wednesday. It is considered as the final item of Routine Proceedings following the rubric "Questions on the *Order Paper*". Ministers are required by statute to table various documents relating to their departmental responsibilities (see section in this chapter on "Tabling of Documents"). On occasion, however, a Member may want to see papers that are not required by law to be tabled. In such instances, the Member may place on the *Notice Paper* notice of a special type of motion requesting that the government compile or produce certain papers or documents and table them in the House. After the 48-hour notice requirement, such notices of motions are transferred to the *Order Paper* under the rubric "Notices of Motions for the Production of Papers".

Historical Perspective

In the early years of Confederation, motions for papers were treated in the same way as other private Members' motions. They were called only on private Members' days and had priority only according to the date on which they were put on the *Order Paper*. Because the House rarely considered these motions, a custom developed whereby motions for papers were called by consent and passed in a block.

In 1910, a new procedure for obtaining papers was introduced.[259] A mechanism was created to allow any Member to move a motion for the production of papers without debate. This was done under "Notices of Motions for the Production of Papers", which had precedence over the existing rubric "Notices of Motion". Notices of motions for the production of papers were disposed of at once when called. If a Member or Minister wished to have a debate on a motion, it would be transferred for debate under "Notices of Motions".

In 1955, an amendment to the Standing Orders listed "Notices of Motions for the Productions of Papers" as a rubric formally on the daily agenda of business. It

---

258. Standing Order 39(5)(*b*).

259. *Journals*, April 29, 1910, pp. 536-7.

also guaranteed that motions for papers would be reached on days designated as Private Members' Days.[260]

Provisional changes to the Standing Orders in 1961,[261] which were made permanent in 1962,[262] provided that "Notices of Motions for the Production of Papers" would be called only on Wednesday at the conclusion of Routine Proceedings. These changes also provided that notices of motions for the production of papers transferred for debate would be listed under a new specific category called "Notices of Motions (Papers)" under Private Members' Business. This procedure is still being used today, although Members have seldom chosen to place notices of motions (papers) on the Order of Precedence for Private Members' Business following the draw.[263]

Manner in Which Notices Are Called

Notices of motions for the production of papers resemble written questions in that they are requests for information from the government. All such motions are worded in the form of either an Order of the House ("That an Order of the House do issue ...") or an Address to the Crown ("That a humble Address be presented to his/her Excellency praying that he/she will cause to be laid before the House of Commons ..."). Thus, a motion, if adopted, becomes either an Order that the government table ("produce") certain documents in the House or an Address to the Governor General requesting that certain papers be sent to the House. An Order of the House is used for papers concerning matters directly related to federal departments. Addresses are formal messages to the Crown through which the House requests the production of documents in the Crown's possession, such as correspondence between the federal and other governments, Orders in Council, and papers concerning the administration of justice, the judicial conduct of judges and the exercise of the prerogatives of the Crown.[264] Motions for papers should be carefully prepared and state clearly and definitely the exact information required.[265] The Speaker is responsible for ensuring that the motion before the House is in proper form; that is, that it is the appropriate motion to do what is sought to be done.[266]

260. *Journals*, July 12, 1955, pp. 888-9.

261. *Journals*, September 26, 1961, pp. 949-50, 953; September 27, 1961, p. 957.

262. *Journals*, April 10, 1962, pp. 338-9; April 12, 1962, p. 350.

263. For examples of notices of motions (papers) placed on the Order of Precedence for Private Members' Business, debated and adopted, see *Journals*, October 2, 1998, p. 1115; November 2, 1998, p. 1221. See also Chapter 21, "Private Members' Business".

264. Prior to 1876, all motions for papers were Addresses to the Governor General (*Bourinot*, 4th ed., p. 245).

265. *Bourinot*, 4th ed., p. 249.

266. *Journals*, February 15, 1960, pp. 137-40, in particular p. 138.

When this rubric is called by the Speaker on Wednesday, one of several outcomes may take place for each of the notices of motions called:[267]

1. Motion acceptable to government

A Minister or a Parliamentary Secretary (usually the Parliamentary Secretary to the Government House Leader)[268] rises and states that the notice of motion is acceptable to the government. The Speaker then asks the House if it wishes to have the motion deemed adopted. If the House agrees, the motion is carried without debate or amendment. This becomes an order for the government to produce the document (a "return") either immediately or at a later date.[269] If the House does not agree, the motion must either be transferred for debate,[270] or be put immediately to the House without debate or amendment.

2. Motion acceptable to government with reservations

A Minister or Parliamentary Secretary rises and states that a notice of motion is acceptable to the government subject to certain reservations (e.g., confidentiality). The Speaker then asks the House if it wishes to have the motion deemed adopted. If the House agrees, the motion is carried without debate or amendment. This becomes an order for the government to produce either immediately or at a later date only those papers or documents not subject to the reservation.[271] If the House does not

---

267. Up until April 1964, when the rubric "Notices of Motions for the Production of Papers" was called, the Speaker would go through the list of motions seriatim. If a motion for papers was adopted, the government would then compile ("produce") the information ordered for presentation on a later date in the House. (See *Bourinot*, 4th ed., pp. 248-9). In 1964, a procedure committee proposed that "Notices of Motions for the Production of Papers" be called on Wednesday and be handled in a manner similar to that being practised with respect to written questions, namely by an announcement that certain ones be accepted, certain ones be accepted subject to qualifications, certain ones might be called and the rest be allowed to stand (*Journals*, April 15, 1964, pp. 213-4; April 20, 1964, pp. 223-6).

268. As with the tabling of documents and replies to questions on the *Order Paper*, today's practice is usually for the Parliamentary Secretary to the Government House Leader to reply on behalf of the government.

269. Standing Order 97(1). See, for example, *Debates*, December 10, 1980, p. 5594; February 4, 1981, pp. 6888-9; June 15, 1983, p. 26414. On at least one occasion, a recorded division was requested after the government had agreed to produce a document (see *Debates*, December 14, 1994, p. 9072) while in another instance a revised return was tabled (*Debates*, October 28, 1981, p. 12281).

270. The procedure by which these motions are debated is examined in Chapter 21, "Private Members' Business".

271. Standing Order 97(1). See, for example, *Debates*, February 4, 1981, p. 6888; February 2, 1983, p. 22431; February 18, 1998, p. 4078; February 25, 1998, p. 4409; April 22, 1998, p. 5964. The Minister's reservation about producing certain documents because of their confidential nature becomes a matter of record (see *Journals*, February 27, 1961, pp. 295-7). In 1981, Speaker Sauvé ruled that the expression "confidential documents" had never been defined and that it would be improper for the Speaker to attempt to do so. She underlined that it is the government's prerogative to decide which documents are of a confidential nature (*Debates*, June 18, 1981, p. 10738).

agree, the motion must either be transferred for debate,[272] or be put immediately to the House without debate or amendment.

3. Motion not acceptable to government; Member is asked to withdraw the notice
A Minister or Parliamentary Secretary rises and states that a notice of motion is not acceptable to the government and asks that the Member withdraw the notice. If the Member agrees, the motion is withdrawn.[273] Otherwise, either the Member sponsoring the item or a Minister may then ask that the motion be transferred for debate.[274] There have been numerous occasions when the sponsor has not been present in the House, but a request was made anyway to have a notice of motion withdrawn. Logically though, a request to withdraw should be made only when the sponsor is present. In the absence of the sponsor, an alternative way of proceeding would be for a Minister, once a notice of motion is called, to immediately request that it be transferred for debate. When a request to transfer is made, the motion is transferred, without debate or amendment, to a heading on the *Order Paper* under Private Members' Business entitled "Notices of Motions (Papers)" on the list of items outside the Order of Precedence. It may be subject to debate at a subsequent time if it is selected by the Member following the draw for the Order of Precedence. If no request is made that the motion once called be transferred for debate, the motion must be put immediately to the House without debate or amendment.[275]

4. Member asks that notice be called
A Member rises and requests the Speaker to call his or her notice of motion. The Member or a Minister may request that it be transferred for debate under Private Members' Business.[276] The motion is then transferred, without debate or amendment, to a heading on the *Order Paper* under Private Members' Business entitled "Notices of Motions (Papers)" on the list of items outside the Order of Precedence. It may be subject to debate at a subsequent time if it is selected by the Member following the draw for the Order of Precedence. If neither the Member nor the Minister requests that it be transferred for debate, the motion must be put immediately to the House without debate or amendment. If the motion is adopted, it becomes an Order of the House that the document be produced either immediately or at a later date.[277]

---

272. The procedure by which these motions are debated is examined in Chapter 21, "Private Members' Business".

273. See, for example, *Debates*, December 17, 1980, p. 5854; March 18, 1981, pp. 8377-8.

274. Standing Order 97(1). See, for example, *Debates*, February 17, 1982, pp. 15107-8; July 14, 1982, p. 19331; February 4, 1998, p. 3328; December 2, 1998, p. 10793. See also ruling of Deputy Speaker Milliken, *Debates*, November 25, 1998, pp. 10436-7. The procedure by which these motions are debated is examined in Chapter 21, "Private Members' Business".

275. See, for example, *Debates*, May 6, 1992, p. 10239.

276. Standing Order 97(1). See, for example, *Debates*, December 9, 1981, p. 13891; December 16, 1981, pp. 14129-30; February 24, 1982, p. 15350; March 31, 1982, pp. 16015-6; August 4, 1982, pp. 20020-1; December 1, 1982, p. 21175; May 30, 1984, pp. 4197-8; April 29, 1998, p. 6297; May 6, 1998, p. 6608; June 3, 1998, pp. 7537-8; November 25, 1998, pp. 10436-7. The procedure by which these motions are debated is examined in Chapter 21, "Private Members' Business".

277. Standing Order 97(1). See, for example, *Debates*, March 31, 1982, p. 16015.

5. Notices allowed to stand

A Minister or Parliamentary Secretary rises and asks that all notices of motions be allowed to stand and retain their place on the *Order Paper.*[278] If some notices have been dealt with, the Minister or Parliamentary Secretary asks that the remaining notices be allowed to stand.

Responses to Orders for the Production of Papers

In 1973, the government tabled in the House of Commons its views on the general principles governing "Notices of Motions for Production of Papers".[279] Although not formally approved by the House, these principles have been followed since then:[280]

General Principle

To enable Members of Parliament to secure factual information about the operations of government to carry out their parliamentary duties and to make public as much factual information as possible consistent with effective administration, the protection of the security of the state, rights to privacy and other such matters, government papers, documents and consultant reports should be produced on Notice of Motion for the Production of Papers unless falling within the categories outlined below, in which case an exemption is to be claimed from production.

Exemptions

The following criteria are to be applied in determining if government papers or documents should be exempt from production:

1. *Legal opinion or advice provided for the use of the government;*

2. *Papers, the release of which would be detrimental to the security of the State;*

3. *Papers dealing with international relations, the release of which might be detrimental to the future conduct of Canada's foreign relations (the release of papers received from other countries to be subject to the consent of the originating country);*

4. *Papers, the release of which might be detrimental to the future conduct of federal-provincial relations or the relations of provinces* inter se *(the release of papers received from provinces to be subject to the consent of the originating province);*

5. *Papers containing information, the release of which could allow or result in direct personal financial gain or loss by a person or a group of persons;*

---

278. Standing Order 42(1). See, for example, *Debates*, March 25, 1998, p. 5341; June 10, 1998, p. 7936.

279. *Journals*, March 15, 1973, p. 187.

280. *Debates*, March 15, 1973, p. 2288. This document was referred to the Standing Joint Committee on Regulations and other Statutory Instruments on March 29, 1973 (*Journals*, p. 226). See also *Debates*, March 29, 1973, pp. 2745-50. In 1974, the President of the Privy Council tabled the guidelines again and they were subsequently referred to the same committee (*Journals*, December 19, 1974, pp. 229, 231). The Committee did not report back to the House on this matter on either occasion.

6. *Papers reflecting on the personal competence or character of an individual;*

7. *Papers of a voluminous character or which would require an inordinate cost or length of time to prepare;*

8. *Papers relating to the business of the Senate;*

9. *Papers, the release of which would be personally embarrassing to Her Majesty or the Royal Family or official representatives of Her Majesty;*

10. *Papers relating to negotiations leading up to a contract until the contract has been executed or the negotiations have been concluded;*

11. *Papers that are excluded from disclosure by statute;*

12. *Cabinet documents and those documents which include a Privy Council confidence;*

13. *Any proceedings before a court of justice or a judicial inquiry of any sort;*

14. *Papers that are private or confidential and not of a public or official character;*

15. *Internal departmental memoranda;*

16. *Papers requested, submitted or received in confidence by the government from sources outside the government.*

Ministers' Correspondence
Ministers' correspondence of a personal nature, or dealing with constituency or general political matters, should not be identified with government papers and therefore should not be subject to production in the House.

Consultant Studies
In the case of consultant studies, the following guidelines are to be applied:

1. *Consultant studies, the nature of which is identifiable and comparable to work that would be done within the Public Service, should be treated as such (the reports and also the terms of reference) when consideration is being given to their release.*

2. *Consultant studies, the nature of which is identifiable and comparable to the kind of investigation of public policy for which the alternative would be a Royal Commission, should be treated as such, and both the terms of reference for such studies and the resulting reports should be produced.*

3. *Prior to engaging the services of a consultant, Ministers are to decide in which category the study belongs and in case of doubts are to seek the advice of their colleagues.*

4. *Regardless of the decision as to which category (1. or 2. above) the consultant report will belong, the terms of reference and the contract for the consultant study are to ensure that the resulting report comprises two or more volumes, one of which is to be the recommendations while the other volume(s) is(are) to be the facts and the analysis of the study. The purpose of this separation is to facilitate the release of the factual and analytical portions (providing that the*

material is not covered by the exemptions listed above) enabling the recommen-
dations (which, in the case of studies under category 1., would be exempt from
production) to be separated for consideration by Ministers.

Despite these principles enunciated by the government, it is not the role of the Chair to decide which documents must be tabled or if all documents have been tabled. If a Member is not satisfied with the response, the Member may pursue the matter by means of another motion.[281]

While there is no time limit on Orders to produce papers, if the House has adopted an Order for the production of a document, the Order should be complied with within a reasonable time.[282] However, the Speaker has no power to determine when documents should be tabled.[283] A prorogation does not nullify an Order for the production of papers.[284]

Government Orders

Each sitting day, a substantial portion of the House's time is devoted to the consideration of Government Orders. It includes any item of business proposed by a Minister for consideration on a certain day.

The rules provide that Government Orders are considered on Monday from 12:00 noon to 2:00 p.m., recommencing following Routine Proceedings until 6:30 p.m. On Tuesday and Thursday, after Routine Proceedings at 10:00 a.m., the House considers Government Orders until 2:00 p.m. and then again following Question Period from 3:00 p.m. to 5:30 p.m., at which time the House considers Private Members' Business. On Wednesday, after Routine Proceedings and "Notices of Motions for the Production of Papers", Government Orders are taken up until 5:30 p.m. when Private Members' Business begins. On Friday, Government Orders are considered from 10:00 a.m. to 11:00 a.m., at which time the House proceeds to Statements by Members. After Routine Proceedings, the House resumes consideration of Government Orders until 1:30 p.m., when Private Members' Business begins.[285] See Figure 10.1 which outlines the daily order of business.

---

281. See, for example, ruling of Speaker Sauvé, *Debates*, November 16, 1982, pp. 20702-3.

282. See, for example, *Debates*, November 21, 1979, pp. 1557-8.

283. See, for example, *Debates*, July 15, 1982, pp. 19361-2.

284. Standing Order 49.

285. Standing Order 30(5) and (6). The time for Government Orders may be increased if a Member moves a motion, without notice, to continue or to extend a sitting beyond the fixed hour of daily adjournment in order to continue the consideration of a particular government order, and the motion is adopted (see Standing Order 26). In addition, as the House moves towards the summer adjournment, a Minister may propose a motion during Routine Proceedings to extend the hours of sitting of the House in the last 10 sitting days of June (see Standing Order 27). These longer hours are typically used for the consideration of government business. See Chapter 9, "Sittings of the House."

Historical Perspective

Historically, there have been many changes to the rules of the House in order to increase the time available to the government and to reduce the proportion of House time devoted to private bills or to matters brought forward by private Members. In 1867, private bills were debated on Monday and for one hour each Wednesday and Friday evening, while notices of motions and public bills were considered on Wednesday and Thursday. Only Tuesday and Friday were reserved for government business. [286]

From 1867 to 1962, the Standing Orders gave precedence to Private Members' Business on particular days each week. However, successive governments found such a distribution inadequate for the conduct of their own legislative programs and regularly gave precedence to their own business via special or sessional orders. In 1962, the House amended its Standing Orders so that government business could be considered each sitting day; only a select number of hours per week were allocated to Private Members' Business. [287] This schedule remained more or less intact until 1982 when the House set aside Wednesday for Private Members' Business. [288] In 1983, the House reverted to the practice of considering Government Orders each day. [289] Today, 23.5 hours a week are set aside for the consideration of government business under normal hours of sitting. [290]

Orders of the Day

When the Speaker calls "Orders of the Day", a Table Officer rises and reads out the motion that the House is to consider at that time. [291] The Orders of the Day are listed in the *Order Paper*.

The sequence of Government Orders as listed on the *Order Paper* does not reflect precedence: it is an administrative breakdown showing the different categories of government business or projected government business in chronological sequence. Items eligible for consideration under Government Orders include all the

---

286. See *Rules, Orders and Forms of Proceeding of the House of Commons of Canada*, 1868, Rule No. 19.

287. *Journals*, April 10, 1962, pp. 338-9; April 12, 1962, p. 350.

288. See the Third Report of the Special Committee on Standing Orders and Procedure, *Minutes of Proceedings and Evidence,* November 4, 1982, Issue No. 7, pp. 14-5, presented on November 5, 1982 (*Journals*, p. 5328), and the motion adopted by the House on November 29, 1982 (*Journals*, p. 5400).

289. See the First Report of the Special Committee on Standing Orders, *Minutes of Proceedings and Evidence,* December 15, 1983, Issue No. 2, pp. 3-4, presented December 15, 1983 (*Journals*, p. 47), and the motion adopted by the House on December 19, 1983 (*Journals*, pp. 55-6).

290. The amount of time available daily to the government for the consideration of its business has fluctuated over the years depending on the hours of sitting and adjournment of the House. For example, in 1990, 18 hours a week were set aside for Government Orders; this grew to 25 hours the following year. In 1994, time available for Government Orders was readjusted when the ordinary hour of daily adjournment was altered and the daily midday interruption for the lunch hour was removed.

291. See *Stewart*, pp. 71-2, for a history of the term "Orders of the Day".

orders made by the House at previous sittings relating to the items of government business then before the House (including, for example, bills introduced and ordered for a second reading, motions which have fulfilled their notice requirements, and any order for resuming debate on an item). These items are listed on the *Order Paper* under the following headings: Supply Proceedings; Ways and Means Proceedings; Government Bills (Commons); Government Bills (Senate); and Government Business. Full descriptions of these items (Government Business excepted) can be found in Chapter 16, "The Legislative Process", and Chapter 18, "Financial Procedures".

Any item of business proposed by a Minister outside of proceedings on Supply, Ways and Means, and bills is listed under the heading "Government Business". They typically include, for example, motions to establish special committees, to refer business to committees, to propose a resolution declaratory of some opinion, or to make arrangements for the conduct of the business of the House. In addition to these items, when debate on motions which have been moved under "Motions" during Routine Proceedings is interrupted or adjourned, the motions are transferred to "Government Business".[292] They typically include motions for concurrence in committee reports.

When Government Orders is called, any item listed may be brought before the House for consideration. Any item that has been called, and on which debate has begun, must be dealt with until adjourned, interrupted or disposed of. If adjourned or interrupted, the item remains on the *Order Paper*.[293] If the item is disposed of, by either an affirmative or negative decision of the House, it is removed from the *Order Paper*.

The business that the House is to consider during Government Orders is determined solely by the government.[294] On occasions when the Opposition has protested

---

292. Standing Order 66. Prior to 1965, resumed debate on motions moved during Routine Proceedings took place under that rubric on the next sitting day. On several occasions, motions to concur in committee reports were debated at length over a number of days, thus preventing the House from considering any further items on the *Order Paper*. In 1965, the Standing Orders were amended in such a way that the government was obliged to call resumed debate on adjourned or interrupted motions as the first item under Government Orders on the next sitting day. This change prevented continued debate on a motion from keeping the House from considering other items of Routine Proceedings or from having a Question Period (*Journals*, June 11, 1965, pp. 224, 226). Three years later, the House concurred in a report from a special committee which recommended that the government be permitted to call such business in the order it chooses without restriction (*Journals*, December 20, 1968, p. 571).

293. See Standing Order 41.

294. Standing Order 40(2). However, in order to be considered, any government business must meet the necessary notice requirement (Standing Order 54). This Standing Order was first included in the rules of the House in 1906 (*Debates*, July 9, 1906, cols. 7477-80; *Journals*, July 10, 1906, pp. 579-80).

a change in the projected order of business for a specific sitting day, the Chair has reminded Members of the government's prerogative.[295]

Information concerning the government's intention to proceed to a specific Order of the Day is conveyed to the Table through the office of the Government House Leader which provides a projected order of business or agenda of orders (bills and motions) the House is to consider that day. The Government House Leader consults regularly and confidentially with the House Leaders of the other recognized parties in the House about the order of business for each day of the week. A weekly statement concerning the projected order of business is traditionally made on Thursday after Question Period.[296] Any last minute changes or additions to the government's agenda are relayed directly to the Table by the Government House Leader or his or her Parliamentary Secretary.

Although the government does not select the subject matter to be debated when the House considers a motion moved on an allotted day pursuant to the Business of Supply, it designates which day the item is to be taken up.[297] The item is considered under Government Orders given that, in moving the motion, a Member of the opposition does so pursuant to the continuing order for Supply moved by the government at the beginning of each session. This order allows the Business of Supply to remain on the agenda for every sitting day of the session thereafter.[298] On an allotted day, the government cannot put aside the Business of Supply and take up other items of Government Orders until all Supply items listed on that day's *Order Paper* have been dealt with.[299]

---

295. In 1987, the Speaker cited this rule when the Opposition challenged the right of the government to call a bill for debate even though, as they claimed, its text was in imperfect form. Despite the charge, the Speaker agreed to allow debate without prejudice to any ruling that might be rendered because, as he stated, under the terms of the rule, the government was within its right to carry on with the debate. See *Debates*, January 23, 1987, pp. 2651-3. See also *Debates*, October 29, 1987, pp. 10508-9; May 25, 1988, pp. 15773-5; April 2, 1993, p. 18002; June 1, 1994, pp. 4709-10.

296. See "Weekly Business Statement" later in this chapter.

297. The hybrid nature of Supply motions, which are formulated by Members of the opposition yet considered under Government Orders, gave rise to one of the few instances in recent years where the Speaker invoked Standing Order 40(2) to resolve a dispute. On February 11, 1982, the Government House Leader announced that a Supply day set for the following day would be postponed by one week. When the opposition objected, the Speaker ruled that as Supply motions fall under Government Orders, they can be "called and considered in sequence as the government determines" (*Debates*, pp. 14896-9).

298. Standing Order 81(1).

299. Standing Order 81(2).

Private Members' Business

Bills and motions sponsored by private Members are taken up individually by the House after several unique requirements are met. (These procedures are discussed in greater detail in Chapter 21, "Private Members' Business".) The House typically devotes one hour of its time each sitting day to the consideration of Private Members' Business.[300] This hour commences at 11:00 a.m. on Monday, 5:30 p.m. on Tuesday, Wednesday and Thursday, and 1:30 p.m. on Friday.[301]

Historical Perspective

From 1867 to 1906, Private Members' Business had precedence over government business on particular days of the week.[302] However, by means of special or sessional orders, the House regularly gave precedence to government business. In 1906, the weekly order of business was officially amended so that Thursday ceased to be a private Members' day four weeks after the start of a session, precedence being given to government business.[303]

Until 1955, there were few changes to the daily order of business, and the use of special and sessional orders continued to appropriate much of the time set aside for private Members. In 1955, amendments to the Standing Orders formalized the practice of giving precedence to government business and guaranteed private Members six Mondays and two Thursdays per session to conduct their business.[304] In 1962, the House abandoned the allocation of a certain number of days each session for Private Members' Business, setting aside instead one hour per day for that purpose.[305] After the hour for Private Members' Business was used 40 times per session on Monday, Tuesday, and Wednesday, it would lapse on those days, only taking place thereafter on Thursday and Friday. In 1968, Private Members' Business was removed from the order of business on Wednesday; the maximum 40 considerations per session for Private Members' Business was retained for Monday and Tuesday only; thereafter, Private Members' Business was held only on Thursday and Friday.[306] This schedule of business remained intact until 1982 when the practice of considering Private Members' Business one hour each day except Wednesday was replaced by a single Private

---

300. At the beginning of a session, Private Members' Business does not take place until the establishment of an Order of Precedence (Standing Order 91).

301. Standing Order 30(6).

302. See *Rules, Orders and Forms of Proceedings of the House of Commons of Canada*, 1868, 1873, 1876, 1880, 1884, 1890, 1893, 1896, 1901, 1904 and 1905, Rule No. 19.

303. See *Debates*, July 9, 1906, cols. 7475-7.

304. See *Journals*, July 12, 1955, pp. 889-93.

305. *Journals*, April 10, 1962, pp. 338-9; April 12, 1962, p. 350.

306. See *Journals*, December 6, 1968, pp. 436-7; December 20, 1968, pp. 563-5.

Members' Day, on Wednesday.[307] This meant a reduction of one hour in debating time per week, from four hours to three. In late 1983, the House reverted to the consideration of Private Members' Business for one hour per day on Monday, Tuesday, Thursday and Friday, without the previous provision for a maximum number of times for consideration on Monday and Tuesday;[308] this meant that the amount of time provided for private Members actually increased. There were no changes to this arrangement until 1991 when amendments to the Standing Orders added an extra hour to the sitting on Wednesday in order to provide another hour of Private Members' Business, thus increasing from four to five the number each week.[309]

Suspension of Private Members' Hour

Consideration of Private Members' Business may be suspended on certain occasions, namely:

- on any day designated for resuming debate on the Address in Reply to the Speech from the Throne;[310]

- on any day designated for the presentation of the Budget Speech if it is scheduled to take place before Private Members' Hour;[311]

- on any day designated for resuming debate on the Budget;[312]

- on any day when an emergency debate takes place before Private Members' Hour;[313]

- when a Minister moves a motion on a matter the government considers to be of an urgent nature, and that debate takes place in the time normally provided for Private Members' Business;[314] and

---

307. See the Third Report of the Special Committee on Standing Orders and Procedure, *Minutes of Proceedings and Evidence*, November 4, 1982, Issue No. 7, pp. 14-5, presented on November 5, 1982 (*Journals*, p. 5328), and the motion adopted on November 29, 1982 (*Journals*, p. 5400).

308. See the First Report of the Special Committee on Standing Orders, *Minutes of Proceedings and Evidence*, December 15, 1983, Issue No. 2, pp. 3-4, presented on December 15, 1983 (*Journals*, p. 47), and the motion adopted by the House on December 19, 1983 (*Journals*, pp. 55-6). In its Tenth Report, presented in the House on September 30, 1983 (*Journals*, p. 6250), the Committee noted that some Members had concerns about one full day being set aside for Private Members' Business because it disrupted the flow of business in the House. The Committee recommended that a more in-depth study be done to determine what day or days should be set aside for Private Members' Business in order to accommodate the largest possible number of Members and to encourage participation. See Special Committee on Standing Orders and Procedure, *Minutes of Proceedings and Evidence,* September 29, 1983, Issue No. 24, p. 7.

309. *Journals*, April 11, 1991, pp. 2905-6, 2908.

310. Standing Order 50(4).

311. Standing Order 83(2).

312. Standing Order 99(1).

313. Standing Order 52(14). See Chapter 15, "Special Debates".

314. Standing Order 99(1). See Chapter 15, "Special Debates".

- on the last allotted day of the Supply period ending June 23, except for Monday when Private Members' Business takes place at the beginning of the sitting.[315]

Because Members must be aware of when particular items are expected to be called for consideration, the Standing Orders require the Speaker to ensure that Members are given at least 24 hours' notice of which item is to be considered during Private Members' Hour on the next sitting day.[316] This notification must be published in the *Notice Paper*.

A Member whose motion or bill is scheduled for consideration during Private Members' Hour and who is unable to be present that day to move the motion may notify the Speaker in writing 48 hours in advance. The Speaker has the authority to arrange an exchange with another item on the Order of Precedence with the permission of the Members involved and Private Members' Hour proceeds as usual.[317] Should such an exchange be impossible, Private Members' Business is suspended for the day, and the House continues with the business previously before it.[318] Should this occur on Monday, the House would then begin consideration of Government Orders at 11:00 a.m. instead of at 12:00 noon.[319]

The Standing Orders also provide that if the Speaker were unable to notify the House at least 24 hours in advance of the item to be considered, then Private Members' Business would be suspended and the House would continue with the business before it.[320] Should this occur on Monday, the sitting would then commence at 11:00 a.m. with Government Orders.

When Private Members' Hour is reached, should a Member be unable to move his or her scheduled item when called, then Private Members' Business is suspended for that day. On Monday, the sitting is suspended until 12:00 noon, at which time the

---

315. Standing Order 99(1).

316. Standing Order 94(1)(*a*).

317. Standing Order 94(2)(*a*).

318. Standing Order 94(2)(*b*). Since the coming into force of this Standing Order, the Chair has instructed, on such occasions, that the item be dropped to the bottom of the Order of Precedence (see, for example, *Debates*, March 23, 1994, p. 2694; April 27, 1995, p. 11911; May 9, 1996, p. 2580; February 4, 1997, p. 7680; March 26, 1998, p. 5442). This practice has been followed since 1986 when the Speaker was asked to clarify the Standing Orders with respect to the disposition of an item of Private Members' Business in the event a Member was unable to move the motion on the designated day. See *Debates*, April 24, 1986, pp. 12624-6; April 25, 1986, pp. 12671-3; May 9, 1986, pp. 13146-7; May 28, 1986, p. 13727; November 17, 1986, pp. 1215-6.

319. Standing Order 99(2). See, for example, *Debates*, November 18, 1994, p. 8004; November 25, 1994, p. 8303; March 10, 1997, p. 8805; May 8, 1998, p. 6736.

320. Standing Order 94(1)(*b*). This provision has been included in the Standing Orders for unforeseen and unexpected circumstances. In practice, this provision is unlikely to be invoked since the Speaker is provided with a mechanism to give notice when an exchange is not possible (Standing Order 94(2)), and since a mechanism is in place to establish the Order of Precedence at the beginning of a session (Standing Order 87(1)) and to maintain it during the session (Standing Order 87(2)).

House commences with Government Orders.[321] On Tuesday, Wednesday and Thursday, the sitting is suspended until the Adjournment Proceedings. When this occurs on Friday, the Speaker adjourns the House.[322]

Finally, as much of Private Members' Hour is suspended as necessary on Tuesday, Wednesday, Thursday and Friday to allow the House to continue Routine Proceedings until the completion of "Introduction of Government Bills".[323]

Private Members' Business may be delayed or interrupted for a number of reasons. Should this occur, the debate on the item of business is then extended or rescheduled to another time.[324] For example, if consideration of Private Members' Business is delayed because of a recorded division,[325] or a ministerial statement,[326] or Royal Assent, or due to an emergency alarm, then Private Members' Hour is extended by a corresponding amount of time.[327] If the delay or interruption extends 30 minutes or more beyond the ordinary ending of Private Members' Hour, the Speaker will add the remaining time or the entire hour to another sitting.[328] The rescheduled debate takes place within 10 sitting days, usually after the ordinary hour of daily adjournment; 24 hours' notice is given.[329]

321. See, for example, *Debates*, February 22, 1993, p. 16247; March 17, 1997, p. 9060; *Notice Paper*, March 17, 1997, p. III.

322. See, for example, *Debates*, April 12, 1991, pp. 19464-5, 19477; March 13, 1992, p. 8236; April 23, 1993, p. 18413.

323. Standing Order 30(4)(*a*).

324. Standing Order 30(7).

325. See *Journals*, May 9, 1996, p. 346.

326. See, for example, *Debates*, September 24, 1991, p. 2657; November 1, 1991, p. 4412; April 18, 1994, p. 3131; May 17, 1996, pp. 2953, 2963; November 6, 1997, pp. 1666, 1684.

327. Prior to February 1994, when Standing Order 30(7) was amended to provide for delays or interruptions in Private Members' Hour for any reason, Private Members' Business could be extended only with the unanimous consent of the House (see, for example, *Debates*, October 2, 1991, p. 3190; June 4, 1992, p. 11438).

328. Standing Order 30(7).

329. As an example, on Tuesday, April 23, 1996, Private Members' Business was scheduled to take place from 5:30 to 6:30 p.m. Because of a ministerial statement, the time for Government Orders was extended by 72 minutes. In addition, at the conclusion of Government Orders, there was a recorded division. Consequently, it was 7:15 p.m., 45 minutes past the time Private Members' Business would normally have ended, when the House was ready to proceed to Private Members' Business. Pursuant to the Standing Order, the Speaker was required to reschedule the debate until another sitting. See *Journals*, April 23, 1996, pp. 244-51; *Debates*, p. 1880. See also *Debates*, June 14, 1995, p. 13853; June 19, 1995, p. 14104; June 20, 1995, p. 14297; May 2, 1996, p. 2283; December 1, 1998, p. 10773; December 7, 1998, p. 10945.

Adjournment Proceedings

The final category of business conducted on a sitting day is the Adjournment Proceedings. A 30-minute period is set aside for Members to seek further information from the government on questions raised. (For further details, see Chapter 11, "Questions".)

In a review of the Standing Orders in 1964, the House adopted a procedure committee proposal for the first-ever Standing Order to regulate Question Period. At the same time, the House agreed to the committee's suggestion that a rule on the Adjournment Proceedings be adopted to complement the Question Period Standing Order. The committee proposed a procedure whereby any Member who felt dissatisfied with an answer given by the government to his or her question during Question Period could give notice that he or she wished to speak further on the subject matter of the question during the Adjournment Proceedings.[330] In addition, since 1991, any Member concerned that a written question he or she submitted for the *Order Paper* has remained unanswered after 45 calendar days may give notice of his or her intention to transfer the question to the Adjournment Proceedings.[331] The question is then removed from the *Order Paper* and the Member's name is placed on a list along with the names of other Members who have given notice of their intention to proceed in the Adjournment Proceedings.

At the conclusion of the sitting, from 6:30 to 7:00 p.m. on Monday, Tuesday, Wednesday and Thursday, a motion to adjourn the House is deemed to have been moved and seconded, and a debate ensues for a maximum of 30 minutes.[332] During this period, up to five topics may be debated. The Speaker must have indicated to the House, at no later than 5:00 p.m., which matter or matters are to be raised.[333] Debate on any one item can last no more than six minutes.[334] Within this six-minute time frame, the Member raising the matter may speak no longer than four minutes with the Minister or Parliamentary Secretary speaking in response thereto for no longer than two minutes.[335] Points of order and questions of privilege may not be raised during this period. After 30 minutes or upon completion of debate, whichever comes first, the motion to adjourn is deemed to have been adopted, and the House is adjourned to the next sitting day.[336] (On Friday and on days where there are no questions

---

330. Standing Order 37(3). See also *Journals*, April 20, 1964, pp. 224-5; *Debates*, p. 2342.

331. Standing Order 39(5)(*b*). See *Journals*, April 11, 1991, pp. 2905, 2909-10. For an example of a Member requesting that his written question be transferred to the Adjournment Proceedings, see *Debates*, November 20, 1992, pp. 13720-1; September 25, 1995, p. 14819.

332. Standing Order 38(1). Because the Adjournment Proceedings are customarily held at the conclusion of the sitting day, this segment of the day is informally known as the "late show".

333. Standing Order 38(4).

334. Standing Order 38(2).

335. Standing Order 38(5).

336. Standing Order 38(5).

scheduled for debate during the Adjournment Proceedings, the Speaker adjourns the House at the conclusion of the sitting.)

Suspension or Delay of the Proceedings

The Adjournment Proceedings may be suspended on certain occasions, namely when the sitting has been extended for an emergency debate,[337] on the day designated for the Budget presentation,[338] or on any day when the House continues to sit beyond the ordinary hour of daily adjournment for the election of a Speaker.[339] The Adjournment Proceedings may be delayed when a sitting is extended due to a ministerial statement[340] or when Private Members' Business has been extended on the second sitting day set aside for the consideration of the report and third reading stages of a bill.[341] The Adjournment Proceedings may also be delayed on the last allotted day in the Supply periods ending December 10, March 26 and June 23.[342] If a motion has been adopted to extend the hours of sitting during the last 10 sitting days in June, the Adjournment Proceedings are delayed until the agreed upon hour of adjournment.[343] If a motion has been adopted to continue a sitting pursuant to Standing Order 26, the Adjournment Proceedings take place at the conclusion of the sitting.[344] On other occasions, when the sitting of the House has been extended for the consideration of legislation or for a special debate, the House has opted to preserve the adjournment debate at its normal time; after the adjournment debate has concluded, instead of being automatically adopted, the motion to adjourn the House has been deemed withdrawn.[345] The Adjournment Proceedings have been interrupted by Royal Assent and resumed upon the return of the House from the Senate following the ceremony.[346]

Weekly Business Statement

Each Thursday, after Question Period, the Speaker recognizes the House Leader of the Official Opposition, or his or her representative, to ask the Government House

---

337. Standing Order 52(12).

338. Standing Order 83(2).

339. Standing Order 2(3).

340. Standing Order 33(2).

341. Standing Order 98(3) and (5).

342. Standing Order 81(17) and (18)(*b*).

343. Standing Order 27(1). See, for example, *Journals*, June 5, 1996, p. 490; June 12, 1996, p. 546.

344. See, for example, *Journals*, May 11, 1998, pp. 772-4. However, whenever a sitting is extended pursuant to Standing Order 26, it is not always possible for those Members scheduled in the Adjournment Proceedings to be available since the beginning of that debate is unknown. See transcript of the meeting of the Standing Committee on Procedure and House Affairs, May 3, 1994, p. 12:18. An announcement by the Speaker may be made, but the Adjournment Proceedings will lapse if Members do not proceed with their questions (see *Debates*, March 13, 1997, p. 9036; *Journals*, pp. 1277-8, 1281).

345. See, for example, *Journals*, November 26, 1992, p. 2242; March 18, 1996, pp. 104, 111.

346. See, for example, *Debates*, November 6, 1990, p. 15236.

Leader, or his or her representative, about the government business to be considered by the House in the succeeding days or week. The Government House Leader then proceeds to outline for the House what business the government intends to bring forward.[347] This practice is commonly known as the "Business Statement" or the "Thursday Statement". The weekly business statement is not referred to in the Standing Orders but is permitted subject to the discretion of the Chair, the government being under no procedural obligation to announce to the House in advance which items of business it intends to call or when.[348] Furthermore, the government is not bound by anything said in the weekly business statement.[349]

The weekly business statement was inaugurated on September 23, 1968, when the then President of the Privy Council, in announcing the business the government intended to call the following day, stated that a new practice would begin whereby on every Thursday the government would outline its intentions for the forthcoming week and then respond to questions.[350] Prior to this, it had been the custom of the Government House Leader to announce, at the close of each sitting day, the business to be considered the next day.[351]

The Chair has stressed on many occasions that the time provided for this statement should not be used by Members as an opportunity to engage in negotiations or debate.[352] The Chair has also not been inclined to consider the question of House business at any time other than on a Thursday during a week of regularly scheduled sittings.[353] On occasion, the Government House Leader has used this period to request the unanimous consent of the House to propose, without notice, motions related to the business of the House.[354]

---

347. Occasionally, following the comments of the Government House Leader, other Members (customarily, but not exclusively, the House Leaders representing parties in opposition) may be recognized to pose brief questions on specific items of business or to clarify information (see *Debates*, November 9, 1995, p. 16443). Although all Members are permitted to participate in posing questions to the Government House Leader, the Speaker has suggested that Members of the opposition should make their representations known to the House through their respective House Leaders (*Debates*, February 14, 1985, p. 2359). See also *Debates*, June 3, 1999, pp. 15814-5.

348. Standing Order 40(2).

349. See *Debates*, June 1, 1994, pp. 4709-10.

350. *Debates*, September 23, 1968, p. 383.

351. The wording of Standing Order 38(6) still refers to the old practice of providing, at the end of a sitting, information about the future business of the House.

352. See, for example, *Debates*, October 11, 1990, p. 14048; November 8, 1991, p. 4838; April 2, 1992, pp. 9262-4; May 7, 1992, pp. 10328-9.

353. *Debates*, April 17, 1984, p. 3144. In ruling out of order a Member attempting to inquire into the business of the House on a day other than Thursday, the Speaker stated: "There is a traditional way of dealing with House business. There are the usual channels by which information is transferred and discussions take place relating to House business." See also *Debates*, May 23, 1984, pp. 3962-3.

354. See, for example, *Debates*, April 21, 1994, pp. 3335-6; March 30, 1995, pp. 11300-1.

11

Questions

If the essence of Parliament is Government accountability, then surely the essence of accountability is the Question Period in the Canadian House of Commons.

SPEAKER JAMES JEROME
(*Mr. Speaker,* p. 51)

he right to seek information from the Ministry of the day and the right to hold that Ministry accountable are recognized as two of the fundamental principles of parliamentary government. Members exercise these rights principally by asking questions in the House. The importance of questions within the parliamentary system cannot be overemphasized, and the search for or clarification of information through questioning is a vital aspect of the duties undertaken by individual Members.[1] Questions may be asked orally without notice or be submitted in writing after due notice.

Each sitting day, time is set aside for the purpose of asking oral questions. This constitutes a unique and distinct part of the daily program of the House. Members who are not satisfied with the answer they receive to an oral question may pursue the matter at greater length during the Adjournment Proceedings, which occur every day except Friday at the end of the sitting.

Written questions, usually more detailed than oral questions, appear on the *Order Paper* after due notice. Responses are provided during Routine Proceedings under the rubric "Questions on the *Order Paper*".

---

1. "Nothing could more weaken the control of Parliament over the executive than the abolition or curtailment of the right of a Member of Parliament to ask a question in the House ...". *Wilding and Laundy*, p. 627.

This chapter will outline the rules and practices of the House regarding oral and written questions, addressing the authority for each, their traditions and unique aspects, the current guidelines under which the House functions, and the role of the Speaker in these matters.

Oral Questions

More than any other segment of the parliamentary day, Question Period serves as a daily snapshot of national political life and is closely followed by Members, the press and the public, each sitting day of the House. It is that part of the parliamentary day where the government is held accountable for its administrative policies and the conduct of its Ministers, both individually and collectively.[2] As has been noted, "Question Period is a free-wheeling affair, with tremendous spontaneity and vitality. The main topics raised are often those on the front pages of the major newspapers or raised on national television news the previous evening."[3] Any Member can ask a question, although the time is set aside almost exclusively for the opposition parties to confront the government and hold it accountable for its actions, and to highlight the perceived inadequacies of the government. "Question Period serves the opposition and to a lesser extent the government well in its present form.... it is not subtle or clever but it is effective in making points—for both sides."[4]

HISTORICAL PERSPECTIVE

For most of the history of parliamentary government in Canada, there were no written rules expressly permitting the asking of oral questions, though the practice did exist. Prior to Confederation, oral questions had been asked essentially by consent and, as responsible government evolved, they became more frequent.[5] When the House of Commons adopted its first set of rules in December 1867, only written questions were provided for.[6] Nevertheless, the practice of oral questions had started even earlier on November 29, 1867, three weeks after the opening of the first session of Parliament, when an oral question was posed, not to a Minister but to the Chairman of the Printing Committee, before Orders of the Day were called.[7]

By 1878, oral questions had become a frequent enough practice to warrant comment by Speaker Anglin: "It is customary for hon. members to ask the Government for any special information between the various calls from the Chair for the day, before Notices of Motion or the Orders of the Day. I am not aware that any hon.

---

2. *Stewart*, p. 56.
3. *Franks*, p. 146.
4. *Franks*, p. 155.
5. *O'Brien*, p. 362.
6. *Rules, Orders and Forms of Proceeding of the House of Commons of Canada*, 1868, Rule No. 29.
7. *Debates*, November 29, 1867, p. 157.

member has a positive right even to do that; but I think he must confine himself entirely to asking the information from the Government, and he must not proceed to descant on the conduct of the Government."[8] In the following years, the practice of Members asking oral questions in the House on matters deemed urgent[9] became established as a right by convention. This practice would continue largely unregulated until 1964.

Over time, informal standards and guidelines developed and, by the 1940s, oral questions ("Questions on Orders of the Day" as it was then referred to) had become an established part of the parliamentary day. However, oral questions were still not sanctioned by any written rules. The legitimacy of the convention was augmented through statements made by Speakers in the House concerning guidelines, interpretations and advice on what kinds of questions and replies were acceptable.[10] Furthermore, in the 1940s, procedure committees began to look at the practice of oral questions in an effort to recognize formally the *de facto* procedure by establishing rules to regulate its proceedings.

The first attempt of the House to codify the practice of oral questions occurred in 1944 when a special committee noted, "The custom of asking questions before the orders of the day are proceeded with has taken such a development that it is now part of our parliamentary practice. It is neither possible nor advisable to do away with it."[11] The committee proposed that a formal rule be adopted permitting oral questions to be asked with a minimum one hour's notice to be followed by no more than three supplementary questions each;[12] however, its report containing the new rule was never adopted. During the next few years, other committee reports proposed rules along similar lines but again none of them were adopted by the House.[13] Meanwhile, beginning in 1947, the heading "Inquiries of the Ministry" appeared in the *Debates* when oral questions were posed in the House.

The continued absence of any rule governing oral questions necessitated further statements from the Chair on Question Period and, in 1955, resulted in the modification of the procedure for starred questions (written questions requiring oral answers). This was intended to reduce the number of oral questions on Orders of the

---

8. *Debates*, March 20, 1878, p. 1269.

9. *Bourinot*, 4th ed., p. 315.

10. See, for example, *Journals*, July 15, 1940, pp. 216-8; March 15, 1943, pp. 160-1; *Debates*, February 16, 1944, p. 548.

11. *Journals*, March 3, 1944, p. 151.

12. *Journals*, March 3, 1944, p. 151. The text of the proposed Standing Order stated: "A question of urgent character may be addressed orally to a Minister on the orders of the day being called, provided a copy thereof has been delivered to the Minister and to the Clerk of the House at least one hour before the meeting of the House. Such a question shall not be prefaced by the reading of telegrams, newspaper extracts, letters or preambles of any kind. The answer shall be oral and may be immediately followed by supplementary questions limited to three in number, without debate or comment, for the elucidation of the information given by the Minister."

13. *Journals*, December 5, 1947, pp. 17-20; June 25, 1948, p. 680.

Day,[14] but in fact, Question Period continued to grow as a proceeding. In the early 1960s, however, the nature of Question Period was briefly changed when the Chair began to enforce several long-standing unwritten rules regarding question content, many of which were outdated.[15] The resulting furor eventually led to the adoption, in 1964, of the first-ever codification of Question Period rules.[16]

The urgency requirement was incorporated in the Standing Orders adopted by the House in 1964.[17] It was also established that the House would begin its consideration of oral questions at the conclusion of Routine Proceedings and immediately before Orders of the Day were called. At that time, every sitting started at 2:30 p.m. with Routine Proceedings. Therefore, Question Period was always at approximately the same time, although it depended on the length of Routine Proceedings. Friday, however, was an exception as the sitting started at 11:00 a.m. with Routine Proceedings. A limit of 30 minutes for the consideration of oral questions on Wednesday was also introduced (no time limit for the remaining weekdays), probably due to the fact that Wednesday was a short day with no evening sitting.[18] At the same time, a new procedure was established whereby Members who were dissatisfied with responses given to their questions during Question Period, or who were told by the Speaker that their question was not urgent, could raise these matters at the adjournment of the House.

In addition to the Standing Order changes, the House simultaneously approved content guidelines for oral questions and the answers to them.[19] The guidelines stemmed from precedents which were still considered valid but had not been codified. Questions were to be asked on matters of sufficient importance requiring immediate, but not lengthy and detailed answers; there could be no questions in regard to statements made in newspapers; questions involving legal opinions or on *sub judice* matters were not permitted; and questions could not raise matters of policy too large to be dealt with as an answer to a question. Answers to questions were to be as brief

---

14. *Journals*, July 12, 1955, p. 912. See also *Dawson*, p. 151.

15. *Journals*, October 31, 1963, pp. 509-13.

16. *Journals*, April 20, 1964, pp. 224-5.

17. *Journals*, April 20, 1964, p. 224. The text of the Standing Order stated in part: "Before the Orders of the Day are proceeded with, questions on matters of urgency may be addressed orally to Ministers of the Crown, provided however that if in the opinion of Mr. Speaker a question is not urgent, he may direct that it not be proceeded with or that it be placed on the *Order Paper,* provided also that on any Wednesday the time allowed for a question period prior to the calling of the Orders of the Day shall not exceed thirty minutes."

18. The time limitation was altered the following year when provisions were adopted to limit the time allowed for oral questions to not more than 30 minutes each day with the exception of Monday when the time allowed for oral questions was not to exceed one hour (*Journals*, June 11, 1965, p. 226). These changes also authorized the Speaker to refer oral questions deemed to be of a non-urgent nature to the *Order Paper*. In 1966, the time limitation was extended to 40 minutes on Tuesday, Thursday and Friday (*Journals*, January 21, 1966, p. 34). In 1968, the Standing Orders were further amended to provide a period of 40 minutes each sitting day for the consideration of oral questions (*Journals*, December 20, 1968, p. 568).

19. *Journals*, April 20, 1964, p. 225.

as possible, deal with the matter raised and not provoke debate. Other issues, including the number of supplementaries, for example, were left entirely to the Speaker, who could direct that a question not be proceeded with or that it be placed on the *Order Paper* after due notice.

In 1975, a set time frame was established for Question Period. Originally Question Period came after Routine Proceedings and could begin anywhere from 2:00 p.m. on. As a result of the House concurring in a procedure committee's report in March 1975, Question Period was placed before Routine Proceedings where it would begin without fail at 2:15 p.m. daily. [20]

At the time of these rule changes, Speaker Jerome made a statement in the House which affects the conduct of Question Period to this day. As he explained in his autobiography, *Mr. Speaker,* when he assumed the Chair in 1974 the only guidance he had for conducting Question Period were precedents ruling questions out of order. [21] He established that asking oral questions was a right, not a privilege of the Members, and he identified several principles for the conduct of Question Period. [22] He also reiterated that the question and answer content requirements would continue to apply and added to them those which had evolved since 1964.

However, after 1975, Question Period became an increasingly open forum where questions of every description could be asked, often without regard to some of the guidelines that had been issued and, as well, without regard to the urgency requirement in the Standing Order. This was coupled with an apparent reluctance on the part of successive Speakers to use their discretionary powers to direct that non-urgent questions be placed on the *Order Paper*. In addition, the introduction of television to the House in 1977 affected the conduct of Members during Question Period:

> *It has also been argued that television has contributed to some less than positive developments. Perhaps the most common complaint is that television has led to the over-emphasis on Question Period. It is also felt that individual Members tend to play to the cameras—that they grandstand—in the hopes of getting a 15-second clip on the evening news.* [23]

In 1986, following a period of acrimonious and disorderly Question Periods during which several Members were named and suspended for the remainder of the sitting day, Speaker Bosley made a statement similar to that of Speaker Jerome in

20. *Journals*, March 14, 1975, p. 373; March 24, 1975, p. 399.

21. *Jerome*, p. 54.

22. *Journals*, April 14, 1975, pp. 439-41.

23. "Watching the House at Work," Ninth Report of the Standing Committee on Elections, Privileges, Procedure and Private Members' Business, December 1989, p. 7 (presented in the House on January 22, 1990 (*Journals*, p. 1078)).

1975.[24] As explained later in this chapter, Speaker Bosley set down four principles for Question Period and its attendant guidelines, which are widely adhered to today.

In 1997, a further change was made to the guidelines for Question Period. Speaker Parent indicated to the House that he would no longer apply the long-established practice of ruling out of order questions anticipating an order of the day. Previously, questions in anticipation of an order of the day were disallowed to prevent the time of the House from being taken up with business to be discussed later in the sitting.[25] In 1975, Speaker Jerome included this restriction in the list of guidelines for Question Period.[26] However, during the budget debate and the debate on the Address in Reply to the Speech from the Throne, the Chair permitted some relaxation of the rules as long as questions on these matters did not monopolize the limited time available.[27] In 1983, Speaker Sauvé ruled that questions relating to opposition motions on Supply days could also be put.[28] In 1997, after a point of order had been raised in the House about the guideline,[29] the Standing Committee on Procedure and House Affairs presented a report in which it recommended that the Speaker "no longer apply this guideline and that questions that anticipate Orders of the Day should not be ruled out of order on this basis alone."[30] On April 7, 1997, Speaker Parent informed the House that the Chair would follow the advice of the Committee.[31]

ROLE OF THE SPEAKER DURING QUESTION PERIOD

Presiding over the daily Question Period is regarded as one of the most onerous and difficult tasks undertaken by the Speaker.[32] The Speaker ensures that Question Period is conducted in a civil manner, that questions and answers do not lead to

---

24. *Debates*, February 24, 1986, pp. 10878-9.

25. *Beauchesne*, 1st ed., p. 98; *Beauchesne*, 4th ed., pp. 147-8. See, for example, *Debates*, February 12, 1970, p. 3508; May 7, 1974, p. 2096.

26. *Journals*, April 14, 1975, p. 441.

27. *Journals*, June 26, 1975, p. 665.

28. *Debates*, February 24, 1983, pp. 23181-3.

29. *Debates*, March 4, 1997, pp. 8594-5. John Williams (St. Albert) asked the Speaker to advise the House, and in particular the opposition parties, on how to formulate questions so as not to encroach on this guideline. Speaker Parent responded that "if a question is of a general nature and not hitting on the bill directly", he would allow it.

30. *Journals*, March 21, 1997, p. 1334. In his testimony before the Standing Committee on Procedure and House Affairs, the Clerk of the House, Robert Marleau, pointed out that the government has the prerogative to change the order of the day without notice and that the Speaker is not always aware what business the House will be discussing following Question Period. Consequently, the Speaker may unintentionally rule out of order a question on the basis that it anticipated the order of the day (see Standing Committee on Procedure and House Affairs, *Evidence*, March 18, 1997, Issue No. 37, pp. 9-10).

31. *Debates*, April 7, 1997, p. 9377.

32. See *Laundy*, p. 129; *Jerome*, pp. 51-69; *Fraser*, pp. 51-2.

debate and that both sides of the House get to participate. As Speaker Fraser noted in *The House of Commons at Work:*

> *Question Period places heavy demands on the Speaker of the House. He must at all times remain keenly alert and attentive, keep a perceptive eye on the whole assembly, be aware of the mood of the House and be familiar with the national and international issues likely to be raised. Insofar as possible, he must be aware of the inter-party tensions over particular issues.* [33]

The Speaker has implicit discretion and authority to rule out of order any question posed during Question Period if satisfied that it is in contravention of House rules of order, decorum and procedure. [34] In ruling a question out of order, the Chair may suggest that it be rephrased in order to make it acceptable to the House. [35] Or, the Speaker may recognize another Member to pose the next question. [36] In cases where such a question has been posed, if a Minister wishes to reply, the Speaker, in order to be equitable, has allowed the Minister to do so.

The Speaker has in the past directed that certain questions posed during Question Period should be placed on the *Order Paper*. [37] These are questions which, in the opinion of the Chair, are not urgent or are of such a technical or detailed nature as to require a similar response. In recent years, the Speaker has not invoked this procedure, opting instead to suggest to the Member asking the question that perhaps it would be more appropriately posed in written form. [38]

Given that only 45 minutes are set aside each day for Question Period, the Speaker has often expressed concern that shorter questions and answers would allow more Members to participate. Since the Speaker retains sole discretion in determining the time that individual questions and answers may take, the Chair may interrupt any Member consuming more than a reasonable share of time in posing or responding to a question. [39] While it is not the Chair's responsibility to determine the length of answers given during Question Period, [40] the Speaker has pointed out to the House that, in the interests of fairness, questions should be as concise as possible in order

---

33. *Fraser*, p. 124.

34. See, for example, *Debates*, February 10, 1994, p. 1184; February 12, 1997, p. 8014; November 18, 1997, p. 1846.

35. See, for example, *Debates*, October 2, 1997, p. 407.

36. See, for example, *Debates*, November 25, 1997, p. 2181; May 25, 1999, p. 15258.

37. Standing Order 37(1). This authority was first incorporated into the Standing Orders in 1964 (*Journals*, April 20, 1964, p. 224).

38. See, for example, *Debates*, February 11, 1993, pp. 15784-5; March 18, 1994, p. 2487; October 1, 1997, p. 334.

39. In response to a point of order raised by a Member who was unable to ask a question during Question Period because of the amount of time taken up with lengthy preambles, Speaker Fraser noted that it was up to the House to change the practice from lengthy preambles to short preambles (*Debates*, November 21, 1991, p. 5157).

40. *Debates*, June 13, 1980, pp. 2084-5.

to encourage answers of similar brevity and thereby allow the Chair to recognize as many Members as possible.[41]

CONDUCT OF QUESTION PERIOD

On each sitting day at no later than 2:15 p.m. (11:15 a.m. on Friday), the 45-minute Question Period begins.[42] At this time, the Speaker recognizes the Leader of the Opposition, or the lead questioner for his or her party, for a round of three questions. From the start of the Thirty-First Parliament in 1979 to the end of the Thirty-Fifth Parliament in 1997, the practice had been to allow the party leader of any other officially recognized party in the House, or his or her representative, to pose an initial question followed by two other questions as supplementary to the initial question.[43] At the beginning of the Thirty-Sixth Parliament in 1997, a new arrangement for the conduct of Question Period was put in place by the Speaker after consultations with the House Leaders of all five officially recognized parties in the House. The lead questioner of the Official Opposition poses an initial question followed by two other questions. The lead questioners of the other officially recognized parties are permitted an initial question and only one additional question. Throughout the rest of Question Period, the same pattern of questioning[44] also applies to other Members representing parties in opposition to the government.[45]

Members representing the governing party are also recognized to ask questions though not as often as opposition Members. During the final minutes of Question Period, the Speaker will normally not permit any Member an additional question in order to allow as many Members as possible the opportunity to ask a question that day.[46]

Participation in Question Period is managed to a large extent by the various caucuses and their Whips and can be the subject of negotiations among the parties.[47]

---

41. *Debates*, February 3, 1997, pp. 7580-1. At the start of the Thirty-Sixth Parliament in 1997, the Speaker announced his intention to shorten the length of time for both questions and answers to allow more questions to be put (*Debates*, September 24, 1997, p. 23). With Members allowed approximately 35 seconds to pose questions and Ministers approximately 35 seconds to respond (see *Debates*, October 30, 1997, p. 1366), between 38 and 42 questions are being asked daily as opposed to the 22 to 24 questions asked each day during the Thirty-Fifth Parliament (1994-1997) (see *Debates*, November 18, 1997, pp. 1848-9). See also *Debates*, February 24, 1998, pp. 4370-1; May 6, 1998, p. 6604.

42. Standing Order 30(5).

43. See, for example, *Debates*, October 10, 1979, pp. 21-2; April 15, 1980, pp. 15-7; November 28, 1995, pp. 16901-3.

44. Speaker Parent has allowed additional questions which were not supplementary to the initial question. For examples of variations in the pattern of questions, see *Debates*, October 28, 1997, p. 1235; October 29, 1997, pp. 1284-5; November 5, 1997, p. 1580; November 6, 1997, p. 1660.

45. See, for example, *Debates*, October 23, 1997, pp. 1042-6; February 26, 1998, pp. 4496-9. An agreement was also reached whereby during the twelfth rotation of questions, the Bloc Québécois is allowed only one question (see, for example, *Debates*, September 30, 1997, p. 289; November 28, 1997, p. 2441).

46. See, for example, *Debates*, October 11, 1991, p. 3649; December 12, 1994, p. 8944.

47. *Fraser*, pp. 124-5. See also *Debates*, January 19, 1994, p. 17.

Each party decides daily which of its Members will participate in Question Period and provides the Speaker with a list of the names and the suggested order of recognition of these Members.[48] Each party's list is typically compiled by the Whip or the Member or Members managing that party's strategy for Question Period. Although the Speaker is under no obligation to use such lists, it has become an accepted practice of the House.[49] With this list as a guide, the Speaker uses his or her discretion in recognizing Members to ask questions. The recognition pattern varies depending on party representation in the House and the number of Members in each party. These factors often determine the number of questioners recognized and the number of questions allowed each party. Since the start of the Thirty-First Parliament (1979), Speakers have recognized, as the questioner immediately following the Leader of the Opposition, a Member also representing the Official Opposition to proceed to the next round of questioning.[50]

Members of a political party not officially recognized in the House and Independent Members are permitted to ask questions although not as frequently as those Members belonging to recognized parties. During the Thirty-Fifth Parliament (1994-97), when their numbers climbed as high as 17 over the life of the Parliament, the Speaker attempted to recognize at least one of them every other Question Period, if not every day, generally towards the end of the proceedings.[51]

While the rules place no restriction on who may ask questions during Question Period, by convention only private Members do so. Members must be in their own seats to be recognized to pose questions.[52] Members have been recognized more than once to ask questions in the same Question Period.[53] Ministers do not ask oral questions either of other Ministers or of private Members. Because of their responsibilities in answering questions on behalf of the government, Parliamentary Secretaries

---

48. See *Jerome*, pp. 53-4 and pp. 61-3; *Fraser*, pp. 124-5.

49. The origins of the Question Period list is recounted in former Speaker James Jerome's autobiography, *Mr. Speaker*, pp. 61-2. In recent years, the use of the list has often become a subject of concern to back-benchers who have objected to its use, believing it has limited their opportunity to be recognized by the Chair during Question Period (*Debates*, June 19, 1991, pp. 2071-2).

50. See, for example, *Debates*, October 12, 1979, p. 122.

51. *Debates*, June 16, 1994, pp. 5437-40, in particular p. 5439; November 7, 1996, pp. 6269-72. On one occasion, Members complained that an Independent Member posed a question at a time when the floor should have been given to a Member of a recognized party. See *Debates*, December 12, 1996, pp. 7470-3, for a discussion on this issue.

52. *Debates,* October 10, 1997, pp. 784-5; October 24, 1997, p. 1101.

53. See, for example, *Debates*, October 30, 1996, pp. 5885-6; November 6, 1996, pp. 6186, 6188-9; April 16, 1997, pp. 9796-9.

do not pose questions during Question Period.[54] Finally, the Speaker neither poses nor responds to oral questions.[55]

POINTS OF ORDER AND QUESTIONS OF PRIVILEGE DURING QUESTION PERIOD

Generally, points of order or questions of privilege are not entertained during Question Period.[56] In his 1975 statement concerning the conduct of Question Period, Speaker Jerome indicated that any points of order or questions of privilege arising out of the proceedings of Question Period should be raised at the end of Question Period.[57] Despite this directive, there have been instances of points of order or questions of privilege being raised during Question Period, but they have been deferred, at the request of the Chair, until after Question Period.[58] However, if a situation arises during Question Period that the Speaker believes to be sufficiently serious to require immediate consideration, for example, unparliamentary language, then the matter is addressed at that time.[59]

PRINCIPLES AND GUIDELINES FOR ORAL QUESTIONS

The guidelines which govern the form and content of oral questions are based on convention, usage and tradition. The written rules state only that oral questions are to be based on "matters of urgency" and that a specific period of time is to be set aside each sitting day for that purpose.[60] There is no formal notice requirement for the posing of oral questions, although some Members, as a courtesy, inform the Minister of the question they intend to ask. Practice, precedents and statements made by

54. For many years prior to a definitive ruling on the subject by Speaker Jerome, Parliamentary Secretaries had been allowed to pose oral questions (*Debates*, November 5, 1974, pp. 1059-64). In ruling that Parliamentary Secretaries possessed the right to ask oral questions, Speaker Lamoureux nonetheless questioned the propriety of this procedure given that Parliamentary Secretaries might be placed "in the position of both answering and asking questions, to the extent where we might have a Parliamentary Secretary asking a question of another Parliamentary Secretary" (*Debates*, March 6, 1973, pp. 1932-3). Speaker Fraser conceded that any recognition of Parliamentary Secretaries to ask questions during Question Period had been entirely inadvertent and unintentional on his part (*Debates*, October 1, 1991, p. 3001).

55. *Beauchesne*, 4th ed., p. 314.

56. Standing Order 47 specifies that points of order are not to be considered during Question Period.

57. *Journals*, April 14, 1975, p. 441.

58. See, for example, *Debates*, April 4, 1989, p. 32; February 9, 1993, p. 15637.

59. See, for example, *Debates*, March 24, 1993, p. 17482. The matter was eventually resolved at the conclusion of Question Period (see *Debates*, pp. 17486-8).

60. Standing Order 37(1).

various Speakers in the House have helped over time to define the conduct of Question Period. While the rules concerning oral questions and Question Period have not changed since 1975, such has not been the case for the various sets of guidelines that have governed the form and content of oral questions. Even the interpretation of "urgent" in the Standing Order has evolved. Each Speaker has felt the need to comment on the way he or she would conduct Question Period.

There exists a vast body of traditional guidelines, many of which are no longer valid or have fallen into disuse.[61] Because of the difficulty in distinguishing between valid and outdated precedents, Speaker Bosley addressed this question in 1986,[62] stating that the appropriate rules for Question Period should recognize the following principles:

- Time is scarce and should, therefore, be used as profitably as possible by as many as possible.

- The public in large numbers do watch, and the House, recognizing that Question Period is often an intense time, should be on its best possible behaviour.

- While there may be other purposes and ambitions involved in Question Period, its primary purpose must be the seeking of information from the government and calling the government to account for its actions.

- Members should be given the greatest possible freedom in the putting of questions that is consistent with the other principles.

Drawing in part on the statement from Speaker Jerome in 1975, Speaker Bosley elaborated further:

> *Mr. Speaker Jerome, in his statement 11 years ago, put his view with regard to the first principle of brevity so well that I would merely quote it:*
>
> > *There can be no doubt that the greatest enemy of the Question Period is the Member who offends this most important principle. In putting the original question on any subject, a Member may require an explanatory remark, but there is no reason for such a preamble to exceed one, carefully drawn sentence.*
> >
> > *It is my proposal to ask all Hon. Members to pay close attention to this admonition and to bring them to order if they fail to do so. It bears repeating that the long preamble or long question takes an unfair share of the time, and invariably, in provoking the same kind of response, only compounds the difficulty.*

---

61. On April 1, 1993, the Standing Committee on House Management recommended a new set of guidelines respecting Question Period which would have superseded all previous guidelines. The report was not considered by the House (see Eighty-First Report of the Standing Committee on House Management, pp. 15-6, presented in the House on April 1, 1993 (*Journals*, p. 2774)).

62. *Debates*, February 24, 1986, pp. 10878-9.

I agree with these comments and would add that such comments obviously also apply to answers by Ministers. I would also endorse Mr. Speaker Jerome's view that supplementary questions should need no preambles; they should flow from the Minister's response and be put in precise and direct terms without any prior statement or argument. It is the Chair's view that it equally follows from the first principle, that time is scarce, that Members should seek to avoid merely repeating questions that have already been asked. I do not mean that other questions on the same subject should not be asked—as apparently I have been interpreted—just that subsequent questions should be other than ones already asked.

For similar reasons it has always been a fundamental rule of questioning Ministers that the subject matter of the question must fall within the collective responsibility of the Government or the individual responsibility of one of its Ministers. This is the only basis upon which Ministers can be expected to answer questions. [63]

These two statements, along with some of the guidelines adopted by the House in 1965, are used today by the Speaker as a reference in managing the Question Period. In summary, when recognized in Question Period, a Member should

- ask a question;
- be brief;
- seek information; [64]
- ask a question that is within the administrative responsibility of the government or the individual Minister addressed. [65]

    Furthermore, a question should not

- be a statement, representation, argument or an expression of opinion; [66]

63. *Debates*, February 24, 1986, p. 10879.

64. See, for example, *Debates*, February 12, 1992, p. 6860.

65. See, for example, *Debates*, June 13, 1996, p. 3824; June 17, 1996, p. 3926; October 3, 1997, pp. 459-60; May 25, 1999, pp. 15254-5. In 1986, opposition Members attempted to ask the Regional Industrial Expansion Minister Sinclair Stevens questions relating to an alleged conflict of interest. The Speaker ruled the questions out of order on the grounds that they did not pertain to Mr. Stevens' responsibilities as a Minister. He further clarified that questions of a purely personal nature are out of order, even if the borderline between what is personal and what is ministerial is not always evident (*Debates*, May 8, 1986, pp. 13081-2).

66. See, for example, *Debates*, November 5, 1990, p. 15127.

- be hypothetical;[67]
- seek an opinion, either legal or otherwise;[68]
- seek information which is secretive in its nature, such as Cabinet proceedings or advice given to the Crown by Law Officers;[69]
- reflect on the character or conduct of Chair occupants, Members of the House and of the Senate or Members of the judiciary;[70]
- reflect on the Governor General;[71]
- refer to proceedings in the Senate;[72]
- refer to public statements by Ministers on matters not directly related to their departmental duties;[73]
- address a Minister's former portfolio or any other presumed functions, such as party or regional political responsibilities;[74]
- be on a matter that is *sub judice;*[75]
- deal with the subject matter of a question of privilege previously raised, on which the Speaker reserved his decision;[76]
- create disorder;[77]
- make a charge by way of a preamble to a question;[78]
- be a question from a constituent.[79]

Finally, all questions and answers must be directed through the Chair.[80]

---

67. While the Speaker has occasionally ruled hypothetical questions out of order (see, for example, *Debates*, May 16, 1995, p. 12681), Members are often asked to rephrase their question (see, for example, *Debates*, November 29, 1990, p. 15980). The Speaker has also given a Minister the option to reply or not to the question (see, for example, *Debates*, October 7, 1991, p. 3387; April 14, 1994, p. 3048; December 3, 1997, p. 2652).

68. See, for example, *Debates*, September 21, 1995, p. 14726.

69. See, for example, *Debates*, June 5, 1991, p. 1201.

70. Standing Order 18. See, for example, *Debates*, July 25, 1988, p. 17914; October 5, 1990, p. 13858; December 13, 1990, p. 16693; September 19, 1991, p. 2401.

71. Standing Order 18. See, for example, *Debates*, September 27, 1990, p. 13513; February 24, 1994, pp. 1799-800.

72. See, for example, *Debates*, February 3, 1994, pp. 892-3; October 16, 1995, p. 15399.

73. See, for example, *Debates*, May 2, 1994, pp. 3762-3.

74. See, for example, *Debates*, February 28, 1983, pp. 23278-9; June 10, 1993, p. 20692; May 2, 1994, pp. 3762-3; November 3, 1997, p. 1474; September 28, 1998, p. 8469.

75. See, for example, *Debates*, April 6, 1995, pp. 11618-9; February 13, 1998, p. 3854. This topic is discussed in greater detail later in this chapter.

76. See, for example, *Debates*, April 14, 1987, p. 5144.

77. See, for example, *Debates*, August 22, 1988, pp. 18615-6.

78. See, for example, *Debates*, September 26, 1988, p. 19618.

79. In early 1994, Randy White (Fraser Valley West) asked Finance Minister Paul Martin a question on behalf of one of his constituents. Speaker Parent advised the Member that questions should not be posed by people who are not Members (*Debates*, January 24, 1994, pp. 234-5).

80. See, for example, *Debates*, April 29, 1996, p. 2067; September 30, 1997, p. 289.

Sub judice *Convention*

Over the years, a practice has developed in the House whereby Members are expected to refrain from discussing matters before the courts or under judicial consideration in order to protect those involved in a court action or judicial inquiry against any undue influence through the discussion of the case. This practice is referred to as the *sub judice* convention and it applies to debate, statements and Question Period.[81] It is deemed improper for a Member, in posing a question, or a Minister, in responding to a question, to comment on any matter that is *sub judice*.

In December 1976, a special committee was established to review the rights and immunities of Members.[82] The Committee decided to study how Members' freedom of speech was affected by the *sub judice* convention. Its First Report remains the definitive study of the convention.[83] In the report, the Committee stated: "It is the view of your Committee that the responsibility of the Chair during the question period should be minimal as regards the *sub judice* convention, and that the responsibility should principally rest upon the Member who asks the question and the minister to whom it is addressed."[84] The Committee clarified further that while all Members share in the responsibility of exercising this restraint, the Speaker is the final arbiter in determining whether a subject matter raised during the consideration of oral questions is *sub judice*. As Speaker Parent noted in a 1995 ruling, the approach of most Chair occupants has been to discourage all comments on *sub judice* matters, rather than to allow Members to experiment within the limits of the convention and to test the Speaker's discretion, given that it is speculative to determine how a comment might influence a matter before the courts.[85] Although Members themselves customarily observe the convention during Question Period, the Speaker has ruled out of order questions concerning criminal cases, noting that the Chair has the duty to balance the legitimate right of the House with the rights and interests of the ordinary citizen undergoing the trial.[86] However, as the Committee noted in 1977, if a question to a Minister touches upon a matter that is *sub judice*, it

---

81. However, the House of Commons retains the right to raise and discuss any matter it deems necessary and appropriate. See *Debates*, April 6, 1995, p. 11618.

82. *Journals*, December 13, 1976, p. 230.

83. *Journals*, April 29, 1977, pp. 720-9. The *sub judice* convention is discussed in greater detail in Chapter 13, "Rules of Order and Decorum".

84. *Journals*, April 29, 1977, p. 728.

85. *Debates*, April 6, 1995, pp. 11618-9. A Member had raised a point of order contending that the Minister of Justice had contravened the *sub judice* convention during Question Period by commenting on a case under appeal in the Alberta courts. The Speaker concluded that the Minister had not contravened the convention when he stated that the federal government disagreed with the court's decision and planned to challenge it. See also *Debates*, October 20, 1997, pp. 829-30.

86. *Debates*, November 7, 1989, pp. 5654-7. On this occasion, Bob Kaplan (York Centre) had asked the Speaker to suspend the convention in relation to a criminal case before the courts involving the 1989 federal budget leak, arguing that his questions were not material to the criminal proceedings. The Chair did not accept that the proceedings in a criminal trial could be split into two parts, with the convention only applying to one of the parts.

is likely that the Minister will have more information concerning the matter than the Speaker and can determine whether answering the question might cause prejudice. The Minister could refuse to answer the question as is his or her prerogative.[87]

Questions Concerning the Administration of the House

The Speaker is the Chairman of the Board of Internal Economy, the body which oversees the administration of the House. It had been the practice that no questions dealing with the management and administration of the House could be put to the Speaker during Question Period even though he or she was the chair of the Board. Questions on these matters, it was held, could be dealt with by communicating directly with the Speaker.[88] In June 1985, the House adopted a new rule allowing questions concerning matters of financial or administrative policy affecting the House itself to be directed not to the Speaker, but to those members of the Board of Internal Economy designated by the Board to respond on its behalf.[89] In explaining the procedure for such questions to the newly elected Members of the Thirty-Fifth Parliament (1994-97), the Speaker stated: "All questions relating to the internal and financial management of the House of Commons fall within the statutory responsibilities of the Board of Internal Economy ... Such matters do not fall within the administrative responsibilities of the government. That is why responses to these questions cannot be expected from the ministry."[90]

Questions Concerning Matters Before Committees

Questions seeking information about the schedule and agenda of committees may be directed to chairs of committees.[91] Questions to the Ministry or a committee chair concerning the proceedings or work of a committee may not be raised.[92] Thus, for example, a question would be disallowed if it dealt with a vote in committee,[93] with the attendance of Members at a committee meeting,[94] or with the content of a committee report.[95] Questions to the Ministry on legislation or on a subject matter that is before a committee, when appropriately cast, are normally permitted as long as the

---

87. *Journals*, April 29, 1977, p. 728. See, for example, *Debates*, December 18, 1990, pp. 16901, 16905-6.

88. *Beauchesne*, 4th ed., p. 314.

89. Standing Order 37(2) was adopted on June 27, 1985 (*Journals*, pp. 914, 919). For examples of questions addressed to the Board of Internal Economy, see *Debates*, March 11, 1992, p. 7979; November 19, 1992, p. 13654; February 2, 1994, pp. 791-2.

90. *Debates*, January 31, 1994, p. 637.

91. *Debates*, May 20, 1970, pp. 7126-7; November 4, 1981, p. 12499; March 9, 1987, p. 3955; May 20, 1992, p. 10934.

92. *Debates*, May 30, 1990, p. 12048; June 4, 1991, p. 1148; March 16, 1994, p. 2361; April 27, 1994, p. 3574; September 19, 1994, p. 5816; October 2, 1998, pp. 8700-1; June 3, 1999, p. 15807.

93. See, for example, *Debates*, April 18, 1985, pp. 3865-6; January 17, 1986, p. 9881.

94. See, for example, *Debates*, September 20, 1983, pp. 27295-6.

95. See, for example, *Debates*, November 27, 1989, pp. 6263, 6266.

questioning does not interfere with the committee's work or anticipate its report.[96] When a question has been asked about a committee's proceedings, Speakers have encouraged Members to rephrase their questions.[97]

Supplementary Questions

Members may seek to clarify the answer to a question or solicit further information through the use of supplementary questions. A supplementary question is posed immediately following a response to an initial question. In conformity with parliamentary tradition, the Speaker retains the authority to determine when supplementary questions may be permitted.[98] The same guidelines which apply to initial questions apply to supplementary questions. They are to be constructed as "a follow-up device flowing from the response and ought to be a precise question put directly and immediately to the Minister, without any further statement".[99] In the past, Speakers used their discretion to insist that a supplementary question be on the same subject and as a general rule be asked of the same Minister.[100] However, at the beginning of the Thirty-Sixth Parliament in 1997, Speaker Parent allowed the practice to be modified by not insisting that an additional question be, strictly speaking, supplementary to the main question.[101] He indicated that he would find it acceptable for a party to split a round of questioning between two Members, with each one asking a different question to a different Minister.[102]

As a supplementary question is meant to flow from or be based upon the information given to the House in the response of the Minister or Parliamentary Secretary to the initial or preceding question, the Speaker has indicated that supplementary questions should not be permitted when a Minister or Parliamentary Secretary, in responding to the question, informs the House that the question will be taken under advisement.[103] However, Members are occasionally permitted to put a supplementary question even under these circumstances.[104]

Historical Perspective

The guidelines for supplementary questions have evolved in much the same way as those for oral questions. The practice of asking supplementary questions began in the

---

96. See, for example, *Debates*, June 4, 1991, p. 1148; May 17, 1995, p. 12725.

97. See, for example, *Debates*, June 5, 1984, p. 4378; January 17, 1986, p. 9881.

98. *Debates*, January 15, 1986, p. 9793.

99. *Debates*, April 14, 1975, p. 440. See also *Debates*, March 25, 1991, p. 18936; October 21, 1994, p. 7033.

100. *Debates*, May 9, 1984, pp. 3552-4.

101. See, for example, *Debates*, October 28, 1997, p. 1235; October 29, 1997, pp. 1284-5; November 5, 1997, p. 1580; November 6, 1997, p. 1660.

102. *Debates*, November 6, 1997, p. 1662.

103. *Debates*, March 4, 1986, pp. 11168-9. In ruling on the acceptability of supplementary questions, the Speaker stated that "when a question is taken on notice, the Chair's practice, which I think is reasonable, is to say that if that is what is being done then it does not make much sense to allow supplementary questions".

104. See, for example, *Debates*, September 27, 1994, pp. 6217-8.

early 1940s, despite the Speaker's disapproval.[105] In 1943, Speaker Glen stated that supplementary questions would only be allowed where "explanations or statements by ministers might reasonably be requested, in circumstances where the minister would no doubt wish to have his remarks made as clearly as possible".[106] In 1944, a procedure committee recommended that the number of supplementary questions be limited to three for each original question; although this proposal was considered in a Committee of the Whole, no decision was made.[107] In 1948, another procedure committee recommended that an oral question be followed by such supplementary questions as necessary to clarify the answer given by the Minister; the report was not considered by the House.[108]

During the 1950s and early 1960s, the continued absence of any rule governing oral questions necessitated a number of statements from various Chair occupants who included remarks on supplementary questions. Some Chair occupants allowed up to two supplementary questions for each initial question; others used their own discretion in permitting a supplementary question.[109] In 1964, when the rules for Question Period were finally codified, some practices, including the number of supplementary questions, were still left to the discretion of the Speaker.

In 1975, Speaker Jerome stated that there should be no preambles to supplementary questions and that they should flow from the Minister's response and be put in precise and direct terms without any prior statement or argument.[110] In a 1984 ruling, Speaker Francis reiterated these remarks,[111] and in 1986, Speaker Bosley further clarified that Members should avoid merely repeating questions that have already been asked, given that the time in Question Period was scarce.[112]

REPLIES TO ORAL QUESTIONS

There are no explicit rules which govern the form or content of replies to oral questions. According to practice, replies are to be as brief as possible, to deal with the subject matter raised and to be phrased in language that does not provoke disorder

---

105. *Debates*, May 8, 1941, p. 2651.

106. *Debates*, May 28, 1943, p. 3126.

107. *Journals*, March 3, 1944, p. 151.

108. *Journals*, June 25, 1948, p. 680.

109. *Journals*, March 16, 1956, pp. 299-305; February 26, 1959, p. 172; October 31, 1963, pp. 509-13 (in particular p. 513).

110. *Journals*, April 14, 1975, p. 440.

111. *Debates*, May 17, 1984, p. 3832.

112. *Debates*, February 24, 1986, p. 10879.

in the House. As Speaker Jerome summarized in his 1975 statement on Question Period, several types of responses may be appropriate. Ministers may

- answer the question;
- defer their answer;
- take the question as notice;
- make a short explanation as to why they cannot furnish an answer at that time;
- say nothing. [113]

Questions, although customarily addressed to specific Ministers, are directed to the Ministry as a whole. It is the prerogative of the government to designate which Minister responds to which question. [114] The Prime Minister (or the Deputy Prime Minister or any other Minister acting on behalf of the Prime Minister) may respond to any or all questions posed during Question Period. [115] Only one Minister may respond to a question, and it need not be the one to whom the question is addressed who actually answers it. [116] A different Minister may, under certain circumstances, reply to a supplementary question. [117] The Speaker has no authority to compel a particular Minister to respond to a question. [118]

As all Members are bound by the rules to attend the sittings of the House unless otherwise occupied with parliamentary activities and functions or on public or official business, [119] no roster system exists to determine which Ministers will be in attendance on a given day. [120] In general, most Ministers are present during Question Period. If a question is asked pertaining to the portfolio of a Minister who is absent from the House, it may be answered by the Prime Minister, another Minister or a

---

113. *Journals*, April 14, 1975, p. 439. See also *Debates*, May 6, 1986, p. 13002; March 13, 1992, pp. 8189, 8192.

114. *Debates*, May 6, 1986, p. 13002; November 3, 1997, p. 1463.

115. *Debates*, May 6, 1986, p. 13001. See *Debates*, June 4, 1982, p. 18105, for an example of a question addressed to an Acting Prime Minister.

116. See *Fraser*, p. 125.

117. Speaker Francis stated in 1984 that another Minister may answer a supplementary question if the first Minister claims that that Minister is concerned with the subject matter of a question; the redirection must be clearly linked to the answer in the first question (*Debates*, May 17, 1984, p. 3832).

118. *Debates,* May 8, 1986, pp. 13081-2.

119. Standing Order 15.

120. A "roster system" of ministerial attendance for Question Period, modelled very loosely on the British House of Commons, was attempted by the Trudeau Ministry during the Twenty-Eighth Parliament (1968-72). The experiment was not a success and was abandoned with the Twenty-Ninth Parliament (1973-74) (see *Stewart*, p. 57).

Parliamentary Secretary.[121] However, if the Minister to whom the question is addressed is present, his or her Parliamentary Secretary may not answer it.[122]

Members may not insist on an answer[123] nor may a Member insist that a specific Minister respond to his or her question.[124] A Minister's refusal to answer a question may not be questioned or treated as the subject of a point of order or question of privilege.[125]

The Speaker ensures that replies adhere to the dictates of order, decorum and parliamentary language. The Speaker, however, is not responsible for the quality or content of replies to questions.[126] In most instances, when a point of order or a question of privilege has been raised in regard to a response to an oral question, the Speaker has ruled that the matter is a disagreement among Members over the facts surrounding the issue.[127] As such, these matters are more a question of debate and do not constitute a breach of the rules or of privilege.

ADJOURNMENT PROCEEDINGS

Any Member who is dissatisfied with the response given to his or her question during Question Period, or who has been told by the Speaker that a question is not urgent, may give notice to speak on the subject matter of the question during a portion of time reserved at the conclusion of most sitting days. This period of House business, known as the Adjournment Proceedings, is also commonly referred to as the "late show".[128] In addition, any Member who is concerned that a written question he or she has submitted for the *Order Paper* has not been responded to within 45 days may give notice of his or her intention to transfer the question to the Adjournment Proceedings.[129] The Member's name is then placed on a list along with the names of

---

121. In the past, Members have noted the absence of Ministers and the Speaker has reminded the House of the prohibition against commenting on the presence or absence of Members. Members have raised questions of privilege concerning the absence of Ministers during Question Period. On January 31, 1986, John Nunziata (York South–Weston) rose on a question of privilege following Question Period to argue that the absence of the Prime Minister affected his privileges because he was unable to pose questions to the government about a particular matter. The Speaker ruled that the government answers questions as a "collegial system of Cabinet responsibility" and that since the government was present during Question Period, no question of privilege existed (see *Debates*, January 31, 1986, p. 10348).

122. *Debates*, August 26, 1987, p. 8429.

123. *Debates*, October 10, 1962, p. 347.

124. *Debates*, May 8, 1986, p. 13082.

125. *Debates*, March 10, 1976, pp. 11669-70.

126. *Debates,* October 9, 1997, p. 735; March 25, 1999, p. 13513.

127. See, for example, *Debates*, March 4, 1988, p. 13420; February 12, 1992, pp. 6859-60; March 27, 1992, pp. 8937-8; October 6, 1994, pp. 6597-8.

128. Standing Order 37(3). Because the Adjournment Proceedings customarily occur at the end of the sitting day, the phrase "late show" was coined before the elimination of night sittings in 1982.

129. Standing Order 39(5)(*b*). This procedure is discussed in greater detail later in the chapter.

other Members who have given such notice. At the commencement of this 30-minute period, from 6:30 p.m. to 7:00 p.m. Monday through Thursday (there are no Adjournment Proceedings on Friday), a motion to adjourn the House is deemed to have been moved and seconded; no mover or seconder is required.[130] After debate, the motion to adjourn is deemed carried and the House adjourns.

The adjournment debate is used as a vehicle for brief exchanges (questions from Members and responses from Ministers or Parliamentary Secretaries) on predetermined topics. Several topics stemming from questions either first raised during Question Period or written questions transferred from the *Order Paper* may be debated. A question ruled out of order during Question Period for any reason other than its lack of urgency is not admissible for debate during the Adjournment Proceedings.[131] Questions addressed to committee chairs during Question Period may also not be the subject of debate during the Adjournment Proceedings.[132]

Historical Perspective

In a review of the Standing Orders in 1964, the House adopted a procedure committee proposal for the first-ever Standing Order to regulate Question Period. At the same time, the House agreed to the committee's suggestion that a rule on the Adjournment Proceedings be adopted to complement the Question Period Standing Order.[133]

The committee's rationale in proposing the Adjournment Proceedings Standing Order was that

> ... *merely to impose restrictions on the Orders of the Day Question Period, by itself, ... would not retain the rights that are inherent in the asking of questions. We therefore propose ... that on three nights in the week, Monday, Tuesday and Thursday, there be available a possible half hour period during which there might be short submissions on three different subjects on each of these three nights. Our proposal is that if during the Question Period a Member feels dissatisfied with the answer he gets from the government, ... he may give notice that he wishes to raise that matter at the time of adjournment.*[134]

By the 1970s, the "late show" had become a popular vehicle for Members wishing to discuss at greater length matters initially raised during Question Period. With

---

130. Standing Order 38(1). On occasion, no Members have risen to participate in the adjournment debate and the Chair has adjourned the House until the following sitting day (see, for example, *Debates*, February 28, 1995, p. 10181). On other occasions, after the motion was deemed moved, Members have risen on points of order to conduct different business or to ask for an extension to continue debate. The Chair has ruled that once debate on the adjournment motion has begun, the proceedings cannot be interrupted (see, for example, *Debates*, February 2, 1993, p. 15313). See also *Debates*, May 19, 1992, p. 10914; May 20, 1992, p. 10935.

131. *Debates*, April 27, 1964, pp. 2581-2.

132. *Debates*, May 7, 1986, p. 13048.

133. *Journals*, April 20, 1964, pp. 223-5.

134. *Debates*, April 20, 1964, p. 2342.

the number of notices given for debate far exceeding the time available, several suggestions were periodically made: to reduce by half the time allotted to each Member participating in the Adjournment Proceedings;[135] to extend the time allotted to late show questions to allow for the number of topics to be debated to increase from three to five and to permit the lapsing of uncalled items after 20 sitting days;[136] and to hold the Adjournment Proceedings at 6:00 p.m. even though the applicable adjournment hour was 10:00 p.m.[137] Eventually, in 1982, the decision to eliminate evening sittings resulted in 6:00 p.m. late shows[138] and, in 1991, the Standing Orders were amended to allow a maximum of five topics to be debated.[139]

Notice

Members who wish to raise, during the Adjournment Proceedings, the subject matter of a question originally posed during Question Period must provide the Table with written notice of their desire to do so, no later than one hour following the conclusion of Question Period on the day the question was raised.[140]

A Member may also be included on the list to take part in the adjournment debate by giving oral notice in the House with reference to a question on the *Order Paper* not being answered within the required 45-day period.[141] This is done when the rubric "Questions on the *Order Paper*" is called during Routine Proceedings.

If, for whatever reason, the subject matter of a question has not been debated during the Adjournment Proceedings 45 sitting days following the notice given by a Member, the notice is deemed withdrawn.[142]

Selection of Questions to Be Raised

The Speaker typically receives more notices to debate a matter during the Adjournment Proceedings than there is time available for debate. Consequently, the subject matter for which notice has been given may not be raised during the Adjournment Proceedings on the same day. Needless to say, when no notices have been filed with the Table, or when no Members are prepared to proceed on a particular day, the Adjournment Proceedings do not take place.

---

135. *Debates*, March 9, 1973, pp. 2075-6.

136. See Appendix "J", Standing Committee on Procedure and Organization, *Minutes of Proceedings and Evidence*, September 30, 1976, Issue No. 20, pp. 57-8; *Journals*, November 1, 1976, pp. 90-1.

137. *Debates*, November 8, 1979, p. 1081.

138. See the *Permanent and Provisional Standing Orders of the House of Commons*, 1982, Standing Order 45(1).

139. *Journals,* April 11, 1991, p. 2909. Originally, the Standing Orders permitted debate to last no more than ten minutes for each topic. Under this time limit, only three topics were debated each "late show". Members were permitted to speak no longer than six minutes, with the Minister or Parliamentary Secretary speaking in response for no longer than four minutes.

140. Standing Order 37(3) is quite clear that oral notice is not sufficient (see, for example, *Debates*, May 30, 1990, p. 12052).

141. See, for example, *Journals*, November 20, 1992, p. 2096.

142. Standing Order 37(3).

The Speaker has the discretionary power to determine the specific questions to be raised and the order of their consideration. The Chair, when making this decision, considers the order in which notices were given, the urgency of the matters raised and the apportioning of opportunities to Members of the various parties in the House to debate such matters.[143] The Speaker may also discuss with and consider the advice of party representatives in arriving at a sequence for the consideration of notices received.[144] In practice, debates during the Adjournment Proceedings are arranged by procedural staff on behalf of the Speaker.

At no later than 5:00 p.m. on Monday, Tuesday, Wednesday and Thursday, the Speaker rises and indicates to the House which matter or matters are to be raised that day at the adjournment of the House.[145] The Speaker retains the authority to control the order of debate during the Adjournment Proceedings and may change the order of those scheduled to speak should the need arise.[146]

Length of Debate

During this 30-minute period, debate on any one item can last no longer than six minutes.[147] Within this six-minute time frame, the Member raising the matter may speak for no longer than four minutes, with the Minister or Parliamentary Secretary speaking in response thereto for no longer than two minutes.[148] However, a Minister or a Parliamentary Secretary is not compelled to respond to any question raised at this time. Any Minister or Parliamentary Secretary may answer on behalf of the government, and the answer, or refusal to answer, may not normally be the subject of a point of order or a question of privilege.[149]

The time limits for these debates are strictly enforced by the Chair and extensions are neither requested nor granted. The full 30-minute period need not be completely used.[150] If the full period is not used, the remaining time lapses and the House is adjourned. After 30 minutes or upon completion of debate, whichever comes first, the motion to adjourn is deemed to have been adopted and the House is adjourned to the next sitting day.[151] If Members fail to proceed with their question during the Adjournment Proceedings on their scheduled day, then the time provided is reduced accordingly.

---

143. Standing Order 38(3).

144. Standing Order 38(3).

145. Standing Order 38(4).

146. *Debates*, May 11, 1993, p. 19297.

147. Standing Order 38(2).

148. Standing Order 38(5).

149. See Speaker's ruling, *Debates*, February 11, 1970, pp. 3465-6.

150. *Debates*, May 15, 1964, p. 3301.

151. Standing Order 38(5). In December 1997, the House adopted a motion to extend the Adjournment Proceedings by 12 minutes to permit debate on seven topics (see *Journals*, December 9, 1997, p. 366; *Debates*, pp. 2954-5).

Suspension or Delay of the Proceedings

Until 1994, the Adjournment Proceedings were cancelled whenever any specified business was to be disposed of or concluded in that sitting or to be continued beyond the ordinary time of daily adjournment. This requirement was deleted from the Standing Orders in June 1994.[152] Since then, the Adjournment Proceedings are suspended pursuant to the Standing Orders only when the sitting has been extended for an emergency debate,[153] on the day designated for the budget presentation,[154] or on any day when the House continues to sit beyond the ordinary hour of daily adjournment for the election of a Speaker.[155]

The Adjournment Proceedings may be delayed until later in the day when a sitting is extended due to a ministerial statement[156] or when Private Members' Business has been extended on the second sitting day set aside for the consideration of the report and third reading stages of a bill.[157] The Adjournment Proceedings may be delayed similarly on the last allotted day in the Supply periods ending March 26, June 23 and December 10.[158] If a motion has been adopted to extend the hours of sitting during the last ten sitting days in June, the Adjournment Proceedings are delayed until the agreed-upon hour of adjournment.[159] If a motion has been adopted to continue a sitting pursuant to Standing Order 26, the Adjournment Proceedings would take place at the end of the extension.[160] On other occasions when the adjournment of the House has been extended for the consideration of legislation or for a special debate, the House has opted to preserve the adjournment debate at its normal time and, after the debate, to deem the motion to be withdrawn.[161] The Adjournment Proceedings have been interrupted by Royal Assent and resumed upon the return of the House from the Senate following the ceremony.[162]

---

152. See *Journals*, June 8, 1994, p. 545; June 10, 1994, p. 563. See also the Twenty-Seventh Report of the Standing Committee on Procedure and House Affairs presented to the House on June 8, 1994.

153. Standing Order 52(12).

154. Standing Order 83(2).

155. Standing Order 2(3).

156. Standing Order 33(2).

157. Standing Order 98(3) and (5). This Standing Order has not been invoked since its adoption in 1986.

158. Standing Order 81(17) and (18)(*b*).

159. Standing Order 27(1). See, for example, *Journals*, June 5, 1996, p. 490; June 12, 1996, p. 546.

160. See transcript of the meeting of the Standing Committee on Procedure and House Affairs of May 3, 1994, p. 18. The time the Adjournment Proceedings are to commence would not be known in this case. The Speaker would still announce the matters to be raised that day (or the announcement may have already been made) but if Members fail to proceed with their questions, the Adjournment Proceedings lapse. See, for example, *Debates*, May 4, 1995, pp. 12211, 12216, 12235; March 13, 1997, pp. 9036, 9044, 9058.

161. See, for example, *Journals*, November 26, 1992, p. 2242; March 18, 1996, p. 104.

162. See, for example, *Debates*, November 6, 1990, p. 15236.

Points of Order and Questions of Privilege

Points of order and questions of privilege may not be raised during the Adjournment Proceedings.[163] The only matters to be considered during this 30-minute period are questions previously raised during Question Period or transferred for debate from the *Order Paper* and on this basis the House operates without a quorum. Speakers have been reluctant to deal, at that time, with points of order and questions of privilege because these matters could affect the whole House. For the same reason, the Speaker would not propose to the House at this time a motion moved by unanimous consent. Aside from unparliamentary language which, on occasion, has been dealt with immediately by the Speaker without any point of order being raised,[164] Speakers have ruled that matters arising from the conduct of the Adjournment Proceedings are to be deferred until the next sitting day.[165] Nonetheless, Speakers have allowed Members on occasion to raise a point of order.[166]

Written Questions

While oral questions are posed without notice on matters deemed to be of an urgent nature, written questions are placed after notice on the *Order Paper* with the intent of seeking from the Ministry detailed, lengthy or technical information relating to "public affairs".[167] The rule states that written questions may also be addressed to private Members concerning any bill, motion or other public matter connected with the business of the House with which such Members may be concerned. However, despite the rule, the practice is that recipients of inquiries by way of written questions have always been Ministers. The Standing Order is mostly silent on how answers to questions addressed to private Members are to be provided. Indeed, there are no known precedents of written questions being addressed to private Members. Any attempt to do so would be contrary to the long-established practice and to the real purpose of asking questions of the Ministry.

---

163. See, for example, *Debates*, November 17, 1969, p. 920; June 29, 1981, p. 11070; December 5, 1991, p. 5892; June 2, 1992, p. 11283; October 6, 1997, p. 567; December 10, 1997, pp. 3064-5.

164. *Debates*, June 13, 1986, p. 14372; March 5, 1987, p. 3882; December 9, 1997, p. 3018. See also *Debates*, April 2, 1998, pp. 5743.

165. *Debates*, April 30, 1964, pp. 2799-802.

166. In 1983, the Chair allowed a Member to rise on a point of order to apologize for unintentionally impugning the character of another Member (*Debates*, July 19, 1982, pp. 19490-1). In 1986, the Speaker permitted a Member to rise on a point of order when confusion arose over which question was to be answered that day (*Debates*, November 3, 1986, p. 1033).

167. Standing Order 39(1).

HISTORICAL PERSPECTIVE

Provisions allowing for written questions to be posed to the Ministry and to private Members have been included in the rules of the House of Commons since 1867.[168] The rule, virtually identical to today's Standing Order, provided then, as it does now, that questions could be asked of private Members as well as Ministers, although it appears that, from the beginning, the practice saw questions directed to Ministers.[169] That practice has continued to this day, and has been periodically reinforced with additions to the Standing Order referring to the manner that answers are to be provided to *Order Paper* questions; in each case, questions to Ministers appear to be assumed.[170]

Between 1867 and 1896, when a written question was called for consideration, the Member in whose name the question stood would rise and read the question, to which the Minister responsible would furnish a response. When a question was called and a response provided, the exchange was printed in full in the *Debates*; supplementary questions were not allowed.[171] Any questions called and not answered were automatically dropped from the *Order Paper* and had to be renewed if a Member still wanted a response.[172]

Beginning in 1896, reforms were made to the practice to shorten the time taken by the House to consider written questions. A numbering process for written questions was instituted removing the necessity of a Member reading in full the text of the question when called for consideration.[173] In 1906, written questions likely to require lengthy responses could be transferred without debate to another section of the *Order Paper* as notices of motions.[174] This rule was adopted because it was thought that too much time was being taken up with reading the answers to the questions in the House. Also at this time, questions that had been called for consideration but not answered could be allowed, at the government's request and with the consent of the Members involved, to stand and retain their place on the *Order Paper* instead of being automatically dropped.[175] In 1910, the rules were amended to allow Ministers to have their answers appear in the *Debates* as if they were read; Members who wished to receive an oral response to a written question could do so by marking it with an asterisk. At the same time, a new rule made it possible for the government to table lengthy or detailed responses to questions. These tabled responses were

---

168. *Rules, Orders and Forms of Proceeding of the House of Commons of Canada*, 1868, Rule No. 29.

169. *Bourinot*, 1st ed., p. 321.

170. See Standing Order 39(3), (5), (6) and (7).

171. *Debates*, May 31, 1895, cols. 1882-3.

172. *Rules, Orders and Forms of Proceeding of the House of Commons of Canada*, 1876, Rule No. 25.

173. *Debates*, September 16, 1896, cols. 1303-4. This change was made at the direction of the Speaker and was not formalized into the rules. A written question would be read if any Member so requested (*Debates*, March 21, 1900, cols. 2367-97).

174. *Debates*, July 10, 1906, cols. 7602-3.

175. *Rules, Orders and Forms of Proceeding of the House of Commons of Canada*, 1906, Rule No. 31.

called "Orders for Return".[176] In most cases, the returns were tabled immediately after the order was deemed made. These responses became sessional papers and were not printed in the *Debates*.

The procedure for answering written questions changed relatively little until 1963 when the process was further refined in order to allow the House to deal specifically with those questions that the government was ready to answer and prepared to make public. In order to dispose of the available responses, the new practice permitted the House, rather than forcing it to proceed through every written question on the *Order Paper,* to consider only those questions to be answered that day by the government. Once these were dealt with, the government would request that all remaining questions be allowed to stand.[177] In 1986, the House agreed to a limit of four questions per Member on the *Order Paper* at any one time,[178] three of which could be answered orally in the House,[179] while also codifying the right of Members to request a reply to a written question within 45 calendar days of its filing.[180] In 1991, the rules were again amended to allow Members whose questions had remained unanswered after 45 days to take the matter up during the Adjournment Proceedings.[181]

GUIDELINES FOR WRITTEN QUESTIONS

In general, written questions are lengthy, often containing two or more subsections, and seek detailed or technical information from one or more government departments or agencies. Restrictions governing the form and content of written questions are found both within the rules and as a result of custom, usage and tradition. Several traditional guidelines and conditions date back to Confederation. With time and following several Speakers' decisions, the list of restrictions grew very long.[182] Concurrently, some became outdated or irrelevant. Thus, a very large measure of responsibility for ensuring the regularity of written questions fell to the Clerk. Aside from a 1965 Speaker's statement, indicating that some of these restrictions no longer

---

176. *Debates*, April 29, 1910, cols. 8367-9.

177. *Debates*, July 17, 1963, p. 2295. Until then, when the House reached "Questions on the *Order Paper*", the Speaker called each question in turn with the Minister or Parliamentary Secretary interrupting occasionally to say "Answered" when they wished to send an answer to the Table (*Stewart*, p. 65).

178. Standing Order 39(4).

179. Standing Order 39(3)(*a*).

180. Standing Order 39(5)(*a*). See *Journals*, February 6, 1986, pp. 1653-4; February 13, 1986, p. 1710. This was to prevent the practice of placing numerous questions on the *Order Paper* and consequently lengthy delays in the provision of responses.

181. *Journals*, April 11, 1991, pp. 2905, 2909-10.

182. See list of restrictions published in successive editions of *Bourinot* and *Beauchesne*.

applied,[183] there is no definitive breakdown of which are still valid.[184] However, as conceded by the Chair, many of these restrictions have become inoperable over time.[185]

A written question is judged acceptable if it satisfies the general guidelines for oral questions and the restrictions provided in the rules. The purpose of a written question is to obtain information, not to supply it to the House. A question must be coherent and concise and the subject matter must pertain to "public affairs"; "no argument or opinion is to be offered, nor any facts stated, except so far as may be necessary to explain the same".[186]

Acting on the Speaker's behalf, the Clerk has full authority to ensure the questions placed on the *Notice Paper* conform with the rules and practices of the House.[187] Given that the purpose of a written question is to seek and receive a precise, detailed answer, it is incumbent on a Member submitting a question for the *Notice Paper* "to ensure that it is formulated carefully enough to elicit the precise information sought".[188] The Clerk may split a question into two or more questions if it is too broad.[189] If there are any irregularities in a question, the Clerk communicates this to the Member who then has the opportunity to amend the question.[190]

Forty-eight hours' notice is required before a question may be placed on the *Order Paper*.[191] A Member may indicate that he or she wishes to receive an oral reply to the question during Routine Proceedings by marking the written question with an asterisk at the time it is submitted.[192] Questions so designated are known as "starred questions". Members are permitted a maximum of three starred questions out of the allowed maximum of four on the *Order Paper* at any one time.[193] All questions are assigned a number when they are submitted.

---

183. *Journals*, March 30, 1965, pp. 1191-4, in particular pp. 1193-4.

184. See *Beauchesne*, 6th ed., pp. 124-6, which lists numerous restrictions covering the form and content of questions.

185. *Journals*, March 30, 1965, pp. 1193-4.

186. Standing Order 39(1) and (2).

187. Standing Order 39(2).

188. See *Debates*, February 9, 1995, pp. 9425-7, in particular p. 9426. Speaker Parent was responding to a question of privilege raised in regard to a reply to a written question which a Member felt was inaccurate. The Speaker ruled that it was a matter of interpretation of the wording of the question placed on the *Order Paper*.

189. Standing Order 39(2). See Speaker Parent's ruling, *Debates*, February 8, 1999, pp. 11531-3, in particular p. 11532.

190. *Bourinot*, 4th ed., p. 313.

191. Standing Order 54.

192. Standing Order 39(3)(*a*).

193. Standing Order 39(3)(*a*).

Withdrawal of a Written Question

A Member may withdraw a written question from the *Order Paper* by advising the Clerk of the House in writing that he or she wishes the question to be withdrawn. A Member may also rise in the House to request that the Speaker withdraw the question. [194]

REPLIES

Replies to written questions are presented each sitting day during Routine Proceedings under the rubric "Questions on the *Order Paper*". [195] A Member, usually the Parliamentary Secretary to the Government House Leader, rises to announce the numbers of the questions being answered that day and to provide oral responses to starred questions. [196] At the same time, the Parliamentary Secretary may also seek the consent of the House to deem a starred question answered orally without actually reading aloud the text of the answer or to provide a very lengthy reply to a question by tabling the response as a document, a process known as transforming a reply into an Order for Return. [197] This is done by the Speaker asking the House whether there is agreement to proceed in that way. [198] In the case of a starred question, if there is no agreement, then the government would proceed to read the answer. In the case of a request for tabling, if there is no agreement, then the government would either not proceed with the question on that day, [199] or alternatively have a Minister table the answer. Finally, the Parliamentary Secretary requests that any remaining unanswered questions be allowed to stand and retain their place on the *Order Paper*. This request is routinely made and granted. [200] The Speaker has indicated that, as this procedure

194. *Journals*, January 13, 1910, p. 154. See, for example, *Debates*, March 14, 1956, p. 2124; May 3, 1993, pp. 18822-3; February 11, 1998, p. 3740. The authorities in the Privy Council Office co-ordinating responses are informed when questions are withdrawn.

195. Standing Order 30(3).

196. See, for example, *Debates*, May 15, 1989, p. 1694; May 14, 1990, pp. 11372-3. The text of the question and of the answer appears in the *Debates* of that day.

197. Although the practice is almost invariably to deem a starred question answered orally, the Speaker, in response to a point of order, indicated that, strictly speaking, the rule requires oral responses to be given to written questions and must be observed unless it is the disposition of the House to dispense with this procedure (*Debates*, May 24, 1989, p. 2102). If a starred question is deemed answered orally, the text of the answer is printed in the *Debates* as if the Minister to whom the question was directed had actually stood in the House and given a full reply.

198. See, for example, *Debates,* December 12, 1991, p. 6181; December 7, 1994, p. 8760.

199. See, for example, *Debates*, March 13, 1995, p. 10397; March 17, 1995, p. 10671.

200. Standing Order 42(1) reads: "Questions put by Members and notices of motions not taken up when called may (upon the request of the government) be allowed to stand and retain their precedence; otherwise they will disappear from the *Order Paper*. They may, however, be renewed." See *Debates*, February 28, 1977, pp. 3473-4; May 27, 1977, p. 6015.

has evolved to become an automatic proceeding, this request is not debatable.[201] If consent were refused by a Member, his or her questions would be dropped from the *Order Paper* exactly as would happen if the government had not made the request. The Member would have to resubmit any questions with appropriate notice. If no questions are to be answered that day, the Parliamentary Secretary to the Government House Leader requests that all questions be allowed to stand on the *Order Paper*.

The guidelines that apply to the form and content of written questions are also applicable to the answers provided by the government. As such, no argument or opinion is to be given, and only the information needed to respond to the question is to be provided in an effort to maintain the process of written questions as an exchange of information rather than an opportunity for debate.[202] It is acceptable for the government, in responding to a written question, to indicate to the House that it cannot supply an answer.[203] On occasion, the government has supplied supplementary replies to questions already answered.[204] The Speaker, however, has ruled that it is not in order to indicate in a response to a written question the total time and cost incurred by the government in the preparation of that response.[205]

There are no provisions in the rules for the Speaker to review government responses to questions. Nonetheless, on several occasions, Members have raised questions of privilege in the House regarding the accuracy of information contained in responses to written questions; in none of these cases was the matter found to be a *prima facie* breach of privilege.[206] The Speaker has ruled that it is not the role of the Chair to determine whether or not the contents of documents tabled in the House are accurate nor to "assess the likelihood of an Hon. Member knowing whether the facts contained in a document are correct".[207]

---

201. *Debates*, May 12, 1971, p. 5733.

202. Standing Order 39(1).

203. *Debates*, May 5, 1971, p. 5515. See also *Debates*, February 25, 1991, p. 17590; March 8, 1991, p. 18237.

204. See, for example, *Debates*, November 18, 1994, p. 7993-4; December 13, 1994, pp. 9003-6; December 15, 1994, pp. 9116-8.

205. *Debates*, October 2, 1991, p. 3147. The government has circumvented this procedural limitation by having a government Member place a question on the *Order Paper* requesting cost amounts for the preparation of responses to written questions for specified time periods (see, for example, *Debates*, April 7, 1992, pp. 9410-1; May 8, 1992, p. 10435; June 19, 1992, p. 12455; April 26, 1993, p. 18462).

206. *Debates*, February 21, 1990, p. 8618; May 15, 1991, p. 100; February 9, 1995, pp. 9425-7; May 27, 1998, pp. 7281-3; February 8, 1999, pp. 11531-3. In the 1995 case, John Cummins (Delta) raised a question of privilege on December 13, 1994, in regard to the accuracy of the response he had received to a written question on November 18, 1994 (*Debates*, November 18, 1994, pp. 7993-4; December 13, 1994, pp. 9003-6). Two days later, the government supplied the Member with a supplementary answer to his question (*Debates*, December 15, 1994, pp. 9116-8). Later that same day, Mr. Cummins rose on a question of privilege to protest that the supplemental answer contained discrepancies (*Debates*, December 15, 1994, pp. 9153-5). On February 9, 1995, the Speaker ruled that it was a matter of interpretation of the wording of the question placed on the *Order Paper* which had subsequently led to a disagreement over certain facts in the answer supplied by the government (*Debates*, pp. 9425-7).

207. *Debates*, February 28, 1983, p. 23278.

Questions Not Responded to Within Forty-five Calendar Days

When filing questions, Members may request that the Ministry respond within 45 calendar days.[208] However, there is no procedural device in the rules compelling the Ministry to reply within this time, and Members have raised this complaint in the House on numerous occasions when the government has not responded to written questions within 45 days. The government has countered that the volume and complexity of questions sometimes requires it to exceed this time frame.[209] In these discussions, the Chair has indicated that it has no power under the rules to order the government to produce an answer within the allotted 45 days.[210] Nonetheless, the Speaker has admonished "those who are asked to prepare these answers to look at this rule and realize that when they do not get the answer back to their Minister in time, they are putting [Members] through a lot of difficulty and taking up the time of the House ..."[211] Members may raise the subject matter of a written question during the Adjournment Proceedings if the written question has not been answered within the required 45-day period.[212]

Orders for Return

In some cases, long and complex questions which require information from a number of government departments, or which would require lengthy replies not compatible with printing in the *Debates,* are transformed to become Orders for Return (that is, documents that must be provided following an order adopted by the House). Although the rule specifies that it is a Minister who must be of the opinion that a reply to a question should be in the form of a return, and that it is a Minister who must state that he or she has no objection to laying such a return upon the Table,[213] in practice the Parliamentary Secretary to the Government House Leader assumes the responsibility of communicating that opinion to the House. The agreement of the House is requested and usually granted.[214] The return is tabled and becomes a sessional paper.[215] As such, it is available to all Members on request from

---

208. Standing Order 39(5)(*a*).

209. The rule change limiting the number of questions to four may have contributed to broader questions requiring more extensive research.

210. *Debates*, May 18, 1989, p. 1891; March 10, 1992, p. 7938; May 6, 1996, pp. 2366-7; February 8, 1999, pp. 11531-3.

211. *Debates*, May 18, 1989, p. 1890.

212. Standing Order 39(5)(*b*). The Adjournment Proceedings are discussed in detail earlier in this chapter.

213. Standing Order 39(7).

214. Consent has been denied on occasion (*Debates*, June 1, 1992, pp. 11169-70; March 13, 1995, p. 10397). The same request was later made and granted (*Debates*, June 5, 1992, p. 11477; March 17, 1995, p. 10671).

215. See, for example, *Journals*, September 23, 1994, p. 725; December 13, 1996, pp. 1018-9. The government has also presented a revised return (see *Journals*, April 2, 1998, p. 664).

the Clerk, but is not printed in the *Debates*. It is not necessary for the return to answer every part of the original question.[216]

The rules also provide the Speaker with the authority to transform a written question into a notice of motion, if he or she believes that a question would require a lengthy reply and if he or she is asked by the government to have the question stand as a notice of motion.[217] Such a notice of motion could then be considered only under "Private Members' Business". However, in a ruling by Speaker Fraser in 1989, the Chair refused a request to transform a written question into a notice of motion.[218] In choosing not to proceed with the government's request, the Speaker stated that the Chair was "unable to comply with the terms of the Standing Order in today's context without prejudicing the right of private Members to control fully their business by choosing for themselves how best to seek information: by placing questions on the *Order Paper*, perhaps requesting an answer from the government within a 45-day period; or by having a Notice of Motion, if chosen after a draw, debated during Private Members' Business". The Speaker remarked that the rule, adopted by the House in 1906, had been unused for many years and, as a result, its invocation decades later would be counter to the series of reforms concerning written questions that had been implemented since then. The Speaker suggested that the government, in responding to a written question requiring a lengthy or detailed response, could make it an Order for Return, a procedurally acceptable and widely used practice. The Chair also submitted that the government may decline to answer a written question but, at the same time, may furnish a reason for its refusal. Similarly, the government may provide a reason why the response could not be provided within 45 days.

Transfer of Unanswered Written Questions to Adjournment Proceedings

As has been discussed earlier in this chapter, if a written question on the *Order Paper* (to which a response within 45 days has been requested) remains unanswered after 45 days, the Member who posed the question may rise in the House during Routine Proceedings after the rubric "Questions on the *Order Paper*" has been called and give notice of his or her intention to transfer the question to the Adjournment Proceedings.[219] The question is then removed from the *Order Paper* and is taken up during the Adjournment Proceedings. This rule was adopted by the House on April 11, 1991, in response to Members' growing frustration over their inability to receive

---

216. *Journals*, November 16, 1962, pp. 285-7, in particular p. 286. See also *Debates*, November 22, 1994, pp. 8077-8, where a Member rose on a point of order to complain that the government had tabled only one part of an answer to his question and the government responded that the responses would not be forthcoming because they were substantial. The Parliamentary Secretary to the Government House Leader suggested that if the Member insisted on additional information, the question could be placed again on the *Order Paper*.

217. Standing Order 39(6). The rule has been invoked only once, on February 16, 1923 (*Debates*, pp. 343-4).

218. *Debates*, June 14, 1989, pp. 3023-6. See also *Debates*, May 30, 1989, pp. 2333-44.

219. Standing Order 39(5)(*b*). See, for example, *Debates*, November 20, 1992, p. 13720; September 25, 1995, p. 14819.

timely answers to written questions. [220] This new procedure also gave Members who have the maximum of four questions on the *Order Paper* the option of transferring one or more of their questions for debate in order to submit other questions for the *Order Paper*. [221]

EFFECT OF PROROGATION ON WRITTEN QUESTIONS

Prorogation of a session of Parliament clears the *Order Paper* and cancels any requests for information contained under the rubric "Questions on the *Order Paper*". Members who wish to pursue their requests for information from the Ministry must resubmit their questions in order for them to be reconsidered in a new session. [222]

---

220. *Journals*, April 11, 1991, pp. 2904-10, in particular pp. 2909-10.

221. For a discussion on this matter, see *Debates*, March 10, 1992, pp. 7936-8.

222. *Debates*, April 12, 1991, p. 19459.

12

The Process of Debate

The principle underlying parliamentary procedure is that the minority should have its say and the majority should have its way.

PHILIP LAUNDY
(*Parliaments in the Modern World,* p. 95)

The process of debate begins when the Speaker, upon receipt of a motion in writing, duly seconded, submits it to the House and proposes the question to determine if the House wishes to adopt the motion. If the motion is one that is debatable, Members may then be recognized to make speeches. The process of debate ends after the motion has been considered, including amendments and sub-amendments, and the original or amended motion is reread by the Speaker and the question for its adoption is put to the House for a decision. The basic components in this process are the "motion" and the "question"—the motion being a proposal that the House do something or express an opinion with regard to some matter; the "question" being the mechanism used to ask the House if it agrees with the motion, first, when it is proposed by the Speaker and, second, when it is put to the House for a decision at the conclusion of debate.

As with all deliberative bodies, discussion in the House of Commons must always be relevant to some definite proposal (or motion).[1] The House makes up its mind on these specific proposals by deciding on questions put to it by the Speaker. Without a motion and a question, there

---

1. *Stewart*, p. 34.

can be no debate.[2] Once a question has been proposed by the Speaker, debate may take place. The Speaker has extensive powers to enforce the rules of debate—which are, in general, limitations on what may be said, when and by whom, and for how long—in order to guide the flow of debate and protect it from excess.[3]

During the process of debate, the House follows a basic sequence of steps: providing notice of the motion, moving and seconding the motion, proposing the question from the Chair, debating the motion, putting the question on the motion, and arriving at a decision on the motion. This chapter describes the steps of this sequence, including rules and practices of the House in connection with each one.

Motions

In order to bring a proposal before the House and obtain a decision on it, a motion is necessary.[4] A motion is a proposal moved by one Member in accordance with well-established rules that the House do something, or order something done or express an opinion with regard to some matter.[5] A motion initiates a discussion and gives rise to the question to be decided by the House.[6] This is the process followed by the House when transacting business.

While there may be many items on the *Order Paper* awaiting the consideration of the House, only one motion can be debated in the House at any one time.[7] After a motion has been proposed to the House by the Chair, the House is formally seized of it. A motion may be debated, amended, superseded, adopted, negatived or withdrawn.[8]

A motion is adopted if it receives the support of the majority of the Members present in the House at the time the decision on it is made. Every motion, once adopted, becomes either an order or a resolution of the House. Through its orders, the House regulates its proceedings or gives an instruction to its Members or officers, or one of its committees. A resolution of the House makes a declaration of opinion or purpose;[9] it does not have the effect of requiring that any action be taken—nor is it binding. The House has frequently brought forth resolutions in order to show support for some action.[10]

---

2. *Redlich*, Vol. III, p. 51.

3. See Chapter 13, "Rules of Order and Decorum".

4. *Bourinot*, 4th ed., p. 292.

5. *Beauchesne*, 4th ed., p. 163.

6. *Stewart*, p. 35.

7. Motions in amendment to a bill at report stage are the exception. The Speaker has the authority to group motions in amendment at the report stage of a bill for debate and decision (Standing Orders 76(5) and 76.1(5)).

8. *Bourinot*, 4th ed., p. 297.

9. *May*, 22nd ed., p. 365.

10. See, for example, *Debates*, September 30, 1998, pp. 8582-3.

A motion must be drafted in such a way that, should it be adopted by the House, "it may at once become the resolution … or order which it purports to be".[11] For example, it is usual for the text of a motion to begin with the word "That". Examples may be found of motions with preambles, but this is considered out of keeping with usual practice.[12] It is customary for motions to be expressed in the affirmative. A motion should not contain any objectionable or irregular wording. It should not be argumentative or written in the style of a speech. [13]

DEBATABLE AND NON-DEBATABLE MOTIONS

Before 1913, the rules provided that a limited number of matters were to be decided without debate; however, the general practice until then was that all motions were debatable barring the existence of some rule or practice to the contrary.[14] In 1913, the Standing Orders were amended to specify that all motions were to be decided without debate or amendment unless specifically recognized as debatable in the text of the rule.[15] The Standing Orders therefore list those motions which are debatable and state that all others, unless otherwise provided in the Standing Orders, are to be decided without debate or amendment.[16]

Debatable motions generally include:

- motions of which written notice is required;

- all Orders of the Day, with the exception of the concurrence in a Ways and Means motion;

- motions taken up during Routine Proceedings under the rubric "Motions"; and

- adjournment motions for the purpose of emergency debates.

---

11. *Bourinot*, 4th ed., p. 316.

12. *Bourinot*, 4th ed., p. 317.

13. *Beauchesne*, 4th ed., pp. 166-7.

14. Examples of matters decided without debate were motions that a Member be now heard, appeals from Speakers' decisions (abolished in 1965), and motions that a Member have leave to move the adjournment of the House to discuss an urgent matter (see 1912 rules 17, 18 and 39).

15. In moving the adoption of the new text on April 9, 1913, Prime Minister Borden claimed that its objective was to give full opportunity of debate upon every substantial motion and to provide that motions which ought to be regarded as purely formal would no longer be debatable (see *Debates*, April 9, 1913, cols. 7403-6). This change was brought forward as part of the government's effort to break an impasse created by an opposition filibuster against a government bill; the changes were adopted on April 23, 1913, after heated debate over several sittings (see *Debates*, April 9, 10, 11, 14, 15, 16, 22 and 23).

16. See Standing Order 67.

As a general rule, every question that is debatable is amendable. Exceptions are the motion to adjourn the House for the purpose of an emergency debate and the previous question (the motion "That this question be now put").

Motions decided without debate or amendment generally include:

- motions that the House do now adjourn;
- motions to proceed to the Orders of the Day;
- motions that the House proceeds to another order of business;
- motions that the debate be now adjourned; and
- motions that the question be postponed to a specific day.

CLASSIFICATION OF MOTIONS

There is no exact way of classifying motions.[17] Generally, they may be grouped into those motions which are self-contained and require notice and those which are dependent on some other proceeding or motion and do not require any notice. In the first group are found substantive motions. In the second group are found subsidiary (or ancillary) and privileged motions. (See Figure 12.1, Classification of Motions.)

SUBSTANTIVE MOTIONS

Substantive motions are independent proposals which are complete by themselves, not incidental to or dependent on any proceeding before the House. They are used to elicit an opinion or action of the House. They are amendable and must be drafted in such a way as to enable the House to express agreement or disagreement with what is proposed. Such motions normally require written notice before they can be moved in the House. They include, for example, private Members' motions, opposition motions on Supply days and government motions.

SUBSIDIARY MOTIONS

Subsidiary motions, also known as ancillary motions, are procedural in nature, dependent on an order already made by the House, and are used to move forward a question then before the House.[18] For example, motions for the second and third

---

17. *Beauchesne* (6th ed., pp. 173-4) classifies motions as either substantive, privileged, incidental or subsidiary. *May* (22nd ed., pp. 328-9) divides motions into two categories: substantive and subsidiary. Subsidiary motions are then divided into three categories—ancillary, superseding and motions dependent on other motions (such as amendments).

18. *Beauchesne*, 4th ed., p. 166; see also *May*, 22nd ed., pp. 328-9.

Figure 12.1   *Classification of Motions*

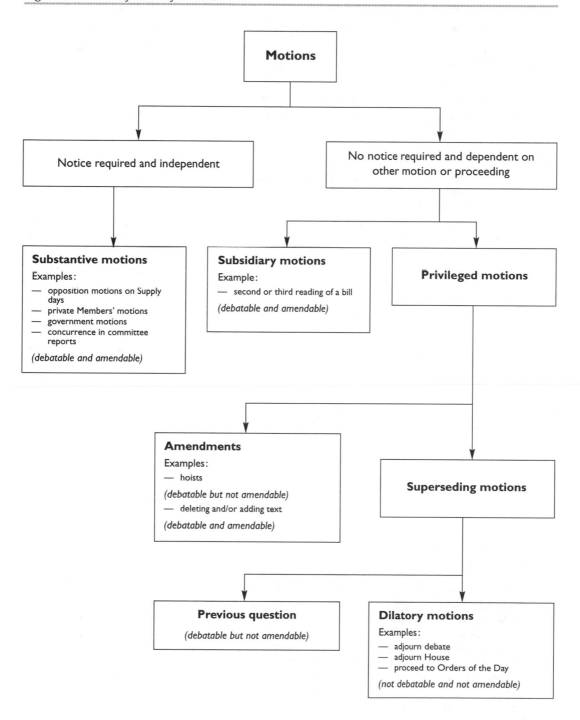

readings of bills, and motions to commit (i.e., to refer a matter to a Committee of the Whole or other committee) are subsidiary motions which are debatable and amendable.[19] Like privileged motions, they may be moved without notice.[20]

PRIVILEGED MOTIONS

A privileged motion (not to be confused with a motion based on a question of privilege) differs from a substantive motion in that it arises from and is dependent on the subject under debate. A privileged motion may be moved without notice when a debatable motion is before the House; the privileged motion then takes precedence over the original motion under debate. Privileged motions can either be amendments or superseding motions. Both types seek to set aside the question under consideration and may be moved only when that question is under debate.

Amendments

A motion in amendment arises out of debate and is proposed either to modify the original motion in order to make it more acceptable to the House or to present a different proposition as an alternative to the original. It requires no notice[21] and is submitted in writing to the Chair. The provision that a motion be in writing ensures that, if the motion is in order, it is proposed to the House in the exact terms of the mover. After the amendment has been moved, seconded and examined as to its procedural acceptability, the Chair submits it to the House. Debate on the main motion is set aside and the amendment is debated until it has been decided, whereupon debate resumes on the main motion and other amendments may be proposed. Just as the text of a main motion may be amended, an amendment may itself be amended. A sub-amendment is an amendment proposed to an amendment. In most cases, there is no limit on the number of amendments which may be moved; however, only one amendment and one sub-amendment may be before the House at any one time.[22]

---

19. See Standing Order 63.

20. The motion for leave to introduce a bill requires notice, but the subsequent motions in the legislative process, with the exception of report stage amendments, require no notice to be filed by a Member—they are automatically inserted on the *Order Paper* (see Standing Orders 54(1), 76(2)and 76.1(2)).

21. If a Member has indicated an intention to propose an amendment, the Member is not entitled to any precedence in debate and must wait to be recognized on debate before moving the amendment (*Bourinot*, 4th ed., p. 316).

22. In some cases, such as the Budget debate and the debate on the Address in Reply to the Speech from the Throne, the Standing Orders set limits on the number of amendments and sub-amendments which can be moved. There are also special provisions so that motions to amend a bill at report stage may be grouped for purposes of debate. For further information on amendments in these circumstances, see Chapter 15, "Special Debates", Chapter 16, "The Legislative Process" and Chapter 18, "Financial Procedures".

An amendment must be relevant to the main motion. It must not stray from the main motion but aim to further refine its meaning and intent.[23] An amendment should take the form of a motion to:

- leave out certain words in order to add other words;
- leave out certain words; or
- insert or add other words to the main motion.

An amendment should be framed so that, if agreed to, it will leave the main motion intelligible and consistent with itself.[24]

An amendment is out of order procedurally, if:

- it is not relevant to the main motion[25] (i.e., it deals with a matter foreign to the main motion or exceeds the scope of the motion,[26] or introduces a new proposition which should properly be the subject of a substantive motion with notice[27]);
- it raises a question substantially the same as one which the House has decided in the same session or conflicts with an amendment already agreed to;[28]
- it anticipates a notice of motion on the *Order Paper*;[29]
- it is the direct negative of the main motion and would produce the same result as the defeat of the main motion;[30] or
- one part of the amendment is out of order.[31]

When an amendment is being debated, the mover of that amendment may not move an amendment to his or her amendment. If the Member wishes to amend the amendment, he or she must seek the consent of the House to withdraw the original amendment and propose a new one.[32]

---

23. See Speaker Parent's ruling, *Debates*, December 5, 1995, p. 17197.

24. "All motions should properly commence with the word 'That'. In this way if a motion meets the approbation of the House, it may at once become the resolution, vote or order which it purports to be" (*Bourinot*, 4ᵗʰ ed., p. 316). See also *Debates*, March 9, 1998, pp. 4566, 4571-2.

25. See, for example, *Debates*, June 17, 1996, pp. 3944-5.

26. See, for example, *Debates*, April 29, 1988, pp. 14985, 14988; March 26, 1992, pp. 8876-7.

27. See, for example, *Debates*, May 6, 1966, p. 4795; December 17, 1987, pp. 11882-3.

28. See, for example, *Journals*, February 13, 1913, p. 247; May 17, 1954, pp. 616-20; see also Speaker Lamoureux's comments in *Journals*, March 6, 1973, pp. 165-7, in which the decision was to allow some degree of latitude for opposition motions on Supply days.

29. *Bourinot*, 4ᵗʰ ed., pp. 301, 320. See also *Journals*, April 1, 1889, p. 214; *Debates*, February 23, 1905, col. 1632; *Journals*, November 21, 1966, pp. 999-1001, and the reference in this ruling to *Journals*, February 7, 1955, pp. 119-20.

30. Expanded negative amendments strike out all the words after "That" in a motion in order to substitute a proposition with the opposite conclusion of the original motion (see, for example, *Journals*, June 6, 1923, pp. 437-8; October 16, 1970, p. 28; *Debates*, August 11, 1988, pp. 18192, 18212-3; October 29, 1991, pp. 4189, 4192).

31. See, for example, *Journals*, April 29, 1970, p. 732.

32. See, for example, *Debates*, November 3, 1989, p. 5541; May 26, 1993, p. 19858.

Sub-amendments

Most of what applies to amendments also applies to sub-amendments. Sub-amendments must be strictly relevant to the amendment and seek to modify the amendment, not the original question;[33] they cannot enlarge on the amendment, introduce new matters foreign to the amendment or differ in substance from the amendment.[34] They cannot strike out all the words in an amendment and thus deny it; the Speaker has ruled that the proper course in such a case would be for the House to defeat the amendment.[35] Debate on a sub-amendment is restricted to the words added to or left out of the original motion by the amendment. Since sub-amendments cannot be further amended, a Member wishing to change one under debate must wait until it is defeated and then offer a new sub-amendment.

Superseding Motions

A superseding motion is one which is moved for the purpose of superseding (or replacing) the question before the House. There are two types of superseding motions: the previous question[36] and several motions known collectively as dilatory motions. While the text of an amendment is dependent on the main motion, the text of a superseding motion is predetermined and proposed with the intention of putting aside further discussion of whatever question is before the House.

Superseding motions can be moved without notice when any other debatable motion is before the House. The Member moving a superseding motion can do so only after having been recognized by the Speaker in the course of debate. It is not in order for such a motion to be moved when the Member has been recognized on a point of order or during the period for questions and comments.[37] With the exception of the previous question, superseding motions are not debatable and cannot be applied to one another.

The Previous Question

When debate on a motion concludes (i.e., no further Member wishes to speak, or the House has ordered debate to conclude), the question is put by the Chair, enabling the House to agree or disagree with the proposition before it. The act of putting the question assumes that the House has finished debate and wants to make a decision. Normally, this is implicit in the process, as seen when the Chair asks if the House is "ready for the question"; however, it can be tested by asking the House to make a formal decision as to whether or not the question should be put. In such a case, a

---

33. See, for example, *Journals*, January 18, 1973, pp. 48-9; *Debates*, February 10, 1998, pp. 3650, 3653, 3656. The Speaker has ruled that where a sub-amendment is found to be in the nature of an amendment to the main motion, its sponsor must wait until the first amendment is negatived before reoffering the motion as another amendment (*Journals*, November 29, 1944, pp. 933-5).

34. See, for example, *Journals*, March 8, 1937, p. 208; *Debates*, April 21, 1986, p. 12500; June 12, 1987, pp. 7060-2; January 16, 1991, pp. 17124-5; October 24, 1996, p. 5659.

35. See, for example, *Journals*, March 14, 1947, p. 198.

36. See Standing Order 61.

37. See, for example, *Journals*, December 30, 1971, p. 1014; *Debates*, November 20, 1996, p. 6503.

decision is required prior to the one on the main motion. This is achieved by proposing, "That this question be now put", a motion known as the previous question.[38]

The previous question has been used irregularly since Confederation. There are only four recorded instances of its use in the nineteenth century.[39] In 1913, a noteworthy event occurred in relation to the previous question when the government, seeking means to bring an end to the lengthy debate on its Naval Aid Bill, moved a motion introducing three new Standing Orders—including the closure rule—and then precluded any possibility of amendment by moving the previous question immediately thereafter.[40] The rules were adopted after days of acrimonious debate[41] and the immediate effect was the application of the closure rule to the Naval Aid Bill.[42] In the late 1920s, and afterwards in the 1940s and early 1950s, the previous question was used fairly regularly and, following an almost 19-year lapse in which it was not used at all,[43] it came into more frequent use in the 1980s and 1990s.[44]

The motion, "That this question be now put", has two functions:

- to supersede the question under debate since, if negatived, thus resolving that the question be *not now* put, the Speaker is bound not to put the main question at that time, and the House proceeds to its next item of business; and

- to limit debate since, until it is decided, it precludes all amendment to the main motion.[45] If adopted, thus resolving that the original question be *now* put, it forces the House to proceed to an immediate decision on the main question.[46]

---

38. Standing Order 61(1). The wording of the previous question has not been altered since its introduction into the rules of the House in 1867. In the British House, the previous question is worded in the negative: "That this question be not now put". If carried, the question under debate drops (but may be brought forward again another day) and the House proceeds to its next business; if negatived, the original question must be put immediately, without further debate. See *May*, 22nd ed., pp. 341-2.

39. *Journals*, May 31, 1869, pp. 163-4; April 28, 1870, pp. 254-5; March 11, 1879, p. 77; March 12, 1886, p. 45.

40. *Journals*, April 9, 1913, pp. 451-3.

41. *Journals*, April 23, 1913, pp. 507-9.

42. For a description of events in the House at the time, see *Dawson*, pp. 122-3.

43. The previous question was moved in 1964 (see *Journals*, December 16, 1964, p. 1016) and then not until 1983 (see *Journals*, February 9, 1983, p. 5587).

44. In many of the post-1980 cases, the previous question was moved in respect to a government bill, often at second reading, seemingly for the purpose of curtailing the debate (see Chapter 14, "The Curtailment of Debate").

45. Standing Order 61(1).

46. Standing Order 61(2).

The previous question has been applied to many substantive motions before the House. For example, it has been moved to the Address in Reply to the Speech from the Throne,[47] to the various stages of a bill,[48] to motions for concurrence in reports from committees[49] and to motions sponsored by private Members[50] and the government.[51]

The previous question cannot be proposed by the mover of the main motion; nor can it be moved by a Member who has been recognized on a point of order. It can only be moved by a Member recognized to speak in the regular course of debate. The previous question is a debatable[52] superseding motion which is given priority once it is proposed during debate. The same time limits for speeches and questions and comments during debate on the main motion apply to the debate on the previous question. It cannot be proposed while an amendment to the main question is being considered, but once the amendment is disposed of by the House and debate resumes on the main motion itself, amended or not, the previous question can then be moved.[53] While the previous question is debatable, it is not amendable[54] and can be only withdrawn by unanimous consent.[55] The previous question cannot be moved in a Committee of the Whole nor in any committee of the House.[56]

A unique feature of the previous question is that it does nothing to hinder debate on the original motion. What is relevant to the previous question is also relevant to the original motion. Nonetheless, after the previous question has been moved, it constitutes a new question before the House and Members may participate in debate even if they have already spoken on the main motion or any amendment which has been disposed of.[57]

---

47. *Journals*, February 16, 1926, pp. 98-9; July 5, 1943, pp. 583-4.

48. *Journals*, May 9, 1928, pp. 371-2 (third reading of a private bill); February 9, 1983, p. 5587 (second reading of a private Member's public bill); August 28, 1987, p. 1397 (Senate amendments to a government bill); November 26, 1998, p. 1316 (second reading of a government bill).

49. *Journals*, December 17, 1964, p. 1016.

50. *Journals*, March 4, 1907, pp. 229-30; April 6, 1959, p. 289.

51. *Journals*, April 9, 1913, pp. 451-3; March 27, 1990, p. 1420; January 16, 1991, p. 2571; December 11, 1992, p. 2394.

52. Standing Order 67(1)(*c*).

53. *Bourinot*, 4th ed., p. 327. See also *Debates*, November 21, 1986, pp. 1413, 1415. For example, the previous question was moved after a six-month hoist amendment had been moved and disposed of (*Journals*, November 16, 1998, p. 1260; November 26, 1998, p. 1316).

54. *Bourinot*, 4th ed., p. 326.

55. See, for example, *Journals*, May 4, 1948, p. 536; December 17, 1964, p. 1016; February 9, 1983, p. 5587; May 10, 1990, p. 1685.

56. *Bourinot*, 4th ed., p. 328. See *Debates*, December 11, 1979, p. 2246, when a Member attempted to move the previous question in a Committee of the Whole and was ruled out of order by the Chair.

57. See, for example, *Debates*, April 6, 1959, p. 2286.

The previous question not being a substantive motion, its mover is not granted the right to speak a second time in reply. [58]

Debate on the previous question may be superseded by a motion to adjourn the debate, a motion to adjourn the House or a motion to proceed to the Orders of the Day; [59] however, such motions are not in order once the House has adopted the motion for the previous question. [60] If debate on the previous question is adjourned or interrupted by the adjournment of the House or otherwise, debate on the previous question and the original motion ceases and both are retained on the *Order Paper*. [61] In some of these cases, the main motion and previous question were again brought before the House and decided; in others, there was no further debate or decision and the motions lapsed when the session ended. [62]

When debate on the motion for the previous question has been concluded, the question is put to the House. [63] Members moving the previous question have, when a recorded division was held, voted in favour, against or not voted at all. [64] If the previous question is resolved in the affirmative, the Chair immediately, without further

58. Standing Order 44(2).

59. See Speaker Lemieux's comments in *Debates*, May 26, 1928, pp. 3419-20; on this occasion, the previous question was moved and a subsequent motion to adjourn the debate was defeated. In 1995, after the previous question was moved, a motion to adjourn the debate was moved and negatived (*Journals*, May 9, 1995, p. 1449; May 10, 1995, pp.1459-60).

60. *Bourinot*, 4th ed., pp. 327-8.

61. Standing Order 41. In 1980, for example, debate on the previous question was interrupted when the time provided for Private Member's Business expired (*Journals*, May 13, 1980, p. 163) and subsequently both motions were carried on the *Order Paper* (*Order Paper and Notice Paper*, May 20, 1980, p. 58). In 1998, debate on the previous question was interrupted when the time provided for Government Orders expired; likewise, both motions were entered on the next day's *Order Paper* (*Journals*, October 2, 1998, p. 1115; *Order Paper and Notice Paper*, October 5, 1998, p. 16). If a recorded division is demanded on the motion for the previous question, and the House decides to defer the vote, both motions are carried on the *Order Paper* (see, for example, *Journals*, October 29, 1998, p. 1214; *Order Paper and Notice Paper*, October 30, 1998, p. 15).

62. This happened in 1928 (third reading of a private bill—*Journals*, May 26, 1928, pp. 461-2); in 1949 (second reading of a private bill—*Journals*, December 2, 1949, pp. 319-20); in 1959 (private Member's motion—*Journals*, April 6, 1959, p. 289); in 1963 (second reading of a private Member's public bill—*Journals*, November 1, 1963, p. 516); and in 1980 (second reading of a private Member's public bill—*Journals*, May 13, 1980, p. 163).

63. On three occasions, motions for closure were applied to curtail debate on the previous question (*Journals*, March 2, 1926, p. 123; March 29, 1932, p. 177; October 26, 1989, pp. 754-5). In each case, the closure motion was adopted.

64. *Bourinot* states that Members "proposing and seconding the previous question generally vote in its favour, but there is no rule to prevent them from voting against their own motion" if their intention is to supersede the question (4th ed., p. 327, which refers to the Speaker's remarks in *Debates*, March 13, 1879, pp. 407-9). See, for example, *Journals*, May 31, 1869, pp. 163-4 (mover voted nay); March 10, 1950, p. 96; April 17, 1950, pp. 236-7 (mover and seconder not recorded as voting); December 1, 1998, p. 1342 (mover and seconder voted yea).

debate or amendment, puts the question on the original motion.[65] If negatived,[66] resolving that the question be *not now* put, the Speaker is bound not to put the main question at that time; the main motion is superseded, the House proceeds to its next item of business, and the main motion is removed from the *Order Paper.*

A recorded division on the previous question may be deferred.[67] However, when a deferred division on the previous question is held and the motion is adopted, the question is put immediately on the main motion and the vote cannot be further deferred.[68]

Dilatory Motions

Dilatory motions are superseding motions designed to dispose of the original question before the House either for the time being or permanently. Although dilatory motions are often used for dilatory tactics and resorted to for the express purpose of causing delay, they may also be used to advance the business of the House. Thus, dilatory motions are used both by the government and the opposition.

Dilatory motions can only be moved by a Member who has been recognized by the Chair in the regular course of debate, and not on a point of order.[69] Dilatory motions include motions:[70]

- to proceed to the Orders of the Day;
- to proceed to another order of business;
- to postpone consideration of a question until a later date;
- to adjourn the House;[71]
- to adjourn the debate.

The Standing Orders indicate that dilatory motions are receivable "when a question is under debate";[72] however, they have also been moved when there was no

---

65. Standing Order 61(2). See also *Bourinot*, 4th ed., pp. 327-8, and *Debates*, November 26, 1998, p. 10472.

66. The previous question was negatived on four occasions (*Journals*, May 31, 1869, pp. 163-4; April 28, 1870, pp. 254-5; June 1, 1928, p. 489; April 15, 1929, p. 242).

67. See, for example, *Journals*, May 26, 1988, pp. 2730, 2732.

68. Standing Order 45(5)(*d*). An exception occurred on March 27, 1991, when a vote on the main motion was deferred to later in the sitting by unanimous consent (*Journals,* p. 2839).

69. See, for example, *Debates*, October 25, 1989, p. 5097; June 21, 1994, p. 5698.

70. Standing Order 58.

71. Adjournment motions are referred to as dilatory motions only when they are used to stop a debate and supersede the original question before the House (*Beauchesne*, 6th ed., p. 173). See section below, "Motion to Adjourn the House".

72. Standing Order 58.

question under debate during Routine Proceedings.[73] The Chair has found in order motions that the House proceeds to the next item under Routine Proceedings,[74] and that the House proceeds to the Orders of the Day.[75] However, a motion to move to another item under Routine Proceedings, other than the next one in the sequence, was ruled out of order on the grounds that the House should proceed from item to item in the usual order.[76] Unlike the previous question, dilatory motions may be proposed when an amendment to a motion is under debate.[77]

When a dilatory motion is moved and seconded, its text must be provided to the Chair in writing.[78] Dilatory motions do not require notice, are not debatable or amendable and, if in order, are put by the Chair immediately. Until 1913, dilatory motions were debatable and the consideration of the superseded question would be delayed by the debate and decision on the dilatory motion.[79] When a dilatory motion is now moved, a recorded division is usually demanded and only the time used to summon the Members and take the vote serves to delay debate on other matters before the House. Obviously, when a motion to adjourn the House is adopted, the time remaining in the sitting day is also lost.

A motion to proceed to the Orders of the Day or to proceed to another order of business, while classed as a dilatory motion, is often used by the government during Routine Proceedings to counteract dilatory tactics or to advance the business of the House. A motion to proceed to the Orders of the Day, if adopted, supersedes

---

73. See Standing Order 30(3) for the list of items under Routine Proceedings, and Chapter 10, "The Daily Program" for further information on Routine Proceedings. There are many examples of motions moved during Routine Proceedings (see events during Routine Proceedings on November 6, 7, 19, 20, 21, 24 and 25, 1986, as well as in April 1987, when the House was debating a contentious bill amending the *Drug Patent Act* (Bill C-22)). On April 13, 1987, the government attempted to move a motion to supersede certain items under Routine Proceedings (*Debates*, pp. 5071-82). The next day, Speaker Fraser ruled to allow the motion, in this instance only, emphasizing that the decision was not to be viewed as a precedent. The Speaker agreed that, on the basis of his ruling of November 24, 1986 (*Debates*, p. 1435), the superseding of items under Routine Proceedings was not in order. Nonetheless, he felt that the interests of the House would be best served if (given the various tactics of obstruction used over a period of weeks, which had blocked debate on the bill) the government were allowed to proceed with its motion (*Debates*, April 14, 1987, pp. 5119-24).

74. See, for example, *Debates*, November 25, 1986, pp. 1485-8.

75. See, for example, *Debates*, November 24, 1986, pp. 1435-7; January 30, 1990, pp. 7588-9.

76. See, for example, *Debates*, November 24, 1986, p. 1435.

77. See, for example, *Journals*, March 9, 1998, p. 540.

78. See, for example, *Debates*, June 21, 1994, p. 5698.

79. See, for example, *Journals*, April 9, 1913, pp. 451-3; April 23, 1913, pp. 507-09.

whatever is then before the House and causes the House to proceed immediately to the Orders of the Day, skipping over any intervening matters on the agenda.[80]

• Motions to Proceed to the Orders of the Day

The motion "That the House do now proceed to the Orders of the Day" may be moved by any Member prior to the calling of Orders of the Day; however, once the House has reached this point, the motion is redundant.[81] The Chair has ruled that a motion to proceed to the Orders of the Day is in order during Routine Proceedings[82] which, in recent practice, is the only time that it is proposed.[83] If the motion is adopted, the item of Routine Proceedings then before the House (and all further items under Routine Proceedings) and requests for emergency debates are superseded and stood over until the next sitting while the House moves immediately to the Orders of the Day.[84] Furthermore, if a motion is being debated at the time a motion to proceed to the Orders of the Day is moved and adopted, it will be dropped from the *Order Paper*. If the motion to proceed to the Orders of the Day is defeated, the House continues with the business before it at the time the motion was moved. This motion has been moved by both the government and the opposition as either a dilatory tactic or to counter dilatory tactics.[85]

• Motions to Proceed to Another Order of Business

A motion "That the House proceed to (name of another order)", if adopted, supersedes whatever is then before the House. The House proceeds immediately to the consideration of the order named in the motion. If a motion to proceed to another order is defeated, debate on the main motion or question before the House continues.

When the House is considering Government Orders, a motion to proceed to another Government Order is not in order if moved by a private Member, since the

---

80. Standing Order 59. See, for example, *Journals*, December 13, 1988, pp. 14-5; December 15, 1988, pp. 33-4; December 20, 1988, pp. 60-1; December 21, 1988, pp. 66-7. The same motion was used by the government in the Pipeline debate of 1956, when debate on a motion to concur in a committee report was superseded so that the government's pipeline bill could move forward (*Journals*, June 5, 1956, pp. 696-9).

81. See, for example, *Journals*, June 29, 1971, p. 759.

82. See, for example, *Debates*, November 24, 1986, p. 1437; January 30, 1990, pp. 7587-9.

83. A motion to proceed to the Orders of the Day has been moved during Routine Proceedings under "Presenting Petitions" (*Journals*, November 6, 1986, pp. 180-1); under "Tabling of Documents" (*Journals*, January 30, 1990, pp. 1132-3); under "Presenting Reports from Committees" (*Journals*, February 5, 1993, pp. 2461-2); under "Motions" (during debate on a motion to concur in a committee report, *Journals*, June 22, 1994, p. 655; and when no question was before the House, *Journals*, March 20, 1997, pp. 1321-2). On February 9, 1987, a motion to proceed to the Orders of the Day was moved at the beginning of the sitting (*Journals*, p. 464).

84. See, for example, *Debates*, December 13, 1988, p. 23; March 6, 1990, pp. 8844-6.

85. There have been many such occasions. See, for example, *Journals,* November 24, 1986, pp. 229-30; April 9, 1987, p. 730; June 2, 1998, pp. 920-1.

government is entitled to call its business in the sequence it wants.[86] On one occasion during Government Orders, a motion was moved proposing that the House proceed to consider an item of Private Members' Business. The Speaker ruled that while the House may move from one item to another within the same type of order, a motion to move from one type of order (Government Orders, in the case at hand) to another in a different section of the *Order Paper* (Private Members' Business, in this case) is seeking to suspend the normal course of House business and, as such, is a substantive motion which could only be moved after providing notice.[87]

A motion to proceed to another order has been interpreted to allow the House to move from one rubric or item of Routine Proceedings to the next in the sequence of items under Routine Proceedings, even though there may be no substantive motion before the House.[88] Use of this motion has become obsolete outside of Routine Proceedings as the sequence of business during Government Orders and Private Members' Business is now determined by various Standing Orders. The House tends to proceed by unanimous consent when it wishes to vary the order of business as set out in the rules.

• Motions to Postpone Consideration of a Question Until a Later Date

The purpose of the non-debatable motion "That consideration of the question be postponed to (date)" is to delay the question until the day specified in the motion. It is linked to an old practice of the House, whereby each order was called each day and then postponed if it was not to be considered that day. This motion has rarely been used in the House of Commons[89] and is now totally obsolete.

• Motion to Adjourn the House

The Standing Orders provide for the House to adjourn every day at a specified time.[90] However, a Member may move a motion "That the House do now adjourn" at some other time during the sitting. If the motion is agreed to, the House adjourns immediately until the next sitting day. With the exception of non-votable items of Private Members' Business, the motion under consideration by the House at the time is not dropped from the *Order Paper,* but is simply put over to the next sitting day when it may be taken up again.[91]

---

86. Standing Order 40(2). See also rulings by Speakers, *Journals*, May 14, 1956, p. 543; April 18, 1967, pp. 1733-4; October 23, 1968, pp. 156-7.

87. See Speaker Lamoureux's ruling, *Journals*, March 29, 1966, pp. 363-4.

88. See, for example, *Debates*, November 24, 1986, p. 1435; November 25, 1986, p. 1488.

89. See, for example, *Journals*, April 29, 1874, p. 133; April 3, 1875, p. 350; April 28 and 29, 1930, pp. 240, 246.

90. Standing Order 24(2).

91. Standing Order 41(2). Prior to April 1991, a dilatory motion to adjourn the House, if agreed to, superseded the motion under debate, which was dropped from the *Order Paper* (*Bourinot*, 4th ed., p. 323*).

Motions to adjourn are referred to as dilatory motions when they are used as a dilatory tactic to supersede and delay the proceedings of the House. However, motions to adjourn are not to be referred to as dilatory motions when they are used by the government for the management of the business of the House. A motion to adjourn the House may be proposed by the government simply to end a sitting.[92] For example, this motion has been used by the government to adjourn late in the sitting but before the scheduled hour of adjournment, rather than call another item of business;[93] or to adjourn because of extraordinary circumstances.[94] A motion to adjourn the House is not debatable. The House has nonetheless used this motion, by unanimous consent or special order, as the vehicle for a debate on a matter deemed important but which was not necessarily connected to any business before the House.[95] In addition, the motion to adjourn the House is debatable when used to hold an emergency debate[96] or, at the end of a sitting, for the adjournment proceedings.[97]

A motion to adjourn the House[98] is in order when moved by a Member who has been recognized by the Speaker to take part in debate on a motion before the House,[99] or to take part in business under Routine Proceedings.[100] A motion to adjourn the House is not in order if conditions are attached to the motion (e.g., where

92. *May,* 22nd ed., pp. 318-9.

93. See, for example, *Journals*, October 30, 1995, p. 2063.

94. For example, it is usual for a motion to adjourn the House to be moved and adopted when news of the death of a sitting Member reaches the House during a sitting (*Debates*, November 17, 1970, p. 1228; see, for example, *Journals*, December 16, 1976, p. 251). In 1998, a Member was stricken in the Chamber and the House adjourned by unanimous consent; the next day, the House met for Routine Proceedings, after which an adjournment motion was moved and adopted "out of respect for the memory" of the deceased Member (*Journals*, December 9, 1998, p. 1430; December 10, 1998, p. 1438). Motions to adjourn the House were also adopted, in 1896, after several Ministers resigned (*Debates*, January 7 to 15, 1896, cols. 5-71); in 1926, when Prime Minister Mackenzie King tendered his resignation as Prime Minister (*Journals*, June 28, 1926, p. 483); and in 1968, following the defeat of a tax bill at third reading (*Journals*, February 20, 1968, p. 705; February 21, 1968, p. 707).

95. In 1954, for example, the House agreed that a motion to adjourn would be the basis of a general debate on foreign policy (*Debates*, January 28, 1954, p. 1580; January 29, 1954, pp. 1584-1622). In 1971, another such debate took place by special order of the House and was conducted similarly to an emergency debate (*Journals*, October 14, 1971, pp. 870-1; *Debates*, October 14, 1971, pp. 8659-60, 8688-734).

96. Standing Order 52. For further information on emergency debates, see Chapter 15, "Special Debates".

97. Standing Order 38. For further information on the adjournment proceedings, see Chapter 11, "Questions".

98. Standing Order 60.

99. See, for example, *Journals*, February 19, 1998, p. 506, when the motion to adjourn the House was moved during debate at second reading of a government bill.

100. See, for example, *Journals*, November 19, 1986, pp. 212-3, and January 22, 1988, pp. 2051-2, when the motion was moved under the rubric "Presentation of Petitions" during Routine Proceedings.

a specific time of adjournment is included), since this transforms it into a substantive motion which may only be moved after notice.[101] In addition, a motion to adjourn the House may not be moved in the following circumstances:

- during Statements by Members or Question Period;[102]
- during the question and comment period following a speech;[103]
- on a point of order;[104]
- by a Member moving a motion in the course of debate (the same Member cannot move two motions at the same time);[105]
- during the election of the Speaker;[106]
- during emergency debates or the Adjournment Proceedings since, at these times, the House is already considering a motion to adjourn;[107]
- on the final allotted day of a Supply period;[108]
- during debate on a motion that is the object of closure;[109]
- when a Standing or Special Order of the House provides for the completion of proceedings on any given business before the House, except when moved by a Minister;[110] or
- during proceedings on any motion proposed by a Minister in relation to a matter the government considers urgent.[111]

If a motion to adjourn is defeated, a second such motion may not be moved until some intermediate proceeding or item of business has been considered.[112] Members may move repeatedly and alternately the motions to adjourn the debate and to

---

101. See, for example, *Debates*, May 23, 1985, p. 4992. See also *Bourinot*, 4ᵗʰ ed., p. 324.

102. See, for example, *Debates*, February 21, 1979, p. 3457; December 7, 1979, pp. 2132-4.

103. See, for example, *Debates*, March 14, 1985, pp. 3029-30.

104. See, for example, *Debates*, December 20, 1978, p. 2320.

105. See, for example, *Debates*, June 21, 1994, p. 5698.

106. Standing Order 2(3).

107. See Standing Orders 38 and 52.

108. Standing Order 81(17) and (18). On June 5, 1984, which was the final allotted day for the Supply period, the Speaker did not accept a motion to adjourn the House (*Debates*, p. 4381).

109. Standing Order 57.

110. Standing Order 25. On one occasion, the Chair ruled a motion to adjourn out of order because the House had agreed to the presentation of the Budget later in the sitting (*Debates*, May 23, 1985, p. 4984). In other instances, an order having been adopted to extend the sitting, the Speaker refused to put the motion to adjourn (*Debates*, December 7, 1990, p. 16470; October 20, 1997, p. 866).

111. Standing Order 53(3)(*d*).

112. Standing Order 60. "Intermediate proceeding" is defined as a "proceeding that can properly be entered on the journals" (*Bourinot*, 4ᵗʰ ed., pp. 322-3). See, for example, *Journals*, March 10, 1966, pp. 274-6.

adjourn the House, as these motions do not have the same effect and are considered intermediate proceedings.[113]

• Motion to Adjourn the Debate

The purpose of a motion to adjourn a debate is to set aside temporarily the consideration of a motion. It can be used as a dilatory tactic or for the management of the business of the House. If the House adopts a motion "That the debate be now adjourned", then debate on the original motion stops and the House moves on to the next item of business. However, the original motion is not dropped from the *Order Paper*; it remains on the House agenda and is put over to the next sitting day when it may be taken up again. Thus, the adoption of a motion to adjourn the debate has the effect of delaying further debate on a motion on that day.[114] If the motion to adjourn the debate is defeated, then debate on the original motion continues.

A motion to adjourn the debate is in order when moved by a Member who has been recognized by the Speaker to take part in debate on a question before the House[115] (but unlike a motion to adjourn the House, it may not be moved during Routine Proceedings except during debate on motions moved under the rubric "Motions"). The other restrictions which apply to motions to adjourn the House also apply to motions to adjourn the debate.[116]

Notice of a Motion

In order to bring a substantive proposal before the House, a notice of motion must generally be given. This is to provide Members and the House with some prior warning so that they are not called upon to consider a matter unexpectedly.[117]

In most cases, notices of motions are required to be submitted in writing and printed in the *Notice Paper*.[118] Generally, the written notices of motions which are

---

113. See *Bourinot*, 4th ed., p. 323.

114. In a Committee of the Whole, the motion that the committee rise and report progress is the equivalent of the motion to adjourn debate. See Chapter 19, "Committees of the Whole House".

115. See, for example, *Journals*, June 21, 1994, pp. 633-4, 637-8, when a motion to adjourn the debate was moved during report stage of a bill which had been time allocated under Standing Order 78; March 12, 1996, pp. 79-80, and March 9, 1998, p. 540, when it was moved during debate on a motion in relation to a matter of privilege; March 26, 1998, pp. 633-4, when, in Routine Proceedings, it was moved during debate on a motion to concur in a committee report.

116. See section above, "Motion to Adjourn the House".

117. Notice requirements have been part of the Standing Orders since Confederation. For a description of the operation of notice in the British House, as it developed rules and principles to organize and arrange the "introduction, treatment and disposal" of the large amount of business before it, see *Redlich*, Vol. III, pp. 8-26.

118. Standing Order 54. For further information on the *Notice Paper*, see Chapter 24, "The Parliamentary Record".

printed in the *Notice Paper* are for substantive motions—self-contained motions which are not dependent on any other question before the House. There are also provisions where notices of motions are simply given orally during a sitting of the House.[119] However, some other types of motions do not require any notice.[120]

Depending on the type of motion and who is moving it, the notice period can vary from one hour to two weeks.[121] It is also possible to have more than one notice on the same subject (with the exception of items of Private Members' Business[122]); but once one of the motions is moved and the House makes a decision on it, any discussion or decision on the others is precluded.[123]

NOTICE IN WRITING

Written notice is required for the following motions or items of business:

- motions for leave to present a government or private Members' bill;[124]
- motions for the appointment of a committee;[125]
- motions for concurrence in committee reports (including those reports for which the concurrence of the House gives rise to an order revoking a regulation or statutory instrument[126]);
- opposition motions on Supply days;[127]
- notice of opposition to any item in the Estimates;[128]
- motions to concur in interim Supply, Main Estimates, supplementary or final Estimates, or to restore or reinstate any item in the Estimates;[129]
- report stage motions for amendments to bills;[130]
- motions of instruction to committees;

---

119. For example, notices of motions for closure (Standing Order 57) and notices of motions for time allocation where there is not agreement among party representatives (Standing Order 78(3)).

120. For example, no notice is required for a motion to adjourn a debate or to amend a motion.

121. See section below, "Specific Notice Requirements".

122. The Speaker has the discretionary power (Standing Order 86(5)) to refuse the most recent notice, to so inform the sponsoring Member and to return the item to the sponsor (see *Debates*, November 2, 1989, pp. 5474-5); see also Chapter 21, "Private Members' Business".

123. See Speaker Lamoureux's ruling, *Debates*, September 14, 1973, pp. 6589-90.

124. Standing Order 54.

125. Standing Order 54.

126. Standing Order 123(4).

127. Standing Order 81(14)(*a*).

128. Standing Order 81(14)(*a*).

129. Standing Order 81(14)(*a*).

130. Standing Orders 76(2), 76.1(2).

- motions respecting Senate amendments to bills;[131]
- items to be considered during Private Members' Business;[132] and
- motions dealing with the conduct of Members, Presiding Officers of the House, judges or the Governor General.[133]

When the House is sitting, a Member giving notice must either table the notice (present it to a Table Officer in the Chamber) or file it with the Clerk (submit it to the Journals Branch), before 6:00 p.m. Monday through Thursday, or before 2:00 p.m. on Friday, for it to be effective on that sitting day; the item will then appear in the *Notice Paper* (which is appended to the *Order Paper*) on the next sitting day.[134] On the last sitting day prior to any of the adjournment periods, the 6:00 p.m. and 2:00 p.m. deadlines do not apply. Notice for that day may be filed with the Clerk at any time up to 6:00 p.m. on the Thursday before the next scheduled sitting of the House. These notices are then printed in the *Notice Paper* for the day the House resumes sitting.[135] If the daily deadline for giving notice is not met, the notice becomes effective at the following sitting of the House.

Members must sign any notices they are submitting for the *Notice Paper* in order to prevent the unauthorized use of their names and as authentication of the Member's intentions. A notice sent by facsimile or electronic mail will be taken as an indication of a Member's intentions; however, it must be followed up by the official notice bearing the Member's original signature before the deadline in order to be included in the *Notice Paper*.[136]

If necessary, the procedural staff of the Clerk of the House will consult with the sponsoring Member when any modifications are needed to the text of the motion in

---

131. Standing Order 77(1).

132. Standing Order 94(1)(*a*).

133. *Bourinot*, 4th ed., pp. 300-1.

134. See Standing Order 54(1). The *Order Paper and Notice Paper* is published daily when the House sits. The *Notice Paper* lists all notices of bills, motions and questions which Members may wish to bring before the House. The *Order Paper* is the official House agenda and lists all items of business which may be brought forward on a given day. Until 1971, the *Notice Paper* was appended to the then *Votes and Proceedings* (now the daily *Journals*), so that each notice given by a Member was printed with the *Votes and Proceedings* of the sitting at which the notice was given. See Chapter 24, "The Parliamentary Record".

135. Standing Order 54(2). Adjournment periods are defined by reference to Standing Order 28(2).

136. In 1993, a Member's notice of a motion (to amend a bill at report stage) was refused for inclusion on the next day's *Notice Paper* because it had been faxed. A point of order was raised and, in his ruling, the Speaker advised that, in addition to having been received after the 6:00 p.m. deadline, the notice was inadmissible because notices submitted for the *Notice Paper* are not considered official until an original document with the Member's signature is received (*Debates*, February 15, 1993, pp. 15899-900).

order to make it procedurally conform with the rules and practice of the House.[137] Rarely has the Speaker been called on to intervene.[138] The notice is inserted under the appropriate heading in the *Notice Paper*. When several notices in the same category are received, they are inserted in the *Notice Paper* in the order they are received.

A long-standing practice exists whereby any Member giving notice of a motion may put it under embargo—that is, he or she may instruct the Table Officers to withhold explicit information about the content of the motion until that day's deadline for filing of notices, or until the publication the following morning of the *Order Paper and Notice Paper* containing the notice. In 1990, when an embargo was placed on the notice of a votable Supply day motion, to be debated and voted on a Friday, an objection was raised on the basis that the embargo had the effect of reducing the 48-hour notice period required in the circumstances.[139] In his ruling, Speaker Fraser reviewed the practice with regard to embargoes and concluded that the notice requirements in this case were met and that, while placing an embargo could potentially have serious consequences, the decision is in the hands of the motion's sponsor, and the Chair and the Table Officers are bound to follow usual practice.[140]

Members have raised points of order about the procedural acceptability of motions on the *Notice Paper*; at times, the Chair has refused to comment until the motions are actually before the House (i.e., called as an Order of the Day);[141] at other times, the Chair has ruled before the motion was before the House.[142]

Removal of Notice

As long as a motion has not been proposed to the House, it remains a notice of motion and the sponsor may secure its withdrawal unilaterally, without seeking the consent of the House.[143] To do so, the Member either requests in writing that the Clerk withdraw it or rises in the House to withdraw the notice orally.[144] The item is then removed from the *Notice Paper* or the *Order Paper*. Alternatively, if the sponsor declines to move the motion when the order is called, it would be dropped from the *Order Paper*.[145] Notices have also been removed from the *Order Paper and Notice*

---

137. This procedure has been followed since Confederation (see *Bourinot*, 1ˢᵗ ed., pp. 308-9).

138. See, for example, *Journals*, January 14, 1953, p. 127.

139. See *Debates*, March 22, 1990, pp. 9613-24, 9628-9.

140. *Debates*, March 26, 1990, pp. 9758-61.

141. See, for example, *Debates*, May 24, 1988, pp. 15697-703.

142. See, for example, *Debates*, June 19, 1990, pp. 12963-7; May 28, 1991, pp. 702-3.

143. See Speaker Fraser's ruling, *Debates*, December 7, 1989, p. 6584.

144. See, for example, *Debates*, February 12, 1993, p. 15851.

145. Standing Order 42(1).

Paper on the Speaker's initiative, following the death or resignation of the sponsoring Member.[146]

A motion or notice of motion is considered to be in the possession of the House under the following conditions:

- once a motion has been moved;

- once a private Member's motion has been selected following the draw for the establishment of the Order of Precedence;[147] or

- once an Order of the Day has been designated for a government notice of motion[148] or notice of a Ways and Means motion.[149]

Such a motion or notice of motion cannot then be removed from the *Order Paper* unless the House so decides. The sponsoring Member or Minister must request that it be withdrawn and the House must give unanimous consent to the request.[150]

Alteration to Notice

A modification to a notice of motion standing on the *Notice Paper* is permitted if the alterations are editorial in nature and no change is brought to the substance or scope of the original notice.[151] In order to bring a substantive change to an item on notice, it is necessary to replace it with a fresh notice which is then subject to the applicable notice requirement.[152]

ORAL NOTICE

Some items of business do not require 48 hours' written notice, but only oral notice to be provided during a sitting of the House. For example, at least 24 hours' oral notice is required before a Minister is permitted to move a motion for closure,[153] or time allocation where there is no agreement among the parties in the House.[154]

---

146. For example, notices sponsored by Jean-Claude Malépart (Laurier–Sainte-Marie) (died November 16, 1989), Catherine Callbeck (Malpeque) (resigned January 25, 1993) and Stephen Harper (Calgary West) (resigned January 14, 1997) were withdrawn. They included notices of motions for Private Members' Business, notices of written questions and notices of motions for the production of papers. Private Members' bills awaiting introduction and notices of motions under Routine Proceedings would also be withdrawn in such circumstances.

147. Standing Order 87. See Chapter 21, "Private Members' Business".

148. Standing Order 56(1).

149. Standing Order 83(2).

150. *Bourinot*, 4th ed., pp. 296-7. See also Standing Order 64. See, for example, *Debates*, March 12, 1993, pp. 16925-6; May 11, 1994, p. 4211.

151. *May*, 22nd ed., p. 332. See also *Bourinot*, 4th ed., p. 299.

152. See Speaker Lemieux's ruling, *Journals*, March 26, 1928, pp. 200-1.

153. Standing Order 57. For further information on closure, see Chapter 14, "The Curtailment of Debate".

154. Standing Order 78(3). For further information on time allocation, see Chapter 14, "The Curtailment of Debate".

NO NOTICE

As a general rule, there are no notice requirements for motions (called "subsidiary" motions) which are dependent on other business of the House. Other motions are also exempt from notice requirements either as a result of practice or a specific Standing Order. These include, for instance:

- motions dealing with the progress of a bill after its introduction;[155]
- motions to commit (i.e., refer a matter to a Committee of the Whole or other committee);
- motions for the previous question;[156]
- motions to adjourn the House;[157]
- motions to adjourn the debate;
- motions for another Member to "be now heard";[158]
- motions to proceed to the Orders of the Day;[159]
- motions to amend a question already before the House;
- motions to postpone the question to a specific day;[160]
- motions to proceed to another order of business;
- motions for time allocation to a bill, when there is complete or majority agreement among party representatives;[161]
- motions for the fixing of sitting days and the hours of meeting[162] or adjournment;
- motions to continue or extend a sitting;[163]
- government motions to suspend the rules governing notice and times of sitting, in connection with matters considered urgent;[164]
- government motions dealing with routine matters, for which unanimous consent is required but has been denied;[165]
- motions based on a *prima facie* question of privilege;[166]

---

155. Standing Order 54. See Chapter 16, "The Legislative Process".

156. Standing Order 61.

157. Standing Order 60.

158. Standing Order 62.

159. Standing Order 59.

160. Standing Order 58.

161. Standing Order 78(1), (2).

162. Standing Order 54 refers to the "times of meeting" which has been interpreted as the hours of sitting. See Speakers' rulings, *Debates*, May 21, 1920, pp. 2625-6; *Journals*, December 20, 1951, pp. 345-7.

163. Standing Order 26(1). See Chapter 9, "Sittings of the House".

164. Standing Order 53. See Chapter 15, "Special Debates".

165. Standing Order 56.1.

166. Standing Order 48. See Chapter 3, "Privileges and Immunities".

- motions to correct the records of the House;
- traditional motions disposed of by the House on the opening day of a session;[167]
- motions to select a Deputy Speaker, a Deputy Chairman of Committees of the Whole, and an Assistant Deputy Chairman of Committees of the Whole; and
- motions for the observance of the proprieties of the House.

PUBLICATION OF A *SPECIAL ORDER PAPER AND NOTICE PAPER*

Either before a session begins or when the House stands adjourned, the government may wish that the House, when it resumes sitting, give immediate consideration to a matter or matters for which notice would have to be provided. In these circumstances, the government communicates its intentions to the Speaker, who then directs that a *Special Order Paper and Notice Paper* be published, listing notices of any government measures requiring immediate consideration by the House.[168] The Speaker also ensures that the *Special Order Paper and Notice Paper* is circulated to all Members at least 48 hours before the sitting. A *Special Order Paper and Notice Paper* has been printed and circulated on more than a dozen occasions.[169]

SPECIFIC NOTICE REQUIREMENTS

The length of the notice period (i.e., the time which must elapse before the item can be considered by the House) varies, depending on the type of motion. Most notices appear in the *Notice Paper*; however, others may be given to the Speaker in writing or given to the House orally. A 48-hour notice period applies in most cases;[170] other requirements range from one hour to two weeks.

Forty-Eight Hours' Notice

In practice, the 48 hours' notice requirement is not exactly 48 consecutive hours, but refers instead to the publication of the notice once in the *Notice Paper* and its transfer the next day to the *Order Paper*. For example, a Member might give notice at 6:00 p.m. on a Tuesday and be free as early as 10:00 a.m. on Thursday to proceed with his or her motion (the notice having appeared in the *Notice Paper* on

---

167. See Chapter 8, "The Parliamentary Cycle".

168. Standing Order 55(1). See, for example, the *Special Order Paper and Notice Paper* published prior to the opening of the Second Session of the Thirty-Fifth Parliament (1996-97). This has also happened when the House has been recalled (see Chapter 8, "The Parliamentary Cycle"). For further information on the *Special Order Paper and Notice Paper*, see Chapter 24, "The Parliamentary Record".

169. For examples of its publication during recalls, see Appendix 13, "Recalls of the House of Commons During Adjournment Periods Since 1867". Since 1991, it has been the practice to include the time the notice was received in the *Special Order Paper and Notice Paper*. This serves to demonstrate that the 48-hour notice requirement has been met.

170. See Standing Order 54.

Wednesday and in the *Order Paper* on Thursday).[171] Furthermore, a Member giving notice of a motion on a Friday before 2:00 p.m. may propose the motion to the House on the following Monday, the minimum notice period (48 hours) having elapsed over the weekend.[172]

Forty-eight hours' written notice is required for:

- leave to introduce a bill; leave to present a resolution or address; for the appointment of any committee or to place a written question on the *Order Paper*;[173]

- notices to oppose any item in the Estimates, during the Supply period ending June 23;[174]

- motions in amendment at the report stage of a bill that has not yet received second reading;[175]

- motions for concurrence in any committee report (including those reports seeking an order to revoke a regulation or statutory instrument[176]); and

- motions to concur in interim Supply, the Main Estimates, and supplementary or final Estimates, or to restore or reinstate any item in the Estimates.[177]

Twenty-Four Hours' Notice

Some items of business require a notice period of 24 hours. Like the 48 hours' notice, it is not timed by the clock. For written notices, the 24-hour notice requirement simply means that a motion may be proposed once it appears in the *Notice Paper* and *Order Paper*. (The text of the motion appears simultaneously in the *Order Paper* and the *Notice Paper*.) For example, if it is filed at 6:00 p.m. on Monday, it may be taken up at 10:00 a.m. on Tuesday. For oral notices, if it is given at any time during a sitting of the House, the motion may be taken up on the next sitting day.

Twenty-four hours' written notice is required for:

- opposition motions on Supply days;[178]

---

171. See *Journals*, October 6, 1970, pp. 1417-20.

172. The same applies when the House sits on a Saturday. Notices filed on a Saturday appear in the *Order Paper* on Monday (see *Bourinot*, 4ᵗʰ ed., p. 296; see also Speaker Michener's ruling, *Journals*, May 8, 1961, p. 516).

173. Standing Order 54(1).

174. Standing Order 81(14)(*a*). At other times, a 24-hour notice period applies. See also Chapter 18, "Financial Procedures".

175. Standing Order 76(2).

176. Standing Order 123(4). See also Chapter 17, "Delegated Legislation".

177. Standing Order 81(14)(*a*).

178. Standing Order 81(14)(*a*).

- motions respecting Senate amendments to a bill;[179]
- motions in amendment to a bill at report stage following second reading;[180]
- notices to oppose any item in the Estimates, except during the Supply period ending June 23;[181]
- the item from the Order of Precedence which is to be considered during Private Members' Hour;[182] and
- meetings of any committee considering a private bill originating in the Senate.[183]

  Twenty-four hours' oral notice is required for:

- motions for closure;[184] and
- motions for time allocation to a bill, when there is no agreement among party representatives.[185]

Two Weeks' Notice

Private Members' motions require a written notice period of at least two weeks. A Member can propose the motion only if it is selected following the draw for the establishment of the Order of Precedence and after the two-week period has elapsed.[186] Private Members' public bills, like other bills, require 48 hours' written notice before the sponsoring Member may ask leave of the House to introduce it. Once the bill is read a first time and printed, second reading is subject to the same requirements of selection after the draw and a two-week notice.[187]

One Week's Notice

Written notice of one week is required for the meeting of any committee considering a private bill originating in the House of Commons.[188]

---

179. Standing Order 77(1).

180. Standing Order 76.1(2).

181. Standing Order 81(14)(*a*). During the Supply period ending June 23, a 48-hour notice period applies. See also Chapter 18, "Financial Procedures".

182. Standing Order 94(1)(*a*)(i). See also Chapter 21, "Private Members' Business".

183. Standing Order 141(2)(*a*).

184. Standing Order 57. See Chapter 14, "The Curtailment of Debate".

185. Standing Order 78(3). See Chapter 14, "The Curtailment of Debate".

186. Standing Order 86(2). See Chapter 21, "Private Members' Business".

187. Standing Order 88.

188. Standing Order 141(2)(*a*).

One Hour's Notice

There are two situations in which Members must provide at least one hour's written notice to the Speaker; this is required if a Member wishes to:

- raise a question of privilege on a matter which has not arisen out of the proceedings in the Chamber during the course of a sitting;[189] or

- request permission to move a motion for the adjournment of the House for the purpose of debating "a specific and important matter requiring urgent consideration" (request for an emergency debate).[190]

Moving a Motion

A Member launches the process of debate in the Chamber by proposing or moving a motion. Where notice of a motion has been given, the Speaker will first ensure that the Member wishes to proceed with moving the motion. If the sponsor of a motion chooses not to proceed with a motion (either by not being present[191] or by being present but declining to move the motion), then the motion is not proceeded with and is dropped from the *Order Paper,* unless allowed to stand at the request of the government.[192] If the sponsor wishes to proceed and nods in agreement, the Speaker then ascertains whether there is a seconder. All motions in the House require a seconder;[193] if none is found, the Speaker will not propose the question to the House and no entry appears in the *Journals* as the House is not in possession of it.[194] Any Member may act as a seconder, even for government motions which may be moved only by Ministers.[195] Once a motion is moved and seconded, it is still not properly before the House—that is, it may not be debated—until it has been proposed and read from the Chair.[196]

For motions which do not require notice, a Member will typically move the motion at the end of his or her speech. Before recognizing another Member on debate, the Speaker first asks if there is a seconder for the motion. If there is a seconder, and after the motion is received in writing, the Speaker proposes and reads the motion to the House.

---

189. Standing Order 48(2). See, for example, *Debates*, April 21, 1989, pp. 799-800; February 22, 1990, p. 8663. A question of privilege arising out of House proceedings may be raised without notice. A Member wishing to raise a question of privilege may also place a notice on the *Notice Paper* pursuant to Standing Order 54 or 86(2). See also Chapter 3, "Privileges and Immunities".

190. Standing Order 52(2). See also Chapter 15, "Special Debates".

191. See, for example, *Debates*, May 1, 1985, pp. 4313-4; May 4, 1992, p. 10011.

192. Standing Order 42(1).

193. Standing Order 65. The requirement that a motion be seconded does not apply in any House committee (see Standing Order 116).

194. *Bourinot*, 4th ed., p. 297.

195. *Debates*, January 25, 1983, p. 22176; October 28, 1991, pp. 4070-2, 4076.

196. Standing Order 65.

The provision that a motion be in writing applies to all motions, whether or not they require notice, as well as to amendments and sub-amendments, both in the House and its committees. When notice of a motion has been given, the provision for it to be in writing is automatically met since the text of the motion appears on the *Order Paper*. In all other instances when the motion does not appear on the *Order Paper* or has not been printed and distributed to Members, the Speaker must receive a written copy of the motion before proposing it to the House prior to debate. The Member will also affix his or her signature to the text of the motion.

Before reading a motion to the House, it is the Speaker's duty to ensure that the motion is procedurally in order. This is done by verifying that the notice requirement (if any) was satisfied; that the wording of the motion corresponds with the notice; and that it contains no objectionable or irregular wording. Any part of a motion found out of order will render the whole motion out of order.[197] If the Chair finds the form of the motion to be irregular, he or she has the authority to modify it in order to ensure that it conforms to the usage of the House.[198] This is usually done with the concurrence of the mover.[199] If a motion is ruled out of order, a Member may move it again after the necessary corrections have been made and the notice requirements satisfied; it is then treated as a new motion.

In ruling a motion out of order, the Speaker informs the House of the reasons and quotes the Standing Order or authority applicable to the case.[200] The motion is not proposed to the House and is dropped from the *Order Paper*.

If the motion is found to be in order, and has been moved and seconded, the Speaker proposes the motion to the House. Once the Speaker has read the motion in the words of its mover, it is considered to be before the House. Every motion found to be in order and proposed from the Chair is entered in the *Journals*. (See Figure 12.2, Moving a Motion.)

The motion is read in English and in French by the Speaker; if the Speaker is not familiar with both languages, he or she reads the motion in one language and directs the Clerk to read it in the other.[201] In practice, the provision that all motions be read in their entirety is regularly relaxed, particularly for lengthy motions. The Speaker will read the first words and then ask, "Shall I dispense (with reading the entire text)?", to which the response from Members is usually affirmative.[202] Likewise, the provision that all motions be read in both languages is also regularly relaxed, given the existence of simultaneous interpretation on the floor of the House and the

---

197. *Journals*, May 31, 1954, pp. 674-5; see also *May*, 22ⁿᵈ ed., p. 337.

198. *Journals*, April 28, 1924, pp. 186-7; May 31, 1954, pp. 674-5.

199. Members wishing to make amendments to the substance of their own motions have sought the unanimous consent of the House to do so (*Bourinot*, 4ᵗʰ ed., p. 299). See, for example, *Journals*, October 28, 1998, p. 1206.

200. Standing Order 10. See, for example, *Debates*, December 5, 1995, pp. 17197, 17217-8.

201. Standing Order 65.

202. There have been occasions when the Chair has not received unanimous consent to dispense with the reading of a motion (see, for example, *Debates*, June 2, 1987, p. 6618; April 3, 1990, p. 10156; March 26, 1991, pp. 19025-7; June 2, 1992, pp. 11249-51).

Figure 12.2   *Moving a Motion*

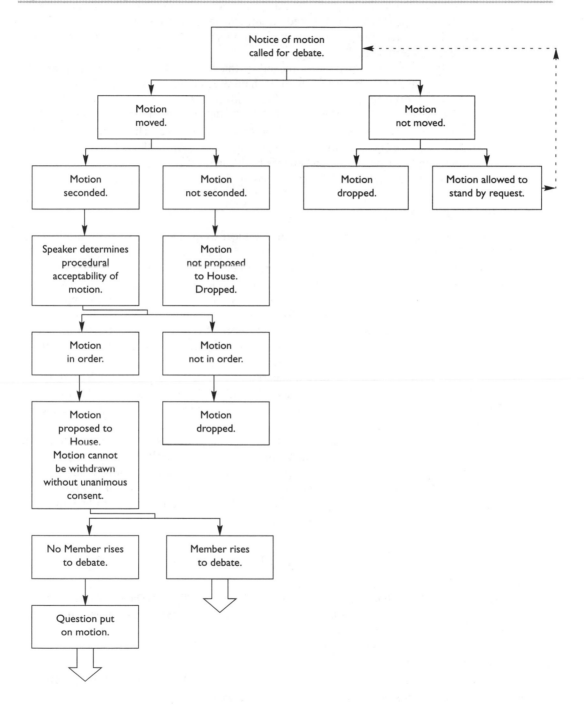

immediate availability of the text of the motion in both official languages on the *Order Paper* or *Notice Paper*. When a motion does not appear on the *Order Paper* or has not been printed and distributed, Members may request at any time during debate that the Chair read the question aloud, so long as no Member speaking to the matter is thereby interrupted.[203]

After a motion has been proposed to the House, the Speaker recognizes the mover as the first to speak in debate. If the mover chooses not to speak, he or she is nonetheless deemed to have spoken (by nodding, the Member is considered to have said "I move" and this is taken as speech in the debate).[204] The Member who seconds a motion is not required to speak to it at this point, but may choose to do so later in the debate. The one exception occurs during the debate on the Address in Reply to the Speech from the Throne, when it is traditional for the seconder to be recognized to speak immediately after the mover has spoken.[205]

THE RULE OF ANTICIPATION

The moving of a motion was formerly subject to the ancient "rule of anticipation" which is no longer strictly observed. According to this rule, which applied to other proceedings as well as motions, a motion could not anticipate a matter which was standing on the *Order Paper* for further discussion, whether as a bill or a motion, and which was contained in a more effective form of proceeding.[206] (For example, a bill or any other Order of the Day is more effective than a motion, which in turn has priority over an amendment, which in turn is more effective than a written or oral question.) If such a motion were allowed, it could indeed forestall or block a decision from being taken on the matter already on the *Order Paper*.

While the rule of anticipation is part of the Standing Orders in the British House of Commons, it has never been so in the Canadian House of Commons. Furthermore, references to attempts made to apply this British rule to Canadian practice are not very conclusive.[207]

The rule is dependent on the principle which forbids the same question from being raised twice within the same session. It does not apply, however, to similar or identical motions or bills which appear on the *Notice Paper* prior to debate.[208] The rule of anticipation becomes operative only when one of two similar motions on the *Order Paper* is actually proceeded with.[209] For example, two bills similar in

203. Standing Order 46.

204. *Debates*, March 19, 1992, pp. 8479-80, 8490-1. See also Chapter 13, "Rules of Order and Decorum".

205. For further information on the Address in Reply to the Speech from the Throne, see Chapter 15, "Special Debates".

206. *May*, 22ⁿᵈ ed., pp. 334-5; *Beauchesne*, 4ᵗʰ ed., pp. 116-7.

207. *Beauchesne*, 6ᵗʰ ed., p. 154.

208. See, for example, *Journals*, March 13, 1959, p. 238; July 3, 1969, pp. 1289-90; July 7, 1969, pp. 1316-8.

209. See, for example, *Journals*, February 24, 1936, pp. 67-8; January 23, 1961, pp. 176-7.

substance will be allowed to stand on the *Order Paper* but only one may be moved and disposed of. If the first bill is withdrawn, the second may be proceeded with. If a decision is taken on the first bill, the other may not be proceeded with. A point of order regarding anticipation may be raised when the second motion is proposed from the Chair, if the first has already been proposed to the House and has become an Order of the Day.

An exception has been allowed, however, in the case of an opposition motion on a Supply day related to the subject matter of a bill already before the House. Under the normal application of the rule, the Chair would refuse the motion because it ranks as inferior to a bill. The Speaker has nonetheless ruled that the opposition prerogative in the use of an allotted day is very broad and ought to be interfered with only on the clearest and most certain procedural grounds.[210]

At one time, Members were also prohibited from asking a question during Question Period if it was in anticipation of an Order of the Day; this was to prevent the time of the House being taken up with business to be discussed later in the sitting.[211] In 1975, the rule was relaxed in regard to questions asked during Question Period when the Order of Day was either the Budget debate or the debate on the Address in Reply to the Speech from the Throne, as long as questions on these matters did not monopolize the limited time available during Question Period.[212] In 1983, the Speaker ruled that questions relating to an opposition motion on a Supply day could also be put during Question Period.[213] In 1997, the Standing Committee on Procedure and House Affairs recommended, in a report to the House, that questions not be ruled out of order on this basis alone.[214] The Speaker subsequently advised the House that the Chair would follow the advice of the Committee.[215]

WITHDRAWAL OF MOTION

Once a motion has been proposed from the Chair, it is in the possession of the House and may be debated. A Member who has moved a motion may request that it be withdrawn, but this can only be done with the unanimous consent of the House.[216] If any Member objects or rises to speak to the original motion, the Speaker deems that unanimous consent has been withheld. Conversely, if no dissenting voice is heard,

---

210. However, the Speaker advised the House that neither the consideration of the opposition motion nor the vote taken on it could prejudice in any way the progress of the bill to which the motion related; see *Journals*, November 14, 1975, pp. 861-2.

211. *Beauchesne*, 4ᵗʰ ed., pp. 147-8. See also Speaker's ruling on the conduct of Question Period, *Journals*, April 14, 1975, pp. 439-41, in particular p. 441.

212. See Speaker's ruling, *Journals*, June 26, 1975, p. 665.

213. *Debates*, February 24, 1983, pp. 23181-3.

214. *Debates*, March 4, 1997, pp. 8594-5; *Journals*, March 21, 1997, p. 1334.

215. *Debates*, April 7, 1997, p. 9377. For additional information, see Chapter 11, "Questions".

216. Standing Order 64. See, for example, *Journals*, November 25, 1992, p. 2213 (withdrawal of a private Members' motion); March 11, 1999, p. 1594 (withdrawal of a motion for the production of papers).

the Speaker declares the motion withdrawn and an entry to that effect appears in the *Journals*. Any motion thus withdrawn may again be put on notice and moved at a later date;[217] it will be treated as a new motion. An amendment and a sub-amendment may also be withdrawn in this manner.[218]

Similarly, a Member wishing to withdraw his or her motion, amendment or sub-amendment and to alter or replace it with another must request and obtain unanimous consent to do so.[219] However, no motion or amendment may be withdrawn if an amendment or sub-amendment to it is before the House. Members have received the consent of the House for the withdrawal of motions (or amendments) moved by other Members.[220]

The term "withdraw" is commonly used when Members seek to remove a motion from the consideration of the House after it has been moved and has been ordered for further consideration (as in the case of a bill awaiting second reading). In such cases, since the item is subject to an order of the House, it cannot be withdrawn until the order of the House has been discharged.[221] The House must first consent to the discharge of the order and then to the withdrawal of the item.

DIVIDING A MOTION

When a complicated motion comes before the House (for example, a motion containing two or more parts each capable of standing on its own), the Speaker has the authority to modify it and thereby facilitate decision-making for the House. When any Member objects to a motion that contains two or more distinct propositions, he or she may request that the motion be divided and that each proposition be debated and voted on separately. The final decision, however, rests with the Chair. On a

---

217. See, for example, *Journals*, April 7, 1941, p. 260.

218. See, for example, *Journals*, June 22, 1988, p. 2950 (withdrawal of amendments to a government motion).

219. See, for example, *Debates*, April 29, 1980, p. 542; May 26, 1993, p. 19858; May 5, 1994, p. 3958. Even corrections to apparent errors in wording require unanimous consent (see, for example, *Debates*, May 3, 1993, pp. 18783-4; November 24, 1994, p. 8255), unless accomplished by means of an amendment moved by another Member.

220. *Bourinot* states that no motion can be withdrawn in the absence of the Member who proposed it; in current practice, however, it is more a matter of courtesy to do so in the presence of the sponsoring Member. See, for example, *Debates*, March 3, 1997, p. 8482 (Member sought and received unanimous consent to withdraw report stage motions in the names of Members of his party); March 4, 1997, p. 8643 (Member sought and received unanimous consent to withdraw another Member's motion under Private Members' Business); February 16, 1999, p. 11982 (Government House Leader, with sponsoring Member's consent, sought and received unanimous consent to withdraw her private Member's bill). Another practice exists whereby a Minister may request the withdrawal of a motion in the absence of the sponsoring Minister (*Bourinot*, 4th ed., p. 300); see, for example, *Debates*, November 13, 1981, p. 12743).

221. See, for example, *Journals*, March 12, 1993, p. 2627 (unanimous consent to discharge the order for second reading and referral to committee of a private Members' bill, and to withdraw the bill).

related matter, the Speaker has ruled that the practice of dividing substantive motions has never been extended to bills and that the Chair has no authority to do so.[222]

The matter of dividing a complicated motion has arisen in the House on at least three occasions. In 1964, a complicated government notice of motion was divided and restated when the Speaker found that the motion contained two propositions which many Members objected to considering together.[223] In 1966, faced with a similar request, the Speaker ruled against taking such an action, stating that only in exceptional circumstances should the Chair make this decision on its own initiative.[224] In 1991, in response to a request to divide a motion dealing with proposed amendments to the Standing Orders, the Speaker undertook discussions with the leadership of the three parties in the House, subsequently ruling that, for voting purposes, the motion would be divided into three groupings, in addition to the paragraphs relating to the coming into force of the motion.[225]

Decisions of the House

The will of the House is ascertained by means of a vote. Once debate on a motion has concluded, the Speaker puts the question and the House pronounces itself on the motion.[226] A simple majority of the Members present and voting is required to adopt or defeat a question. The *Constitution Act, 1867* provides that:

> *Questions arising in the House of Commons shall be decided by a Majority of Voices other than that of the Speaker, and when the Voices are equal, but not otherwise, the Speaker shall have a Vote.*[227]

A decision on a motion before the House can be made with no dissenting voices, in which case the motion is adopted and no division is taken.[228] When there are

---

222. See Chapter 16, "The Legislative Process".

223. *Journals*, June 15, 1964, pp. 427-31.

224. *Journals*, March 23, 1966, p. 334.

225. *Debates*, April 10, 1991, p. 19312.

226. Some types of motions do not result in a vote; debate on these motions expires at the end of the time provided without the Speaker putting the question. For example: non-votable opposition motions on Supply days (Standing Order 81(19)); non-votable items of Private Members' Business (Standing Order 96(1)).

227. R.S.C. 1985, Appendix II, No. 5, s. 49.

228. Although no longer used, motions have been recorded as being adopted by the House *nemine contradicente*, that is, without dissenting voice. From 1867 to 1909 and from 1916 to 1917, the *Journals* routinely used the term for entries related to the election of the Speaker (see, for example, *Journals*, November 6, 1867, p. 2; January 12, 1916, p. 6). This term was also used in the *Debates* for entries relating to the Speaker beginning in 1891 until 1980 (see *Debates*, April 29, 1891, col. 3; April 14, 1980, p. 2). See also the *Journals* for November 21, 1979, where it is recorded that the House agreed *nemine contradicente* to a resolution respecting former Prime Minister Trudeau (p. 244).

dissenting voices, a vote (or division) is taken. This can be either a voice vote or a recorded vote [229] where the House is called on to divide into the "yeas" and the "nays". [230]

TERMINATION OF DEBATE

When debate on a motion appears to be finished (i.e., when no Member rises to be recognized for debate), the Speaker asks if the House is ready for the question—that is, if the House is ready to come to a decision. If no Member rises to speak, the Speaker puts the question to the House for a decision.

Some Standing Orders provide for deadlines within which the Speaker can or must proceed with putting the question on specific matters, unless debate on the motion has already collapsed or unless there is no provision for debate. For instance:

- motions to extend the sitting hours during the last 10 sitting days in June; [231]
- sub-amendments, amendments and the main motion for an Address in Reply to the Speech from the Throne; [232]
- closured motions; [233]
- when the motion for the previous question is adopted, the question on the main motion must be decided immediately without debate or amendment; [234]
- motions for time allocation; [235]
- opposition motions and Supply motions on the last allotted day of each Supply period; [236]
- the main Budget motion and any amendment or sub-amendment; [237]
- votable items of Private Members' Business; [238] and
- motions for the production of papers. [239]

---

229. Standing Order 45(1). When selecting a Speaker, the House makes its choice by secret ballot (Standing Order 4); see Chapter 7, "The Speaker and Other Presiding Officers of the House".

230. In the British House of Commons, a division entails a physical separation into two lobbies of those voting for a question (yeas) and those voting against it (nays); see *May*, 22nd ed., pp. 350-2.

231. Standing Order 27(2). See Chapter 9, "Sittings of the House".

232. Standing Order 50 (5), (6) and (8). See also Chapter 15, "Special Debates".

233. Standing Order 57. See also *Journals*, December 14, 1964, p. 1000. For additional information on the closure rule, see Chapter 14, "The Curtailment of Debate".

234. Standing Order 61.

235. Standing Order 78. See also Chapter 14, "The Curtailment of Debate".

236. Standing Order 81(17), (18). See also Chapter 18, "Financial Procedures".

237. Standing Order 84(4), (5) and (6). See also Chapter 18, "Financial Procedures".

238. Standing Orders 93 and 98(4)). See also Chapter 21, "Private Members' Business".

239. Standing Order 97(2). See also Chapter 21, "Private Members' Business".

In addition, special orders may also contain provisions for the Speaker to put a question at a specific time.

PUTTING THE QUESTION

When the House appears ready to come to a decision, the Speaker will ask, "Is the House ready for the question?" If no Member rises to speak, the Speaker is then satisfied that the debate has concluded and puts the question to dispose of the motion. If debate terminates pursuant to a predetermined deadline, the Speaker interrupts the proceedings to put the question, in accordance with the terms of the Standing Order or the special order.

"Putting the question" means that the Speaker reads the main motion, followed by any proposed amendment or sub-amendment in order.[240] The Speaker then asks, "Is it the pleasure of the House to adopt the motion?" In the absence of any dissenting voice, he or she will declare the motion carried; in this way, a question can be decided without resorting to a vote. If the Speaker hears a dissenting voice, he or she may first verify whether the House wishes to have the motion declared carried or negatived simply "on division". Alternatively, the Speaker will proceed to conduct a voice vote and then, if it is demanded, a recorded vote. (See Figure 12.3, Putting the Question.)

When a motion, an amendment, and a sub-amendment have been proposed, the question is put first on the sub-amendment:

- If the sub-amendment is negatived, debate may then resume on the amendment, another sub-amendment may be moved and debated, or the question is put on the amendment;

- If the sub-amendment is adopted, debate may then resume on the amendment as amended, another sub-amendment may be moved and debated, or the question is put on the amendment as amended.

The question is then put on the amendment (or the amendment as amended):

- If the amendment (or the amendment as amended) is negatived, debate may then resume on the main motion and a new amendment and sub-amendment may be moved and debated, or the question is put on the main motion;

- If the amendment (or the amendment as amended) is adopted, debate may then resume on the main motion as amended, and a new amendment and sub-amendment may be moved and debated, or the question is put on the main motion as amended.

When all sub-amendments and amendments are disposed of and debate on the main motion (or the main motion as amended) concludes, the question is put on the main motion.

---

240. The Speaker will reread the question after Members have been summoned for a recorded division.

Figure 12.3   *Putting the Question*

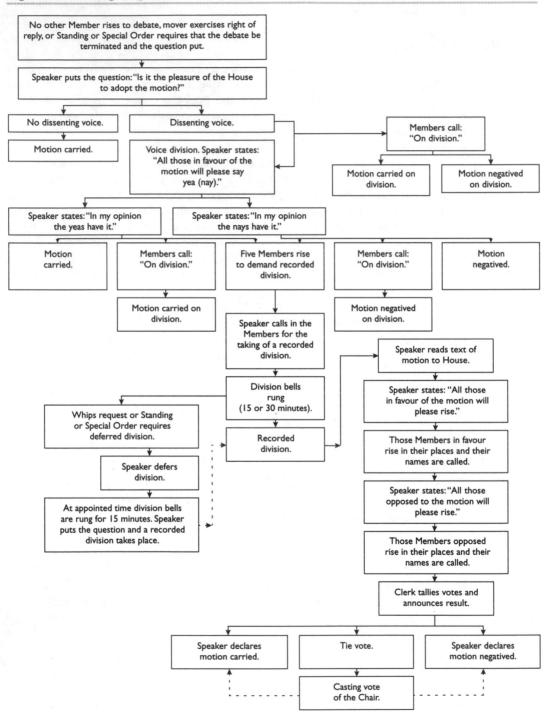

On Division

Members who do not wish a motion to be carried or lost unanimously, but who do not want a recorded division, may indicate their position by simply stating "on division" after the Speaker has asked if it is the pleasure of the House to adopt the motion. The Speaker will then declare the motion carried or lost on division.

Voice Vote

When it is obvious that the House wishes to divide on the question (i.e., dissent is expressed when the Speaker asks if it is the pleasure of the House to adopt the motion), the Speaker will take a voice vote. He or she will ask for the decision of the House by saying, "All those in favour of the motion will please say 'yea'"; and then, "All those opposed will please say 'nay'". The Speaker listens to both responses, judges the voices and the sense of the House, and states his or her opinion as to the result: "In my opinion, the yeas (nays) have it". If there is no objection, the Speaker then declares the motion carried or lost, as the case may be; however, if five or more Members rise to signal a demand for a recorded vote, the Speaker will say, "Call in the Members".[241] If fewer than five Members rise, the Speaker concludes that the initial assessment is correct and declares the motion carried or negatived on division. It sometimes happens that, after the yeas and nays have been called, Members have said "on division" to indicate that the question was not decided unanimously, without resorting to a recorded vote.[242]

Requirement to Vote

There is no rule requiring a Member to vote.[243] A Member may abstain from voting simply by remaining seated during the vote. Such abstentions are of an unofficial status and are not recorded although, on occasion, Members have risen following a vote to offer an explanation as to why they had abstained,[244] or how they would have voted had they been present when the question was put.[245]

---

241. Standing Order 45(1). When a question arose as to whether or not Members rising to request a recorded division were required to do so from their assigned places in the House, the Deputy Speaker stated that the rule does not impose such a requirement (*Debates*, June 23, 1992, p. 12686).

242. See, for example, *Debates*, November 7, 1997, p. 1721.

243. During the first 60 years following Confederation, Members were required to vote if they were in the House during a division (*Bourinot*, 4th ed., p. 381). In 1928, Speaker Lemieux ruled first that Members must vote and then later amended his decision, indicating that not to vote was acceptable (*Debates*, March 27, 1928, p. 1755; May 26, 1928, p. 3420; February 19, 1929, pp. 266-7). In 1931, a committee was set up to consider the question of voting, but made no recommendations regarding compulsory voting (*Debates*, June 26, 1931, pp. 3076-7). In 1944, a procedure committee proposed that voting be made obligatory and explicit in the Standing Orders, but the House did not adopt the committee's report (*Journals*, March 3, 1944, p. 149). In subsequent years, the Chair stated that there was no obligation for Members to vote (see, for example, *Debates*, September 28, 1945, p. 541; June 24, 1963, pp. 1522-3; March 26, 1965, p. 12857).

244. See, for example, *Debates*, December 5, 1990, p. 16325 (act of protest); February 24, 1993, p. 16425 (chairing the legislative committee to which a bill was being referred).

245. See, for example, *Debates*, November 4, 1997, p. 1557.

Direct Pecuniary Interest

No Member is entitled to vote on any question in which he or she has a direct pecuniary interest, and any vote cast in these circumstances is to be disallowed.[246] For a Member to be disqualified from voting, the monetary interest must be direct and personal. A Member's personal interests would not be challenged on questions of public policy, which have a broad application. Even voting a pay increase to Members themselves does not amount to a case of direct monetary interest because it applies to all Members, rather than just one, or to certain Members but not to others.[247]

Where a Member has a direct pecuniary interest in a question, he or she simply abstains from voting.[248] If a Member's vote is questioned, it is the practice to accept the Member's word.[249] If the House wishes to pursue the issue, notice must be given of a substantive motion to disallow a Member's vote.[250] While several Members have voluntarily abstained from voting, or have had their votes questioned, no Member's vote has ever been disallowed on grounds of direct monetary interest.

RECORDED DIVISIONS

Once the Speaker has ordered that the Members be called in for a recorded vote, the division bells are rung and the party Whips assemble their Members. The Sergeant-at-Arms is responsible for ensuring that the division bells are rung in all the buildings of the parliamentary precinct. While the division bells ring, a Presiding Officer remains in the Chair waiting for the Members to assemble for the vote. During this period, the proceedings of the House are effectively suspended; debate has ceased, and no Member can be recognized by the Chair for whatever reason. Committees may voluntarily suspend their meetings so that Members may respond to the bells.[251]

---

246. Standing Order 21. This Standing Order, derived from British practice, has remained unchanged since 1867. See *Debates*, May 27, 1996, p. 3041, when the House was informed that a Member's vote on one question would not be applied to another question in which the Member had a personal interest.

247. *Bourinot*, 4th ed., pp. 387-8. See *Debates*, July 9, 1906, cols. 7470-3, for a wide-ranging discussion on this topic.

248. See, for example, *Debates*, September 10, 1985, p. 6473; November 25, 1985, p. 8794.

249. See, for example, *Debates*, May 3, 1886, p. 1011; June 4, 1900, cols. 6607-8.

250. See Speaker Beaudoin's ruling, *Debates*, May 22, 1956, pp. 4244-5; on this occasion, a Member's vote was challenged but the matter was not taken up by the House.

251. See Speaker Fraser's ruling, *Debates*, March 20, 1990, pp. 9512-3.

Length of Bells

Depending on the type of motion being debated and the conditions surrounding the taking of the vote, division bells can ring for a maximum of either 15 or 30 minutes:[252]

- 15-minute bells—Whenever the Speaker is obliged under the rules or by a special order to put a question or questions at a specific time and a recorded division has been requested, the division bells are rung for not more than 15 minutes;[253]

- 30-minute bells—The bells calling in the Members for a vote on a non-debatable motion or for an unscheduled vote on a debatable motion are rung for not more than 30 minutes.[254]

For example, the bells ring for 15 minutes for votes scheduled to be taken during the debate on the Address in Reply to the Speech from the Throne and during the Budget debate and at the conclusion of debate on a motion subject to a time allocation order. The bells would also ring for up to 15 minutes for recorded divisions demanded on opposition motions on Supply days. If two or more recorded divisions are to be held successively without intervening debate, the division bells are sounded only once to call the Members in.[255]

Appearance of the Whips

When the Government and Opposition Whips conclude that their respective Members are ready to vote, the Whips make a ceremonial return to the House, and the bells stop ringing. They enter together, proceed up the aisle towards the Chair, bow to the Speaker and to each other and resume their seats. This convention provides a signal to the Speaker that the House is ready to proceed with the vote. Once the Whips have taken their seats, the Speaker calls the House to order and immediately puts the question.

The party Whips may return to the Chamber before the bells are due to stop ringing. On occasion, this has occurred with the prior knowledge and consent of the House;[256] at other times, the vote was taken before the bells had rung for the

---

252. The rules pertaining to the length of time the division bells are rung arose from the bell-ringing episode of March 1982. At that time, the Standing Orders provided no time limit for bells rung for unscheduled votes. A recorded vote was demanded on a motion to adjourn. The Opposition Whip refused to accompany the Government Whip into the Chamber to indicate to the Speaker their readiness to proceed with the vote; the government and opposition parties were involved in a dispute over a controversial bill and each side demanded concessions before allowing the vote to take place. Consequently, the division bells rang continuously for over 14 days *(Debates,* March 2, 1982, pp. 15539-41; March 18, 1982, pp. 15555-7). As a result of this episode, the Standing Orders were amended.
253. Standing Order 45(3).
254. Standing Order 45(4) and (5)(*a*)(i).
255. Standing Order 45(8).
256. See, for example, *Debates,* January 22, 1991, p. 17567.

maximum period of time and Members voiced their objection by raising points of order.[257] The Speaker has ruled that the Standing Orders stipulate only that the bells ring for "not more than" 15 or 30 minutes, as the case may be, and that it is therefore possible for the division bells to ring for a shorter period of time.[258] In one case, a 15-minute bell lasted 30 minutes pending the arrival of the Whips and this became the subject of a point of order. On that occasion, the Chair stated that the House should maintain the delicate balance which respects the spirit of the Standing Orders with regard to the designated time of division bells, without infringing upon the traditional role of the Whips.[259] On occasion, a vote was taken even if one of the Whips had not appeared after the bells rang for the maximum prescribed length of time.[260] In each case, the Government Whip re-entered the Chamber but the Opposition Whip, as an act of protest, remained outside the Chamber (sometimes with the entire caucus).

The Speaker has also ruled that it is within the authority of the Chair to intervene during the ringing of division bells should the terms of the motion for which a recorded division has been demanded become inoperable or moot. For example, if a motion to adjourn the House, to adjourn the debate or to proceed to Orders of the Day has been moved and a recorded division demanded but not taken by the ordinary hour of daily adjournment, then the Speaker may order the bells silenced and adjourn the House since those motions are inoperable beyond the ordinary hour of adjournment.[261]

Deferred Divisions

A recorded division on a debatable motion, if demanded, need not be held immediately; it may be deferred to a later time pursuant to various provisions in the Standing Orders or by a special order of the House.

A recorded division on a debatable motion may be deferred to a designated time at the request of the Chief Government Whip or the Chief Opposition Whip, either of whom is acting alone.[262] One of the Whips may approach the Speaker, after the question has been put and while the division bells are ringing, to ask that the vote be deferred. The Speaker stops the ringing of the bells and then informs the House that the recorded vote is deferred until the time requested by the Whip—later in the same

---

257. See, for example, *Debates*, December 11, 1991, pp. 6164-6; March 13, 1997, pp. 8995-6. On October 30, 1991, one Member rose to object and physically attempted to prevent the Mace from leaving the Chamber at the end of the sitting (*Debates*, pp. 4269-70).

258. *Debates*, March 20, 1990, pp. 9512-3; see Standing Order 45.

259. *Debates,* September 15, 1987, pp. 8958-9. In his ruling, the Speaker referred to a similar incident which had occurred on November 2, 1982 (see *Debates*, pp. 20332-3).

260. Although this was not recorded in the *Debates*, votes were taken in the absence of one of the Whips on June 1, 1956; February 3, 1987; October 8, 1997; March 1, 1999.

261. See Speaker Fraser's ruling, *Debates*, April 15, 1987, pp. 5187-8.

262. Standing Order 45(5)(*a*)(ii). However, if the vote concerns a motion to concur in a report to revoke a regulation or statutory instrument, it is automatically deferred to the ordinary hour of daily adjournment the same day (Standing Order 126(1)(*c*) and (2)). See Chapter 17, "Delegated Legislation".

sitting or to a specific time not later than the ordinary hour of adjournment on the next sitting day that is not a Friday.[263] If both Whips make a request for the deferral of a vote to different times, the Speaker makes the final decision.[264]

Alternatively, after a recorded division has been demanded and the division bells are ringing, the Chief Government Whip may, with the agreement of the Whips of all the recognized parties, approach the Chair and ask the Speaker to defer the division to an agreed-upon date and time that may even be beyond the ordinary hour of adjournment on the next sitting day.[265] If the vote is on an item of Private Members' Business, the item's sponsor must also agree. Likewise, recorded divisions already deferred to a specific date and time may further be deferred to any other date and time.

Recorded divisions on debatable motions demanded on a Friday are automatically deferred until the ordinary hour of daily adjournment on the next sitting day; similarly, when on Thursday, a recorded division is deferred to Friday, it is automatically deferred further to the next sitting day—usually the following Monday—at the ordinary hour of daily adjournment.[266]

On Supply days, a recorded division on a votable opposition motion by a Member of a recognized party other than the Official Opposition may also be deferred at the request of the Whip of that party.[267] However, recorded divisions on votable opposition motions on the last allotted day in a Supply period cannot be deferred,[268] except with the agreement of the Whips of all recognized parties.[269] Recorded divisions on opposition motions are deferred from a Friday to a Monday if Friday is not the last allotted day in the Supply period.[270] On one occasion, the House made an exception and adopted a special order providing for the deferral of divisions on the Business of Supply on the last allotted day in the Supply period which was a Friday.[271]

During the report stage of a bill, recorded divisions on motions in amendment may be deferred at the Speaker's discretion, from sitting to sitting if necessary,

263. Standing Order 45(5)(*a*)(ii) and (6)(*a*).

264. On Thursday, June 15, 1995, the Government Whip requested a deferral to later that day and the Opposition Whip requested a deferral to 5:30 p.m. the following day. The Speaker asked that the parties consult; but when no agreement was reached, the Speaker declared that the vote would be deferred to the following Monday (*Debates*, June 15, 1995, pp. 13905-6, 13908, 13927). In 1996, faced with similar conflicting requests, the Speaker deferred the vote to the following day (*Debates*, September 24, 1996, p. 4639).

265. Standing Order 45(7).

266. Standing Order 45(6)(*a*). See Speaker's ruling, *Debates*, October 23, 1995, p. 15706.

267. Standing Order 45(5)(*a*)(iii). See, for example, *Debates*, March 10, 1997, p. 8868.

268. Standing Order 45(5)(*b*) and (6)(*a*).

269. Standing Order 45(7).

270. See, for example, *Journals*, May 8, 1992, p. 1424; November 20, 1992, p. 2096.

271. *Journals*, December 6, 1995, pp. 2215-6; December 8, 1995, p. 2224.

until all motions or a certain number of them have been considered by the House.[272] When all report stage motions have been considered, the House then proceeds to the taking of the deferred divisions; either the Chief Government Whip or Chief Opposition Whip may further defer the vote to no later than the ordinary hour of adjournment on the next sitting day. On Friday only, a recorded division on the motion to concur in a bill at report stage, while being a non-debatable motion, is nonetheless automatically deferred.[273]

At the end of the time provided for the consideration of a votable item of Private Members' Business, a recorded division may not be deferred except by agreement of the Whips of all recognized parties and the sponsor of the item.[274] If debate is concluded prior to the time provided in the Standing Orders, either the Chief Government Whip or the Chief Opposition Whip may defer the vote.

A recorded division on a bill which is under a time allocation order may be deferred by the Chief Government Whip or the Chief Opposition Whip only if debate collapses prior to the time set out in the time allocation order.

The rules of the House restrict the further deferral of a deferred division,[275] except with the agreement of the Whips of all the recognized parties.[276] After the deferral of a vote, the House continues with the business before it.[277]

When the time arrives to take one or more deferred divisions, the Speaker interrupts the proceedings at the time set down in the Standing Orders or ordered by the House, informs the House that the deferred vote or votes will now be held, and orders that Members be called in. The division bells are rung for not more than 15 minutes.[278] Once the Whips have appeared, the Speaker proceeds immediately to put the question. When there are several votes to be taken, the House may first agree to the sequence in which they will be taken; otherwise, the questions are put in the order in which they came before the House and were deferred.[279]

In recent practice, a large percentage of recorded divisions are deferred, tending to be clustered and taken seriatim on Tuesday and Wednesday at the end of the time provided for Government Orders or at the ordinary hour of daily adjournment.[280]

---

272. Standing Orders 76(8) and 76.1(8).

273. Standing Order 45(6)(*b*).

274. Standing Order 45(7).

275. Standing Order 45(5)(*c*).

276. Standing Order 45(7).

277. Standing Order 45(5)(*c*).

278. Standing Order 45(5)(*a*)(ii), (6)(*a*) and (7).

279. See, for example, *Debates*, April 21, 1998, p. 5931, when the House agreed to a sequence in which to take five deferred recorded divisions.

280. In the Thirty-Fifth Parliament (1994-97), there were 1294 recorded votes; 73 percent of these recorded votes were deferred, and over 63 percent of all recorded votes were held on Tuesday or Wednesday.

CALLING THE VOTE AND ANNOUNCING THE RESULTS

When the Whips have returned to the Chamber and the division bells have stopped ringing, the Speaker calls the House to order, rises and reads the motion, adding, "The question is on the main motion (or amendment). All those in favour of the motion (or the amendment) will please rise". The "yeas" are recorded first. As each Member rises and bows to the Speaker, his or her name is called by the Table Officers recording the votes. Members resume their seats after casting their votes. When the "yeas" have voted, the Speaker says, "All those opposed to the motion (or the amendment) will please rise". The "nay" votes are taken in the same manner as the "yea" votes.

Recorded divisions may be conducted in one of two ways: as a party vote or as a row-by-row vote. Generally, a recorded division on government business is conducted as a party vote,[281] and a recorded division on Private Members' Business is conducted as a row-by-row vote.

Conducting a Party Vote

In conducting a party vote, Members' votes are taken by party, in order relative to each party's strength in the House and in rows according to the party seating arrangements, starting with the party leaders. If a Member wishes to vote in a different fashion to his or her party, the Member must rise when the "yeas" (or "nays", as the case may be) are called.

Conducting a Row-by-Row Vote

The calling of a recorded division row-by-row does not proceed by party but rather by the seating rows in the Chamber.[282] In conducting a row-by-row vote, the Speaker first calls for the "yeas". Members in the first row to the right of the Speaker and who are in favour of a motion are requested to rise. After the Table Officers call their names, starting with the Member closest to the Chair, Members resume their seats. Members in the second row who are in favour of the motion then rise. After all Members to the right of the Chair who are in favour of the motion have risen and voted, Members to the left of the Chair who are in favour rise to vote in rows regardless of party affiliation. The same procedure is followed for those who oppose the motion (the "nays"). When a recorded division is taken on an item of Private Members' Business, the vote of the Member sponsoring the bill or motion is recorded first, if he or she is present, followed by the votes of the other Members on the same side of the House, starting with the back row, who are in favour of the bill or motion and

---

281. This is sometimes referred to as a "whipped" vote, meaning that the party Whips marshal their Members to vote as a bloc, in accordance with party policy. In British practice, Whips inform their Members about forthcoming House business, indicating when their attendance is requested (a one-line whip), when it is expected as there is to be a vote (a two-line whip), and when their attendance is required on vital business (a three-line whip); see *Griffith and Ryle*, p. 113; *Wilding and Laundy*, pp. 785-6. This terminology is not used in Canadian practice.

282. The Speaker has explained the process of conducting a row-by-row vote; see, for example, *Debates*, November 23, 1967, p. 4605; June 22, 1976, pp. 14740-1; June 29, 1987, pp. 7817-8.

then the Members on the other side of the House, starting with the back row, who are in favour of the item. Votes against are recorded in the same order.[283]

Free Votes

There are no rules or Standing Orders defining what constitutes a free vote in the House of Commons. Simply defined, a free vote takes place when a party decides that, on a particular issue, its Members are not required to vote along party lines, or that the issue is not a matter of party policy and its Members are free to vote as they choose. A free vote may be allowed by one or more parties or it may be allowed by all parties.[284] Where all parties propose a free vote, the recorded division may be called as a row-by-row vote or in the normal manner of a party vote. The decisions taken by the parties (as to whether or not a matter should be decided in a free vote) are not issues on which the Speaker could be asked to rule.

In the Canadian system of responsible government, free votes have a special relationship to the confidence convention. The principle underlying this convention is simply that the government must enjoy the support of the majority of Members of the House of Commons and be responsible for its actions to this elected body. The confidence convention holds that where a motion does not contain an explicitly worded condemnation of the government, or where the government has not declared a particular vote to be a question of confidence, or where there is no implicit vote of non-confidence (such as in a motion to adopt the Budget, the Address in Reply or the granting of Supply), then the government is at liberty to interpret the result of the vote in any manner it wishes.[285] Consequently, when under such conditions the government declares that it will treat a matter as a free vote, the convention holds that the defeat of the item does not amount to a vote of non-confidence in the government.[286]

---

283. See the Thirteenth Report of the Standing Committee on Procedure and House Affairs, presented on November 26, 1997, and concurred in on November 4, 1998 (*Journals*, November 4, 1998, p. 1238). Prior to the adoption of this report, votes were taken in the same manner but starting with the front row. See the Twenty-Fourth Report of the Standing Committee on House Management presented on February 14, 1992, and concurred in on April 29, 1992 (*Journals*, February 14, 1992, p. 1025; April 29, 1992, p. 1337; see also Standing Committee on House Management, *Minutes of Proceedings and Evidence*, February 14, 1992, Issue No. 24, p. 17). Prior to 1992, votes were taken along party lines unless a Member sought and received unanimous consent to have the vote taken row-by-row.

284. For further analysis of free votes in the House of Commons, see "A Larger Role for the House of Commons, Part 2 – Voting" by Peter Dobell and John Reid in *Parliamentary Government*, Issue No. 40, April 1992, pp. 11-6; and "Free Votes in the House of Commons: A Problematic Reform" by C.E.S. Franks in *Policy Options*, November 1997, Vol. 18, pp. 33-6.

285. For further information on the confidence convention, see "Origins of the Confidence Convention" by Gary O'Brien in *Canadian Parliamentary Review*, Autumn 1984, pp. 11-4; "Government Defeats in the House of Commons: The British Experience" by Philip Norton in *Canadian Parliamentary Review*, Winter 1985-1986, pp. 6-9. See also Chapter 1, "Parliamentary Institutions", and Chapter 2, "Parliaments and Ministries".

286. There have also been instances where the government freed its backbenchers but demanded Cabinet solidarity. Cabinet solidarity was demanded during debate and voting on Bill C-43, *An Act respecting abortion*, during the Second Session of the Thirty-Fourth Parliament. See *Debates*, November 28, 1989, pp. 6343-4.

It is not clear when the first free vote was held in the House of Commons; however, since the 1946 free vote on milk subsidies,[287] there have been several free votes on government business. For example, free votes were held on the issues of the selection of a national flag,[288] capital punishment,[289] abortion,[290] the prohibition of discrimination on the basis of sexual orientation[291] and constitutional amendments.[292]

Announcing the Results

Regardless of how a recorded vote is conducted, the results are always announced in the same way. When the votes have been recorded and the "yeas" and "nays" counted, the Clerk rises and reports the result of the vote to the Speaker. The Speaker then declares the motion (or amendment) carried (or lost).

The Clerk of the House has the responsibility for taking and recording all votes. The Clerk sits at the head of the Table in preparation for a vote. A Table Officer stands to the right of the Clerk, facing the House, ready to call out the names of the Members as they rise and vote. Other Table Officers sit on either side of the Clerk recording the number of Members voting "yea" or "nay". Any discrepancy between the tallies must be reconciled before the result of the vote is announced to the Chair by the Clerk.

During a recorded division, if the Speaker's attention is drawn to the fact that the sum of the votes and the number of Members present who did not vote (including the Speaker) do not total at least 20, then the question remains undecided; the usual quorum procedure is then triggered.[293] If no objection is raised at the time the result of the vote is read to the House, the Speaker simply confirms the result and business proceeds as though there were a quorum.[294]

Votes Held Successively

Where Members are prepared to vote on more than one question, the House proceeds immediately to the next question after the taking of the first vote. This usually arises

---

287. The issue was whether or not to continue providing milk subsidies instituted during the war years; see *Debates,* August 27, 1946, p. 5431.

288. See *Debates,* August 21, 1964, pp. 7109-13.

289. See *Debates*, March 23, 1966, pp. 3067-9 (sponsored by four private Members representing three parties); November 9, 1967, p. 4077; January 26, 1973, pp. 687-8; February 19, 1976, pp. 11120-1; April 27, 1987, p. 5212.

290. See *Debates,* February 25, 1969, pp. 5912, 5919; July 26, 1988, p. 17966; November 7, 1989, pp. 5639, 5650.

291. See references in *Debates*, May 9, 1996, p. 2565.

292. See *Debates*, May 31, 1996, pp. 3246, 3268; *Journals*, November 18, 1997, pp. 229-30.

293. For further information on quorum, see Chapter 9, "Sittings of the House".

294. For examples where recorded votes did not total 20 Members and no objection was taken in the House, see *Journals*, June 15, 1988, p. 2893, and May 26, 1989, p. 274. See also Speaker Sauvé's ruling of July 12, 1982, where it was stated that since no one, according to the record of the proceedings, had asked for a quorum call, "a quorum did exist" (*Debates*, July 9, 1982, p. 19201; July 12, 1982, pp. 19214-5).

as a consequence of deferring votes to a particular time.[295] In recent years, an old practice has been revived whereby the results of one vote are applied to others.[296] Normally, the Chief Government Whip will request the unanimous consent of the House to have the results of one vote directly applied—or on occasion applied in reverse—to subsequent divisions and recorded separately.[297] The Whips of the other parties and Members without party affiliation usually rise to indicate their agreement. The Speaker then declares the motions as being either carried or lost. This manner of proceeding is considered to result in an appreciable saving of the time of the House.[298]

Since the beginning of the Thirty-Fifth Parliament (1994-97), another practice which has developed often occurs in concert with applied voting when there are several motions to vote on at one sitting. Following a recorded division which establishes the Members who are present and how they voted, the Chief Government Whip will rise to request that unanimous consent be given to record the names of Members who voted on the previous motion as having voted on the next motion with government Members being recorded under the "yeas" or "nays". The Whips of the other parties then rise and declare how their parties wish to be recorded as having voted for the motion;[299] finally, Members without party affiliation indicate how they wish to be recorded. Any Member wishing to vote differently from his or her party may rise on a point of order to state how he or she wants to be recorded as voting. Once the new voting pattern has been tabulated by the Table Officers, the Clerk rises and reports the results to the Speaker who will then declare the motion carried or lost. Again, this manner of proceeding is considered to result in appreciable savings of the time of the House.

Pairing of Members

Pairing is a practice whereby the party Whips arrange for two Members from opposite sides of the House to agree that they will abstain from voting on a particular occasion to permit one or both to be absent from the House. In this way, their votes are effectively neutralized and the relative strength of their parties in the House maintains its balance.[300] Until recently, pairing had no official standing and was considered a private arrangement between Members.[301]

---

295. See, for example, Standing Orders 45, 76(8) and 76.1(8).

296. For reference to the old practice, see *Dawson*, p. 184.

297. See, for example, *Debates*, March 24, 1994, p. 2772. In 1984, unanimous consent was refused for applying votes on a contentious piece of legislation and the division process subsequently took more than eight hours (*Debates*, June 20, 1984, pp. 4918-83).

298. For example, during the Thirty-Fifth Parliament (1994-97), 1294 questions were decided by recorded division; 70 percent of these were applied votes.

299. See, for example, *Debates*, December 15, 1994, pp. 9106-11.

300. *Redlich*, Vol. II, pp. 110-1. Pairing is said to have originated in Britain during the time of Cromwell (*Wilding and Laundy*, p. 515).

301. *Bourinot*, 4th ed., p. 382. For one vote in 1946, 124 Members were listed as paired in the *Debates* (*Debates*, May 24, 1946, pp. 1874-5).

In 1991, these arrangements were somewhat formalized. The Standing Orders now provide for the establishment of a Register of Paired Members which is kept at the Table.[302] To indicate that they will not take part in any recorded divisions held on a particular date, Members have their names entered together in the Register by their respective Whips. Independent Members sign for themselves. The names of Members so paired are printed in the *Debates* and in the *Journals* immediately following the entry for any recorded division held on that day.[303]

The Standing Orders are silent on the question of a broken pair, which occurs when a paired Member votes. As Speaker Fraser noted in 1992, notwithstanding the newly formalized way of arranging pairs, agreements to pair still are private arrangements between Members and not matters in which the Speaker or the House can intervene.[304] Members who inadvertently vote when paired must seek the unanimous consent of the House to rescind their votes.

The Casting Vote

The Speaker may not participate in the debates of the House; but in the event of a tie vote, the Speaker has a deciding or casting vote.[305] When using the casting vote, the Speaker may briefly explain the reasons for voting in a given manner. The reasons are then entered in the *Journals*. For further details, see Chapter 7, "The Speaker and Other Presiding Officers of the House".

Decorum During the Taking of a Vote

When Members have been called in for a division, no further debate is permitted.[306] From the time the Speaker begins to put the question until the results of the vote are announced, Members are not to enter, leave or cross the House, or make any noise or disturbance.[307]

Members must be in their assigned seat in the Chamber and have heard the motion read in order for their votes to be recorded.[308] Any Member entering the Chamber while the question is being put or after it has been put cannot have his or her vote counted.[309] Members must remain seated until the result is announced by the Clerk.[310] Members' votes have been questioned because they left the Chamber

---

302. Standing Order 44.1(1).

303. Standing Order 44.1(2).

304. *Debates*, June 11, 1992, p. 11789.

305. *Constitution Act, 1867*, R.S.C. 1985, Appendix II, No. 5, s. 49; see also Standing Order 9.

306. Standing Order 45(2).

307. Standing Order 16(1). See, for example, *Debates*, June 22, 1988, pp. 16731-2; April 9, 1990, p. 10390; November 27, 1991, p. 5458. See also Chapter 13, "Rules of Order and Decorum".

308. See, for example, *Debates,* March 31, 1924, p. 889; *Journals*, October 27, 1949, pp. 168-9.

309. See, for example, *Debates*, February 14, 1983, pp. 22822-3; June 9, 1986, p. 14140. Members' votes have been disallowed when it was pointed out that a Member had left his seat immediately after voting (*Debates*, June 25, 1986, p. 14830) or a Member had entered the House while the division was in progress (*Debates*, May 29, 1990, p. 12011).

310. See Speakers' rulings, *Journals*, April 18, 1956, p. 416; *Debates*, October 28, 1997, p. 1258.

immediately after voting and before the results of the vote were announced, or because they did not remain seated throughout the process.[311] However, if a Member's presence is disputed and the Member in question asserts that he or she was present when the motion was read, convention holds that the House accepts the Member's word.[312]

When breaches of decorum have been drawn to the attention of the Chair, the Speaker has reminded Members of the need for order in the House while votes are being taken.[313] When there is disorder in the galleries during a division, the Speaker may interrupt the proceedings until the galleries are cleared, and then continue with the taking of the vote.[314]

Points of Order and Questions of Privilege

Although the Standing Orders do not expressly forbid the raising of points of order and questions of privilege during divisions, the general practice has been to proceed with the vote and to hear its result before bringing forward any points of order or questions of privilege.[315] There have been occasions when Members have attempted to bring some matter to the attention of the Speaker in the course of a vote (after the Members have been called in and before the result is declared), and the Chair has declined to interrupt the voting process in favour of hearing the point of order or question of privilege.[316] More recently, however, points of order related to the recording of the vote were heard and addressed during the voting process.[317] Immediately

---

311. *Debates*, January 27, 1881, p. 724; May 3, 1951, pp. 2663-4; October 6, 1971, p. 8495; June 20, 1984, pp. 4939-40. In 1959, a Member was formally granted permission to leave before the vote result was announced (*Debates*, April 21, 1959, p. 2919). See also *Debates*, March 13, 1990, pp. 9265-6, and June 9, 1998, p. 7890, when Members' votes were not counted because they had entered or left the Chamber while voting was in progress.

312. See, for example, *Debates*, April 28, 1988, pp. 14942-3; April 2, 1990, p. 10116.

313. See, for example, *Debates*, June 20, 1984, p. 4940 (a series of votes was being taken and a Member rose on a point of order to say that other Members had left their seats before the results of the previous vote were announced); April 9, 1990, p. 10390 (a Member complained that other Members were moving about the Chamber during the votes). More recently, the Speaker interrupted the calling of a vote to request that the leader of an opposition party remove a prop on the grounds that it was creating disorder in the Chamber (*Debates,* June 22, 1995, pp. 14465-6).

314. See, for example, the proceedings during the taking of the vote on third reading of Bill C-43, *An act respecting abortion* (*Debates*, May 29, 1990, pp. 12009-11).

315. *Beauchesne*, 4th ed., p. 53.

316. See, for example, *Debates*, February 19, 1929, p. 266; December 7, 1945, pp. 3133-4; April 4, 1946, p. 572; April 12, 1962, p. 2909; November 26, 1996, p. 6770.

317. See, for example, *Debates*, August 9, 1977, p. 8173 (a Member was misidentified in the course of the vote and the matter was raised and addressed after the taking of the vote and before the announcement of the result); June 14, 1995, p. 13853 (a question as to whether a Member's vote had been recorded was raised and addressed after the taking of the vote and before the announcement of the result); November 20, 1996, p. 6502 (a question as to a Member's eligibility to vote was raised and addressed after Members were called in and prior to the taking of the vote). On two recent occasions, the taking of the vote was interrupted when points of order as to voting intentions were raised and resolved (*Debates*, February 10, 1997, p. 7918, Members voted "yea" when their intention was to vote "nay"; March 9, 1998, p. 4586, Members voted "nay" when their intention was to vote "yea").

after the announcement of the result of a vote, Members who were unable to be in the Chamber for a vote sometimes rise on a point of order to explain how they would have voted had they been present.[318]

Corrections in a Vote

A vote once taken and recorded stands as a decision of the House; a Member's vote cannot be changed. However, Members have risen after a vote to indicate an error or to request a change either because inadvertently they voted contrary to their intentions or voted when paired. In some instances, a vote was changed;[319] in others, the request was denied.[320]

A Member whose name has been missed or incorrectly called may correct the error either before the result of the vote is announced, if the error is noted at the time the vote is taken, or as soon thereafter as the error is noted.[321] If the correction is made after the *Journals* are printed, a *corrigendum* appears in the *Journals* of the next sitting.

A Decision Once Made Must Stand

A decision once made cannot be questioned again but must stand as the judgement of the House.[322] Thus, for example, if a bill or motion is rejected, it cannot be revived in the same session.[323] This is to prevent the time of the House from being used in the discussion of motions of the same nature with the possibility of contradictory decisions being arrived at in the course of the same session. It is not in order for Members to "reflect" on (i.e., to reconsider or go back upon) votes of the House, and

---

318. See, for example, *Debates*, October 29, 1991, p. 4176; February 23, 1994, p. 1729.

319. See, for example, *Debates*, March 26, 1930, p. 962; May 23, 1946, pp. 1793-4; February 1, 1994, p. 751. On June 1, 1954, the Speaker even took the initiative in the matter and had a Member's vote corrected before the Clerk announced the results of the vote (*Debates*, June 1, 1954, p. 5348).

320. See, for example, *Debates*, October 15, 1919, p. 1014; July 1, 1926, pp. 5311-2; June 9, 1998, p. 7907. In the 1926 example, a Member inadvertently voted when paired, and the Speaker ruled that the vote must stand. The newly formed government of Prime Minister Meighen was thus defeated on an important vote and the Fifteenth Parliament was dissolved on July 2, 1926.

321. See, for example, *Debates*, March 19, 1992, pp. 8532, 8534. In 1993, a Member rose on a point of order immediately following the announcement of the results of a vote to clarify that the votes of some Members of the House had been misinterpreted. The following day the same Member raised a question of privilege to object to the tallying of the vote and its recording in the *Debates*. The Speaker subsequently ruled that a *corrigendum* would be issued to correct the vote (see *Debates*, April 20, 1993, pp. 18183-4; April 21, 1993, pp. 18226-7; April 22, 1993, pp. 18323-4).

322. Standing Order 18; *Bourinot*, 4th ed., pp. 328-9.

323. *Bourinot* also notes that a motion that has been negatived cannot be proposed later as an amendment to a question, nor may an amendment that has been negatived be proposed on a future sitting day (*Bourinot*, 4th ed., p. 330).

when this has occurred, the Chair has been quick to call attention to it.[324] Members have also occasionally called attention to the rule.[325]

The House may reopen discussion on an earlier decision (i.e., a resolution or an order of the House) only if the intention is to revoke it;[326] this requires notice of a motion to rescind the resolution or discharge the order, as the case may be.[327] This allows the House to reconsider an earlier resolution or order and, if the original resolution or order is in fact rescinded or discharged, the way is then clear for the House to make a second decision on the same question. A number of instances of orders of the House discharged have concerned arrangements made by the House for the scheduling of its sittings,[328] or for the withdrawal of bills and motions.[329]

The Issue of Electronic Voting

The suggestion to install a system for electronic voting in the Chamber has been put forward over the years as a way to improve the management of the time of the House.[330] In 1985, the Second Report of the McGrath Committee recommended computerized electronic voting, which it felt would reduce the amount of time taken by the House for recorded votes.[331] In the government's response to the report, there was agreement in principle to the recommendation; but the matter was not taken up by the House.[332] In 1995, the Standing Committee on Procedure and House Affairs noted that changes in the way that recorded votes are organized and arranged had significantly altered the context for consideration of electronic voting (this refers to the practices of deferring several votes to the same day and time, and of applying results or votes, which the Committee found to have "greatly speeded up the voting process"). The Committee's recommendation was that the House not proceed at that time to a system of electronic voting.[333] In the First Session (1997-99) of

---

324. See, for example, *Journals*, June 1, 1955, pp. 654-7; *Debates*, May 19, 1960, p. 4025; October 20, 1970, p. 402; May 11, 1983, pp. 25363-6; November 3, 1983, p. 28661; September 24, 1996, p. 4656; May 7, 1998, p. 6690. While this rule refers to decisions of the House rather than votes of individual Members, the Chair has also cautioned Members against commenting on how other Members voted (see, for example, *Debates*, May 22, 1991, p. 385; May 4, 1993, p. 18921; April 6, 1995, p. 11612).

325. See, for example, *Debates*, June 1, 1982, p. 17973; March 1, 1996, pp. 187-8.

326. Standing Order 18.

327. In December 1988, however, the House passed a special order which included a provision allowing a Minister to move without notice a motion to "rescind the order" (see *Journals*, December 16, 1988, pp. 48-9; December 23, 1988, p. 80).

328. See, for example, *Journals*, May 27, 1898, p. 269; August 1, 1942, p. 708; November 22, 1944, p. 923; November 24, 1944, p. 927.

329. See, for example, *Journals;* May 7, 1987, p. 890; June 6, 1988, p. 2796; March 11, 1999, p. 1594.

330. See, for example, *Debates*, February 10, 1959, p. 895; March 31, 1960, pp. 2641-2; May 26, 1965, pp. 1623-4.

331. See pages 119 and 120 of the Second Report of the Special Committee on Reform of the House of Commons, presented on March 26, 1985 (*Journals*, p. 420).

332. See pages 1 and 2 of the Response to the Second Report of the Special Committee on Reform of the House of Commons, tabled on October 9, 1985 (*Journals*, p. 1082).

333. See the Sixty-Ninth Report of the Standing Committee on Procedure and House Affairs, presented on March 24, 1995 (*Journals*, p. 1274). The report was not taken up by the House.

the Thirty-Sixth Parliament, the Committee briefly considered the question of electronic voting, but did not report to the House.[334]

Unanimous Consent

At times, the House may choose to depart from, vary, or abridge, the rules it has made for itself. When the House has made substantial or permanent modifications to its procedures or practices, it has usually proceeded by way of motion preceded by notice; *ad hoc* changes, on the other hand, are often made by obtaining the consent of all Members present in the House at the time the departure from the rules or practices is proposed. Such a suspension of the rules or usual practices is done by what is termed "unanimous consent".[335] When unanimous consent is sought, the Chair takes care to determine that no voice is raised in opposition; if there is one single dissenting voice, there can be no unanimity.[336] Whenever the House proceeds by unanimous consent, the fact is noted in the official record.[337]

Perhaps the most common application of unanimous consent is to escape the notice provisions of the Standing Orders.[338] For example, unanimous consent is sought to waive the notice requirement applicable to a substantive motion[339] and, once it is granted, a motion can be brought forward for a decision by the House. Bills have been introduced without the requisite notice;[340] likewise, motions authorizing committees to travel or to change their membership (so-called "housekeeping" matters) have been introduced without notice by unanimous consent and then decided.[341] Neither is it a rare occurrence for a committee report to be presented

---

334. See Standing Committee on Procedure and House Affairs, *Minutes of Proceedings* and *Evidence,* November 6, 1997.

335. *Bourinot*, 4th ed., p. 203.

336. See, for example, *Debates*, December 11, 1997, p. 3139.

337. The *Journals* note only that unanimous consent existed for a given proceeding; it may be necessary to refer to *Debates* in order to learn what rule or practice was circumvented by the use of unanimous consent.

338. At one time, there was a rule whereby, with the unanimous consent of the House, motions could be proposed without notice (see 1978 Standing Order 43); it was removed in 1982 (*Journals*, November 29, 1982, p. 5400). For information on the former Standing Order 43 as an antecedent of the current Members' statements pursuant to Standing Order 31, see Chapter 10, "The Daily Program".

339. Standing Order 54.

340. See, for example, *Journals*, June 14, 1977, p. 1128.

341. See, for example, *Debates,* February 12, 1999, p. 11843 (unanimous consent to change committee membership); December 19, 1990, pp. 6952-3 (no unanimous consent for committee travel); May 19, 1995, pp. 12850, 12862 (unanimous consent for committee travel, given on second request).

and, by unanimous consent, concurred in on the same day.[342] Unanimous consent has also been sought to move, without notice, a motion proposing changes to the Standing Orders; it was granted and the motion was adopted without debate.[343]

For the most part, unanimous consent is used as a means of expediting the routine business of the House or as a means of extending the courtesies of the House. During debate, unanimous consent has been sought to extend briefly the length of speeches or the length of the questions and comments period following speeches;[344] to permit the sharing of speaking time;[345] to permit a Member who has already spoken once to a question to make additional comments;[346] and even to alter the usual pattern of rotation of speakers.[347]

The arrangement of House business is also commonly achieved by unanimous consent. This may involve changes to the order of business,[348] the suspension of sittings,[349] alterations in adjournment hours or sitting days[350] and special orders respecting procedures for individual events.[351] The established order of the daily agenda of the House, particularly with respect to the sequence in which items are taken up during Routine Proceedings, is often altered by seeking unanimous consent to revert to an item in Routine Proceedings.[352] Thus, Members who may have inadvertently missed their cues under rubrics such as "Tabling of Documents", "Presenting Reports from Committees", "Introduction of Private Members' Bills" and "Petitions" routinely seek and are often granted unanimous consent to return to the appropriate item.

342. See, for example, *Debates*, June 21, 1985, p. 6093; November 5, 1997, pp. 1583-4.

343. *Journals*, November 30, 1998, p. 10620.

344. See, for example, *Debates*, October 25, 1990, pp. 14704-5.

345. An existing practice was codified in the Standing Orders in 1991, so that a 20-minute speaking time can be divided into two if the party Whip so indicates to the Chair (Standing Order 43(2)). Unanimous consent has been sought for other such divisions of speaking time (see, for example, *Debates*, November 2, 1989, p. 5461; February 12, 1992, pp. 6864-5).

346. See, for example, *Debates*, May 18, 1983, p. 25550.

347. See, for example, *Debates*, March 17, 1998, p. 5009.

348. See, for example, *Debates*, August 14, 1987, pp. 8081-2 (for consideration of a bill at second reading, including the vote and suspension of Private Members' Business for that sitting); *Journals*, June 5, 1998, p. 942 (to adjourn the debate, to see the clock as at the time scheduled for Private Members' Business, and to proceed to Private Members' Business).

349. See, for example, *Debates*, May 9, 1994, pp. 4086-7.

350. See, for example, *Debates*, November 7, 1986, p. 1202 (not to sit on what would ordinarily be a sitting day); October 28, 1994, p. 7386 (to proceed with Private Members' Business in advance of the usual time).

351. See, for example, *Debates*, December 4, 1985, p. 9120 (special arrangements for the consideration of a bill); June 12, 1998, p. 8109 (arrangements for the joint address of the President of the Republic of South Africa to the House of Commons and Senate).

352. See, for example, *Debates*, November 8, 1990, p. 15336 (to revert to "Statements by Ministers"); February 11, 1999, p. 11788 (to revert to "Presenting Reports from Committees").

With unanimous consent, bills have been advanced through more than one stage in a single day and referred to a Committee of the Whole rather than a standing committee[353] and have even been amended by unanimous consent.[354]

During divisions, unanimous consent has been sought to apply the results of one vote to another vote,[355] or to vote row-by-row,[356] or to apply Members' votes to subsequent divisions.[357] By unanimous consent, recorded divisions have been deemed demanded and deemed deferred.[358] A private Member may seek unanimous consent to table a document referred to in debate, which is precluded in normal practice.[359]

Less common uses of unanimous consent can also be identified. For example, at the beginning of the Third Session (1991-93) of the Thirty-Fourth Parliament, two bills from the previous session were, by unanimous consent, reinstated on the *Order Paper* at the same stage that they were at when Parliament was prorogued;[360] committees have been reinstated, by unanimous consent, for the sole purpose of completing projects begun in the previous session.[361]

There are two Standing Orders which explicitly recognize the use of unanimous consent. The first provides that "a Member who has made a motion may withdraw the same only by the unanimous consent of the House".[362] The substance of this rule has been in place since Confederation and is based on the principle that any motion once moved becomes the property of the House. It also applies to amendments and sub-amendments.

353. During a labour dispute in 1966, for example, the House was recalled from an adjournment; with unanimous consent, back-to-work legislation was introduced without notice and proceeded with at second reading later in the sitting (*Journals*, August 29, 1966, pp. 785-9). See also *Journals*, December 7, 1998, pp. 1402, 1404-5, when unanimous consent was granted for the consideration at all stages of a Senate public bill.

354. See, for example, *Debates*, June 23, 1987, p. 7534-5; see also Speaker's remarks in *Debates*, June 10, 1985, p. 5593.

355. See, for example, *Debates*, March 24, 1994, pp. 2771-3.

356. See, for example, *Debates*, June 8, 1987, pp. 6864-5.

357. See, for example, *Debates*, December 6, 1994, pp. 8726-7.

358. See, for example, *Journals*, April 2, 1998, p. 666.

359. See, for example, *Debates*, January 27, 1983, p. 22274; June 4, 1996, pp. 3427-8. See also Chapter 10, "The Daily Program".

360. *Journals*, May 17, 1991, pp. 44-5; May 23, 1991, p. 59. Unanimous consent was denied with respect to the reinstatement of five other bills from the previous session. These five other bills were subsequently reinstated by Order of the House following the adoption of a government motion (*Journals*, May 29, 1991, pp. 102-9).

361. *Journals*, May 17, 1991, pp. 42-3.

362. Standing Order 64.

The second rule provides that if, at any time during a sitting of the House, unanimous consent is denied for the presentation of a "routine motion", then a Minister may request, during Routine Proceedings, that the Speaker propose the question on the motion.[363] This request can be made later in the same sitting or at a subsequent sitting of the House.[364] When the request is made, the question is put forthwith on the motion without debate or amendment.[365] If 25 or more Members rise to oppose the motion, it is deemed withdrawn; otherwise, it is adopted.[366] The routine motions to which this process applies include motions for:

- the observance of the proprieties of the House;
- the maintenance of its authority;
- the management of its business;
- the arrangement of its proceedings;
- the establishment of the powers of its committees;
- the correctness of its records; and
- the fixing of its sittings or the times of its meetings or adjournments.[367]

This Standing Order was the object of procedural challenges prior to its adoption in 1991[368] and on the first two occasions it was invoked.[369] Since then, it has been

---

363. Standing Order 56.1. This rule was introduced as part of a package of government-sponsored amendments to the Standing Orders, adopted in April 1991 following the use of closure (*Journals*, April 11, 1991, pp. 2898-932). See also Chapter 14, "The Curtailment of Debate".

364. See, for example, *Journals*, June 8, 1995, p. 1594 (motion adopted after unanimous consent withheld the previous day; see *Debates*, June 7, 1995, p. 13375); *Journals*, April 12, 1999, p. 1687 (motion adopted after unanimous consent withheld earlier in the sitting; see *Debates*, April 12, 1999, pp. 13552, 13573).

365. Standing Order 56.1(2).

366. Standing Order 56.1(3).

367. Standing Order 56.1(1)(*b*).

368. A lengthy point of order was made on the proposed rule change (*Debates*, March 26, 1991, pp. 19042-6). In his ruling, the Speaker pointed to the limited range of motions to which the rule could apply and indicated that there were in the Standing Orders similar procedures with respect to other types of motions. Given this and recognizing the House's privilege to set its own binding rules of procedure, the Speaker declined to rule the proposed Standing Order out of order (*Debates*, April 9, 1991, pp. 19233-7).

369. Both instances concerned motions authorizing committees to travel. Objection was taken to "the use of this very draconian Standing Order in this rather casual way" as, it was argued, there would have been sufficient time to give notice of the motions in the usual way (*Debates*, December 12, 1991, pp. 6173-5).

invoked on a number of occasions after routine motions were refused unanimous consent.[370]

Limitations on the Use of Unanimous Consent

Despite the variety of uses to which it has been put, it should not be assumed that unanimous consent can be utilized to circumvent any and every rule or practice of the House. Limitations do exist. For example, unanimous consent may not be used to set aside provisions of the *Constitution Act* or any other statutory authority. A statutory requirement supersedes any order of the House to which it applies.[371] Members have frequently noted in the course of debate that the House cannot do by unanimous consent that which is illegal.[372]

The workings of this prohibition are seen in matters relating to the Royal Recommendation. Section 54 of the *Constitution Act, 1867* stipulates that a Royal Recommendation[373] must be provided for every vote, resolution, address or bill for the appropriation of public revenues. This constitutional provision is reiterated in the Standing Orders.[374] While the Standing Order, being a House-made rule for its own guidance, could be overcome by unanimous consent, the constitutional provision cannot. This point has been made in a number of Speakers' rulings.[375]

Role of the Speaker

The mechanics of requesting and granting unanimous consent must be carefully observed. The Chair must be meticulous in presenting the request for unanimous consent to the House. For example, a Member wishing to waive the usual notice requirement before moving a substantive motion would ask the unanimous consent of the House "for the following motion", which is then read *in extenso*. The Speaker then asks if the House gives its unanimous consent to allow the Member to move the motion. If a dissenting voice is heard, the Speaker concludes that there is no unanimous consent and the matter goes no further, though it is permissible to make further

---

370. See, for example, *Journals*, December 12, 1991, p. 935 (committee travel—two motions); March 16, 1995, p. 1226 (suspension of sitting for Royal Assent); March 23, 1995, p. 1265 (hours of sitting); December 1, 1997, pp. 290-1 (readings of a bill in one sitting; adjournment of sitting); February 9, 1998, p. 430 (debatable motion to adjourn the House); June 9, 1998, p. 954 (discharge an order of the House—deemed withdrawn); *Debates*, March 22, 1999, pp. 13231-2 (consideration of a bill—deemed withdrawn); *Journals*, April 12, 1999, p. 1687 (debate on an item of government business).

371. *Bourinot*, 4th ed., p. 204.

372. See, for example, *Debates*, April 24, 1985, p. 4067; October 28, 1986, p. 823; March 26, 1991, pp. 19044-5.

373. For further information, see Chapter 18, "Financial Procedures".

374. Standing Order 79(1).

375. See, for example, *Journals*, November 9, 1978, pp. 130-3; *Debates*, November 3, 1983, p. 28655.

attempts for unanimous consent.[376] If no dissent is detected, the Speaker concludes that there is unanimous consent for the moving of the motion, and then asks if it is the pleasure of the House to adopt the motion. At this point, the practice has been for the House to make its decision on the motion; though technically, debate on the motion is still possible.[377]

If the wish of the House is not clear, the Speaker asks again if there is unanimous consent.[378] A single dissenting voice, if heard by the Chair, is sufficient to defeat a request for unanimous consent and the Speaker has reminded Members to make their intentions clear when they do not wish to give consent.[379] The Chair is concerned only with determining whether or not there is unanimity; if there is dissent, it is not proper to speculate on, or attempt to identify, its source.[380]

Decision Not a Precedent

Nothing done by unanimous consent constitutes a precedent. However, orders or resolutions presented or adopted by unanimous consent express the will of the House and are as equally binding as any other House order or resolution. Unanimous consent provides a means for the House to act immediately; for example, once unanimous consent is granted to move a motion without notice, the House must then decide on the motion in the same way as it would for any other motion before it.

---

376. See, for example, *Debates*, March 23, 1999, pp. 13367-9, when, after four attempts, unanimous consent was granted to allow, despite the rule, a questions and comments period following the speech of a Minister moving a government order. See also Speaker Fraser's comments, *Debates*, October 30, 1991, pp. 4221-2.

377. *Debates*, June 11, 1985, p. 5650; December 11, 1997, p. 3071.

378. See *Debates*, November 17, 1975, p. 9101; December 19, 1990, p. 16952. On one occasion in 1966, it appeared that there was unanimous consent to introduce a bill without notice and to proceed to second reading later in the same sitting (*Journals*, August 29, 1966, pp. 786-7); Members later claimed that they were not heard and that there had been no unanimous consent to proceed to second reading of the bill; an agreement was reached after further discussion of the matter (see *Debates*, August 29, 1966, pp. 7766-70).

379. See, for example, *Debates*, March 15, 1996, p. 787. See also *Debates*, March 8, 1993, p. 16631, when the Chair indicated that dissent might be expressed in a non-verbal manner.

380. *Debates*, July 27, 1973, p. 6056; March 23, 1999, p. 13369.

13

Rules of Order and Decorum

Regardless of how dramatically our opinions may diverge or how passionately we hold to convictions that our political opponents do not share, civility must be respected in the House of Commons. This means that each member is entitled to speak and each member can expect a fair hearing, whether or not we agree with what they say or what they stand for.

SPEAKER GILBERT PARENT
(*Debates,* March 16, 1998, p. 4902)

O ne of the basic principles of parliamentary procedure is that proceedings in the House of Commons are conducted in terms of a free and civil discourse. In order that debate on matters of public policy be held in a civil manner, the House has adopted rules of order and decorum for the conduct of Members towards each other and towards the institution as a whole. Members are to show respect for one another and for different viewpoints; offensive or rude behaviour or language is not tolerated. Emotions are to be expressed in words rather than acted out; opinions are to be expressed with civility and freely, without fear of punishment or reprisal.[1]

---

1. *Franks*, pp. 124-5.

Freedom of speech is one of the most important privileges enjoyed by Members of Parliament.[2] This freedom is circumscribed, however, by the necessity of maintaining order and decorum when debate is taking place. Thus, the right to speak is tempered by the written rules of the House which are, in general, limitations on what may be said, and when, by whom and for how long.

The Speaker is charged with maintaining order in the Chamber by ensuring that the House's rules and practices are respected.[3] He or she ensures that the rules are followed respecting proper attire, the quoting and tabling of documents in debate, the application of the *sub judice* convention to debates and questioning in the House, and the civility of remarks directed towards both Houses, Members and Senators, representatives of the Crown, judges and courts. In addition, the Speaker has the duty to maintain an orderly conduct of debate by repressing disorder when it arises either on the floor of the Chamber or in the galleries and by ruling on points of order raised by Members. The Speaker's disciplinary powers ensure that the debate is focussed and permit the Chair to remove Members who persist in behaving inappropriately. Nonetheless, while it is the Speaker who is charged with maintaining the dignity and decorum of the House, Members themselves must take responsibility for their behaviour and conduct their business in an appropriate fashion.

This chapter examines the practices and rules pertaining to debate in the Chamber and the powers of the Speaker to enforce order and decorum when breaches occur.

Recognition to Speak

With few exceptions, a Member may speak to any motion that has been proposed to the House and which is open to debate.[4] In managing the debate on a motion, the Speaker is responsible for deciding the order in which Members are recognized and for applying the rules of debate which deal with such matters as speaking once to a motion, the right of reply and unwarranted interventions.

---

2. Freedom of speech permits Members to speak in the House (and in its committees) without inhibition, to refer to any matter or express any opinion as they see fit, and to say what they feel needs to be said in the furtherance of the national interest and the aspirations of their constituents without fear of legal prosecution. For further information on freedom of speech, see Chapter 3, "Privileges and Immunities."

3. Standing Orders 10 and 11. See also Chapter 7, "The Speaker and Other Presiding Officers of the House".

4. There are also some procedures where no motion is proposed to the House and Members may be recognized by the Speaker to speak (e.g., Statements by Members, Question Period, Routine Proceedings (including Statements by Ministers), and on questions of privilege). During the Adjournment Proceedings, only those Members who were notified earlier in the sitting and the Ministers or Parliamentary Secretaries responding on their behalf are recognized to speak. For information on debatable and non-debatable motions, see Chapter 12, "The Process of Debate".

USUAL ORDER OF SPEAKING

There is no official order for the recognition of speakers laid down in the Standing Orders; the Chair relies on the practice and precedents of the House when recognizing Members to speak. The Standing Orders simply authorize the Speaker to recognize for debate the Member who seeks the floor by rising in his or her place.[5] The Member who is "seen" first is given the right to speak. This is commonly referred to as "catching the Speaker's eye". This expression has become an established phrase in parliamentary terminology and dates back to early British procedure.[6] Although the Whips of the various parties each provide the Chair with a list of Members wishing to speak, these lists are used only as a guide.[7] By tradition, some Members of the House such as Party Leaders, Ministers when appropriate,[8] and often opposition critics or spokespersons are given some priority to speak. A limited number of Members, including the Prime Minister and the Leader of the Opposition, have special rights accorded to them in the Standing Orders, but these rights relate only to the length of their speeches.[9] While the Speaker has complete discretion in recognizing Members,[10] the Chair may follow such informal arrangements as may be made[11] or the Chair may be bound by an Order of the House setting down a specific speaking order.[12]

In the usual order of speaking, after a motion has been proposed to the House, the Speaker recognizes the mover of the motion as the first to speak in debate. If the mover chooses not to speak, he or she is nonetheless deemed to have spoken—by simply nodding, the Member is considered to have said "I move" and this is taken as

---

5. Standing Orders 17 and 62.

6. As noted in *Wilding and Laundy*, p. 81: "Up to 1625, when several members stood up, the House itself had decided whom they wanted to hear, but in that year the House resolved that 'if two rise up at once, the Speaker does determine. He that his eye saw first, has the precedence given.'"

7. See comments of the Chair, *Debates*, May 5, 1994, p. 3925; November 29, 1994, pp. 8406-7.

8. Chair occupants have ruled on numerous occasions that priority of speaking is given to a Minister when a Minister rises at the same time as a Member to be recognized (see, for example, *Debates*, May 16, 1984, p. 3784; April 15, 1987, pp. 5191, 5201; December 19, 1990, p. 16954). See also *Bourinot*, 4th ed., p. 334. In addition, *Beauchesne* (4th ed.) states: "By old parliamentary usage, a member who wishes to make his maiden speech enjoys the privilege of being first seen by the Speaker, if he rises at the same time as other members ..." (p. 111).

9. Standing Order 43 stipulates that the Prime Minister, the Leader of the Opposition, the Minister moving a government order and the Member speaking in reply immediately after the Minister may speak for more than 20 minutes in any debate. In response to a point of order raised by an independent Member who had sat in the House for many years as a Member of a recognized party, the Speaker ruled that length of service in the House is not a criterion for recognition (*Debates*, February 22, 1993, p. 16283).

10. This has been supported by numerous Speaker's rulings (see, for example, *Debates*, October 27, 1970, p. 635; January 27, 1983, p. 22303; May 20, 1986, p. 13443).

11. See, for example, *Debates*, May 17, 1991, pp. 291-2; September 8, 1992, p. 12723.

12. See, for example, *Journals*, June 11, 1991, p. 164; June 18, 1991, p. 217; September 17, 1992, pp. 2011-2.

speech in the debate.[13] The Member who seconds a motion is not required to speak to it at this point, but may choose to do so later in the debate.[14]

The Speaker subsequently "sees" Members from opposite sides of the House in a reasonable rotation, bearing in mind the membership of the various recognized parties in the House,[15] the right of reply,[16] and the nature of the proceedings. For example, during the first round of debate on Government Orders, a representative from the government and from each of the recognized opposition parties are recognized by the Speaker if they rise to seek the floor in debate. For subsequent rounds, the Speaker alternates between Members on the government and opposition benches. The Speaker has given the floor to independent Members and Members of unrecognized parties only after Members of recognized parties have participated in debate in proportion to their membership in the House.[17] During Private Members' Business, the Speaker exercises greater discretion in recognizing Members, ensuring that all parties and groups in the House are heard and that all sides of the issue under debate are expressed. On Supply days, the Chair may recognize Members from the party sponsoring the opposition motion more frequently.[18]

During the 10-minute period for questions and comments following most speeches,[19] Members may direct questions to the Member who has just completed his or her speech, or may make brief comments on that speech. When recognizing Members, the Chair gives preference to Members of parties other than that of the original speaker, but not to the exclusion of Members from the speaker's party.[20] If the questions and comments period is interrupted by another proceeding, when debate resumes on the motion, the questions and comments period will only continue if the Member who made the initial speech is present.[21] Since there is no precise time set aside for the length of each individual question or comment, the Chair will sometimes determine how many Members are interested in participating in the questions and comments period and then apportion the time for each intervention accordingly. Members recognized during the questions and comments period are

---

13. *Debates*, March 19, 1992, pp. 8479-80, 8490-1.

14. During the debate on the Address in Reply to the Speech from the Throne, it is traditional for the seconder to be recognized to speak after the mover has spoken. See Chapter 15, "Special Debates".

15. For a definition of a recognized party for procedural purposes, see Chapter 1, "Parliamentary Institutions".

16. Standing Order 44(2). The right of reply is discussed in detail later in this chapter.

17. See, for example, *Debates*, February 22, 1993, pp. 16282-3; March 14, 1995, p. 10446.

18. For additional information, see Chapter 18, "Financial Procedures".

19. Standing Order 43(1). The House adopted this provision in 1982 (*Journals*, November 29, 1982, p. 5400).

20. See, for example, *Debates*, May 22, 1992, p. 11108; February 20, 1995, p. 9851; June 9, 1998, p. 7842; November 5, 1998, p. 9925.

21. See, for example, *Debates*, October 28, 1985, p. 8075; February 11, 1986, p. 10688; March 3, 1986, p. 11126.

not allowed to move dilatory motions,[22] to propose amendments,[23] or to move motions to extend the hours of sitting.[24]

Motion That a Member Be Now Heard

The Speaker's decision as to who has the right to speak during debate may be altered by the House on a motion that another Member "be now heard". A decision on this motion settles the order of debate immediately.

When two Members rise simultaneously to "catch the Speaker's eye", the Speaker will recognize one of them to speak. By rising on a point of order, another Member may move that the Member who had not been recognized be given the floor.[25] The moving of the motion "that a Member be now heard" is an exception to the rule that a motion cannot be moved on a point of order. The motion may not be moved if the Member first recognized by the Speaker has already begun to speak.[26] If the motion is ruled in order by the Speaker, the question on the motion is put forthwith without debate. A recorded division may take place. If carried, the Member named in the motion may speak.[27] If the motion is defeated, the Member originally recognized retains the right to speak.[28] A second motion "that a Member be now heard" may only be moved after the Member recognized has completed his or her speech.[29] Thus, it is impossible to move a succession of these motions in order to prevent one particular Member from speaking. In addition, the motion cannot be moved:

- if no debatable motion is before the House;[30]

- if no one has yet been given the floor;[31]

---

22. See, for example, *Debates*, March 14, 1985, p. 3029. See also Chapter 12, "The Process of Debate".

23. See, for example, *Debates*, June 9, 1986, p. 14128.

24. See, for example, *Debates*, February 17, 1987, p. 3541.

25. Standing Order 62. This motion has been used as a dilatory tactic (see, for example, *Debates*, February 3, 1987, pp. 3086-7; October 3, 1990, pp. 13755-7, 13761-2). On one occasion, when the Speaker had recognized a Member on a question of privilege, another Member rose on a point of order to move this motion. The Speaker did not accept the motion "that a Member be now heard" because such a motion is traditionally moved during the course of a debate, and a question of privilege has precedence over any other matter. See *Debates*, April 27, 1989, p. 1003.

26. See, for example, *Debates*, June 18, 1987, p. 7305; January 26, 1990, pp. 7528-9; May 12, 1995, p. 12528. On one occasion, after a motion for second reading of a bill had been proposed to the House, a Member moved that a specific Member "be now heard". The Speaker would not allow the motion to be put because only the mover of the motion could be recognized at that time (*Debates*, November 20, 1986, p. 1368).

27. See, for example, *Debates*, October 28, 1987, p. 10497; March 19, 1997, pp. 9227-9.

28. See, for example, *Debates*, January 26, 1990, pp. 7528-9; November 20, 1997, pp. 6503-5.

29. See, for example, *Debates*, October 28, 1987, p. 10497.

30. See, for example, *Debates*, January 31, 1990, p. 7660. There are instances, however, when the Chair has accepted such motions during Routine Proceedings when no motion was under debate (*Journals*, November 7, 1986, pp. 188-9; April 8, 1987, pp. 722-3).

31. See, for example, *Debates*, November 7, 1986, p. 1191.

- if the Member named in the motion did not originally rise to be recognized;[32]
- to give the floor to a Member whose speech would close the debate;[33]
- during the period for questions and comments following a speech;[34] and
- if the House has adopted an order specifying the speaking order to be followed during debate.[35]

Recognition to Speak When Order Next Called

A Member whose speech is interrupted either pursuant to a Standing or Special Order,[36] or by the adoption of a motion to adjourn the debate, may continue speaking to the full amount of his or her allotted time when debate on the motion resumes. Likewise, should the proceedings be suspended, the Member who had the floor at the time of the suspension retains the right to speak when the proceedings resume.[37] Should this Member not be present in the Chamber when the House resumes debate, the Member is considered to have lost the floor and to have finished speaking.[38] This principle also applies to the questions and comments period: if the Member who made the speech is not present upon resumption of debate, the questions and comments period does not continue and another Member is recognized on debate.[39]

Retention of Right to Speak After a Royal Assent Ceremony

If the Usher of the Black Rod arrives at the door of the House with a message from the Governor General summoning the House to the Senate for a Royal Assent

---

32. See, for example, *Debates*, January 31, 1990, p. 7661; September 24, 1990, pp. 13244-5.

33. See, for example, *Debates*, December 5, 1963, p. 5471.

34. See, for example, *Debates*, October 30, 1991, p. 4231.

35. See, for example, *Debates*, June 19, 1991, p. 2109. In 1979, after the leaders of the three recognized parties had spoken on an opposition motion, Speaker Jerome explained his reasons for recognizing next in debate, Fabien Roy, the leader of the Social Credit Party, which held only five seats in the House. As Fabien Roy, began to speak, Yvon Pinard (Drummond) rose on a point of order to move that another Member "be now heard". The Speaker ruled that the Member did not have the floor to move his motion. The following day, in response to a question of privilege, Speaker Jerome clarified that he had interpreted the moving of the motion to be an appeal against the ruling he had just given. See *Debates*, November 6, 1979, pp. 1008-10; November 7, 1979, pp. 1048-9.

36. For example, when a Member's speech is interrupted because of Statements by Members and Question Period, or when the debate is interrupted because of Private Members' Business or the ordinary hour of adjournment. See *Debates*, March 17, 1997, pp. 9091-2, when a Member rose to complain that he was being denied the right to continue his speech because the government called a different Order after Question Period.

37. See, for example, *Debates*, May 25, 1990, p. 11910; May 29, 1990, p. 12011; April 6, 1992, pp. 9359-60; September 29, 1994, p. 6348; September 22, 1995, p. 14759.

38. See, for example, *Debates*, December 18, 1990, p. 16906.

39. See, for example, *Debates*, October 28, 1985, pp. 8075-6; December 11, 1986, pp. 2025-6; February 3, 1994, p. 896; February 27, 1995, p. 10084; February 17, 1998, p. 4033.

ceremony, the business of the House is interrupted.[40] No Member will be recognized to speak on a point of order or a question of privilege.[41] The business before the House continues when the House returns from the Senate and the sitting resumes; the Member whose speech was interrupted upon the arrival of the Usher of the Black Rod is recognized to continue his or her speech.[42]

Recognition to Speak Before and After Divisions

Once the Speaker has put a question to the House, no further debate is permitted. No points of order or questions of privilege are allowed.[43] Indeed, Members must remain seated until the result of the vote is announced. After the result of a recorded division has been announced, Members have, however, risen on points of order to explain why they abstained from voting;[44] or how they would have voted if they had been present in the Chamber to hear the question put;[45] or how they wish to have their votes recorded for subsequent divisions for which the results are to be applied.[46] On occasion, Members have risen on a point of order after a recorded division to seek unanimous consent to change their votes.[47] However, a Member should not raise a point of order to reflect on how another Member voted.[48]

SPEAKING ONCE TO A MOTION

In order to expedite the transaction of House business, the Standing Orders provide that no Member may speak twice during debate on any motion.[49] If a Member inadvertently rises to speak a second time, the Speaker will interrupt the Member and recognize another to speak.[50]

A motion, an amendment and a sub-amendment are three separate questions and are treated as such for the purposes of the rule of speaking only once to a

---

40. *Bourinot*, 4th ed., p. 353.

41. *Debates*, December 17, 1990, pp. 16829-30.

42. See, for example, *Debates*, June 15, 1994, pp. 5364-5; November 24, 1994, pp. 8255-7; March 11, 1999, pp. 12775-6.

43. See, for example, *Debates*, March 20, 1990, pp. 9557-8.

44. See, for example, *Debates*, June 22, 1988, p. 16729; February 24, 1992, p. 7546; March 19, 1992, p. 8522; February 24, 1993, p. 16425.

45. See, for example, *Debates*, June 16, 1994, p. 5403; June 21, 1994, p. 5665; November 1, 1994, p. 7539.

46. See, for example, *Debates*, October 18, 1994, p. 6883; December 15, 1994, p. 9104.

47. See, for example, *Debates*, February 1, 1994, p. 751; December 9, 1997, p. 3011.

48. See, for example, *Debates*, May 4, 1993, p. 18921.

49. Standing Order 44(1). "It is essential to the dispatch of business, that the rule and order of the House, 'That no Member should speak twice to the same question', should be strictly adhered to; and it is the duty of the Speaker to maintain the observance of this rule, without waiting for the interposition of the House; which, in calling to order, seldom produces any thing but disorder" (*Hatsell*, Vol. II, p. 105).

50. See, for example, *Debates*, March 16, 1993, pp. 17091-2; February 3, 1998, p. 3288; May 12, 1998, p. 6826; May 25, 1998, p. 7107. In a Committee of the Whole, Members may speak as often as they wish (Standing Order 101(1)).

question.[51] However, an amendment is not a separate question until the Speaker proposes it to the House. This means that the Member who moves an amendment is deemed to have spoken not only to the amendment, but also to the main motion.[52] Similarly, the Member who moves a sub-amendment is deemed to have spoken also to the amendment and cannot do so again, although this does not affect the Member's right to speak to the main motion.[53] After an amendment (or sub-amendment) has been moved, seconded and proposed to the House, any Member rising to speak addresses the amendment (or sub-amendment). When an amendment (or sub-amendment) has been disposed of, either in the affirmative or in the negative, any Member who has not yet spoken to the main motion (or amendment) may speak to it. An amended main motion is not considered a new question; only those Members who have not yet spoken to the main motion may speak to the amended motion.[54]

Any Member who rises to move a debatable motion must indicate the name of a second Member who formally supports the motion. A government order must be moved by a Minister, but it may be seconded by any Member of the House.[55] If the mover of the motion chooses not to speak immediately after the motion has been proposed to the House, he or she loses the right to speak to the motion except in reply.[56] The seconder may be recognized to speak to the motion later in the debate.[57]

If a Member moves a motion during his or her speech (e.g., an amendment or a motion to adjourn debate), the act of moving the motion will terminate the Member's speech.[58] A Member who has already spoken to a question may not rise again to propose or second an amendment or move a motion to adjourn the debate or the House, although the Member may speak to an amendment if it has been moved by another Member.[59] If the House should negative a motion to adjourn the debate, the mover of the motion will be deemed to have exhausted his or her right of speaking to the main question.[60] However, if the motion is adopted, the mover is allowed to speak

---

51. *Journals*, March 14, 1928, pp. 154-5.

52. See, for example, *Journals*, February 10, 1953, p. 232; November 5, 1991, p. 4609. See also *Bourinot*, 4th ed., p. 345. The same rule applies with the previous question ("That the question be now put"): the Member who moves the previous question is deemed to have spoken to both the previous question and the original motion. For further information, see Chapter 12, "The Process of Debate".

53. See, for example, *Journals*, May 30, 1960, pp. 514-5.

54. *Beauchesne*, 4th ed., p. 138.

55. See, for example, *Debates*, January 25, 1983, p. 22176; January 31, 1985, p. 1845. Upon commencing debate at second or third reading of a government bill, a parliamentary secretary often speaks on behalf of the Minister after the Minister has moved the motion. See, for example, *Debates*, October 6, 1997, p. 495.

56. See, for example, *Debates*, September 26, 1967, pp. 2484, 2486; November 18, 1997, p. 1824; March 19, 1998, p. 5138.

57. It is only during the debate on the Address in Reply to the Speech from the Throne when the seconder speaks immediately after the mover. See Chapter 15, "Special Debates".

58. See, for example, *Debates*, December 11, 1990, p. 16563; May 11, 1998, p. 6814.

59. *Bourinot*, 4th ed., pp. 345-6.

60. *Bourinot*, 4th ed., p. 346.

first the next time the Order is called. If the Member does not then rise, he or she forfeits the opportunity to speak.[61]

The House will occasionally grant a Member unanimous consent to speak a second time to a motion.[62] The Standing Orders also provide for exceptions to the rule of only speaking once to a question. First, although rarely invoked since the implementation in 1982 of the 10-minute questions and comments period,[63] a Member may be allowed to speak a second time in order to explain a material part of his or her speech which may have been misquoted or misunderstood.[64] In doing so, the Member must rise on a point of order and must limit the intervention to an explanation of the alleged misquotation or misunderstanding and cannot introduce any new material.[65] Second, the Standing Orders also allow the movers of certain kinds of motions a right to speak a second time when no other Members wish to speak.[66] This is known as the "right of reply".

THE RIGHT OF REPLY

Any Member who has moved a substantive motion has the right to speak a second time to close the debate.[67] By custom, this right has also been extended to the Member who moved a motion for second reading of a bill, but it does not pertain to movers of amendments, the previous question, an instruction to a committee, or third reading of a bill.[68] The right of reply gives the mover of a substantive motion an opportunity to rebut the criticisms and arguments used against his or her motion, and

---

61. *Bourinot*, 4th ed., p. 346.

62. See, for example, *Debates*, September 24, 1991, p. 2672; November 28, 1991, pp. 5481-2; November 18, 1997, p. 1824.

63. Standing Order 43(1).

64. Standing Order 44(1).

65. See, for example, *Debates*, March 1, 1991, pp. 17872-3; November 27, 1991, p. 5433. In the past, Members frequently abused this right by going beyond the provisions of the Standing Order which prohibited the introduction of "new matter" when an explanation was given. See *Bourinot*, 4th ed., pp. 350-1, for an enumeration of the many types of violations of this rule.

66. Standing Order 44(2).

67. Standing Order 44(2). A substantive motion is a self-contained proposal not dependent on another motion or proceeding. Normally such motions require notice before they can be moved in the House. For further information, see Chapter 12, "The Process of Debate". See also the Chair's remarks in *Debates*, October 4, 1994, p. 6548; October 17, 1994, p. 6752.

68. Standing Order 44(2). Until 1906, the Standing Order only allowed Members who had moved substantive motions the right of reply. In 1906, the rule was amended to extend the right of reply to the mover of second reading of a bill, even though it was well understood that a second reading motion was not a substantive motion. The reason was given by Prime Minister Wilfrid Laurier, who explained that "When a Bill is moved for the first time the member who introduces the Bill may make his speech upon it. Our practice generally is to have that explanation on the second reading." Thus the exception was a way of guaranteeing the mover of a bill two opportunities to speak during debate on second reading. See *Debates*, July 9, 1906, cols. 7467-70. The right of reply does not apply to the third reading motion (*Debates*, May 4, 1990, p. 11034).

its effect is to close the debate. So that no Member wishing to participate in a debate is prevented from doing so by a sudden or unannounced exercise of the right of reply, the Speaker must inform the House that the reply of the mover of the original motion closes the debate.[69]

If a Member moves a motion on behalf of another Member, a later speech by either will close the debate.[70] However, during the debate on the second reading motion of a government bill, a parliamentary secretary may close the debate on behalf of the Minister who moved the motion only with the unanimous consent of the House.[71]

Although Ministers may exercise the right of reply,[72] it is typically only private Members who now make use of the right of reply. Indeed, this right is entrenched in two additional Standing Orders respecting Private Members' Business. The mover of a non-votable item of Private Members' Business is entitled to speak in reply for not more than five minutes at the conclusion of debate.[73] During Private Members' Business, when debate on a motion for the production of papers under "Notices of Motions (Paper)" has taken place for a total of one hour and 30 minutes, a Minister may speak for not more than five minutes, whether or not he or she has previously spoken, and the mover may close the debate by speaking for not more than five minutes.[74]

INTERVENTIONS

When a Member is addressing the House, no other Member may interrupt except to raise a question of privilege which has arisen suddenly or to raise a point of order.[75] Prior to 1982 and the advent of the period for questions and comments following most speeches,[76] if a Member wanted to ask a question during debate, he or she first

---

69. Standing Order 44(3). See, for example, *Debates*, May 28, 1984, pp. 4122-3; October 4, 1994, p. 6548; April 4, 1995, pp. 11516-7; February 15, 1999, p. 11866; February 19, 1999, p. 12201.

70. See, for example, *Journals*, February 7, 1961, p. 226.

71. See, for example, *Debates*, November 7, 1957, pp. 877-8; February 11, 1985, pp. 2219-20. This rule has had a varied history and, as late as 1984, a parliamentary secretary was allowed the right of reply to close off debate without seeking the unanimous consent of the House (*Debates*, June 8, 1984, p. 4492).

72. If a Minister were to exercise his or her right of reply, the length of time he or she would be allowed to speak would depend on the rules being applied at that time. For example, if a Minister chose to close the debate during the first five hours of debate on a second reading motion, he or she would be entitled to speak for 20 minutes. If a Minister chose to close the debate after the first five hours, he or she would get 10 minutes to reply. For an example of a Minister closing off debate on a second reading motion, see *Debates*, January 25, 1971, p. 2726.

73. Standing Order 95(2). This Standing Order was adopted on October 10, 1997 (*Journals*, p. 107). See, for example, *Debates*, October 31, 1997, p. 1433.

74. Standing Order 97(2). See, for example, *Debates*, November 2, 1998, pp. 9676-7.

75. Standing Orders 16(2) and 48.

76. Standing Order 43(1).

had to obtain the consent of the Member who was speaking.[77] The Member allowing the interruption was under no obligation to reply, and was often reluctant to do so, as the time taken up in this way was subtracted from his or her speaking time.

Manner of Speaking

PLACE OF SPEAKING

Any Member who wishes to participate in the proceedings must stand and be in his or her designated place to be recognized and to speak.[78] Exceptions to these two conditions have occurred but only rarely and in unusual circumstances, for example, when a Member has been unable to rise as a result of an injury or illness.[79] When the Chair occupant rises, a Member must sit down.[80] Members have been discouraged from sitting on chair arms or on desks with their backs to the House. When the House sits as a Committee of the Whole, a Member may rise and speak from any seat.

REMARKS ADDRESSED TO THE CHAIR

Any Member participating in debate must address the Chair, not the House, a particular Minister or Member, the galleries, or the television audience. Since one of the basic principles of procedure in the House is that the proceedings be conducted in terms of a free and civil discourse,[81] Members are less apt to engage in direct heated exchanges and personal attacks when their comments are directed to the Chair rather than to another Member. If a Member directs remarks towards another Member and not the Speaker, he or she will be called to order and may be asked to rephrase the remarks.[82] In a Committee of the Whole, Members must direct their comments to the Chairman.[83]

---

77. *Beauchesne*, 4th ed., pp. 113-4.

78. Standing Order 17. See, for example, *Debates*, January 24, 1994, p. 251; November 29, 1994, pp. 8406-7; October 10, 1997, pp. 784-5. Members have been permitted to speak from a place other than their own, but only by consent of the House (see, for example, *Debates*, April 9, 1962, p. 2629).

79. See, for example, *Debates*, November 24, 1992, p. 13977; January 24, 1994, pp. 215, 218; February 2, 1998, p. 3181; October 21, 1998, p. 9229.

80. See, for example, *Debates*, February 24, 1993, p. 16404.

81. *Franks*, p. 124.

82. See, for example, *Debates*, November 28, 1991, p. 5475; April 18, 1996, pp. 1628-9; March 19, 1998, p. 5115.

83. See, for example, *Debates*, February 8, 1994, pp. 1083, 1084.

PROPER ATTIRE

While there is no Standing Order setting down a dress code for Members participating in debate,[84] Speakers have ruled that to be recognized to speak in debate, on points of order or during Question Period, tradition and practice require all Members, male or female, to dress in contemporary business attire.[85] The contemporary practice and unwritten rule require, therefore, that male Members wear a jacket, shirt and tie as standard dress. Clerical collars have been allowed, although ascots and turtlenecks have been ruled inappropriate for male Members participating in debate.[86] The Chair has even stated that wearing a kilt is permissible on certain occasions (for example, Robert Burns Day).[87] Members of the House who are in the armed forces have been permitted to wear their uniforms in the House.[88]

In certain circumstances, usually for medical reasons, the Chair has allowed a relaxation of the dress standards allowing, for example, a male Member whose arm was in a cast to wear a sweater in the House instead of a jacket.[89]

---

84. Until 1994, the Standing Orders did contain one rule respecting a dress code: when participating in any proceedings, Members were required to rise "uncovered", that is, to remove their hats. The Speaker allowed Members to wear hats as long as they removed the head gear before rising to speak. See *Debates*, March 17, 1971, p. 4338; June 20, 1983, pp. 26564-6; June 3, 1992, pp. 11348-9. However, since Members are no longer in the habit of wearing hats in the Chamber, this aspect of the Standing Order had become anachronistic and was finally deleted in June 1994. See the Twenty-Seventh Report of the Standing Committee on Procedure and House Affairs (*Minutes of Proceedings and Evidence*, June 9, 1994, Issue No. 16, p. 3), presented on June 8, 1994 (*Journals*, p. 545), and adopted June 10, 1994 (*Journals*, p. 563).

85. See, for example, *Debates*, October 19, 1979, pp. 405-6; December 10, 1981, pp. 13920-1; September 12, 1983, pp. 26977-8; August 10, 1988, p. 18176; August 11, 1988, pp. 18208-9; April 5, 1990, p. 10206; June 3, 1992, pp. 11348-9; November 20, 1992, p. 13745; April 19, 1996, p. 1703.

86. See, for example, *Debates*, November 29, 1974, p. 1795; February 19, 1990, pp. 8485-6, and Speaker Fraser's ruling, *Debates*, May 3, 1990, pp. 10941-2. On occasion, male Members not wearing a tie have been permitted to vote. See, for example, *Debates*, March 31, 1987, pp. 4726-7; April 5, 1990, p. 10206.

87. See, for example, *Debates*, January 25, 1985, pp. 1685-6.

88. See, for example, *Debates*, February 4, 1943, p. 162.

89. See, for example, *Debates*, April 5, 1990, pp. 10242-3.

LANGUAGE OF DEBATE

The *Constitution Act, 1867* guarantees that a Member may address the House in either English or French.[90] Given the bilingual nature of the House and the existence of simultaneous interpretation,[91] Members rarely have difficulty expressing their views and having those views understood in the Chamber. In addition, all parliamentary publications, such as the *Journals,* the *Debates,* and the *Order Paper and Notice Paper*, are printed in both official languages.

Other languages are occasionally used in debate, but not at great length[92] and a Member will sometimes provide the *Debates* editor with a translation of his or her remarks.[93] As the Speaker has noted, however, serious difficulties could arise in maintaining order in debate (and by extension accurate records of the House) if languages other than English or French were used to any great extent.[94] A Member has also used sign language to make a statement and to ask a question during Question Period.[95]

---

90. R.S.C. 1985, Appendix II, No. 5, s. 133. The *Constitution Act, 1982* also stipulates that the English and French languages have "equality of status and equal rights and privileges as to their use in all institutions of the Parliament and government of Canada" (s. 16(1)) and that everyone has the "right to use English or French in any debates and other proceedings of Parliament" (s. 17(1)). The only references to language requirements in the Standing Orders are found in Standing Orders 7(2), 32(4) and 65. Standing Order 7(2) stipulates that the Deputy Speaker must have a full and practical knowledge of the official language which is not that of the Speaker. Standing Order 32(4) requires that documents distributed or tabled in the House be in both official languages. Standing Order 65 requires motions that are seconded to be read in English and French. See also *Debates*, November 25, 1998, pp. 10432-3.

91. In 1958, the House agreed to the installation in the Chamber of a system for simultaneous interpretation in both official languages (*Journals*, August 11, 1958, p. 402). See also *Debates*, August 11, 1958, pp. 3331-40. On occasion, there have been minor mechanical problems with the simultaneous interpretation system, but debate has not been unduly hampered because of this inconvenience to Members (see, for example, *Debates*, November 1, 1994, p. 7473; March 23, 1999, p. 13311; April 29, 1999, p. 14503).

92. On one occasion, a Member rose on a point of order to complain about another Member who had spoken in Inuktitut. The Chair responded that there was no rule preventing a Member from using a language other than French or English (*Debates*, June 12, 1995, p. 13605). See also *Debates*, June 13, 1995, p. 13702, where the Speaker requested that a Member who had made a speech in Inuktitut consider answering questions in one of the two official languages. The Member complied. Other languages which have been used in debate include Dene-North Slavey (see, for example, *Debates*, October 21, 1991, pp. 3699, 3702), Italian (see, for example, *Debates*, September 10, 1992, p. 12928; September 15, 1992, p. 13164), Punjabi (see, for example, November 19, 1991, p. 5067), Cree (see, for example, *Debates*, June 12, 1998, p. 8119; November 5, 1998, p. 9893), Ojibway (see, for example, *Debates*, November 5, 1998, p. 9893) and Salishan (see, for example, *Debates*, November 5, 1998, p. 9893). On one occasion, there was an exchange between two Members in Latin and Greek (*Debates*, February 18, 1983, p. 22983).

93. See, for example, *Debates*, June 4, 1993, pp. 20356-61; June 13, 1995, p. 13700; March 18, 1998, p. 5041; March 24, 1998, p. 5278; June 9, 1998, p. 7806.

94. *Debates*, December 8, 1964, p. 10926.

95. See, for example, *Debates*, May 13, 1998, pp. 6918-9; May 6, 1999, p. 14381.

READING OF SPEECHES

While not formally prohibited by a Standing Order, practice holds that when addressing the House, Members should not read from a written, prepared speech.[96] A Member may, however, use notes when delivering a speech. The purpose of this rule, which derived from British practice, is to maintain the cut and thrust of debate, which depends upon successive speakers addressing to some extent in their speeches the arguments put forward by previous speakers.[97]

Although the tradition of not reading speeches existed at Confederation, in 1886 the House adopted the following resolution:

> ... *the growing practice in the Canadian House of Commons of delivering speeches of great length, having the character of carefully and elaborately prepared written essays, and indulging in voluminous and often irrelevant extracts, [which] is destructive of legitimate and pertinent debate upon public questions, is a waste of valuable time, unreasonably lengthens the Sessions of Parliament, threatens by increased bulk and cost to lead to the abolition of the official report of the Debates, encourages a discursive and diffuse, rather than an incisive and concise style of public speaking, is a marked contrast to the practice in regard to debate that prevails in the British House of Commons, and tends to repel the public from a careful and intelligent consideration of the proceedings of Parliament.*[98]

Despite this resolution, over the years several Speakers expressed concern that Members were not delivering speeches extemporaneously. Attempts to enforce the rule failed and resulted in a number of Speaker's statements and rulings on this matter.[99] In 1956, Speaker Beaudoin received the consent of the House to have printed in the *Journals* a statement on the rule regarding the reading of speeches. In the statement, he examined the rule as established by the authorities on procedure (i.e., *May, Bourinot,* and *Beauchesne* and various Speakers) and the practice of the House under the rule. He then summarized the practice which is still being followed today:

> *A Member addressing the House may refer to notes. The Prime Minister, the cabinet ministers, the Leader of the Opposition, the leaders of other parties or Members speaking on their behalf, may read important policy speeches.*

---

96. The one notable exception to this practice is when the Minister of Finance is presenting a Budget.

97. *May,* 22nd ed., p. 372. See also *Bourinot,* 4th ed., p. 335. In 1947, Speaker Fauteux noted: "If the rule were otherwise members might read speeches written by other people and the time of the house [would] be taken up considering the arguments of persons who are not properly elected representatives of the people." *Debates,* May 29, 1947, pp. 3567-8.

98. *Journals,* April 19, 1886, pp. 167-8.

99. See, for example, *Debates,* June 14, 1940, p. 781; September 20, 1942, pp. 730-1; September 11, 1945, p. 66; May 29, 1947, pp. 3567-8; February 20, 1951, pp. 496-7; May 29, 1951, pp. 3494-5.

> *New Members may read their [maiden] speeches. The Members speaking in a language other than their mother tongue, the Members speaking in debates involving matters of a technical nature, or in debates on the Address in Reply to the Speech from the Throne and on the Budget may use full notes or, if they wish, read their speeches.*[100]

Other than in the most blatant cases, the Chair has shown a disinclination to insist that Members refrain from reading from a written speech, preferring to wait until attention is drawn to a transgression on a point of order, at which time the Chair typically rules that it is permissible for a Member to refer to notes.[101]

USE OF LECTERN

Members are not permitted to use a lectern when delivering a speech in the Chamber, with the sole exception of the Minister of Finance, who may use one during the presentation of the Budget. Chair occupants have, however, indicated that it is acceptable for Members to lay their notes on books.[102]

CITATION OF DOCUMENTS

There is no Standing Order which governs the citation of documents; the House is guided mainly by custom and precedents. Generally, the reading of articles from newspapers, books or other documents by a Member during debate has become an accepted practice and is not ruled out of order provided that such quotations do not reflect on past proceedings in the House,[103] do not refer to or comment on or deny anything said by a Member,[104] or use language which would be out of order if spoken by a Member.[105]

A speech should not consist of a single long quotation or a series of quotations joined together with a few original sentences.[106] Members may not quote from the "blues" (the unedited preliminary version of *Hansard*) nor may they quote from correspondence when there is no way of ensuring the authenticity of the signature.[107] They may quote from private correspondence as long as they identify the sender by

---

100. See Speaker's statement on reading of speeches, *Journals*, January 31, 1956, pp. 92-102, in particular p. 97.

101. See, for example, *Debates*, September 21, 1983, p. 27358; November 20, 1990, p. 15456; June 18, 1991, p. 1931; May 22, 1992, p. 11117; December 9, 1992, p. 14934.

102. See, for example, *Debates*, April 16, 1970, p. 5937; December 4, 1990, pp. 16245-6.

103. *Bourinot*, 4th ed., p. 336. See also *Journals*, June 21, 1960, p. 675.

104. *Bourinot*, 4th ed., p. 336.

105. *Bourinot*, 4th ed., p. 336. See, for example, *Debates*, February 25, 1998, p. 4407; April 22, 1999, p. 14202.

106. See, for example, *Debates*, July 23, 1963, p. 2549.

107. See, for example, *Debates*, May 31, 1928, p. 3604.

name or take full responsibility for its contents.[108] Finally, Members may not quote from the proceedings of a committee before it has reported to the House.[109]

TABLING OF DOCUMENTS AND SPEECHES

Any document quoted by a Minister in debate or in response to a question during Question Period must be tabled.[110] Indeed, a Minister is not at liberty to read or quote from a despatch (an official written message on government affairs) or other state paper without being prepared to table it if it can be done without injury to the public interest.[111] As Speaker Glen noted in a 1941 ruling, "an honourable member is not entitled to read from communications unless prepared to place them on the Table of the House. The principle upon which this is based is that where information is given to the House, the House itself is entitled to the same information as the honourable member who may quote the document."[112] A public document referred to but not cited by a Minister need not be tabled; only the document cited by a Minister is tabled.[113] If a Minister quotes a private letter in debate, the letter becomes a public document and must be tabled on request.[114] However, a Minister is not obliged to table personal notes referred to during debate or Question Period.[115] All documents tabled in the House by a Minister are required to be tabled in both official languages.[116]

---

108. See, for example, *Debates*, May 16, 1928, p. 3073; May 14, 1973, pp. 3725-7; April 9, 1976, pp. 12682-3; February 14, 1984, pp. 1361-3. See also *Debates*, February 1, 1954, pp. 1644-5, 1647-8, where the Speaker defines an unsigned or anonymous letter.

109. *Debates*, April 14, 1943, p. 2179; September 29, 1994, p. 6314.

110. *Bourinot*, 4th ed., p. 337; *Beauchesne*, 4th ed., pp. 134-5. See, for example, *Debates*, October 2, 1997, p. 415; October 29, 1997, p. 1287; November 5, 1997, pp. 1582-3, 1586; February 6, 1998, pp. 3499-500; February 23, 1998, p. 4289; April 29, 1998, p. 6293. See Chapter 10, "The Daily Program", for additional information on the tabling of documents required by statute or in respect to administrative responsibilities by Ministers during Routine Proceedings under the rubric "Tabling of Documents".

111. *Beauchesne*, 4th ed., p. 134. See also *Debates*, October 28, 1983, pp. 28455-6; November 2, 1983, pp. 28627-31; October 17, 1995, p. 15488.

112. *Journals*, March 7, 1941, pp. 171-2.

113. See, for example, *Journals*, November 16, 1971, p. 922; *Debates*, March 4, 1975, p. 3755; February 11, 1983, p. 22755; November 14, 1984, pp. 219-20; February 4, 1992, p. 6376.

114. See, for example, *Journals*, February 22, 1972, p. 15.

115. See, for example, *Debates*, October 13, 1987, pp. 9898-9.

116. Standing Order 32(4). There have been occasions when a document has been tabled in only one language. See, for example, *Journals*, February 24, 1998, p. 526; March 17, 1998, p. 574; March 16, 1999, p. 1618. See also *Debates*, February 19, 1998, p. 4125, when the Parliamentary Secretary to the Government House Leader sought unanimous consent to table a newspaper article which was quoted by a Minister and which was available in English only. Consent was given.

There has been a long-standing practice in the House that private Members may not table documents, official or otherwise.[117] Speaker Lamoureux submitted that while Ministers must table official documents cited in debate in support of an argument, this rule has never been interpreted to apply to a document, official or otherwise, referred to by private Members. In 1974, when a Member attempted to seek unanimous consent to table a document, Speaker Lamoureux stated that there was "no provision in the rules for a private Member to table or file documents in any way." The Speaker concluded by suggesting that Members "could presumably make them public in a number of other ways".[118] However, since the mid-1980s, Members have been allowed on occasion to table documents or material to which they may have referred during their speeches or during Question Period with the unanimous consent of the House.[119] These documents (often copies of correspondence or advertisements) have typically been tabled in only one language.[120] Private Members sometimes place material for the information of all Members on the Table, although this is not considered an official tabling.[121]

In order that the *Debates* be as accurate a record as possible of what has been spoken in the House, Members are not permitted to table speeches for printing in *Hansard*.[122] On rare occasions, a Member has received the consent of the House to

---

117. *Journals*, April 6, 1971, pp. 475-6. For cases where the Speaker has refused requests by private Members for unanimous consent to table a document, see *Debates*, February 1, 1985, p. 1914; February 13, 1985, p. 2313; March 25, 1985, pp. 3326-7; September 23, 1985, p. 6864; June 27, 1986, p. 15006.

118. *Debates*, December 3, 1974, p. 1882.

119. See, for example, *Debates*, June 8, 1989, pp. 2812-3; December 5, 1990, p. 16330; November 30, 1992, p. 14276; February 1, 1994, p. 690; October 17, 1995, p. 15488; October 2, 1997, p. 415; December 4, 1997, pp. 2706-7; February 13, 1998, p. 3866; March 17, 1998, p. 5029; November 24, 1998, p. 10388; February 16, 1999, p. 11980. The first time a private Member was allowed to seek unanimous consent to table a document occurred on November 15, 1978 (*Debates*, pp. 1160-1). During the Thirty-Second Parliament (1980-84), the Chair discouraged Members from tabling material by unanimous consent, but allowed the request to be made (*Debates*, January 18, 1983, pp. 21954-5; May 6, 1983, pp. 25229-30, February 14, 1984, pp. 1362-3; April 18, 1984, p. 3185). In 1986, in allowing a Member to table a document by unanimous consent, Speaker Fraser advised the House while he would abide by its wishes, "the House has quite clearly decided to move outside the usual practice" (*Debates*, October 24, 1986, pp. 709-10).

120. See, for example, *Journals*, December 5, 1990, p. 2379; November 30, 1992, p. 2254; February 1, 1994, p. 88; March 16, 1994, p. 260; March 20, 1997, p. 1325; October 2, 1997, p. 70; February 16, 1999, p. 1514; March 11, 1999, p. 1596.

121. See, for example, *Debates*, June 13, 1991, p. 1646. See also Speaker's comments, *Debates*, February 24, 1992, p. 7531. In 1992, the House adopted a special order allowing Members to table documents as sessional papers during a debate on proposals for reform of the constitution (*Journals*, February 5, 1992, p. 975).

122. See, for example, *Debates*, June 3, 1971, p. 6359; December 3, 1990, p. 16085. See also *House of Representatives Practice*, 3rd ed., pp. 466-9.

have long lists, statistics or similar material printed in the *Debates* as part of a speech.[123] There have also been instances when the House has given its consent to have documents or exchanges of letters printed as a formal appendix to the *Debates* for the information of the House.[124]

DISPLAYS, EXHIBITS, PROPS

Speakers have consistently ruled out of order displays or demonstrations of any kind used by Members to illustrate their remarks or emphasize their positions. Similarly, props of any kind, used as a way of making a silent comment on issues, have always been found unacceptable in the Chamber. Members may hold notes in their hands, but they will be interrupted and reprimanded by the Speaker if they use papers, documents or other objects to illustrate their remarks.[125] Exhibits have also been ruled inadmissible.[126] During the debate on the flag in 1964, the Speaker had to remind Members on numerous occasions that the display of competing flag designs was not permissible.[127] Small Canadian flags and desk flags have been disallowed when they have been used to cause disorder in the House for the purpose of

---

123. See, for example, *Debates*, December 8, 1997, pp. 2851-2.

124. See, for example, *Debates*, February 8, 1994, pp. 1030, 1095; March 25, 1994, pp. 2812, 2821-2. The Speaker has refused to ask the House for unanimous consent to include as an appendix to *Hansard* the text of a speech given outside the House (*Debates*, April 2, 1981, p. 8876). Nonetheless, the House has agreed to append to the *Debates* a speech made by the Prime Minister in the Senate for the installation of a Govenor General (*Debates*, February 8, 1995, pp. 9334, 9367-70) and remarks made by the Governor General at the funeral service of a former Member (*Debates*, January 20, 1994, pp. 112, 133-5).

125. See, for example, *Debates*, February 11, 1986, p. 10687; February 9, 1993, p. 15637; March 23, 1994, pp. 2671, 2674; December 8, 1995, p. 17444; May 7, 1999, p. 14886. Examples of printed material used as a prop and ruled out of order include advertisements, newspapers, books and money (*Debates*, April 26, 1989, pp. 994-5; March 14, 1990, p. 9277; March 6, 1991, p. 18111; May 25, 1993, p. 19679; November 1, 1994, p. 7497; April 24, 1996, p. 1889).

126. These include produce, samples of grain, detergent boxes, boxes of letters and petitions, a wig and a pen (see, for example, *Debates*, June 16, 1969, p. 10156; October 29, 1969, p. 237; June 10, 1980, p. 1967; June 2, 1982, p. 18022; February 15, 1985, pp. 2387, 2404; May 5, 1987, p. 5763; March 13, 1995, p. 10383; March 5, 1997, p. 8649). On one occasion, a Member, who had been recognized to ask a question to the Minister of Health, held up a toy. The Speaker reprimanded the Member and ruled the question out of order (*Debates*, November 18, 1997, p. 1846). On another occasion, a petition in the form of a birthday card was deemed an exhibit and ordered removed from the Chamber (*Debates*, July 5, 1982, p. 18990). Another time, a Member held up a sign when the Minister of Finance was making a statement during Statements by Ministers and having ignored the Chair's request that the display be removed, the Member was ordered suspended from the service of the House for the remainder of the day's sitting (*Debates*, June 27, 1985, p. 6270).

127. See, for example, *Debates*, May 12, 1964, p. 3165; June 12, 1964, p. 4237; June 16, 1964, pp. 4352-3; August 17, 1964, p. 6926.

interrupting a Member's speech.[128] While political buttons and lapel pins have not been considered exhibits as long as they do not cause disorder,[129] the Speaker has interrupted a division to request that certain Members remove "props" from their lapels.[130]

MAIDEN SPEECH

A Member's first speech in the House is referred to as his or her maiden speech. Traditionally, the House extends certain concessions or courtesies to a Member delivering a maiden speech. On such occasions, the Speaker may recognize that Member in preference to others rising at the same time; however, this privilege will not be granted unless claimed within the Parliament to which the Member was first elected.[131] The Member is permitted to read his or her speech[132] and, by courtesy, is not interrupted. Additional time beyond that allotted by the rules is sometimes granted by the Chair to permit a Member to complete his or her speech.[133] Since consideration of the Address in Reply to the Speech from the Throne is normally the first extensive debate in a new session, many new Members take advantage of the occasion to make their first speeches.[134]

Rules Regarding the Contents of Speeches

REFERENCES TO MEMBERS

During debate, Members do not refer to one another by their names but rather by title, position or constituency name in order to guard against all tendency to personalize debate.[135] A Minister is referred to by the portfolio he or she holds.[136] The two

---

128. See, for example, *Debates*, December 14, 1994, p. 9057. On February 26, 1998, some Members used desk flags to demonstrate their opposition to certain remarks previously made by Suzanne Tremblay (Rimouski – Mitis). The Chair found that such use of the flag created disorder in the House and asked Members that the flags be put back in their desks (*Debates*, p. 4488). When Mrs. Tremblay was recognized later in the sitting, Members began singing the national anthem (*Debates*, p. 4503). A point of order was raised (*Debates*, pp. 4509-12) and, in his subsequent ruling, Speaker Parent underlined that the ruling was not about the flag or the national anthem. It was about "order and decorum and the duty of the Speaker to apply the rules and practices of the House." The Speaker concluded that, until the House decided otherwise, no such displays would be allowed (*Debates*, March 16, 1998, pp. 4902-3).

129. See, for example, *Debates*, December 10, 1984, p. 1064; October 18, 1995, pp. 15537-8.

130. *Debates*, June 22, 1995, pp. 14465-6. See also *Debates*, September 18, 1995, p. 14508; October 2, 1995, pp. 15108-9.

131. *Beauchesne*, 3rd ed., pp. 91-2.

132. See section above, "Reading of Speeches".

133. See, for example, *Debates*, February 25, 1994, p. 1882; April 14, 1994, p. 3027.

134. See, for example, *Debates*, September 25, 1997, pp. 69-71; September 26, 1997, pp. 164-6.

135. *Beauchesne*, 4th ed., p. 126. See, for example, *Debates*, March 10, 1994, p. 2101; October 30, 1997, p. 1388; February 23, 1998, p. 4312; April 2, 1998, p. 5685.

136. *Beauchesne*, 4th ed., p. 126. See, for example, *Debates*, October 6, 1997, p. 530.

main party leaders are generally referred to as the Right Honourable Prime Minister and the Honourable Leader of the Opposition, and other party leaders are identified with their parties.[137] Former Prime Ministers sitting in the House are also referred to as Right Honourable, as are other Members with this designation. Parliamentary Secretaries, House Leaders and Party Whips are typically designated by the posts they hold.

The Speaker will not allow a Member to refer to another Member by name even if the Member is quoting from a document such as a newspaper article. As the Chair noted, a Member "cannot do indirectly what cannot be done directly."[138]

It is unacceptable to allude to the presence or absence of a Member or Minister in the Chamber.[139] The Speaker has traditionally discouraged Members from signalling the absence of another Member from the House because "there are many places that Members have to be in order to carry out all of the obligations that go with their office."[140]

Remarks directed specifically at another Member which question that Member's integrity, honesty or character are not in order.[141] A Member will be requested to withdraw offensive remarks, allegations, or accusations of impropriety directed towards another Member.[142] The Speaker has no authority to rule on statements made outside the House by one Member against another.[143]

REFLECTIONS ON THE HOUSE AND THE SENATE

Disrespectful reflections on Parliament as a whole, or on the House and the Senate as component parts of Parliament are not permitted.[144] Members of the House and the Senate are also protected by this rule. In debate, the Senate is generally referred to as "the other place" and Senators as "members of the other place".[145] References

---

137. *Beauchesne*, 4th ed., p. 126.

138. *Debates*, November 29, 1985, p. 8991. See also *Debates*, January 26, 1988, pp. 12282-5; October 26, 1990, pp. 14767-8; March 17, 1998, p. 4960; March 1, 1999, p. 12262.

139. See, for example, *Debates*, February 18, 1994, pp. 1553-4; June 21, 1994, p. 5674; December 5, 1995, pp. 17207-8; February 6, 1998, p. 3479; February 16, 1999, p. 11941; April 22, 1999, p. 14214; May 5, 1999, p. 14715.

140. *Debates*, April 3, 1987, p. 4875.

141. Standing Order 18.

142. *Bourinot*, 4th ed., p. 361. *Beauchesne*, 4th ed., p. 115. See, for example, *Debates*, June 15, 1994, p. 5377; September 29, 1994, p. 6311; June 9, 1995, p. 13517; October 29, 1996, pp. 5868-9, 5875; October 6, 1998, p. 8832. See also *Debates*, November 4, 1987, p. 10741; September 30, 1994, p. 6371; February 10, 1999, p. 11727. The use of unparliamentary language is discussed in detail later in the chapter.

143. *Debates*, February 11, 1993, pp. 15792-3.

144. Standing Order 18. See also *Bourinot*, 4th ed., pp. 360-1. See, for example, *Debates*, December 20, 1989, pp. 7247-8; June 8, 1990, pp. 12522-3, 12533-4; June 13, 1995, pp. 13734-5; June 14, 1995, p. 13872; September 24, 1998, p. 8354; February 5, 1999, pp. 11515-6.

145. See, for example, *Debates*, January 21, 1994, p. 170; June 8, 1994, pp. 5015-7.

to Senate debates and proceedings are discouraged[146] and it is out of order to question a Senator's integrity, honesty or character.[147] This "prevents fruitless arguments between Members of two distinct bodies who are unable to reply to each other, and guards against recrimination and offensive language in the absence of the other party."[148]

REFLECTIONS ON THE CHAIR

Reflections must not be cast in debate on the conduct of the Speaker or other presiding officers.[149] It is unacceptable to question the integrity and impartiality of a presiding officer and if such comments are made, the Speaker will interrupt the Member and may request that the remarks be withdrawn.[150] Only by means of a substantive motion for which 48 hours' written notice has been given, may the actions of the Chair be challenged, criticized and debated.[151] Reflections on the character or actions of the Speaker or other presiding officers have been ruled to be breaches of privilege.[152]

REFERENCES TO THE SOVEREIGN, ROYAL FAMILY, GOVERNOR GENERAL AND MEMBERS OF THE JUDICIARY

Members are prohibited from speaking disrespectfully of the Sovereign, the Royal Family, the Governor General or the Administrator of the Government of Canada (in the absence of the Governor General).[153] In the same way, a reference to anyone of

---

146. *Bourinot*, 4th ed., p. 357. See, for example, *Debates*, December 5, 1985, pp. 9204-5. It is acceptable to refer to the official printed records of the Senate even though they may not have been formally asked for and communicated to the House.

147. See, for example, *Debates*, October 1, 1990, pp. 13607, 13621-2; March 12, 1993, p. 16913.

148. *May*, 22nd ed., p. 381.

149. *Beauchesne*, 4th ed., p. 114.

150. See, for example, *Debates*, January 17, 1991, pp. 17294-5, 17304-5; May 25, 1993, p. 19709.

151. See, for example, *Debates*, June 1, 1956, pp. 4537-39; *Journals*, June 4, 1956, pp. 692-3; June 8, 1956, pp. 725-6; *Debates*, March 13, 1964, p. 916; *Journals*, March 18, 1964, pp. 103-4; March 19, 1964, pp. 106-7; *Debates*, March 9, 1993, p. 16685. For further information on motions of censure against the Speaker, see Chapter 7, "The Speaker and Other Presiding Officers of the House".

152. In 1981, the Leader of the Opposition made remarks which constituted an attack on the authority and impartiality of the Speaker. The following day, a Minister raised a question of privilege on the matter. The Leader of the Opposition subsequently withdrew his remarks and the matter was closed (*Debates*, January 21, 1981, p. 6410; January 22, 1981, pp. 6455-7). In 1993, a *prima facie* breach of privilege was found when a Member refused to withdraw disparaging remarks about a Chair occupant (*Journals*, March 23, 1993, p. 2688; *Debates*, pp. 17403-5). Two days later, the Member apologized and the matter was closed (*Debates*, March 25, 1993, p. 17537). See also *Debates*, May 14, 1996, p. 2721.

153. Standing Order 18. For examples of disrespectful references to the Governor General, see *Debates*, May 23, 1958, p. 406; March 12, 1959, p. 1869; September 27, 1990, pp. 13509, 13513; February 24, 1994, pp. 1799-1800. Discourteous references to Lieutenant-Governors have also been ruled out of order (see, for example, *Debates*, June 20, 1958, p. 1462; March 12, 1959, p. 1870).

these persons is also prohibited when it appears to be used to influence the work of the House. [154] As noted in *May*: "… Her Majesty cannot be supposed to have a private opinion, apart from that of her responsible advisers; and any attempt to use her name in debate to influence the judgement of Parliament is immediately checked and censured. This rule also extends to other members of the royal family, but it is not strictly applied in cases where one of its members has made a public statement on a matter of current interest so long as comment is made in appropriate terms." [155]

All attacks and censures of judges and courts by Members in debate have always been considered unparliamentary and, consequently, treated as breaches of order. [156] As Acting Speaker McClelland explained to the House, "This is a longstanding tradition in our Parliament that we be cautious when we attack individuals or groups, particularly in the judiciary, and those who are unable to come in here and have the same right of free expression as we enjoy with impunity here." [157] While it is permissible to speak in general terms about the judiciary or to criticize a law, it is inappropriate to criticize or impute motives to a specific judge or to criticize a decision made under the law by a judge. [158]

REFERENCE BY NAME TO MEMBERS OF THE PUBLIC

Members are discouraged from referring by name to persons who are not Members of Parliament and who do not enjoy parliamentary immunity, except in extraordinary circumstances when the national interest calls for the naming of an individual. The Speaker has ruled that Members have a responsibility to protect the innocent, not only from outright slander but from any slur directly or indirectly implied, and has stressed that Members should avoid as much as possible mentioning by name people from outside the House who are unable to reply and defend themselves against innuendo. [159]

REFERENCE TO PREVIOUS DEBATES AND PROCEEDINGS

In the past, reference to prior debates of the current session were generally discouraged in order to economize the time of the House and to prevent Members from reviving a debate that had concluded, unless the remarks were relevant to the matter

---

154. *Bourinot*, 4th ed., pp. 338-9. See, for example, *Debates*, March 9, 1910, cols. 5100-1.

155. *May*, 22nd ed., p. 382.

156. *Beauchesne*, 4th ed., pp. 128-9; 6th ed., pp. 150-1;. See, for example, *Debates*, May 16, 1986, p. 13353; September 19, 1991, p. 2401; November 28, 1996, p. 6854; June 8, 1998, pp. 7680, 7691; June 9, 1998, p. 7835. However, Members are not prohibited from giving notice of a substantive motion concerning the conduct of a judge (*Debates*, February 18, 1926, p. 1106).

157. *Debates*, April 1, 1998, pp. 5653-4. See also *Debates*, April 2, 1998, p. 5743.

158. See, for example, *Debates*, December 1, 1986, p. 1636; June 4, 1998, p. 7575.

159. See, for example, *Debates*, May 26, 1987, pp. 6375-6; November 28, 1991, pp. 5509-10; see also *Debates*, December 21, 1984, p. 1447.

under discussion.[160] Today, the Speaker's attention is rarely, if ever, drawn to breaches of this rule. Generally, Members should not quote from their former speeches or from the speeches of their colleagues made during the current session;[161] the rule does not apply to speeches on different stages of a bill.[162] Direct reference is permitted, however, when a Member wishes to complain of something said or to clear up a misrepresentation or make a personal explanation.[163]

Members may not speak against or reflect upon any decision of the House.[164] This stems from the well-established rule which holds that a question, once put and carried in the affirmative or negative, cannot be questioned again. Such reflections are not in order because the Member is bound by a vote agreed to by a majority.[165] The Chair has been quick to call attention to reflections on votes.[166] However, if a Member gives notice of his or her intention to move a motion that a vote be rescinded, the House may reconsider an earlier resolution or order.[167]

UNPARLIAMENTARY LANGUAGE

The proceedings of the House are based on a long-standing tradition of respect for the integrity of all Members. Thus, the use of offensive, provocative or threatening language in the House is strictly forbidden. Personal attacks, insults and obscene language or words are not in order.[168] A direct charge or accusation against a Member may be made only by way of a substantive motion for which notice is required.[169]

If language used in debate is questionable, the Speaker will intervene. Nonetheless, any Member who feels aggrieved by a remark or allegation may also bring the matter to the immediate attention of the Speaker on a point of order. Points of order

---

160. *Bourinot*, 4th ed., p. 357. It is also irregular to refer to discussions held in a Committee of the Whole.

161. See, for example, *Debates*, December 4, 1984, p. 896. In practice, this rule is often disregarded by the Chair.

162. *Bourinot*, 4th ed., p. 358.

163. *Beauchesne*, 6th ed., p. 141.

164. Standing Order 18.

165. *May*, 22nd ed., p. 380.

166. See, for example, *Journals*, June 1, 1955, pp. 654-7, in particular p. 656; *Debates*, May 19, 1960, p. 4025; October 20, 1970, p. 402; May 11, 1983, pp. 25363-6; November 3, 1983, p. 28661; May 4, 1993, p. 18921; May 14, 1993, pp. 19470-1; April 6, 1995, pp. 11608, 11612; September 24, 1996, p. 4656; May 7, 1998, p. 6690; May 11, 1999, p. 15001.

167. Standing Order 18. This topic is also discussed in Chapter 12, "The Process of Debate".

168. Standing Order 18. See, for example, *Debates*, February 25, 1998, pp. 4401-2; October 28, 1998, p. 9512 .

169. See Speaker Michener's ruling, *Journals*, June 19, 1959, pp. 581-6; see also Speaker Fraser's ruling, *Debates*, December 11, 1991, pp. 6141-2.

may not be raised during Members' Statements or Question Period, [170] however, the Speaker may address a matter of unparliamentary language at once if he or she believes the matter to be sufficiently serious to require immediate attention. [171] Normally, the matter is resolved at the conclusion of Question Period. [172] Since the Speaker must rule on the basis of the context in which the language was used, points of order raised in regard to questionable language must be raised as soon as possible after the irregularity has occurred. [173]

If the Speaker did not hear the alleged unparliamentary language or if there is a dispute as to the words actually used, the Chair may set aside the matter pending a review of the record and, if necessary, return to the House at a later time with a ruling. [174] The Speaker has also ruled that if the Chair did not hear the offensive word or phrase and if the offensive language was not recorded in *Debates,* the Chair cannot be expected to rule where there is no record. [175]

In dealing with unparliamentary language, the Speaker takes into account the tone, manner and intention of the Member speaking; the person to whom the words were directed; the degree of provocation; and, most importantly, whether or not the remarks created disorder in the Chamber. [176] Thus, language deemed unparliamentary one day may not necessarily be deemed unparliamentary the following day. The codification of unparliamentary language has proven impractical as it is the context in which words or phrases are used that the Chair must consider when deciding whether or not they should be withdrawn. [177] Although an expression may be found to be acceptable, the Speaker has cautioned that any language which leads to disorder in the House should not be used. Expressions which are considered unparliamentary when applied to an individual Member have not always been considered so when applied "in a generic sense" or to a party. [178]

---

170. Standing Order 47.

171. See, for example, *Debates*, March 24, 1993, p. 17482; October 22, 1997, p. 964.

172. See, for example, *Debates*, March 24, 1993, pp. 17486-8; October 22, 1997, pp. 971-2; April 22, 1999, pp. 14225, 14229.

173. See, for example, *Debates*, March 26, 1986, p. 11899; June 13, 1986, pp. 14370-2; March 5, 1987, p. 3882; December 9, 1997, p. 3018.

174. See, for example, *Debates*, February 5, 1997, pp. 7716-7; February 17, 1999, pp. 12000-1.

175. *Debates*, December 12, 1991, pp. 6218-9. See also *Debates*, February 10, 1998, pp. 3714-5, when a Member accused another Member of an obscene gesture. The Speaker indicated that it would be difficult to check because the gesture would not be recorded and he did not see it. He cautioned Members to refrain from making gestures which are offensive to other Members.

176. See Speaker Parent's remarks, *Debates*, February 17, 1997, pp. 8200-1; September 25, 1997, pp. 103-4; September 30, 1997, p. 256; June 8, 1998, p. 7707; October 7, 1998, p. 8885; November 5, 1998, pp. 9917-8; March 18, 1999, pp. 13092-3.

177. Lists of terms ruled unparliamentary have been included in the index to the *Debates* in *Bourinot* (4th ed., pp. 361-4) and in *Beauchesne* (6th ed., pp. 142-50).

178. See, for example, *Debates*, November 4, 1987, p. 10741; November 18, 1987, pp. 10927-8; December 14, 1987, pp. 11761-2; October 26, 1998, p. 9379; February 18, 1999, p. 12094.

Should the Speaker determine that offensive or disorderly language has been used, the Member will be requested to withdraw the unparliamentary word or phrase. The Member must rise in his or her place to retract the words unequivocally. The Member's apology is accepted in good faith and the matter is then considered closed.[179] However, if the Member persists in refusing to obey the directive of the Speaker to retract his or her words, the Chair may refuse to recognize the Member until the words have been withdrawn[180] or may "name" the Member for disregarding the authority of the Chair and order him or her to withdraw from the Chamber for the remainder of the sitting.[181]

In 1991, following several incidents of unparliamentary language,[182] a government motion respecting decorum and civility was brought before the House. The motion was debated on three occasions but never came to a vote.[183]

REPETITION AND RELEVANCE IN DEBATE

The rules of relevance and repetition[184] are intertwined and mutually reinforcing. The requirement of relevance is necessary in order that the House might exercise its right to reach a decision and to exclude from debate any discussion which does not contribute to that process. The rule against repetition ensures that once all that is relevant to the debate has been presented, the question will be determined once and for all, at least during the current session. To have one rule without the other would seriously limit the ability of the House to use its time efficiently.

The rules respecting relevance and repetition are somewhat difficult to define and enforce. The rule against repetition can be invoked by the Speaker to prevent a Member from repeating arguments already made in the debate by other Members or the same Member.[185] The rule of relevance, on the other hand, is used to keep a Member from straying from the question before the House or committee. It is not always possible to judge the relevance (or the repetition) of a Member's remarks

---

179. See, for example, *Debates*, September 18, 1991, pp. 2299-300; October 9, 1991, p. 3515; September 25, 1998, p. 8401; October 30, 1998, p. 9641; February 16, 1999, pp. 11972-3; March 25, 1999, pp. 13483-4.

180. On one occasion, when Jim Fulton (Skeena) refused to retract his remarks, Speaker Fraser chose not to recognize the Member until a withdrawal was made three weeks later (*Debates*, October 29, 1987, pp. 10542-3; October 30, 1987, pp. 10583-4; November 18, 1987, pp. 10927-8).

181. See, for example, *Debates*, February 12, 1997, pp. 8016-7; October 1, 1997, pp. 332, 334-5; October 2, 1997, p. 367; December 1, 1998, pp. 10726-7, 10730-1. See also section below, "Naming".

182. See, for example, *Debates*, September 17, 1991, pp. 2235-6, 2261-3; September 18, 1991, pp. 2299-300; September 23, 1991, pp. 2522-3; October 9, 1991, pp. 3515-6; October 10, 1991, pp. 3560-4.

183. See *Journals*, October 23, 1991, pp. 521-2; October 25, 1991, pp. 535-6; November 21, 1991, pp. 703-4.

184. Standing Order 11(2).

185. *Dawson* highlighted the difficulty in enforcing this rule by noting that, "the whole system of procedure is based on an assumption of repetition" and referred to three readings given to a bill (p. 108).

until he or she has made some progress in or completed his or her remarks.[186] In practice, the Speaker allows some latitude—if the rules are applied too rigidly, they have the potential for severely curtailing debate; if applied too loosely and precious debating time is lost, they may prevent other Members from participating in debate. Individual circumstances, the mood of the House and the relative importance of the subject of debate will influence how strictly the Speaker interprets these rules.

In exercising the power to maintain the rules against irrelevance and repetition, the Speaker can call a Member to order and, if necessary, warn the Member that he or she risks being directed to discontinue his or her speech. Such warnings are usually sufficient. However, should the Member continue being irrelevant or repetitious, the Speaker can proceed to recognize another Member or, if no other Member wishes to speak, to put the question. In the event that the Member should disregard the Speaker's instruction or direction, the Speaker has the authority to "name" the Member.[187]

Historical Perspective

It is not certain when the British House of Commons originally adopted the practice of restraining debate that was either repetitious or irrelevant. However, it seems to have been well established by the end of the sixteenth century. A manual of procedure dating from the era of the Elizabethan Parliaments listed among the powers of the Speaker the right to call a Member to order when "any speak to a Bil[sic] and be out of the matter".[188] During the same period, Speaker Popham, upon his election to the Chair in 1580, requested that Members "speak to the matter ... and not to spend too much time in unnecessary motions or superfluous argument".[189] The *Journals* for 1604 suggest that the rule of relevance was adopted that year as an order of the House and Hatsell cited it in this form: "That if any man speak impertinently, or beside the question in hand, it stands with the orders of the House for the Speaker to interrupt him, and to know the pleasure of the House, whether they will further hear him."[190] In addition to this rule, the House soon thereafter adopted another prohibiting repetition.[191] Both rules were difficult to enforce, particularly that on relevance which obliged the Speaker to obtain the support of the House in order to direct a

---

186. *Bourinot*, 1ˢᵗ ed., p. 349. See also the Chair's remarks, *Debates*, June 17, 1992, p. 12297; June 23, 1992, p. 12641.

187. Standing Order 11(2). For examples where the Speaker has directed a Member to discontinue his speech, see *Debates*, May 26, 1947, pp. 3450-1; August 25, 1958, p. 4073. If a Member persists in breaching the repetition or irrelevance rule in a Committee of the Whole, he or she is reported to the House by the Chairman if the committee so directs. For additional information, see Chapter 19, "Committees of the Whole House".

188. Vernon F. Snow, *Parliament in Elizabethan England: John Hooker's Order and Usage*, New Haven: Yale University Press, 1977, p. 169.

189. *Hatsell*, Vol. II, p. 232.

190. *Hatsell*, Vol. II, p. 230.

191. The entry in the *Journals* reads: "... if any superfluous motion, or tedious speech be offered in the House, the party is to be directed and ordered by Mr. Speaker". See *Hatsell*, Vol. II, p. 230.

Member to keep to the subject of debate. During the eighteenth century, interventions by Speakers were so rare that Members sometimes resented interruptions when they did take place. Even so formidable a character as Speaker Arthur Onslow could not manage to enforce the rule by his own authority.[192]

When in 1867, the Canadian House of Commons adopted its rules, no reference was made to repetition in debate, and the rule on relevance was mentioned only in the context of a general order of debate which enjoined Members not to "speak beside the question in debate".[193] Beyond advising the Member to speak to the subject, the Speaker depended almost entirely upon the support of the House and the goodwill of the Members to uphold the rule.

In a revision of the rules in 1910, the power of the Speaker was augmented. The Chair was empowered to direct a Member to discontinue his or her speech if the Chair deemed it either irrelevant or repetitious after having called the attention of the House to the matter.[194] In moving the adoption of this rule, Prime Minister Wilfrid Laurier observed that it was "the English rule copied word for word".[195] This was hardly less true of the rule which dealt with relevance in a Committee of the Whole and which was adopted at the same time: "Speeches in Committee of the Whole must be strictly relevant to the item or clause under consideration."[196]

When the rules were revised in 1927, the role of the Speaker was further clarified. Anticipating the circumstances when a Member might refuse to accept the direction of the Speaker, a special committee on procedure provided for that event by giving the Speaker the power to "name" the recalcitrant Member or, if in committee, to permit the Chairman to report the Member to the House. These changes were accepted by the House without amendment or debate and have remained unchanged to the present time.[197]

The Rule Against Repetition

The rule prohibiting repetition is designed primarily to safeguard the right of the House to reach a decision and to guard against the inefficient use of the time of the House. Although the principle is clear and sensible, it has not always been easy to apply.[198] The scope of the rule permits the Speaker to exercise considerable

---

192. P.D.G. Thomas, *The House of Commons in the Eighteenth Century*, Oxford: Clarendon Press, 1971, pp. 217-8.

193. *Rules, Orders and Forms of Proceedings of the House of Commons of Canada*, 1876, Rule No. 13.

194. *Rules of the House of Commons of Canada*, 1910, Rule No. 19.

195. *Debates*, April 29, 1910, col. 8377.

196. *Rules of the House of Commons of Canada*, 1910, Rule No. 13(5).

197. *Debates*, March 18, 1927, p. 1351.

198. In more blatant cases, the Speaker has been able to cite the date and page where the same speech has been given previously. In one instance, the Speaker was able to predict that the Member was about to begin paragraph six of his speech and, in another, the Speaker cited five instances in which the same appeal was made (*Debates*, June 9, 1955, p. 4610; April 19, 1956, p. 3073). On another occasion when a Member stated that he was going to repeat some of the material he had previously used in the same debate, the Speaker would not allow the Member to proceed (*Debates*, February 17, 1956, p. 1290). See also Speaker Beaudoin's remarks, *Debates*, May 24, 1955, p. 4065.

discretion. The Chair can use the rule to curtail prolonged debate by limiting Members' speeches to points which have not already been made.[199] In the context of the legislative process, this latter restriction applies to the Members' remarks only within the same stage of debate on a bill. Arguments advanced at one stage may legitimately be represented at another. The purpose of the rule is to safeguard the right of the House to reach a decision. The freedom of debate enjoyed by Members does not extend to the right to repeat arguments that have already been heard.[200]

Finally, the rule against repetition has been used by Speakers in various other ways to assist the House in making efficient use of its time. Speakers have ruled out of order the tedious reading of letters even when they were used to support an argument;[201] the asking of a question during Question Period which was similar to another already asked that day;[202] and the repeating of questions of privilege on the same subject matter.[203]

The Rule of Relevance

Although the House now has rules to limit the length of speeches, at one time there were few limits and debate often strayed beyond the subject in question. In 1882, Bourinot felt the need to add this comment to his study on parliamentary practice:

> *A just regard to the privileges and dignity of Parliament demands that its time should not be wasted in idle and fruitless discussion; and consequently every member, who addresses the house, should endeavour to confine himself as closely as possible to the question under consideration.*[204]

This advice still applies today as the business of government is much more complex and the time of the House is limited. Thus, should a Member stray from the question before the House, the Speaker invokes the rule of relevance. In many instances, the Speaker has done this by indicating to a Member who has been called to order, the proper subject matter of the debate and how the Member's remarks were irrelevant.[205] In particular, during the 10-minute questions and comments period following

---

199. See, for example, *Debates*, June 9, 1955, p. 4609. On one occasion, a Member was chided because his remarks were "not much more than a repetition of what has been said by others who preceded him." Consequently, the Member was directed to shorten his remarks so that the House could "get down to the work properly before [it]." See *Debates*, August 31, 1917, p. 5237.

200. See, for example, *Debates*, May 24, 1955, p. 4065.

201. See, for example, *Debates*, April 19, 1922, p. 944.

202. See, for example, *Debates*, November 21, 1977, p. 1063. In 1986, Speaker Bosley established that since time is scarce during Question Period, Members should avoid merely repeating questions that have already been asked, although Members may ask other questions on the same issue (*Debates*, February 24, 1986, p. 10879).

203. *Debates*, June 27, 1978, p. 6769.

204. *Bourinot*, 1st ed., p. 349.

205. See, for example, *Debates*, November 5, 1990, pp. 15159-60; February 4, 1992, p. 6343; April 28, 1999, p. 14450; April 29, 1999, pp. 14492, 14497.

most speeches, if a Member does not address his or her remarks to the arguments expressed in the speech, the Chair will invoke the rule of relevance.[206] Despite such instances, Speakers tend to be mindful of the need for some leniency in applying the rule.[207] Speakers have allowed reference to other matters in debate, if they were made in passing and were not the principal theme of the speech.[208]

The rule of relevance applies not only to debate on a main motion but also to any proposed amendments to the main motion.[209] Should an amendment be proposed to a motion, the rule of relevance requires that debate be limited to that amendment until it is disposed of by the House.[210] Arguments ruled irrelevant during debate on a main motion are similarly irrelevant if introduced as the substance of an amendment. Even if the amendment proposes to replace all the words in the main motion after "that" and substitute an alternative proposition, debate is restricted to the main motion and the amendment; further alternative propositions are irrelevant.[211] Once an amendment is disposed of by the House, it then becomes possible to debate the main motion in its full scope or to consider another amendment.

The previous question has a character that is exceptional with respect to the rule of relevance. "That the question be now put" does nothing to hinder debate on the original motion. On the contrary, Members who have already participated in the debate may speak on the motion again, after the previous question has been moved.[212] However, care must be taken to avoid repetition.

Bills

The relevance of debate to a motion before the House applies especially to the consideration of bills as they proceed through the several stages prior to their adoption. According to the practice which developed originally in the British House of Commons, "each stage is regarded as having its own peculiar function and to a certain extent its more or less limited range of debate."[213] These functions, in turn, provide

---

206. See, for example, *Debates*, February 6, 1987, pp. 3195-6, where the Chair ruled the remarks out of order and recognized another Member. See also *Debates*, September 17, 1992, pp. 13307-8; June 7, 1994, p. 4930.

207. See, for example, *Debates*, May 19, 1992, pp. 10910-1; February 8, 1993, pp. 15520, 15523.

208. See, for example, *Debates*, April 9, 1919, p. 1330; May 4, 1920, p. 1954; March 22, 1921, p. 1193. Alternatively, Speakers have sometimes suggested that a matter raised outside the question in a debate would more properly "form by itself a subject of a special substantive motion". See *Debates*, March 27, 1923, p. 1553.

209. *May*, 22nd ed., p. 346: "Stated generally, no matter ought to be raised in debate on a question which would be irrelevant if moved as an amendment, and no amendment should be used for importing arguments which would be irrelevant to the main question."

210. See, for example, *Debates*, June 2, 1914, p. 4647.

211. *May*, 22nd ed., p. 346.

212. For a discussion of the previous question, see Chapter 12, "The Process of Debate", and Chapter 14, "The Curtailment of Debate".

213. *May*, 20th ed., p. 527.

both the Speaker and the House with guidelines by which to apply the rule of relevance. Thus, for example, the second reading stage of a bill is limited to debate on its principle, whereas debate at report stage treats only motions offered in amendment to a bill. Despite the several occasions allowed to the House to discuss a bill, the scope of debate is supposed to be different at each stage.

• Second Reading

During debate on second reading, there is a frequent temptation to delve into the clauses of a bill instead of considering the principle of the bill. Such debate is in breach of the rule of relevance. Most interruptions made by the Speaker are usually directed at preventing Members from discussing specific provisions of the bill rather than its principle.[214] In one ruling, the Speaker stated quite clearly that "on a motion for second reading it is out of order to discuss the clauses of the bill."[215] When the House is considering an amending bill, the rule requires that debate at second reading be limited to the principle of the amending bill and not the subject matter of the Act which it is amending.[216]

• Committee Stage

The referral of a bill to a committee opens the way for close examination of its contents, clause by clause. Today, most bills are sent to standing committees for study, but in the past, the consideration of bills more often took place in a Committee of the Whole and it was in this larger forum that the practice governing the scrutiny of bills developed. Pursuant to the Standing Orders, speeches made in a Committee of the Whole must be strictly relevant to the item or clause under consideration.[217] Chairmen have frequently cited this rule and requested that Members observe it.[218] The same practice applies in standing, special or legislative committees considering bills.

An important exception to the rule of relevance in committee is found in the wide-ranging debate permitted on Clause 1, or that clause which follows the short title clause. Although there is no provision for this practice in the Standing Orders, it has become an accepted practice since at least the 1930s.[219] Over the years, Chairmen have grappled with the rules of debate on Clause 1 and have established certain limitations. These include proscriptions against repetition of second reading debate

---

214. See, for example, *Debates*, April 2, 1913, col. 7014; March 25, 1920, pp. 734, 750-1; May 26, 1978, p. 5795.

215. *Debates*, February 16, 1979, p. 3321. See also *Debates*, October 28, 1991, p. 4085.

216. *Beauchesne*, 6th ed., pp. 199-200. This is a position which has been maintained by the Speaker on several occasions (*Journals*, November 14, 1949, pp. 237-8; *Debates*, May 6, 1959, p. 3402; *Journals*, October 15, 1962, pp. 76-7).

217. Standing Order 101(2). For additional information, see Chapter 19, "Committees of the Whole House".

218. *Debates*, November 30, 1977, pp. 1418-20; November 30, 1978, pp. 1657, 1665-6; December 10, 1979, p. 2213; December 11, 1979, pp. 2239, 2244; September 30, 1991, pp. 2937, 2979.

219. It is not exaclty clear when this practice started; however, several Members claim that it was a custom which had grown during the years prior to the Second World War. See *Debates*, June 6, 1947, p. 3878; June 30, 1947, p. 4845; July 14, 1947, p. 5570.

and against the anticipation of clause by clause debate.[220] Moreover, general debate on Clause 1 cannot extend outside the contents of the bill.[221] A further limitation arises when an amendment has been proposed to Clause 1. In the words of a Chairman who ruled on the issue: "Once an amendment has been moved, I think discussion should be confirmed [sic] to the amendment until the matter has been disposed of but, afterward, other general remarks can be made."[222] This judgement has been confirmed by practice and by a later ruling.[223]

• Report Stage

According to *Beauchesne,* the report stage of a bill "is one of reconsideration of events which have taken place in committee. The consideration of a bill is now a more formal repetition of the committee stage with the applicable rules of debate which are proper when the Speaker is in the Chair."[224] Report stage motions are amendments to clauses in a bill which seek to change, to delete or to restore those clauses. To avoid excessive repetition of debate, the Speaker has the power to select and to combine motions in amendment.[225] The Speaker can also control debate through the use of the relevance rule as applied to debate on clauses of a bill. Despite the resemblance of debate at report stage to that at committee stage, there is no allowance for a wide-ranging discussion of a bill as occurs by practice in committee on study of Clause 1.[226]

• Third Reading

Debate on third reading is designed to review the legislative measure in its final form and is strictly confined to the contents of the bill.[227] If an amendment is moved, debate should be relevant to that amendment until the House disposes of it.[228]

Debates on the Address in Reply and the Budget

The traditions and practices of the House allow for the rule of relevance to be relaxed somewhat during debate on the motion for an Address in Reply to the Speech from the Throne. During the days allotted to the debate on this motion, Members have the

---

220. *Debates*, May 11, 1960, pp. 3783-4, 3788-9.

221. *Debates*, March 23, 1965, p. 12693.

222. *Debates*, August 2, 1960, p. 7418.

223. See, for example, *Debates*, November 30, 1978, pp. 1657, 1665.

224. *Beauchesne*, 6th ed., p. 211.

225. Standing Orders 76(5) and 76.1(5).

226. See, for example, *Debates*, June 4, 1981, p. 10263.

227. *Beauchesne*, 6th ed., p. 214; *May*, 22nd ed., p. 544.

228. On one occasion, the Speaker corrected a Member who had assumed that he could talk on the amendment as if it were the third reading motion: "My ruling is that a member should only address himself to the last question submitted to the House … the fact that a member has not spoken to the third reading of the Bill is no justification for his travelling over the same ground on this question (the amendment) that he would have covered if he had spoken to the third reading of the Bill" (*Debates*, June 2, 1914, p. 4647).

opportunity "to bring forward topics of their own choosing".[229] Consequently, debate tends to be very wide-ranging and the Speaker usually makes no effort to apply the rule of relevance. This is not the case, however, when the House is debating the Budget. The remarks of Members must be relevant to the motion before the House. All the same, the terms of the motion (i.e., that the House approves of the general budgetary policy of the government) are sufficiently broad to permit Members great latitude in their remarks without violating the principle of the rule.[230]

THE *SUB JUDICE* CONVENTION

During debate, restrictions are placed on the freedom of Members of Parliament to make reference to matters awaiting judicial decisions in the interests of justice and fair play. Such matters are also barred from being the subject of motions or questions in the House. While precedents exist for the guidance of the Chair, no attempt has ever been made to codify the practice known as the "*sub judice* convention".[231] The interpretation of this convention is left to the Speaker since no "rule" exists to prevent Parliament from discussing a matter which is *sub judice,* that is, "under the consideration of a judge or court".

The *sub judice* convention is first and foremost a voluntary restraint on the part of the House to protect an accused person, or other party to a court action or judicial inquiry, from suffering any prejudicial effect from public discussion of the issue.[232] Secondly, the convention also exists, as Speaker Fraser noted, "to maintain a separation and mutual respect between legislative and judicial branches of government".[233] Thus, the perception and reality of the independence of the judiciary must be jealously guarded. However, as Speaker Sauvé explained, the *sub judice* convention has never stood in the way of the House considering a *prima facie* matter of privilege vital to the public interest or to the effective operation of the House and its Members.[234]

---

229. *Beauchesne*, 6ᵗʰ ed., p. 82.

230. See, for example, *Debates*, March 10, 1992, pp. 7949-50.

231. On December 13, 1976, the House appointed a special committee "to review the rights and immunities of Members of the House of Commons, to examine the procedures by which such matters are dealt with by the House, and to report on any changes it may be desirable to make" (*Journals*, p. 230). The Committee held three meetings during which it studied how the rights and immunities of Members are affected by the *sub judice* convention. The First Report to the House of the Special Committee on the Rights and Immunities of Members, presented on April 29, 1977 (*Journals*, pp. 720-9), remains the definitive study of the *sub judice* convention in Canada and is still used today by the Speaker when dealing with such matters arising in the House.

232. See Philip Laundy, "The *Sub Judice* Convention in the Canadian House of Commons", *The Parliamentarian*, Vol. 57, No. 3, July 1976, pp. 211-4.

233. *Debates*, March 8, 1990, p. 9007.

234. *Debates*, March 22, 1983, pp. 24027-8.

There are some situations in which the application of the *sub judice* convention has been fairly straightforward. The convention has been applied to motions, references in debates, questions and supplementary questions.[235] It has also been applied consistently in criminal cases. However, the convention does not apply to bills, as the right of Parliament to legislate must not be limited.[236] If the *sub judice* convention were to apply to bills, the whole legislative process could be stopped simply by the initiation of a writ or legal proceedings in one or other of the courts of Canada.

Criminal and Civil Cases

No distinction has ever been made in Canada between criminal courts and civil courts for the purpose of applying the convention, and it has also had application to certain tribunals other than courts of law. The *sub judice* convention exists to guarantee everyone a fair trial and to prevent any undue influence prejudicing a judicial decision or a report of a tribunal of inquiry. Indeed, in the view of the Special Committee on the Rights and Immunities of Members, "prejudice is most likely to occur in respect of criminal cases and civil cases of defamation where juries are involved."[237]

Where criminal cases are concerned, the precedents are consistent in barring reference to such matters before judgement has been rendered and during any appeal. Members are expected to refrain from discussing matters that are before a criminal court, not only in order to protect those persons who are undergoing trial and stand to be affected whatever its outcome, but also because the trial could be affected by debate in the House.[238] It has been established that the convention would cease to apply, as far as criminal cases are concerned, when judgement has been rendered.[239] The Speaker has confirmed that a matter becomes *sub judice* again if an appeal is entered following a judgement.[240]

---

235. See, for example, *Debates*, March 5, 1984, p. 1766; December 6, 1990, p. 16411; February 3, 1993, p. 15368.

236. See Speaker Lamoureux's ruling, *Debates*, October 4, 1971, pp. 8395-6; and Speaker Sauvé's ruling, *Debates*, March 31, 1981, pp. 8793-4.

237. *Journals*, April 29, 1977, p. 728.

238. See Speaker Fraser's rulings, *Debates*, June 1, 1989, p. 2419; November 7, 1989, p. 5655; and Deputy Speaker Milliken's ruling, *Debates*, March 16, 1999, p. 12911.

239. See Speaker Lemieux's ruling, *Debates*, February 10, 1928, p. 366.

240. See Speaker Lamoureux's ruling, *Debates*, May 2, 1966, pp. 4583-4. In 1995, a Member rose on a point of order to contend that a Minister had contravened the convention during Question Period by commenting on a case under appeal in the Alberta courts. The Minister maintained that there was a difference between commenting on the facts of a case before the courts and stating the government's opinion on a ruling rendered by the courts. In his response to the point of order, Speaker Parent ruled that he could not conclude that the Minister had contravened the convention by stating that the government disagreed with the ruling and planned to challenge the decision (*Debates*, April 6, 1995, pp. 11618-9).

The precedents are not as consistent where civil cases are concerned. The convention has been applied on some occasions[241] and not on others.[242] However, in 1976, the Speaker ruled that no restriction ought to exist on the right of any Member to put questions respecting any matter before the courts, particularly those relating to a civil matter, unless and until that matter is at least at trial.[243] Although nothing resembling a settled practice has developed in relation to civil cases, the Chair has warned on various occasions of the need for caution in referring to matters pending judicial decisions whatever the nature of the court.[244]

Courts of Record and Royal Commissions

From the precedents, it is clear that the application of the convention is limited to tribunals designated by statute as courts of record.[245] (A court of record is defined as follows: "A court that is required to keep a record of its proceedings, and that may fine or imprison. Such record imports verity and cannot be collaterally impeached."[246]) The *sub judice* convention does not apply, however, to matters referred to royal commissions, although the Chair has cautioned against making reference to the proceedings, evidence, or findings of a royal commission before it has made its report.[247]

The Role of the Speaker

Since the *sub judice* convention is not codified and is voluntary, the jurisdiction of the Speaker in such matters is somewhat difficult to outline. The Speaker's discretionary authority over matters *sub judice* derives from his or her role as guardian of free speech in the House. The Chair has the duty to balance the rights of the House

---

241. See, for example, *Debates*, June 7, 1938, p. 3625.

242. See, for example, *Debates*, May 22, 1973, pp. 3990-1; July 9, 1973, pp. 5402-3.

243. See Speaker Jerome's ruling, *Debates*, February 11, 1976, p. 10844. This view was reiterated in a ruling given in 1987, although Speaker Fraser cautioned that a contrary ruling could be made if the Chair felt the question was about to prejudice the rights of either litigant (*Debates*, December 7, 1987, p. 11542). See also *Debates*, April 11, 1991, pp. 19316-7.

244. See, for example, *Debates*, April 6, 1995, pp. 11618-9; March 16, 1999, p. 12911.

245. See Speakers' rulings, *Debates*, March 5, 1947, pp. 1051-2; June 12, 1951, p. 3975; November 2, 1951, p. 662. In a 1933 incident, a Member attempted to debate charges brought against a county court judge whose conduct had been referred to a commission of inquiry. Speaker Black did not allow the discussion, even though the commission was not defined as a court of record. See *Debates*, March 30, 1933, pp. 3558-9.

246. *Black's Law Dictionary*, 5th ed., St. Paul, Minnesota: West Publishing Co., 1979, p. 319.

247. *Debates*, March 21, 1950, p. 949; October 17, 1957, p. 119; May 2, 1966, pp. 4589-90; *Journals*, November 9, 1978, p. 128. Speaker Jerome noted that "the body carrying out [the inquiry] is an investigatory body and not a judicial body coming to decision. … no decision of that body could in any way be prejudiced, surely, by a debate or discussion here" (*Debates*, October 31, 1977, p. 433).

with the rights and interests of the ordinary citizen undergoing trial. Indeed, the Speaker exercises discretion in exceptional cases only where it is clear that to do otherwise would be harmful to specific individuals. The problem facing a Speaker is that determining when a comment will have a tendency to influence is speculative business—it cannot be done until after the remarks have been made.

In its inquiry, the Special Committee on the Rights and Immunities of Members recommended that when there is doubt in the mind of the Chair, a presumption should exist in favour of allowing debate and against the application of the convention.[248] The Committee concluded that while there can be no substitute for the discretion of the Chair, in the last resort all Members of the House should share in the responsibility of exercising restraint when it seems called for.[249] A Member who feels that there could be a risk of causing prejudice in referring to a particular case or inquiry should refrain from raising the matter. Furthermore, a Member who calls for the suppression of discussion of a matter on grounds of *sub judice* should be obliged to demonstrate to the satisfaction of the Chair that he or she has reasonable grounds for fearing that prejudice might result.[250]

It was also the view of the Committee that the responsibility of the Chair particularly during Question Period should be minimal in regard to the *sub judice* convention, and that the responsibility should principally rest upon the Member who asks the question and the Minister to whom it is addressed. Should a question to a Minister touch upon a matter *sub judice,* it is likely that the Minister involved will have more information covering the matter than the Speaker, and the Minister might be better able to judge whether answering the question might cause prejudice. In such a situation, the Minister could refuse to answer the question on these grounds, bearing in mind that refusal to answer a question is his or her prerogative. From the precedents, this appears to be the approach the Chair has taken.[251] The Speaker has interrupted only if he or she has felt the *sub judice* convention was being breached.[252]

PERSONAL EXPLANATIONS

The Chair may occasionally grant leave to a Member to explain a matter of a personal nature although there is no question before the House. This is commonly referred to by Members as "a point of personal privilege" and is an indulgence granted by the Chair. There is no connection to a question of privilege, and one Speaker noted, "There is no legal authority, procedural or otherwise, historic or

---

248. *Journals*, April 29, 1977, p. 728. For an example of when the Speaker has applied this principle, see *Debates*, June 8, 1987, pp. 6817-20 (opposition motion on a Supply day).

249. *Journals*, April 29, 1977, p. 728.

250. See Speaker Bosley's ruling, *Debates*, January 27, 1986, p. 10194.

251. See, for example, *Debates*, February 14, 1986, pp. 10828-9; December 18, 1990, pp. 16901, 16905-6; October 11, 1991, p. 3643; December 4, 1996, p. 7087.

252. See, for example, *Debates*, June 1, 1989, p. 2422; November 7, 1989, pp. 5654-6; June 12, 1996, p. 3711; October 20, 1997, pp. 829-30; February 13, 1998, p. 3854.

precedential, that allows this."[253] Consequently, such occasions are not meant to be used for general debate and Members have been cautioned to confine their remarks to the point they wish to make.[254] When granted, they have been used by Members notably to announce a resignation[255] or to explain changes in party affiliation, matters affecting them which have occurred outside the Chamber or misinterpreted statements.[256]

Points of Order

A point of order is a question raised by a Member who believes that the rules or customary procedures of the House have been incorrectly applied or overlooked during the proceedings. Members may rise on points of order to bring to the attention of the Chair any breach of the relevance or repetition rules, unparliamentary remarks, or a lack of quorum.[257] They are able to do so at virtually any time in the proceedings, provided the point of order is raised and concisely argued[258] as soon as the irregularity occurs.[259] Points of order respecting procedure must be raised promptly and before the question has passed to a stage at which the objection would be out of place. As a point of order concerns the interpretation of the rules of procedure, it is the responsibility of the Speaker to determine its merits and to resolve the issue.[260]

Although Members frequently rise claiming a point of order, genuine points of order rarely occur. Indeed, points of order are often used by Members in an attempt to gain the floor to participate in debate; in such cases, the Speaker will not allow the Member intervening to continue.[261] One point of order must be disposed of before

---

253. *Debates*, November 21, 1990, p. 15526.

254. In 1996, Speaker Parent advised the House that Jean-Marc Jacob (Charlesbourg) would be rising to make a solemn declaration to the House. The Speaker cautioned Members that the statement was not to incite debate. The Speaker subsequently interrupted Mr. Jacob and ruled that "the words being used [in the statement] tend more toward a debate than a solemn declaration." The Member was not allowed to continue. See *Debates*, June 18, 1996, p. 4027. In 1989, a Minister rose on a matter of personal privilege to clarify a statement which he had made the previous day. Following the Minister's statement, Speaker Fraser recognized the critic from the Official Opposition to respond to the statement. However, when the Minister began to engage in a debate with the opposition Member, the Speaker closed off the remarks and advised the House that Members could seek further information from the Minister on another occasion. See *Debates*, May 11, 1989, pp. 1571-3.

255. See, for example, *Debates*, March 15, 1984, pp. 2138-9; May 12, 1986, p. 13149; February 3, 1988, p. 12581; September 24, 1990, p. 13215.

256. See, for example, *Debates*, November 21, 1990, pp. 15526-9; April 9, 1991, pp. 19231-2; February 18, 1992, p. 7205; November 26, 1992, pp. 14113-5; January 24, 1994, p. 197.

257. See, for example, *Debates*, March 17, 1998, p. 4970.

258. *Redlich*, Vol. II, p. 146.

259. See Speaker Marcil's ruling, *Journals*, February 20, 1911, p. 190.

260. Standing Order 10.

261. See, for example, *Debates*, March 30, 1992, pp. 9036-7; November 17, 1994, p. 7951; October 23, 1997, p. 1031; February 16, 1998, p. 3947; March 16, 1999, p. 12913.

another one is raised. Should a point of order be raised during consideration of a question of privilege, the point of order will be given precedence until the Chair has determined whether or not a rule has been breached and the matter settled.[262] The Speaker has, on occasion, refused to hear a point of order during the consideration of a question of privilege.[263] The necessity to control disorder either on the floor or in the galleries would oblige the Speaker to put aside a point of order temporarily.

RAISING A POINT OF ORDER

Any Member can interrupt a Member who has the floor of the House during debate and bring to the Chair's attention a procedural irregularity the moment it occurs, in which case the Member who has the floor resumes his or her seat until the matter is resolved or disposed of.[264] When recognized on a point of order, a Member should only state which Standing Order or practice he or she considers to have been breached; if this is not done, the Speaker may request that the Member do so.

Under the Standing Orders, a brief debate on the point of order is possible at the Speaker's discretion.[265] This rule was carried over at Confederation from the Legislative Assembly of the Province of Canada.[266] Many Members interpreted the rule to mean that any question of order was to be discussed before the Speaker ruled. In fact, the practice and rule did not coincide until 1906, when the rule was amended to legitimize the custom of allowing debate on points of order at the discretion of the Speaker.[267] In the early 1980s, there were increasingly prolonged discussions on points of order, and Chair occupants felt compelled to intervene and sometimes to

---

262. See, for example, *Debates*, April 27, 1989, p. 1003; June 4, 1992, p. 11372.

263. See *Debates*, March 23, 1999, p. 13372.

264. Standing Order 19. In the early years after Confederation, the rule was not specific about who called Members to order and, as a result, Members called each other to order (see, for example, *Debates*, March 23, 1868, pp. 387-8; March 7, 1878, p. 808), but the practice eventually evolved to the less direct method of Members raising points of order for decision by the Chair. It was not until 1925 that a special committee recognized that "This rule seems to state that a member may be called to order by another member ..." (*Journals*, May 29, 1925, p. 353). The committee recommended clarification of the rule. The rule was eventually changed in 1927 to its present form (*Journals*, March 22, 1927, pp. 326-7).

265. Standing Order 19.

266. The rule read as follows: "A Member called to Order shall sit down, but may afterwards explain. The House, if appealed to, shall decide on the case, but without debate. If there be no appeal, the decision of the Chair shall be final." (*Rules, Orders and Forms of Proceeding of the House of Commons of Canada,* 1868, Rule No. 12.)

267. See *Debates*, July 9, 1906, cols. 7465-7.

refuse to recognize Members on points of order.[268] Despite pressure from Members, successive Speakers relied more and more on the literal meaning of the Standing Order and, while still allowing debates on points of order, limited these considerably. When a point of order is raised during a speech, the Speaker will decide whether the intervention is included in the amount of time allotted to that particular stage of debate.[269]

There are numerous exceptions to the rule that a point of order must be raised at the moment a procedural irregularity occurs. Points of order arising out of the debate on the adjournment motion (Adjournment Proceedings) are taken up on the next sitting day.[270]

Points of order arising out of Question Period or the time set aside for Statements by Members are usually delayed until after Question Period.[271] From Confederation until 1975, it was the practice of the House that points of order were raised as soon as the procedural irregularities on which they were based occurred, including during Question Period.[272] In 1975, however, as part of a reform in the sequencing of House business and the conduct of Question Period, the House agreed that points of order should not be raised during Question Period.[273] Although the decision of the House in this regard resulted in only a provisional understanding, successive Speakers upheld its spirit, despite strong objections from Members, even after it ceased to be in effect in October 1977 when the House failed to make certain sessional orders permanent. The Speaker nevertheless continued this new practice.[274] The condition was also applied, in 1982, to the time for Members' Statements.[275] The practice was finally codified in the Standing Orders in 1986.[276] If a Member rises on a point of order during Statements by Members or Question Period, the Speaker advises that he will hear the Member after Question Period.[277]

---

268. See, for example, *Debates*, February 11, 1982, pp. 14899-904; February 12, 1982, pp. 14969-70; March 2, 1982, pp. 15532-9; February 14, 1983, p. 22816; October 27, 1983, pp. 28361-77. In one instance, a Member was named and ejected from the House over the issue (*Debates*, October 31, 1983, pp. 28591-4).

269. See, for example, *Debates*, December 8, 1995, p. 17446; March 16, 1999, p. 12913.

270. For more information on points of order during the Adjournment Proceedings, see Chapter 11, "Questions".

271. Standing Order 47.

272. See, for example, *Debates*, January 14, 1971, p. 2401.

273. See Item Nos. 3, 4 and 5 of the Second Report of the Standing Committee on Procedure and Organization, presented on March 14, 1975 (*Journals*, p. 373), and concurred in on March 24, 1975 (*Journals*, p. 399). See also Speaker Jerome's ruling, *Journals*, April 14, 1975, pp. 439-41.

274. See, for example, *Debates*, December 7, 1977, pp. 1649-52; December 7, 1979, pp. 2134-5.

275. See, for example, *Debates*, April 19, 1983, pp. 24624-6.

276. *Journals*, February 6, 1986, p. 1648; February 13, 1986, p. 1710.

277. See, for example, *Debates*, April 4, 1989, p. 32; June 19, 1992, pp. 12437, 12448-9; February 9, 1993, p. 15637.

Any other matter being raised as a point of order should be brought to the Speaker's attention after Routine Proceedings (held at 10:00 a.m. on Tuesday and Thursday, at 3:00 p.m. on Monday and Wednesday, and at 12:00 noon on Friday),[278] although the Speaker now typically invites Members to raise such points of order following Question Period.

A Member may not direct remarks to the House or engage in debate by raising a matter under the guise of a point of order.[279] A Member may not rise on a point of order to move the adjournment of the House,[280] the adjournment of debate, or the extension of the sitting[281] or to proceed to the Orders of the Day.[282] In addition, Members may not rise on a point of order during a quorum count.[283] Despite the rule that Members may not rise on a point of order to move a substantive motion,[284] Members frequently rise on points of order to seek the unanimous consent of the House to move such a motion.[285] During Routine Proceedings, Members have been permitted to rise on points of order to ask about the status of a question on the *Order Paper*[286] or of a notice of motion for the production of papers.[287] Members have also risen on points of order to seek unanimous consent to extend the time for questions and comments following a speech[288] or to proceed to Private Members' Business before the designated hour.[289]

A Minister may rise on a point of order at any time during a sitting to table a notice of a Ways and Means motion, although the Chair has suggested that such notices should be tabled at the end of Government Orders and before the start of Private Members' Hour, or after a Member has resumed his or her seat and before another Member is recognized during debate.[290] A Minister may also rise on a point

278. Standing Order 47.

279. See, for example, *Debates*, September 27, 1990, p. 13481; March 16, 1999, p. 12913; April 30, 1999, p. 14552; May 3, 1999, p. 14628; May 4, 1999, p. 14680.

280. See, for example, *Debates*, December 4, 1992, p. 14633; June 21, 1994, p. 5698.

281. See, for example, *Debates*, February 14, 1969, p. 5560; March 9, 1993, p. 16747. For information on extending a sitting, see Chapter 9, "Sittings of the House". For information on the moving of dilatory motions, see Chapter 12, "The Process of Debate".

282. See, for example, *Debates*, June 15, 1983, pp. 26394-5.

283. See, for example, *Debates*, May 5, 1982, p. 17067.

284. See, for example, *Debates*, September 24, 1998, p. 8350.

285. See, for example, *Debates*, May 3, 1999, p. 14573; May 4, 1999, p. 14689.

286. See, for example, *Debates*, May 3, 1999, p. 14603.

287. See, for example, *Debates*, February 18, 1998, p. 4079; March 24, 1999, p. 13449.

288. See, for example, *Debates*, May 3, 1999, p. 14608.

289. See, for example, *Debates*, April 30, 1999, p. 14550.

290. See, for example, *Debates*, September 11, 1985, p. 6498.

of order at any time during the proceedings to give oral notice of a time allocation[291] or closure[292] motion.

A point of order may be raised after debate has concluded but before the Speaker puts the question, or after the vote has been taken, but a Member may not interrupt the Speaker when he or she is putting the question to the House.[293] There have been occasions when the Chair was obliged to refuse points of order either after calling in the Members for a vote or before declaring the result of the division.[294] If attention is called to a breach of order during the course of a division, the division is completed before the point of order is dealt with.[295] Points of order related to the vote are typically raised immediately after the announcement of the result of the vote.[296]

RULING ON A POINT OF ORDER

The Speaker has the duty to preserve order and decorum and to decide any matter of procedure that may arise.[297] The Chair is bound to call the attention of the House to an irregularity in debate or procedure immediately, without waiting for the intervention of a Member. In addition, the Speaker decides questions of order once they arise and not in anticipation. Though raised on a point of order, hypothetical queries on procedure cannot be addressed to the Speaker nor may constitutional questions or questions of law.[298]

When a point of order is raised, the Speaker attempts to rule on the matter immediately. However, if necessary, the Speaker may take the matter under advisement and come back to the House later with a formal ruling.[299] In doubtful cases, the Speaker may also allow discussion on the point of order before coming to a decision

---

291. See, for example, *Debates*, June 19, 1992, pp. 12472-3; March 5, 1999, p. 12508; April 23, 1999, p. 14287.

292. See, for example, *Debates*, October 25, 1989, p. 5096; June 19, 1995, p. 14150; March 13, 1996, p. 666.

293. See, for example, *Debates*, November 26, 1996, p. 6770.

294. See, for example, *Debates*, February 19, 1929, pp. 266-7; December 7, 1945, pp. 3133-4; April 4, 1946, pp. 572-3; April 12, 1962, p. 2909. For an exception to this rule, see *Debates*, March 9, 1998, p. 4586.

295. *Beauchesne*, 4th ed., p. 53.

296. Points of order have sometimes been resolved prior to the announcement of the result of the vote (see, for example, *Debates*, July 10, 1956, p. 5845; June 20, 1995, pp. 14259-60). Members who were unable to be in the Chamber for a vote sometimes take the opportunity to rise on points of order after the vote to explain how they would have voted had they been present (see, for example, *Debates*, October 29, 1991, p. 4176; February 23, 1994, p. 1729). For additional information, see Chapter 12, "The Process of Debate".

297. Standing Order 10.

298. See, for example, *Journals*, July 8, 1969, pp. 1319-20.

299. See, for example, *Debates*, October 4, 1995, pp. 15219-21; October 23, 1995, pp. 15671-2.

but the comments must be strictly relevant to the point raised.[300] When a decision on a question of order is reached, the Speaker supports the decision with quotations from the Standing Orders or the authorities, or simply by citing the number of the applicable Standing Order.[301] Once the decision is rendered, the matter is no longer open to debate or discussion and the ruling cannot be appealed to the House.[302] A Member may not rise on a point of order to discuss a matter which the Speaker has already ruled was not a question of privilege[303] or to raise a matter as a question of privilege after the Speaker has ruled that it was not a point of order.[304]

Rules of Decorum

A number of rules and traditions are enforced by the Speaker in order to ensure that debate proceeds in a civil and orderly manner. A Member must be in his or her place to take part in any proceedings in the House and address his or her remarks to the Chair.[305] In order to prevent unnecessary interruptions when a Member is speaking, no other Member is to cross between the Chair and the Member who is addressing the Chair.[306] The only interruption permitted is for a Member to raise a point of order.[307]

As nothing should come between the Speaker and the symbol of his or her authority (the Mace), no Member is to pass between the Chair and the Table, or between the Chair and the Mace when the Mace is being taken off the Table by the Sergeant-at-Arms.[308] A Member must sit down when the Chair occupant rises.[309] When Members cross the floor of the House, or otherwise leave their places, they should bow to the Speaker. When the House adjourns, Members are expected to stay in their seats until the Speaker has left the Chair, although in practice most Members merely pause, whether standing or sitting, during the procession out of the Chamber.[310]

---

300. Standing Order 19.

301. Standing Order 10. See, for example, *Debates*, February 10, 1998, pp. 3647-8; February 12, 1998, pp. 3765-6; May 27, 1998, pp. 7276-7, 7283.

302. Standing Order 10. While it has never been the practice to debate Speakers' rulings on matters of order, it was possible until 1965 for any Member who disagreed with a Speaker's decision to appeal it immediately to the House. For a detailed discussion of this matter, see Chapter 7, "The Speaker and Other Presiding Officers of the House".

303. See, for example, *Debates*, May 7, 1998, pp. 6674-6.

304. See, for example, *Debates*, October 3, 1995, pp. 15186.

305. Standing Order 17.

306. Standing Order 16(2). The Speaker will reprimand Members who have distracted the Member speaking by passing between him or her and the Chair. See *Debates*, October 16, 1970, p. 219; January 25, 1984, p. 738; April 30, 1985, pp. 4269, 4273; August 26, 1987, p. 8431; September 27, 1991, p. 2825.

307. Standing Order 16(2).

308. Standing Order 16(3). See, for example, *Debates,* October 29, 1997, p. 1309.

309. See, for example, *Debates*, February 24, 1993, p. 16404.

310. Standing Order 16(4).

In the Chamber, Members may refresh themselves with glasses of water during debate, but the consumption of any other beverage or food is not allowed.[311] Smoking has never been permitted in the Chamber. The use of cellular phones is not allowed in the Chamber.[312] Since 1994, Members have been permitted to use laptop computers in the Chamber provided that their use does not cause disorder or interfere with the Member who has the floor.

The Speaker usually turns a blind eye to the many incidental interruptions, such as applause,[313] shouts of approval or disapproval, or heckling[314] that sometimes punctuates speeches, as long as disorder does not arise.[315] Members have been called to order for whistling and singing during another Member's speech.[316] Excessive interruptions are swiftly curtailed, particularly when the Member speaking requests the assistance of the Chair.[317] Speakers have consistently attempted to discourage loud private conversations in the Chamber and have urged those wishing to carry on such exchanges to do so outside the Chamber.[318]

DECORUM DURING THE TAKING OF A VOTE

During the taking of a vote, no Member is permitted to enter, walk out of or across the House or make any noise or disturbance from the time the Speaker begins to put the question until the results of the vote are announced.[319] Members must be in their

---

311. See, for example, *Debates*, October 5, 1990, p. 13892; September 30, 1997, p. 320.

312. See, for example, *Debates*, April 27, 1993, p. 18495; March 23, 1999, p. 13311.

313. In the past, it was the custom for Members to pound their desks to signify approval, but after the House proceedings began to be televised in 1977 and the public voiced its displeasure with this custom, Members took to applauding instead.

314. On occasion, the Speaker has asked Members not to heckle (see, for example, *Debates*, September 16, 1991, p. 2190; March 7, 1994, p. 1887; April 5, 1995, p. 11552), while in other instances, the Speaker has indicated that heckling is part of debate (see, for example, *Debates*, April 1, 1992, p. 9193).

315. See *Debates*, February 19, 1998, p. 4156, when Speaker Parent admonished Members that their applause for their colleagues prevented others from hearing Members' statements. See also *Debates*, December 21, 1988, pp. 554-5.

316. *Debates*, October 10, 1990, pp. 14010-1; September 30, 1994, p. 6373. On February 26, 1998, Suzanne Tremblay (Rimouski – Mitis) was prevented from speaking by the singing of the national anthem (*Debates*, p. 4503). The House Leader of the Bloc québécois (Michel Gauthier) subsequently raised a point of order about the disorder (*Debates*, pp. 4509-12). Speaker Parent ruled on March 16, 1998 (*Debates*, pp. 4902-3), that the event had been out of order: "Our law guarantees the right of all duly elected members to speak: our practice guarantees their right to be heard. It is the duty of the Speaker to guarantee that those rights are respected by guaranteeing that the House's rules and practices are respected."

317. See, for example, *Debates*, April 1, 1992, p. 9193; March 20, 1996, p. 986.

318. See, for example, *Debates*, February 9, 1994, p. 1147; June 10, 1994, p. 5169; November 28, 1994, pp. 8384-5; February 9, 1995, p. 9446.

319. Standing Order 16(1). See, for example, *Debates*, June 22, 1988, pp. 16731-2; April 9, 1990, p. 10390; November 27, 1991, p. 5458; October 28, 1997, p. 1258; June 9, 1998, p. 7884. For additional information on the taking of divisions, see Chapter 12, "The Process of Debate".

seats to vote and must remain seated until the result of the vote is announced.[320] Members who enter the Chamber while the question is being put, or after it has been put, cannot have their vote counted.[321] As is the rule in the House during a recorded division, no Member may enter a Committee of the Whole while a division is in progress.[322]

On one occasion, the Speaker interrupted the calling of a vote to request that a leader of an opposition party remove a prop because of the disorder it was creating in the Chamber.[323] The Speaker has also asked Members standing in the middle aisle to take their seats or to leave the Chamber in order that the House could proceed with the taking of a vote.[324]

Powers of the Chair to Enforce Order and Decorum

The Speaker ensures that debate conforms to the rules and practices that the House has adopted in order to protect itself from excesses. While the House is the master of its own proceedings and the Speaker its servant, the Speaker has extensive powers to enforce rules of debate and maintain order so that the House can conduct its business in an orderly fashion. Indeed, the Standing Orders state explicitly that the Speaker shall preserve order and decorum, and decide questions of order.[325] In addition, the Standing Orders empower the Speaker to call a Member to order if the Member persists in repeating an argument already made in the course of debate or in addressing a subject which is not relevant to the question before the House.[326]

The preservation of order and decorum has been a duty of the Speaker since 1867, but the task was never as difficult later as it was in the early years of Confederation. Speakers at that time were regularly confronted with rude and disorderly conduct which they were unable to control. The throwing of paper,[327] books,[328] and

---

320. See, for example, *Journals*, April 18, 1956, p. 416; *Debates*, February 16, 1976, p. 10986. Members are not required to be at their allocated desks during a division taken in a Committee of the Whole.

321. See, for example, *Debates*, February 14, 1983, pp. 22822-3; June 9, 1986, p. 14140. In doubtful cases, the Member is asked if he or she has heard the question, and the Chair accepts the word of the Member (see, for example, *Debates*, April 28, 1988, pp. 14942-3; June 9, 1998, p. 7890).

322. For additional information, see Chapter 19, "Committees of the Whole House".

323. *Debates*, June 22, 1995, p. 14466. Just prior to the taking of the vote on a government bill, Speaker Parent had asked Members to refrain from using props—in this instance, buttons decrying Members' pension benefits (*Debates*, p. 14465).

324. *Debates*, March 1, 1999, pp. 12212-3.

325. Standing Order 10.

326. Standing Order 11(2). See section above, "Repetition and Relevance in Debate".

327. See, for example, *Debates*, May 9, 1883, p. 1086.

328. See, for example, *Debates*, April 25, 1892, col. 1636.

other missiles, including firecrackers in one case,[329] combined with the noise Members made imitating cats,[330] making music[331] and generally being loud, made for a very riotous assembly.[332] The early twentieth century House was a much more austere and calm place, although in 1913, during the debate on the naval bill, the House very nearly got out of control.[333] Subsequent occasions of turbulence were infrequent and usually occurred in connection with the imposition of closure.[334] It was not until 1956, during the Pipeline Debate, that the Speaker again had great difficulty preserving order.[335] The 1960s with a succession of minority governments and the late 1970s with the introduction of televised sittings also proved a challenge. Speakers Jerome, Sauvé, Francis and Bosley all had to contend with scores of language breaches and other violations of order and decorum.[336] During the 1990s, both Speaker Fraser and Speaker Parent had to deal with a number of incidents of disruptive behaviour.[337]

---

329. See, for example, *Debates*, May 13, 1882, p. 1520.

330. See, for example, *Debates*, April 27, 1885, p. 1405.

331. See, for example, *Debates*, April 17, 1878, pp. 2063-4.

332. It was often suggested, not without some truth, that the root of the problem of order and decorum lay in the basement of the Parliament Building, just below the Chamber, where a much-frequented public saloon plied "intoxicating liquors" to Members seeking "refreshment" during the lengthy evening debates. In 1874, the House resolved to instruct the Speaker to close down the bar, but the decision was not enforced. This was attempted once more in 1881 but again to no effect. For a discussion on the closing of the bar, see *Debates*, February 28, 1881, pp. 1166-71. The saloon was finally closed when Wilfrid Laurier became Prime Minister (*Debates*, September 15, 1896, col. 1208). See also Norman Ward, "The Formative Years of the House of Commons, 1867-91", *The Canadian Journal of Economics and Political Science*, Vol. 18, No. 4, November 1952, pp. 432-4.

333. See, for example, *Debates*, March 15, 1913, cols. 6015-22.

334. See, for example, *Debates*, September 12, 1917, pp. 5768-71.

335. See, for example, *Debates*, May 24, 1956, pp. 4292-313.

336. Perhaps the worst scene in modern times occurred in 1980 when closure was moved on a motion to establish a committee to study a constitutional resolution. Several Members, angered by the closure motion, stormed the Chair, demanding to be heard. The resulting disorder on the floor of the House led to the entrance, behind the curtains, of members of the protective staff on the orders of the Sergeant-at-Arms. See *Debates*, October 23, 1980, pp. 4049-51; October 24, 1980, pp. 4065, 4068; November 6, 1980, p. 4499; November 7, 1980, pp. 4553-4. Another particularly serious incident occurred on October 16, 1985, when a Member, after asking a question about the British Columbia fishing industry, placed a dead salmon on the Prime Minister's desk (*Debates*, p. 7678).

337. See, in particular, Speaker Fraser's reprimand of Ian Waddell (Port Moody–Coquitlam) who was called to the Bar of the House for physically attempting to prevent the Mace from leaving the Chamber (*Debates*, October 31, 1991, pp. 4271-8, 4279-85, 4309-10), and Speaker Parent's ruling of March 16, 1998, in regard to the disorder which broke out in the Chamber on February 26, 1998, when a Member of the Bloc québécois (Suzanne Tremblay) attempted to speak (*Debates*, March 16, 1998, pp. 4902-3).

Accepted conventions of parliamentary conduct and respect for the authority of the Chair are normally sufficient guarantees that order and decorum are maintained during debate and other proceedings. However, if a rule of debate is being breached,[338] the Speaker will intervene directly to address a Member or the House in general and to call to order any Member whose conduct is disruptive.[339] The Speaker's declarations on disorderly or indecorous conduct are typically made quickly before any discussion takes place.

Members rarely defy the Speaker's authority or risk evoking the Chair's disciplinary powers. If a Member challenges the authority of the Chair by refusing to obey the Speaker's call to order, to withdraw unparliamentary language, to cease irrelevance or repetition, or to stop interrupting a Member who is addressing the House, the Chair has recourse to a number of options. The Speaker may recognize another Member,[340] or refuse to recognize the Member until the offending remarks are retracted and the Member apologizes.[341] As a last resort, the Chair may "name" a Member, the most severe disciplinary power at the Speaker's disposal.

NAMING

Naming describes a disciplinary measure invoked against a Member who persistently disregards the authority of the Chair. If a Member refuses to heed the Speaker's requests to bring his or her behaviour into line with the rules and practices of the House, the Speaker has the authority to name the Member, that is, to address the Member by name rather than by constituency or title as is the usual practice, and to order his or her withdrawal from the Chamber for the remainder of the sitting day.[342] Alternatively, the Speaker may prefer to let the House take any supplementary disciplinary action it may choose. In either case, naming is a coercive measure of last resort.

Historical Perspective

Until 1927, the British practice of naming Members applied in both the Legislative Assembly of the Province of Canada before Confederation and in the House of Commons after Confederation.[343] Although there were instances of naming before

---

338. See, for example, *Debates*, September 25, 1989, p. 3818; September 26, 1996, p. 4715; February 6, 1997, p. 7790; September 24, 1998, p. 8354.

339. See, for example, *Debates*, February 14, 1992, pp. 7039-40; February 15, 1993, pp. 15918-9; February 4, 1997, pp. 7645-6.

340. See, for example, *Debates*, September 26, 1991, p. 2773; March 24, 1994, p. 2738; November 6, 1995, p. 16238; May 8, 1996, p. 2482.

341. See, for example, *Debates*, October 30, 1987, pp. 10583-4; November 18, 1987, pp. 10927-8; January 17, 1991, pp. 17294-5, 17304-5.

342. Standing Order 11(1)(*a*).

343. For an overview of the British practice, see *May*, 6th ed., p. 323; *May*, 22nd ed., pp. 394-5, 397-9. See also *Hatsell*, Vol. II, pp. 230-8, in particular pp. 237-8.

Confederation,[344] from 1867 until 1927 there was only one case. In 1913, Speaker Sproule, who had taken the Chair to quell disorder in a Committee of the Whole, cited a British rule and named Mr. Clark (Red Deer) for "disregarding the authority of the Chair and flagrantly violating the rules of the House."[345] After the Member was named, he apologized to the House and the House considered his explanation satisfactory. No motion to suspend him was proposed.[346] Still, in the 46-year interval between Confederation and 1913 and in the years 1914-27, there were times when the Speaker, facing Members unwilling to respect the Chair's calls to order, might have resorted to naming but did not.[347]

When the naming sanction was formally provided for in the 1927 Standing Orders,[348] it referred simply to the Speaker's power to name a Member who engaged in persistent irrelevance or repetition;[349] no reference was made to naming a Member for refusing to retract unparliamentary language or for disregarding the authority of the Chair. Furthermore, the Standing Orders did not specify the procedure to be followed after a Member had been named.[350] It was not until 15 years later, in 1942, that the first incident of naming occurred under the amended Standing Orders. In this case, after Speaker Glen had named Mr. Lacombe (Laval–Two Mountains), the Minister of Finance immediately moved a motion to suspend Mr. Lacombe. The

---

344. *Journals* of the Legislative Assembly of Canada, September 9, 1852, pp. 125-6; May 9, 1861, p. 270.

345. *Debates*, March 15, 1913, col. 6019.

346. *Debates*, March 15, 1913, cols. 6016-22.

347. See, for example, *Debates*, March 5, 1877, pp. 482-5; May 9, 1890, cols. 4717-8; September 28, 1903, col. 12562; January 18, 1910, col. 2084. In one case, the Speaker did take action, although not by naming a Member: "In the session of 1875 Mr. Domville, member for King's, N.B., made some remarks which appeared to be most insulting to the House as a body. The Speaker called him to order but he persisted in repeating the offensive expressions and the Speaker immediately ordered the Sergeant-at-Arms to take him into custody. Mr. Domville apologized, for in his excitement he did not seem to know what he had been saying. On a subsequent day, whilst the doors were closed, Mr. Speaker stated frankly that he believed he had exceeded his power in ordering the hon. member to be taken into custody." (Handwritten endnote in Bourinot's personal copy of *May*, 6th ed., p. 330d.)

348. *Journals*, March 22, 1927, pp. 326-7.

349. Standing Order 11(2).

350. An interpretation of both these points was advanced in the same year by the Clerk of the House, Arthur Beauchesne, who wrote that a Member's persistent use of unparliamentary language (in addition to repetition or irrelevance) was sufficient reason for the Speaker to name that Member (*Beauchesne*, 2nd ed., p. 89). As to the procedure to be followed after naming, *Beauchesne* cited a British Standing Order: "... the Speaker shall forthwith put the question, on a motion being made... 'That such member be suspended from the service of the house'" (*Beauchesne*, 2nd ed., p. 92).

motion carried easily.[351] Thus, the practice developed that after being named by the Speaker, a Minister, usually the Government House Leader, would move a motion to suspend the Member, typically for the remainder of the day's sitting. Subsequent naming incidents occurred in 1944 (twice), 1956, 1961, 1962 (twice) and 1964.[352]

Beginning in 1978, after television had been introduced in the Chamber, the frequency of naming increased dramatically.[353] Possibly even more significant than the rise in the number of namings was the fact that the House appeared increasingly willing to divide on the subsequent motion to suspend the offending Member. This placed the Speaker in a potentially vulnerable position in that after naming a Member, it was up to a Minister (usually the Government House Leader) to move a motion to suspend the Member, and since the motion was votable, it could be defeated. Thus, the authority of the Speaker depended, in each case of naming, on

---

351. *Debates*, March 24, 1942, pp. 1603-7. The Minister apparently followed the procedure set out in *Beauchesne* (2nd ed., p. 92).

352. *Journals*, July 4, 1944, p. 526; July 31, 1944, pp. 761-2; May 25, 1956, pp. 625-34; February 10, 1961, p. 238; March 16, 1962, pp. 241-2; *Debates*, October 5, 1962, p. 233; *Journals*, June 19, 1964, pp. 456-7. The July 4, 1944, incident is the only case of naming in which a Member was suspended for more than a day (seven days was the penalty). In the July 31, 1944, case, the Chairman of Committees of the Whole House ruled that certain remarks by a Member were unparliamentary and asked the Member to withdraw the words. The Member appealed the Chairman's ruling to the House, Speaker Glen took the Chair, and the House confirmed the Chairman's ruling. The Speaker asked the Member to withdraw until the House decided what it would do. In his absence, the House passed a motion to suspend the Member for the remainder of the sitting day. All this was done without the Member being "named". See *Debates*, July 31, 1944, pp. 5677-84. A similar incident occurred in 1956 when the Chairman of Committees of the Whole reported a Member to the House for not resuming his seat when directed to do so. See *Debates*, May 25, 1956, pp. 4340-52.

353. The broadcasting of House proceedings began in October 1977. There was one naming in 1978 (*Debates*, May 16, 1978, pp. 5455-8) and another in 1979 (*Debates*, March 21, 1979, pp. 4382-5), while two took place in each of the years 1981 (*Debates*, February 23, 1981, pp. 7586-8; December 3, 1981, pp. 13685-7) and 1982 (*Debates*, May 19, 1982, pp. 17593-6; June 16, 1982, pp. 18523-5). Four incidents occurred in each of the years 1983 (*Debates*, March 24, 1983, pp. 24109-10; May 20, 1983, pp. 25628-31; October 19, 1983, pp. 28129-31; October 31, 1983, pp. 28593-4), 1984 (*Debates*, May 25, 1984, pp. 4078-9; June 8, 1984, pp. 4482-3; December 17, 1984, pp. 1292-3; December 19, 1984, pp. 1363-4) and 1985 (*Debates*, May 22, 1985, pp. 4966-7; June 19, 1985, pp. 5973-4; June 27, 1985, p. 6270; October 11, 1985, pp. 7589-91). Five Members were named in 1986 (*Debates*, February 24, 1986, p. 10889; April 23, 1986, pp. 12568-9; May 21, 1986, pp. 13478-9; May 28, 1986, pp. 13713-4; June 11, 1986, pp. 14242-5).

the initial support of the government to move the motion and on the subsequent support of the House to adopt it.[354]

In 1985, as the number of naming incidents continued to increase, the Special Committee on Reform of the House of Commons (the McGrath Committee) addressed the question of "whether the disciplinary powers of the Chair should be clarified and strengthened".[355] The Committee's final report recommended "that the Speaker be empowered to order the withdrawal of a member for the remainder of a sitting ... [and] that the proceedings consequent upon the naming of a member be set out in the Standing Orders."[356] In February 1986, the government tabled proposed amendments to the Standing Orders that went beyond the recommendation of the Committee to include measures that would allow the Speaker, on ordering the withdrawal of a Member for the second or any subsequent occasion during a session, to suspend him or her for a period of five days without resort to motion.[357] During debate on the motion to adopt these new provisions, Members expressed strong support for the concept of granting the Speaker authority to order the withdrawal of a Member for one sitting, but were equally hesitant to extend such power further, preferring to leave subsequent punishments in the hands of the House itself.[358] In February 1986, the House agreed to amendments to the proposed changes to the Standing Orders, and they came into effect that same month.[359] The rule changes left untouched the Standing Order that had existed since 1927[360] but added a new Standing Order granting the Speaker the authority to order the withdrawal of a Member

---

354. Beauchesne appeared to have anticipated this problem as early as 1927: "The vote on the motion that a member be suspended from the service of the House after having been named by the Speaker is a mere formality, as a rejection of the motion would assuredly be followed by an immediate resignation of the Speaker, a circumstance which his complete freedom from partisanship would render unwelcome even to the parties in opposition" (*Beauchesne*, 2nd ed., p. 92). Between 1944 and 1986, there were 19 instances when the Member named was suspended after a recorded division was taken on the motion. On several occasions, the offending Member withdrew from the Chamber after having been named, and the House took no further action (*Debates*, October 5, 1962, p. 233; February 23, 1981, pp. 7586-8; May 20, 1983, pp. 25628-31; May 25, 1984, pp. 4078-9; December 19, 1984, p. 1364). On one occasion, the named Member withdrew, but in the absence of a formal motion for suspension, the Leader of the Opposition insisted that there be one so that his party could vote against it. The Prime Minister refused to move the motion. The House was left with no choice, however, when the named Member returned to the Chamber and resumed his seat. The Member left the Chamber when the suspension motion was finally put and agreed to on a recorded division. See *Debates*, June 19, 1964, pp. 4489-94, 4521-5.

355. See the Special Committee on the Reform of the House of Commons, Third Report, p. 37, presented on June 18, 1985 (*Journals*, p. 839).

356. See the Special Committee on the Reform of the House of Commons, Third Report, p. 38, presented on June 18, 1985 (*Journals*, p. 839).

357. *Journals*, February 6, 1986, pp. 1645-6.

358. See, for example, *Debates*, February 11, 1986, p. 10668.

359. *Journals*, February 13, 1986, p. 1710. These changes were made permanent on June 3, 1987 (*Journals*, p. 1016).

360. Standing Order 11(2).

for the remainder of the sitting.[361] Although the method of naming, followed by a votable motion to suspend the Member for a specified period of time, has not been resorted to since October 1985,[362] it remains a practice which can still be referred to by the Speaker or invoked by the House.

The Process of Naming

The Speaker typically calls upon a Member who has transgressed the established standards of decorum to retract the offending words or otherwise apologize without qualification. Should the Member hesitate or refuse to comply, the Speaker normally repeats the request, often with a warning that the persistent disregard will result in the Member being named. Such exchanges may continue at the Speaker's discretion, but once it is clear that the Member will not comply, the Speaker names him or her, and orders a withdrawal for the remainder of the sitting day. In naming a Member, the Speaker will say:

> (Name of Member), *it is my duty to name you for disregarding the authority of the Chair, and to direct your withdrawal from the House for the remainder of the sitting.*

Alternately, in some circumstances, after naming a Member but before ordering a withdrawal from the House, the Speaker may wish the House to decide what disciplinary action to take against a Member. This option involves a motion, usually proposed by the Government House Leader, to suspend the Member named from the service of the House for a specified period of time. This motion is neither debatable nor amendable. It carries a greater penalty since suspension from the service of the House bars the Member not only from attendance in the Chamber, but also from committees and the proposed suspension may exceed the remainder of the sitting. Notices standing in the name of the suspended Member are removed from the *Notice Paper* for each day that the Member is suspended.[363] The Speaker may also order the Sergeant-at-Arms to take the necessary steps to remove a Member who refuses to leave the Chamber after being ordered to withdraw.[364]

---

361. Standing Order 11(1).

362. *Journals*, October 11, 1985, p. 1094. Under Speaker Fraser (1986-93), only one Member was named (*Debates*, March 24, 1993, pp. 17482, 17486-8). During the Thirty-Fifth Parliament (1994-97), Speaker Parent named six Members, two on the same day (*Debates*, September 30, 1994, pp. 6386-7; May 29, 1995, pp. 12900-3; November 2, 1995, pp. 16144-5; April 24, 1996, p. 1894; February 12, 1997, pp. 8016-7), and during the First Session of the Thirty-Sixth Parliament (1997-99), he named two Members (*Debates*, October 1, 1997, pp. 334-5; December 1, 1998, pp. 10730-1).

363. *Beauchesne*, 4th ed., pp. 44-5.

364. Standing Order 11(1)(*b*). No Member has been physically removed from the Chamber after being named by the Speaker. There have been, however, instances where, at the request of the Speaker, a Member has been escorted from the Chamber by the Sergeant-at-Arms. See *Debates*, July 4, 1944, p. 4514; May 19, 1982, p. 17596.

During debate in a Committee of a Whole, if a Member refuses to obey the warning of the Chairman to discontinue his or her unparliamentary behaviour, the Chairman of the Committee may rise and report the conduct of the Member to the Speaker. The Chairman may do this on his or her own initiative without recourse to a motion from the Committee.[365] The Speaker will deal with the matter as if it had occurred in the House.[366]

---

365. Standing Order 11(2).

366. See, for example, *Debates*, May 25, 1956, pp. 4340-52; March 16, 1962, pp. 1888-90. See also Chapter 19, "Committees of the Whole House". The Chair of any standing, special, joint or sub-committee may not take such action. The Committee may only decide to report these offences to the House.

14

The Curtailment of Debate

... the whole study of parliamentary procedure over the years, indeed over the decades, has been an endeavour to find a balance between the right to speak at as much length as seems desirable, and the right of parliament to make decisions.

STANLEY KNOWLES, M.P. (Winnipeg North Centre)
(*Debates,* May 20, 1965, p. 1530)

One of the fundamental principles of parliamentary procedure is that debate in the House of Commons must lead to an unimpeded decision in a reasonable time.[1] Although what seems reasonable to one party may arguably appear unfair to another, few parliamentarians contest the idea that, at some point, debate must end.[2] While an overwhelming majority of House business is concluded without recourse to special procedures intended to limit or end debate, certain rules exist to "curtail debate" in cases when it is felt a decision would otherwise not be taken in reasonable time, or not taken at all. Despite the fact that Standing Order changes have made systematic obstruction on the part of the

---

1. For further information on debate in the House of Commons, see Chapter 12, "The Process of Debate", and Chapter 13, "Rules of Order and Decorum".

2. The desire to restrict debate on certain questions, though frequently condemned today, is not entirely a new phenomenon. Dawson writes that "unrestricted debate has never existed in Canada and has not existed for several centuries in the United Kingdom" (*Dawson*, p. 3). See also *Franks*, pp. 128-32.

opposition less frequent, a good understanding of parliamentary procedure still enables Members to extend debate on a given item considerably.

The rules pertaining to the "curtailment of debate" invite the House as a whole to pronounce itself on the issue of limiting debate on a particular item of business beyond what the normal rules would otherwise allow. A distinction, however, must be made between "freedom of speech" and a Member's opportunity to take part in "debate". The question of a Member's freedom of speech—a basic parliamentary privilege—has no relevance to this process. (In a parliamentary sense, "freedom of speech" refers to a Member's immunity from legal prosecution for words stated during debate in the House and its committees, rather than the general notion of an unlimited opportunity to speak.) When asked to deal with the receivability of a motion to limit debate, the Speaker does not judge the importance of the issue in question or the "reasonableness" of the time allowed for debate, but strictly addresses the acceptability of the procedure followed.[3] Speakers have ruled that a procedurally acceptable motion to limit the ability of Members to speak on a given motion before the House does not constitute *prima facie* a breach of parliamentary privilege.[4]

At Confederation, few rules existed to curtail debate. Even at that time, it was recognized that unlimited debate was not possible and that some restraint would have to be exercised or some accommodation reached in order for the House to conduct its business with reasonable despatch.[5] For the first 45 years following Confederation, the only tool at the government's disposal was the previous question.[6] Not only was there no other way of putting an end to a specific debate in "reasonable time", but there were no formal time limits of any kind on debates and the length of speeches was unlimited. Working relations in the House were based largely upon a

---

3. Speaker Fraser, addressing the issue of the Chair's "discretionary powers" in protecting the rights of Members to speak freely on matters of "national interest", ruled that "procedurally speaking, as your presiding officer ... I am without authority to intervene when a Standing Order is used according to our rules and practices" (*Debates*, June 29, 1987, pp. 7713-4).

4. The Speaker has ruled on this issue on numerous occasions. See, for example, *Debates*, December 30, 1971, pp. 10846-7; October 24, 1980, pp. 4066-7; June 29, 1987, pp. 7713-4; October 8, 1997, pp. 662-6.

5. In the First Session of the First Parliament, a committee was appointed to consider whether "the despatch of Public Business can be more effectually promoted" (*Journals*, March 31, 1868, pp. 168-9). In 1869, a motion was adopted concerning the times for the assembling of Parliament; during the debate, concern was expressed that important business was rushed through at the end of the session (*Journals*, June 14, 1869, p. 241; *Debates*, June 14, 1869, pp. 779-80). A similar motion was adopted in 1873 (*Journals*, May 12, 1873, p. 330). In 1886, a motion was adopted concerning length of speeches; debate on the motion indicated that, in order to ensure proper attention to business before the House, some plan would have to be adopted to economize time (*Debates*, April 19, 1886, pp. 789-92).

6. For further information on the previous question, see section below.

spirit of mutual fair play where informal arrangements, or "closure by consent", governed the conduct of debate. In the words of Prime Minister Robert Borden:

> *... at a definite stage in a debate, when, in the judgment of the leading men of both sides of the House, it has proceeded far enough, it has been the practice for a consultation to be held and a date to be fixed; and members who are not able to catch the Speaker's eye within the period so fixed are, by arrangements made on both sides of the House, practically excluded from taking part in the debate on that subject and the question is brought to an issue in that way.*[7]

The early rules governing the business of the House apportioned a major share of time to the consideration of private bills and other business sponsored by private Members. The government's role in the economy being limited, government business was but a small part of the House's workload.[8] After 1900, the changing nature of the business coming before the House, especially the growing volume of business initiated by the government, led to a steady increase in the time that the House set aside for Government Orders. The time of the House became a precious commodity and a source of sometimes fierce partisan contention. This was manifested by a growing propensity on the part of the opposition to thwart the passage of government legislation through delay and obstruction.[9]

These changes in parliamentarians' attitudes and government workload led the House to adopt rules and practices that would, on the one hand, facilitate the daily management of its time[10] and, on the other hand, limit debate and expedite the normal course of events in cases deemed of an important or urgent nature. This chapter focusses on this latter aspect and examines how debate is curtailed through the use of the previous question, closure, time allocation, the moving by a Minister

---

7. *Debates*, April 9, 1913, col. 7391.

8. For a discussion on the changes in government workload and its incidence on the time allotment and closure rules in the House of Commons, see *Stewart*, pp. 238-9.

9. This aspect of procedural change has been widely chronicled; see, for example, the observations and analyses of *Dawson*, pp. 127-33; *Franks*, pp. 128-32; and *Stewart*, pp. 239-41.

10. In April 1913, the House adopted amendments to existing Rule 17 which restricted the number of debatable motions, and provided that on two days of the week certain motions which would ordinarily be debatable (specifically, motions for the House to resolve into the Committee of Supply or into the Committee of Ways and Means) would not be debatable (*Journals*, April 23, 1913, pp. 507-9). In 1927, the House adopted a rule to limit the speeches of a majority of Members to 40 minutes each (*Journals*, March 22, 1927, pp. 328-9). Further restrictions were imposed in 1955 when limits were placed on the length of the Address and Budget Debates, on debate in a Committee of the Whole and on debate on the motion for the House to resolve itself into the Committee of Supply (*Journals*, July 12, 1955, pp. 908-9, 922-9). Permanent changes to the Standing Orders in October 1962 provided further limitations on the Address and Budget Debates and on debate during Private Members' Business (*Journals*, April 12, 1962, p. 350). In 1968, amendments were made to the Standing Order limiting speeches in a Committee of the Whole (*Journals*, December 20, 1968, p. 573).

of a "routine motion" to bypass the requirement for unanimous consent,[11] and the moving of a motion to suspend certain Standing Orders in relation to a matter considered to be of an urgent nature.[12]

The Previous Question

There are occasions where Members will move, during a debate on a motion before the House, "That this question be now put".[13] This motion, commonly known as the previous question, may be proposed to substantive debatable motions before the House. There are a number of restrictions placed on the use of the previous question. These are discussed in more detail in Chapter 12, "The Process of Debate". Once the previous question has been moved, debate on the original motion resumes. Although it does not put an immediate end to debate, the previous question restricts debate and expedites the putting of the question in two ways.

First, it precludes the moving of amendments to the main motion and, therefore, any debate that might have ensued on those amendments. Indeed, if the previous question is carried, the Speaker is obliged to put the question on the main motion forthwith.[14] Members who have spoken already to the main motion or any previous amendments may speak again to the previous question. In this sense, the previous question is at best an unpredictable method of curtailing debate. The previous question has been adopted without debate,[15] it has carried after a short debate,[16] or after several days of debate.[17] In instances where the previous question did not appear useful in bringing a question to a vote, a motion to adjourn the

---

11. Standing Order 56.1.

12. Standing Order 53.

13. Standing Order 61. In Canada, the wording of the previous question has remained unaltered since it was first introduced in the House of Commons in 1867. In the Westminster version, the wording of the motion was changed to "That the question be *not* now put" in 1888 to avoid confusion with closure, which employs the same formula (*May*, 19ᵗʰ ed., p. 378).

14. See *Journals*, January 22, 1991, pp. 2592-3.

15. *Journals*, December 5, 1996, pp. 968-9.

16. In 1990, the previous question moved by a Minister on a government initiative was debated for approximately 40 minutes before being adopted (*Debates*, March 27, 1990, pp. 9849-55). For another example of short debate, see *Journals*, March 25, 1993, p. 2598.

17. On September 23, 1991, for example, the previous question was moved on a motion for second reading of a government bill; the debate continued during that sitting and the sittings of September 24, 25 and 27 before the question was put and the vote deferred to September 30 (*Journals*, September 23, 1991, pp. 378, 380; September 24, 1991, p. 388; September 25, 1991, pp. 394-5; September 27, 1991, p. 402; September 30, 1991, pp. 414-5).

debate[18] or a motion of closure[19] has been moved to put an end to a debate on the previous question. When a recorded division is demanded on the previous question, it may be deferred at the request of either the Chief Government Whip or the Chief Opposition Whip[20]; however, once the previous question is adopted, a recorded division on the main motion may not be deferred.[21]

Second, the previous question can have the effect of superseding a motion under debate since, if negatived, the Speaker is bound *not* to put at that time the question on the main motion. In other words, if the motion "that the question be now put" is not adopted, the motion under debate is dropped from the *Order Paper*. Unless revived on a future day and reinstated on the *Order Paper,*[22] the item will not be debated again. In practice, in a majority of instances when the previous question was negatived, the item was revived and eventually adopted, with or without amendment. As a mechanism for limiting debate by causing an item to drop from the *Order Paper,* the previous question has not been very successful. Since Confederation, the motion "that the question be now put" has been negatived four times.[23] It has also been withdrawn by unanimous consent.[24]

While both government and opposition Members may move the previous question,[25] it is used by some in the hope that it will expedite a vote on the main motion, and by others in the hope that it will prevent the Speaker from putting the question *now* on a motion or a bill. Although the previous question can be both a method of forcing a decision on a motion and a way of postponing or delaying a decision, it has in recent years almost exclusively been used by the government to limit debate.

In the past, the use of the previous question has been anything but predictable. Ministers have moved it on private Members' motions[26] and on government motions

---

18. See, for example, *Journals*, May 10, 1995, pp. 1458-9.

19. *Beauchesne*, 6th ed., p. 160. See, for example, *Journals*, March 2, 1926, p. 123.

20. Standing Order 45(5).

21. Standing Order 61(2).

22. *Beauchesne*, 6th ed., p. 160.

23. In 1869, the main motion was not presented to the House again. On the other three occasions, it was. In 1870 and 1929, the revived motions were adopted and, in 1928, no decision was taken (*Journals*, May 31, 1869, pp. 163-4; April 28, 1870, pp. 254-5; June 1, 1928, p. 489; April 15, 1929, p. 242). The frequency of use of the previous question is discussed in Chapter 12, "The Process of Debate".

24. The previous question has been withdrawn, on occasion, when negotiations had led to arrangements between parties. In 1983, for example, the mover of the previous question withdrew it, by unanimous consent, to allow the matter to be referred to a standing committee (*Debates*, February 9, 1983, pp. 22682-6). See also, *Journals*, May 10, 1990, p. 1685.

25. In 1985, Speaker Bosley ruled that "there is no question in my mind from reading the rules that there is no restriction on the moving of this motion in terms of whether it be by a Minister of the Crown, a Parliamentary Secretary or a Private Member" (*Debates*, January 28, 1985, p. 1708).

26. *Journals*, May 31, 1869, p. 163.

and bills. Conversely, private Members have moved the previous question on other private Members' motions[27] as well as on government motions.[28] Perhaps because of the many restrictions that regulate its use, the previous question has been described as the "most ineffective" method of limiting debate.[29]

Closure

Closure is a procedural device used to bring debate on a question to a conclusion by "… a majority decision of the House, although all Members wishing to speak have not done so".[30] The closure rule[31] provides the government with a procedure to prevent the further adjournment of debate on any matter and to require that the question be put at the end of the sitting in which a motion of closure is adopted. Apart from technical changes as to the hour at which debate is to conclude,[32] the rule has remained virtually unchanged since its adoption in 1913.

Closure may be applied to any debatable matter, including bills and motions. The rule was conceived for use in a Committee of the Whole[33] as much as in the House, but it cannot be applied to business being considered in standing, special, legislative or joint committees of the House. When these committees are considering bills, the House may use the time allocation rule[34] to impose a deadline on the committee stage or to force a committee to report the bill to the House.

HISTORICAL PERSPECTIVE

Introduced at Westminster in 1881 and in the Australian House of Representatives in 1905, the closure rule was not adopted by the Canadian House of Commons until

---

27. *Journals,* April 6, 1959, p. 289.

28. *Journals,* December 5, 1996, p. 968. The motivations for using the previous question have not always been the same and do not always involve curtailing debate. For example, Members of the opposition in favour of a government motion have moved the previous question not to cause the item to be dropped from the *Order Paper* but to signal their support for the government initiative and limit debate "by consent." In 1992, just before moving the previous question on a government motion to amend the Constitution, Opposition Leader Jean Chrétien stated that it was "with great pleasure that I support this motion" (*Debates,* December 11, 1992, pp. 15086-7).

29. *Dawson,* p. 119.

30. *Wilding and Laundy,* p. 139.

31. Standing Order 57.

32. Originally the time for putting all questions to dispose of the closured business was set at 2:00 a.m. (*Journals,* April 23, 1913, pp. 507-9). In 1955, it was changed to 1:00 a.m. (*Journals,* July 12, 1955, pp. 881, 910-1, 945) and, in 1991, to 11:00 p.m. (*Journals,* April 11, 1991, pp. 2905, 2913).

33. See, for example, *Debates,* December 21, 1988, p. 541.

34. Standing Order 78.

1913.[35] The idea of closure had, however, been discussed on a number of occasions, but the House had never been able to adopt a closure rule satisfactory to both government and opposition. By 1913, strong and organized opposition had managed to delay the adoption of government legislation on at least four occasions.[36] Speeches from that period allude to the occasional inability of the House to come to a vote on a question and, in 1911, during one of these protracted debates, a Member of the opposition spoke of the possibility of "illimitable discussion".[37] Opposition Leader Robert Borden, who would eventually introduce the new rule, had himself suggested that a closure rule would be "undesirable,"[38] but nearly two years of discussion on naval policy convinced him of the necessity to bring forward a motion which, among other things, would introduce the closure rule. These changes, vigorously attacked by the opposition, were debated for nearly a month before being adopted.[39] The new closure rule was immediately tested by the government only a few days after its adoption, during debate at the Committee of the Whole stage of the Naval Aid Bill.[40]

Used nine times from 1913 to 1932, the closure rule was then not resorted to for 24 years. In May and June 1956, during the Pipeline Debate, closure was invoked at each stage of the legislative process.[41] This episode, which gave rise to much

35. *Journals*, April 23, 1913, pp. 507-9. Although both Westminster and the Canadian House of Commons have closure rules, some differences are worth noting. First, the wording of the British version of the motion is in the affirmative: "that the question be now put". Second, in the United Kingdom, closure is moved without notice, must be decided forthwith and, if adopted, ends debate immediately. Third, unlike in Canada, the Speaker can refuse to put the motion if it appears "that the motion is an abuse of the rules of the House, or an infringement of the rights of the minority." Fourth, at least 100 Members must vote in favour of the closure motion for it to carry. See Standing Orders 35 and 36 of the Standing Orders of the British House of Commons. The Australian House of Representatives makes a distinction between "Closure of Member", which reads: "That the Member from ... be not further heard" (Standing Order 94) and "Closure of Question", which reads: "That the question be now put" (Standing Order 93).

36. These are the franchise bill in 1885, the Manitoba school legislation in 1896, the franchise bill in 1908 and the reciprocity debate in 1911. See *Dawson*, p. 121.

37. "It is therefore altogether probable that, if the government can force the matter to a vote, it will be carried. On the other hand, the opposition can, if it sees fit, probably prevent a vote. There are 300 items which will give opportunity for illimitable discussion" (*Debates*, April 28, 1911, col. 8038).

38. *Debates*, December 14, 1909, cols. 1441-2.

39. *Journals*, April 23, 1913, pp. 507-9. For a detailed account of the Naval Aid Bill episode, see *Robert Laird Borden: His Memoirs*, Vol. I, edited by Henry Borden, Toronto/Montreal: McClelland and Stewart, 1969, pp. 186-99; and *Dawson*, pp. 122-4.

40. *Debates*, May 9, 1913, col. 9445.

41. Between May 15 and June 5, 1956, closure was used at all four stages of the legislative process as it was then: resolution (*Debates*, May 15, 1956, p. 3895); second reading (*Debates*, May 22, 1956, p. 4165); Committee of the Whole (Debates, May 31, 1956, p. 4498) and third reading (*Debates*, June 5, 1956, p. 4689).

analysis and commentary, had lasting repercussions on Members' perception of how the House operates.[42]

The rule has been the subject of scrutiny and discussion on numerous occasions. In December 1957, the new Diefenbaker government placed a notice of motion on the *Order Paper* to repeal the closure rule, but the motion was never debated.[43] In July 1960, Prime Minister Diefenbaker expressed the hope that "the rules committee will give consideration to removing from the rule book the closure procedure".[44] The Committee never acted on that matter. In March 1962, another special committee was set up to consider the procedures of the House and, in particular, "to consider the desirability of repealing" the closure rule;[45] it did not report on this issue. The Throne Speech in September 1962 indicated that the House would be asked to abolish closure, but this also was not acted upon.[46] During the Thirtieth Parliament (1974-79), a sub-committee of the Standing Committee on Procedure and Organization recommended, in its report on the use of time, that a new Standing Order based on the British House of Commons' closure rule be adopted,[47] but this was never recommended to the House. The issue of repealing the closure rule still resurfaces from time to time.[48]

NOTICE OF CLOSURE

Prior to moving a motion for closure, an oral notice of intention to do so must have been given by a Minister at a previous sitting of the House or a Committee of the Whole. The rule is not specific as to when such notice may be given; thus a variety of precedents exist. Notice of intention to move a closure motion has been given: when there was no question before the House;[49] when the motion to be closured was under debate;[50] and when the question before the House was not related to the notice.[51] Notice has been given on the first day of debate on the motion to be

---

42. Some writers have commented that the use of closure during the Pipeline Debate has produced a lingering distaste for the closure rule, already the subject of some disrepute. See, for example, *Stewart*, pp. 242-6; *Laundy*, pp. 112-9.

43. *Journals*, December 9, 1957, p. 255.

44. *Debates*, July 21, 1960, p. 6676.

45. *Journals*, March 26, 1962, p. 277.

46. *Journals*, September 27, 1962, p. 15.

47. Standing Committee on Procedure and Organization, *Minutes of Proceedings and Evidence*, September 30, 1976, Issue No. 20, p. 57.

48. In 1998, the opposition actually managed temporarily to repeal the rule (*Journals*, June 12, 1998, pp. 1027-8).

49. See, for example, *Debates*, October 22, 1980, p. 3934 (during Routine Proceedings).

50. See, for example, *Debates*, March 1, 1926, p. 1431; July 16, 1981, p. 11629.

51. See, for example, *Debates*, April 6, 1981, p. 9014.

closured,[52] and after one or more days of debate.[53] Regardless, debate on the item which is the subject of the notice must have begun before notice of closure may be given.[54]

Although there is no requirement to give notice more than once, Ministers have provided the same notice in several sittings so as to avoid any objection that notice had not been given at the previous sitting.[55] On the other hand, no obligation exists to proceed with moving the closure motion even if notice has been given; there have been cases where the notice was not proceeded with.[56] On one occasion, the government gave notice of closure on four separate bills, all at the same time: three at second reading and one at third reading;[57] however, four motions proposing closure, one for each bill, had to be moved separately.

MOTION OF CLOSURE

After notice has been given of the intention to move a motion of closure, the motion may be moved during a subsequent sitting, whether the following day or later. The motion for closure must be moved by a Minister, and the debate on the motion or bill to which closure is to apply must have been adjourned at least once before a closure motion can be moved.[58] The motion for closure must be moved immediately before the Order of the Day for resuming debate on the item to which the closure motion is to apply is called, either in the House or in a Committee of the Whole.

Closure motions are neither debatable nor amendable and, once moved, the Speaker or the Chairman puts the question immediately, "That debate ... shall not be further adjourned" (or in a Committee of the Whole, "That debate ... shall not be further postponed"). How much debate the government will allow on a measure before moving closure depends on political factors. The Speaker has at times been

---

52. See, for example, *Journals*, August 29, 1917, p. 605; in December 1988, notice of closure was given on the first day of debate at second reading, Committee of the Whole and third reading stages of Bill C-2, *Canada-United States Free Trade Agreement Implementation Act* (*Journals*, December 15, 1988, pp. 36-7; December 20, 1988, p. 61; *Debates*, December 20, 1988, p. 500; *Journals*, December 22, 1988, pp. 72-3).

53. On March 1, 1926, after some 25 days of debate, the government gave notice of closure on the motion for the Address in Reply; the motion was moved and adopted on March 2 (*Journals*, pp. 121, 123).

54. See Speaker Fraser's ruling, *Debates*, December 15, 1988, p. 78.

55. In 1969, three notices of closure were given in respect to a motion for concurrence in the report of a procedure committee (*Journals*, July 22, 1969, pp. 1383; July 23, 1969, p. 1386; July 24, 1969, p. 1393). The closure motion was moved on July 24, 1969 (*Journals*, p. 1396). In 1987, two notices of closure were given on a motion concerning capital punishment (*Journals*, June 18, 1987, p. 1200; June 26, 1987, p. 1263). The closure motion was moved during the following sitting (*Journals*, June 29, 1987, p. 1274).

56. *Journals*, December 4, 1986, pp. 272, 274; August 26, 1987, p. 1384; August 28, 1987, pp. 1396-7.

57. *Debates*, June 16, 1989, pp. 3146-8.

58. See Speaker Fraser's ruling, *Debates*, December 15, 1988, pp. 76-8.

asked to use discretionary authority to refuse to put a closure motion to the House on the ground that a measure had not yet been given enough debating time. Invariably, he or she has declined to interfere with the application of the rule, deciding in each case that the Chair has no authority to intervene in the process when the closure rule is applied properly.[59]

When a motion for closure is adopted, debate resumes on the now-closured business, typically leading to an extended sitting of the House through the evening. The debate becomes subject to the restrictions imposed by the closure rule.[60] No Member (including the Prime Minister and the Leader of the Opposition) may speak more than once, nor for longer than 20 minutes. A Member who has spoken to the main motion prior to the adoption of the closure motion may speak again if an amendment or sub-amendment is moved during the closured debate. However, a Member who speaks to the main motion after the adoption of the closure motion may not speak to any subsequent amendment or sub-amendment. Any Private Members' Business which might have been scheduled is still taken up at its regular time.

All questions necessary to dispose of the closured business are to be put no later than 11:00 p.m., or as soon as possible thereafter, having allowed any Member who might have been recognized prior to 11:00 p.m. to finish speaking.[61] No Member may rise to speak after 11:00 p.m.,[62] at which time the Speaker or the Chairman will put all questions necessary to dispose of the closured business, including any amendments and sub-amendments.[63] If a recorded division is demanded in the House, the bells will sound for up to 15 minutes.[64] Should the debate conclude before 11:00 p.m., the bells for any recorded division will sound for not more than 30 minutes.[65] The wording of the Standing Order is quite clear that the question on

---

59. Following a question of privilege protesting the government's intent to invoke closure on the motion relating to the reinstatement of capital punishment, Speaker Fraser ruled that the timing of closure in a debate is not a procedural matter and that the Chair has no discretionary power to refuse the motion and is without authority to intervene when a Standing Order is used according to the House's rules and practices (*Debates*, June 29, 1987, pp. 7713-4). See also, *Journals*, July 24, 1969, pp. 1397-9; *Debates*, February 7, 1990, pp. 7953-4.

60. Standing Order 57.

61. *Journals*, December 14, 1964, p. 1000.

62. *Debates*, April 13, 1921, p. 2094; October 23, 1980, pp. 4049-53.

63. In 1969, Speaker Lamoureux delivered a ruling in which he reviewed the precedents and concluded that if the debate as a whole is to be closured, then any amendment or other motion applying to the main motion is included in the termination time set out in the closure rule (*Journals*, July 24, 1969, pp. 1393-6).

64. Standing Order 45(3).

65. On occasion, debate on a closured item has collapsed prior to the cut-off time. See, for example, *Journals*, June 26, 1989, pp. 450-3; March 4, 1996, pp. 33-5, 39-42; and *Debates*, March 4, 1996, pp. 270-3.

a closured motion must be "decided forthwith". A recorded division, if demanded, is therefore held immediately unless it is deferred by unanimous consent of the House to a later day, as it was done on occasion,[66] or with the agreement of the Whips of all recognized parties.[67]

In a Committee of the Whole, it is not necessary for all clauses of a bill to be called and then postponed before invoking closure.[68] Furthermore, once closure is adopted, the moment a clause of the bill is called by the Chair, it is deemed to be under consideration.[69] If consideration of one clause ends and debate begins on the next clause, Members have a further 20 minutes to speak to that clause.[70] The adoption of a closure motion in a sitting ensures that the committee stage will be completed in that sitting.[71]

Time Allocation

The time allocation rule allows for specific lengths of time to be set aside for the consideration of one or more stages of a public bill.[72] While the term "time allocation" connotes ideas of time management more than it does closure, a motion to allocate time may be used as a guillotine by the government. Indeed, although the rule permits the government to negotiate with opposition parties towards the adoption of a timetable for the consideration by the House of a bill at one or more stages (including the stage for the consideration of Senate amendments),[73] it also allows the government to impose strict limits on the time for debate.[74] While it has become the most used mechanism to curtail debate, time allocation remains a means of bringing parties together to negotiate an acceptable distribution of the time of the House.

HISTORICAL PERSPECTIVE

Like the closure rule, the time allocation rule came about in the aftermath of a controversy. During the Pipeline Debate of 1956,[75] closure was the only rule the

---

66. See *Journals*, December 6, 1995, pp. 2214-6; March 14, 1996, pp. 94-6.

67. Standing Order 45(7).

68. See, for example, *Debates*, April 1, 1932, p. 1609; May 31, 1956, pp. 4516-7; December 21, 1988, pp. 539-41.

69. *Debates*, May 24, 1956, pp. 4286-93.

70. *Debates*, April 28, 1919, p. 1796.

71. *Debates*, May 15, 1956, pp. 3968-72.

72. Standing Order 78.

73. See, for example, *Journals*, November 28, 1996, p. 930.

74. Since time allocation can be used to curtail debate, it is commonly referred to as "closure" in debate.

75. Between May 15 and June 5, 1956, closure was used at all four stages of the legislative process as it was then: resolution (*Debates*, May 15, 1956, p. 3895); second reading (*Debates*, May 22, 1956, p. 4165); Committee of the Whole (*Debates*, May 31, 1956, p. 4498); and third reading (*Debates*, June 5, 1956, p. 4689).

government could use to advance its legislation. Closure had come to be perceived as somewhat inflexible for the demands of a modern parliamentary democracy and inadequate as a tool with which to conduct the business of the House. Deliberations began, in the House and in committees, with a view to identifying ways in which the time of the House could be allotted for the consideration of specific items of legislation and for the planning of the session's work, something the closure rule could not provide since the process of giving notice, moving the motion and voting on it must be repeated at every stage of a given bill.[76]

Throughout the period of minority governments in the 1960s, the House attempted, unsuccessfully, to establish a procedural mechanism which would have formally structured the time of the House to facilitate the efficient conduct of debate. Members recognized that the amount and complexity of House business was increasing and that measures were necessary to ensure that the business would be expedited within a reasonable amount of time.[77] Throughout these years, the House agreed to establish a number of special committees charged with considering the procedures of the House and making suggestions to expedite public business.[78]

From the very beginning, the committees explored measures that would allow co-operation among parties. In the Tenth Report of the Special Committee on Procedure and Organization, presented to the House in 1964, reference was made to the difficulty of reaching all-party agreement on a proposal to deal with the fundamental question of the allocation of time.[79] Although the Committee indicated it would "continue to explore this basic question", it did not report further on this matter. Early in the following session, the government took the initiative by moving a motion, which, among other proposals, addressed the issue of time allocation. The motion called for a new Standing Order establishing a "Business Committee" comprised of a representative of each party of the House. Upon the request of a Minister, the Business Committee would consider, and, if agreement were reached, would recommend in a report to the House within three sitting days, an allocation of time for the specific item of business or stage of the matter referred to it. A motion could then be presented without notice by a Minister for concurrence in the report, to be

---

76. As comments from that period suggest, Members were eager to see the time of the House used more efficiently. See, for example, *Debates*, May 9, 1960, pp. 3685, 3692; January 18, 1961, p. 1169; March 26, 1962, pp. 2162-6.

77. See comments by Finance Minister Donald Fleming (*Debates*, May 9, 1960, pp. 3685, 3687); by Opposition Leader Lester B. Pearson and CCF Leader Hazen Argue (*Debates*, January 18, 1961, pp. 1169-70); by Opposition Leader John G. Diefenbaker (*Debates*, October 23, 1963, pp. 3925-31) and by Stanley Knowles (Winnipeg North Centre) (*Debates*, May 20, 1965, pp. 1530-1).

78. Motions to appoint the special committees were adopted on May 9, 1960 (*Journals*, p. 434); January 18, 1961 (*Journals*, p. 163); March 26, 1962 (*Journals*, p. 277); October 23, 1963 (*Journals*, p. 482); March 9, 1964 (*Journals*, pp. 76-7); January 25, 1967 (*Journals*, pp. 1227-8); May 8, 1967 (*Journals*, p. 12).

79. *Journals*, August 19, 1964, p. 633.

decided without debate or amendment. If, however, the Business Committee were unable to reach unanimous agreement or if it failed to report within the three-day period, a Minister could then give notice during Routine Proceedings that, at the next sitting of the House, he or she would move a motion allocating the time for the item of business or the stage.[80]

The motion was debated in the House for 12 days[81] and, throughout the debate, specific concerns were expressed with respect to the Business Committee proposal. The proposal was thus separated from the main motion and referred to a special committee for further study.[82] The special committee recommended in its report to the House another version of the time allocation proposal. The report was concurred in and a provisional rule, referred to as Standing Order 15-A, was adopted.[83] It was invoked on only three occasions from 1965 to 1968, but it became clear that the opposition parties were dissatisfied with it and frequent points of order were raised on how to interpret some of its provisions. In 1967, for example, the Speaker ruled that oral notice was sufficient for the purpose of the time allocation rule and that such a notice did not have to appear on the *Notice Paper*.[84]

When the Twenty-Eighth Parliament assembled in September 1968, the House decided that Provisional Standing Order 15-A would not be in effect.[85] A special procedure committee was established shortly thereafter[86] to consider, among other things, the issue of time allocation. In its Fourth Report, the Committee recommended a new rule on time allocation.[87] However, on December 20, 1968, the House agreed again to refer the issue to the new Standing Committee on Procedure and Organization for further consideration.[88]

Tensions continued between the government and the opposition as to the balance to be achieved between debating at length and perceived curtailment brought about by the provisional rules. It was not until 1969 that the House adopted a report recommending a measure for allocation of time, a forerunner to the present rule.[89] In its simplest form, the newly adopted Standing Order envisaged three options under which a time allotment order could be made, ranging from agreement between all

---

80. *Journals*, May 19, 1965, pp. 128-9.

81. See *Journals* for May 19, 20, 21, 25, 26 and 27, and June 1, 2, 3, 4, 7 and 8, 1965.

82. *Journals*, June 8, 1965, pp. 210-1.

83. *Journals*, June 11, 1965, pp. 219-23.

84. Speaker Lamoureux noted that the provisional Standing Order "not only dispenses with the requirement for 48 hours' notice with respect to a motion for time allocation; it also renders inoperative the ordinary machinery for putting a notice on the order paper" (*Debates*, April 20, 1967, pp. 15120-1).

85. *Journals*, September 20, 1968, p. 58.

86. *Journals*, September 24, 1968, p. 68

87. *Journals*, December 6, 1968, pp. 439-40.

88. *Journals*, December 20, 1968, p. 579.

89. The Third Report of the Standing Committee on Procedure and Organization was presented on June 20, 1969 (*Journals*, pp. 1211-2), and adopted on July 24, 1969 (*Journals*, pp. 1393-402), after debate which continued over 12 sitting days and was brought to an end with the aid of closure.

parties to the government acting alone after negotiation had failed to rally the support of any other party. Members of the opposition later expressed dissatisfaction with the interpretation of this Standing Order.[90] The fact that negotiations were to be held between parties, thus excluding independent Members, was also raised.[91]

In November 1975, the President of the Privy Council indicated his intention to bring proposals with implications for time allocation before the Standing Committee on Procedure and Organization.[92] Although it did not report to the House, the Committee created a sub-committee on the use of time which, among other items, reviewed and proposed alternative text to the Standing Order on time allocation.[93]

The wording of the Standing Order continued to cause procedural concern. In December 1978, after a point of order was raised, Speaker Jerome ruled that a time allocation motion could be moved covering both report and third reading stages, even though third reading had not yet been reached.[94] A position paper on reform, tabled by the government in November 1979, noted the ambiguity in the wording of the Standing Order and proposed that it be rewritten.[95] In March 1983, Speaker Sauvé confirmed that notice of intention to move a time allocation motion could be given at any time during the sitting.[96] In October 1983, she ruled that once the question on the motion for time allocation was proposed, the vote would be taken two hours after that proceeding had begun, and any superseding motions proposed during that time period would be disposed of at the end of the two-hour allotment and before voting on the time allocation motion.[97]

From May 1985, a new practice developed whereby time allocation motions were moved and debated following written government notices of motions under Government Orders. This written notice was in addition to the oral notice of intention to move such a motion which had been given to fulfil the requirements of the

---

90. On December 1, 1971, points of order were raised regarding the wording and interpretation of Standing Order 78(3). Speaker Lamoureux ruled that 48 hours' written notice was not required to move a time allocation motion and, furthermore, that it was regular to move such a motion for the disposal of proceedings for the stage being considered by the House (*Journals*, pp. 947-8).

91. In 1971, Speaker Lamoureux ruled that, in essence, independent Members would not receive the recognition accorded to Members represented by a party spokesperson, according to the wording of Standing Order 78(1) (*Journals*, December 30, 1971, pp. 1013-4).

92. *Debates*, November 13, 1975, p. 9022.

93. Standing Committee on Procedure and Organization, *Minutes of Proceedings and Evidence*, September 30, 1976, Issue No. 20, pp. 59-63.

94. *Debates*, December 20, 1978, pp. 2317-20.

95. See pages 20 and 21 of "Position Paper: The Reform of Parliament", tabled on November 23, 1979 (*Journals*, p. 260).

96. *Debates*, March 7, 1983, pp. 23510-1.

97. *Debates*, October 26, 1983, pp. 28357-8.

Standing Order. The new practice was confirmed by Speaker Bosley as an acceptable way of proceeding.[98]

In June 1987, amendments were adopted to provide that time allocation motions, after only oral notice, would be moved under "Government Orders" rather than under "Motions" during Routine Proceedings, as had been the practice. The revisions also provided that debate on the item of business under consideration at the time the motion was moved would be deemed adjourned.[99]

In August 1988, Speaker Fraser ruled that an oral notice of a time allocation motion need only be a notice of intention and not a notice of the text of the motion itself. In the same ruling, the Speaker further stated that the initiative of announcing any agreements (or lack thereof) to allot time rested with a Minister, who had to be a party to any such agreements.[100]

In 1991, following a further change to the Standing Order, the motion for time allocation moved without the agreement of all parties ceased to be a subject of debate or amendment.[101] Until then, such a motion was subject to amendment and could be debated for up to two hours, at which point all questions necessary to dispose of the motion were to be put by the Chair.

THE THREE OPTIONS

The time allocation rule is divided into three distinct sections. Each section specifies the conditions applying to the allocation of time, depending on the degree of support among the representatives of the recognized parties[102] in the House.

1. *All Parties Agree:*   The first section of the rule envisages agreement among the representatives of all the recognized parties in the House to allocate time to the proceedings at any or all stages of a public bill.[103] Notice is not required. In proposing the motion, a Minister first states that such an agreement has been reached[104] and then sets out the terms of the agreement, specifying the number of days or hours of debate to be allocated.[105] The Speaker then puts the question to the House, which is decided without debate or amendment.

---

98. *Debates*, May 16, 1985, pp. 4821-2.

99. *Journals*, June 3, 1987, pp. 1026-7.

100. *Debates*, August 15, 1988, pp. 18309-11; August 16, 1988, pp. 18352-5, 18380-1.

101. *Journals*, April 11, 1991, pp. 2915-6.

102. For a procedural definition of a recognized party, see Chapter 1, "Parliamentary Institutions". See also *Journals*, December 30, 1971, pp. 1013-4; *Debates*, April 2, 1993, p. 18052.

103. Standing Order 78(1).

104. See, for example, *Debates*, July 22, 1977, p. 7916.

105. There are times when, rather than resorting to the written rule, party representatives agree on an allocation of time, which the House then adopts by unanimous consent. See, for example *Journals*, October 26, 1978, pp. 69-70 (timetable for the consideration of a bill, including number of committee meetings, instruction to amend, and committee reporting deadline); March 10, 1987, p. 568 (agreement to complete consideration of two bills at all stages); March 20, 1992, p. 1192 (agreement to consider all stages of a bill).

2. *Majority of Parties Agree:*   The second section of the rule envisages agreement among a majority of the representatives of the recognized parties in the House.[106] In these circumstances, as in the case of all-party agreement, the government must be a party to any agreement reached.[107] The motion may not cover more than one stage of the legislative process. It may, however, apply both to report stage and third reading, if it is consistent with the rule requiring a separate day for debate at third reading when a bill has been debated or amended at report stage.[108] Again, no notice is required. Prior to moving the motion, the Minister states that a majority of party representatives have agreed to a proposed allocation of time.[109] The motion specifies how many days or hours are to be allocated. The day on which the motion is adopted is counted as one sitting day for this purpose, if it is moved and carried at the beginning of Government Orders.[110]

3. *No Agreement:*   The third section of the rule permits the government unilaterally to propose an allocation of time.[111] In this case, an oral notice of intention to move the motion is required.[112] The motion can propose only the allocation of time for one stage of the legislative process, that being the stage then under consideration. However, the motion can cover both report stage and third reading, provided it is consistent with the rule which requires a separate day for third reading when a bill has been debated or amended at report stage.[113] The amount of time allocated for any stage may not be less than one sitting day.

NOTICE

Oral notice is required when the government wishes to propose its own timetable in the absence of any time allocation agreement among representatives from all or a majority of the recognized parties.[114] The notice may be given only after debate has

---

106. Standing Order 78(2).

107. *Debates*, August 16, 1988, pp. 18380-1. On this occasion, the two parties in opposition contended that an agreement had been reached pursuant to the rule, to which the government was not a party; however, the Chair ruled that the initiative of announcing any agreement or lack thereof is clearly with the government (i.e., a Minister), who must be party to any agreement and whose support is signified by his or her rising under the terms of the Standing Order.

108. Standing Order 76.1(10).

109. Standing Order 78(2)(*a*). See, for example, *Journals*, June 21, 1994, pp. 633-7, when no less than four motions were moved and adopted to allocate time in respect to four bills.

110. Standing Order 78(2)(*b*).

111. Standing Order 78(3).

112. See, for example, *Debates*, December 1, 1971, pp. 10050-1.

113. Standing Order 76.1(10).

114. Written notice of a motion for the allocation of time is acceptable when given in addition to oral notice (see Speaker Bosley's ruling, *Debates*, May 16, 1985, pp. 4821-2).

begun on the stage of the bill to which the time allocation motion is to apply.[115] It must be given by a Minister, from his or her place in the House,[116] any time during the course of the sitting;[117] the time allocation motion can then be moved at any future sitting of the House, even several days or weeks later.

The notice is to state that agreement could not be reached under the other provisions of the rule and that the government therefore intends to propose a motion to allocate time in respect of a particular stage of a particular bill.[118] The notice need only express the intention of the government; it need not include the terms of the motion to follow.[119] Once given, a notice of time allocation may be withdrawn; similarly, notice may be given without a motion being moved subsequently.

MOTION TO ALLOCATE TIME

The wording of a motion for time allocation must be specific as to the terms of the allocation of time. In most cases, time is allocated in terms of sitting days or hours; however, on at least one occasion, time was allocated in increments of less than one hour per stage of the affected bill.[120] In all cases, a motion for time allocation must be moved by a Minister in the House, and is neither debatable nor amendable.[121]

In cases when there is agreement among the party representatives, the motion has normally been moved under "Motions" during Routine Proceedings. In circumstances when a majority agree on the allocation of time, or when no agreement has been reached, the motion is moved under Government Orders. Debate on any item of business interrupted by the moving of a motion for time allocation is deemed adjourned.[122] Once the motion is moved, the question is put forthwith.

After the adoption of a motion for time allocation, debate at the stage or stages of the bill in question then becomes subject to the time limits imposed by the motion. The day on which the time allocation motion is adopted may be counted as one sitting day for that purpose, provided the motion is moved and adopted at the beginning

---

115. See, for example, *Debates*, April 2, 1990, pp. 10102-3; April 3, 1990, p. 10124.

116. Standing Order 78(3). The Speaker has ruled that oral notice of an intention to move a motion for time allocation is not covered by the rule pertaining to notice (Standing Order 54(1)) and that 48 hours' written notice is therefore not required (*Journals*, December 1, 1971, p. 948).

117. See, for example, *Debates*, March 7, 1983, p. 23511; October 19, 1983, pp. 28127-9; June 3, 1988, pp. 16127-8.

118. Standing Order 78(3). See, for example, *Debates*, December 1, 1982, p. 21172; *Journals*, December 1, 1982, p. 5408.

119. See Speaker Fraser's ruling, *Debates*, August 16, 1988, pp. 18380-1.

120. In this case, 0.1 hour was allocated to the report stage and 0.25 hour to third reading (all-party agreement) (*Journals*, April 2, 1993, pp. 2791-2).

121. Standing Order 78.

122. Standing Order 78(2)(*a*), (3)(*a*).

of Government Orders and the bill is taken up immediately.[123] The bill may also be taken up at a future sitting of the House.[124] The normal rules of debate apply. At the expiry of the time allocated for a given stage, any proceedings before the House are interrupted, and the Chair puts every question necessary for the disposal of the bill at that stage. If a recorded division is demanded, the bells summoning the Members will ring for not longer than 15 minutes.[125] Recorded divisions on bills under time allocation are not ordinarily deferred, though deferrals may take place by special order,[126] by automatic deferral of the vote pursuant to rules of the House,[127] or by agreement of the Whips of all recognized parties.[128] When debate concludes prior to the end of the allotted time, if a recorded division is demanded, the bells will ring for not more than 30 minutes, and the vote may be deferred by either the Chief Government Whip or the Chief Opposition Whip.[129]

At times, objections have been raised as to the circumstances in which agreement was reached or to the nature of the consultations undertaken by the government. As with closure, the Speaker has ruled that the Chair possesses no discretionary authority to refuse to put a motion of time allocation if all the procedural exigencies have been observed.[130] The Speaker has stated that the wording of the rule does not define the nature of the consultations which are to be held by the Minister and representatives of the other parties, and has further ruled that the Chair has no authority to determine whether or not consultation took place nor what constitutes consultation among the representatives of the parties.[131]

---

123. Standing Order 78(3)(*b*).

124. For example, consideration of Bill C-85 (*Canagrex Act*) was resumed several months after a time allocation motion for both report stage and third reading had been adopted by the House (*Journals*, December 13, 1982, p. 5458 (notice of time allocation given); December 16, 1982, pp. 5470-1 (time allocation motion adopted); June 7, 1983, pp. 5972-87 (report stage); June 13, 1983, pp. 6000-2 (third reading)).

125. Standing Order 45(3).

126. In 1987, for example, the question on the motion for third reading of a bill, under an order for time allocation adopted on June 15 (*Journals*, pp. 1094-5), was put on June 17 and deferred to June 18, pursuant to a special order adopted on June 16 (*Journals*, p. 1175).

127. Standing Order 45(6)(*a*). See, for example, *Journals*, November 27, 1992, p. 2252; December 1, 1995, p. 2199; March 12, 1999, p. 1601.

128. Standing Order 45(7).

129. Standing Order 45(5). See, for example, *Journals*, November 29, 1996, p. 939.

130. *Debates*, April 4, 1990, pp. 10183-5; December 9, 1992, pp. 14917-23; March 31, 1993, pp. 17854-62.

131. *Debates*, June 6, 1988, pp. 16139, 16142-9; August 16, 1988, pp. 18380-1; March 29, 1990, pp. 9916-7; October 1, 1990, p. 13622.

"Routine Motion" by a Minister

If, at any time during a sitting of the House, unanimous consent is denied for the presentation of a "routine motion", a Minister may request during Routine Proceedings that the Speaker put the motion.[132] For that purpose, a "routine motion" refers to motions which may be required for the observance of the proprieties of the House, the maintenance of its authority, the management of its business, the arrangement of its proceedings, the establishment of the powers of its committees, the correctness of its records or the fixing of its sitting days or the times of its meeting or adjournment.[133] The motion, which is neither debatable nor amendable, is immediately put to the House by the Speaker. If 25 Members or more oppose the motion, it is deemed withdrawn;[134] otherwise, it is adopted.[135]

While it appeared at first that the range of motions to which this process could be used would be limited, over the years the rule has been used to extend a sitting in order to sit on the weekend;[136] to extend the sitting to consider Government Orders;[137] to deal with a specific motion under Government Business;[138] to pass a government bill at all stages;[139] to establish the length of speeches during a "take note" debate;[140] and to attempt to rescind an Order of the House.[141] There is no limit on how often the government can resort to this rule during one sitting.

Adopted in 1991,[142] this procedure was relatively unused until the Thirty-Sixth Parliament (1997-   ).[143] Prior to its adoption, it was argued that the new proposed rule would have a negative impact on Members' ability to debate government motions and "override unanimous consent".[144] On April 9, 1991, Speaker Fraser, while pointing out that the range of motions to which the proposed procedure would

---

132. Standing Order 56.1.

133. Standing Order 56.1(1)(*b*).

134. See, for example, *Journals*, March 22, 1999, p. 1645.

135. See, for example, *Journals*, March 16, 1995, p. 1226; April 24, 1997, pp. 1524-5.

136. See, for example, *Journals*, March 23, 1995, p. 1265.

137. See, for example, *Journals*, June 15, 1995, p. 1754.

138. See, for example, *Journals,* April 12, 1999, p. 1687.

139. See, for example, *Journals,* December 1, 1997, pp. 290-1.

140. See, for example, *Journals,* April 12, 1999, p. 1687.

141. See, for example, *Journals,* June 9, 1998, p. 954.

142. *Journals*, April 11, 1991, p. 2913.

143. Practically unused during the Thirty-Fifth Parliament, Standing Order 56.1 was moved six times between September 1997 and June 1999. It could be argued that, because of the 25-Member provision, Standing Order 56.1 is particularly attractive when there are many officially recognized opposition parties.

144. See, for example, *Debates*, March 26, 1991, p. 19044.

apply was very limited, also suggested that the new Standing Order was to be understood as another procedurally acceptable mechanism for limiting debate: "There are certain similarities also between the proposal and existing Standing Order 78 respecting time allocation in that both use a ladder-like type of approach depending upon the extent of agreement forthcoming to securing the right to propose the motion".[145]

Suspension of Standing Orders for Matter of Urgent Nature

When a situation arises that the government considers urgent, a Minister may move that the House suspend certain Standing Orders respecting notice requirements and the times of sitting in connection with that matter.[146] For example, motion can be used to waive notice for the introduction of a bill or for any stage at which a notice is required.[147] In moving the motion, the Minister gives reasons for the urgency of the situation and, after the motion has been seconded, the Speaker immediately proposes the question.[148] In doing so, the Speaker may allow up to one hour of uninterrupted debate.[149] Speeches are limited to 10 minutes each and no amendment is allowed except by another Minister. When putting the question, the Speaker is bound to ask those Members opposed to rise. If fewer than 10 do so, the motion is automatically adopted;[150] if 10 or more do so, it is deemed to have been withdrawn.[151] The resulting order, if the motion is adopted, applies only to the proceedings specified in that order.

This Standing Order is relatively recent and has been invoked infrequently since its adoption in 1968. The reasons for its establishment go back to 1964, when Prime Minister Pearson moved a motion, without notice, to send a Canadian peacekeeping force to Cyprus. Although the motion appeared to have the overall support of the House, some Members objected to the lack of notice. They argued that 48 hours' advance warning was required before such an important matter could be discussed.

---

145. *Debates*, April 9, 1991, pp. 19233-7, especially p. 19236.

146. Standing Order 53.

147. In 1992, Standing Order 53(1) was used to waive the 48-hour notice requirement for the beginning of the report stage of a government bill (*Journals*, June 1, 1992, pp. 1560-1).

148. In 1992, Deputy Speaker Champagne ruled the motion out of order because, contrary to the terms of Standing Order 53(2), the Minister had not stated the reasons for the urgency of the motion when he presented it to the House. See *Debates*, December 11, 1992, pp. 15132-3.

149. See, for example, *Debates*, June 10, 1999, pp. 16227-30.

150. See, for example, *Journals*, March 15, 1995, p. 1219.

151. See, for example, *Journals*, March 20, 1995, p. 1240; June 10, 1999, p. 2097.

Stating that the Prime Minister had obtained "leave", the Deputy Speaker dismissed the objections and allowed the House to proceed with the motion.[152]

Then, in 1966, when the House was asked to deal urgently with a strike by air traffic controllers, the Minister of Public Works suggested a procedural mechanism for the government to deal with urgent matters. As he explained, "… a private member has a right to move the adjournment of the house to consider a matter of urgent public importance. … It is a curious anomaly that there is no corresponding provision enabling the government to bring any proceedings relating to the same matter before the house without notice."[153] Although opposition Members felt action was required, in the end, the Minister's proposal was withdrawn.[154]

When the present rule was agreed to two years later in 1968, it was evident from its wording that the events of 1966 had been taken into account. Indeed, the new rule was similar to the one proposed in 1966. In suggesting the addition of the rule, the Special Committee on Procedure wrote: "… it seems reasonable to expect that the normal requirement of a notice of motion … might be dispensed with for the purpose of dealing with matters of urgency when the overwhelming majority of the House recognizes that it would be desirable to do so. It seems intolerable … that a single dissenting voice should be permitted to frustrate the otherwise unanimous will of the House…."[155] The rule has not been altered except for minor gender reference changes in 1982.

While intended to be used to waive notice requirements and set times of sitting, this Standing Order has been used to outline terms of debate in a manner that resembles time allocation.[156]

---

152. *Debates*, March 13, 1964, pp. 911, 916, 921-2.

153. *Debates*, December 16, 1966, pp. 11230-1.

154. See *Debates*, December 16, 1966, pp. 11229-34.

155. See the Third Report of the Special Committee on Procedure, presented on December 6, 1968 (*Journals*, p. 435).

156. See, for example, *Journals*, September 16, 1991, pp. 270-1.

15

Special Debates

Debate is not a sin, a mistake, an error or something to be put up with in parliament. Debate is the essence of parliament.

STANLEY KNOWLES, M.P. (Winnipeg North Centre)
(*Debates,* December 10, 1968, p. 3763)

From time to time either because of certain parliamentary events or because of some urgency, the House will put aside its normal way of conducting debate in the House to consider matters that are governed by special rules. These rules are found in the Standing Orders in a chapter entitled "Special Debates". Included in this chapter are rules pertaining to the debate on the Address in Reply to the Speech from the Throne (also known as the Throne Speech Debate), emergency debates, debates to suspend certain Standing Orders to consider urgent matters, and the debate to take note of the Standing Orders. These debates and the related Standing Orders are examined here.

Also examined in this chapter are two other types of debates which are not specifically provided for in the Standing Orders, but whose proceedings are sometimes circumscribed by special procedures. On occasion, the government has initiated debates on a number of issues to allow Members to express their views prior to a decision being taken by the government. This has particularly been the case since the beginning of the Thirty-Fifth Parliament in 1994. These debates have been labelled "take note" debates. In addition, statutory debates occasionally take place in the House. A statutory debate occurs when a statute has included provisions for a debate on the floor of the House with regard to an order, regulation, declaration, guideline or other instrument of delegated legislation.

Address in Reply to the Speech from the Throne

DESIGNATING A DAY FOR CONSIDERATION

Traditionally at the beginning of a session, when the House returns from the Senate after the Speech from the Throne, a day is designated for the consideration of that Speech. The Prime Minister moves a motion to consider the Throne Speech either later that day or at the next sitting of the House.[1] This motion does not require notice and, though generally moved and adopted without debate, is debatable and amendable.[2]

INITIATING DEBATE

On the day specified in the motion for the consideration of the Speech from the Throne, a government backbencher moves that an Address be presented to the Governor General (or, depending on who delivered the speech, to the Sovereign or to the Administrator of the Government of Canada) "to offer our humble thanks ... for the gracious speech which Your Excellency has addressed ...". This allows for wide-ranging debate on the government policies announced in the Throne Speech, thus providing a rare opportunity for Members to address topics of their choice.

From 1867 to 1893, the motion for the Address in Reply to the Speech from the Throne typically consisted of several paragraphs, each of which received separate consideration. The paragraphs collectively formed a resolution which was adopted and referred to a select committee. The committee would then report the Address in Reply to the House where it would be agreed to, engrossed (that is, transcribed upon

---

1. See, for example, *Journals*, September 23, 1997, p. 6. It is noted in *Bourinot* (4th ed., p. 95) that other Ministers in the absence of the Prime Minister may move this motion. While infrequent, this has occurred. Examples of this can be found on April 18, 1895, when George Eulas Foster, Minister of Finance and Receiver General in the Cabinet of Prime Minister Mackenzie Bowell, moved the motion (see *Journals*, April 18, 1895, p. 5) and on January 8, 1926, when Ernest Lapointe, Minister of Justice and Attorney General in the Cabinet of Prime Minister William Lyon Mackenzie King, moved the motion (see *Journals*, January 8, 1926, p. 12). Since the 1950s, the Prime Minister has moved the motion. Between 1896 and 1956, the motion appointed a specific day on which consideration of the Speech from the Throne would begin. In 1940, for the Sixth Session of the Eighteenth Parliament, no Address debate was held. The Session lasted only one day, January 25, 1940, with the government using the Speech from the Throne to advise Parliament of its intention to dissolve Parliament in order to hold a general election. Dissolution occurred the same day (see *Journals*, January 25, 1940, pp. 1, 8, 23-5).

2. On at least three occasions debate has occurred. On January 8, 1926, an amendment was moved to the motion to take into consideration the Speech of the Governor General. This amendment was debated over the course of two sittings and negatived on a recorded division (see *Journals*, January 8, 1926, pp. 12-3; January 14, 1926, pp. 28-9). On February 17, 1972, an amendment to the motion to consider the Speech of the Governor General to provide for a 40-minute oral Question Period was proposed. The Speaker ruled the amendment out of order because it was a substantive motion which could not be attached to the motion before the House. The Speaker noted, however, that the motion could be amended if a procedurally acceptable amendment were proposed (see *Journals*, February 17, 1972, pp. 5-6). The third instance of debate on the motion for consideration can be found in *Journals*, December 12, 1988, p. 6.

parchment) and presented to the Governor General. This cumbersome procedure was changed in 1893, when a new practice was adopted whereby the House itself considered the Address in the form of a presentation to the Governor General.[3] It was not until 1903 that the motion for an Address in Reply became one brief paragraph of thanks for the Speech from the Throne.[4]

Following the mover's speech, a second government backbencher (traditionally one who speaks the official language that is not that of the mover) is recognized to speak to and second the motion. Both the mover and seconder are typically chosen from the ranks of those Members most recently elected.[5] Their speeches have not been followed by the usual 10-minute period for questions and comments and, at the conclusion of the seconder's speech, the debate is normally adjourned by the Leader of the Opposition.[6] The usual practice is for the Prime Minister or a Minister, often the Government House Leader or President of the Privy Council, to subsequently move the adjournment of the House.[7]

RESUMING DEBATE ON THE ADDRESS

The Standing Orders provide for six additional days of debate on the motion and on any amendments proposed thereto.[8] These days are designated by a Minister, usually the Government House Leader, and are not necessarily consecutive. Since 1955, the Standing Orders have provided that when the Order of the Day is called to resume debate on the motion for an Address in Reply, the Order takes precedence over all other business of the House, with the exception of the daily routine of business—that

---

3. *Journals*, January 30, 1893, p. 33.

4. *Journals*, March 13, 1903, p. 25.

5. *Bourinot*, 4th ed., p. 97.

6. The Leader of the Opposition has regularly adjourned the debate since 1935 (see, for example, *Debates*, February 27, 1996, p. 26; September 23, 1997, p. 17).

7. See, for example, *Debates*, September 23, 1997, p. 18. From 1904 until 1979 with only a few exceptions, the Prime Minister would move the motion that the House do now adjourn. Since 1980 with one exception, a Minister has moved the adjournment of the House. In 1983, the Parliamentary Secretary to the President of the Privy Council moved the adjournment of the House (see *Journals*, December 8, 1983, p. 21). On April 4, 1989, the House did not adjourn in the traditional way. The Speaker accepted an application for an emergency debate to consider the oil spill which had occurred outside the Port of Valdez, Alaska. That day the motion to adjourn the debate on the Address in Reply was moved by the Leader of the Opposition, the sitting was suspended until 8:00 p.m., and the emergency debate was held pursuant to the Standing Orders. At 2:05 a.m., the Speaker declared the motion carried and the House adjourned (see *Journals*, April 4, 1989, pp. 22-3). Again in 1996, the House did not adjourn in the traditional way: following the motion by the Leader of the Opposition to adjourn the debate, Government Orders were called. An opposition Member (Gilles Duceppe (Laurier–Sainte-Marie)) subsequently rose on a point of order to object to the receivability of a government motion to reinstate a number of items from the previous session. Debate on the point of order continued until the usual hour of daily adjournment, at which time the Deputy Speaker adjourned the sitting until the following day (see *Debates*, February 27, 1996, pp. 26-30).

8. Standing Order 50(1).

is, Routine Proceedings, Statements by Members and Oral Questions.[9] Private Members' Business is also suspended on these days.[10]

RULES OF DEBATE ON THE ADDRESS

Leaders' Day

The first day of resumed debate is known as "Leaders' Day". It is traditional for the Leader of the Opposition to speak first and to move an amendment to the main motion. Normally, the Prime Minister speaks next and that speech is followed by that of the leader of the second largest party in opposition, who may propose an amendment to the amendment. Then other leaders of parties which have official status in the House are recognized in turn.[11] Leaders of parties holding fewer than 12 seats are not automatically recognized for debate on Leaders' Day.[12]

While this has been the customary speaking order, there is no specific rule stating the order in which party leaders are recognized during the debate on the Address in Reply. During the Address in Reply proceedings in 1989, the leader of the second largest party in opposition spoke after the Leader of the Opposition; the Prime Minister delivered his speech the following day.[13] In 1991, when again the Prime Minister did not rise to speak after the speech of the Leader of the Opposition, a complaint was lodged with the Chair by the Opposition House Leader. The Speaker ruled that in the absence of any Standing Order to this effect, Members were not bound to any particular speaking order.[14] The Prime Minister subsequently addressed the House the next day, and the leader of the second largest party in opposition delivered her speech immediately thereafter.

---

9. Standing Order 50(3). See also *Journals*, July 12, 1955, pp. 881-945. Note pp. 908-9. Beginning in the 1890s and until 1950, the House routinely agreed that the debate on the Address in Reply to the Speech from the Throne should have varying degrees of precedence over other business (see, for example, *Journals*, February 7, 1898, p. 23; December 8, 1947, p. 40). Such motions were not moved in 1903, 1905, either session in 1906, 1910, the first session in 1914, 1930, either session in 1932, 1934, 1935, and the second session in 1939 and 1945.

10. Standing Order 50(4).

11. In 1997, the House adopted a motion whereby the House would not adjourn until the leaders of all recognized parties had spoken in the debate on the Address (see *Journals*, September 23, 1997, p. 9).

12. *Debates*, October 10, 1979, pp. 47-51; October 11, 1979, p. 69.

13. See *Debates*, April 5, 1989, p. 131, where New Democratic Party Leader Edward Broadbent spoke after the Leader of the Opposition, John Turner; and *Debates*, April 6, 1989, p. 145, where Prime Minister Brian Mulroney spoke.

14. *Debates*, May 14, 1991, p. 24.

Duration of Debate on the Address

Until 1955, there was no prescribed limit on the length of the debate on the Address in Reply, and debates lasted anywhere from one to a record length of 28 days. [15] In 1955, further to the recommendations of a special committee on procedure, the House first instituted a limit on the length of debate on the Address in Reply when it agreed to a maximum of 10 days of debate and to morning sittings (not then a feature of the regular sitting day) for the duration of the debate. [16] This was further reduced to eight days in 1960, [17] and in 1991 the Standing Orders were again amended to provide for a maximum of six days of debate. [18]

There have been, however, a number of instances where the debate lasted for less than the maximum number of days provided for in the Standing Orders and the House voted on the motion. [19] There have also been instances where the debate was not completed because of either a prorogation or dissolution: in 1988, only the mover and seconder of the motion spoke, no further debate occurred on the Address in Reply and the session was ended by prorogation after only 11 sittings; in 1997, the session ended when Parliament was dissolved for a general election after 164 sittings and only five of the six days provided for the Address debate having been completed. [20]

As indicated in the Standing Orders, any unused days may be added, if the House so agrees, to the number of allotted days for the Supply period in which they occur, although this rule has never been applied since coming into effect in 1968. [21]

Length of Speeches on the Address Debate

Members may speak for a maximum of 20 minutes, followed by a 10-minute period for questions and comments with the exception of the Prime Minister and Leader of the Opposition (who have unlimited time for debate with no period for questions and

---

15. In 1926, the government imposed closure on the 28th day of debate in order to terminate these proceedings so that it could adjourn the House for a brief period to prepare the work of the session (see *Journals*, March 2, 1926, pp. 123-7). The lengthy debate was the result of the challenge by the Conservative Opposition led by Arthur Meighen of the King Government's right to summon Parliament and remain in office following the results of the General Election of October 29, 1925. See the speech of Ernest Lapointe (Leader of the House) in *Debates*, March 2, 1926, pp. 1435-8.

16. *Journals*, July 12, 1955, pp. 881, 908-9.

17. *Journals*, July 25, 1960, p. 825; August 8, 1960, p. 898.

18. Standing Order 50(1). See also *Journals*, April 11, 1991, pp. 2905, 2912.

19. See, for example, Address debates in 1956 (both sessions), 1960 (second session), 1965, 1968 and 1978.

20. This occurred on one other occasion, but before the introduction of time limits. In 1873, the Second Session of the Second Parliament was ended by prorogation before decisions were reached on the sub-amendment, amendment and main motion.

21. Standing Order 81(11). The first occasion when it could have occurred was in 1978 when the Address in Reply debate concluded after only six days of debate. At that time the Standing Order provided for eight days of resumed debate. However, on October 20, 1978, the House adopted a special order designating October 30, 1978, the sixth and final appointed day (see *Journals*, October 20, 1978, p. 42). In the discussion which took place in the House, it was noted and agreed that the two days taken away from the debate would not be added to the number of allotted days (see *Debates*, October 20, 1978, pp. 312-3).

comments).[22] The House has sometimes extended to other party leaders the opportunity to speak longer than 20 minutes with no period for questions and comments following their speeches.[23] Any Member may be recognized to speak in this debate, though the speaking order follows the general rotation reflecting party standings in the House. There has also been a tendency to either reduce the length of speeches, including the period for questions and comments, or to discontinue the questions and comments period altogether, at times during the debate in order to allow as many Members as possible to speak to the motion.[24]

DISPOSAL OF AMENDMENTS AND TERMINATION OF THE DEBATE ON THE ADDRESS

In the early years of Confederation, one view held that attempts to amend the Address in Reply motion ought not to be made.[25] In 1873, the first amendments were moved to the Address in Reply motion when a motion of censure was made against the government for its conduct in the "Pacific Scandal". Although a sub-amendment subsequently proposed an expression of confidence in the government,[26] Parliament was prorogued following a change in government before the amendments were put to a vote. Amendments were moved again in 1893 and 1899.[27] Over the course of the next 40 years, amendments were commonly moved, although not systematically. It was not until World War II that the practice of moving amendments to the Address in Reply motion became more entrenched.

Until 1955, there were no provisions in the Standing Orders dealing with the moving of amendments or when to put the question thereon. As with an amendment to any motion, the question was put when no Member rose to speak to it. In 1955, a new Standing Order was adopted which established a framework for deciding amendments.[28]

---

22. Standing Order 50(2). The length of speeches on the motion for an Address in Reply has been subject to limitation since 1960 when the House adopted amendments to the Standing Orders, which provided for speeches of 30 minutes in length with 40 minutes being granted to the movers of amendments and sub-amendments (see *Journals*, July 25, 1960, p. 825-6; August 8, 1960, p. 898). In 1982, time limits were reduced to their present length (see *Journals*, November 29, 1982, p. 5400, and the Special Committee on Standing Orders and Procedure, Third Report, *Minutes of Proceedings and Evidence,* November 5, 1982, pp. 3, 16-7).

23. See, for example, *Debates*, November 7, 1984, p. 31; October 3, 1986, p. 52; and May 15, 1991, p. 114.

24. See, for example, *Debates*, April 12, 1989, pp. 404-5; May 22, 1991, p. 433; January 28, 1994, p. 594; October 3, 1997, pp. 484, 486. The provisions of Standing Order 43(2) have also been applied to the Address Debate (see, for example, *Debates*, January 20, 1994, p. 72).

25. This emulated British practice. See *Debates*, February 5, 1875, p. 12; February 11, 1878, p. 36; February 17, 1879, p. 24.

26. *Journals*, October 27, 1873, p. 126; October 28, 1873, p. 128.

27. *Journals*, January 30, 1893, pp. 34-5; April 13, 1899, p. 55; April 18, 1899, pp. 64-5.

28. *Journals*, July 12, 1955, pp. 881-945, in particular pp. 908-9.

While there are no rules governing when amendments are to be moved or if they have to be moved at all, the Standing Orders do set out provisions for the disposal of all amendments proposed before the main motion is put to the House: on the second day of the resumed debate, any sub-amendment before the House is disposed of and on the fourth day of debate any amendment and sub-amendment are disposed of. Amendments are prohibited on the last two days of the debate.

Recent practice has been that the Leader of the Opposition moves an amendment on the first day of resumed debate. A sub-amendment is then normally proposed by the leader of the second largest opposition party. It is not unusual, however, for another Member from that party to do so.[29]

The first sub-amendment must be disposed of on the second appointed day when the Speaker interrupts the debate 15 minutes before the ordinary hour of daily adjournment to put the question.[30] Sub-amendments may again be proposed on the third or fourth day. On the fourth day, the Speaker interrupts the debate 30 minutes before the ordinary hour of daily adjournment to dispose of any amendment or sub-amendment before the House.[31] No further amendments are permitted to the main motion on the fifth and sixth days.[32] Finally on the sixth day, unless the debate has previously concluded, the Speaker interrupts the debate 15 minutes before the ordinary hour of daily adjournment to put all the questions necessary to dispose of the main motion.[33] Since the Standing Orders were amended in 1991 to limit the Throne Speech Debate to six days, there have been three instances of a sub-amendment being disposed of on the second day and a sub-amendment and an amendment being disposed of on the fourth day.[34]

Given the general nature of the motion, the rule of relevance is not strictly applied to the proposed amendment (as opposed to the sub-amendments). However, precedents indicate that an amendment should add some distinct element of its own, whereas a sub-amendment must be relevant to the amendment and cannot raise a new issue.[35] A sub-amendment adding words with the effect of making the

---

29. See, for example, *Journals*, May 14, 1991, p. 20.

30. Standing Order 50(5).

31. Standing Order 50(6).

32. Standing Order 50(7).

33. Standing Order 50(8). Although not frequent, there have been instances of recorded divisions on the main motion (see, for example, *Journals*, March 2, 1926, pp. 126-7; January 23, 1957, pp. 69-70; October 11, 1962, pp. 60-1; February 1, 1994, pp. 89-91).

34. Two sub-amendments were moved, one by an independent Member, to the Address in Reply motion during the Third Session of the Thirty-Fourth Parliament (see *Journals*, May 14, 1991, p. 20; May 16, 1991, p. 36). Two sub-amendments were moved by the Members of the Reform Party during the Second Session of the Thirty-Fifth Parliament (see *Journals*, February 28, 1996, pp. 8-9; March 5, 1996, p. 47). During the First Session of the Thirty-Sixth Parliament, one sub-amendment was moved by a Member of the Bloc Québécois (*Journals*, September 24, 1997, p. 20) and the other by a Member of the New Democratic Party (*Journals*, September 29, 1997, p. 39).

35. See, for example, *Journals*, February 19, 1942, pp. 61-3; January 24, 1966, pp. 43-4; January 11, 1973, p. 28.

amendment a motion of non-confidence in the official opposition has been ruled inadmissible since "votes of want of confidence are only directed against the Government of the day".[36] The Speaker has ruled out of order amendments which were not deemed to challenge directly the government's policies[37] or which sought to increase expenditures, a motion which requires a Royal Recommendation.[38] An amendment similar to one on which the House had already expressed a judgement earlier in the debate has also been disallowed.[39]

On only two occasions has the Address in Reply been adopted with an amendment. In each instance an amendment moved by a Member of the Opposition had itself been amended by a sub-amendment moved by a Member of the government party.[40]

ENGROSSING OF ADDRESS

Immediately after the adoption of the motion for the Address in Reply, the House adopts a motion without debate or amendment that the Address be engrossed, that is, transcribed upon parchment, and presented to the Governor General in person by the Speakers of the House of Commons and the Senate.[41] It is customary for the Speakers to be accompanied by a few invited Members (including the mover and seconder of the Address, as well as the House Leaders and the party Whips) and the Clerks of both Houses.

36. *Journals*, February 6, 1934, p. 51.

37. *Journals*, January 30, 1959, pp. 56-7. The amendment in question called upon the government to establish a committee to investigate certain items noted in the amendment.

38. *Journals*, March 5, 1948, pp. 223-5.

39. *Journals*, April 12, 1965, p. 34. Similarly, later during the session, if amendments comparable to those on which the House decided during the Address in Reply debate are moved to other motions, these amendments could be ruled out of order (*Journals*, May 3, 1955, pp. 545-6).

40. *Journals*, April 18, 1899, pp. 64-5; December 5, 1951, pp. 258-62; December 12, 1951, pp. 305-6. In both cases the sub-amendments supported the government. While this may appear to be contradictory to the purposes of such amendments, the effects were minimal. In the first instance which occurred in 1899, the Address in Reply consisted of nine paragraphs. The amendment added a tenth paragraph calling for the appointment of an independent judicial commission to investigate the administration of the Yukon Territory. The sub-amendment noted the speed at which the government had acted on complaints and praised the integrity of the Commissioner appointed. The second example occurred in 1951. To an amendment critical of the government's failure to make a payment to grain producers, a Member of the government party moved a sub-amendment commending the government for its continuing attention to the problems of farmers. A point of order was raised that the proposed sub-amendment was out of order on the grounds that it was in effect not an amendment, but a further motion of approval and approbation of the government. In his ruling, Speaker Macdonald held that the sub-amendment was relevant to the amendment and that it did not constitute either a direct or an expanded negative of the main amendment. He allowed the proposed sub-amendment to stand.

41. See, for example, *Journals*, October 3, 1997, p. 76.

Standing Orders and Procedure

The Standing Orders provide for a one-day special debate on the Standing Orders and procedures of the House and its committees early in each Parliament.[42] This provision was adopted by the House in 1982 on the recommendation of a special committee on procedure which believed an opportunity should be provided for Members to express their views on this matter.[43]

INITIATING DEBATE

The Standing Order in question provides for an automatic debate on the motion "That this House takes note of the Standing Orders and procedures of the House and its committees" on a day designated by a Minister between the sixtieth and ninetieth sitting day of the first session of a Parliament. If no day is designated, the debate is held on the ninetieth sitting day.[44]

This Standing Order was adopted in 1982. Such a debate on the rules and procedures of the House could have first occurred in 1984; however, well before the sixtieth day, the House unanimously agreed to suspend the Standing Order.[45] The next opportunity for the House to hold the debate came in 1988, but the First Session of the Thirty-Fourth Parliament ended after only 11 sitting days, thereby pre-empting the operation of the Standing Order. In 1994, during the First Session of the Thirty-Fifth Parliament, the House agreed to suspend this Standing Order at the same time as it adopted several amendments to the Standing Orders and referred a number of procedural matters to the Standing Committee on Procedure and House Affairs.[46] In 1998, during the First Session of the Thirty-Sixth Parliament, a debate was held pursuant to this Standing Order for the first time.[47]

---

42. Standing Order 51.

43. *Journals*, November 5, 1982, p. 5328; November 29, 1982, p. 5400; Special Committee on Standing Orders and Procedure, *Minutes of Proceedings and Evidence*, November 4, 1982, Issue No. 7, p. 23.

44. Standing Order 51(1). In the First Session of the Thirty-Sixth Parliament (1997-99), the day was designated by the Government House Leader (see *Debates*, March 26, 1998, p. 5422; April 2, 1998, p. 5724). The order was placed on the *Order Paper* under "Orders of the Day" before "Government Orders" (see *Order Paper*, April 21, 1998, p. 13).

45. *Journals*, December 7, 1984, p. 164. On December 5, 1984, a special committee had been established to examine, among other things, the procedures and practices of the House (*Journals*, December 5, 1984, pp. 153-4).

46. *Journals*, February 7, 1994, pp. 112-20.

47. *Journals*, April 21, 1998, pp. 681-2.

RULES OF DEBATE

Debate on the motion takes precedence over all other business and lasts a maximum of one sitting day; the proceedings on the motion expire when the debate has concluded or at the ordinary hour of daily adjournment, whichever comes first.[48] The motion is deemed to have been proposed[49] and, to encourage participation, no Member may speak more than once or longer than 10 minutes.[50]

Emergency Debates

The Standing Orders provide Members with an opportunity to give their immediate attention to a pressing matter by moving a debatable adjournment motion. A Member may request leave from the Speaker "to make a motion for the adjournment of the House for the purpose of discussing a specific and important matter requiring urgent consideration".[51] Furthermore, the matter "must relate to a genuine emergency"[52] and, if the request is granted by the Speaker, the House is permitted to debate the topic at an early opportunity, forgoing the usual 48 hours' notice period.

Until the turn of the century, any Member, at virtually any time in the proceedings, could introduce a new matter for discussion by moving the adjournment of the House. Since the adjournment motion could be moved at any time and was always subject to debate, the result would be an interruption of the business then before the House, often leading to the disruption of the entire day's program. In 1906, the government of the day decided to remedy this situation and implemented a new rule, the ancestor to the present Standing Order, whereby debate would be permitted only on adjournment motions which dealt with definite matters of urgent public importance.[53]

From 1906 to 1968, motions under the emergency debate rule were considered immediately after they had been accepted for debate. This meant that other business was put aside. In December 1968, the House amended the rule to have the debate begin at 8:00 p.m., except on Fridays when it would begin at 3:00 p.m., if proceeded with the same day.[54] This still resulted in a conflict and a displacement of the regular business of the House. When the regular evening sittings of the House were

---

48. Standing Order 51(1) and (2). On April 21, 1998, debate concluded at the end of the time allotted for Government Orders. The House then proceeded to the taking of deferred divisions, Private Members Business and the Adjournment Proceedings. See *Journals*, April 21, 1998, pp. 682-90.

49. Standing Order 51(1). See, for example, *Journals*, April 21, 1998, p. 681. The Government House Leader was the first person recognized on debate (see *Debates*, April 21, 1998, pp. 5863-4).

50. Standing Order 51(3). On April 20, 1998, an order was adopted by unanimous consent allowing the first spokesperson for each recognized party to speak for a maximum of 20 minutes (*Journals*, April 20, 1998, p. 677).

51. Standing Order 52(1).

52. Standing Order 52(6)(*a*).

53. *Journals*, July 10, 1906, p. 580. The first emergency debate held in accordance with the new rules occurred on February 25, 1907, when the topic of discussion was the Trent Valley Canal (see *Debates*, cols. 3627-8).

54. *Journals*, December 20, 1968, pp. 554-79, in particular p. 555.

abolished in 1982,[55] the conflict between emergency debates and the regular business of the House was eliminated except for Fridays.

As one Speaker noted, an emergency debate should be on a topic "that is immediately relevant and of attention and concern throughout the nation".[56] Thus, matters of chronic or continuing concern, such as economic conditions, unemployment rates and constitutional matters, have tended to be set aside whereas topics deemed to require urgent consideration have included work stoppages and strikes, natural disasters, and international crises and events. At various times other topics such as fisheries, forestry, agriculture and the fur trade industry have been judged acceptable; for example, there have been several emergency debates on grain-related topics since 1968, and since 1984 four emergency debates have been held in regard to the fishing industry in Canada. Topics considered highly partisan in nature are not as readily approved.[57]

INITIATING DEBATE

Any Member, be it a private Member or a Minister,[58] who wishes to move the adjournment of the House to discuss a specific and important matter requiring urgent consideration must give the Speaker written notice of the matter he or she wishes to propose for discussion at least one hour prior to rising in the House to make the formal request.[59] At the conclusion of the ordinary daily routine of business,[60] any Member who has filed an application with the Speaker rises to ask the Speaker for leave to move the adjournment of the House to debate the issue outlined in the application.[61] The Member then makes a brief statement, normally by simply reading the text of the application filed with the Speaker.[62] No discussion or argument is allowed in the presentation[63] because, as one Speaker stressed, a lengthy statement may

---

55. *Journals*, November 29, 1982, p. 5400.

56. *Debates*, February 22, 1978, p. 3128.

57. Between 1984 and 1988, for example, there were 21 requests for emergency debates on the Canada-United States Free Trade Agreement; none was granted.

58. Ministers have been granted leave to move the adjournment of the House on two occasions: October 14, 1971 (*Debates*, p. 8688) and November 18, 1991 (*Debates*, p. 4920). On April 2, 1924, the motion to adjourn was moved by the Prime Minister (*Debates*, p. 945).

59. Standing Order 52(2).

60. Standing Order 52(1). The original purpose for delaying the hearing of applications of emergency debates until the conclusion of Routine Proceedings was "to make sure that all business of the House which was not of a controversial nature would be duly attended to" (*Journals*, April 5, 1951, p. 247; see also *Debates*, January 11, 1956, p. 20).

61. In 1988, the Leader of the New Democratic Party filed notice of an application for an emergency debate on minority language rights. Following Routine Proceedings, the NDP House Leader presented the application. In response to a point of order raised as a result of this, the Speaker ruled that while the person giving notice and the person speaking to it should be the same, he had allowed the House Leader to present the application given its subject matter (*Debates*, April 11, 1988, p. 14309).

62. See, for example, *Debates*, December 11, 1987, pp. 11726-7.

63. Standing Order 52(3).

provoke debate.[64] However, occasionally a Member will be permitted to expand on the application if the Chair indicates that the additional information could be of assistance in reaching a decision.[65]

If more than one notice has been forwarded to the Speaker, Members will be recognized in the order applications were received.[66] If the time set aside in the day's order of business for hearing the application is not reached, or if the House decides to proceed to other business, for example, by adopting a motion to move to the Orders of the Day during Routine Proceedings, then the Chair cannot hear applications for emergency debates. These applications must be refiled at the next sitting of the House unless unanimous consent is granted for the Speaker to hear them at some other time during the sitting.[67]

The timeliness of an application is very important. On one occasion, the Speaker advised a Member who had risen to present his application which had been filed on a previous day to refile it.[68] Although the House may grant a Member unanimous consent to present an application which had not been filed that day,[69] the Chair has expressed reservations about holding over applications. One Speaker stated that a matter which requires urgent action one day may not necessarily demand the same attention the next day, or conversely may be even more critical, a determination that should be left to the discretion of the Member who filed the application.[70] On one occasion, applications were filed during a lengthy recess of the House and were heard at the conclusion of the ordinary routine of business the first day the House resumed sitting.[71]

---

64. *Debates*, September 24, 1990, p. 13229.

65. See, for example, *Debates*, May 9, 1989, pp. 1501-2.

66. See, for example, *Debates*, April 20, 1998, pp. 5829-30.

67. See, for example, *Debates*, January 23, 1990, pp. 7363-5.

68. See, for example, *Debates*, January 29, 1990, p. 7559.

69. See, for example, *Debates*, February 4, 1992, p. 6337.

70. *Debates*, March 6, 1990, p. 8845.

71. See *Debates*, September 24, 1990, pp. 13229-32.

DISCRETIONARY RESPONSIBILITY OF THE SPEAKER

Having heard an application for an emergency debate, the Speaker decides without debate whether or not the matter is specific and important enough to warrant urgent consideration by the House.[72] In deciding whether or not to approve a request for an emergency debate, the Chair is guided by the Standing Orders, the authorities and practice.

The Speaker is not required to give reasons when granting or refusing a request for an emergency debate.[73] Nonetheless, from time to time reasons are offered, although Chair occupants have tried to refrain from this practice in order to prevent the build-up of jurisprudence which could itself become a subject of a debate in the Chamber.[74]

Criteria for Decision

Although the Standing Orders give considerable discretion to the Speaker in deciding if a matter should be brought before the House for urgent consideration, certain criteria must be weighed. The Speaker determines whether a matter is related to a genuine emergency which could not be brought before the House within a reasonable time by other means, such as during a Supply day.[75] To do this, consideration is

---

72. Standing Order 52(4). Between 1906 and 1927, the rules stipulated that the Speaker had to decide on whether the matter was in order rather than urgent and this resulted in most requests being accepted. In 1927, the Standing Orders were amended to clarify that the Speaker also had to rule on the urgency of the matter raised. This new power, however, did not prevent Members from challenging the Chair's decision and only when the Standing Orders were amended in 1965 to prohibit appeals to the House of the decisions of the Chair did this practice cease. This change substituted the right of appeal for a process whereby, if the Chair questioned the urgency of a request, Members would first debate the merits of it, which resulted in the loss of valuable House time. In 1968, amendments to the Standing Orders eliminated this stage in the process, but the Member presenting the application was still required to obtain the leave of the House to move the adjournment motion if it had been accepted by the Speaker. This procedure by which the House granted leave was eliminated altogether in 1987.

73. Standing Order 52(7). Between 1927 and 1968, a number of conditions, based on previous rulings, had to be met before the Speaker would grant a request for an emergency debate. In 1968, the Standing Orders were modified so that the Speaker would no longer be obliged to base a decision on these previous rulings, although some precedent-based conditions were incorporated into the Standing Orders (see *Journals*, December 20, 1968, pp. 554-79, in particular pp. 554-6).

74. In 1985, a special committee recommended the adoption of the practice of not giving reasons, and the government in its response to the committee report supported the recommendation (see p. 45 of the Third Report of the Special Committee on the Reform of the House of Commons, June 1985, presented on June 18, 1985 (*Journals*, p. 839); *Journals*, October 9, 1985, p. 1082). See also *Debates*, September 22, 1987, p. 9172.

75. A number of Speakers have refused applications for emergency debates during consideration of the Address in Reply to the Speech from the Throne because the Address debate allows for discussion on a wide range of topics (see, for example, *Debates*, February 18, 1972, p. 18; April 4, 1989, p. 41; September 25, 1997, p. 60). Similarly, a request for an emergency debate on the alleged premature disclosure of the Budget was disallowed because Members would have ample opportunity to discuss the issue during debate on the Budget motion (see *Debates*, April 20, 1983, p. 24685).

given to the importance and specificity of the issue[76] and the degree to which the matter falls within the administrative responsibilities of the government or could come within the scope of ministerial action.[77]

The Speaker then considers whether the request meets certain other criteria. The matter being raised for discussion must contain only one issue.[78] The motion to adjourn the House for an emergency debate cannot revive discussion on a matter previously debated in this way during the session[79] nor may it raise a question of privilege.[80] In addition, the motion cannot deal with a matter normally debatable only by means of a substantive motion for which notice has been given and which calls for a decision of the House.[81]

Other conditions which have evolved from decisions of previous Speakers are also considered. Chair occupants have established that the subject matter proposed should not normally be of an exclusively local or regional interest nor be related to only one specific group or industry,[82] and should not involve the administration of a government department.[83] Applications to debate ongoing matters have been rejected[84] as have applications to debate matters arising out of the business of the same session,[85] Senate proceedings,[86] matters before the courts or other administrative bodies[87] and non-confidence or censure motions.[88] Furthermore, the Chair has ruled that an emergency debate cannot be held to debate the interpretation of a Standing Order[89] nor may it be "used as a vehicle for the purpose of airing statements made outside the House by organizations or people who are not answerable or responsible to this chamber."[90] In addition, one Speaker ruled that the emergency debate provisions cannot be used to debate "items which, in a regular legislative program of the House of Commons and regular legislative consideration, can come

---

76. See, for example, *Debates*, January 23, 1985, p. 1599.

77. Standing Order 52(5).

78. Standing Order 52(6)(*b*).

79. Standing Order 52(6)(*d*). See, for example, *Debates*, January 23, 1990, pp. 7390-1.

80. Standing Order 52(6)(*e*).

81. Standing Order 52(6)(*f*). See, for example, *Debates*, April 20, 1983, p. 24685; February 11, 1985, pp. 2210-1.

82. See, for example, *Debates*, February 13, 1978, pp. 2785-7; December 18, 1984, p. 1351; December 19, 1984, pp. 1366-7; February 6, 1985, p. 2064; February 3, 1986, p. 10381; February 14, 1986, p. 10830; June 11, 1987, p. 6974; June 22, 1987, p. 7418.

83. See, for example, *Debates*, March 27, 1974, p. 906.

84. See, for example, *Debates*, December 13, 1989, pp. 6875-6.

85. See, for example, *Debates*, September 27, 1990, pp. 13485-6; February 6, 1992, pp. 6464, 6505.

86. See, for example, *Debates*, October 5, 1990, pp. 13871-2.

87. See, for example, *Debates*, March 5, 1981, p. 7928; November 20, 1989, p. 5834.

88. See, for example, *Debates*, May 3, 1971, p. 5425; June 29, 1971, pp. 7434-5; June 12, 1973, p. 4658.

89. *Debates*, April 16, 1974, pp. 1454-5.

90. *Debates*, December 13, 1971, p. 10393.

before the House by way of amendments to existing statutes, or in any case will come before it in other ways." [91]

However, in one exceptional circumstance, an application was approved for an emergency debate on "the sudden and unexpected revelation of events which [had] taken place in the past, in that they might precipitate a course of conduct which, if allowed to continue unchecked, would certainly classify itself as an emergency and a matter of urgent consideration." [92]

Finally, the Speaker may take into account the general wish of the House to have an emergency debate and grant a request for an emergency debate. [93] Similarly, the Chair has periodically allowed an emergency debate on an issue which was not necessarily urgent within the meaning conferred by the rule, but was one on which the parliamentary timetable prevented any discussion in a timely manner. [94]

The responsibility of deciding whether or not an issue is an acceptable topic for an emergency debate is occasionally taken out of the hands of the Chair. There have been instances when the House itself has unanimously decided to hold an emergency debate, sometimes by means of a special order. [95] On one noteworthy occasion, the Speaker was not required to render a decision on a number of similar applications because later in the sitting unanimous consent was granted for the introduction of a bill on the same topic, and the House decided to proceed immediately to debate on the motion for the second reading of the bill. [96]

Frequently, the Speaker defers the decision on an application for an emergency debate until later in the day when the proceedings are interrupted for the purpose of announcing the decision. [97] In one exceptional case, the Speaker did not return to the House with a decision until the following day. [98]

The Standing Orders specify that not more than one motion to adjourn the House for an emergency debate may be moved in any sitting; [99] however, more than one application may be made and when this occurs, the Speaker chooses which one, if any, is acceptable. If more than one request for an emergency debate on the same topic is made in the same sitting and found acceptable, the Speaker grants leave to move the adjournment of the House to the Member who first submitted an acceptable application. [100]

---

91. *Debates*, April 30, 1975, p. 5340. See also *Debates*, July 9, 1980, p. 2711; May 4, 1984, p. 3419.

92. This referred to revelations made by the Solicitor General in the House on October 28, 1977, concerning illegal actions committed by the national security forces of the RCMP in 1973. This matter was referred to the McDonald Royal Commission and to the Attorney General of Quebec. See *Debates*, October 28, 1977, pp. 393-6; October 31, 1977, pp. 433-4.

93. See, for example, *Debates*, June 1, 1988, p. 15993.

94. See, for example, *Journals*, April 9, 1974, pp. 108-9; *Debates*, December 18, 1980, pp. 5888-9.

95. See, for example, *Journals*, October 14, 1971, p. 870; October 27, 1983, p. 6356; January 21, 1991, p. 2588; May 5, 1992, p. 1391; February 2, 1998, p. 402.

96. *Debates*, January 19, 1987, pp. 2346-7, 2370.

97. Standing Order 52(8). See, for example, *Debates*, March 18, 1999, pp. 13049, 13079.

98. *Debates*, January 30, 1990, pp. 7589-90; January 31, 1990, p. 7658.

99. Standing Order 52(6)(*c*).

100. See, for example, *Debates*, June 5, 1989, pp. 2523-4, 2591.

TIMING OF DEBATE

The Standing Orders provide that an emergency debate must occur between the hours of 8:00 p.m. and 12:00 midnight on the day a request for one is granted, unless the Speaker directs that the motion be considered the next sitting day at an hour to be specified later.[101] The House has also periodically adopted special orders setting a time for an emergency debate.[102] In one case, an application for an emergency debate was granted at a time when the House had extended its sitting hours in June.[103]

When an emergency debate is scheduled to be held at 8:00 p.m., the sitting is suspended at the ordinary hour of daily adjournment; the House meets again at 8:00 p.m. when the Member who was granted leave moves the motion, "That this House do now adjourn."[104] Practice has been that when an emergency debate is scheduled for 8:00 p.m. on Monday, Tuesday, Wednesday and Thursday, the normal Adjournment Proceedings do not take place, given that the motion before the House is the same. However, such proceedings have been held by unanimous consent; in these cases, following debate on the Adjournment Proceedings, the motion to adjourn has been deemed withdrawn and the sitting suspended until 8:00 p.m.[105] On occasion, unanimous consent has also been granted for the suspension of the sitting prior to the ordinary hour of daily adjournment in order to give Members an opportunity to prepare for an emergency debate.[106]

Except on Friday, emergency debates usually take place outside the normal sitting hours. However, on Friday or if the Speaker sets down a time at the next sitting that is within the normal sitting hours, the Standing Orders provide that emergency debates take precedence. The Speaker would then determine when any other business that has been superseded by an emergency debate should be considered or disposed of.[107]

---

101. Standing Order 52(9). See, for example, *Journals*, February 18, 1992, p. 1037. Prior to 1968, if an application for an emergency debate was approved, the business of the House was immediately put aside and the Member who requested the debate was given leave to move the adjournment of the House. In 1968, the Standing Orders were amended to stipulate that emergency debates would begin at 8:00 p.m. if proceeded with the same day, 3:00 p.m. on Friday. No time limit for these debates was provided in the Standing Orders and Members often seized the opportunity to extend the debates, in one instance for more than 35 hours (see *Journals*, May 4-5, 1982, pp. 4796-800; May 6, 1982, pp. 4802-4).

102. See, for example, *Journals*, January 21, 1991, p. 2588; March 18, 1999, p. 1636. The House has unanimously agreed on occasion to hold an emergency debate from 6:30 p.m. to 10:30 p.m. (see, for example, *Journals*, May 29, 1995, pp. 1509-10; November 30, 1998, pp. 1325-6).

103. A time allocation order on a certain bill had also been invoked that same day. The Speaker set the time for the emergency debate at 10:00 p.m. with the vote on the bill under consideration scheduled for 9:45 p.m. Unanimous consent was subsequently granted to extend the debate past midnight (*Journals*, June 22, 1992, pp. 1823, 1825-6; *Debates*, pp. 12527-8).

104. Standing Order 52(10). Another Member may move the motion in place of the Member who requested the debate (see, for example, *Debates*, November 18, 1991, p. 4946).

105. See, for example, *Journals*, May 5, 1992, p. 1397; March 18, 1999, p. 1637.

106. See, for example, *Journals*, January 21, 1991, p. 2589; *Debates*, p. 17523.

107. Standing Order 52(15). This situation could occur if an emergency debate were to take place on the same day as the consideration of the Business of Supply on the last allotted day in a Supply period. The Speaker would have to resolve the conflicts between Standing Orders 52 and 81.

Emergency debates on Friday begin as soon as the Speaker finds the application acceptable.[108] If the application is made and granted immediately following the conclusion of Routine Proceedings, debate commences at approximately 12:15 p.m. and continues until 4:00 p.m., at which time the motion "That this House do now adjourn" is deemed adopted. Approximately two to two-and-a-half hours of House business are displaced by an emergency debate held on this day because the ordinary hour of adjournment on Friday is 2:30 p.m. Since this Standing Order came into effect in 1987,[109] no emergency debates have been held on Friday, although on two occasions the Speaker has deferred such a debate until the following Monday at 8:00 p.m.[110]

RULES OF DEBATE

During an emergency debate, no Member may speak for more than 20 minutes[111] and there is no questions and comments period.[112] However, frequently by unanimous consent the length of speeches has been reduced to 10 or 15 minutes to allow as many Members as possible to speak.[113] The established rules of debate apply to these emergency debates.[114] As such, as with all other motions to adjourn, the motion to adjourn the House to discuss an important and urgent matter is not amendable.[115]

INTERRUPTION AND TERMINATION OF DEBATE

As noted above, once underway, an emergency debate takes precedence over all other business. From Monday to Thursday, no conflict should arise if the debate takes place after the normal adjournment hour. In the case of a debate taking place on a Friday, in addition to approximately 90 minutes scheduled for Government Business, the debate also displaces one hour of Private Members' Business. This, however, is dealt with in the Standing Orders which specifically prohibit an interruption for Private Members' Business.[116]

---

108. Standing Order 52(11).

109. *Journals*, June 3, 1987, p. 1020.

110. *Journals*, December 15, 1989, p. 1022; November 27, 1998, p. 1323. The last emergency debate held on a Friday occurred in June 1986 (see *Journals*, June 13, 1986, pp. 2317-9).

111. Standing Order 52(13). Members may split their speaking time (see *Debates*, November 30, 1998, p. 10648).

112. *Debates*, November 30, 1998, p. 10683.

113. See, for example, *Journals*, November 5, 1973, p. 619; April 9, 1974, p. 109; October 31, 1974, p. 98; April 4, 1989, p. 23; June 22, 1992, p. 1825.

114. See Chapter 13, "Rules of Order and Decorum".

115. *Debates*, July 16, 1942, p. 4283.

116. Standing Order 52(14).

Since the wording of the motion for an emergency debate is simply, "That this House do now adjourn", at the conclusion of the debate, the House is not required to render a decision on the matter under discussion. [117] At 12:00 midnight (4:00 p.m. on Friday) or when no Member rises to speak, the motion is declared carried by the Speaker and the House adjourns until the next sitting day. [118] If the debate is held during the regular sitting hours of the House and concludes prior to the ordinary hour of adjournment, the motion is deemed withdrawn and the House continues with other business. [119]

The Standing Orders allow a Member to propose a motion to continue the debate beyond 12:00 midnight (4:00 p.m. on Friday) if the motion is moved in the hour preceding the time the debate would normally adjourn, that is, between 11:00 p.m. and midnight (between 3:00 and 4:00 p.m. on Friday). [120] If fewer than 15 Members rise to object to this motion, the motion is deemed adopted. A handful of debates have been extended past midnight pursuant to the Standing Orders, [121] while several have been prolonged by unanimous consent. [122]

There have been occasions when the House has wanted to express itself on the topic of an emergency debate by adopting a motion or resolution. In 1970, the House held an emergency debate on the Nigerian-Biafran conflict; pursuant to a special order made earlier in the sitting, the debate was interrupted at 10:30 p.m., the House adopted a motion on the same subject and then adjourned without question put. [123] In 1983, following an emergency debate regarding the shooting down of a South Korean civilian aircraft by the Soviet Union, the motion to adjourn the House was deemed withdrawn, the House adopted a resolution denouncing the actions of the Soviet government, and then adjourned until the next sitting day by unanimous

---

117. *Debates*, April 20, 1983, p. 24685.

118. These motions have been disposed of in a variety of ways since 1906. Until 1917, motions were generally negatived after a short debate and the House would continue with other business; by 1918, these motions were being withdrawn at the conclusion of debate and the House would move on to other business. In 1927, when the House agreed to adjourn evening sittings no later than 11:00 p.m., adjournment motions for emergency debates were either withdrawn if debate concluded before 11:00 p.m., or the House would adjourn without question put at the ordinary adjournment hour. Motions were negatived by recorded vote in 1916, 1942 and 1957 (*Journals*, May 5, 1916, pp. 334-5; July 16, 1942, pp. 544-5; February 25, 1957, pp. 181-2) and "negatived on division" in 1961 and 1967 (*Journals*, June 14, 1961, pp. 668-9; November 24, 1967, pp. 534-5). Since January 1969, at the conclusion of debate, all such adjournment motions have been declared "carried" by the Speaker.

119. Standing Order 52(12).

120. Standing Order 52(12).

121. See *Journals*, January 28, 1987, p. 413; April 28-29, 1987, p. 796; February 19, 1992, pp. 1043-4. In one instance, an emergency debate was extended for more than 20 hours. At the next sitting, the debate continued for an additional 14 hours after the House unanimously agreed to resume the debate (*Journals*, April 28-29, 1987, pp. 796-7; April 30, 1987, pp. 800-2). Since 1987, only one emergency debate has concluded at midnight (see *Debates*, November 18, 1991, p. 4986).

122. See *Journals*, April 27, 1987, p. 785; June 1, 1988, p. 2773; April 4, 1989, p. 23; June 5, 1989, p. 315; December 18, 1989, p. 1034; January 21, 1991, pp. 2589-90; May 5, 1992, p. 1398; June 22, 1992, p. 1825.

123. *Journals*, January 12, 1970, pp. 291-3.

consent. [124] In 1989, an emergency debate on the Tiananmen Square massacre in Beijing, China, was temporarily interrupted to allow the House to adopt a resolution condemning the massacre. [125]

Motion to Suspend Certain Standing Orders

In relation to any business that the government considers to be urgent, the House may suspend certain Standing Orders in connection with that business, but only under well-defined conditions. [126] Specifically, a motion may be moved by a Minister, at any time when the Speaker is in the Chair, to suspend the Standing Orders respecting notice requirements and the times of sitting. In moving the motion, the Minister gives reasons for the urgency of the situation. After the motion is seconded, the Speaker immediately proposes the question. In doing so, the Speaker may allow up to one hour of uninterrupted debate, in which case the business then before the House is put aside temporarily and a "special" debate on the motion takes place. If no Member rises, the Speaker will put the question immediately. [127]

INITIATING DEBATE

In moving the motion to suspend the Standing Orders, the Minister must inform the House of the reasons for the urgency of such a motion. [128] Once the motion is duly moved and seconded, the Speaker proposes the motion to the House. [129]

Such motions have seldom been proposed. In 1991, a motion was proposed to suspend the Standing Orders related to the hours of sitting of the House in order for the House to sit three evenings until 10:00 p.m. to complete all stages of an item of back-to-work legislation. After debate, the motion was withdrawn when more than 10 Members rose to object. [130] In 1992, a motion to waive the 48 hours' notice

---

124. *Journals*, September 12, 1983, pp. 6134-5, 6140.

125. *Journals*, June 5, 1989, pp. 314-5.

126. Standing Order 53(1).

127. On March 15, 1995, the Hon. Marcel Massé, President of the Queen's Privy Council for Canada, Minister of Intergovernmental Affairs and Minister Responsible for Public Service Renewal, proposed a motion concerning the notice period for the introduction of legislation dealing with a work stoppage in west coast ports and other hours of sitting for that day. The Speaker put the question immediately without debate and the motion was adopted as fewer than 10 Members rose to object. This led to a point of order because no debate had been allowed. The Speaker indicated that as he had seen no Member seeking the floor for debate, he did not call for debate (see *Debates*, March 15, 1995, pp. 10524-6).

128. Standing Order 53(2). On one occasion, debate had already begun on the motion when a Member informed the Chair that the Minister had not stated the reason for its urgency. The motion was ruled out of order and debate resumed on the Orders of the Day (*Debates*, December 11, 1992, pp. 15131-3).

129. See, for example, *Debates*, August 9, 1977, p. 8177; September 16, 1991, p. 2179; June 1, 1992, p. 11172; March 20, 1995, p. 10697.

130. *Journals*, September 16, 1991, pp. 270-1.

requirement for the report stage of a bill to provide for referendums on the Constitution was adopted.[131] In March 1995, a motion requesting a waiver of the 48 hours' notice requirement for introduction of a bill to end a work stoppage and setting the hours of sitting to debate the bill was put to the House and adopted without debate.[132] Later that same month, a similar motion was debated and deemed withdrawn when more than 10 Members rose to object.[133] In June 1999, a motion proposing that the House continue sitting to consider a bill and to suspend the notice requirements of a closure motion was debated and deemed withdrawn when more than 10 Members rose to object.[134]

RULES OF DEBATE

Debate on such motions lasts not more than one hour and may not be interrupted or adjourned by any other proceeding or Order of the House.[135] Members may speak only once and for no longer than 10 minutes.[136] Amendments are not permitted unless proposed by a Minister other than the mover.[137]

TERMINATION OF DEBATE

When the debate is completed or after one hour, as the case may be, the Speaker puts the question on the motion and, in doing so, must ask those Members opposed to the motion to rise.[138] If 10 or more Members rise to object, the motion is deemed withdrawn;[139] otherwise, the motion is adopted[140] and becomes an Order of the House governing only the proceedings specified in the motion.[141]

---

131. *Journals*, June 1, 1992, pp. 1560-1. The government asserted that it was urgent for the House to pass this legislation as quickly as possible in order to allow Elections Canada time to prepare for these referendums.

132. *Journals*, March 15, 1995, p. 1219.

133. *Journals*, March 20, 1995, p. 1240.

134. *Journals*, June 10, 1999, p. 2097.

135. Standing Order 53(3)(*a*).

136. Standing Order 53(3)(*c*). On one occasion, the Speaker allowed each party 10 minutes to speak (see *Debates*, June 10, 1999, pp. 16227, 16230).

137. Standing Order 53(3)(*b*). No amendments have been moved in the debates held to date.

138. Standing Order 53(4).

139. Standing Order 53(4). See, for example, *Journals*, September 16, 1991, p. 271.

140. Standing Order 53(4). See, for example, *Journals*, June 1, 1992, p. 1561.

141. Standing Order 53(5).

"Take Note" Debates

Over the past several years, a number of "take note" motions have been debated in the House. A Minister moves a motion, which includes the words "that the House 'take note' of", to solicit the views of Members on some aspect of government policy. As the Prime Minister noted in the House on January 25, 1994, "take note" debates allow Members to participate in the development of government policy, making their views known before the government makes a decision.[142] A "take note" motion will not usually come to a vote.

Since the beginning of the Thirty-Fifth Parliament in 1994, there have been numerous "take note" debates, the majority of them dealing with Canada's peacekeeping commitments in various trouble spots around the world[143] and the government's budgetary policy.[144] The topics of other "take note" debates have included cruise missile testing, NORAD, violence against women, the reform of Canada's social security programs, and the war in Kosovo.[145]

INITIATING DEBATE

A "take note" debate is initiated by a Minister giving the usual 48 hours' notice required before a substantive motion may be moved in the House. After the motion has been transferred to the *Order Paper* under Government Business, it is taken up for debate at a time of the government's choosing during Government Orders. On several occasions, however, the 48 hours' notice requirement was by-passed when the House unanimously adopted a special order which included the wording of a "take note" motion and the rules governing the debate.[146] In many cases, the sitting was extended so that the debate could be held after the ordinary hour of daily adjournment.[147]

---

142. *Debates*, January 25, 1994, pp. 261-2. A similar practice exists in the British House of Commons. There a Minister may move the motion "That this House do now adjourn" in order to initiate a general debate on a topic which does not require a decision by the House. At the conclusion of debate, the motion is normally withdrawn with the leave of the House. See *May*, 22nd ed., pp. 275-6.

143. See *Journals*, September 21, 1994, p. 714; March 29, 1995, p. 1310; February 28, 1996, p. 10; April 28, 1998, pp. 717-8; February 17, 1999, p. 1519.

144. See *Journals,* November 28, 1994, p. 943; December 9, 1996, p. 977; December 10, 1997, p. 384; December 11, 1997, pp. 393-4, 395.

145. See *Journals*, January 26, 1994, p. 67 (cruise missile testing); October 6, 1994, p. 774 (social security programs); December 6, 1994, p. 983 (violence against women); March 11, 1996, p. 75 (NORAD); April 12, 1999, p. 1688 (Kosovo).

146. See *Journals*, April 21, 1994, pp. 381-2; November 24, 1994, 927-8; March 29, 1995, p. 1308; February 28, 1996, p. 9; April 24, 1998, pp. 701-2; October 7, 1998, p. 1132; February 16, 1999, pp. 1514-5.

147. See *Journals*, April 21, 1994, pp. 381-2; March 29, 1995, p. 1308; February 28, 1996, p. 9; December 6, 1996, p. 973; April 24, 1998, pp. 701-2; October 7, 1998, p. 1132; February 16, 1999, pp. 1514-5.

RULES OF DEBATE

Unless otherwise specified in a special order,[148] the normal rules of debate pertaining to length of speeches, duration of the debate, and amendments[149] apply. On several occasions, however, the House unanimously agreed to sit beyond the ordinary hour of daily adjournment to continue the debate.[150] In all of these cases, the special orders stipulated that dilatory motions and quorum calls were not allowed.

TERMINATION OF DEBATE

It has been the practice that debate on a "take note" motion lasts one sitting day, either during regular sitting hours or during extended hours. There have been occasions when a "take note" debate resumed on a following sitting day.[151] With one exception, no decision has been taken on a "take note" motion.[152] The motion remains on the *Order Paper* under Government Business.[153]

Statutory Debates

Parliament has seen fit to include in several statutes, provisions governing special "statutory" debates. These special debates are a form of parliamentary supervision and review of specific statutory provisions. In some cases, the statutory provision is designed to be permissive; in others, it is mandatory.[154]

---

148. See *Journals*, April 21, 1994, pp. 381-2; March 29, 1995, p. 1308; February 28, 1996, p. 9; December 6, 1996, p. 973; April 24, 1998, pp. 701-2; October 7, 1998, p. 1132; February 16, 1999, pp. 1514-5; April 12, 1999, p. 1687.

149. See *Debates*, April 12, 1999, pp. 13581-2, 13593-4.

150. See *Journals*, January 25, 1994, p. 62; February 1, 1994, p. 89; May 6, 1994, p. 435; September 20, 1994, pp. 708-9; October 5, 1994, p. 769; December 4, 1995, p. 2203.

151. Debate on reforms to Canada's social security programs took place over five days (October 6 and 7, 1994, and November 17, 18, and 21, 1994). Three "take note" debates on budget consultations continued for two days (November 28 and 30, 1994; December 9 and 11, 1996; December 10 and 11, 1997).

152. On November 28 and 30, 1994, the House debated the following motion: "That this House take note of the opinions expressed by Canadians on the budgetary policy of the government and, notwithstanding the provisions of Standing Order 83.1, authorize the Standing Committee on Finance to make a report or reports thereon no later than December 7, 1994." The House adopted the motion on a recorded division (*Journals*, November 30, 1994, pp. 957-9).

153. During the First Session of the Thirty-Fifth Parliament, these motions were routinely removed from the *Order Paper* by unanimous consent (see, for example, *Journals*, February 18, 1994, p. 174; February 7, 1995, p. 1095).

154. For permissive provisions, see *Energy Administration Act*, R.S.C. 1985, c. E-6, ss. 72-78; *International Development (Financial Institutions) Assistance Act*, R.S.C. 1985, c. I-18, ss. 5-11; *Safe Containers Convention Act*, R.S.C. 1985, c. S-1, ss. 8-12.

Statutory debates can be grouped into two broad categories, although the procedures pertaining to the debates are similar. The first category provides for a general review of an Act or a particular aspect of it. The second and most common category provides for a debate to confirm, revoke or amend an order, regulation, declaration, proclamation, guideline or other instrument of delegated legislation issued pursuant to the statute in question. Some of these statutes make regulations subject to affirmative resolution of Parliament. This obliges both Houses to adopt the regulations, ostensibly by holding a debate on them, before they can come into effect.[155] Conversely, regulations subject to negative resolution of Parliament are in effect until revoked by resolution of both Houses, again presumably after a debate.[156]

Since the 1960s, several statutory debates have taken place. In 1971, for example, pursuant to the *Government Organization Act, 1970,* the House considered and adopted a motion to establish a Ministry of State for Science and Technology.[157] In 1974, the House debated a motion requesting the Minister of Veterans Affairs to continue provisions of the *Veterans' Land Act* scheduled to expire on March 31, 1975.[158] One was held in 1977 in an attempt to advance the expiration date of the *Anti-Inflation Act*.[159] Two occurred consecutively in late 1980 when Members sought to revoke two proclamations tabled by the government in relation to the *Petroleum Administration Act:* one proclamation concerned regulations prescribing maximum prices for various qualities and kinds of crude oil, the other proclamation involved regulations prescribing prices for natural gas.[160] Another took place in 1985 when Members invoked a provision in the *Western Grain Transportation Act* to move a motion to use a parliamentary day to examine a progress report on the Act and any outstanding issues of interest to western farmers.[161] One statutory debate took place in September 1992 when, pursuant to the *Referendum Act,* the House adopted a

155. See, for example, *Unemployment Insurance Act*, R.S.C. 1985, c.U-I, ss. 4(2), 6(7).

156. See, for example, *Safe Containers Convention Act*, R.S.C. 1985, c. S-1, s. 12. A number of acts also specify that reports, orders, regulations or notices of intention must be referred to a parliamentary committee for review (see, for example, *Canadian Environmental Protection Act*, S.C. 1988, c. 22, s. 139).

157. *Government Organization Act, 1970*, R.S.C. 1970 (2nd supp.), c. 14, s. 18(2). *Journals*, June 21, 1971, p. 712.

158. *Veterans' Land Act*, S.C. 1974, c. 3, s. 1(3). *Journals*, November 5, 1974, p. 104; November 6, 1974, p. 106.

159. *Anti-Inflation Act*, S.C. 1974-75-76, c. 98, s. 11(1). *Journals*, June 16, 1977, p. 1144.

160. *Petroleum Administration Act*, S.C. 1974-75-76, c. 47, ss. 36 and 52(1). *Journals*, November 12, 1980, p. 690; November 21, 1980, p. 769; November 26, 1980, p. 784.

161. *Western Grain Transportation Act*, S.C. 1980-81-82-83, c. 168, s. 62(6). *Journals*, December 4, 1985, pp. 1315-7.

motion approving the text of a referendum question.[162] The most recent debate occurred in December 1992 when Members sought to amend the *Special Economic Measures (Haiti) Ships Regulations* in accordance with provisions set down in the *Special Economic Measures Act* for amending or revoking orders and regulations regarding economic sanctions programs.[163]

Until 1986, the *Electoral Boundaries Readjustment Act* contained provisions which allowed Members to discuss their objections to a report of an Electoral Boundaries Commission on the floor of the House. Four debates—in 1966, 1973, 1976 and 1983—were held under the Act's provisions.[164] In 1986, the Act was amended so that these reports are now tabled in the House and automatically referred to a parliamentary committee established for the purpose of dealing with electoral matters.[165] Objections are filed with and considered by this committee.

INITIATING DEBATE

The manner in which statutory debates are triggered depends upon the provisions contained in each statute. For statutes which allow a debate to be held, such a debate may be initiated by a Minister who, within a specified time, files a notice of motion with the Speaker for the confirmation of an order, regulation, declaration, proclamation, guideline or other instrument of delegated legislation issued in accordance with the law.[166]

---

162. *Referendum Act*, S.C. 1992, c. 30, s. 5. *Journals*, September 9, 1992, pp. 1956-7; September 10, 1992, pp. 1960-2.

163. *Special Economic Measures Act*, S.C. 1992, c. 17, s. 7. *Journals*, December 8, 1992, pp. 2308-9.

164. *Electoral Boundaries Readjustment Act*, S.C. 1964-65, c. 31, s. 20. Within 30 days of the tabling in the House of such a report, a motion for consideration of an objection to the report signed by not less than 10 Members could be filed with the Speaker. The motion would detail the provisions of the report objected to and the reasons for the objection. Within 15 days of the filing of the motion, time would be set aside under "Government Orders" for Members to voice their concerns about the report. Upon the conclusion of consideration of the objections, the Speaker was required to refer the objections and the relevant *Debates* pages back to the Commission.

165. *Representation Act, 1985*, S.C. 1986, c. 8, ss. 9, 10. On June 10, 1994, the Standing Orders were amended to designate the Standing Committee on Procedure and House Affairs as the parliamentary committee responsible for electoral matters (see *Journals*, June 10, 1994, p. 563; Twenty-Seventh Report, Standing Committee on Procedure and House Affairs, *Minutes of Proceedings and Evidence*, June 9, 1994, Issue No. 16, pp. 7-8). For additional information on electoral matters, see Chapter 4, "The House of Commons and Its Members".

166. See, for example, *International Development (Financial Institutions) Assistance Act*, R.S.C. 1985, c. I-18, s. 5(2)(*a*).

The initiation of a debate to revoke such instruments typically requires that a notice of motion signed by a minimum number of Members or Senators, as the case may be, be filed with the Speaker.[167] Where statutes require that a debate take place on the use of an instrument of delegated legislation, the relevant provisions typically specify that a confirmation motion signed by a Minister must be laid before Parliament within a specified time.[168]

After notice has been filed in accordance with House rules and transferred to the *Order Paper* under the rubric "Statutory Order",[169] debate must take place within a set number of days as prescribed in the given statute. For example, in 1974, debate pursuant to the *Veterans' Land Act* had to take place within 15 days, and the House adopted a motion fixing the dates for the debate.[170] In 1977, debate pursuant to the *Anti-Inflation Act* was required to take place within 15 days of the notice being filed[171] and, in 1980, pursuant to the *Petroleum Administration Act,* within four sitting days.[172] It appears that in both cases the dates for the debate were fixed through all-party consultation. In 1985, pursuant to subsection 62(6) of the *Western Grain Transportation Act,* which stipulated that debate had to take place within 60 days of the notice being filed, the Speaker assigned the day for the debate.[173] In September 1992, pursuant to the *Referendum Act,* the debate on the text of the referendum question took place 24 hours after the notice was given.[174] In December 1992, after a motion for a debate pursuant to the *Special Economic Measures Act* had been placed on the *Order Paper,* the Chair was asked to rule on its procedural acceptability. The Speaker ruled that the motion was acceptable and that pursuant to the Act, the House had to consider the motion within six sitting days.[175] The House agreed to hold the debate later that day.[176]

---

167. While most legislation providing for such statutory debates makes provision for debate in either House, there are some statutes which do not provide for debate in the Senate. See, for example, *Special Economics Measures Act* (s. 7(2)); *Veterans' Land Act* (s. 1(3)); and *Petroleum Administration Act* (s. 35(3)).

168. See, for example, *Emergencies Act*, S.C. 1988, c. 29, s. 58(1).

169. In 1974, the motion was placed under the rubric "Special Order" following the adoption of a Special Order of the House specifying the time and days on which the motion would be considered (see *Journals*, October 31, 1974, p. 97; *Order Paper*, November 5, 1974, p. 4).

170. See *Veterans' Land Act*, s. 1(3); *Journals*, October 31, 1974, p. 97.

171. See *Anti-Inflation Act*, S.C. 1974-75-76, c. 75, s. 46(6).

172. See *Petroleum Administration Act*, ss. 35(3), 52(4).

173. See *Notice Paper*, December 4, 1985, p. XXIII. Pursuant to the Act, Speaker Bosley designated December 4, 1985, to be the day for the debate.

174. See *Referendum Act*, S.C. 1992, c. 30, s. 5(4). Also see *Notice Paper*, September 9, 1992, p. vi.

175. See *Special Economics Measures Act*, s.7(3); *Debates*, December 8, 1992, pp. 14862-4.

176. *Journals*, December 8, 1992, p. 2308.

RULES OF DEBATE

Duration of Debate

The duration of a statutory debate is usually prescribed in the legislation, be it one or more sitting days or only a few hours. On occasion, the House has also adopted motions setting out additional guidelines.[177] For example, pursuant to subsection 1(3) of the *Veterans' Land Act*, the debate was to take place over two days, without interruption, in accordance with the rules of the House; the House subsequently adopted a motion establishing the days of the debate and suspending Private Members' Business on the first day of debate.[178] The debates held pursuant to the *Anti-Inflation Act* and the *Petroleum Administration Act* lasted four and three days respectively, in accordance with the statutes.[179] Subsection 62(6) of the *Western Grain Transportation Act* stipulated that the progress report was to be debated without interruption for "a period not exceeding the duration of the normal business hours of the House on that day". A motion to this effect was adopted by the House.[180] The motion also indicated that the order was to be the first item of business. The debate held in September 1992 pursuant to the *Referendum Act* lasted two sitting days. The *Act* stipulates that a decision must be taken on the motion by the end of the third sitting day of the debate.[181] The House passed a motion, by unanimous consent, to dispose of the motion after two days of debate.[182] The length of the December 1992 statutory debate was set by subsection 7(4) of the *Special Economic Measures Act* which limits debate to not more than three hours, unless the House fixes a longer period by unanimous consent. In this instance, the House adopted a special order which had the effect of terminating debate after only two hours.[183]

A notable exception to the duration of the debate being prescribed in the legislation is found in the *Emergencies Act*. This statute imposes no time limit on debate on a motion for confirmation of a declaration, or continuation of a declaration, of an emergency or for debate on a motion to revoke or amend a regulation or order. The legislation provides that debate continues uninterrupted until such time as the House is ready for the question.[184]

---

177. Once House procedures are prescribed in statutes, any attempt to modify them would normally require a statutory amendment.

178. *Journals*, October 31, 1974, p. 97.

179. See *Anti-Inflation Act*, S.C. 1974-75-76, c. 75, s. 46(7); *Petroleum Administration Act*, ss. 35(4), 52(5).

180. *Journals*, December 4, 1985, pp. 1315-6.

181. *Referendum Act*, S.C. 1992, c. 30, s. 5(5).

182. *Journals*, September 9, 1992, p. 1944.

183. *Journals*, December 8, 1992, p. 2308. The motion also stipulated that any requested recorded division would be deferred until the following day.

184. See *Emergencies Act*, S.C. 1988, c. 29, ss. 58(6), 60(5), 61(8).

Length of Speeches

Unless otherwise specified in the statute, the length of speeches during a statutory debate is determined by the rules of the House.[185] There have been two exceptions: in 1977 and 1985, the House adopted motions restricting the length of speeches.[186]

INTERRUPTION OF DEBATE

Most statutes which prescribe provisions for statutory debates also stipulate that the debate may not be interrupted. With the exception of the *Petroleum Administration Act,*[187] the acts pursuant to which statutory debates have been held in the House contained these "no interruption" provisions. However, in 1977, debate on the motion pursuant to the *Anti-Inflation Act,* which took place over four days, was interrupted on three occasions for the Adjournment Proceedings, after which the motion to adjourn was deemed withdrawn and debate continued, due to an Order of the House adopted on May 30, 1977.[188] In 1985, the debate held pursuant to the *Western Grain Transportation Act* was interrupted for a ministerial statement by the Minister of Finance pursuant to an Order made by the House.[189]

TERMINATION OF DEBATE

A statutory debate concludes in accordance with provisions outlined in the legislation. Typically, if debate has not concluded earlier, the Speaker is required to interrupt the proceedings at the expiration of a given sitting day or hour of debate and put the question on the motion.[190] If a confirmation motion is adopted by the House of Parliament in which it was introduced, the statute will normally prescribe that a message be sent to the other House requesting its concurrence. If the motion is subsequently adopted by the other House, the regulation or Order in Council is

---

185. Standing Order 43(1).

186. See *Journals*, June 16, 1977, p. 1144; December 4, 1985, p. 1315.

187. While the *Petroleum Administration Act* did not contain a "no interruption" provision, the motions before the House pursuant to this Act were always the first item of business under Government Orders and debate was only interrupted for Private Members' Business.

188. See *Journals*, May 30, 1977, p. 874; June 16, 1977, p. 1145; June 20, 1977, p. 1156; June 21, 1977, p. 1177. The motion under consideration was not the first item of business under Government Orders for two of the four days of debate.

189. *Journals*, December 4, 1985, p. 1316. The debate also took place on a Wednesday when less time was allotted for Government Orders.

190. The *Petroleum Administration Act* specified that the proceedings were to be interrupted 15 minutes before the expiry of time for government business in order to put the question on the motion (ss. 35(4) and 52(5)). However, for the two debates held pursuant to this Act, the House unanimously agreed to defer the putting of the question until the expiry of time for government business, at which time the divisions were deferred (see *Journals*, November 25, 1980, p. 779; November 28, 1980, p. 794).

thereby confirmed, amended or revoked.[191] If a revocation motion is not adopted by the House in which it originated or by the House where it was sent for concurrence, the regulation or Order in Council comes into force or remains unaffected as the case may be.[192]

Normally, motions moved and debated in accordance with a statutory provision are voted on at the conclusion of debate.[193] In 1985, the proceedings held pursuant to the *Western Grain Transportation Act* expired at the ordinary hour of daily adjournment: no question was put on the motion nor the amendment thereto.[194]

---

191. See, for example, *Special Economic Measures Act*, s. 7(7).

192. See, for example, *Special Economic Measures Act,* s. 7(8).

193. See, for example, *Journals*, November 6, 1974, p. 106; June 21, 1977, pp. 1177-8; November 26, 1980, pp. 785-6; December 1, 1980, p. 799; September 10, 1992, pp. 1961-2; December 8, 1992, p. 2309.

194. *Journals*, December 4, 1985, p. 1317.

16

The Legislative Process

The average man, bewildered and overpowered by the thousands of laws and regulations which press in upon him and increasingly restrict his freedom, his right to make decisions, would be left absolutely defenceless without an active parliament with the strength and vitality which it must possess.

G.W. BALDWIN, M.P. (Peace River)
(*Debates,* December 10, 1968, p. 3791)

The examination and enactment of legislation are often regarded as the most significant task of Parliament. It is therefore not surprising that the legislative process takes up a major portion of Parliament's time.[1] But what exactly is the legislative process? There are those who have defined it as a series of actions leading to the proclamation of a statute. The parliamentary stages that are the subject of this chapter are the final links in a much longer process that starts with the proposal, formulation and drafting of a bill, normally by extra-parliamentary bodies.

In the Parliament of Canada, as in all legislative assemblies based on the British model, there is a clearly defined method for enacting legislation. A bill must go through a number of very specific stages in the House of Commons and the Senate before it becomes law. In parliamentary jargon, these stages make up what is called the legislative process. When the House of Commons and the Senate pass a bill, they are asking the Crown to proclaim

---

1. Gregory Tardi, *The Legal Framework of Government: A Canadian Guide*, Aurora, Ont.: Canada Law Book Inc., 1992, p. 122.

that this text is the law of the land. Once Royal Assent is given to the bill, it is transformed from a bill to a statute. Because the process by which a legislative proposal becomes first a bill, and then a law, takes place in Parliament, the product—the statute—is often called an "Act of Parliament".[2]

Traditionally, the process begins with a bill being introduced in one of the Houses of Parliament and ends with the ceremony of Royal Assent, which brings together the three constituent elements of Parliament: the Crown, the Senate and the House of Commons. The process is complex, but the validation of a statute is the result of the approval of the same text by the three constituent elements of Parliament.

This chapter will examine the stages that a public bill must go through before becoming law. Private bills follow essentially the same stages, but they must be initiated by a petition and are subject to certain special rules.[3]

Historical Perspective

GREAT BRITAIN

The legislative process comes to us from medieval times. During the early days of the British Parliament, requests by the Commons in relation to legislation were made to the King in the form of petitions.[4] When the King convened Parliament seeking supply, in return the Commons presented the petitions for which they wished to obtain his assent. Petitions could be either oral or in writing. Those that the King decided to grant[5] were then written up by his advisors in the form of statutes[6] which were entered on the *Statute Rolls*. The statutes reproduced the wording of the petition and the King's reply, but the King and his advisors often took the initiative of

---

2. *Stewart*, p. 79.

3. The stages relating to private bills are described in Chapter 23, "Private Bills Practice".

4. See A.R. Myers, "Parliamentary Petitions in the Fifteenth Century," *The English Historical Review*, Vol. LII, (1937), pp. 590-613. For a historical overview of the legislative process in Great Britain, the following texts may be consulted: Sir William R. Anson, *The Law and Custom of the Constitution*, 4th ed., revised edition (1911), Oxford: Clarendon Press, Vol. I, pp. 240-54; Sheila Lambert, "Procedure in the House of Commons in the Early Stuart Period," *The English Historical Review*, Vol. XCV (1980), pp. 753-81.

5. A favourable reply was expressed by the words *le roy le veult*, a negative reply by the words *le roy s'avisera*. Until the latter part of the reign of Edward III (1327-77), all parliamentary proceedings were conducted in French. The use of English was extremely rare until the reign of Henry IV (1399-1413). Beginning with the reign of Henry VII (1485-1509), English was used for all proceedings, with the exception of Royal Assent, which was always expressed in Norman French (*May*, 11th ed., pp. 512-3; 22nd ed., p. 565).

6. The expression "*statut*" is used in French to mean "*loi*" or "law" only in reference to Great Britain and, by extension, to the other Commonwealth Parliaments. However, in Canada, the expression "*loi*" is used in French.

amending the wording of the petition fairly extensively, and in some cases failed to keep to the reply that had been given.[7]

One important step in the process was taken in 1414 when the Commons asked Henry V (1413-22) to be considered "as well Assentirs as Peticioners" and also asked that when their petitions were written in the form of law, they not be altered without their consent.[8] A few years later, during the reign of Henry VI (1422-61; 1470-71), the Commons succeeded in establishing the practice of having their requests in relation to legislation presented to the King in the form of bills, and they obtained the King's assurance that those bills would not be altered without their consent.[9]

The evolution of the role of the Commons in the legislative process was also marked by the changes made to the enacting clause used in statutes. Starting at the beginning of the reign of Edward III (1327-77), the words "at the request of the Commons" were used as the enacting clause. Under Henry VI, the words "by authority of Parliament" first appeared in legislation, reflecting the growing influence of the Commons in the legislative process.[10]

Once it had been agreed that the statutes should accurately reflect Parliament's requests in relation to legislation, it became necessary to make procedural rules to guide the introduction and passage of bills. By the end of the reign of Elizabeth I (1558-1603), the practice of three readings, with no debate on the first reading and reference of the bill to a committee after second reading, was already firmly established.[11]

CANADA

Before Confederation

In the years preceding Confederation, the assemblies of the Canadian colonies relied on British parliamentary traditions in conducting their deliberations. The legislative assemblies of Upper and Lower Canada that were instituted by the *Constitutional*

---

7. A favourable reply did not necessarily mean that the Commons obtained the legislation they wanted from the King. Sometimes, the matter would be forgotten, or intentionally laid aside until the legislature was dissolved. See Ronald Butt, *A History of Parliament: The Middle Ages*, London: Constable, p. 271; *Anson*, p. 247.

8. *Anson*, p. 248.

9. Although Henry VI and Edward IV (1461-70 and 1471-83) occasionally added new provisions to statutes without consulting Parliament, the form of legislating as we know it today has its origin in the reign of Henry VI (*May*, 11th ed., p. 459).

10. *Anson*, p. 249.

11. J.E. Neale, *The Elizabethan House of Commons*, Hammondsworth: Penguin Books, 1st ed. (1949), revised edition (1963), p. 356.

Act, 1791 followed British parliamentary procedure.[12] The legislative process of the Assembly of Upper Canada, however, was not as elaborate as that of the Assembly of Lower Canada, which had adopted a larger number of rules of procedure in 1792 for passing its bills.[13]

The first Canadian code of procedure, which was published in March 1793 under the title *Rules and Regulations of the House of Assembly, Lower Canada,*[14] contained provisions to govern both the introduction and the passage of the bills of that assembly. At that time, committees were often assigned the task of formulating a bill.[15] Every bill had to be introduced by motion, and be given three readings in both languages,[16] and could not be amended or referred to a committee before receiving second reading.[17] Every bill also had to be printed before second reading. After being passed by the Assembly, bills were transmitted to the Legislative Council for adoption by members of the Council and ultimately for Royal Assent.[18]

At the time of the Union of Upper and Lower Canada in 1840, the legislative assemblies had to agree on a common procedure. Most of the rules that were adopted at that time were those in force in the Assembly of Lower Canada.[19] The procedure for the passage of public bills remained essentially the same.[20] However, a number of provisions were adopted to deal with private bills.[21]

---

12. *Bourinot*, 1st ed., p. 19.

13. *O'Brien*, pp. 86-9, 113-4, 173-4.

14. At that time, this was a 73-page document that had been prepared by a committee of the Assembly under the direction of Speaker Jean-Antoine Panet.

15. *O'Brien*, p. 174.

16. To preserve the uniformity of the texts, bills relating to the criminal laws of Great Britain were introduced in English and then translated. Bills relating to the civil laws, customs and rights were introduced in French and then translated. This meant that several days might go by between when the motion to introduce the bill was adopted and the motion for first reading (*O'Brien*, p. 174).

17. At that time, bills were referred to a Committee of the Whole or a select committee. See Chapter 19, "Committees of the Whole House", the section that gives a historical overview of Committees of the Whole in Canada.

18. Every bill first had to be submitted to the Governor, or the Governor's representative, for assent in His/Her Majesty's name. Assent could be given or withheld, or the Governor could reserve assent and submit the bill for the "Signification of his Majesty's Pleasure thereon" (*Constitutional Act, 1791*, R.S.C. 1985, Appendix II, No. 3, ss. XXX, XXXI).

19. *O'Brien*, p. 134.

20. *O'Brien*, pp. 279-80.

21. *O'Brien*, p. 279.

Since Confederation

When the House of Commons of Canada met for the first time on November 6, 1867, it began its proceedings under the rules of the Legislative Assembly of the Province of Canada, which already contained provisions relating to the consideration of bills. On December 20, 1867, it approved the report of a special committee that had been instructed to assist the Speaker in establishing the rules of procedure for the House. The only major change that was made to the rules of the former Legislative Assembly of Canada related mainly to the process for considering private bills.[22] Consequently, the sections that appear in the Rules of the former Legislative Assembly of Canada under the heading "Proceedings on Bills"[23] were reproduced in full in the first edition of the Standing Orders of the House of Commons.

Some of the rules concerning the legislative process that were in effect at Confederation are still in effect today. Some examples are: the Standing Orders prohibiting the introduction of bills in blank or in an imperfect form, and stipulating that all bills be read three times on different days, be printed in both official languages and be certified by the Clerk of the House on each reading.[24]

The rules of procedure governing the legislative process have been amended on several occasions since 1867 with the aim of facilitating the consideration of public bills, expanding the roles of committees and allowing for greater participation by Members of the House of Commons. For instance, until 1913, a Member had to seek leave of the House if he wanted to introduce a bill, and that motion could be debated and amended.[25] In April 1913, the House decided that motions for leave to introduce a bill would no longer be debated or amended.[26] As well, in 1955, it added another provision to the Standing Orders specifying the practice by which a Member who proposed such a motion would be given leave to provide a brief description of the bill.[27] In 1991, the House again amended the Standing Orders to provide that motions for leave to introduce a bill be deemed to be carried, without debate, amendment or question put.[28]

Some procedural rules were also amended to allow the House to expedite its business. From Confederation until 1927, there was practically no time limit on the

---

22. *Debates*, December 20, 1867, p. 333.

23. For a number of years, the expression "Bill" was used in both English and French to refer to bills. The expression "*projet de loi*" was first used in the French version of the Standing Orders of the House in 1982.

24. See rules 40, 43, 44, 48 and 93 of the first edition of the Rules of the House, adopted on December 20, 1867.

25. See, for example, *Journals*, March 4, 1884, pp. 184-5.

26. *Journals*, April 23, 1913, pp. 507-9.

27. *Journals*, July 12, 1955, pp. 930-1.

28. *Journals*, April 11, 1991, p. 2913.

length of Members' speeches. Debates on bills might sometimes go on for several days.[29] In 1927, the House adopted a Standing Order imposing a limit on the speeches of most Members.[30] That fundamental rule remained in effect without amendment until 1982, the year when the House incorporated specific provisions into the legislative process governing the length of speeches and the period for questions and comments.[31]

Over the years, a number of special committees have examined the Standing Orders governing the legislative process.[32] In 1968, the House assigned the Special Committee on Procedure and Organization of the House the task of performing a thorough review of the legislative process.[33] In its Third Report, the Committee recommended changes designed to eliminate obsolete practices,[34] provide more meaningful opportunities for Members to participate in the consideration and shaping of bills, and identify the crucial stages in a bill's passage.[35] The most important provisions adopted at that time include referring bills other than those based on Supply and Ways and Means motions to standing or special committees, reviving the report stage as a debating stage of the legislative process and reducing the maximum length of speeches in debates at the report stage, and giving the Speaker the authority to select and combine amendments.[36]

---

29. See the comments in *Debates,* April 19, 1886, pp. 789-90.

30. *Journals*, March 22, 1927, pp. 328-9. Until 1982, the present Standing Order 43 governed the length of speeches during consideration of bills.

31. *Journals*, November 29, 1982, p. 5400. See also Special Committee on Standing Orders and Procedure, Third Report, presented to the House on November 5, 1982 (*Journals*, p. 5328).

32. See, in particular, the report of the Joint Committee on Legislation. That Committee was established in 1923 to consider various matters, including the form of bills (*Journals*, June 14, 1923, pp. 469-70). See also Special Committee on Procedure and Organization of the House, Report, presented to the House on December 19, 1963, paragraph 2 (*Journals*, pp. 705-6), and Special Committee on Procedure and Organization of the House, First Report, presented to the House on March 25, 1964, paragraph 9 (*Journals*, p. 125).

33. *Journals*, September 24, 1968, p. 68; December 20, 1968, pp. 554-62. See also Special Committee on Procedure and Organization of the House, Fourth Report, presented to the House on March 13, 1968 (*Journals*, pp. 761-7), before the dissolution of the Twenty-Seventh Parliament.

34. See *Journals*, December 6, 1968, p. 432.

35. For example, the first version of Standing Order 69, which was adopted in December 1867, read as follows: "That this bill be now read a first time". That text remained unchanged until the amendments adopted in December 1968, which gave it its present wording: "That this bill be read a first time and printed." The Committee intended the effect of the amendment to be that the passing of the motion would mean only that the House consented to the introduction of the bill without any commitment beyond the fact that it should be made generally available for the information of Parliament and the public. The new version gave effect to some of the objectives of the Committee, which wanted the crucial stages in the passage of a bill to be identified. While it recommended retaining the three readings, the Committee proposed that the motion relating to each reading be rephrased in such a way as to illuminate the philosophy behind each of the stages in that process (*Journals*, December 6, 1968, pp. 432-3; December 20, 1968, p. 576).

36. *Journals*, December 6, 1968, pp. 432-4; December 20, 1968, pp. 554-62.

In the early 1980s, special committees which had been instructed to examine House procedure once again undertook a consideration of the twin issues of expediting and broadening the scrutiny of bills and expanding the work assigned to committees. In March 1983, a report recommended that "legislative committees" be created and given the task of examining each bill in depth.[37] Although the recommendations that came out of that study were not adopted, the Special Committee on the Reform of the House of Commons recommended, in 1984, that legislative committees be created and that bills based on Ways and Means motions also be referred to legislative committees. The Committee also suggested that the scrutiny of such complex bills in small committees composed of a group of specialist Members was preferable to study by a Committee of the Whole.[38] These two recommendations were incorporated into the amendments made to the Standing Orders on June 27, 1985.[39]

A few years later, in April 1991, the House made extensive changes to its Standing Orders. Among the provisions amended were those relating to the automatic adoption of motions for the introduction and first reading of bills; to the referral, by a Minister after consultation, of a bill to a standing or special committee instead of to a legislative committee; to the requirement of a period of two sitting days, as opposed to 48 hours, between the time a bill is reported and the commencement of report stage; and to the requirement of a 24 hours' written notice for any motion respecting Senate amendments to a bill.[40]

At the beginning of the Thirty-Fifth Parliament in 1994, the Standing Orders were once again amended to make the legislative process more flexible.[41] New provisions were added relating to the preparation and bringing in of bills by committees and to the option of referring bills to either standing, special or legislative committees. However, bills based on Supply motions continued to be referred to a Committee of the Whole. In addition, it became possible for a Minister to move that a government bill be referred to a committee before second reading.

Although the House has since returned to the previous practice of referring bills only to standing and special committees, the rules pertaining to the referral of bills to legislative committees have not been changed. They still exist but have not been resorted to since the changes to the Standing Orders in 1994.

---

37. See Special Committee on Standing Orders and Procedure, Sixth Report, presented to the House on March 29, 1983 (*Journals*, p. 5765), Issue No. 19, pp. 3-12.

38. See Special Committee on the Reform of the House of Commons, First Report, presented to the House on December 20, 1984 (*Journals*, p. 211), Issue No. 2, pp. 7-10, 21.

39. *Journals*, June 27, 1985, pp. 918-9.

40. *Journals*, April 11, 1991, pp. 2898-932.

41. *Journals*, January 25, 1994, pp. 58, 61; February 7, 1994, pp. 112-20.

Types of Bills

There are two main categories of bills: public bills and private bills. While public bills deal with questions of national interest,[42] the purpose of private bills is to grant powers, special rights or exemptions to a person or persons, including corporations.[43]

PUBLIC BILLS

Public bills may be initiated by a Minister, in which case they are referred to as "government bills". They may also be initiated by private Members, in which case they are called "private Members' bills".

Government Bills

A government bill is the text of a legislative initiative that the government submits to Parliament to be approved, and possibly amended, before becoming law. Such bills relate to a matter of public interest and may include financial provisions.

Private Members' Bills

A private Member's bill is the text of a legislative initiative that is submitted to Parliament by a Member who is not a Minister to be approved, and possibly amended, before becoming law. Most bills of this type originate in the House of Commons, but some of them are sent to the Commons by the Senate.

Debate on private Member's bills can take place only during the hour set aside for "Private Members' Business".[44] Before this kind of bill can be taken up for debate by the House, it must have been selected following a random draw, as provided by the Standing Orders.[45] At least two weeks must elapse between first and second readings of this type of bill.[46]

---

42. See, for example, Bill C-15, *An Act to amend, enact and repeal certain laws relating to financial institutions* (*Journals*, March 8, 1996, p. 69).

43. See, for example, Bill C-1001, *An Act respecting Bell Canada* (*Journals*, April 12, 1978, p. 638).

44. See Chapter 21, "Private Members' Business".

45. Standing Orders 87 to 99.

46. Standing Order 88.

PRIVATE BILLS

The purpose of a private bill is to exempt a person or group of persons, including a corporate person, from the application of a statute.[47] It may not be introduced by a Minister, and must be founded on a petition signed by the persons who are interested in promoting it. The distinction between a public bill and a private bill is primarily a function of the purpose of the bill.

Most private bills are introduced in the Senate, but they may also be introduced in the House of Commons, although this is a rarer occurrence. Private bills before the House are dealt with as Private Members' Business, since they are moved by Members who do not hold ministerial office. Although private bills must go through the same stages as any other legislative measure, there are other stages that must be completed before they are introduced.[48]

Bills that seem to be both public and private in nature are referred to as hybrid bills. While British parliamentary practice allows this type of bill, that is not the case in the Canadian Parliament.[49] Canadian parliamentary procedure requires that all bills be classified as either public bills or private bills.[50] When a single bill contains both private bill and public bill considerations, it is dealt with as a public bill.[51]

Form of Bills

The enactment of a statute by Parliament is the final step in a long process that starts with the proposal, preparation and drafting of a bill. The drafting of a bill, in particular, is one of the most important stages in the process. At that point, the decision makers and drafters must take into account certain constraints; the failure to abide by these constraints may have consequences in relation to the interpretation and application of the law and the proper functioning of the legislative process.

---

47. Private legislation may be defined as legislation "of a special kind for conferring particular powers or benefits on any person or body of persons, including individuals and private corporations, in excess of or in conflict with the general law" (*Beauchesne*, 6th ed., pp. 285-6).

48. See Chapter 23, "Private Bills Practice".

49. In a ruling dated February 22, 1971, Speaker Lamoureux stated that "the fact that [a bill that has both private and public characteristics] may correspond to what is a hybrid bill in ... the British House, does not mean it should be treated that way in our own Parliament" (*Journals*, p. 351).

50. In a ruling dated March 12, 1875, Speaker Anglin clearly ruled that a bill that involved private considerations could not be introduced as a public bill (*Journals*, p. 213). See also *Journals*, October 23, 1975, pp. 795-6.

51. *Journals*, February 22, 1971, p. 352; *Debates*, April 15, 1985, pp. 3699-700.

LIMITS ON LEGISLATIVE ACTION

The Constitution of Canada sets out a number of rules that define the limits on legislative action and circumscribe what may be done by the government and Parliament.[52] The effect of the legal duality, which is one of the unique characteristics of Canada, may be to create differences in how a federal statute is applied and interpreted, depending on whether the part of Canada where it is being applied is governed by common law or civil law.[53]

Bills must be enacted, published and printed simultaneously in French and English. Section 133 of the *Constitution Act, 1867* requires that bills proceed in both languages through the entire legislative process, including first reading.[54] Section 18 of the *Constitution Act, 1982* further provides that both versions of the statutes are equally authoritative.

DRAFTING BILLS

Government Bills

The production of a government bill begins when the government decides to transform a policy initiative into a legislative proposal.[55] The Department of Justice then prepares a draft bill, following the instructions given by Cabinet.[56] The Minister of Justice is required to examine every bill introduced by a Minister, and to ascertain that it is consistent with the *Canadian Bill of Rights* and the *Canadian Charter of Rights and Freedoms.*[57]

When a bill has been drafted in both official languages, it must be approved by Cabinet before being introduced in Parliament. The Government House Leader is responsible for reviewing the bill and recommending that it be introduced in

---

52. For example, sections 91 and 92 of the *Constitution Act, 1867* establish the legislative authority of the Parliament of Canada and of the provincial legislatures. Sections 53 to 57 set out rules relating to money votes and Royal Assent to bills. The *Canadian Charter of Rights and Freedoms* imposes certain requirements and restrictions on Parliament, specifically in relation to fundamental rights and freedoms.

53. Two legal systems coexist in Canada. Federal law, and the law of all provinces except Quebec, are governed by the common law in the Anglo-Saxon tradition. The law of Quebec follows rules that come down from the Romano-Germanic tradition, which make up what is called the "*droit civil*" or civil law.

54. See the decision of the Supreme Court of Canada in *Re Manitoba Language Rights* [1985], 1 S.C.R. 721, 783, which interprets section 133 of the *Constitution Act, 1867*. See also section 6 of the *Act respecting the Status and Use of the Official Languages of Canada*, S.C. 1988, c. 38.

55. For more information regarding the process of preparing federal laws and the role of the main participants in that process, see the Department of Justice document entitled *A Guide to the Making of Federal Acts and Regulations* (hereinafter referred to as the *Guide*).

56. Prior to 1948, the responsibility for drafting government legislation was left to the department or agency within whose jurisdiction the subject matter in question fell. Draft bills were scrutinized, revised and often redrafted under the direction of the Law Clerk and Parliamentary Counsel of the House of Commons. In 1948, the legislative drafting function was centralized into a single office: the Legislation Section of the Department of Justice.

57. *Department of Justice Act*, R.S.C. 1985 (1st Supp.), c. 31, s. 93. See also *Guide*, pp. 26-9.

Parliament. Generally, the Government House Leader asks Cabinet to delegate this responsibility to him or her. [58]

Private Members' Bills

Members of the House of Commons who are not in Cabinet may introduce bills that will be considered under Private Members' Business. Members have access to legislative services, which are under the authority of the Speaker of the House, for drafting their bills. Before a bill is introduced in the House, the legislative services of the House of Commons will certify that it is acceptable as to its form and compliance with legislative and parliamentary conventions. [59]

Private Bills

A private bill, which is sponsored by a private Member, is founded on a petition which must first have received a favourable report by the Examiner of Petitions or by the Standing Committee on Procedure and House Affairs. [60] While the form of a private bill is similar to that of a public bill, a private bill must have a preamble, which is not mandatory for a public bill. [61] The Standing Orders of the House also provide for certain rules of drafting and, specifically, rules relating to bills for an Act of incorporation and bills amending or repealing existing Acts. [62]

Drafting by a Committee

A committee may be instructed to prepare and bring in a bill [63] or a committee may be appointed for that specific reason. In both cases, a motion for the preparation of a bill by a committee may be moved by either a Minister or a private Member. A committee that has been instructed to prepare a bill shall, in its report, recommend the principles, scope and general provisions of the bill and may, if it deems it

---

58. See *Guide*, pp. 137-9.

59. A Royal Recommendation, which may only come from a Minister, must be provided before the adoption of bills containing provisions that involve the expenditure of public funds. In addition, Members may not introduce bills involving an increase in taxation: such bills must be preceded by a Ways and Means motion, which can only be moved by a Minister.

60. The provisions relating to this type of bill are described in sections 129 to 147 of the Standing Orders. See also Chapter 23, "Private Bills Practice".

61. *Beauchesne*, 6th ed., p. 287.

62. See, in particular, Standing Order 136(2) and (5). See also, in Chapter 23, "Private Bills Practice", the section dealing with the form of private bills.

63. Standing Order 68(4)(*a*) and (*b*). In February 1994, the House added new provisions to its Standing Orders relating to bills to be prepared and brought in by committees (*Journals*, February 7, 1994, pp. 115-6). This option has always been available, but the House has used it only very rarely. See, for example, the motion by G.W. Baldwin (Peace River) in *Routine Proceedings and Orders of the Day* (November 10, 1969, p. 31); the motion moved by Geoff Wilson (Swift Current–Maple Creek) under the rubric of Private Members' Business (*Journals*, December 13, 1985, p. 1390); and the motion of Don Mazankowski (Deputy Prime Minister) (*Journals*, April 27, 1987, pp. 783-5).

appropriate, include recommendations regarding legislative wording.[64] If the House concurs in the committee report, this will be an order of the House to bring in a bill based on the report.

Other Drafting Characteristics

Bills may also have other drafting characteristics, depending on the purpose of the proposed legislation.

- New legislation: Bills resulting from a policy decision or, in some cases, to implement treaties, conventions or agreements, to accept recommendations arising out of a report of a Task Force or Royal Commission of Inquiry, to carry out administrative measures, or to deal with emergencies.[65]

- Major revisions of existing Acts: Bills to revise an Act because it contains a sunset clause (certain Acts provide that they must be revised after a certain period of time) or because of changing economic or social standards or circumstances.[66]

- Amendments to existing Acts: Bills to amend existing Acts. The amendments may be of either a substantive or a housekeeping nature.

- Statute law amendment bills: An initiative for the purpose of eliminating anomalies, inconsistencies, archaisms and errors in existing legislation and to deal with other matters of a non-controversial and uncomplicated nature.[67]

- Ways and Means bills: An initiative based on Ways and Means motions, the purpose of which is to create a new income or other tax, to continue a tax which is expiring, to increase a tax or to extend the scope of a tax. These bills are governed

---

64. Standing Order 68(5).

65. For example, the *Investment Canada Act*, R.S.C. 1985, c. I-21.8 (c. 28 (1st Supp.)); the *Canadian Security Intelligence Service Act*, R.S.C. 1985, c. C-23, which implemented a Royal Commission of Inquiry recommendation; the *Canada-United States Tax Convention Act*, S.C. 1984, c. 20, which resulted from a treaty; the *Western Arctic (Inuvialuit) Claims Settlement Act*, R.S.C. 1985, c. W-6.7 (S.C. 1984, c. 24), which implemented an agreement; and the *Garnishment, Attachment and Pension Diversion Act*, R.S.C. 1985, c. G-2, which was an administrative measure (Department of Justice of Canada, *The Federal Legislative Process in Canada*, 1989, p. 6).

66. For example, the *Juvenile Delinquents Act*, R.S.C. 1970, c. J-3, which was replaced by the *Young Offenders Act*, R.S.C. 1985, c. Y-1 (*The Federal Legislative Process in Canada*, p. 6).

67. Proposed amendments must not be controversial, involve the spending of public funds, prejudicially affect the rights of persons, or create a new offence or subject a new class of persons to an existing offence (*The Federal Legislative Process in Canada*, p. 7).

by specific provisions of the Standing Orders.[68] Only a Minister may introduce a Ways and Means bill.[69]

- Appropriation bills: An initiative introduced in the House in response to the adoption of Main or Supplementary Estimates or Interim Supply. These bills are also governed by specific provisions of the Standing Orders.[70] Only a Minister may introduce an appropriation bill.

- Borrowing authority bills: An initiative to seek authority to raise money when public revenues are not adequate to cover government expenditures.[71]

- *Pro forma* bills: A *pro forma* bill is introduced by the Prime Minister at the beginning of each session. It affirms the right of the House to conduct its proceedings and to legislate, regardless of the reasons stated in the Speech from the Throne for convening the House. The bill is entitled *An Act respecting the Administration of Oaths of Office*; it is numbered C-1 but is not printed. It is given first reading, but not second reading.[72]

- Draft bills: This expression is used to refer to the draft form of a bill that has not yet been introduced in either House. Occasionally, the House may have the draft of a government bill sent to a committee for examination. As the bill has not yet been given first reading, the committee may examine the proposed legislation without being constrained by the rules of the legislative process, and may recommend changes. The government can then take the committee's report into consideration when finalizing the draft of the bill.

- Omnibus bills: Although this expression is commonly used, there is no precise definition of an omnibus bill. In general, an omnibus bill seeks to amend, repeal or enact several Acts, and it is characterized by the fact that it has a number of related but separate parts.[73] An omnibus bill has "one basic principle or purpose

---

68. Standing Order 83. See also Chapter 18, "Financial Procedures".

69. Also called "tax bills". The most important are those that result from the Budget Speech, and particularly amendments to the *Income Tax Act* (*The Federal Legislative Process in Canada*, p. 6). The provisions relating to this type of bill are described in detail in Chapter 18, "Financial Procedures".

70. Standing Orders 73(4), 81 and 82. See also Chapter 18, "Financial Procedures".

71. Standing Order 73(5). See also Chapter 18, "Financial Procedures".

72. See, for example, *Journals*, September 23, 1997, p. 11. The custom is observed in other parliaments where, in most cases, the bill is read a first time and not heard of again until the start of the next session: the Australian House of Representatives refers to its "formal" or "privilege" bill (*House of Representatives' Practice*, 3rd ed., pp. 234-5); in the British House, it is called the Outlawries Bill (*May*, 22nd ed., p. 245). In the Legislative Assembly of British Columbia, the *pro forma* bill is Bill 1, *An Act to ensure the Supremacy of Parliament* (see, for example, *Votes and Proceedings* for March 17, 1992, and March 26, 1998). See also Chapter 8, "The Parliamentary Cycle".

73. See Speaker Parent's ruling, *Debates*, April 11, 1994, p. 2861.

which ties together all the proposed enactments and thereby renders the Bill intelligible for parliamentary purposes".[74] One of the reasons cited for introducing an omnibus bill is to bring together in a single bill all the legislative amendments resulting from a policy decision to facilitate parliamentary debate.[75]

The use of omnibus bills is unique to Canada. The British Parliament does enact this kind of bill, but its legislative practice is different, specifically in that there is much tighter control over the length of debate. In the Australian Parliament, the opposite practice seems to be followed (the procedure allows for related bills to be considered together for the purpose of debate and vote).[76]

It is not known exactly when the first omnibus bills appeared, but as may be seen from the introduction of a private bill to confirm two separate railway agreements, the practice seems to go back to 1888.[77] A number of omnibus bills have been introduced and passed without any procedural objection to their form being made by Members.[78]

It appears to be entirely proper, in procedural terms, for a bill to amend, repeal or enact more than one Act, provided that the necessary notice is given, it is accompanied by the Royal Recommendation (where necessary), and it follows the form

---

74. See Speaker Fraser's ruling, *Debates*, June 8, 1988, p. 16255.

75. See *Debates*, March 1, 1982, pp. 15485-6.

76. *House of Representatives Practice*, 3rd ed., pp. 415-6. It is interesting to note that on two occasions the Canadian House of Commons has used that procedure in examining bills (*Journals*, September 25, 1991, pp. 394-5; November 26, 1991, pp. 758).

77. *Journals*, March 26, 1888, pp. 135-6.

78. The first time that this procedure prompted any reaction was on April 2, 1953, when Brooke Claxton (Minister of National Defence) provided the following explanation regarding the reasons why the government wanted to amend three Acts in a single bill: "We have decided, and the house so far has concurred, that it would meet the convenience of hon. members, as it does very much that of the armed forces, if all amendments to existing legislation relating to the armed forces were contained in a single bill each year. In consequence the *Canadian Forces Act, 1950*; the *Canadian Forces Act, 1951*; the *Canadian Forces Act, 1952* have been enacted. All of these amended a number of different statutes, and this follows that precedent" (*Debates*, p. 3551). The enactment of the following bills, in fact, confirms that members are not always opposed to omnibus bills: Bill C-125, *An Act to amend the Old Age Assistance Act, the Disabled Persons Act and the Blind Persons Act* (S.C. 1963, c. 26); Bill C-40, *Statute Law (Military and Civilian War Pensions, Compensation and Allowances) Amendment Act* (S.C. 1980-1983, c. 19); Bill C-42, *Canada Post Corporation Act* (S.C. 1980-1983, c. 54); Bill C-43, *An Act to amend the Lobbyists Registration Act and to make related amendments to other Acts* (S.C. 1995, c. 12); and Bill C-41, *An Act to amend the Divorce Act, the Family Orders and Agreements Enforcement Assistance Act, the Garnishment, Attachment and Pension Diversion Act and the Canada Shipping Act* (S.C. 1997, c. 1). Members have on occasion commented favourably on certain omnibus bills. See, for example, *Debates,* March 1, 1982, p. 15482.

required.[79] However, on the question of whether the Chair can be persuaded to divide a bill simply because it is complex or composite in nature, there are many precedents from which it can be concluded that Canadian practice does not permit this.[80]

Members have often rejected the government's reasons for introducing omnibus bills and have argued that some omnibus bills are not acceptable. Frequently, they have cited their "ancient privilege" to vote separately on each proposal which is contained in a complex question. However, the Speakers of the House have ruled that their power to divide complex questions could extend only to substantive motions, and not to motions dealing with the progress of bills.[81] In calling for the division of an omnibus bill, Members sometimes argue that the bill contains more than one principle.[82] Occasionally, Members also contend that the long title of an omnibus bill should refer to every act being amended. The Chair has ruled that this is not necessary.[83]

79. When certain sections or parts of the Criminal Code are amended, it is often necessary to amend other Acts as well. This was the situation in the case of Bill C-55 (regarding high risk offenders), which also amended the *Corrections and Conditional Release Act*, the *Criminal Records Act*, the *Prisons and Reformatories Act* and the *Department of the Solicitor General Act* (S.C. 1997, c. 17). It was also the situation in the case of Bill C-95 (regarding criminal organizations), which amended other Acts in consequence (S.C. 1997, c. 23).

80. See, for example, the rulings of Speaker Sauvé (*Debates*, March 2, 1982, p. 15532, and June 20, 1983, pp. 26537-8) and Speaker Fraser (*Debates*, June 8, 1988, pp. 16255-7, and April 1, 1992, pp. 9147-9). On June 8, 1988, when he informed the House that he could not divide Bill C-130, *Canada-United States Free Trade Agreement Implementation Act*, Speaker Fraser ruled as follows: "Until the House adopts specific rules relating to omnibus Bills, the Chair's role is very limited and the Speaker should remain on the sidelines as debate proceeds and the House resolves the issue" (*Debates*, June 8, 1988, p. 16257).

81. As Speaker Jerome explained in a ruling, "... a motion containing two or more substantive provisions is quite distinct from a procedural motion or a motion which is generally described as having only the effect of dealing with the progress of a bill. The practice in respect of substantive motions has never been extended to those motions which relate to the progress of a bill. The use of the omnibus amending bill is well enshrined in our practices, and I really can find no reason to set aside my predecessor's very clear and sound reasoning, or the practice. Nor can I find any authority which would support an order of the Chair at this second reading stage that the bill be divided" (*Debates*, May 11, 1977, p. 5522). The conclusion reached by Speaker Lamoureux on January 23, 1969 (*Journals*, p. 617) was reiterated by Speaker Sauvé on June 20, 1983 (*Debates*, pp. 26537-8) and by Speaker Fraser on June 8, 1988 (*Debates*, pp. 16256-7).

82. See, for example, Speaker Parent's ruling, *Debates*, April 11, 1994, p. 2860.

83. See, for example, Speaker Fraser's ruling, *Debates*, June 8, 1988, p. 16257. The Speaker had invited members to consult the text by Elmer A. Driedger entitled *The Composition of Legislation: Legislative Forms and Precedents* (2nd ed., Ottawa: Department of Justice, 1976). See pp. 153-4 of that text, where the author explains Canadian practice as it relates to long titles. According to the Speaker, Driedger clearly demonstrates that every Act being amended need not be mentioned in the title and that the Canadian practice has evolved differently from British practice by the use of generic language.

Motions to divide omnibus bills have on occasion been moved in committee, but these have been ruled out of order. Unless a committee has received an instruction from the House, it may only report the bill with or without amendment.[84] Committee chairs have also ruled against motions to submit two reports on one bill in which each addressed specific topics in the bill, thus in effect dividing the bill.[85] However, committee chairs have ruled in order motions which would allow a committee to seek an instruction to divide a bill.[86]

Despite the refusal to divide omnibus bills, the Speaker has expressed deep concerns about the right of Members to make themselves heard properly,[87] and so has occasionally felt the need to suggest what remedies Members have to deal with the dilemma of having to approve several legislative provisions at the same time.[88]

While there has never been an occasion when the Chair has decided that a bill should be divided on the ground of complexity, there are however three cases that are of particular interest. In 1981, during examination of Bill C-54, *An Act to amend the statute law relating to income tax and to provide other authority for raising funds,* Speaker Sauvé ordered that Part I of the bill, relating to borrowing authority, be struck because the necessary notice had not been given.[89] Later in the same session, another amending bill that dealt with both taxation and the borrowing authority was introduced (Bill C-93). At the insistence of the opposition, the government decided to withdraw the bill, on May 7, 1982, and introduced two separate pieces of legislation on May 10, 1982.[90] The division of the omnibus bill in this case was brought about by the political process and was not the result of any procedural argument. The most noteworthy case is Bill C-94, *Energy Security Act, 1982*. On March 2, 1982, in response to a point of order raised the day before, asking the Chair to divide the bill, Speaker Sauvé ruled that there were no precedents which would permit her to divide the bill.[91] This led to the famous "bell-ringing" incident, as a result of which the government ultimately moved, and the

---

84. Standing Committee on Miscellaneous Estimates, *Minutes of Proceedings and Evidence*, June 27, 1975, Issue No. 39, p. 106.

85. Standing Committee on Justice and Legal Affairs, *Minutes of Proceedings and Evidence*, May 6, 1976, Issue No. 45, pp. 5-7.

86. Standing Committee on Indian Affairs and Northern Development, *Minutes of Proceedings and Evidence*, June 2, 1970, Issue No. 23, p. 40.

87. See *Journals*, January 26, 1971, p. 284; *Debates*, May 11, 1977, pp. 5522-3.

88. See, for example, *Journals*, January 26, 1971, p. 284; *Debates*, May 11, 1977, pp. 5523-4.

89. *Debates*, January 19, 1981, p. 6319.

90. *Journals*, May 7, 1982, pp. 4806-7; May 10, 1982, p. 4810.

91. *Debates*, March 2, 1982, p. 15532.

House passed, a motion to divide the bill into eight separate pieces of legislation.[92] Once again, the division of the omnibus bill was brought about by political interaction.

Bills in Blank or in an Imperfect Shape

Since Confederation, the Chair has held that the introduction of bills that contain blank passages or are in an imperfect shape is clearly contrary to the Standing Orders.[93] A bill in blank or in an imperfect shape is a bill which has only a title, or the drafting of which has not been completed.[94] Although this provision deals mainly with errors identified when the bill is introduced, Members have brought such defects or anomalies to the attention of the Chair at various stages in the legislative process. In the past, the Speaker has directed that the order for second reading of certain bills be discharged, when it was discovered that they were not in their final form and were therefore not ready to be introduced.[95]

Occasionally, bills contain provisions that refer to legislation that has not yet been enacted. In April 1970, some Members argued that a bill should be regarded as imperfect and should not be debated because it incorporated provisions of two statutes which had not yet been enacted. Although Speaker Lamoureux ruled that the bill was in order, he pointed out that this question could be raised again on third

---

92. *Journals*, March 22, 1982, pp. 4626-8. At that time, the Standing Orders provided no time limit for bells rung for unscheduled votes. A recorded vote was demanded on a motion to adjourn. The opposition Whip refused to accompany the government Whip into the Chamber to indicate to the Speaker their readiness to proceed with the vote; the government and opposition parties each demanded concessions before allowing the vote to take place. Consequently, the division bells rang continuously for over 14 days *(Debates*, March 2, 1982, pp. 15539-41; March 18, 1982, pp. 15555-7).

93. Standing Order 68(3). See Speaker Anglin's ruling, *Debates*, April 2, 1878, p. 1583. On May 16, 1923, the House, with the Senate, appointed a Joint Committee to consider a number of matters, including the form of bills and the best means of making legislation available in both Houses, at all stages of the process (*Journals*, p. 373). Although the existing text of Standing Order 68(3) was not amended at that time, the Committee recommended in its report, and the House agreed, that certain very specific information should appear in the printed version of bills (*Journals*, June 14, 1923, pp. 469-70). The recommendations set out in the report were incorporated into the Senate Rules. However, they have never been incorporated into the Standing Orders of the House. Over the years, Members have occasionally cited the guidelines set out in the report in calling for certain bills to be ruled out of order (*Debates*, May 12, 1931, pp. 1514-7; *Journals*, May 10, 1938, p. 322).

94. In April 1943, the Leader of the Official Opposition, Gordon Graydon, rose to speak against first reading of a bill that had not yet been written. He said that Members were being asked to pass what was just "a blank piece of paper" (*Debates*, April 16, 1943, pp. 2275-7).

95. *Debates*, May 16, 1978, p. 5461; December 15, 1980, p. 5746. On the other hand, in a ruling made on May 17, 1956, the Chair said that a bill had to have blanks when it was introduced and given first reading in order for it to be ruled to be in blank or in an imperfect shape. Speaker Beaudoin then ruled that a bill referring to an agreement that was not included *in extenso* in the bill was in order (*Journals*, pp. 567-9).

reading, if the House was asked at that stage to adopt a bill which was dependent on the adoption of other legislation.[96]

Printing and Reprinting of Bills

Within a few hours after a bill has been introduced and given first reading, it is printed and distributed to Members. Every bill must be printed in both official languages.[97] The bill will be reprinted after the committee stage, if it has been amended and the committee orders that it be reprinted. It is then used as a working document for the House at the report stage. After adoption at third reading, the bill as passed by the House in its final form is reprinted for the Senate's consideration. Ultimately, it is reprinted in the form of an Act after receiving Royal Assent, and it will then be published in the *Canada Gazette* and, at the end of the year, in the *Annual Statutes*.[98]

Clerical Alterations

The Chair has clearly ruled in the past that when a bill is in possession of the House, it becomes its property, and cannot be materially altered, except by the House itself. Only "mere clerical alterations" are allowed.[99] By issuing a *corrigendum* to the bill, the Speaker[100] may correct any obvious printing or clerical error, at any stage of the bill.[101] On the other hand, no substantive change may be made to the manner in which a bill was worded when it was introduced, or when a committee reported on it, otherwise than by an amendment passed by the House.[102]

---

96. *Debates*, April 20, 1970, pp. 6046-8. Similar rulings were made by Speaker Lamoureux (*Debates*, February 24, 1971, p. 3712) and Speaker Fraser (*Debates*, June 8, 1988, pp. 16252-9, and in particular pp. 16257-8; November 28, 1991, pp. 5513-4).

97. Standing Order 70. See Speaker Michener's ruling, *Journals*, January 19, 1960, p. 28.

98. The Department of Justice is responsible for the publication of federal statutes in the *Canada Gazette* and the *Annual Statutes*.

99. *Journals*, May 6, 1882, pp. 405-6.

100. In the British House of Commons, the Speaker is given wide latitude to correct minor errors in motions or bills (*May*, 22nd ed., pp. 332, 336 and 502). See also *Kaul and Shakdher*, p. 518.

101. *May*, 22nd ed., p. 502. In June 1984, the Chair ruled that the presence of blanks in a bill introduced by a Member was the result of a printing error, and the House agreed to proceed with second reading (*Debates*, June 26, 1984, p. 5139). In January 1987, the Standing Order was cited to argue that a government bill contained two flaws: there was a blank where a parliamentary document number should have appeared, and a memorandum of understanding did not appear. Speaker Fraser ruled that these anomalies did not make the Bill defective under Standing Order 68(3) and directed the Clerk to alter the bill to correct the errors. The Speaker pointed out that such errors would have "to be addressed with regard to their impact on the draft legislation before the House and the consequences that will flow therefrom" (*Debates*, January 26, 1987, pp. 2667-9).

102. *May*, 22nd ed., pp. 544-5.

Structure of Bills

A bill is composed of a number of elements, some of which, such as the title, are essential or fundamental, while others, such as the preamble, are optional. The following is a description of the various elements of a bill.

NUMBER

When a bill is introduced in the House, it is assigned a number to facilitate filing and reference.[103] Government bills are numbered consecutively from C-2 to C-200,[104] while private members' bills are numbered consecutively from C-201 to C-1000. Although private bills are rarely introduced in the House, they are numbered beginning at C-1001. In order to differentiate between bills that are introduced in the two Houses of Parliament, the number assigned to bills introduced in the Senate begins with an "S" rather than a "C". Senate bills are numbered consecutively beginning at S-1, whether they are government bills, private Members' bills or private bills, and are not renumbered or reprinted when they are sent to the Commons.

TITLE

The title is an essential element of a bill. A bill may have two titles: a full or long title and a short title.[105] The long title appears both on the bill's cover page, under the number assigned to the bill, and at the top of the first page of the document. It sets out the purpose of the bill, in general terms, and must accurately reflect its content. The short title is used mainly for citation purposes, and does not necessarily cover all aspects of the bill.[106] The first clause of the bill normally sets out the short title (except in the case of bills amending other Acts, which do not have a short title).

---

103. On March 12, 1974, Speaker Lamoureux announced the implementation of the numbering system now in effect in the House (*Journals*, pp. 31-2). At the beginning of each new session the numbering starts over.

104. The number C-1 is reserved for the *pro forma* bill that is traditionally introduced at the beginning of each new session.

105. For example, Bill C-44 (1998) gives the long title as follows: *An Act to authorize remedial and disciplinary measures in relation to members of certain administrative tribunals, to reorganize and dissolve certain federal agencies and to make consequential amendments to other Acts.* The short title reads: *Administrative Tribunals (Remedial and Disciplinary Measures) Act.*

106. See Ruth Sullivan, *Driedger on the Construction of Statutes*, 3rd ed., Toronto: Butterworths, 1994, pp. 253-8. A growing number of legislative assemblies, including some in Canada, are eliminating the use of long titles (*Driedger*, 3rd ed., p. 257, footnote 51).

PREAMBLE

Sometimes a bill has a preamble, which sets out the purposes of the bill and the reasons for introducing it.[107] The preamble appears between the long title and the enacting clause.

ENACTING CLAUSE

The enacting clause is an essential part of the bill. It states the authority under which it is enacted, and consists of a brief paragraph following the long title and preceding the provisions of the bill: *"Her Majesty, by and with the advice and consent of the Senate and House of Commons of Canada, enacts as follows:"*. Where there is a preamble, the enacting clause follows it.[108]

CLAUSE

A clause is a fundamental element of a bill. It may be divided into subclauses, and then into paragraphs and even subparagraphs.[109] A bill may be comprised of parts, divisions and subdivisions, but not necessarily; however, the numbering of the clauses is continuous from beginning to end. A clause should contain a single idea, which is most often expressed in a single sentence. A number of related ideas will be set out in subclauses within a single clause.[110]

INTERPRETATION PROVISIONS

A bill will sometimes include definitions or rules of interpretation,[111] which provide a legal definition of the key expressions used in the legislation and how those expressions apply, and which are often among the initial clauses of a bill. However, there is nothing that requires that a bill include interpretation provisions.

COMING-INTO-FORCE PROVISIONS

A bill may contain a clause, usually at the end of the bill, specifying when the bill or certain provisions of the bill will come into force. Sometimes, legislation is passed

---

107. *Interpretation Act*, R.S.C. 1985, c. I-21, s. 13. Preambles may assist the courts in understanding and construing legislation, and judges sometimes refer to the preamble in writing their judgements (see *Driedger*, 3rd ed., pp. 259-63).

108. *Interpretation Act*, R.S.C. 1985, c. I-21, s. 4.

109. In English, the practice is to use the expression "clause" until a bill becomes law, after which the expression "section" is used. In French, no such distinction is made and the expression "article" is always used.

110. While there is no specific rule regarding the content of bills, there must still be a theme of relevancy among the various issues addressed in the bill. Those issues must be relevant to and subject to the umbrella which is raised by the terminology of the long title of the bill. See the ruling of the Chair, *Journals*, May 6, 1971, pp. 531-2.

111. *Interpretation Act*, R.S.C. 1985, c. I-21, s. 15.

by both Houses of Parliament and receives Royal Assent, but does not come into force immediately if it contains a provision that it will come into force only on a specific date (other than the date of Royal Assent) or a date to be fixed by Order in Council. Otherwise, the bill will come into force on the day it is assented to.

SCHEDULES

A bill may contain schedules which provide details that are essential to certain provisions of the bill. There are two types of schedules:[112] those that contain material that cannot be put into the form of sections, such as, for example, tables, diagrams, lists and maps,[113] and those that reproduce an agreement that falls within Crown prerogative, such as, for example, treaties and conventions.[114]

EXPLANATORY NOTES

When the purpose of a bill is to amend an existing Act, the drafters will insert notes to explain the amendments made by the bill. Among other things, these notes provide the original text of the provisions affected by the bill. They are considered not to be part of the bill, and they disappear from subsequent reprints of the bill.[115]

SUMMARY

The summary is a general description of the bill. It consists of "a clear, factual, nonpartisan summary of the purpose of the bill and its main provisions".[116] The purpose of the summary is to improve the explanatory material that is available to understand better the contents of the bill. The summary is not part of the contents but appears separately at the beginning of the bill. Once the bill has been passed, it will also appear on a page preceding the resulting Act.[117]

---

112. See *Driedger*, 3rd ed., pp. 279-84.

113. See, for example, *An Act respecting Employment Insurance in Canada*, S.C. 1996, c. 23; *Appropriation Act No. 4, 1995-1996*, S.C. 1996, c. 4.

114. See, for example, *Geneva Conventions Act*, S.C. 1990, c. 14.

115. Members have opposed a bill where the explanatory notes appeared to be insufficient. Speaker Lamoureux has rejected the objection, stating that the Standing Orders do not require that an explanatory note accompany a bill (*Debates*, March 29, 1972, pp. 1267-8).

116. *Guide*, p. 128.

117. See, for example, *An Act to amend the Canada Elections Act (Reimbursement of Election Expenses)*, S.C. 1996, c. 26.

MARGINAL NOTES

Marginal notes consist of short explanations that appear in the margin of the bill. They do not form part of the bill, and appear only as readers' aids or for information purposes.[118]

UNDERLINING AND VERTICAL LINES

In a bill that amends an existing Act, the new text is underlined when it consists of long passages, or simply indicated with a vertical line (in the margin beside the new clauses, subclauses or paragraphs). When a bill that has been amended in committee is reprinted, only the additions made since the last printing are indicated in this manner.

HEADINGS

To make the reader's job easier, legislative drafters insert headings throughout the text. However, those headings are not considered to be part of the bill and therefore cannot be amended.[119]

TABLE OF CONTENTS

As an aid to readers, legislative drafters sometimes add a table of contents at the beginning or end of a bill. It is not, however, considered to be part of the bill.

ROYAL RECOMMENDATION

Bills that involve the expenditure of public funds must have a Royal Recommendation.[120] The recommendation is made by the Governor General. Generally, it is communicated to the House before a bill is introduced, and it must be published in the *Notice Paper* and printed in or annexed to the bill.[121] The Royal Recommendation is not part of the bill but appears separately at the beginning of the bill.[122] After the bill is given first reading, the text of the Royal Recommendation is printed in the *Journals*. The Royal Recommendation may only be obtained by the government.

---

118. *Interpretation Act*, R.S.C. 1985, c. I-21, s. 14. Traditionally, the courts have preferred to ignore marginal notes in construing statutes. However, that attitude is changing; in one of its judgements, the Supreme Court relied on marginal notes (see *Driedger*, 3rd ed., pp. 273-5).

119. See *Driedger*, 3rd ed., pp. 268-73.

120. This requirement is consistent with Standing Order 79(1) and Section 54 of the *Constitution Act, 1867*. The wording is as follows: "His/Her Excellency the Governor General recommends to the House of Commons the appropriation of public revenue under the circumstances, in the manner and for the purposes set out in a measure entitled [long title of the bill]". See also Chapter 18, "Financial Procedures".

121. Standing Order 79(2).

122. See, for example, Bill C-2, *Canada Pension Plan Investment Board Act* (First Session, Thirty-Sixth Parliament, 1997-99).

Stages in the Legislative Process

A bill is carried forward through all the stages of the legislative process "by a long chain of standardized motions" which must be adopted by the House before the bill becomes law. [123] It is these motions, and not the bill, that are the subject of the decisions and debates of the House. These stages "constitute a simple and logical process in which each stage transcends the one immediately before it, so that although the basic motions—that the bill be read a first (second or third) time—ostensibly are the same, and seem repetitious, they have very different meanings". [124] Moreover, the House does not commit itself conclusively in favour of a bill until the final stage, when it takes a decision to let the bill pass from the House or not. [125]

The Standing Orders of the House require that every bill receive three readings, on different days, before being passed. [126] The practice of giving every bill three separate readings derives from an ancient parliamentary practice which originated in the United Kingdom. [127] At that time, when the technology was not yet available to reproduce large numbers of copies at low cost, bills were introduced in handwritten form, one copy at a time. In order for Members to know what the content of the bill was, the clerk read the document to them; the idea of "reading" the bill was taken literally. [128]

Today, a bill is no longer read aloud, but the formality of holding a reading is still preserved. When the Speaker declares that the motion for first reading has

---

123. *Stewart*, p. 81.

124. *Stewart*, p. 81.

125. *Stewart*, p. 84.

126. Standing Order 71. The prohibition on giving more than one reading on the same day appears in the *Rules of the Legislative Assembly of the Province of Canada* (rule 43 in the 1866 version). At Confederation, that text became one of the rules of the new House of Commons of Canada. Standing Order 81(17) and (18) allows for an exemption from the rule requiring three readings on separate days in the case of Supply bills; where those bills are considered on the last allotted day in a Supply period, they must be passed in the same sitting.

127. Lord Campion, *An Introduction to the Procedure of the House of Commons*, 3rd ed., London: MacMillan & Co. Ltd., 1958, pp. 22-3. Although the early *Journals* of the House of Commons of the United Kingdom mention the practice of giving a bill three readings on different days, it has never been laid down in the British Standing Orders (*Stewart*, p. 80).

128. Before the reign of Queen Elizabeth I, it was not uncommon for a bill to be read four, five or even six times in the House to keep Members informed of its contents as amendments were made. By the end of the reign of Elizabeth I, the practice of adopting a limit of three readings was already established, and each reading was given to fill a specific need. A bill was given first reading in order to inform the House of its contents; this was generally the first the House knew of the purpose of the bill. Second reading gave interested Members a chance to hear the text of the bill again, in order that an informed debate could take place. If the House approved the legislation overall, but felt that amendments were required, the bill could be referred to a committee at this stage. However, it was not necessary or mandatory for a bill to be examined by a committee. The third reading enabled the House to hear the final, official text of the bill, including the amendments passed by the House. See *Neale*, pp. 356-61.

passed, a clerk at the Table rises and announces *"First reading of this bill"*, thus signifying that the order of the House has been obeyed. That scenario is repeated when the House has ordered a second and then a third reading of the bill.

A certification of reading must be affixed to every bill immediately after each of the three readings is adopted. The Clerk of the House is responsible for certifying each reading, and entering the date it passed at the foot of the bill.[129] A bill remains in the custody of the Clerk throughout all the stages of consideration. No substantive alteration to the bill is permitted without the express authority of the House or a committee, in the form of an amendment. The original bills, certified by the Clerk, form part of the records of the House.[130]

All bills must go through the same stages of the legislative process, but they do not necessarily follow the same route. Since the House adopted new rules to make the legislative process more flexible,[131] three avenues now exist for the adoption of legislation (see Figure 16.1):

- After appropriate notice, a Minister or a private Member may introduce a bill, which will be given first reading immediately. The bill is then debated generally at the second reading stage. It is then sent to a committee for clause-by-clause study.

- A Minister or a private Member may propose a motion that a committee be instructed to prepare a bill. A bill will be presented by the committee and carried through the second reading stage without debate or amendment.

- A Minister may move that a bill be referred to a committee for study before second reading.

Regardless of the avenue that the House decides to take, the bill will then have to be carried through report stage, be read a third time and be sent to the Senate for passage before receiving Royal Assent. At the start of a new session, a public bill may, if it is the same bill as was introduced in the preceding session, be reinstated at the stage it had reached at the time of prorogation. This procedure may be effected either by passing a motion to that effect[132] or, in the case of a private Member's bill, by invoking the provision of a new Standing Order adopted in 1998.[133]

---

129. Standing Order 72.

130. *Beauchesne*, 3rd ed., pp. 239-40.

131. See *Journals*, February 7, 1994, pp. 112-8.

132. This procedure was used at the beginning of the Second Session of the Thirty-Fifth Parliament (see *Journals*, March 4, 1996, pp. 34-5, 39-41). A total of 14 government bills and 11 private Members' bills, which had been introduced during the First Session of the Thirty-Fifth Parliament and had already advanced through certain stages of the legislative process, were reinstated. Bill C-7, respecting controlled drugs and substances, and Bill C-22, respecting the Lester B. Pearson International Airport, which were in the Senate when Parliament was prorogued, were deemed to have been passed at all stages in the House. They were therefore sent directly to the Senate (*Journals*, March 6, 1996, p. 51; April 19, 1996, p. 235). See also Chapter 8, "The Parliamentary Cycle".

133. Standing Order 86.1. See *Journals*, November 30, 1998, pp. 1327-8.

On urgent or extraordinary occasions, if the House so decides, a bill may be given two or three readings on the same day, or advanced two or more stages in one day.[134] This provision of the Standing Orders refers only to the reading stages.[135] It is up to the House itself, and not the Chair, to determine whether the matter is urgent.[136]

The following are the stages that a bill must go through when it is introduced in the House of Commons:

- Notice of motion for leave to introduce and place on the *Order Paper;*
- Preparation of a bill by a committee (where applicable);
- Introduction and first reading;
- Reference to a committee before second reading (where applicable);
- Second reading and reference to a committee;
- Consideration in committee;
- Report stage;
- Third reading (and passage);
- Consideration and passage by the Senate;
- Passage of Senate amendments by the Commons (where applicable);
- Royal Assent;
- Coming into force.

A bill that is introduced in the Senate must go through essentially the same stages, except that it is considered first in the Senate and then in the House of Commons.[137] Most bills may be introduced in either House, with the exception of bills which involve spending or relate to taxation, which must be introduced in the House of Commons.

---

134. Standing Order 71. For example, Bill C-24, *An Act to provide for the resumption and continuation of postal services*, advanced through second reading, consideration in a Committee of the Whole, report and third reading stages on the same day (*Journals*, December 2, 1997, pp. 314-9). Although it seems that the usual and correct practice has been to let a day or two go by between the different stages in the consideration of a bill, the House has often agreed, since the First Parliament, to expedite the passage of bills by circumventing the prohibition in the Standing Orders. (See Edward Blake's remarks in *Debates*, June 1, 1886, p. 1732. In the first three parliaments from 1867 to 1878, bills were expedited on 27 occasions.)

135. In ruling as to the application of this provision of the Standing Orders, successive Speakers have repeatedly observed that it applied to "readings" of bills, and not to the stages of consideration of bills (*Debates*, April 15, 1878, pp. 2006-7; April 24, 1878, p. 2157; October 11, 1949, pp. 667-9; February 24, 1969, pp. 5893-4). In February 1969, in response to a point of order questioning whether a bill could be read the third time on the day when it passed the report stage, Speaker Lamoureux reiterated that the report stage is not a reading. He pointed out that Standing Order 72 (now Standing Order 71) "always prevails. If there has been a previous reading in that sitting there cannot be a subsequent reading on the same day" (*Journals*, February 24, 1969, pp. 738-9) unless, of course, the House decides otherwise.

136. *Bourinot*, 4th ed., p. 540.

137. In 1997, a Member rose on a question of privilege in regard to the matter of introducing government public bills in the Senate. The Speaker ruled that this question could not be regarded as a question of privilege since the Standing Orders of the House allow for bills to be brought down from the Senate (*Debates*, October 9, 1997, pp. 732-5).

Figure 16.1   *The Three Options of the Legislative Process
(Government Bills Originating in the House of Commons)*

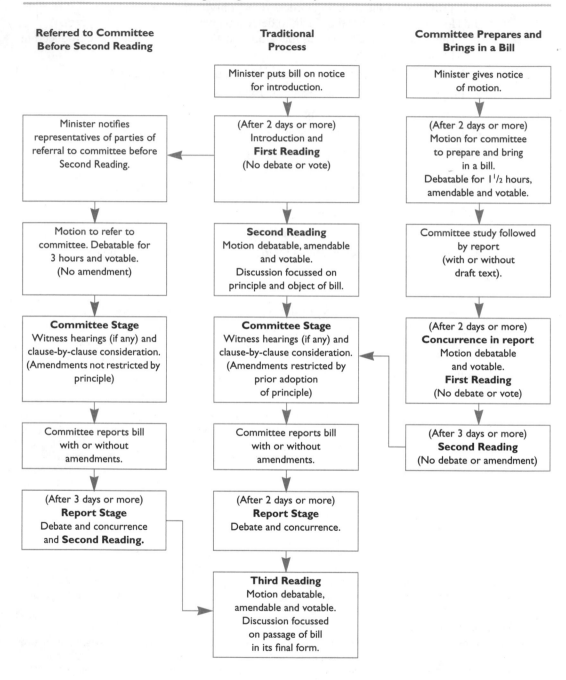

NOTICE OF MOTION FOR LEAVE TO INTRODUCE AND PLACE ON THE *ORDER PAPER*

The introduction of any public bill requires 48 hours' written notice. [138] The notice of motion is a prerequisite in the legislative process. Once notice is given for the introduction of a bill, no further notice is required in respect of the bill at the other stages of consideration (with the exception of motions to amend at the report stage). There are separate requirements that apply in respect of the notice required for private bills. [139]

A private Member or a Minister who intends to introduce a bill in the House of Commons must first give notice to the Clerk of the House before 6:00 p.m. (2:00 p.m. on Friday). [140] The title of the bill to be introduced is then placed on the *Notice Paper*. The day after it appears on the *Notice Paper*, the title will appear in the *Order Paper* in the order that the notices were received, for introduction in the House. This satisfies the 48-hour notice requirement in the Standing Orders. The title of the bill will remain on the *Order Paper* until the day when the private Member or Minister decides to introduce the bill.

There are special rules dealing with the introduction of bills that involve the expenditure of public funds and bills based on Ways and Means motions. Those provisions are described in Chapter 18, "Financial Procedures".

---

138. Standing Order 54. For further information on notice requirements, see Chapter 12, "The Process of Debate".

139. See Chapter 23, "Private Bills Practice".

140. Standing Order 54. A Member who wants to introduce a private Member's bill must ensure that no other Member has already given notice of a bill that is so similar as to be substantially the same. If that has already occurred, the Member could support that bill by asking to be added as "seconder". Up to 20 Members may jointly second a private Member's bill (Standing Order 86(3), (4) and (5)).

PREPARATION OF A BILL BY A COMMITTEE

The Standing Orders provide that a motion to appoint or instruct a committee to prepare a bill [141] may be moved by a Minister [142] or by a private Member. [143] However, the procedures to be followed in each instance are not entirely the same.

A Minister who wants to instruct a committee to prepare and bring in a bill must give 48 hours' written notice of the motion he or she intends to move to do so. [144] Once the notice period has passed, the motion will be placed on the *Order Paper* under "Government Orders". When it is called by the government, it may be debated for a maximum of 90 minutes, after which the Speaker will interrupt debate and put all questions necessary to dispose of the motion. [145]

If a private Member wants to instruct a committee to produce and bring in a bill, the Member must give at least two weeks' written notice of the motion he or she intends to make. [146] When that notice period has passed, the motion will be placed on the *Order Paper* under "Private Members' Business". It will then be governed by all the rules relating to Private Members' Business (that is, it will be subject to the random draw procedure, it will have to be selected as a matter that can be voted on and it will be taken up during the time set aside for Private Members' Business [147]).

The adoption by the House of a motion to concur in a report of a committee instructed to prepare and bring in a bill is an order to bring in the bill. [148] If, at the time the motion for first reading of a bill is moved, the Minister or Member states

---

141. Standing Order 68(4), (5), (6), (7) and (8).

142. On April 19, 1994, pursuant to a motion moved by a Minister, the Standing Committee on Procedure and House Affairs was instructed to prepare and bring in a bill respecting the system of readjusting the boundaries of electoral districts for the House of Commons (*Journals*, p. 363). A few months later, the Committee presented a report to the House which included the text of a draft bill (*Debates*, November 25, 1994, p. 8299). Bill C-69, *An Act to provide for the establishment of electoral boundaries commissions and the readjustment of electoral boundaries*, was given first reading on February 16, 1995 (*Journals*, p. 1141). The bill was passed by the House on April 25, 1995 (*Journals*, pp. 1368-9) but was not passed by the Senate.

143. On October 30, 1997, pursuant to a motion by a private Member, the Standing Committee on Justice and Human Rights was instructed to prepare and bring in a bill, before May 15, 1998, to amend those sections of the Criminal Code which deal with impaired driving (*Journals*, pp. 174-5). On May 15, 1998, the Committee presented a report to the House in which it explained to the House that it was unable to meet the deadline and accordingly the matter was postponed until the fall (*Debates*, p. 7067). On October 22, 1998, the Committee presented another report to the House containing an overview of its activities for the coming months and a commitment to complete its work by May 15, 1999, at the latest (*Debates*, pp. 9304-5). On May 25, 1999, the Committee presented a report to the House containing a draft bill (*Journals*, p. 1905).

144. Standing Order 54(1).

145. Standing Order 68(4)(*a*).

146. Standing Order 86(2).

147. Standing Order 68(4)(*b*). See also Chapter 21, "Private Members' Business".

148. Standing Order 68(6).

that the bill is based on the committee report, the motion for second reading will be moved at a later date, without debate or amendment. Consideration of a government bill at the second reading stage may not begin before the third sitting day after first reading.[149] At least two weeks must elapse between first and second reading of private Member's bills.[150] After second reading, the bill goes through the other ordinary stages for public legislation.

INTRODUCTION AND FIRST READING

The first real stage in the legislative process is the introduction and first reading of the bill in the House. When the notice period has elapsed and the Member or Minister is ready to introduce his or her bill, the Member or Minister informs the Chair of his or her intention to proceed during Routine Proceedings when the item "Introduction of Government Bills" or "Introduction of Private Members' Bills" is called. Leave to introduce a bill is granted automatically, and the motion is deemed carried, without debate, amendment or question put.[151] A Minister does not normally provide any explanation when requesting leave to introduce a bill, but may do so.[152] On the other hand, a private Member normally provides a brief explanation of the bill he or she is introducing in the House.[153]

The purpose of first reading is to allow for the bill to be introduced so that it may be printed and distributed to all Members. It is at that point that a specific bill number is assigned to it. Passage of the motion for first reading simply means that the House agrees to the introduction of the bill without any commitment beyond the fact that it should be made generally available for the information of Parliament and the public.[154] There can be no discussion at this stage. When leave to introduce the bill has been granted, the Speaker proposes the following motion to the House: "That this bill be read a first time and be printed." That motion is deemed carried, without debate, amendment or question put.[155] The Speaker then asks: "When shall the bill

---

149. Standing Order 68(7)(*a*).

150. Standing Order 88.

151. Standing Order 68(2).

152. See the remarks of Speaker Fraser, *Debates*, December 1, 1987, pp. 11343-4; April 7, 1989, pp. 228-9.

153. Standing Order 68(2) provides that any Member must be permitted to give an explanation. That section was incorporated into the Standing Orders in 1955 to "spell out the existing practice" (*Journals*, July 12, 1955, pp. 930-1). In the past, it sometimes happened that after hearing a Member's explanation the House decided to reject the motion for leave (*Debates*, February 22, 1932, pp. 380-4; August 3, 1964, p. 6285; November 13, 1967, pp. 4165-6; December 5, 1967, pp. 5035-6; November 7, 1986, p. 1193). Since 1991, the motion has been deemed carried without debate, amendment or question put (*Journals*, April 11, 1991, pp. 2913-4).

154. Report of the Special Committee on Procedure and Organization of the House, *Journals*, December 6, 1968, pp. 432-3.

155. Standing Order 69(1).

be read a second time?", and answers, "At the next sitting of the House." The question is in fact a formality which enables the bill to be placed on the *Order Paper* under the heading "Government Orders" or "Private Members' Business".[156]

Senate bills are already printed when they are sent to the House of Commons. Accordingly, the request for leave to introduce the bill is not required. The motion for first reading is deemed carried without debate, amendment or question put.[157] Senate bills then go through the same stages as House of Commons bills.

REFERENCE TO COMMITTEE BEFORE SECOND READING

Traditionally, when the House proceeds to second reading of a bill, it is asked to give approval to the principle of the bill. However, the effect of adoption of the principle at this stage of the legislative process is to limit the scope of amendments that may be made during committee study and at report stage. In wishing to provide more flexibility in the legislative process, when the House amended its Standing Orders in 1994,[158] it instituted a new procedure that allows a Minister to move that a government bill be referred to a committee before second reading.[159] This enables Members to examine the principle of a bill before second reading, and to propose amendments to alter its scope.[160] This procedure also applies to bills based on Ways and Means motions.[161]

---

156. See Speaker Fraser's ruling, *Debates*, May 24, 1988, pp. 15722-3.

157. Standing Order 69(2).

158. See *Journals*, February 7, 1994, p. 112. In 1991, the Standing Committee on Consumer and Corporate Affairs and Government Operations had been instructed to do a pre-study, before second reading, of Bill C-22, *An Act to enact the Wage Claim Payment Act, to amend the Bankruptcy Act and to amend other acts in consequence thereof* (*Journals*, June 19, 1991, p. 242). This was the first time that the House had used this procedure, and the initiative was very favourably received by opposition Members (see *Debates*, October 7, 1991, p. 3388). Subsequently, in 1993, in its study of parliamentary reform, the Standing Committee on House Management recommended that government bills be referred to committee after first reading. The Committee argued that this "process ... would assist Members and the House in playing a more meaningful role in the development and passage of legislation" (see Eighty-First Report of the Committee, *Proceedings and Evidence*, April 1, 1993, Issue No. 53, pp. 23-4).

159. Standing Order 73(1). This must not be confused with the pre-study procedure in the Senate, which applies before first reading of a bill. For an overview of the differences between the procedure followed in the House of Commons and the procedure in the Senate, see Roméo LeBlanc (Senator) and Gilbert Parent (Member of the House), " Parliament of Canada: Pre-study of Legislation in the Canadian Parliament", *The Parliamentarian*, Vol. LXXV, No. 3 (July 1994), (Canada Supplement) pp. C3-C6.

160. During the Thirty-Fifth Parliament (1994-97), 25 bills were referred to committees before second reading. Two examples are Bill C-43, *An Act to amend the Lobbyists Registration Act* (*Journals*, June 17, 1994, pp. 608, 611) and Bill C-12, *An Act respecting employment insurance in Canada* (*Journals*, March 7, 1996, p. 59). In the First Session of the Thirty-Sixth Parliament (1997-99) this procedure was not used frequently.

161. See the ruling of the Chair, *Debates*, April 10, 1997, p. 9531.

When the Order of the Day is read for the second reading of a government bill, a Minister may,[162] after notifying representatives of the opposition parties, propose a motion that the bill be forthwith referred to committee before second reading. The Standing Orders are silent as to the manner in which the representatives of the opposition parties are to be notified. However, the practice which has been followed since 1994 is for the Minister to inform the House of the government's intention at the time of the introduction and first reading of the bill. The motion to refer forthwith the bill to committee is not subject to any amendment, and debate is limited to three hours. At the end of the three hours, or when no more Members rise to speak, the Speaker puts the question on the motion.[163] If the motion is adopted, the bill is referred to a standing, special or legislative committee for consideration.

In general, during clause by clause consideration of a bill, the committee follows the same rules and procedures that apply to the consideration of bills in committee after second reading.[164] It may hear witnesses and receive briefs. However, the scope of the amendments that may be made to the bill is much wider, given that the committee study is not limited to the principle of the bill, the principle not having been approved yet by the House. At the end of its study, the committee reports the bill to the House, with or without amendment. The report stage of the bill may not be taken into consideration prior to the third sitting day following the presentation of the report.[165]

When the committee reports the bill to the House, the next stage is essentially a combination of the report stage and second reading. At this stage, Members may propose amendments, after giving written notice two sitting days prior to the bill being called.[166] When consideration of report stage is concluded, a motion "That the bill, as amended, be concurred in at report stage and read a second time" or "That the bill be concurred in at report stage and read a second time" is put and forthwith disposed of by the House, without debate or amendment.[167] Once concurred in at report stage and read a second time, the bill is set down for third reading and passage at the next sitting of the House.

---

162. In 1994, Speaker Parent ruled that only Ministers may refer bills to committee, and that this prerogative "cannot be invoked by private members" (*Debates*, May 11, 1994, pp. 4226-7; June 1, 1994, pp. 4710-1). Subsequently, the Standing Committee on Procedure and House Affairs recommended in its Fifty-Third Report presented to the House on December 9, 1994 (*Journals*, p. 1014) that the Standing Orders be amended to clearly indicate that only government bills can be referred to committee before second reading (Standing Committee on Procedure and House Affairs, *Minutes of Proceedings and Evidence*, December 8, 1994, Issue No. 36, p. 5). The House concurred in the report and the Standing Orders were amended on February 6, 1995 (*Journals*, p. 1081).

163. Standing Order 73(1)(*b*), (*c*) and (*d*).

164. See section below, "Consideration in Committee".

165. Standing Order 76(1).

166. Standing Order 76(2). One sitting day's notice is required for amendments proposed at the report stage of bills that have already been read a second time (Standing Order 76.1(2)).

167. Standing Order 76(9).

SECOND READING AND REFERENCE TO A COMMITTEE

Second reading gives Members an opportunity to hold a general debate on the principle [168] of a bill. Although the Standing Orders of the House make no specific reference to this point, tradition and practice hold that it is at this stage of the legislative process that debate on the general scope of a bill takes place. [169] Consequently, debate must focus on the principle of the bill and not its individual provisions. [170]

Recognition of the importance of this stage of the legislative process has evolved over the years. Traditionally, it was felt that second reading was the most important stage in the legislative process. [171] In 1968, the Special Committee on Procedure and Organization of the House stated in its report, after examining the stages of the process, that the significance of the second reading stage had been exaggerated in the past, and that the decisive stage should occur later in a bill's passage after it had emerged from a committee. [172] In the Committee's view, passage of the motion for second reading simply implied that the House had given preliminary consideration to the bill and that, without any commitment as to the final passage of the bill, it had authorized its reference to a committee for detailed scrutiny. [173]

Second reading of a bill and reference to a committee are moved in the same motion. The motion specifies the committee (standing, special, legislative) to which the bill is referred. [174] The Standing Orders require, in specific cases, that a bill be referred to a Committee of the Whole. [175]

Debate on second reading begins when the Minister or Member, as the case may be, rises when the Order of the Day is read for the second reading of the bill and moves "That Bill _____ be now read a second time and referred to the _____ Committee."

---

168. Other expressions may be used to refer to the "principle" of a bill. Sometimes the expressions "scope", "general scope" and "general objectives" are used. The expression "principle" is also used in the plural. A bill may have "general principles" (See *May*, 22nd ed., p. 468).

169. *Bourinot*, 4th ed., p. 509. The Senate Rules include a provision that the principle of a bill is "usually debated on second reading".

170. See, for example, *Debates*, March 24, 1970, p. 5434; April 27, 1970, p. 6334; June 10, 1970, p. 7973; see also the rulings of the Speaker, *Journals*, November 14, 1949, pp. 237-8; October 15, 1962, pp. 76-7.

171. *May*, 13th ed., p. 389.

172. See *Journals*, December 6, 1968, p. 433. The question of the importance of second reading is also raised in *House of Representatives Practice*, 3rd ed., p. 364.

173. *Journals*, December 6, 1968, p. 433.

174. See Chapter 20, "Committees". While the Standing Orders have provided since 1985 (*Journals*, June 27, 1985, p. 918) for the establishment of legislative committees, it has been the practice since the First Session of the Thirty-Fifth Parliament to refer bills to standing committees.

175. This is the case for Supply bills (Standing Order 73(4)). With the unanimous consent of the House, urgent or non-controversial bills which often go through more than one stage of the legislative process in a single sitting are generally referred to a Committee of the Whole. See also Chapter 19, "Committees of the Whole House".

The Standing Orders contain provisions concerning the length of speeches of Members during debate.[176] There is no time limit for the Prime Minister and the Leader of the Official Opposition. However, no other Member may speak for more than 40 minutes if he or she is the first, second or third Member to speak. In addition, during the five hours of debate that follow the first three Members, no Member may speak for more than 20 minutes, and a period not exceeding 10 minutes is then made available for questions and comments. If there are no questions or comments, or if the time has not been fully used, another Member may then speak. Questions and comments must be relevant to the Member's speech.[177] After five hours of debate, any other Member rising to speak has a maximum of 10 minutes, but no period for questions and comments is provided. The Whip of a party may indicate to the Chair at any time during a debate that one or more of the 20-minute or 10-minute periods of debate allotted to Members of his or her party will be divided in two.[178] By custom, every Member who moves a substantive motion is allowed a reply. Practice is that a Member who proposes a motion for second reading of a bill is also allowed a reply. In the case of government bills, a parliamentary secretary may exercise that right on behalf of the Minister only with the unanimous consent of the House.[179]

The Standing Orders of the House offer the government a mechanism for limiting debate at second reading, and also at other stages of the legislative process, by using time allocation motions.[180] This permits the government to establish a time-table for consideration of a public bill.[181] As well, the government has another mechanism, referred to as "closure", to compel the House to take a decision.[182] However, this latter procedure is rarely used in relation to bills.[183]

At the end of the debate, the Speaker puts the question on the motion "That the bill be now read a second time and referred to the committee". The Speaker asks the House whether it is ready for the question and whether it is the pleasure of the House

---

176. Standing Order 74. These provisions also apply to third reading. Under Standing Order 73(5), a maximum of two sitting days is set aside for the consideration of any bill respecting Borrowing Authority at second reading. Fifteen minutes before the expiry of the time provided for Government Orders, the Speaker interrupts the proceedings and puts forthwith and successively, without further debate or amendment, every question necessary to dispose of the second reading stage of the bill.

177. Standing Order 43(1).

178. Standing Order 74(2). That provision applies to the length of speeches and, where applicable, the period set aside for questions and comments.

179. Standing Order 42(2). See also Chapter 13, "Rules of Order and Decorum".

180. Standing Order 78.

181. See Chapter 14, "The Curtailment of Debate".

182. Standing Order 57.

183. See, for example, *Journals*, December 19, 1988, p. 52; December 23, 1988, p. 78. See also Chapter 14, "The Curtailment of Debate".

to adopt the motion. A recorded division may be requested.[184] Defeat of a motion for second reading results in the withdrawal of the bill; in fact, the bill is deemed to be no longer before the House, and no date is set for consideration of the bill to resume.[185] Once the motion is adopted, the bill is referred to the appropriate committee.

Amendments to the Motion for Reading

A public bill which was not referred to a committee before second reading may not be amended before being read a second time and being referred to committee.[186] However, a motion for second reading of a bill may be amended,[187] but only three types of amendments may be moved without notice: a three months' or six months' hoist; a reasoned amendment; and a referral of the subject matter to a committee.

The Hoist Amendment

The hoist is an amendment that may be moved to a motion for the reading of a bill. Its effect is to prevent a bill from being "now" read a second time, and to postpone the reading for three months or six months.[188] If it is adopted, the bill is withdrawn for the remainder of the current session. If it is defeated, the result of the procedure is nonetheless to have extended the debate and to have allowed Members to speak a second time.

The hoist amendment originated in British practice, where it appeared in the eighteenth century. It enabled the House of Commons to postpone the resumption of the consideration of a bill. It was subsequently agreed that the adoption of such an amendment by the House was tantamount to the rejection of the bill, since the postponement was deliberately set for a date after the end of the session. Normally, if the session went beyond that date, the bill was not placed again on the *Order Paper*.[189]

Historical events were responsible for the establishment of three or six months as the postponement period. A hundred years ago, sessions rarely lasted longer than six months, and so a six months' hoist amendment would be proposed at the beginning of a session, and a three months' hoist in the final weeks of a session. Today, sessions of the House of Commons of Canada are longer, but the length of sessions is neither regular nor fixed in advance.

---

184. If demanded by at least five Members (Standing Order 45(1)).

185. Once a question has been put to and disposed of by the House, it cannot be raised again during the same session (*Bourinot*, 4th ed., pp. 328-9; *May*, 22nd ed., pp. 560-1).

186. Standing Order 73(2). *Debates*, October 28, 1991, p. 4085.

187. *Beauchesne*, 6th ed., p. 199. An amendment to a motion for reading does not affect the provisions of the bill; rather, its purpose is to prevent the House from disposing of the bill, or to delay scrutiny of the bill.

188. Postponement for one month has been ruled in order, as it was regarded, on the whole, as a hoist amendment (*Debates*, November 4, 1985, p. 8331).

189. *May*, 10th ed., p. 446; 22nd ed., p. 504.

An analysis of hoist amendments moved in the House of Commons since Confederation shows that the cases in which this procedure has been used fall into two specific periods. The first was from 1867 to about 1920, and the second from 1920 to the present day.

The first hoist amendment was moved on November 28, 1867.[190] Prior to 1920, it was the government, not the opposition, that used hoist amendments most often.[191] Because the House had only a little time for government business during the short sessions of that era, the government sometimes felt obliged to dispose of a great number of private Members' bills by using the hoist procedure so that it would have more time to devote to its own legislation.

Since 1920, the period set aside for government business has grown to take up the largest share of the time in the House, and hoist amendments have gradually come to be used almost exclusively by the opposition. From an examination of the precedents, it is clear that hoist amendments were moved to motions for second and third reading during periods when there was considerable tension between the parties. Those amendments rarely passed: of the scores of cases recorded in the *Journals*, only four succeeded. In each of those four cases, the hoist amendment was moved by the government with the intent of defeating a private Member's bill.

A hoist amendment must meet a number of requirements if it is to be ruled in order. The purpose of the amendment is to neutralize the word "now" in the motion for reading. It must therefore amend the motion for reading by eliminating all of the words following the word "That" and replacing them with the following proposition: "Bill (number and title) be not now read a second time but that it be read a second time this day three months (or six months) hence." A hoist amendment requires no notice, may be debated and may not be amended.[192]

When a hoist amendment is rejected, debate continues on the main motion; however, no more than one hoist amendment may be moved in respect of the same reading motion.[193] The adoption of a hoist amendment (whether for three months or six months) is tantamount to the postponement of the consideration of the bill for an indefinite period.[194] Consequently, the bill disappears from the *Order Paper* and

---

190. *Journals*, November 28, 1867, p. 40.

191. Of the 62 hoist amendments recorded in the *Journals* for that initial period, no fewer than 44 were moved by the government and passed by the House.

192. *Beauchesne*, 5th ed., p. 225. *Debates*, November 20, 1986, p. 1381; November 21, 1986, p. 1413.

193. "On the rejection of a motion to postpone the second or third reading of a bill for three or six months, no further time amendment was to be permissible" (*Redlich*, Vol. I, p. 195).

194. In the National Assembly of Quebec, an amendment to postpone the consideration of a bill for 20 years was ruled to be out of order (*Journal des Débats*, National Assembly of Quebec, December 14, 1977, pp. 4750-3).

cannot be introduced again, even after the postponement time has elapsed.[195] The bill is accordingly defeated indirectly. It is no longer possible to place the bill back on the *Order Paper,* because to do so would be ruled contrary to the decision of the House. Members have tried to apply the hoist amendment to a resolution[196] or to include it in the text of a reasoned amendment,[197] but these attempts were ruled out of order.

The Reasoned Amendment

The reasoned amendment, another type of amendment that may be moved at second reading of a bill, allows a Member to state the reasons why he or she opposes second reading of a bill, by introducing another relevant proposal to replace the original question.[198] A reasoned amendment, which is introduced in the form of a motion, deletes all the words in the main motion after the word "That" and replaces them with other words.

It is difficult to determine precisely when a reasoned amendment was first moved in the House, but it is believed that the first such amendment was introduced in 1882.[199] An analysis of the reasoned amendments that have been proposed since Confederation shows that there was an initial period, from about 1882 to 1930, which was remarkable for the latitude allowed in the wording of reasoned amendments. In that period, Members were not too concerned with contesting the receivability of reasoned amendments, and the Chair only rarely intervened. In the early 1930s, regular requests began to be made to Speakers to rule as to whether reasoned amendments were in order; during that second period, which lasted until the mid-1960s, a number of precedents were established. Beginning in the 1970s, it became increasingly difficult for Members to move reasoned amendments that were

---

195. It seems that the House of Commons has always observed the principle of postponement for an indefinite period, except in one case. Canadian parliamentary annals contain an old case in which a bill was placed on the *Order Paper* again after expiry of the time for which it had been postponed (*Journals*, March 2, 1882, pp. 96-7). The postponement had been for one month only. The uncertainty surrounding the consequences of the postponement are undoubtedly the reason why the bill was placed back on the *Order Paper* one month later (in April) (*Bourinot*, 4th ed., p. 510). Before and after that one case, passage of a hoist amendment has always resulted in the withdrawal of the bill, which was not placed back on the *Order Paper* afterward.

196. See, for example, *Journals*, March 20, 1924, p. 67. A Member proposed to move an amendment to a government motion creating a special committee by adding the words "in eight months from this day". In making his decision, the Chair stated, "because we do not know whether it will be possible to appoint this committee eight months from now, the same result would be produced if the original motion were simply negatived" (June 21, 1960, pp. 673-4).

197. See, for example, *Journals*, February 24, 1970, pp. 485-7.

198. See, for example, *Debates,* October 21, 1996, p. 5492.

199. *Journals*, May 8, 1882, pp. 410-4.

acceptable in procedural terms.[200] The Chair is therefore now able to refer to a larger body of Canadian precedents in order to determine whether or not a reasoned amendment is in order.

The Standing Orders of the House of Commons contain no provisions respecting reasoned amendments.[201] However, precedents have established rules of procedure over the years that cover both the form and substance of such amendments. Today, a reasoned amendment generally takes the form of a request to the House to decline to give a bill second reading, for a specific reason.[202] There are only two broad categories of reasons that are now cited:

- A reasoned amendment may be declaratory of a principle adverse to or differing from the principles, policy or provisions of the bill; or

- A reasoned amendment may express an opinion as to any circumstances connected with the introduction or consideration of the bill, or with any other initiative opposed to its progress.

For a reasoned amendment to be in order, it must observe the following rules:

- It must be relevant and relate strictly to the bill being considered.[203] A reasoned amendment is not relevant, for example, if it relates to another bill;[204] is intended to divide the bill;[205] proposes that the bill be withdrawn and replaced by another bill,[206]

---

200. As early as 1958, Speaker Michener acknowledged to the House that it was not always easy "to draw the line between an amendment which is simply a negating of the principle of the bill and an amendment which is declaratory of a principle" (*Debates*, September 2, 1958, p. 4477). Similarly, in the early 1970s, Speaker Lamoureux reminded Members that they themselves had admitted that it was "difficult for the Chair to rule on the procedural aspect of reasoned amendments" (*Debates*, September 13, 1971, p. 7771). A few months later, on May 19, 1972 (*Debates*, p. 2433), the Acting Speaker also said that there was little doubt in the mind of the Chair that "a reasoned amendment at the second reading stage of a bill involves one of the more difficult parliamentary procedures".

201. In the past, the Chair has expressed the wish that a committee would look at this matter (see *Debates,* May 19, 1972, p. 2433; October 19, 1978, p. 284).

202. For examples of reasoned amendments that were found to be in order, see *Debates,* February 9, 1990, pp. 8146-7; February 14, 1990, pp. 8329-30; September 17, 1991, p. 2227; May 20, 1992, pp. 10955-6.

203. See, for example, *Journals,* November 20, 1962, pp. 298-9; May 14, 1964, p. 323. In the early 1970s, a number of Members unsuccessfully tried to propose reasoned amendments, which in many cases were nothing more than substantive motions proposed "in the guise of so-called reasoned amendments" (*Debates,* May 8, 1972, p. 2412). Some Members, citing a revision of the Standing Orders and changes to the legislative process, then tried to introduce amendments which quite often had no direct and substantive connection with the principle of the bill (*Debates,* May 19, 1972, pp. 2428-34).

204. See, for example, *Debates,* February 9, 1990, pp. 8109-10, 8134-5.

205. See, for example, *Journals,* May 7, 1971, p. 534.

206. *Journals,* May 14, 1971, pp. 554-5.

relates to the parent Act rather than to the amending bill;[207] goes beyond the scope of the bill;[208] involves the expenditure of funds or proposes changes that go beyond the scope of the royal recommendation.[209]

- It must not be a direct negation of the principle of the bill. The procedure to be followed when a Member does not agree with the principle of a bill and wants to reject it is simply to vote against the motion for second reading of the bill.[210]

- It must not relate to particulars of the bill,[211] if what is sought may be accomplished by amendments in committee.[212]

- It must not attach a condition to the adoption of the second reading motion.[213]

A reasoned amendment which is merely a statement of opposition to portions of the bill is not admissible.[214] On the other hand, a reasoned amendment need not necessarily oppose the principle of a bill in order to be admissible. Opposition to the principle of the bill is only one of the possible conditions for a reasoned amendment to be in order.[215]

Where a reasoned amendment is ruled to be in order, the House must dispose of it. To date, there have been no instances in which the House has decided in favour of a reasoned amendment. If it were to do so, that would end debate on the bill, and the House would have to forego second reading of the bill.[216] The order relating to the bill would disappear from the *Order Paper.*

Referral of the Subject Matter of a Bill to a Committee

During debate on the motion for second reading, a Member may propose an amendment to refer the subject matter of a bill to a committee for it to consider and report on the matter to the House. This type of amendment replaces all the words after "That" with words proposing that the bill be not now read a second time, that the order for second reading be discharged, the bill withdrawn from the *Order Paper* and the subject matter be referred to a committee.[217]

---

207. *Journals,* May 13, 1959, pp. 436-7; October 15, 1962, pp. 76-7.

208. *Journals*, June 5, 1972, p. 354.

209. *Journals,* June 5, 1972, p. 354.

210. See, for example, *Debates,* August 11, 1988, pp. 18212-3; October 3, 1989, pp. 4265, 4272.

211. See, for example, *Journals*, February 2, 1954, p. 257; February 13, 1969, pp. 697-8; January 26, 1971, pp. 285-6.

212. See, for example, *Debates*, February 9, 1990, pp. 8109-10, 8134-5.

213. See, for example, *Debates*, November 28, 1984, pp. 689, 707. *May,* 22nd ed., p. 505.

214. See Speaker Jerome's ruling, *Debates,* February 6, 1975, pp. 2971-2.

215. See, for example, *Debates,* August 30, 1966, p. 7808; March 13, 1995, p. 10363.

216. See *May,* 22nd ed., p. 506.

217. See *Journals,* February 13, 1992, p. 1018; February 24, 1992, p. 1065; September 26, 1995, p. 1952. This type of amendment does not exist in the British and Australian Parliaments (*May,* 22nd ed., p. 504; *House of Representatives Practice*, 3rd ed., p. 368).

Certain conditions must be met, however, for this type of amendment to be in order. First, the subject matter of the bill may not be referred to more then one committee[218] nor to a body not in existence.[219] Second, an amendment that would attach a condition to the adoption of the motion for reading of a bill is out of order.[220] Third, the actual provisions of the bill may not be referred to committee, as this would be tantamount to instructing a committee to consider certain provisions of a bill even before the bill has been read a second time and referred to committee.[221]

Motions of Instruction

Once a bill has been referred to a committee, the House may give the committee an instruction by way of a motion which authorizes it to do what it otherwise could not do, such as, for example, examining a portion of a bill and reporting it separately,[222] examining certain items in particular,[223] dividing a bill into more than one bill,[224] consolidating two or more bills into one bill,[225] or expanding or narrowing the scope or application of a bill.[226] On the other hand, a committee that so wishes may seek an instruction from the House.[227]

The House may give instructions to a Committee of the Whole or any one of its committees. More than one motion of instruction to a committee for the same bill may be proposed, but each motion must be moved separately.[228] Motions of instruction respecting bills are permissive rather than mandatory.[229] It is left to the committee to decide whether or not to exercise the powers given to it by the House.[230]

---

218. *Journals*, January 26, 1971, pp. 285-6.

219. *Journals*, January 21, 1971, pp. 273-4.

220. On February 17, 1970, Speaker Lamoureux ruled out of order an amendment providing that the bill not be read a second time, but that the subject matter of the bill first be put to a referendum (*Journals*, pp. 454-5). See also *Journals*, November 22, 1967, pp. 525-6.

221. *Beauchesne*, 6th ed., p. 201.

222. *May*, 22nd ed., p. 517.

223. See, for example, *Journals*, May 6, 1982, p. 4803.

224. See, for example, *Journals*, March 19, 1948, p. 269 (motion negatived); July 30, 1956, pp. 942-3 (motion negatived).

225. See, for example, *Journals*, April 15, 1920, p. 146.

226. See, for example, *Journals*, March 15, 1948, p. 255 (motion negatived).

227. *Beauchesne*, 4th ed., p. 182.

228. *Bourinot*, 4th ed., p. 516.

229. *Beauchesne*, 3rd ed., p. 152; *Debates*, December 18, 1990, pp. 16916-7. A mandatory instruction is an instruction whose purpose is to direct the deliberations of a committee.

230. *Beauchesne*, 4th ed., p. 183. In one ruling, the Chair clearly decided that whatever effect a permissive instruction given to a committee may have on the committee, it is for the committee to decide what to do with it. What moral weight may be given to a permissive instruction is something for the committee itself to decide, and in his opinion the Chair should not interfere (*Debates*, July 13, 1988, p. 17508).

Motions of instruction derived from British practice during the second half of the nineteenth century. They were incorporated into the practices of the Canadian House of Commons, although they have been used only on rare occasions. Nearly all the precedents on instructions relating to bills took place during a period when bills were referred to a Committee of the Whole after second reading. During debate on the motion "That the Speaker do now leave the Chair", a Member could move an amendment for the purpose of giving an instruction to that committee. Today, when a bill is referred to a Committee of the Whole,[231] the House gives its instructions, if any, by a special order.[232]

Motions of instruction are not admissible as an amendment to the motion for second reading of a bill, and may not be moved while the bill in question is still in the possession of the House.[233] Motions of instruction may be moved immediately after the motion for second reading where it refers the bill to a Committee of the Whole.[234] No notice is required. However, when a motion of instruction is made at this stage of the legislative process, it is not debatable or amendable.[235]

A motion of instruction may also be moved in the form of an independent motion.[236] Forty-eight hours' written notice is required[237] and, when the motion is moved in the House, it may be debated and amended.[238] Debate on a motion of instruction must be strictly relevant to the instruction, and not be directed to the substance of the bill.[239] A motion of instruction may be moved in the House even after a committee has begun its deliberations on the bill.[240]

---

231. The motion "That the Speaker do now leave the Chair" is no longer in use, since Standing Order 100 provides for the Speaker to leave the Chair without question put. See also Chapter 19, "Committees of the Whole House".

232. See, for example, *Journals,* December 2, 1997, pp. 313-4; June 9, 1999, pp. 16123, 16140-1.

233. See Speaker Fraser's ruling, *Debates*, July 13, 1988, p. 17505.

234. See Speaker Fraser's ruling, *Debates*, July 13, 1988, p. 17505. See, for example, *Journals,* March 19, 1948, p. 269. See also the ruling of Speaker Beaudoin, *Journals,* May 23, 1956, pp. 602-3; July 30, 1956, p. 942.

235. See Speaker Fraser's ruling, *Debates*, July 13, 1988, p. 17505. See also Standing Order 56(2).

236. See Speaker Fraser's ruling, *Debates*, July 13, 1988, p. 17505. See, for example, *Journals*, March 26, 1888, p. 136.

237. In 1956, after ruling that notice was not necessary, the Speaker subsequently reversed his ruling and acknowledged that notice was indeed required (*Debates*, May 28, 1956, p. 4370; *Journals*, July 30, 1956, p. 942).

238. *Bourinot*, 4th ed., p. 516. However, amendments must be drafted in such a way that, if accepted, the question as amended would retain the form and effect of an instruction (*May,* 22nd ed., p. 518).

239. *May,* 22nd ed., p. 518.

240. See Speaker Fraser's ruling, *Debates*, July 13, 1988, pp. 15706-7.

Whether proposed by a Minister or a Member, such a motion may be placed under "Motions" in Routine Proceedings on the *Order Paper*. [241] Otherwise, it is placed under Government Business, if the notice is given by a Minister, or under Private Members' Business, if it is given by a private Member. When it is called during the daily period set aside for "Routine Proceedings", a motion of instruction is then dealt with as an independent substantive motion, even though it is only meaningful in connection with the bill in the possession of the committee. If debate on the motion is adjourned or interrupted before the end of the sitting, the motion is transferred to "Government Orders" and the time for resumption of the debate is left to the pleasure of the government. [242]

There are a number of reasons why the Chair may rule a motion of instruction to be out of order. A motion of instruction may not be used to deal with an item in a bill that could properly constitute a distinct measure, or to attempt to interfere in the work of a committee which has not yet reported. [243] A motion of instruction which is not in proper form, or which is not worded in such a way that the committee will clearly understand what the House wants, will also be out of order. [244] A motion of instruction will be ruled out of order if it does not relate to the content of the bill, if it goes beyond the scope of the bill (for example, by embodying in it a principle that is foreign to it or by proposing to amend Acts that are not related to the bill), if it is not sufficiently specific, or if it attempts to delete a portion of the bill. [245] A motion of instruction will also be ruled out of order if it attempts to confer powers to a committee which it already possesses, [246] if it enables a committee to divide a bill that does not lend itself to such division, [247] or if it extends the financial prerogatives of the Crown without a Royal Recommendation for that purpose. [248]

Royal Consent

Royal Consent (which should not be confused with Royal Assent or Royal Recommendation) is taken from British practice and is part of the unwritten rules and customs of the House of Commons of Canada. Any legislation that affects the prerogatives, hereditary revenues, property or interests of the Crown requires Royal Consent, that is, the consent of the Governor General in his or her capacity as representative of the Sovereign. [249] Consent is therefore necessary when property rights of

---

241. See Speaker Fraser's ruling, *Debates*, July 13, 1988, p. 17506.

242. Standing Order 66. See also Speaker Fraser's ruling, *Debates*, July 13, 1988, p. 17506.

243. *Beauchesne*, 6th ed., p. 204.

244. *May*, 22nd ed., p. 517.

245. *May*, 22nd ed., p. 517.

246. *Bourinot*, 4th ed., p. 513. See, for example, *Journals*, May 2, 1872, p. 79; May 23, 1956, pp. 598-603.

247. *May*, 22nd ed., p. 516.

248. *May*, 22nd ed., p. 517.

249. *Bourinot*, 4th ed., p. 413; *May*, 22nd ed., p. 603.

the Crown are postponed, compromised or abandoned, or to waive some prerogative of the Crown.[250] For instance, it was required for bills in connection with railways on which the Crown had a lien,[251] property rights of the Crown (in national parks and Indian reserves),[252] the garnishment, attachment and diversion of pensions[253] and amendments to the *Financial Administration Act.*[254]

However, the consent of the Crown is not required where the bill relates to property that the Crown may hold for the Crown's subjects.[255] The fact that the Crown agrees to give consent does not, however, mean that it approves the substance of the measure; it merely means that it agrees to remove an obstacle to the progress of the bill so that it may be considered by both Houses, and ultimately submitted for Royal Assent.[256]

Although Royal Consent is often given when a bill is read for the second time,[257] it may be signified at any stage before final adoption.[258] It may be given in the form of a special message,[259] but normally it is transmitted by a Minister[260] who rises in the House and states: "His/Her Excellency the Governor General has been informed of the purport of this bill and has given his/her consent, as far as Her Majesty's prerogatives are affected, to the consideration by Parliament of the bill, that Parliament may do therein as it thinks fit". If consent has not been given, the Speaker will refuse to put the question for passage at third reading.[261] If, through inadvertence, a bill requiring Royal Consent were to pass all its stages in the House without consent being given, the proceedings in relation to the bill would be declared null and void.[262]

250. *May*, 11ᵗʰ ed., pp. 448, 561 (cited by Speaker Sévigny, *Journals,* March 29, 1916, p. 207).

251. *Bourinot*, 4ᵗʰ ed., pp. 414-5 and footnotes.

252. *Journals*, April 21, 1955, p. 418; July 14, 1959, pp. 706-7.

253. *Journals*, November 25, 1983, p. 6598.

254. *Journals*, June 13, 1961, p. 664.

255. *Journals*, December 14, 1970, pp. 201-2.

256. *Bourinot*, 4ᵗʰ ed., p. 413.

257. *Bourinot*, 4ᵗʰ ed., p. 414. The consent of the Crown may also be required for an amendment to an existing Act (*Journals*, April 26, 1978, p. 696).

258. *Bourinot*, 4ᵗʰ ed., p. 413.

259. *Bourinot*, 4ᵗʰ ed., p. 413.

260. A parliamentary secretary may not perform this function on behalf of a Minister. (See *Debates*, April 9, 1992, p. 9606; June 18, 1992, p. 12424; *Journals*, June 18, 1992, p. 1801.) When a private Member wishes to obtain Royal Consent, he or she must ask the House to agree to an address for leave to seek Royal Consent before the introduction of his or her bill (*Bourinot*, 4ᵗʰ ed., pp. 413-4).

261. *Bourinot*, 4ᵗʰ ed., p. 414. See also Speaker Lamoureux's ruling, *Journals*, April 25, 1966, pp. 434-5.

262. *Bourinot*, 4ᵗʰ ed., p. 414; *Journals*, April 25, 1966, pp. 434-5.

CONSIDERATION IN COMMITTEE

During consideration in committee, Members examine the clauses of the bill in detail. It is at this stage that they have their first opportunity to propose amendments to the text of the bill. It is also at this stage that witnesses may be invited to present their views and to appear before the committee to answer Members' questions. A bill is referred to a standing, special or legislative committee for consideration,[263] normally *after* the adoption of second reading in the House, but sometimes *before* second reading.[264] Occasionally, bills are referred to a Committee of the Whole. Any bill based on a Supply motion must be referred to a Committee of the Whole.[265] As well, with the unanimous consent of the House, an urgent or non-controversial bill may be referred to a Committee of the Whole,[266] most often after having gone through more than one stage of the legislative process in a single sitting.[267] The House may also decide, by adopting a special order, to refer a bill to a Committee of the Whole.[268]

Mandate of the Committee

A bill that is referred to a committee comprises the order of reference to the committee. The committee's sole mandate is to examine the bill and report it to the House, with or without amendment.[269] If the bill has already received second reading, the committee is bound by the decision of the House and may not amend the bill contrary to its principle.[270] This is not the case when the committee is considering a bill that has not yet been given second reading.[271]

---

263. Standing Order 73(3). While the Standing Order provides for the creation of legislative committees, practice since the opening of the First Session of the Thirty-Fifth Parliament in 1994 has been to refer bills to standing committees. Bills have also been referred to joint committees. See, for example, Bill C-136 (*Canada Pension Plan Act*) (*Journals*, November 16, 1964, p. 876); Bill C-170 (*Public Service Staff Relations Act*) (*Journals*, April 25, 1966, p. 437; May 9, 1966, p. 519); and Bill C-70 (*Act to amend the Public Service Staff Relations Act*) (*Journals*, July 15, 1975, p. 711). During the Third Session of the Thirty-Fourth Parliament (1988-1993), a special joint committee was created to examine Bill C-116 (*Conflict of Interests of Public Office Holders Act*). In its report to the House on June 3, 1993, the committee agreed that the study of the bill should be abandoned (*Journals*, March 30, 1993, pp. 2742-3; June 3, 1993, p. 3107).

264. Standing Order 73(1).

265. Standing Order 73(4).

266. See Chapter 19, "Committees of the Whole House".

267. See, for example, Bill C-10, *An Act to provide for the maintenance of west coast ports operations* (*Journals*, February 8, 1994, pp. 131-2) and Bill C-13, *An Act to amend the Parliament of Canada Act* (*Journals*, October 29, 1997, pp. 166-7).

268. See, for example, *Journals*, March 23, 1999, pp. 1649-63.

269. Standing Order 75(2). See also Speaker Fraser's ruling, *Debates*, April 28, 1992, p. 9801.

270. *May*, 22nd ed., p. 519.

271. Standing Order 73(1).

During consideration of a bill, a committee may receive clarification from the House regarding its order of reference. The "instructions" from the House may expand the committee's mandate by giving it additional powers.[272]

A committee may be asked by the House to reconsider a bill which it has already reported. This reference is normally proposed in the form of an amendment to the motion for third reading of the bill. The House may refer a bill back to a committee to have only certain clauses amended or reviewed; it may refer the bill several times, and it may refer it with or without any limitation. In the latter case, the whole bill is open to reconsideration. When a bill is referred with limitations, the committee can consider only the clauses or amendments referred to it.[273]

Role of a Committee on a Bill

The role of the committee at this stage of the legislative process is to consider a bill clause by clause and, if necessary, word by word, and to approve the text or to modify it to reflect the committee's intentions.[274]

The committee has the power to change the provisions of a bill to such an extent that when it is reported to the House it may be completely different in substance from the bill which was referred to the committee.[275] For example, the committee may, if it so decides, negative a clause or clauses of a bill (to the extent that nothing is left of the text of the bill) and report the bill to the House with amendments; the committee may also negative all the clauses of a bill and substitute new clauses, as long as the new clauses respect the rules of admissibility.[276]

Length of Speeches

Every member of a committee may speak as often as he or she wishes and may also speak as long as he or she wishes, subject to the practice that the committee adopts in that respect.[277] Frequently, a committee will pass motions to govern its proceedings, such as motions to regulate the length of time that members of the committee may speak, to establish the rotation of speakers (usually according to political parties) and to impose time limits for the proposal of certain types of motions or amendments.[278] As well, the length of speeches may be governed by constraints imposed

---

272. For example, authority to travel, to broadcast meetings or to divide a bill. See the section above entitled "Motions of Instruction".

273. *Beauchesne*, 4th ed., p. 287.

274. *May*, 22nd ed., p. 519.

275. *Beauchesne*, 5th ed., p. 231.

276. *May*, 22nd ed., p. 520.

277. Standing Order 116 provides that the Standing Orders of the House apply in a standing committee so far as may be applicable, except the Standing Orders as to certain matters including the length of speeches.

278. For further information, see Chapter 20, "Committees".

by an order of the House[279] or, in the case of a private Member's public bill, by the Standing Orders.[280]

A committee itself may also limit the time it will spend on consideration of a bill by adopting a motion to that effect. Such a motion may be debated and amended. A committee may also pass the equivalent of a time allocation motion, that is, allotting time for the examination of each clause,[281] or terminating consideration of a bill at a particular time or date.[282]

---

279. The House may adopt a time allocation motion (Standing Order 78) which applies to the committee stage of a bill (see, for example, *Journals*, March 22, 1995, pp. 1259-60; April 25, 1996, pp. 260-1). The House may also adopt a special order to that effect (see, for example, *Journals*, March 22, 1982, pp. 4626-8).

280. Standing Order 97.1.

281. Standing Committee on Industry, *Minutes of Proceedings*, March 23, 1999, Meeting No. 104.

282. Standing Committee on Justice and Legal Affairs, *Minutes of Proceedings*, December 4, 1995, Issue No. 115, p. 16; Standing Committee on Human Resources Development, *Minutes of Proceedings*, November 28, 1996, Issue No. 36, p. 33; Standing Committee on Finance, *Minutes of Proceedings*, October 15, 1997, Meeting No. 3; April 2, 1998, Meeting No. 67; May 5, 1998, Meeting No. 80. On occasion, a committee's examination of bills may become particularly acrimonious and the committee may find that it has reached a deadlock. On March 19, 1990, when the Standing Committee on Finance was considering Bill C-62, *An Act to implement the goods and services tax,* a motion was made to establish a timetable for completing the examination of the bill which resulted in a debate that went on for 31 hours. The Chair then decided to terminate the debate and imposed a form of closure. His action was based on a case which occurred in the Standing Committee on Justice and Legal Affairs in 1984, where the Chair had made an identical ruling in similar circumstances (see Standing Committee on Justice and Legal Affairs, *Minutes of Proceedings and Evidence*, June 6, 1984, Issue No. 36, pp. 3-7). The Chair's right to make such a ruling was challenged and appealed, but the ruling was upheld by a majority of the Committee. The Finance Committee then commenced its consideration of the bill, in accordance with the ruling of the Chair (Standing Committee on Finance, *Minutes of Proceedings and Evidence*, March 19, 1990, Issue No. 103, pp. 665-9). Later, when the action of the Chair was challenged in the House, the Speaker ruled that this was a matter within the competence of the Finance Committee, and stated that it was not the role of the Speaker to supervise committee chairmen (*Debates*, March 26, 1990, pp. 9756-8). The Standing Committee on Finance subsequently presented a report in the House in which it asked that the Standing Committee on Privileges and Elections examine the rules and procedures as they relate to the limitation of debate in cases where a committee has reached an impasse. The House concurred in the report and, consequently, the Committee on Privileges and Elections undertook the study in question (*Journals*, April 30, 1990, pp. 1612-3; Standing Committee on Finance, *Minutes of Proceedings and Evidence*, April 30, 1990, Issue No. 111, pp. 3-7). In its Twenty-Fifth Report, presented to the House on March 20, 1991, the Standing Committee on Privileges and Elections indicated that Standing Order 78 on time allocation is the appropriate mechanism to limit debate on a bill when there is an impasse in committee. The report was never adopted by the House (*Journals*, March 20, 1991, p. 2727; Standing Committee on Privileges and Elections, *Minutes of Proceedings and Evidence*, March 14, 1991, Issue No. 41, pp. 3-15).

Hearing of Witnesses

A committee to which a bill is referred usually chooses to hold public hearings.[283] The steering committee of the committee (referred to as the sub-committee on agenda and procedure) may discuss a timetable for meetings and a list of witnesses whom the members wish to invite to appear, and may present its recommendations to the whole committee in the form of a report. The committee may then adopt the report with any amendments deemed necessary. The committee may decide to call on the services of the research officers of the Library of Parliament,[284] or to retain any other specialist it considers necessary to assist in its work.[285]

Before proceeding with the clause by clause examination of the bill, the Chair of the committee calls Clause 1 for debate (or Clause 2, if Clause 1 contains the short title[286]) to allow the members of the committee to hold a general discussion on the bill and to question witnesses, if any witnesses are appearing. The practice is that the first witness to appear before the committee is either the sponsor of the bill or the Minister responsible for the bill (or the Minister's parliamentary secretary). Other witnesses may then be invited to express their views on the bill. Those witnesses may include individuals, experts or representatives of organizations that would be affected by the legislative measure. At this stage, discussion is very open, and relates to both the general principle and the details of the bill. Later, when the committee undertakes its clause by clause consideration of the bill, the Minister responsible, or the Minister's parliamentary secretary, may return to address the committee.[287] The officials of the department will also make themselves available during this phase, to provide explanations of certain complex or technical aspects of the legislative measure.[288]

---

283. For a variety of reasons, some committees have not heard any witnesses other than the Minister and his or her officials, and have immediately commenced clause by clause consideration of the bill (see, for example, Legislative Committee on Bill C-124, *Minutes of Proceedings and Evidence*, May 9, 1988, Issue No. 1, p. 5; Standing Committee on National Defence and Veterans Affairs, *Minutes of Proceedings*, February 18, 1999, Meeting No. 90). An uncontroversial bill may be considered at a single meeting (see, for example, Standing Committee on Finance and Economic Affairs, *Minutes of Proceedings and Evidence*, June 27, 1984, Issue No. 24, pp. 5-7; March 29, 1988, Issue No. 149, p. 5; April 28, 1988, Issue No. 159, p. 5; Legislative Committee on Bill C-91, *Minutes of Proceedings and Evidence*, December 15, 1987, Issue No. 1, p. 5).

284. In addition to offering the services of research officers, the Library of Parliament produces "legislative summaries". These documents provide Members of Parliament with explanatory information on most government bills. In addition, the departments often provide members of the committee and their staffs with very detailed information packages on the bill.

285. Standing Order 120.

286. In that case, examination of Clause 1 is postponed, as provided by Standing Order 75(1).

287. See, for example, for the appearance of a Minister during clause by clause consideration: Special Committee on Electoral Reform, *Minutes of Proceedings and Evidence*, March 15, 1993, Issue No. 16, pp. 3, 7; for the appearance of a Minister's parliamentary secretary during clause by clause consideration: Standing Committee on Agriculture and Agri-Food, *Minutes of Proceedings*, November 6, 1997, Meeting No. 9.

288. In general, officials who are specialists in the matters affected by the bill regularly attend all meetings of the committee devoted to the consideration of the bill.

On occasion, committees have considered more than one bill at a single meeting to take advantage of the presence of a Minister and witnesses so that they can be questioned on all bills at the same time.[289] The bills in question had points in common, so that it was practical to undertake consideration of both simultaneously. However, at the clause by clause stage, the bills were examined separately.[290] A committee has also considered both a bill that had been referred to it and the subject matter of another bill.[291]

Clause by Clause Consideration

Once the witnesses have been heard, the committee proceeds to clause by clause consideration of the bill. It is during this phase of the committees' deliberations that members may propose amendments to the bill.

Order in Which the Elements of the Bill Are Examined

Unless the committee decides otherwise, clause by clause consideration of the bill follows the following order:

- Clauses;
- Clauses allowed to stand (if any);
- Schedules;
- Clause 1 (short title);
- Preamble (if any);
- Title.

The elements of a bill must be considered in a prescribed order: consideration of the preamble (if the bill has one) is postponed until after the clause by clause examination;[292] consideration of Clause 1, if that clause contains only the short title,

---

289. In 1987, the Standing Committee on Transport, by unanimous consent, and in anticipation of hearing witnesses, considered Bills C-18 and C-19 at the same time; the first bill dealt with transportation in general, and the second with motor vehicle transportation (*Minutes of Proceedings*, February 17, 1987, Issue No. 11, p. 4). Again in anticipation of hearing witnesses, the Standing Committee on Finance and Economic Affairs, by unanimous consent, undertook simultaneous consideration of Bill C-42 that same year, *An Act respecting financial institutions and the deposit insurance system*, and Bill C-56, *An Act to amend certain Acts relating to financial institutions* (*Minutes of Proceedings*, June 2, 1987, Issue No. 59, p. 4).

290. See, for example, Legislative Committee on Bill C-66 and Bill C-67, *Minutes of Proceedings and Evidence*, May 22, 1990, Issue No. 1, p. 7; June 11, 1990, Issue No. 6, p. 3; June 12, 1990, Issue No. 7, p. 5; Standing Committee on Justice and Legal Affairs, *Minutes of Proceedings and Evidence*, November 24, 1994, Issue No. 65, p. 3; March 15, 1995, Issue No. 89, p. 3; March 16, 1995, Issue No. 91, p. 3.

291. Standing Committee on Justice and Legal Affairs, *Minutes of Proceedings*, June 17, 1996, Issue No. 32, pp. 1-2.

292. During its consideration of Bill C-32 (*Canadian Environmental Protection Act 1998*), the Standing Committee on Environment and Sustainable Development decided to examine the preamble before considering the clauses. The Committee had first decided, on unanimous consent, to allow the clauses and schedules to stand. A general discussion of the preamble was held, and no amendments were proposed. The preamble was then allowed to stand and examination of the preamble resumed at the end of the process, at which time amendments to it were proposed (Standing Committee on Environment and Sustainable Development, *Minutes of Proceedings*, November 3, 1998, Meeting No. 79).

is also postponed; the other clauses and the schedules are considered in the order in which they appear in the printed version of the bill. [293] The new clauses and new schedules are considered in the order in which they would appear in the bill. While some authorities on parliamentary procedure recommend a different order for examining new clauses and schedules, [294] several years ago, committees adopted the practice of proceeding with new clauses and new schedules in the same manner as for proposed amendments to clauses, that is, in the order in which they would appear in the bill. Committees consider that this approach facilitates clause by clause consideration; it has been used to such an extent that it is now solidly entrenched in the practice of the House of Commons. [295] Once all the provisions have been decided, the committee returns to consider Clause 1 (if it was postponed), the preamble and, finally, the title. [296]

Consideration of the Clauses

Each clause of the bill is a distinct question and must be considered separately. The committee Chair calls each clause successively by its number and, after discussion, puts the question on the clause if no amendment is proposed. If an amendment is proposed, the Chair gives the floor to the member, who reads the amendment. A new question is then placed under consideration and there is a new debate. When debate has concluded, the Chair puts the question on the amendment to the clause and, once decided, puts the question on the clause itself (as amended, if applicable). Once the clause is carried, it may not be discussed again without unanimous consent. [297]

The committee may pass a motion to divide a clause in order to debate the parts separately or to put the question on the parts separately. [298]

---

293. Standing Order 75(1). See also *Journals*, October 9, 1964, p. 780.

294. *Beauchesne*, 5ᵗʰ ed., pp. 231, 234; *May*, 22ⁿᵈ ed., pp. 520, 531-2.

295. See, for example, Standing Committee on Transport, *Minutes of Proceedings*, May 7, 1996, Issue No. 10, pp. 3-4, 9-13; Standing Committee on Justice and Human Rights, *Minutes of Proceedings*, March 26, 1998, Meeting No. 47.

296. During its consideration of Bill C-32 (*Canadian Environmental Protection Act 1998*), the Standing Committee on Environment and Sustainable Development examined the preamble and, after it was carried, began its consideration of an element of the bill called the "Declaration"; it then went on to examine the title (*Minutes of Proceedings*, March 25, 1999, Meeting No. 116).

297. See, for example, Standing Committee on Canadian Heritage, *Minutes of Proceedings*, November 19, 1997, Meeting No. 8; Standing Committee on Environment and Sustainable Development, *Minutes of Proceedings*, November 19, 1998, Meeting No. 83.

298. See, for example, Standing Committee on Miscellaneous Estimates, *Minutes of Proceedings and Evidence*, September 29, 1983, Issue No. 132, pp. 8, 48.

Clauses Allowed to Stand

The committee may, by motion, decide to stand a clause, provided that the committee has not already adopted or negatived an amendment to the clause in question.[299] If, however, an amendment has been proposed and withdrawn, the clause may be stood. In practice, however, committees often decide, by unanimous consent, to postpone examination of a clause even if an amendment to the clause has been proposed. A committee may also stand part of a bill, or a consecutive group of clauses *en bloc*. However, a motion to stand part of a clause, or to postpone consideration of the only effective clause of a bill until the subordinate clauses have been considered, is out of order.[300]

Debate on a motion to postpone consideration of a clause is limited to the issue of postponement, and may not be extended to the merits of the bill or the clause in question. Unless provision to the contrary is made in the motion, clauses which were allowed to stand are considered after all the other clauses of the bill have been disposed of.[301]

Amendments

Proposed during debate on a clause, an amendment attempts to amend the text of the clause under consideration so that it will be more acceptable, or to propose a new text to the committee. An amendment must be relevant to the clause it is proposed to amend,[302] and must therefore relate to only one clause of the bill and not to two or more clauses at once.[303] However, for practical reasons, the Chair may permit debate to range over several other amendments which are interconnected or which raise different aspects of the amendment under consideration.[304] The purpose of a sub-amendment is to alter an amendment to make it clearer. A sub-amendment must relate to the amendment; it may not enlarge upon the scope of the amendment by bringing up a matter that is foreign to it.[305] A committee may consider only two amendments at a time, that is, an amendment to a clause and a sub-amendment to the amendment. Once an amendment has been proposed, it may be withdrawn only at the request of the member who moved it and with the unanimous consent of the members of the committee.[306]

---

299.   See, for example, Standing Committee on Justice and Legal Affairs, *Minutes of Proceedings and Evidence*, April 8, 1982, Issue No. 75, pp. 13-4.

300.   *May,* 22nd ed, p. 521.

301.   *May,* 22nd ed., p. 522.

302.   *May,* 22nd ed., p. 346.

303.   *Beauchesne*, 5th ed., p. 232.

304.   *May,* 22nd ed., pp. 524-5.

305.   See, for example, Standing Committee on Transport, *Minutes of Proceedings and Evidence*, May 14, 1985, Issue No. 12, p. 6.

306.   *May,* 22nd ed., p. 524. See, for example, Standing Committee on Justice and Human Rights, *Minutes of Proceedings*, March 26, 1998, Meeting No. 47.

Only a member of the committee, or his or her designated substitute,[307] is entitled to move an amendment or vote on an amendment.[308] The Chair of the committee, like the Speaker of the House, may not move motions or vote, except in the case of an equality of voices.[309] It is generally acknowledged that in the case of an equality of voices, a Chair should vote in such a way as to permit the discussion to continue. A Chair is not required to state reasons for his or her casting vote, or to explain it.[310] However, when a private bill is before a committee, the Chair may vote on any matter concerning the bill and even has a casting vote if there is an equality of voices.[311]

Legislative drafting services are available to committee members who wish to move amendments to a bill. Each amendment must be submitted in writing to the Chair of the committee and may be moved in either official language. Unlike the rules that apply to motions presented in the House, it is not necessary for a motion moved in a committee to be seconded.[312]

Although a member who intends to move amendments to a bill does not have to provide notice, the normal practice is for the member to communicate with the Chair and clerk of the committee in order to arrange for the translation, compilation and circulation of the amendments to the other members of the committee.[313] If the Chair has advance notice, he or she will then be able to ensure that a proposed amendment is considered in the right place during consideration of the bill. To ensure that clause by clause consideration proceeds in an orderly manner, a committee may pass a motion setting a deadline for the acceptance of proposed amendments.[314]

Order in Which Amendments Are Considered
Three types of amendments may be moved during consideration of a clause of a bill:[315]

---

307. Standing Order 114.

308. Standing Order 119. See, for example, Legislative Committee on Bill C-6, *Minutes of Proceedings and Evidence*, October 29, 1986, Issue No. 1, p. 95; Standing Committee on Transport, *Minutes of Proceedings and Evidence*, March 18, 1993, Issue No. 33, pp. 18-9.

309. Standing Order 9.

310. See, for example, Standing Committee on Environment and Sustainable Development, *Minutes of Proceedings*, March 16, 1999, Meeting No. 109. For further information regarding the casting vote, see Chapter 7, "The Speaker and Other Presiding Officers of the House".

311. Standing Order 141(3).

312. Standing Order 116.

313. *Beauchesne*, 5th ed., p. 232. See also *May*, 22nd ed., p. 522.

314. See, for example, Standing Committee on Environment and Sustainable Development, *Minutes of Proceedings*, November 26, 1998, Meeting No. 86. The Chair of the committee may also simply urge timely submission of amendments (see, for example, Legislative Committee on Bill C-126, *Minutes of Proceedings and Evidence*, May 27, 1993, Issue No. 3, p. 29).

315. *May*, 22nd ed., p. 345.

- an amendment to leave out certain words in order to insert or add others;

- an amendment to leave out a word or words;

- an amendment to insert or add other words, or to add new clauses or schedules to the bill.

The committee Chair calls the proposed amendments in the order in which they should appear in the bill. However, when several amendments are moved to the same clause, an amendment to leave out words and insert other words takes precedence over an amendment to leave out words. The Chair may rule that an amendment is not moved in the right place, or that it should be moved as a new clause.[316]

Amendments should be proposed following the order of the text to be amended. If part of a clause has already been amended by the committee, a member may not move an amendment to an earlier part of the clause.[317]

Admissibility of Amendments

Amendments and sub-amendments that are moved in committee must comply with certain rules of admissibility. It is incumbent upon the Chair to decide on the admissibility of amendments. An amendment must first be moved by a member before the Chair rules as to whether it is admissible; the Chair does not rule on hypothetical motions. When the Chair has to rule on the admissibility of an amendment, he or she relies on the procedural rules that have been established as precedents over the years and on the authorities in parliamentary procedure and practice.

Unlike the situation in the House, where there is no appeal from the Speaker's decisions,[318] the decision of a Chair may be appealed to the committee by motion.[319] However, neither the decision of the Chair nor the motion to appeal may be debated. The Chair's decision may be reversed only by a majority vote. Consequently, if a motion asking that the Chair's decision be upheld results in a tie, the decision is upheld.[320]

---

316. *Beauchesne*, 5th ed., p. 232.

317. *Beauchesne*, 5th ed., p. 232. See, for example, Legislative Committee on Bill C-55, *Minutes of Proceedings and Evidence*, September 11, 1987, Issue No. 10, p. 24.

318. Standing Order 10.

319. Standing Order 117. For examples of decisions regarding the admissibility of amendments that have been appealed, see Standing Committee on Human Resources and the Status of Persons with Disabilities, *Minutes of Proceedings*, April 30, 1998, Meeting No. 33; Standing Committee on National Resources and Government Operations, *Minutes of Proceedings*, November 24, 1998, Meeting No. 47.

320. See, for example, Standing Committee on Citizenship and Immigration, *Minutes of Proceedings and Evidence,* May 18, 1995, Issue No. 47, p. 7.

If, during debate, the Chair determines that an amendment that was moved (but on which no decision has yet been made) is out of order, the Chair so informs the committee and halts consideration of the motion by the committee.[321]

• Rules

The rules concerning the admissibility of amendments are essentially the same for a bill referred to a committee before or after second reading, or for a bill being considered at report stage.[322] However, the rules respecting the principle or scope of a bill do not apply to a bill referred to a committee before second reading, since the principle of the bill has not yet been adopted by the House.

The rules governing the admissibility of amendments to the clauses of a bill may be grouped according to the following characteristics and elements:

Principle and Scope: An amendment to a bill that was referred to a committee *after* second reading is out of order if it is beyond the scope and principle of the bill.[323] (This rule does not apply to a bill referred to a committee *before* second reading, since the principle of the bill has not yet been adopted by the House.) As well, an amendment which is equivalent to a simple negative of the bill or which reverses the principle of the bill as agreed to at second reading[324] is out of order.

Relevance: An amendment to a bill must be relevant; that is, it must always relate to the subject matter of the bill or the clause under consideration. For a bill referred to a committee *after* second reading, an amendment is inadmissible if it amends a statute that is not before the committee[325] or a section of the parent Act unless it is being specifically amended by a clause of the bill.[326] An amendment of that nature would be admissible, however, in the case of a bill referred to a committee *before* second reading, as long as it was relevant. In that case, the principle and scope of the bill have not yet been defined, and so a broader examination is possible.

---

321. *May*, 22nd ed., p. 529.

322. For more information regarding report stage, see the section below entitled "Report Stage".

323. *May*, 22nd ed., pp. 525-6; see, for example, the decision of the Chair: Legislative Committee on Bill C-144, *Minutes of Proceedings and Evidence*, September 9, 1988, Issue No. 7, pp. 8, 10.

324. *May*, 22nd ed., p. 526; see, for example, decisions of the Chair: Standing Committee on Health, Welfare and Social Affairs, *Minutes of Proceedings and Evidence*, December 13, 1982, Issue No. 52, pp. 5, 82-3; Standing Committee on Transport, *Minutes of Proceedings and Evidence*, August 31, 1983, Issue No. 124, pp. 8-9; September 14, 1983, Issue No. 134, p. 5; September 19, 1983, Issue No. 138, pp. 3-4.

325. *Beauchesne*, 5th ed., p. 233; see, for example, decisions of the Chair: Standing Committee on Transport, *Minutes of Proceedings and Evidence*, September 8, 1983, Issue No. 129, p. 4; Standing Committee on Communications and Culture, *Minutes of Proceedings and Evidence*, November 20, 1985, Issue No. 29, pp. 3-4, 29-30; Legislative Committee on Bill C-58, *Minutes of Proceedings and Evidence*, July 5, 1988, Issue No. 3, p. 9.

326. *Beauchesne*, 5th ed., p. 233; see, for example, the decision of the Chair: Legislative Committee on Bill C-84, *Minutes of Proceedings and Evidence*, August 25, 1987, Issue No. 9, p. 9.

Consistency: The committee's decisions concerning a bill must be consistent; they must be compatible with earlier decisions made by the committee. An amendment is therefore out of order if it is contrary to or inconsistent with the provisions of the bill that the committee has already agreed to, if it is inconsistent with a decision that the committee has made regarding a former amendment,[327] or if it is governed[328] or dependent on[329] amendments which have already been negatived.

Financial Initiative of the Crown: An amendment must not offend the financial initiative of the Crown. An amendment is therefore inadmissible if it imposes a charge on the Public Treasury,[330] or if it extends the objects or purposes or relaxes the conditions and qualifications as expressed in the Royal Recommendation.[331] An amendment is also inadmissible if it goes beyond the scope of the Ways and Means motion on which a bill is based, or if it creates a new charge on the people[332] that is not preceded by the adoption of a Ways and Means motion or not covered by the terms of a Ways and Means motions already adopted.[333]

---

327. *May*, 22nd ed., p. 526; see, for example, decisions of the Chair: Standing Committee on Communications and Culture, *Minutes of Proceedings and Evidence*, November 21, 1985, Issue No. 30, pp. 5-6; Standing Committee on Justice and Solicitor General, *Minutes of Proceedings and Evidence*, April 28, 1992, Issue No. 50, pp. 8-9.

328. *May*, 22nd ed., p. 526; see, for example, decisions of the Chair: Legislative Committee on Bill C-62, *Minutes of Proceedings and Evidence*, January 23, 1986, Issue No. 13, pp. 3, 6-7; January 28, 1986, Issue No. 14, p. 7; Legislative Committee on Bill C-144, *Minutes of Proceedings and Evidence*, September 9, 1988, Issue No. 7, pp. 8, 11.

329. *May*, 22nd ed., p. 526; see, for example, decisions of the Chair: Standing Committee on Regional Economic Expansion, *Minutes of Proceedings and Evidence*, April 17, 1985, Issue No. 24, pp. 15-6.

330. *Beauchesne*, 5th ed., p. 233; see, for example, decisions of the Chair: Standing Committee on Transport, *Minutes of Proceedings and Evidence*, July 10, 1980, Issue No. 12, p. 11; Standing Committee on Health, Welfare and Social Affairs, *Minutes of Proceedings and Evidence*, March 13, 1984, Issue No. 20, p. 5; Standing Committee on Justice and Legal Affairs, *Minutes of Proceedings and Evidence*, June 5, 1995, Issue No. 111, pp. 64-6; Standing Committee on Agriculture and Agri-Food, *Minutes of Proceedings and Evidence*, October 8, 1996, Issue No. 36, p. 2; November 27, 1996, Issue No. 50, p. 3; December 12, 1996, Issue No. 6, p. 5; Standing Committee on National Defence and Veterans Affairs, *Minutes of Proceedings*, February 18, 1999, Meeting No. 90.

331. See, for example, decisions of the Chair: Standing Committee on Labour, Manpower and Immigration, *Minutes of Proceedings and Evidence*, February 2, 1982, Issue No. 19, p. 6; Standing Committee on Transport, *Minutes of Proceedings and Evidence*, September 19, 1983, Issue No. 138, p. 4; Standing Committee on Health, Welfare and Social Affairs, *Minutes of Proceedings and Evidence*, March 13, 1984, Issue No. 19, p. 6; Standing Committee on Finance, Trade and Economic Affairs, *Minutes of Proceedings and Evidence*, April 18, 1985, Issue No. 27, pp. 3-4; Standing Committee on Agriculture and Agri-Food, *Minutes of Proceedings and Evidence*, October 22, 1996, Issue No. 4, p. 10.

332. See Chapter 18, "Financial Procedures".

333. *May*, 22nd ed., p. 527. See, for example, decisions of the Chair: Standing Committee on Consumer and Corporate Affairs and Government Operations, *Minutes of Proceedings and Evidence*, December 3, 1991, Issue No. 29, pp. 4-6, 16-32.

Form: An amendment is out of order if it simply attempts to delete a clause, since in that case all that needs to be done is to vote against the adoption of the clause in question.[334] An amendment is also out of order if it is moved at the wrong place in the bill, if it is tendered in a spirit of mockery, or if it is vague or trifling.[335] As well, an amendment is out of order if it refers to, or is not intelligible without, subsequent amendments or schedules of which notice has not been given, or if it is otherwise incomplete.[336] Lastly, an amendment which would make a clause unintelligible or ungrammatical is also out of order.[337]

Interpretation Clause: The interpretation clause of a bill is not the place to propose a substantive amendment to a bill.[338] In addition, an amendment to the interpretation clause of a bill that was referred to a committee *after* second reading must always relate to the bill and not go beyond the scope of or be contrary to the principle of the bill. This rule does not apply to a bill that has been referred to a committee *before* second reading.[339]

---

334. *May*, 22ⁿᵈ ed., pp. 526-7; see, for example, decisions of the Chair: Standing Committee on Transport, *Minutes of Proceedings and Evidence*, July 8, 1980, Issue No. 11, p. 8; Legislative Committee on Bill C-144, *Minutes of Proceedings and Evidence*, September 9, 1988, Issue No. 7, p. 20; Standing Committee on Justice and Solicitor General, *Minutes of Proceedings and Evidence*, November 7, 1991, Issue No. 12, pp. 18, 29-30; Standing Committee on Human Resources and the Status of Persons with Disabilities, *Minutes of Proceedings*, April 30, 1998, Meeting No. 33; Standing Committee on National Resources and Government Operations, *Minutes of Proceedings*, November 24, 1998, Meeting No. 47. See also the decision of the chairman: Standing Committee on Labour, Manpower and Immigration, *Minutes of Proceedings and Evidence*, December 13, 1978, Issue No. 20, pp. 5-6.

335. *Beauchesne*, 5ᵗʰ ed., p. 233; *May*, 22ⁿᵈ ed., p. 527; see, for example, decisions of the Chair: Standing Committee on Transport, *Minutes of Proceedings and Evidence*, July 7, 1982, Issue No. 75, p. 4; Legislative Committee on Bill C-79, *Minutes of Proceedings and Evidence*, November 7, 1985, Issue No. 7, p. 4; Legislative Committee on Bill C-45, *Minutes of Proceedings and Evidence*, June 10, 1986, Issue No. 8, pp. 7-8.

336. *May*, 22ⁿᵈ ed., p. 526; see, for example, decisions of the Chair: Standing Committee on Health, Welfare and Social Affairs, *Minutes of Proceedings and Evidence*, March 13, 1984, Issue No. 19, pp. 4-5.

337. *May*, 22ⁿᵈ ed., p. 527; see, for example, decisions of the Chair: Standing Committee on Communications and Culture, *Minutes of Proceedings and Evidence*, March 18, 1986, Issue No. 40, p. 7.

338. See Speaker Lamoureux's ruling, *Journals*, May 21, 1970, pp. 835-7. See, for example, decisions of the Chair: Standing Committee on Transport, *Minutes of Proceedings and Evidence*, August 31, 1983, Issue No. 124, p. 5; September 21, 1983, Issue No. 143, pp. 14-5; Legislative Committee on Bill C-45, *Minutes of Proceedings and Evidence*, June 10, 1986, Issue No. 8, pp. 5-6; Legislative Committee on Bill C-37, *Minutes of Proceedings and Evidence*, March 24, 1987, Issue No. 10, p. 4; Legislative Committee on Bill C-55, *Minutes of Proceedings and Evidence*, September 10, 1987, Issue No. 9, pp. 3-4; Standing Committee on Industry, *Minutes of Proceedings*, December 4, 1997, Meeting No. 16.

339. See, for example, Standing Committee on Agriculture and Agri-Food, *Minutes of Proceedings and Evidence*, November 28, 1996, Issue No. 51, p. 1.

Marginal Notes and Headings: Because the marginal notes attached to each of the clauses of a bill are not part of the text, they cannot be amended, nor can the headings of the various parts of a bill be amended.[340]

Coming into Force Clause: An amendment to alter the coming into force clause of a bill, making it conditional, is out of order.[341] This type of amendment goes beyond the scope of the bill and is an attempt to introduce a new question into the bill.

Schedules: An amendment may generally be moved to a schedule, and it is also possible to propose new schedules.[342] However, there is an exception in the case of a bill to give effect to an agreement (a treaty or convention) that is within the prerogatives of the Crown. If the schedule to such a bill contains the Agreement itself, the schedule cannot be amended. However, amendments may be proposed to the clauses of the bill, as long as they do not affect the wording of the Agreement in the schedule, and even if the consequence of the amendments is to withhold legislative effect from the Agreement or its parts.[343]

Preamble: In the case of a bill that has been referred to a committee *after* second reading, a substantive amendment to the preamble is admissible only if it is rendered necessary by amendments made to the bill.[344] In addition, an amendment to the preamble is in order when the purpose is to clarify it or make the English and French uniform.[345] If the bill does not contain a preamble, it is not competent for the committee to introduce one.[346] In the case of a bill that has been referred to a committee *before* second reading, if there is not already a preamble, one may be presented as

---

340. *May*, 22nd ed., p. 525; *Beauchesne*, 5th ed., p. 220; *Journals*, May 17, 1956, p. 568; *Debates*, July 13, 1981, p. 11463. See, for example, the decision of the Chair: Sub-committee (of the Standing Committee on Communications and Culture) on Bill C-62, *Minutes of Proceedings and Evidence*, May 12, 1993, Issue No. 9, pp. 51-3. Nonetheless, this kind of technical drafting change may be made in a subsequent reprinting of the bill, to reflect amendments to the bill and changes in the order of clauses and schedules (*May*, 22nd ed., p. 525). Editorial and technical amendments are not the responsibility of Parliament. That task falls instead to the legislative revisors who verify the accuracy of the marginal notes and headings before the statute is published.

341. See the ruling of the Acting Speaker, *Journals*, May 14, 1970, p. 807; the ruling of Speaker Jerome, *Journals*, October 16, 1975, pp. 772-3; the ruling of Speaker Fraser, *Debates*, August 15, 1988, p. 18308; the decision of the Chair, Standing Committee on Labour, Manpower and Immigration, *Minutes of Proceedings and Evidence*, December 13, 1978, Issue No. 20, pp. 5-6.

342. *Beauchesne*, 5th ed., p. 232.

343. *Beauchesne*, 5th ed., p. 235.

344. *May*, 22nd ed., p. 533.

345. See Speaker Lamoureux's ruling, *Journals*, January 19, 1970, pp. 322-3.

346. *May*, 22nd ed., p. 533. See, for example, decisions of the Chair: Standing Committee on National Resources and Public Works, *Minutes of Proceedings and Evidence*, June 25, 1981, Issue No. 69, pp. 82-3; Legislative Committee on Bill C-18, *Minutes of Proceedings and Evidence*, December 14, 1989, Issue No. 11, pp. 4-5.

long as the proposal is relevant to the bill; in addition, substantive amendments to an existing preamble are admissible.[347]

The Enacting Formula: The enacting formula is not submitted for the approval of the committee or the House and therefore may not be debated or amended.[348]

The Title: The long title is postponed until consideration of the bill is concluded.[349] The title may be amended only if the bill has been so altered as to necessitate such an amendment.[350] Any change made to the title by a committee becomes effective when the bill is adopted by the House at report stage.[351]

Putting the Question on Amendments

When an amendment and a sub-amendment have been moved in committee, the Chair of the committee puts the question first on the sub-amendment. If it is negatived, the question is then put on the amendment; if the sub-amendment is carried, the question is then put on the amendment, as amended. Sometimes, with unanimous consent, the committee may arrange a group of amendments to be disposed of as if each amendment had been moved and voted on separately.[352]

Adoption of the Bill

Once the committee has concluded its clause by clause consideration, the bill in its entirety, with or without amendments, is submitted for the approval of the committee.

Leave to Report to the House

After the bill is adopted, the Chair asks the committee for leave to report the bill to the House. The standard formula is as follows: "Shall I report the bill (as amended) to the House?" If the committee agrees, the Chair reports the bill to the House as soon as possible. However, if a committee does not agree to report the bill immediately, it must do so later.

---

347. See, for example, Standing Committee on Transport, *Minutes of Proceedings and Evidence*, May 7, 1996, Issue No. 10, p. 14.

348. *Beauchesne*, 6th ed., p. 193. See Speaker Lamoureux's ruling, *Journals*, June 11, 1973, pp. 394-5, and the decision of the Chair, Standing Committee on Health, Welfare and Social Affairs, *Minutes of Proceedings and Evidence*, May 15, 1973, Issue No. 11, p. 3.

349. Standing Order 75(1). It was only in 1964 that the House adopted a rule providing that the question be called on the title at the end of the consideration of the bill (*Journals*, October 9, 1964, p. 780).

350. *Beauchesne*, 6th ed., p. 209. See, for example, *Journals*, February 13, 1970, pp. 433-4. See also Speaker Sauvé's rulings, *Debates*, July 30, 1982, p. 19866; August 3, 1982, pp. 19958-9; the ruling of the Chair, *Debates,* July 7, 1988, p. 17287; the decision of the Chair, Standing Committee on Canadian Heritage, *Minutes of Proceedings*, December 1, 1998, Meeting No. 57.

351. *Beauchesne*, 6th ed., p. 209. See *Journals*, February 20, 1970, p. 477.

352. See, for example, Standing Committee on Industry, *Minutes of Proceedings*, November 5, 1998, Meeting No. 70; Standing Committee on Environment and Sustainable Development, *Minutes of Proceedings*, November 17, 1998, Meeting No. 81.

Reprinting of the Bill

If the number of amendments made by the committee necessitates it, the committee generally orders that the bill be reprinted for the use of the Members who will have to consult it at report stage.[353]

Report to the House

The committee is bound by its Order of Reference—the bill—and may only report the bill with or without amendment to the House.[354] Consequently, the committee may not include substantive recommendations in its report.[355] On several occasions in the House, the Speaker has ruled a report containing recommendations[356] or a motion to adopt a report containing recommendations out of order.[357] In 1973, Speaker Lamoureux ruled that "... there is no authority to support the contention that a committee of the House when considering a bill should report anything to the House except the bill itself".[358]

On the other hand, after a bill has been reported, there is nothing to prevent a standing committee, under its permanent mandate in the Standing Orders, from presenting another report in which it sets out substantive recommendations concerning that bill.[359]

Obligation to Report

Every committee is bound to report to the House on a bill and the amendments which have been made to the bill,[360] and every bill reported from any committee, whether amended or not, must be received by the House.[361] However, a committee has no authority to submit two reports to the House on one bill, as the effect of this would be to divide the bill.[362] A committee may negative all the clauses, the title, and even

---

353. See *Debates*, April 6, 1970, p. 5520; *Beauchesne*, 6th ed., p. 209.

354. *Beauchesne*, 6th ed., p. 233.

355. See, for example, Standing Committee on Finance, Trade and Economic Affairs, *Minutes of Proceedings and Evidence*, April 13, 1976, Issue No. 99, p. 4; Legislative Committee on Bill C-79, *Minutes of Proceedings and Evidence*, November 7, 1985, Issue No. 7, pp. 13-5, 19-20; Standing Committee on Finance and Economic Affairs, *Minutes of Proceedings and Evidence*, December 10, 1986, Issue No. 17, pp. 26-30; Legislative Committee on Bill C-130, *Minutes of Proceedings and Evidence*, August 4, 1988, Issue No. 23, pp. 19-20.

356. See, for example, *Debates*, June 29, 1983, p. 26943; June 13, 1984, p. 4624.

357. See, for example, *Journals*, December 20, 1973, pp. 774-5; December 9, 1974, pp. 179-81.

358. *Journals*, December 20, 1973, p. 774. See also *Journals*, December 13, 1973, p. 745.

359. Standing Order 108(2). See, for example, the Eighth and Ninth Reports of the Standing Committee on Industry on Bill C-20, *An Act to amend the Competition Act and to make consequential and related amendments to other Acts* (*Journals*, May 27, 1998, p. 896).

360. *Bourinot*, 4th ed., pp. 520-1.

361. Standing Order 75.

362. Standing Committee on Justice and Legal affairs, *Minutes of Proceedings and Evidence*, May 6, 1976, Issue No. 45, pp. 5-7.

reject the bill. The committee then reports the bill with amendments, although the only thing which may be left is the number.[363]

Unless an order of the House[364] or a provision in the Standing Orders[365] imposes a deadline by which a committee must report a bill to the House, it is up to the committee to decide when it reports the bill.[366] The House always has the right to modify the terms of the committal of a bill to a committee. If a Minister or a Member believes that a committee to which a bill has been referred is defying the authority of the House by refusing to consider the bill or report it to the House, he or she may choose to bring this fact to the attention of the House and propose that the committee be given a time limit. This may be done by placing on notice a motion to require the committee to report by a certain date. The notice may, where appropriate, be placed under "Government Orders" or "Private Members' Business". The Speaker may also allow such a motion to be placed under the rubric "Motions" and be dealt with under Routine Proceedings, on the condition that it is strictly limited to the terms of the committal of a bill to the committee and is not an attempt to interfere with the committee's proceedings. In so doing, the House would have an opportunity to determine whether the bill should remain in committee or be reported back.[367]

- Private Member's Public Bill

A committee to which a private Member's public bill has been referred must, within 60 sitting days from the date of the bill's reference to the committee, either report the bill to the House with or without amendment or present a report containing a recommendation not to proceed further with the bill[368] or requesting a single extension of 30 sitting days to consider the bill, giving the reasons therefor. If no bill or report is presented by the end of the 60 sitting days, or the 30 sitting day

---

363. See, for example, Standing Committee on Justice and Human Rights, *Minutes of Proceedings*, March 24, 1999, Meeting No. 130; *Journals*, April 19, 1999, p. 1733. See also Legislative Committee on Bill C-289, *Minutes of Proceedings and Evidence*, February 18, 1993, Issue No. 3, pp. 4-5; *Journals*, February 23, 1993, p. 2546 (the Committee reported solely to inform the House that it disagreed to all the clauses, the title and the bill itself); Standing Committee on Justice and Legal Affairs, *Minutes of Proceedings and Evidence*, December 7, 1995, Issue No. 115, pp. 20-2 (the Committee decided not to report a bill that it had negatived, with all its clauses and its title).

364. For example, an order made after the adoption of a motion to allot time that applies to the committee stage of a bill (Standing Order 78).

365. Standing Order 97.1.

366. See Speaker Parent's ruling, *Debates*, September 23, 1996, p. 4561.

367. See Speaker Parent's ruling, *Debates*, September 23, 1996, p. 4561.

368. See, for example, the Twentieth Report of the Standing Committee on Justice and Human Rights, presented to the House on May 12, 1999 (*Journals*, p. 1864).

extension if approved by the House, the bill is deemed to have been reported without amendment.[369]

- Abandonment of a Bill

On a number of occasions, a committee has presented a report to the House either recommending that a bill be withdrawn[370] or informing the House that the committee has agreed that the bill not be further proceeded with.[371] As well, a committee will occasionally decide not to proceed with the consideration of a bill, without reporting it to the House.[372]

In those circumstances, the final decision as to the fate of a bill lies with the House as a whole, and not solely with the committee, whose function is to carry out the mandate it was given by the House and report the bill. The House alone has the power to prevent the adoption of a bill or to order its withdrawal.[373] While reminding the House that the Chair does not become involved in matters within a committee, Speaker Fraser pointed out that there is nothing to prevent any Member or Minister from placing on notice a motion to have the House exercise its authority by ordering the committee to resume its consideration of the bill and report it to the House.[374]

Report Containing Inadmissible Amendments

Since a committee may appeal the decision of its Chair[375] and reverse that decision, it may happen that a committee will report a bill with amendments that were initially ruled by the Chairman to be out of order. The admissibility of those amendments, and of any other amendments made by a committee, may therefore be challenged on procedural grounds when the House resumes its consideration of the bill at

---

369. Standing Order 97.1. This version of the Standing Order came into force on the first sitting day of 1999 (*Journals*, November 30, 1998, p. 1329).

370. See, for example, *Journals*, April 20, 1909, p. 312; March 16, 1915, pp. 140-1; June 26, 1919, p. 467; May 16, 1929, p. 415; April 4, 1939, p. 297.

371. See, for example, Special Joint Committee on Bill C-116 *(Conflicts of Interests of Public Holders Act), Minutes of Proceedings and Evidence*, June 2, 1993, Issue No. 5, p. 4; *Journals*, June 3, 1993, p. 3107; *Debates*, June 3, 1993, p. 20292.

372. See, for example, Legislative Committee H on Bill C-203, *Minutes of Proceedings and Evidence*, February 18, 1992, Issue No. 10, p. 3 (the Committee adjourned its proceedings *sine die*); Standing Committee on Justice and Legal Affairs, *Minutes of Proceedings and Evidence*, May 14, 1996, Issue No. 17, pp. 2-4; May 16, 1996, Issue No. 18, p. 1; June 18, 1996, Issue No. 35, pp. 1-2; October 21, 1996, Issue No. 54, p. 34; December 4, 1996, Issue No. 89, pp. 26-7 (the Committee decided not to report to the House).

373. *Bourinot*, 4th ed., pp. 520-1.

374. *Debates*, February 26, 1992, p. 7624. See also Speaker Parent's ruling, *Debates*, September 23, 1996, pp. 4560-2.

375. Standing Order 117.

report stage.[376] The admissibility of the amendments is then considered by the Speaker of the House, whether in response to a point of order[377] or on his or her own initiative.[378]

In a 1992 decision, Speaker Fraser ruled: "When a bill is referred to a standing or legislative committee of the House, that committee is only empowered to adopt, amend or negative the clauses found in that piece of legislation and to report the bill to the House with or without amendments. The committee is restricted in its examination in a number of ways. It cannot infringe on the financial initiative of the Crown, it cannot go beyond the scope of the bill as passed at second reading, and it cannot reach back to the parent act to make further amendments not contemplated in the bill no matter how tempting this may be."[379]

Presentation of Report

The report of a committee which has completed its examination of a bill is presented to the House by the Chairman of the committee,[380] during Routine Proceedings, when the rubric "Presenting Reports from Committees" is called.[381] No debate is permitted at that point.

REPORT STAGE

After a bill is examined in committee, it is considered by the House. At this stage (called "report stage"), Members—particularly those who were not on the committee—may propose amendments, after giving written notice, to the text of the bill as it was presented by the committee. Those motions are then debated.

---

376. In 1993, the members of a committee rejected the decision of their Chair, who had ruled three proposed amendments to a bill to be out of order (Standing Committee on Agriculture, *Minutes of Proceedings and Evidence*, March 31, 1992, Issue No. 35, pp. 4-5, 38-43, 48). The amendments were then adopted by the Committee and included in the report to the House. Following a point of order raised in the House in respect of this matter, the Speaker upheld the ruling of the Chair and ordered that the three amendments be struck from the bill. The House subsequently agreed to two of the three amendments, by unanimous consent (*Journals,* April 28, 1992, pp. 1326-7; *Debates,* April 28, 1992, pp. 9801-2).

377. In 1975, a point of order was raised in the House dealing with the admissibility of one of the amendments to a bill contained in the report of the Standing Committee on Miscellaneous Estimates (*Debates*, April 22, 1975, pp. 5072-8*).* Speaker Jerome ruled the amendment out of order because it exceeded the original Royal Recommendation that accompanied the bill, and ordered that the amendment be removed from the bill, and that the bill be reprinted (*Journals*, April 23, 1975, pp. 467-9).

378. In 1981, Deputy Speaker Francis, on his own initiative (that is, no point of order having been raised in this respect), ruled an amendment agreed to by the Standing Committee on Miscellaneous Estimates to be out of order, as it went beyond the terms of the original Royal Recommendation and offended the financial initiative of the Crown (*Journals*, April 7, 1981, p. 1671).

379. *Debates*, April 28, 1992, p. 9801.

380. A member of the committee may be designated by the Chair of the committee to present the report. See, for example, *Journals*, October 30, 1998, p. 1218.

381. See, for example, *Journals*, March 5, 1999, p. 1562; April 15, 1999, p. 1720.

Historical Perspective

At Confederation, the Standing Orders of the House already laid down the procedure to be followed for the consideration of bills in committee and the presentation of reports to the House. Although bills could be referred to a standing or special committee, they then had to be re-examined by a Committee of the Whole.[382] The amendments made in committee had to be communicated to the House, which received them immediately. In addition, the Standing Orders provided that if bills were reported with amendments by a Committee of the Whole, they could be debated and amended before the House ordered third reading. If bills were not amended during consideration in a Committee of the Whole, third reading would proceed forthwith at a time to be set by the House.

Over the years, it was observed that amendments were being proposed only in committee, and that when they were presented to the House, a motion to concur in the amendments was made and the question on the motion called immediately.[383] In 1955, the House amended its Standing Orders to reflect this practice. It was agreed that amendments had to be presented to the House and that the motion for concurrence in the amendments had to be disposed of forthwith before the bill was ordered for third reading at the next sitting of the House.[384] The effect of these amendments to the Standing Orders was to eliminate what then constituted the equivalent of report stage. In 1968, the House performed a thorough revision of its legislative process. After that revision, all bills, except for those based on Supply or Ways and Means motions, were to be referred to standing or special committees, and would not be reconsidered by a Committee of the Whole House. In addition, the House revived report stage and gave the Speaker the power to select and group amendments. It also adopted provisions relating to notice of amendments and the length of speeches at this stage of the legislative process.[385]

In recommending that report stage be revived, the 1968 Special Committee on Procedure considered that stage to be essential in order to provide all Members of the House, and not merely members of the committee, with an opportunity to express their views on the bills under consideration and to propose amendments, where appropriate. However, the intent of the Committee was not for this stage to become a repetition of committee stage. Unlike committee stage where the bill is considered clause by clause, there was not to be any debate at report stage unless notices of amendment were given, and then debate would have to be strictly relevant to those proposed amendments.

---

382. See, for example, *Debates*, May 26, 1954, p. 5115; see also *Stewart*, p. 85 and Chapter 19, "Committees of the Whole House".

383. *Dawson*, p. 234.

384. *Journals*, July 12, 1955, pp. 932-3.

385. *Journals*, December 6, 1968, pp. 432-4; December 20, 1968, pp. 554-62.

The provisions relating to report stage have been amended slightly since 1968. The House has made changes in respect of the length of speeches,[386] and clarified the purpose of report stage and the factors by which the Speaker is to be guided in selecting and grouping amendments.[387] Other changes were also made in 1994 to reflect the new procedure which allows a Minister to propose that a government bill be referred to a committee before second reading.[388]

Notice of Amendment

In order that a motion to amend a bill[389] may be considered at report stage, notice must be given in writing[390] at least one sitting day prior to the commencement of report stage, if the bill was referred to committee after second reading,[391] and two sitting days before, if the bill was referred to committee before second reading.[392] Notice must be received by the Clerk of the House before 6:00 p.m. Monday to Thursday, and before 2:00 p.m. on Friday, to appear on the *Notice Paper* for the next sitting day.[393] During an adjournment period, the deadline for giving notice is

---

386. Between 1968 and 1982, Standing Order 76(7) imposed a 20-minute limit on speeches at report stage, but provided certain exemptions. In 1982, the House decided to limit all speeches to 10 minutes at this stage (*Journals*, November 5, 1982, p. 5328; November 29, 1982, p. 5400; see also the Third Report of the Special Committee on Standing Orders and Procedure, presented to the House on November 5, 1982, Issue No. 7, pp. 3, 18).

387. *Journals*, February 6, 1986, pp. 1665-6; February 13, 1986, p. 1710.

388. *Journals*, February 7, 1994, p. 112. Sections (1) to (10) of the present Standing Order 76 were added at that time.

389. This means "… any motion to amend [see, for example, *Journals*, May 25, 1998, p. 841], delete [see, for example, *Journals*, December 2, 1998, p. 1360], insert [see, for example, *Journals*, November 17, 1998, p. 1264] or restore [see, for example, *Journals*, May 26, 1999, pp. 1917-9] any clause in a bill" (Standing Orders 76(2) and 76.1(2)).

390. Notice sent by facsimile is not proper notice. In 1993, Speaker Fraser ruled: "… all notices submitted for the *Notice Paper* and received by fax … are accepted as advance notice and cannot be considered official unless supported by the member's original signature on the document in question …" (*Debates*, February 15, 1993, pp. 15899-900).

391. Standing Order 76.1(2).

392. Standing Order 76(2).

393. Standing Order 54(1).

6:00 p.m. on the Thursday before the House resumes sitting.[394] No notice may be given on the day on which consideration of report stage of a bill commences, or on the days following.[395]

Amendment as to Form Only

The Standing Orders provide one exception to the notice requirements. A Minister may propose an amendment without notice, if the amendment is in relation only to the form of a government bill.[396] In that case, debate must relate solely to the amendment. The purpose of this rule is to facilitate the incorporation into a bill of amendments that are made necessary by the acceptance of other amendments. It is then up to the Chair to determine whether the amendment is of a strictly consequential nature flowing from the acceptance of another amendment, or if it would change the intent of the bill.

Notice of Royal Recommendation

In the case of an amendment containing financial implications which requires a Royal Recommendation,[397] the Standing Orders provide that notice of the Royal Recommendation must be given no later than the sitting day before report stage is to commence. The notice must be printed on the *Notice Paper* along with the amendment to which it pertains.[398]

Admissibility of Motions in Amendment

It is up to the Speaker to decide what amendments will be considered at report stage. The Speaker does not rule on whether the purport of the amendment or its substance is worthy of debate. The Speaker decides only whether the amendment is procedurally acceptable within the framework of the rules established for the admissibility of amendments presented at report stage.[399]

At report stage, a bill is examined as a whole and not clause by clause as is the case at committee stage. Generally, the rules relating to the admissibility of amendments presented at committee stage also apply to motions in amendment at report

---

394. Standing Orders 28(2) and 54(2).

395. In practice, this may create a problem for Members because, with the exception of the minimum notice of two or three sitting days required by Standing Orders 76(1) and 76.1(1), the day on which consideration of the report stage commences is normally unknown. To overcome this difficulty, most notices are filed as soon as possible after the report of the committee is presented. In 1970, when a Member tried to move an amendment after consideration of report stage had commenced, the Chair refused to accept the motion, pointing out that the Chair's task of selecting and grouping amendments at report stage would be "practically impossible" if the Chair "were faced a few days later with a discussion on another series of similar motions" (*Journals*, June 2, 1970, pp. 908-9).

396. Standing Orders 76(4) and 76.1(4). See also the ruling of the Chair, *Debates*, December 30, 1971, pp. 10886-7.

397. See Chapter 18, "Financial Procedures".

398. Standing Orders 76(3) and 76.1(3). See, for example, *Notice Paper*, March 3, 1997, p. XXVI.

399. See Speaker Fraser's rulings, *Debates*, September 21, 1987, p. 9142; June 2, 1992, p. 11247.

stage.[400] However, certain rules apply only to report stage. For instance, since 1968 when the rules relating to report stage came into force, a motion in amendment to delete a clause from a bill has always been considered by the Chair to be in order, even if such a motion would alter or go against the principle of the bill as approved at second reading;[401] and a motion to amend a number of clauses of a bill is out of order.[402]

At report stage, the Speaker has ruled out of order a motion in amendment that offended the financial initiative of the Crown;[403] that proposed to alter an agreement that was within the prerogatives of the Crown;[404] and that proposed to alter the long title of a bill, when no substantial changes had been made to the bill that would have necessitated a change in the title.[405]

The Chair has also ruled out of order motions in amendment to a bill that was referred to a committee *after* second reading, although the same motions in amendment would have been admissible if the bill had been referred to a committee *before* second reading. For example, the Speaker has ruled out of order a motion in amendment that went beyond the scope of the bill or the clause in question;[406] that was contrary to the principle of the bill as adopted at second reading;[407] that proposed to change the interpretation clause by making a substantive amendment which exceeded the scope of the bill;[408] that would amend a statute not contemplated by the bill;[409] that would amend, not a clause of the bill amending the parent Act, but a

---

400. See the section above entitled "Rules".

401. See, for example, *Notice Paper*, June 11, 1999, pp. V-IX. See also Speaker Jerome's ruling, *Debates*, June 29, 1976, pp. 14961-5.

402. *Debates*, June 20, 1969, p. 10497.

403. A motion in amendment that requires the expenditure of additional public funds, and is not accompanied by a Royal Recommendation, is out of order (*Debates*, August 15, 1988, p. 18307; May 2, 1996, p. 2214). An amendment that would in some way change the objects, purposes, conditions and qualifications of the Royal Recommendation is also out of order (*Debates*, February 5, 1973, pp. 957-8; March 31, 1987, pp. 4744-5), as is an amendment that would impose a tax on the population that was not preceded by the adoption of a Ways and Means motion or that exceeds the scope or limitations of that motion (*Debates*, December 19, 1984, p. 1380). In the past, with the unanimous consent of the House, a new Ways and Means motion has been adopted and a Minister has moved amendments to bills that exceeded the provisions of the original Ways and Means motion. For an example in which the House gave unanimous consent at report stage, see *Debates*, May 26, 1981, pp. 9931-2, 9948.

404. *Debates*, August 15, 1988, p. 18306.

405. *Debates*, October 3, 1983, p. 27675.

406. See, for example, *Debates*, April 16, 1969, pp. 7604-5; October 16, 1975, p. 8290; June 23, 1977, pp. 7052-3; July 15, 1977, pp. 7717, 7727; July 15, 1988, p. 17617; December 9, 1997, p. 2947.

407. See, for example, *Debates*, July 20, 1973, pp. 5841-2; June 29, 1976, pp. 14960-1.

408. See, for example, *Debates*, May 21, 1970, pp. 7166-7; September 27, 1971, pp. 8189-90; August 15, 1988, p. 18306.

409. See, for example, *Debates*, June 7, 1971, pp. 6435-6; March 19, 1993, p. 17290; April 2, 1993, p. 18003.

section of the parent Act itself;[410] and that was equivalent to a simple negative of the bill.[411]

The Chair has also ruled that because report stage is not a reading stage, motions in amendment cannot be moved in the form of reasoned amendments, as such amendments can only be moved on second and third reading of a bill.[412]

Since motions in amendment at report stage are open to debate, they fall into the category of substantive motions that are subject to amendment and sub-amendment.[413] An amendment to a report stage motion must be strictly relevant to that motion[414] and the debate thereon is limited to the amendment itself. An amendment with the same objective as a motion already at report stage has been ruled out of order, because it was in reality a new substantive motion for which notice should have been given before report stage commenced.[415]

Power of the Speaker to Select Amendments

In 1968, fearing that Members would take advantage of report stage to move similar amendments of little importance or which were dilatory in nature,[416] the Special Committee on Procedure recommended in its report that a rule be adopted to permit the Speaker "to select and combine the amendments of which notice had been given".[417] Such a rule was then adopted.[418]

In 1985, the Special Committee on the Reform of the House of Commons (McGrath Committee) deplored the fact that "[a]lthough successive Speakers since 1968 have used the power under the Standing Order to combine amendments, they have never used the power to select".[419] The Committee specifically recommended that the Speaker use the power to select motions in amendment at report stage. In 1986, the House decided to add a note to that effect to the Standing Order in question.[420]

410. See, for example, *Debates*, June 19, 1970, pp. 8368-9; June 11, 1973, pp. 4624-5.

411. See, for example, *Debates*, April 2, 1974, pp. 1101-2.

412. See Speaker Lamouroux's rulings, *Debates*, April 16, 1969, pp. 7601-2; April 25, 1969, p. 7963.

413. Standing Orders 76(6) and 76.1(6). See the rulings of the Chair, *Debates*, April 28, 1969, p. 8068; November 28, 1973, p. 8233. See, for example, *Journals*, June 15, 1995, p. 1766; November 4, 1996, p. 818; December 9, 1997, pp. 365-6.

414. See Speaker Lamoureux's ruling, *Debates*, April 29, 1969, pp. 8147-8.

415. See the ruling of the Chair, *Debates*, June 11, 1973, pp. 4647-8.

416. *Stewart*, p. 86.

417. *Journals*, December 6, 1968, p. 434.

418. See the present Standing Order 76.1(5).

419. See the Third Report of the Special Committee on the Reform of the House of Commons, presented to the House on June 18, 1985 (*Journals*, p. 839), pp. 40-2, and more specifically p. 41.

420. *Journals*, February 13, 1986, p. 1710. See also *Journals*, February 6, 1986, pp. 1665-6; page 6 of the Response of the Government to the Third Report of the Special Committee on the Reform of the House of Commons, tabled on October 9, 1985 (*Journals*, p. 1082).

Under the Standing Order, the Speaker thus has the power to select or group motions in amendment to be proposed at report stage.[421] The process of selecting and grouping motions in amendment has been refined since the 1970s. In the early years of the new rule, Speaker Lamoureux regularly consulted the House before making a final decision as to the admissibility and grouping of amendments.[422] Over the years, however, Speakers started to consult the House only when they were experiencing difficulties as to whether an amendment was in order. As Speaker Fraser explained in a ruling, the Chair followed a review process whereby motions in amendment were the subject of very extensive discussion, in some cases, between the Member filing the motion and the Clerk's staff.[423] Until 1994, all motions in amendment proposed by Members appeared on the *Notice Paper,* even the ones that were out of order. In June 1994, the Standing Orders were changed to provide that only those motions found to be in order by the Speaker were to appear on the *Notice Paper.*[424] When a motion is found to be out of order, the Member is informed of the reasons for the decision by letter.

Normally, the Speaker will not select a motion in amendment previously ruled out of order in committee, unless the reason for it being ruled out of order was that it required a Royal Recommendation.[425] As well, the Speaker should only select motions in amendment that were not or could not be presented in committee.[426] A motion previously defeated in committee will only be selected if the Speaker judges it to be of such significance as to warrant a further consideration at report stage.[427] For the purpose of debate, the Speaker will also group motions that have the same intent and are interrelated. In so doing, the Speaker will consider whether individual Members will be able to express their concerns during the debate on another motion.

On the other hand, the Speaker may, if he or she thinks fit, call upon any Member who has given notice of an amendment to give such explanation of the subject of the amendment as may enable the Speaker to form a judgement upon it. When an amendment is selected that has been submitted by more than one Member, the Speaker, after consultation, will designate which Member will propose it (normally, the Member who first gave notice of the motion).[428]

---

421. Standing Orders 76(5) and 76.1(5) (see, more specifically, the notes accompanying those Standing Orders).

422. See, for example, *Debates*, May 21, 1970, pp. 7166-7; June 11, 1973, pp. 4624-5.

423. *Debates*, December 6, 1990, p. 16357.

424. Standing Orders 76(2) and 76.1(2). See also Standing Committee on Procedure and House Affairs, *Minutes of Proceedings and Evidence*, June 9, 1994, Issue No. 16, p. 6; *Journals*, June 8, 1994, p. 545; June 10, 1994, p. 563.

425. In this case, the amendment may be selected if notice of the recommendation has been given in accordance with Standing Order 76(3) or 76.1(3).

426. Note accompanying Standing Orders 76(5) and 76.1(5).

427. Note accompanying Standing Orders 76(5) and 76.1(5). See, for example, *Debates*, August 28, 1987, p. 8559; August 15, 1988, p. 18306 (motions defeated in committee and not selected by the Speaker).

428. Standing Orders 76(5) and 76.1(5) were amended to this effect on February 7, 1994 (*Journals*, pp. 113-4).

The Speaker's decision on the grouping of motions in amendment at report stage addresses two matters: the grouping for debate and the voting arrangements.

Motions in amendment are grouped for debate according to two factors: the content and the place where they are to be inserted in the bill. Motions are grouped according to content if they could form the subject of a single debate; if, once adopted, they would have the same effect in different places of the bill; or if they relate to the same provision or similar provisions of the bill. Motions in amendment are combined according to the place where they are to be inserted in the bill when they relate to the same line (or lines). These motions in amendment will then be part of a single scheme for voting purposes.

When the Speaker selects and groups motions in amendment, he or she also decides on how they will be grouped for voting, that is, the Speaker determines the order in which the motions in amendment will be called and the consequences of one vote on the others. The purpose of the voting scheme is to avoid the House having to vote twice on the same issue.

The Speaker delivers his or her decision regarding the grouping of motions in amendment after the order for the consideration of report stage of the bill has been read. The Speaker informs the House of the motions in amendment that he or she has selected and grouped for debate as well as the voting arrangements[429] and, where applicable, of the motions in amendment that have not been selected, stating the reasons.[430]

Debate

When the Order of the Day for the consideration of report stage is called, the House commences its consideration of any amendment of which notice has been given, and each amendment is open to debate and amendment.[431] However, if no notice of amendment has been given at report stage, no debate is held.[432]

The report stage of any bill that has already been adopted at second reading cannot be taken into consideration prior to the second sitting day following the presentation of the committee's report.[433] The report stage of a bill that has not yet been adopted at second reading cannot be taken into consideration prior to the third sitting day following the presentation of the report.[434] The minimum number of sitting days between the presentation of the committee's report and commencement of debate at report stage must be strictly observed.[435]

---

429. See, for example, *Debates*, November 17, 1998, pp. 10055-6; December 2, 1998, p. 10794.

430. See, for example, *Debates*, December 12, 1996, p. 7435 (the Royal Recommendation was not obtained for an amendment that required such a recommendation); April 28, 1999, p. 14454 (the same amendments had been negatived in committee).

431. Standing Orders 76(6) and 76.1(6).

432. See the rulings of the Chair, *Debates*, February 3, 1969, pp. 5084-5; November 17, 1982, p. 20746.

433. Standing Order 76.1(1).

434. Standing Order 76(1).

435. See Speaker Lamoureux's ruling, *Journals*, October 6, 1970, pp. 1417-20; and Speaker Jerome's rulings, *Debates*, July 15, 1977, p. 7712; March 9, 1979, pp. 3999-4000.

After ruling on the grouping of motions for debate, the Chair reads the motions in the first group (or the motion in that group, if there is only one). The motions that have been moved and seconded are then debated. Once a motion has been moved, it may be withdrawn only with unanimous consent.[436]

When the Member who gave notice of a motion in amendment is absent, the motion may not be debated unless it is moved by another Member with the unanimous consent of the House.[437] When notice of a motion in amendment is given by the government, it may be moved by any Minister in the absence of the Minister responsible.

During debate at this stage, no Member may speak more than once or longer than 10 minutes on any motion in amendment or group of motions.[438] Unlike second reading and third reading stages, Members' speeches are not followed by a questions and comments period.[439] Of course, debate at report stage is subject to the general rules of debate, such as the rule of relevance.[440]

Deferral of Recorded Division

When a recorded division is demanded on any motion in amendment proposed during report stage of a bill, the Speaker may defer the calling in of the Members for the vote until some or all subsequent motions in amendment to the bill have been debated. In practice, the Speaker defers all recorded divisions that are demanded until the consideration of report stage has been completed. A recorded division, or divisions, is deferred in this manner from sitting to sitting.[441] In cases where there are an unusually large number of motions in amendment for consideration at report stage, the Speaker may, after consulting with the representatives of the parties, direct that deferred divisions be held before all motions in amendment have been taken into consideration.[442]

---

436. See, for example, *Debates*, June 14, 1995, p. 13847.

437. See, for example, *Debates*, February 12, 1993, p. 15828; June 5, 1995, p. 13267; November 26, 1998, p. 10525. For examples of motions that were not debated in the absence of the Member, see *Debates*, March 23, 1992, p. 8592; November 27, 1995, p. 16846; March 4, 1997, pp. 8603, 8613. For examples of motions that were not debated in the absence of the Member and where the House did not consent to the amendments being moved by another Member, see *Debates*, June 3, 1992, p. 11366; April 24, 1997, pp. 10156-7.

438. Standing Orders 76(7) and 76.1(7).

439. See, for example, *Debates*, April 12, 1994, pp. 2912, 2940.

440. See the rulings of the Chair, *Debates*, May 17, 1972, p. 2360; April 1, 1974, p. 1039. For more information on the rules of debate, see Chapter 13, "Rules of Order and Decorum".

441. Standing Orders 76(8) and 76.1(8).

442. Note accompanying Standing Order 76(8) and Note accompanying Standing Order 76.1(8). During the 1970s, recorded divisions were held on a number of motions in amendment at report stage before consideration of all of the motions moved at that stage had been concluded. See, for example, *Journals*, July 8, 1976, pp. 1410-5; July 9, 1976, pp. 1417-9; July 13, 1977, pp. 1350-63; July 14, 1977, pp. 1371-8.

Concurrence at Report Stage

The report stage of a bill that has not yet been read a second time is an integral part of the second reading stage of the bill.[443] At the end of report stage, a motion "That the bill, as amended, be concurred in at report stage and be read a second time" or "That the bill be concurred in at report stage and read a second time" is moved, the question is put on the motion, and the House disposes of it forthwith, without amendment or debate.[444]

At the end of report stage of a bill that has already been read a second time, the motion for concurrence at report stage is also put forthwith, without amendment or debate. The wording of the concurrence motion will vary, depending on whether the original bill has been amended or not, and depending on the stage at which the amendments were made. If, for example, a bill was not amended in committee or at report stage, the motion is as follows: "That the bill be concurred in at report stage." However, if a bill was amended in committee, but not at report stage, the motion will read as follows: "That the bill, as amended, be concurred in at report stage." When the bill was amended at report stage, but not in committee, the motion is as follows: "That the bill be concurred in at report stage, with amendments". Lastly, if the bill was amended in committee and at report stage, the following motion is made: "That the bill, as amended, be concurred in at report stage, with further amendments".

If no motion in amendment is moved at report stage of a bill that has already been read a second time, no debate may take place and consideration of report stage becomes a mere formality preceding third reading.[445] A bill that is reported from a Committee of the Whole, with or without amendments, may not be debated or amended at report stage.[446] The House must dispose of the bill at report stage as soon as it is received from a Committee of the Whole.[447]

THIRD READING (AND PASSAGE)

Third reading is the final stage that a bill must pass in the House of Commons. It is at this point that Members must decide whether the bill should be adopted, and ultimately become law. Although third reading is often regarded as a mere formality, it is still a decisive stage in the legislative process. In the case of a highly controversial bill, it could be a most crucial debating stage for Members.[448]

---

443. Standing Order 76(10).

444. Standing Order 76(9). See, for example, *Debates*, March 25, 1996, p. 1207.

445. Standing Order 76.1(11). See, for example, *Journals*, March 11, 1999, p. 1595.

446. Standing Order 76.1(12).

447. See, for example, *Journals*, October 6, 1998, pp. 1125-6.

448. The Special Committee on Procedure (1968) believed it to be very important that there be an opportunity for debate at this stage of the legislative process (*Journals*, December 6, 1968, p. 433).

Third reading and passage of a bill are moved in the same motion. They may take place in the same sitting as report stage if no amendment has been proposed at that stage or if the bill has been reported from a Committee of the Whole, with or without amendment.[449] When debate has taken place on a bill at the report stage, it may not be presented for third reading and passage before the next sitting of the House.[450] As well, when a bill has been considered by a committee before second reading and the report and second reading stages have then been combined, it may not proceed to third reading and passage until the next sitting of the House.[451]

Debate on third reading commences when the Order of the Day is read for third reading and the Minister or Member, as the case may be, moves: *"That the bill be now read a third time and do pass."*[452] The rules relating to the length of speeches during debate are the same as the rules governing the length of speeches and questions and comments at second reading.[453]

Debate at this stage of the legislative process focusses on the final form of the bill. The amendments that are admissible at this stage are exactly the same as those that were admissible at second reading stage.[454] It is in order to propose an amendment for a three- or six-month hoist,[455] as well as a reasoned amendment.[456] However, at third reading stage, reasoned amendments must deal strictly with the bill and not be contrary to the principle of the bill as adopted at second reading.[457]

An amendment to refer the subject matter of a bill to a committee at second reading stage becomes, at third reading, an amendment to recommit the bill to a committee with instructions to reconsider certain clauses for a specific purpose.[458] The purpose of such an amendment may be to enable the committee to add a new

---

449. Standing Order 76.1(11). See, for example, *Journals*, October 5, 1995, p. 2002. See also Speaker Lamoureux's ruling, *Journals*, February 24, 1969, pp. 738-9. However, the interpretation of this provision must take into account the prohibition in Standing Order 71, which provides that the three readings of a bill must take place on different days.

450. Standing Order 76.1(10).

451. Standing Order 76(10).

452. See, for example, *Journals*, April 16, 1997, p. 1474.

453. Standing Order 74.

454. *Beauchesne*, 4ᵗʰ ed., p. 288.

455. See, for example, *Debates*, September 19, 1996, pp. 4467-8.

456. See, for example, *Debates*, November 9, 1995, p. 16402.

457. *Beauchesne*, 4ᵗʰ ed., p. 288. See, for example, the rulings of the Chair, *Debates*, March 2, 1967, p. 13658; March 24, 1969, p. 7055; May 12, 1969, p. 8595; December 11, 1969, pp. 1858-60; December 16, 1971, pp. 10545-7.

458. See, for example, *Debates*, November 24, 1970, pp. 1416-7; *Journals*, April 23, 1993, p. 2854.

clause, to reconsider a specific clause of the bill or to reconsider previous amendments.[459] However, an amendment to recommit a bill should not seek to give a mandatory instruction to a committee.[460] In addition, an amendment to recommit a bill to a committee other than the committee which previously considered it has been ruled out of order by the Chair.[461] If the amendment to recommit a bill back to the committee is carried, the committee may consider only the part of the bill that is specified in the order of reference.

When the motion for third reading has been carried, the Clerk of the House certifies that the bill has passed, with the date, at the foot of the bill.[462] The bill is then sent to the Senate for approval. Defeat of a motion for third reading will result in the withdrawal of the bill.[463]

CONSIDERATION AND PASSAGE BY THE SENATE

Once the House of Commons has passed a bill, a message is sent to the Senate asking it to pass the bill as well.[464] When the Senate considers a bill, it follows a legislative process that is very similar to the one in the House of Commons. When the Senate has passed a bill, it so informs the House of Commons by message.

Because most government bills originate in the House of Commons, the Senate is sometimes asked to expedite its consideration of a bill. The Senate Rules provide for a procedure known as pre-study, which involves referring the subject matter of a bill that has been introduced in the House of Commons, but has not yet been adopted at first reading in the Senate, to a standing committee.[465] In this way, the Senate may consider the bill and form its opinion even before the bill is sent to it by the House of Commons. Then, when the bill is received, the Senate is in a position to adopt or amend it in a very short time.

---

459. *Debates*, December 20, 1966, p. 11427; March 1, 1967, pp. 13636-7.

460. *Debates*, December 18, 1990, pp. 16916-7.

461. *Journals*, March 9, 1999, pp. 1580-1; *Debates*, March 9, 1999, p. 12646.

462. Standing Order 72.

463. In 1968, a tax bill introduced by the Pearson government was defeated at third reading (*Journals*, February 19, 1968, pp. 702-3). See also *Journals*, February 23, 1968, p. 713; *Debates*, February 23, 1968, p. 6923; *Journals*, February 28, 1968, pp. 719-21.

464. See, for example, *Senate Journals*, October 31, 1995, p. 1235. The Senate may defeat a bill (see, for example, Bill C-43, *An Act respecting Abortion*, *Senate Debates*, January 31, 1991, p. 5307) and even, although it rarely does so, refuse to consider a bill (see, for example, Bill C-280, *An Act to amend the Canada Pension Plan Act (disability pension)*, *Senate Journals*, February 13, 1992, pp. 528-31; *House of Commons Journals*, February 13, 1992, p. 1020).

465. Senate Rule 74(1). This procedure arose during the 1940s, when the Estimates were examined by the Senate Finance Committee even before the subsequent Supply bills were sent to the Senate. During the 1970s, this practice was extended to other bills at the initiative of Senator Hayden, and since then it has also been referred to as the "Hayden formula".

PASSAGE OF SENATE AMENDMENTS (IF ANY)
BY THE HOUSE OF COMMONS

When the Senate adopts a bill without amendment, a message is sent to the House of Commons to inform it that the bill has been passed[466] and Royal Assent is normally given very shortly afterwards, or in the following few days. The bill itself is not sent back to the House, unless it is a Supply bill.[467] However, when the Senate amends the bill, it informs the House of the amendments in the message it sends to the House,[468] and sends the bill back to the House. The Senate sometimes sends the House messages containing the observations or recommendations of the Senate committee that examined the bill.[469] Messages from the Senate are printed in the *Journals* when they are received by the House.

When the House receives amendments to a bill from the Senate, the amendments are then submitted to the House for consideration. It is not for the Speaker of the House of Commons to rule as to the procedural regularity of proceedings in the Senate and of the amendments it makes to bills.[470] Rather, it is for the House itself to decide whether it accepts or rejects the amendments proposed by the Senate, and if the House so desires it may state the reasons for rejecting or amending them. A motion for the consideration of Senate amendments requires 24 hours' written notice.[471] The sponsor of a bill may use such a motion to move that the House concur in,[472] amend or reject[473] the amendments made by the Senate. The motion may at the same time reject certain amendments made by the Senate, and concur in or amend others. The motion must relate exclusively to the Senate amendments, and not to other provisions of the bill that are not contemplated by the amendments. The House may want to reject the Senate amendments for a variety of reasons, for instance, because it believes that they are in contradiction to the principle of the bill[474] or infringe the financial initiative of the Crown and the House of Commons.[475]

The motion will appear on the *Notice Paper* under the heading "Motions Respecting Senate Amendments to Bills". The motion will be considered during

---

466. See, for example, *Journals*, April 9, 1997, p. 1369.

467. *Bourinot*, 4ᵗʰ ed., p. 446; *May*, 22ⁿᵈ ed., p. 485. See also Chapter 18, "Financial Procedures".

468. See, for example, *Journals*, April 16, 1997, pp. 1479-80.

469. See, for example, *Journals*, January 23, 1990, pp. 1091-101.

470. See Speaker Fraser's rulings, *Debates*, July 11, 1988, pp. 17382-5; April 26, 1990, pp. 10719-26. See also Speaker Parent's ruling, *Debates*, November 19, 1996, pp. 6410-11, and the ruling of Deputy Speaker Milliken, *Debates*, June 9, 1999, pp. 16104-5.

471. Standing Order 77(1). It was not until 1991 that a provision relating to the consideration of Senate amendments was incorporated into the Standing Orders (*Journals*, April 11, 1991, p. 2915).

472. See, for example, *Debates*, December 4, 1998, p. 10901.

473. See, for example, *Debates*, August 21, 1987, pp. 8283-4.

474. See, for example, *Debates*, August 21, 1987, pp. 8283-4.

475. See, for example, *Journals*, July 18, 1959, pp. 750-1; May 8, 1990, p. 1661.

Government Orders, if the bill in question is a government bill, or during Private Members' Business, if it is a private Member's bill.

The Senate makes amendments to bills fairly often, and the House is normally quite disposed to accept them, since the amendments generally involve corrections to drafting errors or improvements to administrative aspects.[476] When debate takes place on Senate amendments, Members who speak must confine themselves to the amendments being considered and may not address other aspects of the bill, or the bill as a whole.[477] The motion for the consideration of Senate amendments itself is open to amendment and sub-amendment during debate.[478] With the exception of the Prime Minister and Leader of the Opposition, no Member may speak for more than 20 minutes.[479] Following each 20-minute speech, a period not exceeding 10 minutes is made available for questions and comments. Motions for time allocation[480] and for closure[481] may be moved by the government to limit or close debate.

When the House agrees to the Senate amendments, a message to that effect is sent to the Senate and the bill is sent back to it while awaiting Royal Assent. If the House amends or rejects the Senate amendments, it so acquaints the Senate by message as well. The Senate may then reconsider its amendments, having regard to the message from the House. It may decide to accept the decision of the House, to reject that decision and insist that its amendments be maintained, or to amend what the House has proposed. Regardless of what the Senate decides, it sends another message to the House to inform it of the decision. Communication between the two Houses goes on in this way until they ultimately agree on a text. If it is impossible for an agreement to be reached by exchanging messages, the House that has possession of the bill may ask that a conference be held.

Conference Between the Houses

When a disagreement arises between the House of Commons and the Senate as to the amendments to be made to a bill, there are two possible ways of proceeding: the disagreement may be communicated in a message (this is normally the first step taken), or an attempt may be made to resolve it by holding a conference. Although

---

476. See, for example, *Debates*, June 11, 1996, p. 3642.

477. *Bourinot*, 4th ed., p. 535.

478. See, for example, *Journals*, July 12, 1988, p. 3160; May 8, 1990, p. 1663. Speaker Parent ruled that a sub-amendment requesting the Senate to respond to a message from the House within a specific time was out of order because it went outside the scope of the amendment (*Debates*, November 19, 1996, p. 6452).

479. Standing Order 43(1).

480. Standing Order 78. See *Debates*, November 28, 1996, pp. 6831-2; *Journals*, March 20, 1997, pp. 1322-3.

481. Standing Order 57. See *Journals*, March 13, 1990, pp. 1331-2; June 20, 1995, pp. 1817-8.

this practice has fallen into disuse,[482] a conference may be requested by either of the two Houses in the following cases: to communicate a resolution or an address to which the concurrence of the other House is desired; to discuss the privileges of Parliament; to discuss any matter that warrants the use of this procedure; to require or to communicate statements of facts on which bills have been passed by either House; to offer reasons for disagreeing to, or insisting on, amendments to a bill.[483]

Either of the two Houses may request that a conference be held, as long as it is in possession of the bill or other matter that is to be the subject of the conference.[484] The Standing Orders of the House stipulate that the House is required to prepare and agree to the reasons to be given before a message is sent to the Senate requesting that a conference be held.[485] However, the terms and conditions regarding consent to and preparation for the holding of the conference, and the course of proceedings at conferences, are governed by custom and tradition rather than by the Standing Orders.[486]

Until 1906, the process relating to the holding of conferences was rather complex. The role of representatives at the conference was limited to communicating the reasons to the representatives of the other House. There could be no discussion. In October 1903, three conferences were held, only one of which was a free conference, to resolve a dispute regarding amendments that the Senate wished to make to a bill from the House.[487] The process was found to be so complex that new rules were incorporated into the Standing Orders in 1906,[488] following the passage of a joint resolution of the two Houses the preceding year.[489] The purpose of that amendment to the Standing Orders was to make conferences "free"[490] to facilitate agreement.

482. The last conference was held in 1947 (*Journals*, July 14, 1947, p. 905).

483. *Bourinot*, 4th ed., p. 274.

484. *Bourinot*, 4th ed., p. 278.

485. Standing Order 77(4).

486. See *May*, 1st ed., pp. 249-58; *Campion*, 3rd ed., pp. 227-32; *Hatsell*, Vol. IV, pp. 1-55; *Redlich*, Vol. II, pp. 79-88; *Bourinot*, 4th ed., pp. 274-80; F.A. Kunz, *The Modern Senate of Canada 1925-1963, A Re-Appraisal*, Toronto: University of Toronto Press, 1965, pp. 347-65; Blair Armitage, "Parliamentary Conferences," *Canadian Parliamentary Review*, Summer 1990, pp. 29-30.

487. The first conference, which was held at the initiative of the House, took place at 8:30 p.m. on October 22, 1903 (*Journals*, p. 716); the second, at the initiative of the Senate, took place a little later in the evening, at 11:00 p.m. (*Journals*, p. 723). After hearing the report of the representatives when they returned from the second conference, the House asked that a third, *free*, conference be held "forthwith" (*Journals*, October 23, 1903, p. 727). The representatives at that conference reported to the House on October 23 (*Journals*, October 23, 1903, p. 758) and the issue was resolved on October 24 (*Journals*, October 24, 1903, p. 759).

488. *Journals*, July 10, 1906, pp. 579-80. At the time of Confederation, there was only one Standing Order providing that when the House requested a conference with the Senate, the reasons for disagreement had first to be "prepared and agreed to before a Message" was to be sent "forthwith".

489. *Journals*, July 12, 1905, pp. 500-1.

490. Standing Order 77(3).

The representatives (who are called managers) were thereby given the freedom to talk and negotiate as they saw fit.[491]

Although the two Houses frequently transmit messages to each other, they have rarely held conferences. No conference has taken place since 1947, and there have been only 16 since 1903.[492] Of these 16 conferences, 13 were held after the provisions relating to the holding of free conferences came into effect in 1906.[493] All of these "free" conferences were held at the request of the House of Commons, and they were all held to resolve disputes in respect of bills.

Over the years, the exchange of messages and the appearance of Ministers before House and Senate committees have considerably reduced the need to use this procedure.[494] However, if the two Houses were to reach a deadlock because of a disagreement respecting amendments to be made to a bill, a Member, usually the Member responsible for the bill, could propose that a message be sent to the Senate asking it to participate in a free conference on the amendment or amendments in dispute.[495] Once the message was approved and sent to the Senate, the Senate in turn would send a message to the House to inform the House of its response. If the Senate agreed to participate in the conference, a message would also be sent to the House of Commons to inform it of the time and place chosen for the conference, and of the names of the Senators (who are called managers) who would be acting for the Senate.

---

491. *Bourinot*, 4th ed., p. 280.

492. A review of the indexes to the *Journals* does not reveal a single instance of a conference being held between 1867 and 1902.

493. These 13 conferences were held on the following dates: *Journals*, May 4, 1910, pp. 619-20; June 18, 1919, p. 386; July 4, 1919, p. 521; May 27, 1921, p. 382, and May 28, 1921, p. 385; June 27, 1922, p. 519 (two conferences); July 16, 1924, p. 572; June 25, 1925, p. 532; May 27, 1933, p. 650; June 29, 1934, p. 562; June 24, 1938, p. 522; July 31, 1940, p. 307; July 14, 1947, p. 905. On one occasion, the Senate declined an invitation to participate in a free conference (*Journals*, July 19, 1924, p. 653).

494. In the British Parliament, the exchange of messages between the Commons and the House of Lords has made conferences obsolete (*May*, 22nd ed., p. 610, note 4). In Canada, in recent years, the Senate has tried to revive the procedure on two occasions. On November 18, 1987, the Senate passed a motion that the Leader of the government in the Senate ask his Cabinet colleagues whether they would agree to a conference on Bill C-22, *An Act to amend the Patent Act*. On November 19, the Leader of the government in the Senate informed the Senators that the government would not recommend such a conference to the House of Commons (*Senate Debates*, November 18, 1987, pp. 2179-2184; November 19, 1987, pp. 2212-3). On May 22, 1990, when the Senate was examining the possibility of sending to the House a message respecting the amendments it wished to make to Bill C-21, *An Act to amend the Unemployment Insurance Act*, Senator Allen MacEachen moved that the motion being considered be referred to a conference between the two Houses of Parliament. Senator MacEachen's amendment was negatived on October 22, 1990 (*Senate Journals,* May 22, 1990, pp. 991-2; October 22, 1990, pp. 1848-9).

495. In 1995, following an exchange of messages between the House and the Senate concerning Bill C-69, *Electoral Boundaries Readjustment Act*, the Standing Committee on Procedure and House Affairs expressed its serious concerns in its 108th Report to the House regarding the handling of Bill C-69 by the Senate Standing Committee on Legal and Constitutional Affairs (see Standing Committee on Procedure and House Affairs, *Minutes of Proceedings and Evidence*, Issue No. 54, pp. 8-9; *Debates*, December 8, 1995, p. 17445).

A similar motion would be moved in the House of Commons to designate the representatives of the House (who normally include the Member responsible for the bill)[496] and order that a message to this effect be sent to the Senate.

At the time agreed upon, the managers would meet to try to get the two Houses out of the deadlock. The records of proceedings show that in the event that the House was sitting at the time chosen for the conference, the Speaker would rise and announce that the time had come to hold the conference, and the Clerk would give the names of the managers who would then go to the Senate.[497] When the House managers arrived in the Senate, the Speaker of the Senate would announce the names of the Senate managers, and they would leave the Senate chamber. Since no official report or minutes were prepared for those conferences, there is very little information available as to how free conferences were held in the past and on the other people who attended them in addition to the managers from the two Houses.

A free conference means that the discussion continues until an agreement is reached, but there are three possible outcomes: the conference fails; a compromise is reached; the House accepts the Senate amendments, or the Senate accepts the House amendments, as the case may be. If the conference fails, the matter is closed and the bill simply remains on the *Order Paper* where it dies at the end of the session.[498] During that time, no new bill may be introduced in the House in respect of the same subject matter and containing similar provisions. If a compromise is reached, one of the representatives of the House submits a report to the Members concerning the conference and moves that the report be approved and a message be sent to the Senate so informing the Senate. Lastly, if the House decides not to press for its amendments to be approved, it accepts the Senate amendments and sends a message to the Senate to so notify it.

ROYAL ASSENT

Royal Assent brings all three constituent elements of Parliament together (the Crown, the Senate and the House of Commons). Royal Assent, which is an integral part of the legislative process, is the stage that a bill must complete before officially becoming an Act of Parliament. A version of the bill that is identical to the version passed by the two Houses is approved by a representative of the Crown and is given "the complement and perfection of a law".[499] This essentially ceremonial procedure takes place in the presence of Members and Senators, after the Members have been

---

496. The number of managers has varied for each conference. For the conferences held in 1903, the numbers of Members and Senators were twelve and six respectively. For the conferences held in 1919, the numbers were eleven and eight; in 1922, eight and five; and in 1924, five and three. In each of the other conferences, the numbers of Members and Senators were equal. For five of the fourteen free conferences, the breakdown was three managers from each House.

497. The records of proceedings show that the House adjourned for only four of the fourteen free conferences. In the other cases, the House continued to sit, had not yet been convened or had suspended the sitting for dinner.

498. *Bourinot*, 4ᵗʰ ed., p. 275.

499. *May*, 22ⁿᵈ ed., p. 563.

summoned by the Usher of the Black Rod to go to the Senate to attend the Royal Assent ceremony.

The origins of Royal Assent go back to the time of Henry VI (1422-61; 1470-1).[500] Under his reign, it became practice to introduce bills in both Houses in the form of complete statutes, and not in the form of petitions as had been the case since the early days of the constitution of the British Parliament. Royal Assent was given by the Sovereign in person until 1541; in that year, to spare King Henry VIII the indignity of having to give Royal Assent to the bill for the execution of his wife, Katharine Howard, the task was assigned for the first time to a royal commission.[501] It then became common practice to appoint Lords Commissioners with responsibility for giving Royal Assent on behalf of the Sovereign. The last time that the Monarch granted Royal Assent in person in Great Britain was on August 12, 1854, under the reign of Victoria.[502] In 1967, the British Parliament passed the *Royal Assent Act* which now allows a bill to acquire the force of law on simple report of Royal Assent by the Speakers of the two Houses.[503] This procedure eliminates the need for holding a ceremony.[504]

---

500. *May*, 11th ed., p. 459.

501. P.D.G. Hayter, "Royal Assent: A New Form", *The Table*, Vol. XXXVI, 1967, pp. 53-4.

502. For a description of the ceremony in the presence of a monarch, see *May*, 22nd ed., p. 565, note 4. King George VI gave Royal Assent in person to certain bills of the Parliament of Canada (*Journals*, May 8, 1939, p. 437; May 19, 1939, pp. 525-6).

503. *May*, 22nd ed., pp. 564-5. In 1965, an incident occurred in the British Parliament that led to the abolition of the ceremony of Royal Assent. While the House was engaged in passionate debate, Black Rod knocked on the door of the House of Commons. A number of Members protested and rushed the Bar of the House to prevent him from entering. They refused to attend the ceremony and continued to debate, even after the Speaker had left the chair (*Hayter*, p. 54).

504. However, the adoption of this procedure did not lead to the abolition of the traditional ceremony, which the British Parliament still uses at the time of prorogation, nor does it offend the Queen's prerogatives in this regard (*Hayter*, pp. 55-7).

In the Canadian House of Commons, the ceremony of Royal Assent has sometimes been criticized,[505] but Parliament has remained faithful to the conventions of Royal Assent, the rules of which come down directly from the rules that were in effect in Great Britain at the time of Confederation.[506] Neither the Standing Orders of the House nor the *Constitution Act* specifically mention the precise procedure for giving Royal Assent. Initially, the practice was for Royal Assent to be deferred to the end of a parliamentary session, when the Governor General was present for the prorogation of Parliament. This practice gradually disappeared over time, and today Royal Assent is given to bills at any time during a session.[507] As well, during adjournments of the House, the Speaker may,

---

505. *Debates*, March 30, 1933, pp. 3551-2; March 29, 1984, p. 2544. In the last 15 years, there have been a number of proposals for reforming the procedure for giving Royal Assent. In 1985, the Special Committee on Reform of the House of Commons (McGrath Committee) recommended that a formula be adopted for Royal Assent to be given in writing (see the Second Report of the Committee, p. 118, presented to the House on March 26, 1985 (*Journals*, p. 420)). In its response to the Committee's report, the government at the time indicated that it wanted to modernize the procedure for signifying Royal Assent, in consultation with the Senate (*Journals*, October 9, 1985, p. 1082). The Committee's recommendation was supported by the Board of Internal Economy at its meeting on June 11, 1986 (*Journals*, October 10, 1986, p. 72). In 1993, the Standing Committee on House Management presented a report on parliamentary reform. In its 81st Report, the Committee agreed to act on the recommendation in the McGrath Report (Standing Committee on House Management, *Minutes of Proceedings and Evidence*, Issue No. 53, April 1, 1993, p. 31). The Senate has also expressed interest in reforming Royal Assent. In 1985, the Fourth Report of the Senate Standing Committee on Standing Rules and Orders recommended that a simplified procedure be adopted (*Senate Debates*, November 6, 1985, pp. 1448, 1469). That report prompted a debate (*Senate Debates*, November 7, 1985, pp. 1480-2; January 22, 1986, pp. 1860-2; January 23, 1986, pp. 1873-5) and was followed by the introduction of a government bill, Bill S-19, *Royal Assent Act*, which was debated at second reading in July and September 1988, a few days before dissolution of the Thirty-Third Parliament (*Senate Debates*, July 26, 1988, pp. 4122-3; September 20, 1988, pp. 4463-4). On April 2, 1998, another bill (Bill S-15) to reform Royal Assent was introduced in the Senate, this time by the Leader of the Opposition in the Senate, Senator Lynch-Staunton (*Senate Journals*, p. 576). After being debated at second reading, the bill was referred to the Senate Standing Committee on Legal and Constitutional Affairs on June 9, 1998 (*Senate Journals*, p. 788). The Committee reported it with amendments on June 18, 1998 (*Senate Journals*, pp. 862-3; 898-9). On December 8, 1998, after being debated, the bill was withdrawn (*Senate Journals*, pp. 1170-2). On March 10, 1999, Senator Lynch-Staunton introduced a new bill (S-26) that was virtually identical to the former Bill S-15, as amended by the Committee (*Senate Journals*, p. 1334).

506. According to some observers, the Canadian ceremony seems to be the one that most closely resembles the original ceremony (*Wilding and Laundy*, 3rd ed., 1968, p. 642). Most countries with a parliamentary system on the British model have abandoned the ceremony of Royal Assent. In the Australian Parliament, the ceremony has not taken place since the early years of the Australian Commonwealth. The usual practice is for the chamber that has initiated the bill to transmit copies of it to the residence of the Governor General, who affixes his or her signature. In New Zealand, the Governor General has not attended in person to assent to bills since 1875. The Governor General simply signs the two copies presented and returns them to the House with a message informing the House that assent has been given.

507. Normally, assent is given only once in a sitting. There was a deviation from this practice on July 17, 1980, when the House was called to the Senate at noon and again at 9:00 p.m. in order for other bills to be assented to as well (*Debates,* July 17, 1980, pp. 2998, 3044-5, 3051).

at the request of the government, give notice that the House will meet at an earlier time for the purposes of Royal Assent; being convened "for those purposes only", the House cannot proceed to any other business.[508]

When the House is sitting and there are bills that require Royal Assent, the House may suspend its proceedings until a specific time,[509] until the call of the Chair[510] or until the call of the bell.[511] In the absence of any special arrangements to extend the sitting, the proceedings are interrupted at the normal hour of adjournment and the House stands adjourned until the next sitting day.[512] If the ceremony is scheduled for the same time as other items of business, a decision must be made as to which matter will take precedence.[513]

In the Canadian Parliament, the Governor General will normally give Royal Assent in person, in the case of laws of great importance and when Parliament is to be prorogued. At other times, it is given by a deputy: the Chief Justice of the Supreme Court of Canada or one of the other judges of the Supreme Court.

The Ceremony

When a bill has been passed by both Houses of Parliament and is ready to receive Royal Assent, a special copy is printed on parchment. The Clerk of the House and the Clerk of the Senate both sign the back of it. The Governor General's residence then informs the Speaker of the House that the Governor General or the Deputy Governor will be going to the Senate to give Royal Assent to bills. The Speaker of the House then relays the message to the Members.[514]

---

508. Standing Order 28(4). This provision was added to the Standing Orders in June 1994 (Standing Committee on Procedure and House Affairs, *Minutes of Proceedings and Evidence*, Twenty-Seventh Report, June 9, 1994, Issue No. 16, p. 3; *Debates*, June 8, 1994, p. 4997; June 10, 1994, p. 5183).

509. See, for example, *Debates*, March 9, 1966, pp. 2472-3; February 27, 1969, p. 6034.

510. See, for example, *Debates*, July 12, 1940, p. 1644; March 29, 1985, p. 3547; June 27, 1986, p. 14997.

511. See, for example, *Debates*, March 9, 1966, p. 2472; July 14, 1966, p. 7728; March 24, 1975, p. 4446; December 20, 1975, p. 10257; October 22, 1976, pp. 390-1; June 27, 1985, pp. 6331-2; December 19, 1986, pp. 2337-8.

512. For example, on December 14, 1990, Deputy Speaker Champagne adjourned the House at the normal hour of daily adjournment even though the House had already been informed that the Royal Assent ceremony would soon take place and that the Usher of the Black Rod was on his way to request the attendance of the House (*Debates*, pp. 16787, 16797-9).

513. On June 23, 1971, a recorded division and Royal Assent were both scheduled for the same time, 5:45 p.m. A member rose on a point of order, and it was decided to proceed with the vote first, and then go to the Royal Assent ceremony (*Debates*, June 23, 1971, p. 7265).

514. See, for example, *Debates*, March 28, 1996, p. 1386.

At the appointed time, the Usher of the Black Rod of the Senate informs the House that the Governor General or the Deputy Governor has asked them to proceed to the Senate. Before entering the Commons chamber, he or she knocks three times on the door.[515] Debate that is then taking place is interrupted by the Speaker.[516] Quorum is not required to receive the message from the Usher of the Black Rod.[517] The Sergeant-at-Arms announces to the Speaker that the messenger from the Senate wishes to enter. The Speaker replies: "Admit the messenger", after which the doors are opened to allow the Usher of the Black Rod to enter. Because the House cannot always arrange for its order of business to coincide with the time when Royal Assent is to be given, it sometimes has to make the messenger wait. This situation has prompted considerable discussion regarding the use of the House's time, particularly in respect of the appropriateness of moving on to other business while the House is waiting for the Senate messenger.[518]

When the Usher of the Black Rod has entered and bowed three times, he or she goes forward to the Table and acquaints the Speaker that it is the desire of the Governor General or his or her Deputy that the House attend him or her immediately in the Senate.[519] The Usher of the Black Rod then leads the House to the Senate, followed, in order, by the Sergeant-at-Arms bearing the Mace, the Speaker, the Clerk and the Table Officers, and the Members.

While the Speaker and the Members gather at the Bar of the Senate, the Usher of the Black Rod moves towards the far end of the Senate Chamber. He or she bows to the Governor General or the Deputy Governor and says: "*Order!*" The Speaker of the House then raises his or her hat and bows to the Governor General (or the Deputy Governor). A clerk who is at the Table in the Senate then reads the titles of the bills that are to receive Royal Assent, in English and French, with the exception of Supply bills. The Clerk of the Senate displays the bills and states: "In Her Majesty's name, His/Her Excellency the Governor General (the Honourable the Deputy of the Governor General) doth assent to these bills."

If there is a Supply bill to be assented to, the Speaker of the House of Commons brings it into the Senate Chamber and reads a message, in both official languages, asking that it be given Royal Assent, using the following formula:

---

515. The origins of this practice go back to 1641 when the Gentleman Usher of Great Britain received a reprimand for entering the House before being expressly invited to do so (*The Table*, Vol. XLVI, 1978, p. 129).

516. Occasionally, the interruption of debate has prompted reaction from Members (*Debates*, December 16, 1953, pp. 1012-5; March 31, 1954, p. 3547).

517. Standing Order 29(5).

518. *Debates*, February 19, 1981, pp. 7483-7; March 31, 1982, pp. 16029-32; November 3, 1982, pp. 20383-5. On occasion, Members have challenged the custom that the Usher be admitted to the House immediately (see *Debates*, February 16, 1972, pp. 10959-60).

519. It is the custom that the House should go to the Senate for Royal Assent only when it is invited to do so by the Usher of the Black Rod. However, the Commons has occasionally attended at the bar of the Senate without being accompanied by the Usher. One such incident occurred on June 12, 1925, when the office of the Black Rod was vacant (*Debates*, June 12, 1925, p. 438).

May it Please Your Excellency (Honour[520]): The Commons of Canada have voted supplies to enable the Government to defray certain expenses of the public service. In the name of the Commons, I present to Your Excellency (Honour) the following Bill: (title), to which Bill I humbly request Your Excellency's (Honour's) Assent.

A Senate clerk at the Table goes to the Bar, where the Speaker of the House of Commons gives the clerk the Supply bill, and then returns to the Table. After reading the title of the Supply bill in both official languages, the Clerk of the Senate reads the Royal Assent, using the following formula:

In Her Majesty's name, His/Her Excellency the Governor General (the Honourable the Deputy to the Governor General) thanks her loyal subjects, accepts their benevolence and assents to this Bill.

The representative of the Crown consents to the enactment of all of the bills by nodding his or her head. This is the act by which Royal Assent is officially given and as of that moment the bills have the force of law, unless the bills provide another date on which they are to come into force.[521] The Usher of the Black Rod then turns to face the exit from the Senate, indicating that the ceremony is concluded. The Speaker of the House raises his or her hat, bows to the representative of the Crown, and withdraws from the Chamber with the Members returning to the House of Commons.

Upon returning to the House, the Speaker takes the Chair and informs the Members that the Governor General was pleased to give, in Her Majesty's name, Royal Assent to certain bills. The House resumes the business that had been interrupted, or adjourns if the hour for adjournment has already passed. Normally, the ceremony lasts no more than 20 minutes.[522]

A bill may not be given Royal Assent if it has not gone through all of the stages of the legislative process in both Houses. However, a bill may be read three times and be given Royal Assent at the same sitting.[523] The *Constitution Act, 1867* provides for the circumstances in which statutes may be disallowed or Royal Assent withheld, but does not specify the procedure to be followed.[524]

---

520. "Your Honour" is used to refer to the Deputy Governor.

521. The other date, which is fixed by the Governor in Council, is published in Part II of the *Canada Gazette*.

522. After the ceremony, the Clerk of the Senate, who is also the Clerk of the Parliaments, endorses on every Act, immediately after its title, the day, month and year when the Act was assented to in Her Majesty's name, and the endorsement is a part of the Act, in accordance with Section 5(1) of the *Interpretation Act*, R.S.C. 1985, c. I-21. When a bill has been initialled, it is sent to the residence of the Governor General to be signed on the back by the Governor General, after which it is sent to the Senate where it is kept in a vault. Because it is a single bilingual document, the new Act carries only one signature. The Clerk of the Senate then informs the *Canada Gazette* that bills have been given Royal Assent.

523. See, for example, *Journals*, August 9, 1977, pp. 1542-7; October 23, 1978, pp. 50-3.

524. R.S.C. 1985, Appendix II, No. 5, ss. 55-7.

COMING INTO FORCE

A distinction must be made between the date on which a legislative measure is enacted by Parliament and the date on which it comes into force. The *Interpretation Act* contains provisions governing the coming into force of statutes.[525] A bill becomes law after it has been passed by both Houses in the same form, but the Act comes into force either when it receives Royal Assent, if no date of commencement is provided for in the Act,[526] or on another date provided for in the Act. Accordingly, an Act may come into force on one or more dates specified in the Act itself or fixed by an order of the Governor in Council.

---

525. R.S.C. 1985, c. I-21.

526. *Interpretation Act*, R.S.C. 1985, c. I-21, s. 5(2).

17

Delegated Legislation

... the central problem relating to legislative review of executive and administrative law-making is the degree to which Parliament should involve itself in attempting to influence and control the course of administration. If Parliament goes too far into the substance of day-to-day administration, it defeats many of the underlying reasons for delegating powers to make laws in the first place....

SPECIAL COMMITTEE ON STATUTORY INSTRUMENTS,
Third Report (*Journals,* October 22, 1969, p. 1482)

Some acts of Parliament delegate to Ministers, departments, agencies, boards or other authorities the power to make and apply subordinate legislation described only in general terms in the acts. Delegated legislation is a term used to describe these regulations, orders, rules, by-laws and other instruments. Parliament scrutinizes most delegated legislation to ensure that their provisions do not exceed the powers approved by Parliament itself.

This responsibility to scrutinize delegated legislation has been assigned to the Standing Joint Committee for the Scrutiny of Regulations. In addition to the terms of reference set out by the House itself, this Committee's mandate is in part described by an act of Parliament.[1] Its activities sometimes lead to the invocation of special procedures in the House when the Committee makes a report to the House advocating the revocation of a regulation.

---

1. *Statutory Instruments Act*, R.S.C. 1985, c. S-22, s. 19.

This chapter discusses the mandate of the Standing Joint Committee for the Scrutiny of Regulations and the procedures the House follows to adopt or reject a report recommending the revocation of a statutory instrument.

Historical Perspective

Systematic parliamentary scrutiny of delegated legislation is a relatively modern phenomenon. In the early years of Confederation, parliamentary scrutiny consisted of addresses for papers whereby Parliament obtained the information it desired, and on which it could act if it chose to.[2] Perhaps this lack of regularized oversight was understandable since, as one expert put it, "with the exception of the wartime period 1914-19 it could not be said that before 1939 the scope of the activities of the federal government was such that Parliament lacked adequate time to act as a watch-dog of the executive."[3] This is not to say that the quantity of delegated legislation was low. Indeed, the number of regulations and orders was sufficiently large to warrant the publication in 1889 of *The Consolidated Orders in Council of Canada,* which ran to two volumes and 1,126 pages.[4] In 1914, Parliament passed the *War Measures Act, 1914,* one of the most extreme examples of a statute delegating legislative authority to Cabinet. This Act empowered the Governor in Council to proclaim a state of "real or apprehended war, invasion or insurrection" and "to make from time to time such orders and regulations, as he may by reason of the existence of real or apprehended war, invasion or insurrection, deem necessary or advisable for the security, defence, peace, order and welfare of Canada".[5] At the outbreak of World War II, again the volume of decisions that had to be made in a timely manner was considerable and as a result, Ministers, government departments, boards and crown agencies were given increasing authority to make regulatory decisions.[6] It was during this period that a suggestion was first made that since the role of Parliament was to support and control the executive in order to keep it responsible, Orders in Council having a legislative effect should be regularly tabled in the House and referred to a parliamentary committee for scrutiny.[7]

The postwar years saw a growth in government and a steady escalation in the use of Orders in Council to regulate public affairs. Although the practice of tabling regulations continued after the War, there was much criticism of "government by Order in Council." In 1950, Parliament adopted the *Regulations Act,* which decreed that all "orders, regulations and proclamations made or issued in the exercise of

---

2. *Bourinot,* 2nd ed., pp. 332-3, 808-10.

3. J.R. Mallory, "Delegated Legislation in Canada: Recent Changes in Machinery," *Economics and Political Science: The Journal of the Canadian Political Science Association*, Vol. 19, No. 4 (November 1953), p. 462.

4. Harris H. Bligh, Q.C., *The Consolidated Orders in Council of Canada* (Ottawa, 1889) (published under the authority and direction of the Governor General). See also the Orders in Council printed in the front of the statutes during this period.

5. *War Measures Act,* S.C. 1914, c. 2, s. 6.

6. *Mallory,* pp. 462-3. See also *Dawson's The Government of Canada,* p. 224.

7. *Debates,* February 9, 1943, p. 296.

legislative powers delegated by Parliament" would be systematically and uniformly published and tabled in the House.[8] While regulations and orders were then being examined by the Privy Council Office for uniformity and clarity, the *Regulations Act* did not contain any provision for holding the executive accountable to Parliament for the subordinate laws it had made.

In 1964, the Special Committee on Procedure and Organization recommended the establishment of a parliamentary committee to review regulations made as a result of delegated legislative power and to report to Parliament any regulations or instruments which the Committee believed exceeded the authority delegated by statute.[9] However, no action was taken on this recommendation. In 1968, the Special Committee on Statutory Instruments was mandated to "report on procedures for the review of this House of instruments made in virtue of any statute of the Parliament of Canada".[10] After an extensive examination of the *Regulations Act* and scrutiny procedures in other Commonwealth Parliaments, the Committee presented its Third Report in October 1969.[11] Reiterating the recommendation that a parliamentary committee be established to scrutinize delegated legislation, it also advocated many amendments to the *Regulations Act* and new procedures for the drafting and publication of regulations. In 1970, the government announced its proposed course of action to respond to the report: the replacement of the *Regulations Act* by the *Statutory Instruments Act,* new Cabinet directives for the drafting and publication of regulations, and amendments to the Standing Orders for the establishment of a scrutiny committee.[12]

Standing Joint Committee for the Scrutiny of Regulations

In 1971, pursuant to the *Statutory Instruments Act,*[13] the House and the Senate established the Standing Joint Committee for the Scrutiny of Regulations.[14] It sat a few times between 1973 and 1974 for organizational purposes and began to scrutinize

---

8. *Debates*, May 31, 1950, p. 3039. See also *Regulations Act*, S.C. 1950, c. 50.

9. See Special Committee on Procedure and Organization, Fifteenth Report, *Journals*, December 14, 1964, p. 988.

10. *Journals*, September 30, 1968, p. 82.

11. *Journals*, October 22, 1969, pp. 1411-508.

12. *Debates*, June 16, 1970, pp. 8155-6.

13. *Statutory Instruments Act*, S.C. 1970-71-72, c. 38, s. 26.

14. *Journals*, October 14, 1971, p. 870. This Committee was originally called the Standing Joint Committee on Regulations and Other Statutory Instruments. Its name was changed briefly in 1987 to the Standing Joint Committee for Regulatory Scrutiny (*Journals*, December 7, 1987, p. 1934; December 18, 1987, p. 2017) before its present name was adopted in June 1988 (*Journals*, June 2, 1988, p. 2778). The House attempted to amend the Committee's name to "Standing Joint Committee on Scrutiny of Regulations" in January 1994 (*Journals*, January 25, 1994, pp. 58-61). However, since the Senate did not also amend its rules to reflect this change, the Committee's name remained unchanged.

statutory instruments in earnest in 1974 during the First Session of the Thirtieth Parliament (September 1974 to October 1976).[15]

MANDATE

The Committee's mandate is defined by the *Statutory Instruments Act,* the *Statute Revision Act* and the Standing Orders. Pursuant to the *Statutory Instruments Act,* the Committee can scrutinize any statutory instrument made on or after January 1, 1972.[16] A statutory instrument is "any rule, order, regulation, ordinance, direction, form, tariff of costs or fees, letters patent, commission, warrant, proclamation, by-law, resolution or other instrument issued, made or established ... in the execution of a power conferred by or under an Act of Parliament. ..."[17] The *Statutory Instruments Act* further requires that regulations (with certain exceptions) be published in the *Canada Gazette* and referred to the parliamentary committee charged with the scrutiny of delegated legislation.[18]

The *Statute Revision Act* authorizes the Committee to scrutinize any regulation found in the *1978 Consolidated Regulations of Canada* or other Consolidated Regulations prepared pursuant to that Act, even if that regulation were made prior to the coming into force of the *Statutory Instruments Act* in 1972.[19] The Standing Orders expand on the mandates found in these two Acts by authorizing the Committee to examine any other matter referred to it by both Houses.[20]

Since 1979, the House and the Senate have routinely renewed at the beginning of each session an additional order of reference authorizing the Committee to:

... study the means by which Parliament can better oversee the government regulatory process and in particular to enquire into and report upon:

---

15. The Committee also dealt with other matters. On March 29, 1973, the House referred a document regarding guidelines for the production of papers to the Committee. The Committee was to determine if the guidelines were sound in principle and how they were to be administered (see *Journals*, p. 226; *Debates*, pp. 2745-50). This matter, along with the subject matter of a bill respecting access to information, was referred again to the Committee on December 19, 1974 (*Journals*, p. 231). The Committee reported back to the House on December 16, 1975 (*Journals*, p. 943).

16. *Statutory Instruments Act*, R.S.C. 1985, c. S-22, s. 19. On June 29, 1988, the Committee informed the House that it would not be reviewing and scrutinizing statutory instruments made by the Supreme Court of Canada or the Tax Court of Canada because, it felt, statutory courts enjoyed the same degree of independence as that guaranteed superior courts by the *Constitution Act, 1867*. However, the Committee continues to scrutinize rules of practice and procedures of tribunals whose members are not appointed during good behaviour, e.g., National Transportation Agency and the Labour Relations Board (see *Journals*, June 29, 1988, p. 3017; Standing Joint Committee for the Scrutiny of Regulations, *Minutes of Evidence and Proceedings*, June 23, 1988, Issue No. 28, pp. 9-10).

17. *Statutory Instruments Act*, R.S.C. 1985, c. S-22, s. 2.

18. *Statutory Instruments Act*, R.S.C. 1985, c. S-22, ss. 11(1), 19.

19. *Statute Revision Act*, R.S.C. 1985, c. S-20, s. 19(3).

20. Standing Order 108(4)(*c*).

1) the appropriate principles and practices to be observed

    a) in the drafting powers enabling delegates of Parliament to make subordinate laws;

    b) in the enactment of statutory instruments;

    c) in the use of executive regulation—including delegated powers and subordinate laws;

and the manner in which parliamentary control should be effected in respect of the same;

2) the role, functions and powers of the Standing Joint Committee for the Scrutiny of Regulations. [21]

MEMBERSHIP

The Standing Joint Committee for the Scrutiny of Regulations is composed of eight Senators and a proportionate number of Members of the House.[22] There are two Joint Chairs. Traditionally, one Joint Chair has been from the Senate representing the government party and one Joint Chair has been from the House representing the Official Opposition.[23] The Committee's Vice-Chair is usually a Member of the House from the government benches.

POWERS

The Committee enjoys the same powers other standing committees have. It may sit while the House is sitting[24] and when the House stands adjourned; print papers and evidence; send for persons, papers and records; and delegate to a subcommittee all or any of its powers (except the power to report directly to the House). It may also table reports in the House and request government responses to them.[25] In addition,

---

21. See, for example, *Journals*, February 16, 1979, p. 382; February 21, 1979, p. 401; November 20, 1979, p. 237; April 24, 1996, p. 254; May 29, 1996, p. 457; November 4, 1997, p. 185. The Committee has reported back twice to the House on this matter—in 1980 and 1984 (*Journals*, July 17, 1980, pp. 396-467, and April 17, 1984, p. 386). On November 20, 1980, the House referred the subject matter of enabling clauses of the *Canada Post Corporation Act* to the Committee (*Journals*, p. 762; see also *Journals*, December 15, 1980, pp. 852-65).

22. Standing Order 104(3)(*c*) and Senate Rule 86(1)(*d*). During the Thirty-Fifth Parliament (1994-97), eight Members of the House were appointed to the Committee (see, for example, *Journals*, March 1, 1996, p. 30). During the First Session of the Thirty-Sixth Parliament (1997-99), 17 Members of the House were appointed to the Committee (see *Journals*, September 30, 1997, p. 51; October 1, 1998, p. 1109).

23. In 1997, two Members of the Official Opposition declined the nomination to be the Joint Chair of the Committee; a Member of the governing party was subsequently elected Joint Chair. A Member of the Official Opposition was elected to the position of Vice-Chair. See Standing Joint Committee for the Scrutiny of Regulations, *Minutes of Proceedings and Evidence*, October 23, 1997.

24. In its first report each session, the Committee adds a paragraph to the copy of the report to be tabled in the Senate, requesting the power to sit during sittings of the Senate. Rule 95(4) of the Senate stipulates that a select committee shall not sit during a sitting of the Senate.

25. See, for example, *Journals*, March 22, 1999, pp. 1644-5; June 7, 1999, p. 2060. When the Committee presents a report to the Senate to which a government response is requested, the Senate copy indicates that this request has been made in the report presented to the House.

the Committee has the "power to engage the services of such expert staff, and such stenographic and clerical staff as may be required."[26] Finally, the Committee has the power to initiate the revocation of a statutory instrument.[27] This power is discussed in greater detail below.

REVIEW CRITERIA

The Committee reviews only matters of legality and the procedural aspects of regulations—their merits and the policies they reflect are disregarded.[28]

The Committee reviews all statutory instruments referred to it on the basis of 13 criteria which it provides to both Houses at the beginning of each session in its first report.[29] The criteria found in the report are as follows:[30]

Your Committee informs both Houses of Parliament that the criteria it will use for the review and scrutiny of statutory instruments are the following:

Whether any regulation or statutory instrument within its terms of reference, in the judgement of the Committee,

1. is not authorized by the terms of the enabling legislation or has not complied with any condition set forth in the legislation;[31]

---

26. In 1974, the Committee requested the power to engage additional legal and clerical staff because of the volume of statutory instruments to be scrutinized (*Journals*, April 30, 1974, p. 151). This request was concurred in on May 3, 1974 (*Journals*, p. 161) and since then the Committee has routinely sought and obtained a similar power at the beginning of each session even though on the House side the power is provided by Standing Order 120. See, for example, Standing Joint Committee for the Scrutiny of Regulations, First Report, presented to the House on April 24, 1996 (*Journals*, p. 254).

27. Standing Order 123(1).

28. On various occasions, the Committee has indicated to the House that it would like its mandate expanded to include the scrutiny of the policy or merits of subordinate legislation and the examination of bills after second reading for subordinate lawmaking powers (see, for example, *Journals*, July 17, 1980, p. 435; April 17, 1984, p. 386; Standing Joint Committee for the Scrutiny of Regulations and Other Statutory Instruments, *Minutes of Proceedings and Evidence*, April 12, 1984, Issue No. 4, pp. 11, 37, 45).

29. These 13 criteria were first adopted by the House on December 17, 1986 (*Journals*, p. 337). While the Committee has frequently recommended that the review criteria be written into the Standing Orders, this request has not been agreed to. However, on one occasion, the review criteria were appended to the *Debates* by means of a motion (see *Journals*, November 21, 1978, p. 170; *Debates*, pp. 1323-4).

30. See, for example, Standing Joint Committee for the Scrutiny of Regulations, First Report, presented on April 24, 1996 (*Journals*, p. 254).

31. When the Committee first began to scrutinize delegated legislation, the members found that regulations did not state precisely the authority pursuant to which they were made. Departments and other authorities now routinely disclose this information. One of the more common defects the Committee now encounters is subdelegation: "a person to whom legislative powers have been delegated by Parliament may not in turn delegate the exercise of those powers to another person" (see *Journals*, March 27, 1991, p. 2833; Standing Joint Committee for the Scrutiny of Regulations, *Minutes of Proceedings and Evidence*, March 26, 1991, Issue No. 25, p. 9).

2. *is not in conformity with the Canadian Charter of Rights and Freedoms or the Canadian Bill of Rights;*[32]

3. *purports to have retroactive effect without express authority having been provided for in the enabling legislation;*[33]

4. *imposes a charge on the public revenues or requires payment to be made to the Crown or to any other authority, or prescribes the amount of any such charge or payment, without express authority having been provided for in the enabling legislation;*[34]

5. *imposes a fine, imprisonment or other penalty without express authority having been provided for in the enabling legislation;*

6. *tends directly or indirectly to exclude the jurisdiction of the courts without express authority having been provided for in the enabling legislation;*

7. *has not complied with the Statutory Instruments Act with respect to transmission, registration or publication;*

8. *appears for any reason to infringe the rule of law;*[35]

9. *trespasses unduly on rights and liberties;*[36]

10. *makes the rights and liberties of the person unduly dependent on administrative discretion or is not consistent with the rules of natural justice;*[37]

11. *makes some unusual or unexpected use of the powers conferred by the enabling legislation;*[38]

---

32. This criterion originated with the passage of the *Constitution Act, 1982* (*Journals*, May 26, 1982, p. 4876; Standing Joint Committee on Regulations and Other Statutory Instruments, *Minutes of Proceedings and Evidence*, May 20, 1982, Issue No. 64, p. 3) and was cited in the Committee's disallowance report regarding the Public Works Nuisances Regulations (Standing Joint Committee for the Scrutiny of Regulations, *Minutes of Proceedings and Evidence*, November 19, 1992, Issue No. 17, pp. 8-22).

33. See, for example, the Committee's Seventh Report, *Journals*, June 26, 1986, p. 2433; Standing Joint Committee on Regulations and other Statutory Instruments, *Minutes of Proceedings and Evidence*, June 26, 1986, Issue No. 33, pp. 4-5.

34. See, for example, the Committee's Sixth Report, *Journals*, June 7, 1999, p. 2060.

35. See, for example, the Committee's Ninth Report, *Journals*, June 3, 1993, p. 3113; *Debates*, p. 20293.

36. See, for example, the Committee's Sixth Report, *Journals*, November 19, 1992, p. 2078; Standing Joint Committee for the Scrutiny of Regulations, *Minutes of Proceedings and Evidence*, November 19, 1992, Issue No. 17, pp. 8-22.

37. See, for example, the Committee's Sixth Report, *Journals*, April 16, 1986, pp. 1996-7; Standing Joint Committee on Regulations and Other Statutory Instruments, *Minutes of Proceedings and Evidence*, April 15, 1986, Issue No. 29, pp. 3-5. See also *Debates*, April 22, 1986, pp. 12507-22.

38. This is the criterion which has been cited most often in reports of the Committee. See, for example, *Journals*, February 27, 1992, p. 1084; Standing Joint Committee for the Scrutiny of Regulations, *Minutes of Proceedings and Evidence*, April 9, 1992, Issue No. 11, pp. 6-9.

12. *amounts to the exercise of a substantive legislative power prop-erly the subject of direct parliamentary enactment;*[39]

13. *is defective in its drafting or for any other reason requires eluci-dation as to its form or purport.*[40]

The Committee's scrutiny criteria are very similar to those used by the Clerk of the Privy Council to verify proposed regulations[41] and those recommended by the Special Committee on Statutory Instruments in 1969.[42]

Revocation of a Statutory Instrument

For the first 15 years of its existence, the Committee had statutory power to scruti-nize delegated legislation, but no power to revoke a subordinate law. The Special Committee on Statutory Instruments did not propose a general disallowance proce-dure,[43] and no such procedure was provided for in the *Statutory Instruments Act.* As a result, requests made by the Committee to government departments and other authorities to amend or revoke regulations which it felt were *ultra vires* (beyond legal authority) often produced little or no results. The only recourse the Committee had to publicly discuss these regulations was to present reports in the House and move a motion of concurrence in them.[44]

In 1985, the Committee approached the Special Committee on the Reform of the House of Commons with recommendations regarding the disallowance of statutory instruments.[45] The Committee proposed, among other matters, that all subordinate legislation not subject to a statutory affirmative procedure be subject to being disallowed on resolution of either House and that the Executive be barred from remaking any statutory instrument so disallowed for a period of six months from its

---

39. See, for example, the Committee's Third Report, *Journals*, April 17, 1984, p. 386; Standing Joint Committee on Regulations and Other Statutory Instruments, *Minutes of Proceedings and Evidence,* April 12, 1984, Issue No. 4, pp. 12-3.

40. Since the Privy Council Office issued guidelines entitled *Directives on Submissions to the Governor in Council and Statutory Instruments*, this criterion has rarely been cited.

41. See *Debates*, January 25, 1971, p. 2735. See also *Statutory Instruments Act*, R.S.C. 1985, c. S-22, s. 3.

42. *Journals*, October 22, 1969, pp. 1507-8.

43. See Special Committee on Statutory Instruments, Third Report, *Journals*, October 22, 1969, p. 1508 (Rec-ommendation 21).

44. Reform proposals tabled in the House in 1979 included changes to the Standing Orders to increase oppor-tunities to affirm or negative delegated legislation (see *Journals*, November 23, 1979, p. 260; *Position Paper: The Reform of Parliament*, pp. 18-20). Parliament was dissolved, however, before these reforms were discussed in the House.

45. See Special Committee on the Reform of the House, Third Report, pp. 83-4, presented on June 18, 1985 (*Journals*, p. 839). Previous to this, the Committee had recommended to the House on various occasions that a disallowance procedure be established (see, for example, *Journals*, February 3, 1977, p. 407; July 17, 1980, pp. 435-7; April 17, 1984, p. 386; see also Standing Joint Committee on Regulations and Other Statutory Instruments, *Minutes of Proceedings and Evidence,* April 12, 1984, Issue No. 4, pp. 45-7).

disallowance. Subsequently, in its Third Report to the House, the Special Committee recommended that "the House of Commons adopt a mandatory procedure for affirming or disallowing delegated legislation and regulations made pursuant to an act of Parliament."[46] In its response to the recommendation, the government proposed an alternative, the power to revoke by House Order.[47] This was agreed to by the House in 1986 by means of amendments to the Standing Orders.[48] The House now has procedures which allow it to adopt or reject a report presented by the Committee that advocates the revocation of a statutory instrument because it is not in keeping with the intentions of the Act from which it is derived. The government also made a policy commitment to "consider itself bound by any such report of the Committee" and would therefore follow through with the revocation.[49]

REPORT OF THE COMMITTEE

Should the Committee conclude that a regulation or some other statutory instrument is not in keeping with the intentions of an Act as passed by Parliament, it may make a report to the House on the matter. Such a report must contain only a resolution which, if concurred in, results in a House Order to the government to revoke an offending regulation or statutory instrument.[50] One report is needed for each regulation or statutory instrument for which the Committee is seeking to revoke by House Order, but only one such report may be received in any given sitting of the House.[51]

When this kind of report is presented, the Member presenting it must advise the House of its nature, indicate which regulation or statutory instrument the Committee wishes revoked and state that the relevant text of the regulation or statutory instrument in question is included in the report.[52]

---

46. See Special Committee on the Reform of the House of Commons, Third Report, p. 36, presented on June 18, 1985 (*Journals*, p. 839) (Recommendation 6.1).

47. *Journals*, October 9, 1985, p. 1082 (page 5 of the Government Response).

48. *Journals*, February 6, 1986, pp. 1652-3; February 13, 1986, p. 1710.

49. Standing Joint Committee on Regulations and Other Statutory Instruments, *Minutes of Proceedings and Evidence*, April 15, 1986, Issue No. 29, pp. 11, 22.

50. Since Standing Order 123(1) was amended on December 18, 1987 (*Journals*, December 18, 1987, p. 2017), the report contains a short text including a "resolution" to revoke a statutory instrument, followed by two appendices. Appendix A reproduces the text of the provision to be disallowed and Appendix B gives the reasons of the Committee in support of disallowance (see, for example, *Journals*, May 11, 1995, pp. 1462-3; Standing Joint Committee for the Scrutiny of Regulations, *Minutes of Proceedings and Evidence,* Thursday, May 11, 1995, Issue No. 20, pp. 9-15).

51. Standing Order 123(2). See *Journals*, February 11, 1999, p. 1500 and February 12, 1999, p. 1504 for an example of the Committee presenting two disallowance reports on consecutive days in order to comply with this requirement.

52. Standing Order 123(3). See, for example, *Debates*, February 19, 1987, p. 3584 (Fruit, Vegetables, and Honey Regulations); October 10, 1991, p. 3557 (Agriculture Exhibitions Loans Order); November 19, 1991, p. 4987 (Indian Health Regulations); November 19, 1992, p. 13605 (Public Works Nuisances Regulations); May 11, 1995, p. 12445 (National Capital Commission Traffic and Property Regulations); February 11, 1999, p. 11788 (Narcotic Control Regulations); February 12, 1999, p. 11843 (Food and Drug Regulations).

Once such a report has been presented in the House, notice of a motion for concurrence in the report is automatically placed on the *Notice Paper* by the Clerk of the House in the name of the Member who presented the report.[53] Only one notice of motion for concurrence in the report may be placed on the *Notice Paper* for each report of this nature. After 48 hours, the notice of motion is transferred to the *Order Paper* under the rubric "Motions".

CONCURRENCE IN THE REPORT

The motion for concurrence in the report may either be automatically adopted or disposed of after consideration.

Automatic Adoption

The Standing Orders provide that a motion for concurrence in a report is deemed moved and adopted on the fifteenth sitting day after it first appears on the *Order Paper* (unless a Minister requests that it be debated).[54] The motion is deemed moved and adopted just before the House adjourns on that sitting day, and automatically results in an Order of the House to the responsible authority (usually the Governor in Council) to revoke the subordinate legislation in question.[55] If the House adjourns prior to the ordinary hour of daily adjournment, the report is still deemed adopted.[56]

Consideration of the Concurrence Motion

If requested by a Minister, the concurrence motion is set down for consideration. In a marked departure from the usual practices of the House, the Standing Orders provide that such a concurrence motion may only be called for consideration by a Minister (*any* Minister), and that *any* Member can move the motion on behalf of its

---

53. Standing Order 123(4).

54. Standing Order 125.

55. Sections of the Agriculture Exhibitions Loans Order (*Journals*, November 18, 1991, p. 677), the Indian Health Regulations (*Journals*, December 12, 1991, p. 938), the Public Works Nuisances Regulations (*Journals*, February 1, 1993, p. 2426), the National Capital Commission Traffic and Property Regulations (*Journals*, June 12, 1995, p. 1709), and the Narcotic Control Regulations and the Food and Drug Regulations (*Journals*, March 15, 1999, p. 1614) were revoked without debate. In the case of the Public Works Nuisances Regulations, the statutory instrument in question was revoked before the 15 sitting days had elapsed. The Public Works Nuisances Regulations designated specific areas of Parliament Hill for holding demonstrations and other activities and allowed the Minister of Public Works or a peace officer to prohibit or evict any persons not complying with this order. The Regulations were designed to improve control of disruptive noise during times the House was sitting and to improve control of access to the Parliament Buildings. The Committee objected to these regulations, arguing that they were in breach of the *Canadian Charter of Rights and Freedoms*. Although the Public Works Minister had assured the Committee that these regulations were not being enforced, only when the disallowance report was tabled in the House were the regulations revoked (see Standing Joint Committee for the Scrutiny of Regulations, *Minutes of Proceedings and Evidence*, March 18, 1993, Issue No. 24, p. 8).

56. See, for example, *Journals*, December 12, 1991, p. 938; *Debates*, pp. 6215-6.

sponsor.[57] Several unique conditions apply to the manner in which the motion is taken up and disposed of.

First, the Minister must call for its consideration within 15 sitting days of the notice for concurrence in the report appearing on the *Order Paper* by giving at least 48 hours' written notice.[58] Once this requirement is fulfilled, notice of the debate is immediately placed on the *Order Paper*.[59] The motion is automatically slated for consideration at 1:00 p.m. on the first Wednesday following the expiry of the 48-hour written notice for consideration.[60] The debate must, however, take place by the end of the fifteenth sitting day or the report is automatically deemed adopted. Thus, the time frame for holding the debate varies considerably depending on when the fifteenth sitting day falls. Since the debate must be held on a Wednesday, the time frame for the Minister to act could be much shorter than the 15-day period.

Although only one report may be presented in a sitting and only one motion for concurrence in that report may be placed on the *Order Paper,* the presentation of several reports on successive days can result in more than one concurrence motion being considered on the same Wednesday. The sequence for consideration is determined by a Minister and all concurrence motions are grouped for debate but voted on *seriatim.*[61]

Whether one or several such concurrence motions are called on a particular Wednesday, only one hour between 1:00 p.m. and 2:00 p.m. is made available for their consideration, and they are the only items of business that can be taken up.[62] Members participating in the debate may speak only once and for a maximum of 10 minutes.[63] Points of order about the procedural acceptability of any report may be raised only after the Chair has proposed to the House all questions on the motions for concurrence. If a report is thereafter found to be irreceivable, the motion for concurrence is deemed to have been withdrawn.[64]

---

57. Standing Order 124.
58. Standing Orders 54(1) and 124.
59. See, for example, *Order Paper*, March 17, 1987, p. 8.
60. Standing Order 128(1).
61. Standing Order 127.
62. Standing Orders 126(1) and 128(2).
63. Standing Order 126(1)(*a*).
64. Standing Order 126(1)(*b*). In 1987, Speaker Fraser questioned the form of the first disallowance report (Fruit, Vegetables, and Honey Regulations) presented in the House before the concurrence motion was put to the House. In particular, the Speaker advised the House that if it agreed to the concurrence motion as written, the House would not be ordering the Ministry to revoke a regulation, but rather would only be agreeing that the Committee could move a motion to revoke a regulation, a mechanism not provided for in the Standing Orders. However, the Chair advised that for this report only, he would accept that concurrence in the report would result in an Order of the House to the Ministry to revoke the regulations. The Chair also requested that the Standing Committee on Elections, Privileges and Procedure look into the ambiguity of the Standing Orders (see *Debates*, March 18, 1987, p. 4285). Standing Order 123(1) was subsequently amended to indicate that the report contain only a resolution which, if adopted, would become an Order of the House to revoke a statutory instrument (see *Journals*, December 18, 1987, p. 2017).

Unless the motion or motions have already been disposed of when the hour set aside for their consideration has elapsed (or slightly earlier so as not to impinge on the time allotted for Members' Statements), the Speaker is obliged to interrupt the proceedings and put all questions necessary to complete the proceedings on them.[65] If a concurrence motion is adopted, the resolution as set out in the report concerned becomes an Order of the House that a given instrument of delegated legislation be revoked. If the motion is defeated, the matter is dropped.[66] If requested, recorded divisions are automatically deferred until the ordinary hour of daily adjournment, at which time the bells sound no longer than 15 minutes.[67] Once deferred, divisions cannot be further deferred by a party Whip[68] and the Standing Orders related to the ordinary hour of daily adjournment are suspended until all questions have been decided.[69] When deliberations on a motion or motions for concurrence are completed before 2:00 p.m., the Speaker suspends the sitting until that time.[70]

---

65. Standing Order 128(2)(*b*).

66. In 1986, the Minister responsible for Regulatory Affairs assured the Committee that votes taken pursuant to Standing Order 126(1) would not be considered matters of confidence in the government (see Standing Joint Committee on Regulations and Other Statutory Instruments, *Minutes of Proceedings and Evidence*, April 15, 1986, Issue No. 29, p. 27).

67. Standing Order 126(1)(*c*).

68. Standing Order 126(2). It is, however, permissible for all Whips together to further defer divisions pursuant to Standing Order 45(7).

69. Standing Order 126(3).

70. Standing Order 128(2)(*a*). A motion to concur in such a committee report has been debated only once, in March 1987. After a short debate, an amendment to refer the report back to the Committee for further consideration was adopted. The main motion as amended was then agreed to. The sitting was suspended at 1:25 p.m. See *Journals*, March 18, 1987, p. 610; *Debates*, pp. 4285-8.

18

Financial Procedures

If committees are going to do a better job of examining the Estimates, they need more opportunities to influence expenditure, more authority, and better information. Once improvements have been made, committees should be able to bring new attitudes and approaches to their study of the Estimates.

STANDING COMMITTEE ON PROCEDURE AND HOUSE AFFAIRS, Fifty-First Report (*The Business of Supply: Completing the Circle of Control*) presented to the House on December 10, 1998 (*Journals,* p. 1435)

The development of parliamentary procedure is closely bound up with the evolution of the financial relationship between Parliament and the Crown. As the Executive power,[1] the Crown is responsible for managing all the revenue of the state, including all payments for the public service.[2] The Crown, on the advice of its Ministers, makes the financial requirements of the government known to the House of Commons which, in return, authorizes the necessary "aids" (taxes) and "supplies" (grants of money). No tax may be imposed, or money spent, without the consent of Parliament.

The direct control of national finance has been referred to as the "great task of modern parliamentary

---

1. The *Constitution Act, 1867* invests the "Executive Government and Authority of and over Canada" in the Crown, its governor general and the Privy Council for Canada (ss. 9-11), and the lieutenant-governors advised by the Executive Council for each province (ss. 58-67). Appointed by the Crown's representative, the federal cabinet constitutes the *de facto* or effective federal executive. However, it has *de jure* or statutory existence only as the effective part of the Privy Council for Canada (*McMenemy,* p. 105).

2. *May,* 6th ed., p. 546.

government".[3] That control is exercised at two levels. First, Parliament must assent to all legislative measures which implement public policy and the House of Commons authorizes both the amounts and objects or destination of all public expenditures. Second, through its review of the annual departmental performance reports, the Public Accounts and the reports of the Auditor General, the House ascertains that no expenditure was made other than those it had authorized.[4]

The practices and procedures which govern how Parliament deals with the nation's finances are set out principally in the *Constitution Act, 1867*,[5] the *Financial Administration Act*,[6] unwritten conventions, and the rules of the House of Commons and the Senate.

BASIC COMPONENTS OF FINANCIAL OPERATIONS

The basic components of parliamentary financial procedure may be succinctly described as follows:

Consolidated Revenue Fund: the account into which the government deposits taxes, tariffs, excises and other revenues, once collected, and from which it withdraws the money it requires to cover its expenditures.[7]

Royal Recommendation: the instrument by which the Crown advises Parliament of its intent to introduce a legislative measure having an impact on the Consolidated Revenue Fund.[8] Under the Constitution, all such legislative measures must be initiated by the Crown and originate in the House of Commons.

Supply: the process by which the government submits its projected annual expenditures (the Estimates) for parliamentary approval.

Borrowing Authority: the authorization required by the government to make up any shortfall between revenues and expenditures.

Ways and Means: the process by which the government sets out its economic policy (the Budget) and obtains necessary authority to raise revenues through taxation.

Public Accounts: the annual statement and review of the government's expenditures.

---

3. *Redlich*, Vol. III, p. 160. For a detailed description of the development in Canada of the various practices and institutions relevant to the Canadian version of parliamentary control of finance, see Norman Ward, *The Public Purse: A Study in Canadian Democracy*, Toronto: University of Toronto Press, 1962.

4. *May*, 22nd ed., pp. 732-3. See also *Ward*, pp. 3-10.

5. R.S.C. 1985, Appendix II, No. 5.

6. R.S.C. 1985, c. F-11.

7. *Constitution Act, 1867*, R.S.C. 1985, Appendix II, No. 5, s. 103.

8. *Constitution Act, 1867*, R.S.C. 1985, Appendix II, No. 5, s. 54.

THE FINANCIAL CYCLE

The fiscal year of the Government of Canada runs from April 1 to March 31.[9] However, the planning for the fiscal year begins much earlier with the preparation of departmental expenditure plans, which are developed in accordance with the government's policy and budgetary priorities, and the pre-budget consultations by the Standing Committee on Finance.[10] The expenditure plans are submitted to the House in their consolidated form as the "Main Estimates". At the same time, the Department of Finance is compiling the information taken in during the pre-budget consultations and preparing its economic forecasts. The government's efforts to reconcile its spending obligations and revenue projections are reflected in the Budget.

The Budget outlines the government's fiscal, social and economic policies and priorities, while the Estimates set out, in detail, its projected expenditures for the upcoming fiscal year. Typically, the Budget is presented in the second half of February, although the government is under no obligation to do so.[11] Under normal circumstances, the Main Estimates are tabled in the House on or before March 1 and submitted for concurrence by the House no later than June 23.[12]

Should the government require funds while waiting for, or in the absence of, income from taxes and other revenue sources, it will seek authority to borrow. Should there be a change in the government's requirements as set out in the Main Estimates, Parliament will be asked to approve "supplementary" Estimates.

---

9. *Financial Administration Act*, R.S.C. 1985, c. F-11, s. 2. Until 1906, the fiscal year ran from July 1 to June 30. (See *Debates*, May 10, 1906, col. 3065; *Journals*, June 19, 1906, p. 400, and July 13, 1906, pp. 589-90).

10. See Standing Order 83.1.

11. There is no requirement that the government present an annual Budget; however, this has been the practice followed since the mid-1980s. In an effort to introduce an element of certainty into the timing of the Budget, governments have tried, wherever possible, to present their Budget in mid-February, before the Main Estimates are tabled. (Michael Wilson, Minister of Finance, *The Canadian Budgetary Process: Proposals for Improvement,* Ottawa, Department of Finance, May 1985, pp. 1-8; and Treasury Board of Canada, *The Expenditure Management System of the Government of Canada,* Ottawa, Supply and Services Canada, 1995, p. 4.) See section below on the "Budget".

12. Standing Orders 81(4) and 81(18). Standing Order 81 sets out a precise House schedule for the consideration and disposal of the Business of Supply. If the March 1 deadline is met, the House typically considers and disposes of the Main Estimates for the then fiscal year before it adjourns for the summer. If, because of an unscheduled adjournment or a prorogation or dissolution of Parliament, the March 1 deadline is not met or the Main Estimates are not concurred in by the end of June, the government proposes a new Supply schedule for the approval of the House, usually after negotiations with the parties in opposition. (See, for example, *Journals*, April 29, 1980, pp. 95-6; April 4, 1989, pp. 20-1; March 4, 1996, pp. 34-5, 39-41; September 23, 1997, p. 14.)

The tabling of the *Public Accounts of Canada* and the *Annual Report* of the Auditor General, and their review by the Standing Committee on Public Accounts, completes the government's annual cycle of financial transactions. [13]

Figure 18.1   *The Financial Cycle*

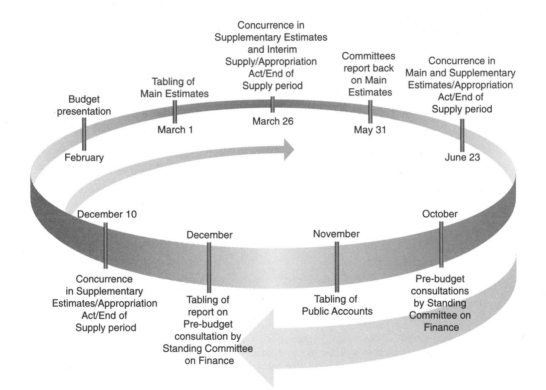

HISTORICAL PERSPECTIVE

The manner in which Canada deals with public finance derives from British parliamentary procedure, as practised at the time of Confederation.[14] The financial procedures adopted by the Canadian House of Commons in 1867 were formed by the following principles:

- that although Parliament alone might impose taxes and authorize the use of public money, Parliament can do this only on the recommendation of the Crown (royal recommendation), in Canada represented by the Governor General;

- that the House of Commons has the right to have its grievances addressed before it considers and approves the financial requirements of the Crown;

- that the House of Commons has exclusive control over the business of public finance (taxing and spending) and all such business is to be initiated in the lower house;[15] and

- that all legislation sanctioning expenditure or initiating taxation is to be given the fullest possible discussion, both in the House and in committee.[16]

British Precedents

The whole law of finance, and consequently the whole British constitution, is grounded upon one fundamental principle, laid down at the very outset of English parliamentary history and secured by three hundred years of

---

14. This is signified by the Preamble to the *British North America Act,* which decreed that Canada was to have a constitution similar in principle to that of the United Kingdom. Consequently, the rules of parliamentary procedure as practiced in Britain at that time would serve also to guide proceedings in the Canadian Houses of Parliament. The Act was renamed the *Constitution Act, 1867,* in 1982. (See also Chapter 1, "Parliamentary Institutions".)

15. Since 1625, the British Commons' exclusive right to grant monies has been fully recognized and, since 1678, the Commons have also claimed the sole right to direct how those monies will be spent (*Redlich,* Vol. III, pp. 115-6). This fundamental principle was firmly established in 1860 when the British Commons refused to acquiesce in the Lords' rejection of one of its money bills. The House subsequently adopted a resolution affirming its sole right to grant aids and supplies. (*Redlich*, Vol. III, pp. 116-9. See also section below on "The Commons' Claim to Predominance in Financial Matters".)

16. A Commons rule that all legislation sanctioning expenditure or initiating taxation must be based on resolutions passed in a committee of the Whole House was introduced in the British Parliament in 1667. During the civil wars, these discussions had been undertaken in select committees to escape pressure and management by the Speakers, acting on the King's behalf. The House of Commons again reverted to Committees of the Whole House because select committees were seen to be too easily swayed by privy councillors and other prominent Members. The 1667 rule actually read: "If any motion be made in the House for any public aid or charge upon the people, the consideration and debate thereon ought not presently to be entered upon but adjourned to such further day as the House shall think fit to appoint; and then it ought to be referred to the Committee of the whole House and their opinion to be reported thereupon, before any resolution or vote of the House do pass therein" (*Stewart*, p. 99). At Confederation, that rule had been revised to read: "If any motion be made in the house for any aid, grant, or charge upon the public revenue, whether payable out of the consolidated fund, or out of monies to be provided by Parliament, or any charge upon the people . . ." (*May*, 6th ed., p. 549).

mingled conflict with the Crown and peaceful growth. All taxes and public burdens imposed upon the nation for purposes of state, whatsoever their nature, must be granted by the representatives of the citizens and taxpayers, i.e., by Parliament.[17]

The requirement that legislation sanction all public spending and taxation has a long constitutional history.[18] In medieval England, the King was expected to meet most public expenses (the court, the clergy and the military) out of his personal revenues. Where this was not possible, he was obliged to seek funds by summoning the common council of the realm, or parliament, to discuss what aids (taxes and tariffs) should be supplied to support the Crown. Even in the earliest days of these assemblies, it was generally recognized that, when "aids" or "supplies" were required, the King should seek consent not only to impose a tax, but also for the manner in which the revenues from that tax might be spent. In 1295, the writ of summons for one of these councils, later known as the "Model Parliament", proclaimed: "What touches all should be approved by all".

Early British Parliaments were not legislative bodies as we understand them today, but petitioning bodies. They presented petitions to the King and agreed to taxes (i.e., money granted to the Crown), on the condition that certain problems (or grievances) outlined in the petitions would be addressed or concessions made. By 1400, the Commons insisted that the King respond to their petitions before any grant of money was made. When the King refused, they adopted the practice of delaying the grant until the last day of the session.

The "councils" subsequently divided into two "Houses" based on their communities of interest: the House of Lords and the House of Commons. In principle, each House taxed itself independently; for this reason it was not considered appropriate that the Lords determine what the Commons should contribute. Moreover, because the greater part of the tax burden fell to the Commoners, grants to the Monarch came to be *made* by the Commons "with the advice and consent" of the Lords. The dominant position of the Commons in terms of deciding matters of taxation was firmly established early in the fifteenth century when Henry IV conceded that any grant to the Sovereign must be agreed upon by both the Lords and the Commons and must be communicated to the Crown by the Speaker of the House of Commons.[19]

Initially, the Commons were content simply to have grants of Supply originate in their House. However, over time the Lords began "tacking on" additional legislative provisions to Commons "money bills", by way of amendments. This was viewed by the House as a breach of its prerogative to originate all legislation which imposed a charge either on the public or the public purse, and led the Commons, in 1678, to resolve that:

---

17. *Redlich*, Vol. III, p. 114.

18. Most of the historical background has been summarized from an article by Elmer A. Driedger entitled "Money Bills and the Senate", *Ottawa Law Review*, Vol. 3 (Fall 1968), pp. 25-46. See also *May*, 6th ed.

19. Ordinance of 1407 on "The Indemnity of the Lords and Commons" (quoted in *Driedger*, p. 31).

All aids and supplies, and aids to his Majesty in Parliament, are the sole gift of the Commons; and all Bills for the granting of any such aids and supplies ought to begin with the Commons: and that it is the undoubted and sole right of the Commons to direct, limit, and appoint, in such Bills, the ends, purposes, considerations, conditions, limitations, and qualifications of such grants; which ought not to be changed or altered by the House of Lords.[20]

By the end of the seventeenth century, the principles of modern financial procedure—most particularly the annual treatment of finance by the House of Commons and the notion of effective and permanent House control over all public expenditure—were well established. Their evolution had taken several centuries and was related to the rise and gradual abolition of the Civil List, the creation of the Consolidated Fund and the growth of the "estimates" system, whereby the government receives annual operating grants from Parliament.

The Civil List
The Civil List[21] was initially a list of all non-military personnel in the service of the Crown for whom remuneration was paid by Parliament.[22] These included individuals in the personal employ of the Sovereign, such as domestic servants, people in the diplomatic service and various public officials and civil servants. Previously, the Crown had covered these expenses out of the Sovereign's hereditary revenues and certain taxes voted to the Sovereign for life by Parliament.

Initially, Parliament did not concern itself with how the funds were spent. In general, it was felt that, while the Crown was not entitled to increase its revenue without the Parliament's consent, it was perfectly free to dispose of, as it pleased, any funds properly in its possession. However, the amounts voted by Parliament were frequently insufficient and the House was increasingly asked for additional grants to discharge debts which the Sovereign had incurred to cover the shortfall. So emerged the practice of allocating to the Crown funds for specific purposes.

With the accession of Queen Victoria to the throne in 1837, Civil List expenditures were reduced to those required solely to meet the personal needs of the Sovereign and her family. All other civil expenses were taken over by the national treasury and paid out of the Consolidated Fund.

The Consolidated Fund
During the seventeenth and eighteenth centuries, the raising and spending of public money were intimately connected. Requests from the Crown for money, in estimated

---

20. *Hatsell*, Vol. III, pp. 122-3. This is the origin of the Canadian House of Commons' Standing Order 80(1) which reads: "All aids and supplies granted to the Sovereign by the Parliament of Canada are the sole gift of the House of Commons, and all bills for granting such aids and supplies ought to begin with the House, as it is the undoubted right of the House to direct, limit, and appoint in all such bills, the ends, purposes, considerations, conditions, limitations and qualifications of such grants, which are not alterable by the Senate."

21. The term "Civil List" was used also in the Canadian colonies.

22. *Redlich*, Vol. III, pp. 161-2.

amounts for specified purposes, were considered and approved by a Committee of the Whole House. This phase concluded, a second Committee of the Whole considered the recommended "ways and means" for raising the money required to cover the amounts approved. The work of the first committee, which came to be known as the Committee on Supply, led directly to the work of the second, the Committee on Ways and Means. Only when the latter came to a decision, would a bill be introduced which empowered the Crown to raise money in the amount and in the manner approved by the Committee on Ways and Means and to spend up to the amount approved, and only for the purposes designated, by the Committee on Supply.

The close coupling of taxing and spending continued until 1786 when the establishment of the Consolidated Fund[23] abolished the need to match a particular outlay with a specified revenue.[24] Once the Committee of Supply had agreed to the expenditure of certain sums, the Ways and Means Committee would look to the Consolidated Fund to pay for the approved expenditures. The concept of an *appropriation* bill was introduced to set aside from the Fund the amounts required for the purposes designated. Appropriation bills merely set aside funds; they do not require the Crown to spend all or any of the money which has been appropriated. Furthermore, appropriations are always made with a time limit; the spending authorization provided under an appropriation act expires at the end of the fiscal year to which the Act applies.[25]

Thus, two distinct kinds of government financial business emerged: the business of Supply, which approved expenditures and their purposes, and resulted in the passing of appropriation bills; and the business of Ways and Means, which resulted in the taxation bills used to raise the monies needed to replenish the Consolidated Fund.

Since the institution of the Consolidated Fund, all expenses of the state have been authorized either by specific statute (ongoing and permanent) or by way of an annual appropriation. It is the annual appropriations, or supply grants, which come before the House for discussion each year.

The Estimates

As the seventeenth century drew to a close, England's continuing colonial disputes with France and Spain and the recent experience of two civil wars made evident the need to maintain a national standing army under the control of Parliament. Previously, the Monarch had simply raised armies to fight wars, as required.

The institution of a permanent military establishment carried with it the requirement for grants to cover the cost of personnel, wars and fortifications.[26] In 1689, the British Parliament passed the *Mutiny Act,* legislation which had to be renewed

---

23. In Canada, this fund is known as the Consolidated Revenue Fund.

24. In 1715, an Aggregate Fund, which was to be fed by definite sources of income and to bear definite charges of a permanent nature, was instituted under George I. However, it was only with the creation of the Consolidated Fund, in 1786, that the whole revenue of the state would flow into one receptacle from which all expenditures of the state would be discharged (*Redlich,* Vol. III, pp. 163-4).

25. *Stewart,* p. 109.

26. *Redlich,* Vol. III, p. 165.

yearly. The Act restricted the use of martial law and gave authorization for a definite number of military personnel. The Act also authorized a grant of funds sufficient to cover military wages, ordnance and shipbuilding for that year. This, then, was the means by which Parliament undertook the regular annual charge of Supply for the army and navy, and from which emerged the parliamentary practice of granting annual appropriations for the operations of government. The principles governing that practice hold that the government may spend on public administration no more than the amounts (estimates) approved by Parliament and is similarly prohibited from using funds voted for one purpose to pay for another (engaging in *virement*).[27] As the scope of civil government expanded, civil expenditure came to comprise a number of expenses funded solely by annual parliamentary grants.[28]

Financial Procedure in Colonial Canada

By the end of the eighteenth century, most of the British North American colonies had acquired representative political institutions.[29] For many years, colonial governance was fraught with dissension as a result of the often irreconcilable interests of appointed governors and elected representatives. Much of that conflict arose over the issue of who should control the public purse.[30] However, by the time of Confederation, the popular assemblies of British North America had asserted their right to decide what taxes should be raised and where they would be spent, thus fulfilling the principle of responsible government, which holds that the executive may only govern while it enjoys the confidence or support of the House of Commons. Parliament's rights and role in the processes of taxing and spending may be found in the various rules and procedures of the legislatures from which they derive.[31] In 1867, the Canadian House of Commons adopted the rules of the former Legislative Assembly of the Province of Canada, including those covering the process of taxing and spending.[32]

Upper Canada

Initially, the colonial administration of Upper Canada was paid for entirely by the British Parliament. However, in 1817, the Executive asked the Assembly for a grant of money to cover certain administrative costs which exceeded the amount authorized by Westminster. Previously, Britain had covered any excesses; but, in view of the growing wealth and relative prosperity of the colony, the local community was asked to subsidize these expenditures. Not surprisingly, the elected representatives demanded a say in how the money would be spent. Moreover, they asked that the

---

27. *Redlich*, Vol. III, pp. 167-8.

28. *Redlich*, Vol. III, p. 165.

29. See also Chapter 1, "Parliamentary Institutions".

30. *Bourinot*, 4th ed., p. 8.

31. See *O'Brien,* pp. 89-93, 175-80, 286-92 and 361-63; and *Bourinot*, 4th ed., pp. 9-11.

32. *Journals*, November 7, 1867, p. 5.

Governor and his Executive Council not spend money which the Assembly had not authorized, nor for purposes other than those it had designated.

Supply (the authority to spend) was rarely withheld.[33] Even when it was withheld (in 1818, 1825 and 1836), it was inconsequential. In fact, the Crown appeared relatively indifferent to the sums voted by the House. Nonetheless, the House continued to take the Supply process seriously, resolving that the misapplication of parliamentary appropriations was a "high crime" and affirming the undoubted right of the elected House to determine how, and how much, public money was spent.

By 1840, Supply proceedings in the Assembly had become relatively formalized. Estimates were referred upon presentation to a permanent Select Committee on Finance. The committee's report would be referred to a Committee of Supply (a Committee of the Whole House)[34] which, in turn, would report back to the House a number of resolutions, each of which recommending that money be appropriated for some item. Once adopted, these resolutions would be referred to a special committee of two members charged with drafting the bills based thereon. A number of bills would then be presented.

Lower Canada

Prior to 1818, the Executive Council requested no funds from the House of Assembly of Lower Canada, with the result that no Estimates were tabled. Nevertheless, the House attempted to exert some financial control by way of its annual review of the public accounts. Until 1812, the accounts were examined in a Committee of the Whole, after which they were referred to a special committee of five members. Beginning in 1818, Estimates were also referred to this committee. The committee's frequent criticisms of the administration for appropriating money without the consent of the House of Assembly prompted the House to resolve that the appropriation of the public revenue without legislation was "a breach of the privileges of this House, and subversive of the Government of this Province, as established by Law". The House further warned that it would hold the Receiver General responsible for all monies levied.[35]

The House of Assembly used various other procedures in its efforts to control the administration, including refusing Supply, refusing to deal with all legislation until basic grievances were met and "tacking" on clauses to bills appropriating revenue for which there was no existing statute, a practice which forced the Executive to choose between enacting the additional clauses or losing Supply.

The Province of Canada

In 1840, the British Parliament passed the *Union Act* uniting Upper and Lower Canada.[36] With its enactment came the acknowledgement that a government should

---

33. *O'Brien*, pp. 92-3.

34. The Assembly sitting as a committee. See also Chapter 19, "Committees of the Whole House".

35. *O'Brien*, p. 176.

36. *Union Act, 1840*, R.S.C. 1985, Appendix II, No. 4.

enjoy the confidence of the people's representatives.[37] It is also by the *Union Act* that the royal prerogative in right of financial legislation was first introduced into Canadian parliamentary law. Prior to 1840, any elected member in the legislatures of Canada could introduce a bill with financial implications for consideration of the assembly. This practice was much frowned upon by governors on the grounds that it interfered with the efficient operation of government.[38] Lord Durham felt strongly that "The prerogative of the Crown which is constantly exercised in Great Britain for the real protection of the people, ought never to have been waived in the Colonies; and [that if] introduced ... it might be wisely employed in protecting the public interests, now frequently sacrificed in that scramble for local appropriations, which chiefly serves to give an undue influence to particular individuals or parties."[39]

Provision was made for a Consolidated Revenue Fund against which would be charged all expenses related to the collection, management and receipt of revenue, all interest on the public debt and remuneration of the clergy and officials included on the civil list.[40] Any surplus remaining in the fund after these charges had been deducted could be used for the service of the public, as the legislature thought fit.[41] All votes, resolutions or bills involving expenditure of public funds were to be first recommended by the governor general.[42]

There were still disputes over the control of money. However, no administration was defeated over an appropriation act; in fact, even when governments changed, a supply bill was often taken over and carried through by the succeeding administration.[43] By 1867, the vote of confidence had virtually replaced withholding Supply as the preferred mechanism by which the Assembly sought control over the administration of government.

Financial Procedure in the Canadian House of Commons

The *Constitution Act, 1867* provided that any bill appropriating any part of the public revenue or imposing a tax or duty must originate in the House of Commons.[44] Furthermore, the Act made it unlawful for the House to pass any measure to appropriate public revenues or impose a tax or duty which had not first been recommended by

---

37. *Bourinot*, 4th ed., p. 12. Bourinot goes on to recount how, in 1849, Nova Scotia Governor Sir John Harvey was instructed by the Colonial Office that it was "neither possible nor desirable to carry on the government of any of the British provinces in North America in opposition to the opinions of the inhabitants".

38. *Bourinot*, 1st ed., p. 463.

39. *Lord Durham's Report: An Abridgement*, edited by G.M. Craig, Ottawa: Carleton University Press, 1992, pp. 144-5.

40. *Union Act, 1840*, R.S.C. 1985, Appendix II, No. 4, Arts. L-LVI.

41. *Union Act, 1840*, R.S.C. 1985, Appendix II, No. 4, Art. LVII.

42. *Union Act, 1840*, R.S.C. 1985, Appendix II, No. 4, Art. LVII.

43. *O'Brien*, p. 361.

44. *Constitution Act, 1867*, R.S.C. 1985, Appendix II, No. 5, s. 53. The language of Section 53 was first written into Canada's constitutional documents in the *Union Act, 1840*, R.S.C. 1985, Appendix II, No. 4, Art. LVII.

the Governor General in the Session in which the measure was proposed.[45] Additional clauses provided for the creation and use of a Consolidated Revenue Fund by the Parliament of Canada for the public service.[46]

Standing Orders (1867-1968)

The first Standing Orders of the House of Commons codified long-established rules of parliamentary practice and procedure, which were rooted in British parliamentary history and, subsequently, also in the rules and procedures of the different colonial legislatures.

The cardinal principle governing Parliament's treatment of financial measures was that they be given the fullest possible consideration in committee and in the House. This was to ensure that "parliament may not, by sudden and hasty votes, incur any expenses, or be induced to approve of measures, which may entail heavy and lasting burthens upon the country".[47] To satisfy the requirement for debate, the 1867 rules required that financial business be considered first in a Committee of the Whole before being debated in the House.[48] In 1874, the House agreed to appoint, henceforth, at the beginning of each session, a Committee of Supply and a Committee of Ways and Means.[49] The Committee of Supply approved the annual Estimates of government expenditure, while the Committee of Ways and Means considered the government's proposals to raise revenue and approved necessary withdrawals from the Consolidated Revenue Fund for the measures in the Estimates. Yet another measure safeguarding the House from hasty financial decisions was the rule that the debate on any motion proposed "for any public Aid or Charge upon the people" would not proceed immediately, but would be adjourned to a subsequent sitting day.[50] This was done so that "no member may be forced to come to a hasty decision, but that every one may have abundant opportunities afforded him of stating his reasons for supporting or opposing the proposed grant".[51]

The first Standing Orders also included, directly under the heading "Aid and Supply", a note in reference to the *Constitution Act, 1867,* which required that any measure seeking to raise or spend public money be initiated by the Crown. The rules provided further that all legislation respecting charges upon the public revenue

---

45. *Constitution Act, 1867*, R.S.C. 1985, Appendix II, No. 5, s. 54.

46. *Constitution Act, 1867*, R.S.C. 1985, Appendix II, No. 5, ss. 102 to 106. A similar system was in use in the United Province of Canada at the time of Confederation.

47. *Bourinot*, 4th ed., pp. 404-5.

48. *Rules, Orders and Forms of Proceeding of the House of Commons of Canada, 1868,* Rule 88.

49. *Journals*, March 31, 1874, p. 10; see also 1876 House of Commons Rule 87. Until 1874, the House was first required to agree to a motion, "That supply be granted to Her Majesty". That motion, proposed immediately following the order to begin debate on the Throne Speech, was the mechanism used to designate a Committee of Supply and to place the Business of Supply on the House agenda. (See also *Bourinot*, 1st ed., p. 477.)

50. *Rules, Orders and Forms of Proceeding of the House of Commons of Canada, 1868,* Rule 88.

51. *Bourinot*, 1st ed., pp. 462-3.

(expenditure) or on the public (taxation) be introduced first in the House of Commons, that is, the Commons alone grants supply.[52]

In general, the financial procedures set out under these rules remained the same for the next hundred years.[53] However, financial procedures came to be used by successive oppositions as a means of obstructing, delaying, and even preventing the government from passing financial business. As a consequence, beginning in the late 1960s, financial procedures, which had remained virtually unchanged for a century, were drastically revised and streamlined. These revisions had to recognize and protect two contradictory principles: that the government is entitled to get its financial legislation through Parliament; and that the opposition is entitled to identify, draw attention to, delay, and debate, items that it feels need attention and discussion.

THE ROYAL RECOMMENDATION

Under the Canadian system of government, the Crown alone initiates all public expenditure and Parliament may only authorize spending which has been recommended by the Governor General.[54] This prerogative, referred to as the "financial initiative of the Crown", is the basis essential to the system of responsible government and is signified by way of the "royal recommendation". With this prerogative, the government is assigned the responsibility for preparing a comprehensive budget, proposing how funds shall be spent, and actually handling the use of funds. The *Constitution Act, 1867,* states that "It shall not be lawful for the House of Commons to adopt or pass any Vote, Resolution, Address, or Bill for the Appropriation of any Part of the Public Revenue, or of any Tax or Impost, to any Purpose that has not been first recommended to that House by Message of the Governor General in the Session in which such Vote, Resolution, Address, or Bill is proposed".[55] The language of the Constitution is echoed in the Standing Orders of the House.[56]

For the first hundred years following Confederation, any bill or clause appropriating money had to be preceded by a House resolution, whose wording defined precisely the amount and purpose of any appropriations sought. The resolution was moved by a Minister of the Crown and was recommended by the Governor General.[57] Every appropriating clause of the subsequent bill had to conform to the provisions outlined in the resolution, and no Member could move amendments to the legislation that would have the effect of increasing the amount or altering the purposes which

---

52. *Rules, Orders and Forms of Proceeding of the House of Commons of Canada, 1868,* Rule 89.

53. In 1968, the House modified its Standing Orders to incorporate a fixed, annual schedule for the consideration of the Business of Supply. See sections below on "The Business of Supply".

54. *Bourinot*, 1st ed., p. 462. Public expenditure is that deemed to be a charge upon the public revenue. See also ruling of Speaker Parent, *Debates*, February 12, 1998, p. 3765.

55. *Constitution Act, 1867*, R.S.C. 1985, Appendix II, No. 5, s. 54.

56. Standing Order 79(1).

57. See, for example, *Journals*, April 24, 1873, pp. 205-6; May 8, 1873, pp. 302-4; May 20, 1873, pp. 396-9; June 2, 1960, pp. 527-8; June 7, 1960, pp. 539-40.

the resolution had authorized.[58] To alter an appropriating clause, the government had first to obtain a new resolution from the House, again recommended by the Governor General, embodying the change.

Because the debate on the financial resolution was often repeated at the second reading stage of the bill, the House eliminated the resolution stage in 1968.[59] The Crown's recommendation would now be conveyed to the House as a printed notice which would appear in the *Notice Paper* and again in the *Journals* when the bill was introduced, and be printed in or appended to the text of the bill.[60] The rule change did not alter the constitutional requirement for a royal recommendation, nor its form, only the procedure to be followed.

In 1994, the Standing Orders were again amended to remove the requirement that a royal recommendation had to be provided to the House before a bill could be introduced.[61] The royal recommendation can now be provided after the bill has been introduced in the House, as long as it is done before the bill is read a third time and passed. However, the government has maintained the practice of providing the royal recommendation to their own bills at the moment they are put on notice for introduction in the House.[62] The royal recommendation accompanying a bill must still be printed in the *Notice Paper,* printed in or annexed to the bill and recorded in the *Journals.*

In general, there are two types of bills which confer parliamentary authority to spend and therefore would require a royal recommendation[63]:

---

58. See, for example, *Journals*, April 11, 1939, p. 325.

59. See the Fifth Report of the Special Committee on Procedure of the House, *Journals*, December 20, 1968, pp. 562, 573 and 579.

60. The rule was as follows: "The message and recommendation of the Governor General in relation to any bill for the appropriation of any part of the public revenue or of any tax or impost shall be printed on the *Notice Paper* and in the *Votes and Proceedings* when any such measure is to be introduced and the text of such recommendation shall be printed with or annexed to every such bill." (See the 1968 Standing Order 61(2), *Journals*, December 20, 1968, p. 573.)

61. Standing Order 79(2). See the Twenty-Seventh Report of the Standing Committee on Procedure and House Affairs, June 9, 1994, Meeting No. 16, pp. 6-7. See also *Journals*, June 8, 1994, p. 545; June 10, 1994, p. 563.

62. See, for example, Bills C-14, *An Act respecting the safety and effectiveness of materials that come into contact with or are used to treat water destined for human consumption* (*Journals*, October 30, 1997, p. 173) and C-15, *An Act to amend the Canada Shipping Act and to make consequential amendments to other Acts* (*Journals*, October 30, 1997, p. 173). Occasionally, the government has provided a royal recommendation after first reading. See, for example, Bill C-45, *An Act to amend the Criminal Code (judicial review of parole ineligibility) and another Act,* introduced and given first reading on June 11, 1996 (*Journals*, p. 510) and royal recommendation given at second reading stage on June 14, 1996 (*Journals*, p. 553).

63. For a discussion on the requirement of a royal recommendation, see R.R. Walsh, "Some Thoughts on Section 54 and the Financial Initiative of the Crown", *Canadian Parliamentary Review*, Summer 1994, p. 24. In recent years, borrowing authority bills have also been accompanied by a royal recommendation (see, for example, *Journals*, February 23, 1994, p. 188; February 27, 1995, p. 1174; March 6, 1996, p. 55).

- Appropriation acts, or supply bills which authorize charges against the Consolidated Revenue Fund up to the amounts approved in the Estimates; and

- Bills which authorize new charges for purposes not anticipated in the Estimates.[64] The charge imposed by the legislation must be "new and distinct"; in other words, not covered elsewhere by some more general authorization.[65]

An appropriation accompanied by a royal recommendation, though it can be reduced, can neither be increased nor redirected without a new recommendation.[66] Because financial legislation must originate in the House of Commons, bills that require a royal recommendation may not be introduced in the Senate.[67]

A royal recommendation not only fixes the allowable charge, but also its objects, purposes, conditions and qualifications. An amendment which either increases the amount of an appropriation, or extends its objects, purposes, conditions and qualifications is inadmissible on the grounds that it infringes on the Crown's financial initiative.[68] However, a royal recommendation is not required for an amendment whose effect is to reduce taxes otherwise payable.[69]

The rules regarding the royal recommendation also apply to a bill sponsored by a private Member.[70] In the past, when such a bill infringed on the financial initiative of the Crown, the Speaker has not allowed it to go forward.[71] However, since the rule change of 1994, private Members' bills involving the spending of public money have been allowed to be introduced and to proceed through the legislative process, on the assumption that a royal recommendation would be submitted by a Minister of the Crown before the bill was to be read a third time and passed.[72] If a royal recommendation

64. *May,* 22nd ed., p. 733. See also Standing Senate Committee on National Finance, *Proceedings,* March 21, 1990, Issue No. 20, p. 6.

65. *May,* 22nd ed., p. 763. Speaker Parent has ruled that, where statutory authority exists to cover the payment of compensation for something for which the government is authorized to assume liability, extending the liability does not itself require a royal recommendation (*Debates,* February 12, 1998, p. 3766). "Where sufficient statutory authority already exists for payments to which bills relate, no further . . . recommendation is required" (*May,* 21st ed., p. 717). See also Speaker Parent's ruling, *Debates,* February 10, 1998, pp. 3647-8.

66. See Speaker Lamoureux's ruling, *Journals,* June 21, 1972, p. 396.

67. *Constitution Act, 1867,* R.S.C. 1985, Appendix II, No. 5, s. 53, and Standing Order 80(1). See, for example, Speaker Lamoureux's rulings, *Journals,* November 12, 1969, pp. 79-80; June 12, 1973, pp. 401-2. See also Speaker Parent's ruling, *Debates,* February 12, 1998, p. 3765.

68. See *Journals,* April 11, 1939, p. 325. See also rulings of Speaker Lamoureux, *Journals,* June 21, 1972, p. 396; February 5, 1973, p. 93.

69. Ruling of Speaker Parent, *Debates,* October 16, 1995, p. 15410.

70. For further information on private Members' bills, see Chapter 16, "The Legislative Process", and Chapter 21, "Private Members' Business".

71. For examples of private Members' bills ruled out of order because they infringed on the financial initiative of the Crown, see *Debates,* April 20, 1971, pp. 5093-4, 5096-7; February 6, 1973, p. 1018; September 18, 1973, p. 6690.

72. See, for example, *Journals,* December 6, 1994, p. 997; *Debates,* December 6, 1994, p. 8734.

were not produced by the time the House was ready to decide on the motion for third reading of the bill, the Speaker would have to stop the proceedings and rule the bill out of order. The Speaker has the duty and responsibility to ensure that the Standing Orders on the royal recommendation as well as the constitutional requirements are upheld. There is no provision under the rules of financial procedure which would permit the Speaker to leave it to the House to decide or to allow the House to do so by unanimous consent.[73]

THE COMMONS' CLAIM TO PREDOMINANCE IN FINANCIAL MATTERS

The Constitution and the Standing Orders of the House of Commons require that bills which appropriate (impose a charge on the public revenue) or levy any tax or duty (impose a charge upon the people) must first be introduced and passed in the House of Commons.[74] The Speaker has ruled that a Senate bill which appropriated public money could not be introduced in the House and directed that the notice for the first reading of the bill be removed from the *Order Paper*.[75] The Speaker has also ruled that a Senate bill which had been read a first time in the House was in fact imposing a tax and should have originated in the Commons; the proceedings on the bill were declared null and void and the bill was ordered withdrawn from the *Order Paper*.[76]

Financial legislation is, in the opinion of the House, not alterable by the Senate.[77] Since Confederation, the Senate has regularly asserted the right to amend money bills.[78] Most of the disagreements between the two Chambers arise over the extent of the Senate's authority to amend financial legislation. On the one hand, it has been argued that the Senate is restricted to passing or rejecting such bills.[79] Others maintain that the Senate has full powers to amend, provided that it not increase appropriations or the amount of taxation.[80] The issue is whether a money bill is one that includes any financial provisions or whether its purpose must be primarily or solely financial; and, consequently, whether any restrictions on the Senate's power to amend should extend to the whole bill or simply to its financial aspects. A further

---

73. See ruling of Deputy Speaker Laniel, *Debates*, November 9, 1978, pp. 975-7. See also ruling of Deputy Speaker Francis, *Debates*, November 3, 1983, pp. 28655-7.

74. *Constitution Act, 1867*, R.S.C. 1985, Appendix II, No. 5, s. 53. Standing Order 80(1).

75. See ruling of Speaker Lamoureux, *Journals*, November 12, 1969, pp. 79-80.

76. See ruling of Speaker Parent on Bill S-13, *Debates*, December 2, 1998, pp. 10788-91.

77. Standing Order 80(1).

78. In 1918, the Senate established a Special Committee to consider its rights with respect to money bills, under the chairmanship of Senator Ross. The Committee's report was presented in the Senate on May 15, 1918. See Second Report of the Special Committee on the question of the rights of the Senate respecting Financial Legislation (Money Bills) (Ross Report), *Senate Journals*, May 15, 1918, pp. 193-204. See also James Robertson, *Financial Legislation and the Senate*, Library of Parliament, April 19, 1990.

79. This argument posits that a financial bill amended by the Senate becomes a different bill and is not the same as that which originated in the House of Commons (*Dreidger*, p. 41).

80. See the Ross Report, presented in the Senate on May 15, 1918 (*Senate Journals*, pp. 193-204), and adopted on May 22, 1918 (*Senate Journals*, p. 241). See also *Robertson*, pp. 10-12.

question is whether or not the Senate can propose amendments to bills amending existing financial legislation.[81] In some instances, the House of Commons has rejected the Senate's amendments and claimed their financial privilege.[82] On other occasions, however, the House has waived its privileges and accepted the Senate amendments.[83] Where the Commons choose to accept a Senate amendment (to a bill appropriating funds or imposing a tax), they usually waive their financial prerogative, while insisting that their decision in this instance does not constitute a precedent.[84] However, the House has, on occasion, accepted or rejected amendments with no reference made to its privileges, whatsoever.[85] On at least two occasions, the Speaker has refused to lay aside Senate amendments to financial legislation, maintaining that it is the responsibility of the Commons, not the Chair, to invoke or waive the privileges claimed by the House.[86] Although the Chair has acknowledged its responsibility for directing the House's attention to any Senate bill or amendment which breaches its privileges,[87] the Speaker does not rule on the right of the Senate to amend financial legislation on the grounds that this is a constitutional issue.[88] Senate bills, on the other hand, have been laid aside on the grounds that they contravened the constitutional principles that financial bills originate in the Commons and are introduced at the initiative of the Crown.[89]

---

81. This arose with respect to Bill C-21, *An Act to amend the Unemployment Insurance Act* (Second Session (1989-91), Thirty-Fourth Parliament).

82. See, for example, *Journals*, May 23, 1873, pp. 429-30; July 18, 1959, pp. 750-1; July 6, 1961, p. 812; July 18, 1988, pp. 3210 and 3223-4; May 9, 1990, pp. 1668-70.

83. See, for example, *Journals*, May 23, 1874, pp. 335-6; September 15, 1917, pp. 662-3; May 23, 1918, p. 333; June 11, 1941, p. 491; and March 20, 1997, pp. 1326-7. The requirement that bills which appropriate or impose a tax originate in the Commons is included in the Constitution and may not be waived by the House; whereas the principle that such bills are not alterable by the Senate is a privilege claimed by the Commons (Standing Order 80(1)) and, as such, may be waived by the House.

84. The Speaker has ruled that to waive its privileges respecting financial legislation the House must suspend Standing Order 80(1). Typically, this is done with the consent of the House. However, where consent is denied, a motion to suspend must be proposed and decided, after appropriate notice of the motion has been given (see Speaker Michener's ruling, *Journal*, July 14, 1959, pp. 708-10; see also *Debates*, July 14, 1959, pp. 5977-85).

85. See, for example, *Journals*, May 15, 1989, pp. 222-3.

86. See Speaker Fraser's ruling, *Debates*, July 11, 1988, p. 17384; April 26, 1990, p. 10723. See also Speaker Rhode's ruling, *Journals*, September 15, 1917, pp. 662-3.

87. See Speaker Michener's ruling, *Journals*, July 14, 1959, p. 708.

88. See Speakers' rulings: *Journals*, September 15, 1917, p. 663; July 14, 1959, p. 708; *Debates*, July 11, 1988, p. 17384; April 26, 1990, p. 10722.

89. See Speaker Lamoureux's ruling, *Journals*, November 12, 1969, p. 80; June 12, 1973, p. 402, and Speaker Parent's ruling, *Debates,* December 2, 1998, pp. 10788-91.

The House will allow the Senate to include or alter pecuniary penalties in bills, where such penalties seek only to punish or prevent crimes or offences and do not have the effect of incurring a public expenditure or imposing a tax on the people.[90]

The Business of Supply

The Business of Supply is the process by which the government asks Parliament to appropriate the funds required to meet its financial obligations and to implement programs already approved by Parliament. The Crown, acting on the advice of its responsible Ministers, transmits to the House of Commons the government's projected annual expenditures, or "estimates", for parliamentary scrutiny and approval. The House of Commons has sole authority to grant the "supplies" needed to satisfy the government's demands. All financial legislation (which includes all government expenditures) must originate in the House of Commons.[91] Once Supply is granted, the government can draw on the Consolidated Revenue Fund to meet its financial obligations.[92]

HISTORICAL PERSPECTIVE

The Supply procedures established in 1867 remained basically unchanged for the first hundred years following Confederation. Deriving from a long-standing rule of the British House of Commons,[93] the Business of Supply was considered in a Committee of the Whole House, called the Committee of Supply.[94]

From Confederation to 1968

Prior to 1968, the Supply proceedings consisted of the process of entering *into* Committee of Supply and the study of the annual Estimates or government spending proposals *in* Committee of Supply. Before the Committee of Supply could begin its work, the Finance Minister had to table the Estimates along with the message from

---

90. Standing Order 80(2).

91. *Constitution Act, 1867,* R.S.C. 1985, Appendix II, No. 5, s. 53; Standing Order 80(1).

92. The *Financial Administration Act* states that no payment shall be made out of the Consolidated Revenue Fund without the authority of Parliament (R.S.C. 1985, c. F-11, s. 26).

93. See *May,* 5th ed., p. 547; Rule 88, *Rules, Orders and Forms of Proceeding of the House of Commons of Canada, 1868.* See also Chapter 19, "Committees of the Whole House".

94. Beginning in 1874, the Committee of Supply and the Committee of Ways and Means were struck at the same time. (*Journals,* March 31, 1874, p. 10; Rule 87, *Rules, Orders and Forms of Proceeding of the House of Commons of Canada, 1876.*) Prior to 1874, the Committee of Supply was struck during the debate on the Speech from the Throne (see, for example, *Journals,* November 19 and 20, 1867, p. 25; April 20, 1869, p. 25; March 1 and 3, 1870, p. 31; April 19, 1872, p. 28). The Committee of Ways and Means was not struck until the House had concurred in a resolution or resolutions reported from the Committee of Supply. (See, for example, *Journals,* December 11, 1867, p. 64; May 4, 1869, p. 58; April 5, 1870, p. 150; April 29, 1872, p. 60.) See also Chapter 19, "Committees of the Whole House".

the Governor General signifying the recommendation of the Crown.[95] The Minister then moved that the message and recommendation, together with the Estimates, be referred to the Committee of Supply.[96]

When the Order of the Day was read for the House to resolve itself into the Committee of Supply,[97] the motion, "That the Speaker do now leave the Chair" was proposed to the House.[98] This initiated the first phase of the Supply proceedings; it was an opportunity for Members to debate and, if they chose, amend the motion that the Speaker leave the Chair. The rules pertaining to relevance were relaxed and Members used amendments to the motion as the mechanism to raise their issues and debate them in the House. In addition, the Opposition could use the threat of delaying Supply to obtain concessions from the Executive. The practice of allowing every description of amendment to be moved,[99] coupled with great latitude permitted in the debate and the lack of time limits, reflected the ancient tenet of parliamentary government which held that the Crown should respond to the grievances of the people before the people granted Supply.[100]

Once having agreed to the motion for the Speaker to leave the Chair, the House was then sitting as the Committee of Supply. Each Estimate was considered as a separate resolution or motion, "that a certain sum be granted to Her Majesty for …" Amendments to the motion were permitted and no time limits were placed on the debate. If decided in the affirmative, the resolutions were reported to the House for its concurrence. This was accomplished by "reading" the resolution twice. The first reading was purely formal; however, the motion for second reading was debatable and amendable. Reports from the Committee of Supply were usually not received or taken up by the House on the same day they were reported, but were ordered to be received at a subsequent sitting of the House. Upon reporting, the Committee

---

95. All financial measures were to be initiated by the Crown (*Constitution Act, 1867*, R.S.C. 1985, Schedule II, No. 5, s. 54).

96. *Bourinot*, 1st ed., p. 477.

97. No motion to grant Supply could be taken up in the Committee of Supply during the same sitting day in which it was proposed (*May*, 5th ed., p. 547; Rule 88, *Rules, Orders and Forms of Proceeding of the House of Commons of Canada, 1868*).

98. This is the same motion that was proposed whenever the House wished to resolve into a Committee of the Whole, as Committees of the Whole are not presided over by the Speaker. Since 1968, however, when the order is called for the House to resolve itself into a Committee of the Whole, the Speaker leaves the Chair without the question being put. (See *Journals*, December 20, 1968, pp. 562 and 572; Standing Order 100. See also Chapter 19, "Committees of the Whole House".)

99. One amendment to the motion was permitted. However, if that amendment were withdrawn, another might be proposed. No sub-amendments were receivable (*Bourinot*, 1st ed., pp. 478-9).

100. This "airing of grievances" is now achieved through what are variably referred to as "supply, allotted or opposition days", when the opposition determines the subject of debate for that day.

requested leave "to sit again", without which permission the Committee of Supply, as an entity, would have ceased to exist.[101]

When the Order of the Day was read to report the resolutions approved in Committee, a formal motion for their first reading was proposed. The motion was never debated or amended. If the House agreed, each resolution was then read separately a second time, after which the Speaker put the question for concurrence. Both the debate and any amendment had to be relevant to the proposed resolution.[102]

When all the Estimates had passed through the Committee of Supply, the Finance Minister would move a motion for the House to resolve into the Committee of Ways and Means to consider resolutions to authorize the necessary withdrawals from the Consolidated Revenue Fund.[103] Again, each sum was proposed as a separate resolution, considered and, if agreed to, reported to the House. Once the resolutions had been read a second time, they formed the basis for the Appropriation or Supply Bill, which set aside (or appropriated) from the Consolidated Revenue Fund the amounts required to fund the programs and activities approved in the Estimates. Supply Bills were often introduced and passed through two or more legislative stages in a single day.[104] Once it had been passed by the House, the Supply Bill was sent to the Senate where it was given three readings and passed before being returned to the House.

The debate on the motion "That the Speaker do now leave the Chair" often resulted in Supply being considered very late in the session, and often late at night. Consequently, by the time the Estimates were actually discussed in the Committee, they tended to be given relatively short examination, provoking frequent criticism of the lack of effective parliamentary oversight of government expenditure.[105]

In 1913, the Standing Orders of the House were modified: henceforth, when the order for the House to go into the Committee of Supply was called on Thursday and Friday, the motion "That the Speaker do now leave the Chair" would be deemed adopted without question put.[106] This change represented the first encroachment on the Members' previously unfettered right to air grievances before considering the government's financial requirements. The effect of the adoption of the change was that from 1913 to 1955, only 132 amendments to the motion were moved, while in the period 1867 to 1913, 271 amendments had been moved. By guaranteeing the

---

101. Constituting the Committee of Supply was the mechanism by which the House might consider supply. Today, the House passes a "continuing order of supply" at the beginning of each session which authorizes it to consider supply at any time. (See *Journals*, May 13, 1991, p. 13; January 18, 1994, p. 19; February 27, 1996, p. 4; September 23, 1997, p. 14.)

102. *Bourinot*, 1st ed., p. 491.

103. *Bourinot*, 1st ed., pp. 496-7.

104. See *Bourinot*, 1st ed., pp. 497-8.

105. See, for example, *Debates*, July 10, 1905, col. 9085-105.

106. *Journals*, April 9, 1913, pp. 451-2; *Debates*, April 9, 1913, col. 7409-10; *Journals*, April 23 and 24, 1913, pp. 507-9.

government at least two days a week on which its financial requirements could be taken up by the House, the new rule introduced the first real constraint on the opposition's capacity to delay Supply.

There were no further modifications until 1927[107] when the House agreed to allow a sub-amendment to the motion for the Speaker to leave the Chair to go into the Committee of Supply or the Committee of Ways and Means when proposed on a day other than a Thursday or Friday.[108]

Opinion soon began to differ as to whether Estimates should continue to be considered in a Committee of the Whole or be referred to a standing committee.[109] In 1955, the House agreed to establish a Special Committee on Estimates.[110] Initially, the Committee lacked the authority to send for persons, papers and records; however, changes to the Standing Orders in 1958 gave the committee the necessary powers.[111]

Additional changes, approved provisionally in 1967, made it possible for standing committees to examine the Estimates and limited to four the number of occasions in any session on which the House could debate the motion to go into the Committee of Supply or the Committee of Ways and Means.[112] A maximum of 30 days in each session was allocated for the consideration of the Business of Supply.[113]

---

107. Proposals to improve Supply procedures were discussed on a number of occasions between 1913 and 1927 (see, for example, *Debates*, April 18, 1921, pp. 2193-211; *Journals*, June 6, 1922, pp. 301-5; *Debates*, March 5, 1923, pp. 856-7, and March 19, 1923, pp. 1299-307).

108. *Journals*, March 22, 1927, pp. 342-3.

109. In 1925, a special committee was established to consider revisions to all Standing Orders. During debate on the motion to appoint the committee, Members expressed concerns regarding parliamentary control over public expenditure, the study of Estimates in Committee and the rules applying to amendments to motions that the Speaker leave the Chair for the House to resolve into the Committee of Supply or the Committee of Ways and Means (*Debates*, February 23, 1925, pp. 412-29). The issue of referring Estimates to standing committees was revived in 1930, 1933 and 1936, and throughout the war years, criticism continued that large sums of money were being spent annually with very little detailed parliamentary scrutiny. (See, for example, *Journals*, February 15, 1933, p. 227; *Debates*, June 23, 1936, pp. 4123-6, and July 24, 1943, pp. 5382-6; *Journals*, March 3, 1944, pp. 146-52; April 10, 1946, pp. 125-6; December 5, 1947, pp. 13-17.)

110. *Journals*, February 8, 1955, pp. 127-8.

111. *Journals*, May 30, 1958, p. 71.

112. *Journals*, April 26, 1967, pp. 1769-74. These temporary changes reflected a consensus with regard to the various House decisions and recommendations of procedure committees which had been tabled throughout the period 1964-67. See, for example, the Fifteenth Report of the Special Committee on Procedure and Organization, presented on December 14, 1964 (*Journals*, pp. 985-96); the Nineteenth Report of the Special Committee on Procedure and Organization, presented on March 26, 1965 (*Journals*, pp. 1176-7); and the motion concerning Supply proceedings adopted on June 8, 1965 (*Journals*, pp. 210-1).

113. For the purpose of the 30 days, the Business of Supply was defined as consisting of "main estimates; interim supply; and supplementary or additional estimates excepting supplementary or additional estimates introduced after the main estimates have been approved, and excepting always the final supplementary or additional estimates" (*Journals*, June 8, 1965, p. 210).

Supply Proceedings Since 1968

In 1968, changes were recommended by the Special Committee on Procedure and Organization. The Committee had described Supply procedures as "time-consuming, repetitive and archaic", claiming they did not permit an effective scrutiny of the Estimates, did not provide the House with the means of organizing meaningful debate on pre-arranged subjects, had failed to preserve effective parliamentary control over expenditures and had failed to guarantee an expeditious decision on appropriation bills. The Committee found that the traditional Supply procedures were irrelevant to the realities of government in the present day.[114] The House agreed to alter substantially its financial procedures.[115] The Committee of Supply was abolished, along with the Committee of Ways and Means. All Estimates would be referred now to standing committees before they were taken up in the House. Under the revised rules, the Main Estimates would be tabled and referred on or before March 1 of each year. Committees were required to report back the Estimates, or would be deemed to have reported them back, no later than May 31.[116]

The House agreed to establish, at the beginning of each session, a continuing order for the consideration of Supply on the House agenda under Government Business.[117] Unlike the order for the House to go into the Committee of Supply, which lapsed once the committee had reported the Estimates back to the House, the continuing order remains on the agenda as an item of government business and may be taken up at any time at the government's discretion.

The new rules divided the parliamentary calendar into three periods, during which 25 days would be allotted to the Business of Supply. Five allotted days were set aside in the Supply period ending December 10, seven days in the period ending March 26 and an additional thirteen days in the period ending June 30. Opposition or Supply motions could be moved only by Members in opposition to the

---

114. See *Journals*, December 6, 1968, pp. 429-31.

115. See *Journals*, December 20, 1968, pp. 554-73.

116. Standing Order 81(4). In March 1975, the House agreed to a provisional Standing Order permitting opposition Members, on allotted days, to select certain items in the Estimates to be considered in a Committee of the Whole. (See the Second Report of the Standing Committee on Procedure and Organization, presented to the House on March 14, 1975 (*Journals*, pp. 372-6) and concurred in on March 24, 1975 (*Journals*, p. 399)) Although this procedure was followed on nine occasions over the next fifteen months, the provision lapsed at the end of the session and the experiment was not renewed. Study of specific items of the Main and Supplementary Estimates was carried out in a Committee of the Whole on May 9, 12, 13, 22, 28 and June 5 and 17, 1975, and on May 20 and 26, 1976.

117. Standing Order 81(1).

government and might be related to any matter within the jurisdiction of the Parliament of Canada.[118]

In addition, the new rules stipulated that in any period, the opposition could ask that up to two of its allotted day motions be brought to a vote and that these could be designated as votes of non-confidence in the government. Since the requirement that the Executive retain the confidence of the House is a matter of convention, many questioned why votable opposition motions should be termed "no-confidence" motions.[119] In March 1975, the Standing Orders were provisionally modified so that votes on opposition supply motions would no longer, *ipso facto,* be considered an expression of confidence in the government.[120] The provisional rules lapsed at the beginning of the following Session and the term "no-confidence" found its way back into the 1977 version of the Standing Orders. Amendments to the Standing Orders in June 1985 again removed the non-confidence provision from the rules on opposition motions.[121]

In 1986, provision was made for the Leader of the Opposition to extend the committee consideration of the Main Estimates of one department or agency beyond the

---

118. Standing Order 81(13). On one occasion, the House considered specific items in the Estimates on a Supply day. (See Speaker Lamoureux's ruling, *Journals*, June 26, 1973, pp. 435-6.)

119. The question of what constitutes a lack of confidence in the government is of a political nature and not one the Speaker should decide. (See, for example, Speaker Lamoureux's ruling, *Journals*, May 4, 1970, pp. 742-3. See also the ruling of Deputy Speaker Champagne, *Debates*, September 19, 1991, pp. 2374-6.) Many see the combination of the confidence convention and strong party discipline as a principal reason for the weak scrutiny of government expenditure currently exercised by the Canadian House of Commons. (See the Fifty-First Report of the Standing Committee on Procedure and House Affairs (*The Business of Supply: Completing the Circle of Control*), and in particular Section IX, "The Confidence Convention and the Business of Supply", presented to the House on December 10, 1998 (*Journals*, p. 1435). In its response to the Fifty-First Report, tabled on May 7, 1999 (*Journals*, p. 1839, Sessional Paper No. 8512-361-131), the government expressed the view that "the proposal to use confidence sparingly on supply matters would not be in keeping with our tradition and would be extremely difficult to implement".)

120. See the Second Report of the Standing Committee on Procedure and Organization, *Journals*, March 14, 1975, pp. 372 and 375, and March 24, 1975, p. 399. The House adopted the first opposition motion on an allotted day on February 12, 1976 (*Journals*, p. 1016, and *Debates*, p. 10883). At the time, the government found the wording of the motion acceptable (*Debates*, February 11, 1976, p. 10842).

121. *Journals*, June 27, 1985, pp. 910, 914-5 and 919. This change was recommended in the First Report of the Special Committee on the Reform of the House of Commons (McGrath Committee), presented to the House on December 20, 1984 (*Journals*, p. 211). The government had responded that it supported the proposal on the grounds that it provided an opportunity for the government and the Opposition to discuss and debate policy without the sometimes rigid restriction of the non-confidence motion (*Debates*, April 18, 1985, p. 3869). This amendment was made permanent two years later (*Journals*, June 3, 1987, pp. 1016 and 1023). On one occasion, a Member proposed a motion which specified that it was not to be considered a question of confidence in the government. A point of order having been raised, the Deputy Speaker declared that the determination of confidence in the government is not a question of procedure and therefore not an issue to be ruled on by the Speaker (*Debates*, September 19, 1991, pp. 2374-6).

May 31 deadline, for a period not exceeding 10 further sitting days.[122] In addition, the new rules set aside the last allotted day in the Supply period ending June 30 to debate the motion to concur in the Main Estimates, instead of the usual opposition motion, and extended the sitting hours on that day until 10:00 p.m. In 1991, the end date for that period was changed to June 23 and, as a result of a reduction of the number of sittings days in the year, the total number of allotted days over a year was reduced from 25 to 20.[123] Provision was also made to increase or decrease the number of allotted days in a Supply period in relation to the total number of sitting days in the period,[124] and to limit the number of allotted days falling on Wednesday and Friday.[125] Finally, in 1998, the total number of allotted days was increased to 21, and the last allotted day in June again provided for the consideration of an opposition motion.[126] However, the consideration of the opposition motion on this last allotted day is not to go beyond 6:30 p.m. and is to be followed with the necessary motions to concur in the Main Estimates.

THE CONTINUING ORDER FOR SUPPLY

In the Speech from the Throne, which begins each new session of Parliament, the Governor General traditionally advises Members of the House of Commons that they will be asked to appropriate (approve the spending of) the funds required to carry on the services and payments authorized by Parliament.[127]

Among its first items of business after the Speech from the Throne, the House considers a motion usually proposed by the Minister serving as President of the Treasury Board: *"That the business of Supply be considered at the next sitting of the House"*.[128] By long-established practice, the motion is not debatable and is traditionally decided without dissent. Once agreed to, the motion is an order of the House to

---

122. *Journals*, February 6, 1986, pp. 1644 and 1655-6, and February 13, 1986, p. 1710. See Standing Order 81(4). This rule change was recommended in the Third Report of the Special Committee on the Reform of the House of Commons (McGrath Committee), June 1985, p. 20.

123. *Journals*, April 11, 1991, p. 2917.

124. *Journals*, April 11, 1991, p. 2917.

125. *Journals*, February 7, 1994, pp. 112 and 117.

126. *Journals*, June 12, 1998, pp. 1027-8. See, for example, *Journals*, June 8, 1999, pp. 2064-6.

127. See, for example, *Journals*, January 18, 1994, p. 17, and *Debates*, February 27, 1996, p. 6. There have been occasions where the traditional request for funds was not included in the Speech from the Throne: September 8, 1930; January 25, 1940; October 9, 1951; December 12, 1988; and April 3, 1989. On the latter occasion, a question of privilege was raised contending that, since the Crown had not requested Supply, the House had no obligation to consider it (*Debates*, April 6, 1989, p. 177). In his ruling, Speaker Fraser noted that the Standing Orders do not require that a request for funds be included in the Throne Speech and that its inclusion has been a matter of tradition, not procedural necessity (*Debates*, May 2, 1989, p. 1177).

128. Standing Order 81(1). See, for example, *Journals*, May 13, 1991, p. 13; January 18, 1994, p. 19; February 27, 1996, p. 4; September 23, 1997, p. 14.

add the Business of Supply on the *Order Paper* for the remainder of the session.[129] This process has the effect of establishing a continuing order of the day for the purposes of considering Supply, which enables the government to call Supply on any sitting day, within the framework laid out in the Standing Orders.

The Business of Supply consists of the consideration of motions:

- to concur in Interim Supply;
- to concur in Main and Supplementary Estimates;
- to restore or reinstate any item in the Estimates;
- to introduce or pass at all stages any bill or bills based thereon;
- to be proposed by the opposition on allotted days.[130]

In any calendar year, 21 days are set aside under the Standing Orders for consideration of the Business of Supply and, on these days, Supply have precedence over all other government business.[131] The Business of Supply can be divided into a general debate phase and a legislative phase. The general debate phase is taken up with the consideration of opposition motions proposed on allotted days.[132] During the legislative phase, the House considers and votes on the government's proposed annual spending plans (the Main and Supplementary Estimates)[133] and the legislation (appropriation bills) needed to authorize all consequential withdrawals from the Consolidated Revenue Fund.

---

129. On March 30, 1990, an allotted day, the House was adjourned for lack of quorum. At that time, the lack of quorum and the subsequent adjournment of the sitting superseded the Supply proceedings then underway (*Debates,* p. 10050). The continuing order for Supply was lost and removed from the *Order Paper.* Speaker Fraser subsequently ruled that losing the order for Supply did not nullify all of the House's previous decisions respecting Supply. The order could be redesignated on a non-debatable motion proposed by a Minister of the Crown (*Debates*, April 3, 1990, pp. 10119-21). A motion to redesignate the continuing order for supply was moved and agreed to (see *Journals*, April 3, 1990, p. 1486). In 1991, the Standing Orders were amended so that loss of quorum no longer had the effect of superseding proceedings then before the House (*Journals*, April 11, 1991, p. 2910). For more information on quorum and superseded orders, see Chapter 9, "Sittings of the House", and Chapter 12, "The Process of Debate".
130. Standing Order 81(3).
131. Standing Order 81(2) and (10)(*a*).
132. Standing Order 81(3).
133. Standing Order 81(7) also permits standing committees of the House to consider projected departmental expenditures for future fiscal years. Although this was previously possible under the provisions of Standing Order 108(2), the general mandate of standing committees, Standing Order 81(7) explicitly includes consideration of future government spending plans under the Business of Supply.

GENERAL DEBATE PHASE

Allotted Days

The setting aside of a specified number of sitting days on which the opposition chooses the subject of debate derives from the tradition which holds that Parliament does not grant Supply until the opposition has had an opportunity to demonstrate why it should be refused. Of the twenty-one days allocated in each annual Supply cycle for the House to consider the Business of Supply, seven days are allotted during the period ending December 10, seven during the period ending March 26 and seven during the period ending June 23. Of these twenty-one days, no more than four may fall on a Wednesday and no more than four on a Friday (the shortest sitting days of the week).[134] The twenty-one days are designated as "allotted days". On each of these days, the House will debate an opposition motion.[135]

The normal Supply cycle can be disrupted by an extended adjournment, a prorogation or a dissolution. In these cases, the number of opposition days in each Supply period may be increased or decreased. If, for any reason, the number of sitting days in any Supply period is fewer than the number prescribed under the parliamentary calendar, the number of allotted days in that period will be reduced by an amount proportional to the number of sitting days the House stood adjourned. The Speaker will determine and announce to the House the reduction in the number of allotted days for that period.[136] Conversely, should the House sit more than the prescribed number of sitting days, the total number of allotted days will be increased by one day for every five additional days the House sits.[137] The House may also decide that any unused days from the six days allotted to the debate on the Address in Reply to the Speech from the Throne, or from the four days allotted to the Budget

---

134. Standing Order 81(10)(*a*). When the new Supply procedures were introduced in 1969, the rules provided for 25 allotted days: five in the period ending December 10, seven in the period ending March 26 and thirteen in the period ending June 30 (*Journals*, December 20, 1968, pp. 554 and 557). Effective June 8, 1987, the distribution was changed to six, nine and ten respectively (*Journals*, June 3, 1987, pp. 1016 and 1023). In 1991, the end date of the third period was changed to June 23 from June 30, the number of days was reduced from 25 to 20 and the distribution was changed to five, seven and eight, effective May 13, 1991 (*Journals*, April 11, 1991, pp. 2905-6, 2917 and 2931). The total number of days was increased to 21 to accommodate four opposition parties, seven to be allotted in each of the three periods, effective September 21, 1998 (*Journals*, June 12, 1998, p. 1028).

135. Standing Order changes approved in 1998 (*Journals*, June 12, 1998, pp. 1027-8) made provision to discuss an opposition motion on the last Supply day in the period ending June 23. Before this change, that day was set aside entirely for the consideration of a motion or motions to concur in the Main Estimates.

136. Standing Order 81(10)(*b*). See, for example, *Journals*, November 16, 1992, p. 2053, and February 27, 1996, p. 4.

137. Standing Order 81(10)(*c*). See, for example, *Journals*, September 16, 1992, p. 1999, and February 4, 1994, p. 107. The number of days the House sits is determined according to the parliamentary calendar set out under Standing Order 28(2).

Debate, be added to the number of allotted days in the Supply period in which they would have been taken up.[138]

If, in the Supply period ending June 23, concurrence is sought in Supplementary Estimates for the previous fiscal year, a further three sitting days will be allocated in that period for the consideration of a motion to concur in those Estimates and for the passage at all stages of the related supply bill.[139] On occasion, changes have been made, with the consent of the House, to the length of a Supply period or to the number of allotted days. For example, the House has agreed to extend the length of a Supply period;[140] to add Supply days;[141] and to transfer unused Supply days from one period to the next.[142] The House has also agreed that an allotted day in one Supply period be deemed disposed of and one additional allotted day be designated in the subsequent Supply period.[143]

Designating an Allotted Day

The government designates the days allotted to the consideration of the Business of Supply. The established practice is for a Minister of the Crown, usually the Government House Leader, to rise in the House and designate the following day or a subsequent day as an allotted day;[144] allotted days may also be designated during the "Thursday Statement" on the House business for the following week.[145] However, the date so designated is not binding on the government and may, like the scheduling of any other Government Order, be revised at any time.[146] If the government fails to designate the prescribed number of allotted days, the remaining days in that period will be designated by default.[147] When the sitting on a day designated as an allotted day ends before the House has reached Orders of the Day, the allotted day has not

---

138. Standing Order 81(11).

139. Standing Order 81(12).

140. See, for example, *Journals*, November 30, 1970, p. 164; *Debates*, November 30, 1970, p. 1598.

141. See, for example, *Journals*, March 14, 1975, p. 376; June 17, 1975, p. 641; April 30, 1993, p. 2884; September 23, 1997, p. 14.

142. See, for example, *Journals*, June 2, 1971, p. 600; December 4, 1975, p. 911. See also *Debates*, March 14, 1975, p. 4115; June 17, 1975, p. 6829.

143. *Journals*, June 3, 1991, p. 132.

144. See, for example, *Debates*, October 26, 1983, p. 28349. Supply days have been designated by a Minister rising on a point of order (see, for example, *Debates*, October 15, 1990, p. 14165; September 21, 1998, p. 8189). On one occasion, the House agreed to consider the Business of Supply although the day had not been designated previously (see *Debates*, May 28, 1987, p. 6467).

145. See, for example, *Debates*, May 28, 1998, p. 7362; October 1, 1998, p. 8656. In the "Thursday Statement", the Government House Leader rises in response to a question from the House Leader of the Official Opposition to advise the House of the business the government intends to call over the following week. (See also Chapter 10, "The Daily Program".)

146. See ruling of Speaker Sauvé, *Debates*, February 11, 1982, pp. 14899-900; ruling of Deputy Speaker Francis, October 27, 1983, p. 28375. See also ruling of Speaker Fraser, *Debates*, March 26, 1990, p. 9759.

147. See ruling of Speaker Fraser, *Debates*, March 22, 1990, p. 9628.

commenced, and therefore the sitting does not count as one of the days designated for the consideration of an opposition motion.[148] On the other hand, once the order for Supply has been called, an allotted day is deemed completed if, subsequently, the proceedings are superseded.[149]

Opposition Motions

Opposition motions have precedence over all government Supply motions on allotted days.[150] However, on the last allotted day for the period ending June 23, at not later than 6:30 p.m., the Speaker interrupts the proceedings on the opposition motion and puts, without further debate or amendment, every question necessary to dispose of the motion. Any recorded division requested is deferred to the end of the Supply proceedings on that day, but not later than 10:00 p.m. Meanwhile, the House proceeds to consider a motion or motions to concur in the Main Estimates.[151]

Members in opposition to the government may propose motions for debate on any matter falling within the jurisdiction of the Parliament of Canada, as well as on committee reports concerning Estimates.[152] The Standing Orders give Members a very wide scope in proposing opposition motions on Supply days and, unless the motion is clearly and undoubtedly irregular (e.g., where the procedural aspect is not open to reasonable argument), the Chair does not intervene.[153]

Notice

Before an opposition motion can be taken up on an allotted day, a 24-hour written notice of the motion must be given.[154] A notice which is not filed by 6:00 p.m. (or 2:00 p.m. on a Friday) on the day before a designated allotted day will not appear on the *Order Paper* the following day.[155] A Member may put an opposition motion on notice even though an allotted day has not yet been designated.[156] However, a decision by the government not to proceed with a designated allotted day is not in itself a reason for the Chair to remove a notice of an opposition motion from the *Notice*

---

148. See ruling of Speaker Fraser, *Debates*, December 4, 1986, pp. 1811-2.

149. See, for example, ruling of Speaker Fraser, *Debates*, April 3, 1990, pp. 10119-20.

150. Standing Order 81(15).

151. Standing Order 81(15) and (18).

152. Standing Order 81(13).

153. See ruling of Speaker Lamoureux, *Journals*, March 6, 1973, pp. 166-7; ruling of Speaker Jerome, *Journals*, November 14, 1975, p. 862; ruling of Speaker Fraser, *Debates*, June 8, 1987, p. 6820.

154. Standing Order 81(14)(*a*). The suspension of a sitting, as opposed to an adjournment, does not prevent Members from filing notices of motions. (See ruling of Speaker Lamoureux, *Debates*, January 27, 1969, p. 4813.)

155. An opposition motion which had not been filed in time to appear on the *Order Paper* was taken up with the agreement of the House. (See *Order Paper*, October 5, 1998, p. 13; *Debates*, October 5, 1998, p. 8729.)

156. See ruling of Speaker Fraser, *Debates*, December 7, 1989, pp. 6583-4.

Paper.[157] It can remain on the *Notice Paper* until it is proceeded with later or withdrawn by the sponsor. Only the sponsor can have it removed, and the consent of the House to do so is not required.[158]

Speaker's Power to Select

The Standing Orders are silent on the method of apportioning allotted days between the parties, when two or more recognized parties form the opposition. Although the government designates which days shall be used for the Business of Supply, the opposition parties decide among themselves which party will sponsor the motion and whether or not, subject to the provisions of the Standing Orders, that motion will be brought to a vote. The distribution has reflected the proportion of seats each recognized party occupies in the Chamber. It is not the purview of the Official Opposition to determine unilaterally who can propose a motion on an allotted day.[159] Notices of more than one motion may be given by one or several opposition parties.[160] Where notice of two or more opposition motions appears on the *Order Paper* for consideration on an allotted day and there is no agreement among the opposition parties as to which shall be taken up, the Speaker must decide which motion shall be given precedence.[161] Generally, in making their decision, Speakers will take into consideration the following: representation of the parties in the House; the distribution of sponsorship to date; fair play towards small parties; the date of notice; the sponsor of the motion; the subject matter; whether or not the motion is votable; and what has happened, by agreement among the parties, in the immediate past Supply periods.[162]

---

157. See ruling of Speaker Sauvé, *Debates*, February 15, 1982, pp. 14997-8.

158. See ruling of Speaker Fraser, *Debates*, December 7, 1989, p. 6584.

159. See ruling of the Acting Speaker, *Debates*, November 22, 1983, p. 29061, and ruling of Speaker Francis, *Debates*, May 31, 1984, pp. 4223-4.

160. See ruling of Speaker Fraser, *Debates*, December 7, 1989, p. 6584.

161. Standing Order 81(14)(*b*). See rulings of Speaker Lamoureux, *Debates*, March 3, 1969, p. 6121, and *Journals*, December 10, 1973, p. 734. See also ruling of the Acting Speaker, *Debates*, November 22, 1983, p. 29061, and ruling of Speaker Francis, *Debates*, May 31, 1984, pp. 4223-4.

162. See ruling of Speaker Fraser, *Debates*, December 7, 1989, p. 6584. See also ruling of the Acting Speaker, *Debates*, November 22, 1983, p. 29061, and ruling of Speaker Francis, *Debates*, May 31, 1984, pp. 4223-4.

Votable Motions

For each annual Supply cycle, not more than 14 opposition motions considered on allotted days may be brought to a vote.[163] For the purpose of calculating votable motions, the period ending December 10 is deemed to be the first period in the Supply cycle.[164] The allocation of the 14 votable motions is worked out in an informal agreement among the opposition parties.[165] However, except in a situation where the limit of allowable votable motions in a Supply period or in any year has been reached, it is not within the competence of the Chair to rule whether or not a particular motion should be votable.[166] Although it happens infrequently, some opposition motions on allotted days have been agreed to by the House.[167]

Proceedings on an Opposition Motion

Proceedings on non-votable opposition motions expire at the conclusion of the debate or at the expiry of the time provided for Government Orders.[168] However, a motion can be moved to extend the sitting beyond the hour of daily adjournment.[169] In the case of votable motions, the Speaker will interrupt the debate 15 minutes before the expiry of the time provided for Government Orders and proceed to put, without further debate or amendment, every question necessary to dispose of the motion.[170] When a recorded division on a votable opposition motion is demanded on a Friday, the division is automatically deferred until the ordinary hour of daily

---

163. Standing Order 81(16). Initially, only two votable motions were provided for in each Supply period. That was changed in 1987 to provide for a maximum of eight in any annual Supply cycle but not more than four in any Supply period (*Journals*, June 3, 1987, pp. 1016 and 1023). That was changed again in 1991 to reduce to three the maximum number of votable opposition motions that could be considered in any Supply period (*Journals,* April 11, 1991, pp. 2905-6 and 2918). The House has, on occasion, agreed to increase the number of votable opposition motions in a Supply period. (See, for example, *Journals*, September 23, 1997, p. 14.) When the Standing Orders in relation to Supply were changed in 1968, the wording respecting votable opposition motions referred to motions of "no-confidence" in the government. However, this is no longer the case. In June 1985, the House introduced changes to the Standing Orders which modified the wording to remove the reference to "no-confidence" (*Journals,* June 27, 1985, pp. 910, 914 and 919). For further information on non-confidence opposition motions, see section entitled "Supply Proceedings Since 1968".

164. See ruling of Speaker Fraser, *Debates*, March 26, 1990, p. 9760.

165. The Speaker has ruled that it is not the right of the Official Opposition to decide which party may put a votable motion on notice (*Debates*, May 31, 1984, pp. 4223-4).

166. See ruling of Speaker Lamoureux, *Journals*, May 4, 1970, pp. 742-3.

167. See, for example, *Journals*, February 12, 1992, pp. 1010-2; March 8, 1994, pp. 220-2; October 28, 1997, pp. 155-7; October 30, 1997, p. 175; February 9, 1999, pp. 1482-3; June 8, 1999, pp. 2064-6, 2069-71.

168. Standing Order 81(19). On occasion, the question on a non-votable motion was put by unanimous consent and agreed to. (*Journals*, May 14, 1987, pp. 917-8; November 24, 1989, pp. 880-2; *Debates*, May 14, 1987, p. 6093. See also ruling of Speaker Fraser, *Debates*, May 14, 1987, p. 6112.)

169. See, for example, *Journals*, March 18, 1969, p. 807 (deemed withdrawn); June 23, 1969, p. 1223 (deemed withdrawn); March 19, 1976, p. 1134 (adopted).

170. Standing Order 81(16).

adjournment on the next sitting day; however, a recorded division demanded on the last allotted day of a Supply period may not be deferred.[171]

The proceedings on a votable opposition motion may continue for more than one allotted day;[172] usually, such proceedings have taken place over two consecutive sitting days where both have been designated together as allotted days.[173] The duration of such proceedings must be stated in the notice respecting the day or days set aside.[174]

The mover of the motion, who is a Member of the opposition, speaks first on an opposition day. No Member may speak for more than twenty minutes; a ten-minute period is also provided for questions and comments.[175] It is often the case that two Members of the same party will agree to share the twenty minutes, with each speaker receiving five minutes for questions and comments.[176] On allotted days, the party of the opposition Member sponsoring the motion may be recognized more frequently on debate than otherwise might be warranted, given their relative numbers in the House.

Only one amendment and one sub-amendment are permitted to opposition motions considered on an allotted day.[177] Amendments which have the effect of providing the basis for an entirely different debate are not in order.[178] When a party has been allocated an allotted day and a subject has been proposed for debate by way of

---

171. Standing Order 45(6)(*a*).

172. Standing Order 81(16).

173. See, for example, *Debates*, January 23, 1969, p. 4716; *Journals*, January 29, 1969, p. 637; January 30, 1969, p. 646; *Debates*, November 17, 1970, p. 1250; *Journals*, November 18, 1970, p. 113; November 19, 1970, pp. 116-7; *Debates*, April 20, 1989, pp. 739-40, 760; *Journals*, April 21, 1989, pp. 124, 128; April 24, 1989, pp. 132, 134-5.

174. Standing Order 81(16). (See, for example, *Notice Paper*, April 21, 1989, p. v.)

175. During the Supply period ending December 10, 1997, when five recognized parties were present in the House, the time allocated to all speakers in the first round of debate, with the exception of the Member proposing the motion, was reduced to ten minutes, with a five-minute period reserved for questions and comments (*Journals*, September 26, 1997, p. 30). Subsequently, the House agreed to continue that order indefinitely during the session (*Journals*, February 9, 1998, p. 427).

176. See, for example, *Debates*, February 2, 1990, p. 7755; February 8, 1990, p. 8070; March 15, 1990, p. 9315; October 20, 1998, p. 9136; October 26, 1998, p. 9372; November 19, 1998, pp. 10174-7. On many occasions, where a party has signalled to the House that Members will be sharing their time, the Member following the Member who moved the motion has proposed an amendment to the motion. (See, for example, *Debates*, October 20, 1998, pp. 9136-9; October 26, 1998, pp. 9372-6; March 15, 1999, p. 12839.)

177. Standing Order 85.

178. See, for example, *Debates*, March 16, 1971, p. 4306; November 3, 1971, pp. 9304-6; October 12, 1989, p. 4588; February 1, 1990, p. 7731; March 12, 1991, p. 18378.

an opposition motion, the day should not be taken away by way of an amendment.[179] The House has consented, despite the rules, to allow amendments which had been ruled inadmissible by the Chair.[180]

LEGISLATIVE PHASE

Main Estimates

The Main Estimates provide a breakdown, by department and agency, of planned government spending for the coming fiscal year. The Estimates are expressed as a series of "Votes", or resolutions, which summarize the estimated financial requirements in a particular expenditure category, such as operations, capital or grants.[181] The Votes are expressed in dollar amounts, the total of which, once agreed to, should satisfy all the budgetary requirements of a department or agency in that category, with the exception of any expenditures provided for under other statutory authority. Each budgetary item, or Vote, has two essential components: an amount of money and a destination (a description of what the money will be used for). Should the government wish to change the approved amount or destination of a Vote, it must do so either by way of a "supplementary" Estimate or by way of new or amending legislation.

The Main Estimates are presented in two parts. Part I, the *Government Expenditure Plan,* gives an overview of the government's projected total expenditures for the new fiscal year. Part II contains the *Main Estimates,* which summarize the budgetary and statutory expenditures for all government ministries and agencies for the same period. It also contains an introductory section, which explains the different kinds of Votes[182] and other elements making up the Estimates, as well as any changes to the content with respect to that found in previous fiscal years. Part II outlines spending according to departments, agencies and programs and contains the proposed wording of the conditions governing spending which Parliament will be asked to

---

179. See, for example, *Debates*, March 16, 1971, p. 4306; November 3, 1971, pp. 9304-6; December 10, 1984, p. 1071; March 26, 1992, p. 8877.

180. See, for example, *Debates*, February 12, 1992, p. 6878; April 2, 1992, p. 9268.

181. A Vote in the Estimates may be referred to variously as a "vote", an "estimate" or an "item". The Votes for each Department or Agency are numbered consecutively 1, 5, 10, 15, etc. Supplementary Votes which modify an appropriation authorized under the Main Estimates will bear the same number followed by the letter which corresponds to the particular set of Supplementary Estimates in question (i.e., typically "a", "b" or "c"). Entirely new Votes included in the Supplementary Estimates will be numbered 2 through 4, 6 through 9, 11 through 14, etc., for each department or agency.

182. The *Main Estimates* include: Program Expenditure Votes; Operating Expenditure Votes; Capital Expenditure Votes; Grants and Contributions Votes; Non-Budgetary Votes (identified by the letter L); Special Votes: Crown Corporation Deficits and Separate Legal Identities; Special Votes: Treasury Board Centrally Financed Votes. (See *1998-99 Estimates, Part II, The Main Estimates*, "Preface".)

approve.[183] The information provided in Part II directly supports the Schedule of the *Appropriation Act*. Statutory items are expenditures authorized under separate legislation and, because already approved by the statute, they do not require further approval by Parliament. They are identified in the Estimates with an "S" and are included for information purposes only.[184] Part I is now combined with Part II in the volume known historically as the "Blue Book".[185]

The form and content of the Main Estimates have been modified on only four occasions since Confederation: in 1938, 1970, 1981 and, most recently, in 1997.[186] In each instance, the impetus behind the reforms was a desire to improve the quality and utility of the information provided to Members of Parliament. In 1938, the Minister of Finance included in the Estimates, for the first time, a breakdown of departmental operating costs by function.[187] Still greater precision was introduced in 1970, when departmental expenditures were linked to programs and activities. An explanatory forward clarifying the technical terms used was added and, for the first time, the Blue Book was printed in bilingual format.[188]

As the scope of the federal government widened and government operations grew increasingly complex, compressing all government expenditure information into a single document became more and more impractical. In 1981, following a comprehensive review of financial management and accountability in the federal government, two new documents were introduced. The old Blue Book became known as Part II, *Estimates,* and a new Part I and Part III were added.[189] Part I provided an overview of federal spending, along with information about planned future activities which could not be included along with the annual appropriations and statutory spending set down in the Blue Book. Part II continued to list in detail the

---

183. See *1998-99 Estimates: Parts I and II, The Government Expenditure Plan and Main Estimates*, inside cover.

184. Statutory items are expenditures which have been authorized by legislation other than appropriation acts, i.e., programs which have been provided with a continuing authority to spend and which do not require an annual appropriation from Parliament. (See the Ninth Report of the Standing Senate Committee on National Finance, March 21, 1990, Issue No. 20, p. 15.) However, because statutory items are not referred to committees for study, they may not be the object of any motion, vote or recommendation. Questions requesting information on statutory items are nevertheless allowed.

185. Until 1997, each department and agency also tabled, along with its Main Estimates, an individual expenditure plan, known as the Part III. Part IIIs were referred, along with the items in the Estimates, to the appropriate standing committees.

186. See *1992 Report of the Auditor General of Canada to the House of Commons*, Supply and Services Canada, November 1992, Chapter 6, pp. 165-6.

187. See *Debates*, February 3, 1938, pp. 148-9.

188. *Debates*, February 11, 1970, p. 3468.

189. For comments on the new format, see, for example, *Debates*, February 26, 1981, pp. 7721-2.

resources that individual departments and agencies required for the upcoming year. Finally, Part III, the *Departmental Expenditure Plan,* was a collection of separate books each providing additional details about the programs and activities of a single department or agency. The first Part IIIs were tabled with the 1982-83 Main Estimates.[190]

In Chapter 6 of the 1992 *Annual Report to Parliament,* the Auditor General addressed the issue of departmental reporting. It was noted that much of the government's financial activity was not expressed as spending and, for this reason, not captured in the information Members of Parliament used when considering and approving Supply.[191] In the view of the Auditor General, information to Parliament should include a description of the organization's mission, its major lines of business, the way it is structured, the instruments it uses, its strategic targets and objectives for achieving the mission, as well as performance reports on the extent to which these objectives have been met.[192] In 1997, the House decided to undertake a pilot project to split the Part III departmental expenditure plans into the *Report on Plans and Priorities* and the *Performance Report.* Beginning in fiscal year 1997-98, the Part IIIs were replaced by two documents, the *Report on Plans and Priorities* to be tabled on or before March 31 and the *Performance Report* to be tabled in the fall.[193]

The *Report on Plans and Priorities* describes a department's (or agency's) mandate, mission and strategic objectives, and provides detailed information about the business line structure, expected results and performance-measurement strategy.[194] The reports are tabled in Parliament by the President of the Treasury Board on behalf of the responsible Minister.[195] *Performance Reports* are individual departmental and

---

190. *Debates*, February 23, 1982, p. 15289. On February 22, 1990, the President of the Treasury Board tabled in the House Parts I and II of the Estimates and 73 out of 87 departmental plans of Part III with the promise that the remaining 14 plans would be tabled by March 12 (*Debates*, pp. 8651-3). A point of order was raised arguing that the adoption by the House of the Twelfth Report of the Standing Committee on Public Accounts (*Journals*, December 17, 1981, p. 4460, and June 23, 1982, p. 5075) obliged the President of the Treasury Board to table all departmental Expenditure Plans (Part IIIs) by March 1. Speaker Fraser ruled that the Standing Orders only require that Part II of the Estimates be tabled by March 1 (*Debates*, March 16, 1990, pp. 9381-3). Nonetheless, he did indicate that since the standing committees require Part III in order to understand the Votes in Part II adequately, Part IIIs should be tabled with Part II.

191. *1992 Report of the Auditor General of Canada*, paras. 6.21 to 6.23, p. 167.

192. *1992 Report of the Auditor General of Canada*, para. 6.26, pp. 167-8.

193. See *Journals,* April 24, 1997, p. 1533. See also the Fifty-First Report of the Standing Committee on Procedure and House Affairs (*The Business of Supply: Completing the Circle of Control*), and in particular Section IV, "Completing the Circle: New Procedures for the Business of Supply", presented to the House on December 10, 1998 (*Journals*, p. 1435).

194. *1998-99 Estimates: Parts I and II, The Government Expenditure Plan and Main Estimates*, p. vii.

195. See, for example, *Journals*, March 25, 1998, pp. 617-20.

agency accounts of achievements, measured against planned performance expectations as set out in their *Report on Plans and Priorities*.[196] These too are tabled by the President of the Treasury Board on the Ministers' behalf and referred to the appropriate standing committee.[197] With regard to the Administration of the House of Commons, the annual *Report on Plans and Priorities,* as well as the annual *Performance Report,* are tabled in the House by the Speaker.[198]

The Main Estimates for an incoming fiscal year must be referred to the standing committees on or before March 1 of the expiring fiscal year. The Estimates are presented by a Minister of the Crown, normally the President of the Treasury Board, and are accompanied by a recommendation from the Governor General, which the Speaker reads aloud in the House.[199] The Main Estimates are typically referred to standing committees as soon as they are tabled.[200] Any Minister may move a motion during Routine Proceedings that an item or items in the Main Estimates be referred to any standing committee or committees; the motion is decided without debate.[201]

Interim Supply

Since the fiscal year begins on April 1 and the normal Supply cycle only provides for the House to decide on Main Estimates in June, the government would appear to be without funds for the interim three months. For this reason, the House authorizes an advance on the funds requested in the Main Estimates to cover the needs of the public service from the start of the new fiscal year to the date on which the Appropriation Act based on the Main Estimates of that year is passed. This is known as "Interim Supply",[202] a spending authority made available to the government pending approval of the Main Estimates.

---

196. *1998-99 Estimates: Parts I and II, The Government Expenditure Plan and Main Estimates*, p. vii.

197. See, for example, *Journals*, November 6, 1997, pp. 199-202; October 29, 1998, pp. 1207-11.

198. See, for example, *Journals*, March 25, 1998, p. 620; November 18, 1998, p. 1271; March 5, 1999, p. 1561. The Standing Committee on Procedure and House Affairs is normally charged with the consideration of the House's Estimates.

199. *Constitution Act,* 1867, R.S.C. 1985, Appendix II, No. 5, s. 54; Standing Order 79. See, for example, *Debates*, May 14, 1991, p. 54; February 26, 1998, p. 4456.

200. See, for example, *Journals*, February 26, 1998, pp. 534-5. The tabling and referral of the Estimates have also occurred on different days. (See, for example, *Journals,* February 23, 1972, p. 17, and February 28, 1972, pp. 29-31.) For further information on Committee consideration of Estimates, see section entitled, "Consideration of Estimates in Committee".

201. Standing Order 81(6).

202. See, for example, *Journals*, March 20, 1996, pp. 122-3; March 12, 1997, pp. 1262-3; March 17, 1998, pp. 581-3; March 16, 1999, pp. 1626-8.

The government gives notice of a motion setting out in detail the sums of money it will require, expressed in twelfths of the amounts to be voted in the Main Estimates.[203] Most are three-twelfths of the total amount, corresponding to the three-month hiatus between the beginning of the new fiscal year and the final passage of the Main Estimates, but the government may request more.[204] The motion for Interim Supply is considered on the last allotted day of the period ending March 26. Concurrence in the motion is followed by the consideration and passage at all stages of an appropriation bill based on Interim Supply and authorizing the prescribed withdrawals from the Consolidated Revenue Fund.[205] The granting of Interim Supply does not necessarily constitute immediate House approval for the programs to which it applies in the Main Estimates.

Supplementary Estimates

Should the amounts voted under the Main Estimates prove insufficient, or should new funding or a reallocation of funds between Votes or programs be required during a fiscal year, the government may ask Parliament to approve additional expenditures set out in Supplementary Estimates. The government may introduce as many sets of Supplementary Estimates in a year as it deems necessary, although the practice has been to limit such requests to two or three.

The Supplementary Estimates are tabled as a document in the same form as Part II of the Main Estimates. However, instead of being expressed as summary Votes (i.e., where a Vote summarizes all the anticipated disbursements in a particular expenditure category), each Supplementary Estimate or Vote relates to a specific program or financial transaction. The information included in the Supplementary Estimates will become a Schedule in the subsequent Appropriation Act authorizing the prescribed withdrawals from the Consolidated Revenue Fund.

As with the Main Estimates, each set of Supplementary Estimates is presented normally by the President of the Treasury Board and is accompanied by a recommendation from the Governor General, which the Speaker reads aloud in the House.[206] Supplementary Estimates are referred to the relevant standing committees immediately after their tabling in the House.[207] The reference motion is moved by a Minister of the Crown during Routine Proceedings and is decided without debate.[208] The Supplementary Estimates must be reported back, or are deemed to have been

---

203. See, for example, *Notice Paper*, March 20, 1996, pp. IV-V; March 12, 1997, p. IV; March 17, 1998, pp. IV-V; March 16, 1999, p. V.

204. See, for example, *Debates*, March 20, 1975, pp. 4357-8; *Journals*, March 20, 1996, pp. 122-3; March 12, 1997, pp. 1262-3.

205. Standing Order 81(17).

206. See, for example, *Journals*, October 29, 1998, pp. 1211-2.

207. Standing Order 81(5).

208. See, for example, *Journals*, October 29, 1998, pp. 1212-4.

reported back, not later than three sitting days before the last allotted day, or the last sitting day, of the Supply period in which they were tabled.[209]

Final Supplementary Estimates

Where concurrence in final Supplementary Estimates cannot be obtained before March 31 of the fiscal year to which they relate, the Standing Orders provide for approval to be sought in the next Supply period, which is the first Supply period of the subsequent fiscal year. In such cases, three days will be added to the Supply period ending not later than June 23 to consider the motion that the House concur in those final Estimates for the previous fiscal year and to pass at all stages any bill based thereon.[210]

Dollar Items

Supplementary Estimates often include what are known as "one dollar items", which seek an alteration in the existing allocation of funds as authorized in the Main Estimates. The purpose of a dollar item is not to seek new or additional money, but rather to spend money already authorized for a different purpose. Since "estimates" are budgetary items, they must have a dollar value. However, because no new funds are requested, the "one dollar" is merely a symbolic amount. Dollar items may be used to transfer funds from one program to another;[211] to write-off debts;[212] to adjust loan guarantees;[213] to authorize grants;[214] or to amend previous appropriation acts.[215]

The inclusion of one dollar items in the Estimates also gave rise to the issue of using Estimates to "legislate" (i.e., Estimates going beyond simply appropriating funds and attempting to obtain new legislative authority which would otherwise require separate enabling legislation through the regular legislative process, outside the Supply procedure).[216]

---

209. Standing Order 81(5).

210. Standing Order 81(12).

211. See, for example, *Appropriation Act No. 4, 1996-97* (S.C. 1997, c. 7, pp. 4-5), Schedule (Supplementary Estimates (B)), Canadian Heritage, Votes 5b and 40b.

212. See, for example, *Appropriation Act No. 4, 1996-97* (S.C. 1997, c. 7, p. 11), Schedule (Supplementary Estimates (B)), Indian Affairs and Northern Development, Vote 36b.

213. See, for example, *Appropriation Act No. 3, 1996-97* (S.C. 1996, c. 29, p. 14), Schedule (Supplementary Estimates (A)), Transport, Vote 33a.

214. See, for example, *Appropriation Act No. 4, 1996-97* (S.C. 1997, c. 7, p. 8), Schedule (Supplementary Estimates (B)), Health, Vote 25b.

215. See ruling of Speaker Jerome, *Journals*, December 7, 1977, p. 185; rulings of Speaker Sauvé, *Debates*, March 25, 1981, p. 8601, and June 12, 1981, p. 10546. See also, for example, *Appropriation Act No. 3, 1996-97* (S.C. 1996, c. 29, p. 13), Schedule (Supplementary Estimates (A)), Public Works and Government Services, Vote 19a.

216. See, for example, *Debates*, March 31, 1952, pp. 966-73; March 27, 1961, pp. 3368-75; April 1, 1964, pp. 1678-95.

Prior to 1968, Supply procedures afforded ample opportunity for the House to debate individual items in the Estimates. Those of a legislative nature (virtually always "one dollar items") were regularly included in Appropriation Acts.[217] However, this practice was not accepted readily by the House and Members did question the regularity of these items.[218] The 1968 changes to the rules governing Supply, which provided for the abolition of the Committee of Supply and the reference of Estimates to standing committees for detailed study, had the effect of reducing significantly the time allocated for the House to consider the Supplementary Estimates (where most dollar items are found). Moreover, the Supplementary Estimates are often tabled fairly late in the Supply period allowing relatively little time for committee consideration. As a result, soon after the 1968 changes, the Speaker was called on increasingly to decide questions concerning the admissibility of dollar items.[219] The rulings by Speakers of the House have clarified what is, and what is not, procedurally acceptable in regard to dollar items.

Speakers have often indicated that Members should take the initiative in bringing to the attention of the Chair any procedural irregularities with regard to the Estimates.[220] They have also repeatedly asked that Members raise questions about the

---

217. In some cases, the wording of the dollar item would specify the statute it was amending or superseding. See, for example, *Appropriation Act No. 5, 1963*, Schedule B (Supplementary Estimates (A), 1963-64), Finance, Votes 58a, 59a and 64a, and Schedule E (Supplementary Estimates (D) 1963-64), Public Works, Vote 178d (S.C. 1963, c. 42, pp. 40-1 and 54); *Appropriation Act No.10, 1964*, Schedule B (Supplementary Estimates (A) 1964-65), Labour, Vote 7a and Schedule D (Supplementary Estimates (C) 1964-65), Finance, Vote L18c (S.C. 1964-65, c. 34, pp. 31 and 44); *Appropriation Act No. 2, 1965*, Schedule (Supplementary Estimates (D) 1964-65), External Affairs, Vote 33d and Transport, Vote 73d (S.C. 1964-65, c. 50, pp. 5 and 13).

218. Items were challenged by Members in opposition (see, for example, the debate on a "one dollar" item respecting the *Unemployment Insurance Act* (*Debates*, April 1, 1964, pp. 1678-95)). On April 2, 1965, three "one dollar" items having the effect of amending the *Public Service Superannuation Act* were challenged in the House and subsequently withdrawn by the government (see *Debates*, April 2, 1965, pp. 13125-32), even though similar items had been approved in previous Appropriation Acts (see, for example, *Appropriation Act No. 5, 1963*, Schedule B (Supplementary Estimates (A), 1963-64), Finance, Votes 58a and 64a (S.C. 1963, c. 42, pp. 37, 40-1). See also ruling of Speaker Lamoureux, *Journals*, March 10, 1971, pp. 395-7. In 1969, the Standing Committee on Miscellaneous Estimates expressed its concern over the extensive use of one dollar items for the purpose of statutory amendments (see the Fourth Report of the Committee, *Journals*, February 28, 1969, p. 756).

219. See rulings of Speaker Lamoureux, *Journals*, March 10, 1971, p. 396; Speaker Jerome, *Journals*, March 22, 1977, pp. 604-8, and December 7, 1977, p. 184; Speaker Sauvé, *Debates*, March 25, 1981, pp. 8600-1.

220. See, for example, ruling of Speaker Jerome, *Journals*, March 22, 1977, pp. 606-7.

procedural acceptability of Estimates as early as possible so that the Chair has time to give "intelligent" consideration to these questions.[221]

The Chair has maintained that Estimates with a direct and specific legislative intent (those clearly intended to amend existing legislation) should come to the House by way of an amending bill.[222] Speaker Jerome stated in a ruling: "… it is my view that the government receives from Parliament the authority to act through the passage of legislation and receives the money to finance such authorized action through the passage by Parliament of an appropriation act. A supply item in my opinion ought not, therefore, to be used to obtain authority which is the proper subject of legislation."[223] He also said in a further ruling: "… supply ought to be confined strictly to the process for which it was intended; that is to say, for the purpose of putting forward by the government the estimate of money it needs, and then in turn voting by the House of that money to the government […] legislation and legislated changes in substance are not intended to be part of supply, but rather ought to be part of the legislative process in the regular way which requires three readings, committee stage, and, in other words, ample opportunity for Members to participate in debate and amendment."[224]

Consideration of Estimates in Committee

When the Estimates are tabled in the House, they are referred to standing committees for consideration.[225] When a committee decides to consider Estimates, each budgetary item, or "Vote", is called, proposed and debated as a distinct motion. A Vote can be agreed to (the budget item is approved), reduced[226] (but, as the case may be, no lower than the amount already approved in interim supply) or negatived[227] (the budget item is not approved).[228] Calling a Vote is the mechanism by which the

---

221. Speaker Jerome's suggestion that such points of order be taken up on the next to last allotted day of a Supply period was supported by Speaker Sauvé. (See ruling of Speaker Jerome, *Journals*, March 22, 1977, pp. 607-8, and ruling of Speaker Sauvé, *Debates*, June 21, 1982, pp. 18646-7.) See also ruling of Speaker Parent, *Debates*, November 25, 1997, p. 2208.

222. See ruling of Speaker Lamoureux, *Journals*, December 10, 1973, p. 737. Even where legislative authority exists, the Speaker has suggested that where a matter involves not only money but also a question of principle, it was preferable that it be brought to the House in the form of a separate bill (see ruling of Speaker Jerome, *Journals*, June 22, 1976, p. 1368).

223. *Journals*, March 22, 1977, p. 607. See also rulings of Speaker Sauvé, *Debates*, March 25, 1981, p. 8601; June 12, 1981, p. 10546; June 21, 1982, p. 18646; March 21, 1983, p. 23968; ruling of Speaker Francis, *Debates*, March 21, 1984, p. 2308; ruling of Speaker Fraser, *Debates*, March 20, 1991, pp. 18731-2; and ruling of Speaker Parent, *Debates*, November 25, 1997, p. 2208.

224. *Journals*, December 7, 1977, p. 184.

225. Standing Order 81(4) and (5).

226. See, for example, *Journals*, May 31, 1973, p. 359. An Estimate should not be reduced by a trifling amount (*Beauchesne*, 5th ed., cit. 497(3), p. 171).

227. See, for example, *Journals*, March 21, 1973, p. 200, and December 7, 1979, p. 324.

228. See ruling of Speaker Lamoureux, *Journals*, June 18, 1973, p. 420.

committee opens debate on the program expenditures to which that Vote pertains. Committees considering Estimates may invite witnesses to appear; these typically include the Minister, departmental or agency officials, and interested individuals or groups.

The discussion on Vote 1 in the Main Estimates (generally departmental administration or operations) is traditionally wide-ranging. Typically, questions on departmental policy are directed to the responsible Minister; questions of a more technical or administrative nature may be referred through the Minister to departmental officials. Chairs have generally exercised considerable latitude in the nature of the questioning permitted on Estimates.[229]

A committee may not increase the amount of a Vote, change the destination of a grant or change the destination or purpose of a subsidy, as this would exceed the terms of the royal recommendation and infringe on the financial initiative of the Crown.[230] A committee may move to reduce a Vote by an amount equal to that set aside in the Estimates for a program or activity to which the committee is opposed.[231] Members cannot propose a motion to reduce a Vote by its full amount; the procedure is simply to vote against the question, "Shall the Vote carry?"

Statutory expenditures are provided for on an ongoing basis by way of legislation other than the Appropriation Act and are identified in the Main Estimates for information purposes only.[232] Motions or recommendations respecting statutory expenditures listed in the Main Estimates are not allowed, although questions requesting information are acceptable. Statutory items may be modified only by way of amending legislation.

Report to the House

A committee is under no obligation to report the Estimates back to the House; however, in the case of Main Estimates, committees that do not report are deemed to have done so on May 31 and, in the case of Supplementary Estimates, they are deemed to have done so on the third sitting day before the last allotted day or the last sitting day in the Supply period.[233] Where a committee chooses to report on the estimates, the Chair, or any member of the committee acting on behalf of the Chair, rises during "Routine Proceedings", when the Speaker calls "Presenting Reports from Committees", for the purpose of presenting the report.

---

229. See also Chapter 20, "Committees".

230. See ruling of Speaker Lamoureux, *Journals*, March 24, 1970, p. 637. See also *Bourinot*, 4ᵗʰ ed., p. 427.

231. See, for example, *Journals*, May 31, 1973, p. 359.

232. See "Preface", *1998-99 Estimates: Parts I and II, The Government Expenditure Plan and Main Estimates*, pp. 1-2.

233. Standing Order 81(4) and (5).

The rules provide for one exception to the May 31 reporting deadline for Main Estimates. The Leader of the Opposition may give, not later than the third sitting day prior to May 31, notice of a motion to extend the committee consideration of the Main Estimates of a named department or agency.[234] The motion is deemed adopted when called under "Motions" during Routine Proceedings on the last sitting day prior to May 31.[235] Adoption of the motion allows the committee to continue its consideration of Main Estimates for that department or agency and to delay the presentation of its report for up to 10 sitting days, but not later than the ordinary hour of daily adjournment on the sitting day immediately preceding the final allotted day in the Supply period.[236] If the committee has not reported by this time, it is deemed to have done so. Where the designated committee chooses to report, the Chair, or any member of the committee acting on behalf of the Chair, may rise on a point of order, at any time prior to the reporting deadline, and the House will revert immediately to "Presenting Reports from Committees" for the purpose of receiving the report.[237]

The report of a committee on Estimates ought to correspond, both in its form and as to its substance, with the authority with which the committee is invested.[238] As it is the Estimates which have been referred to the committee by the House, it is the Estimates (as agreed to, reduced or negatived) which should be reported back to the House. In making other substantive recommendations, the committee is clearly going beyond the scope of its order of reference, which was to deal with the Estimates.[239] The Speaker has expressed strong reservations regarding the inclusion of substantive recommendations in committee reports on Estimates.[240] A standing committee wishing to make substantive recommendations respecting the Estimates which it has considered may do so under its permanent authority to study and report on any matter relating to the mandate, management and operation of the departments or agencies it oversees.[241] A motion to concur in a committee report on Estimates can only be considered on an allotted day as part of the Business of Supply.[242]

---

234. Standing Order 81(4)(*a*). See, for example, *Notice Paper*, May 26, 1998, p. III. In 1999, the Leader of the Opposition chose not to exercise his power to give notice of a motion to extend the consideration of Main Estimates by a committee (see point of order raised by Peter MacKay (Pictou–Antigonish–Guysborough), *Debates*, May 27, 1999, pp. 15351-2, and ruling of Acting Speaker, *Debates*, May 28, 1999, pp. 15429-30).

235. See, for example, *Journals*, May 28, 1998, p. 902.

236. Standing Order 81(4)(*b*).

237. Standing Order 81(4)(*c*).

238. See ruling of Speaker Lamoureux, *Journals*, June 18, 1973, p. 420.

239. See ruling of Speaker Jerome, *Debates*, December 10, 1979, p. 2189.

240. See ruling of Speaker Jerome, *Debates*, December 10, 1979, p. 2189.

241. Standing Order 108(2).

242. Standing Order 81(9). See rulings of Speaker Lamoureux, *Journals*, June 18, 1973, p. 420, and December 6, 1973, p. 725; ruling of Speaker Jerome, *Debates*, December 10, 1979, p. 2189. For examples of a committee report on Estimates being the subject matter of an opposition motion on an allotted day, see *Journals*, March 3, 1969, p. 762; *Debates*, June 19, 1969, p. 10410.

A committee may also report on the expenditure plans and priorities in future fiscal years of the departments and agencies whose Main Estimates are before the committee for consideration.[243] Such reports must be presented to the House not later than the last sitting day in June, as provided for in the parliamentary calendar, and any concurrence motion can only be considered by the House on an allotted day.[244]

Concurrence in Estimates

The Estimates, as reported or deemed reported by the standing committees, must be concurred in by the House in order for the government to introduce the appropriation bill authorizing the necessary withdrawals from the Consolidated Revenue Fund. Any motions to concur in Estimates are proposed on the final allotted day of a Supply period, once the proceedings related to an opposition motion are completed. In a normal Supply cycle, concurrence motions would occur as follows:[245]

- On the last allotted day in the Supply period ending December 10, a motion or motions to concur in Supplementary Estimates would be considered, if any were tabled by the government during the period;

- On the last allotted day in the Supply period ending March 26, a motion or motions to concur in Supplementary Estimates would be considered first, if any were tabled by the government during the period, followed by a motion to concur in Interim Supply for the next fiscal year;

- On the last allotted day in the Supply period ending June 23, a motion or motions to concur in the Main Estimates would be considered first, followed by a motion or motions to concur in Final Supplementary Estimates relating to the preceding fiscal year and a motion or motions to concur in Supplementary Estimates for the current fiscal year, if any were tabled by the government during the period.

A motion to concur in the Main or Supplementary Estimates is a motion to concur in the Estimates as reported or deemed reported by the standing committees. The government, usually through the President of the Treasury Board, will give 48 hours' written notice of a motion or motions to concur in the Estimates.[246] Should a committee have reduced or negatived a Vote or Votes in those Estimates, the government

---

243. Standing Order 81(7).
244. Standing Order 81(8).
245. Standing Order 81(17) and (18).
246. Standing Order 81(14)(*a*). See, for example, *Notice Paper*, November 27, 1998, p. III.

may move that they be restored or reinstated.[247] Forty-eight hours' written notice is also required for any motions to restore or reinstate Estimates which have been reduced or negatived in committee.[248]

Furthermore, any Member may give notice to oppose any item in the Estimates before the House: such items are then referred to as "opposed items" in the Estimates. The notice period for opposed items is 24 hours in the Supply periods ending December 10 and March 26, and 48 hours in the Supply period ending June 23.[249] Members give notice of opposed items to express opposition to the total amount of a Vote[250] or to a specified portion of that amount.[251] A notice to oppose an item in the Estimates is not a motion.[252] Because the government may propose in one motion the concurrence in all the Votes in the Estimates,[253] the notice to oppose an item is rather a mechanism by which Members force the government to propose a separate motion for the concurrence in each Vote that is the subject of total or partial opposition.[254] The wording of the general concurrence motion is then changed to exclude those Votes.[255] On one occasion, Members who had filed notices of opposed items in the Estimates informed the Clerk of the House that they did not wish to proceed with their notices. Thus, the separate motions were not put to the House, and the Votes that had been opposed were reintegrated in the general concurrence motion.[256]

---

247. For example, the Standing Committee on Justice and Legal Affairs reduced Vote 1 under SOLICITOR GENERAL in Main Estimates 1973-74 (*Journals*, May 31, 1973, pp. 358-9). Vote 1 was later restored by the House (*Journals*, June 26, 1973, pp. 438-9), and the full amount was included in the Schedule of the *Appropriation Act No. 4, 1973* (*Journals*, June 28, 1973, p. 447; S.C. 1973-74, c. 16, Schedule, p. 44). On one occasion, the government chose not to move to reinstate Vote 16b under FINANCE in Supplementary Estimates (B) 1972-73, that had been negatived by the Standing Committee on Miscellaneous Estimates (see *Journals*, March 21, 1973, pp. 199-200, and March 26, 1973, p. 214; *Appropriation Act No. 2, 1973*, S.C. 1973-74, c. 4, Schedule, p. 4).

248. Standing Order 81(14)(*a*). See, for example, *Notice Paper*, December 14, 1979, pp. IX-X.

249. Standing Order 81(14)(*a*).

250. See, for example, Notice of opposition to the total amount of Vote 1 under JUSTICE, $193,805,000 (*Notice Paper*, June 9, 1998, p. III).

251. See, for example, Notice of opposition to a sum of $3,765,000 in Vote 1 under INDIAN AFFAIRS AND NORTHERN DEVELOPMENT in the amount of $63, 272,000 (*Notice Paper*, June 9, 1998, p. VIII).

252. See rulings of Speaker Lamoureux, *Journals*, June 22, 1972, pp. 401-2; February 7, 1973, p. 102; December 10, 1973, pp. 736-7.

253. Standing Order 81(20).

254. See ruling of Speaker Jerome, *Journals*, March 24, 1976, pp. 1144-5. A Vote in Supplementary Estimates, for which a notice of opposition had been given, was defeated in the House (see *Debates*, March 26, 1973, pp. 2620-7).

255. See, for example, *Notice Paper*, September 18, 1996, p. VI, and *Journals*, September 18, 1996, pp. 639-40.

256. See *Notice Paper*, June 8, 1999, pp. VII-LIV; *Debates*, June 8, 1999, pp. 16069, 16079-81.

On the last allotted day of each Supply period, once the proceedings on the opposition motion are completed, motions to restore or reinstate Votes in the Estimates are considered first, followed by motions to concur in each of the Votes for which a notice of opposition has been given, and the motion to concur in altogether the remaining unopposed Votes[257] before proceeding to the appropriation bill based on those Estimates. For that purpose, the House may sit beyond the normal hour of adjournment for that day.[258]

In principle, all the motions are debatable and amendable.[259] However, in practice, on the last allotted day in each of the Supply periods ending December 10 and March 26, the debate on the opposition motion, which has precedence over all government motions to dispose of the Business of Supply, continues throughout the day and is interrupted by the Speaker at 15 minutes before the time provided for Government Orders expires. At that time, all the motions, starting with the opposition motion, are decided in sequence without further debate or amendment.[260]

On the last allotted day in the Supply period ending June 23, unless previously disposed of, at 6:30 p.m., the Speaker interrupts the proceedings on the opposition motion. If the opposition motion is not a motion that must come to a vote, proceedings on the motion expire at the conclusion of the debate and the House proceeds to consider a motion or motions relating to the Main Estimates.[261] If the opposition motion is a motion that must come to a vote, the Speaker must put forthwith and without further debate or amendment, every question necessary to dispose of the proceedings and any recorded division requested is deferred to the end of the consideration of a motion or motions relating to the Main Estimates.[262] At 10:00 p.m., the Speaker must interrupt any proceedings then before the House, proceed first to the taking of any deferred division or divisions necessary to dispose of the opposition motion,[263] as the case may be, and subsequently put forthwith, without further debate or amendment, every question necessary to dispose of the motion or motions relating to the Main Estimates. Immediately thereafter, the Speaker must put successively and without debate every question necessary to dispose of any business relating to the final Estimates for the preceding fiscal year or for any Supplementary Estimates, the restoration or reinstatement of any Vote in the final or Supplementary Estimates, or any opposed item in the final or Supplementary Estimates.

---

257. See, for example, *Journals*, June 8, 1994, p. 551, and September 18, 1996, pp. 639-40.

258. Standing Order 81(17) and (18)(*d*).

259. See, for example, *Journals*, June 8, 1994, pp. 546-7.

260. Standing Order 81(17). See also ruling of Speaker Lamoureux, *Journals*, December 10, 1973, p. 736.

261. Standing Order 81(18)(*a*).

262. Standing Order 81(18)(*b*). See, for example, *Journals*, June 8, 1999, pp. 2064-6.

263. See, for example, *Journals*, June 8, 1999, pp. 2066, 2069-71.

The Supply Bill or Appropriation Act

Concurrence in the Estimates or in Interim Supply is an order of the House to bring in an appropriation bill or bills giving effect to the spending authority (amounts and their destinations) that the House has approved.[264] Once adopted, the legislation will authorize the government to withdraw from the Consolidated Revenue Fund amounts up to, but not exceeding, the amounts set out in the Estimates for the purposes specified in the Votes.

Supply bills must be based on the Estimates or Interim Supply as concurred in by the House.[265] They bear the standard title: *An Act for granting to Her Majesty certain sums of money for the public service of Canada for the financial year ending March 31 (year).*[266] They begin with a preamble which cites both the message from the Governor General recommending the Estimates to the House, and the purpose of the Estimates, which is *"to defray certain expenses of the public service of Canada, not otherwise provided for"* for a specified fiscal year. The Chair has cautioned that an Appropriation Act gives authority only for a single year and is therefore not appropriate for expenditure which is meant to continue for a longer period, or indefinitely.[267] On one occasion, Speaker Parent expressed strong reservations about the reference to two fiscal years in the long title of a Supply bill.[268] He qualified the reference as "not needed" and "misleading". Although a separate statute may grant a government agency legislative authority to carry the unexpended balance of money appropriated for a fiscal year over to the end of the following year,[269] the appropriation itself is and must be for one year only and not be referred to as a multi-year appropriation.

The destinations and the amounts attributable to each spending item, or Vote, are set out in the schedules attached to each bill. These provide the governing conditions

---

264. Standing Order 81(21).

265. Standing Order 81(21).

266. See, for example, Bill C-45, *An Act for granting to Her Majesty certain sums of money for the public service of Canada for the financial year ending March 31, 1999* (*Journals*, June 9, 1998, pp. 984-5).

267. See ruling of Speaker Lamoureux, *Journals*, December 10, 1973, p. 737; ruling of Speaker Fraser, *Debates*, March 20, 1991, p. 18732; ruling of Speaker Parent, *Debates*, June 8, 1999, p. 16065. See also *Bourinot*, 4th ed., p. 417; *Debates*, April 30, 1879, p. 1668; *Journals*, April 30, 1879, p. 335; May 6, 1879, p. 367.

268. See the point of order raised by John Williams (St. Albert) on Bill C-86 (*An Act for granting to Her Majesty certain sums of money for the public service of Canada for the financial years ending March 31, 2000 and March 31, 2001*) and the ruling of Speaker Parent (*Debates*, June 8, 1999, pp. 16053, 16065-6).

269. See *Debates*, June 8, 1999, p. 16082.

under which expenditures may be made. The schedules are organized alphabetically, by department, in both the English and French versions of the bill.[270]

Supply bills are considered on the last allotted day in each Supply period, at the end of the day, after the Speaker has interrupted the proceedings on the opposition motion or the Main Estimates, as the case may be, in order for the House to go through all the remaining steps to complete the Business of Supply for the period. At that time, the House must proceed through all the motions related to the Estimates, the Interim Supply and the Supply bills without further debate or amendments.[271] As all bills are printed and made available once they have received first reading, Members would not normally be made aware of the content of the Supply bills until late in the day, at a time when the proceedings are dealt with expeditiously in the House. To compensate for this lack of time, the practice established in recent years is therefore to allow for an early distribution of the draft copy of the bills to Members at the beginning of the Supply proceedings on that day. The House invariably gives its consent to that special arrangement.[272]

Like all public bills, Supply bills are "read" twice, considered in committee, and read a third time before going to the Senate.[273] Because concurrence in the Estimates or in Interim Supply is an order of the House to bring in the appropriation bill, first reading proceeds forthwith, without the formality of introduction, and a motion is proposed that it be read a second time and referred to a Committee of the Whole.[274]

Although, theoretically, a Supply bill is debatable, and therefore amendable, at all stages after first reading, it generally passes without debate or amendment on the last allotted day.[275] However, if time for debate were to remain on that day, and

---

270. From 1867 to 1939, the Estimates were published separately in English and French, with neither version ordered alphabetically. From 1939 to 1970, the Estimates continued to be published separately but each version listed the departments alphabetically, according to their English titles. In 1970, the first bilingual edition of the Estimates was published, in tumble format and ordered alphabetically according to their title in the language in which they were printed. Only the schedules in the Supply bills continued to list the departments alphabetically in the English text, with the French translation of those schedules appearing on the opposite pages. Following complaints by Members (see, for example, *Debates,* February 16, 1973, pp. 1385-6; June 26, 1973, p. 5098; December 10, 1973, p. 8609; December 6, 1989, pp. 6581-2), departments began to be listed alphabetically in the schedules, in each language. The first such bill was *Appropriation Act No. 2, 1990-91*, S.C. 1990, c. 33 (see remarks by Marcel Prud'homme (Saint-Denis), *Debates*, June 6, 1990, pp. 12420-1).

271. Standing Order 81(17) and (18).

272. See, for example, *Debates*, June 9, 1998, p. 7795.

273. See also Chapter 16, "The Legislative Process".

274. Standing Orders 81(21) and 73(4). See also Chapter 19, "Committees of the Whole House".

275. On occasion, through special orders, the House has agreed to debate a Supply bill at the second reading stage (see, for example, *Journals*, March 21, 1977, p. 598; March 24, 1977, p. 621; June 22, 1989, p. 431; June 27, 1989, p. 467) and at the Committee of the Whole stage (see, for example, *Debates*, October 23, 1974, p. 639; *Journals*, October 23, 1974, p. 82; October 24, 1974, p. 83; October 25, 1974, p. 86).

debate were to occur at the second and third reading stages of the bill, speeches would be limited to 20 minutes, followed by a period not exceeding 10 minutes for questions and comments.[276] In a Committee of the Whole, the bill is considered clause by clause and then reported back to the House.[277] It is at the Committee of the Whole stage that a Member of the opposition usually seeks assurance from the President of the Treasury Board that the Supply bill is in its usual form.[278] Bills reported from a Committee of the Whole are concurred in without debate or amendment.[279] Once the bill has been read the third time, it is forwarded to the Senate, where it must be given a further three readings before receiving Royal Assent and becoming law.

Normally, bills which have passed in both Houses of Parliament are held by the Clerk of the Parliaments (the Clerk of the Senate) until the Governor General (or a deputy) grants them Royal Assent. However, because the granting of Supply is a prerogative of the House of Commons, Supply bills are always returned to the House and taken by its Speaker to the Senate Chamber to receive Royal Assent. The Speaker, as spokesperson for the House, assembles with Members from the House of Commons, at the bar of the Senate Chamber. The Speaker addresses the Crown's representative, saying:

> *May it please Your Excellency (Honour[280]): The Commons of Canada have voted Supplies required to enable the Government to defray certain expenses of the public service. In the name of the Commons, I present to Your Excellency (Honour) the following Bill: (title), To which Bill I humbly request Your Excellency's (Honour's) Assent.*

The Speaker presents the bill to the Clerk of the Senate who reads out the title of the bill, to which the Governor General (or a deputy) nods consent. The Royal Assent is then pronounced by the Clerk of the Senate in the following words:

> *In Her Majesty's name, (the Honourable the Deputy to) His/Her Excellency the Governor General thanks Her Loyal Subjects, accepts their benevolence, and assents to this Bill.*

---

276. Standing Order 81(22).

277. See also Chapter 19, "Committees of the Whole House".

278. See *Debates,* June 9, 1998, p. 7908; June 8, 1999, p. 16082.

279. Standing Order 76.1(12).

280. The Deputy to the Governor General is referred to as "Your Honour".

The *Journals* of the House of Commons carries the text of the Speaker's address, together with the response from the Crown's representative in granting Assent, and the title of the bill.[281]

DEVIATIONS FROM SUPPLY CYCLE

From time to time, circumstances may require a deviation from the normal Supply process and cycle. For example, because of an unscheduled adjournment or a prorogation or dissolution of Parliament, the Main Estimates might not be tabled and referred to standing committees before the March 1 deadline, or the Interim Supply or the Main Estimates might not be concurred in by the June 23 deadline. In those cases, the Standing Order provisions relating to the Business of Supply no longer apply (such as those respecting the timetable for the tabling of Estimates, their reference to standing committees and their return to the House, the concurrence motions and the appropriation bills).

Such situations may be dealt with by temporarily suspending the relevant Standing Orders. There may be an arrangement worked out between the government and the opposition parties to finalize Supply as expeditiously as possible. Typically, this involves adopting a special order[282] which, depending on the situation, might address the following matters: length of Supply period;[283] number of allotted days in the period;[284] number of votable opposition motions;[285] committee referral and reporting date for Main or Supplementary Estimates;[286] date of concurrence in Estimates;[287] and debating time allotted to the appropriation bill.[288]

Where the government feels that there is a matter of urgency and it cannot wait until the end of a Supply period, it may use its own time to consider the Estimates. The Standing Orders specifically provide a mechanism in the event of an emergency where a motion to concur in the Estimates and the subsequent appropriation bill may

---

281. See, for example, *Journals*, December 10, 1998, p. 1440. On May 17, 1995, the House concurred in the Seventy-Seventh Report of the Standing Committee on Procedure and House Affairs requiring that the *Journals* reproduce the form of words used by the Speaker and the Clerk of the Senate (see the Seventy-Seventh Report presented to the House on May 10, 1995 (*Journals*, p. 1456) and concurred in on May 17, 1995 (*Journals*, p. 1492)).

282. See, for example, *Journals*, April 29, 1980, pp. 95-6; April 4, 1989, pp. 20-1; May 23, 1991, p. 59; March 4, 1996, pp. 34-5, 39-41; September 23, 1997, p. 14.

283. See, for example, *Journals*, April 4, 1989, p. 20.

284. See, for example, *Journals*, September 23, 1997, p. 14.

285. See, for example, *Journals*, September 23, 1997, p. 14.

286. See, for example, *Journals*, April 4, 1989, pp. 20-1; May 23, 1991, p. 59; March 4, 1996, pp. 34-5; September 23, 1997, p. 14.

287. See, for example, *Journals*, April 4, 1989, p. 21; September 23, 1997, p. 14.

288. See, for example, *Journals*, June 22, 1989, p. 431.

be taken under "Government Orders" and not on days allotted for Supply.[289] The concurrence motion and the bill are then treated like any other item of government business and are therefore debatable. There is no automatic time limit on the debate and the days used for that purpose are not considered as allotted days and may not be deducted from the number of days allocated to the Business of Supply.[290] Apart from these two exceptions, the rules respecting the consideration of Supply under Government Orders are the same as those governing proceedings on any allotted day.[291]

Borrowing Authority

Borrowing powers are needed by the government to cover any shortfall between its revenues and its expenditures. The government borrows principally by issuing treasury bills, marketable bonds and Canada Savings Bonds, on domestic and foreign markets. The *Financial Administration Act* states: "No money shall be borrowed or security issued by or on behalf of Her Majesty without the authority of Parliament",[292] and the authority to borrow sufficient new money to cover estimated financial requirements, together with a margin for contingencies, is normally sought and granted early on in the financial cycle for each new fiscal year.[293] These requests refer to new authority to borrow, since the *Financial Administration Act* already authorizes borrowing for the purpose of refinancing maturing debt.[294] Unused borrowing authority lapses at the end of a fiscal year and must be replaced by new authority.

The government borrows when there is a shortfall between its expenditures, as authorized by Parliament in the Main and Supplementary Estimates and in Interim Supply, and its revenues, whose projected levels are also approved by Parliament. Prior to 1975, it was the custom to include requests for borrowing authority in one of the first appropriation or Supply bills of a new fiscal year. Where circumstances necessitated increasing the level of borrowing authority, the increases were sought by way of subsequent appropriation bills, such as appropriation bills enacting Supplementary Estimates or Interim Supply. The primary justification for including new borrowing authority in an appropriation act was the contention that borrowing powers to cover any shortfall between revenues and expenditures should be authorized

---

289. Standing Order 82.

290. See ruling of Speaker Lamoureux, *Journals,* February 7, 1973, pp. 102-3. See also *Debates*, February 7, 1973, pp. 1052-61.

291. See ruling of Speaker Lamoureux, *Journals*, February 7, 1973, p. 103.

292. R.S.C. 1985, c. F-11, s. 43.

293. See *Debates*, December 16, 1975, pp. 10054-5.

294. R.S.C. 1985, c. F-11, s. 46. See also *Debates*, March 24, 1977, p. 4298.

relatively automatically, given that both the shortfall and the borrowing requirements were a consequence of actions already approved by Parliament.

The 1968 changes to Supply procedures made the inclusion of borrowing authority in appropriation bills problematic.[295] The revised process usually offered no opportunity for Members to debate the borrowing provisions; the borrowing clause was not part of the Estimates, which were discussed in standing committees, and the Supply bills containing the borrowing clauses were generally passed without debate. In 1975, the Speaker ordered a borrowing clause struck from a Supply bill related to Supplementary Estimates on the grounds that, under the rules, its inclusion in a Supply bill based on Supplementary Estimates virtually precluded discussion of the borrowing provisions.[296] Later, in 1981, the Speaker found no objection to including a request for borrowing authority in a tax bill based on a Ways and Means motion, provided that the government also gave the regular 48 hours' notice for the introduction of a bill in order to cover the borrowing provisions.[297]

Borrowing authority is now sought by way of a bill which follows the normal legislative process, with the exception that debate at second reading is limited to a maximum of two sitting days.[298] The recent practice has been for the government to introduce borrowing authority legislation, if required, either when the Budget is presented or shortly thereafter.[299] In theory, if additional borrowing requirements are needed to deal with unforeseen circumstances, then a Supplementary Borrowing Authority Bill would be introduced.

---

295. See *Debates*, December 10, 1974, pp. 2138-9; December 11, 1974, p. 2143; March 20, 1975, pp. 4357-62; March 21, 1975, pp. 4364-5.

296. See ruling of Speaker Jerome, *Journals*, December 9, 1975, p. 924. See also *Debates*, December 9, 1975, pp. 9880-3. In 1977, the House agreed to a debate at second reading of a Supply bill, based on Interim Supply, which contained a borrowing clause. (See *Debates*, March 24, 1977, p. 4298; *Journals*, March 21, 1977, p. 598; March 22, 1977, pp. 610-1; March 24, 1977, p. 621.)

297. See ruling of Speaker Sauvé, *Debates*, January 19, 1981, p. 6319. See also ruling of Speaker Sauvé, *Debates*, February 16, 1982, p. 15053.

298. Standing Order 73(5). See, for example, *Journals*, February 27, 1995, p. 1174; March 2, 1995, p. 1195; March 3, 1995, pp. 1199 and 1202. For more information, see Chapter 16, "The Legislative Process".

299. In 1985, the Minister of Finance tabled a paper which set out recommendations aimed at improving the borrowing process based on the basic principle that the government should not seek borrowing authority for a fiscal year without first providing Parliament with all relevant details relating to the financial requirements. (See *Journals*, May 23, 1985, pp. 648-9. See also *The Canadian Budgetary Process—Proposals for Improvement*, pp. 9-12.)

Governor General's Special Warrants

In a very special circumstance, the *Financial Administration Act* allows the Governor in Council to ask the Governor General to issue a Special Warrant[300] permitting the government to make charges not otherwise authorized by Parliament on the Consolidated Revenue Fund, provided that the following conditions are met:[301]

- Parliament is dissolved;

- A Minister has reported that an expenditure is *urgently required for the public good*; and

- The President of the Treasury Board has reported that there is no appropriation for the payment.

This provision of the Act makes it possible for the government to continue its work during a dissolution. Special Warrants may be used only from the date of dissolution until 60 days following the date fixed for the return of the writs after a general election. Furthermore, no Special Warrants may be issued during that period if Parliament stands prorogued.[302]

The *Financial Administration Act* requires that every Special Warrant be published in the *Canada Gazette* within 30 days of its issue. Notification of the amount

---

300. It is important to differentiate between Governor General's Warrants and the Governor General's Special Warrants. Every time an Appropriation Act receives Royal Assent, the Governor General must sign a Warrant before the government can make the authorized withdrawal from the Consolidated Revenue Fund; these are referred to as Governor General's Warrants. (See ruling of Speaker Fraser, *Debates*, May 2, 1989, p. 1177.) The 1878 *Consolidated Revenue and Audit Act* first authorized the use of Governor General's Special Warrants. The original intent was to allow payment for urgent or unexpected matters when the House was not sitting. In the early years following Confederation, when Parliament sat for only a few weeks or months of the year, it was difficult to convene quickly and the need for such a device was obvious. For most of their history, Special Warrants have been used solely for authorizing emergency expenditures, usually while Parliament was dissolved to allow for a general election. However, in 1988, the House of Commons reconvened in December following a general election and subsequently adjourned. The House did not consider the Business of Supply during the short time it sat. Parliament was then prorogued and a new session began on April 3, 1989, a new fiscal year. During the period of adjournment, and subsequent prorogation, the government resorted to the use of Special Warrants on three occasions. Although the Speaker concluded that the government had met all the requirements—the warrants were tabled in the House within the first 15 days following the commencement of the next session, and retroactively included in the next Appropriation Act—there remained concerns about the legitimacy and propriety of this practice. (See *Debates*, April 6, 1989, pp. 175-84. See also ruling of Speaker Fraser, *Debates*, May 2, 1989, pp. 1175-9.) In 1997, a private Member's bill, sponsored by Peter Milliken (Kingston and the Islands), was enacted. It amended the *Financial Administration Act* and limited the government's use of Special Warrants solely to the period of dissolution (*An Act to amend the Financial Administration Act (session of Parliament)*, S.C. 1997, c. 5).

301. *Financial Administration Act*, R.S.C. 1985, c. F-11, s. 30, as amended, S.C. 1997, c. 5.

302. *Financial Administration Act*, R.S.C. 1985, c. F-11, s. 30(1.1), as amended, S.C. 1997, c. 5, s. 1. See also Chapter 8, "The Parliamentary Cycle".

authorized under such a Warrant must also be tabled in the House within 15 days of the commencement of the next Session of Parliament[303] and authorization must be included retroactively in the first Appropriation Act passed in that Session.

The Business of Ways and Means

The business of "Ways and Means" is the process by which the government sets out its economic policy through the presentation of a Budget and obtains parliamentary approval to raise the necessary revenues through taxation. The most important revenue-raising statutes (i.e., those which replenish the Consolidated Revenue Fund) are the *Income Tax Act,* the *Excise Tax Act,* the *Excise Act* and the *Customs Tariff.*

A principle fundamental to the Ways and Means process is the requirement that taxation originate in the House of Commons. The *Constitution Act, 1867,* provides that "Bills for appropriating any Part of the Public Revenue, or for imposing any Tax or Impost, shall originate in the House of Commons",[304] a requirement echoed in the Standing Orders of the House.[305]

There are two types of Ways and Means proceedings:

- the debate on a motion to approve in general the budgetary policy of the government (the Budget presentation followed by the four-day ensuing debate); and

- the consideration of legislation (bills based on Ways and Means motions already approved by the House) which imposes a tax or other charge on the taxpayer.

A Ways and Means motion proposes that a particular financial measure be considered by the House. For a Budget, the motion seeks to approve the budgetary policy of the government; for legislation, the motion sets out the terms and conditions of the proposed measures, most notably the rates and incidence of taxation. While a Budget is normally followed by the introduction of Ways and Means bills, such bills do not have to be preceded by a Budget presentation. Generally, taxation legislation can be introduced at any time during a session; the only prerequisite being prior concurrence in a Ways and Means motion.

The Crown, on the advice of its responsible Ministers, initiates all requests to impose or increase a tax on the public and the House either grants or withholds its consent.[306] A Ways and Means motion may therefore only be moved by a Minister of

---

303. See, for example, *Journals*, April 12, 1989, pp. 88-9, and *Appropriation Act No. 1, 1989-90*, S.C. 1989, c. 1, s. 3.

304. R.S.C. 1985, Appendix II, No. 5, s. 53.

305. Standing Order 80(1): "All aids and supplies granted to the Sovereign by the Parliament of Canada are the sole gift of the House of Commons, and all bills for granting such aids and supplies ought to begin with the House, as it is the undoubted right of the House to direct, limit, and appoint in all such bills, the ends, purposes, considerations, conditions, limitations and qualifications of such grants, which are not alterable by the Senate."

306. *May,* 22nd ed., p. 732.

the Crown. Once adopted, a Ways and Means motion forestalls the passage of any amendment that would infringe on the financial initiative of the Crown. [307]

WAYS AND MEANS PROCEEDINGS (1867-1968)

Initially, the business of Ways and Means involved the consideration and authorization of measures to raise revenue and measures to appropriate, or set aside, from the Consolidated Revenue Fund, the funds approved in the Estimates by the Committee of Supply.[308] Ways and Means procedures remained essentially unchanged for the first hundred years following Confederation. Measures were proposed in the form of resolutions, each of which had to be debated and adopted formally in the Committee of Ways and Means, then reported to the House. Once reported, the resolutions were read a first and second time and agreed to, before being embodied in one or more bills which then passed through the same legislative stages as other bills.[309]

Over the years, the major business of Ways and Means became the consideration and adoption of resolutions emanating from the Budget speech. However, the financial statement by the Minister of Finance, and opposition responses, could hardly be termed a debate. On a designated day, the Minister of Finance would rise in the Chamber and address the House on the "financial condition of the Dominion". Once the opposition had been given an opportunity to reply, the House would go into the Committee of Ways and Means and consider any resolutions respecting taxation or tariffs which the Minister had proposed in the Budget. At first, consideration of the Budget speech and consequential Ways and Means resolutions accounted for only a small proportion of the work of the Committee; the bulk of its time was occupied with appropriating the funds voted under Supply. Gradually, however, the financial statement evolved into a major political event. Debate on the Budget lengthened as the opposition used it both to challenge the government's financial policy and, through the use of amendments, to draw attention to specific government actions and programs.

For many years after Confederation, the Minister of Finance followed no established procedure when presenting the Budget. Sometimes, the presentation was made on the motion for the House to resolve itself into the Committee of Supply[310] and, on other occasions, while the House was sitting as the Committee of Ways and

---

307. *May*, 22ⁿᵈ ed., p. 776. The Royal Recommendation has the same limiting effect with respect to amendments relating to spending. (See section above on "The Royal Recommendation".)

308. The Committee of Supply and the Committee of Ways and Means were Committees of the Whole House. The rules held that all financial measures—to tax as well as to spend—should be given the fullest possible consideration, both in committee and in the House (*Rules, Orders and Forms of Proceeding of the House of Commons of Canada (1868)*, Rule 88).

309. *Bourinot*, 1ˢᵗ ed., p. 495.

310. This occurred in 1867, 1868, 1875, 1878, 1889, 1892, 1896 and 1911.

Means.[311] From 1912 to 1968, the Budget statement was presented on the motion for the House to resolve itself into the Committee of Ways and Means. As with Supply, the motion for the Speaker to leave the Chair to go into the Committee of Ways and Means was debatable, amendable and not subject to time limitations. This meant that Budget proposals were debated initially on the motion to resolve into the Committee of Ways and Means, debated in the form of resolutions in the Committee, debated when the resolutions were reported to and read in the House, and debated again as bills passed through the normal legislative process. This practice was not modified until 1913, at which time the House resolved that, when the order was read to consider Ways and Means on a Thursday or a Friday, the motion for the Speaker to leave the Chair would be decided without debate or amendment.

Following changes to the Standing Orders in 1955,[312] there was no longer any debate on the motion for the Speaker to leave the Chair for the House to go into the Committee of Ways and Means, except on occasions when a Budget was to be presented. In such cases, the motion, together with any amendments, could be debated for a total of eight sitting days. Any sub-amendment would be disposed of on the fifth day of debate; any amendment on the seventh.[313] In the early 1960s, the House further limited the Budget debate to six days,[314] with the sub-amendment and amendment disposed of on the second and fourth day, respectively. Speeches, with the exception of those of the Minister of Finance, the Prime Minister, the Leader of the Opposition and the Member speaking first on behalf of the opposition, were limited to 30 minutes; the Member moving the sub-amendment could speak for 40 minutes.[315]

Before the 1968 changes to the Standing Orders, tax changes could only be introduced in a Budget. Most felt this procedure was ill-suited to the modern context

---

311. This occurred in 1870, 1874 and 1879.

312. See *Journals*, July 12, 1955, pp. 881, 922-7. See also *Debates*, July 1, 1955, pp. 5558-65.

313. Criticism of Ways and Means proceedings focussed on two concerns: the right to move sub-amendments to the motion to resolve into Committee, and the length of debate on the motion applying to the Budget presentation. The first was resolved in 1927, when the House agreed to the right to move a sub-amendment (*Journals*, March 22, 1927, pp. 316-68). The second issue—the length of debate—was more complex. The questions of limiting individual speeches and the overall proceedings were often discussed in the context of time allotment for debate in general. (See, for example, the resolution debated and adopted April 19, 1886 (*Journals*, pp. 167-8).) In 1927, a new rule limited speeches to 40 minutes on most occasions and for most speakers (*Journals*, March 22, 1927, pp. 328-9), although some Members attempted unsuccessfully to exempt the Budget debate from the application of these limits (*Debates*, March 18, 1927, pp. 1352-7, 1364-71).

314. *Journals*, July 25, 1960, p. 826; August 8, 1960, p. 898.

315. These changes were introduced provisionally at first and made permanent on April 12, 1962 (see *Journals*, April 12, 1962, p. 350). They remained in force until 1968.

in which government saw fiscal policy as its prime instrument for influencing economic activity and needed the flexibility to respond quickly to changing economic conditions.[316]

WAYS AND MEANS PROCEEDINGS (1968 TO PRESENT)

In 1968, the House agreed to abolish the Committee of Ways and Means,[317] to do away with the Committee's role in considering resolutions to authorize any withdrawals from the Consolidated Revenue Fund following the adoption of Supply, and to eliminate the repetitive process of debating Budget proposals initially on the motion to resolve *into* the Committee of Ways and Means, again *in* the Committee of Ways and Means, and yet again during the various stages of the bills subsequently introduced.[318] Ways and Means bills, however, continued to be considered in a Committee of the Whole until 1985.[319]

As a result of these changes, the Budget debate takes place on a generally worded motion respecting the budgetary policy of the government. Ways and Means motions (proposals respecting changes to government revenues) resulting from the Budget are proposed to the House once the Budget debate has concluded and are decided without debate or amendment. Detailed consideration of the proposed Ways and Means measures takes place only during the debate on the bills brought forward to implement them.[320]

In 1982, the time limit for all Members speaking on the Budget motion, except the Minister of Finance, the Member speaking first on behalf of the Opposition, the Prime Minister and the Leader of the Opposition, was reduced from 30 to 20 minutes and a 10-minute period for questions and comments was set aside following each 20-minute speech.[321] In 1991, the total number of sitting days allocated to the Budget debate was reduced from six to four.[322]

---

316. See *Stewart*, pp. 102-4.

317. *Journals*, December 20, 1968, pp. 554-79, and in particular pp. 559-60.

318. In its Third Report, presented to the House on December 6, 1968, the Special Committee on Procedure of the House declared the existing Ways and Means procedure "if anything, even less readily comprehensible than that relating to supply", with an underlying purpose which appeared "to be lost in obscurity" (*Journals*, December 6, 1968, pp. 429, 431-2). See also *Stewart*, pp. 102-4.

319. In 1985, amendments were made to the Standing Orders whereby Ways and Means bills would no longer be dealt with in a Committee of the Whole, but would be referred after second reading to a legislative committee (*Journals*, June 27, 1985, p. 919). Standing Order 73 was further amended in 1994 to allow for all bills, except Supply bills, to be referred after second reading either to a standing, special, or legislative committee (*Journals*, February 7, 1994, pp. 112-20).

320. See the Fourth Report of the Special Committee on Procedure of the House, *Journals*, December 20, 1968, pp. 559-60.

321. See *Journals*, November 29, 1982, p. 5400.

322. *Journals*, April 11, 1991, pp. 2905, 2919.

THE BUDGET

The term "budget" derives from Budge, an anglicized form of the French word Bouge, which denotes a small bag. A 1733 satirical pamphlet, *The Budget Opened,* caricatures Sir Robert Walpole, then British Prime Minister and Chancellor of the Exchequer, "explaining his financial measures as a quack doctor opening a bag filled with medicines and charms".[323] The term "budget" appears to have acquired its current meaning around this time.

By tradition, the Minister of Finance annually makes a formal Budget presentation, offering a comprehensive assessment of the financial standing of the government and giving an overview of the nation's economic condition.[324] The Minister also declares if and where the burden on the taxpayer will be increased or reduced.

The Budget Speech

Whenever the government wishes to make a Budget presentation, a Minister[325] will rise in the House to request that an Order of the Day be designated for this purpose; the Minister will also specify the date and time of the presentation.[326] Traditionally, the Minister of Finance makes the announcement during "Oral Questions" in the House, in response to a question from a Member of the Official Opposition.[327] However, a Minister may do so at any time while the House is sitting. The Minister's announcement has been deemed to be the request that a day be designated pursuant to the requirements of the Standing Orders; no notice is required. The Order of the Day is also deemed to be an Order of the House to sit beyond the ordinary hour of daily adjournment if required.[328]

---

323. *Wilding and Laundy*, p. 61.

324. In the United Kingdom, a general Finance Act must be enacted annually because certain taxes, most notably the income tax, are authorized for one year only. Since Canadian taxation statutes continue in effect from year to year without need of renewal, there is no obligation on the part of the government to present a budget at all although one is normally presented once a year. (For more detail, see *Stewart*, p. 101.) In 1987, the Minister of Finance announced that henceforth the Budget would be presented during the middle weeks of February each year, just prior to the beginning of the new fiscal year (*Debates*, January 30, 1987, p. 2924). There have been exceptions to this commitment: April 27, 1989 (*Journals*, p. 150), April 26, 1993 (*Journals*, p. 2859), and March 6, 1996 (*Journals*, p. 54).

325. It does not have to be the Minister of Finance; see, for example, *Debates*, April 19, 1989, p. 690; February 24, 1992, p. 7522; April 23, 1993, p. 18385.

326. Standing Order 83(2).

327. See, for example, *Debates*, February 11, 1994, p. 1235; February 21, 1995, p. 9901; February 28, 1996, p. 42; February 3, 1997, p. 7579; February 10, 1998, p. 3686. The question has also been asked by a Member from the government side (*Debates*, February 5, 1999, p. 11508).

328. Standing Order 83(2). The provision for the House to sit beyond the ordinary hour of daily adjournment for a Budget presentation was added to the Standing Orders in 1991 (*Journals*, April 11, 1991, pp. 2905, 2918-9) and eliminated the requirement for the House to pass a special order to suspend the regular schedule of business to allow the Minister of Finance to deliver the Budget (see, for example, *Journals*, January 30, 1987, p. 425; February 8, 1988, pp. 2158-9; April 19, 1989, p. 116).

At the specified time on the designated day, typically in the late afternoon after the financial markets have closed, the Speaker interrupts any proceedings then before the House, which are deemed adjourned,[329] and the House proceeds to the consideration of the Order of the Day for the Budget presentation. The Minister of Finance then rises in the House to move a Ways and Means motion, "That this House approves in general the budgetary policy of the Government"[330] and to deliver the Budget speech. The Minister may also table notices of Ways and Means motions setting out the various taxation and other financial measures that will be needed to implement the Budget provisions and ask that an Order of the Day be designated for the consideration of each of these motions. However, concurrence in any of these motions, or of any Ways and Means motions tabled at any other time during the session, may not be proposed until the Ways and Means proceeding on the Budget itself is completed. This is to allow the House to pronounce itself on the budgetary policy of the government before considering any taxation measures.[331]

Convention dictates that taxation proposals are effective as soon as the Minister tables a notice of a Ways and Means motion, even though the government's taxation plans have not yet been officially adopted by way of legislation.[332]

Budget Secrecy

There is a long-standing tradition of keeping the contents of the Budget secret until the Minister of Finance actually presents it in the House. Respect for a Budget's impact on financial markets has often been used as the basis of questions of privilege or points of order respecting the validity of Budget proceedings where there has been a Budget "leak".[333] However, Speakers of the Canadian House have maintained that secrecy is a matter of parliamentary convention, rather than one of privilege.[334] Speaker Sauvé noted that while a breach of Budget secrecy "... might have a very

---

329. Standing Order 83(2).

330. Standing Order 84(1).

331. Standing Order 83(3).

332. It is the long-standing practice of Canadian governments to put tax measures into effect as soon as notice of the Ways and Means motions on which they are based are tabled in the House of Commons, with the result that taxes are collected as of the date of this notice, even though it may be months, if not years, before the implementing legislation is actually passed by Parliament (*The Canadian Budgetary Process: Proposals for Improvement*, p. 15).

333. In 1989, the House had agreed by special order that the Budget would be delivered at 5:00 p.m. on April 27. Following a significant Budget leak in the late afternoon of April 26, the substance of the Budget speech was presented in a televised press conference on that evening, at a time when the House had already adjourned for the day despite an earlier attempt by the Government House Leader to continue the sitting beyond the ordinary hour of daily adjournment (*Debates*, April 26, 1989, p. 1001). The next day, the Opposition tried unsuccessfully to withdraw their consent for the special order authorizing the Budget presentation, on the grounds that it had already been presented. However, the Speaker ruled that the Chair was bound by the order of the House, as previously agreed to (see ruling of Speaker Fraser, *Debates*, April 27, 1989, p. 1060).

334. See, for example, ruling of Speaker Jerome, *Debates*, April 17, 1978, p. 4549; ruling of Speaker Sauvé, *Debates*, November 18, 1981, p. 12898; ruling of Speaker Fraser, *Debates*, June 18, 1987, p. 7315.

negative impact on business or on the stock market [and] might cause some people to receive revenues which they would not otherwise have been able to obtain ... [it has] no impact on the privileges of a member. [It] might do harm—irrevocable in some cases—to persons or institutions, but this has nothing to do with privilege. It has to do with the conduct of a Minister in the exercise of his administrative responsibility."[335] In order that Members of Parliament and the news media are able to respond to the Budget speech, a closed-door informal session, or "lock-up", is usually provided for Members of Parliament and the news media by Finance Department officials several hours before the actual Budget presentation in the House.[336] Although questions of privilege have been raised concerning lock-ups, the Speaker has ruled that admission to lock-ups and the nature of lock-ups are not a matter for the Chair to decide.[337]

Pre-Budget Consultations

With a growing emphasis on consultation, many of the Budget's financial provisions have been discussed publicly before the Budget is ever drafted.[338] Since 1994, the Standing Committee on Finance has been specifically empowered to hold "pre-budget" consultations.[339] Prior to this, only the Minister and the Department of Finance had consulted with the government's economic and social partners during the Budget preparation process. The Finance Committee already had the authority to undertake this type of consultative study.[340] However, the inclusion of an explicit Standing Order for this purpose indicates the House's willingness to receive and consider a report on the matter. Under the Standing Orders, the Committee may report the outcome of its budgetary consultations to the House up to and including the tenth sitting day prior to the last scheduled sitting day in December as provided for in the parliamentary calendar.[341] Although there is no requirement for the House

---

335. See *Debates*, November 18, 1981, p. 12898.

336. Journalists are informed in advance that they will not be permitted to leave the briefing room until after the Budget presentation has begun in the House. Members in attendance, however, may not be prevented from leaving the room in order to attend to their official business (see ruling of Speaker Jerome, *Debates*, November 27, 1978, p. 1515).

337. See ruling of Speaker Jerome, *Debates*, November 27, 1978, pp. 1518-9; ruling of Speaker Sauvé, *Debates*, February 25, 1981, p. 7670; ruling of Speaker Francis, *Debates*, January 19, 1984, p. 563; ruling of Speaker Parent, *Debates*, March 6, 1997, p. 8693.

338. See, for example, comments of Speaker Francis, *Debates*, January 19, 1984, p. 563; and Speaker Parent, *Debates*, March 6, 1997, p. 8693.

339. Standing Order 83.1. (See *Journals*, February 7, 1994, pp. 117 and 119-20.) The actual wording authorizes the Committee to consider and make reports on proposals regarding the budgetary policy of the government. (For example of reports presented to the House, see *Journals*, December 8, 1994, p. 1004; December 12, 1995, p. 2241; December 5, 1996, p. 967; December 1, 1997, p. 290; December 4, 1998, p. 1397.)

340. Such a study could be undertaken under the provisions of Standing Order 108(2), which gives the Committee authority to review the mandate and operations of the Department of Finance.

341. Standing Order 83.1. In some cases, the Committee was authorized by the House to present its report past the deadline (see *Journals*, November 30, 1994, pp. 957-8; December 8, 1994, p. 1004; November 21, 1995, pp. 2135-6; December 12, 1995, p. 2239; February 2, 1996, p. 2273; November 23, 1998, p. 1288; November 25, 1998, p. 1313; December 4, 1998, p. 1397).

to do so, on each occasion that a report has been presented, either the report itself, or the subject matter of the consultations, became the object of a debate in the Chamber. The practice has been that a special "take note" debate is held under Government Orders some time before the Budget is actually presented.[342]

Financial Statement

On occasion, the Minister of Finance has also made an economic statement to the House, generally referred to as a "mini-budget". Unlike a Budget presentation, these statements were delivered without notice and did not precipitate a Budget debate. Notices of Ways and Means motions have also been tabled on these occasions. Such statements have been made in the course of debate during consideration of the Address in Reply to the Speech from the Throne,[343] on a motion to adjourn the House for an emergency debate,[344] during Routine Proceedings under "Statements by Ministers",[345] and on moving the motion for second reading of a borrowing authority bill.[346] The rules of debate pertinent to each situation have applied.[347]

The Budget Debate

At the conclusion of the Budget presentation,[348] the Speaker recognizes a representative of the Official Opposition, usually the finance critic, who, after a brief speech, moves the adjournment of the debate, which is then deemed adopted. In doing so, that Member reserves the right to speak first when debate on the motion resumes at a subsequent sitting. The Speaker then adjourns the House until the next sitting day.[349]

---

342. See *Journals*, November 28, 1994, p. 943; November 30, 1994, p. 957; December 14, 1995, pp. 2262-4; December 9, 1996, pp. 977-9; December 11, 1996, p. 996; December 10, 1997, pp. 384-5; December 11, 1997, pp. 393-5; February 1, 1999, pp. 1442, 1446; February 2, 1999, p. 1461.

343. *Journals*, October 20, 1977, p. 19; April 21, 1980, pp. 61-2. See also *Debates*, October 20, 1977, pp. 98-102; April 21, 1980, pp. 242-8.

344. *Journals*, October 14, 1971, pp. 870-1; *Debates,* October 14, 1971, pp. 8688-90.

345. *Debates*, October 27, 1982, p. 20077.

346. See, for example, *Debates*, December 2, 1992, pp. 14417-27.

347. On November 7, 1984, however, the House adopted a special order enabling the Minister of Finance to make an economic statement and providing for replies from representatives of recognized parties following the example used for ministerial statements (see *Journals*, November 7, 1984, pp. 32-3; November 8, 1984, pp. 37-8).

348. In 1990, in response to a point of order raised seeking clarification as to whether or not Members could question the Minister following the Budget speech, the Speaker ruled that since 1984 the practice of the House had been to not allow a 10-minute questions and comments period following this speech (see *Debates*, February 20, 1990, pp. 8578-9).

349. Standing Order 83(2). See also, for example, *Journals*, February 18, 1997, p. 1147, and February 24, 1998, p. 527.

Duration of Debate

Once the Budget has been presented, the Standing Orders provide for a maximum of four additional days of debate on the Budget motion and any amendments proposed thereto.[350] The four days of debate do not have to be consecutive[351] and, if few Members wish to speak, the debate can be less than four days. The unused days may be added, if the House so agrees, to the number of opposition days in the same Supply period, as suggested by the Standing Orders.[352]

Since the rule changes in 1955, there have been seven cases where Budget debates have not continued for the full amount of time provided for in the Standing Orders.[353] In 1962, the Budget was presented and Parliament was dissolved before any debate on the Budget could take place.[354] The House adopted Special Orders providing for fewer days of debate in 1966 and 1969.[355] Another two debates (in 1974 and 1979) were cut short when the Prime Minister sought and was granted a dissolution of Parliament after sub-amendments were adopted.[356] In early 1991, when the Standing Orders required that there be six days of debate, only four days of debate were held on the Budget presented on February 26; both the amendment and the sub-amendment were negatived and debate on the main motion was not resumed before prorogation occurred in May.[357] In 1993, only two days of debate took place on the Budget presented on April 26; the sub-amendment was negatived and debate on the amendment and the main motion was not resumed before dissolution occurred in September 1993.[358]

Precedence of Debate

In 1955, the House established that debate on the Budget motion should be given precedence over all other orders.[359] When an Order of the Day is called for resuming debate on the Budget motion, pursuant to the Standing Orders it stands as the first

350. Standing Order 84(2). See *Journals*, April 11, 1991, p. 2919.

351. Standing Order 40(2).

352. Standing Order 81(11). This has never occurred.

353. Prior to 1955, only one Budget debate did not terminate with a decision by the House. The Twentieth Parliament dissolved on April 30, 1949, without votes being held on the sub-amendment, amendment or main motion.

354. *Journals*, April 10, 1962, p. 344.

355. *Journals*, April 21, 1966, p. 428; June 5, 1969, p. 1121.

356. On May 8, 1974, following the sub-amendment being agreed to (*Journals*, pp. 175-6), Prime Minister Trudeau sought a dissolution; the Twenty-Ninth Parliament was dissolved the next day. On December 13, 1979, following the sub-amendment being agreed to (*Journals*, pp. 345-6), Prime Minister Clark sought a dissolution; the Thirty-First Parliament was dissolved the next day.

357. *Journals*, February 28, 1991, pp. 2639-40; March 4, 1991, pp. 2653-4.

358. *Journals*, April 28, 1993, pp. 2874-5.

359. *Journals*, July 12, 1955, p. 926.

item of business for the sitting and no other government business may be considered during that sitting, unless the proceedings on the Budget motion are completed.[360]

Length of Speeches

The Minister of Finance, the Prime Minister, the Member speaking first on behalf of the Opposition and the Leader of the Opposition have unlimited speaking time and their speeches are not followed by a 10-minute questions and comments period.[361] All other Members may speak for not more than 20 minutes with their speeches subject to a 10-minute period for questions and comments. The general nature of the Budget motion allows for a wide-ranging debate, during which the rules of relevance are generally relaxed.

Disposal of Amendments and Termination of Debate

Only one amendment and one sub-amendment may be proposed to the Budget motion.[362] This is contrary to the usual rules of debate where Members are permitted to move an unlimited number of amendments and sub-amendments, provided that each one has been disposed of before the next is proposed. On the first day of resumed debate on the Budget motion, the Opposition speaker who had previously moved the adjournment of the Budget debate continues with his or her speech and traditionally moves an amendment at the end of the speech. The next speaker, a Member of the next largest opposition party, typically moves a sub-amendment at the end of his or her speech. Occasionally, no sub-amendment is proposed.[363] There is no rule preventing the amendment or the sub-amendment from being moved on a day after the first day of resumed debate (although this has not occurred since the number of days of resumed debate was reduced to four in 1991).[364]

The Standing Orders define the exact procedures to be followed for the disposal of the amendment and sub-amendment. On the second day of resumed debate, if a sub-amendment has been proposed, the Speaker will interrupt the proceedings 15 minutes before the expiry of time provided for government business to put the question to dispose of the sub-amendment.[365] On the third day of resumed debate, the Speaker will interrupt the proceedings, as on the second day, and put the question on the amendment under consideration.[366] Finally, on the fourth day of resumed debate,

---

360. Standing Order 84(3).

361. Standing Order 84(7). See also *Debates*, February 20, 1990, pp. 8578-9.

362. Standing Order 85.

363. See, for example, the debates on the Budgets presented on June 13, 1963, and March 29, 1966.

364. Amendments to the Budget motion are rarely disallowed, the most recent example occurring in 1978 when a sub-amendment "modif[ied] the first proposition completely" (see *Debates*, November 17, 1978, p. 1250). Other amendments deemed inadmissible include those dealing with matters before the House or already decided upon by the House (see, for example, *Journals*, May 15, 1934, pp. 332-3; July 1, 1942, pp. 454-6) or one of its committees (see, for example, *Journals*, May 7, 1934, pp. 311-2) and those which are not relevant to the question on which the amendment is proposed (see, for example, *Journals*, March 8, 1937, p. 208).

365. Standing Order 84(4).

366. Standing Order 84(5).

unless the debate has been previously concluded, the Speaker will likewise interrupt the proceedings to put the question on the main motion.[367] During the 1970s, the main motion was frequently adopted on division,[368] but since the 1980s, with one exception,[369] Members have requested recorded divisions.

BUDGET PRESENTATION AND DEBATE

Budget Presentation	Budget Debate *Maximum of 4 days*			
	Day 1	Day 2	Day 3	Day 4
Minister of Finance makes presentation normally in late afternoon	Amendment and sub-amendment normally moved	Sub-amendment—question put 15 min. before the end of Government Orders	Amendment—question put 15 min. before the end of Government Orders	Main motion—question put 15 min. before the end of Government Orders

As with amendments moved to the Address in Reply to the Speech from the Throne, proposed amendments to the Budget motion are opportunities for expression of non-confidence in the government. On several occasions since 1930, proposed amendments to the Budget motion have been worded as explicit statements of non-confidence in the government.[370] In two cases in the 1970s, the adoption of amendments was followed by the Prime Minister seeking a dissolution of Parliament.[371]

THE LEGISLATIVE PHASE

The legislation required to give effect to taxation proposals, whether outlined in a Budget or initiated independently of a Budget during the course of a session, must go through a unique preliminary step in the legislative process. The House must first adopt a Ways and Means motion before a bill which imposes a tax or other charge on the taxpayer can be introduced. Charges on the people, in this context, refer to new taxes, the continuation of an expiring tax, an increase in the rate of an existing tax, or an extension of a tax to a new class of taxpayers. Industry levies and service fees imposed by departments do not constitute charges on the people in the context

---

367. Standing Order 84(6).

368. See *Journals*, April 23, 1970, p. 711; November 27, 1974, p. 150; July 4, 1975, p. 685; June 10, 1976, p. 1341; April 20, 1978, p. 668; November 24, 1978, p. 184.

369. *Journals*, March 7, 1986, p. 1777.

370. *Journals*, May 15, 1930, p. 318; April 11, 1933, p. 401; May 27, 1948, p. 485; March 31, 1949, p. 290 (Parliament was dissolved before the amendment came to a vote); December 21, 1960, p. 138; June 22, 1961, pp. 707-8; May 7, 1974, p. 169; April 19, 1977, p. 680; June 29, 1982, p. 5101; February 16, 1984, p. 180.

371. *Journals*, May 8, 1974, pp. 175-6; December 13, 1979, pp. 345-6.

of Ways and Means.[372] Legislative proposals which are not intended to raise money but rather to reduce taxation need not to be preceded by a Ways and Means motion before being introduced in the House.[373]

Ways and Means Motions

Before taxation legislation can be read a first time, a notice of a Ways and Means motion must first be tabled in the House by a Minister of the Crown; this may be done at any time during a sitting.[374] On the day the notice is tabled or at some other time during the session, a Minister of the Crown may make a request to the Speaker that an Order of the Day be designated for the consideration of the motion at a subsequent sitting, that is, to put it on the *Order Paper*.[375] Although there are virtually no restrictions on when a notice can be tabled, a Ways and Means motion cannot be moved during the same sitting in which the notice is tabled,[376] or when the Ways and Means proceedings regarding the Budget have yet to be completed.[377] When the Order of the Day is called, a Minister moves that the motion be concurred in. The motion for concurrence must then be decided immediately without debate or amendment.[378] The adoption of a Ways and Means motion stands as an order of the House either to bring in a bill or bills based on the provisions of that motion or to propose an amendment or amendments to a bill then before the House.[379]

---

372. *May*, 22nd ed., pp. 777-82. See also rulings of Speaker Parent, *Debates*, February 12, 1998, p. 3765, and December 2, 1998, pp. 10789-91.

373. See ruling of Speaker Michener, *Journals*, December 9, 1957, p. 254; ruling of Speaker Lamoureux, *Journals*, March 27, 1972, p. 223. See also *May*, 22nd ed., p. 781.

374. Standing Order 83(1). See, for example, *Debates*, January 30, 1985, p. 1832. While the Standing Orders explicitly permit the tabling of notices of Ways and Means motions at any time during a sitting regardless of the business then before the House, the Speaker has clearly indicated that such tabling is more appropriate during certain proceedings than others. For instance, it would not be appropriate during Question Period or when another Member is speaking unless the House was about to adjourn. (See ruling of Speaker Bosley, *Debates*, September 11, 1985, p. 6498.) Prior to 1968, the practice was for notices of Ways and Means motions to be given only during the Budget speech. It is now procedurally acceptable for a Minister to introduce Ways and Means legislation based on Budget proposals presented in a previous session. (See ruling of Speaker Lamoureux, *Journals*, March 20, 1972, p. 202, and *Debates*, March 20, 1972, pp. 963-5.)

375. Standing Order 83(2). See, for example, October 7, 1997 (*Debates*, p. 569, and *Journals*, p. 83), and December 2, 1998 (*Debates*, p. 10791, and *Journals*, p. 1357).

376. Standing Order 83(1). This restriction has been circumvented with the consent of the House. (See, for example, *Debates*, January 19, 1987, pp. 2368-70).

377. Standing Order 83(3).

378. See, for example, *Journals*, October 22, 1997, p. 136.

379. Standing Order 83(4). (See, for example, *Journals*, April 8, 1997, pp. 1354-5, and April 9, 1997, pp. 1362-3.) On occasion, two or more Ways and Means motions were adopted and a single bill was introduced. (See, for example, *Journals*, February 16, 1971, p. 334, and April 3, 1973, p. 237.)

Ways and Means motions can be expressed in general terms,[380] or be very specific, as in the form of draft legislation.[381] In either case, they establish limits on the scope—specifically tax rates and their applicability—of the legislative measures they propose. Neither the provisions of a Ways and Means bill nor any amendment subsequently proposed to the bill may exceed the limits imposed in the Ways and Means motion. In particular, they may not increase the amount of a tax or extend the incidence of a tax or the applicable tax base.[382] Should this occur, either a new Ways and Means motion must be adopted authorizing the exceptions before those provisions may be considered in committee, or the offending provisions must be amended to conform to the resolution on which the bill is based.[383] To proceed otherwise would infringe on the financial initiative of the Crown in taxation measures. "The terms of the Ways and Means motion are a carefully prepared expression of the financial initiative of the Crown and frequent departures from them can only invite deterioration of that most important power."[384] When a new Ways and Means motion is required, it must also be adopted rather than simply tabled.[385] Should a bill be found not to conform to the provisions of a Ways and Means motion, a new motion will be required before the non-conforming provision can be considered and a decision taken.[386]

A Ways and Means motion often refers to more than one legislative proposal; it can encompass more than one provision in a bill and may seek to introduce more than one bill or a bill amending more than one statute. There are essentially no procedural restrictions on the motion's wording or content.[387]

WAYS AND MEANS BILLS

Concurrence in a Ways and Means motion constitutes an order to bring in a bill or bills based on the provisions of the motion.[388] A Ways and Means bill must be "based

---

380. See, for example, *Journals*, December 11, 1996, p. 992 (Sessional Paper 8570-352-14).

381. See, for example, *Journals*, October 23, 1996, p. 763 (Sessional Paper 8570-352-8).

382. *May*, 22nd ed., p. 794.

383. See, for example, rulings of Speaker Jerome, *Journals*, July 15, 1975, p. 710; May 19, 1978, p. 786; *Debates*, June 7, 1978, p. 6155.

384. Speaker Jerome, *Journals*, December 18, 1974, p. 224. See also *Journals,* July 14, 1975, p. 707; May 19, 1978, p. 784.

385. See ruling of Speaker Jerome, *Debates*, June 7, 1978, p. 6155.

386. See ruling of Speaker Jerome, *Journals*, May 19, 1978, p. 786.

387. See ruling of Speaker Lamoureux, *Journals*, December 13, 1973, pp. 746-7; ruling of Speaker Fraser, *Debates*, January 29, 1990, pp. 7546-9.

388. Standing Order 83(4). This allows for debate on Ways and Means bills to begin one sitting day earlier than the debate on other government bills.

on" but not necessarily "identical to" the provisions of its Ways and Means motion.[389] Such a bill can then be read the first time and ordered to be printed, immediately after the motion is concurred in or at a subsequent sitting of the House.[390] From this point on, the legislative steps for Ways and Means bills are exactly the same as those followed for other public bills.[391] Like all tax measures, bills imposing a charge upon the people, and thereby requiring a Ways and Means motion, must originate in the House of Commons.[392]

Amendment in Committee and at Report Stage

No amendment may be proposed to the text of a bill until the bill is considered in committee. Amendments to Ways and Means bills are subject to the normal rules respecting legislation.[393] Amendments which exceed the scope of the motion on which the bill is based are procedurally unacceptable unless a new Ways and Means motion is concurred in prior to the amendment being moved.[394] Since Ways and Means motions may only be proposed by a Minister of the Crown, and since Ministers do not usually sit on committees, any amendment exceeding the provisions of the authorizing Ways and Means motion may only be proposed and considered at report stage. If the House has concurred in the required Ways and Means motion prior to the bill reaching report stage, the Minister may put amendments on notice and they will be considered with any other report stage amendments. If the debate at report stage has begun before the required Ways and Means motion has been concurred in, the Minister will require the House's consent to table and decide on the Ways and Means motion and to proceed to consider the amendments.

---

389. See, for example, rulings of Speaker Jerome, *Journals*, December 18, 1974, pp. 224-5; July 14, 1975, pp. 706-7; May 19, 1978, pp. 784-6.

390. On one occasion, a Ways and Means bill was introduced and read the first time without prior concurrence in the Ways and Means motion, and the proceedings on the bill were declared null and void. (See ruling of Speaker Fraser, *Debates*, October 9, 1986, p. 246.)

391. See Chapter 16, "The Legislative Process".

392. Speaker Parent ruled that a Senate bill imposed a tax and thus should have been preceded by a Ways and Means motion. The bill was deemed to be improperly presented before the House and the first reading proceedings were declared null and void. (See *Debates*, December 2, 1998, p. 10791, and *Journals*, December 2, 1998, p. 1360.)

393. See Chapter 16, "The Legislative Process".

394. See, for example, *Debates*, December 19, 1984, p. 1380; Standing Committee on Consumer and Corporate Affairs and Government Operations, *Minutes of Proceedings and Evidence*, December 3, 1991, Issue No. 29, pp. 16-35, and in particular pp. 30-1. On occasion, with the unanimous consent of the House, a new Ways and Means motion has been concurred in, and a Minister of the Crown has proposed amendments to bills which went beyond the provisions of the original Ways and Means motion. Consent to move these amendments was usually requested either in a Committee of the Whole or during report stage. (For examples of where the House has proceeded by way of unanimous consent in a Committee of the Whole, see *Debates*, April 9, 1973, p. 3121, and January 7, 1974, p. 9115. For an example of where the House has proceeded by unanimous consent at report stage, see *Debates*, May 26, 1981, pp. 9931-2, 9948.)

Ways and Means Bills Requiring a Royal Recommendation

If a bill based on a Ways and Means motion also contains provisions relating to government expenditure, the bill will also require a royal recommendation.[395] In such cases, the House must both adopt the Ways and Means motion authorizing the government to proceed with the taxation measures, and give leave, after the normal 48-hour notice period, to introduce those spending provisions which are subject to the royal recommendation, before proceeding to the first reading of the bill.[396]

In the event that the notice requirements for the royal recommendation are not met, the offending bill must be withdrawn and the order for second reading of the bill discharged and removed from the *Order Paper;* this would not affect the validity of any Ways and Means motion previously concurred in by the House.[397]

The Accounts of Canada

The financial role of the House of Commons does not end with voting supply or authorizing measures to raise revenue. The House also acts as a "watchdog" to ensure that federal money is spent in the amounts and for the purposes authorized by Parliament.[398] This monitoring function (often described as "closing the loop") is delegated largely to the Standing Committee on Public Accounts, which examines and reports on the *Public Accounts of Canada,* as well as on all reports of the Auditor General of Canada.[399]

THE PUBLIC ACCOUNTS OF CANADA

Under the *Financial Administration Act,* the Receiver General[400] is responsible for ensuring that accounts are kept for each department and agency of the Government of Canada. These accounts must show all expenditures made under each appropriation, all government revenues, and all other payments into and out of the

---

395. See, for example, *Journals*, November 5, 1976, p. 114; October 20, 1978, p. 42; April 9, 1997, pp. 1362-3.

396. See ruling of Speaker Fraser, *Debates*, June 8, 1988, pp. 16254-5. Despite the fact that two different procedures are invoked, such bills are acceptable providing the notice provision is respected (see rulings of Speaker Sauvé, *Debates*, January 19, 1981, p. 6319, and February 16, 1982, p. 15053; ruling of Speaker Francis, *Debates*, January 18, 1984, p. 526).

397. See ruling of Speaker Francis, *Debates*, January 18, 1984, p. 526.

398. As early as 1341, Edward III had conceded the principle that grants to the Crown should be audited to ensure they were spent for the purposes intended (*Dreidger*, p. 30).

399. Standing Order 108(3)(*e*). See also the Final Report of the Royal Commission on Financial Management and Accountability (Lambert Commission), March 1979 (Supply and Services Canada), and especially Part V, "Accountability to Parliament: Closing the Loop", pp. 367-419.

400. The Minister of Public Works and Government Services Canada also serves as Receiver General for Canada (*Department of Public Works and Government Services Act*, S.C. 1996, c. 16, s. 3(3)).

Consolidated Revenue Fund,[401] together with whatever assets, liabilities and related reserves are deemed necessary to present a fair picture of the country's financial position.[402] The accounts of each individual department and agency are rolled up into the Accounts of Canada.

Each year, the President of the Treasury Board tables a detailed report of the financial transactions of all government departments and agencies, entitled the *Public Accounts of Canada*. The report must be tabled[403] on or before December 31 next following the end of the fiscal year to which the accounts apply; or, if the House is not sitting, on any of the next 15 sitting days of the House.[404] As a matter of tradition only, the Public Accounts are addressed to the Governor General.

The fundamental purpose of the *Public Accounts of Canada* is to provide information to Parliament, and thus to the public, which will enable them to understand and evaluate the financial position and transactions of the government. Two constitutional principles underly the public accounting system: that duties and revenues accruing to the Government of Canada form one Consolidated Revenue Fund, and that the balance of the Fund after certain prior charges is appropriated by the Parliament of Canada for the public service.[405]

Responsibility for the form and content of the *Public Accounts of Canada* rests with the President of the Treasury Board[406] and the Minister of Finance.[407] The financial statements are prepared under the joint direction of the President of the Treasury Board, the Minister of Finance and the Receiver General for Canada.[408] By law, the Accounts must include, for the fiscal year to which they apply, a statement of all the government's financial transactions; a statement of all expenditures and revenues; a

---

401. *Financial Administration Act*, R.S.C. 1985, c. F-11, s. 63(1).

402. *Financial Administration Act*, R.S.C. 1985, c. F-11, s. 63(2).

403. The *Public Accounts of Canada* are usually deposited with the Clerk of the House and the tabling is recorded in the *Journals*. (See, for example, *Journals*, October 18, 1994, p. 801; October 22, 1996, pp. 761-2; October 28, 1997, p. 163.) However, the report has also been tabled by a Minister directly on the floor of the House. (See, for example, *Journals*, October 31, 1978, p. 94; December 11, 1979, p. 336.) For more information on the tabling of documents, see Chapter 10, "The Daily Program".

404. *Financial Administration Act*, R.S.C. 1985, c. F-11, s. 64(1).

405. *Constitution Act, 1867*, R.S.C. 1985, Appendix II, No. 5, ss. 102-6. See also "Preface to the Financial Statements of the Government of Canada", *Public Accounts of Canada, 1998*, p. 1.2.

406. The Treasury Board is a committee of Cabinet chaired by the Minister designated as the President of the Treasury Board. There are five other Ministers on the Board, including the Minister of Finance. The Treasury Board is responsible for the management of the public service, including administrative policy and financial management practices. The Treasury Board also acts as the federal employer and represents the government in all matters respecting the federal workforce. The Treasury Board Secretariat is the central staff agency which serves the Treasury Board. Its executive head is designated as the Secretary of the Treasury Board (*McMenemy*, pp. 304-5). Since 1993, the Secretary of the Treasury Board has also borne the title of Comptroller General of Canada. The Comptroller General is the federal official responsible for standards of financial controls, reporting systems and program evaluation of federal departments and agencies (*McMenemy*, p. 52).

407. *Financial Administration* Act, R.S.C. 1985, c. F-11, s. 64(2).

408. "Statement of Responsibility", *Public Accounts of Canada, 1998*, p. 1.4.

statement of the assets and direct and contingent liabilities of Canada; the Auditor General's opinion on the Accounts, pursuant to the *Auditor General Act*; and whatever other accounts and information the President of the Treasury Board and the Minister of Finance deem necessary to represent fairly the financial position of Canada at the close of the year.[409]

Currently, the *Public Accounts of Canada* are divided into two volumes published in three separately bound books. *Volume I* contains the opinion of the Auditor General; the financial statements of Canada on which the Auditor General has expressed an opinion; a 10-year summary of the government's financial transactions; analyses of revenues and expenditures, and of asset and liability accounts; and a variety of government-wide summaries of revenues, expenditures, loans and investments. *Volume II* is divided into two parts: the first gives details of the government's financial operations, segregated by ministry; and the second provides additional information and analyses, such as the financial statements for revolving funds, transfer payments and public debt charges.[410]

Until 1993, the Public Accounts included a third volume which contained financial information on Crown corporations. *Volume III* has been replaced by the *Annual Report to Parliament: Crown Corporations and Other Corporate Interests of Canada,* a consolidated report on the businesses and activities of all parent Crown corporations and other corporate interests of the Government of Canada.[411] The Annual Report is prepared by the Treasury Board Secretariat for the President of the Treasury Board, who tables it in the House.[412]

THE AUDITOR GENERAL OF CANADA

The Auditor General of Canada is an officer of Parliament, appointed by the Governor in Council under the *Auditor General Act,* to audit the accounts of Canada and investigate the financial affairs of the federal government.[413] The Auditor General holds office for a period of 10 years, or until the age of 65, whichever comes first. The term is not renewable. The position was first established in the *Audit Act,*

---

409. *Financial Administration Act,* R.S.C. 1985, c. F-11, s. 64(2) and *Auditor General Act*, R.S.C. 1985, c. A-17, s. 6.

410. "Introduction to the *Public Accounts of Canada:* Nature of the *Public Accounts of Canada*", *Public Accounts of Canada 1998*, Vol. II, Part I.

411. A Crown corporation is an organization with the structure of a private-sector enterprise but which is established by legislation and is owned by the Crown. Although they report to the legislature through a designated Minister, Crown corporations are not subject to direct ministerial control (*McMenemy*, p. 73).

412. *Financial Administration Act*, R.S.C. 1985, c. F-11, ss. 151 and 152. Like the *Public Accounts* of *Canada*, this report is usually deposited with the Clerk of the House and the tabling is recorded in the *Journals*. See, for example, *Journals*, January 20, 1994, p. 43; December 15, 1994, p. 1074; December 7, 1995, p. 2222; December 10, 1996, p. 989; December 11, 1997, p. 396.

413. *McMenemy*, pp. 6-7. An officer of Parliament is an appointed official who is responsible to Parliament for carrying out duties assigned by statute. For terms of appointment and tenure of office, see *Auditor General Act*, R.S.C. 1985, c. A-17, s. 3.

1878.[414] That legislation was replaced in 1886 and in 1931 by the *Consolidated Revenue and Audit Act,*[415] which, in turn, was repealed by the *Financial Administration Act, 1951.*[416] Initially, the Auditor General was responsible only for auditing expenditures; before they were made (pre-payment audit) and after they were made (post-payment audit). In 1977, Parliament enacted the current *Auditor General Act* which broadened the Auditor General's mandate beyond attesting to the accuracy of the government's financial statements, to examining how well the government managed its financial affairs.[417]

As auditor of the Accounts of Canada, the Auditor General examines the government's financial statements to ensure that the information is presented fairly, in accordance with stated accounting policies, and on a basis consistent with the previous accounting year. Additional responsibilities for special examinations of Crown corporations are set out in the *Financial Administration Act.*[418] The Auditor General is empowered to undertake whatever examinations and inquiries are deemed necessary to produce the reports required under the terms of the *Auditor General Act.*[419]

The Office of the Auditor General carries out three types of audits—attest audits, compliance audits and value-for-money audits. Attest auditing verifies that

---

414. *An Act to provide for the better auditing of the Public Accounts*, S.C. 1878, c. 7, ss. 11-56.

415. *An Act respecting the Public Revenue, the raising of loans authorized by Parliament, and the auditing of the Public Accounts*, R.S. 1886, c. 29, ss. 21-59; *The Consolidated Revenue and Audit Act, 1931*, S.C. 1931, c. 27.

416. *An Act to Provide for the Financial Administration of the Government of Canada, the Audit of the Public Accounts and the Financial Control of Crown Corporations*, S.C. 1951, c. 12, ss. 65-75.

417. *Auditor General Act*, R.S.C. 1985, c. A-17, ss. 7(2)(*b*)-(*e*). In 1995, a point of order was raised in the House about the receivability of the Auditor General's annual report on the grounds that the Auditor General had exceeded his mandate under the *Auditor General Act* by including "politically biased statements" about the role of Parliament in relation to the national debt (*Debates*, October 18, 1995, pp. 15530-1). Speaker Parent responded that he had no authority in regard to matters of law and therefore could neither interpret whether what was contained in the report was in conformity with the criteria set out under the Act nor, consequently, rule the report out of order (*Debates*, October 25, 1995, pp. 15812-3).

418. *Financial Administration Act*, R.S.C. 1985, c. F-11, ss. 134(1)-(4). In addition to annual financial audits of those Crown corporations for which the Office is responsible, the Auditor General may carry out special examinations which evaluate whether the systems and practices of Crown corporations provide reasonable assurance that assets are safeguarded, resources are managed economically and efficiently, and operations are carried out effectively (*Office of the Auditor General; 1998-99 Estimates; Part III – Report on Plans and Priorities*, p. 5).

419. *Auditor General Act*, R.S.C. 1985, c. A-17, ss. 5 and 6, and *Financial Administration Act*, R.S.C. 1985, c. F-11, s. 64.

the government is keeping proper accounts and records and that it is presenting its overall financial information fairly.[420] Compliance auditing ensures that the government collects and spends only those amounts of money authorized by Parliament and only for the purposes approved by Parliament. Finally, value-for money auditing assesses whether or not government programs were run economically and efficiently, with due regard to their environmental effects. They also assure Parliament that the government has the means in place to measure the effectiveness of its programs.[421] Since 1995, the Office has been responsible also for evaluating the extent to which department activities meet their environmental and sustainable development objectives.[422]

Where such an assignment does not interfere with the primary responsibilities of the office, the Auditor General may also be asked by the Governor in Council to inquire into and report on any matter related to the financial affairs of Canada or to public property, or to inquire into and report on any person or organization that is seeking or has received financial aid from the Government of Canada.[423]

The Annual Report

The Auditor General must report annually to the House of Commons, drawing the House's attention to any cases where:

- accounts have not been properly maintained or money not properly accounted for;
- the accounting procedures used are insufficient to safeguard the collection and spending of public money;
- money has been spent without due regard for economy and efficiency, or other than for the purposes appropriated by Parliament; or
- appropriate procedures to measure and report program effectiveness have not been implemented.[424]

The *Auditor General Act* requires that each annual report be submitted to the Speaker of the House of Commons on or before December 31 in the year to which

---

420. *Office of the Auditor General; 1998-99 Estimates; Part III – Report on Plans and Priorities*, p. 5. See, for example, "Opinion of the Auditor General on the Financial Statements of the Government of Canada", *Public Accounts of Canada, 1998*, p. 1.5.

421. *Office of the Auditor General; 1998-99 Estimates; Part III – Report on Plans and Priorities*, p. 5. Value-for-money audits are sometimes called performance audits.

422. *An Act to amend the Auditor General Act*, S.C. 1995, c. 43. This act established the position of Commissioner of the Environment and Sustainable Development within the Office of the Auditor General of Canada ("Creation of the Position of Commissioner of the Environment and Sustainable Development", media release, Office of the Auditor General, December 15, 1995).

423. *Auditor General Act*, R.S.C. 1985, c. A-17, s. 11. Such authority would be required for the Auditor General to undertake an audit assignment which did not otherwise fall within the statutory authority of the Office. The authority under section 11 is conferred by way of an Order in Council.

424. *Auditor General Act*, R.S.C. 1985, c. A-17, s. 7(2).

the report relates and that, upon receipt of the Report, the Speaker table it forthwith. If the House is not sitting at that time, the Annual Report is tabled on any of the next 15 sitting days of the House.[425] At the request of the Auditor General, the Speaker has frequently agreed to table the Report in the House at a predetermined time, usually just before "Members' Statements", although there is no requirement that it be tabled at that time.[426] Once tabled, the Report is automatically referred to the Standing Committee on Public Accounts.[427] Prior to the tabling of the Report in the House, the Auditor General typically gives a briefing on its contents to members of the Public Accounts Committee, at an *in camera* session. In addition, the Chairman of the Committee will normally invite Members to a "lock-up",[428] during which they may examine the Report to be tabled later in the day and be briefed in advance by officials. A lock-up for the media is also normally arranged.

Changes to the Act introduced in 1994 authorized the Auditor General to make up to three reports each year over and above the *Annual Report,* any special report on matters of pressing importance or urgency, or any special report on the funding of the Auditor General's Office.[429] Where such an additional report is to be tabled, the Speaker must be advised in writing of the subject matter, and the report itself is submitted to the Speaker 30 days after the notice is sent, or after any longer period which may be specified in the notice.[430] The Speaker is required to table the report

425. *An Act to amend the Auditor General Act* (*Reports*), S.C. 1994, c. 32.

426. "Members' Statements" takes place Monday through Thursday at 2:00 p.m., and Friday at 11:00 a.m. (Standing Order 30(5)). See, for example, *Journals*, October 7, 1997, p. 85; December 2, 1997, p. 314; April 28, 1998, p. 711.

427. Standing Order 108 (3)(*e*).

428. A lock-up is a closed-door or *in camera* information session immediately prior to the presentation of a major initiative, such as a Budget or the Auditor General's Report. Because the information in the Report is confidential until presented in the House, no copy may be removed from the lock-up before it has been tabled. While Members are free to leave the lock-up at any time, they must agree not to give interviews on or divulge the contents of the Report prior to tabling. Members' research staff are usually allowed to attend the lock-up; however, they must be sponsored by a specific Member and must remain in the room until the Report has been tabled. On November 27, 1978, a Member contended that the conditions for participating in the lock-up violated his parliamentary privileges. (See *Debates*, November 27, 1978, pp. 1514-7.) The Speaker stated then, and consistently since, that lock-ups are not a requirement for Members to participate in parliamentary proceedings either in the Chamber or in committee; access or lack of access to a lock-up cannot constitute grounds for a question of privilege. (See ruling of Speaker Jerome, *Debates*, November 27, 1978, pp. 1518-9; rulings of Speaker Sauvé, *Debates*, February 25, 1981, p. 7670, and February 26, 1981, p. 7714; and ruling of Speaker Parent, *Debates*, March 6, 1997, p. 8693.) However, Members may not be prevented from leaving a lock-up room. (See ruling of Speaker Jerome, *Debates*, November 27, 1978, p. 1515.)

429. *Auditor General Act*, R.S.C. 1985, c. A-17, ss. 7(1), 8 (1) and 19(2). The authority to submit several reports was conferred by way of *An Act to amend the Auditor General Act (reports)*, S.C. 1994, c. 32. The Office of the Auditor General views the authority for additional reports as an opportunity to improve the timeliness and relevance of the information it provides to Parliament. Efforts are made by the Auditor General to table the documents one month before a scheduled adjournment of the House and no sooner than two weeks after the House resumes sitting ("Foreword", *Report of the Auditor General of Canada*, May 1995, p. 5).

430. *Auditor General Act*, S.C. 1994, c. 32, ss. 2(4) and (5).

forthwith or, if the House is not sitting, on any of the next 15 sitting days of the House.

Since the enactment of the 1994 provisions, the Auditor General's *Annual Report* has been submitted to the House in several volumes; the first of which has been tabled in the spring, a second in the fall and a final volume in November or December.[431] The final volume tabled continues to be known as the "annual" report and contains the sections on "Matters of Special Importance", as well as follow-ups to previous audits. Each volume contains a foreword from the Auditor General, in addition to the individually numbered chapters[432] reporting on the various studies undertaken and the value-for-money audits of departments and agencies. Audit notes and observations may be included in any or all of the volumes, where deemed appropriate.

THE STANDING COMMITTEE ON PUBLIC ACCOUNTS

Under the Standing Orders, all reports of the Auditor General, as well as the *Public Accounts of Canada,* are deemed permanently referred to the Standing Committee on Public Accounts as soon as they are tabled in the House.[433] Since 1987, the Committee has also been responsible for scrutinizing the annual Estimates for the Office of the Auditor General.

Since 1958, the Committee has been chaired by a Member of the Official Opposition, while the parties are represented in proportion to their voting strength in the House.[434] The Committee's main functions are to ensure that public money is spent for the purposes authorized by Parliament, that extravagance and waste are minimized and that sound financial practices are encouraged in estimating and contracting, and in administration generally. The Committee does not concern itself with the appropriateness of government policy; rather, it focusses on the economy and efficiency of its administration. The Committee regularly reports its findings to the House. The reports typically state conclusions and recommendations on matters pertaining to the improvement of managerial and financial practices and controls of government departments, agencies and Crown corporations.

---

431. See, for example, 1995 Report, *Journals*, May 11, 1995, p. 1463; October 5, 1995, p. 2002; November 21, 1995, p. 2136; and 1996 Report, *Journals*, May 7, 1996, p. 307; September 26, 1996, p. 683; November 26, 1996, p. 918. In 1997, a general election delayed the tabling of the spring volume, with the result that both the April and October volumes were tabled in the fall as Volume 1. Volume 2 was tabled in December (*Journals*, October 7, 1997, p. 85; December 2, 1997, p. 314).

432. Chapters are numbered sequentially by year, not by volume.

433. Standing Order 108(3)(*e*). See also Chapter 20, "Committees".

434. A commitment to having a Member of the Official Opposition chair the Public Accounts Committee was made in the 1958 Throne Speech (see *Debates*, May 12, 1958, p. 6). See also remarks by Prime Minister John Diefenbaker, *Debates*, May 13, 1958, p. 34. See also *Ward*, pp. 218-9.

19

Committees of the Whole House

There is as little sense of reality in appointing a committee of sixty members as there is in having a Committee of the Whole of 265: it is hopeless to expect a committee of such size to accomplish any useful work.

W. F. DAWSON
(*Procedure in the Canadian House of Commons*, p. 209)

A Committee of the Whole is the entire membership of the House of Commons sitting as a committee.[1] Each time the House resolves itself into a Committee of the Whole to deliberate on a specific matter, a new committee is created. Once that committee has completed its business, it ceases to exist. Over the span of a session, many Committees of the Whole can be created on an *ad hoc* basis.

A meeting of a Committee of the Whole is held in the Chamber itself and presided over by the Deputy Speaker, as Chairman of Committees of the Whole, or by the Deputy Chairman[2] or Assistant Deputy Chairman of Committees of the Whole. Whoever is presiding sits at the Table, in the Clerk's chair, while the Speaker's chair remains vacant; the Mace is removed from the top of the Table to signal that the House itself is no longer in session. The Mace rests on the lower brackets at the end of the Table during the entire time that the House sits as a Committee of the Whole.

---

1. See *Wilding and Laundy*, pp. 149-52.

2. When Shirley Maheu (Saint-Laurent–Cartierville) was appointed Deputy Chairman of Committees of the Whole for the First Session of the Thirty-Fifth Parliament (1994-96), she asked to be referred to as Deputy Chairperson of Committees of the Whole.

"The function of a Committee of the Whole is deliberation, not enquiry".[3] Unlike standing committees which have the authority to initiate studies of continuing concern to the House, a Committee of the Whole may only consider questions and bills which the House decides should be dealt with in that forum. At one time, the House sat frequently as a Committee of the Whole to examine the Estimates,[4] appropriation bills[5] and all taxation bills[6] at the committee stage. In addition, most bills that had received a second reading were referred to a Committee of the Whole for consideration and review. Today, although the Standing Orders still provide for a Committee of the Whole to examine appropriation bills[7] and, from time to time, by special order or unanimous consent, other bills which are referred to a Committee of the Whole for consideration, the House spends little time sitting as a Committee of the Whole.[8] Indeed, the expeditious passage of legislation is now the predominant reason for the House resolving into a Committee of the Whole.[9]

Since the membership of a Committee of the Whole is identical to that of the House, one might expect the rules in both forums to be the same. While there are similarities, the rules in a Committee of the Whole are less formal than those which apply when the House is in session and the Speaker is in the Chair. For example, Members may speak more than once on any item.[10] This chapter will examine the role of Committees of the Whole and discuss the rules and practices pertaining to proceedings in a Committee of the Whole.

---

3. *Beauchesne*, 6th ed., p. 249.

4. The Estimates are the expenditure plans of all government departments, consisting of Main Estimates, tabled annually, and Supplementary Estimates, tabled as required. Consideration of the Estimates is a major component of the Business of Supply. See Chapter 18, "Financial Procedures", for additional information.

5. An appropriation bill is a bill authorizing government expenditures, introduced in the House by a Minister following concurrence in the Main or Supplementary Estimates or Interim Supply.

6. A taxation bill is a public bill introduced in the House by a Minister and authorizing the government to raise revenues.

7. Standing Order 73(4). See, for example, *Journals*, March 12, 1997, pp. 1262-3.

8. See, for example, *Journals*, April 20, 1994, pp. 375-6; June 22, 1994, p. 660; April 17, 1997, p. 1485.

9. Since 1980, while a significant number of bills have been referred to Committees of the Whole for examination after second reading, very little time has been spent in this forum debating those bills, with the exception of the Committee of the Whole consideration of Bill C-2, *An Act to implement the Free Trade Agreement between Canada and the United States of America*, in December 1988 (see *Debates*, December 20, 1988, pp. 408-19, 433-517; December 21, 1988, pp. 532-87).

10. See Standing Order 101(1).

Historical Perspective

GREAT BRITAIN

In the British Parliament, two sorts of committees began to evolve in the sixteenth century: small committees composed of no more than 15 members known as "select committees", and large committees whose membership numbered between 30 and 40 called "standing committees". Bills were often considered in detail in select committees and only members appointed to these committees were allowed to participate. In contrast, it became common in standing committees to allow whoever attended to speak. These standing committees eventually evolved into "general" or "grand" committees comprising as many members as the House itself. During the reigns of James I (1603-25) and Charles I (1625-49), they became known as Committees of the Whole.[11] These committees were established as forums for discussing bills of great interest (such as bills to impose a tax or constitutional questions prevalent during the Parliaments of the Stuarts) and provided members the opportunity to speak to a question as often as they wanted.[12] A further reason for considering bills in this forum was the greater freedom of debate secured by the removal of the "constraining presence of the Speaker, who was at this period expected to look after the interests of the King".[13] By the beginning of the eighteenth century, it had become common to refer all bills to grand committees for detailed discussion following second reading.[14] This development proved to be an efficient method of discussing matters of detail and, in the latter half of the century, for the House to establish its control over financial matters.[15]

CANADA

In Canada, the colonial legislatures generally modelled their procedures on those of the British House. The Assemblies of Upper Canada and Lower Canada adopted, in 1792, the British practice of resolving into a Committee of the Whole to consider legislation, or procedural and constitutional matters. Nonetheless, the Upper Canada Assembly made wider use of its select committee system than Great Britain at the time and many bills were referred to select committees after second reading.[16] Beginning in 1817 in Lower Canada, four committees whose membership was composed of all Members were appointed at the commencement of each session and

---

11. See *Bourinot*, 4th ed., pp. 391-2. The earliest references to general committees and grand committees comprising the total membership of the House can be found during the reign of Elizabeth I (*Wilding and Laundy*, p. 152).

12. *Redlich*, Vol. II, p. 208.

13. Lord Campion, *An Introduction to the Procedure of the House of Commons*, 3rd ed., London: MacMillan & Co. Ltd., 1958, p. 27. See also *Griffith and Ryle*, p. 269.

14. *Redlich*, Vol. II, p. 210.

15. *Campion*, pp. 28-9.

16. *O'Brien*, p. 103.

were directed by the Assembly to sit on certain days in each week. They were called the Grand Committees for grievances, courts of justice, agriculture and commerce. In 1840, after the union of Upper and Lower Canada, most of the parliamentary rules that had been in place in Lower Canada were adopted,[17] and the Legislative Assembly of the Province of Canada continued to do a significant part of its business in Committees of the Whole.[18]

At Confederation in 1867, the House of Commons adopted the rules of the former Legislative Assembly of the Province of Canada, including the procedures and practices pertaining to Committees of the Whole.[19] Thus, all matters affecting trade, taxation or the public revenue had to be first considered in a Committee of the Whole House before any resolution or bill could be passed by the House of Commons.[20] Addresses to the Crown were also frequently founded on resolutions first considered in a Committee of the Whole.[21]

From 1867 to 1968, there were three types of committees composed of the membership of the whole House: the Committee of Supply, the Committee of Ways and Means and Committees of the Whole House. The Committee of Supply would debate each request for Supply (Interim Supply, Main Estimates and Supplementary Estimates), item by item.[22] When that Committee recommended to the House that the Supply requested be granted, and the House had concurred, the Members went into the Committee of Ways and Means.[23] The Committee of Ways and Means would subsequently consider resolutions to authorize the expenditures from the Consolidated Revenue Fund;[24] once the resolutions were reported from the Committee of Ways and Means, and concurred in by the House, an appropriation bill based on the resolutions would then be introduced in the House.[25] The Committee of Ways and Means would also give preliminary authorization to taxation proposals outlined in the Minister of Finance's budget.[26] A Committee of the Whole would routinely debate resolutions preceding bills involving the expenditure of public monies.[27] It would only debate the advisability of the measure proposed since the details of the bill would not yet be known. Debate could be very lengthy. After the resolution was

---

17. *O'Brien*, p. 256. O'Brien notes that parliamentary procedure in Lower Canada was more comprehensive and better suited to a larger assembly than that in Upper Canada.

18. *Bourinot*, 1st ed., p. 414.

19. *Bourinot*, 1st ed., p. 212.

20. *Bourinot*, 1st ed., p. 416.

21. *Bourinot*, 1st ed., p. 416.

22. See, for example, *Journals*, October 27, 1967, pp. 418-20.

23. See, for example, *Journals*, March 26, 1964, pp. 133-4.

24. See, for example, *Journals*, March 26, 1964, p. 134; June 18, 1965, p. 278.

25. See, for example, *Journals*, March 26, 1964, p. 134. For additional information on the Committee of Supply and the Committee of Ways and Means, see Chapter 18, "Financial Procedures".

26. See, for example, *Journals*, April 29, 1964, pp. 266-71; December 14, 1967, pp. 595-600.

27. Resolutions relating to the expediency of introducing a bill involving the expenditure of public monies and couched in general rather than specific terms would be proposed to the House and referred to a Committee of the Whole for consideration.

approved, the House would proceed with the introduction and first reading of the bill.[28] A Committee of the Whole would also consider in detail most bills after second reading,[29] and other matters such as reports from committees appointed to review House rules and procedures,[30] and resolutions concerning international treaties and conventions.[31] Few government bills (typically non-contentious ones) were sent to standing or special committees for consideration. At that time, the work of standing and special committees was investigative, not legislative. Standing committees were not given the power to adopt clauses of the bill. After a standing or special committee had made its report, the proposed text of the bill had to be reconsidered again, clause by clause, in a Committee of the Whole. It was the Committee of the Whole's report that the House concurred in at report stage.[32]

Only minor changes to Committee of the Whole proceedings were made during the first hundred years of Confederation. In 1910, the House adopted rules codifying the requirement for relevance during debate in a Committee of the Whole and empowered the Chairman of Committees of the Whole House to direct a Member who persisted in irrelevance or repetition to discontinue his or her speech, the rule being copied verbatim from the British House of Commons' rules.[33] In 1955, the House adopted a committee report recommending restrictions on the length of debate in a Committee of the Whole and on the motion for the House to resolve into Committee of Supply.[34] In October 1964, rules were adopted pertaining to the limitation of debate on a resolution preceding bills involving the expenditure of public monies, and to the rearrangement of the order of consideration of a bill in a Committee of the Whole.[35]

In 1968, a special committee appointed to revise the rules of the House[36] criticized, among other things, the study of legislation in a Committee of the Whole. It argued such studies were too cumbersome and inefficient to handle the increased volume and complexity of legislation and public spending. The special committee

---

28. See, for example, *Journals*, July 3, 1961, pp. 795-6; July 13, 1964, pp. 526-7.

29. See, for example, *Journals*, November 13, 1964, p. 872; November 27, 1967, pp. 537-8.

30. See, for example, *Journals*, April 29, 1910, pp. 535-7; July 12, 1955, p. 881.

31. See, for example, *Journals*, May 1, 1925, pp. 234-6; June 8, 1942, p. 367.

32. See *Stewart*, p. 85. See also, for example, *Journals*, October 6, 1966, pp. 833-4; March 1, 1967, pp. 1459-60; March 15, 1967, p. 1538; March 16, 1967, pp. 1540, 1542; March 17, 1967, p. 1546; March 20, 1967, p. 1556; March 21, 1967, p. 1584.

33. *Journals*, April 29, 1910, pp. 535-7, in particular p. 537. See also British House of Commons Standing Order 42.

34. *Journals*, July 12, 1955, pp. 881, 920, 922-3, 928-9. Speeches were limited to 30 minutes at a time (except for the Prime Minister and Leader of the Opposition who had unlimited time) and the motion for the Speaker to leave the Chair was to be decided without debate or amendment.

35. *Journals*, October 9, 1964, pp. 779-80. Debate on such resolutions was limited to one day. In addition, the length of speeches was reduced to no more than 20 minutes solely during consideration of such resolutions in a Committee of the Whole. Consideration of Clause 1 of a bill was postponed until all other clauses had been considered if Clause 1 contained only the short title of the bill.

36. *Journals*, September 24, 1968, p. 68.

recommended the elimination of the preliminary resolution stage in a Committee of the Whole for taxation bills, and the reference of all bills, except those based on Supply and Ways and Means motions, to standing committees, where the clauses could be meticulously examined. It also recommended that bills referred to standing committees not be reconsidered in a Committee of the Whole, that bills considered in a Committee of the Whole not be debatable at report stage, and that all speeches in that forum be limited to 20 minutes.[37] The House subsequently adopted new Standing Orders which implemented these recommendations.[38]

In 1975, provisional amendments were made to the Standing Orders concerning Supply proceedings whereby selected items in the Estimates could be withdrawn from standing committees and examined in a Committee of the Whole.[39] This provisional Standing Order was continued for the following session through agreement,[40] but was not renewed thereafter. Changes to Committee of the Whole procedures occurred again in 1985 when the House amended its Standing Orders provisionally to reflect a recommendation made by the Special Committee on the Reform of the House of Commons. The Committee recommended that bills based on Ways and Means motions be referred to legislative committees, established specifically to examine bills in detail, rather than a Committee of the Whole. Only bills based on a Supply motion to concur in Estimates or Interim Supply would be referred to a Committee of the Whole.[41] This change was adopted permanently in 1987.[42] Today, any public bill, except one based on such a Supply motion, stands referred to either a standing, special or legislative committee.[43]

Presiding Officers

A Committee of the Whole is not chaired by the Speaker. Instead, it is chaired by the Chairman of Committees of the Whole. In his or her absence, the Chair is taken by the Deputy Chairman of Committees of the Whole, or the Assistant Deputy

---

37. *Journals*, December 6, 1968, pp. 429-64, and in particular pp. 432-3, 436. The Prime Minister and the Leader of the Opposition continued to have unlimited time.

38. *Journals*, December 20, 1968, pp. 554-79, and in particular pp. 560, 562, 572-3.

39. *Journals*, March 14, 1975, pp. 372-6; March 24, 1975, p. 399. In its Second Report, the Standing Committee on Procedure and Organization had expressed the view that the examination of selected items in the Estimates in a Committee of the Whole would permit the House to perform more effectively.

40. *Journals*, October 12, 1976, p. 12.

41. See Special Committee on the Reform of the House of Commons (the McGrath Committee), *Minutes of Proceedings and Evidence,* December 19, 1984, Issue No. 2, pp. 3-23, and in particular p. 21. See also *Journals,* December 20, 1984, p. 211; June 27, 1985, pp. 918-9.

42. *Journals*, June 3, 1987, pp. 1002-3, 1016.

43. For information on the referral of bills, see Chapter 16, "The Legislative Process".

Chairman of Committees of the Whole; alternatively, the Speaker may call upon any Member to chair the proceedings in a Committee of the Whole.[44]

SELECTION

At the beginning of each Parliament, the House selects from among its Members a Chairman of Committees of the Whole who also acts as Deputy Speaker in the absence of the Speaker.[45] The selection of the Chairman of Committees of the Whole proceeds as follows: a Member, usually the Prime Minister, moves that a particular Member of the House be selected Chairman of Committees of the Whole, the Member proposed usually coming from the government side of the House.[46] The motion is moved following the Speaker's report to the House on the Speech from the Throne and is often agreed to without discussion or dissent.[47] The Member selected acts in that capacity until the end of the Parliament, unless a vacancy arises during the course of the Parliament, at which time a successor is chosen.[48] A Deputy Chairman and an Assistant Deputy Chairman may also be selected in the same manner as the Chairman, except that their terms of office are effective only for the session in which they are chosen.[49]

AUTHORITY

The Standing Orders empower the Chairman of Committees of the Whole to maintain order and decorum in the Committee just as the Speaker does in the House and to decide questions of order.[50] However, the Chairman does not possess the authority to name a Member and order him or her to withdraw from the Chamber for the remainder of the day. That power can only be exercised by the Speaker in the House upon receiving a report from the Chairman of Committees of the Whole.[51] Both the Deputy Chairman and the Assistant Deputy Chairman of Committees of the Whole have the same powers as the Chairman.[52]

---

44. Standing Order 7(4). In practice, the person presiding over the House proceedings (other than the Speaker) will also chair the Committee when the House goes into a Committee of the Whole (see, for example, *Debates*, March 15, 1995, p. 10559; April 21, 1997, p. 10000).

45. Standing Order 7(1). For additional information on the selection of presiding officers, see Chapter 7, "The Speaker and Other Presiding Officers of the House".

46. The Deputy Speaker and Chairman of Committees of the Whole is required to be fluent in the official language which is not that of the Speaker. See Standing Order 7(2).

47. See, for example, *Journals*, January 18, 1994, p. 18; September 23, 1997, p. 13.

48. Standing Order 7(3). See, for example, *Journals*, May 15, 1990, pp. 1704-5.

49. Standing Order 8. There have been instances when debate has occurred and recorded divisions have been taken on these appointment motions (see, for example, *Journals*, October 2, 1990, p. 2050; February 27, 1996, pp. 3-4; February 28, 1996, pp. 9-10; October 28, 1996, pp. 778-9; October 29, 1996, pp. 784-9).

50. Standing Order 12.

51. Standing Order 11. See Chapter 7, "The Speaker and Other Presiding Officers of the House", and Chapter 13, "Rules of Order and Decorum". The topic of disorderly conduct in a Committee of the Whole is also discussed later in this chapter under "Conduct of Debate in a Committee of the Whole".

52. Standing Order 8.

APPEALS TO THE CHAIRMAN'S RULINGS

Members may appeal a ruling of the Chairman of Committees of the Whole to the Speaker.[53] (Rulings of the Speaker ceased to be subject to an appeal to the House in 1965.[54]) After the Chairman has made a ruling, a Member may rise on a point of order and appeal the ruling to the Speaker.[55] Such an appeal is not subject to debate. The Chairman immediately leaves the Chair at the Table, the Mace is placed back on the Table, and the Speaker resumes the Chair. (In the absence of the Speaker, the Chairman may take the Chair and decide the appeal to his or her own ruling.[56]) The Chairman stands in front of the Speaker's Chair and reports the incident and the ruling which has been appealed to the Speaker.[57] The Speaker may hear from other Members on the matter before ruling.[58]

As with all Speaker's rulings, after it has been delivered by the Speaker, there is no appeal and no discussion is allowed.[59] Only on rare occasions has a Chairman's ruling been overturned.[60] Since the Committee has not risen and reported progress, as soon as the appeal proceedings have been completed, the Speaker leaves the Chair, the Mace is removed from the Table and the Committee of the Whole resumes its deliberations.[61]

---

53. Standing Order 12.

54. See *Journals*, June 11, 1965, p. 224. For an example of appeals to the House prior to 1965, see *Debates*, May 31, 1956, pp. 4498-4534; June 1, 1956, pp. 4537-9, 4551-70, 4576-82.

55. See, for example, *Debates*, December 21, 1988, p. 541.

56. The Deputy or Acting Speaker hears the report from another Member whom he or she has designated. See, for example, *Journals*, June 25, 1965, pp. 303-4. In this instance, the Deputy Speaker confirmed his own ruling. In February 1971, when a Chairman's ruling was appealed to the Speaker, the Chairman advised the Committee that the Speaker was not in the building and that he did not wish to hear the appeal to his own ruling. By unanimous consent, the Committee agreed to continue its consideration of the legislation before it until the Speaker was available to hear the appeal. The Speaker subsequently sustained the ruling of the Chairman. See *Debates*, February 17, 1971, pp. 3495-6, 3498-501.

57. For practical reasons, the report is presented orally to the Speaker. For examples of recent appeals of Chairman's rulings, see *Journals*, April 6, 1971, pp. 475-6; December 21, 1988, pp. 67-8.

58. In 1971, the Speaker permitted Members to present their arguments to him before he ruled on the matter (*Debates*, April 6, 1971, pp. 4969-71).

59. Standing Orders 10 and 12.

60. When the Standing Orders allowed appeals to be decided by the House, rulings by Chairmen were overturned on at least three occasions (*Journals*, March 6, 1913, p. 323; March 22, 1948, pp. 275-6; December 13, 1957, p. 270).

61. See, for example, *Debates*, April 6, 1971, p. 4971; December 21, 1988, p. 541.

Resolving into a Committee of the Whole

When the Order of the Day is read for the House to go into a Committee of the Whole to consider a resolution or motion[62] or when it is ordered that a bill be considered in a Committee of the Whole,[63] no question is put.[64] The Speaker leaves the Chair and exits the Chamber.[65] The Chair of the Committee is taken by the Chairman, Deputy Chairman or Assistant Deputy Chairman of Committees of the Whole. The Chairman of the Committee sits in the Clerk's chair at the head of the Table, and the Table Officers sit to the right and left of the Chairman. One of the Table Officers acts as the clerk of the Committee.[66]

If legislation is being discussed in a Committee of the Whole, the Minister or Parliamentary Secretary responsible for the legislation sits at one of the front row desks on the government side of the Chamber. The Minister acts both as a witness, by answering any questions Members may have, and as a member of the Committee, participating in debate, voting and moving amendments to the bill, should he or she wish to do so. The Minister may be assisted by one or two departmental officials who are seated at a small table on the floor of the House in front of the Minister. Before proceedings begin, the officials are escorted by a senior page to their place; they are escorted out of the Chamber immediately after the Committee rises and before the

---

62. See, for example, *Debates*, May 9, 1975, p. 5646; January 28, 1988, p. 12362.

63. See, for example, *Debates*, November 24, 1997, p. 2105.

64. Standing Order 100. In addition, pursuant to Standing Order 56(2), any government motion seeking to have the House resolve itself into a Committee of the Whole on the next sitting day is put without debate or amendment. Prior to 1955, as a general rule, whenever the House desired to resolve itself into a Committee of the Whole, the motion "That Mr. Speaker do now leave the Chair" was moved. In some instances, if the motion was for the House to resolve itself into the Committee of Supply or into the Committee of Ways and Means, it was debatable; in other instances, the House would resolve itself into Committee without putting the question. (In 1913, the House had adopted an amendment to the rules which provided that if an Order of the Day were called to go into the Committee of Supply or of Ways and Means on a Thursday or Friday, the Speaker left the Chair without putting any question (*Journals*, April 23, 1913, pp. 507-9)). In 1955, the special committee appointed to consider the procedures of the House recommended a new Standing Order to clarify what had become the "general practice" by that time. The House adopted the rule which specified that except for the particular circumstances of motions to resolve into the Committee of Supply or the Committee of Ways and Means, all motions for the House to resolve itself into a Committee of the Whole on any matter would be decided without debate or amendment (*Journals*, July 12, 1955, pp. 920-1). The wording of the rule remained unchanged until December 1968. Since the Committees of Supply and of Ways and Means were abolished at that time, the Standing Order was rephrased to stipulate that when an Order of the Day was read for the House to go into a Committee of the Whole or when it was ordered that a bill be considered in a Committee of the Whole, no question would be put. The Speaker would simply leave the Chair upon the order being read (*Journals*, December 20, 1968, p. 572).

65. Although the Speaker has participated in debate in a Committee of the Whole (see, for example, *Debates*, April 7, 1927, pp. 2034-8), this is not the modern practice.

66. According to *Beauchesne*, 4th ed. (p. 195), the Clerk also leaves the Chamber when the Speaker exits and returns when the Committee rises. In practice, the Clerk will leave the Chamber along with the Speaker but may reappear to take the place of one of the Table Officers.

Speaker takes the Chair. This is the only occasion when persons other than Members and House staff are permitted on the floor of the Chamber when the House is sitting.

Conduct of Debate in a Committee of the Whole

Proceedings in a Committee of the Whole are governed by the Standing Orders as far as may be applicable and by long-established practice.[67] While Members must be recognized by the Chairman before speaking or moving a motion, discussions are less formal; Members may occupy, speak and vote from places other than those regularly assigned to them,[68] and they may be recognized to speak more than once to a question,[69] although they may not share their speaking time.[70] The Prime Minister and Leader of the Opposition have unlimited time.[71] Members have 20 minutes at a time to make speeches, to ask questions and to receive replies.[72] The Chairman must apply the 20-minute limit to ensure the Minister or sponsor has an opportunity to answer a final question within the 20 minutes. As in the House, where all remarks are addressed to the Speaker, all remarks must be addressed to the Chairman.[73] However, in practice, Members often address one another, ask questions and receive answers directly.[74] In these exchanges, Members should nevertheless always refer to one another by the names of their ridings as is done in the House.[75]

The same rules and practices that apply to motions in the House generally apply in a Committee of the Whole, except that motions do not require a seconder.[76] The

---

67. Rules in a Committee of the Whole are similar to those in standing, special and legislative committees. The Standing Orders apply, except those relating to the seconding of motions, limiting the number of times of speaking, and the length of speeches. See Standing Orders 101 and 116. See also Chapter 20, "Committees".

68. *Debates*, October 15, 1987, p. 10064; October 16, 1987, pp. 10089-90.

69. Standing Order 101(1).

70. Standing Order 43(2) stipulates that only when the Speaker is in the Chair may Members split their speaking time. When the House has resolved into a Committee of the Whole, the Speaker is not in the Chair.

71. Standing Order 101(3).

72. Standing Order 101(3). See also *Debates*, May 26, 1982, p. 17802; March 8, 1983, p. 23550; September 30, 1991, p. 2946; March 21, 1996, p. 1068. This is in contrast to when the Speaker is in the Chair. Pursuant to Standing Order 43(1), when the Speaker is in the Chair, no Member may speak longer than 20 minutes; following each 20-minute speech, there is a 10-minute period for Members to ask questions and comment on the speech.

73. See Standing Order 17. See also *Debates*, February 8, 1994, p. 1084.

74. See *Debates*, April 21, 1997, p. 10001.

75. See, for example, *Debates*, December 2, 1997, p. 2613.

76. Standing Order 101(1).

motions "that the Chair rise and report progress"[77] and "that the Chairman leave the Chair"[78] are unique to a Committee of the Whole and are decided without debate or amendment. Once proposed, motions may be withdrawn only by the mover and only with the unanimous consent of the Committee.[79] When an amendment is moved, debate must proceed on the amendment until it is disposed of.

QUORUM

Under the *Constitution Act, 1867,* and the Standing Orders of the House, a quorum of 20 Members, including the Speaker, is required to "constitute a meeting of the House for the exercise of its powers".[80] Twenty Members is also the quorum for a Committee of the Whole.[81] If a Member draws to the attention of the Chairman a lack of quorum in a Committee of the Whole, the Chairman counts the Members.[82] If 20 Members are not present, the Chairman rises without seeking leave to report progress and sit again. The Speaker takes the Chair,[83] the House is resumed, the Chairman reports the lack of a quorum and the Speaker counts the number of Members in the Chamber. If the Speaker finds a quorum, the Committee resumes its deliberations.[84] If there is no quorum, the bells are rung until there is a quorum, at which time the Committee resumes its deliberations. If after 15 minutes the bells are still ringing, the Speaker adjourns the House until the next sitting day.[85] Any proceedings which are brought to a close by a lack of quorum in the House are allowed to stand and retain their precedence on the *Order Paper* for the next sitting when the Order is called for the House to resolve into a Committee of the Whole.[86] At that time, the Committee resumes its work from the point of interruption.

---

77. See, for example, *Debates*, November 8, 1919, pp. 1992-3; March 17, 1966, p. 2825; November 30, 1978, p. 1679.

78. See Standing Order 102(1).

79. See, for example, *Debates*, December 2, 1997, p. 2615.

80. *Constitution Act, 1867*, R.S.C. 1985, Appendix II, No. 5, s. 48; Standing Order 29(1).

81. *Bourinot*, 4th ed., p. 218; *Beauchesne*, 6th ed., p. 250.

82. See, for example, *Debates*, May 19, 1966, p. 5323; March 14, 1967, pp. 13993-4.

83. The Chairman may also take the Chair as Deputy Speaker (see, for example, *Debates*, June 6, 1899, col. 4461).

84. See, for example, *Debates*, June 6, 1899, col. 4461; March 30, 1915, pp. 1780-1; May 13, 1919, p. 2361; February 29, 1968, pp. 7131-2; October 29, 1968, p. 2180.

85. Standing Order 29(3). See Chapter 9, "Sittings of the House", for additional information on quorum.

86. Standing Order 41(2). Since this Standing Order was first adopted in 1991, proceedings in a Committee of the Whole have not been interrupted because of a lack of quorum. On June 9, 1938, the House was adjourned because of a lack of quorum in the Committee of Supply (see *Journals*, June 9, 1938, p. 434; *Debates*, p. 3704). The following day the Prime Minister moved a motion that the House resolve itself into the Committee of Supply. The motion was adopted and the House went into Committee of Supply. See *Journals*, June 10, 1938, p. 436; *Debates*, pp. 3705-6.

RELEVANCE AND DISORDER IN A COMMITTEE OF THE WHOLE

Speeches in a Committee of the Whole must be strictly relevant to the item or clause under consideration.[87] If a Member's speech is not relevant to the debate, the Chairman is empowered to call the Member to order and if, necessary, warn that he or she risks being reported to the House.[88] An exception which has developed to the rule of relevance is the wide-ranging debate permitted on Clause 1 (or Clause 2 if Clause 1 only contains the short title of a bill).[89] Certain limits have nonetheless been established for consideration of Clause 1, including proscriptions against repetition of second reading debate and against anticipation of clause-by-clause debate.[90] Moreover, debate must be confined to the contents of the bill.[91] A further limitation arises when an amendment has been proposed to Clause 1: remarks must be restricted to the amendment until it has been disposed of.[92]

The Chairman is empowered to maintain order in a Committee of the Whole and to decide all questions of order.[93] However, if a Member persists in irrelevance or repetition, refuses to withdraw unparliamentary remarks or to resume his or her seat when so requested, or if the proceedings become disorderly and the Chairman is unable to restore decorum in the Committee, the Chairman may rise and report the incident to the Speaker without seeking leave of the Committee.[94] The Speaker takes the Chair, receives the report of the Chairman, and deals with the matter as if the

---

87. Standing Order 101(2).

88. Standing Order 11(2). See, for example, *Debates*, September 30, 1991, pp. 2937, 2979; March 15, 1995, p. 10566.

89. There is no provision for this practice in the Standing Orders; nonetheless, it has become an accepted practice over the years. See *Debates*, November 30, 1978, pp. 1657, 1665. See Chapter 13, "Rules of Order and Decorum", for additional information on relevance.

90. See Chairman's ruling, *Debates*, May 11, 1960, pp. 3783-4, 3788-9.

91. See Chairman's ruling, *Debates*, March 23, 1965, p. 12693.

92. See Chairman's rulings, *Debates*, August 2, 1960, p. 7418; December 11, 1979, p. 2239.

93. Standing Order 12.

94. Standing Order 11(2). See, for example, *Debates*, July 31, 1944, pp. 5681-2; May 25, 1956, pp. 4340-1; March 16, 1962, p. 1889. Standing Order 12 stipulates that disorder in a Committee of the Whole can only be censured by the House after the Speaker has received a report from the Chairman. In practice, since 1986 the Speaker has had the authority, under Standing Order 11, to "name" a Member without putting a motion to the House; the Chairman is not vested with the authority to "name" a Member in a Committee of the Whole. See *Journals*, February 6, 1986, pp. 1644-66 and in particular pp. 1645-6; February 13, 1986, p. 1710; June 3, 1987, p. 1016. See also Chapter 13, "Rules of Order and Decorum", for additional information on "naming". Also see *Bourinot*, 4th ed., p. 397.

incident had happened in the House and may subsequently name the Member.[95] In the case of unparliamentary language, the Speaker may request the Member to withdraw the remarks. After the matter has been dealt with, the Committee resumes its deliberations without a motion to this effect. In extreme cases of disorder in a Committee of the Whole, the Speaker has taken the Chair without waiting for the Chairman to report.[96]

QUESTIONS OF PRIVILEGE

Given that the House rarely sits as a Committee of the Whole and that when it does, the proceedings are typically completed in a matter of minutes, questions of privilege are not often raised today in a Committee of the Whole. The practice regarding the raising of questions of privilege in a Committee of the Whole is, nonetheless, identical to that for any standing, legislative or special committee. The Chairman has no authority to rule that a breach of privilege has occurred.[97] The Chairman hears the question of privilege and may entertain a motion that certain events which occurred in the Committee should be reported to the House.[98] If the Committee decides that

---

95. Standing Order 11(2). A Member has never been named for persisting in irrelevance or repetition in a Committee of the Whole. In 1944, the Chairman reported to the Speaker that a Member refused to withdraw the word "bribe". After refusing the Speaker's request that he withdraw his remarks, under the rules in place at the time, the Member was named and ordered to withdraw from the Chamber (see *Debates*, July 31, 1944, pp. 5680-4). In 1956, when the Chairman was addressing the Committee, a Member rose on a question of privilege. When the Chairman asked the Member to resume his seat, the Member refused. The Chairman reported the incident to the Speaker. Under the procedures in place at that time, after debate on the matter, the House voted to suspend the Member from the service of the House for the remainder of the sitting (see *Debates*, May 25, 1956, pp. 4340-52). In 1962, when the House was in Committee of Supply, a Member implied in his remarks that the Chairman was not being impartial when recognizing Members on debate. The Chairman asked the Member to withdraw his comments. When the Member refused, the Chairman reported the incident to the Speaker. Again, under the procedures in place at that time, the House subsequently ordered the Member to withdraw from the Chamber for the remainder of the sitting (see *Debates*, March 16, 1962, pp. 1888-90). On one occasion, disorder ensued when a Member refused to resume his seat when the Chairman would not hear him on a point of order because of the hour of sitting (pursuant to the rules at the time, the Chairman was not permitted to recognize any Member after 1:00 a.m.). The Chairman reported the incident to the Speaker who advised the House to resolve the matter itself. After debate, the House resolved back into the Committee of the Whole and heard the Member's point of order (see *Debates*, May 15, 1956, pp. 3967-9).

96. In 1913, grave disorder in Committee prompted the Speaker to take the Chair twice without hearing a report from the Chairman (*Debates*, March 15, 1913, cols. 6016-22). This incident was procedurally unique in that the Speaker took the Chair on his own initiative before the Committee had reported. Without direction from the House, the Speaker named a Member for disregarding the authority of the Chair. The offending Member subsequently withdrew his remarks and apologized to the Chair and the House. This incident marked the first occasion of "naming" in the House of Commons.

97. See Chapter 3, "Privileges and Immunities". See also *Maingot*, 2nd ed., p. 221.

98. Often, when a Member rises on a question of privilege in a Committee of the Whole, the Chairman rules that the matter raised is more appropriately a point of order or a matter of debate. See, for example, *Debates*, November 23, 1970, p. 1373; November 8, 1971, p. 9435; October 23, 1974, p. 665; May 22, 1975, pp. 6012-3; December 20, 1983, pp. 379-90.

the matter should be reported, then the Chairman rises, the Speaker resumes the Chair, and the Chairman reports the question of privilege.[99] The Speaker then deals with the matter. If a *prima facie* case of privilege is found by the Speaker, a Member may move a motion dealing with the matter.[100]

The Speaker will entertain a question of privilege in regard to a matter that occurred in a Committee of the Whole, only if the matter has been dealt with first in the Committee of the Whole and reported accordingly to the House.[101]

When the House is in a Committee of the Whole, a Member may not rise on a question of privilege affecting the privileges of the House in general; however, a Member may move a motion for the Committee to rise and report progress in order that the Speaker may hear the question of privilege.[102]

INTERRUPTIONS

When proceedings in a Committee of the Whole are interrupted in order for the House to proceed with scheduled items of daily business (for example, at 2:00 p.m. Monday, Tuesday and Thursday, and 11:00 a.m. on Friday, for Statements by Members and Question Period; or an interruption for a scheduled recorded division in the House) or if the Committee is unable to complete its business at the conclusion of the time allotted for Government Orders,[103] the Chairman interrupts the proceedings and rises. The Speaker takes the Chair and the Committee reports progress to the House and requests leave to consider its business again later that day or at the next sitting of the House. The report is then received by the House and the Committee is

---

99. *Beauchesne*, 4th ed., p. 95. See also Chapter 3, "Privileges and Immunities". A question of privilege was raised in a Committee of the Whole in 1987 when John Nunziata (York South–Weston) rose to complain that a Member had assaulted him because he was not in his own seat. He requested an apology, but the Member refused. Although the Chairman advised that he would report on the matter to the full House, only the bill as amended was reported later that day (*Journals*, October 15, 1987, pp. 1688-9). The following day, Mr. Nunziata raised his question of privilege in the House. The Member apologized and the Speaker declared the matter closed (*Debates*, October 15, 1987, p. 10064; October 16, 1987, pp. 10089-90).

100. For further information, see Chapter 3, "Privileges and Immunities".

101. See *Debates*, June 12, 1980, pp. 2030-1; December 20, 1983, pp. 364-9. In the 1983 instance, a Member argued that because the Committee had risen and reported progress, the House was apprised of the circumstances surrounding the question of privilege. The Speaker ruled that the Committee had only risen, reported progress and asked for leave to sit again. The Committee had not reported the bill nor any concerns to the House.

102. See *Debates*, April 30, 1964, p. 2782; October 29, 1964, pp. 9561-2; June 2, 1966, pp. 5908-9.

103. See, for example, *Debates*, December 20, 1988, pp. 419, 517.

granted leave to sit again later that day or at the next sitting of the House.[104] After the interruption, the Committee may resume sitting if the Order is called.[105]

If business arises which requires the attention of the House (for example, a Royal Assent ceremony), the Speaker takes the Chair immediately without waiting for the Committee to rise and report progress.[106] When the matter which led to the interruption has been dealt with, the Committee resumes sitting. Messages received from the Senate will not interrupt the proceedings of the Committee; these messages are only reported to the House by the Speaker after the Committee has risen and reported and before another Order of the Day is taken up by the House.[107]

EXTENSION OF DEBATE

Only when the Speaker is in the Chair, may a Member move a motion, without notice, to extend the sitting beyond the ordinary hour of daily adjournment to continue consideration of a particular item of business.[108] When the House is in a Committee of the Whole, a Member must indicate his intention to move such a motion; the Chairman interrupts the proceedings and, without reporting progress, rises so that the motion can be properly moved and disposed of with the Speaker in the Chair.[109] The motion cannot be debated or amended.[110] It carries automatically unless at least 15 Members who object to it rise in their places when the Speaker puts the question, in which case the motion is deemed withdrawn.[111] On occasion, the House has adopted special orders extending a sitting in order to complete consideration of a bill in a Committee of the Whole.[112]

---

104. See, for example, *Journals*, September 30, 1991, pp. 412, 414; April 21, 1997, p. 1494; *Debates*, December 20, 1988, pp. 419, 517; September 30, 1991, pp. 2904, 2950; April 21, 1997, p. 9984.

105. See, for example, *Debates*, September 30, 1991, pp. 2924, 2954; April 21, 1997, p. 10000.

106. *Bourinot*, 4th ed., p. 397. See, for example, *Journals*, May 9, 1933, pp. 537-8; June 20, 1951, pp. 581-2.

107. *Bourinot*, 4th ed., pp. 401-2.

108. Standing Order 26(1). The motion must be proposed during the hour prior to consideration of the item of business being interrupted by the beginning of Private Members' Business, by the dinner break, or by the ordinary hour of adjournment, as the case may be.

109. Standing Order 26(1)(a). See, for example, *Debates*, March 13, 1969, pp. 6606-7; March 20, 1969, p. 6933; November 9, 1970, pp. 1030-1; November 16, 1970, pp. 1222-3; November 17, 1970, p. 1270. In 1992, such a motion was moved and carried, but only after the Chairman had risen, reported progress and requested leave to consider a bill at the next sitting of the House. After the hour for Private Members' Business had been completed, the House resumed sitting in a Committee of the Whole to consider the bill (see *Debates*, December 11, 1992, p. 15145; *Journals*, pp. 2400-1).

110. Standing Order 26(1)(*c*).

111. Standing Order 26(2).

112. See, for example, *Journals*, June 8, 1987, p. 1052; October 15, 1987, p.1687; September 17, 1991, pp. 354-5.

CLOSURE

The Standing Orders provide the government with a procedural device to force a decision by the House on any motion or bill under debate. This device is known as closure. [113] Although the limited use of Committees of the Whole in modern practice has substantially reduced the use of closure there, it may still be invoked. Once debate has begun in a Committee of the Whole, closure may be applied to a motion; to the whole committee stage of a bill; to its title, preamble or its clauses, individually or in groups; or to amendments or sub-amendments. Furthermore, closure may be moved on clauses of a bill which have not yet been called. [114]

Before invoking closure of a matter being considered in a Committee of the Whole, a notice must be given orally at a previous sitting by a Minister. This notice is normally, but not necessarily, given while a Committee of the Whole is considering the matter to be closured. [115] If notice is to be given at some other time, the consistent practice is then to wait for debate on that matter to have been initiated, either on a previous day or earlier on the same day. When oral notice has been properly given, a Minister may then move "that the further consideration of any resolution or resolutions, clause or clauses, section or sections, preamble or preambles, or title or titles, shall be the first business of the Committee, and shall not further be postponed". [116] Such a closure motion is moved before the Committee resumes consideration of the Order to which closure would apply.

---

113. Standing Order 57. Closure was first introduced in 1913 (*Journals*, April 23, 1913, pp. 507-9) and applied in a Committee of the Whole during consideration of the Naval Aid Bill (*Debates*, May 9, 1913, col. 9445). See Chapter 14, "The Curtailment of Debate", for additional information on closure.

114. On four occasions, in 1913, 1917 (twice) and 1919, all clauses had been called and postponed before closure was moved (*Debates*, May 9, 1913, col. 9445; August 28, 1917, p. 5016; September 12, 1917, p. 5707; April 28, 1919, p. 1797). In three other cases, in 1932, 1956 and 1988, closure was applied to clauses which had not been called (*Debates*, April 1, 1932, p. 1609; May 31, 1956, p. 4498; June 1, 1956, pp. 4554-6; December 21, 1988, p. 541). When closure was moved in 1988, during debate in the Committee of the Whole on Bill C-2, *An Act to implement the Free Trade Agreement between Canada and the United States of America*, Peter Milliken (Kingston and the Islands) raised a point of order questioning the form of the motion, and arguing that the closure motion was not procedurally acceptable because it attempted to closure parts of the bill which had not been debated or postponed. The Chairman of Committees of the Whole ruled that on the basis of the 1932 and 1956 precedents, closure may be applied in a Committee of the Whole to parts of a bill not yet debated. The Chairman's ruling was subsequently appealed to the Speaker who sustained the decision (*Debates*, December 21, 1988, pp. 532-41; *Journals*, pp. 67-8).

115. Standing Order 57. The Standing Order is not specific when oral notice has to be given. For examples of notices in a Committee of the Whole, see *Debates*, May 8, 1913, col. 9444; August 27, 1917, p. 5015; September 11, 1917, p. 5702; April 25, 1919, p. 1789; March 31, 1932, p. 1605; May 30, 1956, pp. 4464-5; December 20, 1988, p. 500.

116. Standing Order 57.

Once moved, a closure motion is decided without debate or amendment.[117] The question is put on the motion and a division may take place. If the motion is adopted, Members' participation in the debate is restricted: they may speak only once on the question to which closure has been applied, and for no longer than 20 minutes.[118] The sitting may be extended but debate concludes no later than 11:00 p.m. that same day, at which time the Chairman puts all the necessary questions to dispose of the matter.[119]

After the consideration of a closured bill is completed, the Chairman reports the bill back to the House with or without amendment. A motion for concurrence in the bill at report stage is moved and put without debate.[120] If the bill is concurred in at report stage and the sitting has not gone beyond the time normally provided for Government Orders, the House can then proceed immediately to the third reading stage of the bill.[121] If the bill is concurred in at report stage and the sitting has been extended beyond the ordinary hour of daily adjournment, the bill is then ordered for third reading at the next sitting and the House adjourns.[122]

TIME ALLOCATION

The Standing Orders provide a mechanism, referred to as time allocation, for restricting the length of debate on bills.[123] Although there are certain elements of closure in time allocation, it allows the government to negotiate with the opposition parties to establish, in advance, a timetable for the consideration of a public bill at one or more legislative stages, including debate at the Committee of the Whole stage. Time allocation has been imposed rarely in a Committee of the Whole; this stems from the fact that bills which are referred to a Committee of the Whole are generally of a non-controversial nature and tend to generate little discussion, or deal with

---

117. Standing Order 57. See, for example, *Debates*, May 9, 1913, col. 9445; August 28, 1917, p. 5016; September 12, 1917, p. 5707; April 28, 1919, p. 1797; April 1, 1932, p. 1609; May 15, 1956, p. 3895. On two occasions, points of order were raised immediately after the closure motion was proposed, the question on the motion was put in both instances only after the Chairman's ruling had been appealed to the Speaker and sustained. See *Debates*, May 31, 1956, pp. 4498-528; June 1, 1956, pp. 4554-6; December 21, 1988, pp. 532, 541.

118. Standing Order 57. See, for example, *Debates*, December 21, 1988, pp. 573, 575.

119. See, for example, *Debates*, December 21, 1988, p. 585. In 1988, the wording of Standing Order 57 stipulated that debate was to conclude at 1:00 a.m. This was changed to 11:00 p.m. in 1991.

120. Standing Order 76.1(12). See, for example, *Debates*, December 21, 1988, pp. 587-9.

121. Standing Order 76.1(11). In 1932, a bill that had been closured in a Committee of the Whole was read a third time at the same sitting because the Committee reported back to the House before the normal hour of adjournment (*Debates*, April 1, 1932, pp. 1609-37).

122. See, for example, *Journals*, June 1, 1956, p. 689; December 21, 1988, pp. 68-9.

123. See Standing Order 78. See Chapter 14, "The Curtailment of Debate", for detailed information on time allocation.

matters of political importance on which arrangements have been made on the use of House time.[124]

PROHIBITION AGAINST THE "PREVIOUS QUESTION"

The motion "That this question be now put" is referred to as the "previous question". Its purpose, when moved and debated in the House, is to achieve one of two possible objectives: either to prevent any amendment to the main motion and force a direct vote on it, or to delay a vote on the main motion by prolonging debate.[125]

The moving of the previous question is prohibited in a Committee of the Whole as it is in any committee.[126] Given that a bill is referred to a Committee of the Whole for clause-by-clause consideration, the moving of the previous question would prevent Members from proposing amendments and considering the legislation to the fullest extent possible.

ADJOURNMENT OF DEBATE

A Committee of the Whole has no power to adjourn its own sitting or to adjourn consideration of any matter to a future sitting.[127] If its consideration of a matter is not concluded by the ordinary hour of daily adjournment, or if the House is scheduled to proceed with Private Members' Business or the Adjournment Proceedings, the Chairman interrupts the proceedings and rises. The Speaker takes the Chair and the Committee reports progress to the House and requests leave to consider its business again at the next sitting.[128] The Speaker asks, as a matter of form, "When shall the

---

124. Between 1971 and 1997, time allocation was applied to the Committee of the Whole stage on eight occasions. In six of the cases, debate had already begun in a Committee of the Whole when a Minister advised the House that an agreement could not be reached with respect to a timetable and gave notice that a time allocation motion would be proposed at the next sitting of the House. See *Debates*, December 1, 1971, pp. 10046-7; January 28, 1977, pp. 2495-6; December 2, 1977, p. 1498; June 12, 1978, p. 6298; December 5, 1979, p. 2040; March 14, 1983, p. 23750. The following sitting day, the Minister moved the time allocation motion during Routine Proceedings. See *Debates*, December 2, 1971, pp. 10076-7; January 31, 1977, p. 2534; December 5, 1977, p. 1545; June 13, 1978, p. 6355; December 7, 1979, p. 2148; March 15, 1983, p. 23798. In the other two instances, a time allocation motion was moved to provide for the completion of debate at all stages of a bill, including the Committee of the Whole stage, in the same sitting. See *Journals*, June 27, 1980, pp. 310, 312; March 15, 1995, pp. 1219-23. By unanimous consent, the House has adopted motions limiting debate in Committees of the Whole to a specific number of hours or sitting days. See, for example, *Journals*, May 7, 1982, pp. 4806-7; September 17, 1991, pp. 354-5. See also *Debates*, September 30, 1991, pp. 2902-3; June 10, 1998, p. 7941.

125. See Standing Order 61. See also Chapter 12, "The Process of Debate", and Chapter 14, "The Curtailment of Debate", for more information on the "previous question".

126. See *Bourinot*, 1st ed., p. 421. This rule appeared as far back as the first edition of *May* (p. 225). See also *May*, 22nd ed., p. 691; *Bourinot*, 4th ed., p. 328. See also *Journals*, May 7, 1913, pp. 560-1; *Debates*, May 7, 1913, cols. 9330-40.

127. *Bourinot*, 4th ed., p. 399.

128. See, for example, *Debates*, December 20, 1988, p. 517; December 11, 1992, p. 15145.

report be received? Now. When shall the Committee have leave to sit again? At the next sitting of the House. So ordered."

During consideration of a bill or motion in a Committee of the Whole, a Member may move "That the Chairman rise and report progress".[129] A motion that "the Chairman report progress" has the same effect as a motion for the House to adjourn debate.[130] In other words, if this motion is adopted, no further debate can occur on the matter under consideration that day. If this motion is rejected, the Committee continues sitting and the question cannot be put again until some intermediate proceeding has taken place.[131]

After a Committee of the Whole has risen, reported progress and received leave to sit again at the next sitting of the House, when the Order is next called, the House goes into a Committee of the Whole and the Committee resumes its business.[132]

TERMINATION OF DEBATE

The proceedings in a Committee of the Whole may be brought abruptly to a close if a Member moves a motion "That the Chairman leave the Chair" and the motion is adopted. Such a motion is always in order, is not debatable and, if adopted, supersedes the question then before the Committee.[133] If the motion is put and agreed to, the Committee rises without a report to the House, and the matter before the

---

129. See, for example, *Debates*, November 8, 1919, pp. 1992-3; March 17, 1966, p. 2825; November 30, 1978, p. 1679.

130. *Bourinot*, 4th ed., p. 399.

131. *Bourinot*, 4th ed., p. 400. According to *Beauchesne*, 3rd ed., "the term 'intermediate proceeding' ... means a proceeding that can properly be entered on the journals. The true test is that if any parliamentary proceeding takes place, the second motion is regular, and the clerk ought to enter the proceedings to show that the motion in question is regular" (p. 74). In a Committee of the Whole, an intermediate proceeding could be the moving of an amendment, the disposal of a clause or the motion that "the Chairman leave the Chair".

132. *Bourinot*, 4th ed., p. 397.

133. Standing Order 102(1). For the first 45 years of Confederation, it was more common for Members to move simply "That the Committee do now rise." The motion was debatable and had the effect of superseding whatever matter was then before the Committee (see, for example, *Debates*, May 19, 1869, pp. 393-4; March 5, 1884, p. 671; May 9, 1892, cols. 2294-305). In 1913, the House adopted a Standing Order which attempted to list all debatable motions (see current Standing Order 67). Omissions in this list provoked discussions about what motions were in fact debatable; one such discussion in 1916 concerned the motion "That the Chairman leave the Chair". In ruling that this motion was correctly omitted from the list, and that as a result debate could not take place on it, the Chairman also established that the correct motion to move was "That the Chairman leave the Chair" and not "That the Committee do now rise." See *Debates*, April 3, 1916, pp. 2449, 2453-4. In 1927, the Standing Order was formally amended to prohibit debate (see *Standing Orders of the House of Commons*, 1927, Standing Order 59).

Committee disappears from the *Order Paper*.[134] If the Committee rejects the motion for the Chairman to leave the Chair, the question cannot be put again without some intermediate proceeding having taken place.[135]

DIVISIONS

When the Chairman puts the question on a bill, clause or motion, if one or more Members object, they may request that a division, or standing vote, take place;[136] if no such request is made, the Chairman declares the bill, clause or motion carried/ adopted or negatived, on division (that is, signalling opposition without calling for a standing vote).[137] It is not necessary to have five Members rise to force a standing vote as is required in the House.[138] In a Committee of the Whole, the names of Members voting for or against an item are not recorded and no bells are rung to call Members in to vote.[139] Those Members present in the Chamber simply rise in rows and are counted by a Table Officer. Members do not have to be in their allocated places. As is the case with a vote in the House, no Member may enter the Chamber while a division is in progress in a Committee of the Whole,[140] nor will the Chairman hear a point of order during a vote.[141] Those in favour of the motion to the right of the Chair rise first and after each row has been counted, the Chair asks the Members in that row to sit. The same procedure is followed for those in favour to the left of the Chair. The procedure is repeated for those opposed to the motion. After the count, the Table Officer stands at the end of the Table and reports the number of "yeas" and "nays"

---

134. *Bourinot*, 4th ed., pp. 400, 527. On a number of occasions during the early years of Confederation, Committees of the Whole either rose without reporting progress on a bill or adopted motions to the effect that the Chairman now leave the Chair (see, for example, *Journals*, May 19, 1869, p. 106; May 23, 1874, p. 326; March 29, 1883, p. 157; April 7, 1886, p. 126). The matter under consideration would disappear from the *Order Paper*. In 1883, the Speaker ruled that a committee could not extinguish a bill and that a bill which had disappeared from the *Order Paper* in this manner could be revived by a motion, moved without notice, that the bill be considered in a committee on a future day (*Journals*, March 30, 1883, pp. 159-60; *Debates*, pp. 331-2).

135. Standing Order 102(2).

136. See, for example, *Debates*, December 20, 1983, p. 352.

137. See, for example, *Debates*, December 21, 1988, p. 586.

138. See Standing Order 45(1).

139. See *Debates*, September 30, 1991, p. 2952.

140. *Debates*, April 17, 1962, p. 3080. This rule has been difficult to enforce because the procedures for a division are less formal when the House sits as a Committee of the Whole: there are no division bells calling Members to vote; the Whips do not signal to the Chair that Members are ready; and Members do not have to be standing at their desk. See, for example, *Debates*, December 1, 1971, pp. 10072-4; December 2, 1971, pp. 10075-6; December 20, 1983, pp. 352-4, 382-3, 388, 390.

141. *Debates*, December 20, 1983, p. 352.

to the Chairman. The Chairman declares the motion carried or negatived. [142] Pairs are not declared when there is a vote in a Committee of the Whole because no record is kept of the names of Members who voted one way or the other. [143]

The Chairman does not vote in a Committee of the Whole, but in the event of a tie, he or she has a casting vote and is governed by the same rules as the Speaker under similar conditions. [144] The general principle guiding a Chairman of a Committee of the Whole is to vote in such a manner as to preserve the matter for further consideration (that is, in such a way as to maintain the status quo). [145]

Consideration of Bills in a Committee of the Whole

After a bill has been read a second time, the House may order it referred to a Committee of the Whole for consideration either pursuant to the Standing Orders [146] or by unanimous consent [147] or pursuant to a special order of the House. [148]

Following concurrence in the Main and Supplementary Estimates and Interim Supply, all appropriation or Supply bills (bills authorizing the actual withdrawal of funds from the Consolidated Revenue Fund for government expenditures) are

---

142. Standing votes have taken place in Committees of the Whole on a number of occasions. Examples can be found in *Debates*, December 21, 1988, pp. 585-7; September 30, 1991, p. 2997. See *Debates*, December 21, 1988, p. 587, and December 2, 1997, p. 2617, for examples of applied votes in a Committee of the Whole.

143. *Debates*, March 8, 1935, pp. 1541-2. Pairing is an arrangement whereby two Members on opposite sides of the House agree not to vote for a specific period of time. The arrangement which permits Members to be absent on other business is worked out either by the respective Whips or by the Members themselves. For additional information on pairing, see Chapter 12, "The Process of Debate".

144. Standing Order 9. See *Bourinot*, 4th ed., p. 398. See also *Debates*, June 20, 1904, col. 5164; April 15, 1920, p. 1265; June 23, 1922, p. 3473; March 26, 1928, p. 1681. As noted in *Dawson* at page 183, there has been a lack of consistency in this practice. In 1904, a Chairman voted against a motion to report progress and ask leave to sit again. In 1920 and 1928, the Chairman voted against amendments to a clause of a bill in order to leave the matter open. In 1922, the Chairman voted for an amendment without giving reasons. The casting vote of the Chair is also discussed in Chapter 7, "The Speaker and Other Presiding Officers of the House", and Chapter 12, "The Process of Debate".

145. *Bourinot*, 4th ed., p. 384.

146. Standing Order 73(4). See also Chapter 16, "The Legislative Process".

147. See, for example, *Journals*, June 20, 1994, pp. 617-8; April 17, 1997, pp. 1485-6. On a number of occasions, two or more public bills or resolutions have been referred and considered jointly in a Committee of the Whole in the same sitting by unanimous consent (see, for example, *Journals*, June 29, 1934, p. 565; March 23, 1942, pp. 182-3; May 26, 1954, p. 658; March 9, 1978, p. 468).

148. For example, in 1988, the House adopted a motion to suspend, for the duration of the First Session of the Thirty-Fourth Parliament, certain Standing Orders including the provisions respecting the committee stage of bills. This order also stipulated that one bill in particular, Bill C-2 (*Canada-U.S. Free Trade Agreement Implementation Act*), was to be referred to a Committee of the Whole after second reading (*Journals*, December 16, 1988, pp. 46-9). See also *Journals*, December 1, 1997, pp. 290-1; December 2, 1997, p. 314.

automatically referred to a Committee of the Whole for consideration.[149] These bills are usually considered at the end of the sitting on the last allotted day in a Supply period when little or no more debating time remains. The Standing Orders provide for the Speaker to interrupt the proceedings at that time and put all questions necessary to dispose of all stages of any Supply bills without further debate. Thus, the committee stage is generally very brief and the bills are reported back to the House without amendment within a matter of minutes.[150]

Often a Committee of the Whole examines non-controversial bills or bills dealing with matters of political importance on which arrangements on the use of House time have been made. Also, by unanimous consent or special order, the House has examined urgent legislation, such as legislation terminating strikes, in a Committee of the Whole.[151] Many of these bills are considered by consent of the House at two or more stages in one sitting.

A bill is dealt with in a Committee of the Whole in much the same way it would be if it were referred to a standing, special or legislative committee.[152] Consideration of the preamble and title (as well as Clause 1 if it only contains the short title of the bill) are postponed.[153] Each clause is a distinct question and is discussed separately in numerical order. Traditionally, when Clause 1 (or Clause 2 if Clause 1 contains only the short title of the bill[154]) is called, the Committee holds a general debate, similar to that at second reading, covering the principles and details of the bill. After Clause 1 (or Clause 2) is disposed of, debate must be strictly relevant to the clause under consideration.[155] This tends to make debate on subsequent clauses shorter. Amendments and sub-amendments to a clause may be proposed if found

---

149. Standing Order 73(4). The adoption of any motion to concur in the Estimates or Interim Supply is an Order for the House to bring in a bill or bills based thereon. See Standing Order 81(21). See also Chapter 18, "Financial Procedures".

150. Standing Order 81(17)-(18). See, for example, *Debates*, November 25, 1997, p. 2217.

151. See, for example, the passage of the Bill C-74, *An Act respecting the supervision of longshoring and related operations at west coast ports* (*Journals*, March 15, 1995, pp. 1219-22). See also *Journals*, September 17, 1991, pp. 354-5; September 30, 1991, pp. 414, 417-9.

152. See Chapter 16, "The Legislative Process", and Chapter 20, "Committees".

153. This practice extends back to Confederation when consideration of the preamble was postponed while each clause was considered in its proper order; the preamble and title were considered last (see *Rules, Orders and Forms of Proceeding of the House of Commons of Canada,* 1868, Rule No. 46).

154. The Thirteenth Report of the Special Committee on Procedure and Organization recommended that consideration of Clause 1 should be postponed when it contained only a short title. See *Journals*, October 7, 1964, pp. 771-3. The recommendation was adopted on a provisional basis on October 9, 1964 (*Journals*, pp. 777-80), and the provisional changes were extended for the Twenty-Seventh Parliament (1966-68) (*Journals*, January 21, 1966, p. 34; April 26, 1967, pp. 1769-74). Permanent changes to the Standing Orders were adopted in December 1968 (*Journals*, December 20, 1968, pp. 554-62, in particular p. 560).

155. See, for example, *Debates*, September 30, 1991, pp. 2968-9.

procedurally acceptable by the Chair, and after debate they must be disposed of before the next clause may be called.[156] After a clause has been considered, the Chair asks if it shall carry.[157] Once a clause has been disposed of, it may not be discussed again during consideration of another clause. New clauses, schedules, new schedules, Clause 1 (if it contains only the short title of the bill), the preamble and the title are the last items considered.[158] Similar to proceedings in standing, special or legislative committees, consideration of particular clauses may be postponed or stood by decision of the Committee.[159]

Since the House is not supposed to be informed of the proceedings of a committee on a bill until the bill has been reported, Members cannot refer to the bill or proceedings on it during consideration of other matters if the bill is still before a Committee of the Whole.[160] When consideration of a bill in a Committee of the Whole is completed, the Chairman requests leave to report the bill. Often leave is granted automatically, but it is not unusual for a division to take place on the motion.[161] Once leave is granted, the Mace is put back in place on the Table, the Speaker resumes the Chair and the Chairman reports the bill, with or without amendment, to the House.[162] The report is then received by the House and the Speaker

---

156. See, for example, *Debates*, April 16, 1997, pp. 9843-4; November 24, 1997, pp. 2105-13. On one occasion, there was agreement in a Committee of the Whole for amendments to any of the clauses in the bill under consideration to be proposed on Clause 2. A general debate was held on all the amendments, but the question was not put on individual amendments until the clauses to which they applied were called. See *Debates*, March 15, 1995, pp. 10559, 10561.

157. Unanimous consent has been granted for the Chair to call a number of clauses as one group in order to expedite proceedings in a Committee of the Whole. See, for example, *Debates*, April 20, 1994, pp. 3291, 3294; May 25, 1994, p. 4416.

158. See, for example, *Debates*, October 6, 1998, pp. 8854-5.

159. See, for example, *Debates*, November 24, 1997, pp. 2107, 2112.

160. *Beauchesne*, 6th ed., pp. 210, 250.

161. See, for example, *Debates*, September 30, 1991, pp. 2996-7.

162. In practice, if the presiding officer who has chaired the Committee of the Whole takes the Chair of the House as Speaker, he or she may simply invoke *pro forma* the name of another Member as presenting the report from the Committee of the Whole.

immediately puts the question on the motion for the bill to be concurred in at the report stage.[163] No amendments or debate are allowed at this stage.[164]

Should the bill be concurred in at the report stage, the third reading motion may be proposed at the same sitting.[165] However, if the bill had been read a second time that same sitting, the third reading motion may only be moved with the unanimous consent of the House because the Standing Orders dictate that the three readings of a bill should occur on different days.[166] With the consent of the House, the third reading motion may be proposed immediately, which is the usual practice,[167] or later the same sitting. Third reading may also take place at the next sitting of the House.[168]

During consideration of the motion for third reading, an amendment may be proposed that the bill be recommitted to a Committee of the Whole.[169] Such a recommital amendment usually limits consideration in the Committee to certain clauses, or new proposed amendments.[170] In some cases, no limitation is included.[171] If adopted, this motion becomes an instruction to the Committee.[172]

---

163. Standing Order 76.1(12). See, for example, *Debates*, April 20, 1994, p. 3291; December 2, 1997, p. 2618.

164. See, for example, *Journals*, April 20, 1994, pp. 375-6; June 20, 1994, pp. 617-8; March 12, 1997, p. 1262. This practice differs significantly for public bills reported back from standing, special or legislative committees. The Standing Orders require that every bill examined and reported by a committee be considered by the House at report stage. In the case of public bills reported back from a standing, special or legislative committee, report stage cannot begin sooner than the second day after the bill has been reported (see Standing Order 76.1(1)). At Confederation, amendments made in a Committee of the Whole were reported by the Chairman to the House which received the report forthwith (see *Rules, Orders and Forms of Proceeding of the House of Commons of Canada*, 1868, Rule No. 47). The rules then provided for debate and amendments to be moved to the bill before it was ordered for third reading. If the bill had not been amended in the Committee, it would be ordered for third reading at a time decided by the House. It was not until 1955 that the Standing Orders were amended to require a report from the Chairman of a Committee of the Whole to be received and the motion for concurrence in amendments to be disposed of forthwith (*Journals*, July 12, 1955, pp. 932-3).

165. Standing Order 76.1(11).

166. See Standing Order 71. See also *Journals*, February 24, 1969, pp. 738-9.

167. See, for example, *Debates*, April 20, 1994, p. 3291; June 18, 1996, p. 4039.

168. See, for example, *Debates*, December 21, 1988, p. 589; September 30, 1991, p. 2998.

169. An amendment to recommit to a Committee of the Whole a bill that had been considered previously by a standing committee was ruled out of order (see *Debates*, March 9, 1999, pp. 12645-6). For an example of a bill which was examined by a standing committee and recommitted to a Committee of the Whole by unanimous consent, see *Journals*, February 11, 1977, p. 464; July 25, 1977, p. 1441. Also refer to Chapter 16, "The Legislative Process".

170. See, for example, *Journals*, April 3, 1882, pp. 248-9; March 27, 1933, pp. 343-4; April 25, 1952, pp. 231-2; June 27, 1952, pp. 604-5; March 1, 1962, pp. 182-3; July 25, 1977, p. 1441.

171. See, for example, *Journals*, February 17, 1928, p. 83; April 10, 1957, p. 445.

172. An instruction is a direction by the House to a committee, which has already received an order of reference, further defining its course of action or empowering it to do something. See Chapter 16, "The Legislative Process", for more information.

MOTIONS OF INSTRUCTION

Motions of instruction are derived from British practice which was developed in the second half of the nineteenth century and incorporated into Canadian practice, although they have seldom been used. Instructions to a Committee of the Whole dealing with legislation are not mandatory but permissive, that is the Committee has the discretion to decide if it will exercise the power given to it by the House to do something which it otherwise would have no authority to do.[173] However, if the Committee itself wishes to extend its powers, it must request that the House give it an instruction to this effect.[174] Today, given that the House usually refers a bill to a Committee of the Whole to expedite its passage, the House agrees to define the committee's work typically by special order.[175]

In the event the House wishes to instruct a Committee of the Whole to do something, a motion of instruction may be moved without notice immediately after a bill has been read a second time and referred to a Committee of the Whole but before the House has resolved itself into the Committee.[176] An instruction to a Committee of the Whole has also been moved as a substantive motion under the rubric "Motions" during Routine Proceedings when a bill was already before the Committee.[177] A motion of instruction is debatable and amendable.[178] Members have moved motions instructing a Committee of the Whole to divide a bill into several bills,[179] to consolidate several bills into one bill,[180] and to insert new clauses into a bill.[181] A motion of instruction is inadmissible if it seeks to confer upon the Committee powers it already has, such as the authority to amend a bill.[182] Any number of motions of instruction may be moved successively to a bill referred to a Committee of the Whole; however, each motion is a separate and independent motion.[183] Once a motion of instruction is adopted, it becomes an Order of Reference to the Committee.

---

173. *Bourinot*, 4th ed., pp. 395, 517. The object of a mandatory instruction is to define the course of action a committee must take. See also Chapter 16, "The Legislative Process".

174. *Bourinot*, 4th ed., p. 398.

175. See, for example, *Journals*, May 20, 1971, p. 569; March 30, 1984, p. 324; December 2, 1997, pp. 313-4.

176. See, for example, *Journals*, March 19, 1948, pp. 268-9; July 30, 1956, pp. 942-3.

177. See, for example, *Journals*, April 15, 1920, p. 146.

178. Debate on the motion of instruction must be relevant to the object of the instruction and not the content of the bill. Amendments must be worded in such a way that if an amendment were adopted, the question would retain the form and effect of an instruction (*May*, 22nd ed., pp. 518-9).

179. See *Journals*, March 19, 1948, p. 269 (motion negatived); July 30, 1956, pp. 942-3 (motion negatived).

180. See *Journals*, April 15, 1920, p. 146.

181. See *Journals*, March 15, 1948, p. 255 (motion negatived).

182. *Bourinot*, 4th ed., p. 513. See, for example, *Journals*, May 2, 1872, p. 79; May 23, 1956, pp. 598-603.

183. *Beauchesne*, 6th ed., p. 204.

Consideration of Motions in a Committee of the Whole

Although the House now resolves itself into a Committee of the Whole primarily for the consideration of legislation, other matters such as motions, resolutions and addresses have been considered in a Committee of the Whole.[184] Indeed, the potential mandate of a Committee of the Whole is virtually unlimited as it may consider any substantive motion which the House chooses to refer to it.[185] In the past, the consideration of matters other than legislation was largely limited to resolutions preceding bills involving the expenditure of public funds, resolutions relating to trade, and resolutions providing for the grant of public money[186] or for the imposition of a public tax; from time to time, other matters have also been debated in a Committee of the Whole.[187]

When a motion or resolution is referred to a Committee of the Whole for consideration, the Chairman proposes the motion or resolution and asks the Committee if it wishes to adopt it.[188] The sponsor of the resolution or motion opens the debate and other Members then rise to participate in the debate and to ask questions. The normal rules for debate in a Committee of the Whole apply. Amendments and subamendments may be proposed. At the conclusion of debate, the Chairman will put the question on the resolution or motion. If agreed to, the Chairman requests leave to report the resolution or motion to the House. If leave is granted, the Chairman rises, the Mace is put back in place on the Table, the Speaker resumes the Chair, and the Chairman reports the resolution or motion.[189]

---

184. A resolution is a motion adopted by the House in order to make a declaration of opinion or purpose. An address is a formal message to the Crown which may either express a wish or an opinion of the House or make a request. Addresses are used to express congratulations, etc., to the Royal Family and also to request the production of documents in the Crown's possession.

185. In 1991, a Member sought to have the House sit as a Committee of the Whole during the debate on the crisis in the Persian Gulf to maximize the exchanges between Members. Consent was denied. See *Debates*, January 15, 1991, p. 16984.

186. For a brief period between 1975 and 1977, through provisional amendments to the Standing Orders on Supply proceedings, the House reinstated the former practice of referring selected items in the Estimates to a Committee of the Whole, where a resolution was subsequently agreed to and reported to the House for concurrence (*Journals*, March 14, 1975, pp. 372-6; March 24, 1975, p. 399). Though this provisional Standing Order was continued for another session through agreement (*Journals*, October 12, 1976, p. 12), it was not renewed thereafter. As an example, see *Journals*, May 9, 1975, pp. 533-4. This occurred again, most recently, in 1988 (*Journals*, January 28, 1988, p. 2076).

187. Motions which have been debated in a Committee of the Whole in the past have dealt with, among other matters, the naturalization of aliens (*Journals,* April 10, 1873, p. 147; April 5, 1875, p. 355), the establishment of provincial boundaries (*Journals*, April 29, 1889, pp. 383-5), the classification and organization of House of Commons Staff (*Journals*, June 5, 1913, pp. 785-8), and the ratification of agreements, conventions and treaties (*Journals*, March 20, 1925, pp. 148-9; June 8, 1942, p. 367).

188. See, for example, *Debates*, May 9, 1975, p. 5646; January 28, 1988, p. 12362. See *Bourinot*, 4th ed., pp. 425-8, for a description of the consideration of resolutions in a Committee of Supply.

189. See, for example, *Debates*, May 9, 1975, p. 5670; January 28, 1988, p. 12371.

Should a Committee of the Whole report a resolution, the Speaker immediately puts the motion to concur in the resolution, without debate or amendment.[190] Given that the House declares its own opinions and purposes by resolution,[191] if the House agrees with the concurrence motion, it expresses its support for the content of the resolution; if not, the House withholds its support.

Reporting of Proceedings

JOURNALS

Proceedings and decisions taken in a Committee of the Whole are not recorded in the *Journals*.[192] Because the House is not officially informed of the proceedings in a Committee of the Whole until the Committee has reported, note is only made in the *Journals* when the House goes into a Committee of the Whole, when the Committee reports progress and when the Committee reports back a bill with or without amendment. If amendments are adopted to a bill in a Committee of the Whole, they are printed in the *Journals* when the Committee reports the bill back to the House.[193]

---

190. Standing Order 103. This Standing Order was adopted in 1955 to reflect a practice the House had previously followed for a number of years in connection with financial proceedings. For a recent example of the use of this Standing Order, see *Journals,* January 28, 1988, p. 2076. For a historical perspective on procedures relative to resolutions reported back from Committees of Supply and of Ways and Means, see *Bourinot*, 4th ed., pp. 433-9; for reports from a Committee of the Whole, see *Bourinot*, 4th ed., pp. 402-3. See also *Beauchesne*, 4th ed., pp. 207-8.

191. *Beauchesne*, 5th ed., p. 150.

192. *Bourinot*, 4th ed., p. 399. Amendments and divisions have been recorded in the *Journals*, but the practice was exceptional. For an example of proceedings in a Committee of the Whole on a bill in the early years of Confederation, see *Journals*, April 22, 1870, pp. 230-1. Prior to 1968 when resolutions were adopted before the first reading of a bill, proceedings in regard to these resolutions in a Committee of the Whole were also recorded in the *Journals* (see, for example, *Journals*, June 21, 1965, p. 284). Proceedings of Committees of Supply and of Ways and Means were recorded in the *Journals* as were any resolutions providing for the expenditure of public money or the imposition of taxes. See, for example, *Journals*, October 19, 1962, pp. 124-5; May 28, 1965, p. 161. See also *Journals*, January 28, 1988, p. 2076, when the House resolved into a Committee of the Whole to consider an item in the Supplementary Estimates.

193. See, for example, *Journals*, August 27, 1987 pp. 1392-4; September 30, 1991, pp. 418-9; April 16, 1997, pp. 1478-9; December 2, 1997, p. 316; October 6, 1998, p. 2025. In 1971, proposed government amendments to a bill were tabled and printed as an Appendix to the *Votes and Proceedings* (*Journals*, October 13, 1971, p. 868; October 28, 1971, p. 895). The amendments were subsequently moved and printed in the *Debates* the following day (*Debates*, October 22, 1971, pp. 8934-61; October 29, 1971, pp. 9157-70). On another occasion, the Royal Recommendations covering amendments to be proposed in a Committee of the Whole were printed in the *Journals* (June 2, 1983, pp. 5954-7).

DEBATES AND BROADCASTING

Proceedings in a Committee of the Whole are recorded verbatim in the *Debates* of the House. In addition, an audio-visual record (an electronic Hansard) of proceedings in a Committee of the Whole is available with the recorded proceedings of the House of Commons.

20

Committees

Experience has shown that smaller and more flexible committees, when entrusted with interesting matters, can have a very positive impact on the development of our parliamentary system, upgrade the role of Members of Parliament, sharpen their interest and ultimately enable this institution to produce much more enlightened measures that better meet the wishes of the Canadian people.

YVON PINARD, President of the Privy Council
(*Debates,* November 29, 1982, p. 21071)

As with other large deliberative assemblies, the House of Commons has taken advantage of the greater flexibility available in committees to carry out functions which can be better performed in smaller groups. These include the examination of witnesses and the detailed consideration of legislation, estimates and technical matters. Committee work provides detailed information to parliamentarians on issues of concern to the electorate and often provokes important public debate. In addition, because committees interact directly with the public, they provide an immediate and visible conduit between elected representatives and Canadians. With respect to their formal proceedings, committees are microcosms and extensions of the House, limited in their powers by the authority delegated to them. This chapter will examine the history, the rules of procedure and the business conducted by committees of the House of Commons.

Historical Perspective

BRITISH PRECEDENTS

Committees of the British Parliament have existed in some form since the fourteenth century.[1] The precursors to the first parliamentary committees were the individuals selected as Triers and Examiners of petitions,[2] and the earliest duty of committees, as we know them, was to draw up legislation to carry into effect those prayers of petitions to which the Crown had acceded. By the middle of the sixteenth century, committees formed part of the regular machinery of parliament, modifying or "improving" legislation to which the House of Commons had agreed in principle. Committees had their own meeting room in the palace of Westminster and committee practice had acquired many of its modern characteristics, including the more relaxed rules governing debate, the right to appoint sub-committees and the right to summon witnesses. However, the House was always careful to exercise control over, and responsibility for, those matters it referred to committee.

At that time, there were two sorts of committees: large committees of 30 to 40 members, and small committees of up to 15 members. The large committees, often composed of different classes of members (professional, regional, functional), were struck to consider substantive matters. In the beginning, they were always classified as "special" committees, that is, bodies created for a particular purpose and disbanded as soon as that purpose was discharged. Over time, some of these large committees were given sessional orders of reference (or mandates) which remained in effect for the duration of a session. As "standing" committees, they were charged with an area of responsibility, such as the consideration of a class of bills or a particular department of House business.[3] By the middle of the seventeenth century, a fairly elaborate system of standing committees was in place, and that system remained virtually unchanged over the next two centuries.[4]

The smaller committees, composed of only those members who had been specifically named by the House, became known as "select" committees. While any

---

1. For a full description of the evolution of committees in the British Parliament, see *Redlich*, Vol. II, Chapter VII, pp. 203-14.

2. See Chapter 22, "Public Petitions".

3. For the first time, in 1571, committees of this nature were appointed for "the subsidy", grievances and petitions, religion and disputed elections. From 1592 onwards, elections and privileges were considered by a single sessional committee. In 1621, the House instituted a grand standing committee on trade and another on the administration of justice. These along with the committees on religion, grievances and the smaller, that is select, Privileges and Elections Committee, constituted the system of standing committees as it was to remain for two centuries (*Redlich*, Vol. II, pp. 206-8).

4. *Redlich*, Vol. II, p. 208.

Member could attend select committee proceedings, only those specifically named to the committee by the House could participate in the deliberations.[5]

By contrast, it became common in the large committees to allow whoever attended to participate in the discussion. As the practice of allowing any Member to speak in a large committee evolved, they came to be known as the "general" or "grand" committees. Ultimately, the membership of these committees equalled that of the House itself and they were referred to as Committees of the Whole.[6] Grand committees became the preferred forum for the consideration of "bills of great concernment, and chiefly in bills to impose a tax, or raise money from the people ... to the end there may be opportunity for fuller debates, for that at a committee the members have liberty to speak as often as they shall see cause, to one question ..."[7]

Britain's revolutionary Long Parliament (1640-60),[8] which assumed all the powers of administration and government on behalf of the Commonwealth, effectively did away with grand committees and ruled by means of small committees. Committees of the Whole were seen to be "highly inconvenient", affording as they did equal debating rights to the opposition.[9]

With the Restoration,[10] Parliament, in 1661, once again reverted to grand committees to consider its most significant orders of business and, by 1700, it had become common to examine bills in Committees of the Whole House following second reading.[11] Over the years, various committees on reform continued to suggest that legislation again be referred to the small committees; however, the House continued to prefer the greater openness available in the larger forum.

PRE-CONFEDERATION PROCEDURE IN COMMITTEES

Contrary to the United Kingdom practice in the nineteenth century, where the majority of committee work was carried out in Committees of the Whole, the legislatures of Upper and Lower Canada regularly referred bills to select committees for consideration.[12] In fact, the standing committee system in the two Canadas, as it evolved, more closely resembled the committee structure of the American colonial

---

5. *Redlich*, Vol. II, p. 207.

6. See also Chapter 19, "Committees of the Whole House". By 1628, all the standing committees, except that on Privileges, were made Committees of the Whole House. The Committee on Privileges remained a select committee (*Redlich*, Vol. II, p. 209).

7. Scobell quoted in *Redlich*, Vol. II, p. 208.

8. The Long Parliament sat during the period of the Civil War and the Commonwealth in Great Britain. See *The Oxford History of England: The Early Stuarts, 1603-1660*, Oxford University Press, 1937, pp. 97, 172.

9. *Redlich*, Vol. II, p. 210.

10. Charles II was restored to the Throne in Great Britain in 1660. See *The Oxford History of England: The Early Stuarts, 1603-1660*, pp. 256-8.

11. *Redlich*, Vol. II, pp. 210-1.

12. For an expanded description of committees during this period, see *O'Brien*, p. 103.

legislatures and the United States Congress than that of the British Parliament.[13] A fairly sophisticated system of committees emerged over the 1830s.

In 1831, Lower Canada began appointing a number of standing committees (i.e., committees having an on-going mandate) at the beginning of every session. Somewhat later, in 1836, the Assembly of Upper Canada appointed 12 select standing committees, touching virtually all matters of government business, a departure from its usual practice of nominating *ad hoc* or special committees as the need arose.[14]

Committees afforded Members of the Legislative Assemblies a degree of independence from the Executive and reflected their desire to involve themselves more directly in government affairs. For this reason, the Executive Council of Upper Canada discontinued the practice of appointing standing committees following the 1837 rebellion.[15] Similarly, the government of the United Province of Canada (1841-66) refused initially to institute a system of standing committees, contending this would compromise the principle of responsible government.[16]

DEVELOPMENT OF THE RULES RESPECTING COMMITTEES OF THE CANADIAN HOUSE OF COMMONS

The rules respecting committees of the House of Commons in the new Dominion of Canada were inherited from the Province of Canada, and were essentially the same as those used in the legislature of Lower Canada prior to the *Union Act, 1840.*[17] Efforts at reform, both before and since Confederation, have continued to reflect either the desire to improve the efficiency of the legislature, or the perpetual struggle to alter the balance of power between the legislature and the Executive.

Of the original Standing Orders adopted in 1867, few were directly concerned with standing or special committees. The rules did not list which committees should be struck, nor specify their powers, procedures or the authority of the Chair. They did, however, deny committee membership to any individual who had declared against the matter under consideration.[18] A feature of British parliamentary practice since at least the time of Queen Elizabeth I, this rule was not rescinded in Canada until 1955.[19]

---

13. *O'Brien*, p. 106.

14. *O'Brien*, p. 105.

15. *O'Brien*, pp. 107-8.

16. *O'Brien*, pp. 301-2. For information on the principle of responsible government, see Chapter 1, "Parliamentary Institutions".

17. The *Union Act, 1840* joined Upper and Lower Canada into the single Province of Canada. See R.S.C. 1985, Appendix II, No. 4.

18. The Member had to have stated opposition to the principle of the matter, rather than dissatisfaction with particular aspects of it. See *Redlich,* Vol. II, p. 205.

19. *Journals*, July 12, 1955, pp. 930-1.

From 1867 to 1906, the list of House standing committees[20] was established by way of a motion adopted during each session of each Parliament, usually in the first days following the Speech from the Throne.[21] In 1906, the House included in the Standing Orders, for the first time, a list of "standing" committees which the House had decided should be appointed in every session, although even these committees were active only when the House specifically ordered them to consider a particular matter.[22] Special and joint committees, whose number and mandate varied from one year to the next, were also established during the course of each session. Also in 1906, the House instituted a committee of selection charged with nominating the standing committee membership.[23]

Due to the considerable size of most committees in the early years of Confederation (some had over one hundred members), and the rule that a majority of the membership was needed for a quorum, the larger standing committees experienced considerable difficulty gathering together enough members, on a regular basis, to meet and transact business.[24] Consequently, over the years, the size of standing committees declined, falling as low as 15 members during the Twenty-Sixth Parliament

20. Throughout this period, the inventory of standing committees remained virtually unchanged and consisted of the committees on Privileges and Elections, Expiring Laws, Railways, Canals and Telegraph Lines, Miscellaneous Private Bills, Standing Orders, Printing, Public Accounts, Banking and Commerce, and Immigration and Colonization (subsequently renamed Agriculture and Colonization). From 1867 to 1906 as well, the House consistently agreed, by separate motions, to Standing Joint Committees on the Library of Parliament and on the Printing of Parliament. See *Journals*, November 19, 1867, pp. 21-2; December 4, 1867, p. 48; April 14, 1887, pp. 5-6; March 14, 1906, p. 46.

21. In 1867, 1883 and 1891, the Speech from the Throne occurred on the second sitting day (see *Journals*, November 7, 1867, p. 5; February 9, 1883, p. 15; April 30, 1891, p. 5). In all other instances, committees were established on the first day of the new session.

22. Legislation was dealt with in a Committee of the Whole at that time. See Chapter 19, "Committees of the Whole House".

23. Prior to this, the standing committee membership was drawn up and reported by a special committee "composed of leading men of the ministry and opposition ..." Members were generally given one or two days to examine the lists before concurring in the report; however, it was often necessary to ask for immediate concurrence so that the Standing Committee on Standing Orders could consider petitions for private bills. These were receivable only within a limited period after the commencement of the session. The membership list included those committees regularly established since Confederation, excepting the Committee on Expiring Laws, which was dropped, and committees on the Library of Parliament and on the Debates of the House, which were added (*Bourinot*, 2nd ed., pp. 493-4). See, for example, *Journals*, January 21, 1884, p. 22; March 12, 1903, p. 22.

24. In 1887, the Standing Committee on Railways, Canals and Telegraph Lines had a membership of 147 and thus a quorum, by rule, of 74; the Standing Committee on Banking and Commerce had a membership of 104 and thus a quorum, by rule, of 53. The membership of the House in 1887 was 215. See *Journals*, April 18, 1887, pp. 17-9.

(1963-65) and rising again to 16-18 members in the Thirty-Sixth Parliament.[25] On the other hand, the number of House standing committees grew from 10 in 1867 to 25 in 1986, falling back to 17 in the Thirty-Sixth Parliament (1997-   ).[26]

Despite the fact that a standing committee structure was established at Confederation, for the first hundred years, most of the committees did not actually meet from one session to another and most House business was transacted on the floor of the Chamber, often in a Committee of the Whole.[27] The House repeatedly considered enhancing the role of standing committees, particularly in relation to the study of Estimates. On several occasions, Members expressed concern over the lack of detailed scrutiny the Estimates received in the House and suggested they could be studied more effectively by first referring them to standing and select committees for consideration. A proposal to this effect was referred to a special committee in February 1925.[28] Although the proposal was not endorsed by the committee, the issue continued to be raised in the House. In July 1955, the House agreed to a motion providing for the withdrawal of the Estimates from the Committee of Supply and referring them to standing or special committees.[29] In 1958, the House added a Standing Committee on Estimates.[30] In 1964, a Special Committee on Procedure and Organization further proposed that the Main Estimates be referred automatically after tabling to the standing committees.[31]

In 1965, the Standing Orders were modified, on a provisional basis, permitting standing committees to examine the Estimates.[32] However, it was not until 1968 that the House agreed to a permanent restructuring and reorientation of the committee system. Under the new rules, the Main Estimates would be tabled and referred to the standing committees by March 1 of each year, to be reported back (or deemed reported back) to the House by May 31. As well, provision was made for standing

---

25. In 1927, the rules regarding committees were revised. The number of members on each standing committee was cut to roughly half, and the size of the membership was set down in the Standing Orders. Quorum for each committee was set individually (see *Journals*, March 22, 1927, pp. 320-3). Further changes in December 1968 (see *Journals*, December 20, 1968, pp. 554-79) restricted committee membership to between 20 and 30 Members of Parliament, excepting the 12-member Committee on Procedure. The slight increase in membership at the beginning of the Thirty-Sixth Parliament enabled committees to reflect the proportions of party representation in a five-party House. See *Journals*, September 23, 1997, pp. 12-3; October 1, 1997, p. 56.

26. *Journals*, November 7, 1867, p. 5; February 6, 1986, pp. 1656-7; November 4, 1987, p. 1831; September 23, 1997, pp. 12-3.

27. See *Franks*, pp. 162-3. See also Chapter 19, "Committees of the Whole House".

28. *Journals*, February 25, 1925, p. 66.

29. *Journals*, July 12, 1955, pp. 881, 926-7.

30. *Journals*, May 30, 1958, p. 71.

31. *Journals*, December 14, 1964, pp. 985-96.

32. *Journals*, June 11, 1965, pp. 229-30.

committee consideration of all bills (other than those based on Supply, and Ways and Means motions) after second reading.[33]

In 1982, the House again appointed a special committee to review the Standing Orders[34] and proceeded to implement several of its recommendations on a provisional basis. Among the most significant changes were those automatically referring the annual reports of departments, agencies and Crown corporations to standing committees and empowering the committees to initiate their own studies or investigations based on the information in those reports.[35] Early in the subsequent Parliament (1984-88), the House agreed to retain the provisional changes[36] and struck yet another special committee to inquire into the efficacy of all aspects of House procedure and administration.[37] This committee made recommendations to enlarge the scope of committee mandates to give standing committees "broad authority" to look into and report to the House on any matter which was relevant to the departments for which they were responsible; to create a committee structure which reflected, as much as practicable, the organization of government;[38] and to establish a Liaison Committee, consisting of the Chairs of all standing committees and appropriate Chairs or Vice-Chairs of joint committees, charged with the allocation of committee budgets.[39] Provisional changes to the Standing Orders in 1986 incorporated the majority of the Committee's recommendations relating to committees; these changes were made permanent the following year.[40] The House's standing committee structure was readjusted in 1991 and 1994, reflecting changes in government organization.[41]

Apart from these reorganizations of the committee system, there have been two other significant changes to committee practice since the McGrath Committee reforms, both aimed principally at enhancing the profile and effectiveness of committees and backbenchers. In April 1991, the House agreed to allow committees to broadcast their proceedings within guidelines established by the Standing Committee on House Management;[42]

---

33. *Journals*, December 20, 1968, pp. 554-79.

34. The Special Committee on Standing Orders and Procedure. See *Journals*, May 31, 1982, pp. 4892-3. The Committee, chaired by Tom Lefebvre, is commonly referred to as the Lefebvre Committee.

35. Third Report of the Special Committee on Standing Orders and Procedure (Parliamentary reform and changes to the Standing Orders). See *Minutes of Proceedings and Evidence*, November 4, 1982, Issue No. 7, pp. 3-41; *Journals*, November 5, 1982, p. 5328; November 29, 1982, p. 5400.

36. *Journals*, December 7, 1984, p. 164.

37. The Special Committee on Reform of the House of Commons. The Committee, chaired by James McGrath, is commonly referred to as the McGrath Committee (see *Journals*, December 5, 1984, pp. 153-4).

38. The Special Committee on Reform of the House of Commons, Third Report, June 1985, pp. 16-27.

39. The Special Committee on Reform of the House of Commons, Third Report, June 1985, pp. 22-5.

40. *Journals*, February 6, 1986, pp. 1644-66; February 11, 1986, p. 1696; February 13, 1986, p. 1710; June 1, 1987, pp. 968-80; June 2, 1987, pp. 984-97; June 3, 1987, pp. 1002-28.

41. *Journals*, April 11, 1991, pp. 2905-32, in particular pp. 2922-3; January 25, 1994, pp. 58-9.

42. *Journals*, April 11, 1991, pp. 2905-32, in particular p. 2929.

in 1994,[43] the rules were again amended to permit the House to appoint and/or instruct a committee to bring in a bill, and to refer bills to a committee before second reading.[44] The intent of these changes was to give ordinary Members an opportunity to participate in policy development before the government had committed itself to a particular legislative initiative.[45]

Governing Provisions

Committees, as creations of the House of Commons, only possess the authority, structure and mandates that have been delegated to them by the House. These are found in the standing and special orders which the House has adopted concerning committees. The House has specified that, in relationship to standing, special or legislative committees, "the Standing Orders shall apply so far as may be applicable, except the Standing Orders as to the election of a Speaker, seconding of motions, limiting the number of times of speaking and the length of speeches."[46]

With these exceptions, committees are bound to follow the procedures set out in the Standing Orders[47] as well as any specific sessional or special orders that the House has issued to them. Committees are otherwise left free to organize their work. In this sense, committees are said to be "masters of their own proceedings".[48]

EFFECT OF PROROGATION ON COMMITTEES

Committee mandates and powers may derive from standing or special orders, but they are in effect only during a session. When Parliament is prorogued, Members are released from their responsibility to attend the House (and its committees), all orders of reference lapse, and committees effectively cease to exist. The only aspect of a committee's work which survives prorogation is a request for a government response to a committee report.[49]

---

43. See *Journals*, February 7, 1994, pp. 112-8.

44. Standing Orders 68 and 73.

45. See *Debates*, February 7, 1994, pp. 957-62. Prior to this time, there had been occasions where committees were empowered by their orders of reference to draft legislative proposals or to bring in a bill. See, for example, Special Joint Committee on Bill C-43, *Senate and House of Commons Conflict of Interest Act*, *Journals*, November 22, 1991, pp. 717-8.

46. Standing Order 116.

47. Chapter XIII of the Standing Orders deals specifically with procedure related to committees.

48. See, for example, Speaker Parent's ruling, *Debates*, June 20, 1994, pp. 5582-3.

49. Standing Order 109. See Speaker Bosley's ruling, *Debates*, June 27, 1986, p. 14969. While a request for a government response to a committee report survives prorogation, it ceases to have effect on dissolution.

The House may choose to reconstitute a special committee or re-adopt a special order of reference to a standing committee at the beginning of the next session so that the work may be completed. To do this, the House adopts an order of reference containing the same elements as those used originally, along with a provision that evidence adduced in the previous session be referred to the reconstituted committee.[50]

Where bills have been reinstated in a new session, the House has on occasion referred the evidence adduced and the documents received in the previous session to the new legislative or standing committee to which it had referred the reinstated bills.[51]

Structure and Mandate of Committees

Leaving aside Committees of the Whole, which are discussed in detail in Chapter 19, there are several distinct types of committees: standing, legislative, special, joint and sub-committees. All are "select" committees, that is, the House has chosen a limited number of members for each committee from among all the Members of the House.[52] Standing committees are provided for in the Standing Orders; permanent changes to the list of these committees can only be made by amending the Standing Orders. Legislative and special committees are appointed by motion on an *ad hoc* basis to carry out specific tasks and cease to exist when they have tabled their final reports. Joint committees are composed of members from both the House and Senate; they may be either standing or special. Sub-committees are committees struck by committees themselves for various purposes. They may exist for the entire duration of the main committee or may cease to exist when their specific purpose has been accomplished.

STANDING COMMITTEES

Standing committees are permanent committees established by Standing Order.[53] They are mandated by the House to oversee a government department or departments, to review particular areas of federal policy or to exercise procedural and administrative responsibilities related to Parliament. Some committees may have both departmental and policy-area responsibilities. As well as the permanent mandates provided to standing committees by the Standing Orders, other matters are

---

50. See, for example, *Journals*, May 17, 1991, p. 42. The motion to reconstitute a committee may also include a budgetary provision, allocating to the reconstituted committee the unspent remainder of the previous committee's budget. See, for example, *Journals*, May 17, 1991, p. 43.

51. See, for example, *Journals*, October 3, 1986, p. 48; March 1, 1996, pp. 23-4; March 4, 1996, pp. 39-41.

52. In contrast, the membership of a Committee of the Whole is not selected, but consists of all Members of the House.

53. Standing Order 104(2)(*a*)-(*q*) and (3)(*a*)-(*c*).

routinely referred to them by the House for examination: bills,[54] Estimates,[55] Order-in-Council appointments,[56] documents tabled in the House pursuant to statute,[57] and specific matters which the House wishes to have studied.[58] The House refers specific studies to committees by adopting a motion to that effect. The motion, once adopted, becomes an order of the House to a committee, known as an order of reference. In addition to the subject matter of the study, the order of reference may also contain conditions that the committee must comply with in carrying out the study or additional powers which it may require for that purpose.

The majority of standing committees are established to oversee a government department or departments.[59] These committees are charged with the review of the relevant statute law, departmental operations and expenditures, and the effectiveness of the policies and programs of the department.[60] The House adjusts the number and responsibilities of departmental standing committees to reflect changes in the structure of government administration.

The Standing Orders provide for a number of committees to have either particular policy responsibilities which have application throughout the federal administration[61] or responsibility for matters pertaining to the procedures and the

---

54. Standing Orders 68 and 73. Pursuant to Standing Order 73(4), Supply bills are considered in a Committee of the Whole. In addition to having legislation referred to them for study, committees may also be asked to prepare bills for presentation to the House. In the First Session of the Thirty-Fifth Parliament (1994-96), the Procedure and House Affairs Committee was instructed to prepare and bring in a bill "… respecting the system of readjusting the boundaries of electoral districts for the House of Commons by the Electoral Boundaries Commissions …" (*Journals*, April 19, 1994, pp. 369-70). In the First Session of the Thirty-Sixth Parliament (1997-99), the Justice and Human Rights Committee was instructed to prepare and bring in a bill "… to amend those sections of the Criminal Code which deal with impaired driving" (*Journals*, October 30, 1997, p. 175).

55. Standing Order 81(4)-(5).

56. Standing Orders 32(6) and 110.

57. Standing Order 32(5). Before 1982, committees could not study a report, return or other paper tabled in the House without a specific order of reference. In 1982, the referral of such papers became automatic and the referral was made permanent so as not to limit committee study to a specific time frame. Currently, few studies are initiated under this provision; the broader mandate provided in Standing Order 108(2) or 108(3) is used. See, for example, Standing Committee on Procedure and House Affairs, *Minutes*, November 20, 1997, Meeting No. 6.

58. Standing Order 108(1)(*a*).

59. Standing Order 108(2).

60. Standing Order 108(2)(*a*)-(*e*).

61. Standing Order 108(3)(*b*)-(*e*) and 108(4)(*b*) and (*c*). The specific mandates of the Standing Joint Committees on the Library of Parliament, Official Languages and the Scrutiny of Regulations are dealt with below under "Standing Joint Committees".

administration of the House and its committees.[62] These committees may be responsible for overseeing a specific government department as well. The mandates currently are as follows:

- The mandate of the Standing Committee on Canadian Heritage includes the monitoring of federal multicultural policy throughout the Government of Canada to aid in preserving and enhancing Canada's multicultural heritage and to encourage government departments and agencies to reflect that heritage.[63]

- The mandate of the Standing Committee on Finance includes the consideration of and report on proposals regarding the budgetary policy of the government.[64]

- The mandate of the Standing Committee on Human Resources Development and the Status of Persons with Disabilities includes the proposing, promoting, monitoring and assessing of initiatives directed at the social integration of persons with disabilities.[65]

- The mandate of the Standing Committee on Justice and Human Rights includes the review of the reports of the Canadian Human Rights Commission.[66]

- The mandate of the Standing Committee on Procedure and House Affairs[67] includes the review of House administration and the services and facilities provided to Members, as well as those services under the joint administration of the two Houses. It also deals with the review of the Standing Orders, the procedures and practices of the House, all matters relating to the election of Members of the House of Commons, the broadcasting of proceedings and the selection of votable items of Private Members' Business.[68] It is to this Committee that the House ordinarily refers matters relating to parliamentary privilege. The Committee is responsible for nominating the members of House committees and the House membership of standing joint committees, as well as preparing lists of associate members.[69] The

---

62. Standing Order 108(3)(*a*).

63. Standing Order 108(3)(*b*).

64. Standing Order 83.1. This provision, added to the Standing Orders in 1994 (see *Journals*, February 7, 1994, pp. 112-8, in particular p. 117 and pp. 119-20), extends the Finance Committee's permanent mandate beyond overseeing the Finance Department and Revenue Canada to include, in the words used by the Government House Leader in proposing the new standing order, "... an annual public consultation on what should be in the next budget" (*Debates*, February 7, 1994, p. 962).

65. Standing Order 108(3)(*c*).

66. Standing Order 108(3)(*d*).

67. Standing Order 108(3)(*a*).

68. Responsibility for Private Members' Business is delegated to a Sub-committee established for that purpose. See, for example, Standing Committee on Procedure and House Affairs, *Minutes of Proceedings*, September 29, 1997, Meeting No. 1. For the Private Members' Business process, including the workings of the Sub-committee, see Chapter 21, "Private Members' Business".

69. Standing Orders 104 and 107(5). The task of selecting committee members is usually delegated to the whips of the recognized parties. See section below, "Membership".

Committee is also specifically charged with establishing priority of use of committee meeting rooms.[70]

- The mandate of the Standing Committee on Public Accounts includes the review of and report on the Public Accounts of Canada and all reports of the Auditor General of Canada.[71]

Powers

The Standing Orders formerly contained no provisions with respect to the powers of standing committees. Powers were provided in the motion establishing a given committee[72] or, following the inclusion of a list of standing committees in the Standing Orders, by separate motion. The powers given usually included the power to examine and enquire into all such things as the House might refer, the power to report from time to time and the power to send for persons, papers and records.[73] In 1965, the Standing Orders were amended to give powers to standing committees on a permanent basis. In addition to those listed above, the power to print from day to day such papers and evidence as the committee might order was included at that time.[74] Subsequently, this list was extended to include the power to sit when the House is sitting or when it stands adjourned, to delegate powers to sub-committees (except the power to report directly to the House),[75] to sit jointly with other committees of the House, and to append supplementary or dissenting opinions to reports.[76] In addition, standing committees are empowered to broadcast their proceedings in accordance with guidelines prepared by the Procedure and House Affairs Committee.[77] They may retain the services of expert, professional, technical and clerical staff.[78] They are accorded an interim spending authority by the Board of Internal Economy.[79] Finally, standing committees are empowered to meet without a quorum for the purpose of hearing evidence and to publish that evidence. At such meetings, no vote, resolution or other decision may be taken.[80]

---

70. Standing Order 115(4).

71. Standing Order 108(3)(*e*).

72. See, for example, *Journals*, November 7, 1867, p. 5; April 6, 1868, p. 184; January 12, 1905, p. 9.

73. See, for example, *Journals*, November 28, 1910, p. 27.

74. *Journals*, June 11, 1965, p. 228.

75. *Journals*, December 20, 1968, pp. 562-79, in particular p. 575.

76. *Journals*, March 26, 1991, pp. 2801-27, in particular pp. 2819-20; April 11, 1991, p. 2904; May 23, 1991, pp. 61-62.

77. Standing Order 119.1(2). The guidelines were approved by the House on March 27, 1992. See *Journals*, February 14, 1992, p. 1024; March 27, 1992, p. 1230.

78. Standing Order 120.

79. Standing Order 121(1).

80. Standing Order 118(2).

Should a standing committee require additional powers to carry out a particular study, the additional powers may be conferred by the House either by concurring in a report of the committee which contains a request for powers[81] or by simply adopting a motion to confer the desired power.[82] It is left to each standing committee to decide the extent to which it will exercise the powers granted to it by the House.

Liaison Committee

The Liaison Committee is a permanent committee, established pursuant to the Standing Orders, but is not a standing committee. It is made up *ex officio* of the Chairs of all the standing committees and the House Chairs of the standing joint committees. The Liaison Committee is responsible for apportioning funds to standing committees from the money allocated for that purpose by the Board of Internal Economy.[83] It meets *in camera* to deliberate on administrative matters relating to the standing committee system and has a quorum of seven members.[84] It is empowered to report to the House from time to time and has also carried out studies on the effectiveness of the committees of the House.[85]

The Liaison Committee Chair is empowered to request that a list of associate members for the Liaison Committee be prepared and reported to the House by the Procedure and House Affairs Committee.[86] These associate members are deemed to be Liaison Committee members for the purpose of forming sub-committees.[87] Associate members of the Liaison Committee are not committee chairs and may include members from all parties.[88] The Liaison Committee usually establishes a Budget Sub-committee charged with apportioning the funds provided by the Board of Internal Economy to the various standing committees.

LEGISLATIVE COMMITTEES

Legislative committees are a distinct type of committee intended expressly to undertake the consideration of legislation. They were created by amendment to the Standing Orders in 1985 in response to recommendations of the Lefebvre and McGrath

---

81. See, for example, *Journals*, April 24, 1985, p. 506; May 10, 1985, p. 602.

82. See, for example, *Journals*, December 11, 1997, p. 394. Pursuant to Standing Order 108(1)(*a*), any additional powers granted to a standing committee may be delegated by it to a sub-committee.

83. Standing Order 107(1).

84. Standing Order 107(4). For standing, special and legislative committees, Standing Order 118(1) sets quorum at a simple majority of the committee members. Under this rule, the quorum of the Liaison Committee would be 11, rather than seven as set out in Standing Order 107(4).

85. Standing Order 107(3). See *Journals*, April 2, 1993, p. 2784. A report on committee effectiveness prepared by the Liaison Committee in the concluding weeks of the Thirty-Fifth Parliament (1994-97) was not tabled in the House, but was circulated directly to interested parties. See *Parliamentary Government*, No. 4, September 1997.

86. Standing Order 107(5).

87. Standing Order 107(6).

88. See *Journals*, December 8, 1997, p. 358; December 10, 1997, p. 382.

Committees.[89] It was felt at the time that standing committees, with an expanded mandate to initiate studies without a specific reference from the House, would not also be able to readily deal with legislation. The solution proposed to this difficulty was the creation of legislative committees appointed solely to deal with bills.[90] They are appointed by the House on an *ad hoc* basis[91] to deal with particular bills and cease to exist upon the presentation of their report to the House.

A legislative committee is required to be struck once second reading debate has begun on a bill which is to be referred to such a committee, or once debate has begun on a motion to appoint a legislative committee. The Procedure and House Affairs Committee must present a report containing a list of members within five sitting days of the beginning of the debate.[92] The report is deemed adopted the moment it is presented in the House. The Speaker then appoints a Chair for the committee from the Panel of Chairmen.[93] The legislative committee meets for the purpose of organization once the bill has been referred to it by the House. The organization meeting must take place within two days of the naming of the Chair and the adoption of the motion referring the bill to committee or appointing the committee.[94]

Powers

A legislative committee is empowered to examine and enquire into the bill[95] referred to it and to report the same with or without amendments. It is not empowered to present a report containing substantive recommendations concerning the bill.[96] A

---

89. See *Journals*, June 27, 1985, pp. 910-9, in particular pp. 915-6. See also Sixth Report of the Special Committee on Standing Orders and Procedure, *Minutes of Proceedings and Evidence,* April 28, 1983, Issue No. 19, pp. 3-11, and First Report of the Special Committee on the Reform of the House of Commons, *Minutes of Proceedings and Evidence,* December 19, 1984, Issue No. 2, pp. 3-23, in particular pp. 7-10.

90. Legislative committees were active from 1985 to 1993; however, from 1994 to 1999, no bills were sent to legislative committees.

91. A change to the Standing Orders on April 11, 1991 (see *Journals*, pp. 2904-32, in particular pp. 2922-7) provided for a system of eight permanent legislative committees, divided equally among four of the five envelopes into which standing committees were grouped. Bills were referred to one of the two committees in the appropriate envelope and a separate Chair was named to take charge of each Bill. The House modified the Standing Orders to remove the envelope system and reinstate *ad hoc* legislative committees on January 25, 1994 (see *Journals*, pp. 58-61, in particular pp. 60-1).

92. Standing Order 113(1).

93. Standing Order 113(2). The Panel of Chairmen is a group composed of the Chairman, the Deputy Chairman, and the Assistant Deputy Chairman of Committees of the Whole and other Members appointed by the Speaker.

94. Standing Order 113(3).

95. Usually, only one bill is referred to a given legislative committee. On four occasions, either two related bills were referred to a single legislative committee at once, or a second related bill was referred to a legislative committee already in existence. See *Journals,* September 23, 1985, p. 1015; May 26, 1986, p. 2208; November 25, 1987, p. 1882; May 17, 1990, pp. 1715-6.

96. See Speaker Lamoureux's ruling regarding the reporting of bills, *Journals*, December 20, 1973, pp. 774-5. A legislative committee has reported to the House seeking permission to travel; however, the House did not take up this report (see *Journals*, February 3, 1988, p. 2130).

legislative committee may also be created to prepare and to bring in a bill.[97] In its examination, the committee may send for officials of government departments, agencies and Crown corporations and competent technical witnesses.[98] It may send for papers and records, sit while the House is sitting,[99] sit while the House stands adjourned,[100] and print papers and evidence.[101] A legislative committee may also delegate to a sub-committee on agenda and procedure the power to schedule meetings, send for witnesses, papers and records subject to approval by the full committee.[102] The Board of Internal Economy may accord spending authority[103] to legislative committees and a legislative committee may retain such expert, professional, technical and clerical staff as it deems necessary.[104]

Should a legislative committee require additional powers, they can only be obtained by having the House adopt a motion to that effect.[105]

SPECIAL COMMITTEES

Special committees are appointed by the House to carry out specific inquiries, studies or other tasks which the House judges of special importance.[106] Each special

---

97. Standing Order 68(4)-(5).

98. Legislative committees are restricted to calling only technical witnesses since an amendment to the Standing Orders was adopted in 1991 (see *Journals*, April 11, 1991, pp. 2904-32, in particular p. 2927). At that time, the Government House Leader stated, "... when legislation passes at second reading in this House, it has received approval in principle—the principle is approved. The role of the [Legislative] Committee is not to debate again whether the legislation is appropriate in principle, by touring the country and hearing from groups about the principle, but rather to look at all the details" (*Debates*, April 8, 1991, pp. 19137-8). In contrast, standing committees are not restricted by the Standing Orders in the type of witness they may call (see Standing Order 108(1)(*a*)).

99. Standing Order 115(2) gives priority during sittings of the House to committees meeting to study legislation or the Estimates.

100. During periods when the House is not sitting, Standing Order 115(3) gives priority to meetings of standing and special committees over those of legislative committees.

101. Standing Order 113(5).

102. Standing Order 113(6). Legislative committees were not empowered to create sub-committees when the Standing Orders concerning them were first adopted. The power to create a sub-committee on agenda and procedure was added to the Standing Orders in 1986. See *Journals*, February 6, 1986, pp. 1644-66, in particular p. 1659; February 13, 1986, p. 1710.

103. Standing Order 121(1).

104. Standing Order 120.

105. See, for example, *Journals*, February 10, 1988, p. 2166.

106. See, for example, *Journals*, January 25, 1977, pp. 286-7; March 30, 1993, pp. 2742-3; November 18, 1997, pp. 224-5. Between 1979 and 1985, the House made use of a variant of the special committee known as a "task force"; the number of members named to a task force was small, no substitutions were permitted, and a limited length of time was given to carry out their work. A detailed analysis of the House's experience with task forces can be found in Audrey O'Brien, "Parliamentary Task Forces in the Canadian House of Commons: A New Approach to Committee Activity", *The Parliamentarian*, January 1985, Vol. LXVI, No. 1, pp. 28-32.

committee is created by means of a motion agreed to by the House (in the case of special joint committees, by both Houses[107]). This motion defines the committee's mandate and usually enumerates other provisions: its powers, its membership and the deadline for submitting its final report. The actual terms of the motion vary from case to case, to suit the specific task for which the committee is being established by the House.

Special committees cease to exist with the presentation of their final report.[108] Where a special committee has not completed its work by the end of a session, it ceases on prorogation, but it may be revived in a subsequent session.[109]

Powers

Special committees possess only those powers that are provided to them by the House in the order of reference which establishes them[110] or by subsequent motion. Depending on whether its mandate concerns a particular subject matter or consideration of a bill, a special committee may be given the powers of a standing[111] or legislative[112] committee. The House may provide special committees with additional powers such as the power to travel,[113] special broadcasting powers[114] or any other exceptional powers it deems necessary.[115] The Board of Internal Economy may accord special committees spending authority.[116] When a special committee requires additional powers to complete a study, it may, where it has been given the power to report from time to time, make a request for those powers in a report to the House. The House confers the requested powers by concurring in the committee's report.[117] Alternatively, the House may simply adopt a motion to confer the powers which the committee requires.[118]

---

107. See, for example, *Journals*, November 5, 1997, pp. 196-7; November 18, 1997, pp. 224-5.

108. An amendment to the motion to concur in the final report, which seeks to recommit the report to the committee, may be made without the need for a motion to reconstitute the committee. See Speaker Macnaughton's ruling, *Journals,* December 1, 1964, pp. 941-7.

109. See, for example, the Special Joint Committee on a Code of Conduct in the First Session (1994-96) and Second Session (1996-97) of the Thirty-Fifth Parliament, *Journals*, June 19, 1995, pp. 1801-2; March 12, 1996, pp. 83-4.

110. See, for example, *Journals*, January 29, 1988, pp. 2092-3.

111. See, for example, *Journals*, October 29, 1990, p. 2183.

112. See, for example, *Journals*, October 10, 1990, p. 2094.

113. See, for example, *Journals*, February 23, 1994, p. 186.

114. See, for example, *Journals*, March 16, 1994, p. 263. Standing Order 119.1(1) restricts committees to the broadcasting facilities provided by the House.

115. See, for example, the power to request drafting assistance from the government (*Journals*, November 22, 1991, p. 717); the power to advertise using the Parliamentary television channel (*Journals*, April 6, 1990, p. 1511).

116. Standing Order 121(1).

117. See, for example, *Journals,* February 25, 1994, p. 206; March 7, 1994, p. 214.

118. See, for example, *Journals*, April 6, 1990, p. 1511.

JOINT COMMITTEES

Joint committees are composed of members of both the House of Commons and the Senate, and may be standing or special. Standing joint committees are permanent committees established pursuant to the Standing Orders of the House of Commons and the Rules of the Senate.[119] They deal either with administrative matters related to both Houses or with matters having application throughout the federal sphere.

Special joint committees are established by motion of both Houses to deal with matters of great public importance. The House which wishes to initiate a special joint committee first adopts a motion to establish it and includes a provision inviting the other Chamber to participate in the proposed committee's work.[120] In addition to the subject of the study, the motion also includes any directions which the originating House may choose to give to the committee and the list of powers which are being delegated to it. The motion may also appoint the members of the committee or indicate how the membership will be established. Decisions of one House concerning the membership, mandate and powers of a proposed joint committee are communicated to the other House by message. While each House retains control of its own members on the committee, both Houses must be in agreement about the mandate and powers of the committee in order for it to be able to undertake its work. Once a request to participate in a joint committee is received, the other House, if it so desires, adopts a motion to establish such a committee and includes a provision to be returned, stating that it agrees to the request. Once the originating House has been informed of the agreement of the other Chamber, the committee can be organized. A special joint committee ceases to exist when it has presented its final report to both Houses, or at prorogation.

Mandate

Standing Joint Committees

The Standing Orders provide for three standing joint committees: Library of Parliament, Official Languages and Scrutiny of Regulations.[121] The Standing Joint Committee on the Library of Parliament is charged with the review of the effectiveness, management and operation of the Library of Parliament, which serves both the

---

119. See Standing Order 104(3) and Senate Rule 86(1)(*a*)-(*e*).

120. Typically, the motion concludes with a request in the following form: "that a message be sent to the Senate, requesting that House to unite with this House for the above purpose ..." See, for example, *Journals*, March 16, 1994, p. 263.

121. Standing Order 104(3). Since 1867, there have been two other standing joint committees: on Printing and on the Parliamentary Restaurant. Reference to these committees is still found in Senate Rule 86(1). Reference to the Standing Joint Committee on Printing was dropped from the Standing Orders in 1986 (see *Journals*, February 6, 1986, pp. 1644-66, in particular p. 1657, and February 13, 1986, p. 1710). While the Standing Orders have never contained a reference to the Standing Joint Committee on the Restaurant of Parliament, the House began to name members to it in 1909 (see *Journals*, February 10, 1909, p. 69). The last occasion on which members were named to this Committee was during the First Session of the Thirtieth Parliament (see *Journals*, March 14, 1980, pp. 168-70).

House of Commons and the Senate.[122] The mandate of this committee arises from a statutory provision giving direction and control of the Library to the Speakers of the House and Senate, with the provision that they are to be assisted by a joint committee.[123]

The Standing Joint Committee on Official Languages is responsible for reviewing and reporting on official languages policies and programs including the reports of the Commissioner of Official Languages, which are deemed permanently referred to the Committee once they are tabled in the House.[124] The mandate of this Committee arises from a statutory provision requiring that the administration of the *Official Languages Act* and reports made under the Act be permanently reviewed by a committee of one or both Houses.[125]

The Standing Joint Committee for the Scrutiny of Regulations[126] is mandated to review and scrutinize statutory instruments.[127] The Committee's mandate is set out in part in the Standing Orders[128] and in part in the *Statute Revision Act* and the *Statutory Instruments Act*.[129] At the beginning of each session, the Committee presents a report relating to its review of the regulatory process, proposing a more detailed mandate. When the report is concurred in, this proposed mandate then becomes an order of reference to the Committee for the remainder of the session.[130]

Special Joint Committees

The mandate of a special joint committee is contained in the order of reference which establishes the committee. In recent years, special joint committees have been appointed to deal with such subjects as child custody,[131] defence[132] and foreign policy,[133] a code of conduct for Members and Senators[134] and Senate reform.[135] Constitutional matters have often been dealt with by special joint committees.[136] Special

---

122. Standing Order 108(4)(*a*).

123. *Parliament of Canada Act,* R.S.C. 1985, c. P-1, s. 74(1).

124. Standing Order 108(4)(*b*).

125. R.S.C. 1985, c. 31 (4th Supp.), s. 88 as amended by S.C. 1995, c. 11, s. 30.

126. The nature and role of the Standing Joint Committee for the Scrutiny of Regulations are set out in detail in Chapter 17, "Delegated Legislation".

127. A statutory instrument is a rule, order, regulation or other regulatory text as defined in s. 2(1) of the *Statutory Instruments Act*, R.S.C. 1985, c. S-22.

128. Standing Order 108(4)(*c*).

129. R.S.C. 1985, c. S-20, s. 19(3) and c. S-22, s. 19.

130. See, for example, *Journals*, April 24, 1996, p. 254; May 29, 1996, p. 457.

131. *Journals*, November 18, 1997, pp. 224-5.

132. *Journals*, February 23, 1994, pp. 186-7.

133. *Journals*, March 16, 1994, pp. 262-5.

134. *Journals*, March 12, 1996, pp. 83-4.

135. *Journals*, December 22, 1982, pp. 5493-4.

136. *Journals*, October 23, 1980, pp. 601-3; June 16, 1987, pp. 1100-2; December 17, 1990, pp. 2488-90; May 17, 1991, p. 43; June 19, 1991, pp. 226-7; October 1, 1997, pp. 59-61; October 28, 1997, pp. 158-61.

joint committees have also been appointed to deal with legislation, either by being empowered to prepare a bill,[137] or to study a bill following second reading.[138]

Powers

Because a joint committee exists only by order of both Houses, the powers provided to a joint committee by the House of Commons can be exercised by the committee only if a similar empowerment is provided by the Senate.[139] Each House provides certain powers to its committees through the rules which it has adopted; additional powers, where required, must be provided for by special order. The motions conferring powers on a joint committee may vary in their terms as a result of differences in the rules of the two Houses, but in order for a power to be exercised by a joint committee, it must receive the power through orders from both Houses. Notably, Senate Rules prohibit committees from meeting during sittings of the Senate.[140] In order for a joint committee to sit at any time (as it is permitted to do by the House), a special order must be adopted by the Senate.[141]

Standing Joint Committees

The powers accorded to standing joint committees by the House are the same as those accorded to other standing committees of the House:

- to examine and enquire into all such matters as the House may refer to them;
- to report from time to time;
- to send for persons, papers and records;
- to sit when the House is sitting and to sit when the House stands adjourned;
- to sit jointly with other committees of the House;
- to print papers and evidence;
- to delegate to sub-committees all of the other powers except the power to report directly to the House.[142]

---

137. *Journals*, November 22, 1991, pp. 717-8.

138. *Journals*, March 20, 1993, pp. 2742-3.

139. Senate Rule 90 provides a standing committee with the powers "to inquire into and report upon such matters as are referred to it from time to time by the Senate ... to send for persons, papers and records ... and to print from day to day such papers and evidence as may be ordered by it".

140. Senate Rule 95(4).

141. See, for example, *Journals of the Senate,* May 30, 1991, p. 59; May 10, 1994, p. 253.

142. Standing Order 108(1). This Standing Order does not distinguish between standing committees of the House and standing joint committees of the House and Senate.

In addition, the Standing Orders provide standing joint committees with limited spending authority,[143] and the power to broadcast,[144] to hire expert, professional, technical and clerical staff,[145] to establish a reduced quorum[146] for the purpose of hearing testimony[147] and to request a comprehensive response from the government to any report presented to the House.[148]

Special Joint Committees

Special joint committees have only those powers which are set out in the order of reference which establishes each committee. The powers granted to special joint committees vary, depending on the mandate given to them. They may be granted powers similar to those granted to standing joint committees by the Standing Orders.[149] They are often granted additional powers with respect to travel[150] and the broadcasting of their proceedings.[151]

SUB-COMMITTEES

Sub-committees are to committees what committees are to the House; the parent body is relieved of a portion of its workload by delegating some part of its mandate or a particular task to a smaller group. Committees may establish sub-committees only if they have been empowered to do so. The House has, on occasion, established a sub-committee directly or ordered that a particular study be carried out by a sub-committee.[152] Proceedings in sub-committees are of an informal, collegial nature. Their membership is often not proportional to the party representation on the main committee and members other than government members have been selected to chair sub-committees.

---

143. Standing Order 121. The *Financial Policy Manual for Committees* of the House of Commons provides that the budgets of each standing joint committee be shared between the two Houses of Parliament in proportion to the number of members from each House on the committee. See *Financial Policy Manual for Committees*, September 1997, Paragraph A-2.3.

144. Standing Order 119.1.

145. Standing Order 120.

146. Standing Order 118(1) reserves for the House the power to determine, in consultation with the Senate, the quorum in standing joint committees. The quorum is the number of members who must be present in order for the standing joint committee to transact business. A reduced quorum is the number of members, less than a full quorum, authorized by the committee to meet for purposes other than the taking of decisions.

147. Standing Order 118(2).

148. Standing Order 109.

149. See, for example, *Journals*, November 22, 1991, p. 717.

150. See, for example, *Journals*, February 23, 1994, p. 186; March 16, 1994, p. 263; November 18, 1997, p. 225.

151. See, for example, *Journals*, March 26, 1996, p. 84; November 5, 1997, p. 196; November 18, 1997, p. 225.

152. See, for example, *Journals*, August 4, 1982, pp. 5266-7; May 28, 1984, pp. 665-6; October 9, 1986, p. 66.

Standing committees (including, so far as the House is concerned, standing joint committees) are empowered to establish sub-committees.[153] In forming sub-committees, standing committees may draw not only on the members of the main committee but also on its associate members.[154] Special committees may establish sub-committees only if empowered to do so by the orders of reference which established them. The Liaison Committee, despite its limited mandate, is empowered to create sub-committees, drawing their membership both from the main committee and from the list of associate members.[155]

A legislative committee is only permitted to establish a sub-committee on agenda and procedure, to which it may delegate the power to schedule meetings, to call for government officials and technical witnesses and to send for papers and records, subject to the approval of the main committee.[156] As legislative committees have a very specific mandate (i.e., consideration of a bill), they do not require sub-committees for other than planning purposes. Depending on their workload, legislative committees have not always found it necessary to establish a sub-committee.

Most standing and special committees also find it convenient to establish a sub-committee on agenda and procedure, also called the steering committee, for planning purposes.[157] Decisions reached by the sub-committee on agenda and procedure are subject to ratification by the full committee. This is done by means of concurrence in a report from the sub-committee, containing its recommendations on the organization of the committee's work.[158]

Mandate

Sub-committees receive their mandate in the order of reference adopted by the main committee. By practice, certain sub-committees are struck in every session and continue in operation until the end of the session: for example, the sub-committee on agenda and procedure[159] and sub-committees charged with the responsibility for a specific aspect of the committee's overall mandate.[160] Sub-committees may also be

---

153. Standing Order 108(1)(*a*).

154. Standing Order 108(1)(*b*). For further information on associate members, see section below, "Substitutions —Associate Members".

155. Standing Order 107(6).

156. Standing Order 113(6).

157. Committees may decide to forgo a sub-committee on agenda and procedure. See, for example, Standing Committee on National Health and Welfare, *Minutes of Proceedings and Evidence*, October 21, 1986, Issue No. 1, p. 3.

158. See, for example, Standing Committee on Foreign Affairs and International Trade, *Minutes*, October 23, 1997, Meeting No. 4.

159. See, for example, Standing Committee on Agriculture and Agri-food, *Minutes*, October 7, 1997, Meeting No. 1.

160. For example, the Sub-committee on Human Rights and International Development (Standing Committee on Foreign Affairs and International Trade, *Minutes*, October 23, 1997, Meeting No. 4); the Sub-committee on Private Members' Business (Standing Committee on House Management, *Minutes of Proceedings and Evidence*, May 21, 1991, Issue No. 1, p. 5; February 3, 1994, Issue No. 1, p. 9; Standing Committee on Procedure and House Affairs, *Minutes*, February 29, 1996, Meeting No. 1; September 29, 1997, Meeting No. 1).

formed to carry out a specific study;[161] such sub-committees cease to exist once they have made their final report to the main committee. If their work is interrupted by prorogation, the main committee may decide to revive the sub-committee in the subsequent session.[162]

Powers

Sub-committees possess only those powers which are conferred on them by the main committee. Sub-committees to which part of a committee's permanent mandate is delegated, or those undertaking special studies, are usually given the full powers of the main committee.[163] Where the House accords additional powers to a standing committee by special order, these powers may be accorded to sub-committees by the main committee. Special committees may delegate to a sub-committee any of the powers granted to them in the order of reference, including the power to travel or special broadcasting powers.[164] However, sub-committees are restricted from reporting directly to the House.[165]

Depending on the purpose for which it is established, a sub-committee may be given a more restricted list of powers than that possessed by the main committee.[166] Sub-committees on agenda and procedure, as their function is only to plan the work of the main committee, are not ordinarily given powers with respect to the summoning of witnesses or sending for documents.

Where a sub-committee requires additional powers, it may put its request in the form of a report to the main committee. If the powers sought are beyond those that the main committee can delegate, the main committee may request them in a report to the House, or the House may adopt a motion granting them directly.[167]

---

161. See, for example, the Sub-committee for the Study of Sports in Canada (Standing Committee on Canadian Heritage, *Minutes*, November 5, 1997, Meeting No. 5).

162. See, for example, Standing Committee on Aboriginal Affairs and Northern Development, *Minutes*, March 7, 1996, Meeting No. 1.

163. See, for example, Standing Committee on Canadian Heritage, *Minutes*, November 5, 1997, Meeting No. 5.

164. See, for example, *Journals*, March 27, 1990, p. 1417.

165. Standing Order 108(1)(*a*) does not allow standing committees to delegate to a sub-committee the power to report directly to the House. A similar restriction is usually placed in the order of reference establishing a special committee. The House has, on occasion, given a sub-committee the power to report directly. See *Journals*, February 17, 1993, p. 2523; February 23, 1993, p. 2546 (Sub-committee on the recodification of the general part of the Criminal Code of the Standing Committee on Justice and Solicitor General); and *Journals*, April 19, 1993, p. 2796; April 20, 1993, pp. 2812-4; May 28, 1993, pp. 3057-71 (Sub-committee on Bill C-62 (*An Act respecting telecommunications*) of the Standing Committee on Communications and Culture).

166. See, for example, Standing Committee on Foreign Affairs and International Trade, *Minutes*, October 23, 1997, Meeting No. 4.

167. See, for example, *Journals*, April 24, 1985, p. 506; May 10, 1985, p. 602; December 5, 1995, p. 2208.

Membership

GENERAL PROVISIONS

Committees cannot take up the responsibilities assigned to them until their membership has been named. At the commencement of the first session of a Parliament,[168] a motion is typically moved by the Government House Leader[169] to appoint the Standing Committee on Procedure and House Affairs to act as a striking committee,[170] that is, to prepare a list of the members to serve on the standing committees of the House (or, in the case of standing joint committees, the House members on those committees). The Committee is also responsible for naming members to legislative committees and for dealing with changes to the membership of standing committees. It may also be called upon to report a proposed membership for a special committee. The membership of the Standing Committee on Procedural and House Affairs continues from session to session throughout the life of a Parliament. The Committee has chosen to delegate to the whips of the recognized parties the authority to strike the membership of committees.[171]

Committee membership generally reflects the proportions of the various recognized parties in the House. Where the governing party has a majority in the House, it will also have a majority on every House committee. Independent members have not ordinarily been appointed to committees.[172]

The membership of committees must be composed of Members of the House of Commons. They may serve on more than one committee. While no rule prevents any Member from being named to a committee, current practice normally excludes

---

168. Standing Order 104(1). On at least one occasion, the House did not have committees struck during the first session of a Parliament; the striking committee was established at the beginning of the second session. See *Journals*, April 6, 1989, p. 50.

169. See, for example, *Journals,* September 23, 1997, pp. 12-3.

170. Formerly, the House established a committee solely to act as a striking committee. This was last done in 1989 (see *Journals*, April 6, 1989, p. 50). In 1991, the role of striking committee was included in the mandate of the House Management Committee (*Journals*, April 11, 1991, pp. 2905-32, in particular p. 2922) and is now part of the mandate of the Procedure and House Affairs Committee (*Journals*, January 25, 1994, pp. 58-61).

171. By practice, the House names the whips of all parties to the Procedure and House Affairs Committee. The Committee adopts at its organization meeting a motion similar to the following: "That the five Whips be delegated the authority to act as the Striking Committee pursuant to Standing Orders 104, 113 and 114 and, provided that the recommendations are unanimous and a copy of the report is signed by all five Whips, or their representatives, they present their recommendations directly to the Chair of the Committee for presentation to the House on behalf of the Committee" (Standing Committee on Procedure and House Affairs, *Minutes*, September 29, 1997, Meeting No. 1). The number of whips set out in the motion varies from Parliament to Parliament with the number of recognized parties in the House.

172. One independent Member, Anthony Roman (York North), was a member of two committees (see Standing Committee on Public Accounts, *Minutes of Proceedings and Evidence,* March 18, 1986, Issue No. 32, p. 10; Standing Joint Committee on Regulations and other Statutory Instruments, *Minutes of Proceedings and Evidence*, February 5, 1987, Issue No. 4, p. 4).

certain Members who have other parliamentary functions: the Speaker[173] and other Chair occupants,[174] Ministers[175] (including the Prime Minister[176]) and the leaders of recognized parties. Parliamentary Secretaries are usually named to the standing committees having a mandate in their area of responsibility.[177] Lists of the members of standing, legislative and special committees, of sub-committees and of the Liaison Committee are appended weekly to the *Debates* and are available on the Parliamentary Website.[178]

Only members of a committee (or officially designated substitutes) may move motions, vote and be counted as part of the quorum. Other members of the House may attend committee meetings, question witnesses and participate in the committee's public proceedings, unless the House or the committee orders otherwise. They may not, however, move motions, vote or be part of a quorum.[179] The attendance of other Members at *in camera* meetings is a matter for the committee to decide; however, they usually withdraw when the committee deliberates on a report to the House.

---

173. The Speaker was formerly named *ex officio* joint chair of the Standing Joint Committees on the Library and on the Parliamentary Restaurant. The Speaker may, on occasion, chair a special committee. Speaker Jerome served as Chair of the Special Committee on the Rights and Immunities of Members and of the Special Committee on TV and Radio Broadcasting of Proceedings of the House of Commons. See *Journals*, December 13, 1976, p. 230, and January 25, 1977, p. 287-8.

174. Chair occupants, other than the Speaker, may be called upon to act as chairs of legislative committees pursuant to Standing Order 112. Deputy Speaker Danis served as Chair of the Special Committee on the Review of the Parliament of Canada Act (see *Journals*, December 14, 1989, p. 1011).

175. The last Minister to be named to a committee was Alan MacEachern, who was named to replace Mitchell Sharp on the Striking Committee during the Second Session of the Thirtieth Parliament (1976-77) (see *Journals*, November 1, 1976, p. 92). In 1990, Marcel Danis, who, as Deputy Speaker, had been appointed Chairman of the Special Committee on the Review of the Parliament of Canada Act, continued as Chair of the Committee, even after his appointment to Cabinet (*Journals*, March 6, 1990, p. 1290).

176. In the early years of Confederation, the Prime Minister served on a variety of standing committees (see, for example, *Journals*, November 15, 1867, pp. 16, 21-2). The last Prime Minister to be named to a standing committee was William Lyon Mackenzie King, who served on the Standing Joint Committee on the Library of Parliament until 1926 (see *Journals*, March 16, 1926, p. 152).

177. Following a recommendation of the Special Committee on Reform of the House of Commons (the McGrath Committee), Parliamentary Secretaries were prohibited from being members of standing committees in the area of their responsibility (see Third Report, June 1985, p. 18, recommendation 4.5 (*Journals*, February 6, 1986, pp. 1644-66, in particular p. 1657)). The absence of Parliamentary Secretaries deprived the government of an official representative on committees and was considered by some to impede the committee's work (see *Debates*, April 9, 1991, pp. 19194-7). The prohibition on the membership of Parliamentary Secretaries was lifted in 1991 (see *Journals*, April 11, 1991, pp. 2905-32, in particular p. 2923).

178. See, for example, *Debates*, November 20, 1998, Appendix, pp. 17-25. The Website address is «http://www.parl.gc.ca/».

179. Standing Order 119.

Standing Committees

The Standing Orders provide for standing committees to be composed of 16 to 18 members.[180] Within 10 sitting days of its appointment at the beginning of a Parliament, the Standing Committee on Procedure and House Affairs is required to report to the House the list of standing committee members.[181] The list of committee members must be revised annually within the first 10 sitting days following the summer adjournment as provided for in the parliamentary calendar, and again at the beginning of each new session, provided that only one such report is presented by the Committee between the third Monday in September and December 31.[182]

The membership of standing committees comes into effect when the Procedure and House Affairs Committee's report is concurred in by the House.[183] Until such a report is concurred in, the committee membership previously approved by the House, if any, remains in force.[184]

Legislative Committees

The Procedure and House Affairs Committee is also responsible for naming members to legislative committees, which are struck on an *ad hoc* basis. Within five sitting days of the commencement of debate on a motion to establish a legislative committee or to refer a bill to one, the Procedure and House Affairs Committee must meet to establish a membership list of not more than 15 members to serve as the legislative committee.[185] The membership list does not include the Chair of the committee, who is named separately by the Speaker from the Panel of Chairmen.[186] The report, which must be presented in the House no later than the following Thursday,[187] is deemed adopted upon presentation.

Special Committees

The Standing Orders provide that special committees shall have no more than 15 members.[188] The membership of special committees may be established in several

---

180. Standing Order 104(2).

181. Standing Order 104(1).

182. Since the provision prohibiting the presentation of a second report was added to the Standing Orders in 1987 (see *Journals*, June 3, 1987, pp. 1016-28, in particular pp. 1023-4), the situation has not occurred.

183. See, for example, *Journals*, September 30, 1997, pp. 45-52.

184. The Forty-Ninth Report of the Committee, presented on October 5, 1990 (see *Journals*, pp. 2074-8), proposed new memberships for all standing and standing joint committees. No motion to concur in the Forty-Ninth Report was presented prior to prorogation on May 12, 1991, and committees continued to function up to prorogation with the membership as it existed prior to the presentation of the report.

185. Standing Order 113(1).

186. Standing Order 113(2). For further information on the Panel of Chairmen, see section below, "Chairs and Vice-Chairs".

187. For example, the second reading debate on Bill C-79 (*An Act to amend the Canada Elections Act*) was begun on Wednesday, March 16, 1988. The report on the committee membership was presented on Thursday, March 24, 1988. See *Journals*, March 16, 1988, p. 2303; March 24, 1988, pp. 2412-3.

188. Standing Order 105.

ways: the order of reference establishing such a committee may include its members;[189] the membership may be named separately by order of the House;[190] or the order of reference establishing the special committee may contain an instruction to a striking committee to prepare and bring in a list of names of members.[191] The report by a striking committee must be concurred in by the House.

Joint Committees

Joint committees, both standing and special, have memberships proportional to the relative size of both Houses.[192] House membership on joint committees is established following the procedure for the corresponding type of House committee (i.e., standing or special). House membership on standing joint committees is determined by the concurrence in a report from the Procedure and House Affairs Committee.[193] House membership on special joint committees may be included in the order of reference which establishes the committee;[194] or it may be named later either by motion of the House[195] or by concurrence in a report from the Procedure and House Affairs Committee.[196] In every case, the House must inform the Senate of the members who will represent it by way of a message. This may be accomplished either by communicating the original order of reference (if it contains the membership list)[197] or by a separate message.[198]

---

189. See, for example, the Special Committee on Acid Rain (*Journals*, October 9, 1986, pp. 64-5).

190. See, for example, the Special Committee on Pension Reform (*Journals*, March 1, 1983, p. 5654; March 9, 1983, p. 5684).

191. See, for example, *Journals*, March 30, 1993, p. 2742; April 2, 1993, pp. 2784-5. An attempt to depart from an order to bring in a list of names, by presenting a report which provided for a mechanism by which a party whip would designate members from time to time, has been ruled out of order (see *Journals*, June 19, 1991, pp. 226-7; September 25, 1991, p. 393; *Debates*, September 25, 1991, pp. 2712-8; September 27, 1991, pp. 2823-5). In at least one instance in the past, the instruction has provided that the striking committee's report be deemed adopted when presented to the House (*Journals*, March 30, 1993, p. 2742).

192. Standing Order 104(3) stipulates that membership on standing joint committees is proportional; there is no provision in the Standing Orders concerning proportional membership on special joint committees. Given the party representation in the two Houses at any given time, the proportional representation on a particular joint committee may be only approximate. See, for example, *Journals*, June 19, 1991, pp. 226-7.

193. Standing Order 104(3). See, for example, *Journals*, September 30, 1997, pp. 45-52.

194. The order of reference may directly name the membership (*Journals*, December 13, 1983, p. 37) or it may be done by reference. For example, the membership of the Standing Committee on Procedure and House Affairs was designated to represent the House on the Special Joint Committee on a Code of Conduct (*Journals*, March 12, 1996, p. 83).

195. See, for example, *Journals*, December 5, 1997, pp. 353-4.

196. See, for example, *Journals*, March 30, 1993, p. 2742; April 2, 1993, pp. 2784-5.

197. See, for example, *Journals*, December 13, 1983, pp. 37-8.

198. See, for example, *Journals*, April 2, 1993, pp. 2784-5.

Sub-committees

The membership of a sub-committee is usually determined by the main committee. Members of sub-committees may be named directly as part of the order of reference passed by the main committee[199] or by the Chair of the main committee following consultations with the party whips.[200] They can be selected either from the regular members of the committee or from the list of associate members established by the Procedure and House Affairs Committee.[201] The House has, on occasion, named the members of a sub-committee directly.[202] The main committee may alter the composition of a sub-committee it has named, but not that of one whose membership was named by the House.[203]

Where committees have agreed to establish sub-committees on agenda and procedure (steering committees), their memberships have varied considerably to suit the needs of individual committees. This sub-committee typically consists of the Chair of the committee, the Vice-Chairs, representatives of each of the other recognized parties and, on committees having a departmental responsibility, the Parliamentary Secretary.[204]

The membership of a sub-committee need not necessarily reflect the proportions of party membership either on the main committee or in the House itself. For example, the membership of the Sub-committee on Private Member's Business has consisted of a Chair from the government party and a single representative from each recognized party.[205]

Substitutions

In 1985, the McGrath Committee recommended that members be responsible for finding their own replacements when they were unable to attend committee

---

199. See, for example, the Sub-committee on Private Members' Business (Standing Committee on Procedure and House Affairs, *Minutes*, September 29, 1997, Meeting No. 1).

200. The motion to appoint the membership usually reads: "to be named by the Chair following the usual consultations with the whips". Committee members of each party consult as necessary with their party's whip and then inform the Chair of the name of their member or members on the sub-committee (see, for example, Standing Committee on Foreign Affairs and International Trade, *Minutes*, October 23, 1997, Meeting No. 4, and Standing Committee on Canadian Heritage, *Minutes*, November 5, 1997, Meeting No. 5). This procedure permits subsequent changes to the membership of a sub-committee at the discretion of the Whip without the need for an order by the committee.

201. Standing Order 108(1)(*b*). Permission was given to a committee to name to a sub-committee Members of the House who were neither members of the committee nor associate members (*Journals*, March 9, 1983, p. 5684).

202. See, for example, *Journals*, June 27, 1985, p. 907.

203. See, for example, *Journals*, October 1, 1985, p. 1052.

204. See, for example, Standing Committee on Environment and Sustainable Development, *Minutes*, October 7, 1997, Meeting No. 1.

205. See also, for example, the Sub-committee on Sittings of the House and the Sub-committee on Members' Services of the Standing Committee on Procedure and House Affairs (Procedure and House Affairs Committee, *Minutes*, October 28, 1997, Meeting No. 3). See also Chapter 21, "Private Members' Business".

meetings.[206] When members of a standing or standing joint committee are unable to attend committee meetings, the Standing Orders provide for their replacement by designated substitutes.[207] A substitute enjoys the same rights and privileges as the regular member of a committee being replaced. Substitutes are counted for purposes of establishing a quorum; they may participate in debate, move motions and vote.[208] A substitution cannot be in effect while the committee member is present at the meeting. Thus, a member, such as the Parliamentary Secretary, who is called upon to appear as a witness before a committee of which he or she is a member, cannot be substituted at that meeting, but retains his or her right to participate and vote in any decisions the committee may take during the meeting.[209]

Standing committee members may file with the clerk of the committee a list of the names of not more than 14 members of their party who may act as substitutes when required. The list is to be filed within five sitting days of the committee's organization meeting, and amendments to it may be filed at later times as required.[210] Notification of a proposed substitution from a list must be sent by the member to the party whip the day before it is to take effect. After signing the notification, the whip forwards it to the clerk of the committee.[211] If no substitute list is filed with the clerk or no notice has been received by the clerk, the whip may initiate a substitution by filing a notice with the clerk of the committee.[212] For the purpose of substitution, the whip may select any member of his or her party or the independent members listed as associate members of the committee.[213]

---

206. See Special Committee on Reform of the House of Commons, Third Report, June 1985, pp. 18-9. Following the presentation of the Report, a provision was added to the Standing Orders that required members of standing committees to file a list of substitutes. Members failing to file such a list were removed from the committee. (See *Journals*, February 6, 1986, pp.1644-66, in particular pp. 1659-60, and February 3, 1986, p. 1710. For an example of this provision in use, see *Journals*, May 29, 1986, pp. 2234-5.) In 1994, the filing of the list of substitutes was made voluntary, and the provision removing members who failed to do so was deleted (see *Journals*, January 25, 1994, pp. 58-61, in particular p. 61).

207. Where necessary, a series of substitutes may replace a given member during a meeting, but only one substitution may be in effect at any given time. See, for example, Standing Committee on Finance, *Minutes*, May 7, 1998, Meeting No. 82.

208. See Speaker Parent's ruling, *Debates*, November 7, 1996, pp. 6225-6.

209. See, for example, Standing Committee on Consumer and Corporate Affairs, *Minutes of Proceedings and Evidence,* November 27, 1991, Issue No. 28, pp. 3, 39-40.

210. Standing Order 114(2)(*a*).

211. In practice, a substitution is considered effective for any or all meetings of the committee which take place on the date indicated on the notice of substitution, rather than for a single meeting. Independent members are required to send their notices to the Chief Whip of the Official Opposition pursuant to Standing Order 114(2)(*b*).

212. The notice must be in the proper form. A notice that was defective has been held to invalidate the substitution, and the vote of the proposed substitute has been disallowed. See Standing Committee on Communications and Culture, *Minutes of Proceedings and Evidence*, June 17, 1992, Issue No. 50, pp. 6, 44-5.

213. Standing Order 114(2)(*c*). In 1994, Audrey McLaughlin (Yukon), who was not an associate member, was substituted for a regular member of the Aboriginal Affairs and Northern Development Committee and voted. When called upon to rule on the matter, Speaker Parent declared that the vote should be disallowed (*Debates*, June 20, 1994, pp. 5582-4).

The Standing Orders do not provide for substitutions in legislative committees. However, Members who are unable to carry out their duties on a legislative committee may be replaced by filing a change in membership, signed by the party whip, with the clerk of the committee.[214] As there is no limit on the number and frequency of such changes, they serve both to make permanent changes to a committee's membership and as a *de facto* substitution system.

Substitutions are permitted on special committees only where such a power is granted in their order of reference and only in the manner stipulated. The House has permitted substitutions on special committees in a manner similar to that used for standing committees[215] and has also permitted special committee membership to be changed on signed notification of the Chief Whip of a party, as is done for legislative committees.[216] As the order of reference of a special committee usually sets no limit on the number or frequency of such changes, they serve both to make permanent changes to the committee's membership and as a *de facto* substitution system.

Committees do not normally make explicit provision for substitutions when establishing sub-committees. The membership of a sub-committee is often designated by indicating the number of members from each party who will form the sub-committee, rather than designating members by name. This permits any of the regular or associate members of a party on the main committee to attend a given meeting of the sub-committee, up to the maximum stipulated in its order of reference.[217]

ASSOCIATE MEMBERS

In addition to regular committee members, the Standing Orders also provide for associate members. Associate members are eligible to be named to sub-committees and to act as substitutes for regular members who are unable to attend committee meetings. While associate members are serving on sub-committees or as substitutes for regular members, they enjoy all of the rights of regular committee members: they are counted for purposes of establishing a quorum, they may participate in debate, they may move motions and vote.[218] The use of associate members on sub-committees helps to reduce the workload of regular committee members.[219] It also permits

---

214. Standing Order 114(3). See *Journals*, December 10, 1990, pp. 2434-5.

215. See, for example, *Journals*, September 21, 1994, pp. 712-3.

216. See, for example, *Journals*, November 18, 1997, pp. 224-5.

217. See, for example, Standing Committee on Foreign Affairs and International Trade, *Minutes*, October 23, 1997, Meeting No. 4.

218. See Speaker Parent's ruling, *Debates*, November 7, 1996, pp. 6225-6.

219. In order to fulfil their mandates, some committees have adopted an alternative to the establishment of sub-committees with the participation of associate members. These committees divide themselves into "groups", each having responsibility for a share of the committee's mandate. The Standing Committee on Foreign Affairs and International Trade has divided itself into two groups "... to be assigned to meet alternately with visiting delegations ..." (Standing Committee on Foreign Affairs and International Trade, *Minutes*, October 8, 1997, Meeting No. 1). The Finance Committee has divided itself into two groups in order to hold simultaneous hearings in different locations as part of the pre-budget consultation (Standing Committee on Finance, *Minutes*, October 7, 1997, Meeting No. 2).

members with particular interest or expertise in the specific area being examined by the sub-committee to participate in its work, without being obliged to become a regular member of the main committee.

The Procedure and House Affairs Committee, in its capacity as striking committee, is responsible for preparing and bringing in a list of associate members for standing and standing joint committees.[220]

EX OFFICIO MEMBERS

Some committees have appointed "*ex officio* members" who were not Members of the House to participate in various committee studies. These individuals, who represented groups specifically targeted by the studies, were permitted to pose questions to witnesses, participate in the committees' deliberations and in the drafting of reports. They were not permitted to move motions or to vote, nor could they be counted for the purposes of quorum.[221]

CHANGES IN MEMBERSHIP

It is generally accepted that a Member is bound to serve on a committee to which he or she has been duly appointed.[222] Members were formerly excused from service on a committee only if they could show some reason why they were unable to attend.[223] As Members are named to committees by the House, they cannot simply resign. They may only be removed following a membership change or by a decision of the House. Committees themselves have no power to alter their own membership. In order to maintain the relative number of members of each party on a committee, the removal of a member is coupled with the naming of a replacement.

Where a Member wishes to resign from a standing committee, he or she may give notice of that intention in writing to the Procedure and House Affairs Committee. The Committee reports to the House indicating the names of the Member wishing to be removed from the standing committee and the new Member being named to it. The change takes effect when the House has concurred in the Committee's report.[224]

220. Standing Order 104(4). See, for example, *Journals*, October 2, 1998, pp. 1114-5. The membership of the Standing Committee on Procedure and House Affairs is named directly by motion of the House; its associate members are named in the same way. See, for example, *Journals*, September 28, 1998, p. 1086.

221. See Sub-committee on Indian Self-Government, *Minutes of Proceedings and Evidence*, October 6, 1982, Issue No. 1, pp. 8-9, 11; November 18, 1982, Issue No. 6, p. 3; and Sub-committee on Indian Women and the Indian Act, *Minutes of Proceedings and Evidence*, September 8, 1982, Issue No. 1, p. 8. In addition to *ex officio* members, the Sub-committee on Indian Self-Government named "liaison members", also not Members of the House, who were permitted to question witnesses at the discretion of the Chair and to participate in the drafting of the Sub-committee's report.

222. *Bourinot*, 4th ed., p. 462.

223. Members were excused by order of the House for such reasons as ill health or advanced age. See, for example, *Journals*, March 24, 1873, p. 60.

224. Standing Order 114(2)(*d*). See, for example, *Journals*, June 15, 1989, p. 377. Changes to the membership of the Standing Committee on Procedure and House Affairs, which is appointed directly by motion of the House, can only be made by a subsequent motion. See, for example, *Journals*, September 28, 1998, p. 1086.

Changes in the membership of legislative committees are effected by having a notice thereof, signed by the Chief Whip of that member's party, filed with the clerk of the committee. The notice indicates both the member being removed from the committee and the replacement. [225]

Where the House makes provisions for changes to the membership of a special committee in the order of reference creating the committee, such provisions usually parallel those used for legislative committees. [226]

Changes in the House membership of joint committees are made following the procedures used in the corresponding type of House committees (i.e., standing or special). [227]

As the membership of sub-committees is normally established by designating a certain number of members from each party, rather than by naming specific individuals, no special provision is required for membership changes.

Chairs and Vice-Chairs

ROLE OF CHAIRS

The Chair of a committee is responsible for recognizing members and witnesses who seek the floor and ensuring that any rules established by the committee concerning the apportioning of speaking time are respected. Furthermore, the Chair is also responsible for maintaining order in committee proceedings. However, the Chair does not have the power to censure disorder or decide questions of privilege; this can only be done by the House upon receiving a report from the committee. [228]

As the presiding officer of the committee, the Chair does not move motions. Furthermore, the Chair does not vote, except in two situations: when a committee is considering a private bill, the Chair may vote like all other members of the committee; and, in all cases where there is an equality of votes, the Chair has a casting vote.

Reports to the House from the committee are signed by the Chair, who must ensure that the text presented in the House is the one agreed to by the committee. Committee reports to the House are usually presented by the Chair. [229] During the Oral Question Period in the House, a committee Chair may respond to questions,

---

225. Standing Order 114(3). See, for example, *Journals,* April 8, 1991, p. 2848.

226. See, for example, *Journals*, November 18, 1997, p. 225.

227. See, for example, *Journals*, March 12, 1996, pp. 83-4; February 9, 1998, p. 430.

228. Standing Order 117. The Speaker's role in this respect is set out in Standing Order 10.

229. Standing Order 35(1) permits a committee report to be presented by any Member of the House, although practice holds that it is normally limited to members of the committee. Committees usually adopt a motion instructing the Chair to present the report on their behalf (see, for example, Standing Committee on Procedure and House Affairs, *Minutes*, December 3, 1998, Meeting No. 45). The Chair of a sub-committee conducting a special study has presented the resulting report of the main committee to the House (see, for example, *Debates*, December 3, 1998, p. 10825).

provided they deal with the proceedings or schedule of the committee and not the substance of its work. [230]

Any Member of the House may be asked to chair a committee, provided that, for all committees except legislative committees, he or she is a member of that committee. The Speaker and the Deputy Speaker have chaired a variety of committees on matters related to the House. [231] The Deputy Speaker has also been called upon, as an *ex officio* member of the Panel of Chairmen, to chair legislative committees. [232] Ministers, [233] party leaders and independent Members [234] do not normally serve on committees and, hence, do not act as Chairs.

Chairs of standing and special committees also often assume a leadership role in planning and co-ordinating the committee's work and in conducting its investigations.

The Chairs of standing committees (and House Joint Chairs of standing joint committees) are *ex officio* members of the Liaison Committee, responsible for the allocation of funds to standing committees. [235]

Chairs of legislative committees have a role analogous to the Chair of Committees of the Whole House. Selected from the all-party Panel of Chairmen by the Speaker, they preside without participating in the debate on substantive issues. This need for impartiality was cited by both the Lefebvre and the McGrath Committees as the justification for establishing the Panel of Chairmen for legislative committees. [236] Some legislative committee Chairs have cited this principle of impartiality as grounds for abstaining from votes in the House on the bill they were to preside over in committee. [237] Unlike the Chairs of other committees, the Chair of a legislative committee is not considered a member of the committee and is not counted as part of a quorum. [238]

---

230. See, for example, *Debates,* October 24, 1985, p. 7965; March 9, 1987, p. 3955.

231. The Speaker has served as the Chair of the Special Committee on the Rights and Immunities of Members (see *Journals*, March 9, 1978, p. 467) and of the Special Committee on TV and Radio Broadcasting of the Proceedings of the House and its Committees (see *Journals*, October 18, 1977, p. 11). The Deputy Speaker has chaired the Special Committee on the Review of the Parliament of Canada Act (see *Journals*, December 14, 1989, p. 1011). Following his appointment as Minister of State (Youth and Fitness and Amateur Sport) and his resignation as Deputy Speaker, Marcel Danis continued as Chair of this Committee (see *Journals*, March 6, 1990, p. 1290).

232. See, for example, *Journals*, November 23, 1989, p. 878.

233. The last Minister to be elected Chair of a committee was Mitchell Sharp. See Standing Committee on Procedure and Organization, *Minutes of Proceedings and Evidence*, October 17, 1974, Issue No. 1, p. 5.

234. Anthony Roman (York North), an independent Member, served as Chair of a legislative committee in 1987. See *Journals*, November 4, 1987, pp. 1835-6.

235. Standing Order 107.

236. See Special Committee on Standing Orders and Procedure, *Minutes of Proceedings and Evidence*, April 28, 1983, Issue No. 19, pp. 5-6, and Special Committee on Reform of the House of Commons, Third Report, June 1985, p. 102.

237. See, for example, *Debates*, June 26, 1989, p. 3645.

238. Standing Order 118(1).

The Chair of a sub-committee has the same role as the Chair of the main committee. By practice, the Chair of the main committee serves as Chair of the sub-committee on agenda and procedure (the steering committee).

ROLE OF VICE-CHAIRS

The Vice-Chairs of committees serve as replacements, presiding over meetings when the Chair is unable to attend. All of the Chair's powers can be delegated to the Vice-Chair, but the Vice-Chair cannot preside over a committee meeting while the office of Chair is vacant.[239] Normally, Vice-Chairs also serve as members of the sub-committee on agenda and procedure.

ACTING CHAIRS

In the absence of the Chair and the Vice-Chairs of a committee, an Acting Chair must be chosen to preside over a committee meeting. With the committee's consent, the Chair of a standing or special committee will often designate a member to act as Chair. Where no Acting Chair has been designated, the clerk of the committee presides over the election of an Acting Chair at the beginning of the meeting. The Chair of a legislative committee is empowered by Standing Order to designate a member of the committee as an Acting Chair.[240] An Acting Chair has all of the powers and duties of the Chair while presiding but has no power to convene meetings of the committee or to preside when the office of Chair is vacant.

ELECTION OF THE CHAIR AND THE VICE-CHAIR

The election of a committee Chair is the first order of a committee's business. Chairs and Vice-Chairs are elected at the beginning of a session and, as necessary, during the course of a session. The election of the Chair, presided over by the clerk of the committee, proceeds by way of a motion, rather than the balloting procedure employed to elect the Speaker of the House.[241] Where several different motions are proposed, the clerk may take those proposed after the initial motion as notices of motion.[242] The motions are put to the committee *seriatim* until one of the motions is adopted. Only a regular member of the committee may be proposed for the position of Chair, but the member nominated need not be present at the meeting. When a

---

239. See, for example, Standing Committee on Labour, Employment and Immigration, *Minutes of Proceedings and Evidence,* June 11, 1987, Issue No. 40, p. 4.

240. Standing Order 113(4).

241. Committees are exempted from following the rules used for the election of the Speaker by Standing Order 116. For an example of a Chair's election, see Standing Committee on Foreign Affairs and International Trade, *Minutes* and *Evidence*, October 8, 1997, Meeting No. 1.

242. See, for example, Standing Committee on Transport, *Evidence*, March 12, 1996, Meeting No. 1.

committee Chair is elected *in absentia,* the clerk immediately proceeds to the election of an Acting Chair, who presides over the remainder of the meeting.[243]

When a motion for the election of a Chair is made, the clerk will first ask if the committee agrees to the nominating motion and will, if necessary, call for the "yeas" and "nays". Members are free to request that the vote be a recorded vote, that is, that the names of those voting for or against the nominating motion be recorded in the minutes.[244] On occasion, committees have had recourse to a secret ballot.[245] This is done only when the committee members express a unanimous desire to proceed in this manner.[246] As the meeting is called pursuant to Standing Order for the sole purpose of electing a Chair, and since the committee is not properly constituted until the Chair has been selected, the clerk who presides over the election has no authority to hear points of order or to entertain any motion except that for the election of a Chair, not even a motion to establish the manner in which the committee wishes to proceed with that election. As well, in the event of a tie vote, the clerk does not have a casting vote.

If no motion proposing a member for the position of Chair is adopted, no other business can be transacted. When an impasse is evident, the members disperse and must be reconvened by the clerk at a later time, with the election of a Chair remaining their first order of business.[247]

In the event of resignation or removal of the Chair from the committee, a new Chair must be elected before the committee can take up other business.[248] This parallels proceedings in the House, where a vacancy in the office of Speaker necessitates the immediate election of a new Speaker before any other matter can be considered.[249] Where the Chair announces his or her resignation as Chair at a committee meeting, the committee proceeds immediately to the election of a new Chair.[250]

A standing committee must meet to elect a Chair within 10 days of concurrence in the Procedure and House Affairs Committee's report establishing the committee

---

243. See, for example, Standing Committee on Canadian Heritage, *Minutes*, October 7, 1997, Meeting No. 1.

244. See, for example, Standing Committee on Fisheries and Oceans, *Minutes* and *Evidence,* October 7, 1997, Meeting No. 1.

245. See, for example, Standing Committee on Communications and Culture, *Minutes of Proceedings and Evidence*, June 4, 1991, Issue No. 1, p. 5.

246. See, for example, Standing Committee on Fisheries and Oceans, *Evidence*, October 7, 1997, Meeting No. 1.

247. Standing Order 106(1). See, for example, Standing Committee on Public Accounts, *Minutes of Proceedings and Evidence*, December 12, 1995, Issue No. 36, pp. 20-1.

248. See, for example, Standing Committee on Industry, *Minutes of Proceedings and Evidence*, February 9, 1995, Issue No. 32, p. 3.

249. See Standing Order 2(2) and Chapter 7, "The Speaker and Other Presiding Officers of the House".

250. See, for example, Standing Committee on Miscellaneous Estimates, *Minutes of Proceedings and Evidence*, December 9, 1982, Issue No. 100, p. 3.

membership.[251] This normally occurs at the beginning of each session and following the presentation of the new membership report in September. Elections are held after the September report, whether or not there has been any change in committee membership.[252]

Each standing committee elects a Chair and two Vice-Chairs of whom two must be government members and the third a member of the opposition.[253] While the Standing Orders do not require it, the practice has been that the opposition member is from the Official Opposition.[254] As well, the Chairs of standing committees have traditionally been government members, with the exception of the Chair of the Standing Committee on Public Accounts[255] and the House Joint Chair of the Standing Joint Committee for the Scrutiny of Regulations,[256] both of which elect Chairs from the Official Opposition.[257]

The Chair of the committee (or, in the Chair's absence, the Acting Chair) presides over the election of the Vice-Chairs. Where a committee is electing two Vice-Chairs, one from the government party and one from the opposition, there is no set order in which the elections must be held, and each committee is free to arrange its own proceedings. When a secret ballot is requested for the election of a Vice-Chair, the decision is made by adopting or rejecting a motion to that effect. As the committee is, with the election of the Chair, properly constituted, any decisions made with respect to the manner of proceeding are decided by a majority vote of the committee.[258] If a Vice-Chair is elected *in absentia,* it is not necessary to proceed to the election of an Acting Vice-Chair.[259]

The Panel of Chairmen for legislative committees is established at the beginning of each session and is composed of 12 members named by the Speaker in proportion

---

251. Standing Order 106(1).

252. The election, following the September report, has been suspended by special order of the House and incumbent Chairs permitted to continue in office. See *Journals*, September 27, 1991, p. 408.

253. Standing Order 106(2).

254. See, for example, Standing Committee on Aboriginal Affairs and Northern Development, *Minutes of Proceedings and Evidence*, March 7, 1996, Issue No. 1, p. 1.

255. In the case of the Public Accounts Committee, the practice of choosing a Chair from the opposition was part of the government's initial intention in establishing the committee. A commitment to having a member of the opposition chair the committee was made in the 1958 Throne Speech. See *Debates*, May 12, 1958, p. 6.

256. The Scrutiny of Regulations Committee was proposed as one which should operate in a primarily non-partisan manner, aided by a proposal that the committee not be chaired only by government members. See *Debates*, October 14, 1971, pp. 8679-81.

257. A departure from this practice arose in the First Session of the Thirty-Sixth Parliament (1997-99) when the Official Opposition members on the Scrutiny of Regulations Committee declined nominations for the position of Joint Chair. A government member was elected to the position. See Standing Committee for the Scrutiny of Regulations, *Minutes* and *Evidence,* October 23, 1997, Meeting No. 1.

258. See, for example, Standing Committee on Canadian Heritage, *Minutes of Proceedings and Evidence*, February 8, 1994, Issue No. 1, p. 5.

259. See, for example, Standing Committee on Foreign Affairs and International Trade, *Minutes*, October 8, 1997, Meeting No. 1.

to the party standings in the House, along with the Deputy Speaker and Chair of Committees of the Whole House, the Deputy Chair of Committees of the Whole House and the Assistant Deputy Chair of Committees of the Whole House.[260] Unlike the practice with respect to standing and special committees, the Chair of a legislative committee may be a member of any of the parties in the House.[261] The designation of the Chair by the Speaker, rather than his or her election by the committee, assists the Chair of a legislative committee in acting as a neutral arbitrator of the proceedings.[262] The Speaker selects the Chair of a legislative committee once the membership of the committee has been established.[263] Legislative committees do not elect Vice-Chairs. When a replacement for the Chair is necessary at a given meeting, the Chair will designate a committee member to act in that capacity for the meeting.[264]

Chairs of special committees are elected following the procedure used in standing committees.[265] This election takes place as the first order of business at the initial meeting of the committee, convened by the clerk for that purpose.[266]

In standing joint committees, two Joint Chairs are elected, one from each House. The Senate Joint Chair is elected first, followed by the Joint Chair of the House of Commons. The election of each Chair is presided over by the Joint Clerk from the respective House. All committee members are entitled to vote on the motions for the Joint Chairs from each House.[267] The Joint Chairs of special joint committees are elected following the procedure used in standing joint committees.[268]

The practice with respect to the election of Vice-Chairs is variable in joint committees: they may choose not to have any Vice-Chairs, to elect one only, or to elect

---

260. Standing Order 112. See, for example, *Journals*, May 19, 1989, p. 248.

261. See, for example, *Journals,* October 18, 1990, p. 2143.

262. The view of the legislative committee chair as a non-partisan presiding officer stems from a recommendation in the Sixth Report of the Lefebvre Committee, repeated in the First Report of the McGrath Committee, concerning the establishment of a system of legislative committees: "Your Committee believes that Legislative Committees ought to be regarded as smaller versions of the Committee of the Whole House ... (T)he Deputy Speaker, as the Chairman of Committees, is an impartial presiding officer. We believe that the establishment of a Panel of Chairmen would impart these qualities to the committee stage of all legislation. As neutral chairmen, panel members would be able to develop expertise in House procedures and to meet from time to time to ensure consistent chairing practices." See Special Committee on Standing Orders and Procedure, *Minutes of Proceedings and Evidence*, April 28, 1983, Issue No. 19, p. 5, and Special Committee on the Reform of Parliament, *Minutes of Proceedings and Evidence*, December 20, 1984, Issue No. 2, p. 8.

263. Standing Order 113(1) and (2). See, for example, *Journals*, December 7, 1990, p. 2399; December 11, 1990, p. 2438; December 12, 1990, p. 2447.

264. Standing Order 113(4).

265. Chairs may be designated in the order of reference establishing a special committee. See, for example, *Journals*, June 27, 1989, p. 472.

266. See, for example, Special Committee on Electoral Reform, *Minutes of Proceedings and Evidence*, February 26, 1992, Issue No. 1, p. 4.

267. See, for example, Standing Joint Committee on the Library of Parliament, *Minutes*, October 28, 1997, Meeting No. 1.

268. See, for example, Special Joint Committee on Child Custody and Access, *Minutes*, December 11, 1997, Meeting No. 1.

two, who may either be from one or both Houses.[269] In standing joint committees, when the House Joint Chair is a member of the government party, the committee usually chooses a member from the Official Opposition in the House as Vice-Chair. The opposite also holds true. For example, in the Standing Joint Committee for the Scrutiny of Regulations, where the House Joint Chair is traditionally from the Official Opposition, a government member from the House is usually elected as Vice-Chair.[270] Special joint committees rarely elect Vice-Chairs.[271]

In establishing sub-committees, the main committee may either designate a Chair in the initial order of reference[272] or allow the members of the sub-committee to elect the Chair themselves.[273] While most sub-committees are chaired by government members, Chairs have been selected among members of the opposition,[274] including parties other than the Official Opposition.[275] Given the small size of their membership and their limited mandates, sub-committees do not usually find it necessary to elect Vice-Chairs.[276]

RESIGNATIONS

In the event that the elected Chair of a committee resigns or is for any reason unable to carry out his or her duties, the committee must proceed to elect a new Chair as its first order of business. As the committee ceases to be properly constituted until a new Chair has been selected, the election is presided over by the clerk of the committee.

---

269. See, for example, Special Joint Committee on Child Custody and Access, *Minutes*, December 11, 1997, Meeting No. 1; Standing Joint Committee on the Library of Parliament, *Minutes*, October 28, 1997, Meeting No. 1; Standing Joint Committee on Official Languages, *Minutes*, October 21,1997, Meeting No. 1; Special Joint Committee on a Code of Conduct, *Minutes of Proceedings and Evidence*, March 20, 1997, Issue No. 1, p. 71.

270. See, for example, Standing Joint Committee for the Scrutiny of Regulations, *Evidence*, October 22, 1998, Meeting No. 13.

271. For a recent exception, see Special Joint Committee on a Code of Conduct, *Minutes of Proceedings and Evidence*, March 20, 1997, Issue No. 1, p. 71.

272. See, for example, Standing Committee on Procedure and House Affairs, *Minutes*, October 28, 1997, Meeting No. 3.

273. See, for example, Sub-committee on Human Rights and International Development of the Standing Committee on Foreign Affairs and International Trade, *Minutes*, November 3, 1997, Meeting No. 1.

274. For example, the Sub-committee on Members' Services of the Standing Committee on Procedure and House Affairs was chaired by a member of the Official Opposition. See Standing Committee on Procedure and House Affairs, *Minutes*, October 28, 1997, Meeting No. 3.

275. See, for example, Standing Committee on Finance, *Minutes of Proceedings and Evidence*, March 24, 1992, Issue No. 40, p. 3.

276. For a recent exception, see Sub-committee on Members' Services of the Standing Committee on Procedure and House Affairs, *Minutes*, April 9, 1997, Meeting No. 1.

The Vice-Chair has no role to play in the election of a new Chair. When a Vice-Chair is elected Chair of a committee, he or she resigns from the office of Vice-Chair.[277]

In the case of the resignation of a Chair who has been designated either by the Speaker (in the case of a legislative committee) or by the House (in the case of some special committees), a new Chair must be designated before the committee can continue with its work.[278]

The Chair of a committee presides over any election necessitated by the resignation of a Vice-Chair.[279]

Committee Staff

In the execution of its functions, each committee is assisted normally by a clerk and a researcher; the clerk, in turn, receives assistance from the support services of the House.

COMMITTEE CLERK

The clerk of a committee is the procedural advisor to the Chair and all members of the committee and also acts as its administrative officer. The role of the committee clerk is analogous to that which the Clerk of the House has with respect to the Speaker and Members of the House. As a non-partisan and independent officer, the clerk serves equally all members of the committee as well as representatives of all parties; clerks discharge their duties and responsibilities with respect to the committee in consultation with the Chair. The clerk also acts as the committee's liaison with other branches and services of the House of Commons.

RESEARCH STAFF

The Library of Parliament provides research staff to all committees on request. The researchers provide briefing material and other background material to committee members. They may identify potential witnesses for the committee as well as possible lines of questioning during committee hearings and provide assistance to the committee in the drafting of reports to the House. Committees are free to seek additional or more specialized research help from outside the Library of Parliament if they require it. This is done on an *ad hoc* basis and the committee is required to pay for the assistance of outside researchers from its own budget.

---

277. See, for example, Standing Committee on Finance, Trade and Economic Affairs, *Minutes of Proceedings and Evidence*, November 17, 1983, Issue No. 156, p. 3.

278. See, for example, *Journals*, June 12, 1989, p. 358; June 15, 1989, p. 379.

279. See, for example, Standing Committee on Procedure and House Affairs, *Minutes of Proceedings and Evidence*, October 4, 1994, Issue No. 24, pp. 6, 8.

OTHER STAFF

On occasion, committees may engage outside consultants on contract to assist them in a study requiring a particular expertise. They may also hire additional support staff as the need arises.[280] Engaging staff on a contract basis requires the adoption of a motion by the committee, which must specify the mandate and duration of the contract and a maximum rate or amount of remuneration.[281] Outside staff engaged by a committee are paid from the committee's budget, in conformity with the guidelines set out by the Board of Internal Economy.[282]

Meetings

Committees conduct their deliberations and make decisions within the framework of meetings. In order to accommodate the wide variety of subjects that a committee may be called upon to consider, considerable latitude is permitted in the format that committee meetings may take. At the same time, there are a number of rules and practices by which committees are bound in transacting their business.

Meetings of committees usually take place in specially equipped rooms in the Parliament Buildings, but committees may hold meetings elsewhere in Canada. The meeting rooms are usually arranged in an open-rectangle configuration. The Chair sits at one end, flanked by the clerk and the research staff. Government members are at the Chair's right, while opposition members sit on the left. Witnesses, if any, sit at the end of the rectangle opposite the Chair. Members' staff sit behind the members on either side of the room and there is seating for the public and the press at the rear of the room, behind the witnesses. (See Figure 20.1, Committee Room Configuration.)

Committee meetings are ordinarily open to the public and the media. Simultaneous interpretation services are offered to committee members, witnesses and members of the public at all committee meetings. Public meetings are broadcast on the House of Commons' internal audio system to all Members of the House and the Parliamentary Press Gallery and may also be publicly televised over the CPaC network.[283]

TYPES OF MEETINGS

Most committee meetings can be described as evidence-gathering meetings. They have traditionally commenced with presentations made by witnesses, followed by a question and answer period during which committee members have the opportunity to explore selected aspects of an issue in greater detail. In recent years, there has been a growing trend towards gathering evidence in other manners to meet the

---

280. Standing Order 120.
281. See, for example, Special Joint Committee on Child Custody and Access, *Minutes*, February 23, 1998, Meeting No. 5.
282. See *Financial Policy Manual for Committees*, Chapter C-3, Contracts.
283. Standing Order 119.1.

Figure 20.1   *Committee Room Configuration*

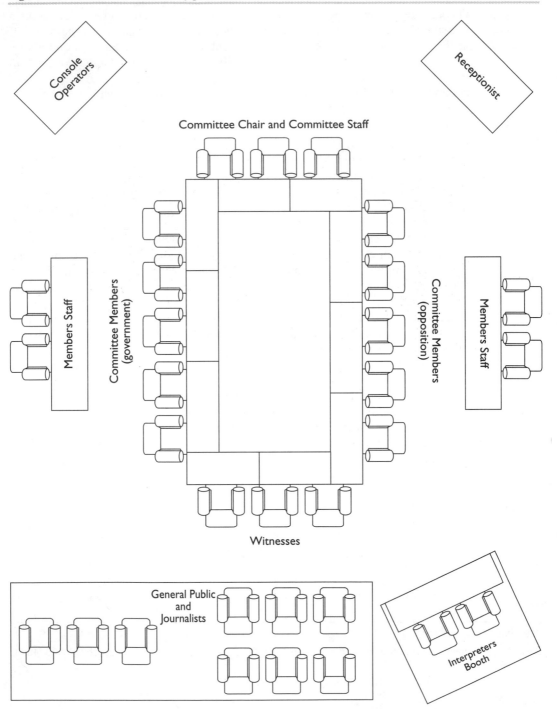

Figure 20.2   *A Committee Room*

changing needs of members and to take the best possible advantage of technological developments. Committees may hold meetings to exchange ideas with panels of witnesses representing different points of views in "round-table" discussions.[284] As well, "town hall" meetings may be organized where members of the public have an opportunity to express their views without making a formal presentation to the committee.[285] Committees have also taken advantage of developing videoconference technology to hear testimony from across the country and internationally.[286] Where a subject is of interest to two or more standing committees, they may decide to hold a joint meeting.[287] While the use of these formats has, for the most part, taken place

---

284. See, for example, Standing Committee on Natural Resources, *Minutes of Proceedings and Evidence*, April 14, 1994, Issue No. 10, p. 3.

285. Town hall meetings are used especially when committees meet outside of the parliamentary precinct. See, for example, Standing Committee on National Defence and Veterans Affairs, *Minutes* and *Evidence*, May 28, 1998, Meeting No. 68.

286. For further information on videoconferencing, see section below.

287. Standing Order 108(1)(*a*). See, for example, Standing Committee on Foreign Affairs and International Trade, *Minutes*, February 9, 1999, Meeting No. 89, and Standing Committee on National Defence and Veterans' Affairs, *Minutes*, February 9, 1999, Meeting No. 88.

within the existing procedural framework, some modification of the Standing Orders has been necessary.[288]

On occasion, a committee may decide to hold an *in camera* meeting to deal with administrative matters, to consider a draft report or to receive a routine background briefing. Committees also meet *in camera* to deal with subject matters requiring confidentiality, such as national security.[289] Often a committee which has several items on its agenda will hold part of a meeting in public and part *in camera*. At *in camera* meetings, neither the public nor the media is permitted, and there is no broadcasting of any kind. The committee decides, either on a case by case basis or as a matter of general policy, whether a transcript of *in camera* proceedings is to be kept.[290] Minutes of *in camera* meetings are publicly available, but certain information usually found in the minutes of committee meetings is not included.[291] Members of the House who are not members of the committee are expected to withdraw when a committee is meeting *in camera*.[292] However, at the discretion of the committee, non-members may remain during *in camera* sessions.[293] Divulging any part of the proceedings of an *in camera* committee meeting has been ruled by the Speaker to constitute a *prima facie* matter of privilege.[294]

---

288. Formerly, committees required special permission of the House to sit jointly. Following the Parliamentary Forum on Global Climate Change in 1990, which permitted several committees to hold joint meetings as well as a plenary session and print a single record of their proceedings, the Standing Orders were modified to permit such joint sittings (see *Journals*, March 28, 1990, p. 1424; Standing Committee on Privileges and Elections, *Minutes of Proceedings and Evidence*, March 19, 1991, Issue No. 42, pp. 3-4; *Journals*, March 20, 1991, p. 2728; April 12, 1991, p. 2943).

289. See, for example, *Journals*, August 1, 1940, pp. 310-6.

290. See, for example, Standing Committee on Aboriginal Affairs and Northern Development, *Minutes of Proceedings and Evidence*, June 22, 1988, Issue No. 45, p. 3.

291. While the text of all motions adopted is included in the minutes of *in camera* meetings, the names of the movers are not included and no information is provided about the numbers of yeas and nays or the names of those voting for or against a motion. See, for example, Standing Committee on Official Languages, *Minutes*, February 11, 1999, Meeting No. 19. The clerk of the committee may be requested to keep more detailed, confidential minutes for the exclusive use of the committee. These detailed minutes, usually referred to as *in extenso* minutes, do not form part of the public record of the committee's proceedings.

292. In the absence of any other direction from the House or the committee, Standing Order 119 permits Members who are not members of a committee to participate only in the public proceedings of the committee.

293. See, for example, Standing Committee on Regional Industrial Expansion, *Minutes of Proceedings and Evidence*, April 28, 1987, Issue No. 13, p. 3.

294. See Speaker Fraser's ruling, *Debates*, May 14, 1987, pp. 6108-11, and the Seventh Report of the Standing Committee on Elections, Privileges and Procedure, *Journals*, December 18, 1987, pp. 2014-6. The case in question involved the divulgation by John Parry (Kenora–Rainy River) of the results of a recorded vote held at an *in camera* meeting of the Standing Committee on Aboriginal Affairs and Northern Development. See *Debates*, March 25, 1987, p. 4540; April 28, 1987, pp. 5329-30; May 5, 1987, pp. 5737-42. A committee may itself decide that a meeting held *in camera* should be declared a public meeting. See, for example, Standing Joint Committee for the Scrutiny of Regulations, *Minutes*, November 5, 1998, Meeting No. 15.

Committees also meet informally with parliamentarians and government officials from other countries.[295] As an informal meeting is not, strictly speaking, a committee meeting, it may take place in a much more relaxed atmosphere. Members are not bound by the ordinary rules and practices that govern committee meetings. The proceedings are not recorded or transcribed, nor is the committee entitled to any of the privileges associated with parliamentary proceedings or to exercise any of the powers which the House has conferred on it.

Meetings Outside the Precinct of Parliament

Committees ordinarily meet on Parliament Hill in the facilities provided for them by the House of Commons. From time to time, committees also travel for the purpose of gathering evidence, consulting or visiting sites related to their study. In order to hold such meetings beyond the parliamentary precinct, a committee must first obtain approval from the Liaison Committee for the necessary travel funds and then the permission of the House to travel.[296] The House may grant permission to travel by adopting a motion to that effect or by concurring in a report recommending that such permission be given.[297]

Committees empowered to hold hearings elsewhere in Canada do so in the same manner as on Parliament Hill. The testimony and deliberations of the committee are recorded and made public, the committee retains all of the powers accorded to it by standing or special orders, and committee members and witnesses are protected by parliamentary privilege.

When travelling outside of Canada, committees have the opportunity to consult with groups and individuals and to visit facilities. When conducting hearings outside the country, committees do not hold formal hearings.[298] The powers which the House

---

295. Committees may also meet in a regular committee setting with such delegations. Even in these cases, however, the usual format is relaxed. The proceedings take more the form of an exchange of views than of the gathering of evidence from witnesses. See, for example, Standing Committee on Foreign Affairs and International Trade, *Minutes*, March 19, 1998, Meeting No. 40.

296. Standing and legislative committees are not accorded the power to travel by the Standing Orders. They are accorded the power to travel by motion of the House or, more rarely, by having the House concur in a committee report recommending that such permission be given. See, for example, *Journals*, February 6, 1986, p. 1644; December 11, 1997, p. 394. Where it seems likely that a special committee will need this power, it is often included in the order of reference which establishes the committee. If a special committee wishes to seek authorization to travel, it may do so by placing a recommendation to that effect in a report to the House. As well, the House may adopt a motion authorizing a committee to travel. Power to travel has also been given directly to a sub-committee. See, for example, *Journals*, June 29, 1983, p. 6116.

297. The motion ordinarily indicates the dates on which the committee is authorized to travel, the locations which it may visit and whether staff will accompany the committee. See, for example, *Journals*, June 21, 1994, pp. 629-30; April 2, 1998, p. 667.

298. In 1996, the Standing Committee on Agriculture and Agri-Food held a formal meeting in the Canadian embassy in Washington. See *Minutes*, May 28, 1996, Meeting No. 23. Where a committee decides to hold formal meetings outside of Canada, they are usually held *in camera*, although the committee may have a transcript of the proceedings made for its own use. See, for example, Special Committee on the Reform of the House of Commons, *Minutes of Proceedings and Evidence*, May 14, 1985, Issue No. 13, p. 5.

delegates to committees are of no force when a committee is outside of Canada, nor are committee proceedings protected by parliamentary privilege.

Videoconferences

As an alternative to committee or witness travel, committees from time to time also make use of videoconferencing technology to hear witnesses from outside Ottawa, either elsewhere in Canada or internationally.[299] Videoconferencing provides for direct audio and video transmission between a committee room on Parliament Hill and a witness in another location. On occasion, several witnesses in different locations are linked with a committee simultaneously. Special permission of the House is not required for committees to hold videoconference meetings.[300]

TIMES OF SITTING AND ROOM ALLOCATION

Standing and legislative committees are empowered to sit either when the House is sitting or when it stands adjourned, and similar powers are usually accorded to special committees in their orders of reference.[301] However, committees may not sit when Parliament is prorogued.[302] During periods when the House is sitting, most committee meetings take place on Tuesdays, Wednesdays and Thursdays. While the average length of a committee meeting is two hours, a committee may choose to meet for a shorter or longer period as it sees fit.[303] While committees usually adjourn or suspend their proceedings when the division bells summon Members to the Chamber for a vote, committees may continue to sit while a vote is being held.[304]

Standing committees are prohibited from sitting at the same time as a legislative committee studying a bill which emanates from, or principally affects, the department for which they are responsible.[305] No such prohibition exists with respect to a

---

299. See, for example, Standing Committee on Foreign Affairs and International Trade, *Minutes*, June 4, 1998, Meeting No. 61.

300. Although videoconferences offer a number of advantages over travel in terms of cost and convenience to Members and witnesses, in some cases, committees may decide that evidence is better gathered through direct contact.

301. The Senate members of joint committees require special permission of the Senate to sit while the Senate is sitting. See, for example, Standing Joint Committee on Official Languages, *Minutes*, October 21, 1997, Meeting No. 1.

302. See *Bourinot*, 4th ed., pp. 467-8.

303. See, for example, Standing Joint Committee on Regulations and Statutory Instruments, *Minutes of Proceedings and Evidence*, February 3, 1983, Issue No. 77, p. 3; Standing Committee on Human Resources Development, *Minutes of Proceedings and Evidence*, April 25, 1996, Issue No. 4, pp. 22-4.

304. See Speaker Fraser's ruling, *Debates*, March 20, 1990, pp. 9512-3.

305. Standing Order 115(1).

standing committee sitting while the House itself is considering such a bill.[306] When the House is actually sitting, committees studying legislation or Estimates have priority over all other committees.[307] When the House is not sitting, priority is given to meetings of standing, special and joint committees in accordance with a schedule established by the Chief Government Whip in consultation with the other parties.[308]

Committee meeting rooms provided by the House of Commons are allocated according to a priority system established by a report of the Standing Committee on Procedure and House Affairs.[309] The Committee's report typically gives each committee priority of access to multi-purpose meeting rooms at set times.[310] The Committee may adjust the room allocation system from time to time, either to reflect changes in committee structure or to take into account requests made by individual committees.[311] Special committees are given priority during periods other than those allotted to standing committees. Committees may meet during any period, even if they do not have priority access to meeting rooms, provided that there is space available. For committees which do not have priority in a given time period, access to meeting rooms is on a first-come-first-served basis, after those entitled to meet at that time.

Committees meeting in locations other than the meeting rooms on Parliament Hill are not bound by the room priorities established by the Standing Committee on Procedure and House Affairs. However, they must still respect the stipulation in the Standing Orders concerning conflicts between standing and legislative committees.[312] Furthermore, any meeting not held in the facilities provided by Parliament entails the expenditure of funds from the committee's budget and requires the permission of the House.[313]

CONVENING A MEETING

Committee members are convened, that is, called together for the purpose of meeting, by the Chair, acting either on a decision made by the committee[314] or on his or

---

306. See Speaker Fraser's ruling, *Debates*, March 20, 1990, pp. 9512-3.

307. Standing Order 115(2).

308. Standing Order 115(3).

309. See Standing Order 115(4), and *Journals*, June 10, 1994, p. 563; September 19, 1994, p. 682.

310. Joint committees may meet in the committee meeting rooms provided either by the House or by the Senate.

311. See, for example, Standing Committee on Procedure and House Affairs, *Minutes*, November 20, 1997, Meeting No. 6.

312. Standing Order 115(1).

313. See, for example, *Journals*, December 5, 1995, p. 2208.

314. The decision may be made by the adoption of a motion in committee or by the concurrence of recommendations of a steering committee. See, for example, Standing Committee on Agriculture and Agri-Food, *Minutes*, October 21, 1997, Meeting No. 2.

her own authority.[315] On rare occasions, the House itself may instruct a committee to meet at a specific time.[316] The clerk of the committee, on instructions from the Chair, sends a notice of each upcoming meeting to all committee members. Where a committee has not made a formal decision concerning the convening of its members, either by adopting a work plan or by concurring in a steering committee report, the Chair usually consults with members informally concerning possible future meetings.

Where a committee decides to sit jointly with another committee or committees, each committee is convened separately by its Chair.[317] Meetings of joint committees are usually convened by one or other of the Joint Chairs.[318] A sub-committee is convened by agreement of its members or by its Chair in the same manner as the main committee. Meetings may be convened on the Chair's instructions when he or she is unavailable to preside, but a Vice-Chair has no power to convene the committee when the office of Chair is vacant.

Notice of Meeting

A committee meeting is convened by a notice sent to the members by the clerk, in accordance with the Chair's instructions. The notice is sent electronically to the Parliament Hill offices of committee members over the House of Commons local area network.[319] The notice indicates the subject matter of the meeting and the authority under which the committee will meet,[320] as well as the time and place of the meeting. The notice also provides other relevant information: the meeting number,[321] whether the meeting is public or *in camera,* whether it will be broadcast on the CPaC television network, and the names of any scheduled witnesses. The notice also indicates whether the witnesses will appear in person or by videoconference and provides the

---

315. See, for example, Standing Committee on Agriculture and Agri-Food, *Minutes*, November 6, 1997, Meeting No. 9. The Chair always acts with the implicit consent of the committee. See Speaker Lamoureux's ruling, *Debates*, March 3, 1967, p. 13704. The exception to the convening of the committee by the Chair is the organization meeting of a standing or special committee, which is convened by the Clerk of the House.

316. See, for example, *Journals*, April 2, 1957, p. 362; April 8, 1957, p. 421.

317. See, for example, Standing Committee on Foreign Affairs and International Trade, *Minutes*, February 4, 1999, Meeting No. 87.

318. Where a joint committee so wishes, it may adopt a motion to govern the manner in which its meetings are to be convened or cancelled, as the case may be. See, for example, Special Joint Committee on Official Languages, *Minutes of Proceedings and Evidence*, March 9-11, 1982, Issue No. 37, pp. 3-4 and 6-13.

319. Prior to February 1996, printed notices were sent via the House of Commons internal mail system or hand delivered by messenger.

320. The subject announced on the notice of meeting is not binding on the committee, which may decide to take up any subject within its mandate at any meeting. See Speaker Fraser's ruling, *Debates*, December 18, 1989, pp. 7059-60; see also *Debates,* October 20, 1989, pp. 4927-33.

321. Meetings of each committee are assigned numbers consecutively, beginning with the first meeting of each session. A committee may hold more than one meeting in a single day, sometimes on unrelated topics.

radio frequencies on which public meetings will be broadcast over the House of Commons' internal network.[322] As well as informing the committee members of an upcoming meeting, the notice also serves to alert the various administrative components of the House which provide logistical support for meetings—maintenance, transcription, interpretation, security and the messenger service. It is sent as well to the Parliamentary Press Gallery.

Meeting Convened at the Request of Four Members

An individual member of a committee, other than the Chair, cannot convene a committee meeting.[323] The Standing Orders provide, however, that four members of a standing committee may make a request in writing that the committee meet. The request must specify the reasons for which the meeting is to be convened, and the Chair must then convene the meeting within 10 sitting days of the receipt of the request. Forty-eight hours' notice of such a meeting must be given to the members.[324]

The matter under consideration at such a meeting is whether or not the committee wishes to take up the requested subject, rather than deliberations on the subject itself. There is no obligation on the committee either to conclude debate on the proposal to study a particular topic or to reach a decision on it. The Chair may agree to consider the matter at a meeting that has already been scheduled, rather than calling a meeting for that purpose alone.[325]

CANCELLING A MEETING

Circumstances sometimes arise which make it necessary to cancel a committee meeting, after a notice convening the committee has been sent. Where a committee has agreed to adjourn to the call of the Chair, the Chair instructs the clerk to send an amendment to the notice convening the members, informing them of the cancellation. Where the meeting has been convened by order of the committee, the Chair consults with representatives of the various parties before sending the cancellation notice. In joint committees, the committee may decide whether a single Joint Chair may convene or cancel meetings or whether both Joint Chairs must act together.[326]

---

322. Notices for all upcoming committee meetings are posted on the Parliamentary Website at «http://www.parl.gc.ca».

323. See Speaker Macnaughton's ruling, *Debates*, October 28, 1963, pp. 4071-2.

324. Standing Order 106(3). See, for example, Standing Committee on Justice and Human Rights, *Minutes*, December 3, 1997, Meeting No. 19. In this case, the notice was sent within the required 10 sitting-day period, and the meeting took place on the eleventh day following receipt of the letter from the four members.

325. See, for example, Standing Committee on Citizenship and Immigration, *Minutes*, March 11, 1998, Meeting No. 14.

326. See, for example, Special Joint Committee on Official Languages, *Minutes of Proceedings and Evidence*, March 11, 1982, Issue No. 37, p. 4.

ADJOURNMENT

Committees most often adjourn to the call of the Chair, that is, the decision as to the exact time of the next meeting is left to the discretion of the Chair.[327] This is done even when the committee has adopted a workplan that lays out in detail its schedule of meetings. In this way, the Chair is given the flexibility to respond effectively to changing events and to the unforeseen availability or unavailability of potential witnesses. Committees may also adjourn to a specific time.[328] This is usually done when the next meeting is scheduled for the immediate future, for example, the next day or later the same day. Committees may, on occasion, adjourn without making any provision for a future meeting, that is, to adjourn *sine die*.[329]

QUORUM

In order to exercise the powers granted to it by the House, a committee is required by the Standing Orders to have a quorum at its meetings. A quorum is the minimum number of committee members who must be present in order for a committee to make decisions. In the case of standing, legislative or special committees, a quorum is a majority of the members.[330] The Chair of a legislative committee, who is named by the Speaker from the Panel of Chairmen, is not counted for the purpose of establishing a quorum. Members of the House who are present at committees are not counted as part of the quorum unless they are either members of the committee or properly designated substitutes. As a courtesy, most committees do not begin their meetings until at least one member of the opposition is in attendance, even if a quorum is present. However, committees may meet and adopt motions in the absence of one or all opposition parties.[331]

The quorum for joint committees is not provided for in the Standing Orders but is established separately. Standing joint committees usually present reports to both Houses recommending the number of their members which should constitute a quorum. The quorum is set when the two Houses concur in the report.[332] The quorum for a special joint committee is usually set out in the order of reference which establishes

---

327. See, for example, Standing Committee on Citizenship and Immigration, *Minutes*, November 17, 1998, Meeting No. 41.

328. See, for example, Standing Committee on Citizenship and Immigration, *Minutes*, October 29, 1998, Meeting No. 39.

329. See, for example, Special Joint Committee on a Renewed Canada, *Minutes of Proceedings and Evidence*, November 13, 1991, Issue No. 19, p. 3. While such adjournments *sine die* may result in a committee not proceeding further with a study ordered by the House, the Speaker has declined to intervene. See *Debates*, February 26, 1992, pp. 7620-4.

330. Standing Order 118(1).

331. See, for example, Standing Committee on Environment and Sustainable Development, *Minutes*, December 4, 1997, Meeting No. 26.

332. See, for example, *Journals*, October 29, 1997, p. 165; November 25, 1997, p. 257.

it.[333] For all joint committees, it is common to stipulate that the quorum requires the presence of members from both Houses.[334]

Meeting Without a Quorum

The Standing Orders permit standing and legislative committees to authorize the Chair of the committee to hold meetings when a quorum is not present, for the purpose of taking evidence.[335] A similar provision is often included in the order by which a special committee is established.[336] In granting permission for such meetings, committees usually stipulate the number of members it wishes to be present for the meeting to take place. The motion granting permission to meet with what is called a "reduced quorum" will usually also indicate any other conditions the committee wishes to have met.[337] No motions may be moved at such meetings nor may any votes be held. Committees do, however, retain the power to publish the evidence received at meetings held with a reduced quorum.[338]

ORGANIZATION MEETING

Before a committee can begin to consider its work, it must be properly constituted, that is, its members must have been appointed and a Chair selected.[339] Where the Chair has not been appointed by the House or named by the Speaker, the election of the Chair takes place at a committee's first meeting,[340] called the "organization" meeting.

A notice of an organization meeting of a standing committee is sent by the clerk in conformity with provisions of the Standing Orders, which require that the committee meet within 10 sitting days of the adoption of the report establishing the membership of the standing committees.[341] Members must be given at least 48 hours'

---

333. See, for example, *Journals*, October 28, 1997, pp. 158-62; November 5, 1997, pp. 196-7.

334. The quorum in joint committees is usually less than a majority of the members. For example, in the case of the Standing Joint Committee on Official Languages, quorum is set at 7, while a simple majority of the members would require a quorum of 13. See Standing Joint Committee on Official Languages, *Minutes*, October 21, 1997, Meeting No. 1.

335. Standing Order 118(2).

336. See, for example, *Journals*, November 5, 1997, p. 196.

337. For House committees, it is often stipulated that a member of the opposition must be present. For joint committees, it is usually required that both Houses be represented in the reduced quorum. See, for example, Standing Committee on Citizenship and Immigration, *Minutes*, October 21, 1997, Meeting No. 2; *Journals*, November 5, 1997, p. 196.

338. Standing Order 118(2).

339. For the manner in which the members of the various types of committees are selected, see section above, "Membership".

340. For the method of electing a committee Chair, see section above, "Election of the Chair and the Vice-Chair".

341. Standing Order 106(1).

notice of this meeting.[342] The authority of the clerk in convening a meeting for the purposes of organization of a standing committee is restricted to the election of the Chair.[343] While a committee may limit its organization meeting to the election of a Chair, in practice it is common to proceed immediately to the election of the Vice-Chairs.[344] The committee may then consider a series of administrative motions, called "routine" motions, to facilitate its work over the course of the session.

As the Chairs of legislative committees are named by the Speaker from the Panel of Chairs, these committees are not required to meet for the purpose of organization. However, they must meet to begin their work within two sitting days of the naming of the Chair and the appointment by the House of their membership or the referral of a bill to the committee.[345] The notice for the first meeting of a legislative committee is thus sent on the Chair's authority.

The Standing Orders contain no provision with respect to when the first meeting of a special committee must take place, nor is it usual to include such a provision in the order of reference which establishes such a committee. When the Chair of a special committee is not named in the order of reference, the organization meeting is convened by the Clerk of the House, following informal consultations among the parties, and the notice is sent by the clerk of the Committee. When the Chair is named in the order of reference, then the meeting is convened by the Chair in the usual fashion.

ROUTINE MOTIONS

As they begin their work, committees find it convenient to adopt a series of motions to deal with items of routine business. Since each committee is free to organize its work as it sees fit, there is no standard list of "routine" motions which every committee must adopt. The following is a list of the principal routine motions which committees have found useful. In many instances, a committee will adapt these motions in order to suit its own particular circumstances.

Examples of each type of routine motion are given in the boxes which follow the description. Note that the examples given below are for purposes of illustration only.

---

342. In practice, 48 hours' notice is taken to mean that the notice is sent on the second day preceding the meeting. The House has, on occasion, suspended this Standing Order with respect to all or some committees to permit them to meet with less than 48 hours' notice. See, for example, *Journals*, September 18, 1995, p. 1891; October 1, 1998, p. 1109.

343. Although standing committees are required to elect Vice-Chairs, the Standing Orders do not give the clerk the authority to include these elections in the notice which convenes the committee. See Standing Order 106(1). Any decision about dealing with matters other than the election of the Chair at an organization meeting is made by the committee with the Chair (or Acting Chair) presiding.

344. Only standing committees are obliged to elect Vice-Chairs. See section above, "Election of the Chair and the Vice-Chair".

345. Standing Order 113(3). When the Legislative Committee on Bill C-72, the *Official Languages Act,* failed to meet within the prescribed period, Speaker Fraser stated that it would not be appropriate for the Speaker to set a date for the first meeting of the Committee. See *Debates*, March 14, 1988, pp. 13706-7.

Sub-committee on Agenda and Procedure

Most committees establish from among their members a sub-committee on agenda and procedure, usually referred to as the "steering committee". The steering committee recommends how the committee should proceed to consider its orders of reference and advises on such topics as the selection of witnesses and the schedule of meetings. The composition of the steering committee may vary from one committee to another and from one Parliament to another. It usually consists of the Chair, the Vice-Chairs, representatives from each of the other parties and, on committees having a departmental responsibility, the Parliamentary Secretary. As a steering committee usually meets *in camera* for the purpose of discussing the future business of the committee, no specific delegation of powers is made in establishing it. Since the recommendations of the steering committee are reported to the main committee and so appear in the *Minutes,* steering committees do not require the power to print and do not publish their own minutes.

> That the Sub-Committee on Agenda and Procedure be composed of the Chair, the Government Vice-Chair, the Parliamentary Secretary, two Liberal members, one member from the Reform Party, one member from the Bloc Québécois Party, one member from the New Democratic Party, and one member from the Progressive Conservative Party.[346]

Research Assistance

In order to carry out their work, committees seek the assistance of expert researchers from the staff of the Library of Parliament. The usual motion leaves the control and co-ordination of the research staff to the Chair of the committee.

> That the Committee retain the services of one or more research officers from the Library of Parliament, as needed, to assist the Committee in its work, at the discretion of the Chair.[347]

Meeting Without a Quorum

Committees may authorize the Chair to hold meetings for the sole purpose of hearing evidence when a quorum is not present.[348] Although the Standing Orders would permit the Chair to hear evidence when no other member is present, it is more usual for the committee to stipulate some minimum number of members who must be present in order for the committee to hear witnesses.[349] This number is referred to as a "reduced quorum". Another element which committees take into consideration in

---

346. Standing Committee on Transport, *Minutes,* October 7, 1997, Meeting No. 1.

347. Standing Committee on Foreign Affairs and International Trade, *Minutes*, October 8, 1997, Meeting No. 1.

348. Standing Order 118(2).

349. See, for example, Standing Committee on Finance, *Minutes*, October 2, 1997, Meeting No. 1.

establishing a reduced quorum is whether any or all of the opposition parties need to be in attendance. [350]

> That the Chair be authorized to hold meetings and to receive evidence when a quorum is not present, provided that at least five members are present, including two members of the opposition. [351]

Time for Opening Remarks and Questioning of Witnesses

When hearing witnesses, committees normally set limits on the time each group or individual is given to make their opening presentation. They also set out the length of time that will be devoted to questioning by committee members and how that time will be divided among the members of the various parties represented on the committee. The division of time for questioning may change from Parliament to Parliament to reflect changes in the number of parties represented on committees. Each committee seeks to balance, as best it can, the desire to ensure that representatives of all parties have the opportunity to put questions. As well, some committees adopt special rules for the questioning of Ministers. [352]

> That witnesses be given five minutes to make their opening statement.
>
> That five minutes be allocated to each questioner in the following order: On the first round of questioning—five minutes each to the Reform and Bloc Québécois parties, five minutes to the Liberal Party and five minutes each to the NDP and Conservative parties. On the following rounds of questioning—five minutes per party alternating between the government and opposition parties.
>
> That the five-minute allocation for questioning be applied for all witnesses, including Ministers. [353]

Witness Expenses

Whether attending meetings held on Parliament Hill or those held while a committee is travelling across Canada, many witnesses incur significant expenses in travelling to appear before committees. As no expenditure can be made from committee funds without committee approval, it is necessary that a motion be adopted setting out the conditions under which witness expenses are to be paid. The Board of Internal Economy has set out guidelines for acceptable levels of reimbursement, but it is up

---

350. In the case of joint committees, it is usual for the motion to require that both Houses be represented. See, for example, Standing Joint Committee on Official Languages, *Minutes*, October 21, 1997, Meeting No. 1.

351. Standing Committee on Citizenship and Immigration, *Minutes*, October 21, 1997, Meeting No. 2.

352. See, for example, Standing Committee on Citizenship and Immigration, *Minutes*, October 28, 1998, Meeting No. 38, and November 17, 1998, Meeting No. 41.

353. Standing Committee on Health, *Minutes*, October 30, 1997, Meeting No. 2.

to each committee to decide under what circumstances they will agree to reimburse witnesses.[354]

> That, as established by the Board of Internal Economy and if requested, reasonable travelling, accommodation and living expenses be reimbursed to witnesses who are invited to appear before the Committee up to a maximum of two representatives for any one organization, and that payment for more than two representatives in exceptional circumstances be at the discretion of the Chair.[355]

Document Distribution

Members of the House of Commons are entitled to receive documents in the official language of their choice. At the same time, members of the public have the right to communicate with a parliamentary committee in either official language.[356] This frequently leads to the situation where a document is presented in a single official language to a committee, while the committee members are entitled to receive it in whichever official language they prefer. Committees must balance the right of members to be treated equally with the benefits they derive from receiving documents in a timely manner. Each committee must decide whether documents submitted to it in only one official language will be distributed to members immediately or once a translation is available.

> That the Clerk of the Committee be authorized to circulate the documents received only when they exist in both official languages.[357]

or

> That the Clerk of the Committee be authorized to distribute documents to the Members of the Committee in the language received, and to ensure that such documents are translated and distributed as promptly as possible.[358]

---

354. Committees routinely pay travel, accommodation and living expenses of witnesses (see *Financial Policy Manual for Committees*, Section C-6, Witness Expenses).

355. Standing Committee on Health, *Minutes*, October 30, 1997, Meeting No. 2.

356. Standing Order 32(4) requires all government documents to be tabled in both official languages. Section 4 of the *Official Languages Act* (R.S.C. 1985, c. 31(4th Supp.)) and section 17 of the *Constitution Act, 1982* (R.S.C. 1985, Appendix II, No. 44, Schedule B) give everyone the right to use either English or French in their dealings with Parliament.

357. Standing Committee on Justice and Human Rights, *Minutes*, November 6, 1997, Meeting No. 5.

358. Standing Committee on Human Resources and the Status of Persons with Disabilities, *Minutes*, October 8, 1997, Meeting No. 1.

Transcripts of In Camera Meetings

While no public record is produced of what is said during *in camera* proceedings, committees often find it useful to have a transcript produced for the private consultation of the members and staff of the committee. In addition to deciding whether or not to keep a transcript of an *in camera* meeting, the committee must also decide how such transcripts will be disposed of at the end of the session (i.e., whether they will be made part of the committee's permanent record for historical purposes, or destroyed). Committees sometimes prefer to deal with the question of the disposal of *in camera* transcripts on a case-by-case basis.[359]

> That *in camera* meetings be transcribed; that the transcription be kept with the Clerk of the Committee for consultation by members of the Committee; and that these transcripts be destroyed at the end of the session.[360]

Staff at In Camera Meetings

Committees normally exclude everyone from *in camera* meetings except members, committee staff and invited witnesses.[361] Members often find it useful, however, to modify this policy by permitting members of their personal office staff to attend. At the same time, it is recognized that the committee may from time to time wish to adopt a more strict interpretation of the *in camera* rule.[362]

> That each Committee member be allowed to have one staff person present at *in camera* meetings, unless there is a decision for a particular meeting to exclude all staff.[363]

Order-in-Council Appointments

The referral of Order-in-Council appointments to committees and their review of such appointments are governed by the Standing Orders. As some committees receive notice of a large number of appointees during the course of a year, it is necessary for

---

359. See, for example, Standing Committee on Communications and Culture, *Minutes of Proceedings and Evidence*, December 17, 1987, Issue No. 73, p. 4.

360. Standing Committee on Industry, *Minutes*, October 2, 1997, Meeting No. 1.

361. Members of the House of Commons who are not members of the committee ordinarily withdraw, although they may remain with the committee's consent. See, for example, Standing Committee on Regional Industrial Expansion, *Minutes of Proceedings and Evidence*, May 6, 1987, Issue No. 13, p. 3.

362. See, for example, Standing Committee on Labour, Employment and Immigration, *Minutes of Proceedings and Evidence*, January 26, 1988, Issue No. 49, p. 3.

363. Standing Committee on Justice and Human Rights, *Minutes*, November 6, 1997, Meeting No. 5.

each committee to decide how it will deal with its responsibility for the consideration of the nominations and the documentation associated with each one. [364]

> That, pursuant to Standing Order 111(4), whenever an Order in Council for appointment or a certificate of nomination for appointment is referred to the Committee, the Clerk shall obtain and circulate to each member of the Committee a copy of the résumé of each appointee. [365]

Notice of Motion

Neither the Standing Orders nor usual practice in committees require the giving of notice prior to presenting a motion in committee. However, in order to better balance their workload and make efficient use of their time, committees sometimes find it appropriate to adopt notice requirements. Thus, when a member wishes to raise a new topic for consideration, committee members have an opportunity to reflect on it beforehand, rather than having the motion placed before the committee without warning. This also prevents undue interruption of a meeting or a series of meetings already planned. [366] Committees may also decide to have such notices considered by the steering committee in proposing a work plan for the committee. Such consideration does not prevent the member who gave notice from moving the motion when the notice period has expired.

In imposing a notice requirement, committees must consider what types of motions will require notice, how notice is to be given (whether orally or in writing) and to whom (the Chair or the clerk). They must also determine how the other members of the committee are to be informed of the proposed motion, as committees do not have a *Notice Paper*.

> That forty-eight (48) hours' notice be given to the members of the Committee before any substantive motion is considered, but this rule does not apply to a motion in amendment to a Bill considered by the Committee....
>
> That the motion be filed with the Clerk of the Committee and circulated to all members in both official languages. Upon receipt of the notice, the Clerk will put the motion on the agenda of the Steering Committee's next meeting. [367]

---

364. Standing Order 111(4) provides that the Minister nominating a person to an Order-in-Council position will supply the committee, to which the nomination is referred, with a copy of the nominee's *curriculum vitae* on request.

365. Standing Committee on Citizenship and Immigration, *Minutes*, October 21, 1997, Meeting No. 2.

366. Committees have varied in their use of notice requirements. In some cases notice has been required for any substantive motion, in others only for new business, unrelated to the subject before the committee at any given time. See, for example, Standing Committee on Canadian Heritage, *Minutes*, October 21, 1997, Meeting No. 2, and Standing Joint Committee on the Library of Parliament, *Minutes*, October 28, 1997, Meeting No. 1.

367. Standing Committee on Justice and Human Rights, *Minutes*, November 6, 1997, Meeting No. 5.

In addition to the routine motions listed above, there are a wide range of motions related to procedure and administration that committees may adopt from time to time. Some are related to particular kinds of committees only, while others deal with specific aspects of a committee's work, such as the preparation of a report to the House. Certain committees routinely adopt motions which relate specifically to their mandate or work methodology, which are not pertinent to other committees.[368]

BUDGETS

Many of the routine operational expenses of committees are borne directly by the House of Commons' administration.[369] Standing committee budgets are drawn up on a project-by-project basis[370] and each budget must be adopted by a committee before it is submitted to the Liaison Committee for approval.[371] Although committees are provided with limited interim spending authority,[372] they require approval of the Liaison Committee for any expenditures which exceed the amount initially allocated.[373] In addition to project funds, all requests for travel funds must be part of a separate budget request, just as the power to travel must be specially sought from the House.[374]

---

368. Other motions used occasionally include: the purchase of documents (see, for example, Standing Committee on Justice and Human Rights, *Minutes*, November 6, 1997, Meeting No. 5); the holding of meetings by videoconference (see, for example, Standing Committee on Aboriginal Affairs and Northern Development, *Minutes*, October 30, 1997, Meeting No. 2); the adoption of a general meeting schedule for the committee (see, for example, Standing Committee on Public Accounts, *Minutes*, October 21, 1997, Meeting No. 3); and working arrangements for lengthy meetings, such as the provision of lunches (see, for example, Standing Committee on Justice and Human Rights, *Minutes*, November 6, 1997, Meeting No. 5). Joint committees must deal with a number of routine matters which are not applicable to standing, legislative and special committees of the House: quorum, times of meeting (see Standing Joint Committee on Official Languages, *Minutes*, October 21, 1997, Meeting No. 1) and mandate (see Standing Joint Committee for the Scrutiny of Regulations, *Minutes of Proceedings and Evidence*, March 24, 1994, Issue No. 1, pp. 4-6 and 9-10).

369. These include, for example, the salaries of committee staff, costs associated with committee meeting rooms, and the production of *Minutes* and *Evidence.* Translation and interpretation services for committees are provided through the Department of Public Works and Government Services. Library of Parliament research staff assigned to committees are paid by the Library (except those permanently assigned to the Standing Joint Committee for the Scrutiny of Regulations, who are paid by the Committee).

370. Project budgets cover such items as witness expenses, report production, consulting contracts, advertising and media relations, temporary administrative support staff, videoconferences and other miscellaneous items, including hospitality expenses. Full details of budgeting are found in the *Financial Policy Manual for Committees*, Chapter B-2, "Preparation of Workplan and Budget".

371. See, for example, Standing Committee on Aboriginal Affairs and Northern Development, *Minutes*, November 17, 1997, Meeting No. 5.

372. Standing Order 121(1).

373. Standing Orders 107(1) and 121(2).

374. See, for example, Standing Committee on Finance, *Minutes*, October 7, 1997, Meeting No. 2.

Special and legislative committees make their budget requests directly to the Board of Internal Economy.[375] The budgets of joint committees are provided by the two Houses in proportion to the size of each House. In order to obtain budgetary approval, it is necessary for standing joint committees to present their budgets to both the Liaison Committee and the Senate Committee on Internal Economy.[376] Special joint committees require budgetary approval from the Board of Internal Economy and the Senate Committee on Internal Economy.[377]

ORDERS OF REFERENCE AND INSTRUCTIONS

An order of reference is an order of the House to a committee instructing it to consider a matter or defining the scope of its deliberations. Committees are provided with orders of reference when they are established and may receive additional orders from time to time.

The Standing Orders provide standing committees with permanent orders of reference by giving them departmental and policy-area responsibilities.[378] In addition, the Standing Orders provide that a number of other matters shall be routinely referred to standing committees for consideration: reports and other documents tabled in the House pursuant to statute,[379] the Estimates,[380] Order-in-Council appointments[381] and legislation.[382] While the Standing Orders provide that these matters shall be referred to committee, the House must specify the committee to which each referral is made by separate motion.[383] With respect to documents, including Order-in-Council appointments, the committee to which they are referred is specified when the documents are tabled. In addition to the orders of reference contained in the Standing Orders, the House reserves the right to refer additional matters to its

---

375. Board of Internal Economy By-law 401, *Committee Finance and Administration By-law.*

376. See, for example, Standing Joint Committee on Official Languages, *Minutes*, February 11, 1999, Meeting No. 19.

377. See, for example, Special Joint Committee on Child Custody and Access, *Minutes*, February 23, 1998, Meeting No. 5.

378. Standing Order 108. Prior to 1986, standing committees received no general mandate from the Standing Orders. They met and began their work once the House had referred a specific matter to them. See *Journals*, February 6, 1986, pp. 1644-66, in particular pp. 1660-2; February 13, 1986, p. 1710.

379. Standing Order 32(5).

380. Standing Order 81(4) and (5).

381. Standing Orders 110 and 32(6).

382. Standing Orders 73(1) to (3) and 141(1).

383. See, for example, *Journals*, October 1, 1997, pp. 57-9; October 2, 1997, pp. 67-8; March 1, 1999, pp. 1545-6; March 5, 1999, pp. 1563-4; March 10, 1999, p. 1592.

committees as it sees fit. Committees may also receive orders of reference which derive from statutes previously passed by Parliament.[384]

When a bill is referred to a committee, the bill itself constitutes the order of reference. When a special committee is established, the order of reference is contained in the motion establishing it.[385] Joint committees receive their orders of reference from both Houses. While the Standing Orders set out mandates for the three standing joint committees,[386] no similar provisions exist in the Rules of the Senate.[387]

Committees are bound by their orders of reference and may not undertake studies or make recommendations to the House which go beyond the limits established by them.[388] In particular, a committee studying a bill may report it with or without amendments, but may not include any comments or recommendations in its report.[389] With the broad powers which standing committees have had since 1986,[390] they may make recommendations to the House related to a bill which has been referred to them. Such recommendations must, however, be presented to the House in a report separate from the report on the bill.[391]

In addition to a committee's initial order of reference, the House may issue further directions to the committee once it has begun a particular study. Directions of this sort are called "instructions" and are sometimes mandatory, but usually permissive. A mandatory instruction is one which directs a committee to deal with a particular issue or to conduct its study in a certain way.[392] A permissive instruction gives a committee the power to do something it would not otherwise be able to do, but does

---

384. A number of statutes contain provisions requiring that they be reviewed by committees. See Legislative Counsel Office, *List of Reports and Returns to be made to the House of Commons*, 1997, pp. 58-9. As with the Standing Orders, statutes do not identify the particular committee to be charged with the review; this decision is left to the House at the time that the review is begun. See, for example, *Canada Business Corporations Act*, S.C. 1994, c. 24, s. 33, and *Journals*, October 1, 1997, p. 55.

385. The motion establishing a special committee usually deals with a number of other matters in addition to the subject of the committee's study: the powers of the committee, its membership and quorum. See, for example, *Journals*, October 1, 1997, pp. 59-61.

386. Standing Order 108(4).

387. Senate Rule 86(1) provides only for the striking of the standing joint committees and indicates the number of Senators who should be named to each one. It gives no indication of each committee's mandate.

388. Committee reports which go beyond the committee's order of reference have been ruled out of order by Speakers. See, for example, *Debates*, June 29, 1983, pp. 26943-4; February 28, 1985, pp. 2602-3.

389. See Speaker Lamoureux's ruling, *Debates*, December 20, 1973, pp. 774-5.

390. Standing Order 108(2).

391. See, for example, *Journals*, June 21, 1995, p. 1827 (substantive report on employment equity), and September 25, 1995, p. 1940 (Bill C-64, *An Act respecting employment equity*).

392. See, for example, *Journals*, June 29, 1983, p. 6116.

not compel the committee to use that power. For example, the House may adopt a motion which provides the committee with the power to travel or to report at a later time than envisaged in the initial order of reference.[393] The Standing Orders contain provisions to permit either a Minister or a private Member to move a motion instructing a standing, special or legislative committee to prepare and bring in a bill.[394]

Conduct of Meetings

In general, the rules governing the process of debate in committees are the same as those in the House of Commons.[395] However, the Standing Orders exempt committees from certain rules which apply in the House: those governing the election of the Speaker, the seconding of motions and limiting the number of times a member may speak on an issue and the length of speeches.[396] This exemption is permissive in nature; each committee may formulate its own rules with respect to these subjects, provided it does not exceed the powers which the House has delegated to it.[397]

Deliberations in committee are often conducted in an informal atmosphere. The much smaller size of committees, in comparison with the House, and the specific mandates they are given have led to certain adaptations of House procedures in order to enhance the effectiveness of deliberations in committee.

Generally, the length of time to be devoted to a particular topic is a matter for the committee to decide. This may be done formally, by adopting a work plan, or by simply allowing committee members to discuss an issue until they are ready to make a decision.[398] Committees routinely limit the amount of time available for presentations by witnesses and allocate time for rounds of questioning by committee members.[399] As there is no limit in committee to the number of times of speaking or the length of speeches, committees may, if they choose, place limits on their own

---

393. See, for example, *Journals*, June 22, 1994, p. 655.

394. Standing Order 68(4)(*a*) and (*b*). See, for example, *Journals*, October 30, 1997, p. 175. For further information on instructions, see Chapter 16, "The Legislative Process".

395. See Chapter 12, "The Process of Debate", and Chapter 13, "Rules of Order and Decorum".

396. Standing Order 116.

397. Although the Speaker will not normally intervene in committee matters in the absence of a report from the committee, this does not extend to circumstances where committees exceed the powers delegated to them. During the First Session of the Thirty-Fifth Parliament (1994-96), the Chair of the Standing Committee on Aboriginal Affairs and Northern Development permitted a Member who was neither a member nor an associate member of the Committee to substitute for one of its associate members. Speaker Parent ruled that a standing committee does not have the authority to establish or modify its own membership, including its associate membership; this power is retained by the House under Standing Order 104(4). See ruling in *Debates*, June 20, 1994, pp. 5582-4.

398. See, for example, Standing Committee on Justice and Human Rights, *Minutes*, October 19, 1998, Meeting No. 87.

399. See section above, "Routine Motions".

deliberations.[400] However, certain matters which are routinely referred to standing committees pursuant to Standing Order contain limits to the length of the committee's consideration. The Standing Orders place limits on committee consideration of a number of matters: the Estimates, the pre-budget consultations of the Finance Committee, private Members' public bills and Order-in-Council appointments. In the case of the Estimates and private Members' bills, the committee must either report by a certain time or it is deemed to have done so, in which case the matter no longer stands referred to the committee. Consideration of Order-in-Council appointments is limited to 10 consecutive sitting days of the House, although the committee is not obliged to report to the House. With respect to pre-budget consultations, reports must be presented by a specific deadline, but there is no obligation on the part of the Committee to report.[401] The House may also, from time to time, impose limits on a committee's consideration of matters referred to it.[402]

AUTHORITY OF THE CHAIR

The Chair presides over the deliberations in committee, recognizing speakers[403] and ensuring that the deliberations adhere to established practices and rules, as well as

---

400. See, for example, Standing Committee on Industry, *Minutes*, March 23, 1999, Meeting No. 104. In 1990, following a lengthy examination of Bill C-62, *An Act to amend the Excise Tax Act, the Criminal Code, the Customs Act, the Customs Tariff, the Excise Act, the Income Tax Act, the Statistics Act, and the Tax Court of Canada Act*, the Chair of the Finance Committee unilaterally terminated debate on a motion to limit further debate and set out a schedule allotting time for the remainder of the Committee's consideration of the Bill. The Chair's decision was appealed and sustained by the Committee. (See Standing Committee on Finance, *Minutes of Proceedings and Evidence*, March 19, 1990, Issue No. 103, pp. 6-9.) In a ruling on a question of privilege related to the Committee Chair's action, Speaker Fraser refused to intervene in the affairs of the Committee and cautioned that, when placing limits on their proceedings, committees are responsible for adhering to the normal procedural means and are expected not to behave in an arbitrary manner. (See Speaker Fraser's ruling, *Debates*, March 26, 1990, pp. 9756-8.) The Committee subsequently made a report to the House outlining its concerns about the manner in which debate had been limited and asking that the matter be referred to the Standing Committee on Privileges and Elections. The House concurred in the report (see *Journals*, April 30, 1990, pp. 1612-3). After study, the Privileges and Elections Committee suggested that Standing Order 78 (time allocation) was the appropriate vehicle to use when proposing a limit on committee consideration of a bill. See Standing Committee on Privileges and Elections, *Minutes of Proceedings and Evidence*, March 14, 1991, Issue No. 41, pp. 3-18, and *Journals*, March 20, 1991, p. 2727.

401. See Standing Orders 81(4) and (5), 83.1, 97.1 and 111(3).

402. Reporting deadlines are frequently included in the orders which establish special committees. See, for example, *Journals*, November 18, 1997, pp. 224-5. The House can impose a limit on the consideration of a bill by a committee through the use of time allocation provisions in Standing Order 78. See, for example, *Journals*, March 22, 1995, pp. 1259-60. The House may, however, simply adopt a motion instructing a committee to report by a certain date. See, for example, *Journals*, May 3, 1994, pp. 419-20.

403. In committee, members do not have fixed or assigned seats. Although government members usually sit to the Chair's right and opposition members to the left, members may be recognized by the Chair from any seat.

to any particular requirements which the committee may have imposed upon itself and its members. The order of speakers may be left to the Chair's discretion; however, committees normally adopt a motion to govern the rotation of questioners, by party, when witnesses appear before them.[404] The Chair also puts the question on all motions before the committee and announces the results of any vote.

The Chair may, at his or her discretion, interrupt a member whose remarks or questions are repetitious, or not relevant to the matter before the committee. If a member's comments continue to be repetitious or irrelevant, the Chair may recognize another member. If the offending member refuses to yield the floor and continues speaking, the Chair may suspend or adjourn the meeting. A point of order calling attention to a departure from the Standing Orders or from the customary manner in which a committee has conducted its proceedings may be raised at any time, by any member of the committee. In doubtful or unprovided cases, the Chair may reserve his or her decision.[405]

While the Chair's rulings are not subject to debate, they may be appealed to the committee.[406] A member appeals a ruling by requesting that the committee vote on the motion, "That the Chair's ruling be sustained."[407] In the event of a tie vote on an appeal, the decision of the Chair is sustained.[408] The overturning of a ruling is not necessarily considered a matter of confidence in the Chair. While the decisions made by a Chair are binding on the committee, they do not, however, constitute precedents which bind other committees, nor do they bind subsequent Chairs of the committee in which they are made.

RIGHT TO SPEAK

Members must be recognized by the Chair before speaking. On occasion, committees place strict limits on the amount of time during which a given item will be considered.[409] In other cases, committee members are free to discuss a matter for as long

---

404. The motion may include the amount of time allotted to each questioner. See section above, "Routine Motions".

405. See, for example, Standing Committee on Natural Resources and Public Works, *Minutes of Proceedings and Evidence*, November 27, 1979, Issue No. 6, p. 3.

406. Standing Order 117. This differs from the procedure in a Committee of the Whole, where the Chair's rulings may be appealed not to the Committee but to the Speaker. See Chapter 19, "Committees of the Whole House".

407. See, for example, Standing Committee on Justice and Legal Affairs, *Minutes of Proceedings and Evidence*, October 17, 1985, Issue No. 47, pp. 3-4; Standing Committee on Finance, *Minutes of Proceedings and Evidence*, March 19, 1990, Issue No. 103, pp. 5, 9.

408. See, for example, Standing Committee on Citizenship and Immigration, *Minutes of Proceedings and Evidence*, May 18, 1995, Issue No. 47, p. 7.

409. Such motions, while directed at the item being considered rather than at members speaking, have the effect of imposing time limits on speeches. See, for example, Standing Committee on Industry, *Minutes*, March 23, 1999, Meeting No. 104.

as they see fit. Members of the House attending committee meetings who are not committee members or substitutes may, at the discretion of the committee, participate in the deliberations. However, they do not have the right to present motions, to vote or to be counted in the quorum.[410] Although they ordinarily withdraw when the committee deliberates *in camera,* they are sometimes permitted to remain at *in camera* meetings.[411]

DISORDER AND MISCONDUCT

Disorder and misconduct in a committee may arise as a result of the failure to abide by the rules and practices of a committee or to respect the authority of the Chair. Disorder and misconduct also include the use of unparliamentary language, failure to yield the floor or persistent interruption of the proceedings in any manner. In the event of disorder, the Chair may suspend the meeting until order can be restored or, if the situation is considered to be so serious as to prevent the committee from continuing with its work, the meeting may be adjourned. Neither committees nor their Chairs have the authority to censure an act of disorder or misconduct.[412] If a committee desires that some action be taken against those disrupting the proceedings, it must report the situation to the House.[413] The House may make a decision on disorder upon receiving such a report.

DECISION-MAKING PROCESS

Decisions in committee are made following the adoption of motions by the majority of the members present. Unless the committee decides otherwise, there is no notice requirement to move a motion.[414] No decision can be made by a committee unless a quorum is present.[415] At the conclusion of debate on debatable motions or when a non-debatable motion has been moved, the Chair first reads the motion and then asks if the committee agrees to it.[416] If there is evident disagreement among the members, the Chair will then call for the yeas and nays. Members vote by raising their hand. When a vote is taken in this way, the number of those voting on each side of the question is recorded in the *Minutes*. If any member requests a recorded division, the clerk will read out the names of the members in alphabetical order, each member replying in turn "yea" or "nay". The results of the vote are announced by the clerk and the

410. Standing Order 119.

411. See, for example, Standing Committee on Regional Industrial Expansion, *Minutes of Proceedings and Evidence*, May 5, 1987, Issue No. 13, p. 3.

412. Standing Order 117.

413. In the absence of a report from the committee, Speakers have consistently refrained from interfering in a committee's work. See, for example, *Journals*, July 1, 1919, p. 498; March 31, 1969, pp. 873-4.

414. See section above, "Routine Motions—Notice of Motion".

415. Standing Order 118(2).

416. Given the less formal atmosphere which is common in committee meetings, proposals, especially those relating to the internal affairs of the committee, are sometimes adopted without the formal reading of the motion by the Chair or the taking of a vote.

Chair declares the motion carried or defeated, as the case may be. The names of the members for and against the motion are listed in the *Minutes*. Unlike the procedure in the House where Members are summoned by division bells, there is no provision for summoning absent committee members to a recorded vote.[417]

When a vote is held at an *in camera* meeting, only the fact that a motion was adopted is recorded in the *Minutes* since adopted motions become orders or resolutions of the committee; the names or number of members voting for or against the motion are not recorded. Motions which have been negatived at an *in camera* meeting are not recorded in the *Minutes* nor are the names or number of members voting for or against the motion; this is to ensure that the deliberations of the committee remain confidential.[418] However, at *in camera* meetings, matters may be recorded in the *Minutes* if the committee expressly decides so.

Casting Vote

Like the Speaker, the Chair of a committee votes only to break a tie, except when a committee is considering a private bill, in which case the Chair votes as a regular member of the committee and, in the event of a tie, has a second, casting vote.[419] The Chair is not bound to give reasons for voting. By convention, the Chair will normally vote in such a way as to maintain the *status quo* or, when no further discussion on the matter is possible, to keep the matter open for further discussion in the committee or at a subsequent proceeding in the House.[420] Where there is a tie vote on an appeal of a Chair's ruling, the Chair traditionally does not vote, but declares the ruling sustained.[421]

Evidence

As part of the consideration of the matters referred to them by the House or taken up as part of the general mandate conferred on them, committees seek information and comment from a wide variety of sources. Briefings and background documents are routinely provided by committee research staff and government departments. Committees also devote considerable effort to gathering the views of those knowledgeable

---

417. There is no set procedure in committee, as there is in the House, for deferring votes, although a committee may decide to hold a matter over for further consideration, rather than put it to a vote at a particular time.

418. See Speaker Fraser's ruling on a question of privilege concerning the disclosure of a vote held at an *in camera* meeting, *Debates*, May 14, 1987, pp. 6108-11.

419. Standing Order 141(3). See also Chapter 23, "Private Bills Practice".

420. For further information on the casting vote, see Chapter 7, "The Speaker and Other Presiding Officers of the House".

421. See, for example, Standing Committee on Citizenship and Immigration, *Minutes of Proceedings and Evidence*, May 18, 1995, Issue No. 47, p. 7.

about or directly concerned by the issue before them. This may range from a relatively small group of technical experts to the Canadian public at large.

Information and comment are generally gathered in two ways: by the direct testimony of witnesses and by the submission of written briefs. The power to send for persons and papers, which is accorded to committees,[422] includes not only the power to invite the appearance of witnesses and the filing of briefs, but also to order, by summons, that individuals appear or that certain documents be filed with the committee.

At the beginning of a study, a committee may take steps to inform the public of its activities and solicit their views. For this purpose, the committee may make use of press releases, newspaper advertisements, announcements placed on the CPaC television network or on the Parliamentary Website.[423]

WITNESSES

A committee may wish to hear testimony from private individuals, representatives of groups, or public officials concerning the matter which it is studying. Witness selection may be carried out in a number of different ways. Normally, witnesses are proposed by individual committee members. The committee may also invite potential witnesses to indicate their interest in appearing. The selection is often delegated to the Sub-committee on Procedure and Agenda, subject to ratification by the full committee.[424] In addition, groups or individuals who are aware of an upcoming committee study may indicate their interest in appearing without any solicitation on the part of the committee. Finally, when holding meetings in the form of "town halls", committees often reserve a period of time when those in the audience have the opportunity to ask questions or make brief comments without having formally arranged for their appearance in advance.

It is the responsibility of the committee as a whole to determine which witnesses it will hear. Practical considerations, such as the length of time allocated for a study,

---

422. In the case of standing and legislative committees, this power is accorded by Standing Orders 108(1) and 113(5). Standing committees may delegate the power to send for persons to sub-committees. Legislative committees are restricted to calling government officials and technical witnesses. A provision empowering special committees to send for persons is ordinarily included in the order which establishes the committee. See, for example, *Journals*, October 1, 1997, pp. 59-61. Committees dealing exclusively with internal, administrative matters may not receive the power to send for persons. No such power is given to the Liaison Committee, nor is it given to steering committees. See Standing Order 107. The power to send for persons goes back at least to the first half of the seventeenth century. See *Redlich*, Vol. II, p. 207.

423. See, for example, Special Committee on the Review of the *Canadian Security Intelligence Service Act* and the *Security Offences Act, Minutes of Proceedings and Evidence*, September 28, 1989, Issue No. 1, p. 7, and Special Committee on the Proposed Companion Resolution to the Meech Lake Accord, *Minutes of Proceedings and Evidence*, April 9, 1990, Issue No. 1, pp. 8-9.

424. See, for example, Standing Committee on Human Resources and the Status of Persons with Disabilities, *Minutes*, October 21, 1997, Meeting No. 2.

limit the number of witnesses the committee will be able to accommodate. While any member of a committee may propose witnesses, the committee makes the final decision as to who will be heard. Witnesses are ordinarily reimbursed for the reasonable expenses which they have incurred in order to appear before the committee.[425]

Summoning Witnesses

In the vast majority of cases, committees are able to obtain the evidence they seek by inviting witnesses to appear before them. However, some witnesses may not agree to appear willingly. When a witness has declined an invitation to appear, a committee may issue a summons to that witness by adopting a motion to that effect.[426] If a proposed witness fails to appear when summoned, the committee may report the fact to the House. The House then takes any action it deems appropriate.[427]

Committees are not empowered to summon Members of the House of Commons or Senators. Should a Member refuse to testify when requested to do so by a committee, the committee can report this to the House which will then decide what action, if any, is necessary. While Senators may appear before House committees voluntarily, their attendance cannot be compelled. If a committee wishes a formal request to be made for a Senator to appear, it must seek the agreement of the House. The House, if it agrees with the committee, sends a message to the Senate requesting that the Senator appear before the committee.[428]

Swearing-in of Witnesses

Any witness appearing before a committee may be required to take an oath or make a solemn affirmation;[429] however, under normal circumstances, witnesses are not sworn in. The decision as to the swearing-in of witnesses is entirely at the discretion

---

425. Committees are authorized to reimburse witnesses, with the exception of those residing in the National Capital Region. The actual level of reimbursement, established from time to time by the Board of Internal Economy, is set out in the *Financial Policy Manual for Committees*. Committees usually limit the number of individuals from a given organization whom they are willing to reimburse. See, for example, Standing Committee on Health, *Minutes*, October 30, 1997, Meeting No. 2. Committees may reimburse witnesses who appear before them in Ottawa or while the committee is travelling. See, for example, Standing Committee on Fisheries and Oceans, *Minutes*, November 27, 1997, Meeting No. 11.

426. While the committee is not obliged to extend an invitation to appear prior to issuing a summons, this is the normal manner of proceeding. See, for example, Standing Committee on Consumer and Corporate Affairs and Government Operations, *Minutes of Proceedings and Evidence*, May 29, 1990, Issue No. 67, p. 4. Prior to an amendment to the Standing Orders in 1994, it was necessary to file a certificate with the Chair of the committee indicating that the evidence of a witness was material and important before a summons could be issued. Since the rule change, a certificate is no longer required prior to the issuing of a summons. See *Journals*, June 8, 1994, p. 545; June 10, 1994, p. 563; and Standing Committee on Procedure and House Affairs, *Minutes of Proceedings and Evidence*, June 9, 1994, Issue No. 16, pp. 3-8, in particular p. 8.

427. See, for example, *Journals*, August 27, 1891, p. 454.

428. See, for example, *Journals,* May 9, 1996, pp. 341-2. When formally requested to appear by the House, Senators may do so only with the permission of the Senate. See Senate Rule 124.

429. See *Parliament of Canada Act*, R.S.C. 1985, c. P-1, ss. 10(3), 11. The form of the oath or solemn affirmation is defined by s. 13(2) of the Act, and is set out in the Schedule attached to it.

of the committee.[430] A witness who refuses to be sworn in might face a charge of contempt.[431] Likewise, the refusal to answer questions or failure to reply truthfully may give rise to a charge of contempt of the House, whether the witness has been sworn in or not.[432] In addition, witnesses who lie under oath may be charged with perjury.[433]

Testimony

Witnesses appearing before committees are usually asked to make a brief opening statement, summarizing their views or the views of the organization they represent, on the subject of the committee's inquiry. Following this opening statement, there is a period for questioning.[434] Questions may be asked by any member of the committee; the Chair may, on occasion, also participate in the questioning of witnesses.[435] Other Members of the House in attendance at committee meetings may also be permitted to pose questions.[436] This depends, in part, on the amount of time the committee has accorded to dealing with each witness and the number of committee members who wish to ask questions. Committee members are usually given priority in the questioning of witnesses.

Witnesses appearing before committees enjoy the same freedom of speech and protection from arrest and molestation as do Members of Parliament.[437] At the committee's discretion, witnesses may be allowed to testify *in camera* when dealing with

---

430. At various times, committees have sworn in the Prime Minister, the Auditor General (an officer of Parliament) and senior public servants. See, for example, Special Committee on Certain Charges and Allegations made by George N. Gordon, *Minutes of Proceedings*, March 3, 1932; Standing Committee on Public Accounts, *Minutes of Proceedings and Evidence*, May 16, 1996, Issue No. 15, p. 1; Standing Committee on Labour, Employment and Immigration, *Minutes of Proceedings and Evidence*, January 28, 1987, Issue No. 20, pp. 3-4, 9-14; and Speaker Fraser's ruling, *Debates*, March 17, 1987, pp. 4265-6.

431. See Speaker Fraser's ruling, *Debates*, March 17, 1987, pp. 4265-6.

432. As in other matters involving privilege, a committee is not empowered to deal with a perceived contempt itself, but must report the matter to the House.

433. *Parliament of Canada Act*, R.S.C. 1985, c. P-1, s. 12.

434. The length of the question period and the order in which questions are asked are matters which must be decided by the committee. See section above, "Routine Motions". Given the less formal atmosphere which prevails in committee, considerable latitude is often shown with respect to these matters.

435. Committees have, on occasion, authorized committee staff to question witnesses. Such cases tend to arise when a technical subject matter is under consideration. See, for example, Standing Committee on Communications and Culture, *Minutes of Proceedings and Evidence*, December 3, 1986, Issue No. 8, p. 3.

436. Standing Order 119 authorizes Members of the House who are not members of the committee to participate in its public proceedings.

437. As with Members, freedom of speech is extended to the testimony given by witnesses before committees and has been held to include protection from any possible prosecution. The House may waive this protection if it sees fit. See, for example, *Journals*, April 12, 1892, pp. 234-5. It is the responsibility of each committee to see that witnesses do not take advantage of this protection to utter defamatory remarks which might give rise to legal proceedings were they made elsewhere. See Speaker Fraser's ruling, *Debates*, March 16, 1993, pp. 17071-2. See also Chapter 3, "Privileges and Immunities".

confidential matters of state or sensitive commercial information.[438] Under special circumstances, witnesses have been permitted to appear anonymously.[439] Tampering with a witness or in any way attempting to deter a witness from giving evidence at a committee meeting may constitute a breach of privilege. Similarly, any interference with or threats against witnesses who have already testified may be treated as a breach of privilege by the House.[440]

Witnesses giving testimony may be assisted by counsel, although permission is seldom sought.[441] Counsel, when permitted, is restricted to an advisory role and may not ask questions or reply on the witness' behalf.

In light of the protection afforded witnesses by Parliament, they are expected to exercise judgement and restraint in presenting their views to committees. Where witnesses persist in making comments which are deemed to be inappropriate by the committee, their testimony may be expunged from the record.[442]

There are no specific rules governing the nature of questions which may be put to witnesses appearing before committees, beyond the general requirement of relevance to the issue before the committee.[443] Witnesses must answer all questions which the committee puts to them.[444] A witness may object to a question asked by an individual committee member. However, if the committee agrees that the question be put to the witness, he or she is obliged to reply.[445] Members have been urged to display the "appropriate courtesy and fairness" when questioning witnesses. Nevertheless, a witness who refuses to answer questions may be reported to the House.[446]

Particular attention has been paid to the questioning of public servants.[447] The obligation of a witness to answer all questions put by the committee must be balanced against the role that public servants play in providing confidential advice

---

438. See, for example, Special Committee on Child Care, *Minutes of Proceedings and Evidence*, June 13, 1986, Issue No. 46, p. 6.

439. See, for example, Standing Committee on Justice and Legal Affairs, *Minutes of Proceedings and Evidence*, June 3, 1996, Issue No. 24, p. 1; June 6, 1996, Issue No. 27, p. 1.

440. See, for example, *Journals*, December 4, 1992, p. 2284; February 18, 1993, p. 2528; February 25, 1993, p. 2568; and Standing Committee on House Management, *Minutes of Proceedings and Evidence*, February 18, 1993, Issue No. 46, pp. 7-11.

441. See, for example, Standing Committee on Elections, Privileges and Procedure, *Minutes of Proceedings and Evidence*, February 23, 1988, Issue No. 24, p. 4.

442. See Speaker Fraser's ruling, *Debates*, March 16, 1993, pp. 17071-2.

443. See, for example, Standing Committee on Elections, Privileges and Procedure, *Minutes of Proceedings and Evidence*, February 3, 1988, Issue No. 20, pp. 3, 25-8.

444. See, for example, Standing Committee on Elections, Privileges and Procedure, *Minutes of Proceedings and Evidence*, February 3, 1988, Issue No. 20, pp. 25-8.

445. *Debates*, December 11, 1986, p. 1999.

446. See *Journals*, February 17, 1913, p. 254.

447. For a discussion, see *Report on Witnesses Before Legislative Committees*, Ontario Law Reform Commission, 1981, pp. 25-45.

to their Ministers. The role of the public servant has traditionally been viewed in relation to the implementation and administration of government policy, rather than the determination of what that policy should be. Consequently, public servants have been excused from commenting on the policy decisions made by the government. In addition, committees will ordinarily accept the reasons that a public servant gives for declining to answer a specific question or series of questions which involve the giving of a legal opinion, or which may be perceived as a conflict with the witness' responsibility to the Minister, or which is outside of their own area of responsibility or which might affect business transactions.[448]

As with the House, committees respect the *sub judice* convention.[449] The convention is applied not only in the discussions held amongst members of the committee but also in the questioning of witnesses.[450]

BRIEFS AND OTHER PAPERS

Most documents which committees seek are provided voluntarily. They include government reports, statistics, correspondance, memoranda and agreements of various sorts, as well as briefs. For committee purposes, a brief is any document presenting the position of an individual, group, organization or government department with respect to a particular issue. Ordinarily, committees are able to obtain the documents they require for their work by simply requesting them.[451] Where a committee meets with a refusal to provide a document it deems essential to its work, the committee may pass a motion ordering its production.[452] If such an order is ignored,

---

448. See, for example, Standing Committee on National Resources and Public Works, *Minutes of Proceedings and Evidence*, November 27, 1979, Issue No. 6, p. 4; Standing Committee on Communications and Culture, *Minutes of Proceedings and Evidence*, February 4, 1988, Issue No. 73, pp. 7, 45; Standing Committee on Canadian Heritage, *Minutes of Proceedings and Evidence*, June 18, 1996, Issue No. 2, p. 7. There has been agreement that Order-in-Council nominees should not be asked questions about their personal lives. See, for example, Standing Committee on Citizenship and Immigration, *Minutes of Proceedings and Evidence*, November 3, 1994, Issue No. 26, p. 4.

449. For a description of the *sub judice* convention, see Chapter 13, "Rules of Order and Decorum".

450. See, for example, Standing Committee on Miscellaneous Estimates, *Minutes of Proceedings and Evidence*, May 10, 1982, Issue No. 84, pp. 30, 34. The House is not prevented from referring a matter to committee because it is *sub judice*. See Speaker Sauvé's ruling, *Debates*, March 22, 1983, pp. 24027-9.

451. See, for example, Standing Committee on Justice and the Solicitor General, *Minutes of Proceedings and Evidence*, May 29, 1990, Issue No. 39, p. 3.

452. See, for example, Standing Committee on Justice and the Solicitor General, *Minutes of Proceedings and Evidence*, December 4, 1990, Issue No. 56, p. 3.

the committee has no power to compel its production, but may report the matter to the House and request that appropriate action be taken. [453]

Although the House has not placed any restrictions on the power to send for papers and records, it may not be appropriate to insist on the production of papers in all cases. In 1991, the Standing Committee on Privileges and Elections pointed out that:

> *The House of Commons recognizes that it should not require the production of documents in all cases; considerations of public policy, including national security, foreign relations, and so forth, enter into the decision as to when it is appropriate to order the production of such documents.* [454]

Where concerns about confidentiality exist, a committee may agree to have documents tabled at an *in camera* meeting. [455] Transcripts of *in camera* meetings and other confidential documents of committees are to be classed as Secret Records by the National Archives for a period of 30 years from the end of the session in which they were created. These documents remain available to Members of the House during that time. [456]

A document submitted to a committee becomes the property of the committee and forms part of the committee's records. Government departments are required to submit documents in both official languages when presenting them to committees. Everyone else, including Members of the House of Commons, may submit written material in either or both official languages. Each committee must decide whether documents submitted to it in only one official language will be distributed to members

---

453. Following the refusal of the Solicitor General to provide two reports to the Standing Committee on Justice and the Solicitor General, citing privacy grounds, the Committee reported the matter to the House. Subsequently, a question of privilege was raised by Derek Lee (Scarborough–Rouge River) concerning the Minister's failure to provide the reports sought by the Committee. No ruling was delivered as to whether the matter constituted a *prima facie* breach of privilege, but the issue was referred to the Standing Committee on Privileges and Elections. Parliament was prorogued before the Committee had completed its deliberations, but the reference was revived in the next session allowing the Committee to conclude its work. The Committee presented a report which concluded that the Standing Committee on Justice and the Solicitor General had been within its rights to insist on the production of the two reports and recommended that the House order the Solicitor General to comply with the order for production. The House subsequently adopted a motion to that effect, with the proviso that the reports be presented at an *in camera* meeting of the Standing Committee on Justice and the Solicitor General. See Standing Committee on Justice and the Solicitor General, *Minutes of Proceedings and Evidence*, May 29, 1990, Issue No. 39, p. 3; December 4, 1990, Issue No. 56, p. 3; December 18, 1990, Issue No. 57, pp. 4-6; *Journals*, December 19, 1990, p. 2508; February 28, 1991, p. 2638; *Debates*, February 28, 1991, pp. 17745-6; *Journals*, May 17, 1991, p. 42; May 29, 1991, pp. 92-9; June 18, 1991, pp. 216-7; and Standing Committee on Justice and the Solicitor General, *Minutes of Proceedings and Evidence*, June 19, 1991, Issue No. 4, pp. 5-6.

454. *Journals*, May 29, 1991, p. 95. The House took note of the Committee's report and referred it to the Standing Committee on House Management for further study. See *Journals*, June 18, 1991, pp. 216-7.

455. See, for example, Standing Committee on Justice and the Solicitor General, *Minutes of Proceedings and Evidence*, November 26, 1992, Issue No. 71, p. 4.

456. For agreement with National Archives, see *Journals*, April 13, 1994, pp. 339-40.

immediately or once a translation is available.[457] The right to submit a document does not, however, imply the right to have the document considered forthwith.

On occasion, a committee will consider a document to be of sufficient importance that it will agree to treat it either as an "Appendix" or an "Exhibit". An Appendix is a document which the committee has ordered to be published appended to the *Evidence* taken at a particular meeting.[458] An Exhibit is any document or item classified as such by the committee and is therefore part of the committee's permanent records.[459] Exhibits are not published or distributed to members but are retained by the clerk and are available for consultation. When a decision is made to designate a document as an Appendix or an Exhibit, the appropriate entry is made in the committee's *Minutes of Proceedings*. Appendices and Exhibits are used, among other purposes, for preserving parts of a presentation to a committee that would otherwise not be included in the *Evidence*. For example, copies of slides or charts used during a presentation may be preserved as Appendices or Exhibits.

COMMITTEE PUBLICATIONS

Like the House, committees publish a number of documents for the use of their members, their staff and the general public.[460] These committee publications parallel, in many respects, those used by the House.[461] They provide a permanent record of evidence received, decisions made and the results of studies carried out. Every committee publishes *Minutes of Proceedings, Evidence* and, from time to time, reports to the House. The *Minutes of Proceedings* are the official record of what the committee has done and are prepared by the clerk of the committee and signed by him or her. The *Minutes* are the equivalent of the *Journals* of the House. The *Evidence* is the transcribed, edited and corrected record of what is said in committee, both by committee members and by witnesses appearing before committees. Reports to the House may be brief documents of less than a page or they may be much larger works, printed and bound separately. All committee publications are prepared in both official languages.

All of the documents published by committees were formerly available in printed format. In 1994, the House began to distribute its publications electronically. Until that time, committees produced a document called *Minutes of Proceedings and*

---

457. Committees usually deal with this question by adopting a motion concerning the general distribution of documents. See section above, "Routine Motions".

458. See, for example, Standing Committee on Aboriginal Affairs and Northern Development, *Minutes*, November 19, 1998, Meeting No. 43.

459. See, for example, Standing Committee on Justice and Human Rights, *Minutes*, November 5, 1997, Meeting No. 4.

460. Standing and legislative committees are empowered by the Standing Orders to print from day to day such papers and evidence as may be ordered by them. See Standing Orders 108(1) and 113(5). A similar provision is usually included in the order establishing a special committee. See, for example, *Journals*, November 18, 1997, pp. 224-5.

461. For a description of the documents produced by the House, see Chapter 24, "The Parliamentary Record".

Evidence, containing the material which is now supplied separately in two documents: *Minutes* and *Evidence.* Reports to the House which were deemed too short to merit separate publication were also included in the *Minutes of Proceedings and Evidence.* Since September 1998, the *Minutes* and *Evidence,* as separate documents, have been available only in electronic format. As the House has moved to the electronic distribution of its publications, the printing of committee documents has, for the most part, been discontinued. They are now available in electronic format at the Parliamentary Website, *Parliamentary Internet Parlementaire.* [462] Committees may still publish major substantive reports in printed format. [463]

Minutes of Proceedings

Minutes of Proceedings are prepared for each meeting of a committee by the clerk, who signs the original copy to attest to its accuracy and authenticity. The original copy of all *Minutes* is kept by the clerk of the committee and is archived along with other committee documents at the end of each session. The *Minutes* record the deliberations and decisions of the committee in a manner similar to the *Journals* of the House. In addition, the *Minutes of Proceedings* indicate the meeting number; [464] the time and place of the meeting; whether the meeting was held in public or was *in camera*; who presided; which members and substitutes were present, whether for all or only part of the meeting. Thus, for a member who attended part of a meeting and was replaced by a substitute for the remainder of it, the *Minutes* will show the member as present and show another member as being a substitute for him or her. [465] The *Minutes* also include the names of other Members and Senators who were in attendance; the names of staff in attendance; the names of witnesses, if any, including their titles and affiliated organizations; the orders of reference that were taken up; and the time of adjournment. The *Minutes* may also contain the text of rulings given by the Chair with respect to the procedural acceptability of motions proposed during the meeting.

Evidence

The *Evidence* is the record of what was said at a committee meeting, corresponding to the *Debates* of the House. It records not only the remarks made by members of the committee but also what was said by witnesses. *Evidence* is published only for

---

462. The Website address is «http://www.parl.gc.ca».

463. See, for example, Standing Committee on Agriculture and Agri-Food, *Minutes*, December 7, 1998, Meeting No. 69.

464. Meetings are numbered consecutively from the beginning of each session. A committee may meet several times in a single day or have a meeting which extends over more than one day. See, for example, Standing Committee on Finance, *Minutes*, June 11, 1998, Meeting Nos. 97-100, and Standing Committee on Human Resources Development, *Minutes of Proceedings and Evidence*, April 25, 1996, Issue No. 4, pp. 22-4.

465. See, for example, Standing Committee on Finance, *Minutes*, November 23, 1998, Meeting No. 162.

public meetings, or for those parts of a meeting which are held in public.[466] It is prepared in a bilingual format, in a process which parallels the production of the House *Debates* from the "blues". Since it has been ruled that the power of a committee to print also includes the power to decide against printing if a committee finds testimony offensive, it may have it expunged from the *Evidence*.[467]

Documents presented at a meeting which a committee considers to be of sufficient importance may be appended to the *Evidence* of that meeting as an Appendix or recorded in the *Minutes* as an Exhibit.[468]

Reports

The observations and recommendations of committees are made known to the House through reports.[469] Reports to the House are available in electronic format and, from time to time, large substantive reports may also be available in printed format. Reports are numbered sequentially by each committee within a session. In addition to observations and recommendations, reports contain a citation to the authority under which the study was conducted, a reference to the relevant *Minutes* of meetings held on the topic, and the signature of the Chair. Attached to the report after the signature of the Chair are any opinions or recommendations dissenting from or supplementary to the report.[470]

BROADCASTING

Committees are permitted to televise their hearings in accordance with the provisions of the Standing Orders,[471] using the facilities provided by the House.[472] Formerly, a committee required special permission of the House to broadcast its proceedings. In 1991, the procedure for obtaining consent to use House facilities for broadcasting was formalized in the Standing Orders. A further change to the

---

466. It is up to each committee to decide whether to meet in public or not. Committees have sometimes decided to make public those deliberations which were originally conducted *in camera*. See, for example, Standing Joint Committee for the Scrutiny of Regulations, *Minutes*, November 5, 1998, Meeting No. 15.

467. As witnesses appearing before committee are protected by parliamentary privilege, it is the responsibility of the committee to see that witnesses do not take advantage of that protection to utter defamatory remarks which might give rise to legal proceedings were they made elsewhere. See Speaker Fraser's ruling, *Debates*, March 16, 1993, pp. 17071-2.

468. See, for example, Standing Committee on Aboriginal Affairs and Northern Development, *Minutes*, November 19, 1998, Meeting No. 43. See section above, "Briefs and Other Papers".

469. For more information on reports, see section below, "Reports to the House".

470. Standing Order 108(1)(*a*).

471. Standing Order 119.1.

472. At the present time, one committee meeting room is permanently equipped for broadcasting purposes. Portable equipment can be set up by House broadcasting services to permit broadcasting from another room, if required.

Standing Orders in 1994 allowed committees to televise their proceedings using House facilities, without the need to seek permission on each occasion.[473] Where a committee wishes to televise using other facilities, special permission is required.[474]

The broadcasting of committee meetings follows guidelines established by the Standing Committee on Procedure and House Affairs which are very similar to those used in broadcasting the proceedings in the House.[475] Only the person recognized by the Chair is shown, and reaction shots are prohibited.

The House also provides facilities for the in-house audio broadcasting of all public committee meetings. The audio broadcast is available to all Members in their Parliament Hill offices as well as to the Press Gallery.

Committee Studies

The role of committees is to examine selected matters in greater depth than is possible in the House and to report any conclusions of those examinations, including recommendations, to the House. Committees undertake studies in four general areas: the Estimates, legislation, Order-in-Council appointments and subject-matter studies (including the review of departmental annual reports). While it may be common for standing committees to conduct studies in all four areas, special committees are normally established to conduct subject-matter inquiries, and legislative committees are charged solely with the examination of legislation.

---

473. See *Journals*, April 11, 1991, pp. 2905-32, in particular p. 2929; Standing Committee on Procedure and House Affairs, *Minutes of Proceedings and Evidence*, June 6, 1994, Issue No. 16, p. 7; *Journals*, June 8, 1994, p. 545; June 10, 1994, p. 563.

474. This includes both broadcasting on Parliament Hill and while sitting outside the parliamentary precinct. See, for example, *Journals*, November 28, 1995, p. 2167; November 21, 1996, p. 880. In addition to being given supplementary broadcasting powers by the House, a committee may need to obtain additional budgetary authorization from the Liaison Committee. Funds for broadcasting purposes are not included in the ordinary budgets of committees.

475. Provisional broadcasting guidelines for committees were tabled as part of the Twenty-Third Report of the Standing Committee on House Management and were approved by the House. The guidelines were made permanent as a result of concurrence by the House in the Eighty-Third Report of the House Management Committee. See Standing Committee on House Management, *Minutes of Proceedings and Evidence*, February 11, 1992, Issue No. 24, pp. 6-13; *Journals*, February 14, 1992, p. 1024; March 27, 1992, p. 1230; Standing Committee on House Management, *Minutes of Proceedings and Evidence*, April 2, 1993, Issue No. 53, pp. 145-7; *Journals*, April 2, 1993, p. 2784; April 28, 1993, p. 2873. In 1998, the Standing Committee on Procedure and House Affairs presented a report which recommended allowing members of the Press Gallery, rather than House Broadcasting Services, to film committee meetings. See Standing Committee on Procedure and House Affairs, *Minutes*, December 3, 1998, Meeting No. 45, and *Journals*, December 8, 1998, p. 1424; April 26, 1999, pp. 1766-7.

Certain items of study, such as the Main Estimates and departmental annual reports, are required to be tabled in the House each year at a specific time and referred to committees. Other items, including Supplementary Estimates, Order-in-Council appointments and legislation, are referred to committees only if and when tabled or introduced in the House. The number of such items varies from year to year, depending on a wide variety of factors including the government's legislative schedule and events outside Parliament.

When a committee receives an order of reference or decides to take up a particular study, the steering committee is usually charged with the responsibility both for establishing a work plan for each study and for co-ordinating the committee's consideration of the variety of topics before it. Standing committees routinely deal with several matters concurrently.[476] While in some cases committees are able to deal with important matters consecutively, time limits imposed by the Standing Orders for consideration of the Main Estimates and Order-in-Council appointments require careful planning to ensure committee effectiveness.[477] One avenue which is often selected by committees having a heavy workload is the delegation of one or several items of study to sub-committees.[478] This allows the committee to share its work by drawing upon the associate members of the committee for the membership of sub-committees.

ESTIMATES

The Main Estimates are the projected government spending for the coming fiscal year broken down by department and program.[479] The Estimates are displayed as a series of budgetary items or "Votes", each of which indicates the amount of money required by the government for a program or function. Normally, a single Vote in the Main Estimates covers a total spending category, such as departmental operations or capital costs, and summarizes all the planned activity or program expenditures for the department or agency in that category. Where additional funds or the reallocation of already appropriated funds is necessary during a fiscal year, the government may table Supplementary Estimates.

The Standing Orders provide for detailed consideration of the Estimates, both Main and Supplementary, by standing committees.[480] Each committee has referred to it those departmental and agency Votes which relate to its mandate. Programs

---

476. See, for example, Standing Committee on Foreign Affairs and International Trade, *Minutes*, October 23, 1997, Meeting No. 4.

477. See Standing Orders 81(4) and 110.

478. The House has occasionally ordered that a particular study be carried out by a sub-committee. See, for example, *Journals*, June 29, 1983, p. 6116.

479. For information on the overall Estimates process, see Chapter 18, "Financial Procedures".

480. Standing Order 81.

whose funding and funding levels are already prescribed by statute are included with the Estimates, marked "S" or "Statutory". As these expenditures have already been approved by the passage of the appropriate legislation, they are not referred to committee for examination, but are provided for information purposes only.

The Estimates for each coming fiscal year are required to be tabled in the House and referred to standing committees no later than March 1 of each year.[481] The Standing Orders do not impose an obligation on committees to consider the Estimates. Where a committee has chosen to study and report on the Estimates, however, it must report them back not later than May 31 of the fiscal year to which they apply. If a committee has not reported the Estimates back by that date, it is deemed to have done so, whether it has actually considered them or not.[482] The Leader of the Opposition may, not later than the third sitting day prior to May 31, ask to extend the reporting deadline respecting committee consideration of the Main Estimates of a named department or agency.[483] A committee studying the Main Estimates of that department or agency must report back, or will be deemed to have reported, no later than the earlier of either 10 sitting days after May 31 or the sitting day prior to the final allotted day in that Supply period.[484] While considering the Main Estimates, committees are also empowered to consider expenditure plans and priorities in future years for the departments and agencies.[485] The deadline for reporting on those plans and priorities is the final sitting day in June.[486]

Supplementary Estimates are referred, upon tabling in the House, to the appropriate standing committees.[487] The deadline for a report on Supplementary Estimates is not later than the third sitting day before the earlier of the final sitting day or the final allotted day in the current Supply period. As with the Main Estimates, if a committee has not reported within the prescribed time, it is deemed to have done so.[488]

---

481. Standing Order 81(4). Since 1968, all Estimates have been referred to standing committees for detailed scrutiny before being considered by the House.

482. Standing Order 81(4). See, for example, Standing Committee on Agriculture and Agri-food, *Minutes*, April 23, 1998, Meeting No. 34, and April 28, 1998, Meeting No. 36. The Committee held no further meetings on the Main Estimates for that year and did not present a report.

483. Standing Order 81(4)(*a*).

484. Standing Order 81(4)(*b*).

485. Standing Order 81(7).

486. Standing Order 81(8).

487. Standing Order 81(5). As Supplementary Estimates deal only with costs in excess of the amounts provided for in the Main Estimates, they relate only to the particular departments or programs having new or additional expenditures. Supplementary Estimates are, therefore, referred only to the standing committees concerned with the Votes they contain. See, for example, *Journals*, May 15, 1998, pp. 835-6.

488. Standing Order 81(5).

Committees consider each Vote separately as a distinct motion, beginning with Vote 1 which covers general departmental administration or operations. Committees usually begin their examination of the Estimates by hearing from the appropriate Minister or the Parliamentary Secretary, accompanied by senior departmental officials.[489] The questioning and discussion at this meeting is generally wide-ranging, although the rule of relevance does apply. Subsequent meetings, if any, are normally held with the senior departmental officials responsible for the areas and programs specifically dealt with in each Vote.[490]

When the committee has completed its consideration of the Estimates, each item is put to a vote separately. Restrictions exist on the power of a committee to amend the Estimates. Amendments may be presented to reduce the amount of an item,[491] but it is not in order to propose an amendment to reduce the amount of a Vote to zero, as the proper course is to vote against the motion "Shall the Vote carry?" It is also out of order to propose an increase in an item, as such a proposal infringes the spending authority of the Crown.[492] Similarly, it is not permitted to attempt to change the way in which funds are allocated, by transferring money from one item to another.[493] Statutory items included in the Estimates for information purposes may not be amended by the committee.[494] Finally, a committee cannot include substantive recommendations in its report on Estimates.[495]

LEGISLATION

Committees play a major role in the legislative process. The Standing Orders provide for all legislation to be considered in committee. Referral to committee may take place either after second reading or before second reading[496] and bills may be

---

489. See, for example, Standing Committee on Human Resources Development and the Status of Persons with Disabilities, *Minutes*, May 5, 1998, Meeting No. 34.

490. See, for example, Standing Committee on Human Resources Development and the Status of Persons with Disabilities, *Minutes*, May 14, 1998, Meeting No. 37.

491. When proposing the reduction of a Vote, it is necessary to take into account the fact that a part of the total amount may already have been approved by the House in granting interim Supply. See, for example, Standing Committee on Citizenship and Immigration, *Minutes of Proceedings and Evidence*, May 18, 1995, Issue No. 47, p. 9. Where a proposal is made to reduce an amount, it must not be for an insignificant amount.

492. See, for example, Standing Committee on National Resources and Public Works, *Minutes of Proceedings and Evidence*, November 27, 1979, Issue No. 6, p. 3. See also *Bourinot*, 4th ed., p. 427.

493. See Speaker Lamoureux's ruling, *Journals*, March 24, 1970, pp. 636-7.

494. See, for example, Standing Committee on Regional Industrial Expansion, *Minutes of Proceedings and Evidence*, May 7, 1986, Issue No. 1, p. 8.

495. See Speaker Lamoureux's rulings, *Journals*, March 24, 1970, pp. 636-7, and June 18, 1973, pp. 419-20; Speaker Jerome's ruling, *Debates*, December 10, 1979, p. 2189. Where a committee does wish to make substantive recommendations concerning the Estimates, it may do so using the mandate provided by Standing Order 108(2).

496. Standing Order 73(1) and (2).

referred to legislative, standing or special committees[497] or to a Committee of the Whole.[498] On rare occasions, the House has referred bills to joint committees.[499] When a bill is referred to a committee, it is the bill itself which constitutes the committee's order of reference. A motion instructing a committee to prepare and bring in a bill may also be proposed by a Minister or by a private Member.[500]

Adoption of a motion for second reading of a bill expresses the House's approval of the principle of the bill. The committee is charged with examining the wording and effect of each clause of the bill in light of the principle; it may propose any modifications deemed necessary or useful in order for the bill to better realize its purpose.[501] When a bill has been referred to a committee following second reading, it is not in order to propose amendments which seek to extend the scope of the bill or alter its principle. It is also not in order to propose amendments to Acts or sections of Acts not affected by the bill itself.[502] When a bill has been referred to a committee prior to second reading, the committee is not bound by the same limitations since the House has not yet approved the bill's principle. While amendments may be proposed which would alter the principle, they must still be relevant to the bill.[503]

Order of Consideration

When a committee studies a bill, consideration of the preamble, if any, is postponed as is consideration of the first clause if it contains only a short title.[504] After Clause 1 has been called by the Chair (or Clause 2, if Clause 1 contains only the short title of the bill), a committee may proceed to hear witnesses, usually beginning with the sponsor of the bill. A legislative committee is restricted to hearing only witnesses on technical matters related to the bill.[505] In addition to hearing witnesses, a committee may receive written briefs related to the bill. At the conclusion of testimony, a committee may invite the sponsor to appear again in order to answer any concerns which have been raised by other witnesses.

A committee then proceeds to clause-by-clause consideration of the bill. Clause-by-clause study involves the consideration of each clause individually and,

---

497. Standing Order 73(3).

498. All bills based on Supply motions are dealt with in a Committee of the Whole (Standing Order 73 (4)). See Chapter 19, "Committees of the Whole House".

499. See *Journals*, November 16, 1964, p. 876; June 22, 1965, pp. 290-1; May 31, 1966, p. 594; July 15, 1975, p. 711; March 30, 1993, pp. 2742-3.

500. Standing Order 68(4)(*a*) and (*b*).

501. For detailed information on amendments to bills in committee, see Chapter 16, "The Legislative Process".

502. See Speaker Fraser's ruling, *Debates*, April 28, 1992, p. 9801.

503. See, for example, Standing Committee on Human Rights and the Status of Persons with Disabilities, *Minutes of Proceedings and Evidence*, April 30, 1995, Issue No. 47, p. 35.

504. Standing Order 75(1).

505. Standing Order 113(5).

if necessary, of each line of the bill. At this stage, each clause is proposed to the committee as a separate question on which it must decide. It is also at this stage that members of the committee have the opportunity to propose amendments to the bill. They may propose that words be added, that certain words be struck out and replaced by others, or that words simply be struck out.[506] During clause-by-clause consideration, it is normal for departmental officials to remain before a committee as witnesses in order to provide technical explanations of the effect of individual clauses of the bill and the technical implications of proposed amendments.[507]

Motions to amend a clause of a bill do not require notice. As a practical matter, proposed amendments are usually forwarded to the clerk of the committee before clause-by-clause consideration begins. The clerk then has the opportunity to place the amendments in the proper sequence for consideration as the committee proceeds through the bill. The proposed amendments received by the clerk are usually circulated to members prior to the beginning of clause-by-clause consideration, for information purposes. At this stage, the amendments are not formally before the committee and the member may move them or not when the committee reaches the appropriate place in the bill.

Time Limits for the Consideration of Bills

The Standing Orders do not set any time limit for the consideration of government bills in committee. Nonetheless, the House may set a reporting deadline by special order[508] or it may invoke the time allocation provisions of the Standing Orders.[509]

Committees are required to report on private Members' public bills within 60 sitting days.[510] The committee must either report the bill to the House with or without amendment, or seek a single 30-day extension to the time provided for consideration of the bill, or present a report containing a recommendation to not proceed further with the bill. If the committee has not reported by the conclusion of the 60-day period (or the 30-day extension, where applicable), the bill is deemed reported back without amendment.

Private bills are to be referred to legislative committees following second reading.[511] However, private bills are often dealt with, by unanimous consent, in a

---

506. For details of the amending process at committee stage, see Chapter 16, "The Legislative Process".

507. See, for example, Standing Committee on Canadian Heritage, *Minutes* and *Evidence*, April 13, 1999, Meeting No. 90.

508. See, for example, *Journals*, May 3, 1994, p. 419.

509. See, for example, *Journals*, April 25, 1996, p. 260. For further information, see Chapter 14, "The Curtailment of Debate".

510. Standing Order 97.1. Formerly, no time limit was placed on the consideration of private Members' bills. This provision was added to the Standing Orders in 1998. See *Journals*, November 30, 1998, pp. 1327-9.

511. Standing Order 141(1).

Committee of the Whole. The particular procedures related to consideration of private bills are found in Chapter 23, "Private Bills Practice".

Adoption and Report

Once a committee has concluded its consideration of the clauses of a bill, a motion is proposed to carry the bill (or the bill, as amended).[512] The committee then adopts a motion, instructing the Chair to report the bill to the House.[513] If the committee has amended the bill, it usually will also order that the bill be reprinted for the use of the House at report stage.[514]

Committee to Prepare and Bring in a Bill

A committee may be given an order of reference to prepare and bring in a bill.[515] The motion proposing such an order is considered under Government Orders, if proposed by a Minister, or under Private Members' Business, if proposed by a private Member.[516] The committee's report recommends the principles, scope and general provisions of the bill and may include proposals for legislative wording.[517]

ORDER-IN-COUNCIL APPOINTMENTS

The government is required to table in the House certified copies of all Order-in-Council appointments to non-judicial posts, not later than five sitting days after they have been published in the *Canada Gazette*.[518] Appointments are effective on the day they are announced by the government, not on the date the certificates are published or tabled in the House. The Standing Orders provide that the certified copies be automatically referred to the standing committee specified at the time of

---

512. See, for example, Standing Committee on Justice and Human Rights, *Minutes,* May 6, 1999, Meeting No. 140. If the bill does not pass, the committee must decide whether to report to the House that the bill not be proceeded with, or to adopt some other course of action. See Chapter 16, "The Legislative Process".

513. See, for example, Standing Committee on Justice and Human Rights, *Minutes*, May 6, 1999, Meeting No. 140.

514. See, for example, Standing Committee on Justice and Human Rights, *Minutes,* May 6, 1999, Meeting No. 140.

515. Standing Order 68(4). See, for example, *Journals*, October 30, 1997, p. 175. This provision was added to the Standing Orders in 1994. See *Journals*, February 7, 1994, pp. 112-20, in particular pp. 115-6.

516. Standing Order 68(4)(*a*) and (*b*).

517. Standing Order 68(5).

518. Standing Order 110(1). See, for example, *Journals*, April 25, 1997, pp. 1551-2. The review of Order-in-Council appointments was recommended in the Third Report of the McGrath Committee. Standing Orders giving effect to the recommendations were adopted provisionally in 1986 and were made permanent in 1987. The review procedure deals only with non-judicial appointments. See Third Report of the Special Committee on Reform of the House of Commons, June 1985, pp. 29-34; *Journals*, February 6, 1986, pp. 1644-66, in particular p. 1664; February 13, 1986, p. 1710; June 3, 1987, pp. 1016-28; *Debates*, October 30, 1986, p. 889.

tabling, normally the committee charged with overseeing the organization to which the individual has been appointed.

A Minister may also table a certificate of nomination to a non-judicial post.[519] Such notices are also referred to the standing committees specified at the time of tabling. Committees have 30 sitting days, following the day of tabling, in which to consider the appointments or nominations.[520] During that period, the committee may call the appointee or nominee to appear before it, for a period not to exceed 10 sitting days,[521] to answer questions respecting his or her qualifications and competence to perform the duties of the post to which he or she has been appointed or nominated.[522] Committees are under no obligation to consider any of the Order-in-Council appointments or nominations which have been referred to them.[523]

Upon written application from the clerk of a committee, the Minister's office must provide the *curriculum vitae* of any Order-in-Council appointee or nominee to any post which falls within the mandate of that standing committee.[524]

The scope of a committee's examination of Order-in-Council appointees or nominees is strictly limited to the qualifications and competence to perform the duties of the post.[525] Questioning by members of the committee may be interrupted by the Chair, if it attempts to deal with matters considered irrelevant to the committee's inquiry. Among the areas usually considered to be outside the scope of the committee's study are the political affiliation of the appointee or nominee, contributions to political parties and the nature of the nomination process itself.[526] Any

---

519. Standing Order 110(2). Nominations are made by Ministers to non-judicial posts in regulatory agencies such as the CRTC. As the wording of the Standing Order indicates, the tabling of certificates of nomination is at the Minister's discretion.

520. Standing Order 110. Where Order-in-Council appointments have been withdrawn from certain committees and referred to other committees, the 30-day period for the committee's study was deemed to have begun with the adoption of the order making the new referral. See, for example, *Debates*, October 30, 1986, p. 889. Committees have used the provisions of Standing Order 108(2) to examine Order-in-Council appointments. See, for example, Standing Committee on Environment, *Minutes of Proceedings and Evidence,* February 18, 1993, Issue No. 56, pp. 3-4; Standing Committee on Natural Resources and Government Operations, *Minutes*, June 4, 1998, Meeting No. 36.

521. Standing Order 111(1).

522. Standing Order 111(2).

523. See Speaker Fraser's ruling, *Debates*, December 11, 1986, p. 1998.

524. Standing Order 111(4).

525. Committees have examined ways in which the process can be used most effectively. See, for example, the Second Report of the Standing Committee on Health, *Minutes of Proceedings and Evidence*, September 29, 1994, Issue No. 13, pp. 3-9.

526. See, for example, Standing Committee on Government Operations, *Minutes of Proceedings and Evidence*, November 27, 1986, Issue No. 4, pp. 4-7; Standing Committee on Citizenship and Immigration, *Minutes of Proceedings and Evidence*, February 13, 1997, Issue No. 6, p. 2. See also Speaker Fraser's ruling, *Debates*, December 11, 1986, p. 1998.

question may be permitted if it can be shown that it relates directly to the appointee's or nominee's ability to do the job.

A committee has no power to revoke an appointment or nomination and may only report that they have examined the appointee or nominee and give their judgement as to whether the candidate has the qualifications and competence to perform the duties of the post to which he or she has been appointed or nominated.[527]

SUBJECT-MATTER STUDIES

Most standing committees are empowered to study and report on any matter relating to the operations and policies of government departments assigned to them. These committee-initiated studies may be directed towards: the relevant statute law; departmental or agency objectives; immediate, medium- and long-term expenditure plans; evaluations of activity against stated objectives; and any other matter relating to departmental or agency mandates or operations.[528] Certain standing committees, including standing joint committees, are accorded specific mandates to initiate studies in well-defined areas of responsibility outlined in the Standing Orders.[529]

A number of committees have permanent orders of reference which give rise to subject-matter studies having particular effect. The Standing Joint Committee for the Scrutiny of Regulations may present reports which initiate a procedure leading to the revocation of government regulations.[530] The Standing Committee on Procedure and House Affairs reports to the House on the selected items of Private Members' Business that have been designated as votable.[531]

As well, the House may strike a special committee[532] or, with the Senate, a special joint committee[533] to inquire into a particular subject matter. In such cases, the order of reference to the committee is usually included in the order which establishes the committee, although the House may refer additional matters to it at a later date.

The House may also refer specific matters to standing committees for consideration.[534] In particular, the House may refer questions arising out of a complaint of

---

527. Standing Order 111(2).

528. Standing Order 108(2). The power to initiate subject-matter studies was accorded to standing committees following the recommendations of the McGrath Committee. See the Third Report of the Special Committee on the Reform of the House of Commons, June 1985, pp. 16-17; *Journals*, February 6, 1986, pp. 1644-66, in particular pp. 1660-1; February 13, 1986, p. 1710.

529. Standing Order 108(3) and (4).

530. Standing Order 123. See Chapter 17, "Delegated Legislation".

531. Standing Orders 92 and 108(3)(*a*)(iv). See Chapter 21, "Private Members' Business".

532. See, for example, *Journals*, October 29, 1990, pp. 2182-3.

533. See, for example, *Journals*, February 23, 1994, pp. 186-7.

534. See, for example, *Journals*, February 8, 1994, pp. 132-4.

breach of privilege to the Standing Committee on Procedure and House Affairs.[535] The Committee will then conduct an inquiry, calling for whatever witnesses and papers it deems appropriate. As with matters related to privilege which occur in any other committee, the Standing Committee on Procedure and House Affairs has no power itself to deal with the matter directly by imposing sanctions of any kind. At the conclusion of its study, the Committee reports to the House, indicating whether, in its opinion, the complaint of breach of privilege was well founded. The Committee also stipulates what, if any, action it feels to be appropriate.[536]

A statute may also require subsequent review by a parliamentary committee of its provisions or operation, requiring the House to designate or establish a committee to carry out the review.[537]

Committees sometimes hold hearings not for the purpose of preparing recommendations for the House but simply in order to stay informed with respect to an important topic within their mandate.[538] In most cases, however, the committee will present a report to the House, outlining the evidence which it received, summarizing its deliberations and presenting its recommendations.

The actual conduct of a subject-matter study varies widely, depending on the topic and the approach selected by the committee. Typically, a committee will begin with a background briefing provided by the committee research staff or departmental officials.[539] The committee will then invite testimony and briefs from interested parties. During the evidence-gathering phase, the committee may travel to broaden the range of witnesses heard and to visit sites and facilities relevant to the study. Following the gathering of evidence, the committee will provide drafting instructions to the staff assigned to prepare the report. Once the draft report has been circulated to members, the committee will meet to consider it and propose any alterations necessary to accurately reflect the committee's views. Committees often consider draft reports at *in camera* meetings,[540] but reports are also considered in public session.[541] Once the committee has agreed to the final version of the report, it is presented to the House.[542]

---

535. See, for example, *Journals*, March 10, 1998, pp. 551-2.

536. See Chapter 3, "Privileges and Immunities".

537. See, for example, *An Act to amend the Canada Business Corporations Act and to make consequential amendments to other Acts,* S.C. 1994, c. 24, s. 33; *Journals*, October 1, 1997, p. 55.

538. See, for example, Standing Committee on Agriculture and Agri-Food, *Minutes*, October 22, 1998, Meeting No. 50.

539. See, for example, Standing Committee on Health, *Minutes* and *Evidence*, November 27, 1997, Meeting No. 7.

540. See, for example, Standing Committee on Health, *Minutes*, October 28, 1998, Meeting No. 51.

541. See, for example, Standing Committee on Procedure and House Affairs, *Minutes*, April 15, 1999, Meeting No. 61.

542. See section below, "Presentation in the House".

Reports to the House

Committees make their views and recommendations known to the House by way of reports. There are several types of reports that committees may present, including: reports dealing with routine matters affecting a committee's operation (such as requesting the extension of a deadline or permission to travel, or drawing the House's attention to irregularities in their proceedings); reports on bills, Estimates or Order-in-Council nominees or appointees; and reports following the completion of an inquiry into some matter referred by the House, or related to the mandate, management or operation of a committee's designated ministry or area of responsibility. This includes not only subject-matter studies but also such topics as the Public Accounts of Canada, delegated legislation and specific procedural issues, such as questions of privilege, referred by the House.

POWER TO REPORT

The power to report their findings to the House is essential to the role of committees. The Standing Orders provide standing committees with the power to report from time to time, enabling them to report to the House as often as they see fit.[543] A similar provision is usually included in the order of reference which establishes a special committee.[544] Legislative committees are only empowered to report the bill or bills referred to them with or without amendment.[545]

Committees are entitled to report to the House only with respect to matters within their mandate. When reporting to the House, committees must indicate the authority under which the study was done (i.e., the Standing Order or the order of reference). If the committee's report has exceeded or has been outside its order of reference, the Speaker has judged such a report, or the offending section, to be out of order.[546]

Although committees have conducted hearings for the sole purpose of receiving a briefing on a certain topic,[547] most committee studies result in reports to the House. A committee may present one or several reports related to a particular study. In addition to any administrative reports dealing with matters such as requests for additional

---

543. Standing Order 108(1)(*a*).

544. See, for example, *Journals*, November 18, 1997, pp. 224-5.

545. Standing Order 113(5). A legislative committee has presented a revised report, subsequent to its initial reporting of a bill to the House, in order to correct technical errors or omissions in the original report. See *Journals*, November 19, 1990, pp. 2260-1; November 21, 1990, pp. 2274-5; *Debates*, November 21, 1990, p. 15529.

546. See, for example, *Debates*, June 13, 1984, p. 4624; *Journals*, December 13, 1984, p. 188; December 14, 1984, p. 192; *Debates*, December 14, 1984, pp. 1242-3; February 28, 1985, pp. 2602-3.

547. See, for example, Standing Committee on Agriculture and Agri-food, *Minutes*, March 26, 1998, Meeting No. 29.

powers or an extension of the final reporting deadline,[548] the committee may present interim reports or a series of reports dealing with various aspects of the subject matter before it.[549]

Sub-committees present their reports to the main committee.[550] The main committee may simply adopt the sub-committee report as its own or amend it before doing so.[551] The report is then presented to the House as a report from the main committee.[552]

A committee may receive an order of reference which includes a reporting deadline. Both Main and Supplementary Estimates, as well as private Member's bills are deemed reported back to the House if the committee does not present its report within the time period set out in the Standing Orders.[553] While no time period is set out with respect to private bills, the Standing Orders require that they be reported to the House in every case.[554] In some cases, statutory reviews also carry reporting deadlines.[555] While a committee ordinarily reports on any matter referred to it by the House, unless the House sets out a specific deadline, the committee may report when it sees fit.[556]

Once committee members have agreed on the contents of the report, it is formally adopted by motion. The committee then specifies clearly and explicitly, by way of a motion, the format of the report.[557] In addition, the committee adopts another motion instructing the Chair to report it to the House.[558] As final changes to

---

548. See, for example, *Journals*, February 3, 1988, p. 2130 (legislative committee seeking travel authority); November 17, 1998, p. 1263 (special committee seeking extension of reporting deadline); March 11, 1999, p. 1593 (standing committee seeking travel authority).

549. For example, the Special Committee on the Reform of the House of Commons presented three substantive reports in the course of fulfilling its mandate. See *Journals*, December 20, 1984, p. 211; March 26, 1985, p. 420; June 18, 1985, p. 839.

550. Standing Order 108(1)(*a*) specifically denies standing committees the power to delegate direct reporting power to a sub-committee. A similar provision is usually included in the order of reference of a special committee. The House has, on occasion, given a sub-committee the power to report directly. See, for example, *Journals*, April 19, 1993, p. 2796.

551. See, for example, Standing Committee on Foreign Affairs and International Trade, *Minutes*, December 9, 1997, Meeting No. 20.

552. See, for example, *Journals*, December 11, 1997, p. 393.

553. See Standing Orders 81(4), (5) and 97.1.

554. Standing Order 141(5).

555. See, for example, *An Act to amend the Criminal Code (mental disorder) and to amend the National Defence Act and the Young Offenders Act in consequence thereof*, S.C. 1991, c. 43, s. 36. The order of reference designating the committee to carry out the statutory review does not usually make explicit reference to the deadline. See, for example, *Journals*, February 4, 1997, p. 1044.

556. See, for example, *Debates,* February 26, 1992, pp. 7620-4.

557. See Speaker Parent's ruling, *Debates*, November 24, 1994, pp. 8252-3.

558. See, for example, Standing Committee on Foreign Affairs and International Trade, *Minutes*, November 24, 1998, Meeting No. 81. The motion instructing the Chair to report to the House may be combined with the motion adopting the report. See, for example, Standing Committee on Aboriginal Affairs and Northern Development, *Minutes*, May 4, 1999, Meeting No. 62.

the report may have been made at the meeting prior to its adoption, it is also usual to adopt a motion giving editorial power to the Chair, to ensure that the final text of the report in both official languages is in conformity with the decisions taken by the committee, provided that no change be made to the substance of the report.[559] The committee may also adopt a motion, requesting that the government provide a response to the committee's report.[560] Finally, the committee may decide to hold a press conference, following the presentation of the report, to publicize the results of their study.[561]

CONTENTS AND FORMAT

Reports to the House can take a variety of formats depending on the subject matter under consideration and the conclusions which the committee has reached. Besides preparing printed versions of their reports, committees have presented reports in Braille, on audiocassette and computer diskette, and in large-print formats.[562] All substantive reports are posted in electronic format at each committee's website. All reports cite the authority under which the study was conducted (either the order of reference from the House or the appropriate Standing Order), and are signed by the Chair of the committee. The *Minutes of Proceedings* relevant to the report are tabled when the report is presented to the House.

Reports on certain subjects, such as the Estimates and Order-in-Council appointments, are restricted in the types of recommendations which can be proposed. In the case of the Estimates, the committee reports the Estimates as adopted, reduced or negatived. Reports on Order-in-Council appointments indicate that the committee has reviewed the appointment and states the committee's view of the qualifications and competence of the appointee. In consequence of this limited scope, reports on these subjects follow brief, established formats. In the case of legislation, the bill itself is reported back to the House, with or without amendments. When a bill is referred to committee, the actual House copy of the bill is delivered to the clerk of the committee. If the committee carries the bill without amendment, it is this copy which is returned to the House, suitably endorsed, as the committee's report. Where the committee has ordered a reprint of the bill, incorporating amendments made by the committee, a copy of the reprint is tabled together with the

---

559. See, for example, Standing Committee on Aboriginal Affairs and Northern Development, *Minutes*, May 4, 1999, Meeting No. 62. In 1968, the failure to report exactly what a committee had adopted was found to be a *prima facie* case of privilege by Speaker Lamoureux. See *Journals*, December 10, 1968, p. 513; February 13, 1969, pp. 695-6.

560. Standing Order 109. For further information, see section below, "Government Response".

561. See, for example, Standing Committee on Environment and Sustainable Development, *Minutes*, May 13, 1998, Meeting No. 52.

562. See, for example, *Journals*, June 16, 1993, p. 3318. Committees have also translated reports into languages other than English and French for distribution to particular audiences. See, for example, Standing Committee on Aboriginal Affairs and Northern Development, *Minutes*, May 4, 1999, Meeting No. 62.

original House copy of the bill. The reprinted copy of the bill clearly indicates the changes which the committee has made to the bill.

Committees also present a variety of procedural or administrative reports from time to time, seeking additional powers not provided in their permanent or special orders of reference. Where a possible breach of privilege related to a committee's work has occurred, the committee is not empowered to deal with the matter itself, but may report the incident to the House.[563]

Substantive Reports

Substantive reports, especially lengthy ones, are often prepared as printed documents with special covers. While committees have considerable latitude in the format of such reports, there are a number of elements which are normally included. The text of the report follows the citation of the authority under which the study was carried out. It outlines the issue or issues dealt with and often includes reference to appropriate portions of the submissions the committee received, both oral and written. For large studies, the text is usually divided into separate chapters, dealing with the various aspects of the subject. Following the text, the committee's recommendations on the subject are listed. Appendices are usually included, listing the witnesses heard and the briefs submitted in the course of the study. If the committee has chosen to request a government response to the report, the request is inserted before the Chair's signature at the end of the report. Any dissenting or supplementary opinions which the committee has agreed to attach appear after the Chair's signature. The relevant minutes of proceedings, relating to the committee's adoption of the report, conclude the document.[564]

Supplementary and Dissenting Opinions

A committee report reflects the opinion of the committee and not that of the individual members. Members of the committee who disagree with the decision of the majority may not present a separate report. There is no provision in the Standing Orders or the practices of the House for presenting minority reports.[565] Where one or several members of a standing committee are in disagreement with the committee's report or wish to make supplementary comments, the committee may decide to

---

563. Committees have reported concerning the revelation of *in camera* proceedings, and the failure of witnesses to appear or to produce papers required by the committee. See, for example, *Journals*, April 28-9, 1987, p. 791; May 13, 1987, p. 909.

564. Copies of the *Minutes* of all meetings relating to the report are tabled in the House along with the report itself. See, for example, *Journals*, May 31, 1999, p. 1968.

565. Speaker Parent pointed out in a 1994 ruling: "Regardless of how the media or members themselves may label such dissent, the House has never recognized or permitted the tabling of minority reports. Speaker Lamoureux twice condemned the idea of minority reports, explaining to the House that what is presented to the House from a committee is a report from the committee, not a report from the majority." See *Debates*, November 24, 1994, p. 8252.

append such opinions to the report,[566] after the signature of the Chair.[567] Dissenting or supplementary opinions may be presented by any member of a committee.[568] Although committees have the power to append these opinions to their reports, they are not obliged to do so.[569] In agreeing to append a dissenting or supplementary opinion, the committee will often specify the maximum length of the text, the deadline for submission to the clerk and whether it is to be submitted in one or both official languages.[570]

PRESENTATION IN THE HOUSE

Committee reports are presented during the Daily Routine of Business, when the Speaker calls, "Presenting Reports from Committees".[571] Reports are ordinarily

---

566. Standing Order 108(1)(a). Prior to the addition of this provision to the Standing Orders in 1991, only the committee report could be presented in the House, and there was no provision for appending the opinions of those members who differed from the majority. See *Journals*, April 11, 1991, pp. 2905-32, in particular p. 2924. On occasion, the House did give consent for dissenting opinions to be presented. See, for example, *Journals*, June 16, 1993, p. 3318; *Debates*, June 16, 1993, p. 20921. Although the current wording of the Standing Order restricts its application to standing committees, Speaker Parent has ruled that, unless the House explicitly directs otherwise, the practice of allowing it to apply to special committees as well will be permitted to continue. See *Debates*, November 24, 1994, p. 8252.

567. On November 16, 1994, Michel Gauthier (Roberval) raised a point of order respecting the receivability of the report of the Special Joint Committee Reviewing Canada's Foreign Policy. The dissenting opinions to the report had been printed in a separate volume from the report itself, and therefore did not immediately follow the Chair's signature. The Member argued that, in the absence of a decision by the Committee, there was no authority to print the report in that format. Speaker Parent ruled that the report's format did not contravene the spirit of the Standing Order, but expressed the view that committees should, in future, "ensure by means of explicit and carefully worded motions in keeping with the terms of Standing Order 108(1)(a) that their members are perfectly clear as to the format in which these reports will be presented to the House". See *Debates*, November 16, 1994, pp. 7859-62; November 24, 1994, pp. 28252-3.

568. Dissenting opinions have been presented by committee Chairs and Parliamentary Secretaries. See, for example, the Seventh Report of the Standing Committee on Public Accounts, March 31, 1998, and the First Report of the Standing Committee on Fisheries and Oceans, March 23, 1998.

569. Committees have negatived motions to append dissenting opinions. See, for example, Standing Committee on Procedure and House Affairs, *Minutes*, November 25, 1997, Meeting No. 7.

570. See, for example, Standing Committee on Environment and Sustainable Development, *Minutes*, May 13, 1998, Meeting No. 52.

571. Standing Orders 30(3) and 35. See Chapter 10, "The Daily Program". If the report relates to the Main Estimates of a department or agency for which consideration has been extended at the request of the Leader of the Opposition, the House may, on the last day provided for the presentation of the report, interrupt its proceedings and revert to "Presenting Reports from Committees" for that purpose (Standing Order 81(4)(c)). The *Centennial Flame Research Award Act*, adopted in 1991, requires the annual tabling of the research paper prepared by the winner of the award for the previous year. While the report is tabled by the Chair of the committee responsible for administering the Act (currently, the Standing Committee on Human Resources Development and the Status of Persons with Disabilities), it is not considered as a report of the Committee. As the Standing Orders do not make provision for the tabling of documents by Members other than Ministers and the Speaker, the presentation of the annual report has varied. It has been presented both under "Tabling of Documents" and "Presenting Reports from Committees", and it has also been filed with the Clerk pursuant to Standing Order 32(1). See S.C. 1991, c. 17, s. 7(1); *Journals*, June 14, 1993, p. 3204; December 13, 1994, p. 1043; April 23, 1997, pp. 1515-6; May 12, 1998, p. 775; June 10, 1999, p. 2090.

presented by the Chair, on instruction from the committee.[572] In the Chair's absence, a report may be presented by another member of the committee. The Member presenting a report may offer a brief explanation of its subject matter.[573] Where a report has supplementary or dissenting opinions appended to it, a committee member from the Official Opposition may offer a succinct explanation.[574] The Standing Orders do not permit any other Member to comment on the report at this time. Where no dissenting or supplementary opinion has been appended, no other Member is permitted to comment on the report when it is presented. On occasion, the House has granted consent to Members from other parties to make a brief statement either concerning a dissenting opinion or on the report itself.[575]

The House sometimes makes provision for the presentation of committee reports during adjournment periods, by having them filed with the Clerk of the House. This has been done both for individual reports and as a general provision for any committee reports completed during the adjournment period.[576]

Committee reports must be presented to the House before they can be released to the public. The majority of committee reports are discussed and adopted at *in camera* meetings. Even when a report is adopted in public session, the report itself is considered confidential until it has actually been presented in the House. In addition, where a committee report has been considered and approved during *in camera* committee meetings, any disclosure of the contents of a report prior to presentation, either by Members or non-Members, may be judged a breach of privilege. Speakers have ruled that questions of privilege concerning leaked reports will not be considered unless a specific charge is made against an individual, organization or group, and that the charge must be levelled not only against those outside the House who

---

572. See, for example, Standing Committee on Environment and Sustainable Development, *Minutes*, December 2, 1997, Meeting No. 23, and *Journals*, December 4, 1997, p. 332. Joint committees present their reports to both Houses. See, for example, *Journals*, June 7, 1999, p. 2060, and *Journals of the Senate*, June 3, 1999, p. 1669.

573. Standing Order 35(1). See, for example, *Debates*, May 7, 1999, p. 14885. This rule resulted from a recommendation of the McGrath Committee that "there should be a better method of bringing (reports) to the attention of the House". See Special Committee on the Reform of the House of Commons, Third Report, June 1985, p. 22.

574. Standing Order 35(2). See, for example, *Debates,* May 14, 1992, pp. 10691-2.

575. See, for example, *Debates*, December 1, 1997, pp. 2503-4; October 31, 1994, p. 7430.

576. See, for example, *Journals*, June 30, 1987, p. 1298; June 18, 1991, p. 219; June 11, 1999, p. 2102. By permitting presentation in this manner, the House enables committees to make their reports public at completion without breaching the privileges of the House or its Members. The House has, on occasion, made specific provision for making public a report prior to its presentation in the House. See, for example, *Journals*, December 22, 1982, pp. 5495-6.

have made *in camera* material public, but must also identify the source of the leak within the House itself.[577]

It is not in order for Members to allude to committee proceedings or evidence in the House until the committee has presented its report to the House. This restriction applies both to references made by Members in debate and during Oral Question Period.[578] If there is an irregularity in the committee's proceedings, the House can only be seized of it once it is reported to the House.[579]

Concurrence

Concurrence in a committee report may be moved by any Member of the House, after 48 hours' notice, during Routine Proceedings. The concurrence motion is moved under the heading "Motions"[580] and is debatable.[581]

A motion to concur in a report on the Estimates can only be debated on an allotted day under the Business of Supply.[582] The Standing Orders also provide a special procedure for concurrence in reports concerning the revocation of a regulation, contained in a report from the Standing Joint Committee for the Scrutiny of Regulations.[583] Where a bill has been reported back from committee, it is subject to the rules and practices governing the legislative process, rather than those relating to committee reports in general.[584]

The House frequently gives its consent to waive the 48 hours' notice required by the Standing Orders[585] in order to concur in a report concerning certain administrative matters, such as changes to the membership of committees. Reports concerning

577. See, for example, Speaker Parent's rulings, *Debates*, November 26, 1998, pp. 10467-8, and December 3, 1998, p. 10866. In response to concerns arising from the leaking of committee reports, the Standing Committee on Procedure and House Affairs studied the issue of confidentiality with respect to *in camera* proceedings and confidential committee documents. In its Seventy-Third Report, the Committee recommended that committees exercise discretion in deciding to meet *in camera*. It also recommended that the reasons for such meetings should be made public, either on the notice of meeting or by the Chair in public session and that the Standing Orders be amended to reiterate that committee reports adopted at *in camera* meetings are confidential until presented in the House. See *Journals*, April 29, 1999, p. 1785.

578. See, for example, *Debates*, September 29, 1994, p. 6314; April 19, 1996, p. 1711.

579. See Speakers' rulings, *Journals*, July 1, 1919, p. 498; March 31, 1969, pp. 873-4.

580. See, for example, *Journals*, April 26, 1999, p. 1766.

581. Standing Order 67(1)(*b*).

582. Standing Order 81(9).

583. See Chapter 17, "Delegated Legislation".

584. See Chapter 16, "The Legislative Process", and Chapter 21, "Private Members' Business".

585. See, for example, *Journals*, June 1, 1999, p. 2032.

the selection of votable items of Private Members' Business and the membership of legislative committees are deemed adopted when presented in the House.[586]

Recommendations in committee reports are drafted in the form of motions so that, if the reports are concurred in, the recommendations become clear orders or resolutions of the House.[587] In framing their recommendations, committees cannot exceed the authority of the House. Most importantly, with respect to the expenditure of funds or the introduction of legislation, committees may recommend only that the government "consider the advisability" of such measures.[588]

When a motion to concur in a report is before the House, it is the concurrence in the report as a whole which the House is considering. No amendment may be presented to the text of the report.[589] A motion may be presented to recommit the report to the committee so that the report may be re-examined.[590]

Government Response

When a report is presented in the House, a standing or special committee may request that the government table a comprehensive response to it within 150 days.[591] The committee may request a response either to the whole report or to one or more parts.[592] The request for a partial response does not prevent the government from responding to the entire report. Speakers have consistently refused to define "comprehensive" in this context, maintaining that the nature of the response must be left to the discretion of the government.[593] When the House is sitting, the response may be tabled by a Minister or a Parliamentary Secretary during Routine Proceedings under "Tabling of Documents" or filed with the Clerk.[594] When the House is adjourned, the response may be filed with the Clerk, or the Minister may wait until

---

586. Standing Orders 92(2) and 113(1).

587. Recommendations not clearly in the form of motions may require further action in order to be implemented. See Speaker Parent's ruling, *Debates*, November 5, 1998, p. 9923.

588. See Speaker Lamoureux's rulings, *Journals*, March 31, 1969, pp. 873-4; April 10, 1973, pp. 257-8.

589. See Speaker Bosley's ruling, *Debates*, December 13, 1985, p. 9476.

590. See, for example, *Journals*, March 18, 1987, p. 610. Following Confederation, amendments to the text of committee reports were occasionally permitted in the House. See, for example, *Journals*, June 21, 1869, p. 304; March 26, 1884, p. 285. In 1919, Speaker Rhodes ruled that it was not in order for the House to amend the report itself. See *Journals*, May 22, 1919, pp. 293-4. Further details on the recommital of bills are given in Chapter 16, "The Legislative Process".

591. Standing Order 109. This provision was added to the Standing Orders following a recommendation in the Third Report of the Lefebvre Committee. See Special Committee on Standing Orders and Procedure, *Minutes of Proceedings and Evidence*, November 4, 1982, Issue No. 7, pp. 21, 29; *Journals*, November 29, 1982, p. 5400.

592. See *Debates*, May 13, 1986, p. 13232.

593. See, for example, *Debates*, April 21, 1986, p. 12480; June 29, 1987, pp. 7749-50; September 24, 1987, pp. 9266-8.

594. Standing Order 32(1). See, for example, *Journals*, March 26, 1998, p. 636; October 5, 1998, p. 118.

the House resumes sitting to table it.[595] The Speaker has ruled that a request for a government response survives a prorogation in the same manner as orders for the production of papers.[596] The Standing Orders do not provide for any sanction should the government fail to comply with the requirement to present a response.[597]

595. See, for example, *Journals*, September 24, 1990, p. 1976; September 21, 1998, p. 1054. For further information on the tabling of documents, see Chapter 10, "The Daily Program".

596. See *Debates*, June 27, 1986, p. 14969. See also Standing Order 49. However, the request lapses on dissolution of a Parliament. Committees have renewed a request for a government response by presenting a report to that effect in the subsequent Parliament. See, for example, *Journals*, November 27, 1997, p. 275.

597. See, for example, *Debates*, September 10, 1992, p. 12977.

21

Private Members' Business

If the private member is to count for anything, there must be a relationship between what the private member and the institution of Parliament can do and what the electorate thinks or expects can be done.

THIRD REPORT OF THE SPECIAL COMMITTEE
ON THE REFORM OF THE HOUSE
(McGrath Committee), June 1985, p. 2

"Private Members" are generally defined as Members of the House of Commons who are not part of the Ministry.[1] While there is no rule specifically excluding Parliamentary Secretaries from this designation, the practice is for them to abstain from sponsoring items under Private Members' Business.[2] In general, Presiding Officers of the

---

1. For information on the Ministry, see Chapter 1, "Parliamentary Institutions". On October 23, 1996, after Don Boudria (Glengarry–Prescott–Russell) was appointed to the Ministry, Speaker Parent directed the Clerk to remove from the *Order Paper* a motion standing in Mr. Boudria's name on the order of precedence for Private Members' Business (*Debates*, p. 5630).

2. Upon being appointed as a Parliamentary Secretary, Members have withdrawn or requested a change in the sponsorship of an item of Private Members' Business brought before the House prior to their appointment (see, for example, *Debates*, April 19, 1988, p. 14634; September 19, 1988, p. 19402; *Journals*, October 28, 1998, p. 1205).

House have also abstained from sponsoring or pursuing private Members' bills or motions.[3]

Each sitting day, one hour is set aside for Private Members' Business, that is, for the consideration of bills and motions presented and sponsored by private Members. Private Members may use the time allotted for the consideration of Private Members' Business to put forth their own legislative and policy proposals, and express their views on a variety of issues.[4] Private Members' proposals can take the form of a bill (either public or private), a motion, or a notice of motion for the production of papers.

A private Member's bill is the text of a legislative initiative sponsored by a private Member. Based on private Members' own ideas and drafted with the aid of legislative counsel, such bills are brought forward by the sponsoring Member. Like government bills, private Members' bills become statutes once they receive Royal Assent.[5] Most private Members' bills are public bills originating in the Commons, but some public bills, and occasionally private bills, sponsored by private Members come to the Commons from the Senate.[6]

A private Member's motion typically proposes that the House declare its opinion on some topic or that the House order a certain course of action to be taken, either by the House itself, or by one of its committees or officers.

A notice of motion for the production of papers is a request that the government compile or produce certain papers or documents and table them in the House.[7]

---

3. For examples of private Members' bills sponsored by Presiding Officers, see *Journals*, October 29, 1970, p. 65 (Gérald Laniel was Deputy Chairman of Committees of the Whole); October 31, 1977, pp. 52-3 (Charles Turner was Deputy Chairman of Committees of the Whole); October 24, 1979, pp. 109, 111, 119 (William C. Scott was Assistant Deputy Chairman of Committees of the Whole); November 28, 1996, p. 935 (Peter Milliken was Deputy Chairman of Committees of the Whole). The sponsorship of another bill standing in the name of Mr. Milliken was transferred to another Member (*Debates*, February 19, 1997, p. 8318).

4. Some important issues first raised by private Members have later reappeared in government legislation. See, for example, Bill C-279, *An Act to amend the Official Languages Act (tabling of documents)* introduced by Jean-Robert Gauthier (Ottawa–Vanier), *Debates*, June 6, 1988, pp. 16179-81.

5. With the exception of bills dealing with changes to the names of electoral districts, relatively few private Members' bills receive Royal Assent. Between 1945 and 1993, 127 private Members' public bills received Royal Assent; only 31 of those bills did not deal with changes to the names of constituencies.

6. Public bills sponsored by Members and introduced first in the House of Commons are numbered consecutively from C-201 to C-1000 in the order of introduction, whereas bills originating in the Senate are numbered from S-1, there being no distinction made as to whether it is a government or private Member's bill.

7. For more information, see Chapter 10, "The Daily Program".

Historical Perspective

FROM 1867 TO 1984

Time Reserved for Private Members' Business

In the early years of Confederation, a large proportion of the time of the House was devoted to private bills or to private Members. In 1867, the Standing Orders gave precedence to Private Members' Business on particular days in each week.[8] However, governments found such a distribution inadequate for the conduct of their own legislative programs, and regularly gave precedence to their own business via special and sessional orders.

Over the years, changes were made to the Standing Orders to give more House time to the government for its own business. By 1906, this pattern had established itself to such a degree that, in that year, the weekly order of business was officially amended so that after four weeks from the start of each session, one of the three private Members' days—Thursday—was given over to government business.[9]

Between 1906 and 1955, the use of special and sessional orders to give precedence to government business had appropriated virtually all the time remaining from private Members. In 1955, amendments to the Standing Orders once again formalized the practice of giving precedence to government business: the number of private Members' days was reduced from each Monday, Wednesday and four Thursdays per session to six Mondays and two Thursdays per session.[10] Depending on the length of each session, this change at least guaranteed that these eight days would not be further nullified by the suspension of private Members' time through the use of special or sessional orders.

In 1962, the House abandoned the allocation of a certain number of days each session for Private Members' Business and, instead, set aside one hour per day for that purpose. However, after this hour had been used 40 times per session, its use on Monday, Tuesday and Wednesday would lapse and Private Members' Business would take place only on Thursday and Friday thereafter.[11] In 1968, Private Members' Business was removed from the order of business on Wednesday, and the rule establishing a maximum 40 considerations per session was retained for Monday and Tuesday only; thereafter, Private Members' Business was only held on Thursday and Friday.[12]

In 1982, the practice of considering Private Members' Business for one hour on certain days was replaced by a single private Members' day on Wednesday. This

---

8. Only Tuesday and Friday were reserved for government business. See *Rules, Orders and Forms of Proceeding of the House of Commons*, 1868, Rule No. 19.

9. *Debates*, July 9, 1906, cols. 7475-7.

10. *Journals*, July 12, 1955, pp. 889, 893, 945.

11. *Journals*, April 10, 1962, pp. 338-9; April 12, 1962, p. 350.

12. *Journals*, December 6, 1968, pp. 429, 436-7; December 20, 1968, pp. 554, 563-5.

resulted in a reduction of one hour of debating time per week, from four hours to three.[13] In late 1983, however, the House reverted to the consideration of Private Members' Business for one hour per day on Monday, Tuesday, Thursday and Friday, without the previous provision for a maximum number of times for consideration on Monday and Tuesday.[14] The omission of this part of the former rule meant that the amount of time provided for Private Members' Business actually increased. (Further changes to the Standing Orders, adopted in April 1991, increased the number of Private Members' Business days from four to five per week, adding an extra hour to the sitting on Wednesday.[15])

Precedence of Items

From Confederation until the late 1950s, the two criteria which determined the order in which items of Private Members' Business were considered were their date of notice and, in the case of bills, their stage in the legislative process. During this period as well, secondary criteria, aimed primarily at distinguishing the different categories of business from one another, also became important.

In 1910, for example, an amendment to the Standing Orders[16] established a higher precedence for unopposed Private Members' Notices of Motions for the Production of Papers. Meanwhile, opposed motions of this kind continued to be considered with other notices of motions until 1961, when they were given a specific category ("Notices of Motions (Papers)") in the order of business and were debated on a designated day.[17]

Similarly, rule changes in 1927 limited each Member to one notice of motion on the *Order Paper* at any one time. Such notices would be dropped from the *Order Paper* if called twice and not proceeded with.[18] In addition, other rules allowed private Members' bills or notices of motions to stand over from one day to the next.[19] These kinds of exceptions to the usual chronological, stage-based ordering, coupled with frequent changes to the day-by-day order of business, eventually led to a fixed sequencing of items for each category of Private Members' Business.[20]

13. The Third Report of the Special Committee on Standing Orders and Procedure, which recommended these changes, was presented to the House on November 5, 1982 (*Journals,* p. 5328), and the motion putting into effect the changes was adopted on November 29, 1982 (*Journals,* p. 5400).

14. The First Report of the Special Committee on Standing Orders, which recommended these changes, was presented to the House on December 15, 1983 (*Journals,* p. 47), and the motion putting into effect the changes was adopted on December 19, 1983 (*Journals,* pp. 55-6).

15. *Journals*, April 11, 1991, pp. 2905-6, 2908.

16. *Journals*, April 29, 1910, pp. 535-7.

17. *Journals*, September 26, 1961, pp. 950, 953; September 27, 1961, p. 957.

18. *Journals,* March 22, 1927, pp. 340-1.

19. See, for example, *Standing Orders of the House of Commons,* 1927, Standing Order 27.

20. See, for example, the day-by-day order of business for 1955 and 1962.

Throughout this period, the volume of Private Members' Business increased, leading to further innovations in procedure. In 1958, Speaker Michener instituted a ballot system for notices of motions.[21] One notice per Member could be submitted at the start of a session and placed in a container. In the presence of the Speaker, the Clerk, and the representatives of the parties, notices of motions were drawn to establish a sequence for consideration. Notices given after the draw were placed on the *Order Paper* after those which had been drawn.

At the start of a subsequent session, a similar practice was extended to private Members' public bills. There were now two draws: one for notices of motions and one for bills. In the latter case, however, each Member could give notice of several bills, there being no limit as with notices of motions. In either case, when an item had been considered but not disposed of, it fell to the bottom of the list. Notices of motions called twice and not proceeded with were dropped from the *Order Paper,* as before.

Members soon realized that by placing several bills on notice, their chances in the draw improved. Inevitably, this approach resulted in some Members receiving more House time than others. To ensure a more equitable distribution, the party Whips limited Members to one bill in the first 50 bills drawn. In a separate development begun in the 1970s, the business to be considered during Private Members' Business was organized by the Office of the Government House Leader, a practice criticized by some Members as undue government interference. Eventually, the Clerk of the House became responsible for the organization of this part of House Business.[22]

The last major change prior to the adoption of the current system for precedence occurred in 1982, when all categories of Private Members' Business (except private bills) were combined into one group, for which a single draw of Members' names was held at the start of each session. A limitation, similar to that which had previously applied to bills, was retained for the first 50 items drawn and, at the same time, the limit of one notice of motion per Member was lifted.[23]

SINCE 1984

The modern rules relating to the conduct of Private Members' Business developed largely from recommendations of the Special Committee on the Reform of the

---

21. Such a procedure was initially proposed in 1925 (*Journals,* May 29, 1925, p. 359).

22. *Debates,* November 28, 1979, p. 1794.

23. The Third Report of the Special Committee on Standing Orders and Procedure, which recommended these changes, was presented to the House on November 5, 1982 (*Journals,* p. 5328), and the motion putting into effect the changes was adopted on November 29, 1982 (*Journals,* p. 5400).

House of Commons (the "McGrath Committee"), established in December 1984. In its final report to the House in June 1985, the Committee made the following observations:

> *The House does not attach any great importance to private members' business as it is now organized (...) members are seldom greatly concerned to claim the priorities they have drawn in the ballot governing the use of private members' time, and this is largely because private members' bills and motions rarely come to a vote.*[24]

The subsequent recommendations in the report resulted in Standing Order amendments adopted provisionally after lengthy debate in the House in February 1986.[25] These amendments to the Standing Orders formed the basis for the modern rules relating to Private Members' Business—the establishment of the order of precedence, the process for determining which items should be made votable, and the manner in which items would be debated. Since February 1986, a number of further adjustments have been made to the rules.

In response to problems caused by the absence of Members whose items were scheduled for debate, a special order was adopted in December 1986 allowing the Speaker to exchange non-votable items should one Member notify the Chair that he or she cannot be present in the House when his or her item is due for consideration.[26]

In June 1987, the provisional Standing Orders were made permanent and other changes were adopted in regard to the order in which items of Private Members' Business were considered.[27] The Speaker was given the power to exchange a non-votable item of a Member who cannot be present with a similar item of a Member who can. In addition, the *Order Paper* was changed to contain all types of items in one list, including private bills and private Members' public bills originating in the Senate.

In 1989, the House adopted a motion to have the Standing Committee on Elections, Privileges, Procedure and Private Members' Business consider and report on various practices and procedures relating to the conduct of Private Members' Business.[28] On December 6, 1989, the Committee presented its Seventh Report, which included several recommendations regarding such matters as the selection of items for the order of precedence, the selection of votable items, and the time limit for debate on votable items.[29] Although the report was not concurred in, it did form the basis of Standing Order amendments adopted on May 10, 1990.[30]

---

24. See the Special Committee on the Reform of the House of Commons, Third Report, p. 40. The Report was presented to the House on June 18, 1985 (*Journals,* p. 839).

25. *Journals*, February 6, 1986, pp. 1648-52; February 13, 1986, p. 1710.

26. *Journals*, December 18, 1986, p. 351.

27. *Journals*, June 3, 1987, pp. 1020-2.

28. *Journals*, October 26, 1989, p. 752.

29. *Journals*, pp. 927-34.

30. *Journals*, pp. 1685-7.

There were several significant changes to the Standing Orders, as recommended by the Standing Committee: Members' names rather than individual items would be drawn, which meant that Members with one motion or bill would have the same chances as those with several motions or bills; separate lists of bills and motions were established, and the number of votable items was set at three bills and three motions; the time for debate on votable items was reduced from five hours to three; and Private Members' Business was suspended on Supply days. The amendments were adopted on a provisional basis until the last sitting day in December 1990.

In December 1990, the Standing Committee on Privileges and Elections, after reviewing the success of the provisional Standing Orders that had been approved in May 1990, recommended in its Twenty-First Report that they be made permanent.[31] It went on to propose a number of other changes, including the exchange of votable items, Private Members' Hour on Monday, and the deferral of any recorded division with respect to Private Members' Business at the request of the Whips. Further changes to the Standing Orders governing Private Members' Business adopted on April 11, 1991, which were largely based on the Twenty-First Report of the Committee, clarified the procedures to be followed in the draw to select items for debate, reduced the number of hours for debate on an item, increased the number of days per week on which Private Members' Business would be considered, and refined the process to be followed for an exchange of items to be debated during Private Members' Hour.[32]

On April 29, 1992, two reports of the Standing Committee on House Management were adopted, thereby amending the Standing Orders to increase the number of votable items and the total number of items on the order of precedence and to clarify the procedures to be followed for deferring recorded divisions on items of Private Members' Business.[33] With the adoption of the Twenty-Fourth Report[34] regarding recorded divisions on private Members' bills or motions, it became the practice for the vote of the sponsoring Member to be recorded first, and then the rest of the votes on that side of the chamber to be recorded before proceeding to the other side. With the adoption of the Twenty-Seventh Report, the order of precedence was increased from 20 to 30 items, draws were to be held before the list dropped below 15 items instead of 10, and the maximum number of votable items increased from three bills and three motions to five of each.[35]

---

31. *Journals*, December 6, 1990, pp. 2385-8.

32. *Journals*, April 11, 1991, pp. 2919-22.

33. *Journals*, April 29, 1992, pp. 1337-8.

34. Standing Committee on House Management, *Minutes of Proceedings and Evidence,* February 11 and 13, 1992, Issue No. 24, p. 17.

35. Standing Committee on House Management, *Minutes of Proceedings and Evidence,* March 12, 1992, Issue No. 26, p. 3.

In 1998, the reference to five bills and five motions was removed so that the reference is now only to ten votable items, and a new procedure was established allowing for a specific item supported by 100 Members to be added to the order of precedence.[36]

Private Members' Bills

Bills sponsored by private Members fall into two categories, public bills and private bills. Public bills deal with matters of public policy under federal jurisdiction, whereas private bills concern matters of a private or special interest to specific corporations and individuals and are designed to grant the beneficiary power to do something which cannot be done otherwise or to exempt the beneficiary from some existing legal obligation. Procedures relating to public bills are discussed in this chapter while those concerning private bills are dealt with in Chapter 23, "Private Bills Practice".

A private Member's bill is typically drafted with the assistance of legislative counsel to ensure that the text conforms with statutory law should it be given Royal Assent. In drafting each legislative proposal, legislative counsel act on Members' clear, written instructions about the purposes and objectives of the proposed legislation and ensure that draft bills are acceptable in terms of their form and compliance with legislative and parliamentary conventions. A private Member's bill is certified by legislative counsel to indicate that the bill is in correct form. The certified copy of the bill is then returned to the Member.

Members also have the option of proposing a motion to have a bill prepared by a standing, special or legislative committee.[37] If such a motion is selected following the draw to establish the order of precedence, it is debated during Private Members' Hour. If selected as a votable motion and later adopted, it becomes an order for a committee to prepare and bring in a bill. If the committee prepares and reports a bill

---

36. *Journals*, November 30, 1998, pp. 1327-9.

37. Standing Order 68(4)(*b*). Prior to this Standing Order being adopted on February 7, 1994 (*Journals,* pp. 112-20), and coming into effect on February 14, 1994, the idea of private Members proposing motions to have a committee prepare a bill did exist (see Speaker Lamoureux's ruling, *Debates*, November 10, 1969, pp. 665-6). For examples of private Members' motions for a committee to bring in a bill, see *Notice Paper*, September 24, 1997, p. XI (M-15); September 29, 1997, p. IV (M-168); November 5, 1997, p. III (M-260). A few of these motions have been placed on the order of precedence (*Order Paper*, October 2, 1997, p. 19 (M-24); May 1, 1998, p. 21 (M-251)). Some of these motions have also been selected as votable (*Order Paper*, October 23, 1997, p. 16 (M-123); May 3, 1999, p. 30 (M-265)). No committee has ever prepared a bill pursuant to a private Member's motion adopted under the terms of Standing Order 68(4)(*b*). However, the adoption of a private Member's motion (penalties for impaired driving) during Private Members' Business (*Journals*, February 7, 1997, pp. 1092-3) eventually led to the adoption of a motion moved by a Minister instructing a committee to prepare a bill in accordance with Standing Order 68(4)(*a*) (*Journals*, October 30, 1997, p. 175). When the committee finally presented its report to the House, a draft bill was included (*Journals*, May 25, 1999, p. 1905).

to the House, a motion to concur in the committee's report may be moved by a private Member during Private Members' Hour if the concurrence motion has also been selected following the draw to establish the order of precedence. However, if a Minister were to move concurrence in the report, the motion would be taken up during Government Orders.[38] The adoption of the motion for concurrence in the committee report constitutes an order to bring in a bill based on the committee's report. If the bill is sponsored by a private Member and is subsequently selected to be votable, when the motion for second reading is proposed to the House, the Speaker immediately puts all questions to dispose of the second reading stage without debate or amendment.[39] If it is not designated votable, the bill is debated for one hour and dropped from the *Order Paper*. If a Minister undertakes to sponsor the bill, it is considered during Government Orders and all questions to dispose of second reading are also put without debate or amendment.

FINANCIAL LIMITATIONS

There is a constitutional requirement that bills proposing the expenditure of public funds must be accompanied by a royal recommendation, which can be obtained only by the government and introduced by a Minister. Since a Minister cannot propose items of Private Members' Business, a private Members' bill should therefore not contain provisions for the spending of funds. However, since 1994, a private Member may introduce a public bill containing provisions requiring the expenditure of public funds provided that a royal recommendation is obtained by a Minister before the bill is read a third time and passed.[40] Before 1994, the royal recommendation had to accompany the bill at the time of its introduction. The Speaker is responsible for

---

38. Standing Order 68(4)(*a*).

39. Standing Order 68(6) and 68(7)(*b*).

40. Standing Order 79(2). See the Twenty-Seventh Report of the Standing Committee on Procedure and House Affairs concurred in by the House on June 10, 1994 (*Journals*, p. 563). For an example of a private Member's bill to which a royal recommendation was attached prior to third reading, see *Journals*, December 6, 1994, p. 997. Bill C-216, *An Act to amend the Unemployment Insurance Act (jury service)*, had been reported back to the House from committee on June 16, 1994, and debate at the third reading stage began on December 6, 1994. The bill was given Royal Assent on March 26, 1995. There have been numerous Speakers' rulings regarding bills and their potential need for an accompanying royal recommendation if the bill involved a charge on the public treasury (see, for example, *Journals*, November 9, 1978, pp. 130-3; February 20, 1979, pp. 393-5; June 6, 1980, pp. 244-5). See also *Debates*, November 1, 1991, pp. 4410-4, where the Chair heard arguments regarding the procedural acceptability of a private Member's bill requiring the expenditure of public funds. One Member argued that on the basis of a ruling made in 1912 (*Journals*, January 16, 1912, pp. 118-9), clauses can be inserted into bills that will prevent funds from being expended unless Parliament appropriates money for the purpose set out in the bill. Because the bill had not been selected to come to a vote, proceedings on the bill expired at the end of Private Members' Hour, and the Speaker never returned to the House with a definitive ruling.

determining whether any bill requires a royal recommendations and the Speaker is empowered to decline to put the necessary questions on bills which require, but have not received, a royal recommendation.[41]

With respect to the raising of revenue, a private Member cannot introduce bills which impose taxes. The power to initiate taxation rests solely with the government and any legislation which seeks an increase in taxation must be preceded by a Ways and Means motion.[42] Only a Minister can bring in a Ways and Means motion. However, private Members' bills which reduce taxes, reduce the incidence of a tax, or impose or increase an exemption from taxation are acceptable.[43]

NOTICE

Once a bill has been drafted, the Member must give 48 hours' notice of his or her intention to introduce the bill, indicating the committee to which the bill will be referred following second reading. The title of the bill and the name of its sponsor are then published in the *Notice Paper*. After the 48-hour notice period has expired, the bill may then be introduced during Routine Proceedings and given first reading whenever the Member is ready to proceed.[44]

SIMILAR ITEMS

If a Member submits notice of a bill which is judged to be substantially the same as another item of Private Members' Business already submitted, the Speaker has the discretionary power to refuse the most recent notice. If the Speaker refuses the notice, the sponsoring Member is advised and the bill is returned.[45] This is intended to prevent a number of similar items from being selected following the draw for the order of precedence. In a 1989 ruling, Speaker Fraser clarified that for two or more items to be substantially the same, they must have the same purpose and they have to achieve their same purpose by the same means.[46] Thus, there could be several bills addressing the same subject, but if their approaches to the issue are different, the Chair could deem them to be sufficiently distinct.

The question has arisen whether a private Member's bill which is similar to a government bill may be placed on the *Order Paper* and debated. The authorities and past rulings show that there is nothing to prevent such similar items from being

---

41. For additional information on the royal recommendation, see Chapter 16, "The Legislative Process", and Chapter 18, "Financial Procedures".

42. *Beauchesne*, 6th ed., p. 265. See also Speaker Parent's ruling, *Debates*, December 2, 1998, pp. 10788-91.

43. *May*, 21st ed., p. 716; *Beauchesne,* 6th ed., p. 267.

44. For information on notices, see Chapter 12, "The Process of Debate".

45. Standing Order 86(5).

46. *Debates*, November 2, 1989, pp. 5474-5.

placed on the *Order Paper* simultaneously. However, because the House cannot take more than one decision on any given matter during a session, a decision on any one of these bills (for example, the adoption or rejection of the second reading motion) will prevent further proceedings on any other similar bills.[47] Consideration of non-votable bills, if dropped from the *Order Paper* after debate, does not preclude consideration of other similar, or even identical, bills since the House does not take a decision on non-votable items.[48]

SECONDERS

A Member who would like to support a bill already appearing on the *Order Paper* may notify the Clerk of the House in writing that he or she wishes to second the bill. The names of the Members wishing to support the bill will be added to the list of seconders on the *Order Paper*.[49] Once the order for second reading has been proposed to the House, no additional names may be appended.[50] No more than 20 Members may jointly second an item under Private Members' Business.[51] The Member who seconds the motions for introduction and first reading of the bill in the House, as well as subsequent stages, need not be one of the seconders listed on the *Order Paper*.

INTRODUCTION AND FIRST READING OF PRIVATE MEMBERS' BILLS

To be eligible for selection following the draw for the order of precedence, private Members' bills must be introduced and given first reading in the House before the draw is held. On the day the Member chooses to introduce the bill, he or she rises during Routine Proceedings when the Speaker calls "Introduction of Private Members' Bills".[52] The Speaker then announces the title of the bill and the motion for leave to introduce the bill is automatically deemed carried, without debate, amendment or question put.[53] The Member is permitted to give a succinct explanation

---

47. *Bourinot*, 4th ed., pp. 547-8. See also Speaker Michener's rulings, *Journals*, October 29, 1957, p. 64; March 13, 1959, p. 238.

48. For example, Bill C-321, which was identical to Bill C-274, was introduced on June 20, 1996, after Bill C-274 was debated at second reading and dropped from the *Order Paper* on June 4, 1996 (*Journals*, June 4, 1996, pp. 486-7; June 20, 1996, p. 592).

49. The list of 20 seconders should not be confused with the 100 signatures of Members who support an item in order that it be placed on the order of precedence (Standing Order 87(6)).

50. Standing Order 86(4).

51. Standing Order 86(3).

52. In order to facilitate the proceedings, Members usually advise the Speaker or the Table Officers in advance that they wish to introduce a bill or bills on a particular day.

53. Standing Order 68(2).

outlining the purpose of the bill.[54] Since no debate is permitted at this time, the Member often simply reads the explanatory note in the bill. The bill is then deemed read a first time and ordered to be printed, also without debate, amendment or question put.[55]

The bill is then transferred to the list of "Private Members' Business—Items Outside the Order of Precedence". This list of items, which may be consulted at the Table in the Chamber or on the electronic version of the *Order Paper,* does not actually appear in the printed publication of the *Order Paper.* Having been placed on this list, the bill is set down for second reading and reference to a committee. When submitting a bill for inclusion on the *Notice Paper,* the sponsor must indicate the standing, special or legislative committee to which the bill is to be referred following second reading. A two-week period must elapse between the first and second reading of the bill.[56]

SENATE PUBLIC BILLS SPONSORED BY PRIVATE MEMBERS

Some private Members' public bills originate in the Senate and are sent to the Commons after passage by the Senate. When the Speaker calls "First Reading of Senate Public Bills" during Routine Proceedings, the Member sponsoring a Senate bill in the House is permitted to give a brief explanation of its purpose, without engaging in debate. The motion for first reading is then deemed carried without debate, amendment or question put, and the bill is automatically added to the bottom of the order of precedence for Private Members' Business without having gone through the draw process.[57]

Private Members' Motions

Private Members' motions are used to introduce a wide range of issues and are framed either as orders or resolutions, depending on their intent.[58] Motions attempting to make a declaration of opinion or purpose, without ordering or requiring a

---

54. While a succinct explanation has traditionally been interpreted to mean 30-60 seconds, it has become more common for Members to speak for longer than 60 seconds since the beginning of the Thirty-Fifth Parliament (1994-97).

55. Standing Order 69(1).

56. Standing Order 88.

57. Since the beginning of 1990, only two Senate public bills sponsored by private Members have received Royal Assent (*Journals*, December 17, 1990, p. 2475; June 22, 1995, p. 1871).

58. Private Members' motions can also propose constitutional amendments. See, for example, Motion M-8 which proposed an amendment to the *Constitution Act* to include property rights (*Journals*, May 2, 1988, pp. 2602-3).

particular course of action, are considered resolutions.[59] Hence, such motions which simply suggest that the government initiate a certain measure are generally phrased as follows: "That, in the opinion of this House, the government should consider …". The government is not bound to adopt a specific policy or course of action as a result of the adoption of such a resolution since the House is only stating an opinion or making a declaration of purpose.[60] This is in contrast to those motions whose object is to give a direction to committees, Members or officers of the House or to regulate House proceedings and, as such, are considered orders once adopted by the House.[61]

No motion sponsored by a Member who is not a Minister can contain provisions for either raising revenue or spending funds, unless it is worded in terms which only suggest that course of action to the government. As an alternative to a bill which might require a royal recommendation obtained only by a Minister, a private Member may choose to move a motion proposing the expenditure of public funds, provided that the terms of the motion only suggest this course of action to the government without ordering or requiring it to do so.[62] Such a motion is normally phrased so as to ask the government to "consider the advisability of …".

NOTICE

A private Member must provide at least two weeks' notice of his or her intention to move a motion.[63] Notice of a private Member's motion appears on the *Notice Paper* for the date on which notice is given and is transferred afterwards to the list of "Private Members' Business—Items Outside the Order of Precedence" which may be consulted at the Table in the Chamber or on the electronic version of the *Order*

---

59. For examples of motions as resolutions, see *Journals,* June 15, 1994, pp. 592-3 (M-89 on non-confidence motions); October 25, 1995, p. 2049 (M-273 on Grandparents' Day); November 5, 1996, p. 831 (M-30 on a Care-Giver Tax Credit); December 4, 1996, p. 964 (M-241 on hazardous materials); May 25, 1998, pp. 887-9 (M-261 on a National Head-Start Program). See also Speaker Parent's rulings on Motion M-266 requesting a conference with the Senate, *Debates,* June 18, 1996, pp. 3981-2; and on Motion M-1 containing allegations of contempt against another Member, *Debates,* June 18, 1996, pp. 4028-31; June 20, 1996, pp. 4183-4.

60. Although the government may not be bound by only an expression of opinion, the adoption of such motions carries the weight of a decision of the House. In the latter half of the 1980s, three statues were erected on Parliament Hill as a result of the adoption of private Members' motions which were framed as resolutions (see *Journals*, February 28, 1985, p. 340 (Rt. Hon. John G. Diefenbaker); February 10, 1987, p. 469 (Rt. Hon. Lester B. Pearson); March 22, 1988, p. 2320 (Her Majesty Queen Elizabeth II)).

61. For examples of motions framed as orders, see *Journals*, April 9, 1997, p. 1366 (M-267 amending the Standing Orders of the House); and *Notice Paper*, September 24, 1997, pp. XII, XXVI (motions M-24 and M-123 for a committee to prepare and bring in a bill).

62. See, for example, Motion M-555 which proposed the restoration of funding for the Canadian Centre for Occupational Health and Safety and which was adopted on April 23, 1990 (*Journals*, p. 1572).

63. Standing Order 86(2).

Paper. The sponsoring Member can move the motion only if the item has been selected following the draw establishing the order of precedence, and only after the two-week notice period has elapsed.

SIMILAR ITEMS

If a Member submits notice of a motion which the Speaker judges to be substantially the same as an item already submitted, the Speaker has the power to refuse the most recent notice, to so inform the Member sponsoring it and to return the motion to him or her. [64]

SECONDERS

A Member who wishes to support a motion already appearing on the *Order Paper* may second that motion by indicating in writing to the Clerk of the House his or her desire to do so. [65] A motion may have up to 20 seconders, although the number of seconders has no bearing on the motion's chances of being selected as a votable item. [66] The names of these seconders are listed with the motion on the *Order Paper*. Once the motion has been proposed to the House, no additional names may be appended. [67] The Member who seconds the motion in the House need not be one of the seconders listed on the *Order Paper*.

Notices of Motions for the Production of Papers

Members may choose to give notice of a motion requesting that certain papers or documents be compiled or produced by the government and tabled in the

---

64. Standing Order 86(5). In 1961, discussion arose in the House on whether a private Member's motion which was similar to two private Members' bills could be debated. Although the Speaker expressed strong reservations that it not become a precedent, debate was allowed to proceed (*Journals*, January 23, 1961, pp. 176-7). In another instance, the Speaker ruled that the House can debate a motion which is similar in substance to a bill already decided upon in the same session since it is unlikely that a bill and motion could substantially raise the same question when the motion is merely affirming the desirability of legislation while the bill is likely to contain qualifying provisions and conditions (*Debates*, May 29, 1984, pp. 4175-6). In 1985, prior to the consideration of a motion similar to a bill which had been adopted at second reading and referred to a standing committee, the Chair cautioned Members to refrain from speaking about the provisions of the bill or the committee's deliberations during debate on the motion (*Debates*, April 18, 1985, p. 3884). In 1992, a Member rose on a point of order to argue the redundancy of debate on a private Member's motion which was similar to the subject matter of a government bill that had been referred to a special committee for pre-study. The Chair ruled that the two items were not identical and that since the motion was a non-votable item, debate could proceed. In closing, the Chair remarked that "a Member's legitimate right to present a motion could be weakened by or violated by an overly strict interpretation of the rule which forbids discussing a bill that is already being considered in committee" (*Debates,* April 1, 1992, pp. 9204-6, 9208-9).
65. Standing Order 86(3).
66. The list of 20 seconders should not be confused with the 100 signatures of Members who support an item in order that it be placed on the order of precedence (Standing Order 87(6)).
67. Standing Order 86(4).

House.[68] Notices of Motions for the Production of Papers resemble written questions in that they are requests for information from the government. All such motions are worded in the form of either an Order of the House ("That an Order of the House do issue ...") or an Address to the Crown, a formal message requesting the production of documents in the Crown's possession ("That a humble Address be presented to His/Her Excellency praying that he/she will cause to be laid before the House of Commons ..."). Thus, a motion, if adopted, becomes either an order that the government table certain documents in the House or an Address to the Governor General requesting that certain papers be sent to the House. An Order of the House is used for papers concerning matters directly related to federal departments or the business of the House. An Address is required for correspondence between federal and provincial governments, federal and foreign governments, the federal government and any company, corporation or individual, Orders in Council, and papers concerning royal commissions, the administration of justice, the judicial conduct of judges or the exercise of Crown prerogatives. It is the responsibility of the Speaker to ensure that the motion proposed is appropriately worded so that it can achieve what it intends to do.[69]

While a number of motions for the production of papers have been transferred for debate in recent years, debate has rarely been held on an item of this nature since 1986.[70] When the House does consider such motions, the debate is restricted to whether or not the papers should be produced rather than the subject matter of the papers.[71]

NOTICE

Members must give 48 hours' written notice of a motion for the production of papers, after which it is transferred from the *Notice Paper* to the *Order Paper* where it appears under the rubric "Notices of Motions for the Production of Papers" on the following Wednesday, the only day of the week such notices of motions can be called.[72]

---

68. For a detailed description of the rules and process concerning Notices of Motions for the Production of Papers, see Chapter 10, "The Daily Program".

69. *Journals*, February 15, 1960, pp. 137-40.

70. In 1986, two motions for the production of papers were debated and concurred in (see *Journals*, June 6, 1986, p. 2281; June 16, 1986, p. 2326; *Debates*, June 16, 1986, pp. 14479-80). Since then, two motions for the production of papers have been debated and concurred in (see *Journals*, October 2, 1998, p. 1115; November 2, 1998, p. 1221) and one was debated and negatived (see *Journals*, April 20, 1999, p. 1739).

71. See *Debates*, March 31, 1966, pp. 3676-7.

72. Standing Order 30(6). See also *Debates*, April 24, 1998, p. 6087; September 28, 1998, pp. 8474-5; February 15, 1999, p. 11893; April 13, 1999, p. 13721.

TRANSFERRED FOR DEBATE

When a Notice of Motion for the Production of Papers is called on a Wednesday following Routine Proceedings, it must be either dealt with immediately, without debate or amendment, or transferred for debate at the request of the sponsoring Member or a Minister.[73] (For further details, see Chapter 10, "The Daily Program".) Once transferred for debate, the motion is placed on the *Order Paper* under the heading entitled "Notices of Motions (Papers)" on the list of items outside the order of precedence. It may be subject to debate at a subsequent time if it is selected by the sponsoring Member following the draw for the order of precedence.

The Order of Precedence

While government bills and motions are called for debate in the order that the government chooses, items of Private Members' Business are called according to their place on the order of precedence; only those items in the order of precedence may be considered during Private Members' Hour.[74] The order of precedence is a list of items sponsored by private Members, established following a random draw of names. A Member's name is entered in the draw provided that he or she does not already have an item in the order of precedence and provided that he or she has at least one item of Private Members' Business on the list of items outside the order of precedence. For the purpose of the draw, the following items are considered to be on the list of items outside the order of precedence:

- a bill, if it has been introduced, read a first time and ordered for a second reading at the time of the draw;

- a notice of motion, if it has been put on the *Notice Paper* not later than the day before the draw;

- a notice of Motion (Papers), if it has been transferred for debate before the draw.

Any item on which a recorded division has been deferred and which would be removed from the order of precedence as a result of the division is not considered to be an item in the order of precedence for the purpose of the draw.[75]

---

73. Standing Order 97(1). See, for example, *Debates*, February 4, 1981, pp. 6888-9; December 14, 1994, p. 9072; December 15, 1994, p. 9103; May 6, 1998, p. 6608; September 30, 1998, p. 8586; November 25, 1998, pp. 10436.

74. Standing Order 87(5). The House may choose, by unanimous consent, to allow debate and possibly even a vote on an item which has not been chosen to be on the order of precedence (see, for example, *Debates,* June 18, 1987, pp. 7345-7).

75. See the Thirteenth Report of the Standing Committee on Procedure and House Affairs, concurred in by the House on November 4, 1998 (*Journals*, p. 1238).

THE DRAW

The draw is organized by the Clerk of the House and is chaired, by practice, by the Deputy Speaker or one of the other Presiding Officers of the House. At least 48 hours before a draw is to be held, the Clerk of the House notifies Members of the date, time and place of the draw.[76] Members or their staff may attend the draw, though their presence is not required. The draw itself is not a formal proceeding of the House; therefore, no formal recording is made in that day's *Journals*. The new items in the order of precedence will appear in the *Order Paper* of the following sitting under the heading "Private Members' Business—Items in the Order of Precedence".

First Draw of a Session

At the beginning of a session, Members are notified of the first draw within two sitting days after 30 or more Members have each placed at least one eligible item of Private Members' Business on the *Order Paper*.[77] The draw is conducted so that the order of precedence contains an equal number of public bills originating in the Commons and motions (including motions for papers), provided there are sufficient numbers of eligible bills and motions.[78] The names of Members with eligible bills are drawn first, followed by the names of Members with eligible motions, for a total of 30 names to be drawn. If a Member's name is drawn for both a bill and a motion, then his or her name is set aside the second time since no Member may have more

---

76. Standing Order 87(1) and (2).

77. Standing Order 87(1)(*a*). In December 1989, the Seventh Report of the Standing Committee on Elections, Privileges, Procedure and Private Members' Business recommended that the order of precedence be determined by drawing lots at random from among the names of those Members with eligible bills or motions instead of drawing from among the eligible bills and motions themselves. In addition, the Committee recommended that the names of Members with eligible bills be drawn separately from the names of Members with eligible motions (including notices of motions (papers)) and that their names be included in the draw no more than once for each type of item of business, regardless of the number of bills or motions which a Member was sponsoring. Thus, there would be no advantage for Members who had introduced large numbers of bills or motions (*Journals*, December 6, 1989, pp. 927-34). See also the Twenty-First Report of the Standing Committee on Privileges and Elections (*Journals*, December 6, 1990, pp. 2385-8) and the motion making extensive changes to the Standing Orders which was adopted by the House on April 11, 1991 (*Journals*, pp. 2919-20).

78. Standing Order 87(1)(*b*). Ideally, the first order of precedence would contain 15 bills and 15 motions. However, if, for example, only four Members had bills eligible for the draw, the names of these Members would be deemed drawn and the bills automatically placed on the *Order Paper*. The other 26 positions on the order of precedence would be filled with motions.

than one motion or bill at second reading on the order of precedence at one time.[79] These 30 names are then redrawn to establish the order of items on the order of precedence.[80]

When a Member whose name has been drawn has more than one eligible item standing in his or her name on the *Order Paper,* the Member must choose which one of these items is to be placed on the order of precedence. The Member must notify the Clerk of the House of his or her choice by the end of the second sitting day after the draw. Should the Member fail to do so within the allotted time, the first item put on the *Order Paper* in the Member's name will be the one placed on the order of precedence.[81] The number of joint seconders influences neither the chances of a bill or a motion being placed on the order of precedence nor of it being selected later as a "votable item".[82] Any private and Senate public bills which have been ordered for a second reading in the House and placed at the bottom of the order of precedence at the time of a draw are not considered to occupy any of the 30 positions on the order of precedence.

Subsequent Draws

The order of precedence may not contain more than 30 motions and public bills originating in the House at the second reading stage, nor fewer than 15 items.[83] Further draws for up to an additional 15 items are held during the session whenever the number of items on the order of precedence is close to 15.[84] The number of bills and motions to be chosen following each draw depends on the number of bills and motions still in the order of precedence at the time of the draw. For example, if there are 10 motions but only five bills on the order of precedence at the time of the draw, five additional motions and 10 additional bills will be chosen. If a Member already has an eligible item on the order of precedence at the time of the draw, his or her name will not be included in the draw, unless it is an item on which a recorded division has been deferred and which would be removed from the *Order Paper* as a result of the vote.[85]

---

79. However, it may happen that a Member has more than one item on the order of precedence at a given time. Bill C-270, standing in the name of Peter Milliken (Kingston and the Islands), was on the order of precedence when Bill S-8, a private bill also standing in his name, was added to the order of precedence pursuant to Standing Order 89 (see *Order Paper*, June 19, 1996, pp. 17, 22). On another occasion, Bill C-235, standing in the name of Dan McTeague (Pickering–Ajax–Uxbridge), was reported back from committee and placed back on the order of precedence on the same day that Bill C-440, also standing in his name on the order of precedence, was referred to committee (see *Journals*, April 16, 1999, pp. 1728-30).

80. Standing Order 87(1)(*c*).

81. Standing Order 87(1)(*d*).

82. Standing Order 92(1).

83. Standing Order 87(3).

84. Standing Order 87(2).

85. Standing Order 87(2). See also the Thirteenth Report of the Standing Committee on Procedure and House Affairs, concurred in by the House on November 4, 1998 (*Journals*, p. 1238).

WITHDRAWAL OF ITEMS

If a Member no longer wishes to proceed with a notice of motion which is on the list of items outside the order of precedence or a bill which has not yet been given first reading, and thus does not wish to see the item placed on the order of precedence, he or she may request to have the item withdrawn from the *Order Paper* by notifying the Clerk of the House in writing. If a Member wishes to withdraw a bill which has been given first reading, he or she must seek the unanimous consent of the House to do so since, having been ordered for a second reading by the House, the bill is then in the possession of the House and only the House can take a further decision on it.[86]

Since the order of precedence is established by the Standing Orders, a Member wishing to withdraw any item which has been placed on the order of precedence must first seek the unanimous consent of the House.[87]

STATUS OF ITEMS NOT CHOSEN

Items not chosen following the draw to establish the order of precedence remain on a list, which may be consulted at the Table in the Chamber or on the electronic version of the *Order Paper*, entitled "Items Outside the Order of Precedence", and are eligible for subsequent draws in the session.[88] Unless chosen following a subsequent draw, items outside the order of precedence do not receive consideration during Private Members' Business. There is no limit to the number of bills and motions a Member may have on the list of items outside the order of precedence.

CERTAIN ITEMS AUTOMATICALLY PLACED ON THE ORDER OF PRECEDENCE

Certain items of Private Members' Business are placed automatically at the bottom of the order of precedence regardless of the results of the draw or the number of items already on the list.[89] These items include:

- orders for consideration of subsequent stages of a bill already debated during Private Members' Business (including bills reported back or deemed to have been reported back from committees[90]);

---

86. See, for example, *Journals,* September 15, 1988, p. 3538; *Debates,* March 12, 1997, p. 8957; June 2, 1998, p. 7470; February 2, 1999, p. 11305; March 11, 1999, p. 12715.

87. See, for example, *Journals,* September 1, 1988, p. 3509; September 18, 1995, p. 1891. On one occasion, with the unanimous consent of the House, a Member withdrew a motion standing in her name on the order of precedence and replaced it with another motion listed in her name on that day's *Notice Paper* (*Journals,* May 5, 1994, p. 430). On another occasion, by unanimous consent, a Member's motion was withdrawn from the order of precedence and substituted with a motion standing in another Member's name (*Journals,* October 2, 1995, p. 1972).

88. Standing Order 87(4).

89. Standing Order 89.

90. Standing Orders 97.1 and 98(1).

- bills on the order of precedence in a previous session which are reinstated;[91]

- consideration of Senate amendments to bills;

- all stages of a private bill;

- private Members' public bills originating in the Senate.

An item supported by 100 Members, including at least 10 Members each from a majority of the recognized parties in the House, is also eligible to be added to the order of precedence if the sponsoring Member does not already have an item on the order of precedence.[92] The order of precedence can contain only one such item at any given time. Thus, it is possible for the total number of items on the order of precedence to exceed 30 since this number applies only to motions and public bills originating in the Commons at second reading.

Selection of Votable Items

MANDATE OF THE STANDING COMMITTEE ON PROCEDURE AND HOUSE AFFAIRS

As soon as practicable after the order of precedence has been established at the beginning of each session, but not later than 10 sitting days after that date, the Standing Committee on Procedure and House Affairs must meet to select from the items placed on the order of precedence as a result of the draw up to 10 items to be designated as "votable items".[93] Being selected as votable should not be construed as a guarantee that the House will adopt the bill or motion.

Certain items which may be selected as votable are nonetheless not to be included as part of the list of 10 votable items, since they were not placed on the order of precedence as a result of the draw:

- bills jointly supported by 100 Members;[94]

- Senate public bills;

---

91. Standing Order 86.1. For an example of a bill reinstated as having been reported back with an amendment, see *Journals*, March 22, 1996, p. 146.

92. Standing Order 87(6). The first such bill added to the order of precedence was Bill C-306, *An Act to amend the Bank Act* (bank charges), on February 1, 1999 (see *Order Paper*, February 2, 1999, pp. 26-7).

93. Standing Order 92(1). In practice, a sub-committee of the Standing Committee on Procedure and House Affairs is created for the purpose of selecting votable items. Reports of the sub-committee must be concurred in by the full Committee before presentation to the House. The sub-committee meets after every draw to consider votable items.

94. See, for example, Bill C-306, *An Act to amend the Bank Act* (bank charges), *Journals*, February 8, 1999, p. 1478.

- bills reinstated from a previous session at the second reading stage.

As well, any item on which a recorded division has been deferred, and which would be removed from the order of precedence as a result of that division, is not to be included as part of the list of 10 votable items.

Furthermore, other items are automatically placed on the order of precedence and automatically made votable but are not to be included as part of the list of 10 votable items:

- all stages of a private bill;[95]

- notices of motions (papers);[96]

- bills reported from committee (or deemed to have been reported from committee);

- bills at the third reading stage;

- consideration of Senate amendments to bills.

CONSULTATION WITH MEMBERS

It has been the practice since 1986 for the Committee to consult with the sponsors of each bill or motion placed on the order of precedence before making its selection of votable items. Each Member sponsoring an item on the order of precedence is invited to appear before the Committee in a public meeting to make a short presentation explaining why his or her item warrants additional debate and being put to a vote in the House. Each presentation may be followed by a brief question-and-answer period. The Committee has traditionally selected votable items by consensus rather than on the basis of votes.[97]

A Member may ask the Committee not to select his or her item as votable by notifying the clerk of the Committee. The item will still remain on the order of precedence and be debated as a non-votable item.

CRITERIA FOR SELECTION

Since 1986, the Committee has based its selection of votable items on specific criteria, the list of which was occasionally modified throughout the years.[98] The most

---

95. Standing Order 92(3).

96. Standing Order 97(2).

97. See the Seventieth Report of the Standing Committee on Procedure and House Affairs presented to the House on April 20, 1999 (*Journals*, p. 1737). One Member introduced the same bill three times before it was selected as votable (see *Journals*, June 4, 1996, pp. 486-7 (Bill C-274); December 3, 1996, p. 955 (Bill C-321); April 22, 1998, p. 692 (Bill C-251)).

98. See *Journals*, May 23, 1986, pp. 2200-1; October 21, 1987, pp. 1717-8. There have been objections raised regarding the Committee's selection of votable items (see *Debates*, November 19, 1986, pp. 1325-34, and Speaker Fraser's ruling, *Debates*, December 4, 1986, pp. 1759-60; see also *Debates*, April 18, 1997, pp. 9919-20; November 4, 1998, pp. 9836-7).

recent list, outlined in the Seventieth Report of the Standing Committee on Procedure and House Affairs in April 1999,[99] contains the following criteria:

- Bills and motions must be drafted in clear, complete, and effective terms;
- Bills and motions must be constitutional and concern areas of federal jurisdiction;
- Bills and motions should concern matters of significant public interest;
- Bills and motions should concern issues that are not part of the government's current legislative agenda and which have not been voted on or otherwise addressed by the House of Commons in the current session of Parliament;
- All other things being equal, higher priority will be given to items which transcend purely local interest, are not couched in partisan terms, or cannot be addressed by the House in other ways.

PRESENTATION OF REPORT

After consulting the Members sponsoring the items on the order of precedence, the Committee meets, *in camera,* to make a final decision. It prepares a report which contains the list of the items selected and the names of the sponsoring Members. Once presented to the House, the report is deemed adopted without debate or amendment.[100]

FURTHER SELECTION OF VOTABLE ITEMS

Further meetings to select items may be held from time to time during the session, usually when the order of precedence has been replenished through subsequent draws. The number of votable items which the Committee can select after a draw will depend on the number of items still on the list from previous selections,

---

99. *Journals*, April 20, 1999, p. 1737.

100. Standing Order 92(2). The first selection of votable items was contained in the First Report of the Standing Committee on Private Members' Business, presented to the House on April 23, 1986 (*Journals*, pp. 2064-5). For other examples, see *Journals*, June 19, 1986, pp. 2366-7; October 22, 1997, pp. 133-4; November 4, 1998, p. 1236; November 17, 1998, pp. 1263-4. In 1994, John Nunziata (York South–Weston) raised a question of privilege in regard to a report on votable items by the Standing Committee on Procedure and House Affairs. The Member argued that the process followed by the Committee for selecting private Members' bills infringed on his "right as a Member of Parliament to advance Private Members' Business." He further stated that it was the Speaker's responsibility to ensure that the process for selecting bills to be voted upon by the House was fair to all Members. The Speaker ruled that there was no question of privilege and advised the Member that the Committee's report in no way prevented him from submitting his bill again for the draw (*Debates,* March 10, 1994, pp. 2129-31).

although no more than 10 items selected as votable can be on the order of precedence at any given time. [101]

Private Members' Hour

Private Members' Business is considered for one hour every sitting day. [102] At the beginning of a session, Private Members' Business is suspended until an order of precedence and a list of votable items have been established. [103] Once this has occurred, the consideration of Private Members' Business begins the following day.

The Speaker must give Members at least 24 hours' notice before an item on the order of precedence can be considered. This notice is published in the *Notice Paper*. [104] During Private Members' Hour, items on the order of precedence are considered in the order in which they are listed and normally only one item is considered each day. [105]

EXCHANGE OF ITEMS

If the sponsor of an item is unable to move his or her motion on the day set by the order of precedence and has given the Speaker at least 48 hours' written notice, the Speaker may arrange to exchange the position of the sponsor's item with that of another Member in the order of precedence, with the permission of the Members involved. [106] The Speaker consults with Members and finds a date that is agreeable to two Members. Members sponsoring items on which debate has previously begun may not request an exchange but may agree to a request for exchange from another sponsoring Member. If no exchange is possible, Private Members' Hour is

---

101. Standing Order 92(1). See also Speaker Parent's ruling, *Debates,* December 5, 1997, pp. 2787-8.

102. The current schedule for Private Members' Hour is as follows: Monday, 11:00 a.m. to 12:00 noon; Tuesday, Wednesday and Thursday, 5:30 p.m. to 6:30 p.m.; and Friday, 1:30 p.m. to 2:30 p.m. This schedule came into effect on February 14, 1994, following the adoption of amendments to the Standing Orders on February 7, 1994 (*Journals*, February 7, 1994, pp. 112-20).

103. Standing Order 91.

104. Standing Order 94(1)(*a*).

105. The Member is advised in advance of the day when his or her item is scheduled for debate. On occasion, two or more items have been considered during Private Members' Hour by unanimous consent (see, for example, *Journals*, July 21, 1988, pp. 3250-1; June 27, 1989, pp. 468-70; June 7, 1990, pp. 1852-5; June 18, 1992, pp. 1800-1; November 28, 1996, p. 935; April 28, 1999, pp. 1780-1). The House has also extended Private Members' Business by 30 minutes in order to have two items considered (*Journals*, March 18, 1997, p. 1310; March 19, 1997, pp. 1319-20).

106. Standing Order 94(2)(*a*). In the First Session (1997-99) of the Thirty-Sixth Parliament, there had been an increasing loss of time for Private Members' Business due to Members not being available for exchanges. This matter was discussed by the Standing Committee on Procedure and House Affairs (see *Evidence*, April 15, 1999; April 20, 1999).

suspended for that day, the House continues with the business before it,[107] and the Member's item is consequently dropped to the bottom of the order of precedence.[108] On Monday, the House takes up Government Orders during that hour.[109]

CANCELLATIONS AND SUSPENSIONS

Although Private Members' Hour is regularly scheduled for each day that the House sits, there are some situations when it may be cancelled or suspended. The cancellation or suspension of the Hour has been a matter of concern to the House ever since the adoption of the modern rules relating to Private Members' Business in 1986.[110]

The consideration of Private Members' Business may be cancelled or suspended for a number of reasons:

- Should the sponsor of an item set for consideration not be present to move the item or should the sponsor decline to move the item, Private Members' Business is cancelled for that day; the Hour cannot be used for other business without the unanimous consent of the House.

- Should Members not have 24 hours' notice of the item to be considered during Private Members' Hour, the Speaker will advise the House that Private Members' Business will be suspended for that day; the House will continue with, or revert to, the business before it prior to the time designated for Private Members' Business.[111] If the Member scheduled to move an item gives the required 48 hours' written notice that he or she is unable to do so on the day scheduled, and no exchange of items is possible, the House also reverts to the business before it prior to Private Members' Business.[112] In both cases, when Private Members'

---

107. Standing Order 94(2)(*b*). See, for example, *Debates*, March 23, 1994, p. 2694.

108. In 1986, the Chair explained, on several occasions, the procedure to be followed when Members were unable to be present to move their item on the day scheduled (see *Debates,* April 24, 1986, pp. 12624-6; April 25, 1986, pp. 12671-3; May 9, 1986, pp. 13146-7; May 28, 1986, p. 13727; November 17, 1986, pp. 1215-6).

109. Standing Order 99(2). See, for example, *Debates*, November 18, 1994, p. 8004; March 7, 1997, p. 8790; May 8, 1998, p. 6736.

110. In its Third Report to the House in June 1986, the Standing Committee on Private Members' Business expressed concerns about the suspension of Private Members' Hour: "Since debate began under the new rules ..., there have been, theoretically, thirty-two hours for Private Members' Business; but only fifteen have been used. Ten were suspended because of allotted days and seven were lost because Members in whose name the motions stood were unable to attend the House" (*Journals*, June 19, 1986, p. 2365).

111. Standing Order 94(1)(*b*). When this occurs, a private Member's motion is dropped from the *Order Paper* (Standing Order 42(1)), whereas a private Member's bill is dropped to the bottom of the order of precedence (Standing Order 42(2)). See, for example, *Journals*, March 13, 1992, p. 1140; February 1, 1993, p. 2416.

112. Standing Order 94(2)(*b*).

Business is suspended on Monday, the House takes up Government Orders during the time designated for Private Members' Business.[113]

- If proceedings under "Introduction of Government Bills" during Routine Proceedings have not been completed on a Tuesday or Thursday prior to Statements by Members, Routine Proceedings will continue immediately after Question Period until the completion of all items under "Introduction of Government Bills", thereby suspending as much of Private Members' Hour as necessary.[114]

- Private Members' Business is cancelled on any day designated for resuming debate on the Budget or the Address in Reply to the Speech from the Throne.[115]

- On the last Supply day in June, the consideration of Private Members' Business is cancelled in order to allow more time to consider and dispose of the Main Estimates.[116]

- Private Members' Business will be cancelled when a Minister moves a motion in relation to a matter the government considers to be of an urgent nature, and debate subsequently takes place during the time scheduled for Private Members' Business.[117] If such a motion is moved during Private Members' Hour, only the remaining time allotted for consideration of the item being debated is suspended. If the maximum one hour of debate allowed on the motion extends into Private Members' Hour, then the beginning of Private Members' Hour is delayed.[118]

- As no emergency debate may be interrupted by Private Members' Business, Private Members' Hour would be cancelled if an emergency debate were to begin prior to the time scheduled for the consideration of Private Members' Business.[119]

---

113. Standing Order 99(2).

114. Standing Order 30(4)(*a*).

115. Standing Orders 50(4) and 99(1). Private Members' Business is cancelled on any day designated for the presentation of the Budget if the presentation is scheduled to take place prior to the time designated for Private Members' Business. Pursuant to Standing Order 83(2), if the House is considering Private Members' Business at the time specified for the presentation of the Budget, the Speaker will interrupt the proceedings and the proceedings will be deemed adjourned.

116. Standing Order 99(1). See also Chapter 18, "Financial Procedures".

117. Standing Orders 53 and 99(1). No debate of this nature has ever led to the cancellation of Private Members' Business. For further information, see Chapter 15, "Special Debates".

118. Standing Order 30(7).

119. Standing Order 52(14). Thus, when an emergency debate takes place on a Friday, Private Members' Hour is cancelled (see, for example, *Debates*, June 13, 1986, p. 14388).

- Private Members' Business is suspended until an order of precedence and a list of votable items are established at the beginning of a session.[120]

- Private Members' Business is suspended when, during the course of a session, the House must proceed to the election of a new Speaker.[121]

- Private Members' Business, or the remainder thereof, is suspended when the House adjourns due to a lack of quorum.[122]

DELAYS AND INTERRUPTIONS

If Private Members' Hour is delayed or interrupted for any reason, the debate is then extended or rescheduled so that no time is lost.[123] For example, if the start of Private Members' Hour is delayed because of deferred divisions or interrupted so that Members may attend the Royal Assent ceremony in the Senate Chamber, Private Members' Hour is extended by the corresponding amount of time. Similarly, when the time provided for Government Orders has been extended by 90 minutes or less because of a ministerial statement, the start of Private Members' Hour will be delayed by a corresponding amount of time.[124] If debate on Private Members' Business does not begin or resume by 30 minutes after the time Private Members' Business would have ordinarily ended, the remaining time or the entire hour is added to another sitting.[125]

RESCHEDULING OF DEBATE

The rescheduling of any unused time of a Private Members' Hour due to a delay or interruption is done at the discretion of the Speaker within 10 sitting days and after consultation with the Member involved.[126] No more than one adjournment period as provided in the parliamentary calendar may intervene in the rescheduling of the debate. The rescheduled business is considered during an additional Private Members' Hour, which is added to the daily schedule of the House.

---

120. Standing Orders 91 and 99.

121. Standing Order 2(3).

122. Standing Order 29(3). See, for example, *Journals*, October 19, 1995, p. 2032.

123. Standing Order 30(7).

124. Standing Order 33(2). See, for example, *Debates*, November 1, 1991, p. 4412.

125. Standing Order 30(7). See, for example, *Debates,* June 14, 1995, p. 13853; December 1, 1998, p. 10773.

126. Standing Order 30(7). See, for example, *Order Paper*, June 15, 1995, p. 21; *Debates*, June 19, 1995, p. 14104; *Order Paper*, December 2, 1998, p. 25; *Debates*, December 7, 1998, p. 10945.

The regular 24 hours' notice of the item to be considered is given to the House. The notice is printed on the *Notice Paper* on the day the additional debate is to take place.[127] The *Order Paper* entry referring to the rescheduled debate, or to a debate awaiting rescheduling, appears at the top of the list of "Items in the Order of Precedence".[128] The Standing Orders do not provide for an exchange between a Member whose item of business has been rescheduled and another Member who has an item on the order of precedence.

On days when Private Members' Business has been rescheduled, the adjournment proceedings are delayed by the amount of time required to complete the rescheduled debate.

Time Limits on Debate

NON-VOTABLE ITEMS

An item of Private Members' Business not selected to come to a vote is debated for up to one hour and, once the debate has concluded or the time for debate has expired, the item is then removed from the *Order Paper*.[129] Debate does not last the full hour allotted for Private Members' Business if no other Member rises to speak on the item, if a quorum is lost, or if a motion to adjourn is carried.

The removal of an item of Private Members' Business from the *Order Paper* does not constitute a decision since a question is not put to the House.[130] Thus, a Member whose non-votable item has been removed may resubmit it by giving notice of the item in the usual manner. It remains on the *Order Paper* on the list of items outside the order of precedence until it is chosen again for inclusion on the order of precedence.[131]

VOTABLE ITEMS

An item of Private Members' Business selected as a votable item is eligible for up to three hours of consideration before the question is put to dispose of it.[132] Votable

---

127. See, for example, *Notice Paper*, June 20, 1995, pp. IV-V; December 8, 1998, p. IV.

128. See, for example, *Order Paper*, June 15, 1995, p. 21; December 8, 1998, p. 21.

129. Standing Order 96(1). On occasion, with the unanimous consent of the House, the order for second reading of a non-votable public bill has been discharged and its subject matter referred to a committee for consideration (see, for example, *Journals*, June 7, 1994, pp. 541-2; June 17, 1994, pp. 611-2). A non-votable item of Private Members' Business has also been designated votable with the unanimous consent of the House (see, for example, *Journals*, May 11, 1994, p. 453; June 1, 1994, p. 519; October 4, 1996, p. 716) and a decision taken at the end of the time provided for debate.

130. Standing Order 96(2).

131. See, for example, *Journals*, June 18, 1991, pp. 215-6; September 23, 1991, p. 379. The bill will be given a different number when reintroduced.

132. Standing Order 93.

items work their way up the order of precedence in the same way that all other items do, but at the end of Private Members' Hour on the day the item is debated, if debate is not concluded, they are placed at the bottom of the order of precedence instead of being removed from the *Order Paper*.[133] The item continues to work its way up to the top of the list again, is debated and then placed at the bottom once more. Unless the item has been disposed of earlier, this continues until exactly two hours and 45 minutes of debate have been completed, at which time the Speaker interrupts the proceedings and puts every question necessary to dispose of the item.

If the votable item is a motion framed as a resolution, the House makes a decision either for or against that item of business and, accordingly, it is disposed of. No further action is required since it is solely an expression of opinion or a declaration of purpose. If the votable item is a motion framed as an order to the House itself, its committees, its Members or officers, again the House makes a decision either for or against and, if agreed to, further action will be required to execute the order.

If the votable item is a bill and second reading is agreed to by the House, the bill is then referred to a committee for study.[134] The committee is obliged, within 60 sitting days from the date of reference, to either report back a bill with or without amendment, or to present to the House a report recommending not to proceed further with a bill or requesting a one-time extension of 30 sitting days to consider a bill. Reasons must be given for either recommendation. Should a committee fail to report back to the House as required, the bill is automatically deemed reported without amendment.[135]

---

133. Standing Order 90.

134. For further information, see Chapter 16, "The Legislative Process".

135. Standing Order 97.1. Until 1997, there was no time limit on committee consideration of a private Member's bill. For example, in 1992, a private Member's bill (Bill C-203) was allowed to die on the *Order Paper* when the legislative committee to which it was referred adopted a motion to adjourn *sine die* its consideration of the bill (Legislative Committee H on Bill C-203, *Minutes of Proceedings and Evidence*, February 18, 1992, Issue No. 10, p. 3; *Debates*, February 26, 1992, pp. 7620-4). On another occasion, Speaker Parent ruled that the decision of a committee not to report a bill back to the House did not constitute a matter of privilege (*Debates*, September 23, 1996, pp. 4560-2) and later ruled in order a motion moved by a private Member under Routine Proceedings to have the same bill reported back to the House within a specified time (*Debates*, November 21, 1996, pp. 6519-20). In April 1997, and again in November 1998, the Standing Orders were amended to specifically require committees considering a private Member's public bill to report back to the House within a time limit (*Journals*, April 9, 1997, pp. 1366-8; November 30, 1998, pp. 1327-9). Some bills have since been reported back with the title and clauses deleted (*Debates*, April 16, 1999, p. 13965; April 19, 1999, p. 14026).

REPORT STAGE AND THIRD READING

When a committee reports a private Member's bill back to the House or is deemed to have reported a bill back, the order for consideration of the report stage is placed at the bottom of the order of precedence.[136] Two Private Members' Hours on separate sitting days are allotted for report stage and third reading consideration.[137] On the first day, if there are no motions in amendment at the report stage on the *Notice Paper*, the motion for concurrence at the report stage is put immediately and, if adopted, the motion for third reading is moved and debate commences at third reading.[138] If there are motions in amendment at the report stage and debate on these motions concludes during the first hour, the question is put on all motions to dispose of the report stage and, if the bill is concurred in at report stage, the House immediately proceeds to the consideration of the third reading stage.[139] At the end of the first Private Members' Hour, unless the bill has been otherwise disposed of, it drops to the bottom of the order of precedence and works its way up to the top for consideration by the House during the second Private Members' Hour. Fifteen minutes before the end of the time provided for this second consideration, all questions necessary to dispose of the bill at the remaining stage or stages are put and the bill, if passed, is sent to the Senate for consideration.[140]

The time provided for the consideration of a private Member's bill at report stage and third reading may be extended by up to five hours on the second day of debate. If a bill is not disposed of within the first 30 minutes of debate on the first day of consideration, during any time then remaining on that day, any Member may propose a motion to extend the debate on the second day for a period not to exceed five consecutive hours.[141] This non-debatable, non-amendable motion is deemed withdrawn if fewer than 20 Members rise to support it.[142] The motion may

---

136. Standing Order 98(1). The bill is set down on the *Order Paper* for consideration at report stage even if the committee reports back the bill with the title and clauses deleted (*Debates*, April 16, 1999, p. 13965; *Order Paper*, April 19, 1999, p. 34; *Debates*, April 19, 1999, p. 14026; *Order Paper*, April 20, 1999, p. 32).

137. Standing Order 98(2).

138. See, for example, *Journals*, May 11, 1992, p. 1428.

139. See, for example, *Journals*, June 13, 1994, p. 568.

140. On occasion, the House has given unanimous consent, during consideration of a private Member's bill at report stage, to refer the bill back to a committee for further consideration (see, for example, *Journals*, March 11, 1993, p. 2623; *Debates*, March 8, 1999, p. 12523). Bills have also been withdrawn, by unanimous consent, when the order for consideration at report stage was called (see, for example, *Debates*, August 11, 1988, p. 18223) and when the order for the consideration of Senate amendments was called (see, for example, *Debates*, September 14, 1987, pp. 8922-3).

141. Standing Order 98(3).

142. Standing Order 98(3)(*a*).

subsequently be proposed again during the time remaining provided an intervening proceeding has occurred.[143] If the motion is adopted and the time for consideration is extended on the second day, the Standing Orders relating to the normal hour of adjournment are suspended.[144] Not later than 15 minutes before the conclusion of the time provided on the second day, the Speaker puts every question necessary to dispose of any remaining stages of the bill.[145] On Monday, the extension of up to five additional hours of debate begins at the ordinary hour of daily adjournment.[146]

SENATE AMENDMENTS TO A PRIVATE MEMBER'S BILL

The order for the consideration of Senate amendments to a private Member's bill is placed at the bottom of the order of precedence when the message is received from the Senate.[147] The Standing Orders do not specify any time limit for the consideration of a motion respecting Senate amendments. When the item reaches the top of the order of precedence, it is considered during Private Members' Hour and, if not disposed of at the end of the hour, it is placed again at the bottom of the order of precedence. This process is repeated until the debate ends and the question can be put on the motion.[148]

NOTICES OF MOTIONS (PAPERS)

Motions for papers may be debated for a total of one hour and 40 minutes before the question is put.[149] Unless otherwise disposed of, the item is placed at the bottom of the order of precedence after the first hour of debate. After the item has worked its way up the order of precedence, it is debated for a further 30 minutes. At that time, the Speaker interrupts the proceedings and allows a Minister to speak for a

---

143. Standing Order 98(3)(*b*).

144. Standing Order 98(5).

145. Standing Order 98(4).

146. Standing Order 98(3).

147. For examples of Senate amendments to private Members' bills considered by the House, see *Debates*, September 14, 1987, pp. 8922-3 (bill withdrawn); *Journals*, March 26, 1991, pp. 2827-8 (amendments concurred in); *Debates*, May 27, 1996, p. 2973 (amendments concurred in); *Debates*, December 12, 1996, pp. 7481, 7495 (amendments concurred in); *Journals*, April 22, 1997, pp. 1512-3, and April 25, 1997, pp. 1554-5 (died on the *Order Paper* at dissolution); *Debates*, June 11, 1998, pp. 8077-8 (amendments concurred in).

148. See *Journals*, April 22, 1997, pp. 1512-3, and April 25, 1997, pp. 1554-5.

149. Standing Order 97(2).

maximum of five minutes, even if he or she has already spoken in debate.[150] The mover of the motion is then permitted to speak for an additional five minutes to close the debate before the Speaker puts the question to the House. If the motion carries, it becomes an order to the government to table the documents requested in the motion.

INDIVIDUAL SPEECHES

During debate on a votable item of Private Members' Business, the sponsor may speak for 20 minutes, while other Members may speak for 10 minutes each.[151] Debate on a non-votable item begins with the mover of the item speaking for up to 15 minutes. Other Members may speak for up to 10 minutes, with the time allotted for 10-minute speeches limited to a maximum of 40 minutes. After 40 minutes, or sooner if no other Member rises to speak, the Member moving the motion has the right of reply to conclude the debate by speaking again for a maximum of five minutes.[152]

Although there is no practice of a fixed pattern for the recognition of Members wishing to speak during Private Members' Business, the Chair seeks to ensure that there is a smooth flow of debate, providing opportunities for all points of view to be expressed.[153] Members speaking during Private Members' Business require the unanimous consent of the House to share their time with another Member.[154] There is no question and comment period after each speech.[155]

Divisions

If consideration of a votable item of Private Members' Business ends before the maximum time allowed for debate, the question is then put and, if a recorded division is demanded, either the Chief Government Whip or the Chief Opposition Whip may ask the Speaker to defer the division.[156] In the event that the time for consideration of a private Member's item has expired and debate is interrupted by the Chair in order to put the question, a recorded division can be deferred only upon the

---

150. Only by unanimous consent may a Parliamentary Secretary speak for a Minister in the closing segment (see, for example, *Debates*, November 8, 1979, p. 1112; April 1, 1982, pp. 16064-5).

151. Standing Order 95(1).

152. Standing Order 95(2). See *Debates*, October 23, 1997, p. 1071; November 26, 1997, p. 2276; February 13, 1998, p. 3887; March 11, 1998, p. 4737; June 2, 1998, p. 7516.

153. See, for example, *Debates*, March 16, 1992, p. 8243; March 18, 1992, p. 8466; November 30, 1992, pp. 14236, 14238; October 18, 1995, p. 15552.

154. See *Debates*, September 19, 1996, p. 4480; March 25, 1998, p. 5356.

155. See, for example, *Debates*, September 28, 1994, p. 6289.

156. Standing Order 45(5)(*a*) (ii).

agreement of all Whips and the Member sponsoring the item upon which a vote is to be taken.[157]

When a recorded division is taken on an item of Private Members' Business, the vote of the Member sponsoring the bill or motion is recorded first, if he or she is present, followed by the votes of the other Members on the same side of the House, starting with the back row, who are in favour of the bill or motion and then the Members on the other side of the House, starting with the back row, who are in favour of the item. Votes against are recorded in the same order.[158]

Management of Private Members' Business

The Speaker is responsible for the orderly conduct of Private Members' Business, ensuring that there is a minimum 24 hours' notice of items to be considered during Private Members' Hour, identifying identical or similar items of Private Members' Business, arranging the exchange of items in the order of precedence and rescheduling debate if Private Members' Hour is delayed for more than 90 minutes.

The Clerk of the House is responsible for most of the administrative and procedural duties associated with Private Members' Business. These include making arrangements for the draws to establish the order of precedence, ensuring that Members and their staff know when their items of business are to be taken up during Private Members' Hour and providing the Standing Committee on Procedure and House Affairs with procedural advice on Private Members' Business.

Legislative counsel assists Members in the drafting of their bills for introduction in the House and in the drafting of amendments to legislation. Priority in the drafting of private Members' bills is accorded to those Members who have not previously had a bill drafted by legislative counsel during that session.[159] Legislative advice usually involves the appropriateness of the proposed legislation, taking into

---

157. Standing Order 45(7). See also the Fifty-Third Report of the Standing Committee on Procedure and House Affairs (*Minutes of Proceedings and Evidence*, December 8, 1994, Issue No. 36, pp. 3-4) presented to the House on December 9, 1994 (*Journals*, p. 1014), and concurred in on February 6, 1995 (*Journals*, p. 1081).

158. See the Thirteenth Report of the Standing Committee on Procedure and House Affairs, presented to the House on November 26, 1997 (*Journals,* p. 270), and concurred in on November 4, 1998 (*Journals*, p. 1238). Prior to the adoption of this report, votes were taken in the same manner but starting with the front row (see the Twenty-Fourth Report of the Standing Committee on House Management (*Minutes of Proceedings and Evidence*, February 11 and 13, 1992, Issue No. 24, p. 17), presented to the House on February 14, 1992 (*Journals,* p. 1025*),* and concurred in on April 29, 1992 (*Journals*, p. 1337). Prior to that, votes were taken by party unless a Member sought and received unanimous consent to have the vote taken row by row. For further information, see Chapter 12, "The Process of Debate".

159. See the Thirteenth Report of the Standing Committee on Procedure and House Affairs, presented to the House on November 26, 1997 (*Journals*, p. 270), and concurred in on November 4, 1998 (*Journals*, p. 1238).

account constitutional requirements or impediments, vested rights issues, drafting conventions, and procedural requirements. While Members may draft their own bills or retain outside counsel for that purpose, before these bills are introduced in the House, they are reviewed by legislative counsel for constitutionality, form and compliance with drafting conventions. In addition, all private Members' bills are certified by legislative counsel before introduction in the House.

22

Public Petitions

All authorities agree that the right of petitioning parliament for redress of grievances is acknowledged as a fundamental principle of the constitution. It has been uninterruptedly exercised from very early times and has had a profound effect in determining the main forms of parliamentary procedure.

SPEAKER GASPARD FAUTEUX
(*Debates,* June 18, 1947, pp. 4278-9)

Simply defined, a petition is a formal request to an authority for redress of a grievance. Public petitions, addressed to the House of Commons and presented to the House by its Members, constitute one of the most direct means of communication between the people and Parliament. Certainly, it is among the most ancient; the act of petitioning has been described as "the oldest of Parliamentary forms, the fertile seed of all proceedings of the House of Commons".[1]

Petitions today may be described as a vehicle for political input, a way of attempting to influence policy-making and legislation and also, judging by their continued popularity, a valued means of bringing public concerns to the attention of Parliament. Petitions also have their place among the tools which Members and Ministers can use to formulate public policy and to carry out their representative duties. In the early 1980s, after many years during which the presentation of petitions appeared to have fallen

---

1. *Redlich*, Vol. II, p. 239.

out of favour, a resurgence of interest occurred which continues without abatement.[2] This is illustrated by Figure 22.1, which indicates the number of petitions presented during each session from the Seventh Session of the Twelfth Parliament (1917) to the Second Session of the Thirty-Fifth Parliament (1997).

Figure 22.1   *Petitions Presented to the House of Commons Since 1917*

Parl. Sess. (year)	Petitions	Parl. Sess. (year)	Petitions	Parl. Sess. (year)	Petitions
12.7(1917)	2 788	18.1(1936)	1	26.3(1965)	3
13.1(1918)	2	18.2(1937)	3	28.2(1969-70)	2
13.2(1919)	364	18.3(1938)	8	28.3(1970-72)	2
13.3(1919)	1	18.4(1939)	10	28.4(1972)	4
13.4(1920)	6	18.5(1939)	10	29.1(1973-74)	4
13.5(1921)	11	19.1(1940)	2	29.2(1974)	1
14.2(1923)	3	19.2(1940-42)	1	30.1(1974-76)	21
14.3(1924)	4	19.3(1942-43)	1	30.2(1976-77)	12
14.4(1925)	5	19.5(1944-45)	22	30.3(1977-78)	7
15.1(1926)	6	20.2(1946)	2	30.4(1978-79)	2
16.1(1926-27)	32	20.3(1947)	8	31.1(1979)	3
16.2(1928)	6	20.4(1947-48)	1	32.2(1983-84)	185
16.3(1929)	584	20.5(1949)	3	33.1(1984-86)	3 899
16.4(1930)	178	21.7(1952-53)	3	33.2(1986-88)	5 575
17.2(1931)	5	22.2(1955)	1	34.1(1988-89)	16
17.3(1932)	3	22.5(1957)	1	34.2(1989-91)	8 928
17.4(1932-33)	9	25.1(1962-63)	1	34.3(1991-93)	5 282
17.5(1934)	12	26.1(1963)	1	35.1(1994-96)	4 271
17.6(1935)	3	26.2(1964-65)	2	35.2(1996-97)	2 361

---

2. This may be attributed in part to the fact that the rules permit Members to initiate petitions, solicit signatures and make an oral presentation in the House; and in part to Members' awareness that presenting large numbers of petitions serve not only to raise issues of public concern, but also to use time and so delay the business of the House (see note 7). Recently, the British House of Commons and the Australian House of Representatives experienced similar renewals of interest in petitioning. See *House of Representatives Practice*, 3rd ed., pp. 734, 812-3; *May*, 21st ed., p. 761, note 3; 22nd ed., p. 816, note 2.

This chapter will concern itself with public petitions, the current rules regarding their form, content and presentation, government responses to petitions, and the role and responsibilities of the Clerk of Petitions. Petitions for private bills are dealt with in Chapter 23, "Private Bills Practice".

Historical Perspective

While the right of the citizen to petition Parliament for redress of a grievance is frequently referred to as fundamental, or as a fundamental principle of the constitution,[3] the constitution is in fact silent on the matter. The recognition of this right is, however, well entrenched, based as it is on centuries-old tradition and established precedent.

Petitioning the Crown (and later Parliament) for redress of a grievance originated in the time of the thirteenth-century monarch Edward I. Petitioners had recourse to the Crown's prerogative power, which was above the law. Petitions granted to individuals and communities were in the nature of private laws; those granted to the nation as a whole made public laws.

In medieval times, before Parliament had assumed its present constitution and when its judicial and legislative functions were as yet undefined, Receivers and Triers of petitions appointed by the Crown travelled the country to hear the complaints of the people. Certain matters would be referred to local courts by the Triers, but others would be found appropriate for consideration by the High Court of Parliament.

As Parliament evolved from a primarily judicial to a predominantly legislative body with its judicial functions taken over by the courts, the character of petitions changed. By the end of the fourteenth century, legislative remedy was sought by individuals and corporations who petitioned Parliament or the House of Commons. At the same time, petitions from the Commons to the Crown—these being of a general nature and expressing national grievances—became frequent. The British Parliament's first legislative acts occurred with the Commons petitioning the King for certain amendments to the law. (This was the precursor to legislation by bill, as later the Commons assumed the task of drafting the desired statute which could then be accepted or rejected—but not amended—by the Crown.) The seventeenth century saw the development of what may be considered the "modern" form of petition—

---

3. See, for example, Speakers' rulings, *Journals*, June 7, 1972, pp. 361-2; *Debates*, June 30, 1987, pp. 7821-2. All six editions of *Beauchesne* describe petitioning as a fundamental principle of the Constitution.

addressed to Parliament, drawn up in a prescribed manner, usually dealing with public grievances.[4]

In Canada, provisions for petitions (long a feature of the pre-Confederation legislative assemblies) have always been part of the written rules of the House.[5] The rules adopted in 1867 were somewhat expanded in 1910, and operated without substantial modification for some 76 years.[6] However, starting in the immediate post-Confederation period, an extensive body of practice began to build, resulting in a collection of form and content requirements which were not codified in the Standing Orders but which had to be met in order for a petition to be acceptable to the House.

In the early and mid-1980s, the resurgence in the use of petitions led to a situation in which the presentation of petitions occupied large amounts of the time of the House, sometimes to the exclusion of other business.[7] As well, the Chair was at times called upon to intervene or rule on matters relating to the admissibility of petitions and the manner of their presentation.[8] As a consequence, the Special Committee on the Reform of the House of Commons (the McGrath Committee) made several recommendations intended to clarify the rules relating to petitions, to promote increased uniformity in their presentation, to ensure their receivability as to content and to provide guidelines as to form and the petitioners' signatures.[9] In 1986, the House adopted amendments to the Standing Orders based on these recommendations.[10]

The most significant of the changes adopted in 1986 was the requirement for certification of petitions by the Clerk of Petitions prior to their presentation in the House. Also included were a number of requirements, some previously uncodified

---

4. *May*, 10th ed., pp. 493-5; *Wilding and Laundy*, pp. 561-3, 620-1; *May*, 22nd ed., p. 809; *Redlich*, Vol. I, pp. 6-25.

5. Certain constituent parts of what is now Standing Order 36 can be traced to Rules 85-7, 80 and 73 used in the United Province in 1860, 1853 and 1841 respectively; and to the 1825 Rule 43 of the Legislative Assembly of Upper Canada (*O'Brien*, p. 442).

6. *Journals*, December 20, 1867, pp. 116-7, 122; April 29, 1910, pp. 535-6; March 22, 1927, p. 339. See also Standing Order 73 in the *Permanent and Provisional Standing Orders of the House of Commons*, September 9, 1985, pp. 67-8.

7. On May 19, 1983, for example, because of the number of petitions presented, the daily routine of business occupied the balance of time available for that day's proceedings (*Journals*, pp. 5910-1; *Debates*, pp. 25591-612). On December 19, 1985, 365 petitions were presented (including 7 filed with the Clerk); this is thought to be the largest number of petitions presented during a single sitting of the House. The daily routine of business was not completed and again the House was not able to return to Orders of the Day (*Journals*, pp. 1444-8; *Debates*, pp. 9631-7). See also, for October 27 and 28, 1983, *Journals*, pp. 6356-59, 6362-67, and *Debates*, pp. 28393-415, 28456-85.

8. See, for example, *Debates*, April 6, 1982, p. 16198; *Journals*, October 5, 1983, pp. 6264-5.

9. See pp. 44-5 of the Third Report of the Special Committee on Reform of the House of Commons, June 1985, presented on June 18, 1985 (*Journals*, p. 839).

10. The motion encompassing the proposals was tabled on February 6, 1986 (*Journals*, p. 1665) and adopted as amended on February 13, 1986 (*Journals*, p. 1710).

but well established by precedent and practice, to be met in order for petitions to be certified correct as to their form and content (for example, petitions must contain a prayer requesting action, must be respectful in tone and must bear original signatures). Guidelines issued by the Speaker made reference to these and to other established practices concerning the presentation of petitions during Routine Proceedings.[11] A new rule provided for mandatory government replies to petitions.

Several changes were adopted in 1987, in particular a new requirement that signatories to petitions must include their addresses.[12] As well, the number and sequence of Routine Proceedings rubrics was revised so that "Presenting Petitions", formerly the fifth of nine items, became the ninth of ten.[13] In 1991, a further amendment set a limit of 15 minutes on the time provided for the presentation of petitions during the daily routine of business.[14] An amendment adopted in 1994 provided that the original petitions be transmitted to the Ministry (Privy Council Office) and that government responses to petitions may be tabled by depositing them with the Clerk of the House.[15]

Current Guidelines for Petitions

Petitions have always been subject to verification by an official of the House of Commons. Amendments to the rules, adopted in 1910, make the first mention of the Clerk of Petitions as the individual charged with this responsibility.[16] Until 1986, such verification took place after Members presented their petitions; the Standing Orders now provide for petitions to be certified correct as to form and content by the Clerk

---

11. On February 26, 1986, the Speaker wrote to all Members, drawing their attention to the changes in the Standing Orders concerning petitions and explaining the process by which petitions would henceforth be certified. The coming into force of the new rules left some Members holding uncertifiable petitions which would have been acceptable under the old rules (*Debates*, March 5, 1986, p. 11208). This difficulty was circumvented by the adoption of a special order allowing Members a limited period of time in which to file these petitions with the Clerk of the House (*Journals*, April 22, 1986, pp. 2048-9).

12. *Journals*, June 3, 1987, pp. 1016, 1026.

13. *Journals*, June 3, 1987, pp. 1016-8.

14. *Journals*, April 11, 1991, pp. 2905, 2908-9. This was one of an extensive package of amendments to the Standing Orders put forward by the government with a view to "modernizing" the rules and improving Parliament as a forum for debate (*Debates*, April 8, 1991, p. 19133). No particular reason was given for this change; however, it is worth noting that the presentation of quantities of petitions had in the past resulted in disruption to the agenda of the House (see note 7); the institution of a time limit eliminated the risk of any recurrence of this.

15. *Journals*, June 10, 1994, p. 563. (See the Twenty-Seventh Report of the Procedure and House Affairs Committee, presented June 8, 1994.)

16. *Debates*, April 29, 1910, cols. 8365-6; *Journals*, April 29, 1910, pp. 535-6. See also *Rules of the House of Commons of Canada*, 1910, Rule 75.

of Petitions prior to their presentation to the House.[17] Petitions not meeting the form and content requirements cannot be certified and only certified petitions can be presented to the House.[18]

Those engaged in drafting petitions may consult the Clerk of Petitions to ensure that the proposed text is in keeping with the rules and practices of the House. Once a petition is signed and ready to be certified, it is sent by a Member to the Clerk of Petitions, accompanied by a written request for certification. The Clerk of Petitions examines each petition received, including its signatures, to ensure that the form and content are in keeping with the requirements. If the petition is in order, a certificate signed by the Clerk of Petitions is attached and the petition is returned to the Member for presentation to the House. If the petition cannot be certified, it is returned to the Member with an explanatory note.

Any forgery or fraud in the preparation of petitions or signatures, or any complicity in or knowledge thereof may be dealt with as a breach of privilege.[19]

FORM

A petition typically begins with a superscription identifying it as a petition and indicating that it is addressed to the House of Commons. This is followed by a statement identifying the petitioners; the petitioners then draw the attention of the House to a statement of grievance which is generally set out in paragraph form. The final and essential part of the petition is a request, called a "prayer", in which the petitioners specify the action they wish the House to take in response to their grievance. Then follow the signatures and addresses of the petitioners. The recommended form of petition is reproduced as Figure 22.2.

Addressed to the House of Commons

As the House of Commons is the body being petitioned, it is therefore the first criterion of acceptability that petitions be addressed to the House of Commons, or to the House of Commons in Parliament assembled,[20] rather than to the Government, to the Prime Minister, to individual Ministers or Members, or to some outside authority. The words "To the House of Commons" or "To the House of Commons in Parliament Assembled" should normally appear at the beginning of the petition.

---

17. Standing Order 36(1).

18. On rare occasions, petitions failing to satisfy form and content requirements (and thus not certified) were presented with the unanimous consent of the House (*Journals,* February 18, 1987, p. 503; *Debates*, February 18, 1987, p. 3568). In an unusual proceeding in 1992, unanimous consent was given for an uncertified petition to be "received" by the House—although the Standing Orders no longer provide for petitions to be received—and referred to a standing committee for consideration (*Journals*, November 18, 1992, p. 2070).

19. *Bourinot*, 4th ed., p. 237. While doubts have been expressed from time to time concerning the authenticity of signatures (see, for example, *Debates*, May 21, 1885, pp. 2023-9; October 28, 1983, pp. 28475-9), no breach of privilege alleging fraud or forgery in the preparation of petitions has yet been found.

20. Standing Order 36(2)(*a*).

Figure 22.2 *Form of a Petition*

First page of petition

PETITION TO THE HOUSE OF COMMONS
IN PARLIAMENT ASSEMBLED

We, the undersigned

{ *Here identify, in general terms, who the petitioners are, for example*
- *citizens (or residents) of Canada*
- *electors of (name of electoral district)*
- *residents of the Province of ....*
- *residents of the City (or Village or Township, etc.) of ....*

draw the attention of the House to the following:

THAT,

{ *Here briefly state the reasons underlying the request for the intervention of the House by outlining the grievance or problem or by summarizing the facts which the petitioners wish the House to consider.*

THEREFORE,
your petitioners

request that Parliament

or

call upon Parliament to

Here set out the "prayer" or request by stating succinctly what action the petitioners wish Parliament to take or what action it should refrain from taking.

Signatures	**Addresses**
(Sign your own name. Do not print.)	(Give your full home address or your city and province.)
_____	_____
_____	_____
_____	_____
_____	_____

Subsequent pages of petition

THEREFORE, your petitioners

Or

Petition concerning

{ *Here repeat the "prayer" or request from the first page of the petition.*

{ *Here state the subject matter of the petition.*

Signatures	**Addresses**
(Sign your own name. Do not print.)	(Give your full home address or your city and province.)
_____	_____
_____	_____
_____	_____
_____	_____

Prayer

Petitions, to be certified for presentation to the House, must contain a prayer; that is, a concise, clearly worded and respectful request that the House take, or refrain from taking, some sort of action in response to an alleged grievance. Petitions without prayers—that is, documents consisting solely of statements of opinion or statements of grievance—cannot be accepted as petitions.[21] The action sought must fall within Parliament's jurisdiction.[22] A petition pertaining to a matter falling outside of Parliament's authority to act—a matter under the jurisdiction of a provincial or municipal government, for example—could not be certified for presentation to the House.[23]

Written, Typewritten or Printed on Paper of Usual Size

To be certified, petitions must be written, typewritten or printed on paper of usual size.[24] The requirement for petitions to be written or printed has been part of the written rules since Confederation.[25] Petitions with photocopied text are acceptable. Paper of "usual size" is interpreted nowadays to mean 21.5 cm × 28 cm (8.5 × 11 inches) or 21.5 cm × 35.5 cm (8.5 × 14 inches) sheets. Petitions produced on materials other than paper do not meet this requirement; likewise petitions of a non-standard size will not be certified.[26]

Erasures or Interlineations

To be certified, a petition must be free of erasures or interlineations in its text;[27] that is, the text of a petition may not be altered by erasing words, crossing out words, or adding words or commentary.

---

21. *Journals*, March 22, 1876, p. 180; *Debates*, April 23, 1879, pp. 1453-4.

22. Standing Order 36(2)(*b*).

23. On one occasion pre-dating the requirement for certification, a Member presented a petition concerning safety at a certain street intersection in her constituency. The Speaker suggested that such petitions be directed to the competent municipal authority. The Clerk of Petitions later reported that this petition had failed to meet the requirements as to form (*Debates,* June 11, 1985, p. 5648; *Journals,* June 12, 1985, p. 796).

24. Standing Order 36(2)(*c*).

25. Rule 86, adopted December 20, 1867 (*Journals,* p. 122).

26. Prior to the adoption of this rule, petitions of unusual style were presented from time to time and judged by the Clerk of Petitions to be in accordance with the prevailing requirements as to form. See, for example, *Debates*, December 10, 1974, p. 2099; *Journals*, December 11, 1974, p. 187; *Debates*, April 6, 1982, p. 16196; *Journals*, April 7, 1982, p. 4698-A.

27. Standing Order 36(2)(*d*).

Attachments, Appendices or Lengthy Extracts

In accordance with a practice established in 1876, a petition is not in order if it has letters, affidavits, or other documents appended or attached to it.[28] Material such as maps, pictures, news articles, explanatory or supporting statements attached or appended to petitions will render them unacceptable for certification and presentation to the House. The proscription on attachments and appendices applies to extraneous matter written, photocopied or affixed on the petition itself.[29] Petitions incorporating lengthy extracts from other documents or publications have also been deemed irregular.[30] A return address, however, may appear on the petition without constituting an obstacle to its certification.

Subject Matter Indicated on Every Sheet

When a petition consists of more than one sheet of signatures and addresses, each succeeding page is to contain an indication of the subject matter of the petition[31] so that petitioners are made fully aware of the nature of the document they are supporting. This is generally achieved by a notation at the top of each additional page, as shown in Figure 22.2.

Language

Petitions may be written in either of the official languages.[32] They should be respectful and temperate in tone, and there should be no disrespect to the Sovereign or offensive imputation on the character or conduct of Parliament, the courts or any other constituted authority.[33] For many years, it was customary for petitions to be written in a formal style of expression, opening with the words *"To the Honourable the House of Commons in Parliament assembled. The Petition of the undersigned ... who now avail themselves of their ancient and undoubted right thus to present a grievance common to your Petitioners in the certain assurance that your honourable House will therefor provide a remedy, humbly sheweth"* and closing with the words *"and your petitioners, as in duty bound, will ever pray"*. A special committee recommended in 1985 that this traditional language, which it saw as archaic, need not be used.[34] While petitions couched in the formal style continue to be presented, petitions employing more contemporary wording are equally acceptable to the House, as long as the import is the same. For example, in Figure 22.2, the opening and closing formulae quoted above do not appear, and the petitioners "request" that Parliament respond to their grievance rather than "humbly pray and call upon Parliament" to do so.

---

28. *Debates*, March 28, 1876, pp. 867-8; February 23, 1978, p. 3200.
29. *May*, 22nd ed., p. 811.
30. *Bourinot*, 4th ed., p. 235.
31. Standing Order 36(2)(*e*).
32. *Bourinot*, 4th ed., p. 235; see also the *Official Languages Act*, R.S.C. 1985, c. 31 (4th Supp.), s. 22.
33. *Bourinot*, 4th ed., p. 231. See, for example, *Journals*, March 30, 1905, p. 234; April 5, 1909, p. 234.
34. See p. 45 of the Third Report of the Special Committee on Reform of the House of Commons, presented on June 18, 1985 (*Journals*, p. 839).

CONTENT

Matters Under the Authority of the House

It has been said that the prayer of a petition must request action which is within the powers of the House to take.[35] Therefore, it follows that the petition as a whole must set forth a case for which the House has the authority to intervene.[36] Matters of provincial or municipal responsibility or those which properly belong before a court of law or tribunal may not be made the subject of a petition to be presented to the House of Commons. Over the years, the House has chosen to delegate certain matters to the courts and other administrative and regulatory bodies. Petitions dealing with matters which the House has delegated to another body have not always been found acceptable.[37]

Requesting Expenditure of Public Funds

Historically, petitions making direct requests for the expenditure of public funds which have not received the recommendation of the Crown (Royal Recommendation) have not been allowed to be presented to the House.[38] At issue is the fundamental principle of the Crown's initiative in respect of the expenditure of public money.[39] Many rulings from the Chair have upheld the practice of rejecting petitions involving the expenditure of public revenue[40] while at the same time seeking to preserve, without setting undue limitation on, the time-honoured right of the citizen to petition the House for redress of a grievance. In 1869, when a petition was called into question because it appeared to request a grant of public funds not recommended by the Crown, the Speaker defined it as a request for legislation rather than money, thus creating a distinction between direct requests, which could not be accepted, and indirect requests (later described as requests for legislation or for "such measures as the

---

35. Standing Order 36(2)(*b*).

36. *Journals*, February 16, 1956, p. 163; June 7, 1972, pp. 361-2.

37. For example, petitions questioning the return of a Member were not received because the House had vested in the courts the responsibility for matters relating to the election of Members (*Journals,* April 20, 1874, p. 82; February 15, 1881, pp. 199-200). On the other hand, petitions concerning the CRTC (Canadian Radio-television and Telecommunications Commission, the independent agency regulating the broadcasting system) have at different times been rejected (*Journals*, June 7, 1972, pp. 361-2; October 24, 1973, pp. 591-2) and accepted (*Debates*, April 30, 1984, p. 3235; *Journals*, May 1, 1984, p. 400).

38. *Journals*, May 7, 1868, p. 297. For historical background on the principles underlying this long-standing convention, see *Redlich*, Vol. III, pp. 119-24.

39. See Section 54 of the *Constitution Act, 1867* (R.S.C. 1985, Appendix II, No. 5), which states that the House shall not adopt or pass any vote, resolution, address or bill for the appropriation of any part of the public revenue that has not been first recommended to the House by a message from the Governor General, that is, by a Royal Recommendation.

40. For example, see *Journals*, February 5, 1912, p. 181; August 24, 1946, p. 767. A petition praying for an increase to the old age pension was allowed because the Royal Recommendation had been granted to a bill having the same purpose (*Journals,* May 19, 1947, p. 423).

House may think expedient to take"), which could be accepted.[41] In 1987, the Speaker upheld the decision of the Clerk of Petitions to reject a petition calling upon Parliament to provide federal funding to the provinces and territories for non-profit child care, but went on to make the following observation:

> *The right to petition Parliament is fundamental to our parliamentary system, and it is not unreasonable to assume that the remedy, in many a situation, could only be found through the expenditure of public funds. A petitioner is entitled to petition for relief in a burdensome situation, so that a mere change in wording could well render a petition in order which might otherwise be out of order. A petition praying for the enactment of a measure which would provide the relief being sought might avoid the restriction imposed by our practice.*[42]

Signatures and Addresses

From 1867 until 1986, it was possible for a lone individual to petition the House. The amendments to the Standing Orders adopted in 1986 introduced a new requirement that a petition, to be certified, would have to contain at least 25 signatures.[43] In 1987, a further amendment added the requirement for addresses as well as signatures.[44] Petitioners must not sign for anyone else. Written addresses may be in the form of complete home addresses or simply the names of the petitioners' town and province of residence. Petitions must contain original signatures written directly on the document and not pasted or otherwise transferred to it.[45] In 1872, a petition received by telegraph was ruled out of order because it contained no original signatures;[46] in 1986, the Speaker ruled that for the same reason, photocopied signatures were unacceptable.[47] A Member may sign a petition but should ask another Member to present it.[48] The signatures of Members inscribed on petitions are not counted towards the required 25 signatures and addresses.[49]

Petitions signed exclusively by non-resident aliens have traditionally been found unacceptable.[50] However in 1984, a petition signed by Canadian citizens as well as by foreigners was received with the unanimous consent of the House;[51] in a similar situation arising in 1990, the Speaker ruled that the right of Canadians to

---

41. *Journals*, April 20, 1869, pp. 22-3.

42. *Debates*, June 30, 1987, p. 7821.

43. *Journals*, February 13, 1986, p. 1710.

44. *Journals*, June 3, 1987, pp. 1016, 1026.

45. Standing Order 36(2)(*f*).

46. *Journals*, May 3, 1872, p. 80.

47. *Debates*, January 24, 1986, p. 10143.

48. *May*, 22nd ed., p. 815.

49. Standing Order 36(2)(*g*).

50. See, for example, *Journals*, October 5, 1983, pp. 6264-5.

51. *Debates*, November 20, 1984, pp. 412-3.

petition their House of Commons would be better served if such petitions, provided they were otherwise in order, could be presented notwithstanding the presence of "the occasional signature of a non-Canadian not resident in Canada".[52]

Presentation of Petitions

As outsiders are not permitted to address the House directly, petitions are presented by Members. Therefore, groups and individuals with petitions for the House must enlist the aid of Members to have their petitions certified and presented. Members are not bound to present petitions and cannot be compelled to do so;[53] nevertheless, it is evident that many Members consider it a duty to present to the House petitions brought forward by citizens.[54] The Member, whose role it is to make the presentation on behalf of the petitioners, is not required to be in agreement with the content of any petition he or she may choose to present, and no such inference is to be drawn.[55]

Once they have been certified by the Clerk of Petitions, petitions are ready for presentation to the House and are returned to the Members who submitted them. A certified petition is not to be altered or tampered with in any way; nor is the certificate to be removed. No rule or practice specifies a time period during which a petition must be presented following its certification; nor must a petition necessarily be presented by the Member who had it certified.[56] The Speaker has observed that various reasons might prevent a Member from presenting a certified petition expeditiously, but has also found merit in the view that petitions ought to be presented promptly after certification so that petitioners may have confidence that petitions brought to the House are answered as quickly as possible.[57]

Petitions are presented by Members, including Ministers.[58] The Speaker traditionally does not present petitions, but instead asks the assistance of another Member to do so. This practice originated in the British House of the late eighteenth century, a time when petitions were routinely debated. Presenting petitions would have led to the Speaker participating in the proceedings of the House, which would have been

---

52. *Debates*, December 19, 1990, pp. 16963-4.

53. *Bourinot*, 4ᵗʰ ed., p. 232.

54. See, for example, the general discussion on petitions on February 13, 1990 (*Debates*, pp. 8233-42). In presenting petitions, Members occasionally make reference to their "duty" in this respect (*Debates,* December 1, 1981, p. 13549; October 20, 1989, p. 4953; March 14, 1994, p. 2226).

55. *Debates*, November 25, 1986, pp. 1501, 1505; February 25, 1994, pp. 1863-4.

56. See *Debates*, October 21, 1997, p. 878 (petitions presented on behalf of a Member who had resigned).

57. *Debates*, May 28, 1987, pp. 6500-1; September 22, 1987, p. 9172; March 8, 1988, p. 13490.

58. See, for example, *Debates*, December 12, 1991, p. 6176.

at odds with the essential neutrality of the Chair.[59] In choosing to present a petition, a Member must be satisfied of its fitness and regularity, for it is a long-standing rule of the House that the Member is answerable for any improprieties and impertinences therein.[60] In addition, every Member presenting a petition must endorse it (i.e., they sign the back of the petition, or the back of the first page).[61]

Certified petitions may be presented in two ways: orally during Routine Proceedings,[62] or by filing them with the Clerk of the House during any sitting of the House.[63] In practice, the majority of petitions are presented during Routine Proceedings.[64]

PRESENTATION DURING ROUTINE PROCEEDINGS

Certified petitions are presented daily during Routine Proceedings, under the rubric "Presenting Petitions". A maximum of 15 minutes is provided for the presentation of petitions.[65] To be recognized, Members must be in their assigned places.[66] Members with more than one petition to present on a given day are advised to present them all when given the floor, as individual Members are recognized by the Chair only once during "Presenting Petitions".[67] This allows more Members to be recognized within the 15-minute time limitation.

No debate is permitted during the presentation of petitions.[68] Any comment on the merits of a petition—even a Member's personal agreement or disagreement with the petitioners—has been deemed to constitute a form of debate and is therefore out of order.[69] Members are permitted a brief factual statement, in the course of which they may allude to the petition being duly certified, to its source, to the subject matter

---

59. *Bourinot*, 4th ed., p. 231. See also *Debates*, April 23, 1879, pp. 1453-4; March 23, 1987, pp. 4433-4. Other Presiding Officers have presented petitions (see, for example, *Journals*, October 26, 1994, p. 829 (Bob Kilger, Assistant Deputy Chairman of Committees of the Whole); June 19, 1995, p. 1784 (Shirley Maheu, Deputy Chairman of Committees of the Whole)).

60. Standing Order 36(3). This has been part of the written rules since Confederation.

61. Standing Order 36(4).

62. Standing Order 36(6).

63. Standing Order 36(5).

64. Statistics compiled by the Clerk of Petitions indicate that 2107 of 2361 petitions presented in the Second Session of the Thirty-Fifth Parliament (1996-97) were presented orally during Routine Proceedings.

65. Standing Order 36(6). Rarely is the entire 15 minutes taken up (see, for example, *Debates*, March 13, 1995, pp.10393-7).

66. Standing Order 36(6).

67. *Debates*, October 28, 1983, p. 28457; June 11, 1985, p. 5649; November 7, 1986, pp. 1190-1.

68. Standing Order 36(7).

69. *Debates*, April 27, 1994, p. 3576; June 22, 1995, p. 14413; November 20, 1995, p. 16547; November 4, 1996, pp. 6068-9. Members had been known to inform the House of their personal views as they presented petitions. See, for example, *Debates*, June 9, 1947, p. 3912; March 29, 1985, p. 3510; April 26, 1994, p. 3483.

of the petition and its prayer, and the number of signatures it carries.[70] In any event, petitions are not to be read in their entirety and Members presenting them should avoid straying into debate or argument.[71] In view of the limited time available and of the number of Members with petitions to present on any given day, the Chair is generally quick to intervene when Members appear to be making speeches, indulging in debate, or launching on the lengthy reading of the full text of a petition.

PRESENTATION BY FILING WITH THE CLERK OF THE HOUSE

Since 1910, Members have had the option of presenting petitions at any time during a sitting of the House, by filing them with the Clerk of the House.[72] The Member may approach the Table, or may hand the certified and endorsed petition to a page, with instructions to deliver it to the Table where it is received by the Clerk or by a Table Officer on behalf of the Clerk.

FOLLOWING PRESENTATION

When petitions are presented during Routine Proceedings, the Members' remarks are recorded, transcribed and printed in the *Debates* for that day. An entry is also made in the *Journals,* the official record of House proceedings. The petitions are listed as having been certified correct and presented pursuant to the Standing Orders. Petitions filed with the Clerk are of course not mentioned in the *Debates,* but they are listed in the *Journals.* Certified petitions once presented to the House (by either method) are then delivered to the Clerk of Petitions who is responsible for their reception and processing.

Petitions have been presented which were later found to be uncertified; in such cases, while the *Debates* contain the transcription of the Members' remarks, the petitions in question are not recorded in the *Journals.*[73] They are examined by the Clerk of Petitions; if in order, they are certified and then filed with the Clerk on the Member's behalf; only then is the presentation noted in the *Journals.* If the petitions cannot be certified, they are returned to the Members. On one occasion, a Member who attempted to present an uncertified petition was called to order and admonished by the Chair.[74]

---

70. *Debates*, April 26, 1989, p. 975.

71. See, for example, *Debates*, April 6, 1982, p. 16198; March 14, 1990, p. 9284; September 16, 1991, p. 2173; December 8, 1992, pp. 14806-7; May 7, 1993, pp. 19111-2; September 28, 1998, p. 8474.

72. Standing Order 36(5).

73. On May 22, 1992, two Members presented petitions which were not recorded in that day's *Journals* (*Debates*, pp. 11088-9; *Journals*, p. 1546).

74. *Debates*, May 15, 1992, p. 10794.

COPIES OF PETITIONS

Anyone who wishes to read or consult a petition after it has been presented may do so by making arrangements with the Clerk of Petitions. A Member who requests a photocopy of a petition, including the signatures, is entitled to receive it.[75]

Government Response to Petitions

Since 1986, the Standing Orders have provided that the Ministry shall respond within 45 calendar days to every petition referred to it.[76] After certified petitions are presented to the House, they are deposited with the Clerk of Petitions. Under the authority of the Clerk of the House, the original petition is forwarded to the Privy Council Office,[77] which makes arrangements with the appropriate government departments and agencies for the preparation and collection of replies. Government responses to petitions are generally tabled in the House during Routine Proceedings, under the rubric "Tabling of Documents", but may also be deposited with the Clerk.[78] Petitions receive individual responses. Any Member who has presented a petition is provided with a copy of the response at the time it is tabled. After being tabled in the House, government responses to petitions (unlike the petitions themselves) become sessional papers.[79]

The tabling of government responses to petitions is entered in the *Journals*. If the tabling is done during Routine Proceedings, the government spokesperson, usually the Parliamentary Secretary to the Government House Leader, simply informs the House that responses to a certain number of petitions are being tabled; no reference is made to specific petitions or the content of the responses, and the intervention is transcribed in the *Debates*.

The Standing Orders provide no sanction to apply in the event the government fails to respond to petitions within the 45-day time frame. Complaints have been raised about breaches of this rule.[80] In 1993, however, the Speaker found a *prima facie* question of privilege concerning the failure to table an Order in Council and in his ruling made reference to earlier complaints that responses to petitions, answers to written questions and responses to committee reports were not always tabled within the prescribed time limits.[81] The matter of timeliness was referred to the committee dealing with matters of privilege, which stated in a report to the House that

---

75. *Debates*, January 20, 1986, p. 9946.

76. Standing Order 36(8).

77. From 1986 to 1994, a copy of each petition was forwarded to the Privy Council Office. Since the Standing Order changes in 1994, the original petition is now transmitted to the Privy Council Office.

78. See, for example, *Journals*, September 19, 1994, pp. 683-5 (depositing with the Clerk); February 6, 1995, p. 1076 (tabling during Routine Proceedings).

79. A sessional paper is any document tabled (or deemed tabled) in the House during a given session and as such is available for public scrutiny.

80. See, for example, *Debates*, February 8, 1993, pp. 15560-2.

81. *Debates*, April 19, 1993, pp. 18104-6.

"statutory and procedural time limits must be complied with ... It may be that the time periods set out in the Standing Orders and certain statutes need to be reviewed ... Until this is done, however, it is essential that the deadlines be respected."[82]

While normally all proceedings would be terminated when Parliament is prorogued, the Speaker has ruled that government responses to petitions have the same status as orders for return (documents which the House has ordered to be produced and presented in the House).[83] Pursuant to the rules, such orders are considered to have been readopted at the start of a new session without a motion to that effect.[84] Thus, government responses to petitions, ordered in a previous session, must be tabled in a new session following a prorogation.[85]

---

82. See the One Hundred and First Report of the Standing Committee on House Management, deemed tabled on September 8, 1993 (*Journals*, p. 3338).

83. *Debates*, June 27, 1986, p. 14969.

84. Standing Order 49.

85. See, for example, *Journals,* February 29, 1996, p. 17, when responses to petitions presented in the First Session of the Thirty-Fifth Parliament were tabled early in the Second Session.

23

Private Bills Practice

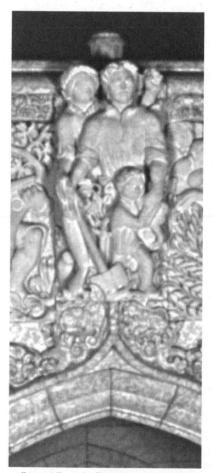

The distinction between public and private legislation has been inherited from British practice.[1] Private bills differ from public bills by their intent, content and method of passage. By definition, the purpose or intent of a private bill is to confer special powers or benefits upon one or more persons or body of persons; or to exclude one or more persons or body of persons from the general application of the law. A public bill may be broadly described as a bill which deals with a matter of public policy for the benefit of the community at large and is introduced directly by a Member of the House. On the other hand, a private bill relates directly to the affairs of an individual or group of individuals,

---

1. Private bills trace their origins to the medieval English parliaments, and their peculiar procedure is explained by that history. In the early history of Parliament, special laws for the benefit of private parties and judicial decrees for the redress of private wrongs were founded on petitions and were not easily distinguishable in principle or in form. When petitions sought remedies which the common law afforded, the parties were referred to the ordinary tribunals. But when an individual or community was unable to obtain relief from the common law courts, the King was petitioned. The manner of receiving and trying petitions was judicial rather than legislative. As noted in *May*, 1st ed. (pp. 301-2): "Receivers and triers of petitions were appointed, and proclamation was made, inviting all people to resort to the receivers. These were ordinarily the clerks of the chancery, and afterwards the masters in chancery (and still later some of the judges), who, sitting in some public place accessible to the people,

including a corporation, named in the bill; the bill seeks something which cannot be obtained by means of the general law and is founded on a petition from an individual or group of individuals.[2]

Private bills must not be confused with private Members' bills. Although private bills are sponsored by private Members, the term "private Member's bill" refers to public bills dealing with a matter of public policy introduced by Members who are not Ministers.

Private bills are subject to special rules in both Houses of Parliament. Since private bills ask Parliament to adjudicate upon the interests of private parties and to be watchful over the interests of the public, they are said to involve Parliament in both a judicial capacity and a legislative capacity.[3] Private bills can originate in either the House of Commons or the Senate, although most private bills originate in

---

received their complaints, and transmitted them to the auditors or triers. The triers were committees of prelates, peers, and judges, who had power to call to their aid the lord chancellor, the lord treasurer, and the serjeants-at-law. By them the petitions were examined; and in some cases the petitioners were left to their remedy before the ordinary courts; in others, their petitions were transmitted to the judges on circuit; and if the common law offered no redress, their case was submitted to the High Court of Parliament.... In the reign of Henry IV, petitions began to be addressed, in considerable numbers, to the House of Commons. The courts of equity had, in the meantime relieved Parliament of much of its remedial jurisdiction; and petitions were now more in the nature of petitions for private bills, than for equitable remedies for private wrongs. Of this character were many of the earliest petitions; and the orders of Parliament upon them can only be regarded as special statutes, of private or local application. As the limits of judicature and legislation became defined, the petitions applied more distinctly for legislative remedies, and were preferred to Parliament through the commons; but the function of Parliament, in passing private bills, have always retained the mixed judicial and legislative character of ancient times."

2. See Speaker Lamoureux's ruling, *Journals*, February 22, 1971, p. 351.

3. *Bourinot*, 4th ed., pp. 558-9. See *Todd's Private Bill Practice*, 3rd ed., Ottawa: John Durie & Son, 1868, pp. 1-2: "In passing Private Bills, while Parliament still exercises its legislative functions, its proceedings also partake also [sic] of a judicial character; the parties interested in such bills appear as suitors, while those who apprehend injury are admitted as adverse parties to the suit. Much of the formality of a Court of Justice is maintained; conditions are required to be observed and their observance proved by the promoters of a bill, and if they abandon it and no other parties take it up, the bill is dropped, however sensible the House may be of its value."

the Senate where the fees and charges imposed on the promoter are less.[4] Private bills must pass through the basic procedural stages common to all legislation; they must also meet certain parliamentary requirements which distinguish them procedurally from all other types of bills.

Private bill procedure is unique in its origins, forms and principles and has changed very little since 1867. While they are now relatively rare, private bills once constituted a large part of the legislative business of the House. In the early years of Confederation, the House dealt with a large volume of private legislation to establish companies to build and operate railways and to incorporate interprovincial companies since no other legal authority allowed such corporations to be formed. In addition, private bills requesting the dissolution of marriages occupied much of the House's time because Parliament had been granted the exclusive jurisdiction to legislate with respect to marriage and divorce.

Today, private legislation accounts for only a minuscule percentage of House business.[5] Most private bills now deal with the incorporation of, or amendments to the acts of incorporation of, religious, charitable and other organizations and of insurance, trust and loan companies.[6] In recent years, private legislation has been used for the amalgamation of insurance companies and the revival of small business

---

4. This was done as a deliberate effort to direct private legislation to the Senate. If the bill originates in the Senate, the promoter only has to pay a fee of $200 (Senate Rule 110) instead of a fee of $500 in the House (Standing Order 134(2)). This difference in fees was first established in 1934 when the Standing Orders of the House were changed to "secure the freedom of this house from the initial consideration of large numbers of private bills by increasing the business that may be presented to the second chamber in the way of private legislation" (see *Debates*, June 30, 1934, pp. 4509-10). This has led to most private bills being introduced in the Senate. Since 1970, only six private bills have originated in the House, the last in 1978: Bill C-164, *An Act to incorporate Unity Bank of Canada*, on March 29, 1972 (*Journals*, p. 232); Bill C-264, *An Act respecting the Eastern Canada Synod of the Lutheran Church in America*, on April 3, 1974 (*Journals*, p. 94); Bill C-1001, *An Act to provide an exception from the general law relating to marriage in the case of Richard Fritz and Marianne Strass*, on July 30, 1975 (*Journals*, p. 750); Bill C-1002, *An Act to incorporate the Northland Bank*, on December 20, 1975 (*Journals*, p. 977); Bill C-1001, *An Act to incorporate the Continental Bank of Canada*, on July 14, 1977 (*Journals*, p. 1371); and Bill C-1001, *An Act respecting Bell Canada*, on April 12, 1978 (*Journals*, p. 638).

5. For example, during the Third Session of the Thirty-Fourth Parliament (May 1991 to September 1993), nine private bills were considered for a total of 1 hour and 54 minutes; during the First Session of the Thirty-Fifth Parliament (January 1994 to February 1996), the House considered three private bills for a total of 1 hour and 20 minutes. See *Statistics Respecting House Business* prepared by the Journals Branch of the House of Commons.

6. See, for example, *An Act to amend the Act of incorporation of the Grand Lodge of the Benevolent and Protective Order of Elks of the Dominion of Canada*, S.C. 1980-81-82-83, c. 186; *An Act to incorporate Green Shield Canada*, S.C. 1992, c. 56; *An Act to amend An Act to incorporate the Royal Society of Canada*, S.C. 1992, c. 58; *An Act to change the name of The Canadian Medical Association*, S.C. 1993, c. 48; *An Act to incorporate the Canadian Association of Lutheran Congregations*, S.C., 1994, c. 49.

corporations which have previously been dissolved.[7] Although the reasons for this decrease in the passage of private bills vary, it is to a large degree due to changes to the general law, such as the *Dissolution and Annulment of Marriages Act* in 1963,[8] and the *Marriage (Prohibited Degrees) Act* in 1990,[9] and administrative mechanisms found in present acts such as the *Canada Business Corporations Act*,[10] the *Canada Corporations Act*[11] and the *Bank Act*.[12]

This chapter explains in general terms the kinds of bills classed as private, describes the principles of private bill procedure and how they are applied, and gives an overview of the particularities of the legislative process for such bills in the House of Commons.

Nature of Private Bills

A private bill may benefit the private interest of a particular individual or group of individuals in one of two ways:[13]

- The bill may supplement the general law by granting the beneficiary power to do something which cannot be done otherwise; or

- The bill may alter the general law by exempting the beneficiary from some existing legal obligation.

---

7. See, for example, *An Act to amend and repeal The Alliance Nationale Consolidated Act, 1945*, S.C. 1986, c. 64; *An Act to revive E.G. Klein Limited and to provide for its continuance under the Canada Business Corporation Act*, S.C. 1980-81-82-83, c. 185; *An Act to revive Yellowknife Electric Limited and to provide for its continuance under the Canada Business Corporation Act*, S.C. 1987, c. 56.

8. S.C. 1963, c. 10. This statute authorized the Senate alone to dissolve or annul marriages by resolution. Prior to the enactment of this Act, the innocent party to divorce in either Newfoundland or Quebec (their provincial courts were not empowered to hear divorce cases) would petition Parliament for a private bill to dissolve the marriage. The petition would allege a matrimonial offense and pray for "relief". Most petitions were first considered in the Senate before its Committee on Divorce (where the fees for a private bill were less than the fees imposed in the House of Commons). The majority of divorce bills were uncontested and passed both Houses without question. However, if any Member questioned the reasons for the divorce or if the participants in the cases wished to be heard, the House of Commons Standing Committee on Miscellaneous Private Bills had the authority to rehear the case. Petitioner and respondent, both represented by counsel, would appear before the committee, which would function as a court of law. The House dealt with the bill when a report was received from the committee. See *Dawson*, p. 243. In 1968, the *Divorce Act* (S.C. 1967-68, c. 24) set up divorce courts in these two provinces, and the Senate was no longer empowered to dissolve or annul marriages.

9. S.C. 1990, c. 46.

10. S.C. 1974-75-76, c. 33.

11. S.C. 1964-65, c. 52.

12. S.C. 1953-54, c. 48, and S.C. 1966-67, c. 87.

13. *May*, 22nd ed., p. 857.

Thus, a bill which allows a group of individuals to form a type of corporation not provided for in the general law would be an example of a bill which supplements the general law.[14] A bill which exempts an existing corporation from a general provision of a statute applicable to all such corporations would be an example of a private bill which derogates from the general law.[15] Legislation which authorizes the marriage of two blood relations would be another example of a bill exempting one or more persons from the general law.[16]

A bill may affect the private interest of an individual or a defined class of individuals and yet not be considered a private bill.[17] In order that a bill be designated as private, it should not and cannot include any feature of public policy because such characterization would transcend any private nature it may have.[18] A bill should be introduced as a public bill when it affects public policy, when it proposes to amend or repeal a public act, or when it affects a large area and multiplicity of interests.[19]

Principles of Private Bill Procedure

As the Speaker noted in 1971, private bill procedure was established to protect the public against the uncontrolled granting of special powers to private interests.[20] The person or organization affected petitions Parliament to grant some extraordinary

---

14. See, for example, *Green Shields Canada Act*, S.C. 1992, c. 56.

15. See, for example, *An Act respecting the acquisition, operation and disposal of the Windsor–Detroit Tunnel by the City of Windsor*, S.C. 1987, c. 55.

16. See, for example, *An Act to provide an exception from the public general law relating to marriage in the case of Gerald Harvey Fudge and Audrey Marie Saunders*, S.C. 1984, c. 52.

17. See, for example, Bill S-25, *An Act respecting Hudson's Bay Company* (*Journals*, June 17, 1970, p. 1026; *Debates*, October 5, 1970, pp. 8797-8800), and Bill C-259, *An Act to extend the term of a patent relating to certain food additives* (*Journals*, June 17, 1987, p. 1184; *Debates*, June 18, 1987, pp. 7346-7). Unlike British parliamentary practice which has provisions for a cross-category of bills having both public and private attributes, these so-termed hybrid bills do not exist in Canadian parliamentary practice. Hybrid bills may be defined as public bills which affect a particular private interest in a manner different from the private interest of other persons or bodies of the same category or class (*May*, 22nd ed., p. 554). As Speaker Lamoureux stated in a 1971 ruling, "We have, according to our standing orders and our long established practice, just two kinds of bills—private bills and public bills". See *Journals*, February 22, 1971, p. 351; *Debates*, pp. 3617-29.

18. See rulings in *Journals*, February 22, 1971, p. 352; *Debates*, April 15, 1985, pp. 3699-700. See also *Debates*, February 2, 1911, cols. 2883-4, where the Speaker ruled that a bill which a Member wished to introduce as a public bill was in fact a private bill and, as such, the Member was instructed that the rules respecting private bills had to be followed. Almost 65 years later, the Speaker made a similar ruling when a private Member attempted to introduce a bill entitled *An Act for the parole of Dr. Henry Morgentaler* as a public bill (see *Journals*, October 23, 1975, pp. 795-6).

19. See *May*, 22nd ed., p. 853. See also *Journals*, February 22, 1971, p. 352.

20. *Journals*, February 22, 1971, p. 351.

favour set down in a bill. The facts upon which the bill is based are examined by both Houses of Parliament. If deemed necessary, the committee to which the private bill is referred may call witnesses to testify, and the committee will adjudicate whether the need for the bill has been demonstrated. Thus, in considering private bills, Parliament acts in both a judicial and legislative capacity. Like a court, Parliament will hear all parties involved and decide whether or not the interests of private parties justify additional rights or exemptions from the general law; as a legislature overseeing the passage of a bill, it is watchful over the interests of the public.[21]

Four fundamental principles underlie and define private bill procedure as set out in the Standing Orders and the procedural authorities.[22] These principles may be expressed in the following terms:

1. A private bill should only be passed at the explicit request of the persons who are to benefit from the legislation.

2. Pertinent information regarding a private bill should be made available to all interested persons.

3. All persons or bodies affected by a private bill should be heard and the need for the bill demonstrated.

4. The financial burden of considering a bill for the benefit of private interests should not be borne solely by the public treasury.

These principles are examined in detail in the pages that follow.

PRINCIPLE 1. A PRIVATE BILL SHOULD ONLY BE PASSED AT THE EXPLICIT REQUEST OF THE PERSONS WHO ARE TO BENEFIT FROM THE LEGISLATION

In the decision to proceed with a private bill, there is a balance to be achieved between the undoubted right of Parliament to initiate legislation and the recognition of the ancient fundamental right to petition Parliament for the redress of grievances.[23] Unlike a public bill, which may be introduced after 48 hours' notice either by the government (in the person of a Minister) or by a private Member, a private bill is only presented after a private Member has filed with the Clerk of the House a

---

21. See Edward P. Hartney, *Manual of Private Bill Practice of the Parliament of Canada,* Ottawa: Maclean, Roger & Co., 1882, p. 2.

22. In the First Parliament, the House of Commons adopted the rules and practice in force in the Province of Canada with regard to private bills. (There had been no clearly defined practice for private bills in the legislatures of Nova Scotia and New Brunswick.) See *Todd*, 3rd ed., p. iii.

23. According to a principle outlined before a special committee of the British House of Commons in 1832, a person should come before Parliament as a suitor only if there was no other way of obtaining some redress for a grievance. This principle was subsequently observed by the Canadian Parliament. See *Beauchesne*, 4th ed., p. 336. See also Chapter 22, "Public Petitions".

petition from the applicant for a private bill.[24] It is well recognized in the Canadian House of Commons that Ministers may not sponsor private bills as the Crown cannot petition itself.[25]

The rules respecting public petitions generally apply to petitions for private bills[26] (see Chapter 22, "Public Petitions"). A private bill petition is presented to the House by a private Member who has signed the back of the petition and who will be acting as sponsor of the private bill.[27] The petition for a private bill sets out the reasons why special legislation is requested, explaining what that legislation is intended to accomplish, and concludes with an explicit request for such legislation to be enacted. The petition must bear the signatures of the persons who are requesting the legislation and who are to benefit from it. The sponsor is responsible for ensuring that the form of the petition complies with the requirements set down in the Standing Orders.[28] The Member may present the petition at any time during a sitting by filing it with the Clerk of the House.[29] The usual practice, however, is for the petitioner for a private bill, or the petitioner's parliamentary agent (see below), to deposit the petition with the Clerk of Petitions (a House official responsible for examining and reporting to the House on the form of petitions) who, after having the petition endorsed by the sponsoring Member, sees that it is filed with the Clerk of the House.

In addition to filing a petition, the applicant must deposit a copy of the bill, in English or French, with the Clerk of the House not later than the first day of the session if the bill is to originate in the House.[30] An official appointed by the Clerk, acting as Examiner of Private Bills, examines and, if necessary, revises the bill before

---

24. A petition may only be presented through a Senator or a Member of the House of Commons. See *Beauchesne*, 4th ed., p. 256. Even if a private bill is to originate in the Senate, the practice has been that individuals interested in obtaining a private bill also petition the House of Commons. The person or corporation seeking passage of a private bill is referred to as the applicant, the petitioner or the promoter of the bill. In one exceptional case in 1989, a Member of the House was the applicant of a private bill for the incorporation of a national passenger rail service and another Member the sponsor. Given that the petition for the bill was not filed within the specified time limit then in force, the two Members were invited to appear before the Standing Committee on Elections, Privileges, Procedure and Private Members' Business. At that meeting, a letter was read into the record from the sponsor indicating that the applicant was no longer interested in proceeding with the bill (see *Journals*, September 29, 1989, p. 555; October 2, 1989, p. 562; October 5, 1989, p. 579; Standing Committee on Elections, Privileges, Procedure and Private Members' Business, *Minutes of Proceedings and Evidence*, October 24, 1989, Issue No. 9, pp. 3-5).

25. *Bourinot*, 4th ed., p. 581.

26. Standing Orders 36 and 131.

27. Standing Order 131(3). On occasion, the name of the sponsor of a private bill has been changed by unanimous consent (see, for example, *Journals*, September 30, 1988, p. 3652).

28. Standing Order 131(2).

29. Standing Order 131(1).

30. Standing Order 134(1).

it is printed to ensure that it is drafted in accordance with the Standing Orders of the House.[31]

Unlike a public bill which is introduced by either a Minister or a private Member and subsequently "belongs" to the House of Commons, a private bill belongs to the applicant and not to the Member of Parliament sponsoring the bill or to the House. Should the applicant decide not to proceed any further with the bill, the committee to which the bill was referred after second reading will report back to the House accordingly.[32]

Although under no obligation to do so, the promoter of a private bill may choose to be represented before the House or any of its committees by someone who may or may not be a member of a provincial bar; this person is known as the promoter's "parliamentary agent". While a Member of Parliament must agree to present the petition and sponsor the bill, a Member cannot serve as parliamentary agent.[33] In order for someone to act as parliamentary agent, that person must be so authorized by the Speaker and is personally responsible to the Speaker for the observance of the rules, practices and procedures of Parliament.[34] The parliamentary agent acts as advisor and counsel for the petitioners throughout the various stages leading to the passage of the private bill and is responsible for the payment of all charges and fees prescribed by the Standing Orders.

No person may act as a parliamentary agent during any session without first paying a fee of $25.[35] The person must also be involved in promoting or opposing a private bill or petition pending in Parliament during that session. However, because most private bills originate in the Senate, the parliamentary agent is registered and pays the $25 fee only if asked to represent the promoter before a House committee.

---

31. Standing Order 136(1). Standing Order 136(2) to (5) sets out the rules for drafting a private bill. (See section on "Form of a Private Bill".) The first mention in the printed text of the Standing Orders of the term "Examiner" with regard to private bill procedure occurred in 1890 and resulted from amendments to the Standing Orders adopted in June 1887 (*Journals*, June 17, 1887, pp. 313-4; June 23, 1887, p. 412). The 1890 version of the Standing Orders stated that the Examiner would report to the Committee on Standing Orders that he had examined the bill and "noted variations from the provisions contained in the Model Bill" before its consideration by the Committee. As well, the Examiner would revise and certify all private bills passed by the Committee and the reports thereon before they are presented to the House "to ensure uniformity". See *Rules, Orders and Forms of Proceeding of the House of Commons of Canada*, 1890, Rule No. 59A.

32. See, for example, *Journals*, December 18, 1963, p. 697. See also Standing Committee on Elections, Privileges, Procedure and Private Members' Business, *Minutes of Proceedings and Evidence*, October 24, 1989, Issue No. 9, pp. 4-5, where the sponsor of a private bill informed the committee considering the promoter's late petition that the promoter did not wish to proceed with his private bill.

33. *Bourinot*, 4th ed., p. 581. Neither Members nor Officers of the House are allowed to transact private business before the House for profit (*Bourinot*, 4th ed., p. 582).

34. Standing Order 146(1).

35. Standing Order 146(3). Prior to 1927, parliamentary agents were not required to pay a sessional fee of $25. In 1927, the Special Committee appointed to revise the rules of the House presented a report. See *Journals*, March 15, 1927, pp. 232-84. Included in this report, which was adopted by the House, was the recommendation that a parliamentary agent pay a fee of $25 for any session in which he had some business before the House. See *Journals*, March 22, 1927, pp. 316-68, in particular pp. 366-7; *Debates*, pp. 1434-5. See also *Standing Orders of the House of Commons*, 1927, Standing Order 119(3).

Any parliamentary agent who willfully violates the Standing Orders or practices of Parliament or who deliberately behaves in an unbecoming manner when conducting proceedings before Parliament is liable to be barred, at the discretion of the Speaker, either permanently or temporarily, from exercising his or her duties as a parliamentary agent.[36]

PRINCIPLE 2. PERTINENT INFORMATION REGARDING A PRIVATE BILL SHOULD BE MADE AVAILABLE TO ALL INTERESTED PERSONS

The procedural requirements found in the Standing Orders respecting notice at various stages of private bills are not only directed towards Members but also to the public. The purpose of these notice provisions is to ensure that any person whose interests may be affected by the requested private legislation is sufficiently notified so that he or she may oppose or support the bill, in whole or in part, before its passage.

At the beginning of each session, the Clerk of the House publishes in the *Canada Gazette*[37] the Standing Order respecting notices of applications for private bills.[38] Thereafter, a note referring to the previous publication of this Standing Order is published each week in the *Canada Gazette*.[39]

The Standing Orders also require that applicants for private bills place a notice of their intention to apply for a bill once a week for four consecutive weeks in the *Canada Gazette*.[40] The published notice should set out the intent of the proposed legislation, indicate during which session it is to be applied for, who the applicant is, and the address of the applicant or the applicant's parliamentary agent.[41] In certain cases, notices must also be sent to certain officials and be published in local newspapers.[42] The applicant must

---

36. Standing Order 146(4).

37. The *Canada Gazette* is a periodical publication of the Government.

38. The notice, which appears in Part 1 of the *Canada Gazette*, is a reprint of Standing Order 130. The notice also advises that further information may be obtained from the Private Members' Business Office at the House of Commons. See, for example, *Canada Gazette*, Part 1, September 27, 1997, pp. 3097-8.

39. Standing Order 129. See, for example, *Canada Gazette*, Part 1, April 25, 1998, p. 920. Prior to March 23, 1990, when the present Standing Order was adopted (see *Journals*, March 23, 1990, p. 1397), the Clerk would have the Standing Orders relating to Private Bills published weekly in the *Canada Gazette* (see, for example, *Canada Gazette*, Part 1, January 7, 1989, pp. 18-26). After the first six weeks of a session, the notice would also indicate when the time limit for filing petitions had expired. See, for example, *Canada Gazette*, Part 1, January 6, 1990, pp. 5-13.

40. Standing Order 130(1), (3). When an application for a private bill originates in Quebec or Manitoba, the notice must be published in English in an English-language newspaper and in French in a French-language newspaper and in both languages in the *Canada Gazette*. Proof that the notice was duly published is established by statutory declaration (an affidavit) sent to the Clerk of the House.

41. Standing Order 130(1).

42. Standing Order 130(2).

provide proof of the publication of the notice by means of a statutory declaration (affidavit) sent to the Clerk of the House.[43]

Since Members of Parliament may be asked to speak on behalf of the promoter or opponent of a bill, certain notices regarding the meetings of the committee on a private bill are posted by the Clerk of the House throughout the parliamentary precinct and appended to the *Journals* for a specified period of time before the committee sits.[44] In the case of a bill originating in the Commons, there must be one week's notice of a committee meeting; in the case of a bill originating in the Senate, the notice period is 24 hours. Lists of all private bills referred to committee, specifying the committee and dates on or after which the bills can be considered, as well as lists of all committee meetings must also be posted.[45] Moreover, no significant amendment to a private bill may be proposed in the House unless one day's notice has been given.[46]

Finally, in addition to the notices, certain records regarding each private bill are kept by the staff of the House, and these records are open for public inspection.[47] Records are kept of general information pertaining to the person or group applying for the bill or to the parliamentary agent, to the fees paid, and to the proceedings on the bill.

PRINCIPLE 3. ALL PERSONS OR BODIES AFFECTED BY A PRIVATE BILL SHOULD BE HEARD AND THE NEED FOR THE BILL DEMONSTRATED

Since a private bill makes certain assertions which are put forth in support of the request for legislation, they should be proven before Parliament agrees to enact the legislation being sought. The legislative function of Parliament demands that each measure be given due deliberation and orderly consideration. The judicial-like proceedings surrounding private bill practice demands, in addition, that those concerned be heard, or at the very least be given the opportunity to be heard.

The decision of the House to give second reading to a private bill does not mean that the House has approved the principle of the bill as is the case for a public bill.

---

43. Standing Order 130(3). On one occasion, when a number of private bills failed to pass because of the dissolution of Parliament, the applicants of the bills attempted to have the same bills considered in the House the following Parliament without first publishing the required notices of intention. This matter was referred to the Select Standing Committee on Standing Orders, which recommended in its First Report that the rules regarding notice be suspended. The Report was subsequently adopted by the House. See *Journals*, February 9, 1927; pp. 88-9; February 18, 1927, pp. 134-5.

44. Standing Order 141(2). The provisions of this Standing Order have been suspended on occasion (see, for example, *Journals*, March 16, 1978, p. 499 (bill originating in the House); *Journals*, July 17, 1980, p. 396 (bill originating in the Senate)).

45. Standing Order 145.

46. Standing Order 142.

47. Standing Order 144.

Rather, the House has given the bill a second reading conditional upon a committee's finding that the assertions contained in the petition and repeated in the bill's preamble have been proven.[48] While a preamble is optional in a public bill, it is essential in all private bills.[49] The procedure thus requires that a private bill be sent to committee so that opponents of the bill may be heard. Another reason why it is sent to committee is so that Parliament can satisfy itself that the matters raised in the preamble of the bill are true and that the provisions of the bill are a proper response to those assertions. The bill as reported from the committee, with or without amendments, may be said to be the committee's decision on the petitioner's request.[50]

Private bills typically relate to subjects of a particular character, some of them purely personal, and thus do not evoke extensive debate in the House. The private interests being asserted by them, however, may occasionally infringe on other private rights. In this respect, the committee on a private bill carries out not just a legislative function but sits in a quasi-judicial capacity, hearing all parties concerned and ruling on whether the petitioner's request should be granted. The committee must also be vigilant in preventing frauds from being perpetrated on Parliament by cross-examining the promoters on their claims made in the bill's preamble.[51]

The committee on a private bill does not hear witnesses in the same sense that a committee studying a public bill does. The promoter of the bill, who may or may not be represented by counsel, appears before the committee as the petitioner for relief of a legislative nature which the courts and governmental agencies cannot provide. The promoter, as opposed to the committee, may call witnesses to support the assertions put forth in the preamble of the bill.[52]

Any opponents of a bill, whether or not represented by counsel, may also address the committee and may call witnesses in support of their position when the committee begins consideration of the particular clause or clauses being opposed.[53] However, before an opponent of a private bill may be heard in committee, a petition against that part of the bill found to be objectionable must first be presented to the House. The petition must state the grounds for the objection; it is presented to the House on the opponent's behalf by a Member who may submit it to the Clerk of the

---

48. *Bourinot*, 4th ed., p. 599.

49. *Beauchesne*, 6th ed., p. 287.

50. *Beauchesne*, 4th ed., p. 336.

51. Prior to Confederation, committees had no power to examine witnesses under oath, but in 1867-68, an Act was passed empowering the committee on any private bill to examine witnesses upon oath to be administered by the Chair or any member of such committee (*Todd*, 3rd ed., p. 68). See *An Act to provide for Oaths to Witnesses being administered in certain cases for the purposes of either House of Parliament*, S.C. 1867-68, c. 24, ss. 2-3.

52. *Beauchesne*, 4th ed., pp. 355-6.

53. *Beauchesne*, 4th ed., pp. 350, 356.

House at any time while the bill is under consideration in the House or in committee. After the Clerk of Petitions has reported that the petition is in conformity with the rules, it is deemed referred to the committee studying the bill.[54] The promoter may challenge the *locus standi,* or right to appear, of any opponent by questioning whether the opponent's interests would really be affected by the proposed legislation. The committee alone has the power to decide whether an opponent has standing and should be heard.[55] If the opponent is heard, the promoter may cross-examine the opponent and the opponent's witnesses, and the opponent may likewise cross-examine the promoter and the promoter's witnesses. However, the opponents may only be heard on the grounds stated in their petition.[56] If the committee does not feel that the grounds stated in the petition are specific enough, the committee may request that the opponent to the bill provide a more specific statement.[57] No petitioners will be heard against the preamble unless in their petition they specifically ask to be heard against it.[58]

When the parliamentary agent is addressing the committee, or while witnesses are under examination, the committee room is an open court, but when the committee deliberates, all the agents, witnesses and strangers are ordered to withdraw and the committee sits *in camera.* When the committee has come to a decision, the doors are opened and the Chair informs the parties of the committee's decision.[59]

PRINCIPLE 4. THE FINANCIAL BURDEN OF CONSIDERING A BILL FOR THE BENEFIT OF PRIVATE INTERESTS SHOULD NOT BE BORNE SOLELY BY THE PUBLIC TREASURY

Since a private bill is for the benefit of private interests, the financial burden of considering such a bill should not be borne solely by the public treasury. It is in recognition of this principle that the Standing Orders set out fees and charges which are imposed on the promoter and which must be paid before the bill can proceed.[60]

---

54. Standing Order 141(1). See, for example, *Journals*, May 29, 1990, p. 1776; May 30, 1990, p. 1784.

55. Petitioners have no *locus standi* before a committee when their property or interests are not directly affected by the bill, or when, for other reasons, they are not entitled to oppose it (*Bourinot*, 4th ed., p. 608).

56. For procedures relative to committee proceedings when a petition against a private bill has been received by a legislative committee, see Legislative Committee on Bill S-10, *An Act respecting the Canadian Institute of Chartered Accountants*, *Minutes of Proceedings and Evidence*, May 22, 1990 and May 30, 1990, Issue No. 1, p. 6.

57. *Todd*, 3rd ed., p. 73.

58. *Todd*, 3rd ed., p. 73; *Bourinot*, 4th ed., p. 606.

59. *Todd*, 3rd ed., p. 79. For a recent example of a committee exercising this quasi-judicial function, see Legislative Committee on Bill S-10, *An Act respecting the Canadian Institute of Chartered Accountants*, *Minutes of Proceedings and Evidence*, May 22, 1990 and May 30, 1990, Issue No. 1, pp. 5-6, 51-3.

60. See Standing Order 134. Section 15 of the *Publication of Statutes Act* (R.S.C. 1985, c. S-21) also provides for the promoter to pay the charges set by the House in which the bill originates. This principle was entrenched in Rule No. 58 of the *Rules of the House of Commons of Canada, 1868*: "The expenses and costs attending on Private Bills giving an exclusive privilege, or for any object of profit, or private, corporate, or individual advantage; or for amending, extending, or enlarging any former Acts, in such manner as to confer additional powers, ought not to fall on the public ..."

Any person who wishes to have a private bill enacted must deposit with the Clerk of the House, on the first day of the session, a copy of the bill in either French or English. A sum of money sufficient to cover the printing and translation costs must be paid at this time.[61] After second reading of the private bill, but before its consideration by a committee, the applicant must pay the cost of printing the Act in the statutes and a fee of $500.[62] If the purpose of the bill is to increase a company's capital stock, additional charges may be levied based on a scale found in the Standing Orders and corresponding to the requested capital stock increase.[63] Other charges, such as for an exemption from a particular Standing Order, or for reprinting a bill amended in committee, may also be levied. A statement of these charges is prepared by a House official[64] and remitted to the promoter or parliamentary agent who subsequently deposits the fees with the Clerk of the House.[65] In practice, however, no additional charges are imposed for most private bills even when committee meetings are held and the proceedings published. The fees paid on a private bill that has not become law may be refunded.[66]

The House has, on occasion, waived its fees for private bills. In the early years of Confederation, fees were frequently waived,[67] especially when no commercial interests were affected.[68] More recently, prior to the rule changes in 1994,[69] when

---

61. Standing Order 134(1).

62. Standing Order 134(2).

63. Standing Order 134(3)-(8). These fees apply also to bills originating in the Senate. The rules on the matter of fees refer to a time when private bills were the usual way for companies to become incorporated or to amend their charters. Such parliamentary procedure is now almost totally superseded by administrative procedure under public general acts such as the *Canadian Business Corporations Act* (R.S.C. 1985, c. C-44).

64. This official is referred to as the Chief Clerk of Private Bills and also acts as the Examiner of Petitions for Private Bills and the Examiner of Private Bills. In 1862, the Legislative Assembly of the Province of Canada appointed the Chief Clerk of the Private Bills Office as its Examiner of Standing Orders, assigning to him the responsibility of examining the facts with regard to notice given on each petition. This practice continued following Confederation in the new Parliament. See *Todd*, 3rd ed., p. 36.

65. Standing Order 134(9). The House has allowed those fees paid in a previous session (when the bill was introduced but had not passed because of a prorogation) to apply to a bill in the following session (see, for example, *Journals*, October 20, 1967, p. 401).

66. *Journals*, June 8, 1892, p. 354; July 2, 1892, p. 417; May 21, 1976, p. 1307; May 26, 1976, p. 1313. See also Speaker's ruling, *Journals*, December 9, 1974, pp. 179-81.

67. *Bourinot*, 2nd ed., p. 730.

68. *Bourinot*, 4th ed., p. 604.

69. Standing Order 132 was deleted on June 10, 1994. See Standing Committee on Procedure and House Affairs, *Minutes of Proceedings and Evidence* (Twenty-Seventh Report), June 9, 1994, Issue No. 16, p. 8. See also *Journals*, June 8, 1994, p. 545; June 10, 1994, p. 563.

petitions for private bills had to be introduced within the first six weeks of a session, the House often saw fit to waive its fees for late petitions.[70]

Form of a Private Bill

The form of a private bill is similar to that of a public bill with the exception that it must have a preamble, containing the following formula:

> *Whereas (the person/corporation named) has by its petition prayed that it be enacted as hereinafter set forth and it is expedient to grant the prayer of the said petition: Therefore Her Majesty, by and with the advice and consent of the Senate and the House of Commons, enacts, as follows:*[71]

In addition to the above wording, the preamble typically spells out in detail the reasons the person or corporation wishes to have a private bill enacted. While in some instances the preamble is short and straightforward,[72] most preambles are lengthy and may include a history of a corporation concerned.[73]

During the first 20 years of Confederation, private bills were drafted in a haphazard way. Members of the House of Commons and the committees to which private bills stood referred complained frequently that private bills were not uniformly framed and often contained provisions which committees had objected to in other private bills. In response to these complaints, the House adopted, in 1883, a recommendation from the Standing Committee on Railways, Canals and Telegraph Lines. It stated that any private acts of incorporation should include specific clauses from the general act relating to such bills.[74] In 1887, after further study by a special committee, a model bill was drawn up to which all bills of incorporation had to conform.[75]

The Standing Orders stipulate that any bill for an Act of incorporation must conform with a model bill, which can be obtained from the Clerk of the House.[76] The objective is to ensure that all pertinent information is made available. Any

---

70. See, for example, *Journals*, March 19, 1990, pp. 1363-4.

71. *Beauchesne*, 6th ed., p. 287.

72. See, for example, *An Act respecting the Canadian Institute of Chartered Accountants*, S.C. 1990, c. 52; *An Act to change the name of The Canadian Medical Association*, S.C. 1993, c. 48.

73. See, for example, *An Act to amalgamate the Alberta corporation known as the Missionary Church with the Canada corporation known as the Evangelical Missionary Church, Canada West District*, S.C. 1995, c. 50; *An Act to dissolve the Nipissing and James Bay Railway Company*, S.C. 1996, c. 38.

74. *Debates*, April 20, 1883, pp. 741-3. Departures from the general form were to be specially noted, and any bill which deviated from this rule would be returned to the promoters (see *Dawson*, p. 246).

75. *Debates*, June 18, 1887, pp. 1115-6. Unusual provisions in the proposed bills were to be marked and were to be clearly specified in the notice of application (*Dawson*, p. 246). Model bills were prepared for the incorporation of banks, trust companies, loan companies, insurance companies and railways.

76. Standing Order 136(2).

provisions in the proposed bill which are not in accord with the model bill must be inserted between brackets or underlined.[77] When a private bill amends an existing Act, the new text must be underlined and the existing text printed in the right-hand page opposite the proposed text.[78] When a private bill proposes to repeal certain clauses or sections of an existing Act, these clauses or sections must be indicated opposite the repealing clause.[79] A brief explanatory note giving the reasons for any clause of an unusual nature or which differs from the model bill clauses must be printed opposite the clause in the bill.[80] Finally, if the bill is for the purpose of confirming any agreement, a verified copy of such agreement must be attached.[81]

If the promoter of any private bill decides to present the bill first in the House of Commons, he or she should meet with a legislative counsel of the House who can assist in the drafting of the bill in accordance with the rules and practices of Parliament.[82] The legislative counsel can also advise the petitioners on the various preliminary stages in the passage of a private bill (for example, when the notices are published in the *Canada Gazette* or in newspapers) and, when requested, advises the committee examining the private bill of any provisions in it which are in variance with the general law and of any unusual provisions deserving special attention.

Legislative Process for Private Bills

Private bills are subject to the same procedural requirements as public bills: they must have three separate readings and be given a detailed study by a committee.[83] Bills originating in the Senate retain their Senate bill number during passage through

---

77. Standing Order 136(2).

78. Standing Order 136(3).

79. Standing Order 136(4).

80. Standing Order 136(5).

81. Standing Order 138.

82. Although in the past a private bill might have been drafted by the promoter's counsel who would then also act as the parliamentary agent, in today's practice a private bill is usually drafted with the assistance of the Law Clerk and Parliamentary Counsel of the Senate because most, if not all, private bills are now introduced in that Chamber. If a bill is to originate in the House of Commons however, pursuant to Standing Order 134(1), a copy of the bill is to be deposited with the Clerk of the House no later than the first day of the session. The bill is then examined by a House official to ensure it satisfies the specific requirements as to form (Standing Order 136(1)).

83. Standing Order 147. In current practice (because most, if not all, private bills originate in the Senate), after the petition and the bill have been received by the House, the House typically proceeds through all stages in the same sitting by unanimous consent. See, for example, *Journals*, March 13, 1997, p. 1281; April 14, 1997, p. 1383; December 9, 1998, p. 1430, March 18, 1999, pp. 1636-7. On one occasion, a petition for a private bill originating in the Senate was filed by a Member, deemed filed within the required time limit and reported on by the Examiner of Petitions; and the bill was read a second time, referred to a Committee of the Whole, reported without amendment, concurred in at the report stage, read a third time and passed, all on the same day. See *Journals*, June 15, 1993, pp. 3309, 3314.

the House.[84] Those private bills originating in the House are numbered consecutively beginning with C-1001. Private bills are considered during the time provided for Private Members' Business. However, as explained earlier in this chapter, while a private bill must be sponsored by a private Member in the House, it is not considered as a private Member's bill because it is introduced at the request of a private person outside Parliament.

FILING OF THE PETITION

As soon as a petition for a private bill is received, the Clerk of Petitions asks the Member who will be acting as the sponsor to endorse the petition by signing the back of it.[85] It is then filed with the Clerk of the House and recorded in that day's *Journals*.[86] The petition must bear the original signatures of the persons who are requesting the legislation and who are to benefit from it.[87] In the case of a petition from a corporation, the petition must bear the corporate seal as well as the signatures of the authorized officials of the corporation. The signatures must appear at the end of the prayer,[88] and where there are three or more petitioners, at least three of the signatures must follow the prayer on the same page.[89]

Although the Standing Orders are not explicit as to whether a petition is required for a private bill originating in the Senate to be considered by the House, the long-established practice is for the promoter of the bill to petition each House separately.[90] With a private bill originating in the Senate, the usual practice is for the Member acting as the sponsor to file the petition with the Clerk of the House after the bill has received second reading in the Senate.

REPORT OF THE CLERK OF PETITIONS

The day after the petition is recorded in the *Journals,* the Clerk of Petitions files a report with the Clerk of the House indicating whether the petition meets the requirements of the Standing Orders and the practices of the House as to form and content.

---

84. Senate bill numbers commence with the letter "S". For further information, see Chapter 16, "The Legislative Process".

85. Standing Order 131(3). Unlike a public petition, a private bill petition is not certified by the Clerk of Petitions before being presented.

86. See, for example, *Journals*, December 1, 1992, p. 2267; June 15, 1993, p. 3314; May 5, 1999, p. 1831.

87. Unlike public petitions, petitioners for a private bill are not required to obtain 25 signatures (see Speaker's ruling, *Debates*, December 1, 1986, p. 1647). See also Chapter 22, "Public Petitions".

88. The prayer is that part of a petition in which the petitioners present their request for some action. The prayer must be clear, proper and respectful, and the action requested must be within the jurisdiction of Parliament.

89. Standing Order 131(4).

90. Between 1920 and 1928, a number of examples can be found in the *Journals* where a private bill originating in the Senate passed through the House of Commons without a petition being presented in the House of Commons; but since 1928, it has been the practice for a petition to be presented in both Houses.

If the petition does meet the requirements, it is deemed read and received[91] and will be deemed referred to the committee which will be studying the private bill after second reading.[92] If the petition is deemed inadmissible, it cannot be received by the House as it stands, and the private bill based thereon cannot be submitted to the House.[93] No debate is allowed on the report of the Clerk of Petitions.[94]

REPORT OF THE EXAMINER OF PETITIONS FOR PRIVATE BILLS

Once the petition for a private bill has been received by the House, an official of the House acting as the Examiner of Petitions for Private Bills examines the petition and the published notices to ensure that the requirements have been met regarding notice and the number of times it has been advertised in the *Canada Gazette*.[95] The Examiner of Petitions for Private Bills then files a report with the Clerk of the House on whether the requirements regarding notice have been observed by the applicant.[96] Should the Examiner report that notice has in some way been deficient or defective

---

91. Standing Order 131(5).

92. Standing Order 141(1).

93. Prior to June 1994, petitions had to be filed within the first six weeks of the session. If they were not filed within this period, the Clerk of Petitions would report that the petition did not meet the requirements in respect to the filing of petitions (see, for example, *Journals*, November 27, 1991, p. 809; April 1, 1992, p. 1250). A motion would then be adopted to refer the petition and the report to the Standing Committee on Procedure and House Affairs. The Committee would recommend the suspension of the Standing Order. If the Committee's report was concurred in by the House, the petition would be received (Standing Order 140) (see, for example, *Journals*, February 14, 1990, p. 1219; March 19, 1990, pp. 1363-4). On occasion, and throughout most of the Third Session of the Thirty-Fourth Parliament (1991-93), unanimous consent would be given to deem that a petition for a private bill had been presented within the required time frame (see, for example, *Journals*, December 4, 1991, p. 846). Since Standing Order 132 concerning the time requirement for the filing of petitions was removed from the Standing Orders in June 1994 (*Journals*, June 10, 1994, p. 563), no petition has been deemed inadmissible. The Committee occasionally recommended that charges be levied for the suspension or modification of the Standing Orders (Standing Order 134(3)(*a*)) (see, for example, *Journals*, July 7, 1981, pp. 2790-1).

94. Standing Order 131(6).

95. The position of Examiner of Petitions for Private Bills first appeared in the text of the written Standing Orders in 1906. In July of that year, the Special Committee to Revise the Rules of the House recommended that such a position be established, the purpose of which would be to consider whether petitions for private bills met the notice requirements and so report to the House. This employee relieved the Committee on Standing Orders of its preliminary responsibility to report to the House on notice requirements. See *Journals*, July 10, 1906, pp. 579-80. In March 1927, a number of amendments were made to the Standing Orders concerning private bills, one of which declared that the Chief Clerk of Private Bills would be the Examiner of Petitions for Private Bills (*Journals*, March 22, 1927, pp. 352-3).

96. Standing Order 133(2). See, for example, *Journals*, June 11, 1992, p. 1696; March 18, 1997, p. 1310. It has happened that the Clerk of Petitions and the Examiner of Petitions for Private Bills have reported the same day (see, for example, *Journals*, June 21, 1994, pp. 651-2; December 13, 1995, p. 2257; April 27, 1999, p. 1775). In case of a railway company, or of a canal company, or for extension of the line of any existing or authorized railway or canal, or for the construction of branches thereto, the Examiner of Petitions can not consider the petition unless a map or plan is also filed (Standing Order 133(4)). If the map or plan is not filed, the Examiner of Petitions will not report, and the matter would not be further proceeded with.

or that there is some doubt in the matter, the Examiner's report and the petition are deemed referred to the Standing Committee on Procedure and House Affairs.[97] If a private bill originating in the Senate is sent to the Commons without being based on a petition received in the House, the Examiner of Petitions compares the terms of the preamble of the bill with the required notices and proceeds exactly as if a petition had been received.[98]

COMMITTEE PROCEEDINGS ON THE PUBLICATION OF NOTICES

If a report of the Examiner of Petitions has been referred to the Standing Committee on Procedure and House Affairs, the Committee may call before it the Member of Parliament who presented the petition for a private bill as well as the applicant or the parliamentary agent. After hearing their explanations, the Committee decides whether or not the petition should be acted on and under what conditions. The Committee presents a report to the House regarding any deficiencies or defects found in the notices and recommends the course it deems appropriate in the circumstances.[99] For example, the Committee may recommend that certain provisions of the Standing Orders be suspended, the grounds for which are included in the report. Should the Committee not recommend that the Standing Orders be suspended, the House cannot consider the bill based on the petition.[100] After the Committee's report has been tabled, the Chair of the Committee or the Member who presented the petition will usually move concurrence in the report.[101]

FIRST READING OF THE BILL

After either the Examiner of Petitions for Private Bills or the Standing Committee on Procedure and House Affairs has reported that the notice requirements have been satisfied (i.e., the applicants published a notice of intent in the *Canada Gazette* and provided proof of this publication), any private bill originating in the Commons may

---

97. Standing Order 133(2). Since 1960, there have been no cases of a report of the Examiner of Petitions for Private Bills being referred to a committee for consideration because of deficiencies in the notice requirements.

98. Standing Order 133(3). See also *Todd*, 3rd ed., p. 118. The Examiner of Petitions for Private Bills examines and reports on the bill after first reading and before the committee stage.

99. Standing Orders 133(2) and 140. If the Committee finds, for example, that the persons affected by the proposed bill had sufficient knowledge of the applicant's intentions or that the applicant alone would be affected, then the Committee may even recommend that the notice requirement be suspended completely. If, when the Committee compares the notice and the petition, it finds that the terms of the notice do not correspond to those of the petition or that the notice fails to indicate clearly the object of the petition, the Committee must conclude that the bill is inadmissible, in whole or in part, and may recommend that the matter not be proceeded with or that certain provisions not included in the notice be struck from the bill (see *Bourinot*, 4th ed., pp. 593-4; *Beauchesne*, 4th ed., p. 344).

100. If the Committee does not recommend that a particular provision of the Standing Orders be suspended, Standing Order 140 implies that no motion for suspension of that provision can be made in the House.

101. Should the Committee receive new information after its report has been tabled, it may present a new report on the matter. For example, new evidence may be received showing that the other interested persons were sufficiently informed or that amended notices or additional notices have since appeared (*Bourinot*, 4th ed., p. 595; *Beauchesne*, 4th ed., p. 349).

be laid upon the Table by the Clerk of the House.[102] It is then deemed to have been read a first time, ordered to be printed, ordered for a second reading and added to the bottom of the Order of Precedence for Private Members' Business.[103] It is designated a votable item for the purposes of Private Members' Business.[104]

A private bill originating in the Senate is deemed to have been read a first time and ordered for a second reading at a subsequent sitting of the House as soon as a message is received from the Senate advising that it has passed the bill.[105] It is also placed at the bottom of the Order of Precedence for Private Members' Business and considered a votable item.[106]

SECOND READING AND REFERENCE TO A COMMITTEE

Unlike a public bill which is founded on reasons of public policy and which the House, in agreeing to its second reading, accepts and affirms in principle, the expediency of a private bill is mainly founded upon assertions to be proven in committee. The practice is for the House to agree to the second reading of a private bill; in doing so, it affirms the principle of the private bill, subject to a committee finding that the assertions set down in the preamble are true.[107] The amendments which can be moved at second reading are the same as those which can be moved to the motion for second reading of a public bill (i.e., a hoist amendment, a reasoned amendment and motion to discharge the order for second reading).[108]

---

102. Standing Order 135(1). In actual practice, an entry of the tabling is recorded in the *Journals* for that day (see, for example, *Journals*, July 9, 1975, p. 691; November 5, 1975, p. 824; November 1, 1976, p. 89; October 21, 1977, p. 24). This procedure differs from that for public bills which are introduced during Routine Proceedings either under the rubric "Introduction of Government Bills" or under the rubric "Introduction of Private Members' Bills". See Chapter 10, "The Daily Program", and Chapter 16, "The Legislative Process", for additional information.

103. Standing Orders 89 and 135(1). These bills are not subject to the random draw procedure.

104. Standing Order 92(3).

105. Standing Order 135(2). See, for example, *Journals*, June 8, 1994, p. 547; May 5, 1999, p. 1812.

106. Standing Order 92(3).

107. *Bourinot*, 4th ed., p. 599. The House may not debate any printed evidence taken by a Senate committee during the second reading stage (see Speaker's ruling, *Journals*, December 4, 1962, pp. 354-5).

108. See Chapter 16, "The Legislative Process", for detailed information on these kinds of amendments. If second reading is delayed three or six months (adoption of the hoist amendment), or if the bill is rejected, no new bill with the same intent may be introduced during the same session (*Beauchesne*, 4th ed., p. 353). An amendment interjecting a matter of public policy into a private bill has been ruled out of order (see Speaker's ruling, *Debates*, March 21, 1927, p. 1419). Similarly, an amendment expanding the scope of a private bill was also ruled out of order. In 1948, a Member moved that a private bill (*An Act respecting The Bell Telephone Company of Canada*) not be read a second time but "that it be resolved that in the opinion of this House no company should ask Parliament for an increase in authorized capital in excess of one hundred per cent". The Deputy Speaker ruled the amendment out of order as it "would affect all bills which will hereafter be introduced into the house ..." See *Debates*, April 30, 1948, pp. 3502-3.

COMMITTEE CONSIDERATION

Although the Standing Orders require that all private bills be referred to a legislative committee after second reading, the House of Commons regularly gives unanimous consent to take the committee stage in a Committee of the Whole since most private bills originate in the Senate.[109] However, where the House has received a petition against the bill or Members feel the bill warrants further examination, it is usually referred to a committee.[110]

The first business of the committee is to prove the preamble of the bill, that is, to substantiate the assertions contained in the bill's preamble and on which the rest of the bill is based. The promoters, or their parliamentary agent, present their case for the accuracy of the assertions and the appropriateness of the solution provided by the provisions of the bill. Any opponents, or their parliamentary agent, may present grounds for opposition to the bill or to some part of it. If any part of the preamble is not proven to the committee's satisfaction, then it may strike from the bill both that part of the preamble and those provisions which pertain to the unproven assertions. The committee may also prefer to report that the preamble was found not proven and that the bill should not be proceeded with. Any such report must include the reason for any material change to the preamble of the bill or why the preamble was found not proven.[111] Finally, the committee may amend the preamble either by striking out or modifying any assertions that may not have been substantiated to their satisfaction or by expunging any assertions the promoters may be desirous of withdrawing.

---

109. Standing Order 141(1). In the first six years of Confederation, the House referred all private bills to the Standing Committee on Private Bills or to the Standing Committee on Banking and Commerce or the Standing Committee on Railways, Canals and Telegraph Lines (*Todd*, 3rd ed., p. 64). This rule was changed in 1873, when the House agreed that private bills should be sent to standing committees after second reading to allow time for the bills to be printed (*Dawson*, p. 247). From 1876 to 1965, all private bills were referred to the Standing Committee on Private Bills or to the Standing Committee on Banking and Commerce, the Standing Committee on Railways, Canals and Telegraph Lines or to the Standing Committee on Miscellaneous Bills. From 1965 to 1986, private bills were referred after second reading to the Standing Committee on Finance, Trade and Economic Affairs, the Standing Committee on Transportation and Communications or to the Standing Committee on Miscellaneous Private Bills. In 1986, the Standing Order was amended to refer all private bills to legislative committees after second reading (*Journals*, February 13, 1986, pp. 1709-10). However, since the beginning of the Thirty-Fifth Parliament (1994-97), all private bills have been considered in Committees of the Whole. See, for example, *Journals*, June 14, 1994, p. 584; June 22, 1994, p. 660; September 17, 1996, p. 633; April 14, 1997, p. 1383. See also *Debates*, May 10, 1966, pp. 4958-9; March 16, 1967, p. 14085, for comments on the consideration of private bills in a Committee of the Whole.

110. For examples of committees examining private bills referred to them, see Legislative Committee on Bill S-9, *An Act to amalgamate the two Corporations known, respectively, as "The Governing Council of the Salvation Army, Canada East" and "The Governing Council of the Salvation Army, Canada West" and to make necessary provisions regarding the charter of the amalgamated corporation, Minutes of Proceedings and Evidence*, February 15, 1990, Issue No. 1; Legislative Committee on Bill S-10, *An Act respecting the Canadian Institute of Chartered Accountants, Minutes of Proceedings and Evidence*, May 22, 1990, and May 30, 1990, Issue No. 1.

111. Standing Order 141(6). See *Journals*, April 7, 1927, p. 476; July 15, 1931, p. 539; August 9, 1958, p. 397; July 17, 1963, p. 221. See also *Beauchesne*, 4th ed., p. 361, for a list of reasons why private bills have been reported back without their preambles having been proven.

After the preamble has been considered and proven to the satisfaction of the committee, it reviews the bill clause by clause and amendments may be moved. The amendments made to a private bill by a committee ought not to be so extensive as to constitute a different bill from that which has been read a second time.[112] All questions before the committee are decided by a majority of votes. The Chair may vote twice: once with the other members of the committee on any question, and then a second time if the first vote results in a tie.[113] The Chair initials the clauses of the bill when they are passed, with or without amendments, and signs the bill.[114]

Once the deliberations on the bill have been completed, the committee is required to report the bill back to the House, with or without amendments.[115]

If a committee reports to the House that the preamble was not proven, the bill is not placed on the *Order Paper* unless by special order of the House.[116] If the committee reports to the House that the bill contains provisions which were not contemplated in the notice or petition, the bill is not placed on the *Order Paper* until the Examiner of Petitions reports on the sufficiency or otherwise of the notice or petition to cover such provisions.[117]

Since the bill belongs to the promoter and not to the Member in charge of ushering the bill through the House, the promoter may inform the committee at any time that he or she does not wish to proceed any further with the bill.[118] This is reported to the House and the bill is withdrawn.[119]

---

112. *Bourinot*, 4th ed., pp. 611-2.

113. Standing Order 141(3). See Legislative Committee on Bill S-10, *An Act respecting the Canadian Institute of Chartered Accountants*, *Minutes of Proceedings and Evidence,* May 22, 1990, and May 30, 1990, Issue No. 1, p. 19, in regard to the Chairman's decision to cast a vote only in the event of a tie.

114. Standing Order 141(7).

115. Standing Order 141(5). For examples of private bills being reported back to the House from committee with amendments, see *Journals*, February 17, 1976, p. 1031 (Bill S-30, *An Act to incorporate Continental Bank of Canada*); April 6, 1978, p. 578 (Bill C-1001, *An Act respecting Bell Canada*). While Standing Orders 141(7) and 141(8) describe the procedures to be followed in regard to the reprint of a private bill, the procedures for clause-by-clause consideration in committee of a private bill and the referral back to the House and reprint of a private bill are the same today as those procedures established for the consideration of a public bill in committee. See Chapter 16, "The Legislative Process", and Chapter 20, "Committees".

116. Standing Order 141(6). See *Journals*, July 16, 1931, p. 552; August 11, 1958, p. 401; July 18, 1963, pp. 225-6. After the bill is reported back to the House with its preamble unproven and if the House wishes to have the bill reconsidered in committee, the motion to refer the bill back to committee is considered during Private Members' Business.

117. Standing Order 141(4). See *Bourinot*, 4th ed., p. 612.

118. See, for example, *Journals*, December 18, 1963, p. 697.

119. In 1968, prior to the House resolving into a Committee of the Whole to consider a private bill, the sponsor of the bill informed the House that the promoters were not in favour of having their bill amended. The sponsor then asked that the order for consideration of the bill in Committee of the Whole be discharged and the bill be withdrawn from the *Order Paper*. The motion was adopted. See *Debates*, March 14, 1968, p. 7641; *Journals*, p. 774. Pursuant to Standing Order 139, if the promoters do not appear before the committee to proceed with the bill on two separate occasions, the committee is to report the bill back with a recommendation that it be withdrawn. This Standing Order stems from the days when committees considered numerous private bills. If the order was called in committee for the consideration of a private bill and the promoters did not appear, the committee would proceed to the next private bill on its agenda. If the promoters did not appear the second time their private bill was scheduled for consideration, the order would be discharged.

REPORT STAGE AND THIRD READING

These two stages are governed by the Standing Orders relating to Private Members' Business (see Chapter 21, "Private Members' Business"). If a private bill is considered at the report stage, one day's notice of all amendments to the bill must be given at this stage of the proceedings.[120] During the third reading stage, the same amendments that may be proposed during third reading of a public bill may be moved (i.e., a hoist amendment, a reasoned amendment and an amendment to recommit the bill to committee).

PASSAGE AND ROYAL ASSENT

If a private bill which has originated in the House is passed in the same form by the Senate, the bill receives Royal Assent and becomes law. If it is amended by the Senate, a message is sent informing the House of the amendments. Between 1945 and 1978 (the last time a private bill originated in the House), no amendments were made by the Senate to private bills originating in the House. In the early years of Confederation, the Senate often amended private bills which had originated in the House. The House would typically read the amendments a second time and pass them.[121] On occasion, if amendments were substantive as opposed to "merely verbal or unimportant", the House would refer the amendments back to the committee which originally studied the bill.[122] If these amendments were agreed to by the committee in a report to the House, they were considered by the House.[123] If the amendments were read a second time and passed by the House, a message was sent informing the Senate accordingly and the bill then received Royal Assent. If the committee disagreed with the amendments, it reported accordingly to the House. The House then sent a message to this effect to the other Chamber if it concurred in the committee's report.[124]

If a private bill which has originated in the Senate is passed by the House in the same form, the bill receives Royal Assent and becomes law. If the House of Commons has passed the bill with amendments, a message is sent to the Senate requesting concurrence in the amendments. Subsequently, a message is received from the Senate agreeing or disagreeing with the amendments. If the amendments are concurred in by the Senate, a message is sent informing the House of its concurrence and the bill then receives Royal Assent.[125] If the Senate does not agree with the amendments, it informs the House accordingly.

---

120. Standing Order 142. See *Journals*, February 26, 1976, p. 1070, where the Speaker ruled that report stage is part of the legislative process for the passage of a private bill. For an example of a private bill being amended at report stage, see *Journals*, October 28, 1971, p. 896; March 16, 1972, p. 195.

121. See, for example, *Journals*, March 15, 1893, p. 161; March 17, 1893, p. 170.

122. Standing Order 143.

123. See, for example, *Journals*, May 4, 1886, p. 215; May 5, 1886, p. 228; May 14, 1886, p. 267; May 17, 1886, p. 275.

124. See, for example, *Journals*, April 15, 1889, pp. 259-61.

125. See, for example, *Journals*, March 13, 1990, p. 1338; March 29, 1990, pp. 1435-6; June 6, 1990, p. 1838; June 12, 1990, pp. 1872-3.

24

The Parliamentary Record

A great speech is not only a news event; it is part of history. As history is written it should also be seen. We should have some way of preserving for those who come after us the words, the faces, the expressions and the emotions of the members of this house.

MAX SALTSMAN, M.P. (Waterloo South)
(*Debates,* June 5, 1967, p. 1158)

he House produces many documents for the use of its Members, their staff and the general public. These documents enable all interested parties to follow parliamentary business; they also provide a permanent record of debate, decisions taken and other business coming before the House and its committees. The House also ensures the broadcasting of the proceedings of the House and its committees.

Parliamentary Publications

The following publications of the House of Commons are described in this chapter:

- *Journals:* The official record of what is done in the House, drawn from the scroll kept by Table Officers during the sittings of the House and signed by the Clerk of the House.

- *Debates:* The transcribed, edited and corrected record of what is said in the House and in a Committee of the Whole.

- *Order Paper and Notice Paper:* The *Order Paper* is the official agenda of the House, produced for each sitting day, and listing all items that may be brought forward in the Chamber on that day. The *Notice Paper* contains notices of items which Ministers and Members may wish to bring before the House.

- *Projected Order of Business:* A document, produced each day the House sits, containing an unofficial forecast of the order of business for the House that day, including such information as the length of speeches and any time limits on debate.

- *Status of House Business:* Updated daily when the House is sitting, this document provides cumulative information on the status of bills and motions.

- *Minutes of Proceedings, Evidence,* and *Reports of Committees:* These three documents form the records produced by parliamentary committees—the "minutes" being the official record of business; the "evidence" being the verbatim transcript of proceedings held in public; and the "reports" containing the observations and recommendations that committees make to the House.

- *Bills:* A bill is a proposed law, submitted to Parliament for its approval.

In 1994, the House began to distribute its publications electronically and the following year, it began the process of making its publications accessible worldwide through the *Parliamentary Internet Parlementaire.*[1] The growing accessibility of official publications by electronic means has meant a rationalization in production and distribution of the printed product.[2]

GOVERNING PROVISIONS

The House of Commons has exclusive control of its publications.[3] These documents are published under the authority of the House (as represented by the Speaker or the Clerk). All parliamentary publications are produced in both official languages. The Constitution and the *Official Languages Act* provide for the use and equal status of the official languages in the "records and journals" of Parliament.[4]

---

1. See Minutes of the meeting of the Board of Internal Economy on June 21, 1995, tabled on October 16, 1995 (*Journals*, p. 2012). The *Parliamentary Internet Parlementaire* (http://www.parl.gc.ca), which provides information on the Parliament of Canada, was created and is maintained jointly by the Senate, the House of Commons and the Library of Parliament.

2. See Minutes of the meeting of the Board of Internal Economy on April 12, 1994, tabled on May 12, 1994 (*Journals*, p. 461), and September 19, 1995, tabled on December 1, 1995 (*Journals*, p. 2199).

3. See *May*, 22nd ed., pp. 84-5; and *Maingot*, 2nd ed., pp. 40-4. For further information, see Chapter 3, "Privileges and Immunities".

4. Section 18(1) of the *Constitution Act, 1982* (R.S.C. 1985, Appendix II, No. 44) states: "The statutes, records and journals of Parliament shall be printed and published in English and French and both language versions are equally authoritative". This repeats a portion of Section 133 of the *Constitution Act, 1867* (R.S.C. 1985, Appendix II, No. 5). See also sections 4(3) and 5 of the *Official Languages Act* (R.S.C. 1985, c. 31 (4th Supp.)).

Many of the Standing Orders of the House of Commons make explicit reference to the *Journals,* the *Debates,* the *Order Paper* and the *Notice Paper.*[5] These publications, along with minutes of committees and bills introduced in the House of Commons, are produced by order of the House, under the authority of the Speaker and are considered as "official" publications. Other unofficial publications (for example, the *Projected Order of Business* and the *Status of House Business*) have come into existence through administrative decisions or following recommendations of committees. They are also published under the authority of the Speaker or of the Clerk of the House.

The Standing Orders confer on the Clerk of the House responsibility for the preparation of House documents, as well as the safekeeping of parliamentary documents and records.[6]

THE *JOURNALS*

The *Journals* record all that is done, or deemed done, by the House. They are the minutes of the meetings of the House[7] and as such, the authoritative record of its proceedings, which may be used as evidence in a court of law.[8] The *Journals* are prepared by House staff under the responsibility of the Clerk. The basis of the *Journals* is the scroll—notes and records kept by the Clerk of the House and other Table Officers in the course of a sitting. Formerly, the House produced daily *Votes and Proceedings* which were not designated as *Journals* until they had been revised and bound at the end of the session. Since September 1994, revised weekly *Journals* have been produced as well as unrevised daily *Journals.*[9]

No explicit authority exists by which the *Journals* are published. At the time of Confederation, the then *Votes and Proceedings* were published under a sessional order[10] which read as follows:

> *That the Votes and Proceedings of this House be printed, being first perused by Mr. Speaker, and that he do appoint the printing thereof, and*

---

5. Most such references are to the *Order Paper* or *Notice Paper* (see Standing Orders 39, 40, 54(1), 55(1), 90, 124, 152); there are also references to the *Journals* (see Standing Orders 9, 29(4), 32(3), 45(1)) and to the *Debates* (see Standing Orders 39(3)(*b*), 44.1(2)).

6. Standing Order 151.

7. Unlike some assemblies, such as the United States House of Representatives, there is no requirement to adopt or approve the minutes at the beginning of the following sitting.

8. *Bourinot,* 4th ed., pp. 186-7.

9. The current system was put into place following decisions taken by the Board of Internal Economy and the adoption of the Twenty-Fourth Report of the Standing Committee on Procedure and House Affairs (*Journals,* June 3, 1994, p. 529). For text of the report, see *Minutes of Proceedings and Evidence,* Standing Committee on Procedure and House Affairs, June 1, 1994, Issue No. 14, pp. 4-5.

10. An order is a decision of the House governing the conduct of House or Committee business. A sessional order is effective for the remainder of the session in which it is adopted.

that no person but such as he shall appoint, do presume to print the same. [11]

The record has since been produced without interruption; by the late 1870s, however, the practice of adopting a sessional order appeared to have fallen into disuse. [12]

When the House is sitting, the unrevised *Journals* for a given sitting are available on the morning of the following weekday; revised compilations are published on a weekly basis. The *Journals* are also available in electronic format on the Internet. At the end of a session, a compilation of the revised *Journals* along with other information is available in a limited number of bound copies [13] and on CD-ROM.

Format and Contents

Until the Second Session of the Thirtieth Parliament (1976-77), the *Journals* were printed in separate English and French editions; thereafter they have been printed in a bilingual side-by-side format. The *Journals* follow the order of proceedings in the House and succinct entries are made of the business conducted and decisions taken by the House.

The Standing Orders expressly state that a record is to be made in the *Journals* when a vote is cast by the Chair and reasons are given; [14] and when documents and papers are tabled, presented or filed, including petitions and reports from committees and parliamentary delegations. [15] In the event the House adjourns for want of a quorum, the names of Members present are to be recorded in the *Journals*. [16] Similarly, when a recorded vote has taken place, and Members have been registered as paired, their names are to be recorded in the *Journals*. [17] When a bill involving expenditure of public funds is before the House, the accompanying Royal Recommendation is

---

11. *Journals*, November 7, 1867, p. 5.

12. Sessional orders for the publication of the *Votes and Proceedings* were also adopted on the following dates: *Journals,* April 15, 1869, p. 8; February 15, 1870, p. 8; February 15, 1871, p. 10; April 11, 1872, p. 8; March 6, 1873, p. 5; March 27, 1874, p. 4; February 4, 1875, p. 54; February 8, 1877, p. 12.

13. The bound *Journals*, produced at the end of a session for use of the Clerk and the Library of Parliament, contain a comprehensive index, lists and other information of general interest:

   • proclamations of the Governor General opening and closing the session;
   • the Ministry in order of precedence, as of the final day of the session;
   • alphabetical list of Members, including constituency names and party affiliations;
   • alphabetical list of constituencies, including Members' names and party affiliations.

14. Standing Order 9. For further information on the casting vote of the Chair, see Chapter 7, "The Speaker and Other Presiding Officers of the House".

15. Standing Order 32(3). It also happens on occasion that papers are tabled by the unanimous consent of the House (see, for example, *Journals*, October 21, 1991, p. 496). For further information on tabling of documents, see Chapter 10, "The Daily Program".

16. Standing Order 29(4). For further information on quorum, see Chapter 9, "Sittings of the House".

17. Standing Order 44.1(2). For further information on recorded votes and pairing, see Chapter 12, "The Process of Debate".

recorded.[18] Also, when the Clerk of Petitions reports to the House following the presentation of a petition for a private bill, the report is printed in the *Journals*[19] and further *Journals* entries are made at subsequent points in the legislative process with regard to private bills.[20]

The *Journals* contain no record of debate in the House, except to note that it took place on a question. Likewise, no record is made of the proceedings or decisions taken in a Committee of the Whole, except to note when a Committee of the Whole sits, reports progress and reports back a bill with or without amendment. When amendments are reported, they are printed in the *Journals*.

Corrections and Alterations

The daily *Journals* are revised and corrections or changes are incorporated prior to publication of the weekly *Journals*. The accuracy of the record has rarely been questioned.[21] Errors or omissions have on occasion been brought to the attention of the House;[22] editorial errors are corrected by those responsible for the publication.[23] On one occasion, the Speaker informed the House that the record of the previous day's proceedings had to be reprinted to correct a number of inaccuracies in voting lists.[24]

THE *DEBATES*

The *House of Commons Debates,* commonly known as the *Debates* or as *Hansard,*[25] is the report *in extenso* of the debates which take place in the House and in a Committee of the Whole, with due regard to necessary grammatical, vocabulary and editorial changes.

---

18. Standing Order 79(2). For further information on the Royal Recommendation, see Chapter 18, "Financial Procedures".

19. Standing Order 131(5). For further information on private bills, see Chapter 23, "Private Bills Practice".

20. Standing Orders 135(1) and (2), and 141(2)*(b)*.

21. On one occasion when this occurred, the Speaker found that the record was correct (*Debates*, June 26, 1985, pp. 6203-4). There have been occasions where the decision was taken to remove items from the *Votes and Proceedings* (as the daily *Journals* were formerly known): on April 6, 1925, for example, the Speaker ruled that the government's answer to a written question contained unnecessary facts and that it should be "expunged from the records" (*Journals*, p. 193); on June 6, 1944, the House ordered that a committee report "presented by mistake" be deleted from the *Votes and Proceedings* (*Journals*, p. 434); on June 7, 1973, the Speaker informed the House that an item in the *Votes and Proceedings* of the previous day would be expunged, a Senate public bill having inadvertently been treated as a private bill (*Journals*, p. 389).

22. See, for example, *Journals*, March 31, 1871, pp. 173-4; *Debates*, November 6, 1996, p. 6191.

23. See, for example, the *corrigendum* appended to the *Votes and Proceedings* for June 10, 1994.

24. *Debates*, June 4, 1992, pp. 11381-2.

25. Hansard is the name of the family responsible for arranging the official reporting of debates in the British House of Commons throughout most of the nineteenth century. The term is now used to refer generally to official reports of parliamentary debates (see *Wilding and Laundy,* pp. 340-5).

In the pre-Confederation assemblies and for some years after Confederation, there was no official reporting of debates in the House of Commons.[26] Contemporary newspapers carried accounts of legislative proceedings including debates, with varying degrees of thoroughness, accuracy and impartiality.

After Confederation, there were attempts to establish a reporting service, which did not succeed as not all Members were convinced of the need.[27] In 1875, reporting of proceedings in the House of Commons began to be carried out on a contract basis, overseen by a committee of the House and in accordance with guidelines meant to ensure the accuracy of the record.[28] Over time, the system of contract reporting was found wanting, and the House came to the view that an improved and comprehensive official parliamentary report was needed.[29] In April 1880, the House concurred in a committee report which recommended, in the interests of "greater permanency" and "a higher state of efficiency", that the House engage its own permanent reporting staff.[30] Thus, verbatim reporting of debates became an official function of the House under the control of a committee of the House. In 1882, with the adoption of a report from a committee appointed to supervise the Official Report of the Debates, the House agreed to produce an index to the *Debates*.[31]

The *Debates* are published under the authority of the Speaker of the House. They are compiled using the audio recording of the proceedings as well as information provided by Hansard staff stationed on the floor of the House. They are produced in both official languages and are available the next day.

Format and Contents

The *Debates* are published under separate cover in each official language, with uniformity of pagination between the two editions.[32] The language used by the Member

---

26. An exception took place in 1865 when, by special order of the United Canada Legislative Assembly, the debates on Confederation were officially recorded. See the history of Canadian parliamentary reporting in the Introduction to the reconstructed *Debates of the Legislative Assembly of United Canada, 1841–1867*, Vol. I, pp. XXVIII-LIV.

27. *Bourinot*, 2nd ed., pp. 227-8. Members argued that the newspaper accounts were adequate, that costs to the House of setting up its own service would be prohibitive, and that official verbatim reporting would encourage excessive verbosity and lead to unnecessary lengthening of parliamentary sessions. See, for example, *Debates*, December 10, 1867, pp. 231-2; March 27, 1868, pp. 409-10; April 25, 1870, pp. 1176-80.

28. See the First and Second Reports of the Committee appointed to report on the subject of a Canadian Hansard (*Journals*, May 8, 1874, pp. 200-1), concurred in on May 18, 1874 (*Journals*, pp. 264-5).

29. See, for example, *Debates*, April 28, 1880, pp. 1815-9.

30. The report was presented on April 26, 1880, and concurred in on April 28, 1880 (*Journals*, pp. 268-9, 281).

31. The report was presented on March 30, 1882 (*Journals*, p. 231), and concurred in on April 3, 1882 (*Journals*, p. 242).

32. In 1965, after a period of experimentation, the House concurred in a recommendation to proceed to uniform pagination between the English and French versions of the *Debates* and other publications (*Journals*, June 1, 1964, pp. 381-2; April 2, 1965, pp. 1211-2).

speaking is indicated.[33] Like the *Journals,* the *Debates* follow the actual order of proceedings in the House, based on the order of business for the sitting; unlike the *Journals,* the *Debates* contain the full deliberations of the House—speeches and statements of Members as well as other comments and interventions made in the Chamber. It is not considered usual or regular to include in the *Debates* material not delivered in the Chamber; however, some exceptions exist. For example, the *Debates* contain:

- division lists, when a recorded division takes place (paired Members are included);[34]
- written answers to questions on the *Order Paper;*[35]
- the text of the Speech from the Throne at the beginning of each session;
- other material specifically ordered by the House.[36]

For information purposes, the House has occasionally agreed to print a text as an appendix to the *Debates.*[37] In certain circumstances, editorial notes may also be inserted.[38] Each Friday,[39] the *Debates* contains an appendix comprising the following lists:

- Chair occupants;
- Members of the Board of Internal Economy;
- Members of the House of Commons listed alphabetically and by province, including constituency name and political affiliation;

---

33. The official language used by a Member is indicated by the marginal notes "English" and "Translation" in the English *Hansard* and "Français" and "Traduction" in the French. Languages other than the two official languages are occasionally used in the House; see Chapter 13, "Rules of Order and Decorum".

34. Standing Order 44.1(2).

35. Standing Order 39(3)*(b).*

36. The House has on more than one occasion consented to dispense with the reading of a motion and to have the text printed in the *Debates* as if read; a recurring example is the typically lengthy motion to refer the main estimates to the various standing committees of the House (see *Debates,* April 30, 1980, pp. 575-6; February 26, 1998, pp. 4457-8).

   Rarely, the House has consented to have material not read in the House incorporated in the *Debates* as part of a Member's speech (see, for example, *Debates,* March 23, 1971, pp. 4533-5; December 8, 1997, pp. 2851-2).

37. The House has agreed to append such documents as Budget documents (see, for example, *Debates,* March 16, 1964, pp. 974, 988-1003), exchanges of correspondence (see, for example, *Debates,* December 4, 1980, pp. 5356, 5394), reports (see, for example, *Journals,* November 15, 1977, p. 102; *Debates,* November 15, 1977, pp. 920-2) and texts of addresses to Parliament by foreign dignitaries (see, for example, *Journals,* June 9, 1992, pp. 1660-1; *Debates,* June 19, 1992, pp. 12480-8). In a very unusual occurrence, the House agreed to append to the *Debates* the texts of a ministerial statement and two opposition responses, none of which was delivered in the House (*Journals,* January 25, 1990, p. 1114).

38. See, for example, *Debates,* May 11, 1970, p. 6796 (disturbance in the galleries); June 4, 1993, p. 20356 (remarks in a language other than English or French); September 29, 1994, p. 6348 (sounding of the fire alarm).

39. Until September 1996, the appendix was attached to Wednesday's *Debates.* It also appears in an electronic version, updated as changes occur.

- Committees and their membership;
- Panel of Chairmen of Legislative Committees;
- the Ministry, with ministerial titles and according to precedence;
- Parliamentary Secretaries.

The *Debates* are also available in electronic format on the Internet, and at the end of each session, a compilation of the revised *Debates* is produced in a limited number of bound copies and also in CD-ROM format.

Corrections and Alterations

The unedited transcripts of *Hansard,* at one time produced on blue paper, continue to be known as the "blues". The Debates Reporting Service sends to a Member who speaks in the House the transcript of his or her intervention.[40] Blues are also sent to the Press Gallery. Question Period blues are sent to the offices of party leaders, party research offices and the office of the Speaker. The blues may also be made available on request to other Members, to the Clerk and to senior House officials. At times, the Chair has referred to the blues in deciding points of order or grievances raised by Members.[41] However, the blues are a preliminary copy and are not to be quoted from during debate.[42]

A Member verifies his or her own intervention and may suggest corrections to errors and minor alterations to the transcription; a Member may not make material changes in the meaning of what was said in the House. It is a long-standing practice of the House that editors of the *Debates* may exercise judgement as to whether or not changes suggested by Members constitute the correction of an error or a minor alteration.[43] The editors may likewise alter a sentence to render it more readable but may not go so far as to change its meaning.[44] Editors must ensure that the *Debates* are a faithful reflection of what was said; any changes made, whether by Members or editors, are for the sole purpose of improving the readability of the text, given the difference between the spoken and written word.

In order for corrections and alterations to be considered, the blues must be returned within stipulated deadlines. Returned blues must be clearly initialed by the Member or a designated agent. If a Member's blues are not returned, it is assumed there are no modifications to be made.

Substantial errors, as opposed to editorial changes, must be brought to the attention of the House by means of a point of order, as soon as possible after the sitting,

---

40. The blues are sent by facsimile and electronic mail and may occasionally be delivered by hand to a Member in the Chamber.

41. See, for example, *Debates*, February 18, 1997, p. 8279.

42. See *Debates*, September 24, 1985, p. 6893. At times, the blues have been referred to by Members raising points of order or questions of privilege (see, for example, *Debates*, March 15, 1996, pp. 786-7).

43. See *Journals*, November 1, 1973, p. 613.

44. See *Debates*, March 20, 1978, p. 3925; September 20, 1983, pp. 27299-300.

if a Member wishes to have the verbatim record changed. Such mishaps may be attributed to a misstatement on the part of the Member, or to transcription error.[45] A Member may correct the record of his or her own statement, but may not correct that of another Member.[46] When a question arises in the House as to the accuracy of the record, it is the responsibility of the Speaker to look into the matter.[47] On occasion the Speaker has seen fit to order the printing of a *corrigendum* to the *Debates*.[48]

Since the advent of broadcasting of House proceedings, occasional points of order have been raised on the basis of discrepancy in the content of the *Debates* and the broadcast tape.[49] While such matters have been resolved as they arose, the Speaker, in 1978, noted:

> *An examination of the record through these electronic recording devices is being resorted to by more and more Canadians all the time. Therefore, additional strain is being put on the reporting staff who have enjoyed this editorial licence in the past. They now find themselves under the constraint of matching their records exactly with the language used on the radio and television.*[50]

In 1986, the Speaker repeated these remarks and suggested that the issue of the official status of the electronic Hansard ought to be clarified.[51] Until this occurs, each discrepancy must be examined on its own merit.[52]

THE *ORDER PAPER AND NOTICE PAPER*

The *Order Paper and Notice Paper* is a single publication, published daily when the House sits. It consists of two parts: the *Order Paper* and the *Notice Paper*. The *Order Paper* is the complete and authoritative agenda of all items of business which may be considered by the House of Commons; unless otherwise provided for in the Standing Orders, only those items may be considered by the House during a sitting.

---

45. See, for example, *Debates*, November 19, 1969, p. 982; September 26, 1990, p. 13455; November 6, 1996, p. 6191.

46. See, for example, *Debates*, July 9, 1980, p. 2705; May 28, 1982, p. 17872.

47. See, for example, *Debates*, October 27, 1994, p. 7318; February 25, 1998, p. 4406. There have been occasions where it was decided to expunge text from the *Debates* (see, for example, *Journals*, April 6, 1925, p. 193; *Debates*, July 27, 1942, p. 4798; December 1, 1960, p. 391; June 30, 1972, p. 3724); however, such instances have not formed part of recent House practice.

48. See, for example, *Debates*, November 15, 1983, p. 28894. In 1995, the Speaker ordered a *corrigendum* to be printed, having found a substantial difference between a Member's remarks in the House and in the *Debates*, and having ruled that the Member's changes to the blues ought not to have been accepted by the Hansard editors (*Debates*, March 16, 1995, pp. 10618-9).

49. See, for example, *Debates*, November 28, 1978, pp. 1569-70; February 2, 1984, p. 1015; June 6, 1986, pp. 14055-6.

50. *Debates*, November 28, 1978, p. 1570.

51. *Debates*, June 6, 1986, pp. 10455-6.

52. In the British House of Commons, it has been established that the authoritative version of its deliberations is the printed *Debates* (*May*, 22nd ed., p. 230).

As its name suggests, the *Notice Paper* contains all items for which notice must be given. Together, these documents contain virtually all items of business which are before the House or which may be brought before the House.

The rules of the House require notice to be given before almost any matter of substance can be raised for consideration by the House.[53] The usual way of giving notice is for the sponsoring Member to send a written and signed notice to the Clerk for inclusion in the *Notice Paper*. Notices given or deemed given on a particular day are printed in that day's *Notice Paper* and transferred to the *Order Paper* after the applicable notice period has elapsed. All items, with the exception of Government Orders, are to be taken up in accordance with the precedence assigned to them on the *Order Paper*.[54] Thus, the *Order Paper* has a double significance. It contains, first, all items of business to be considered (orders) and, second, the sequence in which the orders are to be considered.

The Standing Orders require the Clerk of the House to provide the Speaker, each day before the House meets, with the official agenda of proceedings for the day.[55] This rule has traditionally been interpreted to mean that the Speaker must be in possession of a copy of the *Order Paper and Notice Paper* before the business of the House may proceed.

Historical Perspective

The *Order Paper* originated as a document containing any item of business which the House had ordered to be taken up on a specified day. The *Order Paper* still contains such items;[56] other items are placed on the *Order Paper* not because the House has adopted an order but because the Standing Orders require it, after proper notice.[57]

Formerly, it was the practice for notices submitted by Members to be appended to the *Votes and Proceedings* of the sitting during which the notice was given.[58] The current practice of producing the *Notice Paper* with the *Order Paper* began on

---

53. Standing Order 54. For further information, see Chapter 12, "The Process of Debate".

54. Standing Order 40.

55. Standing Order 152. The rule, which dates from Confederation, has precursors in the pre-Confederation assemblies. *Redlich*, tracing the evolution of British parliamentary practice, refers to the establishment in the seventeenth century of the "custom … of making the daily programme known to the House at the beginning of the sitting …" (Vol. I, p. 47). The 1854 *Rules and Standing Orders of the Legislative Assembly of Canada*, for example, require the Clerk "to lay on the Speaker's table, every morning, previous to the meeting of the House, the order of the proceedings for the day"; and secondly, "that a copy of the same be hung up in the lobby, for the information of Members." This seems to indicate that at that time, the daily distribution of the *Order Paper* to all Members was not possible and that it was produced by the Clerk, primarily for the Speaker.

56. For example, after a bill is read a first time, the Speaker asks when it shall be read a second time, and the usual reply is "At the next sitting of the House". An order for the bill's second reading is then placed on the *Order Paper* so that the bill might, in principle, be taken up at that time.

57. See, for example, Standing Order 56(1).

58. *Bourinot*, 4th ed., pp. 295-6.

October 27, 1969, when the House was in the process of computerizing its production processes for publications.[59]

Role of the Speaker

As with other parliamentary publications, the *Order Paper and Notice Paper* is published under the authority of the Speaker of the House. When a notice is submitted for inclusion on the *Notice Paper*, it is examined by procedural staff of the Clerk. If any procedural irregularity is found, modifications as to the form and content of the notice may then be made in consultation with the sponsoring Member.[60] Where items of Private Members' Business are concerned, it may happen that a certain item for which notice has been given is deemed to be substantially the same as another. In such cases, the rules give the Speaker discretionary power to refuse the most recent notice, inform the Member and return the item.[61]

Format and Contents

The *Order Paper and Notice Paper* is a bilingual publication, available electronically and in a printed version. The part containing the *Order Paper* is divided into sections corresponding to the various categories of orders the House considers:

- Order of Business: Items for which notice has already been given and which are awaiting introduction during Routine Proceedings. They are listed under Introduction of Government Bills, Introduction of Private Members' Bills, First Reading of Senate Public Bills, and Motions (including motions for concurrence in committee reports);

- Government Orders: Items which are already before the House and are awaiting first consideration or resumption of debate. They are listed under Supply Proceedings, Ways and Means Proceedings, Government Bills (Commons), Government Bills (Senate), and Government Business;

- Notices of Motions for the Production of Papers: This list appears only on Wednesdays;[62]

- Private Members' Business: Items in the order of precedence appear in the order in which they are to be considered by the House. The list may change from day to day as items are added or dropped and because the rules allow exchanges of place.[63] The list of items outside the order of precedence is available

---

59. For background information, see Alexander Small, "The Use of Computers in the Bilingual Publishing and Retrieval of Parliamentary Publications," *The Table*, Vol. XLII, 1974, pp. 66-72. The Standing Orders were changed in 1987 to reflect alterations to publications (*Journals*, June 3, 1987, pp. 1002-28; see in particular p. 1022).

60. This practice has a long history; see *Bourinot*, 1st ed., pp. 308-9.

61. Standing Order 86(5). For further information on the interpretation of this rule, see Chapter 21, "Private Members' Business".

62. See Chapter 10, "The Daily Program", and Chapter 21, "Private Members' Business".

63. Standing Order 94(2)*(a)*.

electronically, and an updated copy is kept for consultation at the Table in the House;

- Questions: Written questions are printed only when they appear on the *Notice Paper*. The complete list of questions on the *Order Paper* is also available electronically and at the Table for consultation.

The *Order Paper* also includes the "Weekly Review of Business", a compilation of information on items of business introduced, placed on notice or considered in the House during the course of the week. The Review in Monday's *Order Paper* contains the complete summary for the preceding week. The information is also incorporated in the *Status of House Business,* which is updated daily when the House sits.

Similar to the *Order Paper,* items on the *Notice Paper* are listed under the following categories of business:

- Introduction of Government Bills;
- Introduction of Private Members' Bills;
- Motions (Routine Proceedings);
- Questions;
- Notices of Motions for the Production of Papers;
- Business of Supply;
- Government Business;
- Private Members' Notices of Motions;
- Private Members' Business;
- Report Stage of Bills.

Transfer to Order Paper from Notice Paper

When the notice requirement for a given item has been met, the notice is transferred to the appropriate section of the *Order Paper*. Some particularities found in the *Notice Paper* are worth noting:

- Opposition motions under Supply proceedings, which are to be debated on "allotted" or "opposition" days, require only 24 hours' notice.[64] The motion is usually taken up by the House on the sitting day following the day notice is given. The text of the motion appears simultaneously on the *Order Paper* and on the *Notice Paper.*
- Motions to amend a bill at report stage following second reading also require only 24 hours' notice.[65] In order to keep all such proposed amendments together, the

---

64. Standing Order 81(14)*(a)*.

65. Standing Order 76.1(2). Where report stage precedes second reading, the notice period is 48 hours (Standing Order 76(2)).

list of these notices together with the list of any deferred divisions on report stage motions are kept in the *Notice Paper* even after the notice requirement has been met.

- The rules require that any item of Private Members' Business to be considered on a given day must also appear on that day's *Notice Paper;* if the notice does not appear, no Private Members' Business is taken up that day. [66]

Written questions appear once on the *Notice Paper* when notice is given, and are then moved to the list of questions on the *Order Paper* which is available electronically and at the Table. [67] When a question has been dealt with (answered, made an order for return, withdrawn or transferred [68]), the fact is noted in the *Status of House Business*.

Withdrawing Items from the Order Paper

As long as a motion has not been proposed to the House, it remains a notice and the sponsoring Member is free to withdraw it; the consent of the House is not required. [69] A notice may be withdrawn in one of two ways: the Member either makes a written request to the Clerk to withdraw the notice or rises in the House to withdraw the notice orally. [70] This applies to items on the *Notice Paper* and on the *Order Paper*, as long as the House has not been seized of them—for example, bills not yet introduced, motions not yet moved, [71] and notices of motions for the production of papers. [72] The item is then removed from the *Notice Paper* or the *Order Paper*. In addition, in certain circumstances notices have been removed from the *Order Paper and Notice Paper* by the Speaker when informed, for example, of the death or

---

66. Standing Order 94(1).

67. Under the heading "Questions", the printed *Order Paper* refers readers to the electronic version and to the complete list of questions on the *Order Paper,* which is available for consultation at the Table. At one time all questions were printed on the *Order Paper*. In 1983, in line with the recommendation of a special committee on procedure (see Section 9, Part II in the Third Report of the Special Committee on Standing Orders and Procedure, presented on November 5, 1982 (*Journals*, p. 5328) and the special order adopted by the House on November 29, 1982 (*Journals*, p. 5400)), questions began to be published in a Monthly Supplement to the *Order Paper.* The Monthly Supplement ceased to be published in 1997 when a recommendation of the Procedure and House Affairs Committee (see *Minutes*, Issue No. 3, pp. 26-7) was approved by the Board of Internal Economy (see Minutes of the Board's meeting of March 18, 1997, tabled on April 25, 1997 (*Journals*, p. 1557)).

68. See Chapter 11, "Questions".

69. See Speaker's ruling, *Debates*, December 7, 1989, p. 6584.

70. For Speakers' rulings, see *Journals*, January 13, 1910, p. 154; *Debates*, December 7, 1989, p. 6584.

71. See, for example, *Debates*, June 19, 1991, p. 2111.

72. This is one of the options open to Members when the government is unable to accede to the request for the production of papers. See, for example, *Debates*, March 18, 1981, pp. 8377-8; April 19, 1989, pp. 691-2. For more information on notices of motions for the production of papers, see Chapter 10, "The Daily Program".

resignation of a sponsoring Member.[73] On one occasion, the Speaker informed the House that a revised *Notice Paper* had been prepared, which included notices of report stage amendments inadvertently left off the original.[74]

Once a notice has been transferred to the *Order Paper* and moved in the House,[75] it is considered to be in the possession of the House and can only be removed from the *Order Paper* by an order of the House; that is, the Member who has moved the motion requests that it be withdrawn, and the House must give its unanimous consent.[76]

Special Order Paper

From time to time, a *Special Order Paper* is published.[77] This may happen before the opening of the first or a subsequent session of a Parliament, or when the House stands adjourned and the government wishes the House to give immediate consideration to a matter or matters for which notice would have to be given.[78] Once advised of this, the Speaker ensures that the required notice is published in a *Special Order Paper,* which is circulated to Members at least 48 hours before the session either begins or resumes.

The format of a *Special Order Paper* is like that of a regular *Order Paper*. It contains only the notices of the measure or measures which are to receive the immediate consideration of the House.

THE *PROJECTED ORDER OF BUSINESS*

The *Order Paper* lists all the business which might be taken up by the House on a given day, but it does not indicate which items the government intends, or is likely, to call. The *Projected Order of Business,* published each sitting day, is a tentative working agenda which lists all the government and Private Members' Business

---

73. For example, notices sponsored by Jean-Claude Malépart (Montréal–Sainte-Marie) (died November 16, 1989), Catherine Callbeck (Malpeque) (resigned January 25, 1993) and Stephen Harper (Calgary West) (resigned January 14, 1997) were withdrawn. They included notices of motions for Private Members' Business (including items in the Order of Precedence), notices of written questions and notices of motions for the production of papers. Private Members' bills awaiting introduction and notices of motions under Routine Proceedings would also be withdrawn in such circumstances.

In another instance, the House concurred in a committee report by unanimous consent, following which an earlier notice of motion to concur in the same report was removed from the *Order Paper* (*Order Paper and Notice Paper*, November 25, 1997, p. 9; *Journals*, November 25, 1997, p. 257; *Order Paper and Notice Paper*, November 27, 1997, p. 10).

74. *Debates*, September 27, 1971, p. 8173.

75. In the case of Private Members' Business, it must first be selected following the draw for the Order of Precedence (Standing Order 87(5)).

76. Standing Order 64. See, for example, *Journals*, March 12, 1993, p. 2627; *Debates*, March 12, 1993, pp. 16925-6; *Journals*, May 11, 1994, p. 451; *Debates*, May 11, 1994, p. 4211.

77. Standing Order 55. See also Chapter 12, "The Process of Debate".

78. See, for example, the *Special Order Papers* published on September 23, 1997 (before the opening of a first session), February 27, 1996 (before the opening of a subsequent session), and August 11, 1987 and September 19, 1994 (during an adjournment).

expected to be taken up on a particular day. It was first published in 1983 as a result of a special procedure committee's identification of the need for a "simplified, unofficial, daily agenda, in addition to the *Order Paper,* to indicate the likely order of business for any particular day".[79]

Format and Contents

The *Projected Order of Business* is produced in side-by-side bilingual format. A printed version is available and distributed daily to Members when the House sits; in addition, it is available electronically and may also be viewed on the parliamentary television channel.

Material is organized under a sequence of headings corresponding to the Order of Business for the day, including Government Orders and Private Members' Business. Entries under the headings indicate which items from the *Order Paper* are expected to be taken up when that heading is called by the Chair. When no entry appears under items for which notice is required, it may be taken to mean either that the *Order Paper* has no items listed for that category of business, or that any of the items appearing on the *Order Paper* under that heading may be taken up. Typically, there would be no entries under other items which do not require notice, such as tabling of documents or presenting petitions.

In addition, the *Projected Order of Business* contains notes providing the reader with information, such as length of speeches and any time limits on debate (with reference to the applicable Standing or Special Orders) applying to items expected to come before the House, as well as a projection of business for subsequent days. The projection is based on the order of precedence for Private Members' Business and on the weekly statement on government business.[80]

Subject to Change

Items listed under the heading of Government Orders are included on the basis of the weekly business statements and information provided to the Clerk by the office of the Government House Leader. As indicated on the document itself, the listing is subject to change without notice, as the government retains its right to determine the sequence in which items of government business are called and considered.[81]

---

79. See section 9 in Part II of the Third Report of the Special Committee on Standing Orders and Procedure, presented on November 5, 1982 (*Journals*, p. 5328). Although the report was not concurred in, a motion adopted on November 29, 1982 (*Journals*, p. 5400) put this and other portions of the report into effect. The new document appeared for the first time on January 17, 1983.

80. See Chapter 21, "Private Members' Business"; for further information on the weekly business statement or "Thursday statement", see Chapter 10, "The Daily Program".

81. Standing Order 40(2). This was emphasized in a ruling by the Speaker (*Debates*, March 20, 1997, pp. 9281-2).

THE *STATUS OF HOUSE BUSINESS*

The *Status of House Business* provides a concise history of each item of business which has been considered by the House or which has appeared on the *Order Paper and Notice Paper* since the beginning of the session. Produced under the authority of the Clerk, it is available electronically and updated daily. Until the end of the Thirty-Fifth Parliament (1994-97), the *Status of House Business* was printed approximately once a month when the House was sitting.

Format and Contents

The *Status of House Business* is produced in both official languages and has three parts. Part I contains the legislative history of all the bills in the House (government bills and private Members' bills, as well as bills originating in the Senate). Part II gives similar information with respect to motions (motions under Government Orders, motions for the production of papers, private Members' motions and motions dealing with other business such as the operations of the House and its committees). Part III contains information on written questions submitted by private Members.

The *Status of House Business* is accompanied by an alphabetical, subject-based index. References in this index are to the various items of business and sections of the document. Lists are provided under certain headings, such as bills, government business, Supply proceedings and Ways and Means proceedings.

MINUTES OF PROCEEDINGS, EVIDENCE AND REPORTS OF COMMITTEES

Each committee of the House produces its own records. Since 1995, these records have become available primarily by electronic means. They include three main documents:

- the minutes of proceedings: the formal record of business occurring during a committee meeting;

- the evidence: the *in extenso* transcript of what is said during a meeting;

- reports to the House: the means by which committees make their views and recommendations known.

All committee records are made available electronically under the authority of the Speaker of the House. Under the Standing Orders, committees are empowered to print papers and evidence in accordance with any such decision they may make.[82] However, this authority is somewhat qualified by limitations set by the Board of Internal Economy.[83]

---

82. Standing Orders 108(1)*(a)* and 113(5).

83. For example, committee reports may be printed and distributed from time to time in accordance with guidelines established by the Board of Internal Economy (see Board's decision of October 29, 1986). For further information on this and other powers of committees, see Chapter 20, "Committees".

Corrections and Alterations

Unedited transcripts of committee proceedings, known (as with the *Debates*) as "blues", are made available on request to committee members, usually within 24 hours after a committee meets. Traditionally, minor corrections could be effected by informing the committee clerk, who would have an *erratum* printed; corrections of a more significant nature would be made by the committee itself as a *corrigendum*.[84] In 1993, the decision of a committee to alter its official record by expunging portions of testimony gave rise to a question of privilege in the House. The Speaker's ruling established that a committee's power to print includes the right not to print, which may be extended to a decision to omit evidence from the record.[85]

BILLS

The House of Commons considers proposed laws—or bills—submitted for its approval by Ministers or private Members. Bills originating in the House are published and circulated under the authority of the Speaker; they are also available in electronic format. They are designated by letter and number in accordance with the type of bill and its House of origin. Bills originating in the House and sponsored by Ministers are numbered from C-1 to C-200, in the order of their introduction during the session. Bills originating in the House and sponsored by private Members are likewise numbered from C-201 to C-1000 through the session. All bills originating in the Senate are numbered from S-1. Most private bills originate in the Senate, but any originating in the Commons would be numbered from C-1001. All bills originating in the House are printed in both official languages by order of the House.[86]

Broadcasting Services

HISTORICAL PERSPECTIVE

Prior to the introduction of television in the House of Commons in 1977, only special parliamentary events, such as openings of Parliament and addresses by distinguished visitors,[87] were broadcast. The question of radio and television broadcasting was debated in the House in 1967 and 1969 and referred to a procedure committee in 1970.[88] The committee's report, tabled in 1972, discussed the concept of an

---

84. *Beauchesne*, 6th ed., p. 233.
85. See *Debates*, March 16, 1993, pp. 17071-3. See also Chapter 20, "Committees".
86. Standing Orders 69(1) and 70. See also Chapter 16, "The Legislative Process".
87. For example, the address to both Houses of Parliament in the Commons Chamber by Richard Nixon, President of the United States, on April 14, 1972, was televised.
88. See *Debates*, June 5, 1967, pp. 1157-66; March 26, 1969, pp. 7158-79; *Journals*, March 23, 1970, p. 633.

"electronic Hansard" whereby radio and television coverage would be a faithful record of proceedings and debates in the House, in the same sense as the written *Debates*.[89] This approach was to become a guiding principle in the broadcasting of House proceedings. Parliament was dissolved before the committee's recommendations could be considered. A feasibility study was undertaken in 1974[90] and on January 25, 1977, the House adopted the following motion:

> *That this House approves the radio and television broadcasting of its proceedings and of the proceedings of its committees on the basis of the principles similar to those that govern the publication of the printed official reports of debates; and that a special committee, consisting of Mr. Speaker and seven other members to be named at a later date, be appointed to supervise the implementation of this resolution ...*[91]

The special committee chaired by Speaker James Jerome made the necessary decisions as to lighting, camera placement and other matters. During the summer recess, the Chamber was extensively refitted and on October 17, 1977, gavel-to-gavel coverage of the proceedings of the House of Commons began.[92]

In 1989, a consortium of cable television companies and the Canadian Broadcasting Corporation jointly proposed a new specialty cable channel, to be called the Canadian Parliamentary Channel (CPaC), which would broadcast the House of Commons proceedings as well as other public affairs programming. A committee undertook a study of this proposal within a wide-ranging review of broadcasting and the House of Commons.[93] In its final report,[94] the committee endorsed the CPaC proposal. The committee also found existing camera guidelines unnecessarily strict.[95]

---

89. See *Journals*, June 30, 1972, pp. 471-86.

90. "Television Broadcasting of Parliament: A Feasibility Study," Canadian Broadcasting Corporation, Ottawa, May 1976. The study was done by the Canadian Broadcasting Corporation for the President of the Privy Council. An earlier version, dated April 12, 1976, was tabled in the House (*Journals*, June 8, 1976, p. 1337). See Alistair Fraser, "Televising the Canadian House of Commons", *The Table*, Vol. XLVII for 1979, pp. 66-71.

91. See *Journals*, January 25, 1977, p. 287.

92. *Debates*, October 17, 1977, pp. 8201-2. See also Speaker Jerome's memoir, *Mr. Speaker,* Toronto: McClelland and Stewart Limited, 1985, pp. 113-22.

93. The matter was referred to the Standing Committee on Elections, Privileges, Procedure and Private Members' Business on June 8, 1989 (*Journals*, p. 340).

94. The Committee's Ninth and final report, entitled "Watching the House at Work", was deemed presented on December 29, 1989 (*Journals*, January 22, 1990, p. 1078).

95. In one of its recommendations, the committee suggested that the production and direction of House of Commons broadcasting should be delegated, under the supervision of a House committee, to the programming director who would exercise professional judgement in the choice of camera angles or shots, so as to "convey the full flavour of the House of Commons, and to ensure that the parliamentary broadcasts provide a dignified and accurate reflection of the House". See "Watching the House at Work", the Ninth Report of the Standing Committee on Elections, Privileges, Procedure and Private Members' Business, pp. 3-6, 8-10. (The report was deemed presented on December 29, 1989; see *Journals*, January 22, 1990, p. 1078.)

Although the report itself was not concurred in, a motion endorsing the CPaC proposal in principle was adopted by the House.[96] Further enhancements proposed by the committee were taken up by the House and implemented.[97] In 1992, the House agreed to the use of a greater variety of camera angles during the coverage of Question Period and of recorded votes.[98]

AUTHORITY AND JURISDICTION

At an early stage, well before the House agreed to the broadcasting of its proceedings, it was clear that control of any such broadcasting system, including the safeguarding of the electronic Hansard concept, was to remain with the House and under the supervision of the Speaker acting on behalf of all Members.[99]

In support of this principle, the Standing Committee on Procedure and House Affairs has, as part of its permanent mandate, the duty to review and report on the broadcasting of proceedings of the House and its committees, and to deal with any complaints from Members in connection with such broadcasting.[100]

---

96. *Journals*, February 23, 1990, p. 1277. Later in the session, on June 19, 1990 (*Debates*, pp. 12930-48), a motion to concur in the committee report was debated but not disposed of.

97. An example would be the production of informational videos (see the Nineteenth Report of the Standing Committee on Privileges and Elections presented on November 23, 1990 (*Journals*, p. 2289), and concurred in on December 19, 1990 (*Journals*, p. 2510)).

98. See the Twenty-Second, Forty-Third and Fifty-Seventh Reports of the Standing Committee on House Management, presented on February 12, 1992 (*Journals*, p. 1009), June 5, 1992 (*Journals*, p. 1632), and December 4, 1992 (*Journals*, p. 2285), respectively, and concurred in on April 29, 1992 (*Journals*, p. 1337), June 8, 1992 (*Journals*, p. 1638), and December 11, 1992 (*Journals*, p. 2399), respectively.

99. See, for example, paragraph 74 of the Procedure and Organization Committee's report on broadcasting, presented on June 30, 1972 (*Journals*, pp. 471-86). In 1979, for example, a Member crossed the floor of the House to sit with another party, but the event was not captured by the cameras because to have done so would have contravened the broadcasting guidelines established by the House (*Debates*, March 8, 1979, pp. 3943-4). In another instance, when a point of order was raised as to the style of coverage of a budget presentation, the Speaker ruled that the coverage had not been consistent with previous budget presentations and suggested that the guidelines then in effect be observed until such time as the House decided otherwise (*Debates*, May 28, 1985, pp. 5146-7). In 1995, the House agreed to the temporary installation of stationary television cameras on the floor of the House for the address of the President of the United States (*Journals*, February 20, 1995, p. 1151). Two cameras were placed next to the Bar of the House, one operated by Canadian television networks and one operated by the American networks.

   In a 1993 case before the Supreme Court of Canada, a broadcaster had applied to film the proceedings of a provincial legislature from the public galleries, using its own cameras *(New Brunswick Broadcasting Co. v. Nova Scotia (Speaker of the House of Assembly)* [1993] 1 S.C.R. 319). The Speaker of the Assembly contended that to do so would interfere with the decorum and orderly proceedings of the Assembly, and moreover that the Assembly would have no control over the production or use of the film. The Court ruled in a majority opinion that in excluding the cameras from the gallery, the House of Assembly was exercising its right to control its internal proceedings and its right to exclude strangers from the House and its precinct. Five separate opinions were delivered in the Court's 7-1 decision. They are discussed at length in *Maingot*, 2nd ed.; see in particular pp. 306-18.

100. Standing Order 108(3)*(a)*(v).

CURRENT ARRANGEMENTS

The broadcasting service provided by the House ensures that the daily proceedings of the House are taped, archived and distributed live to the media. In addition, House and committee proceedings are transmitted via satellite and distributed on the Canadian Public Affairs Channel (CPaC),[101] which makes use of the existing national system of cable television channels. CPaC viewers have access to live, gavel-to-gavel proceedings of the House, the daily replay of Question Period, and committee coverage.

The broadcast system is integrated into the architecture of the Chamber so as not to offend existing decor. Committee and House proceedings are broadcast and recorded from the opening of business until adjournment and distributed to outside users without editing or revision.[102]

Chamber Proceedings

The Chamber is equipped with cameras mounted beneath the galleries and operated from a control room constructed over the south gallery, invisible from the floor of the House. The recording of the proceedings is governed by guidelines, intended to preserve the concept of the electronic Hansard, as adopted by the House.[103] The camera focusses on the Speaker, or on the Member who has been recognized by the Speaker. During debate, camera shots are restricted to the head and torso of the Member speaking, and the microphone picks up only his or her voice. Reaction shots, split screens and cutaway shots are not permitted. In order to give viewers a better appreciation of "the context and dynamic of the House", wider camera angles, showing more of the House and its Members, may be used during Question Period and the taking of recorded votes.[104]

Committee Proceedings

The resolution adopted by the House in 1977 also applied to the broadcasting of committee proceedings; however, the special committee implementing radio and television broadcasting determined that further study was necessary before committee proceedings could be televised.[105] In the next Parliament, the Speaker was asked to

---

101. In 1991, the CBC announced that it would no longer fund CPaC and the following year, a new cable consortium formed, called the Cable Parliamentary Channel (CPaC). In 1996, it was renamed the Cable Public Affairs Channel (CPaC).

102. However, the unedited images are "enhanced" by House of Commons broadcast staff. An example would be the insertion of information at the bottom of the screen, such as the name of the Member or committee witness speaking, or the subject of debate.

103. *Journals*, January 25, 1977, p. 287.

104. See the Fifty-Seventh Report of the Standing Committee on House Management (*Minutes of Proceedings and Evidence*, Issue 42, pp. 3-4), presented on December 4, 1992 (*Journals*, p. 2285), and concurred in on December 11, 1992 (*Journals*, p. 2399). The adoption of these new guidelines on wider angles was preceded by a trial period; see the Committee's Twenty-Second and Forty-Third Reports, concurred in on April 29, 1992 (*Journals*, p. 1337), and June 8, 1992 (*Journals*, p. 1638), respectively.

105. In what turned out to be its last report, the special committee raised a concern about the applicability of the "electronic Hansard" concept to broadcasting of committee proceedings and alluded to the need to consider procedures for televising committees (*Journals*, November 23, 1977, p. 130).

rule on the question of whether a committee had the power to televise and decided that since no guidelines had been established, the broadcasting of committee proceedings could only be authorized by the House itself.[106]

Beginning in 1980, a number of committees received permission from the House to broadcast their proceedings on a single-issue basis—that is, to broadcast a single meeting, or all the meetings held with respect to a particular order of reference.[107] In 1991, the House adopted a rule codifying the requirement for committees to seek the consent of the House to use House facilities for broadcasting. This new rule also required the then Standing Committee on House Management to establish experimental guidelines which, when concurred in by the House, would govern the broadcasting of committee meetings.[108] In 1992, the House concurred in the Committee's report recommending the audio broadcast of all public committee meetings and the equipping of one committee room for television broadcasting, with an evaluation to be made by the Committee after six months.[109] In April 1993, the House agreed to continue these broadcasting arrangements on a permanent basis, subject to ongoing review by the Standing Committee on Procedure and House Affairs.[110]

Access to Broadcast Materials

Members may listen to selected committee meetings on an in-house radio network; they may also view the live broadcast of House or committee proceedings on an in-house television network. Both networks provide service in French, English or "floor" sound (the actual language of debate, without interpretation). In addition to providing a live feed which is accessible by other media apart from the parliamentary television channel, the Broadcasting Service of the House maintains a complete video archive dating back to October 1977. Members may request retrieval and replay of any part of the televised proceedings of the House and may also obtain video and/or audio copies of House and committee proceedings.

---

106. See *Debates*, November 6, 1980, pp. 4531-2.

107. A number of these were committees studying constitutional or financial matters. For further information, see the section on broadcasting in Chapter 20, "Committees".

108. Standing Order 119.1, adopted on April 11, 1991 (*Journals*, pp. 2904-5, 2929).

109. See the Twenty-Third Report of the Standing Committee on House Management, presented on February 14, 1992 (*Journals*, pp. 1024-5), and concurred in on March 27, 1992 (*Journals*, p. 1230).

110. The Eighty-Third Report of the then Standing Committee on House Management, presented on April 2, 1993 (*Journals*, p. 2784), was concurred in on April 28, 1993 (*Journals*, p. 2873). See also Chapter 20, "Committees".

Appendices

List of Appendices

Appendix 1

GOVERNORS GENERAL
OF CANADA SINCE 1867

Appointed by the Sovereign on the advice of the Prime Minister, the Governor General usually holds office for five years. However, the term can continue beyond five years and is brought to an end by the installation or the swearing-in of a successor. The *Constitution Act, 1867,* confers upon the Governor General certain basic powers of government: a recommendation from the Governor General must accompany all spending measures introduced in the House; it is the Governor General who gives Royal Assent to legislation; and it is the Governor General who summons, prorogues and dissolves Parliament. However, in administering the executive authority of the Government, the Governor General acts solely upon the advice of the Ministry. In addition to these basic powers of government, the Governor General also has a number of ceremonial responsibilities. The list of Governors General of Canada since Confederation and the information on their appointment and term of office was kindly provided by Rideau Hall.

	Governor General	Appointment Date[2]	Term of Office[1] Installation Date[3]	Last Day in Office[4]
1.	Charles Stanley Monck, **Viscount Monck**	June 1, 1867	July 1, 1867	November 14, 1868
2.	Sir John Young, **Lord Lisgar**	December 29, 1868	February 2, 1869	June 21, 1872
3.	Sir Frederick Temple Blackwood, **The Earl of Dufferin**	May 22, 1872	June 25, 1872	November 14, 1878

	Governor General	Appointment Date[2]	Term of Office[1]	
			Installation Date[3]	Last Day in Office[4]
4.	Sir John Douglas Sutherland Campbell, **The Marquess of Lorne**	October 7, 1878	November 25, 1878	October 22, 1883
5.	Henry Charles Keith Petty-Fitzmaurice, **The Marquess of Lansdowne**	August 18, 1883	October 23, 1883	May 30, 1888
6.	Sir Frederick Arthur Stanley, **Lord Stanley of Preston**	May 1, 1888	June 11, 1888	September 6, 1893
7.	Sir John Campbell Hamilton Gordon, **The Earl of Aberdeen**	May 22, 1893	September 18, 1893	November 12, 1898
8.	Gilbert John Murray Kynynmound Elliot, **The Earl of Minto**	July 30, 1898	November 12, 1898	November 18, 1904
9.	Sir Albert Henry George Grey, **Earl Grey**	September 26, 1904	December 10, 1904	October 12, 1911
10.	H. R. H. Prince Arthur William Patrick Albert, **Field Marshall H.R.H. The Duke of Connaught and Strathearn**	March 6, 1911	October 13, 1911	October 11, 1916

	Governor General	Appointment Date[2]	Term of Office[1]	
			Installation Date[3]	Last Day in Office[4]
	11. Sir Victor Christian William Cavendish, **The Duke of Devonshire**	August 8, 1916	November 11, 1916	July 19, 1921
	12. Sir Julian Hedworth George Byng, **General Lord Byng of Vimy**	August 2, 1921	August 11, 1921	September 29, 1926
	13. Sir Freeman Freeman-Thomas, **The Viscount Willingdon of Ratton**	August 5, 1926	October 2, 1926	January 16, 1931
	14. Sir Vere Brabazon Ponsonby, **The Earl of Bessborough**	March 20, 1931	April 4, 1931	September 29, 1935
	15. Sir John Buchan, **Lord Tweedsmuir of Elsfield**	August 10, 1935	November 2, 1935	February 11, 1940*
	16. Sir Alexander Augustus Frederick William Alfred George Cambridge, **Major General The Earl of Athlone**	June 2, 1940	June 21, 1940	March 16, 1946
	17. Sir Harold Rupert Leofric George Alexander, **Field Marshal The Viscount Alexander of Tunis**	March 21, 1946	April 12, 1946	January 28, 1952

* Died in office.

| | Governor General | Appointment Date[2] | Term of Office[1] | |
			Installation Date[3]	Last Day in Office[4]
18.	**The Rt. Hon. Vincent Charles Massey**	February 1, 1952	February 28, 1952	September 15, 1959
19.	**Major General The Rt. Hon. Georges Philias Vanier**	August 1, 1959	September 15, 1959	March 5, 1967*
20.	**The Rt. Hon. Daniel Roland Michener**	March 29, 1967	April 17, 1967	January 14, 1974
21.	**The Rt. Hon. Jules Léger**	October 5, 1973	January 14, 1974	January 22, 1979
22.	**The Rt. Hon. Edward Richard Schreyer**	December 28, 1978	January 22, 1979	May 14, 1984
23.	**The Rt. Hon. Jeanne Mathilde Sauvé**	January 28, 1984	May 14, 1984	January 29, 1990
24.	**The Rt. Hon. Ramon John Hnatyshyn**	December 14, 1989	January 29, 1990	February 8, 1995

* Died in office.

	Governor General	Appointment Date[2]	Term of Office[1]	
			Installation Date[3]	Last Day in Office[4]
	25. **The Rt. Hon. Roméo Adrien LeBlanc**	January 16, 1995	February 8, 1995	October 7, 1999
	26. **The Rt. Hon. Adrienne Clarkson**	September 8, 1999	October 7, 1999	

1. Term of Office: The appointment of a Governor General is without a specific term and persists legally until brought to an end by the installation or the swearing-in of a successor. By convention, the term has come to be regarded as five years, but its actual length is determined by the Prime Minister's recommendation to the Sovereign on the appointment of a successor.

2. Appointment Date: The appointment is made by the Sovereign on the basis of formal advice submitted by the Prime Minister who recommends the appointment in the form of a commission of appointment and the date of the commission becomes the appointment date. The appointment is then announced simultaneously in London and in Ottawa in the form of a press release issued by the Prime Minister's Office.

3. Installation Date: The swearing-in or installation formalizes the appointment of the Governor General and is the first official day of his/her term of office.

4. Last Day in Office: The last day of the Governor General's term of office is usually the day of the installation or swearing-in of his/her successor. However, in some cases, an Administrator was appointed from the last day in office of the Governor General until the installation of the successor.

Appendix 2

SPEAKERS OF THE HOUSE OF COMMONS SINCE 1867

The Speaker of the House of Commons assumes the position of highest authority in the House and represents the Commons in all its powers, proceedings and dignity. The duties of the Speaker fall into three categories: 1) acting as the spokesperson of the House; 2) presiding over sittings of the House and maintaining order and decorum; and 3) assuming important administrative responsibilities. Provisions for the Speakership are defined in the *Constitution Act, 1867,* in the *Parliament of Canada Act,* and in the Standing Orders of the House of Commons. The election of the Speaker by the House is a constitutional requirement. At the beginning of every Parliament, the House must elect a Speaker from amongst its Members. From Confederation until 1985, Speakers were elected by way of motion usually initiated by the Prime Minister. Provisional rules adopted in June 1985, and made permanent in June 1987, have since provided for the election of the Speaker by secret ballot.

	Speaker (Party)	Date of Election as Speaker	Parliament (Years)
1.	James Cockburn (Conservative)	November 6, 1867	1st Parliament (1867-72)
		March 5, 1873	2nd Parliament (1873-74)
2.	Timothy Warren Anglin [1] (Liberal)	March 26, 1874	1st Session, 3rd Parliament to 4th Session, 3rd Parliament (1874-77)
		February 7, 1878	5th Session, 3rd Parliament (1878)
3.	Joseph-Godéric Blanchet (Liberal-Conservative)	February 13, 1879	4th Parliament (1879-82)

	Speaker (Party)	Date of Election as Speaker	Parliament (Years)
4.	George Airey Kirkpatrick (Liberal-Conservative)	February 8, 1883	5th Parliament (1883-87)
5.	Joseph-Aldéric Ouimet (Liberal-Conservative)	April 13, 1887	6th Parliament (1887-91)
6.	Peter White (Conservative)	April 29, 1891	7th Parliament (1891-96)
7.	James David Edgar[2] (Liberal)	August 19, 1896	1st Session, 8th Parliament to 4th Session, 8th Parliament (1896-99)
8.	Thomas Bain (Liberal)	August 1, 1899	4th Session, 8th Parliament to 5th Session, 8th Parliament (1899-1900)
9.	Louis-Philippe Brodeur[3] (Liberal)	February 6, 1901	1st Session, 9th Parliament to 3rd Session, 9th Parliament (1901-04)
10.	Napoléon-Antoine Belcourt (Liberal)	March 10, 1904	4th Session, 9th Parliament (1904)

	Speaker (Party)	Date of Election as Speaker	Parliament (Years)
11.	Robert Franklin Sutherland (Liberal)	January 11, 1905	10th Parliament (1905-08)
12.	Charles Marcil (Liberal)	January 20, 1909	11th Parliament (1909-11)
13.	Thomas Simpson Sproule[4] (Conservative)	November 15, 1911	1st Session, 12th Parliament to 5th Session, 12th Parliament (1911-15)
14.	Albert Sévigny[5] (Conservative)	January 12, 1916	6th Session, 12th Parliament (1916-17)
15.	Edgar Nelson Rhodes (Conservative)	January 18, 1917 March 18, 1918	7th Session, 12th Parliament (1917) 13th Parliament (1918-21)
16.	Rodolphe Lemieux[6] (Liberal)	March 8, 1922 January 7, 1926 December 9, 1926	14th Parliament (1922-25) 15th Parliament (1926) 16th Parliament (1926-30)
17.	George Black[7] (Conservative)	September 8, 1930	1st Session, 17th Parliament to 5th Session, 17th Parliament (1930-35)

	Speaker (Party)	Date of Election as Speaker	Parliament (Years)
	18. James Langstaff Bowman (Conservative)	January 17, 1935	6th Session, 17th Parliament (1935)
	19. Pierre-François Casgrain[8] (Liberal)	February 6, 1936	18th Parliament (1936-40)
	20. James Glen (Liberal)	May 16, 1940	19th Parliament (1940-45)
	21. Gaspard Fauteux (Liberal)	September 6, 1945	20th Parliament (1945-49)
	22. William Ross Macdonald[9] (Liberal)	September 15, 1949	21st Parliament (1949-53)
	23. Louis-René Beaudoin[10] (Liberal)	November 12, 1953	22nd Parliament (1953-57)
	24. Roland Michener (Progressive Conservative)	October 14, 1957 May 12, 1958	23rd Parliament (1957-58) 24th Parliament (1958-62)

	Speaker (Party)	Date of Election as Speaker	Parliament (Years)
	25. Marcel Lambert (Progressive Conservative)	September 27, 1962	25th Parliament (1962-63)
	26. Alan Macnaughton (Liberal)	May 16, 1963	26th Parliament (1963-65)
	27. Lucien Lamoureux[11] (Liberal)	January 18, 1966 September 12, 1968 January 4, 1973	27th Parliament (1966-68) 28th Parliament (1968-72) 29th Parliament (1973-74)
	28. James Jerome[12] (Liberal)	September 30, 1974 October 9, 1979	30th Parliament (1974-79) 31st Parliament (1979)
	29. Jeanne Sauvé[13] (Liberal)	April 14, 1980	1st Session, 32nd Parliament to 2nd Session, 32nd Parliament (1980-84)
	30. Lloyd Francis (Liberal)	January 16, 1984	2nd Session, 32nd Parliament (1984)
	31. John Bosley[14] (Progressive Conservative)	November 5, 1984	1st Session, 33rd Parliament to 2nd Session, 33rd Parliament (1984-86)

	Speaker (Party)	Date of Election as Speaker	Parliament (Years)
32.	John Fraser[15] (Progressive Conservative)	September 30, 1986	2nd Session, 33rd Parliament (1986-88)
		December 12, 1988	34th Parliament (1988-93)
33.	Gilbert Parent[16] (Liberal)	January 17, 1994	35th Parliament (1994-97)
		September 22, 1997	36th Parliament (1997-)

1. On April 28, 1877, the last sitting day of the Fourth Session of the Third Parliament, the Select Standing Committee on Privileges and Elections presented a report to the House of Commons stating its view that Speaker Anglin had, because of certain commercial dealings with the Government, violated the Independence of Parliament Act and thus his election was void. Although the report was never adopted, during the recess, Mr. Anglin resigned his seat, and thus the Speakership, and was re-elected in a by-election. On the opening of the final session of the Third Parliament, Prime Minister Mackenzie renominated Mr. Anglin who was elected as Speaker although the opposition challenged his eligibility and forced a recorded vote on the question (*Debates*, February 7, 1878, pp. 1-12).

2. Speaker Edgar died in office on July 31, 1899.

3. Speaker Brodeur resigned as a Member, and thus the Speakership, on January 19, 1904, to become Minister of Inland Revenue. Until 1931, Members of the House who accepted Cabinet positions were required, pursuant to the *Senate and House of Commons Act,* to resign their seats and seek re-election.

4. Speaker Sproule was summoned to the Senate on December 3, 1915, during the recess.

5. Speaker Sévigny resigned as a Member, and thus the Speakership, on January 8, 1917, during the recess, to become Minister of Inland Revenue.

6. Speaker Lemieux, elected as a Liberal, continued to serve as Speaker during the Conservative government of Prime Minister Arthur Meighen which had replaced the government of Prime Minister W.L. Mackenzie King on June 29, 1926, during the Fifteenth Parliament.

7. On January 17, 1935, Prime Minister R.B. Bennett announced to the House that Speaker Black had resigned due to illness.

8. Speaker Casgrain was the second Speaker not to have his nomination supported by the entire House. The motion was agreed to, on division (*Journals*, February 6, 1936, p. 8).

9. Speaker Macdonald was appointed to the Senate on June 12, 1953.

10. The motion to nominate Speaker Beaudoin to the Chair was seconded by the Leader of the Opposition, George A. Drew. This marked the first time that anyone other than a Cabinet Minister had seconded the nomination of the Speaker.

11. Speaker Lamoureux resigned his party affiliation and sought and won election to the House of Commons as an independent candidate in the general elections held on June 25, 1968, and October 30, 1972.

12. The election of Speaker Jerome to a second term following the general election of May 22, 1979, marked the first time a Member of an opposition party had been nominated by the governing party to preside over the House of Commons.

13. Speaker Sauvé, the first woman to be elected Speaker of the House of Commons, resigned as Speaker on January 15, 1984, during the Second Session of the Thirty-Second Parliament, after having been designated to become Governor General. On May 14, 1984, Mme Sauvé was sworn in as Canada's first female Governor General.

14. Speaker Bosley resigned the Speakership on September 30, 1986. Two letters dated September 5 and September 25, 1986, and addressed to the Clerk of the House of Commons, were tabled in the House (*Journals*, September 30, 1986, p. 2).

15. With his election to the Speakership on September 30, 1986, Mr. Fraser became the first Speaker to be elected by secret ballot, following amendments to the Standing Orders adopted on June 27, 1985. Speaker Fraser was elected on the eleventh ballot from among an original list of 39 candidates. At the beginning of the Thirty-Fourth Parliament, on December 12, 1988, Mr. Fraser was re-elected as Speaker on the first ballot from among a list of 12 candidates.

16. On January 17, 1994, Speaker Parent was elected on the sixth ballot from among an original list of 12 candidates. At the beginning of the Thirty-Sixth Parliament, on September 22, 1997, Mr. Parent was re-elected as Speaker on the fourth ballot from among an original list of 29 candidates.

Appendix 3

DEPUTY SPEAKERS AND CHAIRMEN OF COMMITTEES OF THE WHOLE HOUSE SINCE 1885

The position of Deputy Speaker and Chairman of Committees of the Whole was created through amendments to the Standing Orders adopted on February 10, 1885, and through the adoption of legislation which was assented to on May 1, 1885. The Statute was entitled *An Act to provide for the appointment of a Deputy Speaker of the House of Commons* (S.C. 1885, c. 1). The Standing Orders require the House to elect, from among its Members, a Deputy Speaker and Chairman of Committees of the Whole at the commencement of every Parliament. The same person performs the duties of both offices and must have full and practical knowledge of the official language which is not that of the current Speaker. The Deputy Speaker is vested with all the powers of the Speaker when the latter is absent from the House, presides over the proceedings of the House, and is responsible for chairing Committees of the Whole House.

	Deputy Speaker (Party)	Date of Appointment	Parliament (Years)
1.	Malachy B. Daly[1] (Liberal-Conservative)	February 10, 1885	3rd Session, 5th Parliament to 4th Session, 5th Parliament (1885-87)
2.	Charles Carroll Colby[2] (Liberal-Conservative)	May 11, 1887	1st Session, 6th Parliament to 3rd Session, 6th Parliament (1887-89)
3.	John F. Wood (Conservative)	January 21, 1890	4th Session, 6th Parliament (1890-91)
4.	J.G.H. Bergeron (Liberal-Conservative)	May 22, 1891	7th Parliament (1891-96)
5.	Louis-Philippe Brodeur[3] (Liberal)	August 27, 1896	8th Parliament (1896-1900)
6.	Peter Macdonald (Liberal)	February 11, 1901	9th Parliament (1901-04)
7.	Charles Marcil[4] (Liberal)	January 16, 1905	10th Parliament (1905-08)
8.	Gilbert H. McIntyre (Liberal)	January 25, 1909	11th Parliament (1909-11)

	Deputy Speaker (Party)	Date of Appointment	Parliament (Years)
9.	Pierre-Édouard Blondin[5] (Conservative)	November 29, 1911	1st Session, 12th Parliament to 4th Session, 12th Parliament (1911-14)
10.	Albert Sévigny[6] (Conservative)	February 9, 1915	5th Session, 12th Parliament (1915)
11.	Edgar Nelson Rhodes[7] (Liberal-Conservative)	February 3, 1916	6th Session, 12th Parliament (1916)
12.	Joseph H. Rainville (Conservative)	February 1, 1917	7th Session, 12th Parliament (1917)
13.	George Henry Boivin[8] (Liberal)	March 21, 1918	13th Parliament (1918-21)
14.	George N. Gordon (Liberal)	March 24, 1922	14th Parliament (1922-25)
15.	William Duff (Liberal)	March 16, 1926	15th Parliament (1926)
16.	John Frederick Johnston (Liberal)	December 14, 1926	16th Parliament (1926-30)
17.	Armand LaVergne[9] (Liberal-Conservative)	September 9, 1930	1st Session, 17th Parliament to 6th Session, 17th Parliament (1930-35)
18.	Raymond Morand (Conservative)	March 11, 1935	6th Session, 17th Parliament (1935)
19.	Frederick George Sanderson (Liberal)	February 13, 1936	18th Parliament (1936-40)
20.	Thomas Vien[10] (Liberal)	May 21, 1940	1st Session, 19th Parliament to 3rd Session, 19th Parliament (1940-42)
21.	Joseph Arthur Bradette (Liberal)	February 25, 1943	4th Session, 19th Parliament to 6th Session, 19th Parliament (1943-45)
22.	William Ross Macdonald[11] (Liberal)	September 27, 1945	20th Parliament (1945-49)
23.	Joseph Alfred Dion[12] (Liberal)	September 15, 1949	1st Session, 21st Parliament to 6th Session, 21st Parliament (1949-52)
24.	Louis-René Beaudoin[13] (Liberal)	April 9, 1952	6th Session, 21st Parliament to 7th Session, 21st Parliament (1952-53)
25.	William Alfred Robinson (Liberal)	November 12, 1953	22nd Parliament (1953-57)
26.	Henri Courtemanche (Progressive Conservative)	October 14, 1957	23rd Parliament (1957-58)

	Deputy Speaker (Party)	Date of Appointment	Parliament (Years)
27.	Pierre Sévigny[14] (Progressive Conservative)	May 12, 1958	1st Session, 24th Parliament to 2nd Session, 24th Parliament (1958-59)
28.	Jacques Flynn[15] (Progressive Conservative)	January 14, 1960	3rd Session, 24th Parliament to 4th Session, 24th Parliament (1960-61)
29.	Paul Martineau[16] (Progressive Conservative)	January 18, 1962	5th Session, 24th Parliament (1962)
30.	Gordon Campbell Chown (Progressive Conservative)	September 27, 1962	25th Parliament (1962-63)
31.	Lucien Lamoureux[17] (Liberal)	May 16, 1963	26th Parliament (1963-65)
32.	Herman Maxwell Batten (Liberal)	January 18, 1966	27th Parliament (1966-68)
33.	Hugh Faulkner[18] (Liberal)	September 12, 1968	1st Session, 28th Parliament to 2nd Session, 28th Parliament (1968-70)
34.	Russell C. Honey (Liberal)	October 5, 1970	2nd Session, 28th Parliament to 4th Session, 28th Parliament (1970-72)
35.	Robert McCleave[19] (Progressive Conservative)	January 4, 1973	29th Parliament (1973-74)
36.	Gérald Laniel[20] (Liberal)	September 30, 1974	30th Parliament (1974-79)
		October 9, 1979	31st Parliament (1979)
37.	Lloyd Francis[21] (Liberal)	April 14, 1980	1st Session, 32nd Parliament to 2nd Session, 32nd Parliament (1980-84)
38.	Eymard Corbin (Liberal)	January 16, 1984	2nd Session, 32nd Parliament (1984)
39.	Marcel Danis[22] (Progressive Conservative)	November 5, 1984	33rd Parliament (1984-88)
		December 12, 1988	1st Session, 34th Parliament to 2nd Session, 34th Parliament (1988-90)
40.	Andrée Champagne[23] (Progressive Conservative)	May 15, 1990	2nd Session, 34th Parliament to 3rd Session, 34th Parliament (1990-93)
41.	David Kilgour (Liberal)	January 18, 1994	35th Parliament (1994-97)
42.	Peter Milliken (Liberal)	September 23, 1997	36th Parliament (1997-)

1. Following the adoption of amendments to the Standing Orders on February 10, 1885, the House resolved that Malachy B. Daly take the Chair as Deputy Speaker and Chairman of Committees of the Whole.

2. Charles Carroll Colby resigned as a Member, and thus as Deputy Speaker, between the Third and Fourth Sessions, upon his appointment as President of the Privy Council on November 28, 1889. Until 1931, Members of the House who accepted Cabinet positions were required, pursuant to the *Senate and House of Commons Act*, to resign their seats and seek re-election.

3. Louis-Philippe Brodeur was elected Speaker in the next Parliament.

4. Charles Marcil was elected Speaker in the next Parliament.

5. Pierre-Édouard Blondin resigned as a Member, and thus as Deputy Speaker, between the Fourth and Fifth Sessions, upon his appointment as Minister of Inland Revenue on October 20, 1914.

6. Albert Sévigny was elected Speaker on January 12, 1916.

7. Edgar Nelson Rhodes was elected Speaker on January 18, 1917.

8. George Henry Boivin, a Liberal Member, served under the Unionist Government of Sir Robert Borden.

9. Armand LaVergne died in office on March 5, 1935.

10. Thomas Vien was summoned to the Senate on October 5, 1942, and became Speaker of the Senate on January 23, 1943.

11. William Ross Macdonald was elected Speaker in the next Parliament.

12. Joseph Alfred Dion was appointed judge and resigned his seat on April 9, 1952.

13. Louis-René Beaudoin was elected Speaker in the next Parliament.

14. Pierre Sévigny was appointed Associate Minister of National Defence on August 20, 1959, during the recess.

15. Jacques Flynn was appointed Minister of Mines and Technical Surveys on December 28, 1961, during the recess.

16. The motion to appoint Paul Martineau was agreed to on a recorded division. This marked the first occasion that there was a recorded division on the appointment of a Deputy Speaker. (*Debates*, January 18, 1962, pp. 5-6.)

17. Lucien Lamoureux was elected Speaker in the next Parliament.

18. Hugh Faulkner was appointed Parliamentary Secretary to the Secretary of State on October 1, 1970.

19. Robert McCleave, a Progressive Conservative Member, served under a Liberal Government.

20. Gérald Laniel, a Liberal Member, served under a Progressive Conservative Government in the Thirty-First Parliament.

21. Lloyd Francis was elected Speaker on January 16, 1984, during the Second Session of the Thirty-Second Parliament.

22. Marcel Danis was appointed Minister of State (Youth) and Minister of State (Fitness and Amateur Sport) and Deputy Leader of the Government in the House of Commons on February 23, 1990. However, although he did not sit in the Chair following his appointment to the Cabinet, Mr. Danis remained Deputy Speaker and Chairman of Committees of the Whole until his official resignation and the appointment to that position of Andrée Champagne on May 15, 1990.

23. First woman to become Deputy Speaker.

Appendix 4

DEPUTY CHAIRMEN OF COMMITTEES OF THE WHOLE HOUSE SINCE 1938

On February 11, 1938, the Standing Orders of the House were amended to provide for the appointment of a Deputy Chairman of Committees of the Whole. The tenure of this office is for a single session rather than for a Parliament. Whenever the Chairman of Committees of the Whole is absent, the Deputy Chairman is entitled to exercise all the powers vested in the Chairman of Committees of the Whole, including the powers as Deputy Speaker. After the first appointment, the position was left vacant for nine years and then from 1947 until 1953, only being filled when necessary. In 1953 and subsequent years, the practice of appointing a Deputy Chairman for a session was firmly established.

	Deputy Chairman of Committees of the Whole (Party)	Date of Appointment	Parliament (Years)
1.	John Frederick Johnston[1] (Liberal)	February 11, 1938	3rd Session, 18th Parliament (1938)
2.	William Henry Golding (Liberal)	March 28, 1947	3rd Session, 20th Parliament (1947)
		December 15, 1947	4th Session, 20th Parliament (1947-48)
		January 27, 1949	5th Session, 20th Parliament (1949)
3.	Louis-René Beaudoin[2] (Liberal)	September 15, 1949	1st Session, 21st Parliament (1949)
		February 21, 1950	2nd Session, 21st Parliament (1950)
		September 5, 1950	3rd Session, 21st Parliament (1950-51)
		January 30, 1951	4th Session, 21st Parliament (1951)
		October 9, 1951	5th Session, 21st Parliament (1951)
		February 29, 1952	6th Session, 21st Parliament (1952)

Deputy Chairman of Committees of the Whole (Party)	Date of Appointment	Parliament (Years)
4. William Alfred Robinson[3] (Liberal)	May 23, 1952	6th Session, 21st Parliament (1952)
	November 20, 1952	7th Session, 21st Parliament (1952-53)
5. Edward T. Applewhaite (Liberal)	December 16, 1953	1st Session, 22nd Parliament (1953-54)
	January 7, 1955	2nd Session, 22nd Parliament (1955)
	January 10, 1956	3rd Session, 22nd Parliament (1956)
	November 26, 1956	4th Session, 22nd Parliament (1956-57)
	January 8, 1957	5th Session, 22nd Parliament (1957)
6. Arza Clair Casselman (Progressive Conservative)	October 15, 1957	23rd Parliament (1957-58)
7. Charles Edward Rea[4] (Progressive Conservative)	May 12, 1958	1st Session, 24th Parliament (1958)
	January 15, 1959	2nd Session, 24th Parliament (1959)
	January 14, 1960	3rd Session, 24th Parliament (1960)
	November 17, 1960	4th Session, 24th Parliament (1960-61)
8. Gordon Campbell Chown[5] (Progressive Conservative)	June 8, 1961	4th Session, 24th Parliament (1961)
	January 18, 1962	5th Session, 24th Parliament (1962)
9. Rémi Paul (Progressive Conservative)	September 27, 1962	25th Parliament (1962-63)
10. Herman Maxwell Batten[6] (Liberal)	May 16, 1963	1st Session, 26th Parliament (1963)
	February 18, 1964	2nd Session, 26th Parliament (1964-65)
	April 5, 1965	3rd Session, 26th Parliament (1965)

	Deputy Chairman of Committees of the Whole (Party)	Date of Appointment	Parliament (Years)
11.	Maurice Rinfret[7] (Liberal)	January 18, 1966	1st Session, 27th Parliament (1966-67)
		May 8, 1967	2nd Session, 27th Parliament (1967-68)
12.	Albert Béchard[8] (Liberal)	September 12, 1968	1st Session, 28th Parliament (1968-69)
		October 23, 1969	2nd Session, 28th Parliament (1969-70)
13.	Gérald Laniel[9] (Liberal)	October 5, 1970	2nd Session, 28th Parliament (1970)
		October 8, 1970	3rd Session, 28th Parliament (1970-72)
		February 17, 1972	4th Session, 28th Parliament (1972)
		January 4, 1973[10]	1st Session, 29th Parliament (1973-74)
		February 27, 1974	2nd Session, 29th Parliament (1974)
14.	Keith Penner[11] (Liberal)	September 30, 1974	1st Session, 30th Parliament (1974-75)
15.	Charles Robert Turner (Liberal)	October 14, 1975	1st Session, 30th Parliament (1975-76)
		October 12, 1976	2nd Session, 30th Parliament (1976-77)
		October 18, 1977	3rd Session, 30th Parliament (1977-78)
		October 11, 1978	4th Session, 30th Parliament (1978-79)
16.	Fred McCain (Progressive Conservative)	October 9, 1979	31st Parliament (1979)
17.	Denis Ethier[12] (Liberal)	April 14, 1980	1st Session, 32nd Parliament (1980-82)
18.	Rod Blaker[13] (Liberal)	July 27, 1982	1st Session, 32nd Parliament (1982-83)
		December 7, 1983	2nd Session, 32nd Parliament (1983-84)
19.	Harold Thomas Herbert (Liberal)	January 16, 1984	2nd Session, 32nd Parliament (1984)

Deputy Chairman of Committees of the Whole (Party)	Date of Appointment	Parliament (Years)
20. Steven Paproski (Progressive Conservative)	November 5, 1984	1st Session, 33rd Parliament (1984-86)
	October 1, 1986	2nd Session, 33rd Parliament (1986-88)
	December 12, 1988	1st Session, 34th Parliament (1988-89)
	April 3, 1989	2nd Session, 34th Parliament (1989-91)
	May 13, 1991	3rd Session, 34th Parliament (1991-93)
21. Shirley Maheu [14] (Liberal)	January 18, 1994	1st Session, 35th Parliament (1994-96)
22. Robert Kilger [15] (Liberal)	February 27, 1996	2nd Session, 35th Parliament (1996)
23. Peter Milliken [16] (Liberal)	October 29, 1996	2nd Session, 35th Parliament (1996-97)
24. Ian McClelland [17] (Reform)	September 23, 1997	1st Session, 36th Parliament (1997-)

1. At the time of the appointment of Mr. Johnston, it was expected that the Deputy Speaker and Chairman of Committees of the Whole would be absent for a period of time. No Deputy Chairman of Committees of the Whole was appointed between 1938 and 1947.

2. Louis-René Beaudoin was appointed Deputy Speaker and Chairman of Committees of the Whole on April 9, 1952. The position of Deputy Chairman of Committees of the Whole remained vacant from that date until May 23, 1952.

3. William Alfred Robinson was selected as Deputy Speaker in the next Parliament.

4. Charles Edward Rea was replaced as Deputy Chairman of Committees of the Whole, due to illness, on June 8, 1961.

5. Gordon Campbell Chown was selected as Deputy Speaker in the next Parliament.

6. Herman Maxwell Batten was selected as Deputy Speaker in the next Parliament.

7. On December 26, 1967, Maurice Rinfret died in office. The position remained vacant during the remainder of the Second Session of the Twenty-Seventh Parliament.

8. Albert Béchard was appointed Parliamentary Secretary to the Minister of Justice on October 1, 1970, and resigned as Deputy Chairman of Committees of the Whole on October 5, 1970.

9. Gérald Laniel was selected as Deputy Speaker in the next Parliament.

10. For the first time, the motion for this position was seconded by a Member of an opposition party.

11. Keith Penner's resignation as Deputy Chairman of Committees of the Whole was announced in the House on October 14, 1975. He had been appointed Parliamentary Secretary to the Minister of Science and Technology on October 10, 1975.

12. On July 21, 1982, the Speaker informed the House that Denis Ethier had resigned as Deputy Chairman of Committees of the Whole, effective July 8, 1982.

13. Rod Blaker resigned as Deputy Chairman of Committees of the Whole on January 15, 1984. He had been appointed Parliamentary Secretary to the Minister for International Trade on January 13, 1984.

14. Shirley Maheu was appointed to the Senate on February 2, 1996.

15. Mr. Kilger's appointment was agreed by the House on a recorded division (*Journals*, February 27, 1996, p. 3). This marked the first occasion that the motion for this position was adopted on a recorded division. Mr. Kilger resigned as Deputy Chairman of Committees of the Whole on October 29, 1996, when he was appointed Government Whip by the Liberal Government.

16. Mr. Milliken's appointment was agreed by the House on a recorded division (*Journals*, October 29, 1996, pp. 787-8). Mr. Milliken was selected as Deputy Speaker in the next Parliament.

17. For the first time, a member of the Official Opposition was appointed to the position.

Appendix 5

ASSISTANT DEPUTY CHAIRMEN OF COMMITTEES OF THE WHOLE HOUSE SINCE 1967

On April 26, 1967, the Standing Orders of the House were amended to provide for the appointment of an Assistant Deputy Chairman of Committees of the Whole. The tenure of this office is for a single session rather than for a Parliament. Whenever the Chairman of Committees of the Whole or the Deputy Chairman is absent, the Assistant Deputy Chairman is entitled to exercise all the powers vested in the Chairman of Committees of the Whole, including the powers as Deputy Speaker. Mr. Paul Tardif was the first such appointee. No Assistant Deputy Chairman of Committees of the Whole was appointed during the First and Second Sessions of the Twenty-Eighth Parliament.

	Assistant Deputy Chairman (Party)	Date of Appointment	Parliament (Years)
1.	Paul Tardif (Liberal)	June 22, 1967	2nd Session, 27th Parliament (1967-68)
2.	Prosper Boulanger (Liberal)	September 30, 1971	3rd Session, 28th Parliament (1971-72)
		February 17, 1972	4th Session, 28th Parliament (1972)
		January 4, 1973	1st Session, 29th Parliament (1973-74)
		February 27, 1974	2nd Session, 29th Parliament (1974)
3.	Albanie Morin [1] (Liberal)	September 30, 1974	1st Session, 30th Parliament (1974-76)
4.	Denis Ethier [2] (Liberal)	October 12, 1976	2nd Session, 30th Parliament (1976-77)
		October 18, 1977	3rd Session, 30th Parliament (1977-78)
		October 11, 1978	4th Session, 30th Parliament (1978-79)
5.	William C. Scott (Progressive Conservative)	October 9, 1979	31st Parliament (1979)

	Assistant Deputy Chairman (Party)	Date of Appointment	Parliament (Years)
6.	Rod Blaker[3] (Liberal)	April 14, 1980	1st Session, 32nd Parliament (1980-82)
7.	Eymard Corbin[4] (Liberal)	July 27, 1982	1st Session, 32nd Parliament (1982-83)
		December 7, 1983	2nd Session, 32nd Parliament (1983-84)
8.	Jacques Guilbault (Liberal)	January 16, 1984	2nd Session, 32nd Parliament (1984)
9.	Jean Charest[5] (Progressive Conservative)	November 5, 1984	1st Session, 33rd Parliament (1984-86)
10.	Andrée Champagne[6] (Progressive Conservative)	October 1, 1986	2nd Session, 33rd Parliament (1986-88)
		December 12, 1988	1st Session, 34th Parliament (1988-89)
		April 3, 1989	2nd Session, 34th Parliament (1989-90)
11.	Denis Pronovost[7] (Progressive Conservative)	May 15, 1990	2nd Session, 34th Parliament (1990)
12.	Charles DeBlois[8] (Progressive Conservative)	October 2, 1990	2nd Session, 34th Parliament (1990-91)
		May 13, 1991	3rd Session, 34th Parliament (1991-93)
13.	Robert Kilger (Liberal)	January 18, 1994	1st Session, 35th Parliament (1994-96)
14.	Pierrette Ringuette-Maltais[9] (Liberal)	February 28, 1996	2nd Session, 35th Parliament (1996-97)
15.	Yolande Thibeault (Liberal)	September 23, 1997	1st Session, 36th Parliament (1997-)

1. Albanie Morin died on September 30, 1976. She was the first woman in Canadian history to officially occupy the Chair of the House of Commons.

2. Denis Ethier was selected as Deputy Chairman of Committees of the Whole on April 14, 1980.

3. Rod Blaker was selected as Deputy Chairman of Committees of the Whole on July 27, 1982.

4. Eymard Corbin was appointed Deputy Speaker and Chairman of Committees of the Whole on January 16, 1984.

5. Jean Charest was appointed Minister of State (Youth) on June 30, 1986.

6. Andrée Champagne was appointed Deputy Speaker and Chairman of Committees of the Whole on May 15, 1990.

7. Denis Pronovost resigned from the position of Assistant Deputy Chairman of Committees of the Whole on May 31, 1990.

8. The motion to appoint Mr. DeBlois was agreed to, on a recorded division. This marked the first occasion of a recorded division on the appointment of an Assistant Deputy Chairman of Committees of the Whole.

9. The motion to appoint Mrs. Ringuette-Maltais was agreed to on a recorded division.

Appendix 6

CLERKS OF THE HOUSE OF COMMONS SINCE 1867

An Order-in-Council appointee by Letters Patent under the Great Seal, the Clerk has traditionally held office at pleasure. While many of the Clerk's functions are defined in the Standing Orders and the *Parliament of Canada Act,* most of the duties have developed as the House itself has evolved. As a commissioner of oaths, the Clerk is one of the officers who administer the oath of allegiance to newly elected Members. The Clerk is the chief advisor to the Speaker and Members of the House of Commons on procedural matters and oversees the general administration of the House. The Clerk has the status of deputy minister and is Secretary to the Board of Internal Economy.

	Name	Date of Order-in-Council Appointment	Date Appointment Entered in *Journals* of the House
1.	William Burns Lindsay[1]	November 2, 1867	November 6, 1867
2.	Alfred Patrick[2]	January 21, 1873	March 5, 1873
3.	John George Bourinot[3]	December 1, 1880	December 9, 1880
4.	Thomas Barnard Flint[4]	November 11, 1902	March 12, 1903
5.	William Barton Northrup	March 11, 1918	March 18, 1918
6.	Arthur Beauchesne[5]	January 7, 1925	February 5, 1925
7.	Léon J. Raymond[6]	August 5, 1949	September 15, 1949
8.	Alistair Fraser	August 6, 1967	September 25, 1967
9.	Charles Beverley Koester	September 1, 1979	October 9, 1979
10.	Robert Marleau	July 2, 1987	September 18, 1987

1. Until his appointment as Clerk of the House of Commons, William Burns Lindsay held the position of Clerk of the Legislative Assembly of the Province of Canada from 1862 to 1867. At Confederation, he became the first Clerk of the House of Commons.

2. Until his appointment as Clerk of the House of Commons, Alfred Patrick held the position of Clerk Assistant in the Legislative Assembly of Canada and the House of Commons.

3. John George Bourinot was the author of *Parliamentary Procedure and Practice in the Dominion of Canada,* the first Canadian treatise on parliamentary procedure and an authoritative work that had four editions published in 1884, 1892, 1903 and 1916.

4. Thomas Barnard Flint was a former Member of Parliament. He was first elected to the House of Commons in 1891 and was re-elected in 1896 and 1900. His resignation as Member of Parliament and subsequent appointment as Clerk of the House of Commons were announced in the House by the Speaker on March 12, 1903 (*Debates*, March 12, 1903, pp. 1-2).

5. Arthur Beauchesne, a public servant, was appointed Clerk Assistant on February 17, 1916. He was also the author of *Rules and Forms of the House of Commons of Canada,* an authoritative work on parliamentary procedure that had six editions published in 1922, 1927, 1943, 1958, 1978 and 1989.

6. Léon J. Raymond was a former Member of Parliament. He was first elected to the House of Commons in 1945 and was re-elected in 1949. His resignation as Member of Parliament and subsequent appointment as Clerk of the House of Commons were announced in the House by the Speaker on September 15, 1949 (*Debates*, September 15, 1949, pp. 4, 11).

Appendix 7

SERGEANTS-AT-ARMS OF THE HOUSE OF COMMONS SINCE 1867

Appointed by Letters Patent under the Great Seal, the Sergeant-at-Arms performs many ceremonial and administrative duties and, as a commissioner of oaths, is one of the officers who may administer the oath of allegiance to newly elected Members. Bearing the Mace, the Sergeant-at-Arms precedes the Speaker as he or she enters and leaves the Chamber each day. The Sergeant-at-Arms occupies a desk at the Bar of the House when the House is sitting. In accordance with the Standing Orders, the Sergeant-at-Arms preserves order in the galleries, lobbies and corridors, and is responsible for taking into custody strangers who misbehave in the galleries. Traditionally, the position has been held by military officers.

	Name	Date of Order-in-Council Appointment
1.	Lieutenant-Colonel Donald William Macdonell[1]	November 2, 1867
2.	Lieutenant-Colonel Henry Robert Smith[2]	January 13, 1892
3.	Lieutenant-Colonel Henry William Bowie[3]	March 5, 1918
4.	Lieutenant-Colonel Henry Judson Coghill[4]	July 26, 1930
5.	Major Milton Fowler Gregg[5]	February 13, 1934
6.	Lieutenant-Colonel William John Franklin	August 24, 1945
7.	Lieutenant-Colonel David Vivian Currie	January 7, 1960
8.	Major-General Maurice Gaston Cloutier	April 27, 1978

1. Until his appointment as Sergeant-at-Arms of the House of Commons, Donald William Macdonell held the position of Sergeant-at-Arms of the Legislative Assembly of the Province of Canada from June 14, 1854, to Confederation. On November 6, 1867, upon the opening of the First Session of the First Parliament, Donald William Macdonell is listed as a Commissioner appointed to administer the Oath to the Members of the House of Commons.

2. Henry Robert Smith held the position of Deputy Sergeant-at-Arms of the House of Commons from 1872 until his appointment as Sergeant-at-Arms.

3. Henry William Bowie held the position of Deputy Sergeant-at-Arms of the House of Commons from 1891 until his appointment as Sergeant-at-Arms.

4. Henry Judson Coghill died on January 9, 1934, while in office.

5. During the Second World War (1939-45), Milton Fowler Gregg was on active service in the Canadian Army. In his place, the Clerk of the House of Commons, Arthur Beauchesne, assumed the duties of the Sergeant-at-Arms of the House of Commons.

Appendix 8

GOVERNMENT MINISTRIES AND PRIME MINISTERS OF CANADA SINCE 1867

The selection of a Ministry is the Prime Minister's responsibility, and the Governor General follows the Prime Minister's advice in formalizing the appointments. The formal initiative in selecting a new Prime Minister rests with the Governor General. The duration of a Ministry is measured by the tenure of its Prime Minister. It is calculated from the day the Prime Minister takes the oath of office to the day the Prime Minister resigns. The resignation of a Prime Minister brings about the resignation of the Ministry as a whole. A Prime Minister who resigns but later returns to form another Ministry is said to be forming a new Ministry. Since Confederation, there have been 26 Ministries.

Number of Ministry	Prime Minister (Party)	Term of Office	Parliamentary Period (Years)	Reasons for Forming Ministry	Reasons for Ending Ministry
First	Sir John A. Macdonald (Liberal-Conservative)	01-07-1867 to 05-11-1873	1st Parliament to 2nd Session, 2nd Parliament (1867-73)	On May 24, 1867, Macdonald was formally commissioned by the Governor General to form the first government under Confederation.	Resignation
Second	Alexander Mackenzie (Liberal)	07-11-1873[1] to 08-10-1878	2nd Session, 2nd Parliament to 3rd Parliament (1873-78)	Called upon by the Governor General to form a ministry following the resignation of Sir John A. Macdonald and his government	Results of general election held on September 17, 1878
Third	Sir John A. Macdonald (Liberal-Conservative)	17-10-1878 to 06-06-1891	4th Parliament to 1st Session, 7th Parliament (1878-91)	Results of general election held on September 17, 1878	Death of Macdonald on June 6, 1891

Number of Ministry	Prime Minister (Party)	Term of Office	Parliamentary Period (Years)	Reasons for Forming Ministry	Reasons for Ending Ministry
Fourth	Sir John Abbott[2] (Liberal-Conservative)	16-06-1891 to 24-11-1892	1st Session, 7th Parliament to 2nd Session, 7th Parliament (1891-92)	Called upon by the Governor General to form a ministry following the death of Sir John A. Macdonald	Resignation
Fifth	Sir John Thompson (Liberal-Conservative)	05-12-1892 to 12-12-1894	3rd Session, 7th Parliament to 4th Session, 7th Parliament (1892-94)	Called upon by the Governor General to form a ministry following the resignation of Sir John Abbott	Death of Thompson on December 12, 1894
Sixth	Sir Mackenzie Bowell[3] (Conservative)	21-12-1894 to 27-04-1896	5th Session, 7th Parliament to 6th Session, 7th Parliament (1894-96)	Called upon by the Governor General to form a ministry following the death of Sir John Thompson	Resignation
Seventh	Sir Charles Tupper (Conservative)	01-05-1896 to 08-07-1896	During a dissolution[4]	Called upon by the Governor General to form a ministry following the resignation of Sir Mackenzie Bowell	Results of general election held on June 23, 1896
Eighth	Sir Wilfrid Laurier (Liberal)	11-07-1896 to 06-10-1911	8th Parliament to 11th Parliament (1896-1911)	Results of general election held on June 23, 1896	Results of general election held on September 21, 1911
Ninth	Sir Robert Borden (Conservative)	10-10-1911 to 12-10-1917	12th Parliament (1911-17)	Results of general election held on September 21, 1911	Formation of a new ministry[5]

Number of Ministry	Prime Minister (Party)	Term of Office	Parliamentary Period (Years)	Reasons for Forming Ministry	Reasons for Ending Ministry
Tenth	Sir Robert Borden[6] (Conservative)	12-10-1917 to 10-07-1920	1st Session, 13th Parliament to 4th Session, 13th Parliament (1917-20)	Re-organization	Resignation
Eleventh	Arthur Meighen[7] (Conservative)	10-07-1920 to 29-12-1921	5th Session, 13th Parliament (1921)	Prime Minister Borden recommended that the Governor General call upon Arthur Meighen to succeed him as Prime Minister.	Results of general election held on December 6, 1921
Twelfth	W.L. Mackenzie King (Liberal)	29-12-1921 to 28-06-1926	14th Parliament to 1st Session, 15th Parliament (1921-26)	Results of general election held on December 6, 1921	Resignation[8]
Thirteenth	Arthur Meighen (Conservative)	29-06-1926 to 25-09-1926	1st Session, 15th Parliament (1926)	With the resignation of W.L. Mackenzie King, the Governor General called upon Arthur Meighen, the Leader of the Opposition, to form a ministry.	Results of general election held on September 14, 1926
Fourteenth	W.L. Mackenzie King (Liberal)	25-09-1926 to 07-08-1930	16th Parliament (1926-30)	Results of general election held on September 14, 1926	Results of general election held on July 28, 1930
Fifteenth	R.B. Bennett (Conservative)	07-08-1930 to 23-10-1935	17th Parliament (1930-35)	Results of general election held on July 28, 1930	Results of general election held on October 14, 1935

Number of Ministry	Prime Minister (Party)	Term of Office	Parliamentary Period (Years)	Reasons for Forming Ministry	Reasons for Ending Ministry
Sixteenth	W.L. Mackenzie King (Liberal)	23-10-1935 to 15-11-1948	18th Parliament to 4th Session, 20th Parliament (1935-48)	Results of general election held on October 14, 1935	Resignation
Seventeenth	Louis St. Laurent (Liberal)	15-11-1948 to 21-06-1957	5th Session, 20th Parliament to 22nd Parliament (1948-57)	On August 7, 1948, St. Laurent was chosen leader of the Liberal Party of Canada at a party leadership convention. On November 15, 1948, upon the resignation of Prime Minister W.L. Mackenzie King, he was sworn in as Prime Minister.	Results of general election held on June 10, 1957
Eighteenth	John Diefenbaker (Progressive Conservative)	21-06-1957 to 22-04-1963	23rd Parliament to 25th Parliament (1957-63)	Results of general election held on June 10, 1957	Results of general election held on April 8, 1963
Nineteenth	Lester B. Pearson (Liberal)	22-04-1963 to 20-04-1968	26th Parliament to 2nd Session, 27th Parliament (1963-68)	Results of general election held on April 8, 1963	Resignation
Twentieth	Pierre E. Trudeau (Liberal)	20-04-1968 to 04-06-1979	2nd Session, 27th Parliament to 30th Parliament (1968-79)	On April 6, 1968, Trudeau was chosen leader of the Liberal Party of Canada at a party leadership convention. On April 20, 1968, upon the resignation of Prime Minister Lester B. Pearson, he was sworn in as Prime Minister.	Results of general election held on May 22, 1979

Number of Ministry	Prime Minister (Party)	Term of Office	Parliamentary Period (Years)	Reasons for Forming Ministry	Reasons for Ending Ministry
Twenty-first	Joseph Clark (Progressive Conservative)	04-06-1979 to 03-03-1980	31st Parliament (1979)	Results of general election held on May 22, 1979	Results of general election held on February 18, 1980
Twenty-second	Pierre E. Trudeau (Liberal)	03-03-1980 to 30-06-1984	1st Session, 32nd Parliament to 2nd Session, 32nd Parliament (1980-84)	Results of general election held on February 18, 1980	Resignation
Twenty-third	John Turner[9] (Liberal)	30-06-1984 to 17-09-1984	2nd Session, 32nd Parliament (1984)	On June 16, 1984, Turner was chosen leader of the Liberal Party of Canada at a party leadership convention. On June 30, 1984, upon the resignation of Prime Minister Pierre E. Trudeau, he was sworn in as Prime Minister.	Results of general election held on September 4, 1984
Twenty-fourth	Brian Mulroney (Progressive Conservative)	17-09-1984 to 25-06-1993	33rd Parliament to 3rd Session, 34th Parliament (1984-93)	Results of general election held on September 4, 1984	Resignation
Twenty-fifth	Kim Campbell (Progressive Conservative)	25-06-1993 to 04-11-1993	3rd Session, 34th Parliament (1993)[10]	On June 13, 1993, Campbell was chosen leader of the Progressive Conservative Party of Canada at a party leadership convention. On June 25, 1993, upon the resignation of Prime Minister Brian Mulroney, she was sworn in as Prime Minister.	Results of general election held on October 25, 1993

Number of Ministry	Prime Minister (Party)	Term of Office	Parliamentary Period (Years)	Reasons for Forming Ministry	Reasons for Ending Ministry
Twenty-sixth	Jean Chrétien (Liberal)	04-11-1993 to present	35th Parliament to present	Results of general election held on October 25, 1993	

1. The government of Sir John A. Macdonald resigned on November 5, 1873, as a result of the exposure in Parliament of the Canadian Pacific Railway scandal. On November 7, 1873, the Liberals under Alexander Mackenzie formed a government.

2. Sir John Abbott served as Prime Minister from the Senate.

3. Sir Mackenzie Bowell served as Prime Minister from the Senate.

4. Sir Charles Tupper served as Prime Minister during the dissolution following the end of the Sixth Session of the Seventh Parliament and before the beginning of the First Session of the Eighth Parliament.

5. The Tenth Ministry was a re-organization of the Ninth Ministry, with the addition of certain Liberal Ministers. All Ministers continuing from the Ninth Ministry and changing office, resigned by Order in Council, were re-appointed by Order in Council and were sworn to their new offices; those continuing in their old offices were not required to be either re-appointed or re-sworn. Sir Robert Borden continued throughout as Prime Minister from his original appointment in 1911.

6. On October 12, 1917, Prime Minister Sir Robert Borden formed a ministry, known as the Unionist government, which brought together Liberal-Conservative and Liberal Members of Parliament who supported conscription during the First World War. According to some sources such as the *Canadian Guide of Electoral History and Leadership (1867-1987)*, edited by Wayne D. Madden and updated by the Library of Parliament, Borden was the leader of the Unionist Party.

7. According to some sources like the *Canadian Guide of Electoral History and Leadership (1867-1987)*, edited by Wayne D. Madden and updated by the Library of Parliament, Meighen was the leader of the Unionist Party.

8. On June 26, 1926, Prime Minister W.L. Mackenzie King requested that the Governor General dissolve Parliament and order a general election. The Governor General declined to do so and, following the resignation of King, on June 28, 1926, called upon the Leader of the Opposition, Arthur Meighen, to form a government. On June 29, 1926, Arthur Meighen formed a government. However, his government faced Parliament for only three days before being defeated in the House on July 1, 1926. The Fifteenth Parliament was dissolved the next day and a general election was called for September 14, 1926.

9. During his tenure as Prime Minister, John Turner did not sit in the House as a Member of Parliament.

10. The House did not meet during her tenure as Prime Minister.

Appendix 9

LEADERS OF THE OFFICIAL OPPOSITION IN THE HOUSE OF COMMONS SINCE 1873

The Member who is the leader of the largest party sitting in opposition to the Government in the House of Commons becomes the "Leader of Her Majesty's Opposition". Provisions governing the position are defined in the *Parliament of Canada Act,* in the Standing Orders and in various practices of the House. To become the Leader of the Official Opposition, a person must hold a seat in the House of Commons. Consequently, in instances where the national leader of a party was not a Member of the House of Commons, another Member of Parliament of that party served as Leader of the Official Opposition. Those instances are indicated with an asterisk.

	Name	Party	Period	Parliament
1.	Alexander Mackenzie	Liberal	1873[1]	1st Session, 2nd Parliament to 2nd Session, 2nd Parliament
2.	Sir John A. Macdonald	Liberal-Conservative	1873-78	2nd Session, 2nd Parliament to 3rd Parliament
3.	Alexander Mackenzie	Liberal	1879-80	1st Session, 4th Parliament to 2nd Session, 4th Parliament
4.	Edward Blake	Liberal	1880-87	2nd Session, 4th Parliament to 1st Session, 6th Parliament
5.	Wilfrid Laurier	Liberal	1887-96	1st Session, 6th Parliament to 7th Parliament
6.	Sir Charles Tupper	Conservative	1896-1901	8th Parliament
7.	Robert Borden	Conservative	1901-11	9th Parliament to 11th Parliament
8.	Sir Wilfrid Laurier	Liberal	1911-19	12th Parliament to 1st Session, 13th Parliament
9.	Daniel McKenzie*	Liberal	1919	2nd Session, 13th Parliament to 3rd Session, 13th Parliament
10.	W.L. Mackenzie King	Liberal	1919-21	4th Session, 13th Parliament to 5th Session, 13th Parliament

	Name	Party	Period	Parliament
11.	Arthur Meighen	Conservative	1921-26	14th Parliament to 1st Session, 15th Parliament
12.	W.L. Mackenzie King	Liberal	1926	1st Session, 15th Parliament
13.	Hugh Guthrie	Conservative	1926-27	1st Session, 16th Parliament
14.	R.B. Bennett	Conservative	1927-30	2nd Session, 16th Parliament to 4th Session, 16th Parliament
15.	W.L. Mackenzie King	Liberal	1930-35	17th Parliament
16.	R.B. Bennett	Conservative	1935-38	1st Session, 18th Parliament to 3rd Session, 18th Parliament
17.	Robert J. Manion	Conservative	1938-40	4th Session, 18th Parliament to 6th Session, 18th Parliament
18.	Richard B. Hanson*	Conservative	1940-43	1st Session, 19th Parliament to 3rd Session, 19th Parliament
19.	Gordon Graydon*	Progressive Conservative	1943-45	4th Session, 19th Parliament to 6th Session, 19th Parliament
20.	John Bracken	Progressive Conservative	1945-48	1st Session, 20th Parliament to 4th Session, 20th Parliament
21.	George Drew	Progressive Conservative	1948-54	5th Session, 20th Parliament to 1st Session, 22nd Parliament
22.	W. Earl Rowe*	Progressive Conservative	1954-55	2nd Session, 22nd Parliament
23.	George Drew	Progressive Conservative	1955-56	2nd Session, 22nd Parliament to 3rd Session, 22nd Parliament
24.	W. Earl Rowe*	Progressive Conservative	1956	3rd Session, 22nd Parliament to 4th Session, 22nd Parliament
25.	John Diefenbaker	Progressive Conservative	1956-57	5th Session, 22nd Parliament
26.	Louis St. Laurent	Liberal	1957-58	1st Session, 23rd Parliament
27.	Lester B. Pearson	Liberal	1958-63	1st Session, 23rd Parliament to 25th Parliament
28.	John Diefenbaker	Progressive Conservative	1963-67	26th Parliament to 2nd Session, 27th Parliament
29.	Michael Starr*	Progressive Conservative	1967	2nd Session, 27th Parliament
30.	Robert Stanfield	Progressive Conservative	1967-76	2nd Session, 27th Parliament to 1st Session, 30th Parliament

	Name	Party	Period	Parliament
31.	Joseph Clark	Progressive Conservative	1976-79	1st Session, 30th Parliament to 4th Session, 30th Parliament
32.	Pierre E. Trudeau	Liberal	1979-80	31st Parliament
33.	Joseph Clark	Progressive Conservative	1980-83	1st Session, 32nd Parliament
34.	Erik Nielsen*	Progressive Conservative	1983	1st Session, 32nd Parliament
35.	Brian Mulroney	Progressive Conservative	1983-84	1st Session, 32nd Parliament to 2nd Session, 32nd Parliament
36.	John Turner	Liberal	1984-90	33rd Parliament to 2nd Session, 34th Parliament
37.	Herb Gray*	Liberal	1990	2nd Session, 34th Parliament
38.	Jean Chrétien	Liberal	1990-93	2nd Session, 34th Parliament
39.	Lucien Bouchard	Bloc Québécois	1993-96	1st Session, 35th Parliament
40.	Gilles Duceppe*	Bloc Québécois	1996	1st Session, 35th Parliament
41.	Michel Gauthier	Bloc Québécois	1996-97	2nd Session, 35th Parliament
42.	Gilles Duceppe	Bloc Québécois	1997	2nd Session, 35th Parliament
43.	Preston Manning	Reform	1997	1st Session, 36th Parliament

1. In the First Parliament, following the general election of 1867, the Members who sat in the House opposite the government of Sir John A. Macdonald did not constitute a party but a coalition of various interests, just as the government did. A number of historians state that John Sandfield Macdonald (Reform Member for Cornwall and the first Premier of Ontario), who had campaigned in alliance with Sir John A. Macdonald in the general election, was appointed Leader of the Opposition by the government. Other historians hold that although Alexander Mackenzie (Lambton) was not formally appointed Leader of the Opposition until March 6, 1873, when he assumed the leadership of the Liberal Party, he was *de facto* Leader of the Opposition as early as 1869. (See William Buckingham and George Ross, *The Hon. Alexander Mackenzie: His Life and Times*, 5th ed., (Toronto: Rose Publishing, 1892), pp. 242, 254, 329; J. C. Courtney, "Party Leadership Selection in the New Dominion", *Canadian Political Party Systems: A Leader*, edited by R. K. Carty (Peterborough: Broadview Press, 1992), p. 108; Donald Creighton, *John A. Macdonald*, Vol. 1: *The Old Chieftain* (Toronto: Macmillan, 1955), p. 4; Joseph Schull, *Edward Blake*, Vol. 1: *The Man of the Other Way (1833-1881)* (Toronto: Macmillan, 1975), p. 46; Dale Thomson, *Alexander Mackenzie: Clear Grit* (Toronto: Macmillan, 1960), p. 103.)

Appendix 10

PARTY LEADERS IN THE HOUSE OF COMMONS SINCE 1867

By tradition, leaders of political parties are expected to have a seat or to seek a seat in the House of Commons as soon as possible. In those instances where a party leader is not a Member of the House, the party usually chooses one of its elected Members to act as the Leader of the party in the House. Parties and party leaders play a significant role in the proceedings of the House. Some statutes require that the government consult with the Leader of the Official Opposition, as well as with other party leaders, when certain actions are contemplated or prior to making certain appointments. The Standing Orders of the House provide an opportunity for opposition parties to respond to Ministers' statements, to propose motions on allotted or opposition days and to participate in the leadership of the standing committees. The leader of a recognized party usually sits in the front row of the Chamber. The party leaders listed below are those who, since Confederation, have officially represented their parties in the House.

Parliament	Party	Leader
1st (1867-72)	• Liberal-Conservative[1]	• Sir John A. Macdonald[2]
2nd (1873-74)	• Liberal-Conservative • Liberal	• Sir John A. Macdonald • Alexander Mackenzie
3rd (1874-78)	• Liberal • Liberal-Conservative	• Alexander Mackenzie • Sir John A. Macdonald
4th (1879-82)	• Liberal-Conservative • Liberal	• Sir John A. Macdonald • Alexander Mackenzie/Edward Blake
5th (1883-87)	• Liberal-Conservative • Liberal	• Sir John A. Macdonald • Edward Blake
6th (1887-91)	• Liberal-Conservative • Liberal	• Sir John A. Macdonald • Edward Blake/Wilfrid Laurier
7th (1891-96)	• Liberal-Conservative • Liberal	• Sir John A. Macdonald • Sir John Thompson[3]/Sir Charles Tupper[4] • Wilfrid Laurier
8th (1896-1900)	• Liberal • Liberal-Conservative	• Sir Wilfrid Laurier • Sir Charles Tupper

Parliament	Party	Leader
9th (1901-04)	• Liberal • Conservative	• Sir Wilfrid Laurier • Robert Borden[5]
10th (1905-08)	• Liberal • Conservative	• Sir Wilfrid Laurier • Robert Borden
11th (1909-11)	• Liberal • Conservative	• Sir Wilfrid Laurier • Robert Borden
12th (1911-17)	• Conservative • Liberal	• Sir Robert Borden[6] • Sir Wilfrid Laurier
13th (1918-21)	• Unionist • Laurier Liberals • Progressive	• Sir Robert Borden[7]/Arthur Meighen • Sir Wilfrid Laurier/Daniel Mackenzie[8] • T.A. Crerar[9]
14th (1922-25)	• Liberal • Progressive • Liberal-Conservative • Labour	• W.L. Mackenzie King • T.A. Crerar/Robert Forke • Arthur Meighen • J.S. Woodsworth
15th (1926)	• Liberal • Conservative • Progressive • Labour	• W.L. Mackenzie King[10] • Arthur Meighen[11] • Robert Forke • J.S. Woodsworth
16th (1926-30)	• Liberal • Conservative • Labour	• W.L. Mackenzie King • Hugh Guthrie[12]/R.B. Bennett • J.S. Woodsworth
17th (1930-35)	• Conservative • Liberal • Labour	• R.B. Bennett • W.L. Mackenzie King • J.S. Woodsworth[13]
18th (1936-40)	• Liberal • Conservative • Social Credit • Co-operative Commonwealth Federation (CCF)	• W.L. Mackenzie King • R.B. Bennett/Robert J. Manion • John H. Blackmore • J.S. Woodsworth
19th (1940-45)	• Liberal • National Government (Conservative) • New Democracy (Social Credit) • Co-operative Commonwealth Federation (CCF)	• W.L. Mackenzie King • Richard B. Hanson[14]/Gordon Graydon • John H. Blackmore/Solon Low • J.S. Woodsworth/M.J. Coldwell[15]
20th (1945-49)	• Liberal • Progressive Conservative • Co-operative Commonwealth Federation (CCF) • Social Credit • Bloc populaire canadien	• W.L. Mackenzie King/Louis St-Laurent • John Bracken/George Drew • M.J. Coldwell • Solon Low • Maxime Raymond

Parliament	Party	Leader
21st (1949-53)	• Liberal • Progressive Conservative • Co-operative Commonwealth Federation (CCF) • Social Credit	• Louis St-Laurent • George Drew • M.J. Coldwell • Solon Low
22nd (1953-57)	• Liberal • Progressive Conservative • Co-operative Commonwealth Federation (CCF) • Social Credit	• Louis St-Laurent • George Drew[16]/John Diefenbaker • M.J. Coldwell • Solon Low
23rd (1957-58)	• Progressive Conservative • Liberal • Co-operative Commonwealth Federation (CCF) • Social Credit	• John Diefenbaker • Louis St-Laurent/Lester B. Pearson • M.J. Coldwell • Solon Low
24th (1958-62)	• Progressive Conservative • Liberal • Co-operative Commonwealth Federation (CCF)	• John Diefenbaker • Lester B. Pearson • Hazen Argue[17]/T.C. Douglas
25th (1962-63)	• Progressive Conservative • Liberal • Social Credit • New Democratic Party	• John Diefenbaker • Lester B. Pearson • Robert Thompson • T.C. Douglas
26th (1963-65)	• Liberal • Progressive Conservative • Ralliement des créditistes • New Democratic Party • Social Credit	• Lester B. Pearson • John Diefenbaker • Réal Caouette[18] • T.C. Douglas • Robert Thompson
27th (1966-68)	• Liberal • Progressive Conservative • New Democratic Party • Ralliement des créditistes • Social Credit	• Lester B. Pearson/Pierre E. Trudeau • John Diefenbaker/Michael Starr[19]/Robert Stanfield • T.C. Douglas • Réal Caouette • Robert Thompson/Alexander Patterson
28th (1968-72)	• Liberal • Progressive Conservative • New Democratic Party • Ralliement des créditistes	• Pierre E. Trudeau • Robert Stanfield • T.C. Douglas/David Lewis[20] • Réal Caouette[21]
29th (1973-74)	• Liberal • Progressive Conservative • New Democratic Party • Social Credit	• Pierre E. Trudeau • Robert Stanfield • David Lewis • Réal Caouette

Parliament	Party	Leader
30th (1974-79)	• Liberal • Progressive Conservative • New Democratic Party • Social Credit	• Pierre E. Trudeau • Robert Stanfield/Joseph Clark • Edward Broadbent[22] • Réal Caouette/André Fortin
31st (1979)	• Progressive Conservative • Liberal • New Democratic Party • Social Credit	• Joseph Clark • Pierre E. Trudeau • Edward Broadbent • Fabien Roy
32nd (1980-84)	• Liberal • Progressive Conservative • New Democratic Party	• Pierre E. Trudeau/John Turner • Joseph Clark/Erik Nielsen[23]/Brian Mulroney • Edward Broadbent
33rd (1984-88)	• Progressive Conservative • Liberal • New Democratic Party	• Brian Mulroney • John Turner • Edward Broadbent
34th (1988-93)	• Progressive Conservative • Liberal • New Democratic Party	• Brian Mulroney • John Turner/Jean Chrétien[24] • Edward Broadbent/Audrey McLaughlin
35th (1994-97)	• Liberal • Bloc Québécois • Reform • New Democratic Party • Progressive Conservative	• Jean Chrétien • Lucien Bouchard/Michel Gauthier/Gilles Duceppe • Preston Manning • Audrey McLaughlin • Jean Charest
36th (1997-)	• Liberal • Reform • Bloc Québécois • New Democratic Party • Progressive Conservative	• Jean Chrétien • Preston Manning • Gilles Duceppe • Alexa McDonough • Jean Charest[25]/Elsie Wayne

1. In 1867, a pre-Confederation coalition of Liberal and Conservative elements formed a permanent national party named the Liberal-Conservative Party. Although formally known as the Liberal-Conservative Party, the party was commonly referred to as the Conservative Party until 1917 and the formation of the Unionist government. With the resignation of Sir Robert Borden and the rise to party leadership of Arthur Meighen in July 1920, the party was officially renamed the National Liberal and Conservative Party. At a party conference in March 1922, the party was renamed the Liberal-Conservative Party. In March 1938, at a party conference, the party was renamed the National Conservative Party. During the general election campaign of 1940, the party was renamed the National Government Party. Following the general election of 1940, the party was again named the National Conservative Party. On December 11, 1942, at a party leadership convention which elected the former Progressive Premier of Manitoba, John Bracken, to the position of party leader, the party was renamed the Progressive Conservative Party.

2. On May 24, 1867, Sir John A. Macdonald was formally commissioned by Lord Monck to form the first government under Confederation. On July 1, 1867, the First Ministry assumed office with Macdonald serving as Prime Minister. Sir John A. Macdonald died while in office on June 6, 1891.

3. Sir John Thompson was the Leader of the Government in the House of Commons between June 16, 1891, and July 9, 1892, while Sir John Abbott governed as Prime Minister from the Senate. Upon the resignation of Abbott, Thompson was called upon to form a government and served as Prime Minister from December 5, 1892 until his death on December 12, 1894. Sir Mackenzie Bowell then occupied the position of Prime Minister from the Senate until 1896. George Foster served as the Leader of the Government in the House of Commons throughout the Fifth Session of the Seventh Parliament, April 18, 1895 to July 22, 1895, and during the Sixth Session of the Seventh Parliament between January 2, 1896 and January 5, 1896, where-upon he resigned from the Cabinet. On January 15, 1896, he was reappointed to Cabinet and again assumed the duties of the Leader of the Government in the House of Commons until February 11, 1896. Sir Adolphe Caron served as the Leader of the Government in the House of Commons from January 7, 1896 until January 15, 1896.

4. Sir Charles Tupper entered the Cabinet of Prime Minister Mackenzie Bowell on January 15, 1896. He became the Leader of the Government in the House of Commons upon his introduction in the House on February 11, 1896 until April 23, 1896. Tupper served as Prime Minister from May 1, 1896 to July 8, 1896, and as Leader of the Opposition throughout the Eighth Parliament, from August 19, 1896 to July 18, 1900. He continued to serve as party leader until February 5, 1901.

5. In the general election held on November 3, 1904, Sir Robert Borden suffered personal defeat. As a result, from January 11, 1905 to February 6, 1905, George Foster served as Acting Leader of the Opposition in the House. Borden was re-elected in a by-election held on February 4, 1905, and returned to the House of Commons on February 7, 1905.

6. Sir George Foster, who had been knighted in 1914, served as Acting Prime Minister from April 19, 1917 to May 15, 1917. During this period, Prime Minister Borden was in attendance at the Imperial War Conference in London. Borden returned to the House of Commons on May 16, 1917.

7. Sir Thomas White served as Acting Prime Minister from February 20, 1919 to May 23, 1919. During this period, Prime Minister Borden was attending the Paris Peace Conference which followed the end of the First World War. Borden returned to the House of Commons on May 26, 1919. Sir George Foster served as Acting Prime Minister from February 26, 1920 to May 12, 1920. During this period, Prime Minister Borden was absent from the House of Commons due to illness. Borden recommended that the Governor General call upon Arthur Meighen to succeed him as Prime Minister. Mr. Meighen was sworn in as Prime Minister on July 10, 1920.

8. On February 17, 1919, Sir Wilfrid Laurier died. On February 25, 1919, Daniel McKenzie was elected by the Liberal caucus to serve as leader of the Liberal Party in the House. On August 7, 1919, at a convention of the Liberal Party, W.L. Mackenzie King was elected leader of the Liberal Party. He was elected to the House on October 20, 1919, and introduced in the House on October 23, 1919. However, he did not assume the duties of leader of the Liberal Party in the House until the opening of the Fourth Session of the Thirteenth Parliament on February 26, 1920. Daniel McKenzie had continued in his duties as Leader of the Opposition and leader of the Liberal Party in the House until the end of the Third Session of the Thirteenth Parliament.

9. On February 26, 1920, at the opening of the Fourth Session of the Thirteenth Parliament, Liberal-Unionist T.A. Crerar assumed the leadership of the Progressive Party until November 11, 1922.

10. In the general election of October 29, 1925, the government of W.L. Mackenzie King was returned to office. Mr. King himself suffered electoral defeat but remained Prime Minister. When the First Session of the Fifteenth Parliament opened on January 7, 1926, Ernest Lapointe served as Leader of the Government in the House. Mr. King was elected in a by-election on February 15, 1926, and returned to the House on March 15, 1926.

11. Sir Henry Drayton served as the Leader of the Government in the House of Commons from June 29, 1926, to July 1, 1926. Drayton assumed this position, when the Prime Minister, Arthur Meighen, resigned his seat in the House of Commons according to law, in order to assume the office of Prime Minister. Until August 3, 1931, and the adoption of an amendment to the *Senate and House of Commons Act* (R.S.C. 1927, c. 147), members of the House were required to resign their seat and seek re-election when appointed to Cabinet.

12. Hugh Guthrie occupied the position of Leader of the Official Opposition following the resignation of the party leader, Arthur Meighen, and prior to the assumption of party leadership by R.B. Bennett.

13. J.S. Woodsworth became president of the Co-operative Commonwealth Federation, known as the CCF, in July 1933. The CCF Party was founded in Calgary on August 1, 1932. At the August 1960 convention, the party constitution was amended to create a new position, that of "national leader".

14. Richard B. Hanson and Gordon Graydon occupied the position of Leader of the Official Opposition because the leaders of the National Party, throughout this period, Arthur Meighen and John Bracken, did not sit in the House.

15. Due to the deteriorating health of party leader J.S. Woodsworth, a CCF caucus meeting on November 6, 1940, elected M.J. Coldwell to serve as acting leader of the party. Shortly after Mr. Woodsworth's death, a caucus meeting held on April 22, 1942, elected Mr. Coldwell permanent leader of the party.

16. On two occasions, W. Earl Rowe assumed the duties of Acting Leader of the Official Opposition due to the illness of the Leader of the Official Opposition, George Drew.

17. Following the defeat of M.J. Coldwell in the federal election of 1958, Hazen Argue occupied the position of leader of the party in the House. Mr. Argue held this position from April 23, 1958 until August 11, 1960, whereupon he became permanent national leader of the CCF at a party leadership convention. On August 3, 1961, at a party leadership convention, the existing party joined with groups representing organized labour to form a new party. As a result, the name of the party was changed from the Co-operative Commonwealth Federation to the New Democratic Party. T.C. Douglas was elected leader of the New Democratic Party. However, Mr. Douglas was not elected to the House until a by-election held on October 22, 1962, and was not introduced in the House until November 2, 1962. During this period, Hazen Argue served as party leader in the House until his resignation from the New Democratic Party on February 18, 1962. The following day, the NDP caucus elected H.W. Herridge to serve as party leader in the House. Herridge occupied this position until November 1, 1962.

18. On September 1, 1963, 13 Members from Quebec left the Social Credit Party and formed the Ralliement des créditistes under the leadership of Réal Caouette. On October 21, 1963, the Ralliement des créditistes was officially recognized as a party by the House of Commons.

19. Michael Starr occupied the position of Leader of the Official Opposition following the resignation of the party leader, John Diefenbaker, and prior to the new party leader, Robert Stanfield, being elected and introduced in the House.

20. T.C. Douglas was defeated in the general election of June 25, 1968. He was re-elected in a by-election held on February 10, 1969, and introduced in the House on February 20, 1969. In his absence from the House, David Lewis led the New Democratic Party Members in the House. David Lewis was formally elected leader of the party at a party leadership convention on April 24, 1971.

21. In 1971, the Ralliement des créditistes, who had elected to the House 14 Members in the previous general election, reunited with the Social Credit Party. On October 10 of that year, Réal Caouette was confirmed as leader of the Social Credit Party.

22. In the general election of July 8, 1974, David Lewis suffered personal defeat. Although Mr. Lewis remained party leader until July 7, 1975, Edward Broadbent served as leader of the party in the House beginning with the opening of the Thirtieth Parliament on September 30, 1974. Mr. Broadbent was formally elected leader of the party at a party leadership convention on July 7, 1975.

23. Erik Nielsen occupied the position of Leader of the Official Opposition following the resignation from that position of Joseph Clark, and prior to the election and introduction to the House of the subsequent party leader, Brian Mulroney.

24. On February 7, 1990, John Turner resigned from his position as Leader of the Official Opposition but remained leader of the Liberal Party. In his place, Herb Gray assumed the duties of Leader of the Official Opposition. On June 23, 1990, at a leadership convention, Jean Chrétien was elected leader of the Liberal Party. Chrétien was elected to the House in a by-election on December 10, 1990, and was introduced in the House and became Leader of the Official Opposition on January 15, 1991.

25. Elsie Wayne served as leader of the party in the House following the resignation of Jean Charest, as leader of the Progressive Conservative Party, on April 2, 1998. On November 14, 1998, Joseph Clark was elected as leader of the Progressive Conservative Party. Since he was not a Member, Elsie Wayne continued to serve as leader of the party in the House.

Appendix 11

GENERAL ELECTION RESULTS SINCE 1867

Since the early days of Confederation, most Members of the House of Commons have been members of political parties. The nature of these political parties has varied with time, and several different parties have had representation in the House. While a majority government is formed by the political party or the coalition of parties holding the majority of the seats in the House, a minority government is formed by one or more parties, but without the majority of seats. Most governments since Confederation have been majority governments formed by a single party having gathered a majority of the seats in a general election. However, the general elections of 1921, 1925, 1957, 1962, 1963, 1965, 1972 and 1979 all resulted in no single party obtaining a majority of seats.

Parlia-ment	Date of Election	Total Number of Seats	Total Number of Seats Won [1]				Results by Party	
			Govern-ment	Opposi-tion	Govern-ment Majority	Govern-ment Minority		
1st	07-08-1867[2] to 20-09-1867	181	101	80	+21		Liberal-Conservative[3] Liberal	101 80
2nd	20-07-1872 to 12-10-1872[4]	200	103	97	+6		Liberal-Conservative Liberal	103 97
3rd	22-01-1874	206	133	73	+60		Liberal Liberal-Conservative Independent	133 72 1
4th	17-09-1878	206	137	69	+68		Liberal-Conservative Liberal	137 69
5th	20-06-1882	210	139	71	+68		Liberal-Conservative Liberal	139 71
6th	22-02-1887	215	123	92	+31		Liberal-Conservative Liberal National-Conservateur	123 89 3
7th	05-03-1891	215	123	92	+31		Liberal-Conservative Liberal National-Conservateur	123 89 3

Parlia-ment	Date of Election	Total Number of Seats	Total Number of Seats Won[1]				Results by Party	
			Govern-ment	Opposi-tion	Govern-ment Majority	Govern-ment Minority		
8th	23-06-1896	213	117	96	+21		Liberal	117
							Conservative	89
							Protestant Protective Association	4
							Patrons of Industry	2
							Independent	1
9th	07-11-1900	214	128	81	+47		Liberal	128
							Conservative	78
							Independent	3
							Other (Vacancy, Dual Representation)	5
10th	03-11-1904	214	139	75	+64		Liberal	139
							Conservative	75
11th	26-10-1908	221	133	88	+45		Liberal	133
							Conservative	85
							Independent	3
12th	21-09-1911[5]	221	133	88	+45		Conservative	133
							Liberal	86
							Independent	2
13th	17-12-1917	235	153	82	+71		Unionist[6] (Conservative and Liberal)	153
							Laurier Liberals[7]	82
14th	06-12-1921	235	117	118		−1[8]	Liberal	117
							Progressive	64
							Liberal-Conservative (Conservative)	50
							Labour	3
							Independent	1
15th	29-10-1925[9]	245	101	144		−43	Conservative	116
							Liberal	101
							Progressive	24
							Labour	2
							Independent	2

Parlia-ment	Date of Election	Total Number of Seats	Total Number of Seats Won[1]				Results by Party	
			Govern-ment	Opposi-tion	Govern-ment Majority	Govern-ment Minority		
16th	14-09-1926	245	125[10]	120	+5		Liberal	116
							Liberal-Progressive	9
							Conservative	91
							Progressive	13
							United Farmers of Alberta	11
							Labour	3
							Independent	2
17th	28-07-1930	245	137	108	+29		Conservative	137
							Liberal	88
							United Farmers of Alberta	9
							Liberal-Progressive	3
							Independent	2
							Progressive	2
							Labour	2
							Independent Labour Party	1
							United Farmers of Ontario	1
18th	14-10-1935	245	173[11]	72	+101		Liberal	171
							Liberal-Progressive	2
							Conservative	39
							Social Credit	17
							Co-operative Common-wealth Federation	7
							Independent Liberal	5
							United Farmers of Ontario – Labour	1
							Reconstruction Party	1
							Independent Conservative	1
							Independent	1
19th	26-03-1940	245	181[12]	64	+117		Liberal	178
							Liberal-Progressive	3
							National Government (Conservative)	39
							New Democracy (Social Credit)	10
							Co-operative Common-wealth Federation	8
							Independent Liberal	3
							Independent	1
							Independent Conservative	1
							Unity-Reform	1
							Unity-Saskatchewan	1

Parlia-ment	Date of Election	Total Number of Seats	Total Number of Seats Won[1]				
			Govern-ment	Opposi-tion	Govern-ment Majority	Govern-ment Minority	Results by Party

20th	11-06-1945	245	125	120	+5		Liberal 125
							Progressive Conservative[13] 67
							Co-operative Common-
							  wealth Federation 28
							Social Credit 13
							Independent 5
							Independent Liberal 3
							Bloc Populaire Canadien 2
							Independent C.C.F. 1
							Labour-Progressive
							  (Communist) 1

21st	27-06-1949	262	190[14]	72	+118		Liberal 189 Liberal-Labour 1 Progressive Conservative 41 Co-operative Common- wealth Federation 13 Social Credit 10 Independent 5 Independent Liberal 3
22nd	10-08-1953	265	171[15]	94	+77		Liberal 170 Liberal-Labour 1 Progressive Conservative 51 Co-operative Common- wealth Federation 23 Social Credit 15 Independent 3 Independent Liberal 2
23rd	10-06-1957	265	112	153		−41	Progressive Conservative 112 Liberal 105 Liberal-Labour 1 Co-operative Common- wealth Federation 25 Social Credit 19 Independent 2 Independent Liberal 1
24th	31-03-1958	265	208	57	+151		Progressive Conservative 208 Liberal 48 Liberal-Labour 1 Co-operative Common- wealth Federation 8

Parlia-ment	Date of Election	Total Number of Seats	Total Number of Seats Won[1]				Results by Party	
			Govern-ment	Opposi-tion	Govern-ment Majority	Govern-ment Minority		
25th	18-06-1962	265	116	149		−33	Progressive Conservative	116
							Liberal	99
							Liberal-Labour	1
							Social Credit	30
							New Democratic Party[16]	19
26th	08-04-1963	265	129[17]	136		−7	Liberal	128
							Liberal-Labour	1
							Progressive Conservative	95
							Social Credit[18]	24
							New Democratic Party	17
27th	08-11-1965	265	131[19]	134		−3	Liberal	130
							Liberal-Labour	1
							Progressive Conservative	97
							New Democratic Party	21
							Ralliement des Créditistes	9
							Social Credit	5
							Independent Prog. Cons.	1
							Independent	1
28th	25-06-1968	264	155[20]	109	+46		Liberal	154
							Liberal-Labour	1
							Progressive Conservative	72
							New Democratic Party	22
							Ralliement des Créditistes	14
							Independent	1
29th	30-10-1972	264	109	155		−46	Liberal	109
							Progressive Conservative	107
							New Democratic Party	31
							Social Credit	15
							Independent	2
30th	08-07-1974	264	141	123	+18		Liberal	141
							Progressive Conservative	95
							New Democratic Party	16
							Social Credit	11
							Independent	1

Parlia-ment	Date of Election	Total Number of Seats	* Total Number of Seats Won [1] — Govern-ment	Opposi-tion	Govern-ment Majority	Govern-ment Minority	Results by Party	
31st	22-05-1979	282	136	146		−10	Progressive Conservative	136
							Liberal	114
							New Democratic Party	26
							Social Credit	6
32nd	18-02-1980	282	147	135	+12		Liberal	147
							Progressive Conservative	103
							New Democratic Party	32
33rd	04-09-1984	282	211	71	+140		Progressive Conservative	211
							Liberal	40
							New Democratic Party	30
							Independent	1
34th	21-11-1988	295	169	126	+43		Progressive Conserva-tive	169[21]
							Liberal	83
							New Democratic Party	43
35th	25-10-1993	295	177	118	+59		Liberal	177
							Bloc Québécois	54
							Reform Party	52
							New Democratic Party	9
							Progressive Conservative	2
							Independent	1
36th	02-06-1997	301	155	146	+9		Liberal	155
							Reform Party	60
							Bloc Québécois	44
							New Democratic Party	21
							Progressive Conservative	20
							Independent	1

1. Source: *Canadian Guide of Electoral History and Leadership (1867-1987),* edited by Wayne D. Madden and updated by the Library of Parliament. The numbers reflecting party strengths indicated in this listing are based on the results immediately following general elections and do not account for any changes in party affiliation that may have occurred between general elections.

2. During the general elections of 1867 and 1872, elections in the constituencies were held at various times between the dates listed. Upon the assent of the *Dominion Elections Act* on May 26, 1874, the holding of all elections on one day became statutory, with certain exceptions because of physical difficulties in some areas.

3. The government that was formed under the leadership of Sir John A. Macdonald as a result of the general election of 1867 was a governing coalition of Liberal and Conservative elements that had initially favoured Confederation. The party retained this Liberal-Conservative base throughout some subsequent elections but was generally referred to as the Conservative Party.

4. In November of 1873, the Macdonald government was forced to resign as a result of the Canadian Pacific Railway scandal. Alexander Mackenzie, leading the Liberals, took office.

5. During the First World War, the term of the Twelfth Parliament was extended beyond five years. On February 8, 1916, the House adopted an Address to His Majesty the King requesting that the term of that Parliament be extended to October 7, 1917 (*Journals*, p. 62).

6. On October 12, 1917, Prime Minister Borden formed a Ministry, known as the Unionist government, which brought together Liberal-Conservative and Liberal Members of Parliament who supported conscription during First World War. These Members campaigned as Unionist candidates in the general election of December 17, 1917.

7. Due to the restructuring of the party system as a result of the conscription issue of 1917, the Liberal candidates elected to the House as a result of the general election of 1917 were known as the Laurier Liberals.

8. As a result of the general election of December 6, 1921, the Liberals gained 117 seats in the House of Commons, one short of a majority. However, with the support of Members of the Progressive Party, W. L. Mackenzie King was able to form a government and was sworn in as Prime Minister on December 29, 1921. The First Session of the Fourteenth Parliament opened on March 8, 1922. Over the course of the Fourteenth Parliament, as a result of Members crossing the floor and by-elections, Mr. King's government fluctuated between minority and majority status in the House.

9. As a result of the general election of October 29, 1925, Liberal representation in the House was reduced to 101 Members. However, with the support of the Progressive Party, W.L. Mackenzie King remained Prime Minister. On June 26, 1926, Mr. King requested that the Governor General dissolve Parliament and order a general election. The Governor General declined to do so and, following the resignation of Mr. King, called upon Arthur Meighen, the leader of the Liberal-Conservatives, to form a government. On June 29, 1926, Arthur Meighen formed a government with the support of a minority of the Members of the House. The distribution of seats was the following: Government: 116; Opposition: 129. His government faced Parliament for only three days before being defeated on July 1, 1926. The Fifteenth Parliament was dissolved the next day and a general election was called for September 14, 1926.

10. Liberal: 116; Liberal-Progressive: 9. The Liberal-Progressives had agreed to join the Liberals to form a majority Government. One of the issues of the 1926 electoral campaign was the break-up of the Progressive Party. Some of its supporters retained the party label while some ran as Liberal-Progressives. Other adopted the banner of the United Farmers of Alberta.

11. Liberal: 171; Liberal-Progressive: 2.

12. Liberal: 178; Liberal-Progressive: 3.

13. The general election of 1945 was the first general election that saw the election to the House of candidates under the banner of the Progressive Conservative Party. The change in the name of the party had been adopted on December 11, 1942, at a party convention.

14. Liberal: 189; Liberal-Labour: 1.

15. Liberal: 170; Liberal-Labour: 1.

16. In 1961, the Co-operative Commonwealth Federation was dissolved and became the New Democratic Party under the leadership of T.C. Douglas.

17. Liberal: 128; Liberal-Labour: 1.

18. On September 1, 1963, 13 Members from Quebec left the Social Credit Party to form the Ralliement des Créditistes under Réal Caouette.

19. Liberal: 130; Liberal-Labour: 1.

20. Liberal: 154; Liberal-Labour: 1.

21. A few days after the general election of 1988, the Member who had been elected for the constituency of Beaver River, Alberta, John Dahmer, died suddenly without having taken his seat in the House. A by-election took place on March 13, 1989. A candidate for the Reform Party, Deborah Grey, was elected.

Appendix 12

PARLIAMENTS SINCE 1867 AND NUMBER OF SITTING DAYS

The length of a Parliament is calculated from the date set for the return of the writs following a general election to its dissolution by the Governor General by speech or proclamation. The *Constitution Act, 1867*, s. 50, and the *Constitution Act, 1982*, ss. 4(1) and 5, provide for a maximum five-year lifespan for the House of Commons from the date fixed for the return of the writs. A Parliament is divided into sessions. A session begins with a Speech from the Throne when Parliament is summoned by proclamation of the Governor General; it ends with a prorogation or dissolution of Parliament. A session is divided into sittings and adjournments. A sitting is a meeting of the House within a session. The Standing Orders provide times and days for the sittings of the House. A sitting is not necessarily synonymous with a "day". Some days may contain more than one sitting; some sittings may extend over more than one day.

Parliament Session	Date of General Election[1]	Date for Return of Writs	Date of Opening	Last Day on Which the House Sat	Date of Prorogation	Date of Dissolution	Number of Sitting Days	Number of Sittings
1st Parliament	07-08-1867 to 20-09-1867	24-09-1867[2]						
1st Session			06-11-1867	22-05-1868	22-05-1868		83	99
2nd Session			15-04-1869	22-06-1869	22-06-1869		49	55
3rd Session			15-02-1870	12-05-1870	12-05-1870		62	62
4th Session			15-02-1871	14-04-1871	14-04-1871		43	43
5th Session			11-04-1872	14-06-1872	14-06-1872	08-07-1872	46	46
2nd Parliament	20-07-1872 to 12-10-1872	03-09-1872[3]						
1st Session			05-03-1873	13-08-1873	13-08-1873		59	59
2nd Session			23-10-1873	07-11-1873	07-11-1873	02-01-1874	11	11

Parliament Session	Date of General Election[1]	Date for Return of Writs	Date of Opening	Last Day on Which the House Sat	Date of Prorogation	Date of Dissolution	Number of Sitting Days	Number of Sittings
3rd Parliament	22-01-1874	21-02-1874[4]						
1st Session			26-03-1874	26-05-1874	26-05-1874		42	42
2nd Session			04-02-1875	08-04-1875	08-04-1875		48	48
3rd Session			10-02-1876	12-04-1876	12-04-1876		46	46
4th Session			08-02-1877	28-04-1877	28-04-1877		59	59
5th Session			07-02-1878	10-05-1878	10-05-1878	16-08-1878	68	68
4th Parliament	17-09-1878	21-11-1878						
1st Session			13-02-1879	15-05-1879	15-05-1879		64	64
2nd Session			12-02-1880	07-05-1880	07-05-1880		57	57
3rd Session			09-12-1880	21-03-1881	21-03-1881		65	65
4th Session			09-02-1882	17-05-1882	17-05-1882	18-05-1882	68	68
5th Parliament	20-06-1882	07-08-1882						
1st Session			08-02-1883	25-05-1883	25-05-1883		73	73
2nd Session			17-01-1884	19-04-1884	19-04-1884		67	67
3rd Session			29-01-1885	20-07-1885	20-07-1885		122	119
4th Session			25-02-1886	02-06-1886	02-06-1886	15-01-1887	65	65
6th Parliament	22-02-1887	07-04-1887						
1st Session			13-04-1887	23-06-1887	23-06-1887		49	49
2nd Session			23-02-1888	22-05-1888	22-05-1888		61	61
3rd Session			31-01-1889	02-05-1889	02-05-1889		65	65
4th Session			16-01-1890	16-05-1890	16-05-1890	03-02-1891	81	81
7th Parliament	05-03-1891	25-04-1891						
1st Session			29-04-1891	30-09-1891	30-09-1891		102	102
2nd Session			25-02-1892	09-07-1892	09-07-1892		87	87
3rd Session			26-01-1893	01-04-1893	01-04-1893		47	47
4th Session			15-03-1894	23-07-1894	23-07-1894		87	89
5th Session			18-04-1895	22-07-1895	22-07-1895		65	68
6th Session			02-01-1896	23-04-1896	23-04-1896	24-04-1896	78	71

Parliament Session	Date of General Election[1]	Date for Return of Writs	Date of Opening	Last Day on Which the House Sat	Date of Prorogation	Date of Dissolution	Number of Sitting Days	Number of Sittings
8th Parliament	23-06-1896	13-07-1896						
1st Session			19-08-1896	05-10-1896	05-10-1896		34	34
2nd Session			25-03-1897	29-06-1897	29-06-1897		65	78
3rd Session			03-02-1898	13-06-1898	13-06-1898		86	98
4th Session			16-03-1899	11-08-1899	11-08-1899		104	102
5th Session			01-02-1900	18-07-1900	18-07-1900	09-10-1900	115	115
9th Parliament	07-11-1900	05-12-1900						
1st Session			06-02-1901	23-05-1901	23-05-1901		73	73
2nd Session			13-02-1902	15-05-1902	15-05-1902		63	63
3rd Session			12-03-1903	24-10-1903	24-10-1903		156	155
4th Session			10-03-1904	10-08-1904	10-08-1904	29-09-1904	103	103
10th Parliament	03-11-1904	15-12-1904						
1st Session			11-01-1905	20-07-1905	20-07-1905		129	129
2nd Session			08-03-1906	13-07-1906	13-07-1906		88	88
3rd Session			22-11-1906	27-04-1907	27-04-1907		95	95
4th Session			28-11-1907	20-07-1908	20-07-1908	17-09-1908	151	150
11th Parliament	26-10-1908	03-12-1908						
1st Session			20-01-1909	19-05-1909	19-05-1909		84	84
2nd Session			11-11-1909	04-05-1910	04-05-1910		103	102
3rd Session			17-11-1910	28-07-1911		29-07-1911	117	117
12th Parliament	21-09-1911	07-10-1911						
1st Session			15-11-1911	01-04-1912	01-04-1912		75	75
2nd Session			21-11-1912	06-06-1913	06-06-1913		121	111
3rd Session			15-01-1914	12-06-1914	12-06-1914		103	103
4th Session			18-08-1914	22-08-1914	22-08-1914		5	5
5th Session			04-02-1915	15-04-1915	15-04-1915		51	51
6th Session			12-01-1916	18-05-1916	18-05-1916		89	88
7th Session			18-01-1917	20-09-1917	20-09-1917	06-10-1917	135	135

Parliament Session	Date of General Election[1]	Date for Return of Writs	Date of Opening	Last Day on Which the House Sat	Date of Prorogation	Date of Dissolution	Number of Sitting Days	Number of Sittings
13th Parliament	17-12-1917	27-02-1918						
1st Session			18-03-1918	23-05-1918	23-05-1918		47	47
2nd Session			20-02-1919	07-07-1919	07-07-1919		93	93
3rd Session			01-09-1919	10-11-1919	10-11-1919		50	50
4th Session			26-02-1920	01-07-1920	01-07-1920		86	86
5th Session			14-02-1921	04-06-1921	04-05-1921	04-10-1921	80	79
14th Parliament	06-12-1921	14-01-1922						
1st Session			08-03-1922	27-06-1922	27-06-1922		75	75
2nd Session			31-01-1923	30-06-1923	30-06-1923		98	98
3rd Session			28-02-1924	19-07-1924	19-07-1924		95	95
4th Session			05-02-1925	27-06-1925	27-06-1925	05-09-1925	98	98
15th Parliament	29-10-1925	07-12-1925						
1st Session			07-01-1926	01-07-1926		02-07-1926	111	111
16th Parliament	14-09-1926	02-11-1926						
1st Session			09-12-1926	14-04-1927	14-04-1927		54	54
2nd Session			26-01-1928	11-06-1928	11-06-1928		93	93
3rd Session			07-02-1929	14-06-1929	14-06-1929		83	83
4th Session			20-02-1930	30-05-1930		30-05-1930	62	62
17th Parliament	28-07-1930	18-08-1930						
1st Session			08-09-1930	22-09-1930	22-09-1930		12	13
2nd Session			12-03-1931	03-08-1931	03-08-1931		96	96
3rd Session			04-02-1932	26-05-1932	26-05-1932		78	78
4th Session			06-10-1932	27-05-1933	27-05-1933		119	119
5th Session			25-01-1934	03-07-1934	03-07-1934		105	105
6th Session			17-01-1935	05-07-1935	05-07-1935	14-08-1935	97	97

Parliament Session	Date of General Election[1]	Date for Return of Writs	Date of Opening	Last Day on Which the House Sat	Date of Prorogation	Date of Dissolution	Number of Sitting Days	Number of Sittings
18th Parliament	14-10-1935	09-11-1935						
1st Session			06-02-1936	23-06-1936	23-06-1936		91	92
2nd Session			14-01-1937	10-04-1937	10-04-1937		62	62
3rd Session			27-01-1938	01-07-1938	01-07-1938		102	102
4th Session			12-01-1939	03-06-1939	03-06-1939		103	103
5th Session			07-09-1939	13-09-1939	13-09-1939		6	6
6th Session			25-01-1940	25-01-1940		25-01-1940	1	1
19th Parliament	26-03-1940	17-04-1940						
1st Session			16-05-1940	05-11-1940	05-11-1940		61	61
2nd Session			07-11-1940	21-01-1942	21-01-1942		105	105
3rd Session			22-01-1942	27-01-1943	27-01-1943		124	124
4th Session			28-01-1943	26-01-1944	26-01-1944		120	120
5th Session			27-01-1944	31-01-1945	31-01-1945		136	136
6th Session			19-03-1945	16-04-1945		16-04-1945	19	19
20th Parliament	11-06-1945	09-08-1945						
1st Session			06-09-1945	18-12-1945	18-12-1945		76	76
2nd Session			14-03-1946	31-08-1946	31-08-1946		118	118
3rd Session			30-01-1947	17-07-1947	17-07-1947		115	115
4th Session			05-12-1947	30-06-1948	30-06-1948		119	119
5th Session			26-01-1949	30-04-1949		30-04-1949	59	59
21st Parliament	27-06-1949	25-08-1949						
1st Session			15-09-1949	10-12-1949	10-12-1949		64	64
2nd Session			16-02-1950	30-06-1950	30-06-1950		90	90
3rd Session			29-08-1950	29-01-1951	29-01-1951		17	17
4th Session			30-01-1951	09-10-1951	09-10-1951		105	105
5th Session			09-10-1951	29-12-1951	29-12-1951		56	56
6th Session			28-02-1952	20-11-1952	20-11-1952		87	87
7th Session			20-11-1952	14-05-1953	14-05-1953	13-06-1953	108	108

Parliament Session	Date of General Election[1]	Date for Return of Writs	Date of Opening	Last Day on Which the House Sat	Date of Prorogation	Date of Dissolution	Number of Sitting Days	Number of Sittings
22nd Parliament	10-08-1953	08-10-1953						
1st Session			12-11-1953	26-06-1954	26-06-1954		139	139
2nd Session			07-01-1955	28-07-1955	28-07-1955		140	141
3rd Session			10-01-1956	14-08-1956	14-08-1956		152	152
4th Session			26-11-1956	08-01-1957	08-01-1957		5	5
5th Session			08-01-1957	12-04-1957		12-04-1957	71	71
23rd Parliament	10-06-1957	08-08-1957						
1st Session			14-10-1957	01-02-1958		01-02-1958	78	78
24th Parliament	31-03-1958	30-04-1958						
1st Session			12-05-1958	06-09-1958	06-09-1958		93	93
2nd Session			15-01-1959	18-07-1959	18-07-1959		127	127
3rd Session			14-01-1960	10-08-1960	10-08-1960		146	146
4th Session			17-11-1960	28-09-1961	28-09-1961		174	174
5th Session			18-01-1962	18-04-1962		19-04-1962	65	65
25th Parliament	18-06-1962	18-07-1962						
1st Session			27-09-1962	05-02-1963		06-02-1963	72	72
26th Parliament	08-04-1963	08-05-1963						
1st Session			16-05-1963	21-12-1963	21-12-1963		117	117
2nd Session			18-02-1964	02-04-1965	03-04-1965		248	248
3rd Session			05-04-1965	30-06-1965		08-09-1965	53	53
27th Parliament	08-11-1965	09-12-1965						
1st Session			18-01-1966	08-05-1967	08-05-1967		250	250
2nd Session			08-05-1967	23-04-1968		23-04-1968	155	155
28th Parliament	25-06-1968	25-07-1968						
1st Session			12-09-1968	22-10-1969	22-10-1969		198	198
2nd Session			23-10-1969	07-10-1970	07-10-1970		155	155
3rd Session			08-10-1970	16-02-1972	16-02-1972		244	244
4th Session			17-02-1972	01-09-1972		01-09-1972	91	91
29th Parliament	30-10-1972	20-11-1972						
1st Session			04-01-1973	26-02-1974	26-02-1974		206	207
2nd Session			27-02-1974	08-05-1974		09-05-1974	50	50

Parliament Session	Date of General Election[1]	Date for Return of Writs	Date of Opening	Last Day on Which the House Sat	Date of Prorogation	Date of Dissolution	Number of Sitting Days	Number of Sittings
30th Parliament	08-07-1974	31-07-1974						
1st Session			30-09-1974	12-10-1976	12-10-1976		343	343
2nd Session			12-10-1976	17-10-1977	17-10-1977		175	175
3rd Session			18-10-1977	10-10-1978	10-10-1978		151	151
4th Session			11-10-1978	26-03-1979		26-03-1979	98	98
31st Parliament	22-05-1979	11-06-1979						
1st Session			09-10-1979	14-12-1979		14-12-1979	49	49
32nd Parliament	18-02-1980	10-03-1980						
1st Session			14-04-1980	30-11-1983	30-11-1983		609	591
2nd Session			07-12-1983	29-06-1984		09-07-1984	116	116
33rd Parliament	04-09-1984	24-09-1984						
1st Session			05-11-1984	24-07-1986	28-08-1986		308	308
2nd Session			30-09-1986	30-09-1988		01-10-1988	390	389
34th Parliament	21-11-1988	12-12-1988						
1st Session			12-12-1988	30-12-1988	28-02-1989		11	11
2nd Session			03-04-1989	08-05-1991	12-05-1991		307	305
3rd Session			13-05-1991	23-06-1993		08-09-1993	268	268
35th Parliament	25-10-1993	15-11-1993						
1st Session			17-01-1994	02-02-1996	02-02-1996		280	280
2nd Session			27-02-1996	25-04-1997		27-04-1997	164	164
36th Parliament	02-06-1997	23-06-1997						
1st Session			22-09-1997	11-06-1999	18-09-1999		239	239

1. In the years following Confederation, the electoral system allowed the voting to be held over more than a single day. See A *History of the Vote in Canada*, Minister of Public Works and Government Services (1997), pp. 42-3.

2. All writs were returnable on September 24, 1867, except those for the electoral districts of Gaspé and of Chicoutimi and Saguenay, which were returnable on October 24, 1867 (*Journals*, Vol. I, 1867-68, pp. vii-viii).

3. All writs were returnable on September 3, 1872, except those for the electoral districts of Gaspé and of Chicoutimi and Saguenay, which were returnable on October 12, 1872, and also those for the Province of Manitoba and the Province of British Columbia, which were returnable on October 12, 1872 (*Journals*, Vol. VI, pp. vi-vii).

4. All writs were returnable on February 21, 1874, except those for the electoral districts of Gaspé and of Chicoutimi and Saguenay, which were returnable on March 12, 1874, and also those for the Province of Manitoba and the Province of British Columbia, which were returnable on March 12, 1874 (*Journals*, Vol. VIII, p. vi).

Appendix 13

RECALLS OF THE HOUSE OF COMMONS DURING ADJOURNMENT PERIODS SINCE 1867

Whenever the House adjourns for a period of time during a session, either pursuant to the Standing Orders or by a special order, the Speaker of the House is empowered to recall the House before the date specified in the motion or order if satisfied by the Government that it is in the public interest to do so. On the day the House resumes sitting, the usual practice is for the Speaker to inform the Members of the reason for recalling the House, the various steps taken for its recall, and the publication of a *Special Order Paper* (if one has been requested by the Government). The following instances occurred when the House was recalled for matters relating to public interest.

Parliament Session	Date	Reason	By What Authority
19.5	November 22, 1944	To consider the resignation of Minister of National Defence (J.L. Ralston) and matters in reference thereto	By the Speaker of the House pursuant to Resolution adopted by the House (August 12, 1944).[1] Notice printed in *Canada Gazette* (November 18, 1944).
21.3	January 29, 1951	To prorogue the Third Session of the Twenty-First Parliament	By the Speaker of the House pursuant to Resolution adopted by the House (September 14, 1950). Notice printed in *Canada Gazette* (January 6, 1951).
27.1	August 29, 1966	To consider Bill C-230, *Maintenance of Railway Operation Act, 1966*	By the Speaker of the House pursuant to Resolution adopted by the House (July 14, 1966). Notice printed in *Canada Gazette* (August 22, 1966).
28.4	August 31, 1972	To consider Bill C-231, *West Coast Ports Operations Act*	By the Speaker of the House pursuant to Resolution adopted by the House (July 6, 1972). Notice printed in *Canada Gazette* (August 29, 1972) and *Special Order Paper* published.

Parliament Session	Date	Reason	By What Authority
29.1	August 30, 1973	To consider Bill C-217, *Maintenance of Railway Operations Act*	By the Speaker of the House pursuant to Resolution adopted by the House (July 27, 1973). Notice printed in *Canada Gazette* (August 28, 1973) and *Special Order Paper* published.
30.2	August 9, 1977	To consider Bill C-63, *Air Traffic Control Services Continuation Act*	By the Speaker of the House pursuant to Resolution adopted by the House (July 25, 1977). Notice printed in *Canada Gazette* (August 6, 1977) and *Special Order Paper* published.
32.1	October 6, 1980	To consider a government motion regarding the establishment of a Special Joint Committee on the Constitution	By the Speaker of the House pursuant to Resolution adopted by the House (July 22, 1980). Notice printed in *Canada Gazette* (October 1, 1980) and *Special Order Paper* published.
33.1	July 24, 1986	To consider amendments made by the Senate to Bill C-67, *Parole and Penitentiary Acts (amdt.)*	By the Speaker of the House pursuant to Standing Order.[2] Notice printed in *Canada Gazette* (July 23, 1986).
33.2	August 11, 1987	To consider Bill C-55, *Immigration Act, 1976 (amdt.)*; Bill C-84, *Immigration Act, 1976 (amdt.)*	By the Speaker of the House pursuant to Standing Order. Notice printed in *Canada Gazette* (August 9, 1987) and *Special Order Paper* published.
34.2	January 15, 1991	To consider government motion regarding the Persian Gulf crisis	By the Speaker of the House pursuant to Standing Order. Notice printed in *Canada Gazette* (January 13, 1991) and *Special Order Paper* published.
34.2	February 25, 1991	To resume House business after adjournment to the call of the Chair	By the Speaker of the House pursuant to Resolution adopted by the House (January 21, 1991) and Standing Order. *Special Order Paper* published.
34.3	September 8, 1992	To consider government motions regarding the Constitution	By the Speaker of the House pursuant to Standing Order. *Special Order Paper* published.

1. On August 3, 1940, a motion for the adjournment of the House included a provision allowing the Speaker to recall the House early if, after consulting with the government, he felt it was in the public interest to do so. In subsequent sessions, similar motions were moved, and soon came to be made routinely when the House adjourned for an extended period of time.

2. On December 22, 1982, a provisional Standing Order came into effect, as a result of recommendations of the Special Committee on Standing Orders and Procedure, authorizing the Speaker to recall the House if, after consultation with the government, he or she felt it was in the public interest to do so. This provision is currently framed as Standing Order 28(3).

Appendix 14

PRIMA FACIE CASES OF PRIVILEGE SINCE 1958

Modern practice in matters of privilege first took root following the publication of the fourth edition of Arthur Beauchesne's *Parliamentary Rules and Forms of the House of Commons of Canada* in 1958. Beauchesne included a new section, taken from *Erskine May*'s 14th edition published in 1946, on the manner of raising questions of privilege. This description of the British procedure soon became a handy reference seized upon by successive Speakers, beginning with Speaker Michener, as a way to curtail spurious interventions by Members on non-privilege matters. It introduced two guiding conditions: whether on the first impression (*prima facie*) the matter raised appeared to be a matter of privilege, and whether the matter was raised as soon as it could have been. Both were to be determined by the Speaker before a debate could proceed. The motions were debatable and amendable and were sometimes negatived. On occasion, the House adopted motions on matters of privilege without a ruling of the Speaker. While not all questions of privilege were referred to a committee, on those occasions when they were, the committee generally reported back that they had studied the matter and that no further action was necessary. In rare circumstances, the House concurred in the Committee report.

The following chart includes all cases of privilege since 1958 that were ruled
prima facie by the Speaker.

Date of Speaker's Ruling	Subject Matter (including Member raising issue)	References	Disposition of Motion	Committee Reference	Report from Committee
February 16, 1960	Alleged improper reproduction of *Hansard* by Sperry and Hutchinson Co. (Murdo Martin (Timmins))	*Debates*, February 16, 1960, pp. 1100-4; *Journals*, February 16, 1960, pp. 156-8	Agreed to	Yes[1]	*Journals*, March 16, 1960, p. 280
November 1, 1962	*Le Devoir* article reporting Bernard Dumont's (Bellechasse) remarks on the attitude of Speaker Lambert concerning questions in the House on bilingualism (Lionel Chevrier (Laurier))	*Debates*, November 1, 1962, pp. 1167-8; *Journals*, November 1, 1962, pp. 201-2	Agreed to[2]	Yes	Committee did not report

Date of Speaker's Ruling	Subject Matter (including Member raising issue)	References	Disposition of Motion	Committee Reference	Report from Committee
November 29, 1962	*La Presse* articles regarding Members' participation in international conferences (Raymond Langlois (Megantic))	*Debates*, November 28, 1962, pp. 2105-6; November 29, 1962, pp. 2132-2; *Journals*, November 29, 1962, p. 334	Agreed to	Yes	Committee did not report
June 18, 1964	Ottawa *Citizen* editorial reflecting on conduct of a Member (Terence Nugent (Edmonton–Strathcona))	*Debates*, June 18, 1964, pp. 4431-5; *Journals*, June 18, 1964, p. 443-5	Negatived on recorded division	N/A	N/A
February 16, 1965	Arrest of Gilles Grégoire (Lapointe) within parliamentary precincts (George McIlraith (Ottawa West))	*Debates*, February 16, 1965, pp. 11356-62; *Journals*, February 16, 1965, pp. 1035-6	Agreed to on division	Yes	*Journals*, March 19, 1965, pp. 1141-2
March 23, 1965	Request that any Member called upon to give evidence before the Dorion Commission be authorized to do so by the House (Erik Nielsen (Yukon))	*Debates*, March 19, 1965, pp. 12555-9; March 22, 1965, pp. 12614-7; March 23, 1965, pp. 12675-7; *Journals*, March 23, 1965, pp. 1159-60	Agreed to	No	N/A
March 23, 1965	Unauthorized reproduction of the cover page of the *Hansard* Index by the Political Action Committee of the Steelworkers Hamilton Council (John Munro (Hamilton East))	*Debates*, March 23, 1965, pp. 12677-9; *Journals*, March 23, 1965, p. 1160	Agreed to	Yes	*Journals*, April 1, 1965, p. 1204
March 10, 1966	Charges made by Pierre Cardin (Minister of Justice) regarding the involvement of certain Members with a spy (Douglas Harkness (Calgary North))	*Debates*, March 10, 1966, pp. 2483-96; *Journals*, March 10, 1996, pp. 268-9	No motion was moved[3]	N/A	N/A

Date of Speaker's Ruling	Subject Matter (including Member raising issue)	References	Disposition of Motion	Committee Reference	Report from Committee
October 24, 1966	Allegations in *Le Droit* that the Member was being directed by someone in the public galleries (Terence Nugent (Edmonton–Strathcona))	*Debates*, October 20, 1966, pp. 8889-91; *Journals*, October 24, 1966, pp. 911-6	Negatived on recorded division	N/A	N/A
March 27, 1969	Refusal of the government to pay the Member the terminal gratuity following his departure from the Public Service (John Roberts (York–Simcoe))	*Debates*, March 27, 1969, pp. 7181-2; *Journals*, March 27, 1969, p. 853	Agreed to	Yes	*Journals*, April 24, 1969, p. 937
September 4, 1973	Interrogation of the Member and her staff in her parliamentary office by police forces (Flora MacDonald (Kingston and the Islands))	*Debates*, September 4, 1973, pp. 6179-80, 6181, *Journals*, September 4, 1973, p. 532	Agreed to	Yes	*Journals*, September 21, 1973, p. 567
October 17, 1973	Electronic surveillance of NDP caucus meeting by a journalist (David Lewis (York South))	*Debates*, October 17, 1973, pp. 6942-4; *Journals*, October 17, 1974, p. 577	Agreed to[4]	No	N/A
December 19, 1974	Remarks by Réal Caouette (Témiscamingue) that Members of Parliament bribed reporters from the Press Gallery (Roch La Salle (Joliette))	*Debates*, December 17, 1974, pp. 2317-21; December 19, 1974, pp. 2383-4; *Journals*, December 19, 1974, p. 228	Agreed to on recorded division	Yes	*Journals*, March 6, 1975, p. 349
July 25, 1975	Montreal *Gazette* article alleging that the Member had advance knowledge of a budget and had conveyed the information to businessmen (John Reid (Kenora–Rainy River))	*Debates*, July 24, 1975, pp. 7886-9; *Journals*, July 25, 1975, pp. 742-3	Motion agreed to, as amended	Yes	*Journals*, October 17, 1975, pp. 781-2

Date of Speaker's Ruling	Subject Matter (including Member raising issue)	References	Disposition of Motion	Committee Reference	Report from Committee
May 7, 1976	Allegations by a former Member that a number of Members of Parliament had been in receipt of bribes (Walter Baker (Grenville–Carleton))	*Debates*, May 7, 1976, pp. 13269-71, 13280-1; *Journals*, May 7, 1976, p. 1275	Agreed to	Yes	*Journals*, May 21, 1976, pp. 1305-7
March 21, 1978	Alleged electronic surveillance by the RCMP (John Rodriguez (Nickel Belt))	*Debates*, March 8, 1978, pp. 3571-6; March 16, pp. 3831-2; March 21, 1978, pp. 3975-6, 3988; *Journals*, March 21, 1978, pp. 520-2, 525	Negatived on recorded division	N/A	N/A
December 6, 1978	Allegation that a letter from the Solicitor General was misleading and obstructed the Member in his duties (Allan Lawrence (Northumberland–Durham))	*Debates,* November 3, 1978, pp. 777-80; November 9, 1978, pp. 964-7; December 6, 1978, pp. 1856-77; December 7, 1978, pp. 1892-925; *Journals*, November 9, 1978, pp. 125-9; December 6, 1978, pp. 221-4; December 7, 1978, p. 228	Negatived on recorded division	N/A	N/A
March 22, 1983	Montreal *Gazette* article alleging that the Member was a paid lobbyist (Bryce Mackasey (Lincoln))	*Debates*, March 16, 1983, pp. 23834-5; March 22, 1983, pp. 24027-30; *Journals*, March 22, 1983, p. 5376	Agreed to	Yes	*Journals*, November 23, 1983, p. 6588
February 20, 1984	Alleged intimidation of a Member by a Canada Post official (Albert Cooper (Peace River))	*Debates*, February 6, 1984, pp. 1101-6; February 9, 1984, pp. 1234-5; February 14, 1984, pp. 1382-4; February 20, 1984, pp. 1559-61; *Journals*, February 20, 1984, pp. 188-9	Negatived on recorded division	N/A	N/A

Date of Speaker's Ruling	Subject Matter (including Member raising issue)	References	Disposition of Motion	Committee Reference	Report from Committee
May 6, 1985	Newspaper advertisement by former Member claiming to be the present Member (Andrew Witer (Parkdale–High Park))	*Debates*, April 25, 1985, pp. 4111-3; May 6, 1985, p. 4439; *Journals*, May 6, 1985, p. 570	Agreed to	Yes	*Journals*, May 30, 1985, pp. 676-7
May 14, 1987	Unauthorized disclosure by John Parry (Kenora–Rainy River) of results of a vote held in an *in camera* sitting of a standing committee[5] (Felix Holtmann (Selkirk–Interlake))	*Debates*, April 28, 1987, pp. 5299, 5329-30; May 5, 1987, pp. 5737-42; May 14, 1987, pp. 6108-11; *Journals*, May 14, 1987, p. 917	Agreed to	Yes	*Journals*, December 18, 1997, pp. 2014-6
October 30, 1989	Access to Parliament Hill blocked by taxis (Herb Gray (Windsor West))	*Debates*, October 30, 1989, pp. 5298-302; *Journals*, October 30, 1989, p. 773	Agreed to[6]	Yes	Committee did not report
November 6, 1990	Disturbance in the gallery. Member claimed involvement of Howard McCurdy (Windsor–St. Clair) in disturbance[7] (Albert Cooper (Peace River))	*Debates*, October 18, 1990, pp. 14359-68; November 6, 1990, pp. 15177-81; *Journals*, November 6, 1990, p. 2228	Agreed to	Yes	*Journals*, March 6, 1991, p. 2666
October 31, 1991	Conduct of Ian Waddell (Port Moody–Coquitlam) in grabbing the Mace (Jesse Flis (Parkdale–High Park))	*Debates*, October 31, 1991, pp. 4271-8; 4279-80; 4309-10; *Journals*, October 31, 1991, p. 574	Agreed to[8]	No	N/A
December 4, 1992	Alleged intimidation of a committee witness by a CBC employee (Don Boudria (Glengarry–Prescott–Russell))	*Debates*, December 4, 1992, pp. 14629-31; *Journals*, December 4, 1992, p. 2284	Agreed to	Yes[9]	*Journals*, February 18, 1993, p. 2528[10]

Date of Speaker's Ruling	Subject Matter (including Member raising issue)	References	Disposition of Motion	Commit-tee Reference	Report from Committee
March 23, 1993	Alleged comments by Benoît Tremblay (Rosemont) about Acting Speaker (Charles DeBlois) casting doubt on the integrity and impartiality of the Speakership (Gilles Bernier (Beauce))	*Debates*, March 16, 1993, p. 17027; March 23, 1993, pp. 17403-5; *Journals*, March 23, 1993, p. 2688	Agreed to[11]	Yes	Committee did not report
April 19, 1993	Failure of the Minister of Finance (Don Mazankowski) to table Order pursuant to *Customs Tariff Act*[12] (Derek Lee (Scarborough–Rouge River))	*Debates*, February 24, 1993, pp. 16393-4; April 19, 1993, pp. 18104-6; *Journals*, April 19, 1993, pp. 2796-7	Agreed to	Yes	*Journals*, September 8, 1993, p. 3338
April 19, 1993	Failure of government to provide response to committee report (Lloyd Axworthy (Winnipeg South Centre))	*Debates*, March 29, 1993, p. 17722; April 19, 1993, pp. 18104-6	Agreed to[13]	Yes	*Journals*, September 8, 1993, p. 3338
March 12, 1996	Communiqué of Jean-Marc Jacob (Charlesbourg) addressed to members of the Canadian Armed Forces in Quebec inviting all francophone members of the Forces to join the Quebec military in the event of a yes vote supporting separation from Canada (Jim Hart (Okanagan–Similkameen–Merritt))	*Debates*, March 12, 1996, pp. 557-67; March 13, 1996, pp. 648-74; March 13, 1996, pp. 680-703, 716-47; March 18, 1996, pp. 854-8; *Journals*, March 18, 1996, pp. 107-110	Agreed to, as amended[14]	Yes[15]	*Journals*, June 18, 1996, pp. 565-6
March 10, 1998	Members' statements in *Ottawa Sun* bringing into question the integrity of the House and the Speaker (Peter MacKay (Pictou–Antigonish–Guysborough))	*Debates*, March 9, 1998, pp. 4560-75; March 10, 1998, pp. 4592-8; *Journals*, March 10, 1998, pp. 550-2	Agreed to, as amended	Yes	*Journals*, April 27, 1998, p. 706[16]

Date of Speaker's Ruling	Subject Matter (including Member raising issue)	References	Disposition of Motion	Committee Reference	Report from Committee
February 17, 1999	Molestation of a Member by PSAC picketers[17] (Jim Pankiw (Saskatoon–Humboldt))	*Debates*, February 17, 1999, pp. 12009-12; *Journals*, February 17, 1999, p. 1517	Agreed to	Yes	*Journals*, April 14, 1999, p. 1714
February 18, 1999	Member was impeded from entering his office by PSAC picketers (John Reynolds (West Vancouver–Sunshine Coast))	*Debates*, February 17, 1999, pp. 12009-12; February 18, 1999, p. 12134; *Journals*, February 18, 1999, p. 1525	Agreed to	Yes	*Journals*, April 14, 1999, p. 1714

1. Until 1992, questions of privilege were referred to the Standing Committee on Privileges and Elections, which for a short period of time was also known as the Standing Committee on Elections, Privileges, Procedure and Private Members' Business.

2. The motion was moved by Leon Balcer and not by Mr. Chevrier who originally raised the issue.

3. The Speaker found a *prima facie* case but ruled that the proposed motion was too general and therefore was not in order. Other Members attempted to move similar or identical motions, but the Speaker ruled them out of order.

4. The motion was not to have the matter referred to a committee but rather to have the tapes in question surrendered to either Mr. Lewis or the Speaker.

5. On April 28, 1987, the Standing Committee on Aboriginal Affairs and Northern Development presented their Third Report concerning the disclosure by Mr. Parry of the results of a vote held during an *in camera* meeting.

6. The matter was referred to the Standing Committee on Elections, Privileges, Procedure and Private Members' Business. On February 16, 1990, the name of this Committee reverted to the Standing Committee on Privileges and Elections.

7. The reference to Mr. McCurdy was removed from the proposed motion, and the matter of the disturbance in the galleries was referred to the Committee.

8. There was no reference to a committee. Mr. Waddell was called to the Bar of the House and admonished by the Speaker.

9. At this point, questions of privilege were referred to the Standing Committee on House Management.

10. The Committee report was concurred in on February 25, 1993 (*Journals*, p. 2568).

11. Mr. Tremblay withdrew the offending remarks on March 25, 1993 (*Debates*, p. 17537).

12. The document was tabled on February 25, 1993. The Speaker ruled this question of privilege *prima facie* as well as that of Mr. Axworthy concerning the delay of the government in responding to a committee report. The motion dealt with the "non-observance of the tabling requirement for Order in Council ... and other documents in the House of Commons ..."

13. The Speaker ruled on this question of privilege at the same time as he ruled on the question of privilege raised by Derek Lee concerning the late tabling of a Customs Tariff Order. Motion dealt with the "non-observance of the tabling requirement for Order in Council … and other documents in the House of Commons …"

14. There were three days of debate before the motion was adopted. Closure was invoked on March 14, 1996, and the motion to refer the matter to the Committee was amended and adopted on March 18, 1996. The amendment removed from the motion the references that the activity was "seditious and offensive".

15. The matter was referred to the Standing Committee on Procedure and House Affairs, which had replaced the Standing Committee on House Management.

16. The Committee report was concurred in on May 5, 1998 (*Journals*, pp. 744-5).

17. The question of privilege was originally raised by Mr. Reynolds (West Vancouver–Sunshine Coast), following which other Members raised related concerns.

Appendix 15

STANDING ORDERS OF THE HOUSE OF COMMONS

The Standing Orders constitute the permanent written rules under which the House of Commons regulates its proceedings. There are more than 150 Standing Orders, each of which is a continuing order of the House for the governance and regulation of its proceedings. The continuing or "standing" nature of the Standing Orders means that they do not lapse at the end of a session or parliament. Rather, they remain in effect until the House itself decides to suspend, change or repeal them. The following are the Standing Orders in force as of October 12, 1999.

UNPROVIDED CASES

Procedure in unprovided cases.

1. In all cases not provided for hereinafter, or by other Order of the House, procedural questions shall be decided by the Speaker or Chairman, whose decisions shall be based on the usages, forms, customs and precedents of the House of Commons of Canada and on parliamentary tradition in Canada and other jurisdictions, so far as they may be applicable to the House.

CHAPTER I

PRESIDING OFFICERS

ELECTIONS AND APPOINTMENTS

First order of business.

2. (1) At the opening of the first session of a Parliament, and at any other time as determined pursuant to section (2) of this Standing Order, the election of a Speaker shall be the first order of business and shall not be interrupted by any other proceeding.

Vacancy in Office of Speaker.

(2) When there is, or is to be, a vacancy in the Office of the Speaker, whether at the opening of a Parliament, or because the incumbent of that Office has indicated his or her intention to resign the Office of Speaker, or for any other reason, the Members, when they are ready, shall proceed to the election of a Speaker.

Precedence over all other business. Adjournment of the House.

(3) The election of a Speaker shall take precedence over all other business and no motion for adjournment nor any other motion shall be accepted while it is proceeding and the House shall continue to sit, if necessary, beyond its ordinary hour of daily adjournment, notwithstanding any other Standing or Special Order, until a Speaker is declared elected, and is installed in the Chair in the usual manner, provided that if the House has continued to sit beyond its ordinary hour of daily adjournment, the Speaker shall thereupon adjourn the House until the next sitting day.

3. (1) During an election of a Speaker the Chair shall be taken by:

Member presiding during election.

(*a*) at the opening of a Parliament, the Member who has had the longest period of unbroken service as determined by reference to his or her position on the list published in the *Canada Gazette,* and who is neither a Minister of the Crown, nor holds any office within the House including that of leader of a party; or,

(*b*) in the case of the Speaker having indicated his or her intention to resign that office, the Speaker; and

(*c*) at other times, in the absence of the Speaker, the Deputy Speaker and Chairman of Committees of the Whole as provided by Statute.

Powers and vote of Member presiding during election.

(2) The Member presiding during the election of a Speaker shall be vested with all the powers of the Chair provided that he or she:

(*a*) shall be entitled to vote in the election of a Speaker; and

(*b*) shall have no casting vote in the event of there being an equality of votes cast for two candidates.

Balloting procedure.

4. The election of a Speaker shall be conducted by secret ballot as follows:

Notification to Clerk when Member does not wish to be considered for election. List of names to be provided to Member presiding during election.

(1) Any Member who does not wish to be considered for election to the Office of Speaker shall, not later than 6:00 p.m. on the day preceding the day on which the election of a Speaker is expected to take place, in writing, so inform the Clerk of the House who shall prepare a list of such Members' names together with a list of the names of all Ministers of the Crown and party leaders, and shall provide the same to the Member presiding prior to the taking of the first ballot.

Ballot papers.

(2) Members present in the Chamber shall be provided with ballot papers by the Clerk of the House.

Announcement of availability of list.

(3) The Member presiding shall announce from the Chair that the list provided pursuant to section (1) of this Standing Order is available for consultation at the Table.

Choice indicated on ballot paper.

(4) Members wishing to indicate their choice for the Office of Speaker shall print the first and last name of a Member on the ballot paper.

Ballot paper deposited in box.

(5) Members shall deposit their completed ballot papers in a box provided for that purpose on the Table.

Counting and destruction of ballot papers.

(6) The Clerk of the House shall, once all Members wishing to do so have deposited their ballot papers, empty the box and count the ballots and being satisfied as to the accuracy of the count, shall destroy the ballots together with all records of the number of ballots cast for each candidate and the Clerk of the House shall in no way divulge the number of ballots cast for any candidate.

Announcement of successful candidate.

(7) In the event of one Member having received a majority of the votes cast, the Clerk of the House shall provide the Member presiding with the name of that Member, whereupon the Member presiding shall announce the name of the new Speaker.

When no majority of votes.

(8) In the event of no Member having received a majority of the votes cast the procedure shall be as follows:

Clerk to provide Member presiding during election with alphabetical list of candidates.

(*a*) the Clerk of the House shall provide the Member presiding the names of the candidates for the next ballot, in alphabetical order, provided that the Clerk of the House shall first determine the number representing the least total number of votes cast and the Clerk shall exclude the names of all Members having received that total number of votes, together with the names of all Members having received five percent or less of the total votes cast, from the list of candidates so provided, and provided that in the event of every candidate receiving the same number of votes no names shall be excluded from the list so provided; and

(*b*) whereupon the Member presiding shall announce the names of the candidates, which shall be the only names thereafter accepted, in alphabetical order, provided that prior to the taking of the second ballot, he or she shall ask that any Member, whose name has been so announced and who does not wish to be further considered for election to the Office of Speaker, state his or her reason therefor.

(9) Subsequent ballots shall be conducted in the manner prescribed in sections (4) through (8) of this Standing Order except that following the second and all subsequent ballots the Member presiding shall not ask the candidates to state their reasons for not wishing to be further considered for election to the Office of Speaker but shall forthwith proceed to the taking of that subsequent ballot and the balloting shall continue, in like manner, until such time as a new Speaker is elected.

(10) During the election of a Speaker there shall be no debate and the Member presiding shall not be permitted to entertain any question of privilege.

5. No Minister of the Crown, nor party leader, shall be eligible for election to the Office of Speaker.

6. The election of a Speaker shall not be considered to be a question of confidence in the government.

7. (1) A Chairman of Committees of the Whole who shall also be Deputy Speaker of the House shall be elected at the commencement of every Parliament; and the Member so elected shall, if in his or her place in the House, take the Chair of all Committees of the Whole.

(2) The Member elected to serve as Deputy Speaker and Chairman of Committees of the Whole shall be required to possess the full and practical knowledge of the official language which is not that of the Speaker for the time being.

(3) The Member so elected as Deputy Speaker and Chairman of Committees of the Whole shall continue to act in that capacity until the end of the Parliament for which he or she is elected, and in the case of a vacancy by death, resignation or otherwise, the House shall proceed forthwith to elect a successor.

(4) In the absence of the Deputy Speaker and Chairman of Committees of the Whole, the Speaker may, in forming a Committee of the Whole, before leaving the Chair, appoint any Member Chairman of the Committee.

8. At the commencement of every session, or from time to time as necessity may arise, the House may appoint a Deputy Chairman of Committees of the Whole and also an Assistant Deputy Chairman of Committees of the Whole, either of whom shall, whenever the Chairman of Committees of the Whole is absent, be entitled to exercise all the powers vested in the Chairman of Committees of the Whole including his or her powers as Deputy Speaker during the Speaker's unavoidable absence.

Order and Decorum

9. The Speaker shall not take part in any debate before the House. In case of an equality of voices, the Speaker gives a casting vote, and any reasons stated are entered in the *Journals*.

Order and decorum. No appeal.

10. The Speaker shall preserve order and decorum, and shall decide questions of order. In deciding a point of order or practice, the Speaker shall state the Standing Order or other authority applicable to the case. No debate shall be permitted on any such decision, and no such decision shall be subject to an appeal to the House.

Naming of a Member.

11. (1)(*a*) The Speaker shall be vested with the authority to maintain order by naming individual Members for disregarding the authority of the Chair and, without resort to motion, ordering their withdrawal for the remainder of that sitting, notwithstanding Standing Order 15.

Removal of Member disregarding Chair's authority.

(*b*) In the event of a Member disregarding an order of the Chair made pursuant to paragraph (*a*) of this section, the Speaker shall order the Sergeant-at-Arms to remove the Member.

Irrelevance or repetition.

(2) The Speaker or the Chairman, after having called the attention of the House, or of the Committee, to the conduct of a Member who persists in irrelevance, or repetition, may direct the Member to discontinue his or her speech, and if then the Member still continues to speak, the Speaker shall name the Member or, if in Committee, the Chairman shall report the Member to the House.

Decorum in Committee of the Whole.

12. The Chairman shall maintain order in Committees of the Whole; deciding all questions of order subject to an appeal to the Speaker; but disorder in a Committee of the Whole can only be censured by the House, on receiving a report thereof. No debate shall be permitted on any decision.

When motion is contrary to rules and privileges of Parliament.

13. Whenever the Speaker is of the opinion that a motion offered to the House is contrary to the rules and privileges of Parliament, the Speaker shall apprise the House thereof immediately, before putting the question thereon, and quote the Standing Order or authority applicable to the case.

Notice of strangers. Question that strangers withdraw. Speaker or Chairman decides.

14. If any Member takes notice that strangers are present, the Speaker or the Chairman (as the case may be) may put the question "That strangers be ordered to withdraw", without permitting any debate or amendment; provided that the Speaker or the Chairman may order the withdrawal of strangers.

CHAPTER II

MEMBERS

Attendance required.

15. Every Member, being cognizant of the provisions of the *Parliament of Canada Act,* is bound to attend the sittings of the House, unless otherwise occupied with parliamentary activities and functions or on public or official business.

Decorum.

16. (1) When the Speaker is putting a question, no Member shall enter, walk out of or across the House, or make any noise or disturbance.

(2) When a Member is speaking, no Member shall pass between that Member and the Chair, nor interrupt him or her, except to raise a point of order.

(3) No Member may pass between the Chair and the Table, nor between the Chair and the Mace when the Mace has been taken off the Table by the Sergeant-at-Arms.

(4) When the House adjourns, Members shall keep their seats until the Speaker has left the Chair.

Rising to be recognized.

17. Every Member desiring to speak is to rise in his or her place and address the Speaker.

Disrespectful or offensive language. Reflection on a vote.

18. No Member shall speak disrespectfully of the Sovereign, nor of any of the Royal Family, nor of the Governor General or the person administering the Government of Canada; nor use offensive words against either House, or against any Member thereof. No Member may reflect upon any vote of the House, except for the purpose of moving that such vote be rescinded.

Point of order. Speaker may allow a debate.

19. Any Member addressing the House, if called to order either by the Speaker or on a point raised by another Member, shall sit down while the point is being stated, after which he or she may explain. The Speaker may permit debate on the point of order before giving a decision, but such debate must be strictly relevant to the point of order taken.

When a Member shall withdraw.

20. If anything shall come in question touching the conduct, election or right of any Member to hold a seat, that Member may make a statement and shall withdraw during the time the matter is in debate.

Pecuniary interest.

21. No Member is entitled to vote upon any question in which he or she has a direct pecuniary interest, and the vote of any Member so interested will be disallowed.

Public registry of Members' foreign travel.

22. The Clerk of the House shall maintain a public registry of foreign travel by Members of Parliament in which Members shall register all visits they make outside Canada, arising from or relating to their membership in the House of Commons where the cost of any such travel is not wholly borne by the Consolidated Revenue Fund, the Member personally, any inter-parliamentary association or friendship group recognized by the House of Commons and any recognized party, together with the name of the sponsoring person or organization which paid for travel to and/or from Canada.

Offer of money to Members.

23. (1) The offer of any money or other advantage to any Member of this House, for the promoting of any matter whatsoever depending or to be transacted in Parliament, is a high crime and misdemeanour, and tends to the subversion of the Constitution.

Bribery in elections.

(2) If it shall appear that any person has been elected and returned a Member of this House, or has endeavoured so to be, by bribery or any other corrupt practices, this House will proceed with the utmost severity against all such persons as shall have been wilfully concerned in such bribery or other corrupt practices.

CHAPTER III

SITTINGS OF THE HOUSE

Times and days of sittings.

24. (1) The House shall meet on Mondays at 11:00 a.m., on Tuesdays, Thursdays and Fridays at 10:00 a.m. and on Wednesdays at 2:00 p.m. unless otherwise provided by Standing or Special Order of this House.

Daily adjournment.

(2) At 6:30 p.m. on any sitting day except Friday and at 2:30 p.m. on Fridays, the Speaker shall adjourn the House until the next sitting day.

When motion to adjourn required.

25. When it is provided in any Standing or Special Order of this House that any business specified by such Order shall be continued, forthwith disposed of, or concluded in any sitting, the House shall not be adjourned before such proceedings have been completed except pursuant to a motion to adjourn proposed by a Minister of the Crown.

Motion to continue or extend sitting.

26. (1) Except during Private Members' Business, when the Speaker is in the Chair, a Member may propose a motion, without notice, to continue a sitting through a dinner hour or beyond the ordinary hour of daily adjournment for the purpose of considering a specified item of business or a stage or stages thereof subject to the following conditions:

Motion to relate to business.

(*a*) the motion must relate to the business then being considered provided that proceedings in any Committee of the Whole may be temporarily interrupted for the purpose of proposing a motion under the provisions of this Standing Order;

When motion to be made.

(*b*) the motion must be proposed in the hour preceding the time at which the business under consideration should be interrupted by a dinner hour, Private Members' Hour or the ordinary hour of daily adjournment; and

No debate.

(*c*) the motion shall not be subject to debate or amendment.

When objection taken.

(2) In putting the question on such motion, the Speaker shall ask those Members who object to rise in their places. If fifteen or more Members then rise, the motion shall be deemed to have been withdrawn; otherwise, the motion shall have been adopted.

Extension of sitting hours in June.

27. (1) On the tenth sitting day preceding June 23 a motion to extend the hours of sitting to a specific hour during the last ten sitting days may be proposed, without notice, by any Minister during routine proceedings.

When question put.

(2) Not more than two hours after the commencement of proceedings thereon, the Speaker shall put every question necessary to dispose of the said motion.

House not to sit.

28. (1) The House shall not meet on New Year's Day, Good Friday, the day fixed for the celebration of the birthday of the Sovereign, St. John the Baptist Day, Dominion Day, Labour Day, Thanksgiving Day, Remembrance Day and Christmas Day. When St. John the Baptist Day and Dominion Day fall on a Tuesday, the House shall not meet the preceding day; when those days fall on a Thursday, the House shall not meet the following day.

House calendar.

(2) When the House meets on a day, or sits after the normal meeting hour on a day, set out in column A, and then adjourns, it shall stand adjourned to the day set out in column B.

A:	B:
The Friday preceding Thanksgiving Day.	The second Monday following that Friday.
The Friday preceding Remembrance Day.	The second Monday following that Friday.
The second Friday preceding Christmas Day.	The first Monday in February.

The Friday preceding the week marking the mid-way point between the first Monday in February and the Friday preceding Good Friday.	The second Monday following that Friday.
The Friday preceding Good Friday.	The Monday following Easter Monday.
The Friday preceding the week marking the mid-way point between the Monday following Easter Monday and June 23.	The second Monday following that Friday or, if that Monday is the day fixed for the celebration of the birthday of the Sovereign, on the Tuesday following that Monday.
June 23 or the Friday preceding if June 23 falls on a Saturday, a Sunday or a Monday.	The second Monday following Labour Day.

Recall of House.

(3) Whenever the House stands adjourned, if the Speaker is satisfied, after consultation with the Government, that the public interest requires that the House should meet at an earlier time, the Speaker may give notice that being so satisfied the House shall meet, and thereupon the House shall meet to transact its business as if it had been duly adjourned to that time. In the event of the Speaker being unable to act owing to illness or other cause, the Deputy Speaker, the Deputy Chairman of Committees or the Assistant Deputy Chairman of Committees shall act in the Speaker's stead for all the purposes of this section.

Royal Assent during adjournments.

(4) During adjournments of the House pursuant to section (2) of this Standing Order, if a bill or bills are awaiting Royal Assent, the Speaker may, at the request of the Government, give notice that the House shall meet at an earlier time for the purposes of Royal Assent. The House shall meet at the specified time for those purposes only; and immediately thereafter the Speaker shall adjourn the House to the time to which it had formerly been adjourned. In the event of the Speaker being unable to act owing to illness or other cause, the Deputy Speaker, the Deputy Chairman of Committees or the Assistant Deputy Chairman of Committees shall act in the Speaker's stead for all the purposes of this section.

Quorum of twenty.

29. (1) The presence of at least twenty Members of the House, including the Speaker, shall be necessary to constitute a meeting of the House for the exercise of its powers.

Lack of quorum.

(2) If at the time of meeting there be not a quorum, the Speaker may take the Chair and adjourn the House until the next sitting day.

Ringing of bells for quorum.

(3) If, during a sitting of the House, the attention of the Speaker is drawn to the lack of a quorum, the Speaker shall, upon determining that a quorum is lacking, order the bells to ring for no longer than fifteen minutes; thereupon a count of the Members present shall be taken, and if a quorum is still lacking, the Speaker shall adjourn the House until the next sitting day.

Recorded in *Journals*.

(4) Whenever the Speaker adjourns the House for want of a quorum, the time of the adjournment, and the names of the Members then present, shall be inserted in the *Journals*.

Speaker to receive Black Rod.

(5) When the Sergeant-at-Arms announces that the Gentleman Usher of the Black Rod is at the door, the Speaker shall take the Chair, whether there be a quorum present or not.

CHAPTER IV

DAILY PROGRAM

Prayers.

30. (1) The Speaker shall read prayers every day at the meeting of the House before any business is entered upon.

Commencement of business.

(2) Not more than two minutes after the reading of prayers, the business of the House shall commence.

Routine Proceedings.

(3) At 3:00 p.m. on Mondays and Wednesdays, at 10:00 a.m. on Tuesdays and Thursdays, and at 12:00 noon on Fridays, the House shall proceed to the ordinary daily routine of business, which shall be as follows:

Tabling of Documents (pursuant to Standing Orders 32 or 109)

Statements by Ministers (pursuant to Standing Order 33)

Presenting Reports from Inter-parliamentary Delegations (pursuant to Standing Order 34)

Presenting Reports from Committees (pursuant to Standing Order 35)

Introduction of Government Bills

Introduction of Private Members' Bills

First Reading of Senate Public Bills

Motions

Presenting Petitions (pursuant to Standing Order 36(6))

Questions on *Order Paper.*

When introduction of Government Bills not completed before statements by Members.

(4)(*a*) When proceedings under "Introduction of Government Bills" are not completed on a Tuesday or Thursday prior to statements by Members, the ordinary daily routine of business shall continue immediately after oral questions are taken up, notwithstanding section (5) of this Standing Order, until the completion of all items under "Introduction of Government Bills", suspending as much of Private Members' Business as necessary.

Before ordinary hour of daily adjournment.

(*b*) When proceedings under "Introduction of Government Bills" are not completed before the ordinary hour of daily adjournment, the House shall continue to sit to complete the ordinary daily routine of business up to and including "Introduction of Government Bills", whereupon the Speaker shall adjourn the House.

Time for statements by Members, Oral Question period and Orders of the Day.

(5) At 2:00 p.m. on Mondays, Tuesdays, Wednesdays and Thursdays, and at 11:00 a.m. on Fridays, Members, other than Ministers of the Crown, may make statements pursuant to Standing Order 31. Not later than 2:15 p.m. or 11:15 a.m., as the case may be, oral questions shall be taken up. At 3:00 p.m. on Tuesdays and Thursdays, and after the ordinary daily routine of business has been disposed of on Mondays, Wednesdays and Fridays, the Orders of the Day shall be considered in the order established pursuant to section (6) of this Standing Order.

Day by day order of business.

(6) Except as otherwise provided in these Standing Orders, the order of business shall be as follows:

(Monday)
(Before the daily routine of business)
   Private Members' Business — from 11:00 a.m. to 12:00 noon:
     Public Bills, Private Bills, Notices of Motions and Notices of Motions (Papers).
   Government Orders.
(After the daily routine of business)
   Government Orders.
(Tuesday and Thursday)
(After the daily routine of business)
   Government Orders.
   Private Members' Business — from 5:30 to 6:30 p.m.:
     Public Bills, Private Bills, Notices of Motions and Notices of Motions (Papers).
(Wednesday)
(After the daily routine of business)
   Notices of Motions for the Production of Papers.
   Government Orders.
   Private Members' Business — from 5:30 to 6:30 p.m.:
     Public Bills, Private Bills, Notices of Motions and Notices of Motions (Papers).
(Friday)
(Before the daily routine of business)
   Government Orders.
(After the daily routine of business)
   Government Orders.
   Private Members' Business — from 1:30 to 2:30 p.m.:
     Public Bills, Private Bills, Notices of Motions and Notices of Motions (Papers).

Delay or interruption of Private Members' Hour.

(7) If the beginning of Private Members' Hour is delayed for any reason, or if the Hour is interrupted for any reason, a period of time corresponding to the time of the delay or interruption shall be added to the end of the Hour suspending as much of the business set out in section (6) of this Standing Order as necessary. If the beginning of Private Members' Hour is delayed or the interruption continues past thirty minutes after the time at which the Hour would have ordinarily ended, Private Members' Hour for that day and the business scheduled for consideration at that time, or any remaining portion thereof, shall be added to the business of the House on a day to be fixed, after consultation, by the Speaker, who shall attempt to designate that day within the next ten sitting days, but who, in any case, shall not permit the intervention of more than one adjournment period provided for in Standing Order 28(2). In cases where the Speaker adjourns the House pursuant to Standing Orders 2(3), 30(4)(b) or 83(2), this section shall not apply.

Statements by Members.

31. A Member may be recognized, under the provisions of Standing Order 30(5), to make a statement for not more than one minute. The Speaker may order a Member to resume his or her seat if, in the opinion of the Speaker, improper use is made of this Standing Order.

Documents deposited pursuant to statutory or other authority.

32. (1) Any return, report or other paper required to be laid before the House in accordance with any Act of Parliament or in pursuance of any resolution or Standing Order of this House may be deposited with the Clerk of the House on any sitting day or, when the House stands adjourned, on the Wednesday following the fifteenth day of the month. Such return, report or other paper shall be deemed for all purposes to have been presented to or laid before the House.

Tabling of documents in the House.

(2) A Minister of the Crown, or a Parliamentary Secretary acting on behalf of a Minister, may, in his or her place in the House, state that he or she proposes to lay upon the Table of the House, any report or other paper dealing with a matter coming within the administrative responsibilities of the government, and, thereupon, the same shall be deemed for all purposes to have been laid before the House.

Recorded in Journals.

(3) In either case, a record of any such paper shall be entered in the *Journals*.

In both official languages.

(4) Any document distributed in the House or laid before the House pursuant to sections (1) or (2) of this Standing Order shall be in both official languages.

Permanent referral to committee.

(5) Reports, returns or other papers laid before the House in accordance with an Act of Parliament shall thereupon be deemed to have been permanently referred to the appropriate standing committee.

Referral to committee in other cases.

(6) Papers required to be laid upon the Table pursuant to Standing Order 110 shall be deemed referred to the appropriate standing committee during the period specified in laying the same upon the Table.

Statements by Ministers.

33. (1) On Statements by Ministers, as listed in Standing Order 30(3), a Minister of the Crown may make a short factual announcement or statement of government policy. A Member from each of the parties in opposition to the government may comment briefly thereon. The time for such proceedings shall be limited as the Speaker deems fit.

Extension of sitting.

(2) A period of time corresponding to the time taken for the proceedings pursuant to section (1) of this Standing Order shall be added to the time provided for government business in the afternoon of the day on which the said proceedings took place. Private Members' Business, where applicable, and the ordinary time of daily adjournment shall be delayed accordingly, notwithstanding Standing Orders 24, 30 and 38 or any Order made pursuant to Standing Order 27.

Reports of Inter-parliamentary delegations.

34. (1) Within twenty sitting days of the return to Canada of an officially recognized inter-parliamentary delegation composed, in any part, of Members of the House, the head of the delegation, or a Member acting on behalf of him or her, shall present a report to the House on the activities of the delegation.

Succinct explanation allowed.

(2) A Member presenting a report, pursuant to section (1) of this Standing Order, shall be permitted to make a succinct oral presentation of its subject-matter.

Reports from committees. Succinct explanation allowed.

35. (1) Reports to the House from committees may be made by Members standing in their places, at the time provided pursuant to Standing Order 30(3) or 81(4)(c), provided that the Member may be permitted to give a succinct explanation of the subject-matter of the report.

Further succinct explanation.

(2) Upon presentation of a report accompanied by supplementary or dissenting opinions or recommendations pursuant to Standing Order 108(1)(a), a committee member of

the Official Opposition representing those who supported the opinion or opinions expressed in the appended material may also rise to give a succinct explanation thereof.

Petitions to be examined by Clerk of Petitions.

36. (1) Prior to presentation, the Clerk of Petitions shall examine all petitions, and in order to be presented, they must be certified correct as to form and content by the said Clerk.

Form of petitions.

(2) In order to be certified, pursuant to section (1) of this Standing Order, every petition shall:

(*a*) be addressed to the House of Commons or to the House of Commons in Parliament assembled;

(*b*) contain a clear, proper and respectful prayer requesting that Parliament see fit to take some action within its authority;

(*c*) be written, typewritten or printed on paper of usual size;

(*d*) be free of erasures and interlineations in its text;

(*e*) have its subject-matter indicated on every sheet if it consists of more than one sheet of signatures and addresses;

(*f*) contain only original signatures and addresses written directly onto the petition and not pasted thereon or otherwise transferred to it; and

(*g*) contain at least twenty-five signatures together with the addresses of the signatories, from persons other than Members of Parliament.

Members answerable.

(3) Members presenting petitions shall be answerable that they do not contain impertinent or improper matter.

Member's endorsement.

(4) Every Member presenting a petition shall endorse his or her name thereon.

Filing with Clerk of the House.

(5) A petition to the House may be presented by a Member at any time during the sitting of the House by filing the same with the Clerk of the House.

Presentation in the House.

(6) Any Member desiring to present a petition, in his or her place in the House, may do so on "Presenting Petitions", a period not to exceed fifteen minutes, during the ordinary daily routine of business.

No debate.

(7) On the presentation of a petition no debate on or in relation to the same shall be allowed.

Ministry's response.

(8) Every petition presented pursuant to this Standing Order shall forthwith be transmitted to the Ministry, which shall, within forty-five days, respond to every petition referred to it; provided that the said response may be tabled pursuant to Standing Order 32(1).

CHAPTER V

QUESTIONS

Oral Questions

Daily question period. Speaker decides urgency.

37. (1) Questions on matters of urgency may, at the time specified in Standing Order 30(5), be addressed orally to Ministers of the Crown, provided however that, if in the opinion of the Speaker a question is not urgent, he or she may direct that it be placed on the *Order Paper.*

Questions to member of Board of Internal Economy.

(2) Questions may also be addressed orally at the time specified in Standing Order 30(5), to a member of the Board of Internal Economy so designated by the Board.

Notice of question for adjournment proceedings.

(3) A Member who is not satisfied with the response to a question asked on any day at this stage, or a Member who has been told by the Speaker that the question is not urgent, may give notice that he or she intends to raise the subject-matter of the question on the adjournment of the House. The notice referred to herein, whether or not it is given orally during the oral question period provided pursuant to Standing Order 30(5), must be given in writing to the Speaker not later than one hour following that period the same day. Unless previously disposed of, the said notice shall be deemed withdrawn after the forty-fifth sitting day from the day of notice.

Adjournment proceedings.

38. (1) Except as otherwise provided in these Standing Orders, at the time of adjournment on Mondays, Tuesdays, Wednesdays and Thursdays, the Speaker may, notwithstanding the provisions of Standing Orders 24(2) and 67(2), deem that a motion to adjourn the House has been made and seconded, whereupon such motion shall be debatable for not more than thirty minutes.

Notice required and time limit.

(2) No matter shall be debated during the thirty minutes herein provided, unless notice thereof has been given by a Member as provided in Standing Order 37(3) or 39(5)(*b*). No debate on any one matter raised during this period shall last for more than six minutes.

Selection of matters to be raised.

(3) When several Members have given notices of intention to raise matters on the adjournment of the House, the Speaker shall decide the order in which such matters are to be raised. In doing so, the Speaker shall have regard to the order in which notices were given, to the urgency of the matters raised, and to the apportioning of the opportunities to debate such matters among the Members of the various parties in the House. The Speaker may, at his or her discretion, consult with representatives of the parties concerning such order and be guided by their advice.

Questions to be announced.

(4) By not later than 5:00 p.m. on any Monday, Tuesday, Wednesday or Thursday, the Speaker shall indicate to the House the matter or matters to be raised at the time of adjournment that day.

Question time: four minutes. Answer time: two minutes.

(5) The Member raising the matter may speak for not more than four minutes. A Minister of the Crown, or a Parliamentary Secretary speaking on behalf of a Minister, if he or she wishes to do so, may speak for not more than two minutes. When debate has lasted for a total of thirty minutes, or when the debate on the matter or matters raised has

ended, whichever comes first, the Speaker shall deem the motion to adjourn to have been carried and shall adjourn the House until the next sitting day.

Time in announcing future business not to count.

(6) The time required for any questions and answers concerning the future business of the House, whether this item takes place before or after the thirty minute period herein provided, shall not be counted as part of the said thirty minutes.

Written Questions

Questions on *Order Paper*.

39. (1) Questions may be placed on the *Order Paper* seeking information from Ministers of the Crown relating to public affairs; and from other Members, relating to any bill, motion or other public matter connected with the business of the House, in which such Members may be concerned; but in putting any such question or in replying to the same no argument or opinion is to be offered, nor any facts stated, except so far as may be necessary to explain the same; and in answering any such question the matter to which the same refers shall not be debated.

Responsibilities of the Clerk.

(2) The Clerk of the House, acting for the Speaker, shall have full authority to ensure that coherent and concise questions are placed on the *Notice Paper* in accordance with the practices of the House, and may, on behalf of the Speaker, order certain questions to be posed separately.

Starred questions. Limit of three.

(3)(*a*) Any Member who requires an oral answer to his or her question may distinguish it by an asterisk, but no Member shall have more than three such questions at a time on the daily *Order Paper*.

Reply printed in Hansard.

(*b*) If a Member does not distinguish his or her question by an asterisk, the Minister to whom the question is addressed hands the answer to the Clerk of the House who causes it to be printed in the official report of the *Debates*.

Limit of four questions on *Order Paper*.

(4) No Member shall have more than four questions on the *Order Paper* at any one time.

Request for ministerial response.

(5)(*a*) A Member may request that the Ministry respond to a specific question within forty-five days by so indicating when filing his or her question.

After forty-five days.

(*b*) If such a question remains unanswered at the expiration of the said period of forty-five days, the Member who put the question may rise in the House under "Questions on *Order Paper*" and give notice that he or she intends to transfer the question and raise the subject-matter thereof on the adjournment of the House.

Transfer of question to Notices of Motions.

(6) If, in the opinion of the Speaker, a question on the *Order Paper* put to a Minister of the Crown is of such a nature as to require a lengthy reply, the Speaker may, upon the request of the government, direct the same to stand as a notice of motion, and to be transferred to its proper place as such upon the *Order Paper,* the Clerk of the House being authorized to amend the same as to matters of form.

Question made order for return.

(7) If a question is of such a nature that, in the opinion of the Minister who is to furnish the reply, such reply should be in the form of a return, and the Minister states that he or she has no objection to laying such return upon the Table of the House, the Minister's statement shall, unless otherwise ordered by the House, be deemed an order of the House to that effect and the same shall be entered in the *Journals* as such.

CHAPTER VI
PROCESS OF DEBATE

Precedence of items on *Order Paper*.

40. (1) All items standing on the Orders of the Day, except Government Orders, shall be taken up according to the precedence assigned to each on the *Order Paper*.

Calling of government business.

(2) Government Orders shall be called and considered in such sequence as the government determines.

Business interrupted.

41. (1) Whenever the business before the House is interrupted pursuant to Standing Order or Special Order, unless otherwise provided, the proceedings then under consideration shall stand over until the next sitting day or later the same sitting day after the period provided pursuant to Standing Order 30(5), as the case may be, when it will be taken up at the same stage where its progress was interrupted.

Order of the Day interrupted by adjournment of the House.

(2) If debate on any Order of the Day be interrupted by the House being adjourned by motion or for want of a quorum, such motion or Order shall be allowed to stand and retain its precedence on the *Order Paper* for the next sitting, provided that if debate on any item of Private Members' Business not selected pursuant to Standing Order 92 is so interrupted, it shall thereupon be dropped from the *Order Paper*.

Questions and notices of motions not taken up.

42. (1) Questions put by Members and notices of motions not taken up when called may (upon the request of the government) be allowed to stand and retain their precedence; otherwise they will disappear from the *Order Paper*. They may, however, be renewed.

When orders may be stood or dropped.

(2) Orders not proceeded with when called, upon the like request, may be allowed to stand retaining their precedence; otherwise they shall be dropped and be placed on the *Order Paper* for the next sitting after those of the same class at a similar stage.

Orders postponed.

(3) All orders not disposed of at the adjournment of the House shall be postponed until the next sitting day, without a motion to that effect.

Time limit and comments on speeches when Speaker in Chair.

43. (1) Unless otherwise provided in these Standing Orders, when the Speaker is in the Chair, no Member, except the Prime Minister and the Leader of the Opposition, or a Minister moving a government order and the Member speaking in reply immediately after such Minister, shall speak for more than twenty minutes at a time in any debate. Following each twenty-minute speech, a period not exceeding ten minutes shall be made available, if required, to allow Members to ask questions and comment briefly on matters relevant to the speech and to allow responses thereto.

Period of debate divided in two.

(2) The Whip of a party may indicate to the Speaker at any time during a debate governed by this Standing Order that one or more of the periods of debate limited pursuant to section (1) of this Standing Order and allotted to Members of his or her party are to be divided in two.

No Member to speak twice. Exception.

44. (1) No member, unless otherwise provided by Standing or Special Order, may speak twice to a question except in explanation of a material part of his or her speech which may have been misquoted or misunderstood, and the Member is not to introduce any new matter, but then no debate shall be allowed upon such explanation.

Right of reply.

(2) A reply shall be allowed to a Member who has moved a substantive motion, but not to the mover of an amendment, the previous question or an instruction to a committee.

Reply closes debate.

(3) In all cases the Speaker shall inform the House that the reply of the mover of the original motion closes the debate.

Register of paired Members.

44.1 (1) The Clerk of the House shall cause to be kept at the Table a Register of Paired Members, in which any Member of the government party and any Member of an Opposition party may have their names entered together by their respective Whips, to indicate that they will not take part in any recorded division held on the date inscribed on that page of the Register; provided that independent Members of Parliament may sign the Register in their own right.

Names to be printed.

(2) On any day on which one or more recorded divisions have taken place, the names of the Members so entered shall be printed in the *Debates* and the *Journals*, immediately following the entry for each of the said divisions.

When vote recorded.

45. (1) Upon a division, the "yeas" and "nays" shall not be entered in the *Journals*, unless demanded by five members.

No debate preparatory to a division.

(2) When Members have been called in, preparatory to a division, no further debate is to be permitted.

15-minute division bell when Speaker has interrupted any proceeding.

(3) When, under the provisions of any Standing Order or other Order of this House, the Speaker has interrupted any proceeding for the purpose of putting forthwith the question on any business then before the House, the bells to call in the Members shall be sounded for not more than fifteen minutes.

30-minute division bell on non-debatable motion.

(4) When the Speaker has put the question on any non-debatable motion, the bells to call in the Members shall be sounded for not more than thirty minutes.

30-minute division bell on debatable motion. Deferring division upon request of a Whip.

(5)(*a*)(i) Except as provided in sections (3) and (6) of this Standing Order, when the Speaker has put the question on a debatable motion and a recorded division has been demanded on the question, the bells to call in the Members are sounded for not more than thirty minutes.

(ii) During the sounding of the bells, either the Chief Government Whip or the Chief Opposition Whip may ask the Speaker to defer the division. The Speaker then defers it to an appointed time, which must be no later than the ordinary hour of daily adjournment on the next sitting day that is not a Friday. At that time, the bells sound for not more than fifteen minutes. Exceptions to this method of deferring recorded divisions are found in paragraph (*b*) of this section, in section (6) of this Standing Order and in Standing Order 126(2).

(iii) In the case of a votable opposition motion proposed by a Member of a party other than the Official Opposition, the Whip of that party also may ask the Speaker to defer the division.

Deferring division on an allotted day.

(*b*) When the Speaker has put the question on a votable opposition motion on an allotted day and a recorded division has been demanded on the question, a deferral of the division may be requested under the terms of paragraph (*a*) of this section, except on the last allotted day of a supply period.

House continues
with business.

(*c*) A recorded division can be deferred, under the terms of paragraph (*a*) of this section or section (6) of this Standing Order, only once. When a recorded division has been deferred, the House continues with the business before it, as set out in Standing Order 30(6).

Business to be
concluded after
deferred division is
taken.

(*d*) If the Speaker has interrupted debate on any item of business that an Order of the House provides must be disposed of in a particular sitting, and one of the divisions involved has been deferred, no further debate can take place on the item once the deferred division has been taken, but everything necessary to dispose of the item must then be done immediately.

Division on
debatable motion
demanded on a
Friday.
Division deferred on
a Thursday.
Exception: division
on the last allotted
day of a supply
period.

(6)(*a*) If, on a Friday, a division is demanded on any debatable motion, the division is deferred until the ordinary hour of daily adjournment on the next sitting day. A division deferred on Thursday is not held on Friday, but is instead deferred to the next sitting day, at the ordinary hour of daily adjournment. The bells for all such deferred divisions sound for not more than fifteen minutes. An exception to this rule is the division on a votable opposition motion on the last allotted day of a supply period, which cannot be deferred, except as provided in Standing Order 81(18)(*b*). Except as provided in section (7) of this Standing Order, in case of conflict this section will prevail over any other provision of the Standing Orders.

Recorded division on
report stage to be
deferred on a Friday.

(*b*) A recorded division on a non-debatable motion to concur in a bill at the report stage under Standing Order 76(9), 76.1(9) or 76.1(12) may be deferred.

Deferring division
upon the agreement
of Whips.

(7) Notwithstanding any other provision of the Standing Orders, at any time after a recorded division has been demanded, the Chief Government Whip, with the agreement of the Whips of all other recognized parties (and, in the case of an item of Private Members' Business, also with the agreement of the Member sponsoring that item), may ask the Speaker to defer or further defer, as the case may be, the division to an appointed date and time. The Speaker then defers the division to that time. The bells for all such divisions sound for not more than fifteen minutes.

Division bells
sounded only once.

(8) If, pursuant to any Standing or Special Order of the House, two or more recorded divisions are to be held successively without intervening debate, the division bells shall be sounded to call in the Members only once.

Reading the question
where not printed.

46. When the question under discussion does not appear on the *Order Paper* or has not been printed and distributed, any Member may require it to be read at any time of the debate, but not so as to interrupt a Member while speaking.

When points of
order to be raised.

47. Where points of order do not arise during debate or during the times provided for statements pursuant to Standing Order 31 and oral questions pursuant to Standing Order 30(5), such matters may be presented to the Speaker immediately following the ordinary daily routine of business. Points of order which arise during the said periods may be presented to the Speaker immediately after the said period provided pursuant to Standing Order 30(5).

Question of
privilege.

48. (1) Whenever any matter of privilege arises, it shall be taken into consideration immediately.

Notice required.

(2) Unless notice of motion has been given under Standing Orders 54 or 86(2), any Member proposing to raise a question of privilege, other than one arising out of proceedings

in the Chamber during the course of a sitting, shall give to the Speaker a written statement of the question at least one hour prior to raising the question in the House.

Prorogation not to nullify order or address for returns.

49. A prorogation of the House shall not have the effect of nullifying an Order or Address of the House for returns or papers, but all papers and returns ordered at one session of the House, if not complied with during the session, shall be brought down during the following session, without renewal of the Order.

CHAPTER VII

SPECIAL DEBATES

Address in Reply to the Speech from the Throne

Six days of debate.

50. (1) The proceedings on the Order of the Day for resuming debate on the motion for an Address in Reply to the Speech from the Throne and on any amendments proposed thereto shall not exceed six sitting days.

Time limit and comments on speeches.

(2) No Member, except the Prime Minister and the Leader of the Opposition, shall speak for more than twenty minutes at a time in the said debate. Following the speech of each Member a period not exceeding ten minutes shall be made available, if required, to allow Members to ask questions and comment briefly on matters relevant to the speech and to allow responses thereto.

Appointed days to be announced. Precedence.

(3) Any day or days to be appointed for the consideration of the said Order shall be announced from time to time by a Minister of the Crown and on any such day or days this Order shall have precedence of all other business except the ordinary daily routine of business.

Private Members' Business suspended.

(4) On any day designated for resuming the Address debate, the consideration of Private Members' Business, if provided for in such sitting, shall be suspended.

Sub-amendment disposed of on second day.

(5) On the second of the said days, if a sub-amendment be under consideration at fifteen minutes before the ordinary hour of daily adjournment, the Speaker shall interrupt the proceedings and forthwith put the question on the said sub-amendment.

Amendments disposed of on fourth day.

(6) On the fourth of the said days, if any amendment be under consideration at thirty minutes before the ordinary hour of daily adjournment, the Speaker shall interrupt the proceedings and forthwith put the question on any amendment or amendments then before the House.

No amendment on or after fifth day.

(7) The motion for an Address in Reply shall not be subject to amendment on or after the fifth day of the said debate.

Main motion disposed of on sixth day.

(8) On the sixth of the said days, at fifteen minutes before the ordinary hour of daily adjournment, unless the said debate be previously concluded, the Speaker shall interrupt the proceedings and forthwith put every question necessary to dispose of the main motion.

Standing Orders and Procedure

Motion to consider
the Standing Orders
and procedure.

51. (1) Between the sixtieth and ninetieth sitting days of the first session of a Parliament on a day designated by a Minister of the Crown or on the ninetieth sitting day if no day has been designated, an Order of the Day for the consideration of a motion "That this House takes note of the Standing Orders and procedure of the House and its Committees" shall be deemed to be proposed and have precedence over all other business.

Expiration of
proceedings.

(2) Proceedings on the motion shall expire when debate thereon has been concluded or at the ordinary hour of daily adjournment on that day, as the case may be.

Time limit on
speeches.

(3) No Member shall speak more than once or longer than ten minutes.

Emergency Debates

Leave must be
requested.

52. (1) Leave to make a motion for the adjournment of the House for the purpose of discussing a specific and important matter requiring urgent consideration must be asked for after the ordinary daily routine of business as set out in sections (3) and (4) of Standing Order 30 is concluded.

Written statement
to Speaker.

(2) A Member wishing to move, "That this House do now adjourn", under the provisions of this Standing Order shall give to the Speaker, at least one hour prior to raising it in the House, a written statement of the matter proposed to be discussed.

Making statement.

(3) When requesting leave to propose such a motion, the Member shall rise in his or her place and present without argument the statement referred to in section (2) of this Standing Order.

Speaker's
prerogative.

(4) The Speaker shall decide, without any debate, whether or not the matter is proper to be discussed.

Speaker to take into
account.

(5) In determining whether a matter should have urgent consideration, the Speaker shall have regard to the extent to which it concerns the administrative responsibilities of the government or could come within the scope of ministerial action and the Speaker also shall have regard to the probability of the matter being brought before the House within reasonable time by other means.

Conditions.

(6) The right to move the adjournment of the House for the above purposes is subject to the following conditions:

(*a*) the matter proposed for discussion must relate to a genuine emergency, calling for immediate and urgent consideration;

(*b*) not more than one matter can be discussed on the same motion;

(c) not more than one such motion can be made at the same sitting;

(*d*) the motion must not revive discussion on a matter which has been discussed in the same session pursuant to the provisions of this Standing Order;

(e) the motion must not raise a question of privilege; and

(*f*) the discussion under the motion must not raise any question which, according to the Standing Orders of the House, can only be debated on a distinct motion under notice.

Speaker not bound to give reasons.

(7) In stating whether or not the Speaker is satisfied that the matter is proper to be discussed, the Speaker is not bound to give reasons for the decision.

Reserving decision.

(8) If the Speaker so desires, he or she may defer the decision upon whether the matter is proper to be discussed until later in the sitting, when the proceedings of the House may be interrupted for the purpose of announcing his or her decision.

Motion to stand over.

(9) If the Speaker is satisfied that the matter is proper to be discussed, the motion shall stand over until 8:00 p.m. on that day, provided that the Speaker, at his or her discretion, may direct that the motion shall be set down for consideration on the following sitting day at an hour specified by the Speaker.

Evening interruption.

(10) When a request to make such a motion has been made on any day, except Friday, and the Speaker directs that it be considered the same day, the House shall rise at the ordinary hour of daily adjournment and resume at 8:00 p.m.

When moved on Friday.

(11) When a request to make such a motion has been made on any Friday, and the Speaker directs that it be considered the same day, it shall be considered forthwith.

Time limit on debate.

(12) The proceedings on any motion being considered, pursuant to sections (9) or (11) of this Standing Order, may continue beyond the ordinary hour of daily adjournment but, when debate thereon is concluded prior to that hour in any sitting, it shall be deemed withdrawn. Subject to any motion adopted pursuant to Standing Order 26(2), at 12:00 midnight on any sitting day except Friday, and at 4:00 p.m. on Friday, the Speaker shall declare the motion carried and forthwith adjourn the House until the next sitting day. In any other case, the Speaker, when satisfied that the debate has been concluded, shall declare the motion carried and forthwith adjourn the House until the next sitting day.

Time limit on speeches.

(13) No Member shall speak longer than twenty minutes during debate on any such motion.

Debate not to be interrupted by Private Members' Business.

(14) Debate on any such motion shall not be interrupted by "Private Members' Business".

Debate to take precedence. Exception.

(15) The provisions of this Standing Order shall not be suspended by the operation of any other Standing Order relating to the hours of sitting or in respect of the consideration of any other business; provided that, in cases of conflict, the Speaker shall determine when such other business shall be considered or disposed of and the Speaker shall make any consequential interpretation of any Standing Order that may be necessary in relation thereto.

Suspension of Certain Standing Orders — Matter of Urgent Nature

Motion by Minister.

53. (1) In relation to any matter that the government considers to be of an urgent nature, a Minister of the Crown may, at any time when the Speaker is in the Chair, propose a motion to suspend any Standing or other Order of this House relating to the need for notice and to the hours and days of sitting.

(2) After the Minister has stated reasons for the urgency of such a motion, the Speaker shall propose the question to the House.

(3) Proceedings on any such motion shall be subject to the following conditions:

(*a*) the Speaker may permit debate thereon for a period not exceeding one hour;

(*b*) the motion shall not be subject to amendment except by a Minister of the Crown;

(*c*) no Member may speak more than once nor longer than ten minutes; and

(*d*) proceedings on any such motion shall not be interrupted or adjourned by any other proceeding or by the operation of any other Order of this House.

(4) When the Speaker puts the question on any such motion, he or she shall ask those who object to rise in their places. If ten or more Members then rise, the motion shall be deemed to have been withdrawn; otherwise, the motion shall have been adopted.

(5) The operation of any Order made under the provisions of this Standing Order shall not extend to any proceeding not therein specified.

CHAPTER VIII

MOTIONS

54. (1) Forty-eight hours' notice shall be given of a motion for leave to present a bill, resolution or address, for the appointment of any committee, for placing a question on the *Order Paper* or for the consideration of any notice of motion made pursuant to Standing Order 123(4); but this rule shall not apply to bills after their introduction, or to private bills, or to the times of meeting or adjournment of the House. Such notice shall be laid on the Table, or filed with the Clerk, before 6:00 p.m. (2:00 p.m. on a Friday) and be printed in the *Notice Paper* of that day, except as provided in section (2) of this Standing Order. Any notice filed with the Clerk pursuant to this Standing Order shall thereupon be deemed to have been laid on the Table in that sitting.

(2) On any sitting day on which the House adjourns pursuant to Standing Order 28(2), the time specified pursuant to section (1) of this Standing Order for the filing with the Clerk of any notice shall not apply. Any such notice may be filed with the Clerk no later than 6.00 p.m. on the Thursday before the next sitting of the House and shall be printed in the *Notice Paper* to be published for that sitting.

55. (1) In the period prior to the first session of a Parliament, during a prorogation or when the House stands adjourned, and the government has represented to the Speaker that any government measure or measures should have immediate consideration by the House, the Speaker shall cause a notice of any such measure or measures to be published on a special *Order Paper* and the same shall be circulated prior to the opening or the resumption of such session. The publication and circulation of such notice shall meet the requirements of Standing Order 54.

When Speaker unable to act.

(2) In the event of the Speaker being unable to act owing to illness or other cause, the Deputy Speaker shall act in his or her stead for the purposes of this order. In the unavoidable absence of the Speaker and the Deputy Speaker or when the Office of Speaker is vacant, the Clerk of the House shall have the authority to act for the purposes of this Standing Order.

Government notices of motions.

56. (1) After notice pursuant to Standing Order 54, a government notice of motion shall be put on the *Order Paper* as an order of the day under Government Orders.

Motion to go into Committee of the Whole decided without debate.

(2) Proposed motions under Government Orders for the House to go into a Committee of the Whole at the next sitting of the House when put from the Chair shall be decided without debate or amendment.

When unanimous consent denied, routine motion by Minister.

56.1 (1)(*a*) In relation to any routine motion for the presentation of which unanimous consent is required and has been denied, a Minister of the Crown may request during Routine Proceedings that the Speaker propose the said question to the House.

(*b*) For the purposes of this Standing Order, "routine motion" shall be understood to mean any motion, made upon Routine Proceedings, which may be required for the observance of the proprieties of the House, the maintenance of its authority, the management of its business, the arrangement of its proceedings, the establishing of the powers of its committees, the correctness of its records or the fixing of its sitting days or the times of its meeting or adjournment.

Question put forthwith.

(2) The question on any such motion shall be put forthwith, without debate or amendment.

Objection by twenty-five or more Members.

(3) When the Speaker puts the question on such a motion, he or she shall ask those who object to rise in their places. If twenty-five or more Members then rise, the motion shall be deemed to have been withdrawn; otherwise, the motion shall have been adopted.

Closure. Notice required. Time limit on speeches. All questions put at 11 p.m.

57. Immediately before the Order of the Day for resuming an adjourned debate is called, or if the House be in Committee of the Whole, any Minister of the Crown who, standing in his or her place, shall have given notice at a previous sitting of his or her intention so to do, may move that the debate shall not be further adjourned, or that the further consideration of any resolution or resolutions, clause or clauses, section or sections, preamble or preambles, title or titles, shall be the first business of the Committee, and shall not further be postponed; and in either case such question shall be decided without debate or amendment; and if the same shall be resolved in the affirmative, no Member shall thereafter speak more than once, or longer than twenty minutes in any such adjourned debate; or, if in Committee, on any such resolution, clause, section, preamble or title; and if such adjourned debate or postponed consideration shall not have been resumed or concluded before 11:00 p.m., no Member shall rise to speak after that hour, but all such questions as must be decided in order to conclude such adjourned debate or postponed consideration, shall be decided forthwith.

Privileged motions.

58. When a question is under debate, no motion is received unless to amend it; to postpone it to a day certain; for the previous question; for reading the Orders of the Day; for proceeding to another order; to adjourn the debate; to continue or extend a sitting of the House; or for the adjournment of the House.

Motion to read
Orders of the Day.

59. A motion for reading the Orders of the Day shall have preference to any motion before the House.

Motion to adjourn.

60. A motion to adjourn, unless otherwise prohibited in these Standing Orders, shall always be in order, but no second motion to the same effect shall be made until some intermediate proceeding has taken place.

The previous
question.

61. (1) The previous question, until it is decided, shall preclude all amendment of the main question, and shall be in the following words, "That this question be now put".

Original question to
be put.

(2) If the previous question be resolved in the affirmative, the original question is to be put forthwith without any amendment or debate.

Motion that Member
"be now heard".

62. When two or more Members rise to speak, the Speaker calls upon the Member who first rose in his or her place; but a motion may be made that any Member who has risen "be now heard", or "do now speak", which motion shall be forthwith put without debate.

Motion to refer a
question to
committee.

63. A motion to refer a bill, resolution or any question to any standing, special or legis-lative committee or to a Committee of the Whole, shall preclude all amendment of the main question.

Unanimous consent
required to
withdraw motion.

64. A Member who has made a motion may withdraw the same only by the unanimous consent of the House.

Motions to be in
writing and
seconded. Read in
both languages.

65. All motions shall be in writing, and seconded, before being debated or put from the Chair. When a motion is seconded, it shall be read in English and in French by the Speaker, if he or she be familiar with both languages; if not, the Speaker shall read the motion in one language and direct the Clerk of the Table to read it in the other, before debate.

When transferred to
Government
Orders.

66. When a debate on any motion made after the start of the sitting (after 2:00 p.m. on Mondays and after 11:00 a.m. on Fridays) and prior to the reading of an Order of the Day is adjourned or interrupted, the order for resumption of the debate shall be trans-ferred to and considered under Government Orders.

Debatable motions.

67. (1) The following motions are debatable:

Every motion:

(*a*) standing on the order of proceedings for the day, except as otherwise provided in these Standing Orders;

(*b*) for the concurrence in a report of a standing or special committee;

(*c*) for the previous question;

(*d*) for the second reading and reference of a bill to a standing, special or legislative committee or to a Committee of the Whole House;

(*e*) for the consideration of any amendment to be proposed at the report stage of any bill reported from any standing, special or legislative committee;

(*f*) for the third reading and passage of a bill;

(*g*) for the consideration of Senate amendments to House of Commons bills;

(h) for a conference with the Senate;

(i) for the adjournment of the House when made for the purpose of discussing a specific and important matter requiring urgent consideration;

(j) for the consideration of a Ways and Means Order (Budget);

(k) for the consideration of any motion under the order for the consideration of the business of supply;

(l) for the adoption in Committee of the Whole of the motion, clause, section, preamble or title under consideration;

(m) for the appointment of a committee;

(n) for reference to a committee of any report or return laid on the Table of the House;

(o) for the suspension of any Standing Order unless otherwise provided; and

(p) such other motion, made upon Routine Proceedings, as may be required for the observance of the proprieties of the House, the maintenance of its authority, the appointment or conduct of its officers, the management of its business, the arrangement of its proceedings, the correctness of its records, the fixing of its sitting days or the times of its meeting or adjournment.

Motions not debatable.

(2) All other motions, unless otherwise provided in these Standing Orders, shall be decided without debate or amendment.

CHAPTER IX

PUBLIC BILLS

Introduction and Readings

Motion for introduction of bills.

68. (1) Every bill is introduced upon motion for leave, specifying the title of the bill; or upon motion to appoint a committee to prepare and bring it in.

Brief explanation permitted.

(2) A motion for leave to introduce a bill shall be deemed carried, without debate, amendment or question put, provided that any Member moving for such leave may be permitted to give a succinct explanation of the provisions of the said bill.

Imperfect or blank bills.

(3) No bill may be introduced either in blank or in an imperfect shape.

Motion by a Minister to prepare and bring in a bill.

(4)(a) A motion by a Minister of the Crown to appoint or instruct a standing, special or legislative committee to prepare and bring in a bill, pursuant to section (1) of this Standing Order, shall be considered under Government Orders. During debate on any such motion no Member shall be permitted to speak more than once or for more than ten minutes. After not more than ninety minutes debate on any such motion, the Speaker shall interrupt debate and put all questions necessary to dispose of the motion without further debate or amendment. A motion by a Minister of the Crown to concur in the report of a committee pursuant to this section or to section (4)(*b*) of this Standing Order shall also be taken up under Government Orders and shall, for the purposes of Standing Order 78, be considered to be a stage of a public bill.

Motion by a Member to prepare and bring in a bill.

(*b*) A motion by a Private Member to appoint or instruct a standing, special or legislative committee to prepare and bring in a bill, pursuant to section (1) of this Standing Order, shall be considered as a motion under Private Members' Business and shall be subject to the procedures in that regard set down in Standing Orders 86 to 99, inclusive. A motion by a Member other than a Minister of the Crown to concur in the report of a committee pursuant to this section or to section (4)(*a*) of this Standing Order shall also be taken up as a motion under Private Members' Business pursuant to the aforementioned Standing Orders in that regard.

Committee's report.

(5) A committee appointed or instructed to prepare and bring in a bill shall, in its report, recommend the principles, scope and general provisions of the said bill and may, if it deems it appropriate, but not necessarily, include recommendations regarding legislative wording.

Order to bring in a bill.

(6) The adoption of a motion to concur in a report made pursuant to section (5) of this Standing Order shall be an order to bring in a bill based thereon.

Second reading stage of the bill. Minister's motion.

(7)(*a*) When a Minister of the Crown, in proposing a motion for first reading of a bill, has stated that the bill is in response to an order made pursuant to section (6) of this Standing Order, notwithstanding any Standing Order, the bill shall not be set down for consideration at the second reading stage before the third sitting day after having been read a first time. The second reading and any subsequent stages of such a bill shall be considered under Government Orders. When a motion for second reading of such a bill is proposed, notwithstanding any Standing Order, the Speaker shall immediately put all questions necessary to dispose of the second reading stage of the bill without debate or amendment.

Second reading stage of the Bill. Member's motion.

(*b*) When a Member other than a Minister of the Crown, in proposing a motion for first reading of a bill, has stated that the bill is in response to an order made pursuant to section (6) of this Standing Order, and if the bill is subsequently selected pursuant to Standing Order 92, when a motion for second reading of such a bill has been proposed, notwithstanding any Standing Order, the Speaker shall immediately put all questions necessary to dispose of the second reading stage of the bill without debate or amendment.

Bill considered under Government Orders.

(8) A Minister of the Crown may propose a motion for first reading of a bill based on an order made pursuant to section (6) of this Standing Order, whether that order was the result of a motion by a Minister or of a private Member, and notwithstanding the provisions of section (4)(*b*) of this Standing Order, any such bill shall thereafter be considered under Government Orders.

Motion for first reading and printing.

69. (1) When any bill is presented by a Member, in pursuance of an Order of the House, the question "That this bill be read a first time and be printed" shall be deemed carried, without debate, amendment or question put.

First reading of Senate public bills.

(2) When any bill is brought from the Senate, the question "That this bill be read a first time" shall be deemed carried, without debate, amendment or question put.

Printed in English and French before second reading.

70. All bills shall be printed before the second reading in the English and French languages.

Three separate readings. Urgent cases.

71. Every bill shall receive three several readings, on different days, previously to being passed. On urgent or extraordinary occasions, a bill may be read twice or thrice, or advanced two or more stages in one day.

Clerk certifies readings.

72. When a bill is read in the House, the Clerk shall certify upon it the readings and the time thereof. After it has passed, the Clerk shall certify the same, with the date, at the foot of the bill.

Motion to refer a government bill to a committee before second reading.

73. (1) Immediately after the reading of the Order of the Day for the second reading of any government bill, a Minister of the Crown may, after notifying representatives of the opposition parties, propose a motion that the said bill be forthwith referred to a standing, special or legislative committee. The Speaker shall immediately propose the question to the House and proceedings thereon shall be subject to the following conditions:

(*a*) the Speaker shall recognize for debate a Member from the party forming the Government, followed by a Member from the party forming the Official Opposition, followed by a Member from each officially recognized party in the House, in order of the number of Members in that party, provided that, if no Member from the party whose turn has been reached rises, a Member of the next party in the rotation or a Member who is not a Member of an officially recognized party may be recognized;

(*b*) the motion shall not be subject to any amendment;

(*c*) no Member may speak more than once nor longer than ten minutes.

(*d*) after not more than 180 minutes of debate, the Speaker shall interrupt the debate and the question shall be put and decided without further debate.

Referral before amendment.

(2) Every public bill, except for bills referred to a committee before being read a second time pursuant to section (1) of this Standing Order, shall be read twice and referred to a committee before any amendment may be made thereto.

Referral to a committee.

(3) Unless otherwise ordered and except for bills referred to a committee before being read a second time pursuant to section (1) of this Standing Order, in giving a bill second reading, the same shall be referred to a standing, special or legislative committee.

Supply bills.

(4) Any bill based on a Supply motion shall, after second reading, stand referred to a Committee of the Whole.

Second reading of borrowing authority bills: two days' consideration.

(5) When an Order of the Day is read for the consideration of any bill respecting borrowing authority, a maximum of two sitting days shall be set aside for the consideration of the bill at second reading. On the second of the said days, at fifteen minutes before the expiry of the time provided for Government Orders, the Speaker shall interrupt the proceedings then in progress and shall put forthwith and successively, without further debate or amendment, every question necessary for the passage of the second reading stage of the bill.

Time limit and comments on speeches during second or third reading of government bill.

74. (1) Unless otherwise provided by Standing Order or Special Order, when second reading or third reading of a government bill is being considered, no Member except the Prime Minister and the Leader of the Opposition shall speak for more than:

(*a*) forty minutes if that Member is the first, second or third speaker;

(*b*) twenty minutes following the first three speakers, if that Member begins to speak within the next five hours of consideration; and following the speech of each Member a period not exceeding ten minutes shall be made available, if required, to allow Members to ask questions and comment briefly on matters relevant to the speech and to allow responses thereto; and

(*c*) ten minutes if a Member speaks thereafter.

Period of debate divided in two.

(2) The Whip of a party may indicate to the Speaker at any time during a debate governed by this Standing Order that one or more of the periods of debate limited pursuant to paragraphs (1)(*b*) and (*c*) of this Standing Order, and allotted to Members of his or her party, are to be divided in two.

Consideration by Committee

Proceedings on bills in any committee.

75. (1) In proceedings in any committee of the House upon bills, the preamble is first postponed, and if the first clause contains only a short title it is also postponed; then every other clause is considered by the committee in its proper order; the first clause (if it contains only a short title), the preamble and the title are to be last considered.

Proceedings reported.

(2) All amendments made in any committee shall be reported to the House. Every bill reported from any committee, whether amended or not, shall be received by the House on report thereof.

Report Stage at Second Reading

Not before third sitting day.

76. (1) The report stage of any bill reported by any standing, special or legislative committee before the bill has been read a second time shall not be taken into consideration prior to the third sitting day following the presentation of the said report, unless otherwise ordered by the House.

Notice to amend.

(2) If, not later than the second sitting day prior to the consideration of the report stage of a bill that has not yet been read a second time, written notice is given of any motion to amend, delete, insert or restore any clause in a bill, it shall be printed on the *Notice Paper*. When the same amendment is put on notice by more than one Member, that notice shall be printed once, under the name of each Member who has submitted it. If the Speaker decides that an amendment is out of order, it shall be returned to the Member without having appeared on the *Notice Paper*.

Recommendation of Governor General.

(3) When a recommendation of the Governor General is required in relation to any amendment of which notice has been given pursuant to section (2) of this Standing Order, notice shall be given of the said Recommendation no later than the sitting day before the day on which the report stage is to commence and such notice shall be printed on the *Notice Paper* along with the amendment to which it pertains.

Amendment as to form only.

(4) An amendment, in relation to form only in a government bill, may be proposed by a Minister of the Crown without notice, but debate thereon may not be extended to the provisions of the clause or clauses to be amended.

NOTE: The purpose of this section is to facilitate the incorporation into a bill of amendments of a strictly consequential nature flowing from the acceptance of other amendments. No waiver of notice would be permitted in relation to any amendment which would change the intent of the bill, no matter how slightly, beyond the effect of the initial amendment.

Speaker's power to select amendments.

(5) The Speaker shall have the power to select or combine amendments or clauses to be proposed at the report stage and may, if he or she thinks fit, call upon any Member who has given notice of an amendment to give such explanation of the subject of the amendment as may enable the Speaker to form a judgement upon it. If an amendment has been selected that has been submitted by more than one Member, the Speaker, after consultation, shall designate which Member shall propose it.

NOTE: The Speaker will not normally select for consideration any motion previously ruled out of order in committee, unless the reason for its being ruled out of order was that it required a recommendation of the Governor General, in which case the amendment may be selected only if such Recommendation has been placed on notice pursuant to this Standing Order. The Speaker will normally only select motions that were not or could not be presented in committee. A motion, previously defeated in committee, will only be selected if the Speaker judges it to be of such exceptional significance as to warrant a further consideration at the report stage. The Speaker will not normally select for separate debate a repetitive series of motions which are interrelated and, in making the selection, shall consider whether individual Members will be able to express their concerns during the debate on another motion.

For greater certainty, the purpose of this Standing Order is, primarily, to provide Members who were not members of the committee with an opportunity to have the House consider specific amendments they wish to propose. It is not meant to be a reconsideration of the committee stage.

Debate on the amendments.

(6) When the Order of the Day for the consideration of a report stage is called, any amendment proposed pursuant to this Standing Order shall be open to debate and amendment.

Limits on speeches.

(7) When debate is permitted, no Member shall speak more than once or longer than ten minutes during proceedings on any amendment at that stage.

Division deferred.

(8) When a recorded division has been demanded on any amendment proposed during the report stage of a bill, the Speaker may defer the calling in of the Members for the purpose of recording the "yeas" and "nays" until more or all subsequent amendments to the bill have been considered. A recorded division or divisions may be so deferred from sitting to sitting.

NOTE: In cases when there are an unusually great number of amendments for consideration at the report stage, the Speaker may, after consultation with the representatives of the parties, direct that deferred divisions be held before all amendments have been taken into consideration.

Motion when report stage concluded.

(9) When proceedings at the report stage on any bill that has not been read a second time have been concluded, a motion "That the bill, as amended, be concurred in and be read a second time" or "That the bill be concurred in and read a second time" shall be put and forthwith disposed of, without amendment or debate.

Third reading.

(10) The report stage of a bill pursuant to this Standing Order shall be deemed to be an integral part of the second reading stage of the bill. When a bill has been concurred in and read a second time in accordance with the procedures set forth in this Standing Order, it shall be set down for a third reading and passage at the next sitting of the House.

Report Stage After Second Reading

Not before second sitting day.

76.1. (1) The report stage of any bill reported by any standing, special or legislative committee after the bill has been read a second time shall not be taken into consideration prior to the second sitting day following the presentation of the said report, unless otherwise ordered by the House.

Notice to amend.

(2) If, not later than the sitting day prior to the consideration of the report stage of a bill that has been read a second time, written notice is given of any motion to amend, delete, insert or restore any clause in a bill, it shall be printed on the *Notice Paper*. When the same amendment is put on notice by more than one Member, that notice shall be printed once, under the name of each Member who has submitted it. If the Speaker decides that an amendment is out of order, it shall be returned to the Member without having appeared on the *Notice Paper*.

Recommendation of Governor General.

(3) When a recommendation of the Governor General is required in relation to any amendment to be proposed at the report stage of a bill that has been read a second time, at least twenty-four hours' written notice shall be given of the said Recommendation and proposed amendment.

Amendment as to form only.

(4) An amendment, in relation to form only in a government bill, may be proposed by a Minister of the Crown without notice, but debate thereon may not be extended to the provisions of the clause or clauses to be amended.

NOTE: The purpose of the section is to facilitate the incorporation into a bill of amendments of a strictly consequential nature flowing from the acceptance of other amendments. No waiver of notice would be permitted in relation to any amendment which would change the intent of the bill, no matter how slightly, beyond the effect of the initial amendment.

Speaker's power to select amendments.

(5) The Speaker shall have power to select or combine amendments or clauses to be proposed at the report stage and may, if he or she thinks fit, call upon any Member who has given notice of an amendment to give such explanation of the subject of the amendment as may enable the Speaker to form a judgement upon it. If an amendment has been selected that has been submitted by more than one Member, the Speaker, after consultation, shall designate which Member shall propose it.

NOTE: The Speaker will not normally select for consideration by the House any motion previously ruled out of order in committee and will normally only select motions which were not or could not be presented in committee. A motion, previously defeated in committee, will only be selected if the Speaker judges it to be of such exceptional significance as to warrant a further consideration at the report stage. The Speaker will not normally select for separate debate a repetitive series of motions which are interrelated and, in making the selection, shall consider whether individual Members will be able to express their concerns during the debate on another motion.

For greater certainty, the purpose of this Standing Order is, primarily, to provide Members who were not members of the committee, with an opportunity to have the House consider specific amendments they wish to propose. It is not meant to be a reconsideration of the committee stage of a bill.

Debate on the amendments.

(6) When the Order of the Day for the consideration of a report stage is called, any amendment of which notice has been given in accordance with this Standing Order shall be open to debate and amendment.

Limits on speeches.

(7) When debate is permitted, no Member shall speak more than once or longer than ten minutes during proceedings on any amendment at that stage.

Division deferred.

(8) When a recorded division has been demanded on any amendment proposed during the report stage of a bill, the Speaker may defer the calling in of the Members for the purpose of recording the "yeas" and "nays" until more or all subsequent amendments to the bill have been considered. A recorded division or divisions may be so deferred from sitting to sitting.

NOTE: In cases when there are an unusually great number of amendments for consideration at the report stage, the Speaker may, after consultation with the representatives of the parties, direct that deferred divisions be held before all amendments have been taken into consideration.

Motion when report stage concluded.

(9) When proceedings at the report stage on any bill that has been read a second time have been concluded, a motion "That the bill, as amended, be concurred in" or "That the bill be concurred in" shall be put and forthwith disposed of, without amendment or debate.

Third reading after debate or amendment.

(10) When a bill that has been read a second time has been amended or debate has taken place thereon at the report stage, the same shall be set down for a third reading and passage at the next sitting of the House.

Third reading when no amendment or after Committee of the Whole.

(11) When a bill that has been read a second time has been reported from a standing, special or legislative committee, and no amendment has been proposed thereto at the report stage, and in the case of a bill reported from a Committee of the Whole, with or without amendment, a motion, "That the bill be now read a third time and passed", may be made in the same sitting.

Report stage of bill from a Committee of the Whole.

(12) The consideration of the report stage of a bill from a Committee of the Whole shall be received and forthwith disposed of, without amendment or debate.

Senate Amendments

Written notice of motion.

77. (1) Twenty-four hours' written notice shall be given by a Member proposing any motion respecting Senate amendments to a bill.

When Senate and House disagree.

(2) In cases in which the Senate disagrees to any amendments made by the House of Commons, or insists upon any amendments to which the House has disagreed, the House is willing to receive the reasons of the Senate for their disagreeing or insisting (as the case may be) by message, without a conference, unless at any time the Senate should desire to communicate the same at a conference.

Conference.

(3) Any conference between the two Houses may be a free conference.

Reasons for
conference.

(4) When the House requests a conference with the Senate, the reasons to be given by this House at the same shall be prepared and agreed to by the House before a message be sent therewith.

Time Allocation

Agreement to allot
time.

78. (1) When a Minister of the Crown, from his or her place in the House, states that there is agreement among the representatives of all parties to allot a specified number of days or hours to the proceedings at one or more stages of any public bill, the Minister may propose a motion, without notice, setting forth the terms of such agreed allocation; and every such motion shall be decided forthwith, without debate or amendment.

Qualified agreement
to allot time.

(2)(*a*) When a Minister of the Crown, from his or her place in the House, states that a majority of the representatives of the several parties have come to an agreement in respect of a proposed allotment of days or hours for the proceedings at any stage of the passing of a public bill, the Minister may propose a motion, without notice, during proceedings under Government Orders, setting forth the terms of the said proposed allocation; provided that for the purposes of this section of this Standing Order an allocation may be proposed in one motion to cover the proceedings at both the report and the third reading stages of a bill if that motion is consistent with the provisions of Standing Order 76.1(10). The motion shall not be subject to debate or amendment, and the Speaker shall put the question on the said motion forthwith. Any proceeding interrupted pursuant to this section of this Standing Order shall be deemed adjourned.

(*b*) If a motion pursuant to this section regarding any bill is moved and carried at the beginning of Government Orders on any day and if the order for the said bill is then called and debated for the remainder of the sitting day, the length of that debate shall be deemed to be one sitting day for the purposes of paragraph (*a*) of this section.

Procedure in other
cases to allot time.

(3)(*a*) A Minister of the Crown who from his or her place in the House, at a previous sitting, has stated that an agreement could not be reached under the provisions of sections (1) or (2) of this Standing Order in respect of proceedings at the stage at which a public bill was then under consideration either in the House or in any committee, and has given notice of his or her intention so to do, may propose a motion during proceedings under Government Orders, for the purpose of allotting a specified number of days or hours for the consideration and disposal of proceedings at that stage; provided that the time allotted for any stage is not to be less than one sitting day and provided that for the purposes of this paragraph an allocation may be proposed in one motion to cover the proceedings at both the report and the third reading stages on a bill if that motion is consistent with the provisions of Standing Order 76.1(10). The motion shall not be subject to debate or amendment, and the Speaker shall put the question on the said motion forthwith. Any proceedings interrupted pursuant to this section of this Standing Order shall be deemed adjourned.

(*b*) If a motion pursuant to this section regarding any bill is moved and carried at the beginning of Government Orders on any day and if the order for the said bill is then called and debated for the remainder of the sitting day, the length of that debate shall be deemed to be one sitting day for the purposes of paragraph (*a*) of this section.

CHAPTER X

FINANCIAL PROCEDURES

Recommendation

Recommendation of Governor General.

79. (1) This House shall not adopt or pass any vote, resolution, address or bill for the appropriation of any part of the public revenue, or of any tax or impost, to any purpose that has not been first recommended to the House by a message from the Governor General in the session in which such vote, resolution, address or bill is proposed.

Recommendation to be printed.

(2) The message and recommendation of the Governor General in relation to any bill for the appropriation of any part of the public revenue or of any tax or impost shall be printed on the *Notice Paper,* printed in or annexed to the bill and recorded in the *Journals.*

Message on Estimates.

(3) When estimates are brought in, the message from the Governor General shall be presented to and read by the Speaker in the House.

Right of the House

Commons alone grant aids and supplies.

80. (1) All aids and supplies granted to the Sovereign by the Parliament of Canada are the sole gift of the House of Commons, and all bills for granting such aids and supplies ought to begin with the House, as it is the undoubted right of the House to direct, limit, and appoint in all such bills, the ends, purposes, considerations, conditions, limitations and qualifications of such grants, which are not alterable by the Senate.

Pecuniary penalties in Senate bills.

(2) In order to expedite the business of Parliament, the House will not insist on the privilege claimed and exercised by them of laying aside bills sent from the Senate because they impose pecuniary penalties nor of laying aside amendments made by the Senate because they introduce into or alter pecuniary penalties in bills sent to them by this House; provided that all such penalties thereby imposed are only to punish or prevent crimes and offences, and do not tend to lay a burden on the subject, either as aid or supply to the Sovereign, or for any general or special purposes, by rates, tolls, assessments or otherwise.

Supply

Order for Supply.

81. (1) At the commencement of each session, the House shall designate, by motion, a continuing Order of the Day for the consideration of the business of supply.

Business of supply takes precedence over government business.

(2) On any day or days appointed for the consideration of any business under the provisions of this Standing Order, that order of business shall have precedence over all other government business in such sitting or sittings.

Business of supply defined.

(3) For the purposes of this Order, the business of supply shall consist of motions to concur in interim supply, main estimates and supplementary or final estimates; motions to restore or reinstate any item in the estimates; motions to introduce or pass at all stages any bill or bills based thereon; and opposition motions that under this order may be considered on allotted days.

Main estimates referred to and reported by standing committees.

(4) In every session the main estimates to cover the incoming fiscal year for every department of government shall be referred to standing committees on or before March 1 of the then expiring fiscal year. Each such committee shall consider and shall report, or shall be deemed to have reported, the same back to the House not later than May 31 in the then current fiscal year, provided that:

Extension of consideration by a committee.

(a) not later than the third sitting day prior to May 31, the Leader of the Opposition may give notice during the time specified in Standing Order 54 of a motion to extend consideration of the main estimates of a named department or agency and the said motion shall be deemed adopted when called on "Motions" on the last sitting day prior to May 31;

Report by the committee.

(b) on the sitting day immediately preceding the final allotted day, but in any case not later than ten sitting days following the day on which any motion made pursuant to paragraph (a) of this section is adopted, at not later than the ordinary hour of daily adjournment, the said committee shall report, or shall be deemed to have reported, the main estimates for the said department or agency; and

Reverting to "Presenting Reports from Committees".

(c) if the committee shall make a report, the Chairman or a member of the committee acting for the Chairman may so indicate, on a point of order, prior to the hours indicated in paragraph (b) of this section, and the House shall immediately revert to "Presenting Reports from Committees" for the purpose of receiving the said report.

Supplementary estimates referred to and reported by standing committees.

(5) Supplementary estimates shall be referred to a standing committee or committees immediately they are presented in the House. Each such committee shall consider and shall report, or shall be deemed to have reported, the same back to the House not later than three sitting days before the final sitting or the last allotted day in the current period.

Motion to refer estimates to standing committees.

(6) A motion, to be decided without debate or amendment, may be moved during Routine Proceedings by a Minister of the Crown to refer any item or items in the main estimates or in supplementary estimates to any standing committee or committees and, upon report from any such committees, the same shall lie upon the Table of the House.

Future expenditure plans and priorities.

(7) When main estimates are referred to a standing committee, the committee shall also be empowered to consider and report upon the expenditure plans and priorities in future fiscal years of the departments and agencies whose main estimates are before it.

Presentation of report.

(8) Any report made in accordance with section (7) of this Standing Order may be made up to and including the last normal sitting day in June, as set forth in Standing

Order 28(2), and shall be deemed to be subject to the provisions of section (9) of this Standing Order.

Motion to concur in a report.

(9) There shall be no debate on any motion to concur in the report of any standing committee on estimates which have been referred to it except on an allotted day.

Supply periods. Allotted days.

(10)(a) In any calendar year, seven sitting days shall be allotted to the business of supply for the period ending not later than December 10; seven additional days shall be allotted to the business of supply in the period ending not later than March 26; and seven additional days shall be allotted to the business of supply in the period ending not later than June 23; provided that the number of sitting days so allotted may be altered pursuant to paragraph (b) or (c) of this section. These twenty-one days are to be designated as allotted days. In any calendar year, no more than one fifth of all the allotted days shall fall on a Wednesday and no more than one fifth thereof shall fall on a Friday.

(b) Notwithstanding paragraph (a), if the House does not sit on days designated as sitting days pursuant to Standing Order 28(2), the total number of allotted days in that supply period shall be reduced by a number of days proportionate to the number of sitting days on which the House stood adjourned, provided that the number of days of the said reduction shall be determined by the Speaker and announced from the Chair.

(c) Notwithstanding paragraph (a), if the House sits, for purposes other than those set out in Standing Order 28(4), on days designated as days on which the House shall stand adjourned pursuant to Standing Order 28(2), the total number of allotted days in that supply period shall be increased by one day for every five such days during which the House sits.

Unused days added to allotted days.

(11) When any day or days allotted to the Address Debate or to the Budget Debate are not used for those debates, such day or days may be added to the number of allotted days in the period in which they occur.

Final supplementary estimates after close of fiscal year.

(12) When concurrence in any final supplementary estimates relating to the fiscal year that ended on March 31 is sought in the period ending not later than June 23, three days for the consideration of the motion that the House concur in those estimates and for the passage at all stages of any bill to be based thereon shall be added to the days for the business of supply in that period.

Opposition motions.

(13) Opposition motions on allotted days may be moved only by Members in opposition to the government and may relate to any matter within the jurisdiction of the Parliament of Canada and also may be used for the purpose of considering reports from standing committees relating to the consideration of estimates therein.

Notice for government motion. Notice for opposition motion.

(14)(a) Forty-eight hours' written notice shall be given of motions to concur in interim supply, main estimates, supplementary or final estimates, to restore or reinstate any item in the estimates. Twenty-four hours' written notice shall be given of an opposition motion on an allotted day or of a notice to oppose any item in the estimates, provided that for the supply period ending not later than June 23, forty-eight hours' written notice shall be given of a notice to oppose any item in the estimates.

Speaker's power of selection.

(*b*) When notice has been given of two or more motions by Members in opposition to the government for consideration on an allotted day, the Speaker shall have power to select which of the proposed motions shall have precedence in that sitting.

Opposition motions have precedence on allotted days.

(15) Opposition motions shall have precedence over all government supply motions on allotted days and shall be disposed of as provided in sections (16), (17), (18) and (19) of this Standing Order.

Number of votable motions allowed. Duration of proceedings.

(16) Not more than fourteen opposition motions in total shall be motions that shall come to a vote during the three supply periods provided pursuant to section (10) of this Standing Order. The duration of proceedings on any such motion shall be stated in the notice relating to the appointing of an allotted day or days for those proceedings. Except as provided for in section (18) of this Standing Order, on the last day appointed for proceedings on a motion that shall come to a vote, at fifteen minutes before the expiry of the time provided for Government Orders, the Speaker shall interrupt the proceedings and forthwith put, without further debate or amendment, every question necessary to dispose of the said proceedings.

When question put in December and March periods.

(17) On the last allotted day in the supply periods ending December 10 and March 26, but, in any case, not later than the last sitting day in each of the said periods, at fifteen minutes before the expiry of the time provided for Government Orders, the Speaker shall interrupt the proceedings then in progress and,

Non-votable motions. Putting of questions seriatim.

(*a*) if those proceedings are not in relation to a motion that shall come to a vote, the Speaker shall put forthwith and successively, without debate or amendment, every question necessary to dispose of any item of business relating to interim supply and supplementary estimates, the restoration or reinstatement of any item in the estimates or any opposed item in the estimates and, notwithstanding Standing Order 71, for the passage at all stages of any bill or bills based thereon; or

Votable motions. Putting of questions seriatim.

(*b*) if those proceedings are in relation to a motion that shall come to a vote, the Speaker shall first put forthwith, without further debate or amendment, every question necessary to dispose of that proceeding, and forthwith thereafter put successively, without debate or amendment, every question necessary to dispose of any item of business relating to interim supply and supplementary estimates, the restoration or reinstatement of any item in the estimates, or of any opposed item in the estimates and, notwithstanding the provisions of Standing Order 71, for the passage at all stages of any bill or bills based thereon.

Ordinary hour of adjournment suspended if necessary.

The Standing Orders relating to the ordinary hour of daily adjournment shall remain suspended until all such questions have been decided.

Opposition Motion and Main Estimates to be considered on last day of June period.

(18) On the last allotted day in the period ending June 23, the House shall consider an opposition motion and any motion or motions to concur in the Main Estimates, provided that:

Non-votable Motion. Expiration of proceedings.

(*a*) if the opposition motion is not a motion that shall come to a vote, proceedings on the motion shall expire when debate thereon has been concluded or at 6:30 p.m., as the case may be, notwithstanding Standing Order 33(2) and the House shall proceed to consider a motion or motions relating to the Main Estimates; or

Votable Motions. Deferral of divisions.

(*b*) if the opposition motion is a motion that shall come to a vote, unless previously disposed of, at 6:30 p.m. the Speaker shall interrupt the proceedings and put forthwith, without further debate or amendment, every question necessary to dispose of the proceedings and any recorded division requested shall be deferred to the conclusion of consideration of a motion or motions relating to the Main Estimates as set out in section (18)(*c*); and

When question put in June period.

(*c*) when proceedings on the opposition motion have been concluded, but in any case not later than 6:30 p.m., the House shall proceed to the consideration of a motion or motions to concur in the Main Estimates, provided that, unless previously disposed of, at not later than 10:00 p.m., the Speaker shall interrupt any proceedings then before the House, and the House shall proceed to the taking of any division or divisions necessary to dispose of the opposition motion deferred pursuant to paragraph (b) of this Standing Order, and the Speaker shall then put forthwith and successively, without further debate or amendment, every question necessary to dispose of the motion or motions to concur in the Main Estimates, and forthwith thereafter put successively, without debate or amendment, every question necessary to dispose of any business relating to the final estimates for the preceding fiscal year or for any supplementary estimates, the restoration or reinstatement of any item in the final or supplementary estimates or any opposed item in the final or supplementary estimates and, notwithstanding Standing Order 71, for the passage at all stages of any bill or bills based on the final, main or supplementary estimates; and

Ordinary hour of adjournment suspended.

(*d*) the Standing Orders relating to the ordinary hour of daily adjournment shall remain suspended until all such questions pursuant to paragraph (c) have been decided.

Expiration of proceedings.

(19) Proceedings on an opposition motion, which is not a motion that shall come to a vote, shall expire when debate thereon has been concluded or at the expiry of the time provided for Government Orders, as the case may be, provided that the expiry of the said time may be delayed pursuant to Standing Order 33(2).

Unopposed items.

(20) The adoption of all unopposed items in any set of estimates may be proposed in one or more motions.

Order to bring in a bill.

(21) The adoption of any motion to concur in any estimate or estimates or interim supply shall be an Order of the House to bring in a bill or bills based thereon.

Time limit and comments on speeches.

(22) During proceedings on any item of business under the provisions of this Standing Order, no Member may speak more than once or longer than twenty minutes. Following the speech of each Member, a period not exceeding ten minutes shall be made available, if required, to allow Members to ask questions and comment briefly on matters relevant to the speech and to allow responses thereto.

Where urgency arises.

82. In the event of urgency in relation to any estimate or estimates, the proceedings of the House on a motion to concur therein and on the subsequent bill are to be taken under Government Orders and not on days allotted pursuant to Standing Order 81.

Ways and Means

Notice of Ways and Means.

83. (1) A notice of a Ways and Means motion may be laid upon the Table of the House at any time during a sitting by a Minister of the Crown, but such a motion may not be proposed in the same sitting.

Order of the Day designated.
Order of the Day for a Budget presentation.

(2) An Order of the Day for the consideration of a Ways and Means motion or motions shall be designated at the request of a Minister rising in his or her place in the House. When such an Order is designated for a Budget presentation, the Minister shall specify the date and time thereof and the Order shall be deemed to be an Order of the House to sit beyond the ordinary hour of daily adjournment, if required. At the specified time, the Speaker shall interrupt any proceedings then before the House and such proceedings shall be deemed adjourned; and the House shall proceed forthwith to the consideration of the Ways and Means motion for the Budget presentation. When a motion for the adjournment of the debate on the Ways and Means motion has been made by a Member of the Official Opposition, it shall be deemed adopted without question put; whereupon the Speaker shall adjourn the House to the next sitting day.

Motion to concur in Ways and Means motion other than Budget.

(3) When an Order of the Day is read for the consideration of any motion of which notice has been given in accordance with section (1) of this Standing Order, a motion to concur in the same shall be forthwith decided without debate or amendment, but no such motion may be proposed during the Budget Debate.

Effect of motion being adopted.

(4) The adoption of any Ways and Means motion shall be an order to bring in a bill or bills based on the provisions of any such motion or to propose an amendment or amendments to a bill then before the House, provided that such amendment or amendments are otherwise admissible.

Budget Debate

Standing Committee on Finance to consider budgetary policy.

83.1 Commencing on the first sitting day in September of each year, the Standing Committee on Finance shall be authorized to consider and make reports upon proposals regarding the budgetary policy of the government. Any report or reports thereon may be made no later than the tenth sitting day before the last normal sitting day in December, as set forth in Standing Order 28(2).

Form of motion Budget.

84. (1) When an Order of the Day is designated pursuant to Standing Order 83(2) for the purpose of enabling a Minister of the Crown to make a Budget presentation, a motion "That this House approves in general the budgetary policy of the Government" shall be proposed.

Budget debate: four days.

(2) The proceedings on the Order of the Day for resuming debate on such Budget motion and on any amendments proposed thereto shall not exceed four sitting days.

Precedence.

(3) When the Order of the Day for resuming the said Budget Debate is called, it must stand as the first Order of the Day and, unless it be disposed of, no other Government Order shall be considered in the same sitting.

When question put on sub-amendment.

(4) On the second of the said days, if a sub-amendment be under consideration at fifteen minutes before the expiry of the time provided for government business in such sitting, the Speaker shall interrupt the proceedings and forthwith put the question on the said sub-amendment.

When question put on amendment.

(5) On the third of the said days, if an amendment be under consideration at fifteen minutes before the expiry of the time provided for government business in such sitting, the Speaker shall interrupt the proceedings and forthwith put the question on the said amendment.

When question put on main motion.

(6) On the fourth of the said days, at fifteen minutes before the expiry of the time provided for government business in such sitting, unless the debate be previously concluded, the Speaker shall interrupt the proceedings and forthwith put the question on the main motion.

Time limit and comments on speeches.

(7) No Member, except the Minister of Finance, the Member speaking first on behalf of the Opposition, the Prime Minister and the Leader of the Opposition, shall speak for more than twenty minutes at a time in the Budget Debate. Following the speech of each Member a period not exceeding ten minutes shall be made available, if required, to allow Members to ask questions and comment briefly on matters relevant to the speech and to allow responses thereto.

Amendments

Amendments: Budget Debate and Supply on allotted days.

85. Only one amendment and one sub-amendment may be made to a motion proposed in the Budget Debate or to a motion proposed under an Order of the Day for the consideration of the business of supply on an allotted day.

CHAPTER XI

PRIVATE MEMBERS' BUSINESS

Notice

Notice of item by one Member.

86. (1) Any one Member may give notice of an item of Private Members' Business.

Two weeks' notice required.

(2) In the case of Private Members' Notices of Motions, at least two weeks' notice shall be given.

More than one seconder.

(3) Notwithstanding the usual practices of the House, not more than twenty Members may jointly second an item under Private Members' Business and may indicate their desire to second any motion in conjunction with the Member in whose name it first appeared on the *Notice Paper*, by so indicating, in writing to the Clerk of the House, at any time prior to the item being proposed.

Appending seconders' names.

(4) Any names received, pursuant to section (3) of this Standing Order, shall be appended to the notice or order as the case may be. Once proposed to the House, Members' names shall not be added to the list of those seconding the said motion or order.

Similar items. Speaker to decide.

(5) The Speaker shall be responsible for determining whether two or more items are so similar as to be substantially the same, in which case he or she shall so inform the Member or Members whose items were received last and the same shall be returned to the Member or Members without having appeared on the *Notice Paper*.

Reinstatement of bills after prorogation.

86.1 During the first thirty sitting days of the second or subsequent Session of a Parliament, whenever a private Member, when proposing a motion for first reading of a public bill, states that the said bill is in the same form as a private Member's bill that he or she introduced in the previous Session, if the Speaker is satisfied that the said bill is in the same form as at prorogation, notwithstanding Standing Order 71, the said bill shall be deemed to have been considered and approved at all stages completed at the time of prorogation and shall stand, if necessary, on the *Order Paper* pursuant to Standing Order 87 after those of the same class, at the same stage at which it stood at the time of prorogation or, as the case may be, referred to committee, and with the designation accorded to it pursuant to Standing Order 92(1) during the previous Session.

Order of Precedence

Establishing order of precedence at beginning of Session.

87. (1)(*a*) At the beginning of a Session, the Clerk of the House, acting on behalf of the Speaker, shall, within two sitting days of the placing on the *Order Paper* of separate items of Private Members' Business from at least thirty Members, notify the Members involved, of the time, date and place of a random draw of thirty Members' names to establish the order of precedence for thirty separate items.

(*b*) To the extent that there is a sufficient number of eligible motions and bills, the draw shall be conducted so that there shall be in the order of precedence an equal number of motions and public bills originating in the House of Commons.

(*c*) The names of Members with bills and those of Members with motions shall be drawn separately to produce the appropriate number of bills and motions. The names first drawn separately shall then be combined and drawn out again to determine the order of precedence for those items.

(*d*) Not later than the ordinary hour of daily adjournment on the second sitting day after the day on which the draw is conducted, each Member whose name has been drawn, and who has given notice of more than one motion, shall file with the Clerk an indication as to which motion is to be placed in the order of precedence. If a Member does not file such an indication within the time specified, the first motion standing on the *Order Paper* in the name of that Member under Private Members' Business will be included in the order of precedence. This requirement applies equally to each Member whose name has been drawn for a public bill.

During a Session.

(2) The Clerk of the House, acting on behalf of the Speaker, shall, when necessary during a Session, conduct a random draw to establish an order of precedence for not more than fifteen additional items of Private Members' Business, in the manner set down in section (1) of this Standing Order. No Member having an item listed in the order of precedence at the time of the draw shall be eligible to have his or her name chosen. Not later than two sitting days prior to the conduct of the draw the Clerk shall inform the Members involved of the time, date and place of the said draw.

Limited number of items.

(3) Notwithstanding sections (1) and (2) of this Standing Order, the order of precedence shall not contain, at any time, more than thirty motions and public bills originating in the House of Commons at second reading placed there as a result of a draw or draws, nor fewer than fifteen items, when there are sufficient items contained in the list which have not been given a position on the order of precedence.

Notice of other items.

(4) The establishment of an order of precedence for Private Members' Business shall not be construed so as to prevent Members from giving notice of items of Private Members' Business.

Order of precedence items only to be considered.

(5) The House shall not consider any order for the second reading and reference to a standing, special or legislative committee or for reference to a Committee of the Whole House of any bill, nor any Notices of Motions or Notices of Motions (Papers) unless the said item has been placed in the order of precedence.

List of 100 Members supporting an item.

(6)(*a*) At any time after the holding of the first draw in a Session, a Member may file with the Clerk a list containing the signatures of one hundred Members, including at least ten Members each from a majority of the recognized parties in the House, who support a specific item, sponsored by the Member, eligible to be placed in the order of precedence.

Item to be placed at bottom of order of precedence

(*b*) Notwithstanding section (3) of this Standing Order, the item for which the list referred to in paragraph (*a*) of this section has been filed shall be added to the bottom of the order of precedence, provided that the Member filing the list does not have an item in the order of precedence and that there shall be only one such item in the order of precedence at any one time.

Two week period.

88. Subject to Standing Order 71, at least two weeks shall elapse between first and second reading of Private Members' Public Bills.

Order of bills on precedence list.

89. The order for the first consideration of any subsequent stages of a bill already considered during Private Members' Business, of second reading of a private bill and of second reading of a private Member's public bill originating in the Senate shall be placed at the bottom of the order of precedence.

On adjournment or interruption.

90. Except as provided pursuant to Standing Order 96, after any bill or other order standing in the name of a private Member has been considered in the House or in any Committee of the Whole and any proceeding thereon has been adjourned or interrupted, the said bill or order shall be placed on the *Order Paper* for the next sitting at the bottom of the order of precedence under the respective heading for such bills or orders.

Suspension of Private Members' Business until order of precedence established.

91. Notwithstanding Standing Order 30(6), the consideration of Private Members' Business shall be suspended and the House shall continue to consider any business before it at the time otherwise provided for the consideration of Private Members' Business until an order of precedence is established pursuant to sections (1) and (2) of Standing Order 87 and the Standing Committee on Procedure and House Affairs has made a report on its selection of votable items, pursuant to Standing Order 92(1).

When Committee to meet for the selection of items as votable items. Report to House.

92. (1) The Standing Committee on Procedure and House Affairs shall meet as soon as practicable after the order of precedence being established pursuant to sections (1) and (2) of Standing Order 87, but in any case not later than ten sitting days after that day, and from time to time thereafter, and may select after consultation with, among others, the Members proposing the items, not more than ten items from among the items in the order of precedence, excluding those items added to it pursuant to Standing Order 86.1, and an appropriate number from among any subsequent items for which the order of precedence is established and such selected items shall be designated as "votable items". In making its selection, the Committee shall not take into account the number of Members jointly seconding an item, but shall allow the merits of the items alone to determine the selection and shall report thereon, from time to time. At no time shall there be more than ten selected items on the order of precedence placed there as a result of a draw or draws.

(2) Reports of the Committee made pursuant to section (1) of this Standing Order shall be deemed adopted when laid upon the Table.

(3) Notwithstanding section (1) of this Standing Order, every private bill which has been placed on the order of precedence shall be deemed to have been selected and designated a "votable item".

93. Unless previously disposed of, selected bills at the second reading stage or selected motions shall receive not more than three hours of consideration and, unless previously disposed of, an item having been once considered, shall be dropped to the bottom of the order of precedence and again considered only when it reaches the top of the said order.

Provided that, unless otherwise disposed of, at not later than fifteen minutes before the end of the time provided for the consideration of the said item, any proceedings then before the House shall be interrupted and every question necessary to dispose of the selected motion or of the selected bill at the second reading stage, shall be put forthwith and successively without further debate or amendment.

94. (1)(*a*) The Speaker shall make all arrangements necessary to ensure the orderly conduct of Private Members' Business including:

(i) ensuring that all Members have not less than twenty-four hours' notice of items to be considered during "Private Members' Hour"; and

(ii) ensuring that the notice required by sub-paragraph (i) of this paragraph is published in the *Notice Paper*.

(*b*) In the event of it not being possible to provide the twenty-four hours' notice required by subparagraph (i) of this section, "Private Members' Hour" shall be suspended for that day and the House shall continue with or revert to the business before it prior to "Private Members' Hour" until the ordinary hour of daily adjournment.

(2)(*a*) When a Member has given at least forty-eight hours' written notice that he or she is unable to be present to move his or her motion under Private Members' Business on the date required by the order of precedence, the Speaker, with permission of the Members involved, may arrange for an exchange of positions in the order of precedence with a Member whose motion or bill has been placed in the order of precedence.

(*b*) In the event that the Speaker has been unable to arrange an exchange, the House shall continue with the business before it prior to "Private Members' Hour".

95. (1) When an item of Private Members' Business that is votable is under consideration, no Member shall speak for more than ten minutes, provided that the Member moving the item may speak for not more than twenty minutes.

(2) When an item of Private Members' Business that is not votable is proposed, the Member moving the item shall speak for not more than fifteen minutes. Thereafter, no Member shall speak for more than ten minutes for a period not exceeding forty minutes. After forty minutes, or earlier if no other Member rises in debate, the Member moving

the said item shall, if he or she chooses, speak again for not more than five minutes and thereby conclude the debate.

Dropped orders.

96. (1) The proceedings on any item of Private Members' Business which is not a votable item selected pursuant to Standing Order 92 shall expire when debate thereon has been concluded or at the end of the time provided for the consideration of such business and that item shall be dropped from the *Order Paper.*

Not to be considered as a decision of the House.

(2) The dropping of an item pursuant to section (1) of this Standing Order shall not be considered a decision of the House.

Not to apply in certain cases.

(3) This Standing Order shall not apply to the consideration of Notices of Motions for the Production of Papers or of Notices of Motions (Papers).

Production of papers.
When debate desired.

97. (1) Notices of motions for the production of papers shall be placed on the *Order Paper* under the heading "Notices of Motions for the Production of Papers". All such notices, when called, shall be forthwith disposed of; but if on any such motion a debate be desired by the Member proposing it or by a Minister of the Crown, the motion will be transferred by the Clerk to the order of "Notices of Motions (Papers)".

Time limits on speeches and debate.

(2) When debate on a motion for the production of papers, under the order "Notices of Motions (Papers)", has taken place for a total time of one hour and thirty minutes, the Speaker shall at that point interrupt the debate, whereupon a Minister of the Crown, whether or not such Minister has already spoken, may speak for not more than five minutes, following which the mover of the motion may close the debate by speaking for not more than five minutes. Unless the motion is withdrawn, as provided by Standing Order 64, the Speaker shall forthwith put the question.

Committee Report.

97.1 A standing, special or legislative committee to which a Private Member's public bill has been referred shall in every case, within sixty sitting days from the date of the bill's reference to the committee, either report the bill to the House with or without amendment or present to the House a report containing a recommendation not to proceed further with the bill and giving the reasons therefor or requesting a single extension of thirty sitting days to consider the bill, and giving the reasons therefor. If no bill or report is presented by the end of the sixty sitting days, or the thirty sitting day extension if approved by the House, the bill shall be deemed to have been reported without amendment.

Bill to be placed at bottom of precedence list after committee stage.

98. (1) When a Private Member's bill is reported from a standing, special or legislative committee or a Committee of the Whole House, or is deemed to have been reported pursuant to Standing Orders 86.1 and 97.1, the order for consideration of the report stage shall be placed at the bottom of the order of precedence notwithstanding Standing Order 87(3).

Two-day debate at certain stages of a bill.

(2) The report and third reading stages of a Private Member's bill shall be taken up on two sitting days, unless previously disposed of, provided that once consideration has been interrupted on the first such day the order for the remaining stage or stages shall be placed at the bottom of the order of precedence, notwithstanding Standing Orders 87(3) and 96 and shall be again considered when the said bill reaches the top of the said order.

Extension of sitting hours. Limited to five hours. (3) When the report or third reading stages of the said bill are before the House on the first of the sitting days provided pursuant to section (2) of this Standing Order, and if the said bill has not been disposed of prior to the end of the first thirty minutes of consideration, during any time then remaining, any one Member may propose a motion to extend the time for the consideration of any remaining stages on the second of the said sitting days during a period not exceeding five consecutive hours, which shall begin at the end of the time provided for Private Members' Business, except on a Monday when the period shall begin at the ordinary hour of daily adjournment, on the second sitting day, provided that:

Support of twenty Members. (*a*) the motion shall be put forthwith without debate or amendment and shall be deemed withdrawn if fewer than twenty members rise in support thereof; and

No subsequent motion unless intervening proceeding. (*b*) a subsequent such motion shall not be put unless there has been an intervening proceeding.

When question put. (4) On the second sitting day provided pursuant to section (2) of this Standing Order, unless previously disposed of, at not later than fifteen minutes before the end of the time provided for the consideration thereof, any proceedings then before the House shall be interrupted and every question necessary to dispose of the then remaining stage or stages of the said bill shall be put forthwith and successively without further debate or amendment.

Suspension of adjournment hour in certain cases. (5) If consideration has been extended pursuant to section (3) of this Standing Order, the Standing Orders relating to the ordinary hour of daily adjournment shall be suspended until all questions necessary to dispose of the said bill have been put.

Suspension

Suspension of Private Members' Business in provided cases. 99. (1) The proceedings on Private Members' Business shall not be suspended except as provided for in Standing Orders 2(3), 30(4), 50(4), 52(14), 83(2), 91 and 94(1)(*b*) or as otherwise specified by Special Order of this House. No Private Members' Business shall be taken up on days appointed for the consideration of business pursuant to Standing Orders 53 and 84(2) nor on days, other than Mondays, appointed for the consideration of business pursuant to Standing Order 81(18).

Suspension on a Monday. (2) Whenever Private Members' Business is suspended or not taken up on a Monday, the House shall meet from 11:00 a.m. to 12:00 noon for the consideration of Government Orders.

CHAPTER XII

COMMITTEES OF THE WHOLE

Order for House in Committee of the Whole. 100. When an Order of the Day is read for the House to go into a Committee of the Whole or when it is ordered that a bill be considered in a Committee of the Whole, the Speaker shall leave the Chair without question put.

Application of Standing Orders.

101. (1) The Standing Orders of the House shall be observed in Committees of the Whole so far as may be applicable, except the Standing Orders as to the seconding of motions, limiting the number of times of speaking and the length of speeches.

Relevancy.

(2) Speeches in Committees of the Whole must be strictly relevant to the item or clause under consideration.

Time limit on speeches.

(3) No Member, except the Prime Minister and the Leader of the Opposition, shall speak for more than twenty minutes at a time in any Committee of the Whole.

Motion to leave the Chair.

102. (1) A motion that the Chairman leave the Chair is always in order, shall take precedence of any other motion, and shall not be debatable.

Intermediate proceeding.

(2) Such motion, if rejected, cannot be renewed unless some intermediate proceeding has taken place.

Resolutions concurred in forthwith.

103. Whenever a resolution is reported from any Committee of the Whole, a motion to concur in the same shall be forthwith put and decided without debate or amendment.

CHAPTER XIII

COMMITTEES

Striking of Committees

Duty of Procedure and House Affairs Committee. Report. No second report during specific period.

104. (1) At the commencement of the first session of each Parliament, the Standing Committee on Procedure and House Affairs, which, notwithstanding section (2) of this Standing Order, shall consist of sixteen Members, and the membership of which shall continue from session to session, shall be appointed to act, among its other duties, as a striking committee. The said Committee shall prepare and report to the House within the first ten sitting days after its appointment, and thereafter, within the first ten sitting days after the commencement of each session and within the first ten sitting days after the second Monday following Labour Day, lists of Members to compose the standing committees of the House pursuant to Standing Order 104(2), and to act for the House on standing joint committees; provided that the Committee shall not present a second report pursuant to this Standing Order between the second Monday following Labour Day and the end of that calendar year.

Membership of standing committees.

(2) The standing committees, which shall consist of the number of Members stipulated below, and for which the lists of members are to be prepared, except as provided in section (1) of this Standing Order, shall be on:

(*a*) Aboriginal Affairs and Northern Development (sixteen Members);

(*b*) Agriculture and Agri-Food (sixteen Members);

(*c*) Canadian Heritage (sixteen Members);

(*d*) Citizenship and Immigration (sixteen Members);

(*e*) Environment and Sustainable Development (sixteen Members);

(*f*) Finance (sixteen Members);

(*g*) Fisheries and Oceans (sixteen Members);

(*h*) Foreign Affairs and International Trade (eighteen Members);

(*i*) Health (sixteen Members);

(*j*) Human Resources Development and the Status of Persons with Disabilities (eighteen Members);

(*k*) Industry (sixteen Members);

(*l*) Justice and Human Rights (sixteen Members);

(*m*) National Defence and Veterans Affairs (sixteen Members);

(*n*) Natural Resources and Government Operations (sixteen Members);

(*o*) Procedure and House Affairs (sixteen Members);

(*p*) Public Accounts (seventeen Members); and

(*q*) Transport (sixteen Members).

Membership of standing joint committees.

(3) The Standing Committee on Procedure and House Affairs shall also prepare and report lists of Members to act for the House on the Standing Joint Committees on:

(*a*) the Library of Parliament;

(*b*) Official Languages; and

(*c*) Scrutiny of Regulations;

Provided that a sufficient number of Members shall be appointed so as to keep the same proportion therein as between the memberships of both Houses.

Associate Members.

(4) The Standing Committee on Procedure and House Affairs shall also prepare lists of associate members for each Standing Committee and Standing Joint Committee referred to in this Standing Order, who shall be deemed to be members of that committee for the purposes of Standing Orders 108(1)(*b*) and 114(2)(*a*) and who shall be eligible to act as substitutes on that committee pursuant to the provisions of Standing Order 114(2)(*b*).

Membership of a special committee.

105. A special committee shall consist of not more than fifteen members.

Clerk of the House to convene meetings.

106. (1) Within ten sitting days following the adoption by the House of a report of the Standing Committee on Procedure and House Affairs pursuant to Standing Order 104(1), the Clerk of the House shall convene a meeting of each standing committee whose membership is contained in that report for the purpose of electing a Chairman, provided that forty-eight hours' notice is given of any such meeting.

Election of Chairman and Vice-Chairmen.

(2) Each standing or special committee shall elect a Chairman and two Vice-Chairmen, of whom two shall be Members of the government party and the third a Member in opposition to the government, in accordance with the provisions of Standing Order 116, at the commencement of every session and, if necessary, during the course of a session.

Chairman to con-
vene meeting upon
written request.
Reasons to be stated
in request. Forty-
eight hours' notice
required.

(3) Within ten sitting days of the receipt, by the clerk of a standing committee, of a request signed by any four members of the said committee, the Chairman of the said committee shall convene such a meeting provided that forty-eight hours' notice is given of the meeting. For the purposes of this section, the reasons for convening such a meeting shall be stated in the request.

Liaison Committee

Membership.

107. (1) The Chairman of each standing committee, together with the Member of the House from each standing joint committee who is the Chairman of the said joint committee, shall form a Liaison Committee, which is charged with making apportionments of funds from the block of funds authorized by the Board of Internal Economy to meet the expenses of committee activities, subject to ratification by the Board.

Election of Chairman and Vice-Chairman of Liaison Committee.
Clerk of the House to convene meeting.

(2) Within five sitting days of the meeting of the last standing committee to elect its Chairman pursuant to Standing Order 106(2), but in any event no later than the twentieth sitting day after the adoption of the report of the Standing Committee on Procedure and House Affairs presented pursuant to Standing Order 104(1), the Clerk of the House shall convene a meeting of the Chairmen, together with any Members of the House elected as Chairman of any joint committees for which such elections have then been held, for the purpose of electing a Chairman and a Vice-Chairman of the Liaison Committee.

Reports.

(3) The Liaison Committee shall be empowered to report from time to time to the House.

Quorum.

(4) Seven members of the Liaison Committee shall constitute a quorum.

Associate Members.

(5) The Standing Committee on Procedure and House Affairs shall, at the request of the Chairman of the Liaison Committee, prepare and report to the House a list of associate members of that Committee, who shall be deemed to be members thereof for the purposes of section (6) of this Standing Order.

Power to create sub-committees.

(6) The Liaison Committee shall be empowered to create sub-committees of which the membership may be drawn from among both the list of members of the Committee and the list of associate members provided for in section (5) of this Standing Order.

Mandate

Powers of standing committees.

108. (1)(a) Standing committees shall be severally empowered to examine and enquire into all such matters as may be referred to them by the House, to report from time to time and to print a brief appendix to any report, after the signature of the Chairman, containing such opinions or recommendations, dissenting from the report or supplementary to it, as may be proposed by committee members, and except when the House otherwise orders, to send for persons, papers and records, to sit while the House is sitting, to sit during periods when the House stands adjourned, to sit jointly with other standing committees, to print from day to day such papers and evidence as may be ordered by them, and to delegate to sub-committees all or any of their powers except the power to report directly to the House.

Power to create sub-committees.

(b) Standing Committees shall be empowered to create sub-committees of which the membership may be drawn from among both the list of members and the list of associate members provided for in Standing Order 104, who shall be deemed to be members of that committee for the purposes of this Standing Order.

Additional powers of standing committees.

(2) The standing committees, except those set out in sections (3)(*a*), (3)(*e*) and (4) of this Standing Order, shall, in addition to the powers granted to them pursuant to section (1) of this Standing Order and pursuant to Standing Order 81, be empowered to study and report on all matters relating to the mandate, management and operation of the department or departments of government which are assigned to them from time to time by the House. In general, the committees shall be severally empowered to review and report on:

(*a*) the statute law relating to the department assigned to them;

(*b*) the program and policy objectives of the department and its effectiveness in the implementation of same;

(*c*) the immediate, medium and long-term expenditure plans and the effectiveness of implementation of same by the department;

(*d*) an analysis of the relative success of the department, as measured by the results obtained as compared with its stated objectives; and

(*e*) other matters, relating to the mandate, management, organization or operation of the department, as the committee deems fit.

Mandates of certain standing committees.

(3) The mandate of the Standing Committee on:

Procedure and House Affairs.

(*a*) Procedure and House Affairs shall include, in addition to the duties set forth in Standing Order 104, and among other matters:

(i) the review of and report on, to the Speaker as well as the Board of Internal Economy, the administration of the House and the provision of services and facilities to Members provided that all matters related thereto shall be deemed to have been permanently referred to the Committee upon its membership having been established;

(ii) the review of and report on the effectiveness, management and operation, together with the operational and expenditure plans of all operations which are under the joint administration and control of the two Houses except with regard to the Library of Parliament and other related matters as the Committee deems fit;

(iii) the review of and report on the Standing Orders, procedure and practice in the House and its committees;

(iv) the selection of items of Private Members' Business pursuant to Standing Order 92, and the consideration of business related to Private Bills;

(v) the review of and report on the radio and television broadcasting of the proceedings of the House and its committees; and

(vi) the review of and report on all matters relating to the election of Members to the House of Commons;

Canadian Heritage.

(b) Canadian Heritage shall include, among other matters, the monitoring of the implementation of the principles of the federal multiculturalism policy throughout the Government of Canada in order:

— to encourage the departments and agencies of the federal government to reflect the multicultural diversity of the nation; and

— to examine existing and new programs and policies of federal departments and agencies to encourage sensitivity to multicultural concerns and to preserve and enhance the multicultural reality of Canada;

Human Resources Development and the Status of Persons with Disabilities.

(c) Human Resources Development and the Status of Persons with Disabilities shall include, among other matters, the proposing, promoting, monitoring and assessing of initiatives aimed at the integration and equality of disabled persons in all sectors of Canadian society;

Justice and Human Rights.

(d) Justice and Human Rights shall include, among other matters, the review and report on reports of the Canadian Human Rights Commission, which shall be deemed permanently referred to the Committee immediately after they are laid upon the Table;

Public Accounts.

(e) Public Accounts shall include, among other matters, review of and report on the Public Accounts of Canada and all reports of the Auditor General of Canada, which shall be severally deemed permanently referred to the Committee immediately after they are laid upon the Table;

and any other matter which the House shall, from time to time, refer to the Standing Committee.

Mandate of Standing Joint Committees.

(4) So far as this House is concerned, the mandates of the Standing Joint Committee on

Library of Parliament.

(a) the Library of Parliament shall include the review of the effectiveness, management and operation of the Library of Parliament;

Official Languages.

(b) Official Languages shall include, among other matters, the review of and report on official languages policies and programs including Reports of the Commissioner of Official Languages, which shall be deemed permanently referred to the Committee immediately after they are laid upon the Table;

Scrutiny of Regulations.

(c) Scrutiny of Regulations shall include, among other matters, the review and scrutiny of statutory instruments which are permanently referred to the Committee pursuant to section 19 of the *Statutory Instruments Act*;

Provided that both Houses may, from time to time, refer any other matter to any of the aforementioned Standing Joint Committees.

Government response to committee reports.

109. Within 150 days of the presentation of a report from a standing or special committee, the government shall, upon the request of the committee, table a comprehensive response thereto.

Tabling of Order in Council appointments. Deemed referred to committee.

110. (1) A Minister of the Crown shall lay upon the Table a certified copy of an Order in Council, stating that a certain individual has been appointed to a certain non-judicial post, not later than five sitting days after the Order in Council is published in the *Canada Gazette*. The same shall be deemed to have been referred to a standing committee specified at the time of tabling, pursuant to Standing Order 32(6), for its consideration during a period not exceeding thirty sitting days.

Tabling of certificate of nomination for appointment. Deemed referred to committee.

(2) A Minister of the Crown may, from time to time, lay upon the Table a certificate stating that a specified individual has been nominated for appointment to a specified non-judicial post. The same shall be deemed to have been referred to a standing committee specified at the time of tabling, pursuant to Standing Order 32(6), for its consideration during a period not exceeding thirty sitting days.

Appearance of appointee or nominee.

111. (1) The committee specified pursuant to Standing Orders 32(6) and 110, during the period of thirty sitting days provided pursuant to Standing Order 110, shall if it deems it appropriate, call the so named appointee or nominee to appear before it during a period not exceeding ten sitting days.

Qualification study of appointee or nominee.

(2) The committee, if it should call an appointee or nominee to appear pursuant to section (1) of this Standing Order, shall examine the qualifications and competence of the appointee or nominee to perform the duties of the post to which he or she has been appointed or nominated.

Time limit for study.

(3) The committee shall complete its examination of the appointee or nominee not later than the end of the ten sitting day period indicated in section (1) of this Standing Order.

Appointee's *curriculum vitae* to be provided.

(4) The office of the Minister who recommended the appointment shall provide the *curriculum vitae* of such an appointee or nominee to the committee upon written application from the clerk of the committee.

Legislative Committees

Chairmen of legislative committees. Panel of Chairmen.

112. At the commencement of each session, the Speaker shall appoint as many as twelve Members, and from time to time additional Members as required, to act as Chairmen of legislative committees, provided that a proportionate number of Members from both the government party and the opposition parties shall be so appointed. The Members appointed under the provisions of this Standing Order, together with the Deputy Speaker and Chairman of Committees of the Whole, the Deputy Chairman of Committees of the Whole and the Assistant Deputy Chairman of Committees of the Whole, shall constitute the Panel of Chairmen for the legislative committees.

Striking of legislative committees.

113. (1) Without anticipating the decision of the House, within five sitting days after the commencement of debate on a motion to appoint a legislative committee or to refer a bill thereto, the Standing Committee on Procedure and House Affairs shall meet to prepare, and shall report not later than the following Thursday, a list of members of such a legislative committee, which shall consist of not more than fifteen Members. Such a committee shall be organized only in the event that the House adopts the motion for appointment or referral. Upon presentation of such a report of the Standing Committee on Procedure and House Affairs, the same shall be deemed adopted.

Appointment of Chairman.

(2) Once the said report is adopted, the Speaker shall forthwith appoint the Chairman of the said committee from the Panel of Chairmen established pursuant to Standing Order 112.

When a legislative committee to meet.

(3) A legislative committee constituted pursuant to sections (1) and (2) of this Standing Order shall meet within two sitting days of the naming of the Chairman and the adoption

of the motion appointing or referring the bill to the committee of which the membership has been reported.

Acting Chairman of legislative committee.

(4) When the Chairman appointed pursuant to section (2) of this Standing Order is unable to act in that capacity at or during a meeting of the legislative committee, the Chairman shall designate a member of the committee to act as Chairman at or during the said meeting and such an acting Chairman shall be vested with all the powers of the Chairman at or during the said meeting.

Powers of a legislative committee.

(5) Any legislative committee shall be empowered to examine and enquire into the bills referred to it by the House and to report the same with or without.amendments, to prepare a bill pursuant to Standing Order 68 and to report thereon and, except when the House otherwise orders, to send for officials from government departments and agencies and crown corporations and for other persons whom the committee deems to be competent to appear as witnesses on technical matters, to send for papers and records, to sit when the House is sitting, to sit when the House stands adjourned, and to print from day to day such papers and evidence as may be ordered by it.

Sub-committee on agenda and procedure of a legislative committee.

(6) Any legislative committee may delegate to a sub-committee on agenda and procedure, its power to schedule meetings of the committee and to call for officials from government departments and agencies and crown corporations and for other persons whom the committee deems competent to appear before it as witnesses on technical matters, or to send for papers and records to be presented to the committee in relation to the bill before the committee, provided that the committee shall retain the power to approve such arrangements.

Membership

Membership of standing and standing joint committees.

114. (1) The membership of standing and standing joint committees shall be set out in the report of the Standing Committee on Procedure and House Affairs, which shall prepare lists of members in accordance with Standing Order 104. Once the report of the Committee is concurred in, the membership shall continue from session to session within a Parliament, subject to such changes as may be effected from time to time.

List of replacements may be filed with the clerk of the committee.

(2)(*a*) Within five sitting days of the organization of any standing or standing joint committee, and from time to time thereafter, any member of every such committee may file with the clerk of the committee a list of not more than fourteen Members selected from Members of his or her own party, who may substitute for him or her during a meeting of the said committee, according to the procedure set out in paragraph (*b*) of this section, provided that they shall not become permanent members of the committee.

Substitutions in membership of standing and standing joint committees.

(*b*) Substitutions in the membership of any standing committee or, so far as the House is represented, on any standing joint committee shall be effective the day after notification thereof is forwarded, by a permanent member of the committee who has filed a list pursuant to paragraph (*a*) of this section, to the Chief Whip of his or her party (or, in the case of independent Members, the Chief Whip of the Official Opposition) for signature who, in turn, will forward the substitution to the clerk of the committee.

Substitutions by Chief Whip when no list filed or no notice received.

(*c*) At any time when no list has been filed with the clerk of the committee pursuant to paragraph (*a*) of this section or when no notice has been received by the clerk of the committee pursuant to paragraph (*b*) of this section, the Chief Whip of any recognized party may effect substitutions by filing notice thereof with the clerk of the committee, having selected the substitutes from among all the Members of his or her party and/or the independent members listed as associate members of the committee pursuant to Standing Order 104(4); and such substitutions shall be effective immediately they are received by the clerk of the committee.

Member's resignation from committee, when effective.

(*d*) When a permanent member of a standing or standing joint committee gives notice in writing to the Chairman of the Standing Committee on Procedure and House Affairs of his or her intention to give up his or her membership, that Member's resignation shall be effective when a report of the Standing Committee on Procedure and House Affairs naming a replacement for him or her has been concurred in by the House.

Changes in membership of legislative committees.

(3) Changes in the membership of any legislative committee shall be effective immediately after notification thereof, signed by the Chief Whip of any recognized party, has been filed with the clerk of the committee.

Changes in membership of standing committees.

(4) Changes in the membership of standing committees shall be effective when a report of the Standing Committee on Procedure and House Affairs to that effect is concurred in by the House.

Meetings

Sittings of committees.

115. (1) Notwithstanding Standing Order 108(1)(*a*), no standing or standing joint committee shall sit at the same time as a legislative committee on a bill emanating from or principally affecting the same department or agency.

Priority during sittings of the House.

(2) During periods coinciding with the hours of sittings of the House, priority shall be given to the meetings of committees considering legislation or Estimates over meetings of committees considering other matters.

Priority during adjournments. Chief Government Whip to set schedules.

(3) During periods when the House stands adjourned, priority shall be given to meetings of standing, special and joint committees, according to the schedule established from time to time by the Chief Government Whip, in consultation with representatives of the other parties.

Priority of use in committee rooms.

(4) Priority of use in committee rooms shall be established from time to time by the Standing Committee on Procedure and House Affairs.

Standing Orders apply generally.

116. In a standing, special or legislative committee, the Standing Orders shall apply so far as may be applicable, except the Standing Orders as to the election of a Speaker, seconding of motions, limiting the number of times of speaking and the length of speeches.

Decorum in committee.

117. The Chairman of a standing, special or legislative committee shall maintain order in the committee, deciding all questions of order subject to an appeal to the committee; but disorder in a committee can only be censured by the House, on receiving a report thereof.

Quorum.

118. (1) A majority of the members of a standing, special or legislative committee shall constitute a quorum; provided that, in the case of a legislative committee, the Chairman is not included in the number of members constituting a quorum. In the case of a joint committee, the number of members constituting a quorum shall be such as the House of Commons acting in consultation with the Senate may determine.

Meetings without quorum.

(2) The presence of a quorum shall be required whenever a vote, resolution or other decision is taken by a standing, special or legislative committee, provided that any such committee, by resolution thereof, may authorize the Chairman to hold meetings in order to receive evidence and may authorize its printing when a quorum is not present.

Only members may vote or move motion.

119. Any Member of the House who is not a member of a standing, special or legislative committee, may, unless the House or the committee concerned otherwise orders, take part in the public proceedings of the committee, but may not vote or move any motion, nor be part of any quorum.

Broadcasting of committee meetings.

119.1 (1) Any committee wishing to have its proceedings televised, other than by means of those facilities provided for that purpose by the House of Commons, shall first obtain the consent of the House thereto.

Report on experimental guidelines. Electronic media.

(2) The Standing Committee on Procedure and House Affairs shall establish, by report to the House of Commons, experimental guidelines governing the broadcasting of committee meetings. After concurrence by the House in such a report, any committee may permit the presence of the electronic media at its meetings, subject to the said guidelines.

Staff and Budgets

Staff of committees.

120. Standing, special or legislative committees shall be severally empowered to retain the services of expert, professional, technical and clerical staff as may be deemed necessary.

Interim spending authority. Budgets submitted to Board of Internal Economy.

121. (1) The Board of Internal Economy may give interim spending authority to standing, special and legislative committees. The committees shall be empowered to expend any amount up to the full spending authority so granted but shall not incur any further expenses until the Chairman of that committee, or a member of the committee acting for the Chairman, has presented to the Board a budget setting forth, in reasonable detail, estimates of its proposed expenditures for a specific period of time together with an account of its expenditures to that date, and until the said budget has been approved by the Board.

Budget and statement of expenditures to be presented as soon as practicable.

(2) Notwithstanding any spending authority granted by the Board of Internal Economy pursuant to section (1) of this Standing Order, the Chairman of each such committee, or a member of the committee acting for the Chairman shall, as soon as practicable, present the budget and statement of expenditures of the committee pursuant to section (1) of this Standing Order for the consideration by the Board.

Supplementary budgets.

(3) When the expenditures of any such committee have reached the limits set forth in any such budget, the committee shall not incur any further expenses until a supplementary budget or budgets has or have been presented to the Board of Internal Economy pursuant to section (1) of this Standing Order, and until the said budgets have been approved in whole or in part by the Board.

Annual financial report on committees.

(4) The Board of Internal Economy shall cause to be tabled in the House an annual comprehensive financial report, outlining the individual expenditures of every standing,

special and legislative committee, provided that the Board may cause such reports to be so tabled at any time with respect to a specific committee.

Witnesses

122. If any Member files a certificate with the Chairman of a committee of the House, stating that the evidence to be obtained from a particular person is, in his or her opinion, material and important, the Chairman shall apprise the committee thereof.

CHAPTER XIV

DELEGATED LEGISLATION

Report may contain a resolution. Order of the House upon adoption.

123. (1) In addition to the powers granted, so far as this House is concerned, to the Standing Joint Committee for the Scrutiny of Regulations, pursuant to Standing Order 108(4), the said Committee shall be empowered to make a report to the House containing only a resolution which, if the report is concurred in, would be an Order of this House to the Ministry to revoke a statutory instrument, or a portion thereof, which the Governor in Council or a Minister of the Crown has the authority to revoke.

Only one report to be presented in the same sitting.

(2) Not more than one report pursuant to section (1) of this Standing Order shall be received during any sitting.

Member presenting report to state that it contains a resolution and shall identify the statutory instrument.

(3) When any report is made pursuant to section (1) of this Standing Order, the Member presenting it shall state that it contains a resolution pursuant to section (1) of this Standing Order, shall identify the statutory instrument, or portion thereof, in relation to which the said report is made, and shall indicate that the relevant text is included in the report.

Motion for concurrence placed on *Notice Paper* in name of Member presenting report. Only one such motion allowed.

(4) Immediately after the said report is received and laid upon the Table, the Clerk of the House shall cause to be placed on the *Notice Paper*, a notice of motion for concurrence in the report, which shall stand in the name of the Member presenting the report. No other notice of motion for concurrence in the report shall be placed on the *Notice Paper*.

Motion for concurrence considered at request of Minister. Any Member may move motion.

124. When a notice given pursuant to Standing Order 123(4) is transferred to the *Order Paper* under "Motions", it shall be set down for consideration only pursuant to Standing Order 128(1) and shall be considered only at the request of a Minister of the Crown, provided that any other Member shall be permitted to propose the motion on behalf of the Member in whose name it stands, notwithstanding the usual practices of the House.

Motion deemed adopted.

125. Except as otherwise provided in any Standing or Special Order of the House, and unless otherwise disposed of, at not later than the ordinary hour of daily adjournment on the fifteenth sitting day following the date on which a notice of motion made pursuant to Standing Order 123(4) appeared on the *Order Paper,* the same shall be deemed to have been moved and adopted by the House.

Time limit on debate.

126. (1) A notice given pursuant to Standing Order 123(4) shall be taken up and considered for a period not exceeding one hour, provided that:

Time limit on
speeches.

(a) during the consideration of any such motion or motions, no Member shall speak more than once or for more than ten minutes;

Procedural
acceptability of a
report. Motion
deemed withdrawn.

(b) for the purposes of this Standing Order and notwithstanding the usual practices of the House, no consideration of the procedural acceptability of any report, for which a notice of motion for concurrence has been given pursuant to Standing Order 123(4), shall be entertained until all such notices of motions of which notice of consideration had previously been given pursuant to Standing Order 54, have been put to the House for its consideration. If any report is thereafter found to be irreceivable, the motion for concurrence in the report shall be deemed to have been withdrawn; and

Putting of questions.
Deferring divisions.
Length of bells.

(c) unless the motion or motions be previously disposed of, not later than the end of the said hour of consideration, the Speaker shall interrupt any proceedings then before the House and put forthwith and successively, without further debate or amendment, every question necessary to dispose of the said motion or motions, provided that any division or divisions demanded in relation thereto shall stand deferred until no later than the ordinary hour of daily adjournment in that sitting, when the bells to call in the Members shall be sounded for not more than fifteen minutes. Any remaining questions necessary to dispose of proceedings in relation to such motion or motions, on which a decision has been deferred until after the taking of such a division, shall be put forthwith and successively, without further debate or amendment.

Division not to be
further deferred.

(2) The provisions of Standing Order 45(5) shall be suspended in the case of any division demanded pursuant to paragraph (c) of section (1) of this Standing Order.

Adjournment hour
suspended.

(3) The Standing Orders relating to the ordinary hour of daily adjournment shall be suspended until all questions have been decided pursuant to paragraph (c) of section (1) of this Standing Order.

Order in which
motions are set
down for
consideration.
Grouping of
motions.

127. The House shall undertake consideration of any motion or motions made pursuant to Standing Order 123(4) in the order in which they may be set down for consideration at the request of a Minister of the Crown, provided that all such motions shall be grouped together for debate.

Motions for
concurrence to be
taken up on a
Wednesday.

128. (1) When a notice or notices of motion for concurrence given pursuant to Standing Order 123(4) has or have been set down for consideration pursuant to Standing Order 124, the House shall meet at 1:00 p.m. on the Wednesday next, at which time the order of business shall be the consideration of the said notice or notices.

Consideration.

(2) When the House meets at 1:00 p.m. on any Wednesday pursuant to section (1) of this Standing Order, the House shall not consider any other item but those provided pursuant to that section, provided that:

(a) if such proceedings are concluded prior to 2:00 p.m. on any such day, the Speaker shall suspend the sitting until that hour; and

(b) all such proceedings shall be concluded except as provided pursuant to Standing Order 126(1)(c) at 2:00 p.m. on the same day.

CHAPTER XV

PRIVATE BILLS

Notices

Publication of Standing Order.

129. At the beginning of a session, the Clerk of the House shall publish in the *Canada Gazette* the Standing Order respecting notices of intended applications for private bills. Thereafter, the Clerk of the House shall publish weekly in the *Canada Gazette* a notice referring to the previous publication of the aforementioned Standing Order.

Publication of notices.

130. (1) All applications to Parliament for private bills, of any nature whatsoever, shall be advertised by a notice published in the *Canada Gazette*; such notice shall clearly and distinctly state the nature and objects of the application, and shall be signed by or on behalf of the applicants, with the address of the party signing the same; and when the application is for an Act of incorporation, the name of the proposed company shall be stated in the notice. If the works of any company (incorporated, or to be incorporated) are to be declared to be for the general advantage of Canada, such intention shall be specifically mentioned in the notice; and the applicants shall cause a copy of such notice to be sent by registered letter to the clerk of each county or municipality which may be specially affected by the construction or operation of such works, and also to the secretary of the province in which such works are, or may be located. Every such notice sent by registered letter shall be mailed in time to reach its destination not later than two weeks before the consideration of the proposed bill by the committee to which it may be referred; and proof of compliance with this requirement by the applicants shall be established by statutory declaration.

Additional notice.

(2) In addition to the notice in the *Canada Gazette* aforesaid, a similar notice shall also be published in some leading newspaper as follows:

In case of incorporation.

(*a*) when the application is for an Act to incorporate:

Railway or canal company.

(i) a railway or canal company: in the principal city, town or village in each county or district, through which the proposed railway or canal is to be constructed;

Telegraph or telephone company.

(ii) a telegraph or telephone company: in the principal city or town in each province or territory in which the company proposes to operate;

Construction of works. Exclusive rights.

(iii) a company for the construction of any works which in their construction or operation might specially affect the particular locality; or obtaining any exclusive rights or privileges; or for doing any matter or thing which in its operation would affect the rights or property of others: in the particular locality or localities in which the business, rights or property of other persons or corporations may be affected by the proposed Act; and

Banking, insurance, trust, loan company or industrial company.

(iv) a banking company; an insurance company; a trust company; a loan company; or an industrial company without any exclusive powers: in the *Canada Gazette* only.

In case of amending Act.

(*b*) when the application is for the purpose of amending an existing Act:

Extension of railway.

(i) for an extension of any line of railway, or of any canal; or for the construction of branches thereto: in the place where the head office of the company is situated, and in the principal city, town or village in each county or district through which such extension or branch is to be constructed;

Extension of time.

(ii) for an extension of time for the construction or completion of any line of railway or of any branch or extension thereof, or of any canal, or of any telegraph or telephone line, or of any other works already authorized: at the place where the head office of the company is situated and in the principal city or town of the districts affected; and

Continuation of charter.

(iii) for the continuation of a charter or for an extension of the powers of the company (when not involving the granting of any exclusive rights) or for the increase or reduction of the capital stock of any company; or for increasing or altering its bonding or other borrowing powers; or for any amendment which would in any way affect the rights or interests of the shareholders or bondholders or creditors of the company: in the place where the head office of the company is situated or authorized to be.

Exclusive rights.

(*c*) when the application is for the purpose of obtaining for any person or existing corporation any exclusive rights or privileges or the power to do any matter or thing which in its operation would affect the rights or property of others: in the particular locality or localities in which the business, rights or property of others may be specially affected by the proposed Act.

Duration of notice.

(3) All such notices, whether inserted in the *Canada Gazette* or in a newspaper, shall be published at least once a week for a period of four consecutive weeks; and when originating in the Province of Quebec or in the Province of Manitoba shall be published in English in an English newspaper and in French in a French newspaper, and in both languages in the *Canada Gazette*, and if there is no newspaper in a locality where a notice is required to be given, such notice shall be given in the next nearest locality wherein a newspaper is published; and proof of the due publication of notice shall be established in each case by statutory declaration; and all such declarations shall be sent to the Clerk of the House endorsed "Private Bill Notice".

Petition

Petition filed with Clerk of the House.

131. (1) A petition for a private bill may be presented by a Member at any time during the sitting of the House by filing the same with the Clerk of the House.

Members answerable.

(2) Members presenting petitions for private bills shall be answerable that such petitions do not contain impertinent or improper matter.

Member's signature.

(3) Every Member presenting a petition for a private bill shall sign his or her name on the back thereof.

Signatures of petitioners.

(4) Petitions for private bills may be either written or printed; provided always that when there are three or more petitioners the signatures of at least three petitioners shall be subscribed on the sheet containing the prayer of the petition.

Report of Clerk of Petitions.

(5) On the next day following the presentation of a petition for a private bill, the Clerk of the House shall lay upon the Table the report of the Clerk of Petitions thereon and such report shall be printed in the *Journals*. Every petition so reported upon, not containing matter in breach of the privileges of this House and which, according to the Standing Orders or practice of this House, can be received, shall then be deemed to be read and received.

No debate on report. Petition may be read.

(6) No debate shall be permitted on the report but a petition referred to therein may be read by the Clerk of the House at the Table, if required.

132. Deleted (*June 10, 1994*).

Examiner of petitions for private bills.

133. (1) The Chief Clerk of Private Bills shall be the Examiner of Petitions for Private Bills.

Report to the House.

(2) Petitions for private bills, when received by the House, are to be taken into consideration by the Examiner who shall report to the House in each case the extent to which the requirements of the Standing Orders regarding notice have been complied with; and in every case where the notice is reported by the Examiner to have been insufficient or otherwise defective, or if the Examiner reports that there is any doubt as to the sufficiency of the notice as published, the petition, together with the report of the Examiner thereon, shall be taken into consideration, without special reference, by the Standing Committee on Procedure and House Affairs, which shall report to the House as to the sufficiency or insufficiency of the notice, and where the notice is deemed insufficient or otherwise defective, shall recommend to the House the course to be taken in consequence of such deficiency or other defect.

Private bills from Senate.

(3) All private bills from the Senate (not being based on a petition which has already been so reported on) shall be first taken into consideration and reported on by the Examiner of Petitions, and when necessary by the Standing Committee on Procedure and House Affairs in like manner, after the first reading of such bills, and before their consideration by any other legislative committee.

Map or plan with petition.

(4) No petition praying for the incorporation of a railway company, or of a canal company, or for an extension of the line of any existing or authorized railway or canal, or for the construction of branches thereto, shall be considered by the Examiner, or by the Standing Committee on Procedure and House Affairs, until there has been filed with the said Examiner a map or plan, showing the proposed location of the works, and each county, township, municipality or district through which the proposed railway or canal, or any branch or extension thereof, is to be constructed.

Fees and Charges

Time limited for depositing bill. Printing and translation cost.

134. (1) Any person desiring to obtain any private bill shall deposit with the Clerk of the House not later than the first day of each session, a copy of such bill in the English or French language, with a sum sufficient to pay for translating and printing the same; the translation to be done by the officers of the House, and the printing by the Department of Public Printing.

Cost of printing the Act.

(2) After the second reading of a bill, and before its consideration by the committee to which it is referred, the applicant shall in every case pay the cost of printing the Act in the Statutes, and a fee of $500.

Other charges.

(3) The following charges shall also be levied and paid in addition to the foregoing:

(*a*) when any Standing Order of the House is suspended in reference to a bill or the petition therefor, for each such suspension $100

(*b*) when a bill is presented in the House after the eighth week of the session and not later than the twelfth week $100

(*c*) when a bill is presented in the House after the twelfth week of the session ... $200

(*d*) when the proposed capital stock of a company does not exceed $250,000 .... $100

(*e*) when the proposed capital stock of a company is over $250,000 and does not exceed $500,000 .... $200

(*f*) when the proposed capital stock of a company is over $500,000 and does not exceed $750,000 .... $300

(*g*) when the proposed capital stock of a company is over $750,000 and does not exceed $1,000,000 .... $400

(*h*) when the proposed capital stock of a company is over $1,000,000 and does not exceed $1,500,000 .... $600

(*i*) when the proposed capital stock of a company is over $1,500,000 and does not exceed $2,000,000 .... $800

(*j*) for every additional million dollars or fractional part thereof $200

Capital increased.

(4) When a bill increases the capital stock of an existing company, the additional charge shall be according to the foregoing tariff, upon the amount of the increase only.

Borrowing powers increased.

(5)(*a*) When a bill increases or involves an increase in the borrowing powers of a company without any increase in the capital stock, the additional charge shall be $300.

Increase of capital and borrowing powers.

(*b*) When a bill increases both the capital stock and the borrowing powers of a company, the additional charge shall be made upon both.

Bill stands until charges are paid.

(6) If any increase in the amount of the proposed capital stock or borrowing powers of a company be made at any stage of a bill, such bill shall not be advanced to the next stage until the charges consequent upon such change have been paid.

Interpretation.

(7) In this Standing Order the term "proposed capital stock" includes any increase thereto provided for in the bill; and where power is taken in a bill to increase at any time the amount of the proposed capital stock, the additional charge shall be levied on the maximum amount of such proposed increase which shall be stated in the bill.

Additional charges apply to Senate bills.

(8) The additional charges provided for in this Standing Order shall also apply to private bills originating in the Senate; provided, however, that if a petition for any such bill has been filed with this House, the additional charges made under paragraphs (b) or (c) of section (3) shall not be levied thereon.

Collection of fees.

(9) The Chief Clerk of Private Bills shall prepare and send to the promoter or parliamentary agent in charge of every private bill a statement of fees and charges payable under this Standing Order, and shall collect all such fees and charges and deposit the same with the accountant of the House and shall send a copy of each such deposit slip to the Clerk of the House.

Introduction and Readings

Private bills introduced on petition.

135. (1) All private bills are introduced on petition, and after such petition has been favourably reported upon by the Examiner of Petitions or by the Standing Committee on Procedure and House Affairs, such bills shall be laid upon the Table of the House by the Clerk, and shall be deemed to have been read a first time and ordered to be printed, and to have been ordered for a second reading when so laid upon the Table, and so recorded in the *Journals*.

Senate bills deemed read a first time.

(2) When the Speaker informs the House that any private bill has been brought from the Senate, the bill shall be deemed to have been read a first time and ordered for a second reading and reference to a legislative committee at the next sitting of the House and so recorded in the *Journals*.

Examiner of private bills.

136. (1) The Chief Clerk of Private Bills shall be the Examiner of Private Bills, and, as such, shall examine and revise all private bills before they are printed, for the purpose of insuring uniformity where possible and of seeing that they are drawn in accordance with the Standing Orders of the House respecting private bills.

Model bill.

(2) Every bill for an Act of incorporation, where a form of model bill has been adopted, shall be drawn in accordance with a model bill (copies of model bills may be obtained from the Clerk of the House). Any provisions contained in any such bill which are not in accord with the model bill shall be inserted between brackets or underlined, and shall be so printed.

Amending bill.

(3) Where a private bill amends any section, subsection or paragraph of an existing Act, such section, subsection or paragraph shall be repealed in the text of the bill and re-enacted as proposed to be amended, the new matter being indicated by underlining; and the section, subsection or paragraph which is to be so repealed, or so much thereof as is essential, shall be printed in the right-hand page opposite such section, subsection or paragraph.

When a repeal is involved.

(4) When a private bill repeals an existing section, subsection, or other minor division of a section, that section, subsection or division, or so much thereof as is essential, shall be printed opposite the clause.

Explanatory note where necessary.

(5) A brief explanatory note giving the reasons for any clause of an unusual nature or which differs from the model bill clauses or standard clauses shall be printed opposite the clause in the bill.

Map or plan with bill.

137. No bill for the incorporation of a railway or canal company, or for authorizing the construction of branch lines or extensions of existing lines of railways or of canals, or for changing the route of the railway or of the canal of any company already incorporated, shall be considered by a legislative committee, until there has been filed with the committee, at least one week before the consideration of the bill, a map or plan drawn upon a scale of not less than half an inch to the mile, showing the location upon which it is intended to construct the proposed work, and showing also the lines of existing or authorized works of a similar character within, or in any way affecting the district, or any part thereof, which the proposed work is intended to serve; and such map or plan shall be signed by the engineer or other person making same.

Bills confirming agreements.

138. When any bill for confirming any agreement is presented to the House, a true copy of such agreement must be attached to it.

Instruction to committees in certain cases.

139. That it be an instruction to all committees on private bills, in the event of promoters not being ready to proceed with their measures when the same have been twice called on two separate occasions for consideration by the committee, that such measures shall be reported back to the House forthwith, together with a statement of the facts and with the recommendation that such bills be withdrawn.

Suspension of rules.

140. No motion for the suspension or modification of any provision of the Standing Orders applying to private bills or to petitions for private bills shall be entertained by the House until after reference is made to the Standing Committee on Procedure and House Affairs, and a report made thereon by the Committee and, in its report, the Committee shall state the grounds for recommending such suspension or modification.

Bills and petitions referred to committee.

141. (1) Every private bill, when read a second time stands referred to a legislative committee, and all petitions for or against the bills are considered as referred to the same committee.

Notice of sitting of committee.

(2)(*a*) No committee on any private bill originating in this House is to consider the same until after one week's notice of the sitting of such committee has been first affixed in the lobby; nor, in the case of any such bill originating in the Senate, until after twenty-four hours' like notice.

Notice to be appended to *Journals*.

(*b*) On the day of the posting of any bill under this section, the Clerk of the House shall cause a notice of such posting to be appended to the *Journals*.

Voting in committee. Chairman votes.

(3) All questions before committees on private bills are decided by a majority of voices including the voice of the Chairman; and whenever the voices are equal, the Chairman has a second or casting vote.

Provision not covered by notice.

(4) It is the duty of the committee to which any private bill may be referred by the House, to call the attention of the House specially to any provisions inserted in such bill that do not appear to have been contemplated in the notice or petition for the same, as

reported upon by the Examiner of Petitions or by the Standing Committee on Procedure and House Affairs; and any private bill so reported shall not be placed on the *Order Paper* for consideration until a report has been made by the Examiner as to the sufficiency or otherwise of the notice to cover such provisions.

All bills to be reported.

(5) The committee to which a private bill may have been referred shall report the same to the House in every case.

When preamble not proven.

(6) When the committee on any private bill reports to the House that they have made any material change in the preamble of a bill, the reasons for making such change shall be stated in their report; and if they report that the preamble of a bill has not been proved to their satisfaction, they must also state the grounds upon which they have arrived at such a decision; and no bill, the preamble of which has been reported as not proven shall be placed upon the Orders of the Day unless by special Order of the House.

Chairman to sign bills and to initial amendments.

(7) The Chairman of the committee shall sign with his or her name at length a printed copy of the bill, and shall also sign with the initials of his or her name, the preamble and the various sections of the bill and also any amendments which may be made or clauses added in committee; and another copy of the bill with the amendments, if any, written thereon shall be prepared by the clerk of the committee, who shall sign the bill with his or her name at length and shall also sign with the initials of his or her name the preamble and the various sections adopted by the committee, and any amendments which may have been made thereto, and shall file the same with the Clerk of the House or attach it to the report of the committee.

Reprinting of bills when amended.

(8) Private bills amended by any committee may be reprinted by order of such committee; or after being reported, and before consideration in the House, may be reprinted in whole or in part as the Clerk of the House may direct; and the cost of such reprinting shall, in either case, be added to the cost of the first printing of the bill and be payable by the promoter of the same.

Notice of amendments.

142. No important amendment may be proposed to any private bill in the House unless one day's notice of the same has been given.

Amendments by the Senate.

143. When any private bill is returned from the Senate with amendments, the same not being merely verbal or unimportant, such amendments are, previous to the second reading, referred to the committee to which such bill was originally referred.

Record and Lists

Record of private bills.

144. A record shall be kept in the private bills office of the name, description, and place of residence of the parties applying for a private bill or of their agent, the amount of fees paid, and all the proceedings thereon, from the time of the deposit of the bill with the Clerk of the House to the passage of the bill; such record to specify briefly each proceeding in the House or in any committee to which the bill or the petition may be referred, and the day on which the committee is appointed to sit; such record shall be open to public inspection during office hours.

List of bills posted in lobbies.

145. (1) Lists of all private bills which have been referred to any committee shall be prepared daily by the Chief Clerk of Private Bills, specifying the committee to which each

bill has been referred and the date on or after which the bill may be considered by such committee, and shall cause the same to be hung up in the lobby.

Publication of committee meetings.

(2) A list of committee meetings shall be prepared from time to time as arranged, by the Chief Clerk of Private Bills, stating the day and hour of each such meeting, and the room in which it is to be held, which list shall be hung up in the lobby on the day previous to that on which the meeting is to be held.

Parliamentary Agent

Authority conferred by the Speaker.

146. (1) No person shall act as parliamentary agent conducting proceedings before the House of Commons or its committees without the express sanction and authority of the Speaker, and all such agents shall be personally responsible to the House and to the Speaker, for the observance of the rules, orders and practice of Parliament and rules pre-scribed by the Speaker, and also for the payment of all fees and charges.

List of agents.

(2) A list of such persons shall be kept by the Chief Clerk of Private Bills and a copy filed with the Clerk of the House.

Fee per session.

(3) No person shall be allowed to be registered as a parliamentary agent during any session unless he or she has paid a fee of twenty-five dollars for such session and is actu-ally employed in promoting or opposing some private bill or petition pending in Parliament during that session.

Liability of agents.

(4) Any parliamentary agent who wilfully acts in violation of the Standing Orders and practice of Parliament, or of any rules to be prescribed by the Speaker, or who wilfully misconducts himself or herself in prosecuting any proceedings before Parliament, shall be liable to an absolute or temporary prohibition to practice as a parliamentary agent, at the pleasure of the Speaker; provided, that upon the application of such agent, the Speaker shall state in writing the ground for such prohibition.

Application of Standing Orders

Standing Orders apply to private bills.

147. Except as herein otherwise provided, the Standing Orders relating to public bills shall apply to private bills.

CHAPTER XVI

HOUSE ADMINISTRATION

Report of the proceedings of Board of Internal Economy.

148. (1) The Speaker shall, within ten days after the opening of each session, lay upon the Table of the House a report of the proceedings for the preceding session of the Board of Internal Economy.

Report on committee budgets.

(2) The Speaker shall, as soon as the Board of Internal Economy has reached a decision concerning any budget or supplementary budget presented to it pursuant to sections (1) and (2) of Standing Order 121, lay upon the Table the record of the Board's decision.

149. Deleted (June 10, 1994).

150. Deleted (June 10, 1994).

151. The Clerk of the House is responsible for the safe-keeping of all the papers and records of the House, and has the direction and control over all the officers and clerks employed in the offices, subject to such orders as the Clerk may, from time to time, receive from the Speaker or the House.

152. The Clerk of the House shall place on the Speaker's table, every morning, previous to the meeting of the House, the order of the proceedings for the day.

153. It is the duty of the Clerk of the House to make and cause to be printed and delivered to each Member, at the commencement of every session of Parliament, a list of the reports or other periodical statements which it is the duty of any officer or department of the government, or any bank or other corporate body to make to the House, referring to the Act or resolution, and page of the volume of the laws or *Journals* wherein the same may be ordered; and placing under the name of each officer or corporation a list of reports or returns required to be made, and the time when the report or periodical statement may be expected.

154. A Clerk of this House may be the bearer of messages from this House to the Senate. Messages from the Senate may be received at the bar by a Clerk of this House, as soon as announced by the Sergeant-at-Arms, at any time while the House is sitting, or in committee, without interrupting the business then proceeding.

155. Deleted (June 10, 1994).

156. Deleted (June 10, 1994).

157. (1) The Sergeant-at-Arms is responsible for the safe-keeping of the Mace.

(2) The Sergeant-at-Arms serves all Orders of the House upon those whom they may concern and is entrusted with the execution of warrants issued by the Speaker. The Sergeant-at-Arms issues cards of admission to, and preserves order in, the galleries, corridors, lobbies and other parts of the House of Commons.

158. (1) Any stranger admitted into any part of the House or gallery who misconducts himself or herself, or does not withdraw when strangers are directed to withdraw, while the House or any Committee of the Whole House is sitting, shall be taken into custody by the Sergeant-at-Arms; and no person so taken into custody shall be discharged without the special Order of the House.

(2) No stranger who has been committed, by Order of the House, to the custody of the Sergeant-at-Arms, shall be released from such custody until he or she has paid a fee of four dollars to the Sergeant-at-Arms.

159. It is the duty of the officers of this House to complete and finish the work remaining at the close of the session.

Index

D

n

Q